Understanding Psychology

FIFTEENTH EDITION

Robert S. Feldman

University of Massachusetts Amherst

UNDERSTANDING PSYCHOLOGY: FIFTEENTH EDITION

Published by McGraw Hill LLC, 1325 Avenue of the Americas, New York, NY 10121. Copyright ©2021 by McGraw Hill LLC. All rights reserved. Printed in the United States of America. Previous editions ©2019, 2017, and 2015. No part of this publication may be reproduced or distributed in any form or by any means, or stored in a database or retrieval system, without the prior written consent of McGraw Hill LLC, including, but not limited to, in any network or other electronic storage or transmission, or broadcast for distance learning.

Some ancillaries, including electronic and print components, may not be available to customers outside the United States.

This book is printed on acid-free paper.

2 3 4 5 6 7 8 9 LKV 24 23 22

ISBN 978-1-260-82946-4 (bound edition)
MHID 1-260-82946-4 (bound edition)
ISBN 978-1-260-40843-0 (loose-leaf edition)
MHID 1-260-40843-4 (loose-leaf edition)

Senior Portfolio Manager: *Ryan Treat*
Product Development Manager: *Dawn Groundwater*
Lead Product Developer: *Cara Labell*
Marketing Manager: *Olivia Kaiser*
Content Project Managers: *Mary E. Powers (core), Jodi Banowetz (assessment)*
Buyer: *Sandy Ludovissy*
Designer: *Beth Blech*
Content Licensing Specialist: *Carrie Burger*
Cover Image: *©gstockstudio/123RF*
Compositor: *Aptara®, Inc.*

All credits appearing on page or at the end of the book are considered to be an extension of the copyright page.

Library of Congress Cataloging-in-Publication Data

Names: Feldman, Robert S. (Robert Stephen), 1947- author.
Title: Understanding psychology / Robert S. Feldman, University of
    Massachusetts Amherst.
Description: Fifteenth editon. | New York, NY : McGraw-Hill Education,
    [2021] | Revised edition of the author's Understanding psychology,
    c2018. | Includes bibliographical references and indexes.
Identifiers: LCCN 2020017621 (print) | LCCN 2020017622 (ebook) | ISBN
    9781260829464 (hardcover) | ISBN 9781260408430 (spiral bound) | ISBN
    9781260408461 (ebook) | ISBN 9781260408508 (ebook other)
Subjects: LCSH: Psychology.
Classification: LCC BF121 .F34 2021 (print) | LCC BF121 (ebook) | DDC
    150–dc23
LC record available at https://lccn.loc.gov/2020017621
LC ebook record available at https://lccn.loc.gov/2020017622

The Internet addresses listed in the text were accurate at the time of publication. The inclusion of a website does not indicate an endorsement by the authors or McGraw Hill LLC, and McGraw Hill LLC does not guarantee the accuracy of the information presented at these sites.

mheducation.com/highered

Dedication

To

Jon, Leigh, Alex, Miles, Josh, Julie, Naomi, Marina, Sarah, Jeff, Lilia, Rose, and Kathy

About the Author

ROBERT S. FELDMAN is Professor of Psychological and Brain Sciences and Senior Advisor to the Chancellor of the University of Massachusetts Amherst. A recipient of the College Distinguished Teacher Award, he teaches psychology classes ranging in size from 15 to nearly 500 students. During the course of more than three decades as a college instructor, he has taught undergraduate and graduate courses at Mount Holyoke College, Wesleyan University, and Virginia Commonwealth University in addition to the University of Massachusetts.

Professor Feldman, who initiated the Minority Mentoring Program at the University of Massachusetts, also has served as a Hewlett Teaching Fellow and Senior Online Teaching Fellow. He initiated distance-learning courses in psychology at the University of Massachusetts.

A Fellow of the American Psychological Association, the Association for Psychological Science, and the American Association for the Advancement of Science, Professor Feldman received a BA with High Honors from Wesleyan University and an MS and PhD from the University of Wisconsin–Madison. He is a winner of a Fulbright Senior Research Scholar and Lecturer Award and the Distinguished Alumnus Award from Wesleyan. He is past President of the Federation of Associations in Behavioral and Brain Sciences (FABBS) Foundation, which advocates for the field of psychology, and is on the board of the Social Psychology Network (SPN). He also chairs the McGraw-Hill Learning Science Advisory Board.

Robert S. Feldman

He has written and edited more than 250 books, book chapters, and scientific articles. He has edited *Applications of Nonverbal Behavioral Theory and Research*, *Improving the First Year of College: Research and Practice*, and, most recently, *Learning Science: Theory Research and Practice*. He is also author of *P.O.W.E.R. Learning: Strategies for Success in College and Life*.

His textbooks, which have been used by more than 2 million students around the world, have been translated into Spanish, French, Portuguese, Dutch, German, Italian, Arabic, Chinese, Korean, and Japanese. His research interests include deception and honesty in everyday life, work that he described in *The Liar in Your Life*. His research has been supported by grants from the National Institute of Mental Health and the National Institute on Disabilities and Rehabilitation Research.

Professor Feldman loves music, is an enthusiastic pianist, and enjoys cooking and traveling. He is chair of the Board of Directors of New England Public Media, representing the major public broadcasting and streaming outlets in western New England. He and his wife, also a psychologist, live in the Pioneer Valley of Massachusetts in a home overlooking the Holyoke mountain range.

Brief Contents

Contents

DGLimages/Shutterstock

CHAPTER 3

Neuroscience and Behavior 53

Prostock Studio/Shutterstock

CHAPTER 4

Sensation and Perception 88

Odua Images/Shutterstock

MJTH/Shutterstock

India Picture/Shutterstock

Maddie Meyer/Getty Images

Gpointstudio/Cultura/age fotostock

Nancy Mao Smith/Shutterstock

santypan/Shutterstock

Alxcrs/Shutterstock

CHAPTER 15

Psychological Disorders 492

Andrey_Popov/Shutterstock

SeventyFour/Shutterstock

Vitalii Nesterchuk/123RF

Rawpixel.com/Shutterstock

McGraw-Hill Education Psychology APA Documentation Style Guide

Instructors: Student Success Starts with You

Tools to enhance your unique voice

Want to build your own course? No problem. Prefer to use our turnkey, prebuilt course? Easy. Want to make changes throughout the semester? Sure. And you'll save time with Connect's auto-grading too.

65%
Less Time Grading

Laptop: McGraw Hill; Woman/dog: George Doyle/Getty Images

Study made personal

Incorporate adaptive study resources like SmartBook® 2.0 into your course and help your students be better prepared in less time. Learn more about the powerful personalized learning experience available in SmartBook 2.0 at **www.mheducation.com/highered/connect/smartbook**

Affordable solutions, added value

Make technology work for you with LMS integration for single sign-on access, mobile access to the digital textbook, and reports to quickly show you how each of your students is doing. And with our Inclusive Access program you can provide all these tools at a discount to your students. Ask your McGraw Hill representative for more information.

Padlock: Jobalou/Getty Images

Solutions for your challenges

A product isn't a solution. Real solutions are affordable, reliable, and come with training and ongoing support when you need it and how you want it. Visit **www.supportateverystep.com** for videos and resources both you and your students can use throughout the semester.

Checkmark: Jobalou/Getty Images

Students: Get Learning that Fits You

Effective tools for efficient studying

Connect is designed to make you more productive with simple, flexible, intuitive tools that maximize your study time and meet your individual learning needs. Get learning that works for you with Connect.

Study anytime, anywhere

Download the free ReadAnywhere app and access your online eBook or SmartBook 2.0 assignments when it's convenient, even if you're offline. And since the app automatically syncs with your eBook and SmartBook 2.0 assignments in Connect, all of your work is available every time you open it. Find out more at **www.mheducation.com/readanywhere**

> *"I really liked this app—it made it easy to study when you don't have your textbook in front of you."*
>
> - Jordan Cunningham,
>   Eastern Washington University

Calendar: owattaphotos/Getty Images

Everything you need in one place

Your Connect course has everything you need—whether reading on your digital eBook or completing assignments for class, Connect makes it easy to get your work done.

Learning for everyone

McGraw Hill works directly with Accessibility Services Departments and faculty to meet the learning needs of all students. Please contact your Accessibility Services Office and ask them to email accessibility@mheducation.com, or visit **www.mheducation.com/about/accessibility** for more information.

Preface

Students First

If I were to encapsulate my goals in writing *Understanding Psychology* across 15 editions, as well as my teaching philosophy, this is what I would say: *Students First.*

I believe that an effective introduction to a discipline must be oriented to students—informing them, engaging them, and exciting them about the field and helping them connect it to their world. It needs to embody the principles of contemporary learning science and present the material in a way that draws students into the field and stimulates their thinking. *Understanding Psychology*, with its focus on *Students First*, seeks to promote success by engaging students' attention and informing them about the field, which results in students deeply learning the course content and—equally important to me—becoming excited about the field of psychology.

To achieve my *Student First* goals, *Understanding Psychology*, 15/e, includes this rich array of features:

MODULAR ORGANIZATION

Each chapter of *Understanding Psychology* is divided into three to five manageable, self-contained sections, called modules, that include learning outcomes and assessment opportunities. Thus, rather than facing a long and potentially daunting chapter, students encounter material that has been organized into manageable portions, which psychological research has found is the optimal way to learn.

A PERSONALIZED EXPERIENCE THAT LEADS TO IMPROVED LEARNING AND RESULTS

McGraw-Hill Education's Connect is a digital assignment and assessment platform that strengthens the link between faculty, students, and course work, helping everyone accomplish more in less time. Connect for Introductory Psychology includes assignable and assessable videos, quizzes, exercises, and interactivities, all associated with learning objectives. Interactive assignments and videos allow students to experience and apply their understanding of psychology to the world with fun and stimulating activities. McGraw-Hill Education's SmartBook helps students distinguish the concepts they know from the concepts they don't, while pinpointing the concepts they are about to forget. SmartBook's real-time reports help both students and instructors identify the concepts that require more attention, making study sessions and class time more efficient. Smart-Book is optimized for mobile and tablet use and is accessible for students with disabilities. Content-wise, measurable and observable learning objectives help improve student outcomes. SmartBook personalizes learning to individual student needs, continually adapting to pinpoint knowledge gaps and focus learning on topics that need the most attention. Study time is more productive and, as a result, students are better prepared for class and coursework. For instructors, SmartBook tracks student progress and provides insights that can help guide teaching strategies.

- SmartBook helps students study more efficiently by highlighting where in the chapter to focus, asking review questions and pointing them to resources until they understand.

- Connect's assignments help students contextualize what they've learned through application, so they can better understand the material and think critically.

- SmartBook will create a personalized study path customized to individual student needs.

- Connect reports deliver information regarding performance, study behavior, and effort, so instructors can quickly identify students who are having issues, or focus on material that the class hasn't mastered.

THE POWER OF DATA

Understanding Psychology harnesses the power of data to improve the instructor and student experiences.

Better Data, Smarter Revision, Improved Results In the past, I began the revision process for a new edition by gathering information from instructors about what they would change and what they would keep. Experts in the field were asked what new material they would like to see added and what dated material I should review. Using this feedback, I would revise the material.

For the 15th edition, however, I used a far better, and revolutionary, revision process made possible by SmartBook, the adaptive learning system that provides students with individualized assessment of their own progress. SmartBook provides me with the previous students' (anonymous) performance data, which I was able to analyze to inform the revisions. Because virtually every text paragraph is tied to several questions that students answer while using SmartBook, I had access to empirical data in the form of a "Heat Map" report to easily pinpoint the concepts with which they were having the most difficulty.

The Power of Student Data Using Heat Maps

Step 1.

Over the course of 2 years, data on students' understanding of text concepts was anonymously collected from SmartBook for the previous edition of *Understanding Psychology.*

Step 2.

The data was provided to me in the form of a **Heat Map,** which graphically illustrated "hot spots" in the text that posed particular difficulty for students.

Step 3.

I then used the **Heat Map** data to refine the content with the goal of reinforcing student comprehension in the new edition. Additional quiz questions and assignable activities were created for use in Connect Psychology to further support student success.

4. RESULT.

Because the **Heat Map** provided empirically based feedback at the paragraph and even sentence level, I was able to develop the new edition to clarify concepts that caused students the most difficulty.

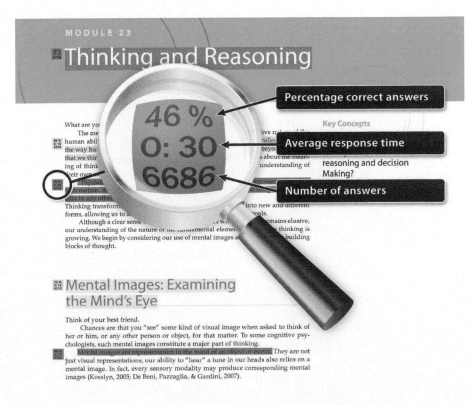

POWERFUL REPORTING

Whether a class is face-to-face, hybrid, or entirely online, McGraw-Hill's Connect provides the tools needed to reduce the amount of time and energy that instructors must spend to administer their courses. Easy-to-use course management tools allow instructors to spend less time administering and more time teaching, while reports allow students to monitor their progress and optimize study time.

- The At-Risk Student Report provides instructors with one-click access to a dashboard that identifies students who are at risk of dropping out of the course due to low engagement levels.
- The Category Analysis Report details student performance relative to specific learning objectives and goals, including APA Learning Goals and Outcomes and levels of Bloom's taxonomy.
- The SmartBook Reports allow instructors and students to easily monitor progress and pinpoint areas of weakness, giving each student a personalized study plan to achieve success.

STUDENT CRITICAL THINKING SKILLS

At the apply and analyze levels of Bloom's taxonomy, **Scientific Reasoning Activities** found in Connect offer in-depth arguments to sharpen students' critical thinking skills and prepare them to be more discerning consumers of psychology in their everyday lives. For each chapter, there are multiple sets of arguments accompanied by auto-graded assessments requiring students to think critically about claims presented as facts. These exercises can also be used in Connect as group activities or for discussion.

Power of Process guides students through the process of critical reading, analysis, and writing. Faculty can select or upload their own content, such as journal articles, and assign analysis strategies to gain insight into students' application of the scientific method. For students, Power of Process offers a guided visual approach to exercising critical thinking strategies to apply before, during, and after reading published research. Additionally, utilizing the relevant and engaging research articles built into Power of Process, students are supported in becoming critical consumers of research.

STUDENT ACTIVE ENGAGEMENT

Students first also means activities that contribute to success in the course. New to this edition: application-based activities and a writing assignment tool.

Application-Based Activities are highly interactive, automatically graded, online learn-by-doing exercises that provide students a safe space to apply their knowledge and problem-solving skills to real-world scenarios. Each scenario addresses key concepts and skills that students must use to work through and solve course-specific problems, resulting in improved critical thinking and development of relevant workplace skills. Topics include the following:

- Drugs and their effects on the brain
- Ethics in research
- Female sexual anatomy
- Gender identity
- Homologous structures
- Male sexual anatomy
- Observational learning
- Reinforcement and punishment
- Research design
- States of consciousness
- Stages of memory
- Stages of sleep
- Structures and functions of the brain
- Theories of emotion
- Theories of motivation
- Types of love
- Types of memory

Power of Process for

PSYCHOLOGY

McGraw Hill Education connect®

Writing Assignments offer faculty the ability to assign a full range of writing assignments to students (both manual-scoring and auto-scoring) with just-in-time feedback. You may set up manually scored assignments in a way that students can

- automatically receive grammar and high-level feedback to improve their writing before they submit a project to you;

- run originality checks and receive feedback on "exact matches" and "possibly altered text" that includes guidance about how to properly paraphrase, quote, and cite sources to improve the academic integrity of their writing before they submit their work to you.

The new writing assignments will also have features that allow instructors to assign milestone drafts (optional), easily re-use your text and audio comments, build/score with your rubric, and view your own originality report of student's final submission.

Concept Clips help students comprehend some of the most difficult ideas in introductory psychology. Colorful graphics and stimulating animations describe core concepts in a step-by-step manner, engaging students and aiding in retention. Concept Clips can be used as a presentation tool in the classroom or for student assessment.

Interactivities, assignable through Connect, engage students with content through experiential activities. New and updated activities include: Understanding Correlations, Heuristics, Gardner's Theory of Multiple Intelligences, Sexual Anatomy, Sexually Transmitted Infections, Personality Assessment Cognitive Dissonance, Explicit and Implicit Bias, and First Impressions and Attraction.

Through the connection of psychology to students' own lives, concepts become more relevant and understandable. Powered by McGraw-Hill Education's Connect Psychology, **NewsFlash** exercises tie current news stories to key psychological principles and learning objectives. After interacting with a contemporary news story, students are assessed on their ability to make the link between real life and research findings.

Introductory Psychology videos show psychological concepts in action. New to this edition are: Neuroscience of Language, Neuroscience of ADHD, Neuroscience of Anxiety, Treating ADHD with Therapy, Neuroscience of Love, History of Psychology, The, Naturalistic Observation in Psychology, The Usefulness of Psychological Research, The Birth of Epigenetics: the Agouti Mouse Study, Conformity – Are You Like a 3 or 7 Year Old?

Psychology at Work videos, assignable and assessable within McGraw Hill Connect™, highlight nine careers in which knowledge of psychology is beneficial in the workplace. Each video introduces a person at work who specifies how knowledge gained from taking introductory psychology in college is applied to the work environment.

Student Tools: Mastering the Material

Student success in psychology means mastering the material at a deep level. These are some additional tools embedded in *Understanding Psychology* that help students maximize their performance:

STUDY ALERTS

Throughout, marginal notes point out important and difficult concepts and topics. These Study Alerts offer suggestions for learning the material effectively and for studying for tests.

APPLYING PSYCHOLOGY IN THE 21ST CENTURY

These boxes—all new in this edition—highlight the relevance of psychology by presenting current and potential applications of psychological theory and research findings to real-world problems. For example, one of the *Applying Psychology in the 21st Century* boxes focuses on the effect of the coronavirus pandemic on stress levels and mental health in young people.

Study Alert
Differentiate the stages of sleep (stage 1, stage 2, stage 3, and REM sleep), which produce different brain-wave patterns.

APPLYING PSYCHOLOGY IN THE 21ST CENTURY

STRESS, CORONAVIRUS, AND YOUNG AMERICANS' MENTAL HEALTH

Are you feeling stressed out, perhaps more than some of the adults around you seem to feel? How did the coronavirus pandemic affect your level of stress? Significantly? If so, you're not alone. Many others of the current generation of college students report feeling the same way, and the stress is taking a toll on their mental health.

Even before the pandemic, a report by the American Psychological Association (2018) detailed the findings of an online survey of over 3,500 adults (plus an additional 300 teens between 15 and 17 years old) investigating their perceived stress levels and mental health. Sixty-four percent of adults reported feeling stressed over money and work. Among Americans aged 15 to 21 (known as Generation Z), 30% reported feeling significantly stressed by housing insecurity, while fully a third were stressed by personal debt. Alarmingly, 28% reported hunger or food insecurity as ongoing sources of stress in their lives.

FROM THE PERSPECTIVE OF...

Every chapter includes questions to help students connect psychological concepts with career realities. Called "From the Perspective of...," this feature helps students understand how psychology relates to various career fields.

From the perspective of...

An Educator How might you use the findings in sleep research to maximize student learning?

Andersen Ross/Blend Images/Getty Images

EXPLORING DIVERSITY

In addition to substantial coverage of material relevant to diversity, including the images that accompany the text, every set of modules also includes at least one special section devoted to an aspect of racial, ethnic, gender, or cultural diversity. These sections highlight the ways in which psychology informs (and is informed by) issues relating to the increasing multiculturalism of our global society. For example, one *Exploring Diversity* section discusses the issue of race and ethnicity in establishing test norms.

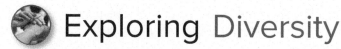

Exploring Diversity

Should Race and Ethnicity Be Used to Establish Test Norms?

The passions of politics may confront the objectivity of science when test norms are established, at least in the realm of standardized tests that are meant to predict future job performance. In fact, a national controversy has developed around the question of whether different test norms should be established for members of various racial and ethnic groups (Manly & Echemendia, 2007; Pedraza & Mungas, 2008; Nettles, 2019).

NEUROSCIENCE IN YOUR LIFE

This feature emphasizes the importance of neuroscientific research within the various subfields of the discipline and in students' lives. Representative brain scans, with both caption and textual explanation, illustrate significant neuroscientific findings that increasingly influence the field of psychology. For example, one *Neuroscience in Your Life* feature explores whether people can develop unusually superior memories:

NEUROSCIENCE IN YOUR LIFE: SUPERIOR MEMORY

Some people have astounding memory and can memorize as many as 100 words in just 5 minutes. But can anyone have superior memory with the appropriate training? Apparently, the answer is yes, for recent research has shown that people's memory can be trained to show significant changes in capacity, and these changes are reflected in changes in the brain. For example, participants in one study spent 30 minutes a day for 6 weeks practicing to improve their memory. Following training, participants were given 10 minutes to remember as many words as they could, and their memory capacity increased from 26 words to 62 words. This improvement was paralleled by increased connectivity between areas of the *medial temporal lobe,* including the hippocampus, and the frontal cortex, similar to what is found in those with strongly superior memories (memory athletes).

FIGURE 2 In this three-stage model of memory, information initially recorded by the person's sensory system enters sensory memory, which momentarily holds the information. The information then moves to short-term memory, which stores it for 15 to 25 seconds. Finally, the information can move into long-term memory, which is relatively permanent. Whether the information moves from short-term to long-term memory depends on the kind and amount of rehearsal of the material that is performed.

Source: Adapted from Dresler, M., Shirer, W. R., Konrad, B. N., Muller, N. C., Wagner, I. C., Fernandez, G., et al. (2017). Mnemonic training reshapes brain networks to support superior memory. *Neuron, 93*(5), 1227-1235 e1226. doi: 10.1016/j.neuron.2017.02.003.

Student Learning: Content and Concepts

Understanding Psychology provides broad coverage of the field of psychology, including the theories, research, and applications that form the core of the discipline. Along with the traditional areas of psychology–neuroscience, sensation and perception, states of consciousness, learning, memory, cognition, human development, personality, psychological disorders and treatment, and social psychology–the applied topics of gender and sexuality and health psychology receive extensive attention.

The new edition continues its commitment to extensive coverage of diversity. A concluding module called "Diversity, Culture, Conflict, and Cooperation" addresses questions of how diversity affects individual behavior, how we observe and understand other people, and how our understandings (and misunderstandings) of our differences can lead to cooperation and/or conflict.

In addition, the 15th edition of *Understanding Psychology* contains a significant amount of new and updated features and content. Hundreds of new citations have been added, and most of them refer to articles and books published since 2019. Finally, the text includes numerous substantive references to the coronavirus pandemic, an event that has played a central role in shaping students' lives since its start. Specifically, the pandemic is discussed in chapters 1, 7, 14, 15, 16, and 17.

The following list of new and revised topics and textual changes, including new definitions and clarifications based on heat map data, provides a good indication of the content's currency and *Student First* focus:

Chapter 1, Introduction to Psychology
- Included new prologue on coronavirus pandemic
- Updated information on diversity of working psychologists
- Noted changes in demographics of early career psychologists
- Updated data on proportion of graduate students by gender, noting that it increases the gender gap favoring women
- Added data on the higher job satisfaction of psychology doctorate degree holders
- Refined definition of behavioral perspective
- Refined explanation of the humanistic perspective
- Clarified individual differences versus universal principles
- Clarified definition of personality psychology
- Added material on psychologists' role in understanding reactions to climate change
- Added material on psychologists' investigation of young adults' connectivity via cellphones

Chapter 2–Psychological Research
- Noted contradictions to traditional bystander effect
- Explained importance of replication
- Discussed the potential replication crisis
- Explained the use of Mechanical Turk for research
- Refined explanation of archival studies
- Clarified explanation of drawbacks to case studies
- Refined definition of a significant outcome
- Clarified the reasons for using nonhumans in research
- Clarified experimenter expectations material
- Refined the criteria to evaluate research studies

Chapter 3–Neuroscience and Behavior
- Redefined neuron
- Refined discussion of neurons' unique communication capabilities
- Clarified direction of neuronal impulses through the neuron
- Clarified distinction between sensory and motor neurons

- Refined the distinction between the somatic and autonomic divisions of the nervous system
- Clarified the distinction between the sympathetic and parasympathetic divisions
- Clarified the purpose of fMRI
- Augmented information on capabilities of PET scans
- Refined discussion and operation of auditory and visual cortex
- Clarified right-hemisphere strengths
- Refined discussion of gender differences in hemispheric specialization
- Added material on females having "younger" brains than males
- Added coverage on control of protheses through brain implants
- Added coverage on brain-machine interface
- Updated information on use of Neuropixels to measure brain activity

Chapter 4–Sensation and Perception
- Added information on techniques for restoring lost sense of smell
- Redefined psychophysics definition
- Redefined definition of absolute threshold
- Added new definition of visual spectrum
- Clarified location of cornea
- Clarified description of rods
- Refined description of cones
- Clarified description of light adaptation
- Refined description of transmission light through rods and cones
- Refined presentation of Gestalt laws of organization
- Explained genetic causes of synesthesia
- Introduced concept of hyperacusis
- Added information on use of medical marijuana for pain reduction
- Introduced information on use of virtual reality immersive therapy for pain relief

Chapter 5–States of Consciousness
- Introduced and evaluated concept of sleep learning
- Added new figure on tweets and happiness
- Discussed mixed evidence on safety of marijuana
- Introduced work on cross-species experience of consciousness

- Added information on screen time, melatonin production, and insomnia
- Redefined rapid eye movement sleep
- Refined description of nightmares
- Clarified description of night terrors
- Refined description of behavior while hypnotized
- Clarified definition of addiction
- Replaced concept of "physiological addiction" with "biological addiction"
- Added new figure on binge drinking
- Clarified effects of binge drinking on lighter drinkers
- Updated statistics on drug use
- Added new figure on drug use
- Revised statistics on heroin-related deaths
- Revised definition of barbiturates
- Added information on use of MDMA
- Discussed creation of creative ideas during daydreaming

Chapter 6–Learning
- Discussed learning for helper animals
- Clarified that UCS doesn't initially lead to desired response
- Refined description of spontaneous recovery
- Clarified description of stimulus generalization
- Refined description of stimulus discrimination
- Refined description of basic assumptions of classical conditioning
- Clarified examples of primary reinforcers
- Clarified presentation of continuous reinforcement schedule
- Clarified presentation of partial reinforcement schedule
- Clarified the distinction between fixed- and variable-interval schedules
- Refined example of genetic constraints on learning
- Refined presentation of cognitive learning theory
- Introduced new studies in support of not spanking children
- Discussed research on violence in video games and mass shooting

Chapter 7–Memory
- Added information on use of brain implants to enhance memory in those with disorders

- Added information on benefits of forgetting
- Discussed the effect of intentional forgetting on improvement of memory for other information
- Discussed testing yourself as a means to better recall
- Added information on transcranial alternating current stimulation (tACS) and its enhancement of memory
- Refined presentation of sensory, short-term, and long-term memory definitions
- Refined explanation of sensory memory
- Clarified rehearsal presentation
- Added discussion concerning recollection of coronavirus memories formed in quarantine
- Refined explanation of semantic networks
- Clarified repressed memories
- Added concept of fake news
- Added new statistics on Alzheimer's disease

Chapter 8–Cognition and Language

- Added feature on use of GPS and its impact on cognitive maps and brain activity
- Added term *mental set*
- Added coverage of AlphaZero chess program strategy
- Included new material on attention span
- Discussed the present-bias heuristic
- Updated section on artificial intelligence
- Introduced the science of fake news
- Discussed the acceptability of good-enough solutions
- Refined definition of availability heuristic
- Clarified description of means-ends analysis process
- Clarified definition of divergent thinking
- Refined description of overgeneralization
- Revised description of cognitive psychologists' critique of Chomsky's language acquisition approach
- Expanded research on biculturalism and it mental health benefits, including an increased sense of well-being

Chapter 9–Intelligence

- Discussed new applications for technology approximating intelligence

- Clarified description of *g*, or *g*-factor
- Refined description of fluid intelligence
- Clarified definition of analytical intelligence
- Updated Galton presentation
- Added new data on correlation between brain size and intelligence
- Clarified findings on culture-fair IQ tests
- Discussed inclusion of racially biased items on statewide high school test

Chapter 10–Motivation and Emotion

- Clarified description of use of language to describe emotions
- Revised statistics on rates of obesity
- Revised material on populations at risk for anorexia nervosa
- Explained consequences of bariatric surgery
- Introduced the concepts of growth mindset, fixed mindset, and grit
- Added genetic evidence for anorexia nervosa
- Discussed the relationship between cutting down on screen time and weight loss
- Discussed the genetic basis for obesity
- Introduced new evidence regarding the degree to which facial expressions reflect emotions
- Refined definition of instincts
- Refined discussion of evidence against drive-reduction theories
- Refined discussion of incentive theories
- Discussed importance of Maslow outside of psychology
- Clarified use of Thematic Apperception Test
- Clarified explanation of visceral experience as arousal of the autonomic nervous system

Chapter 11–Sexuality and Gender

- Added new statistics on prevalence of female circumcision
- Added new statistics on abuse
- Added case study of a transgender woman
- Added new research on the genetic basis of homosexuality
- Refined discussion of double standard
- Clarified multiple motivations for rape
- Added material on repercussions of rape for male victims
- Clarified term *intersex*

- Refined discussion of learning theory as an explanation of sexual orientation
- Clarified summary of sexual-orientation determinants
- Added new statistics on frequency of gay, lesbian, and bisexual behavior
- Refined definition of sexual normality
- Refined discussion of cross-cultural similarities in stereotypes
- Added feature on gender stereotypes driven by sex of virtual assistants
- Added data on Americans having less sex
- Added material on the roots of gender differences: Girls spend more time doing chores than boys but earn less allowance
- Changed definition of bisexuality
- Updated terminology for gender-confirmation surgery

Chapter 12–Development

- Revised statistics on when the United States will become majority minority
- Added material on the success of immigrant children
- Revised information about U.S. divorce rates
- Added material on in vitro fertilization cases
- Added material on the increase in online friendships
- Clarified definition of identical twins
- Clarified drawbacks to longitudinal data
- Refined presentation of vernix
- Refined presentation of attachment
- Introduced the term *parallel play*
- Refined object permanence presentation
- Clarified stage versus continuous theory distinctions
- Refined presentation of adolescence
- Added new statistics on adolescent suicide
- Discussed cluster suicides
- Added material on increase in suicidal thoughts and attempts
- Discussed easy access to weapons as cause for suicide
- Included recommendations for screen time restrictions
- Added information on men's physical declines in middle age

Chapter 13–Personality

- Discussed use of TAT to measure achievement motivation

- Added case study on gangster Whitey Bulger
- Discussed over- and underestimation of traits
- Added information on the Kuder career self-report test
- Discussed Myers-Briggs self-report measure and its shortcomings
- Refined presentation of psychoanalytic theory
- Refined presentation of ego in Freud's theory
- Clarified process of identification
- Refined concept of cardinal trait
- Refined discussion of cognitive-affective processing system (CAPS)
- Refined discussion of self-esteem
- Added new definition of test standardization

Chapter 14–Health Psychology: Stress, Coping, and Well-Being

- Discussed coronavirus pandemic as a source of stress
- Added a case study on vaping addiction
- Added definition of vaping
- Added a new figure on teenage vaping
- Added new research on vaping leading to smoking cigarettes
- Added evidence on dangers of vaping and vaping deaths due to contaminants
- Discussed use of e-cigarettes to quit smoking
- Added new statistics on deaths due to medical error
- Discussed mass shootings in the United States and their relation to stress
- Discussed the knowledge gaps that relate vaccines to autism
- Refined presentation of general adaptation syndrome
- Added new definition of hardiness
- Refined presentation on happiness and control relationship
- Defined subjective well-being
- Introduced information on health benefits of broad social networks

Chapter 15–Psychological Disorders

- Added new statistics on incidence of major depression
- Added new statistics on cost of major depression

- Added new figure on student mental health problems
- Rephrased "deviation from average behavior" as approach to abnormality
- Rephrased "deviation from ideal behavior" as approach to abnormality
- Refined critique of cognitive perspectives of abnormality
- Added new data on race and homelessness
- Discussed coronavirus pandemic and increase in reported mental health issues
- Clarified criticisms of DSM-5
- Refined description of phobias
- Clarified description of somatic disorders
- Added new statistics on worldwide rate of major depressive disorder
- Revised Applying Psychology feature to address impact of the pandemic on stress in young people.
- Refined presentation of causes of mood disorders
- Rephrased predisposition explanations of schizophrenia
- Added new figure on children's disorders
- Added new data/figure on psychological disorders worldwide
- Augmented discussion of signs of need for help with a psychological disorder
- Discussed mass shooters and psychological disorders
- Discussed differing experiences of psychological disorder across cultures

Chapter 16–Treatment of Psychological Disorders

- Added coverage of "boot camp" therapy
- Added case study on psychotropic therapy
- Added information on lowering the stigma of electroshock therapy
- Discussed electroshock therapy used in dementia
- Added information about online therapy
- Refined discussion of most appropriate type of therapist
- Redefined discussion of humanistic therapy
- Introduced mixed scientific evidence for efficacy of Alcoholics Anonymous

- Revised definition of drug therapy
- Refined presentation of electroconvulsive therapy
- Clarified description of biomedical therapy drawbacks
- Added new statistics on mental health and homelessness
- Discussed use of hotlines using phone and text
- Discussed online therapy during the coronavirus pandemic

Chapter 17–Social Psychology

- Discussed negative outcomes of social media use
- Expanded discussion of social media sites
- Discussed use of social media as a news provider
- Introduced information on brain circuits and aggression
- Introduced lost-wallet study and altruism
- Discussed historical changes in implicit attitudes
- Refined presentation of relationship between need for cognition and central/peripheral route processing
- Included new definition of cognitive dissonance
- Refined presentation of cognitive dissonance
- Rephrased explanation of the assumed similarity bias
- Refined discussion of the Asch conformity study procedure
- Refined discussion of door-in-the-face technique
- Modified description of aggressive cues
- Added new definition of diffusion of responsibility
- Included research on impact of discrimination on targets, which includes declines in cognitive functioning
- Added discussion of differential impact of coronavirus pandemic as related to race, ethnicity, and wealth/poverty
- Included research on impact of observing subtle discrimination
- Included research on early preference for same-race faces

McGraw-Hill Psychology APA Documentation Style Guide

- Updated based on the 7th edition of the *Publication of the American Psychological Association.*

SUPPORTING INSTRUCTORS WITH TECHNOLOGY

McGraw-Hill offers additional technology tools for instructors to develop and tailor the course they want to teach. They include the following:

REMOTE PROCTORING

New remote proctoring and browser-locking capabilities are seamlessly integrated within Connect to offer more control over the integrity of online assessments. Instructors can enable security options that restrict browser activity, monitor student behavior, and verify the identity of each student. Instant and detailed reporting gives instructors an at-a-glance view of potential concerns, thereby avoiding personal bias and supporting evidence-based claims.

TAILOR YOUR COURSE

Easily rearrange chapters, combine material from other content sources, and quickly upload content you have written, such as your course syllabus or teaching notes, using McGraw-Hill Education's **Create.** Find the content you need by searching through thousands of leading McGraw-Hill Education textbooks. Arrange your book to fit your teaching style. Create even allows you to personalize your book's appearance by selecting the cover and adding your name, school, and course information. Order a Create book, and you will receive a complimentary print review copy in 3 to 5 business days or a complimentary electronic review copy via email in about an hour. Experience how McGraw-Hill Education empowers you to teach *your* students *your* way: **http://create.mheducation.com.**

TRUSTED SERVICE AND SUPPORT

McGraw-Hill Education's Connect offers comprehensive service, support, and training throughout every phase of your implementation. If you're looking for some guidance on how to use Connect or want to learn tips and tricks from super users, you can find tutorials as you work. Our Digital Faculty Consultants and Student Ambassadors offer insight into how to achieve the results you want with Connect.

INTEGRATION WITH YOUR LEARNING MANAGEMENT SYSTEM

McGraw-Hill integrates your digital products from McGraw-Hill with your school learning management system (LMS) for quick and easy access to best-in-class content and learning tools. Build an effective digital course, enroll students with ease, and discover how powerful digital teaching can be.

Available with Connect, integration is a pairing between an institution's LMS and Connect at the assignment level. It shares assignment information, grades and calendar items from Connect into the LMS automatically, creating an easy-to-manage course for instructors and simple navigation for students. Our assignment-level integration is available with **Blackboard Learn, Canvas by Instructure,** and **Brightspace by D2L,** giving you access to registration, attendance, assignments, grades, and course resources in real time, in one location.

INSTRUCTOR SUPPLEMENTS

Instructor's Manual The instructor's manual provides a wide variety of tools and resources for presenting the course, including learning objectives and ideas for lectures and discussions.

Test Bank and Test Builder By increasing the rigor of the test bank development process, McGraw-Hill Education has raised the bar for student assessment. Organized by chapter, the questions are designed to test factual, conceptual, and applied understanding. All test questions are available within Test Builder software and as Word documents.

New to this edition and available within Connect, Test Builder is a cloud-based tool that enables instructors to format tests that can be printed or administered within a Learning Management System. Test Builder offers a modern, streamlined interface for easy content configuration that matches course needs, without requiring a download. Test Builder enables instructors to:

- Access all test bank content from a particular title
- Easily pinpoint the most relevant content through robust filtering options
- Manipulate the order of questions or scramble questions and/or answers
- Pin questions to a specific location within a test
- Determine your preferred treatment of algorithmic questions
- Choose the layout and spacing
- Add instructions and configure default settings

PowerPoint Presentations The PowerPoint presentations, which are WCAG compliant, highlight the key points of the chapter and include supporting visuals. All of the slides can be modified to meet individual needs.

Image Gallery The Image Gallery features the complete set of downloadable figures and tables from the text. These can be easily embedded by instructors into their own PowerPoint slides.

Acknowledgments

One of the central features of *Understanding Psychology* is the involvement of professionals as well as students in the review process. The 15th edition of *Understanding Psychology* has relied heavily—and benefited substantially—from the advice of instructors and students from a wide range of backgrounds.

Many teachers along my educational path have shaped my thinking. I was introduced to psychology at Wesleyan University, where several committed and inspiring teachers—and in particular, Karl Scheibe—conveyed their sense of excitement about the field and made its relevance clear to me. Karl epitomizes the teacher-scholar combination to which I aspire, and I continue to marvel at my good fortune in having such a role model.

By the time I left Wesleyan, I could envision no other career but that of psychologist. Although the nature of the University of Wisconsin, where I did my graduate work, could not have been more different from the much smaller Wesleyan, the excitement and inspiration were similar. Again, a cadre of excellent teachers—led, especially, by the late Vernon Allen—molded my thinking and taught me to appreciate the beauty and science of the discipline of psychology.

My colleagues and students at the University of Massachusetts Amherst provide ongoing intellectual stimulation, and I thank them for making the university a fine place to work. Several people also provided extraordinary research and editorial help. In particular, I am especially grateful to my superb students, past and present, including Erik Coats, Ben Happ, Sara Levine, Chris Poirier, Jim Tyler, and Matt Zimbler. John Bickford, in particular, provided invaluable editorial input that has enhanced the content considerably. Finally, I am grateful to John Graiff and Michelle Goncalves, whose hard work and dedication helped immeasurably on just about everything involving this material.

I offer great thanks to the McGraw-Hill Education editorial and marketing teams that participated in this new edition. Thanks especially to Katie Stevens, Ryan Treat, and the entire psychology team (2019 Best Team Award winners), who provided encouragement and support as I worked on this revision. I also thank Marketing Managers AJ

Laferrera (2019 Marketing Manager of the Year!) and Olivia Kaiser for their enthusiasm and commitment to this project. I am in awe of their enthusiasm, commitment, and never-ending good ideas. I'm also happy that Cory Reeves provided input about all sorts of topics, and I especially thank him for his mentorship in the realm of all things musical. Finally, the upper management of McGraw-Hill has provided me with ongoing support, encouragement, and inspiration, and I especially thank Mike Ryan, president of the Higher Education group, and Simon Allen, CEO of McGraw-Hill. I thank these folks not only for their superb professionalism, but also for their friendship.

I am very grateful to Susan Messer, product developer on this edition. Susan did a superb job of managing a myriad of details (as well as me), bringing motivation, intelligence, and a fine literary sense to the project. Finally, every reader of this book owes a debt to Rhona Robbin and Judith Kromm, developmental editors on earlier editions of *Understanding Psychology*. Their relentless pursuit of excellence helped form the essence of this book, and they taught me a great deal about the craft and art of writing. Central to the design, production, and marketing process were Program Manager Kelly Heinrichs, Content Project Manager Mary Powers, Content Licensing Specialist Carrie Burger, and Designer Beth Blech, key members of the production group. I am proud to be a part of this world-class McGraw-Hill team.

Finally, I remain completely indebted to my family. My parents, Leah Brochstein and Saul Feldman, provided a lifetime foundation of love and support, and I continue to see their influence in every corner of my life. My extended family also plays a central role in my life. They include, more or less in order of age, my nieces and nephews, my terrific brother, my brothers- and sisters-in-law, and the late Ethel Radler. My mother-in-law, the late Mary Evans Vorwerk, had an important influence on this book, and I remain ever grateful to her.

Ultimately, my children, Jonathan, Joshua, and Sarah; my daughters-in-law Leigh and Julie; my son-in-law Jeffrey; my grandsons Alex and Miles; my granddaughters Naomi, Lilia, Rose, and Marina; and my wife, Katherine, remain the focal points of my life. I thank them, with immense love, and thank my lucky stars that they are in my life.

Robert S. Feldman
Amherst, Massachusetts

Making the Grade: A Practical Guide to Smarter Studying

No matter why you are taking introductory psychology, it's a safe bet you're interested in maximizing your understanding of the material and getting a good grade. And you want to accomplish these goals as quickly and efficiently as possible.

Good news: Several subfields of psychology have identified different ways to help you learn and remember material you will study throughout college. Here's my guarantee to you: If you learn and follow the guidelines in each of these areas, you'll become a better student and get better grades. Always remember that *good students are made, not born.*

Adopt a General Study Strategy: Using the Power Framework

Psychologists have devised several excellent techniques to improve study skills. One of the best, based on a substantial body of research, is "P.O.W.E.R." or *Prepare, Organize, Work, Evaluate,* and *Rethink*

P.O.W.E.R. system entails the following steps:

- **Prepare.** In *Understanding Psychology,* 15th Edition, read the broad questions called *Learning Outcomes* to *Prepare* yourself for the material that follows. *Learning Outcomes* are at the start of each chapter and each module.

- **Organize.** The *Organize* stage involves developing a mental roadmap of where you are headed. *Understanding Psychology* includes an outline at the beginning of each chapter. Read it to get an idea of what topics are covered and how they are organized.

- **Work.** Because of your effort in the *Power* and *Organize* stages, the *Work* stage will be easier. You know what questions the material will answer based on the *Learning Outcomes,* and you know how it is organized based on the outline. Read everything in the content, including the material in boxes and the margins, to fully understand the material.

- **Evaluate.** *Evaluate* provides the opportunity to determine how effectively you have mastered the material. In *Understanding Psychology,* questions at the end of each module offer a rapid check of your understanding of the material. *Evaluate* your progress to assess your degree of mastery.

- **Rethink.** This final stage, *Rethink,* entails reanalyzing,

Comstock/Stockbyte/Getty Images

reviewing, questioning, and challenging assumptions. Rethinking allows you to consider how the material fits with other information you have already learned. Every major section of *Understanding Psychology* ends with a *Rethink* section. Answering its thought-provoking questions will help you think about the material at a deeper level.

Using the P.O.W.E.R. framework will help you maximize the efficiency and effectiveness of your study. In addition, the P.O.W.E.R. framework can be applied beyond the classroom, helping you to achieve success in your career and life.

Manage Your Time

Managing your time as you study is a central aspect of academic success. But remember: The goal of time management is to permit us to make informed choices about how we use our time. Use these time management procedures to harness time for your own advantage.

SET YOUR PRIORITIES. First, determine your priorities. *Priorities* are the tasks and activities you need and want to do, rank-ordered from most important to least important.

The best procedure is to start off by identifying priorities for an entire term. What do you need to accomplish? Rather than making these goals too general, make them specific, such as, "studying 10 hours before each chemistry exam."

IDENTIFY YOUR PRIME TIME. Are you a morning person, or do you prefer studying later at night? Being aware of the time or times of day when you can do your best work will help you plan and schedule your time most effectively.

MASTER THE MOMENT. Here's what you'll need to organize your time:

- *A master calendar* that shows all the weeks of the term on one page. It should include every week of the term and 7 days per week. On the master calendar, note the due date of every assignment and test you will have. Also include important activities from your personal life, drawn from your list of priorities. Add some free time for yourself.

- *A weekly timetable* that shows the days of the week across the top and the hours, from 6:00 a.m. to midnight, along the side. Fill in the times of all your fixed, prescheduled activities–the times that your classes meet, when you have to be at work, the times you have to pick up your child at day care, and any other recurring appointments. Add assignment due dates, tests, and any other activities on the appropriate days of the week. Then add blocks of time necessary to prepare for those events.

- *A daily to-do list* using a small calendar or your smartphone. List all the things that you intend to do during the day and their priority. Start with the things you *must* do and that have fixed times, such as classes and work schedules. Then add in the other things that you *should* accomplish, such as researching an upcoming paper or finishing a lab report. Finally, list things that are a low priority, such as taking in a new movie.

CONTROL YOUR TIME. If you follow the schedules that you've prepared, you've taken the most important steps in time management. Things, however, always seem to take longer than planned.

Stockbyte/Getty Images

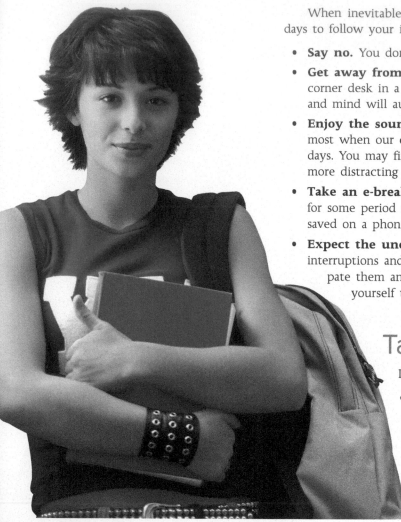

When inevitable surprises occur, there are several ways to take control of your days to follow your intended schedule:

- **Say no.** You don't have to agree to every favor that others ask of you.
- **Get away from it all.** Adopt a specific spot to call your own, such as a corner desk in a secluded nook in the library. If you use it enough, your body and mind will automatically get into study mode as soon as you get there.
- **Enjoy the sounds of silence.** Studies suggest that we are able to concentrate most when our environment is silent. Experiment and work in silence for a few days. You may find that you get more done in less time than you would in a more distracting environment.
- **Take an e-break.** Take an e-break and shut down your communication sources for some period of time. Phone calls, text messages, IMs, and e-mail can be saved on a phone or computer. They'll wait.
- **Expect the unexpected.** You'll never be able to escape from unexpected interruptions and surprises that require your attention. But by trying to anticipate them and thinking about how you'll react to them, you can position yourself to react effectively when they do occur.

F64/Photodisc/Getty Images

Take Good Notes in Class

Let's consider some of the basic principles of notetaking:

- **Identify the instructor's—and your—goals for the course.** The information you get during the first day of class and through the syllabus is critical. In addition to the instructor's goals, you should have your own. How will the information from the course help you to enhance your knowledge, improve yourself as a person, achieve your goals?
  - **Complete assignments before coming to class.**
  - **Listen for the key ideas.** Listen for such phrases as "you need to know . . . ," "the most important thing to consider . . . ," "there are four problems with this approach . . . ," and—a big one—"this will be on the test . . . "; phrases like these should cause you to sit up and take notice. Also, if an instructor says the same thing in several ways, the material being discussed is important.
- **Use short, abbreviated phrases—not full sentences—when taking notes.**
- **Pay attention to PowerPoint slides or what is displayed in class on overhead projectors, whiteboards, or chalk boards. Remember these tips:**
  - Listening is more important than seeing.
  - Don't copy everything that is on every slide.
  - Remember that key points on slides are . . . key points.
  - Check to see if the presentation slides are available online.
  - Remember that presentation slides are not the same as good notes for a class.

Memorize Efficiently

Here's a key principle of effective memorization: Memorize what you need to memorize. *Forget about the rest.*

You have your choice of dozens of techniques of memorization. Also, feel free to devise your own strategies or add those that have worked for you in the past.

REHEARSAL. Say it aloud: rehearsal. Think of this word in terms of its three syllables: re–hear–sal. If you're scratching your head about why you should do this, it's to illustrate the point of *rehearsal:* to transfer material that you encounter into long-term memory.

MNEMONICS. This odd word (pronounced with the "m" silent–"neh MON ix") describes formal techniques used to make material more readily remembered.

Among the most common mnemonics are the following:

- **Acronyms.** *Acronyms* are words or phrases formed by the first letters of a series of terms.

  For example, Roy G. Biv helps people to remember the colors of the spectrum (red, orange, yellow, green, blue, indigo, and violet).

- **Acrostics.** *Acrostics* are sentences in which the first letters spell out something that needs to be recalled. The benefits of acrostics are similar to those of acronyms.

- **Rhymes and jingles.** "Thirty days hath September, April, June, and November." If you know the rest of the rhyme, you're familiar with one of the most commonly used mnemonic jingles in the English language.

USE OF MULTIPLE SENSES. Every time we encounter new information, all of our senses are potentially at work. Each piece of sensory information is stored in a separate location in the brain, and yet all the pieces are linked in extraordinarily intricate ways.

- **When you learn something, use your body.** Move around. Stand up; sit down. Touch the page. Trace figures with your fingers. Talk to yourself. Think out loud. By involving every part of your body, you've increased the number of potential ways to trigger a relevant memory later, when you need to recall it.

- **Draw and diagram the material.** Structuring written material by graphically grouping and connecting key ideas and themes is a powerful technique. Creating drawings, sketches, and even cartoons can help us remember better.

- **Visualize.** Visualization is effective because it helps make abstract ideas concrete; it engages multiple senses; it permits us to link different bits of information together; and it provides us with a context for storing information.

- **Overlearning.** *Overlearning* consists of studying and rehearsing material past the point of initial mastery. Through overlearning, you can recall the information without even thinking about it.

Stockbyte/Getty Images

Study for Tests Strategically

Here are some guidelines that can help you do your best on tests:

KNOW WHAT YOU ARE PREPARING FOR. To find out about an upcoming test, ask if it is a "test," an "exam," a "quiz," or something else. These names imply different things. In addition, each kind of test question requires a somewhat different style of preparation.

- **Essay questions.** The best approach to studying for an essay test involves four steps:

  1. Reread your class notes and any notes you've made on assigned readings that will be covered on the upcoming exam. Also go through the readings themselves, reviewing underlined or highlighted material and marginal notes.

Stockbyte/PunchStock

2. Think of likely exam questions. Some instructors give lists of possible essay topics; if yours does, focus on this list and think of other possibilities.

3. Answer each potential essay question–aloud. You can also write down the main points that any answer should cover.

4. After you've answered the questions, look at the notes and readings again. If you feel confident that you've answered specific questions adequately, check them off. If you had trouble with some questions, review that material immediately. Then repeat step 3, answering the questions again.

• **Multiple-choice, true–false, and matching questions.** Studying for multiple-choice, true-false, and matching questions requires attention to the details. Write down important facts on index cards: They're portable and available all the time, and the act of creating them helps drive the material into your memory.

  • **Short-answer and fill-in questions.** Short-answer and fill-in questions are similar to essays in that they require you to recall key pieces of information, but they don't demand that you integrate or compare different types of information. Consequently, the focus of your study should be on the recall of specific, detailed information.

TEST YOURSELF. When you believe you've mastered the material, test yourself on it. You can create a test for yourself, in writing, making its form as close as possible to what you expect the actual test to be.

DEAL WITH TEST ANXIETY. What does the anticipation of a test do to you? *Test anxiety* is a temporary condition characterized by fears and concerns about test-taking. You'll never eliminate test anxiety completely, nor do you want to. A little bit of nervousness can energize us, making us more attentive and vigilant.

On the other hand, for some students, anxiety can spiral into the kind of paralyzing fear that makes their minds go blank. There are several ways to keep this from happening to you:

• *Prepare thoroughly.*
• *Take a realistic view of the test.*
• *Learn relaxation techniques.*
• *Visualize success.*

FORM A STUDY GROUP. *Study groups* can be extremely powerful tools because they help accomplish several things:

• They help members organize and structure the material to approach their studying in a systematic and logical way.

• They allow students to share different perspectives on the material.

• They make it more likely that students will not overlook any potentially important information.

• They force members to rethink the course material, explaining it in words that other group members will understand. This helps both understanding and recall of the information when it is needed on the test.

• Finally, they help motivate members to do their best. When you're part of a study group, you're no longer working just for yourself; your studying also benefits the other study group members. Not wanting to let down your classmates in a study group may encourage you to put in your best effort.

Rubberball/Getty Images

Ariel Skelley/DigitalVision/Getty Images

CHAPTER 1
Introduction to Psychology

LEARNING OUTCOMES FOR CHAPTER 1

	MODULE 1
LO 1-1 What is the science of psychology?	**PSYCHOLOGISTS AT WORK**
LO 1-2 What are the major specialties in the field of psychology?	The Subfields of Psychology: Psychology's Family Tree
	Working at Psychology
LO 1-3 Where do psychologists work?	

	MODULE 2
LO 2-1 What are the origins of psychology?	**A SCIENCE EVOLVES: THE PAST, THE PRESENT, AND THE FUTURE**
LO 2-2 What are the major approaches in contemporary psychology?	The Roots of Psychology
	Today's Five Major Perspectives
	Applying Psychology in the 21st Century: Psychology Matters

	MODULE 3
LO 3-1 What are psychology's key issues and controversies?	**PSYCHOLOGY'S KEY ISSUES AND CONTROVERSIES**
	Exploring Diversity: Understanding How Culture, Ethnicity, and Race Influence Behavior
LO 3-2 What is the future of psychology likely to hold?	Psychology's Future
	Neuroscience in Your Life: Enhancing Your Mind
	Becoming an Informed Consumer of Psychology: Thinking Critically About Psychology: Distinguishing Legitimate Psychology from Pseudo-Psychology

PROLOGUE *PANDEMIC*

No one is certain how the coronavirus pandemic began. It may have originated with an infected bat or a chicken that passed the disease to a human carrier. We may never know for sure.

The coronovirus, shown here in supermagnification, produced a worldwide pandemic that led to fundamental changes in behavior of people across the globe.
Alissa Eckert, MS; Dan Higgins, MAMS/CDC

What we do know is that the pandemic affected people across the globe in profound ways. Hundreds of thousands became ill and died. In a desperate effort to stop the disease from spreading, government officials across the globe ordered people to remain in their homes, while other potentially infected people self-quarantine. Normal life ground to a halt as people were told to socially distance themselves from others. Health facilities were stretched to their breaking points.

Offices closed, and staff were told to work from home. Public schools were shut down. Colleges canceled face-to-face classes and hastily initiated online instruction.

Consumers engaged in panic buying, emptying grocery shelves of hand sanitizers and food staples. Some merchants took advantage of the demand, raising prices exponentially.

Other people, though, risked their own health, delivering food to those with the virus and tending to the needs of the sick. As some sacrificed their safety to help others, they showed the best of human nature.

LOOKING *Ahead*

From its start, the coronavirus pandemic gave rise to as many psychological issues as it did to medical concerns. For example, consider these questions addressed by psychologists:

- How could health experts and government leaders best guide people in protecting themselves from the virus without causing panic?

- How did people calculate their personal risk of contracting the virus?

- How did people form memories about the pandemic, and how will those memories impact their behavior in the future?

- What were the most effective ways to help people cope with the sudden and unexpected deaths of friends and loved ones due to the pandemic?

- How did parents and teachers explain coronavirus and the pandemic to young children?

- What explains the self-sacrifice shown by health workers and everyday people, and the self-centeredness shown by others in the face of the pandemic?

As you'll soon see, the field of psychology addresses questions like these—and many, many more. In this chapter, we begin our examination of psychology, the different types of psychologists, and the various roles that psychologists play.

Module 1
Psychologists at Work

Psychology is the scientific study of behavior and mental processes. The simplicity of this definition is in some ways deceiving, concealing ongoing debates about how broad the scope of psychology should be. Should psychologists limit themselves to the study of outward, observable behavior? Is it possible to scientifically study thinking? Should the field encompass the study of such diverse topics as physical and mental health, perception, dreaming, and motivation? Is it appropriate to focus solely on human behavior, or should the behavior of other species be included?

Most psychologists would argue that the field should be receptive to a variety of viewpoints and approaches. Consequently, the phrase *behavior and mental processes* in the definition of psychology must be understood to mean many things: It encompasses not just what people do but also their thoughts, emotions, perceptions, reasoning processes, memories, and even the biological activities that maintain bodily functioning.

Psychologists try to describe, predict, and explain human behavior and mental processes, as well as help to change and improve the lives of people and the world in which they live. They use scientific methods to find answers that are far more valid and legitimate than those resulting from intuition and speculation, which are often inaccurate (see Figure 1; Ferguson, 2015).

LEARNING OUTCOMES

LO 1-1 What is the science of psychology?

LO 1-2 What are the major specialties in the field of psychology?

LO 1-3 Where do psychologists work?

psychology The scientific study of behavior and mental processes. (Module 1)

FIGURE 1 The scientific method is the basis of all psychological research and is used to find valid answers. Test your knowledge of psychology by answering these questions.

Source: Adapted from Bensley, Alan D. & Lilienfield, Scott O. (2017). Psychological misconceptions: Recent scientific advances and unresolved issues. *Current Directions in Psychological Science*, 26(4), 377-382, and Lamal, P. A. (1979). College students' common beliefs about psychology. *Teaching of Psychology, 6*, 155–158.

Psychological Truths?

To test your knowledge of psychology, try answering the following questions:

1. Infants love their mothers primarily because their mothers fulfill their basic biological needs, such as providing food. True or false?

2. Geniuses generally have poor social adjustment. True or false?

3. The best way to ensure that a desired behavior will continue after training is completed is to reward that behavior every single time it occurs during training rather than rewarding it only periodically. True or false?

4. People with schizophrenia have at least two distinct personalities. True or false?

5. Parents should do everything they can to ensure their children have high self-esteem and a strong sense that they are highly competent. True or false?

6. Children's IQ scores have little to do with how well they do in school. True or false?

7. Frequent masturbation can lead to mental illness. True or false?

8. Once people reach old age, their leisure activities change radically. True or false?

9. Most people would refuse to give painful electric shocks to other people. True or false?

10. People who talk about suicide are unlikely to actually try to kill themselves. True or false?

Scoring: The truth about each of these items: They are all false. Based on psychological research, each of these "facts" has been proven untrue. You will learn the reasons why as we explore what psychologists have discovered about human behavior.

The Subfields of Psychology: Psychology's Family Tree

As the study of psychology has grown, it has given rise to a number of subfields (described in Figure 2). The subfields of psychology can be likened to an extended family, with assorted nieces and nephews, aunts and uncles, and cousins who, although

Subfield	Description
Behavioral genetics	*Behavioral genetics* studies the inheritance of traits related to behavior.
Behavioral neuroscience	*Behavioral neuroscience* examines the biological basis of behavior.
Clinical psychology	*Clinical psychology* deals with the study, diagnosis, and treatment of psychological disorders.
Clinical neuropsychology	*Clinical neuropsychology* unites the areas of biopsychology and clinical psychology, focusing on the relationship between biological factors and psychological disorders.
Cognitive psychology	*Cognitive psychology* focuses on the study of higher mental processes.
Counseling psychology	*Counseling psychology* focuses primarily on educational, social, and career adjustment problems.
Cross-cultural psychology	*Cross-cultural psychology* investigates the similarities and differences in psychological functioning in and across various cultures and ethnic groups.
Developmental psychology	*Developmental psychology* examines how people grow and change from the moment of conception through death.
Educational psychology	*Educational psychology* is concerned with teaching and learning processes, such as the relationship between motivation and school performance.
Environmental psychology	*Environmental psychology* considers the relationship between people and their physical environment, including climate change issues.
Evolutionary psychology	*Evolutionary psychology* considers how behavior is influenced by our genetic inheritance from our ancestors.
Experimental psychology	*Experimental psychology* studies the processes of sensing, perceiving, learning, and thinking about the world.
Forensic psychology	*Forensic psychology* focuses on legal issues, such as determining the accuracy of witness memories.
Health psychology	*Health psychology* explores the relationship between psychological factors and physical ailments or disease.
Industrial/organizational psychology	*Industrial/organizational psychology* is concerned with the psychology of the workplace.
Personality psychology	*Personality psychology* focuses on the consistency in people's behavior over time and the traits that differentiate one person from another.
Program evaluation	*Program evaluation* focuses on assessing large-scale programs, such as the Head Start preschool program, to determine whether they are effective in meeting their goals.
Psychology of women	*Psychology of women* focuses on issues such as discrimination against women and the causes of violence against women.
School psychology	*School psychology* is devoted to counseling children in elementary and secondary schools who have academic or emotional problems.
Social psychology	*Social psychology* is the study of how people's thoughts, feelings, and actions are affected by others.
Sport psychology	*Sport psychology* applies psychology to athletic activity and exercise.

FIGURE 2 The major subfields of psychology.

(Top): Spencer Grant/Science Source; (Middle): Monkey Business Images/Shutterstock; (Bottom): Don Hammond/Design Pics they may not interact on a day-to-day basis, are related to one another because they share a common goal: understanding behavior. One way to identify the key subfields is to look at some of the basic questions about behavior that they address.

WHAT ARE THE BIOLOGICAL FOUNDATIONS OF BEHAVIOR?

In the most fundamental sense, people are biological organisms. *Behavioral neuroscience* is the subfield of psychology that focuses on the ways in which the brain, the nervous system, and the other biological aspects of the body determine behavior.

Thus, neuroscientists consider how our body influences our behavior. For example, they may examine the link between specific sites in the brain and the muscular tremors of people affected by Parkinson's disease or attempt to determine how our emotions are related to physical sensations.

HOW DO PEOPLE SENSE, PERCEIVE, LEARN, AND THINK ABOUT THE WORLD?

If you have ever wondered why you are susceptible to optical illusions, how your body registers pain, or how to make the most of your study time, an experimental psychologist can answer your questions. *Experimental psychology* is the branch of psychology that studies the processes of sensing, perceiving, learning, and thinking about the world. (The term *experimental psychologist* is somewhat misleading: Psychologists in every specialty area use experimental techniques.)

Several subspecialties of experimental psychology have become specialties in their own right. One is *cognitive psychology*, which focuses on higher mental processes, including thinking, memory, reasoning, problem solving, judging, decision making, and language.

WHAT ARE THE SOURCES OF CHANGE AND STABILITY IN BEHAVIOR ACROSS THE LIFE SPAN?

A baby producing her first smile . . . taking his first step . . . saying her first word. These universal milestones in development are also singularly special and unique for each person. *Developmental psychology* studies how people grow and change from the moment of conception through death. *Personality psychology* focuses on the consistency in people's behavior across their lives, as well as the traits that differentiate one person from another.

HOW DO PSYCHOLOGICAL FACTORS AFFECT PHYSICAL AND MENTAL HEALTH?

Frequent depression, stress, and fears that prevent people from carrying out their normal activities are topics that interest a health psychologist, a clinical psychologist, and a counseling psychologist. *Health psychology* explores the relationship between psychological factors and physical ailments or disease. For example, health psychologists are interested in assessing how long-term stress (a psychological factor) can affect physical health and in identifying ways to promote behavior that brings about good health (Proyer et al., 2013; Sauter & Hurrell, 2017).

Clinical psychology deals with the study, diagnosis, and treatment of psychological disorders. Clinical psychologists are trained to diagnose and treat problems that range from the crises of everyday life, such as unhappiness over the breakup of a relationship, to more extreme conditions, such as profound, lingering depression. Some clinical psychologists also research and investigate issues that vary from identifying the early signs of psychological disturbance to studying the relationship between family communication patterns and psychological disorders.

Study Alert

The subfields of psychology allow psychologists to explain the same behavior in multiple ways. Review Figure 2 for a summary of the subfields.

PsychTech

It's now common knowledge that we cannot safely text and drive at the same time. This awareness came from the work of cognitive psychologists, who demonstrated that it is impossible to do both without a serious and potentially deadly decline in driving ability.

Like clinical psychologists, counseling psychologists deal with people's psychological problems, but the problems they deal with are more specific. *Counseling psychology* focuses primarily on educational, social, and career adjustment problems. Almost every college has a center staffed with counseling psychologists. This is where students can get advice on the kinds of jobs they might be best suited for, on methods of studying effectively, and on strategies for resolving everyday difficulties, such as problems with roommates and concerns about a specific professor's grading practices. Many large business organizations also employ counseling psychologists to help employees with work-related problems.

HOW DO OUR SOCIAL NETWORKS AFFECT BEHAVIOR?

Our complex networks of social interrelationships are the focus for many subfields of psychology. For example, *social psychology* is the study of how people's thoughts, feelings, and actions are affected by others. Social psychologists concentrate on such diverse topics as human aggression, liking and loving, persuasion, and conformity.

Cross-cultural psychology investigates the similarities and differences in psychological functioning in and across various cultures and ethnic groups. For example, cross-cultural psychologists examine how cultures differ in their use of punishment during child-rearing.

EXPANDING PSYCHOLOGY'S FRONTIERS

The boundaries of the science of psychology are constantly growing. Three newer members of the field's family tree—evolutionary psychology, behavioral genetics, and clinical neuropsychology—have sparked particular excitement, and debate, within psychology.

Evolutionary Psychology *Evolutionary psychology* considers how behavior is influenced by our genetic inheritance from our ancestors. The evolutionary approach suggests that the chemical coding of information in our cells not only determines traits such as hair color and race but also holds the key to understanding a broad variety of behaviors that helped our ancestors survive and reproduce.

Evolutionary psychology stems from Charles Darwin's arguments in his groundbreaking 1859 book, *On the Origin of Species*. Darwin suggested that a process of natural selection leads to the survival of the fittest and the development of traits that enable a species to adapt to its environment.

Evolutionary psychologists take Darwin's arguments a step further. They argue that our genetic inheritance determines not only physical traits such as skin and eye color but certain personality traits and social behaviors as well. For example, evolutionary psychologists suggest that behavior such as shyness, jealousy, and cross-cultural similarities in qualities desired in potential mates are at least partially determined by genetics, presumably because such behavior helped increase the survival rate of humans' ancient relatives (Fost, 2015; Lewis et al., 2017; Bhogal, Farrelly, & Galbraith, 2019.

Although they are increasingly popular, evolutionary explanations of behavior have stirred controversy. By suggesting that many significant behaviors unfold automatically because they are wired into the human species, evolutionary approaches minimize the role of environmental and social forces. Still, the evolutionary approach has stimulated a significant amount of research on how our biological inheritance influences our traits and behaviors (Mesoudi, 2011; Flannelly, 2017; Al-Shawaf, Lewis, & Buss, 2018).

Behavioral Genetics Another rapidly growing area in psychology focuses on the biological mechanisms, such as genes and chromosomes, that enable inherited behavior to unfold. *Behavioral genetics* seeks to understand how we might inherit certain behavioral traits and how the environment influences whether we actually display such traits (Vukasović & Bratko, 2015; Krüger, Korsten, & Hoffman, 2017).

Clinical Neuropsychology *Clinical neuropsychology* unites the areas of neuroscience and clinical psychology: It focuses on the origin of psychological disorders in biological factors. Building on advances in our understanding of the structure and chemistry of the brain, this specialty has already led to promising new treatments for psychological disorders as well as debates over the use of medication to control behavior (Boake, 2008; Holtz, 2011; Craig, 2017).

Working at Psychology

Help Wanted: Assistant professor at a small liberal arts college. Teach undergraduate courses in introductory psychology and courses in specialty areas of cognitive psychology, perception, and learning. Strong commitment to quality teaching as well as evidence of scholarship and research productivity necessary.

Help Wanted: Industrial-organizational consulting psychologist. International firm seeks psychologists for full-time career positions as consultants to management. Candidates must have the ability to establish a rapport with senior business executives and help them find innovative and practical solutions to problems concerning people and organizations.

Help Wanted: Clinical psychologist. PhD, internship experience, and license required. Comprehensive clinic seeks psychologist to work with children and adults providing individual and group therapy, psychological evaluations, crisis intervention, and development of behavior treatment plans on multidisciplinary team.

As these job ads suggest, psychologists are employed in a variety of settings. Many doctoral-level psychologists are employed by institutions of higher learning (universities and colleges) or are self-employed, usually working as private practitioners treating clients (see Figure 3). Other work sites include hospitals, clinics, mental health centers, counseling centers, government human-services organizations, businesses, schools, and even prisons. Psychologists are employed in the military, working with soldiers, veterans, and their families, and they work for the federal government Department of

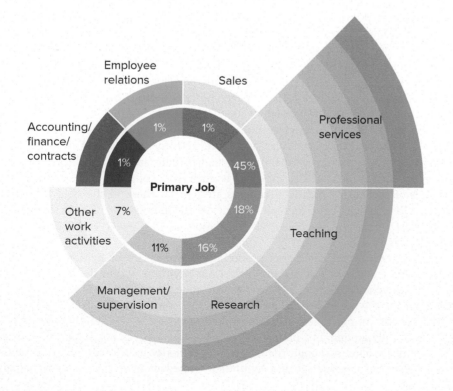

FIGURE 3 The breakdown of where U.S. psychologists (who have a PhD or PsyD) work.
Source: Stamm, K., Lin, Luona, and Cristidis, P. (2016, June). Datapoint. *Monitor on Psychology,* 12.

Homeland Security, fighting terrorism. Psychologists who specialize in program evaluation are increasingly employed by foundations that want to assess the value of programs they fund (American Psychological Association, 2016; DeAngelis & Monahan, 2008; Moscoso, Chaves, & Argilaga, 2013; Urban & Linver, 2019).

Most psychologists, though, work in academic settings, allowing them to combine the three major roles played by psychologists in society: teacher, scientist, and clinical practitioner. Many psychology professors are also actively involved in research or in serving clients. Whatever the particular job site, however, psychologists share a commitment to improving individual lives as well as society in general. In addition, whatever their specialization and subfield, psychologists tend to be happy with their work. In fact, those with doctoral degrees are more likely to report job satisfaction than doctoral degree holders in other fields (Conroy, Lin, & Christidis, 2019).

Moreover, keep in mind that professionals from a variety of occupations use the findings of psychologists. To get a glimpse into how nonpsychologists use psychology in their professions, you will find a feature titled *From the perspective of . . .* throughout the text.

From the perspective of...

An Educator Imagine that a classroom teacher wants to improve the performance of a 10-year-old boy who is not doing well in math. What branches of psychology might she draw on to get ideas about how to help him?

Andersen Ross/Blend Images/Getty Images

PSYCHOLOGISTS: A PORTRAIT

Although there is no "average" psychologist in terms of personal characteristics, we can draw a statistical portrait of the field. Nearly 200,000 active psychologists are working today in the United States, but they are outnumbered by psychologists in other countries. In fact, psychologists in the United States now make up only between 20% to 24% of the world's psychologists. Although most research is conducted in the United States, psychologists in other countries are increasingly influential in adding to the knowledge base and practices of psychology (Rees & Seaton, 2011; American Psychological Association, 2015; Takooshian et al., 2016).

In the United States, women outnumber men in the field, a big change from earlier years, when women faced bias and were actively discouraged from becoming psychologists. Today, for every male psychologist, there are 2.1 female psychologists. And looking at the educational pipeline, women will continue to outnumber men: about 75% of psychology graduate students are female. Those in the field are actively debating whether and how to seek balance in the proportion of men and women psychologists (American Psychological Association, 2018; Fowler et al., 2018; Varma, 2018; Marulanda & Radtke, 2019).

Furthermore, despite the higher proportion of women in the field, women still lag behind when it comes to salaries and high-status positions within the field. For example, female psychologists working in four-year colleges and medical schools earn, on average, 82.7% of what males make (Clay, 2017; Wiedman, 2019).

The majority of psychologists in the United States are white, limiting the diversity of the field. Only around 14% of all professionally active psychologists are members of racial minority groups. Although the numbers of minority individuals entering the field are far greater than a decade ago and continue to grow (among early career psychologists, around a third are members of racial minority groups), the numbers have not kept up with the growth of the minority population at large (American Psychological Association, 2018; Lin, Stamm, & Christidis, 2018; Frost et al., 2019).

The underrepresentation of racial and ethnic minorities among psychologists is significant for several reasons. First, the field of psychology is diminished by a lack of the diverse perspectives and talents that minority-group members can provide. Furthermore, minority group psychologists serve as role models for members of minority communities, and their underrepresentation in the profession might deter other minority-group members from entering the field. Finally, because members of minority groups often prefer to receive psychological therapy from treatment providers of their own race or ethnic group, the rarity of minority psychologists can discourage some members of minority groups from seeking treatment (Bryant et al., 2005; Stevens, 2015; Stewart et al., 2017).

Study Alert

Be sure you can differentiate between a PhD (doctor of philosophy) and a PsyD (doctor of psychology), as well as between psychologists and psychiatrists.

THE EDUCATION OF A PSYCHOLOGIST

How do people become psychologists? The most common route is a long one. Most psychologists have a doctorate, either a *PhD* (doctor of philosophy) or, less frequently, a *PsyD* (doctor of psychology). The PhD is a research degree that requires a dissertation based on an original investigation. The PsyD is obtained by psychologists who want to focus on the treatment of psychological disorders. Note that psychologists are distinct from psychiatrists, who have a medical degree and specialize in the diagnosis and treatment of psychological disorders, often using treatments that involve the prescription of drugs.

Both the PhD and the PsyD typically take 4 or 5 years of work past the bachelor's level. Some fields of psychology involve education beyond the doctorate. For instance, doctoral-level clinical psychologists, who deal with people with psychological disorders, typically spend an additional year doing an internship.

About a third of people working in the field of psychology have a master's degree as their highest degree, which they earn after 2 or 3 years of graduate work. These psychologists teach, provide therapy, conduct research, or work in specialized programs dealing with drug abuse or crisis intervention. Some work in universities, government, and business, collecting and analyzing data.

CAREERS FOR PSYCHOLOGY MAJORS

Although some psychology majors head for graduate school in psychology or an unrelated field, the majority join the workforce immediately after graduation. Most report that the jobs they take after graduation are related to their psychology background.

An undergraduate major in psychology provides excellent preparation for a variety of occupations. Because undergraduates who specialize in psychology develop good analytical skills, are trained to think critically, and are able to synthesize and evaluate information well, employers in business, industry, and the government value their preparation (American Psychological Association, 2011; Geher, 2019).

According to the American Psychological Association, undergraduate psychology programs should instruct students in five domains: (1) the key content of psychology, (2) critical thinking and an understanding of the scientific method, (3) ethical and social responsibility, (4) strong communication skills, and (5) opportunities for professional development. Notably, each of these domains is essential to a career in virtually any field (American Psychological Association, 2013).

The most common areas of employment for psychology majors are in the social services, including working as administrators, serving as a counselors, and providing direct care. Some 20% of recipients of bachelor's degrees in psychology work in the social services or in some other form of public affairs. In addition, psychology majors often enter the fields of education or business or work for federal, state, and local governments (see Figure 4; Murray, 2002; Rajecki & Borden, 2011; Sternberg, 2017).

FIGURE 4 Although many psychology majors pursue employment in social services, a background in psychology can prepare one for many professions outside the social services field. What is it about the science and art of psychology that make it such a versatile field?

Source: Adapted from Kuther, T. L. (2003). *Your career in psychology: Psychology and the law.* New York: Wadsworth and Landrum; R. E. (2018). *What can you do with a bachelor's degree in psychology? Like this title, the actual answer is complicated.* Psychology Student Network. Washington, DC: American Psychological Association; and Geher, G. (2019). *Own your psychology major!* Washington, DC: American Psychological Association.

Positions Obtained by Psychology Majors		
Business Field	**Education/ Academic Field**	**Social Field**
• Administrative assistant	• Administration	• Activities coordinator
• Advertising trainee	• Child-care provider	• Behavioral specialist
• Affirmative action officer	• Child-care worker/ supervisor	• Career counselor
• Benefits manager	• Data management	• Case worker
• Claims specialist	• Laboratory assistant	• Child protection worker
• Community relations officer	• Parent/family education	• Clinical coordinator
• Customer relations	• Preschool teacher	• Community outreach worker
• Data management	• Public opinion surveyor	• Corrections officer
• Employee counselor	• Research assistant	• Counselor assistant
• Employee recruitment	• Teaching assistant	• Crisis intervention counselor
• Human resources coordinator/manager/ specialist		• Employment counselor
• Labor relations manager/ specialist		• Group home attendant
• Loan officer		• Mental health assistant
• Management trainee		• Occupational therapist
• Marketing		• Probation officer
• Personnel manager/ officer		• Program manager
• Product and services research		• Rehabilitation counselor
• Programs/events coordination		• Residence counselor
• Public relations		• Social service assistant
• Retail sales management		• Social worker
• Sales representative		• Substance abuse counselor
• Special features writing/ reporting		• Youth counselor
• Staff training and development		
• Trainer/training office		

RECAP/EVALUATE/RETHINK

RECAP

LO 1-1 What is the science of psychology?

- Psychology is the scientific study of behavior and mental processes, encompassing not just what people do but also their biological activities, feelings, perceptions, memory, reasoning, and thoughts.

LO 1-2 What are the major specialties in the field of psychology?

- Behavioral neuroscientists focus on the biological basis of behavior, and experimental psychologists study the processes of sensing, perceiving, learning, and thinking about the world.
- Cognitive psychology, an outgrowth of experimental psychology, studies higher mental processes, including memory, knowing, thinking, reasoning, problem solving, judging, decision making, and language.
- Developmental psychologists study how people grow and change throughout the life span.
- Personality psychologists consider the consistency and change in an individual's behavior, as well as the individual differences that distinguish one person's behavior from another's.

- Health psychologists study psychological factors that affect physical disease, whereas clinical psychologists consider the study, diagnosis, and treatment of abnormal behavior. Counseling psychologists focus on educational, social, and career adjustment problems.
- Social psychology is the study of how people's thoughts, feelings, and actions are affected by others.
- Cross-cultural psychology examines the similarities and differences in psychological functioning among various cultures.

- Other increasingly important fields are evolutionary psychology, behavioral genetics, and clinical neuropsychology.

LO 1-3 Where do psychologists work?

- Psychologists are employed in a variety of settings. Although the primary sites of employment are private practice and colleges, many psychologists are found in hospitals, clinics, community mental health centers, and counseling centers.

EVALUATE

Match each subfield of psychology with the issues or questions posed below.

a. behavioral neuroscience
b. experimental psychology
c. cognitive psychology
d. developmental psychology
e. personality psychology
f. health psychology
g. clinical psychology
h. counseling psychology
i. educational psychology
j. school psychology
k. social psychology
l. industrial psychology

1. Joan, a college freshman, is worried about her grades. She needs to learn better organizational skills and study habits to cope with the demands of college.
2. At what age do children generally begin to acquire an emotional attachment to their fathers?
3. It is thought that pornographic films that depict violence against women may prompt aggressive behavior in some men.
4. What chemicals are released in the human body as a result of a stressful event? What are their effects on behavior?
5. Luis is unique in his manner of responding to crisis situations, with an even temperament and a positive outlook.
6. The teachers of 8-year-old Jack are concerned that he has recently begun to withdraw socially and to show little interest in schoolwork.
7. Janetta's job is demanding and stressful. She wonders if her lifestyle is making her more prone to certain illnesses, such as cancer and heart disease.
8. A psychologist is intrigued by the fact that some people are much more sensitive to painful stimuli than others are.
9. A strong fear of crowds leads a young man to seek treatment for his problem.
10. What mental strategies are involved in solving complex word problems?
11. What teaching methods most effectively motivate elementary school students to successfully accomplish academic tasks?
12. Jessica is asked to develop a management strategy that will encourage safer work practices in an assembly plant.

RETHINK

Do you think intuition and common sense are sufficient for understanding why people act the way they do? In what ways is a scientific approach appropriate for studying human behavior?

Answers to Evaluate Questions

a-4; b-8; c-10; d-2; e-5; f-7; g-9; h-1; i-11; j-6; k-3; l-12

KEY TERM

psychology

Module 2
A Science Evolves: The Past, the Present, and the Future

LEARNING OUTCOMES

LO 2-1 What are the origins of psychology?

LO 2-2 What are the major approaches in contemporary psychology?

Seven thousand years ago, people assumed that psychological problems were caused by evil spirits. To allow those spirits to escape from a person's body, ancient healers chipped a hole in a patient's skull with crude instruments—a procedure called *trephining*.

According to the 17th-century French philosopher René Descartes, nerves were hollow tubes through which "animal spirits" conducted impulses in the same way that water is transmitted through a pipe. When a person put a finger too close to a fire, heat was transmitted to the brain through the tubes.

Franz Josef Gall, an 18th-century physician, argued that a trained observer could discern intelligence, moral character, and other basic personality characteristics from the shape and number of bumps on a person's skull. His theory gave rise to the field of phrenology, employed by hundreds of practitioners in the 19th century.

Although these explanations might sound far-fetched, in their own times they represented the most advanced thinking about what might be called the psychology of the era. Our understanding of behavior has progressed tremendously since the 18th century, but most of the advances have been recent. As sciences go, psychology is one of the new kids on the block. (For highlights in the development of the field, see Figure 1.)

FIGURE 1 This time line illustrates major milestones in the development of psychology.

(Descartes): Everett - Art/Shutterstock; (Locke): National Gallery of Art; (James): Paul Thompson/FPG/Getty Images; (Pavlov): Bettmann/Getty Images; (Calkins): The Schlesinger Library, Radcliffe Institute, Harvard University; (Watson): George Rinhart/Corbis/Getty Images; (Maslow and Piaget): Bettmann/Getty Images; (Loftus): ©Elizabeth Loftus

The Roots of Psychology

We can trace psychology's roots back to the ancient Greeks, who considered the mind to be a suitable topic for scholarly contemplation. Later philosophers argued for hundreds of years about some of the questions psychologists grapple with today. For example, the 17th-century British philosopher John Locke believed that children were born into the world with minds like "blank slates" (*tabula rasa* in Latin) and that their experiences determined what kind of adults they would become. His views contrasted with those of Plato and Descartes, who argued that some knowledge was inborn in humans.

However, the formal beginning of psychology as a scientific discipline is generally considered to be in the late 19th century, when Wilhelm Wundt established the first experimental laboratory devoted to psychological phenomena in Leipzig, Germany. At about the same time, William James was setting up his laboratory in Cambridge, Massachusetts.

When Wundt set up his laboratory in 1879, his goal was to study the structures of the mind and their relationship to conscious experience—an approach he called structuralism. **Structuralism** focused on uncovering the fundamental mental components of perception, consciousness, thinking, emotions, and other kinds of mental states and activities.

To determine how basic sensory processes shape our understanding of the world, Wundt and other structuralists used a method called introspection. **Introspection** is a procedure in which people are presented with a stimulus such as an image or a sentence—and asked to describe, in their own words and in as much detail as they can, what they were experiencing. Wundt argued that by analyzing people's reports, psychologists could come to a better understanding of the structure of the mind.

Over time, psychologists challenged Wundt's approach. They became increasingly dissatisfied with the assumption that introspection could reveal the structure of the mind. Introspection was not a truly scientific technique because there were few ways an outside

Structuralism focuses on uncovering the fundamental mental components of consciousness, thinking, and other mental states and activities.
Wayhome Studio/Shutterstock

structuralism Wundt's approach, which focuses on understanding the fundamental mental components of consciousness, thinking, and other kinds of mental states and activities. (Module 2)

introspection A procedure used to study the structure of the mind in which a person is asked to describe in detail what they are experiencing when they are exposed to a stimulus. (Module 2)

1924 John B. Watson, an early behaviorist, publishes *Behaviorism*

1928 Leta Stetter Hollingworth publishes work on adolescence

1951 Carl Rogers publishes *Client-Centered Therapy*, helping to establish the humanistic perspective

1953 B. F. Skinner publishes *Science and Human Behavior*, advocating the behavioral perspective

1954 Abraham Maslow publishes *Motivation and Personality*, developing the concept of self-actualization

1957 Leon Festinger publishes *A Theory of Cognitive Dissonance*, producing a major impact on social psychology

1969 Arguments regarding the genetic basis of IQ fuel lingering controversies

1980 Jean Piaget, an influential developmental psychologist, dies

1981 David Hubel and Torsten Wiesel win Nobel Prize for work on vision cells in the brain

1985 Increasing emphasis on cognitive perspective

2000 Elizabeth Loftus does pioneering work on false memory and eyewitness testimony

2020 Subfields such as clinical neuropsychology, environmental psychology, and health psychology develop

Modern Psychology

2000

How do people make choices from an array of possibilities? Introspection sought to determine how individuals could analyze and articulate their internal thought processes when they were making a decision.
Obradovic/E+/Getty Images

observer could confirm the accuracy of others' introspections. Moreover, people had difficulty describing some kinds of inner experiences, such as emotional responses. Those drawbacks led to the development of new approaches, which largely replaced structuralism.

The perspective that replaced structuralism is known as functionalism. Rather than focusing on the mind's structure, **functionalism** concentrated on what the mind *does* and how behavior *functions*. Functionalists, whose perspective became prominent in the early 1900s, asked what role behavior plays in allowing people to adapt to their environments. For example, a functionalist might examine the function of the emotion of fear in preparing us to deal with emergency situations.

William James, an American psychologist, led the functionalist movement. Functionalists examined how people satisfy their needs through their behavior and focused on the purpose of thinking, unlike the structuralists, who were more interested in the structure of the brain. The functionalists also considered how the flexibility of the mind allowed people to continually change their thinking as they interacted with a complex world, something the functionalists discussed as the "stream of consciousness" of the mind The American educator John Dewey drew on functionalism to develop the field of school psychology, proposing ways to best meet students' educational needs.

Another important reaction to structuralism was the development of Gestalt psychology in the early 1900s. **Gestalt psychology** emphasizes how perception is organized. Instead of considering the individual parts that make up thinking, Gestalt psychologists took the opposite tack, studying how people consider individual elements together as units or wholes. Led by German scientists such as Hermann Ebbinghaus and Max Wertheimer, Gestalt psychologists proposed that "The whole is different from the sum of its parts," meaning that our perception, or understanding, of objects is greater and more meaningful than the individual elements that make up our perceptions. Gestalt psychologists have made substantial contributions to our understanding of perception.

functionalism An early approach to psychology that concentrated on what the mind does–the functions of mental activity–and the role of behavior in allowing people to adapt to their environments. (Module 2)

Gestalt psychology An approach to psychology that focuses on the organization of perception and thinking in a "whole" sense rather than on the individual elements of perception. (Module 2)

Study Alert
Knowing the basic outlines of the history of the field will help you understand how today's major perspectives have evolved.

WOMEN IN PSYCHOLOGY: FOUNDING MOTHERS

As in many scientific fields, social prejudices hindered women's participation in the early development of psychology. For example, many universities would not admit women to their graduate psychology programs in the early 1900s.

Despite the hurdles they faced, women made notable contributions to psychology, although their impact on the field was largely overlooked until recently. For example, Margaret Floy Washburn (1871–1939) was the first woman to receive a doctorate in psychology, and she did important work on animal behavior. Leta Stetter Hollingworth (1886–1939) was one of the first psychologists to focus on child development and on women's issues. She collected data to refute the view, popular in the early 1900s, that women's abilities periodically declined during parts of the menstrual cycle (Hollingworth, 1943/1990; Denmark & Fernandez, 1993; Furumoto & Scarborough, 2002).

Mary Calkins (1863–1930), who studied memory in the early part of the 20th century, became the first female president of the American Psychological Association. Karen Horney (pronounced "HORN-eye") (1885–1952) focused on the social and cultural factors behind personality; she also was the founder of the *American Journal of Psychoanalysis*. June Etta Downey (1875–1932) spearheaded the study of personality traits and became the first woman to head a psychology department at a state university. Anna Freud (1895–1982), the daughter of Sigmund Freud, also made notable contributions to the treatment of abnormal behavior, and Mamie Phipps Clark (1917–1983) carried out pioneering work on how children of color grew to recognize racial differences (Lal, 2002; Galdi, 2015).

Today's Five Major Perspectives

The men and women who laid the foundations of psychology shared a common goal: to explain and understand behavior using scientific methods. Seeking to achieve the same goal, the tens of thousands of psychologists who followed those early pioneers embraced—and often rejected—a variety of broad perspectives.

The perspectives of psychology offer distinct outlooks and emphasize different factors. Just as we can use more than one map to find our way around a particular region—for instance, a map that shows roads and highways and another map that shows major landmarks psychologists developed a variety of approaches to understanding behavior. When considered jointly, the different perspectives provide the means to explain behavior in its amazing variety.

Today, the field of psychology includes five major perspectives (summarized in Figure 2). These broad perspectives emphasize different aspects of behavior and mental processes, and each takes our understanding of behavior in a somewhat different direction.

Study Alert
Use Figure 2 to differentiate the five perspectives, which are important, because they provide a foundation for every topic covered throughout the text.

Neuroscience
Views behavior from the perspective of biological functioning

Behavioral
Focuses on observable behavior

Psychodynamic
Believes behavior is motivated by inner, unconscious forces over which a person has little control

Cognitive
Examines how people understand and think about the world

Humanistic
Contends that people can control their behavior and that they naturally try to reach their full potential

FIGURE 2 The major perspectives of psychology.
(Neuroscience): Alfred Pasieka/Science Photo Library/Alamy Stock Photo; (Cognitive): David Sanger/The Image Bank/Getty Images; (Behavioral): Ariel Skelley/Blend Images; (Humanistic): White Packert/The Image Bank/Getty Images; (Psychodynamic): Athanasia Nomikou/Shutterstock

THE NEUROSCIENCE PERSPECTIVE: BLOOD, SWEAT, AND FEARS

neuroscience perspective The approach that views behavior from the perspective of the brain, the nervous system, and other biological functions. (Module 2)

When we get down to the basics, humans are animals made of skin and bones. The **neuroscience perspective** considers how people and nonhumans function biologically: how individual nerve cells are joined together, how the inheritance of certain characteristics from parents and other ancestors influences behavior, how the functioning of the body affects hopes and fears, which behaviors are instinctual, and so forth. Even more complex kinds of behaviors, such as a baby's response to strangers, are viewed as having critical biological components by psychologists who embrace the neuroscience perspective. This perspective includes the study of heredity and evolution, which considers how heredity may influence behavior; and behavioral neuroscience, which examines how the brain and the nervous system affect behavior.

Because every behavior ultimately can be broken down into its biological components, the neuroscience perspective has broad appeal. Psychologists who subscribe to this perspective have made major contributions to the understanding and betterment of human life, ranging from cures for certain types of deafness to drug treatments for people with severe mental disorders. Furthermore, advances in methods for examining the anatomy and functioning of the brain have permitted the neuroscientific perspective to extend its influence across a broad range of subfields in psychology. (We'll see examples of these methods throughout this book in the feature titled *Neuroscience in Your Life.*)

NEUROSCIENCE IN YOUR LIFE: ENHANCING YOUR MIND

Neuroscientists have strived to understand how the normal brain works, as well as what happens to it following injury or disease. Recently, they have begun to use technologies to enhance people's typical existing abilities. For example, researchers are exploring how repetitive transcranial magnetic stimulation (TMS), a form of noninvasive brain stimulation, can enhance cognitive abilities. In one study, researchers used repetitive TMS to stimulate the hippocampus, a brain region involved in memory (see the image below of the area targeted for stimulation). Stimulation over the course of a week led to increased brain connectivity and improved memory (Wang et al., 2014; Yang et al., 2019).

MRI-guided stimulation delivery

THE PSYCHODYNAMIC PERSPECTIVE: UNDERSTANDING THE INNER PERSON

psychodynamic perspective The approach based on the view that behavior is motivated by unconscious inner forces over which the individual has little control. (Module 2)

To many people who have never taken a psychology course, psychology begins and ends with the psychodynamic perspective. Proponents of the **psychodynamic perspective** argue that behavior is motivated by inner forces and conflicts about which we have little awareness or control. They view dreams and slips of the tongue as indications of what a person is truly feeling within a seething cauldron of unconscious psychic activity.

The origins of the psychodynamic view are linked to one person: Sigmund Freud. Freud was an Austrian physician in the early 1900s whose ideas about unconscious determinants of behavior had a revolutionary effect on 20th-century thinking, not just in psychology but in related fields as well. Although some of the original Freudian principles have been roundly criticized, the contemporary psychodynamic perspective has provided a means not only to understand and treat some kinds of psychological disorders but also to understand everyday phenomena such as prejudice and aggression.

THE BEHAVIORAL PERSPECTIVE: OBSERVING THE OUTER PERSON

Whereas the neuroscience and psychodynamic approaches look at what is inside people to determine the causes of their behavior, the behavioral perspective takes a different approach. Proponents of the behavioral perspective rejected psychology's early emphasis on the internal workings of the mind and brain. Instead, the **behavioral perspective** suggests that the focus should be on external behavior that can be directly observed and measured objectively.

John B. Watson was the first major American psychologist to use a behavioral approach. Working in the 1920s, Watson believed that one could gain a complete understanding of behavior by studying the environment in which a person operated.

In fact, Watson believed rather optimistically that it was possible to bring about any desired type of behavior by controlling a person's environment. This philosophy is clear in his own words: "Give me a dozen healthy infants, well-formed, and my own specified world to bring them up in and I'll guarantee to take any one at random and train him to become any type of specialist I might select—doctor, lawyer, artist, merchant-chief, and yes, even beggar-man and thief, regardless of his talents, penchants, tendencies, abilities, vocations and race of his ancestors" (Watson, 1924).

The behavioral perspective was championed by B. F. Skinner, a pioneer in the field. Much of our understanding of how people learn new behaviors is based on the behavioral perspective. As we will see, the behavioral perspective crops up along every byway of psychology. Along with its influence in the area of learning processes, this perspective has made contributions in such diverse areas as treating mental disorders, curbing aggression, resolving sexual problems, and ending drug addiction (Schlinger, 2011; Ruiz, 2015; Fryling, 2017).

THE COGNITIVE PERSPECTIVE: IDENTIFYING THE ROOTS OF UNDERSTANDING

Efforts to understand behavior lead some psychologists straight into the mind. Evolving in part from structuralism and in part as a reaction to behaviorism, which focused so heavily on observable behavior and the environment, the **cognitive perspective** focuses on how people think, understand, and know about the world. The emphasis is on learning how people comprehend and represent the outside world within themselves and how our ways of thinking about the world influence our behavior.

Many psychologists who adhere to the cognitive perspective compare human thinking to the workings of a computer, which takes in information and transforms, stores, and retrieves it. In their view, thinking is *information processing*.

Psychologists who rely on the cognitive perspective ask questions on subjects ranging from how people make decisions to whether a person can watch television and study at the same time. The common elements that link cognitive approaches are an emphasis on how people understand and think about the world and an interest in describing the patterns and irregularities in the operation of our minds.

Sigmund Freud
Ingram Publishing

behavioral perspective The approach that suggests that observable, external behavior, which can be objectively measured and observed, should be the focus of study. (Module 2)

cognitive perspective The approach that focuses on how people think, understand, and know about the world. (Module 2)

From the perspective of...

A Health-Care Provider How can a basic understanding of psychology improve your job performance in the health-care industry?

Tetra Images/Getty Images

THE HUMANISTIC PERSPECTIVE: THE UNIQUE QUALITIES OF THE HUMAN SPECIES

humanistic perspective The approach that suggests that all individuals naturally strive to grow, develop, and be in control of their lives and behavior. (Module 2)

The **humanistic perspective** rejects the view that behavior is determined largely by automatically unfolding biological forces, unconscious processes, or the external world around us. Instead, the humanistic perspective suggests that all individuals naturally strive to grow, develop, and be in control of their lives and behavior. Humanistic psychologists maintain that each of us has the capacity to seek and reach fulfillment.

According to Carl Rogers and Abraham Maslow, who were central figures in the development of the humanistic perspective, people actively strive to reach their full potential. The emphasis of the humanistic perspective is on *free will*, the ability to freely make decisions about one's own behavior and life. The notion of free will stands in contrast to *determinism*, which sees behavior as caused, or determined, by things beyond a person's control.

The humanistic perspective assumes that people have the ability to make their own choices about their behavior rather than relying on societal standards. More than any other approach, it stresses the role of psychology in enriching people's lives and helping them achieve self-fulfillment. By reminding psychologists of their commitment to the individual person in society, the humanistic perspective has been an important influence (Nichols, 2011; Linley, 2013; Hayes, 2015; DeRobertis & Bland, 2019).

Don't let the abstract qualities of the broad approaches we have discussed lull you into thinking that they are purely theoretical: These perspectives underlie ongoing work of a practical nature, as we discuss throughout this book. To start seeing how psychology can improve everyday life, read *Applying Psychology in the 21st Century.*

APPLYING PSYCHOLOGY IN THE 21ST CENTURY

PSYCHOLOGY MATTERS

"Investigators search for clues at site of suicide bombing."

"Eyewitness to killing proves unable to provide reliable clues."

"Social media like Facebook, Twitter, Snapchat, and Instagram change how people interact with others."

"Black suspect in robbery dies after scuffle with police."

"A group of young Americans sue federal government for failing to limit climate change, thereby depriving them of a climate system capable of sustaining human life."

A quick review of any day's news headlines reminds us that the world is beset by a variety of stubborn problems that resist easy solutions. At the same time, a considerable number of psychologists are devoting their energies and expertise to addressing these problems and improving the human condition. Let's consider some of the ways in which psychology has addressed and helped

Concerns about climate change have led to a surge of interest in environmental psychology.
Design Pics/PunchStock

work toward solutions of major societal problems:

- *What are the causes of terrorism?* What motivates suicide bombers? Are they psychologically disordered, or can their behavior be seen as a rational response to a particular system of beliefs? As we'll see when we discuss psychological disorders, psychologists are gaining an understanding of the factors that lead people to embrace suicide and to engage in terrorism to further a cause in which they deeply believe (Post, 2015; Theriault, Krause, & Young, 2017; Choma et al., 2018)

- *How are social media changing the way we live?* Social networking media such as Facebook and Twitter have changed the way people communicate and the way news spreads around the world. How do social media affect the way people relate to each other? How do they affect our perceptions of world events? Psychologists are examining the motivations behind social networking, its influence on individuals and social institutions, and possible beneficial applications of the technology (Kosinski et al., 2015; Young et al., 2017; Zyoud et al., 2018; Parent, Gobble, & Rochlen, 2019).

- *How is information about climate change affecting the way people interact with the environment?* Psychologists are applying their knowledge and skills to addressing environmental issues. How can we encourage behavior that will benefit rather than harm the environment? How do people learn and understand the causes of climate change? How do changes in temperature affect people's lives and psychological health? Work by psychologists will increasingly influence

these vital questions (Abeles et al., 2019; Xiang et al., 2019).

- *Why do eyewitnesses to crimes often remember the events inaccurately, and how can we increase the precision of eyewitness accounts?* Psychologists' research has come to an important conclusion: Eyewitness testimony in criminal cases is often inaccurate and biased. Memories of crimes are often clouded by emotion, and the questions asked by police investigators often elicit inaccurate responses. Work by psychologists has been used to provide national guidelines for obtaining more accurate memories during criminal investigations (Beaudry et al., 2015; Wixted et al., 2015; Kassin et al., 2018).

- *Has the use of smartphones changed the social behavior of young people?* Today's young adults are the first generation to grow up with smartphone technology, which allows them to interact with the world from the confines of their bedroom. Psychologists have turned their attention to determining whether this pervasive connectivity affects adolescents' social relationships, their mental health, and their general preparedness for the challenges of work and adulthood (Twenge, Martin, & Campbell, 2018; Twenge et al., 2019).

- *What are the roots of racism in the United States?* Psychologists have discovered

that even subtle forms of prejudice and discrimination can cause significant harm in recipients. Furthermore, they have learned that people who sincerely believe themselves to not be racist still harbor unconscious racist thoughts that can translate into discriminatory behavior. On the positive side, they are developing strategies that break down racial barriers and heal the hurt and stigma of decades of racism (Fisher et al., 2017; Mason et al., 2017; David & Derthick, 2018).

- *What gives people satisfaction with life and a sense of well being?* Research has found that during difficult economic times, it's important to understand that wealth and possessions don't make people happy. Instead, happiness comes from enjoying life's little moments and finding purpose and meaning in what you do (Pavot & Diener, 2013; Crespo & Mesurado, 2015; Jin & Kim, 2017; Etxeberria, Extebarria, & Urdaneta, 2019).

These topics represent just a few of the issues that psychologists address daily. To further explore the many ways that psychology has an impact on everyday life, check out the American Psychological Association (APA) website, which features psychological applications in everyday life, at www.apa.org.

RETHINK

- What do *you* think are the major problems affecting society today?
- What are the psychological issues involved in these problems, and how might psychologists help find solutions to them?

RECAP/EVALUATE/RETHINK

RECAP

LO 2-1 What are the origins of psychology?

- Wilhelm Wundt laid the foundation of psychology in 1879, when he opened his laboratory in Germany.
- Early perspectives that guided the work of psychologists were structuralism (led by Wilhelm Wundt), functionalism (led by William James), and Gestalt theory.

LO 2-2 What are the major approaches in contemporary psychology?

- The neuroscience approach focuses on the biological components of the behavior of people and animals.
- The psychodynamic perspective suggests that powerful, unconscious inner forces and conflicts about which people have little or no awareness are the primary determinants of behavior.

- The behavioral perspective deemphasizes internal processes and concentrates instead on observable, measurable behavior, suggesting that understanding and control of a person's environment are sufficient to fully explain and modify behavior.
- Cognitive approaches to behavior consider how people know, understand, and think about the world.
- The humanistic perspective emphasizes that people are uniquely inclined toward psychological growth and higher levels of functioning and that they will strive to reach their full potential.

EVALUATE

1. Wundt described psychology as the study of conscious experience, a perspective he called _____.
2. Early psychologists studied the mind by asking people to describe what they were experiencing when exposed to various stimuli. This procedure was known as _____.
3. The statement "In order to study human behavior, we must consider the whole of perception rather than its component parts" might be made by a person subscribing to which perspective of psychology?
4. Jeanne's therapist asks her to recount a violent dream she recently experienced in order to gain insight into the unconscious forces affecting her behavior. Jeanne's therapist is working from a _____ perspective.

5. "It is behavior that can be observed that should be studied, not the suspected inner workings of the mind." This statement was most likely made by someone with which perspective?
   a. cognitive perspective
   b. neuroscience perspective
   c. humanistic perspective
   d. behavioral perspective
6. "My therapist is wonderful! He always points out my positive traits. He dwells on my uniqueness and strength as an individual. I feel much more confident about myself—as if I'm really growing and reaching my potential." The therapist being described most likely follows a _____ perspective.

RETHINK

Focusing on one of the five major perspectives in use today (that is, neuroscience, psychodynamic, behavioral, cognitive, and humanistic), can you describe the kinds of research questions and studies that researchers using that perspective might pursue?

Answers to Evaluate Questions

1. structuralism; 2. introspection; 3. Gestalt; 4. psychodynamic; 5. d; 6. humanistic.

Module 3
Psychology's Key Issues and Controversies

As you consider the many topics and perspectives that make up psychology, ranging from a narrow focus on minute biochemical influences on behavior to a broad focus on social behaviors, you might find yourself thinking that the discipline lacks cohesion. However, the field is more unified than a first glimpse might suggest. For one thing, no matter what topical area a psychologist specializes in, he or she will rely primarily on one of the five major perspectives. For example, a developmental psychologist who specializes in the study of children could make use of the cognitive perspective or the psychodynamic perspective or any of the other major perspectives.

Psychologists also agree on what the key issues of the field are (see Figure 1). Although there are major arguments regarding how best to address and resolve the key issues, psychology is a unified science because psychologists of all perspectives agree that the issues must be addressed if the field is going to advance. As you contemplate these key issues, try not to think of them in "either/or" terms. Instead, consider the opposing viewpoints on each issue as the opposite ends of a continuum, with the positions of individual psychologists typically falling somewhere between the two ends.

Issue 1: *Nature (heredity) versus nurture (environment)* is one of the major issues that psychologists address in trying to determine the causes of behavior. How much of people's behavior is due to their genetically determined nature (heredity), and how much is due to nurture, the influences of the physical and social environment in which a child is raised? Furthermore, what is the interplay between heredity and environment? These questions have deep philosophical and historical roots, and they are involved in many topics in psychology

Issue	Neuroscience	Cognitive	Behavioral	Humanistic	Psychodynamic
Nature (heredity) vs. nurture (environment)	Nature (heredity)	Both	Nurture (environment)	Nurture (environment)	Nature (heredity)
Conscious vs. unconscious determinants of behavior	Unconscious	Both	Conscious	Conscious	Unconscious
Observable behavior vs. internal mental processes	Internal emphasis	Internal emphasis	Observable emphasis	Internal emphasis	Internal emphasis
Free will vs. determinism	Determinism	Free will	Determinism	Free will	Determinism
Individual differences vs. universal principles	Universal emphasis	Individual emphasis	Both	Individual emphasis	Universal emphasis

FIGURE 1 Key issues in psychology and the positions taken by psychologists subscribing to the five major perspectives of psychology.
(Neuroscience): Alfred Pasieka/Science Photo Library/Alamy Stock Photo; (Cognitive): David Sanger/The Image Bank/Getty Images; (Behavioral): Ariel Skelley/Blend Images; (Humanistic): White Packert/The Image Bank/Getty Images; (Psychodynamic): Athanasia Nomikou/Shutterstock

A psychologist's take on this issue depends partly on which major perspective he or she subscribes to. For example, developmental psychologists whose focus is on how people grow and change throughout the course of their lives may be most interested in learning more about hereditary influences if they follow a neuroscience perspective. In contrast, developmental psychologists who are proponents of the behavioral perspective are more likely to focus on environment (Rutter, 2002; Moffitt, Caspi, & Rutter, 2006; Barrett, 2011).

However, every psychologist would agree that neither nature nor nurture alone is the sole determinant of behavior; rather, it is a combination of the two. In a sense, then, the real controversy involves how much of our behavior is caused by heredity and how much is caused by environmental influences.

Issue 2: Conscious versus unconscious causes of behavior. How much of our behavior is produced by forces of which we are fully aware, and how much is due to unconscious activity–mental processes that are not accessible to the conscious mind? This question represents one of the great controversies in the field of psychology. For example, clinical psychologists adopting a psychodynamic perspective argue that psychological disorders are brought about by unconscious factors, whereas psychologists employing the cognitive perspective suggest that psychological disorders largely are the result of faulty thinking processes.

Issue 3: Observable behavior versus internal mental processes. Should psychology concentrate solely on behavior that can be seen by outside observers, or should it focus on unseen thinking processes? Some psychologists, particularly those relying on the behavioral perspective, contend that the only legitimate source of information for psychologists is behavior that can be observed directly. Other psychologists, building on the cognitive perspective, argue that what goes on inside a person's mind is critical to understanding behavior, and so we must concern ourselves with mental processes.

Issue 4: Free will versus determinism. How much of our behavior is a matter of **free will** (choices made freely by an individual), and how much is subject to **determinism,** the notion that behavior is largely produced by factors beyond people's willful control? An issue long debated by philosophers, the free-will/determinism argument is also central to the field of psychology (Goto et al., 2015; Moynihan, Igou, & van Tilburg, 2017; Allakhverdov, 2019).

free will The idea that behavior is caused primarily by choices that are made freely by the individual. (Module 3)

determinism The idea that people's behavior is produced primarily by factors outside of their willful control. (Module 3)

For example, some psychologists who specialize in psychological disorders argue that people make intentional choices and that those who display so-called abnormal behavior should be considered responsible for their actions. Other psychologists disagree and contend that such individuals are the victims of forces beyond their control. The position psychologists take on this issue has important implications for the way they treat psychological disorders, especially in deciding whether treatment should be forced on people who don't want it.

Issue 5: Individual differences versus universal principles. Specifically, how much of behavior is due to the unique and special qualities of each person–the *individual differences* that characterize them–compared with how much stems from the culture and society in which people live, reflecting universal principles that underlie the behavior of all humans?

Psychologists who rely on the neuroscience perspective tend to look for universal principles of behavior, such as how the nervous system operates or the way certain hormones automatically prime us for sexual activity. Such psychologists concentrate on the similarities in our behavioral destinies despite vast differences in our upbringing. In contrast, psychologists who employ the humanistic perspective focus more on the uniqueness of every individual. They consider every person's behavior a reflection of distinct and special individual qualities.

The question of the degree to which psychologists can identify universal principles that apply to all people has taken on new significance in light of the tremendous demographic changes now occurring in the United States and around the world. As we discuss next, these changes raise new and critical issues for the discipline of psychology in the 21st century.

Exploring Diversity

Understanding How Culture, Ethnicity, and Race Influence Behavior

A mother in Burr Ridge, Illinois, helps her son with his math assignment. After he complains that he is "terrible at math," she tries to cheer him up by saying, "Don't feel bad; some people are born to do well in math, and others have a lot of trouble with it. It's just the way things are."

At the same time, on the other side of the world in Taipei, Taiwan, a mother is helping her daughter with her math homework. When the daughter complains that she's no good at math, the mother tells her to keep at it because everyone has pretty much the same ability in math and it is hard work that guarantees success.

These two apparently simple parent-child exchanges reveal a deep difference in perspectives on the world. People in North America and Europe are far more likely to attribute success to what they see as stable, unchanging causes, such as a person's intelligence. In contrast, people in Asia are more likely to attribute school performance to temporary, situational factors, such as the amount of expended effort.

These different perspectives may help explain the fact that Asian students often outperform U.S. students in international comparisons of student achievement. Asian students are taught that hard work and increased effort lead to academic success, and so they may be more willing to put in more effort to achieve success. In contrast, North American students tend to believe that their ability is fixed at birth and largely determines their success, and so they may be less willing to work hard (Chen & Stevenson, 1995; Pearce & Lin, 2007; Yoo & Castro, 2011).

Our knowledge that people in different cultures can have very different views of the world underlines the importance of moving beyond North America and studying other cultural groups to identify universal principles of behavior. Furthermore, broad cultural differences are not the only ones taken into account by psychologists in their attempts to identify general principles of behavior. Subcultural, ethnic, racial, and socioeconomic differences are increasingly important targets of study by psychologists (Tucker & Herman, 2002; Cardemil, Pinedo, & Miller, 2005; Hunt, 2017; Garcia, 2019).

Although the discipline is growing more aware of the importance of taking cultural and subcultural factors into account, progress has not been rapid in actual practice. For example, the amount of research conducted in the United States on groups other than white middle-class college students is woefully small.

Furthermore, there's a lack of clarity on the use of terms such as *race* and *ethnic group*. Race, for instance, originated as a biological concept that, technically, should be used only to refer to classifications based on the physical characteristics of an organism or species. But such a definition has little validity for humans, given that we are all

Members of different cultures attribute academic success to different factors. How might differing cultural perspectives affect the performance of Asian students compared with that of American students?
(Left): Tanya Constantine/Blend Images;
(Right): Ingram Publishing/SuperStock

99.9 percent identical in our genetic makeup. Consequently, today race is generally thought of as a social construction—that is, something defined by people and their beliefs. In contrast, *ethnic group* and *ethnicity* are broader terms that refer to cultural background, nationality, religion, and language (Freeman, 2006; French, Coleman, & DiLorenzo, 2013; Reich, 2018).

To compound the difficulty, there are no universally acceptable names for races and ethnic groups. Psychologists—like other members of U.S. society—are divided on whether they should use the label *African American* (which focuses on geographical origins) or *black* (which focuses on skin color), just as they disagree about whether to use *Caucasian* or *white*, *Hispanic* or *Latino*, and *Native American* or *American Indian* (Council of National Psychological Associations for the Advancement of Ethnic Minority Interests, 2000; Phinney, 2003; Wang & Sue, 2005).

Psychologists also know that the consequences of race cannot be understood without taking into account environmental and cultural factors. People's behavior is a joint product of their race and of the treatment they receive from others because of it. In sum, only by examining behavior across ethnic, cultural, and racial lines can psychologists differentiate principles that are universal from those that are culture-bound.

Psychology's Future

We have examined psychology's foundations, but what does the future hold for the discipline? Although the course of scientific development is notoriously difficult to predict, several trends seem likely:

- As its knowledge base grows, psychology will become increasingly specialized, and new perspectives will evolve. For example, our growing understanding of the brain and the nervous system, combined with scientific advances in genetics and gene therapy, will allow psychologists to focus on *prevention* of psychological disorders rather than only on their treatment (Cuijpers et al., 2008; Goldstein, Ross, & De Luca, 2019).

- The evolving sophistication of neuroscientific approaches is likely to have an increasing influence over other branches of psychology. For instance, social psychologists already are increasing their understanding of social behaviors such as persuasion by using brain scans as part of an evolving field known as *social neuroscience*. Furthermore, as neuroscientific techniques become more sophisticated, there will be new ways of applying that knowledge, as we discuss in *Neuroscience in Your Life* (Cacioppo & Decety, 2009; Di Ieva et al., 2015; Mattan, Kubota, & Cloutier, 2017).

- Psychology's influence on issues of public interest also will grow. The major problems of our time–such as violence, terrorism, racial and ethnic prejudice, poverty, environmental changes, and technological disasters–have important psychological components Already, psychology has had significant influences on social policy, informing lawmakers' decision-making, a trend that is likely to increase (Dweck, 2017; Fiske, 2017).

- Psychologists will follow increasingly strict ethical and moral guidelines. When it was revealed in 2015 that several psychologists participated in the interrogation and torture of military prisoners in the aftermath of the 9/11 terrorist attacks and that some of the leadership of the American Psychological Association (APA) were aware of these activities, a national scandal ensued. As a consequence, the APA adopted strict new guidelines that prohibit psychologists from participating in national security interrogations, and the psychologists who devised the interrogation techniques are being put on trial. In addition, psychologists are barred from working at the Guantánamo base in Cuba and at CIA black sites (Risen, 2015; Fink, 2017).

- The public's view of psychology will become more informed. Surveys show that the public at large does not fully understand the scientific underpinnings of the field. However, as the field itself embraces such practices as using scientific evidence to choose the best treatments for psychological disorders, psychology's reputation will grow (Lilienfeld, 2012; Ferguson, 2015).

- Finally, as the population becomes more diverse, issues of diversity–embodied in the study of racial, ethnic, linguistic, and cultural factors–will become more important to psychologists providing services and doing research. The result will be a field that can provide an understanding of *human* behavior in its broadest sense (Quintana. Aboud, & Chao, 2006; Richmond et al., 2015).

From the perspective of...

A Social Worker Imagine that you have a caseload of clients who come from diverse cultures, ethnicities, and races. How might you consider their diverse backgrounds when assisting them?

Sam Edwards/OJO Images/age fotostock

BECOMING AN INFORMED CONSUMER
of Psychology

Thinking Critically About Psychology: Distinguishing Legitimate Psychology from Pseudo-Psychology

"Expand Your Mind Beyond Virtual Reality . . . & Learn at the Speed of Light!" declares the sales pitch that arrives in the day's spam. "I have an astounding technology I'm going to share with you. Something so profound it will . . . transform your mind and soul forever."

From advertisements to television and radio talk shows to the Internet, we are subjected to a barrage of information about psychology. We are told that we can become better adjusted, smarter, more insightful, and happier individuals by learning the secrets that psychologists have revealed.

However, such promises are usually empty. So how can we separate accurate information, which is backed by science and objective research, from pseudo-psychology based on anecdotes, opinions, and even outright fraud? The best approach is to employ critical thinking techniques. Developed by psychologists who specialize in learning, memory, cognition, intelligence, and education, critical thinking procedures provide the tools to scrutinize assumptions, evaluate assertions, and think with greater precision (Roediger & McCabe, 2007; Meltzoff & Harris, 2018).

We'll be considering ways to boost critical thinking skills in *Becoming an Informed Consumer of Psychology* sections throughout the book. To get started, let's consider what you need in order to evaluate information of a psychological nature, whether the source is an advertisement, a television show, a magazine article, or even a book as seemingly reliable as a college textbook.

- For starters, know who is offering the information and advice. Are the providers of the information trained psychologists? What kinds of degrees do they have? Are they licensed? Are they affiliated with a particular institution? Before seriously relying on experts' advice, check out their credentials.

- Keep in mind that there is no free ride. If it is possible to solve major psychological ills by buying a $29.95 book, why do many people who suffer from such problems typically expend a considerable amount of time and money to obtain help? If you could buy a computer program that would really "unlock the hidden truths" about others, wouldn't it be in widespread use? Be wary of simple, glib responses to major difficulties.
- Be aware that few universal cures exist for humankind's ills. No method or technique works for everyone. The range of difficulties attached to the human condition is so broad that any procedure that purports to resolve all problems is certain to disappoint.
- Finally, remember that no source of information or advice is definitive. The notion of infallibility is best left to the realm of religion; you should approach psychological information and advice from a critical and thoughtful perspective.

RECAP/EVALUATE/RETHINK

RECAP

LO 3-1 What are psychology's key issues and controversies?

- Psychology's key issues and controversies center on how much of human behavior is a product of nature or nurture, conscious or unconscious thoughts, observable actions or internal mental processes, free will or determinism, and individual differences or universal principles.

LO 3-2 What is the future of psychology likely to hold?

- Psychology will become increasingly specialized, will pay greater attention to prevention instead of just treatment, will become more and more concerned with the public interest, and will take the growing diversity of the country's population into account more fully.

EVALUATE

1. The view that behavior is largely produced by factors beyond people's willful control is known as _____.
2. In the nature/nurture issue, nature refers to heredity, and nurture refers to the _____.
3. Race is a biological concept, not a psychological one. True or false?

RETHINK

"The fact that some businesses now promote their ability to help people 'expand their minds beyond virtual reality' shows the great progress psychology has made lately." Criticize this statement in light of what you know about professional psychology and pseudo-psychology.

Answers to Evaluate Questions

1. determinism; 2. environment; 3. true

KEY TERMS

free will   determinism

LOOKING *Back*

EPILOGUE

The field of psychology, as you have seen, is broad and diverse. It encompasses many subfields and specialties practiced in a variety of settings, with new subfields continually arising. You have also seen that even within the subfields, psychologists may adopt different approaches, including the neuroscience, psychodynamic, behavioral, cognitive, and humanistic perspectives.

For all its diversity, though, psychology focuses on certain key issues. These issues will reappear as themes throughout this text as you learn about the work and accomplishments of psychologists in the many subfields of the discipline.

In light of what you've already learned about the field of psychology, reconsider the coronavirus pandemic discussed in the Prologue to this chapter and answer the following questions:

1. What issues would a health psychologist be particularly focused on in addressing the pandemic?
2. What types of psychologists might a national leader consult with in determining how to react to the pandemic?
3. What aspects of people's reaction to the pandemic would most interest a cognitive psychologist? A clinical psychologist? A social psychologist?
4. What are some ways in which both nature and nurture could contribute to a person's reaction to the pandemic?

VISUAL SUMMARY 1 Introduction to Psychology

MODULE 1 Psychologists at Work

Subfields of Psychology

- Biological foundations
  - Behavioral neuroscience
- Sensing, perceiving, learning, and thinking
  - Experimental and cognitive psychology
- Sources of change and stability
  - Development and personality psychology
- Physical and mental health
  - Health, clinical, and counseling psychology
- Social networks
  - Social and cross-cultural psychology
- Expanding frontiers
  - Evolutionary psychology
  - Behavioral genetics
  - Clinical neuropsychology

Working at Psychology

Where U.S. psychologists work

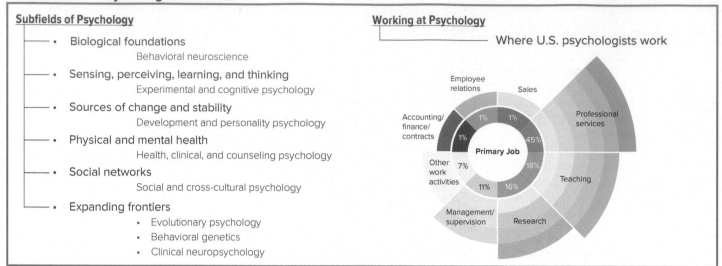

MODULE 2 A Science Evolves

Roots

- Structuralism
- Functionalism

Today's Perspectives: Five major perspectives

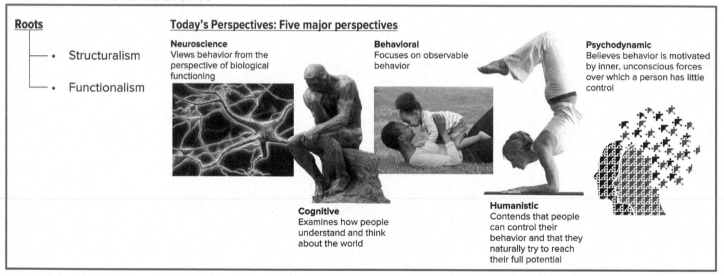

Neuroscience
Views behavior from the perspective of biological functioning

Behavioral
Focuses on observable behavior

Psychodynamic
Believes behavior is motivated by inner, unconscious forces over which a person has little control

Cognitive
Examines how people understand and think about the world

Humanistic
Contends that people can control their behavior and that they naturally try to reach their full potential

MODULE 3 Psychology's Key Issues and Controversies

Issues in psychology and positions psychologists take on them

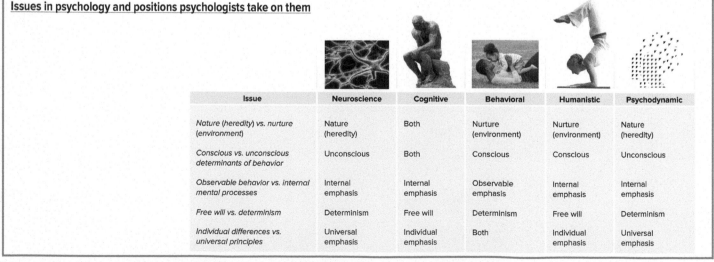

Issue	Neuroscience	Cognitive	Behavioral	Humanistic	Psychodynamic
Nature (heredity) vs. nurture (environment)	Nature (heredity)	Both	Nurture (environment)	Nurture (environment)	Nature (heredity)
Conscious vs. unconscious determinants of behavior	Unconscious	Both	Conscious	Conscious	Unconscious
Observable behavior vs. internal mental processes	Internal emphasis	Internal emphasis	Observable emphasis	Internal emphasis	Internal emphasis
Free will vs. determinism	Determinism	Free will	Determinism	Free will	Determinism
Individual differences vs. universal principles	Universal emphasis	Individual emphasis	Both	Individual emphasis	Universal emphasis

Bill Diodato/Corbis/Getty Images

CHAPTER 2
Psychological Research

LEARNING OUTCOMES FOR CHAPTER 2

		MODULE 4
LO 4-1	What is the scientific method?	**THE SCIENTIFIC METHOD**
LO 4-2	What role do theories and hypotheses play in psychological research?	Theories: Specifying Broad Explanations Hypotheses: Crafting Testable Predictions

		MODULE 5
LO 5-1	What research methods do psychologists use?	**CONDUCTING PSYCHOLOGICAL RESEARCH** Archival Research
LO 5-2	How do psychologists establish cause-and-effect relationships in research studies?	Naturalistic Observation Survey Research The Case Study Correlational Research Experimental Research

LO 6-1 What major issues confront psychologists conducting research?

PROLOGUE *A CRY FOR HELP*

No one can say why 31-year-old Jamel Dunn, a disabled man who walked with a cane, wandered into the waters of a local pond in Florida. But what happened next is indisputable, as it was all captured on video. Dunn quickly found himself in trouble and began flailing in the water. A group of nearby teenagers, one of whom was taking the video, responded by taunting and laughing at him. "Ain't nobody going to help you," shouted one. "You shouldn't have gone in there!" Moments later Dunn could be seen letting out a whimper and sinking below the water to his death as the teenagers continued to laugh at his plight (Chokshi, 2017).

In contrast, consider the response of 36-year-old Antonio Salazar-Garcia to swimmers in distress in Oklahoma. When he heard the screams of a pair of children who were swimming in a dangerous, fast-moving river, he didn't hesitate to jump in to their rescue. When he reached the children, he tried helping one of them but was pushed under water and swept away. Other nearby witnesses managed to rescue the children, but Salazar-Garcia—a true hero—sadly was found dead an hour later (Weaver, 2019).

LOOKING *Ahead*

Why didn't the bystanders in Florida help a man who was clearly in trouble? Why, instead, did they taunt the unfortunate victim? And in the Oklahoma situation, what led the heroic bystander to put his own life in danger without hesitation?

If incidents like the one in Florida were rare, we might be able to attribute the inaction to something particular about the situation or to the specific people involved. However, events such as this one are all too common.

In one infamous case in 1964, a woman named Kitty Genovese was attacked by a man near an apartment building in New York City. At one point during the assault, which lasted 30 minutes, she managed to free herself and screamed, "Oh, my God, he stabbed me. Please help me!"

According to most accounts—although there were significant discrepancies in witness recollections—no fewer than 38 neighbors heard her screams, yet few people intervened. One couple pulled chairs up to the window and turned off the lights so that they could see better. Someone called out, "Let that girl alone." But shouts were not enough to scare off the killer. He chased Genovese, stabbing her eight more times, and sexually molested her before leaving her to die (Griggs, 2015; Kassan, 2017; Pinker, 2019).

Such incidents remain dismaying—and perplexing. Why is it that bystanders frequently don't intervene, particularly when so many are around who could potentially help? And why is it that others unflinchingly risk their lives to intervene?

Psychologists puzzled over the problem for many years. However, after much research, they reached an unexpected conclusion: Kitty Genovese probably would have been better off if only a few people, rather than many, had heard her cries for help. In fact, if only a single, lone bystander had been present, the chances that this person would have intervened might have been fairly high. It turns out that the fewer the witnesses to an assault, the better the victim's chances of getting help.

How did psychologists come to such a curious conclusion? After all, logic and common sense clearly suggest that more bystanders would produce a greater likelihood that someone would help a person in need. This seeming contradiction—and the way psychologists resolved it—illustrates a central challenge for the field of psychology: asking questions about the unknown and getting valid answers.

Like professionals in any science, psychologists are vitally concerned with refining and expanding knowledge within their field. In the following modules, we'll see how psychologists pose questions of interest and answer them through scientific research. We will find that the answers psychologists obtain from their research not only advance our understanding of behavior but also offer the potential to improve the human condition.

Module 4
The Scientific Method

"Birds of a feather flock together" . . . or "Opposites attract"? "Two heads are better than one" . . . or "If you want a thing done well, do it yourself"? "The more the merrier" . . . or "Two's company, three's a crowd"?

If we were to rely on common sense to understand behavior, we'd have considerable difficulty—especially because commonsense views are often contradictory. In fact, one of the major undertakings for the field of psychology is to develop suppositions about behavior and to determine which of those suppositions are accurate (Ferguson, 2015).

Psychologists—as well as scientists in other disciplines—meet the challenge of posing appropriate questions and properly answering them by relying on the scientific method. The **scientific method** is the approach used by psychologists to systematically acquire knowledge and understanding about behavior and other phenomena of interest. As illustrated in Figure 1, it consists of four main steps: (1) identifying questions of interest, (2) formulating an explanation, (3) carrying out research designed to support or refute the explanation, and (4) communicating the findings.

Theories: Specifying Broad Explanations

In using the scientific method, psychologists start by identifying questions of interest. We have all been curious at some time about our observations of everyday behavior. If you have ever asked yourself why a particular teacher is so easily annoyed, why a friend is always late for appointments, or how your dog understands your commands, you have been formulating questions about behavior.

LEARNING OUTCOMES

LO 4-1 What is the scientific method?

LO 4-2 What role do theories and hypotheses play in psychological research?

scientific method The approach through which psychologists systematically acquire knowledge and understanding about behavior and other phenomena of interest. (Module 4)

Identify questions of interest stemming from
- Behavior and phenomenon requiring explanation
- Prior research findings
- Curiosity, creativity, insight

Formulate an explanation
Specify a theory

Develop a hypothesis

Carry out research
Devise an operational definition of the hypothesis

Select a research method

Collect the data

Analyze the data

Communicate the findings

FIGURE 1 The scientific method, which encompasses the process of identifying, asking, and answering questions, is used by psychologists and researchers from every other scientific discipline to come to an understanding about the world. What do you think are the advantages of this method?

Study Alert
Use Figure 1 to remember the four steps of the scientific method (identifying questions, formulating an explanation, carrying out research, and communicating the findings).

Psychologists, too, ask questions about the nature and causes of behavior. They may want to explore explanations for everyday behaviors or for various phenomena. They may also pose questions that build on findings from their previous research or from research carried out by other psychologists. Or they may produce new questions that are based on curiosity, creativity, or insight.

After a question has been identified, the next step in the scientific method is to develop a theory to explain the observed phenomenon. **Theories** are broad explanations and predictions concerning observations of interest. They provide a framework for understanding the relationships among a set of otherwise unorganized facts or principles.

theories Broad explanations and predictions concerning phenomena of interest. (Module 4)

All of us have developed our own informal theories of human behavior, such as "People are basically good" or "People's behavior is usually motivated by self-interest." However, psychologists' theories are more formal and focused. They are established on the basis of a careful study of the psychological literature to identify earlier relevant research and previously formulated theories, as well as psychologists' general knowledge of the field.

Growing out of the diverse approaches employed by psychologists, theories vary both in their breadth and in their level of detail. For example, one theory might seek to explain and predict a phenomenon as broad as emotional experience. A narrower theory might attempt to explain why people display the emotion of fear nonverbally after receiving a threat (Croom, 2015; Smith et al., 2017; Gruber et al., 2019).

Psychologists Bibb Latané and John Darley, responding to the failure of bystanders to intervene when Kitty Genovese was murdered in New York, developed what they called a theory of *diffusion of responsibility* (Latané & Darley, 1970). According to their theory, the greater the number of bystanders or witnesses to an event that calls for helping behavior, the more the responsibility for helping is perceived to be shared by all the bystanders. Thus, the greater the number of bystanders in an emergency situation, the smaller the share of the responsibility each person feels—and the less likely that any single person will come forward to help.

Hypotheses: Crafting Testable Predictions

Although the diffusion of responsibility theory seems to make sense, it represented only the beginning phase of Latané and Darley's investigative process. Their next step was to devise a way to test their theory. To do this, they needed to create a hypothesis. A **hypothesis** is a prediction stated in a way that allows it to be tested. Hypotheses stem from theories; they help test the underlying soundness of theories.

hypothesis A prediction, stemming from a theory, stated in a way that allows it to be tested. (Module 4)

In the same way that we develop our own broad theories about the world, we also construct hypotheses about events and behavior. Those hypotheses can range from trivialities (such as why our English instructor wears those weird shirts) to more meaningful matters (such as what is the best way to study for a test). Although we rarely test these hypotheses systematically, we do try to determine whether they are right. Perhaps we try comparing two strategies: cramming the night before an exam versus spreading out our study over several nights. By assessing which approach yields better test performance, we have created a way to compare the two strategies.

A hypothesis must be stated in a way that will allow it to be tested, which involves creating an operational definition. An **operational definition** is the translation of a hypothesis into specific, testable procedures that can be measured and observed in an experiment.

operational definition The translation of a hypothesis into specific, testable procedures that can be measured and observed in an experiment. (Module 4)

There is no single way to go about devising an operational definition for a hypothesis; it depends on logic, the equipment and facilities available, the psychological perspective being employed, and ultimately the creativity of the researcher. For example, one researcher might develop a hypothesis that uses as an operational definition of "fear" an increase in heart rate. In contrast, another psychologist might use as an operational definition of "fear" a written response to the question "How much fear are you experiencing at this moment?"

Latané and Darley's hypothesis was a straightforward prediction from their more general theory of diffusion of responsibility: The more people who witness an emergency situation, the less likely it is that help will be given to a victim. They could, of course, have chosen another hypothesis (try to think of one!), but their initial formulation seemed to offer the most direct test of the theory.

Psychologists rely on formal theories and hypotheses for many reasons. For one thing, theories and hypotheses allow them to make sense of unorganized, separate observations and bits of data. They permit them to place observations and data within a coherent framework. In addition, theories and hypotheses allow psychologists to move beyond known facts and make deductions about unexplained phenomena and develop ideas for future investigation (van Wesel, Boeije, & Hoijtink, 2013; Barrett & Russell, 2015; Haig, 2018; Laplane et al., 2019).

In short, the scientific method, with its emphasis on theories and hypotheses, helps psychologists pose appropriate questions. With properly stated questions in hand, psychologists then can choose from a variety of research methods to find answers.

Study Alert
Remember that a theory is a broad explanation, whereas a hypothesis is a more narrow prediction.

RECAP/EVALUATE/RETHINK

RECAP

LO 4-1 What is the scientific method?

- The scientific method is the approach psychologists use to understand behavior. It consists of four steps: identifying questions of interest, formulating an explanation, carrying out research that is designed to support or refute the explanation, and communicating the findings.

LO 4-2 What role do theories and hypotheses play in psychological research?

- Research in psychology is guided by theories (broad explanations and predictions regarding phenomena of interest) and hypotheses (theory-based predictions stated in a way that allows them to be tested).
- To test a hypothesis, researchers must formulate an operational definition, which translates the abstract concepts of the hypothesis into the actual procedures used in the study.

EVALUATE

1. An explanation for a phenomenon of interest is known as a _____.

2. To test this explanation, a researcher must state it in terms of a testable question known as a _____.
3. An experimenter is interested in studying the relationship between hunger and aggression. She decides that she will measure aggression by counting the number of times a participant will hit a punching bag. In this case, her _____ definition of aggression is the number of times the participant hits the bag.

RETHINK

Starting with the theory that diffusion of responsibility causes responsibility for helping to be shared among bystanders, Latané and Darley derived the hypothesis that the more people who witness an emergency situation, the less likely it is that help will be given to a victim. How many other hypotheses can you think of that are based on the same theory of diffusion of responsibility?

Answers to Evaluate Questions

1. theory; 2. hypothesis; 3. operational

KEY TERMS

scientific method	theories	hypothesis	operational definition

Module 5
Conducting Psychological Research

LEARNING OUTCOMES

LO 5-1 What research methods do psychologists use?

LO 5-2 How do psychologists establish cause-and-effect relationships in research studies?

Research–systematic inquiry aimed at the discovery of new knowledge–is a central ingredient of the scientific method in psychology. It provides the key to understanding the degree to which hypotheses (and the theories behind them) are accurate.

Just as we can apply different theories and hypotheses to explain the same phenomena, we can use a number of alternative methods to conduct research. As we consider the major tools that psychologists use to conduct research, keep in mind that their relevance extends beyond testing and evaluating hypotheses in psychology. All of us carry out elementary forms of research on our own. For instance, a supervisor might evaluate an employee's performance; a physician might systematically test the effects of different doses of a drug on a patient; a salesperson might compare different persuasive strategies. Each of these situations draws on the research practices we are about to discuss.

Let's begin by considering several types of *descriptive research* designed to systematically investigate a person, group, or patterns of behavior. These methods include archival research, naturalistic observation, survey research, and case studies.

Archival Research

Suppose that, like the psychologists Latané and Darley (1970), you were interested in finding out more about emergency situations in which bystanders did not provide help. One of the first places you might turn to would be historical accounts. By searching newspaper records, for example, you might find support for the notion that a decrease in helping behavior historically has accompanied an increase in the number of bystanders.

archival research Research in which existing data, such as census documents, college records, and newspaper clippings, are examined to test a hypothesis. (Module 5)

Using newspaper articles is an example of archival research. In **archival research**, existing data, such as census documents, college records, online databases, and newspaper articles, are examined to test a hypothesis. For example, college transcripts, stored in college files, may be analyzed and used to determine whether there are gender differences in academic performance. Similarly, Facebook and Twitter provide huge pools of data from millions of users that researchers can use to collect data–though this practice raises serious privacy issues (Fisher & Barnes-Farrell, 2013; Kosinski et al., 2015; Roy et al., 2019).

Archival research is a relatively inexpensive means of testing a hypothesis because someone else has already collected the basic data. Of course, the use of existing data has several drawbacks. For one thing, the data may not be in a form that allows the researcher to test a hypothesis fully. The information could be incomplete, or it could have been collected haphazardly (Riniolo et al., 2003; Vega, 2006; Zickar, 2015).

Most attempts at archival research are hampered by the simple fact that records with the necessary information may not exist. In these instances, researchers often turn to another research method: naturalistic observation.

Naturalistic Observation

naturalistic observation Research in which an investigator simply observes some naturally occurring behavior and does not make a change in the situation. (Module 5)

In **naturalistic observation**, the investigator observes some naturally occurring behavior and does not make a change in the situation. For example, a researcher investigating helping behavior might observe the kind of help given to victims in a high-crime area of a city. The important point to remember about naturalistic observation is that the researcher simply records what occurs, making no modification in the situation that is being observed (Kennison & Bowers, 2011; Haas et al., 2015; Wilson & Joye, 2017).

Observing behavior in its natural habitat, without making any changes in the setting, is characteristic of naturalistic observation.
Suzanne Long/Alamy Stock Photo

Although the advantage of naturalistic observation is obvious—we get a sample of what people do in their "natural habitat"—there is also an important drawback: the inability to control any of the factors of interest. For example, we might find so few naturally occurring instances of helping behavior that we would be unable to draw any conclusions. Because naturalistic observation prevents researchers from making changes in a situation, they must wait until the appropriate conditions occur. Furthermore, if people know they are being watched, they may alter their reactions and produce behavior that is not truly representative.

Survey Research

There is no more straightforward way of finding out what people think, feel, and do than asking them directly. For this reason, surveys are an important research method. In **survey research**, a *sample* of people chosen to represent a larger group of interest (a *population*) is asked a series of questions about their behavior, thoughts, or attitudes. Survey methods have become so sophisticated that even with a very small sample, researchers are able to infer with great accuracy how a larger group would respond. For instance, a sample of just a few thousand voters is sufficient to predict within one or two percentage points who will win a presidential election—if the representative sample is chosen with care (Groves et al., 2004; Igo, 2006; Rea & Parker, 2014).

Researchers investigating helping behavior might conduct a survey by asking people to complete a questionnaire in which they indicate their reluctance for giving aid to someone. Similarly, researchers interested in learning about sexual practices have carried out surveys to learn which practices are common and which are not and to chart changing notions of sexual morality historically (Santelli et al., 2009; Mendoza-Pérez, Ortiz-Hernández, & Lozano-Verduzco, 2019).

Surveys also play a role in driving public policy. For example, a recent survey of U.S. teenagers and young adults found that more than 70% believe that climate change will cause a moderate or great deal of harm to people in their generation. Furthermore, a majority are afraid and angry about it, and 1 in 7 has participated in some sort of demonstration or rally, or has written to a public official to discuss their views on global warming. The results of surveys on such topics can influence lawmakers as well as psychological research on the anxieties of people concerned with climate change. Moreover, psychologists may use such survey data to understand how anxieties about

survey research Research in which people chosen to represent a larger population are asked a series of questions about their behavior, thoughts, or attitudes. (Module 5)

PsychTech

One of the most efficient ways to conduct surveys is via the web. But web surveys may have sampling problems, given that not everyone has easy access to the web, such as people living in poverty. Consequently, web surveys may not be representative of the broader population.

climate change are translated into activism. In short, surveys can spur additional research (Abeles et al., 2019; Bandura & Cherry, 2019; Hamel et al., 2019).

On the other hand, survey research has several potential pitfalls. For one thing, if the sample of people who are surveyed is not representative of the broader population of interest, the results of the survey will have little meaning. For instance, if a sample of voters in a town only includes Republicans, it would hardly be useful for predicting the results of an election in which both Republicans and Democrats are voting. Consequently, researchers using surveys strive to obtain a *random sample* of the population in question, in which every voter in the town has an equal chance of being included in the sample receiving the survey (Davern, 2013; Engel et al., 2015; Nedelec, 2017).

In addition, survey respondents may not want to admit to holding socially undesirable attitudes. (Most racists know they are racists and might not want to admit it.) Furthermore, people may not want to admit they engage in behaviors that they feel are somehow abnormal—a problem that plagues surveys of sexual behavior because people are often reluctant to admit what they really do in private. Finally, in some cases, people may not even be consciously aware of what their true attitudes are or why they hold them.

From the perspective of...

A Marketing Manager How would you design a survey that targets the customers in whom you are most interested?

Jack Hollingsworth/Getty Images

The Case Study

When we hear about the perpetrator of a school shooting, many of us wonder what it is about the shooter's personality or background that leads to such behavior. To answer this question, psychologists might conduct a case study. In contrast to a survey, in which many people are studied, a **case study** is an in-depth, intensive investigation of a single individual or a small group. Case studies might include *psychological testing*, a procedure in which a carefully designed set of questions is used to gain some insight into the personality of the individual or group.

When case studies are used as a research technique, the goal is to use the insights gained from the study of one or a few individuals to improve our understanding of people in general. Sigmund Freud developed his theories through case studies of individual patients. Similarly, case studies of those who commit school shootings might help identify others who are prone to violence.

The drawback to case studies? If the individuals examined are unique in certain ways or if the sample is too small, it is impossible to make valid generalizations to a larger population. Still, case studies sometimes lead the way to better explanations, as well as treatments for psychological disorders.

Correlational Research

In using the descriptive research methods we have discussed, researchers often wish to determine the relationship between two variables. **Variables** are behaviors, events, or other characteristics that can change, or vary, in some way. For example, in a study

case study An in-depth, intensive investigation of an individual or small group of people. (Module 5)

variables Behaviors, events, or other characteristics that can change, or vary, in some way. (Module 5) to determine whether the amount of studying makes a difference in test scores, the variables would be study time and test scores.

In **correlational research**, two sets of variables are examined to determine whether they are associated, or correlated. The strength and direction of the relationship between the two variables are represented by a mathematical statistic known as a *correlation* (or, more formally, a *correlation coefficient*), which can range from +1.0 to −1.0.

A *positive correlation* indicates that as the value of one variable increases, we can predict that the value of the other variable will also increase. For example, if we predict that the more time students spend studying for a test, the higher their grades on the test will be, and that the less they study, the lower their test scores will be, we are expecting to find a positive correlation. (Higher values of the variable "amount of study time" would be associated with higher values of the variable "test score," and lower values of "amount of study time" would be associated with lower values of "test score.") The correlation, then, would be indicated by a positive number, and the stronger the association was between studying and test scores, the closer the number would be to +1.0. For example, we might find a correlation of +.85 between test scores and amount of study time, indicating a strong positive association.

In contrast, a *negative correlation* tells us that as the value of one variable increases, the value of the other decreases. For instance, we might predict that as the number of hours spent studying increases, the number of hours spent partying decreases. Here we are expecting a negative correlation, ranging between 0 and −1.0. More studying is associated with less partying, and less studying is associated with more partying. The stronger the association between studying and partying is, the closer the correlation will be to −1.0. For instance, a correlation of −.85 would indicate a strong negative association between partying and studying.

Of course, it's quite possible that little or no relationship exists between two variables. For instance, we would probably not expect to find a relationship between number of study hours and height. Lack of a relationship would be indicated by a correlation close to 0. For example, if we found a correlation of −.02 or +.03, it would indicate that there is virtually no association between the two variables; knowing how much someone studies does not tell us anything about how tall he or she is.

When two variables are strongly correlated with each other, we are tempted to assume that one variable causes the other. For example, if we find that more study time is associated with higher grades, we might guess that more studying *causes* higher grades. Although this is not a bad guess, it remains just a guess–because finding that two variables are correlated does not mean that there is a causal relationship between them. The strong correlation suggests that knowing how much a person studies can help us predict how that person will do on a test, but it does not mean that the studying *causes* the test performance. Instead, for instance, people who are more interested in the subject matter might study more than do those who are less interested, and so the amount of interest, not the number of hours spent studying, would predict test performance. The mere fact that two variables occur together does not mean that one causes the other.

Similarly, suppose you learned that the number of houses of worship in a large sample of cities was positively correlated with the number of people arrested, meaning that the more houses of worship, the more arrests there were in a city. Does this mean that the presence of more houses of worship caused the greater number of arrests? Almost surely not, of course. In this case, the underlying cause is probably the size of the city: in bigger cities, there are both more houses of worship *and* more arrests.

One more example illustrates the critical point that correlations tell us nothing about cause and effect but only provide a measure of the strength of a relationship between two variables. We might find that children who watch a lot of television programs featuring high levels of aggression are likely to demonstrate a relatively high degree of aggressive behavior and that those who watch few television shows that portray aggression are apt to exhibit a relatively low degree of such behavior (see Figure 1). But we cannot say that the aggression is *caused* by the TV viewing because many other explanations are possible.

correlational research Research in which the relationship between two sets of variables is examined to determine whether they are associated, or correlated. (Module 5)

Study Alert
The concept that "correlation does not imply causation" is a key principle.

Many studies show that the observation of violence in the media is associated with aggression in viewers. Can we conclude that the observations of violence cause aggression?
Maica/Getty Images

FIGURE 1 If we find that frequent viewing of television programs with aggressive content is associated with high levels of aggressive behavior, we might cite several plausible causes, as suggested in this figure. For example, (a) choosing to watch shows with aggressive content could produce aggression; or (b) being a highly aggressive person might cause one to choose to watch televised aggression; or (c) having a high energy level might cause a person to choose both to watch aggressive shows and to act aggressively. Correlational findings, then, do not permit us to determine causality. Can you think of a way to study the effects of televised aggression on aggressive behavior that is not correlational?

For instance, children who have an unusually high level of energy may seek out programs with aggressive content *and* are more aggressive. The children's energy level, then, could be the true cause of the children's higher incidence of aggression. Also, people who are already highly aggressive might choose to watch shows with a high aggressive content *because* they are aggressive. Clearly, then, any number of causal sequences are possible–none of which can be ruled out by correlational research.

The fact that correlational research is unable to demonstrate cause-and-effect relationships is a crucial drawback to its use. There is, however, an alternative technique that does establish causality: the experiment.

Experimental Research

Carrying out experiments is the *only* way psychologists can establish cause-and-effect relationships. In a formal **experiment**, a researcher investigates the relationship between two (or more) variables by deliberately changing one variable in a controlled situation and observing the effects of that change on other aspects of the situation. In an experiment then, the conditions are created and controlled by the researcher, who deliberately makes a change in those conditions in order to observe the effects of that change.

The **experimental manipulation** is the change that a researcher deliberately makes in an experiment. Experimental manipulations are used to detect relationships between different variables (Salazar, Crosby, & DiClemente, 2015).

Several steps are involved in carrying out an experiment, but the process typically begins with the development of one or more hypotheses for the experiment to test. For example, Latané and Darley, in testing their theory of the diffusion of responsibility in bystander behavior, developed this hypothesis: The higher the number of people who witness an emergency situation is, the less likely it is that any of them will help the victim. They then designed an experiment to test this hypothesis.

Their first step was to formulate an operational definition of the hypothesis by conceptualizing it in a way that could be tested. Latané and Darley had to take into account the fundamental principle of experimental research mentioned earlier: Experimenters must manipulate at least one variable in order to observe the effects of the manipulation on another variable while keeping other factors in the situation constant.

experiment The investigation of the relationship between two (or more) variables by deliberately producing a change in one variable in a situation and observing the effects of that change on other aspects of the situation. (Module 5)

experimental manipulation The change that an experimenter deliberately produces in a situation. (Module 5)

However, the manipulation cannot be viewed by itself, in isolation; if a cause-and-effect relationship is to be established, the effects of the manipulation must be compared with the effects of no manipulation or a different kind of manipulation.

EXPERIMENTAL GROUPS AND CONTROL GROUPS

Experimental research requires, then, that the responses of at least two groups be compared. One group will receive some special **treatment**–the manipulation implemented by the experimenter–and another group will receive either no treatment or a different treatment. Any group that receives a treatment is called an **experimental group**; a group that receives no treatment is called a **control group**. (In some experiments, there are multiple experimental and control groups, each of which is compared with another group.)

By employing both experimental and control groups in an experiment, researchers are able to rule out the possibility that something other than the experimental manipulation produced the results observed in the experiment. Without a control group, we couldn't be sure that some other variable, such as the temperature at the time we were running the experiment, the color of the experimenter's hair, or even the mere passage of time, wasn't causing the changes observed.

For example, consider a medical researcher who thinks he has invented a medicine that cures the common cold. To test his claim, he gives the medicine one day to a group of 20 people who have colds and finds that 10 days later all of them are cured.

Eureka? Not so fast. An observer viewing this flawed study might reasonably argue that the people would have gotten better even without the medicine. What the researcher obviously needed was a control group consisting of people with colds who *don't* get the medicine and whose health is also checked 10 days later. Only if there is a significant difference between experimental and control groups can the effectiveness of the medicine be assessed. Through the use of control groups, then, researchers can isolate specific causes for their findings–and draw cause-and-effect inferences.

Returning to Latané and Darley's experiment, we see that the researchers needed to translate their hypothesis into something testable. To do this, they decided to create a false emergency situation that would appear to require the aid of a bystander. As their experimental manipulation, they decided to vary the number of bystanders present. They could have had just one experimental group with, say, two people present and a control group for comparison purposes with just one person present. Instead, they settled on a more complex procedure involving the creation of groups of three sizes–consisting of two, three, and six people–that could be compared with one another.

treatment The manipulation implemented by the experimenter. (Module 5)

experimental group Any group participating in an experiment that receives a treatment. (Module 5)

control group A group participating in an experiment that receives no treatment. (Module 5)

In this experiment, preschoolers' reactions to the puppet are monitored. Can you think of a hypothesis that might be tested in this way?
Thierry Berrod, Mona Lisa Production/Science Source

INDEPENDENT AND DEPENDENT VARIABLES

Latané and Darley's experimental design now included an operational definition of what is called the **independent variable**. The independent variable is the condition that is manipulated by an experimenter. (You can think of the independent variable as being independent of the actions of those taking part in an experiment; it is controlled by the experimenter.) In the case of the Latané and Darley experiment, the independent variable was the number of people present, which was manipulated by the experimenters.

The next step was to decide how they were going to determine the effect that varying the number of bystanders had on behavior of those in the experiment. Crucial to every experiment is the **dependent variable**. The dependent variable is the variable that is measured in a study. The dependent variable is expected to change as a result of the experimenter's manipulation of the independent variable. The dependent variable is dependent on the actions of the *participants* or *subjects*–the people taking part in the experiment.

independent variable The variable that is manipulated by an experimenter. (Module 5)

dependent variable The variable that is measured in an experiment. It is expected to change as a result of the experimenter's manipulation of the independent variable. (Module 5)

Latané and Darley had several possible choices for their dependent measure. One might have been a simple yes/no measure of the participants' helping behavior. But the investigators also wanted a more precise analysis of helping behavior. Consequently, they also measured the amount of time it took for a participant to provide help.

Latané and Darley now had all the necessary components of an experiment. The independent variable, manipulated by them, was the number of bystanders present in an emergency situation. The dependent variable was the measure of whether bystanders in each of the groups provided help and the amount of time it took them to do so. Consequently, like all experiments, this one had both an independent variable and a dependent variable. *All* true experiments in psychology fit this straightforward model.

> **Study Alert**
>
> To remember the difference between dependent and independent variables, recall that a hypothesis predicts how a dependent variable *depends* on the manipulation of the independent variable.

RANDOM ASSIGNMENT OF PARTICIPANTS

To make the experiment a valid test of the hypothesis, Latané and Darley needed to add a final step to the design: properly assigning participants to a particular experimental group.

The significance of this step becomes clear when we examine various alternative procedures. For example, the experimenters might have assigned just males to the group with two bystanders, just females to the group with three bystanders, and both males and females to the group with six bystanders. If they had done this, however, any differences they found in helping behavior could not be attributed with any certainty solely to group size, because the differences might just as well have been due to the composition of the group. A more reasonable procedure would be to ensure that each group had the same composition in terms of gender; then the researchers would be able to make comparisons across groups with considerably more accuracy.

Participants in each of the experimental groups ought to be comparable, and it is easy enough to create groups that are similar in terms of gender. The problem becomes a bit more tricky, though, when we consider other participant characteristics. How can we ensure that participants in each experimental group will be equally intelligent, extroverted, cooperative, and so forth, when the list of characteristics—any one of which could be important—is potentially endless?

random assignment to condition
A procedure in which participants are assigned to different experimental groups or "conditions" on the basis of chance and chance alone. (Module 5)

The solution is a simple but elegant procedure called **random assignment to condition**: Participants are assigned to different experimental groups, or *conditions*, on the basis of chance and chance alone. The experimenter might, for instance, flip a coin for each participant and assign a participant to one group when "heads" came up and to the other group when "tails" came up. The advantage of this technique is that there is an equal chance that participant characteristics will be distributed across the various groups. When a researcher uses random assignment—which in practice is usually carried out using computer-generated random numbers—chances are that each of the groups will have approximately the same proportion of intelligent people, cooperative people, extroverted people, males and females, and so on.

Figure 2 provides another example of an experiment. Like all experiments, it includes the following set of key elements, which you should keep in mind as you consider whether a research study is truly an experiment:

- An independent variable, the variable that is manipulated by the experimenter
- A dependent variable, the variable that is measured by the experimenter and that is expected to change as a result of the manipulation of the independent variable
- A procedure that randomly assigns participants to different experimental groups (called *conditions*) of the independent variable
- A hypothesis that predicts the effect the independent variable will have on the dependent variable

Only if each of these elements is present can a research study be considered a true experiment in which cause-and-effect relationships can be determined. (For a summary of the different types of research that we've discussed, see Figure 3.)

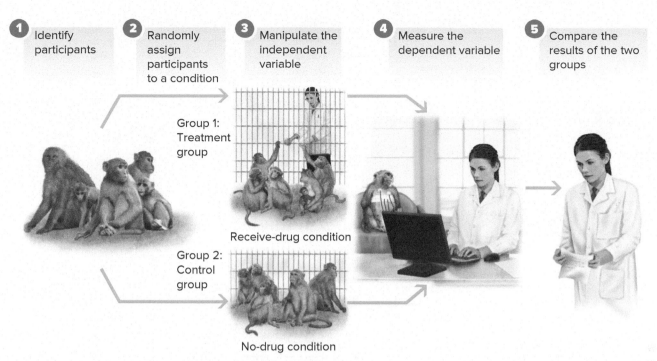

① Identify participants

② Randomly assign participants to a condition

③ Manipulate the independent variable

④ Measure the dependent variable

⑤ Compare the results of the two groups

Group 1: Treatment group

Receive-drug condition

Group 2: Control group

No-drug condition

FIGURE 2 In this depiction of a study investigating the effects of the drug propranolol on heart disease, we can see the basic elements of all true experiments. The participants in the experiment were monkeys that were randomly assigned to one of two groups. Monkeys assigned to the treatment group were given propranolol, hypothesized to prevent heart disease, whereas those in the control group were not given the drug. Administration of the drugs, then, was the independent variable.

All the monkeys were given a high-fat diet that was the human equivalent of two eggs with bacon every morning, and they occasionally were reassigned to different cages to increase their stress. To determine the effects of the drug, the monkeys' heart rates and other measures of heart disease were assessed after 26 months. These measures constituted the dependent variable. The results? As hypothesized, monkeys that received the drug showed lower heart rates and fewer symptoms of heart disease than those that did not.

Source: Based on a study by Kaplan, J. R., & Manuck, S. B. (1989). The effect of propranolol on behavioral interactions among adult male cynomolgus monkeys (Macacafas-cicularis) housed in disrupted social groupings. *Psychosomatic Medicine, 51*, 449–462.

WERE LATANÉ AND DARLEY RIGHT?

To test their hypothesis that increasing the number of bystanders in an emergency situation would lower the degree of helping behavior, Latané and Darley placed the participants in a room and told them that the purpose of the experiment was to talk about personal problems associated with college. The discussion was to be held over an intercom, supposedly to avoid the potential embarrassment of face-to-face contact. Chatting about personal problems was not, of course, the true purpose of the experiment, but telling the participants that it was provided a way of keeping their expectations from biasing their behavior. (Consider how they would have been affected if they had been told that their helping behavior in emergencies was being tested. The experimenters could never have gotten an accurate assessment of what the participants would actually do in an emergency. By definition, emergencies are rarely announced in advance.)

The sizes of the discussion groups were two, three, and six people, which constituted the manipulation of the independent variable of group size. Participants were randomly assigned to these groups upon their arrival at the laboratory. Each group included one trained confederate of the experimenters. A *confederate* is an actor employed by a researcher who participates in a psychological experiment, pretending to be a participant. The researcher trains the confederate to act in a particular way during the experiment.

As the participants in each group were holding their discussion, they suddenly heard through the intercom one of the other participants—but who in reality was the confederate—having what sounded like an epileptic seizure. The confederate then called for help.

The actual participants' behavior was now what counted. The dependent variable was the time that elapsed from the start of the "seizure" to the time a participant began trying to help the "victim." If 6 minutes went by without a participant offering help, the experiment was ended.

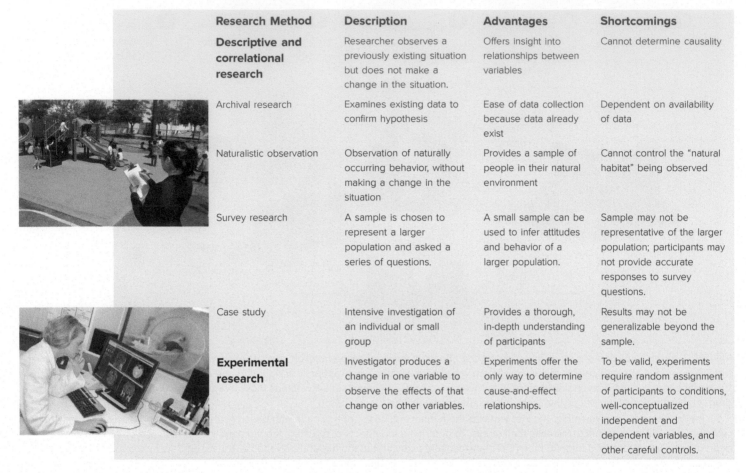

Research Method	Description	Advantages	Shortcomings
Descriptive and correlational research	Researcher observes a previously existing situation but does not make a change in the situation.	Offers insight into relationships between variables	Cannot determine causality
Archival research	Examines existing data to confirm hypothesis	Ease of data collection because data already exist	Dependent on availability of data
Naturalistic observation	Observation of naturally occurring behavior, without making a change in the situation	Provides a sample of people in their natural environment	Cannot control the "natural habitat" being observed
Survey research	A sample is chosen to represent a larger population and asked a series of questions.	A small sample can be used to infer attitudes and behavior of a larger population.	Sample may not be representative of the larger population; participants may not provide accurate responses to survey questions.
Case study	Intensive investigation of an individual or small group	Provides a thorough, in-depth understanding of participants	Results may not be generalizable beyond the sample.
Experimental research	Investigator produces a change in one variable to observe the effects of that change on other variables.	Experiments offer the only way to determine cause-and-effect relationships.	To be valid, experiments require random assignment of participants to conditions, well-conceptualized independent and dependent variables, and other careful controls.

FIGURE 3 Research strategies.
(Top): Bill Aron/PhotoEdit; (Bottom): ALPA PROD/Shutterstock

As predicted by the hypothesis, the size of the group had a significant effect on whether a participant provided help. The more people who were present, the less likely it was that someone would supply help, as you can see in Figure 4 (Latané & Darley, 1970).

Because these results are straightforward, it seems clear that the experiment confirmed the original hypothesis. However, Latané and Darley could not be sure that the results were truly meaningful until they determined whether the results represented what statisticians call a significant outcome.

significant outcome An outcome of a research study in which the observed results are statistically meaningful. (Module 5)

A **significant outcome** indicates that the findings of a research study are statistically meaningful, showing that the differences between conditions are large enough for researchers to feel confident that they have confirmed their hypotheses. Using statistical analysis, researchers can determine whether a numeric difference is a real difference or is due merely to chance. Only when differences between groups are large enough that statistical tests show them to be significant is it possible for researchers to confirm a hypothesis.

MOVING BEYOND THE STUDY

The Latané and Darley study contains all the elements of an experiment: an independent variable, a dependent variable, random assignment to conditions, and multiple experimental groups. Consequently, we can say with some confidence that group size *caused* changes in the degree of helping behavior.

replicated research Research that is repeated, sometimes using other procedures, settings, and groups of participants, to increase confidence in prior findings. (Module 5)

Of course, one experiment alone does not forever resolve the question of bystander intervention in emergencies. Psychologists–like other scientists–require that findings be **replicated**, or repeated, sometimes using other procedures, in other settings, with other groups of participants, before full confidence can be placed in the results of any single experiment.

For example, follow-up research shows that college students aren't the only ones who show the bystander effect; for instance, young children do as well. Furthermore, a procedure called *meta-analysis* permits psychologists to combine the results of many separate studies into one overall conclusion (Kisely et al., 2015; Plotner et al., 2015; Stone & Rosopa, 2017).

On the other hand, some follow-up research shows that in certain cases, the presence of more bystanders may actually lead to help. Using real-life video footage of aggressive interactions in several countries, researchers found that in many cases, the presence of more bystanders was associated with a higher likelihood of intervention. These findings, which are inconsistent with much prior research, show the importance of replication in fully understanding psychological phenomena (Philpot et al., 2019)

In short, replication is a critical activity, and many researchers believe that psychologists need to increase the number of studies that replicate earlier research in order to have greater confidence in their findings. They point to an influential study that attempted to replicate 100 previous findings, resulting in only 36% of the replications yielding similarly significant findings as in the original studies. (Open Science Collaboration, 2015; Card, 2017; Servick, 2018).

In fact, some researchers claim that psychology (and other social sciences) are facing a *replication crisis* because many replication studies have failed to support the original findings. Whether a full blown crisis exists is open to debate, but it is clear that in order to be fully confident about the meaning of research studies, results need to be replicated (Wiggins & Chrisopherson, 2019).

In addition to replicating experimental results, psychologists need to test the limitations of their theories and hypotheses to determine under which specific circumstances they do and do not apply. It seems unlikely, for instance, that increasing the number of bystanders *always* results in less helping.

In fact, follow-up research shows that bystander intervention is more likely to occur in situations viewed as clear-cut and dangerous because bystanders are more likely to perceive that the presence of others will provide resources for helping. In short, it is critical to continue carrying out experiments to understand the conditions in which exceptions to this general rule occur and other circumstances in which the rule holds (Garcia et al., 2002; Fischer et al., 2011; Menolascino & Jenkins, 2018).

Before leaving the Latané and Darley study, note that it represents a good illustration of the basic principles of the scientific method. The two psychologists began with a *question of interest*, in this case stemming from a real-world incident in which bystanders in an emergency did not offer help. They then *formulated an explanation* by specifying a theory of diffusion of responsibility and from that formulated the specific hypothesis that increasing the number of bystanders in an emergency situation would lower the degree of helping behavior. Finally, they *carried out research* to confirm their hypothesis, and they eventually *communicated their findings* by publishing their results. This four-step process embodied in the scientific method underlies all scientific inquiry, allowing us to develop a valid understanding of others'–and our own–behavior.

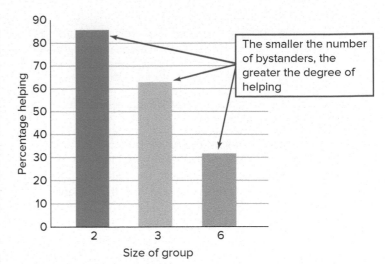

The smaller the number of bystanders, the greater the degree of helping

FIGURE 4 The Latané and Darley experiment showed that as the size of the group witnessing an emergency increased, helping behavior decreased.

Source: Adapted from Darley, J. M., & Latané, B. (1968). Bystanders' intervention in emergencies: Diffusion of responsibility. *Journal of Personality and Social Psychology, 8*, 377–383.

RECAP/EVALUATE/RETHINK

RECAP

LO 5-1 What research methods do psychologists use?

- Archival research uses existing records, such as online databases, newspapers, or other documents, to test a hypothesis. In naturalistic observation, the investigator acts mainly as an observer, making no change in a naturally occurring situation. In survey research, people are asked a series of questions about their behavior, thoughts, or attitudes. The case study is an in-depth interview and examination of one person or group.

- These descriptive research methods rely on correlational techniques, which describe associations between variables but cannot determine cause-and-effect relationships.

LO 5-2 How do psychologists establish cause-and-effect relationships in research studies?

- In a formal experiment, the relationship between variables is investigated by deliberately producing a change—called the experimental manipulation—in one variable and observing changes in the other variable.
- In an experiment, at least two groups must be compared to assess cause-and-effect relationships. The group receiving the treatment (the special procedure devised by the experimenter) is the experimental group; the second group (which receives no treatment) is the control group. There also may be multiple experimental groups, each of which is subjected to a different procedure and then compared with the others.
- The variable that experimenters manipulate is the independent variable. The variable that they measure and expect to change as a result of manipulation of the independent variable is called the dependent variable.
- In a formal experiment, participants must be assigned randomly to treatment conditions, so that participant characteristics are distributed evenly across the different conditions.
- Psychologists use statistical tests to determine whether research findings are significant.

EVALUATE

1. Match the following forms of research to their definitions:
   1. archival research
   2. naturalistic observation
   3. survey research
   4. case study

   a. directly asking a sample of people questions about their behavior

   b. examining existing records to test a hypothesis

   c. looking at behavior in its true setting without intervening in the setting

   d. doing an in-depth investigation of a person or small group

2. Match each of the following research methods with its primary disadvantage:
   1. archival research
   2. naturalistic observation
   3. survey research
   4. case study

   a. The researcher may not be able to generalize to the population at large.

   b. People's behavior can change if they know they are being watched.

   c. The data may not exist or may be unusable.

   d. People may lie in order to present a good image.

3. A friend tells you, "Anxiety about speaking in public and performance are negatively correlated. Therefore, high anxiety must cause low performance." Is this statement true or false, and why?

4. A psychologist wants to study the effect of attractiveness on willingness to help a person with a math problem. Attractiveness would be the _____ variable, and the amount of helping would be the _____ variable.

5. The group in an experiment that receives no treatment is called the _____ group.

RETHINK

Can you describe how a researcher might use naturalistic observation, case studies, and survey research to investigate gender differences in aggressive behavior at the workplace? First state a hypothesis, and then describe your research approaches. What positive and negative features does each method have?

Answers to Evaluate Questions

1. 1-b, 2-c, 3-a, 4-d. 2. 1-c, 2-b, 3-d, 4-a; 3. False. Correlation does not imply causation. Just because two variables are related does not mean that one causes the other. Poor performance may cause people to become more anxious, or a third variable may cause both of these effects; 4. independent; dependent; 5. control

---

KEY TERMS

archival research	correlational research	experimental group	random assignment to
naturalistic observation	experiment	control group	condition
survey research	experimental	independent variable	significant outcome
case study	manipulation	dependent variable	replicated research
variables	treatment		

Module 6
Critical Research Issues

You probably realize by now that there are few simple formulas for psychological research. Psychologists must make choices about the type of study to conduct, the measures to take, and the most effective way to analyze the results. Even after they have made these essential decisions, they must still consider several critical issues. We turn first to the most fundamental of these issues: ethics.

The Ethics of Research

Put yourself in the place of one of the participants in the experiment conducted by Latané and Darley to examine the helping behavior of bystanders in which another "bystander" simulating a seizure turned out to be a confederate of the experimenters (Latané & Darley, 1970). How would you feel when you learned that the supposed victim was in reality a paid accomplice?

Although you might at first experience relief that there had been no real emergency, you might also feel some resentment that you had been deceived by the experimenter. You might also experience concern that you had been placed in an embarrassing or compromising situation—one that might have dealt a blow to your self-esteem, depending on how you had behaved.

Most psychologists argue that deception is sometimes necessary to prevent participants from being influenced by what they think a study's true purpose is. (If you knew that Latané and Darley were actually studying your helping behavior, wouldn't you automatically have been tempted to intervene in the emergency?) To avoid such outcomes, a small proportion of research involves deception.

Nonetheless, because research has the potential to violate the rights of participants, psychologists are expected to adhere to a strict set of ethical guidelines aimed at protecting participants (American Psychological Association, 2002, 2017; Tien et al., 2012; Young, 2017). Those guidelines involve the following safeguards:

- Protection of participants from physical and mental harm
- The right of participants to privacy regarding their behavior
- The assurance that participation in research is completely voluntary
- The necessity of informing participants about the nature of procedures before their participation in the experiment
- All experiments must be reviewed by an independent panel before being conducted (Fisher, 2003; Coventry et al., 2003; Crano, Brewer, & Lac, 2015).

One of psychologists' key ethical principles is **informed consent**. Before participating in an experiment, the participants must sign a document affirming that they have been told the basic outlines of the study and are aware of what their participation will involve, what risks the experiment may hold, and the fact that their participation is purely voluntary, and they may terminate it at any time.

Furthermore, after participation in a study, participants must be given a debriefing in which they receive an explanation of the study and the procedures that were involved. The only time informed consent and a debriefing can be eliminated is in experiments in which the risks are minimal, as in a purely observational study in a public place (Barnett, Wise, & Johnson-Greene, 2007; Nagy, 2011; Hetzel-Riggin, 2017).

LEARNING OUTCOMES

LO 6-1 What major issues confront psychologists conducting research?

Study Alert
Because the protection of experiment participants is essential, remember the key ethical guideline of informed consent.

informed consent A document signed by participants affirming that they have been told the basic outlines of the study and are aware of what their participation will involve. (Module 6)

Although readily available and widely used as research subjects, college students may not represent the population at large. What are some advantages and drawbacks of using college students as subjects?
annedde/E+/Getty Images

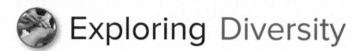 Exploring Diversity

Choosing Participants Who Represent the Scope of Human Behavior

When Latané and Darley, both college professors, decided who would participate in their experiment, they turned to the people most easily available: college students. Using college students as participants has both advantages and drawbacks. The big benefit is that because most research occurs in university settings, college students are readily available. Typically, they cost the researcher very little: They participate for either extra course credit or a relatively small payment.

The problem is that college students may not represent the general population adequately. In fact, undergraduate research participants are typically a special group of people: relative to the general population, college students tend to be from **W**estern, **e**ducated, **i**ndustrialized, **r**ich, and **d**emocratic cultures. That description forms the acronym WEIRD, which led one researcher to apply the nickname to research participants (Jones, 2010; Alper & Yilmaz, 2019; Kupferschmidt, 2019).

Nothing is necessarily wrong with using WEIRD participants. It's just that they may differ from most people who populate the world, and they have different characteristics that could be psychologically relevant. We certainly know that people in other cultures differ in fundamental ways from those in Western culture, such as in terms of generosity or even in the perception of geometric objects. Yet one review found that most research participants do come from the United States, and most of those are psychology majors (Arnett, 2008; Henrich, Heine, & Norenzayan, 2010; Kaiser, Thomas, & Bowers, 2017).

Because psychology is a science whose goal is to explain *all* human behavior generally, its studies must use participants who are fully representative of the general population in terms of gender, age, race, ethnicity, socioeconomic status, and educational level (see *Neuroscience in Your Life* and *Applying Psychology in the 21st Century* features).

To encourage a wider range of participants, the National Institute of Mental Health and the National Science Foundation—the primary U.S. funding sources for psychological research—now require that experiments address issues of diverse populations (Carpenter, 2002; Lindley, 2006; Sierra-Mercdo & Lazaro-Munoz, 2018).

NEUROSCIENCE IN YOUR LIFE: THE IMPORTANCE OF USING REPRESENTATIVE PARTICIPANTS

Most neuroscience research is conducted to understand the brains of all individuals. But even though their brains may be structurally similar, people differ significantly in the way they process information. For example, culture and experiences shape the way our brains process information, as a recent review of seven studies showed. The researchers found that individuals raised in Eastern countries, such as Japan, and individuals raised in Western countries, such as the United States, process information differently during cognitive tasks (Han & Ma, 2014; Russell et al., 2019).

In the images below, each brain indicates a different area in which differences were seen. The key indicates within a brain whether Easterners showed greater activation (green) or whether Westerners did (yellow). Overall, Easterners show more activity in the left hemisphere (green), whereas Westerners show more activity in the right hemisphere (yellow).

Might these differences indicate clear genetic differences between Easterners' and Westerners' brains? Not at all. It is equally plausible that cultural factors (exposure to certain kinds of experiences) cause the brains to develop after birth in different ways. In any case, it is clear that the best research must include participants who represent the rich diversity of humanity (Han & Ma, 2014; Tang et al., 2018).

■ East > West
West > East

Source: Neuroimage, "Cultural differences in human brain activity: a quantitative meta-analysis."

Should Animals Be Used in Research?

Like those who work with humans, researchers who use nonhuman animals in experiments have their own set of exacting guidelines to ensure that the animals do not suffer. Specifically, researchers must make every effort to minimize discomfort, illness, and pain. Procedures that subject animals to distress are permitted only when an alternative procedure is unavailable and when the research is justified by its prospective value. Moreover, researchers strive to avoid causing physical discomfort, but they are also required to promote the *psychological* well-being of some species of research animals, such as primates (Lutz & Novak, 2005; Miller & Williams, 2011; Herzog, 2017).

But why should animals be used for research in the first place? Is it really possible to learn about human behavior from the results of research employing rats, gerbils, and pigeons?

The answer is that psychological research that employs nonhumans is designed to answer questions different from those posed in research with humans and to study those questions in a different way. For example, the shorter life span of animals (rats live an average of 2 years) allows researchers to learn about the effects of aging in a relatively short time frame. It is also possible to provide greater experimental control over nonhumans and to carry out procedures that might ethically not be possible with people. For example, some studies require large numbers of participants that share similar backgrounds or have been exposed to particular environments—conditions that could not practically be met with human beings.

Research involving animals is controversial but, when conducted within ethical guidelines, yields significant benefits for humans.
D-Keine/E+/Getty Images

APPLYING PSYCHOLOGY IN THE 21ST CENTURY

CONDUCTING RESEARCH ON THE INTERNET

Conducting psychological research is certainly exciting and rewarding, but it's rarely convenient, fast, or inexpensive. More specifically, many challenges of doing research come during the data-collection phase. Traditionally, this has entailed recruiting participants and enticing them to come to a research lab, presenting them with stimulus materials, and recording their responses. The participants have commonly been students enrolled in psychology classes or members of the local community, and their motivation is usually extra credit in their class or payment. As you can probably imagine, meeting with them individually or in small groups to conduct the research procedure takes a lot of coordination, time, and effort.

Enter Mechanical Turk, or MTurk. The brainchild of Internet retailer Amazon, MTurk brings together researchers and participants in an online environment where the participants, motivated by payment, can spend all day if they wish participating in studies wherever they can find an Internet connection. Researchers have access to a ready-made pool of motivated participants, and the online system walks them through the procedures and collects their responses in an automated fashion—no appointments or lab assistants required! Furthermore, researchers can collect data from hundreds of participants in a matter of days, or perhaps even hours.

Of course, convenience shouldn't be the primary concern when conducting research, and researchers have expressed some reservations about using MTurk. An early concern was whether MTurk provides sufficient experimental control to trust the data. After

Although research has traditionally been carried out in face-to-face laboratory settings, researchers are now increasingly conducting research online.
Richard T. Nowitz/Science Source

all, researchers aren't present to guide and assist participants, and participants who are participating in studies to rack up payments may not be paying close attention or giving quality responses. Early research showed that results obtained with MTurk do indeed mirror results from lab studies, alleviating some of those concerns. Still, it's hard to know what unsupervised participants are actually doing when they complete the procedures (Buhrmester, Kwang, & Gosling, 2011).

Whether MTurk participants are representative of the larger population is another question, and research suggests that they are not. They tend to be well educated but underemployed young adults, with Asian people overrepresented and other people of color underrepresented. The responses of such a specific group of people might potentially differ in important ways from

those of the general population. On the other hand, the traditional participant pool of college students is also quite distinctive (recall the earlier discussion of WEIRD participants) and in certain ways that overlap with the MTurk participants, such as being younger and better educated than the general population. This isn't necessarily a problem as long as researchers understand and acknowledge the limited generalizability of their sample. A more worrisome question is whether MTurk participants, who may be participating in many studies every day, become so well practiced and so familiar with research materials and procedures that their responses are no longer spontaneous and genuine (Chandler et al., 2015; Stewart et al., 2015).

These considerations aside, many researchers are excited about the potential of MTurk to make research more efficient and cost effective. Concerns can be addressed by, for example, collecting data via both MTurk and more traditional means to ensure that the participants and procedures are comparable. And if nothing else, MTurk is useful for pilot-testing materials and procedures in a cheap and efficient way to be sure that they work properly before committing a larger investment to them. Like all research tools, MTurk offers a profile of advantages and disadvantages that researchers must consider carefully before deciding how best to proceed with their research.

QUESTIONS TO CONSIDER

1. If you were a researcher, what additional concerns might you have about using MTurk? Do you think the benefits outweigh the liabilities?
2. What kinds of research questions do you think might be well suited for answering with MTurk? What kinds of research questions might be better reserved for a traditional participant pool or laboratory environment?

Research with animals has provided psychologists with information that has profoundly benefited humans. For instance, it furnished the keys to detecting eye disorders in children early enough to prevent permanent damage, to communicating more effectively with children with severe intellectual disability, and to reducing chronic pain in people. Still, the use of research using nonhumans is controversial, involving complex moral and philosophical concerns. Consequently, all research involving nonhumans must be carefully reviewed beforehand to ensure that it is conducted ethically (Grundy, 2015; Guidelines for the treatment of animals, 2017; Watts et al., 2019).

Threats to Experimental Validity: Avoiding Experimental Bias

Even the best-laid plans are susceptible to **experimental bias**, meaning factors that distort the way the independent variable affects the dependent variable in an experiment. In one form of experimenter bias, the researcher unintentionally transmits cues to participants about the way the experimenter expects them to behave, thereby affecting the results. That is, the experimenter's expectations actually produce the expected result (Rosenthal, 2003).

A related problem is *participant expectations* about appropriate behavior. If you have ever been a participant in an experiment, you probably developed guesses about what was expected of you. In fact, participants often develop their own hypotheses about what the experimenter hopes to learn from the study. If participants form their own hypotheses and then act on their hunches, it may be their expectations, rather than the experimental manipulation, that produce the results (Rutherford et al., 2009).

To guard against participant expectations biasing the results of an experiment, the experimenter may try to disguise the true purpose of the experiment. Participants who do not know that helping behavior is being studied, for example, are more apt to act in a "natural" way than they would if they knew.

Sometimes it is impossible to hide the actual purpose of research; when that is the case, other techniques are available to prevent bias. Suppose you were interested in testing the ability of a new drug to alleviate the symptoms of severe depression. If you simply gave the drug to half your participants and not to the other half, the participants who were given the drug might report feeling less depressed merely because they knew they were getting a drug. Similarly, the participants who got nothing might report feeling no better because they knew that they were in a no-treatment control group.

To solve this problem, psychologists typically use a procedure in which all the participants receive a treatment but those in the control group receive only a **placebo**—a false treatment, such as a pill, "drug," or other substance that has no significant chemical properties or active ingredient. Because members of both groups are kept in the dark about whether they are getting a real or a false treatment, any differences in outcome can be attributed to the quality of the drug and not to the possible psychological effects of being administered a pill or other substance (Justman, 2011; Keränen et al., 2015; Ćurković, Kosec, & Savic, 2019).

However, there is one more safeguard that a careful researcher must apply in an experiment such as this one. To overcome the possibility that *experimenter* expectations will affect the participant, the person who administers the drug shouldn't know whether it is actually the true drug or the placebo. By keeping both the participant and the experimenter who interacts with the participant "blind" to the nature of the drug that is being administered, researchers can more accurately assess the effects of the drug. This method is known as the *double-blind procedure*.

experimental bias Factors that distort how the independent variable affects the dependent variable in an experiment. (Module 6)

Study Alert

Learn the main types of potential bias in experiments: experimenter expectations, participant expectations, and placebo effects.

placebo A false treatment, such as a pill, "drug," or other substance, without any significant chemical properties or active ingredient. (Module 6)

BECOMING AN INFORMED CONSUMER
of Psychology

Thinking Critically About Research

If you were about to purchase an automobile, you would not likely stop at the nearest car dealership and drive off with the first car a salesperson recommended. Instead, you would probably mull over the purchase, read about automobiles, consider the alternatives, talk to others about their experiences, and ultimately put in a fair amount of thought before you made such a major purchase.

In contrast, many of us are considerably less conscientious when we hear about research findings. People often jump to conclusions on the basis of incomplete and inaccurate information, and only rarely do they take the time to critically evaluate research and data.

Because the field of psychology is based on an accumulated body of research, we must scrutinize thoroughly the methods, results, and claims of researchers. Three questions can help us sort through what is valid and what is not:

- *What was the purpose of the research?* Research studies should evolve from a clearly specified theory. Furthermore, we must take into account the specific hypothesis that is being tested. Unless we know what hypothesis is being examined, we cannot judge how successful a study has been.
- *Was the study conducted appropriately to answer the questions it was intended to address?* Consider who the participants were, how many were involved, what methods were employed, and what problems the researcher encountered in collecting the data. There are important differences, for example, between a case study that reports the comments of a handful of respondents and a survey that collects data from several thousand people.
- *Are the results presented fairly?* The research findings must be assessed in terms of how closely they relate to the way in which a study was carried out and how they reflect what was found. For instance, suppose a drug producer claims that "no other sleeping pill has been shown to be more effective in helping people get a good night's sleep." This does not mean that theirs is the *best* sleeping pill on the market. It just means that no other sleeping pill has been proved *more* effective; other pills may be just as effective. Expressed in the latter fashion, the finding doesn't seem worth bragging about.

These three basic questions can help you assess the validity of research findings you come across—both within and outside the field of psychology. The more you know how to evaluate research, the better you will be able to assess what the field of psychology has to offer.

RECAP/EVALUATE/RETHINK

RECAP

LO 6-1 What major issues confront psychologists conducting research?

- One of the key ethical principles followed by psychologists is that of informed consent. Participants must be informed, before participation, about the basic outline of the experiment and the risks and potential benefits of their participation.
- Although the use of college students as participants has the advantage of easy availability, there are drawbacks, too. For instance, students do not necessarily represent the population as a whole. The use of nonhuman animals as participants may also have costs in terms of the ability to generalize to humans, although the benefits of using animals in research have been profound.
- Experiments are subject to a number of biases, or threats. Experimenter expectations can produce bias when an experimenter unintentionally transmits cues to participants about her or his expectations regarding their behavior in a given experimental condition. Participant expectations can also bias an experiment.

Among the tools experimenters use to help eliminate bias are placebos and double-blind procedures.

EVALUATE

1. Ethical research begins with the concept of informed consent. Before signing up to participate in an experiment, participants should be informed of:
   a. the procedure of the study, stated generally.
   b. the risks that may be involved.
   c. their right to withdraw at any time.
   d. all of these.
2. List three benefits of using animals in psychological research.
3. Deception is one means experimenters can use to try to eliminate participants' expectations. True or false?
4. A false treatment, such as a pill that has no significant chemical properties or active ingredient, is known as a _____.
5. A study has shown that men differ from women in their preference for ice cream flavors. This study was based on a sample of two men and three women. What might be wrong with this study?

RETHINK

A researcher strongly believes that college professors tend to show female students less attention and respect in the classroom than they show male students. He sets up an experimental study involving observations of classrooms in different conditions. In explaining the study to the professors and the students who will participate, what steps should the researcher take to eliminate experimental bias based on both experimenter expectations and participant expectations?

Answers to Evaluate Questions

1. d; 2. (1) We can study some phenomena in animals more easily than we can in people because with animal subjects, we have greater control over environmental and genetic factors. (2) Large numbers of similar participants can be easily obtained. (3) We can look at generational effects much more easily in animals because of their shorter life span than we can with people; 3. true; 4. placebo; 5. There are far too few participants. Without a larger sample, no valid conclusions can be drawn about ice cream preferences based on gender.

KEY TERMS

informed consent   experimental bias   placebo

LOOKING *Back*

EPILOGUE

We have been discussing the ways in which psychologists seek to understand phenomena and answer questions of interest. We examined the scientific method and its reliance on posing good questions, creating productive theories, and crafting testable hypotheses. We also looked at the basic methods psychologists use to conduct research studies and compared correlational methods and experimental methods. Finally, we explored some of the major challenges that psychologists have to deal with when conducting research, including ethical considerations, the use of animals in research, and potential bias.

Before leaving this topic, reconsider the two drowning victims we discussed in the prologue of this chapter. Consider the following questions in light of what you now know about conducting psychological research.

1. Do you think any of the teenagers who watched Jamel Dunn drown might have been more inclined to help if they had been alone rather than with their friends? Do you think that Antonio Salazar-Garcia might have hesitated to jump into dangerous waters if he was among other bystanders?
2. What other factors might have influenced Salazar-Garcia to risk his life and the Florida teenagers to not only avoid helping Jamel Dunn but to actually taunt him? Formulate a hypothesis of your own.
3. How might you go about testing your hypothesis?

VISUAL SUMMARY 2 Psychological Research

MODULE 4 The Scientific Method

Scientific Method

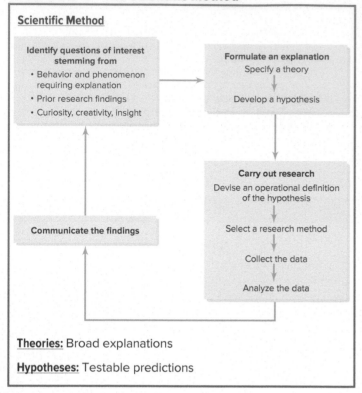

Identify questions of interest stemming from
- Behavior and phenomenon requiring explanation
- Prior research findings
- Curiosity, creativity, insight

Formulate an explanation
Specify a theory

Develop a hypothesis

Carry out research
Devise an operational definition of the hypothesis

Select a research method

Collect the data

Analyze the data

Communicate the findings

Theories: Broad explanations

Hypotheses: Testable predictions

MODULE 5 Conducting Psychological Research

Descriptive Research: Describes associations among variables
- Archival research
- Naturalistic observation
- Survey research
- Case study
- Correlational research
  - Does not explain causality

Possible Cause | Potential Result

(a) Choosing to watch television programs with high aggressive content → High viewer aggression

(b) High viewer aggression → Choosing to watch television programs with high aggressive content

(c) Unusually high energy level → High viewer aggression / Choosing to watch television programs with high aggressive content

MODULE 6 Critical Research Issues

Experimental Research: Assesses cause-and-effect relationships between variables
- Experimental manipulation
- Experimental and control groups
- Independent and dependent variables
- Random assignment of participants

1. Identify participants
2. Randomly assign participants to a condition
3. Manipulate the independent variable
4. Measure the dependent variable
5. Compare the results of the two groups

Group 1: Treatment group
Receive-drug condition

Group 2: Control group
No-drug condition

Ethics of Research

Informed consent

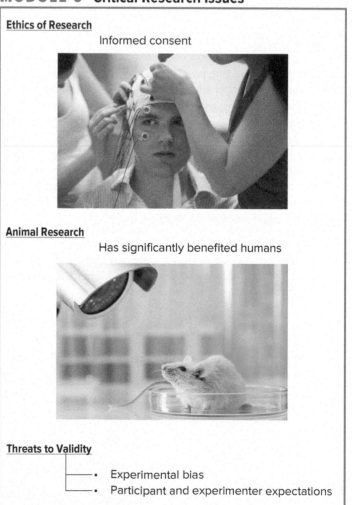

Animal Research

Has significantly benefited humans

Threats to Validity
- Experimental bias
- Participant and experimenter expectations

(Module 5): Source: Psychosomatic Medicine, "The effect of propranolol on behavioral interactions among adult male cynomolgus monkeys (Macacafas-cicularis) housed in disrupted social groupings."; (Module 6): annedde/E+/Getty Images; D-Keine/E+/Getty Images

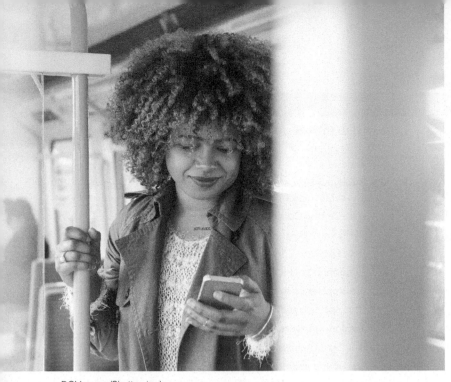

DGLimages/Shutterstock

CHAPTER 3
Neuroscience and Behavior

LEARNING OUTCOMES FOR CHAPTER 3

	MODULE 7
LO 7-1 Why do psychologists study the brain and the nervous system?	**NEURONS: THE BASIC ELEMENTS OF BEHAVIOR** The Structure of the Neuron
LO 7-2 What are the basic elements of the nervous system?	How Neurons Fire Where Neurons Meet: Bridging the Gap Neurotransmitters: Multitalented Chemical Couriers
LO 7-3 How does the nervous system communicate electrical and chemical messages from one part to another?	

	MODULE 8
LO 8-1 How are the structures of the nervous system linked?	**THE NERVOUS SYSTEM AND THE ENDOCRINE SYSTEM: COMMUNICATING WITHIN THE BODY** The Nervous System: Linking Neurons
LO 8-2 How does the endocrine system affect behavior?	The Evolutionary Foundations of the Nervous System The Endocrine System: Of Chemicals and Glands

LO 9-1   How do researchers identify the major parts and functions of the brain?

LO 9-2   What are the major parts of the brain, and for what behaviors is each part responsible?

LO 9-3   How do the halves of the brain operate interdependently?

LO 9-4   How can an understanding of the nervous system help us find ways to alleviate disease and pain?

PROLOGUE *HEALING HER BRAIN*

It happened in the blink of an eye: one moment 28-year-old Molie Wright was on her way to a much-anticipated ski trip with her boyfriend, and the next she was unconscious and close to death, trapped in the wreckage of an auto accident.

Her condition was grim: the vertebrae in her neck were crushed, leaving her internally decapitated: nothing but skin and muscle connected her head to her body. Scans done at the hospital found injuries across many regions of her brain. No one could say whether she would ever awaken from her coma. And even if she did recover, it was unclear whether she would be the same. Would her old personality survive the brain trauma, or would it be forever altered, turning Wright into a stranger, even to her closest family members?

For the first several weeks, Wright lay in her hospital bed completely unresponsive to stimulation. Then, miraculously, she started showing signs of life: a fixed gaze, a spontaneous movement, movement of her eyes.

It would be several months later when Wright regained full consciousness, and many more months still while she relearned to eat, talk, and walk. Although she continues to cope with many challenges, Wright reclaimed a normal life for herself. Just two years after the accident, she was finally able to finish her fateful trip and hit the ski slopes with her boyfriend (Hangley, 2018).

LOOKING *Ahead*

It's hard to believe that someone with severe brain injuries like those Wright sustained could heal so well. But this is just one example of the remarkable capacity of the brain and nervous system to overcome severe injury.

An organ roughly half the size of a loaf of bread, the brain controls our physical, emotional, and intellectual behavior through every waking and sleeping moment. Our movements, thoughts, hopes, aspirations, dreams—our very awareness that we are human—all depend on the brain and the nerves that extend throughout the body, constituting the nervous system.

Because of the importance of the nervous system in controlling behavior and because humans at their most basic level are biological beings, many researchers in psychology and other fields as diverse as computer science, zoology, and medicine have made the biological underpinnings of behavior their specialty. These experts collectively are called *neuroscientists* (Kasemsap, 2017; Vaughan-Graham et al., 2019).

Psychologists who specialize in considering the ways in which the biological structures and functions of the body affect behavior are known as **behavioral neuroscientists** (or *biopsychologists*). They seek to answer several key questions: How does the brain control the voluntary and involuntary functioning of the body? How does the brain communicate with other parts of the body? What is the physical structure of the brain, and how does this structure affect behavior? Are psychological disorders caused by biological factors, and how can such disorders be treated?

As you consider the biological processes that we discuss in this chapter, keep in mind the reason why behavioral neuroscience is an essential part of psychology: Our understanding of human behavior requires knowledge of the brain and other parts of the nervous system. Biological factors are central to our sensory experiences, states of consciousness, motivation and emotion, development throughout the life span, and physical and psychological health. Furthermore, advances in behavioral neuroscience have led to the creation of drugs and other treatments for psychological and physical disorders. In short, we cannot understand behavior without understanding our biological makeup (Schlinger, 2015; Filbey, 2019).

behavioral neuroscientists (or biopsychologists) Psychologists who specialize in considering the ways in which the biological structures and functions of the body affect behavior. (Module 7)

Module 7
Neurons: The Basic Elements of Behavior

Watching Serena Williams hit a stinging backhand, Dario Vaccaro dance a complex ballet routine, or Derek Jeter swing at a baseball, you may have marveled at the complexity—and wondrous abilities—of the human body. But even the most everyday tasks, such as pouring a cup of coffee or humming a tune, depend on a sophisticated sequence of events in the body that is itself truly impressive.

The nervous system is the pathway for the instructions that permit our bodies to carry out such precise activities. Here, we look at the structure and function of neurons, the cells that make up the nervous system, including the brain.

The Structure of the Neuron

Playing the piano, driving a car, or hitting a tennis ball depends, at one level, on exact muscle coordination. But if we consider *how* the muscles can be activated so precisely, we see that more fundamental processes are involved. For the muscles to produce the complex movements that make up any meaningful physical activity, the brain has to provide the right messages to them and coordinate those messages.

Such messages—as well as those that enable us to think, remember, and experience emotion—are passed through specialized cells called neurons. **Neurons,** or nerve cells, are the basic components of the nervous system. Their quantity is staggering: our bodies have perhaps as many as 1 *trillion* neurons.

Although there are several types of neurons, they all have a similar structure, as illustrated in Figure 1. Like most cells in the body, neurons have a cell body that contains a nucleus. The nucleus incorporates the hereditary material that determines

LEARNING OUTCOMES

LO 7-1 Why do psychologists study the brain and the nervous system?

LO 7-2 What are the basic elements of the nervous system?

LO 7-3 How does the nervous system communicate electrical and chemical messages from one part to another?

neurons Nerve cells, the basic components of the nervous system (Module 7)

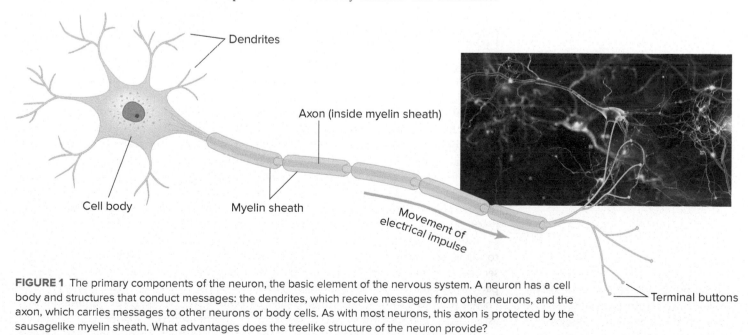

FIGURE 1 The primary components of the neuron, the basic element of the nervous system. A neuron has a cell body and structures that conduct messages: the dendrites, which receive messages from other neurons, and the axon, which carries messages to other neurons or body cells. As with most neurons, this axon is protected by the sausagelike myelin sheath. What advantages does the treelike structure of the neuron provide?
Photo: Whitehoune/Shutterstock

how a cell will function. Neurons are physically held in place by *glial cells*. Glial cells provide nourishment to neurons, insulate them, help repair damage, and generally support neural functioning (Keshavarz, 2017; Gould et al., 2019).

In contrast to most other cells, however, neurons have a distinctive feature: they can communicate with other cells and transmit information across relatively long distances. Many of the body's neurons receive signals from outside the body or relay the nervous system's messages to muscles and other target cells, but the vast majority of neurons communicate only with other neurons in the elaborate information system that regulates behavior.

As shown in Figure 1, there's a cluster of fibers at the end of every neuron that are called dendrites. **Dendrites** are the part of the neuron that receives messages from other neurons. They look like the twisted branches of a tree.

On the opposite side of every neuron is a long, slim, tube-like extension called an axon. The **axon** carries messages received by the dendrites to other neurons. The axon is considerably longer than the rest of the neuron. Although most axons are several millimeters in length, some are as long as 3 feet. Axons end in small bulges called terminal buttons. **Terminal buttons** send messages to other neurons. They look like a small bulge at the end of the axon.

The messages that travel through a neuron are electrical. Those electrical messages, or *impulses*, generally move across neurons in one direction only, as if they were traveling on a one-way street. Impulses follow a route that begins with the dendrites, continues into the cell body, and leads ultimately along the tube-like extension, the axon, to adjacent neurons.

To prevent messages from short-circuiting one another, axons must be insulated in some fashion (just as electrical wires must be insulated). Most axons are insulated by a **myelin sheath,** a protective coating of fat and protein that wraps around the axon like the casing on links of sausage.

The myelin sheath also serves to increase the velocity with which electrical impulses travel through axons. Those axons that carry the most important and most urgently required information have the greatest concentrations of myelin. If your hand touches a painfully hot stove, for example, the information regarding the pain is passed through axons in the hand and arm that have a relatively thick coating of myelin, speeding the message of pain to the brain so that you can react instantly.

How Neurons Fire

Like a gun, neurons either fire–that is, transmit an electrical impulse along the axon– or don't fire. There is no in-between stage, just as pulling harder on a gun trigger doesn't make the bullet travel faster. Similarly, neurons follow an **all-or-none law:** They are either on or off, with nothing in between the on state and the off state. When there is enough force to pull the trigger, a neuron fires.

Before a neuron is triggered–that is, when it is in a **resting state**–it has a negative electrical charge of about −70 millivolts (a millivolt is one 1/1,000 of a volt). This charge is caused by the presence of more negatively charged ions within the neuron than outside it. (An ion is an atom that is electrically charged.) You might think of the neuron as a miniature battery in which the inside of the neuron represents the negative pole and the outside represents the positive pole.

When a message arrives at a neuron, gates along the cell membrane open briefly to allow positively charged ions to rush in at rates as high as 100 million ions per second. The sudden arrival of these positive ions causes the charge within the nearby part of the cell to change momentarily from negative to positive. When the positive charge reaches a critical level, the "trigger" is pulled, and an electrical impulse, known as an *action potential*, travels along the axon of the neuron (see Figure 2).

The **action potential** moves from one end of the axon to the other like a flame moving along a fuse. As the impulse travels along the axon, the movement of ions

---

dendrite A cluster of fibers at one end of a neuron that receive messages from other neurons. (Module 7)

axon The part of the neuron that carries messages to other neurons. (Module 7)

terminal buttons The part of the axon that sends messages to other neurons. They look like a small bulge at the end of the axon. (Module 7)

! **Study Alert**
Remember that dendrites detect messages from other neurons; axons carry signals away from the neuron.

myelin sheath A protective coat of fat and protein that wraps around the axon. (Module 7)

all-or-none law The rule that neurons are either on or off. (Module 7)

resting state The state in which there is a negative electrical charge of about −70 millivolts within a neuron. (Module 7)

action potential An electric nerve impulse that travels through a neuron's axon when it is set off by a "trigger," changing the neuron's charge from negative to positive. (Module 7) causes a change in charge from negative to positive in successive sections of the axon (see Figure 3). After the impulse has passed through a particular section of the axon, positive ions are pumped out of that section, and its charge returns to negative while the action potential continues to move along the axon.

FIGURE 2 Movement of an action potential along an axon. Just before Time 1, positively charged ions enter the cell membrane, changing the charge in the nearby part of the axon from negative to positive and triggering an action potential. The action potential travels along the axon, as illustrated in the changes occurring from Time 1 to Time 3 (from top to bottom in this drawing). Immediately after the action potential has passed through a section of the axon, positive ions are pumped out, restoring the charge in that section to negative. The change in voltage illustrated by the blue line above the axon can be seen in greater detail in Figure 3.

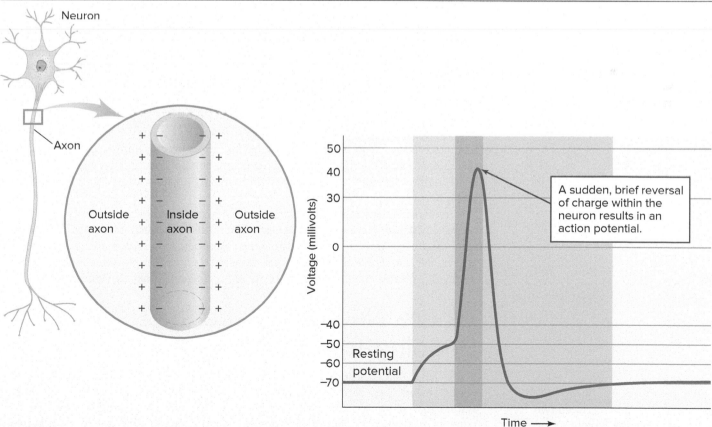

FIGURE 3 Changes in the voltage in a neuron during the passage of an action potential. In its normal resting state, a neuron has a negative charge of about −70 millivolts. When an action potential is triggered, however, the charge becomes positive, increasing from about −70 millivolts to about +40 millivolts. Immediately following the passage of the action potential, the charge becomes even more negative than it is in its typical resting state. After the charge returns to its normal resting state, the neuron will be fully ready to be triggered once again.

Just after an action potential has passed through a section of the axon, the cell membrane in that region cannot admit positive ions again for a few milliseconds, and so a neuron cannot fire again immediately no matter how much stimulation it receives. It is as if the gun has to be reloaded after each shot. There then follows a period in which, though it is possible for the neuron to fire, a stronger stimulus is needed than would be if the neuron had reached its normal resting state. Eventually, though, the neuron is ready to fire again.

SPEED OF TRANSMISSION

These complex events can occur at dizzying speeds, although there is great variation among different neurons. The particular speed at which an action potential travels along an axon is determined by the axon's size and the thickness of its myelin sheath. Axons with small diameters carry impulses at about 2 miles per hour; longer and thicker ones can average speeds of more than 225 miles per hour.

Neurons differ not only in terms of how quickly an impulse moves along the axon but also in their potential rate of firing. Some neurons are capable of firing as many as 1,000 times per second; others fire at much slower rates. The intensity of a stimulus determines how much of a neuron's potential firing rate is reached. A strong stimulus, such as a bright light or a loud sound, leads to a higher rate of firing than a less intense stimulus does. Thus, even though all impulses move at the same strength or speed through a particular axon–because of the all-or-none law–there is variation in the frequency of impulses, providing a mechanism by which we can distinguish the tickle of a feather from the weight of someone standing on our toes.

MIRROR NEURONS

mirror neurons Specialized neurons that fire not only when a person enacts a particular behavior but also when a person simply observes another individual carrying out the same behavior. (Module 7)

Although all neurons operate through the firing of action potentials, there is significant specialization among different types of neurons. For example, neuroscientists have discovered the existence of **mirror neurons,** neurons that fire not only when a person enacts a particular behavior but also when a person simply observes *another* individual carrying out the same behavior (Spaulding, 2013; Brucker et al., 2015; Bonini, 2017).

Mirror neurons may help explain how (and why) humans have the capacity to understand others' intentions. Specifically, mirror neurons may fire when we view someone doing something, helping us to predict what their goals are and what they may do next.

The discovery of mirror neurons suggests that the capacity of even young children to imitate others may be an inborn behavior. Furthermore, mirror neurons may be at the root of empathy–those feelings of concern, compassion, and sympathy for others–and even the development of language in humans (Rogalsky et al., 2011; Lim & Okuno, 2015; Krautheim et al., 2019).

Some researchers suggest an even broader role for mirror neurons. For example, mirror neurons, which respond to sound, appear to be related to speech perception and language comprehension. Furthermore, stimulating the mirror neuron system can help stroke victims as well and may prove to be helpful for those with emotional problems by helping them to develop greater empathy (Gallese et al., 2011; Hoenen, Lübke, & Pause, 2017).

Where Neurons Meet: Bridging the Gap

synapse The space between two neurons where the axon of a sending neuron communicates with the dendrites of a receiving neuron by using chemical messages. (Module 7)

If you have looked inside a computer, you've seen that each part is physically connected to another part. In contrast, evolution has produced a neural transmission system that at some points has no need for a structural connection between its components. Instead, a chemical connection bridges the gap, known as a synapse, between two neurons (see Figure 4). The **synapse** is the space between two neurons where the axon of a sending neuron communicates with the dendrites of a receiving neuron by using chemical messages.

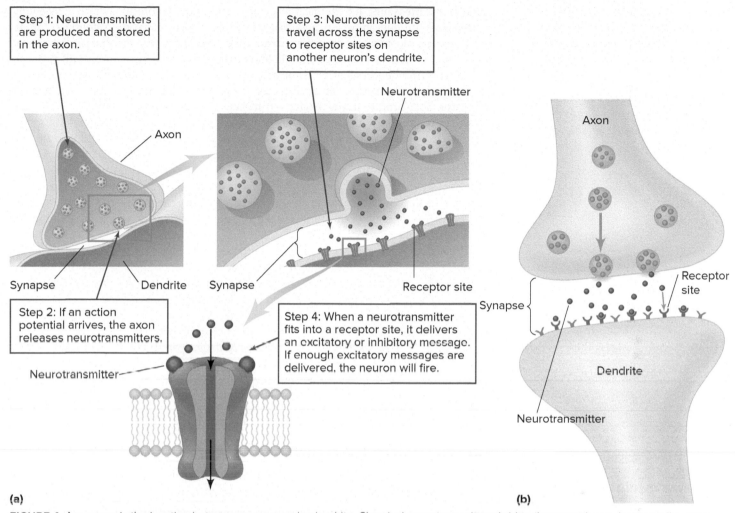

Step 1: Neurotransmitters are produced and stored in the axon.

Step 3: Neurotransmitters travel across the synapse to receptor sites on another neuron's dendrite.

Axon

Neurotransmitter

Synapse   Dendrite   Synapse   Receptor site

Step 2: If an action potential arrives, the axon releases neurotransmitters.

Step 4: When a neurotransmitter fits into a receptor site, it delivers an excitatory or inhibitory message. If enough excitatory messages are delivered, the neuron will fire.

Neurotransmitter

Axon

Receptor site

Synapse

Dendrite

Neurotransmitter

(a)   **(b)**

FIGURE 4 A synapse is the junction between an axon and a dendrite. Chemical neurotransmitters bridge the synaptic gap between the axon and the dendrite (Mader, 2000). (a) Read Step 1 through Step 4 to follow this chemical process. (b) Just as the pieces of a jigsaw puzzle can fit in only one specific location in a puzzle, each kind of neurotransmitter has a distinctive configuration that allows it to fit into a specific type of receptor cell (Johnson, 2000). Why is it advantageous for axons and dendrites to be linked by temporary chemical bridges rather than by the hard wiring typical of a radio connection or telephone hookup?

When a nerve impulse comes to the end of the axon and reaches a terminal button, the terminal button releases a chemical messenger called a neurotransmitter. **Neurotransmitters** carry messages from one neuron to another neuron. Like a boat that ferries passengers across a river, these chemical messengers move from the axon of one neuron to the dendrite of a receiving neurons.

Keep in mind that the chemical mode of message transmission that occurs between neurons differs strikingly from the means by which communication occurs inside neurons: Although messages travel in electrical form *within* a neuron, they move *between* neurons through a chemical transmission system.

There are several types of neurotransmitters, and not all neurons are capable of receiving the chemical message carried by a particular neurotransmitter. In the same way that a jigsaw puzzle piece can fit in only one specific location in a puzzle, each kind of neurotransmitter has a distinctive configuration that allows it to fit into a specific type of receptor site on the receiving neuron (see Figure 4b). It is only when a neurotransmitter fits precisely into a receptor site that successful chemical communication is possible.

If a neurotransmitter does fit into a site on the receiving neuron, the chemical message it delivers is basically one of two types: excitatory or inhibitory.

neurotransmitters Chemicals that communicate messages from one neuron to another neuron across the synapse. (Module 7)

Study Alert

Remember this key fact: Messages inside neurons are transmitted in electrical form, whereas messages traveling between neurons travel via chemical means.

excitatory message A chemical message that makes it more likely that a receiving neuron will fire and an action potential will travel down its axon. (Module 7)

inhibitory message A chemical message that prevents or decreases the likelihood that a receiving neuron will fire. (Module 7)

reuptake The reabsorption of neurotransmitters by a terminal button. (Module 7)

Excitatory messages are chemical messages that make it more likely that a receiving neuron will fire and an action potential will travel down its axon. In contrast, inhibitory messages do just the opposite: **inhibitory messages** provide chemical information that prevents or decreases the likelihood that the receiving neuron will fire.

Because the dendrites of a neuron receive both excitatory and inhibitory messages simultaneously, the neuron must integrate the messages by using a kind of chemical calculator. Put simply, if the excitatory messages ("Fire!") outnumber the inhibitory ones ("Don't fire!"), the neuron fires. In contrast, if the inhibitory messages outnumber the excitatory ones, nothing happens, and the neuron remains in its resting state.

If neurotransmitters remained at the site of the synapse, receiving neurons would be awash in a continual chemical bath, producing constant stimulation or constant inhibition of the receiving neurons. This would make effective communication across the synapse impossible. To avoid this problem, enzymes deactivate the neurotransmitters, or—more commonly—the terminal button sucks them back up in an example of chemical recycling called reuptake.

Reuptake is the process in which a neurotransmitter produced by a terminal button is reabsorbed by the terminal button. Like a vacuum cleaner sucking up dust, neurons reabsorb the neurotransmitters that are now clogging the synapse. All this activity occurs at lightning speed, with the process taking just several milliseconds (Gingrich et al., 2017).

Our understanding of the process of reuptake has permitted the development of a number of drugs used in the treatment of psychological disorders. Some antidepressant drugs, called *SSRIs*, or *selective serotonin reuptake inhibitors*, permit certain neurotransmitters to remain active for a longer period at certain synapses in the brain, thereby reducing the symptoms of depression (Hilton et al., 2013; Leong et al., 2017; Jauhar et al., 2019).

Neurotransmitters: Multitalented Chemical Couriers

Neurotransmitters are a particularly important link between the nervous system and behavior. Not only are they important for maintaining vital brain and body functions, but a deficiency or an excess of a neurotransmitter can produce severe behavior disorders. More than a hundred chemicals have been found to act as neurotransmitters, and neuroscientists believe that more may ultimately be identified. The major neurotransmitters and their effects are described in Figure 5 (Schmidt, 2006).

One of the most common neurotransmitters is *acetylcholine* (or *ACh*, its chemical symbol), which is found throughout the nervous system. ACh is involved in our every physical move because—among other things—it transmits messages relating to our skeletal muscles. ACh also aids in memory capabilities. In fact, diminished production of ACh may be related to Alzheimer's disease (Bazalakova et al., 2007; Van der Zee, Platt, & Riedel, 2011; Betterton et al., 2017).

Another common excitatory neurotransmitter, *glutamate*, plays a role in memory. Memories appear to be produced by specific biochemical changes at particular synapses, and glutamate, along with other neurotransmitters, plays an important role in this process (Micheau & Marighetto, 2011; Solomonia & McCabe, 2015; Jelen et al., 2019).

Gamma-amino butyric acid (GABA), which is found in both the brain and the spinal cord, appears to be the nervous system's primary inhibitory neurotransmitter. It moderates a variety of behaviors, ranging from eating to aggression. Several common substances, such as the tranquilizer Valium and alcohol, are effective because they permit GABA to operate more efficiently (Ball, 2004; Criswell et al., 2008; Lobo & Harris, 2008).

Another major neurotransmitter is *dopamine (DA)*, which is involved in movement, attention, and learning. The discovery that certain drugs can have a significant effect on dopamine release has led to the development of effective treatments for a wide variety of physical and mental ailments. For instance, Parkinson's disease, from which actor Michael J. Fox suffers, is caused by a deficiency of dopamine in the brain. Techniques for increasing the production of dopamine in Parkinson's patients are proving effective (Hanna-Pladdy, Pahwa, & Lyons, 2015; McGuigan et al., 2019).

Actor Michael J. Fox suffers from Parkinson's disease, and he has become a strong advocate for research into the disorder.

Theo Wargo/Getty Images

Neurotransmitter Name	Location	Effect	Function
Acetylcholine (ACh)	Brain, spinal cord, peripheral nervous system, especially some organs of the parasympathetic nervous system	Excitatory in brain and autonomic nervous system; inhibitory elsewhere	Muscle movement, cognitive functioning
Glutamate	Brain, spinal cord	Excitatory	Memory
Gamma-amino butyric acid (GABA)	Brain, spinal cord	Main inhibitory neurotransmitter	Eating, aggression, sleeping
Dopamine (DA)	Brain	Inhibitory or excitatory	Movement control, pleasure and reward, attention
Serotonin	Brain, spinal cord	Inhibitory	Sleeping, eating, mood, pain, depression
Endorphins	Brain, spinal cord	Primarily inhibitory, except in hippocampus	Pain suppression, pleasurable feelings, appetites, placebos

FIGURE 5 Major neurotransmitters.

In other instances, overproduction of dopamine produces negative consequences. For example, researchers have hypothesized that schizophrenia and some other severe mental disturbances are affected or perhaps even caused by the presence of unusually high levels of dopamine. Drugs that block the reception of dopamine reduce the symptoms displayed by some people diagnosed with schizophrenia (Howes & Kapur, 2009; Seeman, 2011; Howes et al., 2017).

PsychTech

A team of Swedish researchers has discovered a way to stimulate specific neurons via chemical neurotransmitters, rather than using earlier technologies involving electrical signals to stimulate them. This discovery opens a novel path to treat those who suffer from severe psychological disorders produced by brain dysfunction.

From the perspective of...

A Health-Care Provider How might your understanding of the nervous system help you explain the symptoms of Parkinson's disease to a patient with the disorder?

Tetra Images/Getty Images

Another neurotransmitter, *serotonin,* is associated with the regulation of sleep, eating, mood, and pain. A growing body of research points toward a broader role for serotonin, suggesting its involvement in such diverse behaviors as alcoholism, depression, suicide, impulsivity, aggression, and coping with stress (Carrillo et al., 2009; Pawluski, Li, & Lonstein, 2019).

Endorphins, another class of neurotransmitters, are a family of chemicals produced by the brain that are similar in structure to painkilling drugs such as morphine. The production of endorphins reflects the brain's effort to deal with pain as well as to elevate mood.

Endorphins also may produce the euphoric feelings that runners sometimes experience after long runs. The exertion and perhaps the pain involved in a long run may stimulate the production of endorphins, ultimately resulting in what has been called "runner's high" (Stanojevic, Mitic, & Vujic, 2007; Stoll, 2019).

Endorphin release might also explain other phenomena that have long puzzled psychologists. For example, the act of taking placebos (pills or other substances that contain no actual drugs but that patients *believe* will make them better) may induce the release of endorphins, leading to the reduction of pain (Crum & Langer, 2007; Bruehl et al., 2017).

RECAP/EVALUATE/RETHINK

RECAP

LO 7-1 Why do psychologists study the brain and nervous system?

- A full understanding of human behavior requires knowledge of the biological influences underlying that behavior, especially those originating in the nervous system. Psychologists who specialize in studying the effects of biological structures and functions on behavior are known as behavioral neuroscientists.

LO 7-2 What are the basic elements of the nervous system?

- Neurons, the most basic elements of the nervous system, carry nerve impulses from one part of the body to another. Information in a neuron generally follows a route that begins with the dendrites, continues into the cell body, and leads ultimately down the tube-like extension, the axon.

LO 7-3 How does the nervous system communicate electrical and chemical messages from one part to another?

- Most axons are insulated by a coating called the myelin sheath. When a neuron receives a message to fire, it releases an action potential, an electric charge that travels through the axon. Neurons operate according to an all-or-none law: Either they are at rest, or an action potential is moving through them. There is no in-between state.
- When a neuron fires, nerve impulses are carried to other neurons through the production of chemical substances called neurotransmitters that bridge the gaps—known as synapses—between neurons. Neurotransmitters may be either excitatory, telling other neurons to fire, or inhibitory, preventing or decreasing the likelihood of other neurons firing.
- Endorphins, another type of neurotransmitter, are related to the reduction of pain. Endorphins aid in the production of a natural painkiller and are probably responsible for creating the kind of euphoria that joggers sometimes experience after running.

EVALUATE

1. The _____ is the fundamental element of the nervous system.
2. Neurons receive information through their _____ and send messages through their _____.
3. Just as electrical wires have an outer coating, axons are insulated by a coating called the _____ _____.
4. The gap between two neurons is bridged by a chemical connection called a _____..
5. Endorphins are one kind of _____, the chemical "messenger" between neurons.

RETHINK

1. How might psychologists use drugs that mimic the effects of neurotransmitters to treat psychological disorders?
2. In what ways might endorphins help to produce the placebo effect? Is there a difference between *believing* that one's pain is reduced and actually *experiencing* reduced pain? Why or why not?

Answers to Evaluate Questions

1. neuron; **2.** dendrites, axons; **3.** myelin sheath; **4.** synapse; **5.** neurotransmitter

KEY TERMS

behavioral neuroscientists (or biopsychologists)	axon	resting state	neurotransmitters
	terminal buttons	action potential	excitatory message
neurons	myelin sheath	mirror neurons	inhibitory message
dendrite	all-or-none law	synapse	reuptake

Module 8

The Nervous System and the Endocrine System: Communicating Within the Body

In light of the complexity of individual neurons and the neurotransmission process, it should come as no surprise that the connections and structures formed by the neurons are complicated. Because each neuron can be connected to 80,000 other neurons, the total number of possible connections is astonishing. For instance, estimates of the number of neural connections within the brain fall in the neighborhood of 10 quadrillion–a 1 followed by 16 zeros–and some experts put the number even higher. However, connections among neurons are not the only means of communication within the body; as we'll see, the endocrine system, which secretes chemical messages that circulate through the blood, also communicates messages that influence behavior and many aspects of biological functioning (Heintz, Brander, & White, 2015).

The Nervous System: Linking Neurons

Whatever the actual number of neural connections, the human nervous system has both logic and elegance. We turn now to a discussion of its basic structures.

CENTRAL AND PERIPHERAL NERVOUS SYSTEMS

As you can see from the schematic representation in Figure 1, the nervous system is divided into two main parts: the central nervous system and the peripheral nervous system. The **central nervous system (CNS)** is composed of the brain and spinal cord. The **spinal cord,** which is about the thickness of a pencil, contains a bundle of neurons that leaves the brain and runs down the length of the back (see Figure 2). As you can see in Figure 2, the spinal cord is the primary means for transmitting messages between the brain and the rest of the body.

However, the spinal cord is not just a communication channel. It also controls some simple behaviors on its own, without any help from the brain. An example is the way the knee jerks forward when it is tapped with a rubber hammer. This behavior is a type of **reflex,** an automatic, involuntary response to an incoming stimulus. A reflex is also at work when you touch a hot stove and immediately withdraw your hand. Although the brain eventually analyzes and reacts to the situation ("Ouch–hot stove–pull away!"), the initial withdrawal is directed only by neurons in the spinal cord.

Several kinds of neurons are involved in reflexes. **Sensory (afferent) neurons** transmit information *from* the perimeter of the body *to* the central nervous system and the brain. For example, touching a hot stove sends a message to the brain (hot!) via sensory neurons. **Motor (efferent) neurons** communicate information in the opposite direction, sending messages *from* the brain and nervous system *to* the muscles

central nervous system (CNS) The part of the nervous system that includes the brain and spinal cord. (Module 8)

spinal cord A bundle of neurons that leaves the brain and runs down the length of the back and is the main means for transmitting messages between the brain and the body. (Module 8)

reflex An automatic, involuntary response to an incoming stimulus. (Module 8)

sensory (afferent) neurons Neurons that transmit information from the perimeter of the body to the nervous system and brain. (Module 8)

motor (efferent) neurons Neurons that communicate information from the brain and nervous system to muscles and glands. (Module 8)

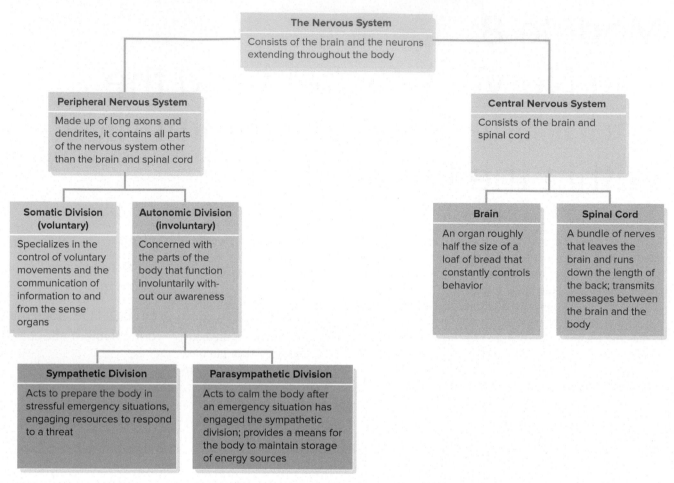

The Nervous System

Consists of the brain and the neurons extending throughout the body

Peripheral Nervous System

Made up of long axons and dendrites, it contains all parts of the nervous system other than the brain and spinal cord

Central Nervous System

Consists of the brain and spinal cord

Somatic Division (voluntary)

Specializes in the control of voluntary movements and the communication of information to and from the sense organs

Autonomic Division (involuntary)

Concerned with the parts of the body that function involuntarily without our awareness

Brain

An organ roughly half the size of a loaf of bread that constantly controls behavior

Spinal Cord

A bundle of nerves that leaves the brain and runs down the length of the back; transmits messages between the brain and the body

Sympathetic Division

Acts to prepare the body in stressful emergency situations, engaging resources to respond to a threat

Parasympathetic Division

Acts to calm the body after an emergency situation has engaged the sympathetic division; provides a means for the body to maintain storage of energy sources

FIGURE 1 A schematic diagram of the relationship of the parts of the nervous system.

FIGURE 2 The central nervous system consists of the brain and spinal cord, and the peripheral nervous system encompasses the network of nerves connecting the brain and spinal cord to other parts of the body.

Photo: Ianych/Shutterstock

Central Nervous System

Brain

Spinal cord

Peripheral Nervous System

Spinal nerves

Study Alert

Use Figures 1 and 2 to learn the components of the central and peripheral nervous systems.

and glands. When the brain sends a message to the muscles of the hand (hot—move away!), the message travels via motor neurons.

The importance of the spinal cord and reflexes is illustrated by the outcome of accidents in which the cord is injured or severed. In some cases, injury results in *quadriplegia*, a condition in which people lose voluntary muscle movement below the neck. In a less severe but still disabling condition, *paraplegia*, people are unable to voluntarily move any muscles in the lower half of the body.

As suggested by its name, the **peripheral nervous system** branches out from the spinal cord and brain and reaches the extremities of the body. Made up of neurons with long axons and dendrites, the peripheral nervous system encompasses all the parts of the nervous system other than the brain and spinal cord. There are two major divisions of the peripheral nervous system—the somatic division and the autonomic division—both of which connect the central nervous system with the sense organs, muscles, glands, and other organs.

The **somatic division** of the peripheral nervous system specializes in the control of voluntary movements, such as the motion of your eyes to read this sentence or those of your hand to scroll down a page. The somatic division also communicates information to and from the sense organs.

The **autonomic division** of the peripheral nervous system controls the parts of the body that automatically function to keep us alive—the heart, blood vessels, glands, lungs, and other organs that function involuntarily without our awareness. As you are reading at this moment, the autonomic division of the peripheral nervous system is pumping blood through your body, pushing your lungs in and out, and overseeing the digestion of your last meal.

ACTIVATING THE DIVISIONS OF THE AUTONOMIC NERVOUS SYSTEM

The autonomic division plays a particularly crucial role during emergencies. Suppose that as you are walking down a street and checking your cell phone, you suddenly see the glint of something that might be a knife. As confusion clouds your mind and fear overcomes your attempts to think rationally, what happens to your body? If you are like most people, you react immediately on a biological level level. Your heart rate increases, you begin to sweat, and you may develop goose bumps all over your body.

The biological changes that occur during a crisis result from the activation of the part of the autonomic nervous system called the sympathetic division. The **sympathetic division** prepares the body for action in stressful situations by engaging all the organism's resources to run away or to confront the threat. This is often called the "fight-or-flight" response.

In contrast, the **parasympathetic division** of the autonomic nervous system acts to calm the body after the emergency has ended. When you find, for instance, that what you thought might be a knife is actually the glint of keys in the stranger's hand, your parasympathetic division begins to take over, lowering your heart rate, stopping your sweating, and returning your body to the state it was in before you became alarmed. The parasympathetic division also directs the body to store energy for use in emergencies.

The sympathetic and parasympathetic divisions work together to regulate many functions of the body (see Figure 3). For instance, sexual arousal is controlled by the parasympathetic division, but sexual orgasm is a function of the sympathetic division. The sympathetic and parasympathetic divisions also are involved in a number of disorders. For example, one explanation of documented examples of "voodoo death"—in which a person is literally scared to death resulting from a voodoo curse—may be produced by overstimulation of the sympathetic division due to extreme fear.

peripheral nervous system The part of the nervous system that includes the autonomic and somatic subdivisions; made up of neurons with long axons and dendrites, it branches out from the spinal cord and brain and reaches the extremities of the body. (Module 8)

somatic division The part of the peripheral nervous system that specializes in the control of voluntary movements and the communication of information to and from the sense organs. (Module 8)

autonomic division The part of the peripheral nervous system that controls involuntary movement of the heart, glands, lungs, and other organs. (Module 8)

sympathetic division The part of the autonomic division of the nervous system that acts to prepare the body for action in stressful situations, engaging all the organism's resources to respond to a threat. (Module 8)

parasympathetic division The part of the autonomic division of the nervous system that acts to calm the body after an emergency has ended. (Module 8)

FIGURE 3 The major functions of the autonomic nervous system. The sympathetic division acts to prepare certain organs of the body for stressful situations, and the parasympathetic division acts to calm the body after the emergency has passed. Can you explain why each response of the sympathetic division might be useful in an emergency?

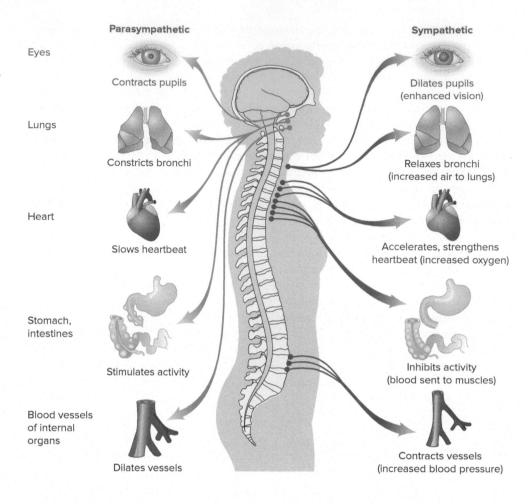

Parasympathetic

Eyes — Contracts pupils

Lungs — Constricts bronchi

Heart — Slows heartbeat

Stomach, intestines — Stimulates activity

Blood vessels of internal organs — Dilates vessels

Sympathetic

Dilates pupils (enhanced vision)

Relaxes bronchi (increased air to lungs)

Accelerates, strengthens heartbeat (increased oxygen)

Inhibits activity (blood sent to muscles)

Contracts vessels (increased blood pressure)

PsychTech
Rob Summers, who was paralyzed when hit by a car at age 20, took his first steps 5 years later after he received an experimental treatment in which electrodes were implanted into his back to stimulate his spinal cord.

From the perspective of...

A Health-Care Provider How would an understanding of the nervous system be valuable in your job as a medical care provider?

Rubberball/Getty Images

The Evolutionary Foundations of the Nervous System

The complexities of the nervous system can be better understood if we take the course of evolution into consideration. The forerunner of the human nervous system is found in the earliest simple organisms to have a spinal cord. Basically, those organisms were simple input-output devices: When the upper side of the spinal cord was stimulated by, for instance, being touched, the organism reacted with a simple response, such as jerking away. Such responses were completely a consequence of the organism's genetic makeup.

Over millions of years, the spinal cord became more specialized, and organisms became capable of distinguishing between different kinds of stimuli and responding appropriately to them. Ultimately, a portion of the spinal cord evolved into what we would consider a primitive brain.

Today, the nervous system is *hierarchically organized*, meaning that relatively newer (from an evolutionary point of view) and more sophisticated regions of the brain regulate the older, and more primitive, parts of the nervous system. As we move up along the spinal cord and continue upward into the brain then, the functions controlled by the various regions become progressively more advanced.

Why should we care about the evolutionary background of the human nervous system? The answer comes from researchers working in the area of **evolutionary psychology,** the branch of psychology that seeks to identify how behavior is influenced and produced by our genetic inheritance from our ancestors.

Evolutionary psychologists argue that the course of evolution is reflected in the structure and functioning of the nervous system and that evolutionary factors consequently have a significant influence on our everyday behavior. Their work, in conjunction with the research of scientists studying genetics, biochemistry, and medicine, has led to an understanding of how our behavior is affected by heredity, our genetically determined heritage.

Evolutionary psychologists have spawned a new and increasingly influential field: behavioral genetics. As we will discuss further in chapter 12 on development, **behavioral genetics** is the study of the effects of heredity on behavior. Consistent with the evolutionary perspective, behavioral genetics researchers are finding increasing evidence that cognitive abilities, personality traits, sexual orientation, and psychological disorders are determined to some extent by genetic factors (Appelbaum, Scurich, & Raad, 2015; Barbaro et al., 2017; Wertz et al., 2019).

evolutionary psychology The branch of psychology that seeks to identify behavior patterns that are a result of our genetic inheritance from our ancestors. (Module 8)

behavioral genetics The study of the effects of heredity on behavior. (Module 8)

The Endocrine System: Of Chemicals and Glands

Another of the body's communication systems, the **endocrine system** is a chemical communication network that sends messages throughout the body via the bloodstream. Its job is to secrete **hormones,** chemicals that circulate through the blood and regulate the functioning or growth of the body. It also influences—and is influenced by—the functioning of the nervous system. Although the endocrine system is not part of the brain, it is closely linked to the hypothalamus.

As chemical messengers, hormones are like neurotransmitters, although their speed and mode of transmission are quite different. Whereas neural messages are measured in thousandths of a second, hormonal communications may take minutes to reach their destination. Furthermore, neural messages move through neurons in specific lines (like a signal carried by wires strung along telephone poles), whereas hormones travel throughout the body, similar to the way radio waves are transmitted across the entire landscape. Just as radio waves evoke a response only when a radio is tuned to the correct station, hormones flowing through the bloodstream activate only those cells that are receptive and "tuned" to the appropriate hormonal message.

A key component of the endocrine system is the tiny **pituitary gland,** which is found near—and regulated by—the hypothalamus in the brain. The pituitary gland has sometimes been called the "master gland" because it controls the functioning of the rest of the endocrine system. But the pituitary gland is more than just the taskmaster of other glands; it has important functions in its own right. For instance, hormones secreted by the pituitary gland control growth. Extremely short people and unusually tall ones usually have pituitary gland abnormalities. Other endocrine glands, shown in Figure 4, affect emotional reactions, sexual urges, and energy levels.

endocrine system A chemical communication network that sends messages throughout the body via the bloodstream. (Module 8)

hormones Chemicals that circulate through the blood and regulate the functioning or growth of the body. (Module 8)

pituitary gland The major component of the endocrine system, or "master gland," that secretes hormones that control growth and other parts of the endocrine system. (Module 8)

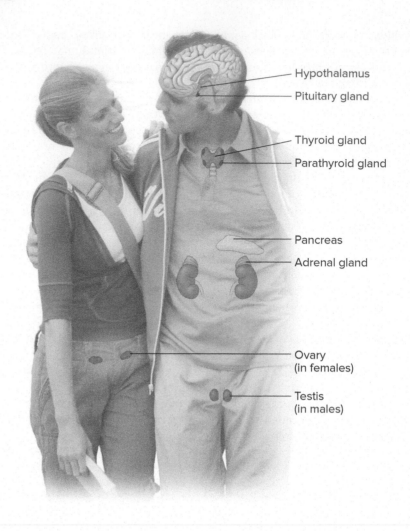

FIGURE 4 Location and function of the major endocrine glands. The pituitary gland controls the functioning of the other endocrine glands and, in turn, is regulated by the hypothalamus.

Photo: Laurence Mouton/PhotoAlto/Getty Images

Hypothalamus

Pituitary gland

Thyroid gland

Parathyroid gland

Pancreas

Adrenal gland

Ovary
(in females)

Testis
(in males)

Study Alert

The endocrine system produces hormones, chemicals that circulate through the body via the bloodstream.

Despite its designation as the "master gland," the pituitary is actually a servant of the brain because the brain is ultimately responsible for the endocrine system's functioning. The brain maintains the internal balance of the body through the hypothalamus.

Individual hormones can wear many hats, depending on circumstances. For example, the hormone oxytocin is at the root of many of life's satisfactions and pleasures. In new mothers, oxytocin produces an urge to nurse newborn offspring. The same hormone also seems to stimulate cuddling between species members. And—at least in rats—it encourages sexually active males to seek out females more passionately and females to be more receptive to males' sexual advances. There's even evidence that oxytocin is related to the development of trust in others, helping to grease the wheels of effective social interaction (De Dreu et al., 2011; de Visser et al., 2017; Berends et al., 2019).

Although hormones are produced naturally by the endocrine system, the ingestion of artificial hormones has proved to be both beneficial and potentially dangerous. For example, before the early 2000s, physicians frequently prescribed hormone replacement therapy to treat symptoms of menopause in older women. However, because recent research suggests that the treatment has potentially dangerous side effects, health experts now warn that in many cases, the dangers outweigh the benefits (Alexandersen, Karsdal, & Christiansen, 2009; Jacobs et al., 2013; Doty et al., 2015).

Steroids can provide added muscle and strength, but they have dangerous side effects. A number of well-known athletes in a variety of sports, such as baseball player Robinson Cano, pictured here, have been accused of using the drugs illegally. In fact, a number of them have publicly said they have used them.
Rich Schultz/Getty Images

The use of testosterone, a male hormone, and drugs known as *steroids*, which act like testosterone, is increasingly common. For athletes and others who want to bulk up their appearance, steroids provide a way to add muscle weight and increase strength. However, these drugs can lead to stunted growth, shrinking of the testicles, heart attacks, strokes, and cancer, making them extremely dangerous. Furthermore, they can even produce violent behavior. For example, in one tragic case, professional wrestler Chris Benoit strangled his wife, suffocated his son, and later hanged himself—acts that were attributed to his use of steroids (Zahnow et al., 2017; Geniole et al., 2019).

RECAP/EVALUATE/RETHINK

RECAP

LO 8-1 How are the structures of the nervous system linked?

- The nervous system is made up of the central nervous system (the brain and spinal cord) and the peripheral nervous system. The peripheral nervous system is made up of the somatic division, which controls voluntary movements and the communication of information to and from the sense organs, and the autonomic division, which controls involuntary functions such as those of the heart, blood vessels, and lungs.
- The autonomic division of the peripheral nervous system is further subdivided into the sympathetic and parasympathetic divisions. The sympathetic division prepares the body in emergency situations, and the parasympathetic division helps the body return to its typical resting state.
- Evolutionary psychology, the branch of psychology that seeks to identify behavior patterns that are a result of our genetic inheritance, has led to increased understanding of the evolutionary basis of the structure and organization of the human nervous system.

LO 8-2 How does the endocrine system affect behavior?

- The endocrine system secretes hormones, chemicals that regulate the functioning of the body, via the bloodstream. The pituitary gland secretes growth hormones and influences the release of hormones by other endocrine glands and in turn is regulated by the hypothalamus.

EVALUATE

1. If you put your hand on a red-hot piece of metal, the immediate response of pulling it away would be an example of a(n) _____.
2. The central nervous system is composed of the _____ and the _____.
3. In the peripheral nervous system, the _____ division controls voluntary movements, whereas the _____ division controls organs that keep us alive and function without our awareness.
4. Maria saw a young boy run into the street and get hit by a car. When she got to the fallen child, she was in a state of panic. She was sweating, and her heart was racing. Her biological state resulted from the activation of what division of the nervous system?
   a. parasympathetic
   b. central
   c. sympathetic

5. The emerging field of _____ studies ways in which our genetic inheritance predisposes us to behave in certain ways.

RETHINK

1. In what ways is the "fight-or-flight" response helpful to humans in emergency situations?
2. How might communication within the nervous system result in human consciousness?

Answers to Evaluate Questions

1. reflex; 2. brain, spinal cord; 3. somatic, autonomic; 4. c. sympathetic; 5. evolutionary psychology

KEY TERMS

central nervous system (CNS)	sensory (afferent) neurons	autonomic division	behavioral genetics
spinal cord	motor (efferent) neurons	sympathetic division	endocrine system
reflex	peripheral nervous system	parasympathetic division	hormones
	somatic division	evolutionary psychology	pituitary gland

Module 9
The Brain

It is not much to look at. Soft, spongy, mottled, and pinkish-gray in color, it hardly can be said to possess much in the way of physical beauty. Despite its physical appearance, however, it ranks as the greatest natural marvel that we know and has a beauty and sophistication all its own.

The object to which this description applies: the brain. The brain is responsible for our loftiest thoughts—and our most primitive urges. It is the overseer of the intricate workings of the human body. If one were to attempt to design a computer to mimic the range of capabilities of the brain, the task would be nearly impossible; in fact, it has proved difficult even to come close. The sheer quantity of nerve cells in the brain is enough to daunt even the most ambitious computer engineer. Many billions of neurons make up a structure weighing just 3 pounds in the average adult. However, it is not the number of cells that is the most astounding thing about the brain but its ability to allow the human intellect to flourish by guiding our behavior and thoughts.

We turn now to a consideration of the particular structures of the brain and the primary functions to which they are related. However, a caution is in order. Although we'll discuss specific areas of the brain in relation to specific behaviors, this approach is an oversimplification. No straightforward, one-to-one correspondence exists between a distinct part of the brain and a particular behavior. Instead, behavior is produced by complex interconnections among sets of neurons in many areas of the brain: Our behavior, emotions, thoughts, hopes, and dreams are produced by a variety of neurons throughout the nervous system working in concert.

LEARNING OUTCOMES

LO 9-1 How do researchers identify the major parts and functions of the brain?

LO 9-2 What are the major parts of the brain, and for what behaviors is each part responsible?

LO 9-3 How do the two halves of the brain operate interdependently?

LO 9-4 How can an understanding of the nervous system help us find ways to alleviate disease and pain?

Studying the Brain's Structure and Functions: Spying on the Brain

The brain has posed a continual challenge to those who would study it. For most of history, its examination was possible only after an individual had died. Only then could the skull be opened and the brain cut into without serious injury. Although informative, this procedure could hardly tell us much about the functioning of the healthy brain.

Today, however, brain-scanning techniques provide a window into the living brain. Using these techniques, investigators can take a "snapshot" of the internal workings of the brain without having to cut open a person's skull. The most important scanning techniques, illustrated in Figure 1, are the electroencephalogram (EEG), positron emission tomography (PET), functional magnetic resonance imaging (fMRI), and transcranial magnetic stimulation imaging (TMS).

The *electroencephalogram (EEG)* records electrical activity in the brain through electrodes placed on the outside of the skull. Although traditionally the EEG could produce only a graph of electrical wave patterns, new techniques are now used to transform the brain's electrical activity into a pictorial representation of the brain that allows more precise diagnosis of disorders such as epilepsy and learning disabilities.

The brain (shown here in cross-section) may not be much to look at, but it represents one of the great marvels of human development. Why do most scientists believe that it will be difficult, if not impossible, to duplicate the brain's abilities with artificial intelligence?
Photo and Dissection by Christine Eckel/McGraw-Hill

(a) EEG

(b) fMRI

(c) PET scan

(d) TMS Apparatus

FIGURE 1 Brain scans produced by different techniques. (a) A computer-produced EEG image. (b) The fMRI scan uses a magnetic field to provide a detailed view of brain activity on a moment-by-moment basis. (c) The PET scan displays the functioning of the brain at a given moment. (d) Transcranial magnetic stimulation (TMS), the newest type of scan, produces a momentary disruption in an area of the brain, allowing researchers to see what activities are controlled by that area. TMS also has the potential to treat some psychological disorders.
(a) SPL/Science Source; (b) Stegerphoto/Getty Images; (c) National Institutes of Health; (d) Amelie Benoist/BSIP/Corbis Documentary/Getty Images

! Study Alert
Remember how EEG, fMRI, PET, and TMS scans differ in the ways that they produce an image of the brain.

Functional magnetic resonance imaging (fMRI) scans provide a detailed, three-dimensional computer-generated image of brain structures and activity by aiming a powerful magnetic field at the brain or other parts of the body. With fMRI scanning, it is possible to produce vivid, detailed images of the functioning and structure of the brain.

Using fMRI scans, researchers are able to view features of less than a millimeter in size and view changes occurring in intervals of one-tenth of a second. For example, fMRI scans can show the operation of individual bundles of nerves by tracing the flow of blood, opening the way for improved diagnosis of ailments ranging from chronic back pain to nervous system disorders such as strokes, multiple sclerosis, and Alzheimer's. Scans using fMRI are routinely used in planning brain surgery because they can help surgeons distinguish areas of the brain involved in normal and disturbed functioning (Hurschler et al., 2015; Sahakian & Gottwald, 2017).

Positron emission tomography (PET) scans show biochemical activity within the brain at a given moment. PET scans begin with the injection of a radioactive (but safe) liquid into the bloodstream, which makes its way to the brain. By locating radiation within the brain, a computer can determine which are the more active regions, providing a striking picture of the brain at work. For example, PET scans may be used to diagnose memory problems, seeking to identify the presence of brain tumors. PET scans can even measure blood flow and oxygen use (Konijnenberg et al., 2019).

Transcranial magnetic stimulation (TMS) uses magnetic fields to produce an understanding of the functioning of the brain. In TMS, a tiny region of the brain is bombarded by a strong magnetic field that causes a momentary interruption of electrical activity. Researchers then are able to note the effects of this interruption on normal brain functioning.

One of the newest procedures used to study the brain, TMS is sometimes called a "virtual lesion" because it produces effects similar to what would occur if areas of the brain were physically cut. The enormous advantage of TMS, of course, is that the virtual cut is only temporary. In addition to identifying areas of the brain that are responsible for particular functions, TMS has the potential to treat certain kinds of psychological disorders, such as depression and schizophrenia, by shooting brief magnetic pulses through the brain (Prasser et al., 2015; Francis et al., 2019).

Future discoveries may yield even more sophisticated methods of examining the brain. For example, the emerging field of *optogenetics* involves genetic engineering and the use of special types of light to view individual circuits of neurons. In addition, researchers are developing *hydrogel-embedding* methods. which allow observation of individual brain cells and the wiring of brain circuitry. Finally, using nonhumans, researchers have developed *Neuropixels,* implanted probes that allow neuroscientists to read activity in hundreds of neurons in multiple parts of the brain simultaneously (Shirai & Hayashi-Takagi, 2017; Yang, Song, & Qing, 2017; Steinmetz et al., 2018; de Sousa et al., 2019).

The Central Core: Our "Old Brain"

Although the capabilities of the human brain far exceed those of the brain of any other species, humans share some basic functions, such as breathing, eating, and sleeping, with more primitive animals. Not surprisingly, those activities are directed by a relatively primitive part of the brain. A portion of the brain known as the **central core** (see Figure 2) is quite similar in all vertebrates (species with backbones). The central core is sometimes referred to as the "old brain" because its evolution can be traced back some 500 million years to primitive structures found in nonhuman species.

If we were to move up the spinal cord from the base of the skull to locate the structures of the central core of the brain, the first part we would come to would be the *hindbrain,* which contains the medulla, pons, and cerebellum (see Figure 3). The

Cerebral cortex
(the "new brain")

Central core
(the "old brain")

FIGURE 2 The major divisions of the brain: the cerebral cortex and the central core.

central core The "old brain," which controls basic functions such as eating and sleeping and is common to all vertebrates. (Module 9)

Hypothalamus
Responsible for regulating basic biological needs: hunger, thirst, temperature control

Pituitary Gland
"Master" gland that regulates other endocrine glands

Pons
Involved in sleep and arousal

Reticular Formation
A network of neurons related to sleep, arousal, and attention

Spinal Cord
Responsible for communication between brain and rest of body; involved with simple reflexes

Cerebral Cortex
The "new brain" responsible for the most sophisticated processing

Corpus Callosum
Bridge of fibers passing information between the two cerebral hemispheres

Thalamus
Relay center for cortex; handles incoming and outgoing signals

Cerebellum
Controls bodily balance

Medulla
Responsible for regulating largely unconscious functions such as breathing and circulation

FIGURE 3 The major structures in the brain.
Photo: Dana Neely/Taxi/Getty Images

medulla controls a number of critical body functions, the most important of which are breathing and heartbeat. The *pons* is a bridge in the hindbrain. Containing large bundles of nerves, the pons acts as a transmitter of motor information, coordinating muscles and integrating movement between the right and left halves of the body. It is also involved in regulating sleep.

cerebellum (ser-uh-BELL-um) The part of the brain that controls bodily balance. (Module 9)

The **cerebellum** extends from the rear of the hindbrain. Without the help of the cerebellum, we would be unable to walk a straight line without staggering and lurching forward, for it is the job of the cerebellum to control bodily balance. It constantly monitors feedback from the muscles to coordinate their placement, movement, and tension. In fact, drinking too much alcohol seems to depress the activity of the cerebellum, leading to the unsteady gait and movement characteristic of drunkenness. The cerebellum is also involved in several intellectual functions, ranging from the analysis and coordination of sensory information to problem solving (Vandervert, Schimpf, & Liu, 2007; Swain, Kerr, & Thompson, 2011; Ronconi et al., 2017).

reticular formation The part of the brain extending from the medulla through the pons; it is related to changes in the level of arousal of the body. (Module 9)

The **reticular formation** is a nerve network in the brain that extends from the medulla through the pons, passing through the middle section of the brain, called the *midbrain*, and into the front-most part of the brain, called the *forebrain*. Like an ever-vigilant guard, the reticular formation produces general arousal of our body. If, for example, we are startled by a loud noise, the reticular formation can prompt a heightened state of awareness to determine whether a response is necessary. The reticular formation also helps regulate our sleep-wake cycle by filtering out background stimuli to allow us to sleep undisturbed.

thalamus The part of the brain located in the middle of the central core that acts primarily to relay information about the senses. (Module 9)

The **thalamus,** which is hidden within the forebrain, acts primarily as a relay station for information about the senses. Messages from the eyes, ears, and skin travel to the thalamus to be communicated upward to higher parts of the brain. The thalamus also integrates information from higher parts of the brain, sorting it out so that it can be sent to the cerebellum and medulla.

hypothalamus A tiny part of the brain, located below the thalamus, that maintains homeostasis and produces and regulates vital behavior, such as eating, drinking, and sexual behavior. (Module 9)

The **hypothalamus** is located just below the thalamus. Although tiny—about the size of a fingertip—the hypothalamus plays an extremely important role. One of its major functions is to maintain *homeostasis*, a steady internal environment for the body. The hypothalamus helps provide a constant body temperature and monitors the amount of nutrients stored in the cells. A second major function is equally important: The hypothalamus produces and regulates behavior that is critical to the basic survival of the species, such as eating, self-protection, and sex.

limbic system The part of the brain that controls eating, aggression, and reproduction. (Module 9)

The Limbic System: Beyond the Central Core

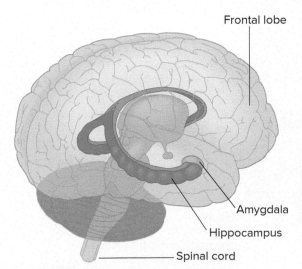

Frontal lobe

Amygdala

Hippocampus

Spinal cord

FIGURE 4 The limbic system is involved in self-preservation, learning, memory, and the experience of pleasure.

In an eerie view of the future, science fiction writers have suggested that people someday will routinely have electrodes implanted in their brains. Those electrodes will permit them to receive tiny shocks that will produce the sensation of pleasure by stimulating certain centers of the brain. When they feel upset, people will simply activate their electrodes to achieve an immediate high.

Although far-fetched—and ultimately improbable—such a futuristic fantasy is based on fact. The brain does have pleasure centers in several areas, including some in the **limbic system.** Consisting of a series of doughnut-shaped structures that include the *amygdala* and *hippocampus*, the limbic system borders the top of the central core and has connections with the cerebral cortex (see Figure 4).

The structures of the limbic system jointly control a variety of basic functions relating to emotions and self-preservation, such as eating, aggression, and reproduction. Injury to the limbic system can produce striking changes in behavior. For example, injury to the amygdala, which is involved in fear and aggression, can turn animals that are usually docile and tame into belligerent savages. Conversely, animals that are usually wild and uncontrollable may become meek and obedient following injury to the amygdala (Gontkovsky, 2005; Smith et al., 2013; Reznikova et al., 2015).

Research examining the effects of mild electric shocks to parts of the limbic system and other parts of the brain has produced some thought-provoking findings. In one classic experiment, rats that pressed a bar received mild electric stimulation through an electrode implanted in their brains, which produced pleasurable feelings. Even starving rats on their way to food would stop to press the bar as many times as they could. Some rats would actually stimulate themselves literally thousands of times an hour—until they collapsed with fatigue (Routtenberg & Lindy, 1965; Fountas & Smith, 2007; Pieper et al., 2019).

Some humans have also experienced the extraordinarily pleasurable quality of certain kinds of stimulation: As part of the treatment for certain kinds of brain disorders, some people have received electrical stimulation to certain areas of the limbic system. Although at a loss to describe just what it feels like, these people report the experience to be intensely pleasurable, similar in some respects to sexual orgasm.

The limbic system and hippocampus, in particular, play an important role in learning and memory. Their importance is demonstrated in certain patients with epilepsy, who, in an effort to stop their seizures, have had portions of the limbic system removed. One unintended consequence of the surgery is that individuals sometimes have difficulty learning and remembering new information. In one case, a patient who had undergone surgery was unable to remember where he lived, although he had resided at the same address for 8 years. Further, even though the patient was able to carry on animated conversations, he was unable, a few minutes later, to recall what had been discussed (Milner, 1966; Grimm, 2011; de Voogd et al., 2017).

The limbic system, then, is involved in several important functions, including self-preservation, learning, memory, and the experience of pleasure. These functions are hardly unique to humans; in fact, the limbic system is sometimes referred to as the "animal brain" because its structures and functions are so similar to those of other mammals. To identify the part of the brain that provides the complex and subtle capabilities that are uniquely human, we need to turn to another structure—the cerebral cortex.

The Cerebral Cortex: Our "New Brain"

As we have proceeded up the spinal cord and into the brain, our discussion has centered on areas of the brain that control functions similar to those found in less sophisticated organisms. But where, you may be asking, are the portions of the brain that enable humans to do what they do best and that distinguish humans from all other animals? Those unique features of the human brain—indeed, the very capabilities that allow you to come up with such a question in the first place—are embodied in the ability to think, evaluate, and make complex judgments. The principal location of these abilities, along with many others, is the **cerebral cortex.**

The cerebral cortex is referred to as the "new brain" because of its relatively recent evolution. It consists of a mass of deeply folded, rippled, convoluted tissue. Although only about one-twelfth of an inch thick, it would, if flattened out, cover an area more than 2 feet square. This configuration allows the surface area of the cortex to be considerably greater than it would be if it were smoother and more uniformly packed into the skull. The uneven shape also permits a high level of integration of neurons, allowing sophisticated information processing.

The cerebral cortex consists of four major sections called **lobes.** Each lobe has specialized areas that relate to particular functions. If we take a side view of the brain, the *frontal lobes* lie at the front center of the cortex and the *parietal lobes* lie behind them. The *temporal lobes* are found in the lower-center portion of the cortex, with the *occipital lobes* lying behind them. These four sets of lobes are physically separated by deep grooves called *sulci.* Figure 5 shows the four areas.

cerebral cortex The "new brain," responsible for the most sophisticated information processing in the brain; contains four lobes. (Module 9)

lobes The four major sections of the cerebral cortex: frontal, parietal, temporal, and occipital. (Module 9)

FIGURE 5 The cerebral cortex of the brain. The major physical structures of the cerebral cortex are called lobes. This figure also illustrates the functions associated with particular areas of the cerebral cortex. Are any areas of the cerebral cortex present in nonhuman animals?
Photo: Ron Krisel/Photodisc/Getty Images

Another way to describe the brain is in terms of the functions associated with a particular area. Figure 5 also shows the specialized regions within the lobes related to specific functions and areas of the body. Three major areas are known: the motor areas, the sensory areas, and the association areas. Although we will discuss these areas as though they were separate and independent, keep in mind that this is an oversimplification. In most instances, behavior is influenced simultaneously by several structures and areas within the brain, operating interdependently. To give one example, people use different areas of the brain when they create sentences (a verbal task) compared with when they improvise musical tunes. Furthermore, when people suffer brain injury, uninjured portions of the brain can sometimes take over the functions that were previously handled by the damaged area. In short, the brain is extraordinarily adaptable (Sacks, 2003; Boller, 2004; Brown, Martinez, & Parsons, 2006).

THE MOTOR AREA OF THE CORTEX

motor area The part of the cortex that is largely responsible for the body's voluntary movement. (Module 9)

If you look at the frontal lobe in Figure 5, you will see a shaded portion labeled **motor area.** This part of the cortex is largely responsible for the body's voluntary movement. Every portion of the motor area corresponds to a specific locale within the body. If we were to insert an electrode into a particular part of the motor area of the cortex and apply mild electrical stimulation, there would be involuntary movement in the corresponding part of the body. If we moved to another part of the motor area and stimulated it, a different part of the body would move.

The motor area is so well mapped that researchers have identified the amount and relative location of cortical tissue used to produce movement in specific parts of the human body. For example, the control of movements that are relatively large scale and require little precision, such as the movement of a knee or a hip, is centered in a very small space in the motor area. In contrast, movements that must be precise and delicate, such as facial expressions and finger movements, are controlled by a considerably larger portion of the motor area (Schwenkreis et al., 2007; Ross et al., 2019).

In short, the motor area of the cortex provides a guide to the degree of complexity and the importance of the motor capabilities of specific parts of the body. In fact, it may do even more: Increasing evidence shows that not only does the motor cortex control different parts of the body, but it may also direct body parts into complex postures, such as the stance of a football center just before the ball is snapped to the quarterback or a swimmer standing at the edge of a diving board (Pool et al., 2013; Massé-Alarie et al., 2017).

Ultimately, movement, like other behavior, is produced through the coordinated firing of a complex variety of neurons in the nervous system. The neurons that produce movement are linked in elaborate ways and work closely together.

THE SENSORY AREA OF THE CORTEX

Given the one-to-one correspondence between the motor area and body location, it is not surprising to find a similar relationship between specific portions of the cortex and specific senses. The **sensory area** of the cortex includes three regions: one that corresponds primarily to body sensations (including touch and pressure), one relating to sight, and a third relating to sound.

For instance, the *somatosensory area* in the parietal lobe encompasses specific locations associated with the ability to perceive touch and pressure in a particular area of the body. As with the motor area, the amount of brain tissue related to a particular location on the body determines the degree of sensitivity of that location. Specifically, the greater the area devoted to a specific area of the body within the cortex, the more sensitive is that area of the body.

For example, our fingers are related to a larger portion of the somatosensory area in the brain and are the most sensitive to touch. The weird-looking individual in Figure 6 shows what we would look like if the size of every external part of our body corresponded to the amount of brain tissue related to touch sensitivity.

The senses of sound and sight are also represented in specific areas of the cerebral cortex. The *auditory area* located in the temporal lobe is responsible for the sense of hearing. If your auditory area were to be stimulated electrically, you would hear sounds such as clicks or hums. It also appears that particular locations within the auditory area respond to specific pitches (Anderson, Lazard, & Hartley, 2017; McKetton, DeSimone, & Schneider, 2019).

The *visual area* in the cortex, located in the occipital lobe, responds in an analogous way to electrical stimulation. Stimulation by electrodes produces the experience of flashes of light or colors, suggesting that the raw sensory input of images from the eyes is received in this area of the brain and transformed into meaningful stimuli. The visual area provides another example of how areas of the brain are intimately related to specific areas of the body: Specific structures in the eye are related to a particular part of the cortex—with, as you might guess, more area of the brain given to the most sensitive portions of the retina (Stenbacka & Vanni, 2007; Libedinsky & Livingstone, 2011).

THE ASSOCIATION AREAS OF THE CORTEX

In a freak accident in 1848, an explosion drove a 3-foot-long iron bar completely through the skull of railroad worker Phineas Gage, where it remained after the accident. Amazingly, Gage survived and, despite the rod lodged through his head, a few minutes later seemed to be fine.

But he wasn't. Before the accident, Gage was hardworking and cautious. Afterward, he became irresponsible, drank heavily, and drifted from one wild scheme to another. In the words of one of his physicians, "He was 'no longer Gage'" (Harlow, 1869).

What had happened to the old Gage? Although we have no way of knowing for sure, we can speculate that the accident injured the region of Gage's cerebral cortex known as the

sensory area The site in the brain of the tissue that corresponds to each of the senses, with the degree of sensitivity related to the amount of tissue. (Module 9)

FIGURE 6 The greater the amount of tissue in the somatosensory area of the brain that is related to a specific body part, the more sensitive is that body part. If the size of our body parts reflected the corresponding amount of brain tissue, we would look like this strange creature.
Natural History Museum, London/Science Source

association areas One of the major regions of the cerebral cortex; the site of the higher mental processes, such as thought, language, memory, and speech. (Module 9)

association areas. The **association areas** are the site of higher mental processes such as thinking, language, memory, and speech.

The association areas make up a large portion of the cerebral cortex. The association areas control *executive functions*, which are abilities that are related to planning, goal setting, judgment, and impulse control.

Much of our understanding of the association areas comes from patients who, like Phineas Gage, have suffered some type of brain injury. For example, when parts of the association areas are damaged, people undergo personality changes that affect their ability to make moral judgments and process emotions. At the same time, people with damage in those areas can still be capable of reasoning logically, performing calculations, and recalling information (Beauchamp et al., 2019).

Injuries to the association areas of the brain can produce *aphasia*, problems with language. In *Broca's aphasia*, speech becomes halting, laborious, and often ungrammatical, and a speaker is unable to find the right words. In contrast, *Wernicke's aphasia* produces difficulties both in understanding others' speech and in the production of language. The disorder is characterized by speech that sounds fluent but makes no sense, as in this example from a Wernicke's patient: "Boy, I'm sweating, I'm awful nervous, you know, once in a while I get caught up, I can't mention the tarripoi, a month ago, quite a little . . ." (Robson et al., 2013; Ardila, 2015; Nielsen et al., 2019). For more about association areas, see the Applying Psychology in the 21st Century feature.

APPLYING PSYCHOLOGY IN THE 21ST CENTURY

BREAKING THE BRAIN-MACHINE BARRIER

A totally paralyzed man in a research lab successfully uses a mechanical arm to lift a bottle of beer to his mouth and drink from it.

Over the past decade, accomplishments such as this have almost become routine, but the case has an additional twist: To initiate and control the movement, he doesn't use a joystick, or a switch, or an eye-tracking device. He merely has to *think* about what he wants his prosthetic arm to do, and it reads his mind.

The man and his mechanical arm use a device called a *brain-machine interface*, or BMI. People who aren't paralyzed can easily move their limbs without having to think about it at all—the intention forms, and the brain just executes it. This kind of seamless integration between intention and action has been the ultimate goal of BMI research for a long time, but the technological challenges have been difficult to surmount. Recently, however, progress has been considerable (Andersen, 2019).

The newest BMI uses an implant that is about 4 square millimeters in size, from which emerges an array of 100 tiny millimeter-long electrodes. The implant can record activity from about 100 to 200 individual neurons in the brain.

The capabilities of brain-activated machines are become increasingly sophisticated.
Aris Suwanmalee/Shutterstock

Sophisticated decoding hardware then uses mathematical formulas to discern the meaning underlying the detected patterns of neural firing and translate it into action.

BMI research usually targets the brain's motor cortex for neural implantation, perhaps not surprisingly, but this strategy presents certain challenges. For instance, the motor cortex for each arm is located in a different hemisphere of the brain, necessitating multiple implants and tricky

coordination if both arms need to be controlled. One research lab, however, is taking a novel approach by targeting an association area of the brain rather than a motor region. Subregions of the association area are activated when an intention to move is formed (Andersen & Buneo, 2002; Sakellaridi et al., 2019).

The next challenge is integrating touch feedback with BMI. When you pick up an object, your motor responses are fine-tuned by feedback from your somatosensory receptors. You can feel how your arm and hand are moving through space, you can feel the shape and texture of the object you're reaching for, and the pressure against your skin tells you how tight you're grasping the object. Implants in the somatosensory cortex are already able to provide this kind of rich tactile feedback, with work underway to integrate it with BMI output. Although the research is promising, it may still be a long while before someone with paraplegia can lift a beer with you at your local bar.

QUESTIONS TO CONSIDER

1. What might be other advantages of using association areas of the brain rather than motor areas for BMI input?
2. As neuroscientists develop increasingly sophisticated ways to control the functioning of the brain, what might be some ethical implications of their scientific advances?

Neuroplasticity and the Brain

Shortly after he was born, Jacob Stark's arms and legs started jerking every 20 minutes. Weeks later he could not focus his eyes on his mother's face. The diagnosis: uncontrollable epileptic seizures involving his entire brain.

His mother, Sally Stark, recalled: "When Jacob was 2½ months old, they said he would never learn to sit up, would never be able to feed himself... . They told us to take him home, love him, and find an institution." (Blakeslee, 1992)

Instead, Jacob had brain surgery when he was 5 months old in which physicians removed 20% of his brain. The operation was a complete success. Three years later, Jacob seemed normal in every way, with no sign of seizures.

The surgery that helped Jacob was based on the premise that the diseased part of his brain was producing seizures throughout the brain. Surgeons reasoned that if they removed the misfiring portion, the remaining parts of the brain, which appeared intact in PET scans, would take over. They correctly bet that Jacob could still lead a normal life after surgery, particularly because the surgery was being done at so young an age.

The success of Jacob's surgery illustrates that the brain has the ability to shift functions to different locations after injury to a specific area or in cases of surgery. But equally encouraging are some new findings about the *regenerative* powers of the brain and nervous system.

Scientists have learned in recent years that the brain continually changes, reorganizes itself, and is far more resilient than they once thought. **Neuroplasticity** refers to the brain's ability to change throughout the life span through the addition of new neurons, new interconnections between neurons, and the reorganization of information-processing areas.

Advances in our understanding of neuroplasticity have changed the earlier view that no new brain cells are created after childhood. The reality is very different: Not only do the interconnections between neurons become more complex throughout life, but it now appears that new neurons are also created in certain areas of the brain during adulthood—a process called *neurogenesis*. Each day, thousands of new neurons are created, especially in areas of the brain related to learning and memory (Shors, 2009; Kempermann, 2011; Apple, Fonseca, & Kokovay, 2017).

The ability of neurons to renew themselves during adulthood has significant implications for the potential treatment of disorders of the nervous system (see *Neuroscience in Your Life*). For example, drugs that trigger the development of new neurons might be used to counter such diseases as Alzheimer's, which are produced when neurons die (Hamilton et al., 2013; Ekonomou et al., 2015; Dard, Dahan, & Rampon, 2019).

Furthermore, specific experiences can modify the way in which information is processed. For example, if you learn to read Braille, the amount of tissue in your cortex related to sensation in the fingertips will expand. Similarly, if you take up the violin, the area of the brain that receives messages from your fingers will grow—but only relating to the fingers that actually move across the violin's strings (Schwartz & Begley, 2002; Kolb, Gibb, & Robinson, 2003).

The future also holds promise for people who suffer from the tremors and loss of motor control produced by Parkinson's disease, although the research is mired in controversy. Because Parkinson's disease is caused by a gradual loss of cells that stimulate the production of dopamine in the brain, many investigators have reasoned that a procedure that would increase the supply of dopamine might be effective. They seem to be on the right track. When *stem cells*—immature cells from human fetuses that have the potential to develop into a variety of specialized cell types, depending on where they are implanted—are injected directly into the brains of Parkinson's sufferers, they take root and stimulate dopamine production. Preliminary results have been promising, with some patients showing great improvement (Parish & Arenas, 2007; Newman & Bakay, 2008; Wang et al., 2011).

Stem cells thus hold great promise. When a stem cell divides, each newly created cell has the potential to be transformed into more specialized cells that have the potential to repair damaged cells. Because many of the most disabling diseases, ranging

neuroplasticity The brain's ability to change throughout the life span through the addition of new neurons, new interconnections between neurons, and the reorganization of information-processing areas. (Module 9)

NEUROSCIENCE IN YOUR LIFE: THE PLASTIC BRAIN

The brain is highly plastic, meaning that it can change in significant ways over the course of the life span. For example, brain plasticity is apparent in patients who lose a limb due to injury. Many such patients experience pain in their missing limb, called phantom limb pain. In a recent study, brain scans of participants with phantom hand pain showed changes in activity within sensory and motor brain regions. For example, regions involved in processing elbow information migrated into regions that previously processed missing hand information.

The images below show brain activity when participants moved their elbows (left) and hands (right; imagined for amputees). In the column labeled elbows, we see differences between activity during movement and rest (yellow indicates the greatest differences) in the same areas as in the column labeled hands, indicating that activity for elbow movements has migrated into regions for hand movements (Raffin et al., 2016).

Source: Adapted from Raffin, E., Richard, N., Giraux, P., & Reilly, K. T. (2016). Primary motor cortex changes after amputation correlate with phantom limb pain and the ability to move the phantom limb. *Neuroimage, 130*, 134-144.

from cancer to stroke, result from cell damage, the potential of stem cells to revolutionize medicine is significant.

However, because the source of implanted stem cells typically is aborted fetuses, their use is controversial. Some critics have argued that the use of stem cells in research and treatment should be prohibited, while supporters argue that the potential benefits of the research are so great that stem cell research should be unrestricted. The issue has been politicized, and the question of whether and how stem cell research should be regulated is not clear (Giacomini, Baylis, & Robert, 2007; Holden, 2007; Towns, 2017).

The Specialization of the Hemispheres: Two Brains or One?

The most recent development, at least in evolutionary terms, in the organization and operation of the human brain probably occurred in the last several million years: a specialization of the functions controlled by the left and right sides of the brain (MacNeilage, Rogers, & Vallortigara, 2009; Tommasi, 2009; Gülbetekin, 2019).

The brain is divided into two roughly mirror-image halves. Just as we have two arms, two legs, and two lungs, we have a left brain and a right brain. Because of the way nerves in the brain are connected to the rest of the body, these symmetrical left and right halves, called **hemispheres,** control motion in—and receive sensation from—the side of the body opposite their location. The left hemisphere of the brain, then, generally controls the right side of the body, and the right hemisphere controls the left side of the body. Thus, damage to the right side of the brain is typically indicated by functional difficulties in the left side of the body.

hemispheres Symmetrical left and right halves of the brain that control the side of the body opposite to their location. (Module 9)

Despite the appearance of similarity between the two hemispheres of the brain, they are somewhat different in the functions they control and in the ways they control them. Certain behaviors are more likely to reflect activity in one hemisphere than in the other, or are **lateralized.**

For example, for most people, language processing occurs more in the left side of the brain. In general, the left hemisphere concentrates more on tasks that require verbal competence, such as speaking, reading, thinking, and reasoning. In addition, the left hemisphere tends to process information sequentially, one bit at a time (Hines, 2004).

The right hemisphere has different strengths, particularly in nonverbal areas such as the understanding of spatial relationships, recognition of patterns and drawings, music, and expression and understanding of emotions. The right hemisphere tends to process information globally, considering it as a whole (Gotts et al., 2013; Longo et al., 2015; Gainotti, 2019).

The degree and nature of lateralization vary from one person to another. If, like most people, you are right-handed, the control of language is probably concentrated more in your left hemisphere. By contrast, if you are among the 10% of people who are left-handed or are ambidextrous (you use both hands interchangeably), it is much more likely that the language centers of your brain are located more in the right hemisphere or are divided equally between the left and right hemispheres.

Keep in mind that despite the different strengths of the two hemispheres, the differences in specialization between the hemispheres are not great. Furthermore, the two hemispheres of the brain function in tandem. It is a mistake to think of particular kinds of information as being processed solely in the right or the left hemisphere. The hemispheres work interdependently in deciphering, interpreting, and reacting to the world.

In addition, people who suffer injury to the left side of the brain and lose linguistic capabilities often recover the ability to speak: The right side of the brain often takes over some of the functions of the left side, especially in young children; the extent of recovery increases the earlier the injury occurs (Johnston, 2004; Chang et al., 2018).

Furthermore, not every researcher believes that the differences between the two hemispheres of the brain are terribly significant. According to neuroscientist Stephen Kosslyn, a more critical difference occurs in processing between the upper and lower halves of the brain. In his theory, the top-brain system of the brain specializes in planning and goal-setting. In contrast, the bottom-brain system helps classify information coming from our senses, allowing us to understand and classify information. It is still too early to know the accuracy of Kosslyn's theory, but it provides an intriguing alternative to the notion that left-right brain differences are of primary importance (Kosslyn & Miller, 2013).

In any case, evidence continues to grow that the differences between processing in the left and right hemispheres are meaningful. For example, researchers have unearthed evidence that there may be subtle differences in brain lateralization patterns between males and females and members of different cultures, as we see in *Exploring Diversity.*

lateralization The dominance of one hemisphere of the brain in specific functions, such as language. (Module 9)

Study Alert
Although the hemispheres of the brain specialize in particular kinds of functions, the degree of specialization is not great, and the two hemispheres work interdependently.

PsychTech
Using a procedure called *hemispherectomy,* in which an entire hemisphere of the brain is removed, surgeons ended Christina Santhouse's seizures, which occurred at the rate of hundreds a day. Despite the removal of the right side of her brain, Christina recently completed a master's degree in speech pathology.

From the perspective of...

An Office Worker Could personal differences in people's specialization of right and left hemispheres be related to occupational success? For example, might a designer who relies on spatial skills have a different pattern of hemispheric specialization than does a lawyer?

Caia Images/Glow Images

Exploring Diversity

Human Diversity and the Brain

The interplay of biology and environment in behavior is especially clear when we consider evidence suggesting that even in brain structure and function, there are both sex and cultural differences. Let's consider sex differences first. Accumulating evidence seems to show intriguing differences in males' and females' brain lateralization, weight, and processing (Clements, Rimrodt, & Abel, 2006; Joel & McCarthy, 2017).

For instance, the two sexes show differences in the speed at which their brains develop. For example, the frontal lobes, which control aggressiveness and language, develop earlier in girls than boys. On the other hand, boys' brains develop faster in the region that facilitates visual and spatial tasks such as geometry. And even in adulthood, sex differences exist: for example, women's brains seem to age more slowly than those of men (Raznahan et al., 2010; Tanaka et al., 2012; Goyal et al., 2019).

Furthermore, most males tend to show greater lateralization of language in the left hemisphere. For them, language is clearly relegated largely to the left side of the brain. In contrast, women display less lateralization, with language abilities apt to be more evenly divided between the two hemispheres. Such differences in brain lateralization may account, in part, for the superiority often displayed by females on certain measures of verbal skills, such as the onset and fluency of speech (Petersson et al., 2007; Mercadillo et al., 2011; Hirnstein, Hugdahl, & Hausmann, 2019)).

Other research suggests that men's brains are somewhat bigger than women's brains, even after taking differences in body size into account. In contrast, part of the *corpus callosum,* a bundle of fibers that connects the hemispheres of the brain, is proportionally larger in women than in men. In addition, there are differences in brain responses between males and females who are frequent videogame players, particularly in parts of the brain related to the processing of rewards and cravings. These differences might account for sex differences in the use of technology (Smith et al., 2007; Taki et al., 2013; Dong et al., 2018).

However, the meaning of such sex differences is far from clear. Consider one possibility related to differences in the proportional size of the corpus callosum: Its greater size in women may permit stronger connections to develop between the parts of the brain that control speech. In turn, this would explain why speech tends to emerge slightly earlier in girls than in boys.

Before we rush to such a conclusion, though, we must consider an alternative hypothesis: The reason verbal abilities emerge earlier in girls may be that infant girls receive greater encouragement to talk than do infant boys. In turn, this greater early experience may foster the growth of certain parts of the brain. Hence, physical brain differences may be a *reflection* of social and environmental influences rather than a *cause* of the differences in men's and women's behavior. At this point, it is impossible to know which of these alternative hypotheses is correct.

Culture also gives rise to differences in brain size and lateralization. For example, the volume of gray-matter material in the cortex is greater in higher-income adolescents than in low-income adolescents. Furthermore, brain development is related to differences in academic achievement between students of different income levels. Specifically, the brain's cortex is thicker in higher-income students than in lower-income students, and cortex configuration is related to their academic achievement (Mackey et al., 2015; Dufford, Bianco, & Kim, 2019).

Clearly, our brains reflect a combination of genetically determined structure and functioning. But they also reflect the impact of the social and cultural experiences to which we are exposed.

The Split Brain: Exploring the Two Hemispheres

When Vicki visited her neurologist, she was desperate: Her frequent and severe epileptic seizures weren't just interfering with her day-to-day life—they were putting her in danger. She never knew when she might just collapse suddenly, making many mundane situations such as climbing stairs potentially life-threatening for her.

Vicki's neurologist had a solution, but a radical and potentially dangerous one: surgically severing the bundle of fibers connecting the two hemispheres of her brain. This procedure would stop the firestorms of electrical impulses that were causing Vicki's seizures, but it would also have its own curious effects on her day-to-day functioning.

In the months after the surgery, Vicki was relieved to be free of the seizures that had taken over her life. But she had new challenges to overcome. Simple tasks such as food shopping or even dressing herself became lengthy ordeals–not because she had difficulty moving or thinking but because the two sides of her brain no longer worked in a coordinated way. Each side directed its half of the body to work independently of the other (Wolman, 2012).

People like Vicki, whose corpus collosums have been cut or injured, are called *split-brain patients*. They offer a rare opportunity for researchers investigating the independent functioning of the two hemispheres of the brain. For example, psychologist Roger Sperry–who won the Nobel Prize for his work–developed a number of ingenious techniques for studying how each hemisphere operates (Sperry, 1982; Savazzi et al., 2007; Bagattini et al., 2015).

In one experimental procedure, patients who were prevented from seeing an object by a screen touched the object with their right hand and were asked to name it (see Figure 7). Because the right side of the body corresponds to the language-oriented left side of the brain, split-brain patients were able to name it. However, if patients touched the object with their left hand, they were unable to name it aloud, even though the information had registered in their brains. When the screen was removed, patients could identify the object they had touched. Information can be learned and remembered, then, using only the right side of the brain. (By the way, unless you've had split-brain surgery, this experiment won't work with you because the bundle of fibers connecting the two hemispheres of a normal brain immediately transfers the information from one hemisphere to the other.)

Site where corpus collosum is severed

Corpus collosum

Right cerebral hemisphere

Left cerebral hemisphere

A

Screen prevents participant from seeing objects

B

FIGURE 7 Hemispheres of the brain. (a) The corpus callosum connects the cerebral hemispheres of the brain, as shown in this cross section. (b) A split-brain patient is tested by touching objects behind a screen. Patients could name the objects they touched with their right hand but couldn't name them when they touched them with their left hand. If a split-brain patient with her eyes closed was given a pencil to hold and called it a pencil, what hand was the pencil in?

It is clear from experiments like this one that the right and left hemispheres of the brain specialize in handling different sorts of information. At the same time, it is important to realize that both hemispheres are capable of understanding, knowing, and being aware of the world, in somewhat different ways. The two hemispheres, then, should be regarded as different in terms of the efficiency with which they process certain kinds of information, rather than as two entirely separate brains. The hemispheres work interdependently to allow the full range and richness of thought of which humans are capable.

BECOMING AN INFORMED CONSUMER
of Psychology

Learning to Control Your Heart—and Mind—Through Biofeedback

When Tammy DeMichael was involved in a horrific car accident that broke her neck and crushed her spinal cord, experts told her that she was doomed to be a quadriplegic for the rest of her life, unable to move from the neck down. But they were wrong. Not only did she regain the use of her arms, but she also was able to walk 60 feet with a cane.

biofeedback A procedure in which a person learns to control through conscious thought internal physiological processes such as blood pressure, heart and respiration rate, skin temperature, sweating, and the constriction of particular muscles. (Module 9)

The key to DeMichael's astounding recovery: biofeedback. **Biofeedback** is a procedure in which a person learns to control through conscious thought internal physiological processes such as blood pressure, heart and respiration rate, skin temperature, sweating, and the constriction of particular muscles. Although it traditionally had been thought that heart rate, respiration rate, blood pressure, and other bodily functions are under the control of parts of the brain over which we have no influence, psychologists have discovered that these responses are actually susceptible to voluntary control (Cho, Holyoak, & Cannon, 2007; Badke et al., 2011; Arena & Tankersley, 2018).

In biofeedback, a person is hooked up to electronic devices that provide continuous feedback relating to the physiological response in question. For instance, someone trying to control headaches through biofeedback might have electronic sensors placed on certain muscles on her head and learn to control the constriction and relaxation of those muscles. Later, when she felt a headache starting, she could relax the relevant muscles and abort the pain (Nestoriuc et al., 2008; Magis & Schoenen, 2011; Esparham & Dilts, 2019).

DeMichael's treatment was related to a form of biofeedback called *neurofeedback*, in which brain activity is displayed for a patient. Because not all of her nervous system's connections between the brain and her legs were severed, she was able to learn how to send messages to specific muscles, "ordering" them to move. Although it took more than a year, DeMichael was successful in restoring a large degree of her mobility.

Although the control of physiological processes through the use of biofeedback is not easy to learn, it has been employed with success in a variety of ailments, including emotional problems (such as anxiety, depression, phobias, tension headaches, insomnia, and hyperactivity), physical illnesses with a psychological component (such as asthma, high blood pressure, ulcers, muscle spasms, and migraine headaches), and physical problems (such as DeMichael's injuries, strokes, cerebral palsy, and curvature of the spine) (Reiner, 2008; Dias & van Deusen, 2011).

RECAP/EVALUATE/RETHINK

RECAP

LO 9-1 How do researchers identify the major parts and functions of the brain?

- Brain scans take a "snapshot" of the internal workings of the brain without having to cut surgically into a person's skull. Major brain-scanning techniques include the electroencephalogram (EEG), positron emission tomography (PET), functional magnetic resonance imaging (fMRI), and transcranial magnetic stimulation imaging (TMS).

LO 9-2 What are the major parts of the brain, and for what behaviors is each part responsible?

- The central core of the brain is made up of the medulla (which controls functions such as breathing and the heartbeat), the pons (which coordinates the muscles and the two sides of the body), the cerebellum (which controls balance), the reticular formation (which acts to heighten arousal and sudden awareness), the thalamus (which communicates sensory messages to and from the brain), and the hypothalamus (which maintains homeostasis, or body equilibrium, and regulates behavior related to basic survival). The functions of the central core structures are similar to those found in other vertebrates. This central core is sometimes referred to as the "old brain."
- The cerebral cortex–the "new brain"–has areas that control voluntary movement (the motor area); the senses (the sensory area); and thinking, reasoning, speech, and memory (the association areas). The limbic system, found on the border of the "old" and "new" brains, is associated with eating, aggression, reproduction, and the experiences of pleasure and pain.

LO 9-3 How do the two halves of the brain operate interdependently?

- The brain is divided into left and right halves, or hemispheres, each of which generally controls the opposite side of the body. Each hemisphere can be thought of as being specialized in the functions it carries out: The left specializes in verbal tasks, such as logical reasoning, speaking, and reading; the right specializes in nonverbal tasks, such as spatial perception, pattern recognition, and emotional expression.

LO 9-4 How can an understanding of the nervous system help us to find ways to alleviate disease and pain?

- Biofeedback is a procedure by which a person learns to control internal physiological processes. By controlling involuntary responses, people are able to relieve anxiety, tension, migraine headaches, and a wide range of other psychological and physical problems.

EVALUATE

1. Match the name of each brain scan with the appropriate description:

   a. EEG
   b. fMRI
   c. PET

   1. By locating radiation within the brain, a computer can provide a striking picture of brain activity.
   2. Electrodes placed around the skull record the electrical signals transmitted through the brain.
   3. This technique provides a three-dimensional view of the brain by aiming a magnetic field at the body.

2. Match the portion of the brain with its function:

   a. medulla
   b. pons
   c. cerebellum
   d. reticular formation

   1. Maintains breathing and heartbeat
   2. Controls bodily balance
   3. Coordinates and integrates muscle movements
   4. Activates other parts of the brain to produce general bodily arousal

3. A surgeon places an electrode on a portion of your brain and stimulates it. Immediately, your right wrist involuntarily twitches. The doctor has most likely stimulated a portion of the _____ area of your brain.
4. Each hemisphere controls the _____ side of the body.
5. Nonverbal realms, such as emotions and music, are controlled primarily by the _____ hemisphere of the brain, whereas the _____ hemisphere is more responsible for speaking and reading.

RETHINK

1. Before sophisticated brain-scanning techniques were developed, behavioral neuroscientists' understanding of the brain was based largely on the brains of people who had died. What limitations would this pose, and in what areas would you expect the most significant advances once brain-scanning techniques became possible?
2. Could personal differences in people's specialization of right and left hemispheres be related to occupational success?

Answers to Evaluate Questions

1. a-2, b-3, c-1; 2. a-1, b-3, c-2, d-4; 3. motor; 4. opposite; 5. right, left

---

KEY TERMS

central core	thalamus	lobes	neuroplasticity
cerebellum	hypothalamus	motor area	hemispheres
(ser-uh-BELL-um)	limbic system	sensory area	lateralization
reticular formation	cerebral cortex	association areas	biofeedback

LOOKING *Back*

EPILOGUE

In our examination of neuroscience, we've traced the ways in which biological structures and functions of the body affect behavior. Starting with neurons, we considered each of the components of the nervous system, culminating in an examination of how the brain permits us to think, reason, speak, recall, and experience emotions—the hallmarks of being human.

Before proceeding, turn back for a moment to the chapter prologue about Molie Wright, a woman who recovered from severe brain injuries after an auto accident. Consider the following questions:

1. How would you explain Wright's ability to recover her lost brain function?

2. Do you think that a recovery such as Wright experienced would be more or less likely if she had been a young girl? An older woman? Why do you think so?

3. Did Wright's family have good reason to worry that even if she recovered from her injuries she might not be the same person as before her accident? Explain.

Design Elements: Woman with laptop: Dragon Images/Shutterstock.com; Exclamation point: McGraw-Hill; Smartphone: and4me/Shutterstock.com; Hands: Nattanon Kanchak/Shutterstock.

VISUAL SUMMARY 3 Neuroscience and Behavior

MODULE 7 Neurons: The Basic Element

Neuron Structure

Dendrites

Axon (inside myelin sheath)

Cell body

Myelin sheath

Movement of electrical impulse

Terminal buttons

Neuron Function

Time 1 — Voltage

Time 2 — Voltage

Time 3 — Voltage

■ Positive charge
☐ Negative charge
→ Direction of impulse

Axon

Receptor site

Synapse

Dendrite

Neurotransmitter

Synapse

Neurotransmitters
- Acetylcholine
- Serotonin
- Dopamine
- Endorphins

MODULE 8 Nervous System

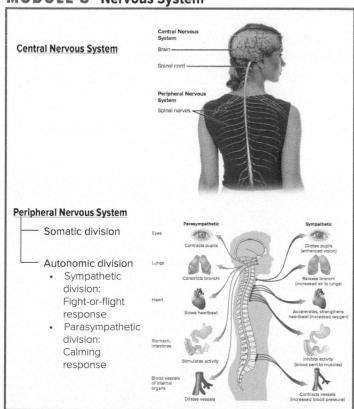

Central Nervous System

Central Nervous System

Brain

Spinal cord

Peripheral Nervous System

Spinal nerves

Peripheral Nervous System

- Somatic division

- Autonomic division
  - Sympathetic division: Fight-or-flight response
  - Parasympathetic division: Calming response

Parasympathetic — Eyes — Contracts pupils

Sympathetic — Dilates pupils (enhanced vision)

Lungs — Constricts bronchi — Relaxes bronchi (increased air to lungs)

Heart — Slows heartbeat — Accelerates, strengthens heartbeat (increased oxygen)

Stomach, intestines — Stimulates activity — Inhibits activity (blood sent to muscles)

Blood vessels of internal organs — Dilates vessels — Contracts vessels (increased blood pressure)

MODULE 9 The Brain

Areas of the Brain

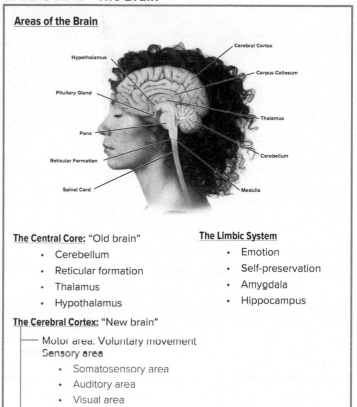

Hypothalamus

Cerebral Cortex

Corpus Callosum

Pituitary Gland

Thalamus

Pons

Cerebellum

Reticular Formation

Medulla

Spinal Cord

The Central Core: "Old brain"
- Cerebellum
- Reticular formation
- Thalamus
- Hypothalamus

The Cerebral Cortex: "New brain"
- Motor area: Voluntary movement
- Sensory area
  - Somatosensory area
  - Auditory area
  - Visual area
- Association areas
  - Executive functions
  - Personality

The Limbic System
- Emotion
- Self-preservation
- Amygdala
- Hippocampus

Brain Features
- Neuroplasticity
- Lateralization: Two hemispheres with specialized functions
- The Split Brain: Corpus callosum with independent hemispheric functions

(Module 7): Whitehoune/Shutterstock; (Module 8): Ianych/Shutterstock; (Module 9): Dana Neely/Taxi/Getty Images; Source: Freeman, "Brain, Mind and Behavior."

Prostock Studio/Shutterstock

CHAPTER 4
Sensation and Perception

LEARNING OUTCOMES FOR CHAPTER 4

	MODULE 10
LO 10-1 What is sensation, and how do psychologists study it?	**SENSING THE WORLD AROUND US**
	Absolute Thresholds: Detecting What's Out There
LO 10-2 What is the relationship between a physical stimulus and the kinds of sensory responses that result from it?	Difference Thresholds: Noticing Distinctions Between Stimuli
	Sensory Adaptation: Turning Down Our Responses

	MODULE 11
LO 11-1 What basic processes underlie the sense of vision?	**VISION: SHEDDING LIGHT ON THE EYE**
	Illuminating the Structure of the Eye
	Neuroscience in Your Life: Recognizing Faces
LO 11-2 How do we see colors?	Color Vision and Color Blindness: The 7-Million-Color Spectrum

	MODULE 12
LO 12-1 What role does the ear play in the senses of sound, motion, and balance?	**HEARING AND THE OTHER SENSES**
	Sensing Sound
	Smell and Taste
LO 12-2 How do smell and taste function?	**Applying Psychology in the 21st Century:** Restoring a Lost Sense of Smell: Aromatherapy?
LO 12-3 What are the skin senses, and how do they relate to the experience of pain?	The Skin Senses: Touch, Pressure, Temperature, and Pain
	Becoming an Informed Consumer of Psychology: Managing Pain
	How Our Senses Interact

LO 13-1 What principles underlie our organization of the visual world and allow us to make sense of our environment?

LO 13-2 How are we able to perceive the world in three dimensions when our retinas are capable of sensing only two-dimensional images?

LO 13-3 What clues do visual illusions give us about our understanding of general perceptual mechanisms?

PERCEPTUAL ORGANIZATION: CONSTRUCTING OUR VIEW OF THE WORLD

The Gestalt Laws of Organization

Top-Down and Bottom-Up Processing

Depth Perception: Translating 2-D to 3-D

Perceptual Constancy

Motion Perception: As the World Turns

Perceptual Illusions: The Deceptions of Perceptions

Exploring Diversity: Culture and Perception

PROLOGUE *I FEEL YOUR PAIN, I TASTE YOUR WORDS*

When Jo Cameron was expecting to give birth, she wasn't particularly worried about the pain. Even though friends who had experienced childbirth described the event as intensely painful, Cameron declined painkillers. She later described the sensation as a tickle—certainly nothing to fear.

Cameron's cavalier attitude toward the pain of childbirth was nothing new for her. Throughout her life, Cameron had been largely impervious to pain. Cuts, bone fractures, even burns didn't bother her. In fact, she often didn't even realize she had injured herself until she saw blood or smelled the burning of her own flesh. Not that any of this concerned Cameron very much; indeed, pretty much nothing does. In much the same way that she doesn't feel pain, she also simply doesn't feel anxiety.

So it wasn't until late in life that Cameron's unusual condition came to the attention of medical researchers. When she refused pain medication after a hand operation because it simply didn't cause her any pain, the anesthetist couldn't understand why. A research team discovered what made Cameron so unusual: a rare mutation in a gene associated with the experience of pain. Cameron's father had the same condition, and her son inherited a milder form of it, too. Cameron's rare genetic condition is of great interest to researchers who are investigating the genetic basis of pain and who hope one day to use this information to develop new and better treatments for pain and anxiety (Murphy, 2019).

LOOKING *Ahead*

Cameron's experience illustrates how complex and mysterious our senses are and how central they are to normal functioning. Our senses offer a window to the world, not only providing us with an awareness, understanding, and appreciation of the world's beauty but also alerting us to its dangers. Our senses enable us to feel the gentlest of breezes, see flickering lights miles away, and hear the soft murmuring of distant songbirds.

In the upcoming modules, we focus on the field of psychology that is concerned with the ways our bodies take in information through the senses and the ways we interpret that information. We explore both sensation and perception. *Sensation* encompasses the processes by which our sense organs receive information from the environment. *Perception* is the brain's and the sense organs' sorting out, interpretation, analysis, and integration of stimuli.

Although perception clearly represents a step beyond sensation, in practice it is sometimes difficult to find the precise boundary between the two. Indeed, psychologists—and philosophers as well—have argued for years over the distinction. The primary difference is that sensation can be thought of as an organism's first encounter with a raw sensory stimulus, whereas perception is the process by which it interprets, analyzes, and integrates that stimulus with other sensory information.

For example, if we were considering sensation, we might ask about the loudness of a ringing fire alarm. If we were considering perception, we might ask whether someone recognizes the ringing sound as an alarm and identifies its meaning.

To a psychologist interested in understanding the causes of behavior, sensation and perception are fundamental topics because so much of our behavior is a reflection of how we react to and interpret stimuli from the world around us. The areas of sensation and perception deal with a wide range of questions—among them, how we respond to the characteristics of physical stimuli; what processes enable us to see, hear, and experience pain; why visual illusions fool us; and how we distinguish one person from another. As we explore these issues, we'll see how the senses work together to provide us with an integrated view and understanding of the world.

Module 10
Sensing the World Around Us

LO 10-1 What is sensation, and how do psychologists study it?

LO 10-2 What is the relationship between a physical stimulus and the kinds of sensory responses that result from it?

! Study Alert
Remember that *sensation* refers to the activation of the sense organs (a physical response), whereas *perception* refers to how stimuli are interpreted (a psychological response).

sensation The activation of the sense organs by a source of physical energy. (Module 10)

perception The sorting out, interpretation, analysis, and integration of stimuli by the sense organs and brain. (Module 10)

stimulus Energy that produces a response in a sense organ. (Module 10)

psychophysics The study of the relationship between the physical aspects of a stimulus and people's psychological experience of the stimulus. (Module 10)

absolute threshold The lowest intensity of a stimulus that an organism can detect. (Module 10)

As Isabel sat down to Thanksgiving dinner, her father carried the turkey in on a tray and placed it squarely in the center of the table. The noise level, already high from the talking and laughter of family members, grew louder still. As Isabel picked up her fork, the smell of the turkey reached her, and she felt her stomach growl hungrily. The sight and sound of her family around the table, along with the smells and tastes of the holiday meal, made Isabel feel more relaxed than she had since starting school in the fall.

Put yourself in this setting and consider how different it might be if any one of your senses were not functioning. What if you were blind and unable to see the faces of your family members or the welcome shape of the golden-brown turkey? What if you had no sense of hearing and could not listen to the conversations of family members or were unable to feel your stomach growl, smell the dinner, or taste the food? Clearly, you would experience the dinner very differently than someone whose sensory apparatus was intact.

Moreover, the sensations mentioned above barely scratch the surface of sensory experience. Although perhaps you were taught, as I was, that there are just five senses—sight, sound, taste, smell, and touch—that enumeration is too modest. Human sensory capabilities go well beyond the basic five senses. For example, we are sensitive not merely to touch but to a considerably wider set of stimuli—pain, pressure, temperature, and vibration, to name a few. In addition, vision has two subsystems—relating to day and night vision—and the ear is responsive to information that allows us not only to hear but also to keep our balance.

To consider how psychologists understand the senses and, more broadly, sensation and perception, we first need a basic working vocabulary. In formal terms, **sensation** is the activation of the sense organs by a source of physical energy. **Perception** is the sorting out, interpretation, analysis, and integration of stimuli carried out by the sense organs and brain. A **stimulus** is any passing source of physical energy that produces a response in a sense organ.

Stimuli vary in both type and intensity. Different types of stimuli activate different sense organs. For instance, we can differentiate light stimuli (which activate the sense of sight and allow us to see the colors of a tree in autumn) from sound stimuli (which, through the sense of hearing, permit us to hear the sounds of an orchestra). In addition, stimuli differ in intensity, relating to how strong a stimulus needs to be before it can be detected.

Questions of stimulus type and intensity are considered in a branch of psychology known as psychophysics. **Psychophysics** is the study of the relationship between the actual physical aspects of a stimulus and our psychological experience of that stimulus. Psychophysics played a central role in the development of the field of psychology. Many of the first psychologists studied issues related to psychophysics, and there is still an active group of psychophysics researchers (Acuna et al., 2015; Jack & Schyns, 2017; Vicario, Kuran, & Urgesi, 2019).

Absolute Thresholds: Detecting What's Out There

Just when does a stimulus become strong enough to be detected by our sense organs? The answer to this question requires an understanding of the concept of absolute threshold. An **absolute threshold** is the lowest intensity of a stimulus that an organism can detect (Aazh & Moore, 2007).

FIGURE 1 This test can shed some light on how sensitive the human senses are.

Source: Galanter, Eugene. "Contemporary psychophysics." In New directions in psychology, Edited by R. Brown, E. Galanter, E. Hess, & G. Maroler. New York: Holt, 1962.

How Sensitive Are You?

Take this true/false quiz to test your awareness of the capabilities of your senses:

1. On a clear, dark night, you can see a candle flame from a distance of 30 miles.
   ☐ True   ☐ False

2. A single drop of perfume can be detected over the area of a 3-room apartment.
   ☐ True   ☐ False

3. Under quiet conditions, the ticking of a watch can be heard from 20 feet away.
   ☐ True   ☐ False

4. You would need 2 tablespoons of sugar to detect its taste when dissolved in 2 gallons of water.
   ☐ True   ☐ False

Scoring: For questions 1–3, the answer is **True**. Question 4 is **False**. It takes only 1 teaspoon of sugar for its taste to be detected when dissolved in 2 gallons of water.

Despite the "absolute" in absolute threshold, things are not so cut and dried. As the strength of a stimulus increases, the likelihood that it will be detected increases gradually. Technically, then, an absolute threshold is the stimulus intensity that is detected 50% of the time.

It often takes a very small stimulus to produce a response in our senses. For example, the sense of touch is so sensitive that we can feel a bee's wing falling on our cheeks when it is dropped from a distance of 1 centimeter. Test your knowledge of the absolute thresholds of other senses by completing the questionnaire in Figure 1.

In fact, our senses are so fine-tuned that we might have problems if they were any more sensitive. For instance, if our ears were slightly more acute, we would be able to hear the sound of air molecules in our ears knocking into the eardrum—a phenomenon that would surely prove distracting and might even prevent us from hearing sounds outside our bodies.

Of course, the absolute thresholds we have been discussing are measured under ideal conditions. Normally our senses cannot detect stimulation quite as well because of the presence of noise. *Noise*, as defined by psychophysicists, is background stimulation that interferes with the perception of other stimuli. Hence, *noise* refers not just to auditory stimuli, as the word suggests, but also to unwanted stimuli that interfere with other senses.

For example, picture a talkative group of people crammed into a small, crowded room at a party. The din of the crowd makes it hard to hear individual voices. In this case, the crowded conditions would be considered "noise," because they are preventing sensation at more discriminating levels. Similarly, we have limited ability to concentrate on several stimuli simultaneously.

PsychTech

Our inability to focus on multiple stimuli simultaneously is the reason why texting while driving is so dangerous. One study mounted video cameras inside trucks and found that truckers were 23 times more likely to be in a collision while texting than while not texting.

Crowded conditions, sounds, and sights can all be considered as noise that interferes with sensation. Can you think of other examples of noise that is not auditory in nature?
Praetorianphoto/E+/Getty Images

Difference Thresholds: Noticing Distinctions Between Stimuli

Suppose you wanted to choose the six best apples from a supermarket display—the biggest, reddest, and sweetest apples. One approach would be to compare one apple with another systematically until you were left with a few so similar that you could not tell the difference between them. At that point, it wouldn't matter which ones you choose.

difference threshold (just noticeable difference) The smallest level of added or reduced stimulation required to sense that a change in stimulation has occurred. (Module 10)

Psychologists have discussed this comparison problem in terms of the **difference threshold,** the smallest level of added or reduced stimulation required to sense that a *change* in stimulation has occurred. Thus, the difference threshold is the minimum change in stimulation required to detect the difference between two stimuli, and so it also is called a **just noticeable difference** (Heath & Manzone, 2017; Ozana & Ganel, 2019).

The size of a stimulus that constitutes a just noticeable difference depends on the initial intensity of the stimulus. The relationship between changes in the original size of a stimulus and the degree to which a change will be noticed forms one of the basic laws of psychophysics: Weber's law, discovered by psychophysicist E. H. Weber (*Weber* is pronounced "VAY-ber"). **Weber's law** states that a just noticeable difference is a *constant proportion* of the intensity of an initial stimulus (rather than a constant amount).

Weber's law A basic law of psychophysics stating that a just noticeable difference is a constant proportion to the intensity of an initial stimulus (rather than a constant amount). (Module 10)

For example, Weber found that the just noticeable difference for weight is 1:50. Consequently, it takes a 1-ounce increase in a 50-ounce weight to produce a noticeable difference, and it would take a 10-ounce increase to produce a noticeable difference if the initial weight were 500 ounces. In both cases, the same proportional increase is necessary to produce a just noticeable difference (1:50 = 10:500). Similarly, the just noticeable difference distinguishing changes in loudness between sounds is larger for sounds that are initially loud than it is for sounds that are initially soft, but the *proportional* increase remains the same.

Study Alert
Remember that Weber's law holds for every type of sensory stimuli: vision, sound, taste, and so on.

Weber's law helps explain why a person in a quiet room is more startled by the ringing of a cellphone than is a person in an already noisy room. To produce the same amount of reaction in a noisy room, a cellphone ring would have to be set to a much higher level. Similarly, when the moon is visible during the late afternoon, it appears relatively dim. On the other hand, the moon appears much brighter when it is in the dark night sky.

From the perspective of...

A Software Designer How might you use principles of psychophysics to direct the attention of a software user to a particular part of the computer screen?

Rubberball/Getty Images

Sensory Adaptation: Turning Down Our Responses

You enter a movie theater, and the smell of popcorn is everywhere. A few minutes later, though, you barely notice the smell. The reason you become accustomed to the odor is sensory adaptation. **Adaptation** is an adjustment in sensory capacity after prolonged exposure to unchanging stimuli. Adaptation occurs as people become accustomed to a stimulus and change their frame of reference. In a sense, our brain mentally turns down the volume of the stimulation that it's experiencing (Carbon & Ditye, 2011; Erb et al., 2013; Nourouzpour et al., 2015).

One example of adaptation is the decrease in sensitivity that occurs after repeated exposure to a strong stimulus. If you were to hear a loud tone over and over, eventually it would begin to sound softer. Similarly, although jumping into a cold lake may be temporarily unpleasant, eventually you probably will get used to the temperature.

This apparent decline in sensitivity to sensory stimuli is due to the inability of the sensory nerve receptors to fire off messages to the brain indefinitely. Because these receptor cells are most responsive to *changes* in stimulation, constant stimulation is not effective in producing a sustained reaction (Wark, Lundstrom, & Fairhall, 2007; Summers et al., 2017).

adaptation An adjustment in sensory capacity after prolonged exposure to unchanging stimuli. (Module 10)

Although initially difficult to tolerate, exposure to cold temperatures eventually becomes less unpleasant due to the phenomenon of adaptation.
papa1266/123RF

Judgments of sensory stimuli are also affected by the context in which the judgments are made. This is the case because judgments are made not in isolation from other stimuli but in terms of preceding sensory experience. You can demonstrate this for yourself by trying a simple experiment:

Take two envelopes, one large and one small, and put 15 nickels in each one. Now lift the large envelope, put it down, and lift the small one. Which seems to weigh more? Most people report that the small one is heavier, although, as you know, the weights are nearly identical. The reason for this misconception is that the visual context of the envelope interferes with the sensory experience of weight. Adaptation to the context of one stimulus (the size of the envelope) alters responses to another stimulus (the weight of the envelope) (Coren, 2004; Han et al., 2019).

RECAP/EVALUATE/RETHINK

RECAP

LO 10-1 What is sensation, and how do psychologists study it?

- Sensation is the activation of the sense organs by any source of physical energy. In contrast, perception is the process by which we sort out, interpret, analyze, and integrate stimuli to which our senses are exposed.

LO 10-2 What is the relationship between a physical stimulus and the kinds of sensory responses that result from it?

- Psychophysics studies the relationship between the physical nature of stimuli and the sensory responses they evoke.
- The absolute threshold is the smallest amount of physical intensity at which a stimulus can be detected. Under ideal conditions, absolute thresholds are extraordinarily sensitive, but the presence of noise (background stimuli that interfere with other stimuli) reduces detection capabilities.
- The difference threshold, or just noticeable difference, is the smallest change in the level of stimulation required to sense that a change has occurred. According to Weber's law, a just noticeable difference is a constant proportion of the intensity of an initial stimulus.
- Sensory adaptation occurs when we become accustomed to a constant stimulus and change our evaluation of it. Repeated exposure to a stimulus results in an apparent decline in sensitivity to it.

EVALUATE

1. _____ is the stimulation of the sense organs; _____ is the sorting out, interpretation, analysis, and integration of stimuli by the sense organs and the brain.
2. The term *absolute threshold* refers to the _____ intensity of a stimulus that must be present for the stimulus to be detected.
3. Weber discovered that for a difference between two stimuli to be perceptible, the stimuli must differ by at least a _____ proportion.
4. After completing a very difficult rock climb in the morning, Carmella found the afternoon climb unexpectedly easy. This example illustrates the phenomenon of _____.

RETHINK

1. How might it be possible to have sensation without perception? Conversely, might it be possible to have perception without sensation?
2. How is sensory adaptation essential for everyday psychological functioning?

Answers to Evaluate Questions

1. Sensation, perception; 2. smallest; 3. constant; 4. adaptation

KEY TERMS

sensation	psychophysics	difference threshold (just	Weber's law
perception	absolute threshold	noticeable difference)	adaptation
stimulus			

Module 11
Vision: Shedding Light on the Eye

If, as poets say, the eyes provide a window to the soul, they also provide us with a window to the world. Our visual capabilities permit us to admire and to react to scenes ranging from the beauty of a sunset, to the configuration of a lover's face, to the words written on the pages of a book.

Vision starts with *light*, the physical energy that stimulates the eye. Light is a form of electromagnetic radiation waves. Like ocean waves, light is measured in *wavelengths*, the distance between peaks of the lightwaves.

The *visual spectrum* is the range of wavelengths that is visible to the human eye. As shown in Figure 1, the visible spectrum that humans can see includes the wavelengths that make up the colors of a rainbow, from the shortest wavelength of violet blue to the longest wavelength of red. Compared to that of nonhumans, the visual spectrum in humans is relatively restricted. For instance, some reptiles and fish sense energies of longer wavelengths than humans do, and certain insects sense energies of shorter wavelengths than humans do.

Light waves coming from some object outside the body (such as the tree in Figure 2) are sensed by the only organ that is capable of responding to the visible spectrum: the eye. Our eyes convert light to a form that can be used by the neurons that serve as messengers to the brain. The neurons themselves take up a relatively small percentage of the total eye. Most of the eye is a mechanical device that is similar in many respects to a nonelectronic camera that uses film, as you can see in Figure 2.

Despite the similarities between the eye and a camera, vision involves processes that are far more complex and sophisticated than those of any camera. Furthermore, once an image reaches the neuronal receptors of the eye, the eye/camera analogy ends, for the processing of the visual image in the brain is more reflective of a computer than it is of a camera.

LEARNING OUTCOMES

LO 11-1 What basic processes underlie the sense of vision?

LO 11-2 How do we see colors?

Illuminating the Structure of the Eye

The ray of light being reflected off the tree in Figure 2 first travels through the *cornea*, a transparent, protective window at the front of the eye. The cornea, because of its curvature, bends (or *refracts*) light as it passes through, playing a primary role in focusing the light more sharply. After moving through the cornea, the light traverses the

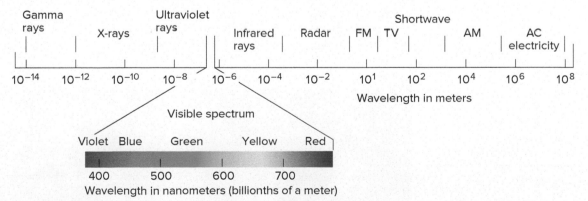

FIGURE 1 The visible spectrum—the range of wavelengths to which people are sensitive—is only a small part of the kinds of wavelengths present in our environment. Is it a benefit or disadvantage to our everyday lives that we aren't more sensitive to a broader range of visual stimuli? Why?

A camera's lens focuses the inverted image on the film in the same way the eye's lens focuses images on the retina.

Fovea

Cornea

Optic nerve

Iris

Blind spot

Pupil

Retina

Lens

Nonsensor cells of retina

FIGURE 2 Although human vision is far more complicated than the most sophisticated camera, in some ways basic visual processes are analogous to those used in photography. Like the automatic lighting system of a traditional, nondigital camera, the human eye dilates to let in more light and contracts to block out light.

pupil. The *pupil* is a dark hole in the center of the *iris,* the colored part of the eye, which in humans ranges from a light blue to a dark brown. The size of the pupil opening depends on the amount of light in the environment. The dimmer the surroundings are, the more the pupil opens to allow more light to enter.

Why shouldn't the pupil be open completely all the time, allowing the greatest amount of light into the eye? The answer relates to the basic physics of light. A small pupil greatly increases the range of distances at which objects are in focus. With a wide-open pupil, the range is relatively small, and details are harder to discern. The eye takes advantage of bright light by decreasing the size of the pupil and thereby becoming more discriminating. In dim light, the pupil expands to enable us to view the situation better–but at the expense of visual detail. (Perhaps one reason candlelight dinners are thought of as romantic is that the dim light prevents one from seeing a partner's physical flaws.)

Once light passes through the pupil, it enters the *lens,* which is directly behind the pupil. The lens acts to bend the rays of light so that they are properly focused on

Like the automatic lighting system on a camera, the pupil in the human eye expands to let in more light (left) and contracts to block out light (right). Can humans adjust their ears to let in more or less sound in a similar manner?
(Both): Biophoto Associates/Science Source

the rear of the eye. The lens focuses light by changing its own thickness, a process called *accommodation:* It becomes flatter when viewing distant objects and rounder when looking at closer objects.

REACHING THE RETINA

Having traveled through the pupil and lens, the image of the tree finally reaches its ultimate destination in the eye: the retina. The **retina** is the part of the eye that converts the electromagnetic energy of light to electrical impulses for transmission to the brain.

Interestingly, as the image travels through the lens, it has reversed itself. Consequently, the image reaches the retina upside down (relative to its original position). Although it might seem that this reversal would cause difficulties in understanding and moving about the world, this is not the case. The brain automatically interprets the image in terms of its original position.

The retina consists of a thin layer of nerve cells at the back of the eyeball (see Figure 3). There are two kinds of light-sensitive receptor cells in the retina. The names they have been given describe their shapes: rods and cones. **Rods** are thin, cylindrical

retina The part of the eye that converts the electromagnetic energy of light to electrical impulses for transmission to the brain. (Module 11)

rods Thin, cylindrical receptor cells in the retina that are highly sensitive to light. (Module 11)

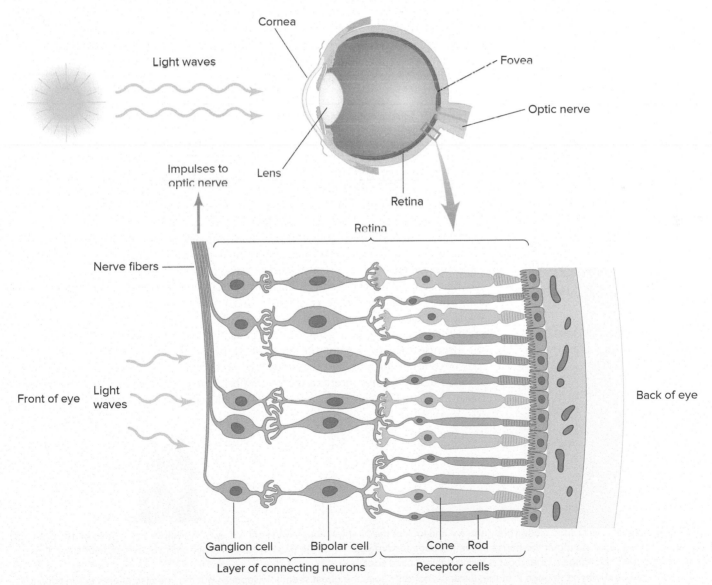

FIGURE 3 The basic cells of the eye. Light entering the eye travels through the ganglion and bipolar cells and strikes the light-sensitive rods and cones located at the back of the eye. The rods and cones then transmit nerve impulses to the brain via the bipolar and ganglion cells.

cones Cone-shaped, light-sensitive receptor cells in the retina that are responsible for sharp focus and color perception, particularly in bright light. (Module 11)

receptor cells in the retina that are highly sensitive to light. **Cones** are cone-shaped, light-sensitive receptor cells in the retina that are responsible for sharp focus and color perception, particularly in bright light. The rods and cones are distributed unevenly throughout the retina. Cones are concentrated on the part of the retina called the *fovea*. The fovea is a particularly sensitive region of the retina. If you want to focus on something of particular interest, you will automatically try to center the image on the fovea to see it more sharply.

The rods and cones not only are structurally dissimilar, but they also play distinctly different roles in vision. Cones are primarily responsible for the sharply focused perception of color, particularly in brightly lit situations; rods are related to vision in dimly lit situations and are largely insensitive to color and to details as sharp as those the cones are capable of recognizing. The rods play a key role in *peripheral vision*—seeing objects that are outside the main center of focus—and in night vision.

Rods and cones also are involved in *dark adaptation*, the phenomenon of adjusting to dim light after being in brighter light. (Think of the experience of walking into a dark movie theater and groping your way to a seat but a few minutes later seeing the seats quite clearly.) The speed at which dark adaptation occurs is a result of the rate of change in the chemical composition of the rods and cones. Although the cones reach their greatest level of adaptation in just a few minutes, the rods take 20 to 30 minutes to reach the maximum level.

An analogous phenomenon describes how we adapt to bright light. *Light adaptation* is the process of adjusting to bright light after being in dim light. Light adaptation occurs much faster than dark adaptation, taking only a minute or so.

SENDING THE MESSAGE FROM THE EYE TO THE BRAIN

When light energy strikes the rods and cones, it starts a chain of events that transforms light into neural impulses that can be communicated to the brain. Even before the neural message reaches the brain, however, some initial coding of the visual information takes place.

What happens when light energy strikes the retina depends in part on whether it encounters a rod or a cone. Rods contain *rhodopsin*, a complex reddish-purple protein whose composition changes chemically when energized by light. The substance in cone receptors is different, but the principles are similar. Stimulation of the rods and cones in the eye triggers a neural response that is transmitted to other nerve cells in the retina called *bipolar cells* and *ganglion cells*.

Bipolar cells receive information directly from the rods and cones and communicate that information to the ganglion cells. The ganglion cells collect and summarize visual information, which is then moved out the back of the eyeball and sent to the brain through a bundle of ganglion axons called the **optic nerve**.

optic nerve A bundle of ganglion axons that carry visual information to the brain. (Module 11)

Because the opening for the optic nerve passes through the retina, there are no rods or cones in the area, and that creates a blind spot. Normally, however, this absence of nerve cells does not interfere with vision because you automatically compensate for the missing part of your field of vision. (To find your blind spot, see Figure 4.)

FIGURE 4 To find your blind spot, close your right eye and look at the haunted house with your left eye. You will see the ghost on the periphery of your vision. Now, while staring at the house, move the page toward you. When the page is about a foot from your eye, the ghost will disappear. At this moment, the image of the ghost is falling on your blind spot.

But also notice how, when the page is at that distance, not only does the ghost seem to disappear, but the line also seems to run continuously through the area where the ghost used to be. This simple experiment shows how we automatically compensate for missing information by using nearby material to complete what is unseen. That's the reason you never notice the blind spot. What is missing is replaced by what is seen next to the blind spot. Can you think of any advantages that this tendency to provide missing information gives humans as a species?

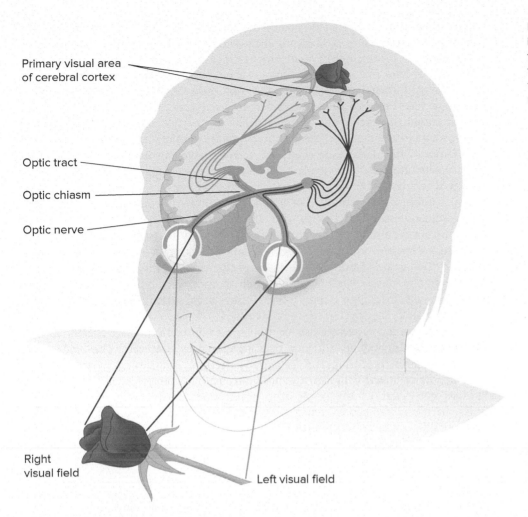

Primary visual area
of cerebral cortex

Optic tract

Optic chiasm

Optic nerve

Right
visual field

Left visual field

FIGURE 5 Because the optic nerve coming from the eye splits at the optic chiasm, the image to a person's right eye is sent to the left side of the brain, and the image to the person's left is transmitted to the right side of the brain.

Once beyond the eye itself, the neural impulses relating to the image move through the optic nerve. As the optic nerve leaves the eyeball, its path does not take the most direct route to the part of the brain right behind the eye. Instead, the optic nerves from each eye meet at a point roughly between the two eyes—called the *optic chiasm* (pronounced KI-asm)—where each optic nerve then splits.

When the optic nerves split, the nerve impulses coming from the right half of each retina are sent to the right side of the brain, and the impulses arriving from the left half of each retina are sent to the left side of the brain. Because the image on the retinas is reversed and upside down, however, those images coming from the right half of each retina actually originated in the field of vision to the person's left, and the images coming from the left half of each retina originated in the field of vision to the person's right (see Figure 5).

PROCESSING THE VISUAL MESSAGE

By the time a visual message reaches the brain, it has passed through several stages of processing. One of the initial sites is the ganglion cells. Each ganglion cell gathers information from a group of rods and cones in a particular area of the eye and compares the amount of light entering the center of that area with the amount of light in the area around it. Some ganglion cells are activated by light in the center (and darkness in the surrounding area). Other ganglion cells are activated when there is darkness in the center and light in the surrounding areas. The outcome of this process is to maximize the detection of variations in light and darkness. The image that is passed on to

PsychTech

New technologies are helping the blind to see. For example, by surgically implanting electrodes into the eyes and using a nose-mounted camera and a video processor strapped to the waist, previously totally blind individuals can differentiate plates from cups and can identify large letters.

feature detectors Specialized neurons that are activated only by visual stimuli having specific features, such as a particular shape or pattern. (Module 11)

the brain, then, is an enhanced version of the actual visual stimulus outside the body (Grünert et al., 2011; Sanes & Masland, 2015; Prayag, Najjar, & Gronfier, 2019).

The ultimate processing of visual images takes place in the visual cortex of the brain, and it is here that the most complex kinds of processing occur. Psychologists David Hubel and Torsten Wiesel won the Nobel Prize in 1981 for their discovery of feature detectors. **Feature detectors** are specialized neurons that are activated only by visual stimuli having certain features, such as a particular shape or pattern. For instance, some feature detectors are activated only by lines of a particular width, shape, or orientation. Other feature detectors are activated only by moving, as opposed to stationary, stimuli (Hubel & Wiesel, 2004; Sebastiani, Castellani, & D'Alessandro, 2011; Jacoby & Schwartz, 2017).

Visual information coming from individual neurons is combined and processed in extraordinarily specialized ways, and different parts of the brain jointly process nerve impulses according to the attributes of an image. For instance, one brain system processes shapes, one processes colors, and others process movement, location, and depth. The specialization goes further: specific parts of the brain are involved in the perception of certain *kinds* of stimuli, such as reacting to human faces, nonhuman animal faces, and inanimate stimuli (Zvyagintsev et al., 2013; Stevens, 2015; Ptak & Lazeyras, 2019).

If separate neural systems exist for processing information about specific aspects of the visual world, how are all these data integrated by the brain? The brain makes use of information regarding the frequency, rhythm, and timing of the firing of particular sets of neural cells. Furthermore, the brain's integration of visual information does not occur in any single step or location in the brain but rather is a process that occurs on several levels simultaneously. The ultimate outcome, though, is indisputable: a vision of the world around us (also see the *Neuroscience in Your Life* feature).

NEUROSCIENCE IN YOUR LIFE: RECOGNIZING FACES

The ability to recognize faces is important for social bonding in humans as well as other animals. Although it has long been believed that face processing in the brain is genetically determined, recent evidence shows that experience plays an important role as well. To examine whether innate face-processing regions of the brain exist, researchers kept one group of monkeys from seeing faces during development. When the monkeys were approximately 200 days old, the researchers measured their brain activity while they viewed faces and other common objects. Compared to normal monkeys (labeled the controls), those that were face-deprived show less activity for faces (red/yellow areas) compared to objects (purple areas) in visual regions of the brain (the circled regions in the images below). These results show that early sensory experience is important for the development of face recognition and has important implications for those who suffer from prosopagnosia, an inability to recognize faces (Arcaro et al., 2017).

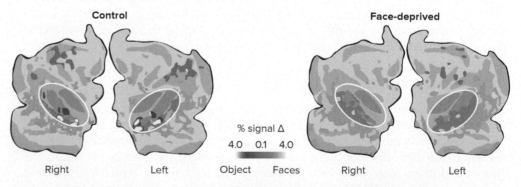

Source: Arcaro, M. J., Schade, P. F., Vincent, J. L., Ponce, C. R., & Livingstone, M. S. (2017). Seeing faces is necessary for face-domain formation. *Nature Neuroscience, 20*(10), 1404-1412.

Color Vision and Color Blindness: The 7-Million-Color Spectrum

Although the range of wavelengths to which humans are sensitive is relatively narrow, at least in comparison with the entire electromagnetic spectrum, the portion to which we are capable of responding allows us great flexibility in sensing the world. Nowhere is this clearer than in terms of the number of colors we can discern. A person with normal color vision is capable of distinguishing no less than 7 million different colors (Rabin, 2004).

Although the variety of colors that people are generally able to distinguish is vast, there are certain individuals whose ability to perceive color is quite limited–the color blind. Interestingly, the condition of these individuals has provided some of the most important clues to understanding how color vision operates (Nijboer, te Pas, & van der Smagt, 2011; Alfaro et al., 2015).

From the perspective of...

A Graphic Designer How might you market your products to those who are color blind versus those who have normal color vision?

Zoonar GmbH/Alamy Stock Photo

Approximately 7% of men and 0.4% of women are color blind. For most people with color-blindness, the world looks dull and lacks contrast (see Figure 6). Red fire engines appear yellow, green grass seems yellow, and the three colors of a traffic light all look yellow. In fact, in the most common form of color-blindness, all red and green objects are seen as yellow. In other forms of color-blindness, people are unable to tell the difference between yellow and blue. In the most extreme cases of color-blindness, which are quite rare, people perceive no color at all. To such individuals, the world looks something like the picture on an old black-and-white TV.

EXPLAINING COLOR VISION

To understand why some people are color blind, we need to consider the basics of color vision. Two processes are involved. The first process is explained by the **trichromatic theory of color vision,** which was first proposed by Thomas Young and extended

trichromatic theory of color vision The theory that there are three kinds of cones in the retina, each of which responds primarily to a specific range of wavelengths. (Module 11)

FIGURE 6 Those with color blindness see a very different view of the world (left) compared to those who have normal vision (right).
(Both): Jr. Ralph C. Eagle /Science Source

by Hermann von Helmholtz in the first half of the 1800s. This theory suggests that there are three kinds of cones in the retina, each of which responds primarily to a specific range of wavelengths. One is most responsive to blue-violet colors, one to green, and the third to yellow-red (Brown & Wald, 1964). According to trichromatic theory, perception of color is influenced by the relative strength with which each of the three kinds of cones is activated. If we see a blue sky, the blue-violet cones are primarily triggered, and the others show less activity.

However, there are aspects of color vision that the trichromatic theory is less successful at explaining. For example, the theory does not explain what happens after you stare at something like the flag shown in Figure 7 for about a minute. Try this yourself and then look at a blank white page: You'll see an image of the traditional red, white, and blue U.S. flag. Where there was yellow, you'll see blue, and where there were green and black, you'll see red and white.

The phenomenon you have just experienced is called an *afterimage*. It occurs because activity in the retina continues even when you are no longer staring at the original picture.

However, the fact that the colors perceived in the afterimage differ from those in the original image calls into question the validity of the trichromatic theory. To explain this failure of the trichromatic theory, alternative explanations for color vision have been developed. One alternative is the opponent-process theory.

opponent-process theory of color vision The theory that receptor cells for color are linked in pairs, working in opposition to each other. (Module 11)

According to the **opponent-process theory of color vision,** first proposed by German physiologist Ewald Hering in the 19th century, receptor cells are linked in pairs, working in opposition to each other. Specifically, there are a blue-yellow pairing, a red-green pairing, and a black-white pairing. If an object reflects light that contains more blue than yellow, it will stimulate the firing of the cells sensitive to blue, simultaneously discouraging or inhibiting the firing of receptor cells sensitive to yellow—and the object will appear blue. If, in contrast, a light contains more yellow than blue, the cells that respond to yellow will be stimulated to fire while the blue ones are inhibited, and the object will appear yellow (Robinson, 2007).

The opponent-process theory provides a good explanation for afterimages. When we stare at the yellow in the figure, for instance, our receptor cells for the yellow component of the yellow-blue pairing become fatigued and are less able to respond to yellow stimuli. In contrast, the receptor cells for the blue part of the pair are not tired because they are not being stimulated. When we look at a white surface, the light reflected off it would normally stimulate both the yellow and the blue receptors equally. But the fatigue of the yellow receptors prevents this from happening. They temporarily do not respond to the yellow, which makes the white light appear to be

FIGURE 7 Stare at the dot in this flag for about a minute and then look at a piece of plain white paper. What do you see? Most people see an afterimage that converts the colors in the figure into the traditional red, white, and blue U.S. flag. If you have trouble seeing it the first time, blink once and try again.

blue. Because the other colors in the figure do the same thing relative to their specific opponents, the afterimage produces the opponent colors–for a while. The afterimage lasts only a short time because the fatigue of the yellow receptors is soon overcome, and the white light begins to be perceived more accurately.

We now know that both opponent processes and trichromatic mechanisms are at work in producing the perception of color vision but in different parts of the visual sensing system. Trichromatic processes work within the retina itself, whereas opponent mechanisms operate both in the retina and at later stages of neuronal processing (Horiguchi et al., 2013; Bunce, 2015).

RECAP/EVALUATE/RETHINK

RECAP

LO 11-1 What basic processes underlie the sense of vision?

- Vision depends on sensitivity to light, electromagnetic waves in the visible part of the spectrum that are either reflected off objects or produced by an energy source. The eye shapes the light into an image that is transformed into nerve impulses and interpreted by the brain.
- As light enters the eye, it passes through the cornea, pupil, and lens and ultimately reaches the retina, where the electromagnetic energy of light is converted to nerve impulses for transmission to the brain. These impulses leave the eye via the optic nerve.
- The visual information gathered by the rods and cones is transferred via bipolar and ganglion cells through the optic nerve, which leads to the optic chiasm–the point where the optic nerve splits.

LO 11-2 How do we see colors?

- Color vision seems to be based on two processes described by the trichromatic theory and the opponent-process theory.
- The trichromatic theory suggests that there are three kinds of cones in the retina, each of which is responsive to a certain range of colors. The opponent-process theory presumes pairs of different types of cells in the eye that work in opposition to each other.

EVALUATE

1. Light entering the eye first passes through the _____, a protective window.

2. The structure that converts light into usable neural messages is called the _____.
3. A woman with blue eyes could be described as having blue pigment in her _____
4. What is the process by which the thickness of the lens is changed in order to focus light properly?
5. The proper sequence of structures that light passes through in the eye is the _____, _____, _____, and _____
6. Match each type of visual receptor with its function.

   a. rods   **1.** used for dim light, largely insensitive to color
   b. cones   **2.** detect color, good in bright light

7. _____ theory states that there are three types of cones in the retina, each of which responds primarily to a different color.

RETHINK

1. If the eye had a second lens that "unreversed" the image hitting the retina, do you think there would be changes in the way people perceive the world?
2. From an evolutionary standpoint, why might the eye have evolved so that the rods, which we rely on in low light, do not provide sharp images? Are there any advantages to this system?

Answers to Evaluate Questions

1. cornea; 2. retina; 3. iris; 4. accommodation; 5. cornea, pupil, lens, retina; 6. a-1, b-2; 7. Trichromatic

KEY TERMS

retina	optic nerve	trichromatic theory of	opponent-process theory
rods	feature detector	color vision	of color vision
cones			

Module 12
Hearing and the Other Senses

LEARNING OUTCOMES

LO 12-1 What role does the ear play in the senses of sound, motion, and balance?

LO 12-2 How do smell and taste function?

LO 12-3 What are the skin senses, and how do they relate to the experience of pain?

The blast-off was easy compared with what the astronaut was experiencing now: space sickness. The constant nausea and vomiting were enough to make him wonder why he had worked so hard to become an astronaut. Even though he had been warned that there was a two-thirds chance that his first experience in space would cause these symptoms, he wasn't prepared for how terribly sick he really felt.

Whether or not the astronaut wishes he could head right back to Earth, his experience, a major problem for space travelers, is related to a basic sensory process: the sense of motion and balance. This sense allows people to navigate their bodies through the world and keep themselves upright without falling. Along with hearing–the process by which sound waves are translated into understandable and meaningful forms–the sense of motion and balance resides in the ear.

Sensing Sound

Although many of us think primarily of the outer ear when we speak of the ear, that structure is only one simple part of the whole. The outer ear acts as a reverse megaphone, designed to collect and bring sounds into the internal portions of the ear (see Figure 1). The location of the outer ears on different sides of the head helps with *sound localization,* the process by which we identify the direction from which a sound is coming. Wave patterns in the air enter each ear at a slightly different time, and the brain uses the discrepancy as a clue to the sound's point of origin. In addition, the two outer ears delay or amplify sounds of particular frequencies to different degrees (Schnupp, Nelken, & King, 2011; Tolnai, Beutelmann & Klump, 2017).

sound The movement of air molecules brought about by a source of vibration. (Module 12)

Sound is the movement of air molecules brought about by a source of vibration. Sounds travel through the air in wave patterns similar in shape to those made in water when a stone is thrown into a still pond. Sounds, arriving at the outer ear in the form of wavelike vibrations, are funneled into the *auditory canal,* a tube-like passage that leads to the eardrum. The **eardrum** is the part of the ear that vibrates when sound waves hit it. The more intense the sound, the more the eardrum vibrates. These vibrations are then transferred into the *middle ear,* a tiny chamber containing three bones (the *hammer,* the *anvil,* and the *stirrup*) that transmit vibrations to the oval window, a thin membrane leading to the inner ear. Because the hammer, anvil, and stirrup act as a set of levers, they not only transmit vibrations but also increase their strength. Moreover, because the opening into the middle ear (the eardrum) is considerably larger than the opening out of it (the *oval window*), the force of sound waves on the oval window becomes amplified. The middle ear, then, acts as a tiny mechanical amplifier.

eardrum The part of the ear that vibrates when sound waves hit it. (Module 12)

The *inner ear* is the portion of the ear that changes the sound vibrations into a form in which they can be transmitted to the brain. (As you will see, it also contains the organs that allow us to locate our position and determine how we are moving through space.) When sound enters the inner ear through the oval window, it moves into the **cochlea,** a coiled tube that looks something like a snail and is filled with fluid that vibrates in response to sound. Inside the cochlea is the **basilar membrane,** a structure that runs through the center of the cochlea, dividing it into an upper chamber and a lower chamber. The basilar membrane is covered with **hair cells.** When the hair cells are bent by the vibrations entering the cochlea, the cells send a neural message to the brain (Zhou, Liu, & Davis, 2005; Møller, 2011; Curthoys, 2017).

cochlea (KOKE-lee-uh) A coiled tube in the ear filled with fluid that vibrates in response to sound. (Module 12)

basilar membrane A vibrating structure that runs through the center of the cochlea, dividing it into an upper chamber and a lower chamber and containing sense receptors for sound. (Module 12)

hair cells Tiny cells covering the basilar membrane that, when bent by vibrations entering the cochlea, transmit neural messages to the brain. (Module 12)

FIGURE 1 The major parts of the ear.

THE PHYSICAL ASPECTS OF SOUND

As we mentioned earlier, what we refer to as sound is actually the physical movement of air molecules in regular, wavelike patterns caused by a vibrating source. Sometimes it is even possible to see these vibrations: If you have ever seen an audio speaker that has no enclosure, you know that, at least when the lowest notes are playing, you can see the speaker moving in and out. Less obvious is what happens next: The speaker pushes air molecules into waves with the same pattern as its movement. Those wave patterns soon reach your ear, although their strength has been weakened considerably during their travels. All other sources that produce sound work in essentially the same fashion, setting off wave patterns that move through the air to the ear. Air–or some other medium, such as water–is necessary to make the vibrations of objects reach us. This explains why there can be no sound in a vacuum.

We are able to see the audio speaker moving when low notes are played because of a primary characteristic of sound called frequency. *Frequency* is the number of wave cycles that occur in a second. At very low frequencies, there are relatively few wave cycles per second (see Figure 2). These cycles are visible to the naked eye as vibrations in the speaker. Low frequencies are translated into a sound that is very low in pitch. (*Pitch* is the characteristic that makes sound seem "high" or "low.") For example, the lowest frequency that humans are capable of hearing is 20 cycles per second. Higher frequencies are heard as sounds of higher pitch. At the upper end of the sound spectrum, people can detect sounds with frequencies as high as 20,000 cycles per second.

Amplitude is a feature of wave patterns that allows us to distinguish between loud and soft sounds. Amplitude is the spread between the up-and-down peaks and valleys of air pressure in a sound wave as it travels through the air. Waves with small peaks and valleys produce soft sounds; those with relatively large peaks and valleys produce loud sounds.

We are sensitive to broad variations in sound amplitudes. The strongest sounds we are capable of hearing are over a trillion times as intense as the very weakest sound

FIGURE 2 The sound waves produced by different stimuli are transmitted—usually through the air—in different patterns, with lower frequencies indicated by fewer peaks and valleys per second.

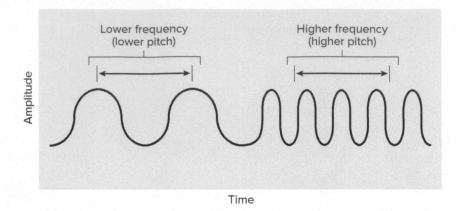

we can hear. This range is measured in *decibels*. When sounds get higher than 120 decibels, they become painful to the human ear.

Our sensitivity to different frequencies changes as we age. For instance, as we get older, the range of frequencies we can detect declines, particularly for high-pitched sounds. This is why high school students sometimes choose high-pitched ring tones for their cell phones in settings where cell phone use is forbidden: the ringing sound goes undetected by their older teachers (Vitello, 2006; Moreno-Gómez et al., 2017; Winberg, 2019) (See Figure 3.)

In addition, some individuals are particularly sensitive to sound. In a rare disorder known as *hyperacusis*, a person is acutely sensitive to sounds that others find tolerable. A doorbell ring or even the crumpling of a paper can be extremely painful. Hyperacusis can be brought on by too much exposure to loud sounds, and there is no known cure (Fagelson & Baguley, 2018; Owen, 2019).

Explaining Hearing: Listen to the Theories of Sound How are our brains able to sort out wavelengths of different frequencies and intensities? One important clue comes from studies of the basilar membrane, the area in the cochlea that translates physical vibrations into

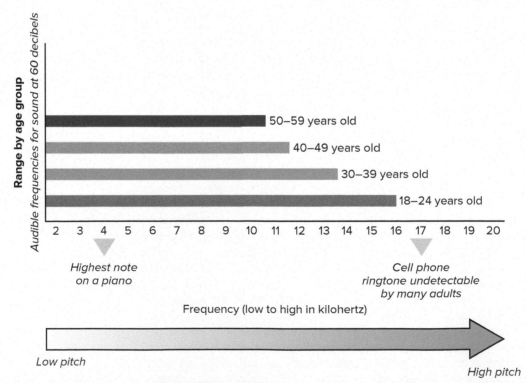

FIGURE 3 Some teenagers set their text-message ring tone to a frequency too high for most adults to hear, allowing them to use cell phones where they are prohibited. Similarly, some organizations use high-frequency sounds to discourage teenage loitering.
Source: Vitello, P. (2006, June 12). A ring tone meant to fall on deaf ears. *The New York Times*, A1.

nerve impulses. It turns out that sounds affect different areas of the basilar membrane according to the frequency of the sound wave reaching it. The part of the basilar membrane nearest to the oval window is most sensitive to high-frequency sounds. In contrast, the part of the basilar membrane nearest to the cochlea's inner end is most sensitive to low-frequency sounds. This finding has led to the **place theory of hearing,** which states that different areas of the basilar membrane are specialized to respond to different sound frequencies.

However, place theory does not tell the full story of hearing because of a significant fact: Very low frequency sounds trigger neurons across such a wide area of the basilar membrane that no single site is involved. Consequently, an additional explanation for hearing has been proposed: frequency theory. The **frequency theory of hearing** suggests that the entire basilar membrane acts as a microphone, vibrating as a whole in response to a sound. According to this explanation, the nerve receptors send out signals that are tied directly to the frequency (the number of wave crests per second) of the sounds to which we are exposed, with the number of nerve impulses being a direct function of a sound's frequency. Thus, the higher the pitch of a sound (and therefore the greater the frequency of its wave crests), the greater the number of nerve impulses that are transmitted up the auditory nerve to the brain.

Ultimately, it seems that we need both place theory and frequency theory to understand the process of hearing. Specifically, place theory provides a better explanation for the sensing of high-frequency sounds, whereas frequency theory explains what happens when low-frequency sounds are encountered. Medium-frequency sounds incorporate both processes (Hudspeth, 2013; Vadivel & Ganesh, 2019).

Regardless of whether we employ place theory or frequency theory, we know that after an auditory message leaves the ear, it is transmitted to the auditory cortex of the brain through a complex series of nerve interconnections. And similar to visual nerve cells in the brain that respond to specific kinds of stimuli, auditory neurons respond to specific types of sounds. For example, certain neurons respond selectively to clicks and whistles. Other neurons respond only to a specific sound pattern, such as a steady tone but not an intermittent one. Furthermore, specific neurons transfer information about a sound's location through their particular pattern of firing (Wang et al., 2005; Alho et al., 2006; Romero-Guevara et al., 2015).

If we were to analyze the configuration of the cells in the auditory cortex, we would find that neighboring cells are responsive to similar frequencies. The auditory cortex, then, provides us with a "map" of sound frequencies, just as the visual cortex furnishes a representation of the visual field. In addition, because of the asymmetry in the two hemispheres of the brain, the left and right ears process sound differently. The right ear reacts more to speech, whereas the left ear responds more to music (Sininger & Cone-Wesson, 2006; McCulloch et al., 2017).

Speech perception requires that we make fine discriminations among sounds that are quite similar in terms of their physical properties. Furthermore, not only are we able to understand *what* is being said from speech, we also can use vocal cues to determine who is speaking, whether they have an accent and where they may be from, and even their emotional state. Such capabilities illustrate the sophistication of our sense of hearing (Ross et al., 2011; Mattys et al., 2013; Gordon et al., 2019).

Scientists are also beginning to investigate how we use sound to navigate through our environment. *Echolocation* is the use of sound waves and echoes to determine where objects are. It is the navigational technique that bats use, and some people with impaired vision have learned to use echolocation by generating sounds (such as snapping their fingers or making clicking noises) and using the echoes that bounce off objects to navigate. Although psychologists are early in their research on the phenomenon, it may provide a window into sensory processes and ultimately improve the lives of those with sensory impairments (Thaler, 2015; Salles, Bohn, & Moss, 2019).

Balance: The Ups and Downs of Life Several structures of the ear are related more to our sense of balance than to our hearing. Collectively, these structures are known as the *vestibular system,* which responds to the pull of gravity and allows us to maintain our balance, even when standing in a bus in stop-and-go traffic.

place theory of hearing The theory that different areas of the basilar membrane respond to different frequencies.

frequency theory of hearing The theory that the entire basilar membrane acts like a microphone, vibrating as a whole in response to a sound. (Module 12)

Study Alert
Be sure to understand the differences between the place and frequency theories of hearing.

Zero gravity presents numerous challenges. For example, the weightlessness of the ear's otoliths produces space sickness in most astronauts.
Dusan Petkovic/Shutterstock

semicircular canals Three tube-like structures of the inner ear containing fluid that sloshes through them when the head moves, signaling rotational or angular movement to the brain. (Module 12)

The main structure of the vestibular system is formed by the **semicircular canals** of the inner ear (refer to Figure 1), which consist of three tubes containing fluid that sloshes through them when the head moves, signaling rotational or angular movement to the brain. The pull on our bodies caused by the acceleration of forward, backward, or up-and-down motion, as well as the constant pull of gravity, is sensed by the *otoliths*, tiny, motion-sensitive crystals in the semicircular canals. When we move, these crystals shift as sands do on a windy beach, contacting the specialized receptor *hair cells* in the semicircular canals. The brain's inexperience in interpreting messages from the weightless otoliths is the cause of the space sickness commonly experienced by two-thirds of all space travelers, mentioned at the start of this module (Yoder et al., 2015; Macauda et al., 2019).

Smell and Taste

Until he bit into a piece of raw cabbage on that February evening . . ., Raymond Fowler had not thought much about the sense of taste. The cabbage, part of a pasta dish he was preparing for his family's dinner, had an odd, burning taste, but he did not pay it much attention. Then a few minutes later, his daughter handed him a glass of cola, and he took a swallow. "It was like sulfuric acid," he said. "It was like the hottest thing you could imagine boring into your mouth." (Goode, 1999)

More than 1,000 olfactory receptor cells, like this one in the center of the scan, are spread across the nasal cavity. The cells are specialized to react to particular odors. Do you think it is possible to "train" the nose to pick up a greater number of odors?
Professor Pietro M. Motta/Science Source

It was evident that something was very wrong with Fowler's sense of taste. After extensive testing, it became clear that the nerves involved in his sense of taste had been damaged, probably because of a viral infection or a medicine he was taking. (Luckily for him, a few months later, his sense of taste returned to normal.)

Even without disruptions in our ability to perceive the world such as those experienced by Fowler, we all know the important roles that taste and smell play. We'll consider these two senses next.

SMELL

Although many animals have keener abilities to detect odors than we do, the human sense of smell (*olfaction*) permits us to detect more than 10,000 separate smells. We also have a good memory for smells, and long-forgotten events and memories—good and bad—can be brought back with the mere whiff of an odor associated with a memory (Schroers, Prigot, & Fagen, 2007; Arshamian et al., 2013; Glachet et al., 2019).

Results of "sniff tests" have shown that women generally have a better sense of smell than men do (Engen, 1987). People also have the ability to distinguish males from females on the basis of smell alone. In one experiment, blindfolded students who were asked to sniff the breath of a female or male volunteer who was hidden from view were able to distinguish the sex of the donor at better-than-chance levels. People can also distinguish happy from sad emotions by sniffing underarm smells, and women are able to identify their babies solely on the basis of smell just a few hours after birth (Doty et al., 1982; Fusari & Ballesteros, 2008; Flohr et al., 2017).

The sense of smell is sparked when the molecules of a substance enter the nasal passages and meet *olfactory cells*, the receptor neurons of the nose, which are spread across the nasal cavity. More than 1,000 separate types of receptors have been identified on those cells so far. Each of these receptors is so specialized that it responds only to a small band of different odors. The responses of the separate olfactory cells are then transmitted to the brain, where they are combined into recognition of a particular smell (Marshall, Laing, & Jinks, 2006; Zhou & Buck, 2006; Jia & Hegg, 2015).

Smell may also act as a hidden means of communication for humans. It has long been known that nonhumans release *pheromones*, chemicals they secrete into the environment that produce a social response in other members of the same species. Pheromones transmit messages such as alarm ("danger—predators are close by!") or sexual availability ("I'm interested in sex"). For instance, the vaginal secretions of female monkeys contain pheromones that stimulate the sexual interest of male monkeys (Brennan, 2011; Zizzari et al., 2017; Romero-Lebrón et al., 2019).

The degree to which pheromones are part of the human experience remains an open question. Some psychologists believe that human pheromones affect emotional responses, although the evidence is inconclusive. For one thing, it is not clear what specific sense organ is receptive to pheromones. In nonhumans, it is the *vomeronasal organ* in the nose, but in humans, the organ appears to recede during fetal development (Haviland-Jones & Wilson, 2008; Hummer & McClintock, 2009; Gelstein et al., 2011); also see *Applying Psychology in the 21st Century*.

PsychTech

When male participants in a study sniffed women's tears, fMRI brain scans showed reduced activity in the parts of the brain associated with sexual arousal. Apparently, tears contain a chemical signal.

TASTE

The sense of taste (*gustation*) involves receptor cells that respond to four basic stimulus qualities: sweet, sour, salty, and bitter. A fifth category also exists, a flavor called *umami*, although there is controversy about whether it qualifies as a fundamental taste. *Umami* is a hard-to-translate Japanese word, although the English "meaty" or "savory" comes close. Chemically, umami involves food stimuli that contain amino acids (the substances that make up proteins) (Erickson, 2008; Nakamura et al., 2011; Cecchini et al., 2019).

Although the specialization of the receptor cells leads them to respond most strongly to a particular type of taste, they are capable of responding to other tastes as well. Ultimately, every taste is simply a combination of the basic flavor qualities, in the same way that the primary colors blend into a vast variety of shades and hues (Yeomans, Tepper, & Ritezschel, 2007; Spence, Auvray, & Smith, 2015).

The receptor cells for taste are located in roughly 10,000 *taste buds*, which are distributed across the tongue and other parts of the mouth and throat. The taste buds wear out and are replaced every 10 days or so. That's a good thing because if our taste buds weren't constantly reproducing, we'd lose the ability to taste after we'd accidentally burned our tongues.

There are 10,000 taste buds on the tongue and on other parts of the mouth. Taste buds wear out and are replaced every 10 days. What would happen if taste buds were not regenerated?
Omikron/Science Source

APPLYING PSYCHOLOGY IN THE 21ST CENTURY

RESTORING A LOST SENSE OF SMELL: AROMATHERAPY?

Sensory impairments are more common than you may think. Many people live with some form of impaired vision or hearing, yet they get by just fine with the assistance of corrective medical devices such as eyeglasses, contact lenses, or hearing aids. But what would life be like with an impaired sense of smell, and can that also be corrected?

This isn't a trivial question. Although you may think an impaired sense of smell wouldn't be a very big deal, it has some serious consequences. Examples include difficulty detecting threats such as fires, gas leaks, or spoiled food; impaired ability to taste food; and even chronic self-consciousness about one's own scent. And it's not an uncommon condition. Whether from injury, illness, or aging, nearly 25% of adults over 40–and more than 60% of those over 80– live with an impaired sense of smell. And in part because research on the sense of smell lags behind other senses, options for correcting an impairment have been limited. One approach entails relearning to identify specific scents through repeated exposure, but this isn't helpful for people

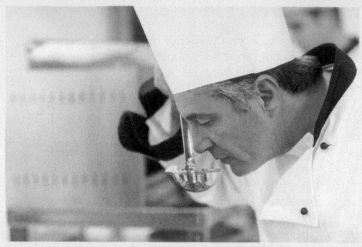

A lost sense of smell is a disastrous disability for a chef.
Wavebreak/iStock/Getty Images

with severe or total loss of smell (Costanzo & Miwa, 2006; Seow, Ong, & Huang, 2016).

Restoring a lost sense isn't impossible. For example, for those with hearing loss, a device called a cochlear implant produces partial restoration by converting sounds into neural impulses, much as a normally functioning inner ear would do. Medical researchers are working to develop a

similar kind of device that would sit under the nose, or perhaps in a pair of glasses, to translate scent molecules into neural impulses via a microprocessor.

Technology that detects scent molecules already exists and is used for such applications as bomb-sniffing. Researchers are working on ways to miniaturize such technology to make surgical implantation possible. They also need to figure out how to interface the device's output with the region of the brain called the olfactory bulb, which responds to scent. Success likely won't come for years, but it's within reach. The technology exists. The challenge is to adapt it for medical use and then perhaps one day restore a missing piece of sensory experience to those who have lost their ability to detect smell (Holbrook et al., 2018; Weintraub, 2019).

RETHINK

- What challenges might researchers have to overcome in developing a scent-detecting implant?
- How might your understanding of the world be different if you had no sense of smell?

The sense of taste differs significantly from one person to another, largely as a result of genetic factors. Some people, dubbed "supertasters," are highly sensitive to taste; they have twice as many taste receptors as "nontasters," who are relatively insensitive to taste. Supertasters (who, for unknown reasons, are more likely to be female than male) find sweets sweeter, cream creamier, and spicy dishes spicier, and weaker concentrations of flavor are enough to satisfy any cravings they may have (Pickering & Gordon, 2006; Cornelis et al., 2017).

Supertasters–who make up about 15% of the U.S. population–may even be healthier than nontasters. Because supertasters find fatty foods distasteful, they are thinner than the general population. In contrast, because they aren't so sensitive to taste, nontasters may seek out relatively sweeter and fattier foods in order to maximize the taste. As a consequence, they may be prone to obesity (Reddy, 2013).

Are you a supertaster? To find out, complete the questionnaire in Figure 4.

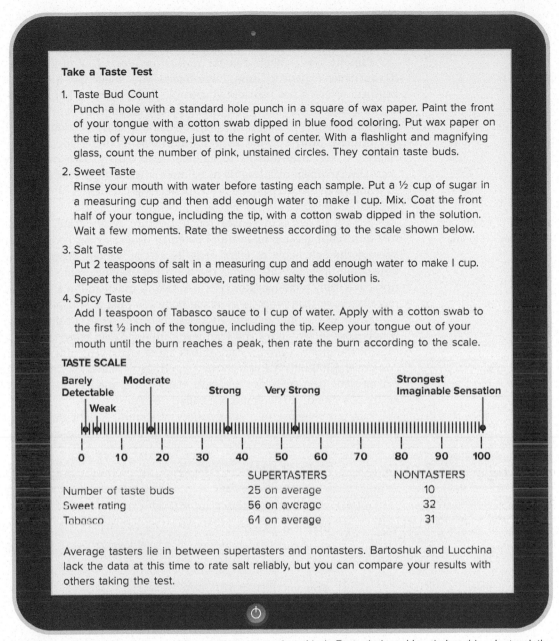

Take a Taste Test

1. **Taste Bud Count**
   Punch a hole with a standard hole punch in a square of wax paper. Paint the front of your tongue with a cotton swab dipped in blue food coloring. Put wax paper on the tip of your tongue, just to the right of center. With a flashlight and magnifying glass, count the number of pink, unstained circles. They contain taste buds.

2. **Sweet Taste**
   Rinse your mouth with water before tasting each sample. Put a ½ cup of sugar in a measuring cup and then add enough water to make I cup. Mix. Coat the front half of your tongue, including the tip, with a cotton swab dipped in the solution. Wait a few moments. Rate the sweetness according to the scale shown below.

3. **Salt Taste**
   Put 2 teaspoons of salt in a measuring cup and add enough water to make I cup. Repeat the steps listed above, rating how salty the solution is.

4. **Spicy Taste**
   Add I teaspoon of Tabasco sauce to I cup of water. Apply with a cotton swab to the first ½ inch of the tongue, including the tip. Keep your tongue out of your mouth until the burn reaches a peak, then rate the burn according to the scale.

TASTE SCALE

Barely Detectable — Weak — Moderate — Strong — Very Strong — Strongest Imaginable Sensation

0 10 20 30 40 50 60 70 80 90 100

	SUPERTASTERS	NONTASTERS
Number of taste buds	25 on average	10
Sweet rating	56 on average	32
Tabasco	64 on average	31

Average tasters lie in between supertasters and nontasters. Bartoshuk and Lucchina lack the data at this time to rate salt reliably, but you can compare your results with others taking the test.

FIGURE 4 All tongues are not created equal, according to taste researchers Linda Bartoshuk and Laurie Lucchina. Instead, they suggest that the intensity of a flavor experienced by a given person is determined by that person's genetic background. This taste test can help determine if you are a nontaster, average taster, or supertaster.

Sources: Bartoshuk, L., & Lucchina, L. (1997, January 13). Are you a supertaster? *U.S. News & World Report*, 58–59, and Science Buddies (2012). Super-Tasting Science: Find Out If You're a "Supertaster"! *Scientific American*.

The Skin Senses: Touch, Pressure, Temperature, and Pain

It started innocently when Jennifer Darling hurt her right wrist during gym class. At first, it seemed like a simple sprain. But even though the initial injury healed, the excruciating, burning pain accompanying it did not go away. Instead, it spread to her other arm and then to her legs. The pain, which Jennifer described as similar to "a hot iron on your arm," was unbearable—and never stopped.

The source of Darling's pain turned out to be a rare condition known as *reflex sympathetic dystrophy syndrome*, or RSDS. RSDS is a disease characterized by constant, intense pain that is out of proportion to any injury. For a victim of RSDS, a stimulus as mild as a gentle breeze or the touch of a feather can produce agony. Even bright sunlight or a loud noise can trigger intense pain (Coderre, 2011; Harden et al., 2013).

Pain such as Darling's can be devastating, yet a lack of pain can be equally bad. If you never experience pain, for instance, you might not notice that your arm had brushed against a hot pan, and you would suffer a severe burn. Similarly, without the warning sign of abdominal pain that typically accompanies an inflamed appendix, your appendix might eventually rupture, spreading a fatal infection throughout your body.

Pain has other benefits, as well. Pain helps us better appreciate pleasurable experiences. It also may lead us to affiliate more closely with others, by arousing their empathy. And pain may lead us to be more vigilant about our surroundings as we seek to avoid or moderate pain we are experiencing (Bastian et al., 2014; Cameron, Spring, & Todd, 2017; Liu et al., 2019).

skin senses The senses of touch, pressure, temperature, and pain. (Module 12)

In fact, all our **skin senses**–touch, pressure, temperature, and pain–play a critical role in survival, making us aware of potential danger to our bodies. Most of these senses operate through nerve receptor cells located at various depths throughout the skin, distributed unevenly throughout the body. For example, some areas, such as the fingertips, have many more receptor cells sensitive to touch and as a consequence are notably more sensitive than other areas of the body (Gardner & Kandel, 2000) (see Figure 5).

Probably the most extensively researched skin sense is pain, and with good reason: People consult physicians and take medication for pain more than for any other symptom or condition. Chronic pain afflicts more than 116 million American adults and costs over $600 billion a year in the United States alone. Fifty million Americans report having some pain every day or almost every day in the past six months (Robinson-Papp et al., 2015; Carr, 2019; Smith & Hillner, 2019).

Pain is a response to a great variety of stimuli. A light that is too bright can produce pain, and sound that is too loud can be painful. There are also multiple forms of

> **Study Alert**
> Remember that there are multiple skin senses, including touch, pressure, temperature, and pain.

FIGURE 5 Skin sensitivity in various areas of the body. The lower the average threshold is, the more sensitive a body part is. The fingers and thumb, lips, nose, cheeks, and big toe are the most sensitive. Why do you think certain areas are more sensitive than others?

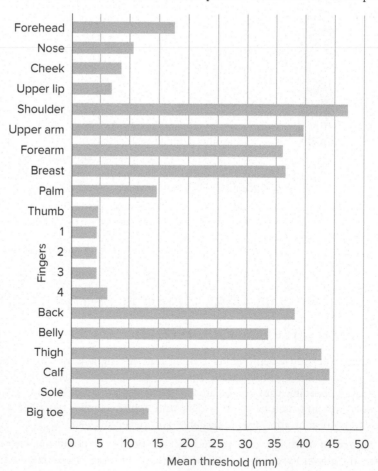

pain; even itching can be considered a form of pain (Papoiu et al., 2013; Bautista, Wilson, & Hoon, 2014; Sutherland, 2016.)

One explanation for pain is that it is an outcome of cell injury; when a cell is damaged, regardless of the source of damage, it releases a chemical called *substance P* that transmits pain messages to the brain.

Some people are more susceptible to pain than others. For example, women experience painful stimuli more intensely than men do. These gender differences are associated with the production of hormones related to menstrual cycles. In addition, certain genes are linked to the experience of pain, so that we may inherit our sensitivity to pain (Kim, Clark, & Dionne, 2009; Park, 2011; Berke et al., 2017).

But the experience of pain is not determined by biological factors alone. For example, women report that the pain experienced in childbirth is moderated to some degree by the joyful nature of the situation. In contrast, even a minor stimulus can produce the perception of strong pain if it is accompanied by anxiety (for example, during a visit to the dentist). Clearly, then, pain is a perceptual response that depends heavily on our emotions and thoughts (Lang, Sorrell, & Rodgers, 2006; Kennedy et al., 2011; Jensen & Turk, 2014).

From the perspective of...

A Medical or Dental Services Provider How would you handle a patient who is anxiously awaiting treatment and complaining that her pain is getting worse?

Robert Daly/age fotostock

According to the **gate-control theory of pain,** particular nerve receptors in the spinal cord lead to specific areas of the brain related to pain. When these receptors are activated because of an injury or problem with a part of the body, a "gate" to the brain is opened, causing us to experience the sensation of pain (Vasudeva et al., 2015; Penlington, Urbanek, & Barker, 2019).

But the gate that produces pain does not necessarily remain open. Specifically, another set of neural receptors can, when stimulated, close the "gate" to the brain, thereby reducing the experience of pain.

The gate can be shut in two ways. First, other impulses can overwhelm the nerve pathways relating to pain, which are spread throughout the brain. In this case, non-painful stimuli compete with and sometimes displace the neural message of pain, thereby shutting off the painful stimulus. This explains why rubbing the skin around an injury (or even listening to distracting music) helps reduce pain. The competing stimuli can overpower the painful ones (Somers et al., 2011; Lunde et al., 2019).

Second, the neural gate producing pain can be shut by psychological factors relating to an individual's current emotions, interpretation of events, and previous experience. Specifically, the brain can close a gate by sending a message down the spinal cord to an injured area, producing a reduction in or relief from pain. Thus, soldiers who are injured in battle may experience no pain—the surprising situation in more than half of all combat injuries. The lack of pain probably occurs because a soldier experiences such relief at still being alive that the brain sends a signal to the injury site to shut down the pain gate (Gatchel & Weisberg, 2000; Pincus & Morley, 2001).

Gate-control theory also may explain cultural differences in the experience of pain. Some of these variations are astounding. For example, in India, people who participate in the "hook-swinging" ritual to celebrate the power of the gods have steel hooks embedded

gate-control theory of pain The theory that particular nerve receptors in the spinal cord lead to specific areas of the brain related to pain. (Module 12)

PsychTech
Researcher Sean Mackey exposed participants in a study to a painful stimulus while watching an fMRI scan of their brain. Mackey found that the participants could be trained to exert control over the region of the brain activated by the pain, thereby reducing their experience of pain.

The ancient practice of acupuncture is still used in the 21st century. How does the gate-control theory of pain explain how acupuncture works?
Fuse/Corbis/Getty Images

under the skin and muscles of their backs. During the ritual, they swing from a pole, suspended by the hooks. What would seem likely to induce excruciating pain instead produces a state of celebration and near euphoria. In fact, when the hooks are later removed, the wounds heal quickly, and after 2 weeks, almost no visible marks remain (Melzack & Katz, 2001; Krupić et al., 2019).

Gate-control theory suggests that the lack of pain is due to a message from the participant's brain that shuts down the pain pathways. Gate-control theory also may explain the effectiveness of *acupuncture*, an ancient Chinese technique in which sharp needles are inserted into various parts of the body. The sensation from the needles may close the gateway to the brain, reducing the experience of pain. It is also possible that the body's own pain-killers—called *endorphins*—as well as positive and negative emotions, play a role in opening and closing the gate (Witt, Jena, & Brinkhaus, 2006; Cabioglu, Ergene, & Tan, 2007; Khedr et al., 2017).

Although the basic ideas behind gate-control theory have been supported by research, other processes are involved in the perception of pain. For instance, it appears that there are multiple neural pathways involved in the experience of pain. Furthermore, the suppression of pain can occur through the natural release of endorphins and other compounds that produce a reduction of discomfort and a sense of well-being. Finally, cognitive factors—such as people's expectations and their prior learning about pain—play a significant role in the perception of pain (Grahek, 2007; Wiech, 2016).

BECOMING AN INFORMED CONSUMER
of Psychology

Managing Pain

Are you one of the more than 116 million people in the United States who suffers from chronic pain? Psychologists and medical specialists have devised several strategies to fight pain. Among the most important approaches are these:

- *Medication.* Painkilling drugs are the most popular treatment in fighting pain, despite the dangers of overuse that many see as the source of the current opioid crisis. Drugs range from those that directly treat the source of the pain—such as reducing swelling in painful joints—to those that work on the symptoms. Medication can be in the form of pills, patches, injections, or liquids. In a recent innovation, drugs are pumped directly into the spinal cord. Increasing evidence also indicates that medical cannabis (marijuana) can be an effective painkiller (Bagnall, 2010; Jain et al, 2019; Wallis, 2019).
- *Nerve and brain stimulation.* Pain can sometimes be relieved when a low-voltage electric current is passed through the specific part of the body that is in pain. For example, in *peripheral-nerve stimulation,* a tiny battery-operated generator is implanted in the lower back. In even more severe cases, electrodes can be implanted surgically directly into the brain, or a handheld battery pack can stimulate nerve cells to provide direct relief (Landro, 2010; Tan et al., 2011; Conforto et al., 2019).
- *Light therapy.* One of the newest forms of pain reduction involves exposure to specific wavelengths of red or infrared light. Certain kinds of light increase the production of enzymes that may promote healing (Evcik et al., 2007; de Sousa et al., 2019).
- *Hypnosis.* For people who can be hypnotized—and not everyone is susceptible—hypnosis can greatly relieve pain. In fact, it can affect the brain and spinal-cord functioning in injured people, actually improving their physical functioning (Accardi & Milling, 2009; Lee & Raja, 2011; Jensen & Patterson, 2014).

- *Biofeedback and relaxation techniques.* Using *biofeedback*, people learn to control what are usually involuntary functions such as heartbeat, respiration, blood pressure, and muscle tension. Through biofeedback, a person can learn to control the stimulus that is causing the pain. For instance, people with tension headaches or back pain can be trained to relax their bodies to bring themselves relief (Sielski, Rief, & Glombiewski, 2017; McKenna et al., 2019).
- *Surgery.* In one of the most extreme methods, specific nerve fibers that carry pain messages to the brain can be cut surgically. Still, because of the danger that other bodily functions will be affected, surgery is a treatment of last resort, used most frequently with dying patients (Amid & Chen, 2011).
- *Cognitive restructuring.* Cognitive treatments are effective for people who continually say to themselves, "This pain will never stop," "The pain is ruining my life," or "I can't take it anymore," and are thereby likely to make their pain even worse. By substituting more positive ways of thinking, people can increase their sense of control—and actually reduce the pain they experience (Liedl et al., 2011; Ehde, Dillworth, & Turner, 2014; Nowakowski, McCabe, & Busse, 2019).
- *Virtual reality therapy.* In one of the newest treatments, pain sufferers wear a headset that creates an entertaining, relaxing, and interactive virtual reality environment. The experience is so rich in stimulation that the brain has no capacity to process pain sensations at the same time (Brody, 2019: Fusaro, Tieri, & Aglioti, 2019).

How Our Senses Interact

When Matthew Blakeslee shapes hamburger patties with his hands, he experiences a vivid bitter taste in his mouth. Esmerelda Jones (a pseudonym) sees blue when she listens to the note C sharp played on the piano; other notes evoke different hues–so much so that the piano keys are actually color-coded, making it easier for her to remember and play musical scales. (Ramachandran & Hubbard, 2006)

The explanation? Both of these people have an unusual condition known as synesthesia. *Synesthesia* is a perceptual phenomenon in which the stimulation of one sensory system (such as hearing) involuntarily leads a person to experience an additional sensory response in a different sensory system (such as vision).

The origins of synesthesia are not totally clear, although some research suggests it is genetically inherited. Also, people with synesthesia may have unusually dense neural linkages between the sensory areas of the brain. Another hypothesis is that they lack the neural controls that usually inhibit connections between sensory areas (Deroy & Spence, 2013; Meier & Rothen, 2015; Jewanski et al., 2019).

Whatever the reason for synesthesia, it is a rare condition. (If you'd like to check out this phenomenon, see Figure 6.) Even so, the senses of all of us do interact and integrate in a variety of ways. For example, the taste of food is influenced by its texture

 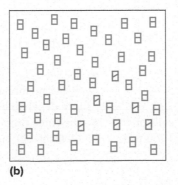

(a)   (b)

FIGURE 6 (a) Try to pick out the 0s in the display. (Note: each 0 appears as a rectangular "ø" with a slash through it.) Most people take several seconds to find them buried among the 8s and to see that the øs form a triangle. People with certain forms of synesthesia, however, find this easy because they perceive the numbers in contrasting colors as in (b).

(a and b): Sources: Adapted from Ramachandran, V. S., & Hubbard, E. M. (2006). Hearing colors, tasting shapes. *Scientific American, 16,* 76–83, and Safran, A. B., & Sanda, N. (2015). Color synesthesia. Insight into perception, emotion, and consciousness. *Current Opinion in Neurology, 28*(1), 36–44 and temperature. We perceive food that is warmer as sweeter (think of the sweetness of steamy hot chocolate compared with cold chocolate milk). Spicy foods stimulate some of the same pain receptors that are also stimulated by heat—making the use of *hot* as a synonym for *spicy* quite accurate (Balaban, McBurney, & Affeltranger, 2005; Brang et al., 2011; Alfaro et al., 2015).

It's important, then, to think of our senses as interacting with one another. For instance, brain imaging studies show that the senses work in tandem to build our understanding of the world around us. We engage in *multimodal perception*, in which the brain collects the information from the individual sensory systems and integrates and coordinates it (Macaluso & Driver, 2005; Paulmann, Jessen, & Kotz, 2009; Gruber & Block, 2017).

Moreover, despite the fact that very different sorts of stimuli activate our individual senses, they all react according to the same basic principles that we discussed at the start of this chapter. For example, our responses to visual, auditory, and taste stimuli all follow Weber's law involving our sensitivity to changes in the strength of stimuli.

In short, in some ways our senses are more similar to one another than different. Each of them is designed to pick up information from the environment and translate it into usable information. Furthermore, individually and collectively, our senses help us to understand the complexities of the world around us, allowing us to navigate through the world effectively and intelligently.

RECAP/EVALUATE/RETHINK

RECAP

LO 12-1 What role does the ear play in the senses of sound, motion, and balance?

- Sound, motion, and balance are centered in the ear. Sounds, in the form of vibrating air waves, enter through the outer ear and travel through the auditory canal until they reach the eardrum.
- The vibrations of the eardrum are transmitted into the middle ear, which consists of three bones: the hammer, the anvil, and the stirrup. These bones transmit vibrations to the oval window.
- In the inner ear, vibrations move into the cochlea, which encloses the basilar membrane. Hair cells on the basilar membrane change the mechanical energy of sound waves into nerve impulses that are transmitted to the brain. The ear is also involved in the sense of balance and motion.
- Sound has a number of physical characteristics, including frequency and amplitude. The place theory of hearing and the frequency theory of hearing explain the processes by which we distinguish sounds of varying frequency and intensity.

LO 12-2 How do smell and taste function?

- Smell depends on olfactory cells (the receptor cells of the nose), and taste is centered in the taste buds on the tongue and mouth.

LO 12-3 What are the skin senses, and how do they relate to the experience of pain?

- The skin senses are responsible for the experiences of touch, pressure, temperature, and pain. Gate-control theory suggests that particular nerve receptors, when activated, open a "gate" to specific areas of the brain related to pain and that another set of receptors closes the gate when stimulated.
- Among the techniques used frequently to alleviate pain are medication, hypnosis, biofeedback, relaxation techniques, surgery, nerve and brain stimulation, and cognitive therapy.

EVALUATE

1. The tube-like passage leading from the outer ear to the eardrum is known as the _____ _____.
2. The purpose of the eardrum is to protect the sensitive nerves underneath it. It serves no purpose in actual hearing. True or false?
3. The three middle ear bones transmit their sound to the _____ _____.
4. The _____ theory of hearing states that the entire basilar membrane responds to a sound, vibrating more or less, depending on the nature of the sound.
5. The three fluid-filled tubes in the inner ear that are responsible for our sense of balance are known as the _____ _____.

6. The _____ _____ theory states that when certain skin receptors are activated as a result of an injury, a "pathway" to the brain is opened, allowing pain to be experienced.

sensitive than normal)? What benefits might this ability bring? What problems might it cause?

2. Why might sensitivity to pheromones have evolved differently in humans than in other species? What cultural factors might have played a role?

RETHINK

1. Much research is being conducted on repairing faulty sensory organs through devices such as personal guidance systems and eyeglasses, among others. Do you think that researchers should attempt to improve normal sensory capabilities beyond their "natural" range (for example, make human visual or audio capabilities more

Answers to Evaluate Questions

1. auditory canal; 2. False: It vibrates when sound waves hit it and transmits the sound; 3. oval window; 4. frequency; 5. semicircular canals; 6. gate-control

---

KEY TERMS

sound	basilar membrane	frequency theory of	skin senses
eardrum	hair cells	hearing	gate-control theory of pain
cochlea (KOKE-lee-uh)	place theory of hearing	semicircular canals	

Module 13
Perceptual Organization: Constructing Our View of the World

LEARNING OUTCOMES

LO 13-1 What principles underlie our organization of the visual world and allow us to make sense of our environment?

LO 13-2 How are we able to perceive the world in three dimensions when our retinas are capable of sensing only two-dimensional images?

LO 13-3 What clues do visual illusions give us about our understanding of general perceptual mechanisms?

Gestalt (geh-SHTALLT) laws of organization A series of principles that describe how we organize bits and pieces of information into meaningful wholes. (Module 13)

Consider the vase shown in Figure 1a for a moment. Or is it a vase? Take another look, and instead you may see the profiles of two people.

Now that an alternative interpretation has been pointed out, you will probably shift back and forth between the two interpretations. Similarly, if you examine the shapes in Figure 1b long enough, you will probably experience a shift in what you're seeing. The reason for these reversals is this: Because each figure is two-dimensional, the usual means we employ for distinguishing the figure (the object being perceived) from the *ground* (the background or spaces within the object) do not work.

The fact that we can look at the same figure in more than one way illustrates an important point. We do not just passively respond to visual stimuli that happen to fall on our retinas. Rather, we actively try to organize and make sense of what we see.

We turn now from a focus on the initial response to a stimulus (sensation) to what our minds make of that stimulus (perception). Perception is a constructive process by which we go beyond the stimuli that are presented to us and attempt to construct a meaningful situation.

The Gestalt Laws of Organization

Some of the most basic perceptual processes can be described by a series of principles that focus on the ways we organize bits and pieces of information into meaningful wholes. These principles, known as the **Gestalt laws of organization,** were set forth in the early 1900s by a group of German psychologists who studied patterns, or *gestalts* (Wertheimer, 1923). Those psychologists discovered a number of important principles that are valid for visual (as well as auditory) stimuli, illustrated in Figure 2: closure, proximity, similarity, and simplicity.

Figure 2a illustrates *closure*: We usually group elements to form enclosed or complete figures rather than open ones. We tend to ignore the breaks in Figure 2a and concentrate on the overall form. Figure 2b demonstrates the principle of *proximity*: We perceive elements that are closer together as grouped together. As a result, we tend to see pairs of dots rather than a row of single dots in Figure 2b.

FIGURE 1 When the usual cues we use to distinguish figure from ground are absent, we may shift back and forth between different views of the same figure. In (a), you can see either a vase or the profiles of two people. In (b), the shaded portion of the figure, called a Necker cube, can appear to be either the front or the back of the cube.

(a)

(b)

(a) Closure   **(b)** Proximity   **(c)** Similarity   **(d)** Simplicity

FIGURE 2 Organizing these various bits and pieces of information into meaningful wholes constitutes some of the most basic processes of perception, which are summed up in the gestalt laws of organization. How might we determine if any other species share this organizational tendency?

Elements that are *similar* in appearance we perceive as grouped together. We see, then, horizontal rows of circles and squares in Figure 2c, rather than vertical mixed columns. Finally, in a general sense, the overriding Gestalt principle is *simplicity*: When we observe a pattern, we perceive it in the most basic, straightforward manner that we can. For example, most of us see Figure 2d as a square with lines on two sides, rather than as the block letter *W* on top of the letter *M*. If we have a choice of interpretations, we generally opt for the simpler one.

Although Gestalt psychology no longer plays a prominent role in contemporary psychology, its legacy endures. One fundamental Gestalt principle that remains influential is that two objects considered together form a whole that is different from the simple combination of the objects. Gestalt psychologists argued that the perception of stimuli in our environment goes well beyond the individual elements that we sense. Instead, it represents an active, constructive process carried out within the brain (Wagemans et al., 2012; Chiu, Lo, & Hsieh, 2017) (see Figure 3).

Top-Down and Bottom-Up Processing

Ca- yo- re-d t-is -en-en-e, w-ic- ha- ev-ry -hi-d l-tt-r m-ss-ng? It probably won't take you too long to figure out that it says: "Can you read this sentence, which has every third letter missing?"

FIGURE 3 Although at first it is difficult to distinguish anything in this drawing, keep looking, and eventually you may see the figure of a dog—or actually, several dogs. Each dog represents a Gestalt, or perceptual, whole, which is something greater than the sum of the individual elements.
Gandee Vasan/Stone/Getty Images

FIGURE 4 The power of context is shown in this figure. Note how the B and the 13 are identical.
Source: Coren, S., Ward, L. M. (1989). Sensation and perception (3rd ed.). San Diego, CA: Harcourt Brace Jovanovich.

A B C D E F
9 10 11 12 13 14

If perception were based primarily on breaking down a stimulus into its most basic elements, understanding the sentence, as well as other ambiguous stimuli, would not be possible. The fact that you were probably able to recognize such an imprecise stimulus illustrates that perception proceeds along two different avenues, called top-down processing and bottom-up processing.

In **top-down processing,** perception is guided by higher-level knowledge, experience, expectations, and motivations. You were able to figure out the meaning of the sentence with the missing letters because of your prior reading experience and because written English contains redundancies. Not every letter of each word is necessary to decode its meaning. Moreover, your expectations played a role in your being able to read the sentence. You were probably expecting a statement that had *something* to do with psychology, not the lyrics to a Lady Gaga song.

Top-down processing is illustrated by the importance of context in determining how we perceive objects. Look, for example, at Figure 4. Most of us perceive that the first row consists of the letters *A* through *F*, while the second contains the numbers 9 through 14. But take a more careful look, and you'll see that the B and the 13 are identical. Clearly, our perception is affected by our expectations about the two sequences—even though the two stimuli are exactly the same.

However, top-down processing cannot occur on its own. Even though top-down processing allows us to fill in the gaps in ambiguous and out-of-context stimuli, we would be unable to perceive the meaning of such stimuli without bottom-up processing. **Bottom-up processing** consists of the progression of recognizing and processing information from individual components of a stimuli and moving to the perception of the whole. We would make no headway in our recognition of the sentence without being able to perceive the individual shapes that make up the letters. Some perception, then, occurs at the level of the patterns and features of each of the separate letters.

Top-down and bottom-up processing occur simultaneously and interact with each other in our perception of the world around us. Bottom-up processing permits us to process the fundamental characteristics of stimuli, whereas top-down processing allows us to bring our experience to bear on perception. As we learn more about the complex processes involved in perception, we are developing a better understanding of how the brain continually interprets information from the senses and permits us to make responses appropriate to the environment (Westerhausen et al., 2009; Falasca et al., 2015; Riener, 2019).

Depth Perception: Translating 2-D to 3-D

As sophisticated as the retina is, the images projected onto it are flat and two-dimensional. Yet the world around us is three-dimensional, and we perceive it that way. How do we make the transformation from 2-D to 3-D?

The ability to view the world in three dimensions and to perceive distance—a skill known as **depth perception**—is due largely to the fact that we have two eyes. Because there is a certain distance between the eyes, a slightly different image reaches each retina. The brain integrates the two images into one view, but it also recognizes the difference in images and uses this difference to estimate the distance of an object from us. The difference in the images seen by the left eye and the right eye is known as *binocular disparity* (Gillam, Palmisano, & Govan, 2011; Valsecchi et al., 2013; Gao, Schneider, & Li, 2017; Campagnoli & Domini, 2019).

top-down processing Perception that is guided by higher-level knowledge, experience, expectations, and motivations. (Module 13)

bottom-up processing Perception that consists of the progression of recognizing and processing information from individual components of a stimuli and moving to the perception of the whole. (Module 13)

depth perception The ability to view the world in three dimensions and to perceive distance. (Module 13)

Railroad tracks that seem to join together in the distance are an example of linear perspective.
Fuse/Getty Images

To get a sense of binocular disparity, hold a pencil at arm's length and look at it first with one eye and then with the other. There is little difference between the two views relative to the background. Now bring the pencil just 6 inches away from your face, and try the same thing. This time you will perceive a greater difference between the two views.

The difference between the images in the two eyes provides us with a way of determining distance. If we view two objects and one is considerably closer to us than the other is, the retinal disparity will be relatively large. That disparity leads us to have a greater sense of depth between the two. However, if two objects are a similar distance from us, the retinal disparity will be minor. Therefore, we will perceive them as being a similar distance from us.

In some cases, certain cues permit us to obtain a sense of depth and distance with just one eye. These cues are known as *monocular cues*.

For example, *motion parallax* is the monocular cue in which a change in position of an object on the retina allows the perception of movement. For example, suppose you are a passenger in a moving car and you focus your eye on a stable object such as a tree. Objects that are closer than the tree will appear to move backward, and the nearer the object is, the more quickly it will appear to move. In contrast, objects beyond the tree will seem to move at a slower speed but in the same direction as you are. Your brain is able to use these cues to calculate the relative distances of the tree and other objects.

Similarly, the monocular cue of *relative size* reflects the assumption that if two objects are the same size, the object that makes a smaller image on the retina is farther away than the one that makes a larger image. But it's not just size of an object that provides information about distance; the quality of the image on the retina helps us judge distance. The monocular cue of *texture gradient* provides information about distance because the details of things that are far away are less distinct (Proffitt, 2006).

Finally, anyone who has ever seen railroad tracks that seem to come together in the distance knows that distant objects appear to be closer together than are nearer ones, a phenomenon called linear perspective. *Linear perspective* is a type of perspective in which objects in the distance appear to converge. We use linear perspective as a monocular cue in estimating distance, allowing the two-dimensional image on the retina to record the three-dimensional world (Shimono & Wade, 2002; Bruggeman, Yonas, & Konczak, 2007).

From the perspective of...

A Computer Game Designer What are some techniques you might use to produce the appearance of three-dimensional terrain on a two-dimensional computer screen? What are some techniques you might use to suggest motion?

Sam Edwards/age fotostock

Perceptual Constancy

Consider what happens as you finish a conversation with a friend and she begins to walk away from you. As you watch her walk down the street, the image on your retina becomes smaller and smaller. Do you wonder why she is shrinking?

Of course not. Despite the very real change in the size of the retinal image, because of perceptual constancy, you factor into your thinking the knowledge that your friend is moving farther away from you. **Perceptual constancy** is the recognition that physical objects are consistent and do not vary, even though our sensory input about them changes.

Perceptual constancy allows us to view objects as having an unchanging size, shape, color, and brightness, even if the image on our retina changes. For example, despite the varying size or shape of the images on the retina as an airplane approaches, flies overhead, and then disappears, we do not perceive the airplane as changing shape or size. Experience has taught us that the plane's size remains constant (Garrigan & Kellman, 2008; Sachse et al., 2017; Sato, Matsuo, & Kitazaki, 2019).

In some cases, though, our application of perceptual constancy can mislead us. One good example of this involves the rising moon. When the moon first appears at night, close to the horizon, it seems to be huge—much larger than when it is high in the sky later in the evening. You may have thought that the apparent change in the size of the moon was caused by the moon's being physically closer to the earth when

perceptual constancy Our understanding that physical objects are consistent and do not vary, even though sensory input about them may vary. (Module 13)

Despite the moon appearing very large when it is close to the horizon, perceptual constancy helps us to know that the moon's size has not changed and remains the same.

Paul Souders/The Image Bank/Getty Images

it first appears. In fact, though, this is not the case at all: the actual image of the moon on our retina is the same, whether it is low or high in the sky.

There are several explanations for the moon illusion. One suggests that the moon appears to be larger when it is close to the horizon primarily because of perceptual constancy. When the moon is near the horizon, the perceptual cues of intervening terrain and objects such as trees on the horizon produce a misleading sense of distance, leading us to misperceive the moon as relatively large.

In contrast, when the moon is high in the sky, we see it by itself, and we don't try to compensate for its distance from us. In this case, then, perceptual constancy leads us to perceive it as relatively small. To experience perceptual constancy, try looking at the moon when it is relatively low on the horizon through a paper-towel tube; the moon suddenly will appear to "shrink" back to normal size (Kaufman, Johnson, & Liu, 2008; Rogers & Naumenko, 2015; Francis et al., 2019).

Perceptual constancy is not the only explanation for the moon illusion, and it remains a puzzle to psychologists. It may be that several different perceptual processes are involved in the illusion (Gregory, 2008; Kim, 2008).

Motion Perception: As the World Turns

When a batter tries to hit a pitched ball, the most important factor is the motion of the ball. How is a batter able to judge the speed and location of a target that is moving at some 90 miles per hour?

The answer rests in part on several cues that provide us with relevant information about the perception of motion. For one thing, the movement of an object across the retina is typically perceived relative to some stable, unmoving background. Moreover, if the stimulus is heading toward us, the image on the retina expands in size, filling more and more of the visual field. In such cases, we assume that the stimulus is approaching—not that it is an expanding stimulus viewed at a constant distance.

It is not, however, just the movement of images across the retina that brings about the perception of motion. If it were, we would perceive the world as moving every time we moved our heads. Instead, one of the critical things we learn about perception is to factor information about our own head and eye movements along with information about changes in the retinal image.

Sometimes we perceive motion when it doesn't occur. Have you ever been on a stationary train that feels as if it is moving because a train on an adjacent track begins to slowly move past? Or have you been in an IMAX movie theater in which you feel as if you were falling as a huge image of a plane moves across the screen? In both cases, the experience of motion is convincing. *Apparent movement* is the perception that a stationary object is moving. It occurs when different areas of the retina are quickly stimulated, leading us to interpret motion (Lindemann & Bekkering, 2009; Brandon & Saffran, 2011; Luo et al., 2019).

Perceptual Illusions: The Deceptions of Perceptions

If you look carefully at the Parthenon, one of the most famous buildings of ancient Greece, still standing at the top of an Athens hill, you'll see that it was built with a bulge on one side. If it didn't have that bulge—and quite a few other architectural "tricks" like it, such as columns that incline inward—it would look as if it were crooked and about to fall down. Instead, it appears to stand completely straight, at right angles to the ground.

The fact that the Parthenon appears to be completely upright is the result of a series of visual illusions. **Visual illusions** are physical stimuli that consistently produce errors in perception. In the case of the Parthenon, the building appears to be completely

visual illusions Physical stimuli that consistently produce errors in perception. (Module 13)

(a)

(b)

(c)

FIGURE 5 (a) In building the Parthenon, the Greeks constructed an architectural wonder that looks perfectly straight, with right angles at every corner. (b) However, if it had been built with completely true right angles, it would have looked as it does here. (c) To compensate for this illusion, the Parthenon was designed to have a slight upward curvature, as shown here.

(a) Mlenny Photography/E+/Getty Images; (b and c) Luckiesh, M, Scientific American Monthly, 3, p 497-501 (1921).

square, as illustrated in Figure 5a. However, if it had been built that way, it would look to us as it does in Figure 5b. The reason for this is an illusion that makes right angles placed above a line appear as if they were bent. To offset the illusion, the Parthenon was constructed as in Figure 5c, with a slight upward curvature.

The *Müller-Lyer illusion* (illustrated in Figure 6) has fascinated psychologists for decades. Although the two lines are the same length, the one with the arrow tips pointing outward, away from the vertical line (Figure 6a, left) appears to be shorter than the one with the arrow tips pointing inward (Figure 6a, right).

Although all kinds of explanations for visual illusions have been suggested, most concentrate either on the physical operation of the eye or on our misinterpretation of the visual stimulus. For example, one explanation for the Müller-Lyer illusion is that eye movements are greater when the arrow tips point inward, making us perceive the line as longer than it is when the arrow tips face outward. In contrast, a different explanation for the illusion suggests that we unconsciously attribute particular significance to each of the lines (Gregory, 1978). When we see the left line in Figure 6a, we tend to perceive it as if it were the relatively close outside corner of a rectangular object, such as the outside corner of the room illustrated in Figure 6b. In contrast, when we view the line

!**Study Alert**

The explanation for the Müller-Lyer illusion is complicated. Figure 6 will help you master it.

FIGURE 6 In the Müller-Lyer illusion (a), the vertical line on the left appears shorter than the one on the right, even though they are identical in length. One explanation for the Müller-Lyer illusion suggests that the line on the left (with arrow points directed outward) is perceived as the relatively close corner of a rectangular object, such as the building corner in (b), and the line on the right (with the arrow points directed inward) is interpreted as the inside corner of a rectangular object, such as the room extending away from us (c). Our previous experience with distance cues leads us to assume that the outside corner is closer than the inside corner and, consequently, the inside corner must be longer.

(a)

(b)

(c)

Optical illusions have been used to slow traffic, as these virtual speed bumps in Iceland illustrate. Although they appear to be hovering aboveground, in fact they are flush to the ground.
Thorir Ingvarsson/Shutterstock

on the right in Figure 6a, we perceive it as the relatively more distant inside corner of a rectangular object, such as the inside room corner in Figure 6c. Because previous experience leads us to assume that the outside corner is closer than the inside corner, we make the further assumption that the inside corner must therefore be longer.

Despite the complexity of the latter explanation, a good deal of evidence supports it. For instance, cross-cultural studies show that people raised in areas where there are few right angles—such as the Zulu in Africa—are much less susceptible to the illusion than are people who grow up where most structures are built using right angles and rectangles (Segall, Campbell, & Herskovits, 1966; Fujita et al., 2017).

Exploring DIVERSITY

Culture and Perception

As the example of the Zulu indicates, the culture in which we are raised has clear consequences for how we perceive the world. Consider the drawing in Figure 7. Sometimes called the "devil's tuning fork," it is likely to produce a mind-boggling effect, as the center tine of the fork alternates between appearing and disappearing.

Now try to reproduce the drawing on a piece of paper. Chances are that the task is nearly impossible for you—unless you are a member of an African tribe with little exposure to Western cultures. For such individuals, the task is simple; they have no trouble reproducing the figure. The reason is that Westerners automatically interpret the drawing as something that cannot exist in three dimensions, and they therefore are inhibited from reproducing it. The African tribal members, in contrast, do not make the assumption that the figure is "impossible" and instead view it in two dimensions, a perception that enables them to copy the figure with ease (Deregowski, 1973).

Cultural differences are also reflected in depth perception. A Western viewer of Figure 8 would interpret the hunter in the drawing as aiming for the antelope in the foreground, while an elephant stands under the tree in the background. A member of an isolated African tribe, however, interprets the scene very differently by assuming that the hunter is aiming at the elephant. Westerners use the difference in sizes between the two animals as a cue that the elephant is farther away than the antelope (Hudson, 1960; deBruïne, Vredeveldt, & van Koppen, 2018).

FIGURE 7 The "devil's tuning fork" has three prongs . . . or does it have two?

FIGURE 8 Is the man aiming for the elephant or the antelope? Westerners assume that the difference in size between the two animals indicates that the elephant is farther away and, therefore, the man is aiming for the antelope. In contrast, members of some African tribes, not used to depth cues in two-dimensional drawings, assume that the man is aiming for the elephant. Do you think people who view the picture in three dimensions could explain what they see to someone who views the scene in two dimensions and eventually get that person to view it in three dimensions?

Source: Hudson, W. (1960). Pictorial depth perception in subcultural groups in Africa. *Journal of Social Psychology, 52,* 183–208.

Does this mean that basic perceptual processes differ among people of different cultures? No. Variations in learning and experience produce cross-cultural differences in perception, and the underlying psychological processes involved in perception are similar (McCauley & Henrich, 2006).

Although visual illusions may seem like mere psychological curiosities, they actually illustrate something fundamental about perception. There is a basic connection between our prior knowledge, needs, motivations, and expectations about how the world is put together and the way we perceive it. Our view of the world is very much an outcome, then, of fundamental psychological factors. Furthermore, each person perceives the environment in a way that is unique and special (Repp & Knoblich, 2007; Phillips, 2019).

SUBLIMINAL PERCEPTION

Can stimuli that we're not consciously aware of change our behavior? In some ways, yes.

Subliminal perception refers to the perception of messages about which we have no awareness. The stimulus could be a written word, a sound, or even a smell that activates the sensory system but that is not intense enough for a person to report having experienced it. For example, in some studies, people are exposed to a descriptive label—called a *prime*—about a person (such as the word *smart* or *happy*) so briefly that they cannot report seeing the label. Later, however, they form impressions that are influenced by the content of the prime. Somehow, they have been influenced by the prime that they say they couldn't see, providing some evidence for subliminal perception (Kawakami & Miura, 2015; Lucini et al., 2019).

Although subliminal messages (which social psychologists refer to as *priming*) can influence behavior in subtle ways, there's little evidence that they can lead to *major* changes in attitudes or behavior. Most research suggests that they cannot. For example, people who are subliminally exposed to an image of a Coke can and the word *thirst* do later rate themselves as thirstier, and they actually do drink more when given the opportunity. However, they don't particularly care if they drink Coke or some other liquid to quench their thirst (Dijksterhuis, Chartrand, & Aarts, 2007; Parkinson et al., 2017).

In short, although we are able to perceive at least some kinds of information of which we are unaware, there's little evidence that subliminal messages can change our attitudes or behavior in substantial ways. At the same time, subliminal perception does have at least some consequences. If our motivation to carry out a behavior is already high and the appropriate stimuli are presented subliminally, subliminal perception may have at least some effect on our behavior (Pratkanis, Epley, & Savitsky, 2007; Randolph-Seng & Nielsen, 2009; Gafner, 2013).

EXTRASENSORY PERCEPTION (ESP)

Psychologists are highly skeptical of reports of *extrasensory perception*, or ESP–perception that does not involve our known senses. Although almost half of the general population of the United States believes it exists, most psychologists reject the existence of ESP, asserting that there is no sound documentation of the phenomenon (Moore, 2005).

However, a debate in one of the most prestigious psychology journals, *Psychological Bulletin*, heightened interest in ESP in the early 2000s. According to proponents of ESP, reliable evidence existed for an "anomalous process of information transfer," or *psi*. These researchers, who painstakingly reviewed considerable evidence, argued that a cumulative body of research shows reliable support for the existence of psi (Storm & Ertel, 2001; Parra & Argibay, 2007;Storm & Rock, 2015).

Ultimately, their conclusion was challenged and largely discredited for several reasons. For example, critics suggested that the research methodology was inadequate and that the experiments supporting psi are flawed (Kennedy, 2004; Rouder, Morey, & Province, 2013).

Because of questions about the quality of the research, as well as a lack of any credible theoretical explanation for how extrasensory perception might take place, almost no psychologists would claim that there is reliable scientific support for ESP. Still, the topic continues to inspire research, which is the only way the issue will be fully settled (Wiseman & Greening, 2002; Bem, 2012; Huang, 2019).

RECAP/EVALUATE/RETHINK

RECAP

LO 13-1 What principles underlie our organization of the visual world and allow us to make sense of our environment?

- Perception is a constructive process in which people go beyond the stimuli that are physically present and try to construct a meaningful interpretation.
- The Gestalt laws of organization are used to describe the way in which we organize bits and pieces of information into meaningful wholes, known as Gestalts, through closure, proximity, similarity, and simplicity.
- In top-down processing, perception is guided by higher-level knowledge, experience, expectations, and motivations. In bottom up processing, perception consists of the progression of recognizing and processing information from individual components of a stimuli and moving to the perception of the whole.

LO 13-2 How are we able to perceive the world in three dimensions when our retinas are capable of sensing only two-dimensional images?

- Depth perception is the ability to perceive distance and view the world in three dimensions, even though the images projected on our retinas are two-dimensional. We are able to judge depth and distance as a result of binocular disparity and monocular cues, such as motion parallax, the relative size of images on the retina, and linear perspective.
- Perceptual constancy permits us to perceive stimuli as unvarying in size, shape, and color despite changes in the environment or the appearance of the objects being perceived.
- Motion perception depends on cues such as the perceived movement of an object across the retina and information about how the head and eyes are moving.

LO 13-3 What clues do visual illusions give us about our understanding of general perceptual mechanisms?

- Visual illusions are physical stimuli that consistently produce errors in perception, causing judgments that do not reflect the physical reality of a stimulus accurately. One of the best-known illusions is the Müller-Lyer illusion.
- Visual illusions are usually the result of errors in the brain's interpretation of visual stimuli. Furthermore, culture clearly affects how we perceive the world.
- Subliminal perception refers to the perception of messages about which we have no awareness. The reality of the phenomenon, as well as of ESP, is open to question and debate.

EVALUATE

1. Match each of the following organizational laws with its meaning:

   a. closure
   b. proximity
   c. similarity
   d. simplicity

   1. Elements close together are grouped together.
   2. Patterns are perceived in the most basic, direct manner possible.
   3. Groupings are made in terms of complete figures.
   4. Elements similar in appearance are grouped together.

2. _____ analysis deals with the way in which we break an object down into its component pieces in order to understand it.
3. Processing that involves higher functions such as expectations and motivations is known as _____, whereas processing that recognizes the individual components of a stimulus is known as _____.
4. When a car passes you on the road and appears to shrink as it gets farther away, the phenomenon of _____

_____ permits you to realize that the car is not in fact getting smaller.
5. _____ _____ is the ability to view the world in three dimensions instead of two.
6. The brain makes use of a phenomenon known as _____ _____, or the difference in the images the two eyes see, to give three dimensions to sight.

RETHINK

1. In what ways do painters represent three-dimensional scenes in two dimensions on a canvas? Do you think artists in non-Western cultures use the same or different principles to represent three-dimensionality? Why?
2. Can you think of examples of the combined use of top-down and bottom-up processing in everyday life? Is one type of processing superior to the other?

Answers to Evaluate Questions

1. a-3, b-1, c-4, d-2; 2. Feature; 3. top-down, bottom-up; 4. perceptual constancy; 5. Depth perception; 6. binocular disparity

KEY TERMS

Gestalt (geh-SHTALLT) laws of organization	top-down processing bottom-up processing	depth perception perceptual constancy	visual illusions

LOOKING *Back*

EPILOGUE

We have noted the important distinction between sensation and perception, and we have examined the processes that underlie both of them. We've seen how external stimuli evoke sensory responses and how our different senses process the information contained in those responses. We also have focused on the physical structure and internal workings of the individual senses, including vision, hearing, balance, smell, taste, and the skin senses, and we've explored how our brains organize and process sensory information to construct a consistent, integrated picture of the world around us.

Before ending our discussion of sensation and perception, let's reconsider Jo Cameron, whom we met in the prologue and who doesn't feel pain or anxiety. Using your knowledge of sensation and perception, answer these questions:

1. What might be some downsides to Cameron's inability to feel pain?
2. If Cameron can't feel anxiety, do you think she can ever feel excitement or other positive emotions? Explain why you think so.
3. Do you think Cameron's condition supports or contradicts the gate-control theory of pain? Why?

VISUAL SUMMARY 4 Sensation and Perception

MODULE 10 Sensing the World

Absolute thresholds

Difference thresholds

- Just noticeable difference

- Weber's law

Sensory Adaptation

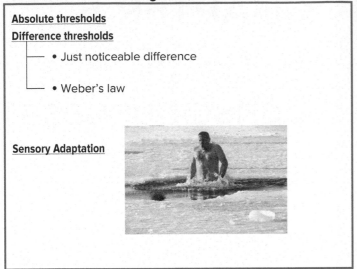

MODULE 11 Vision

Eye Structure

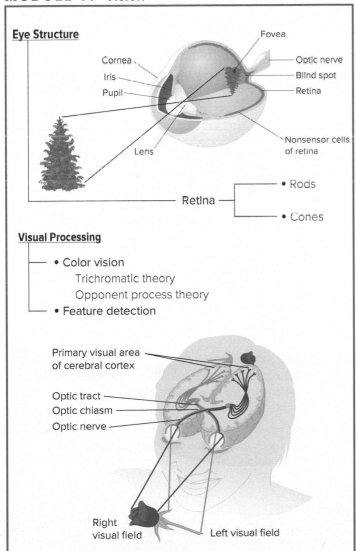

Cornea
Iris
Pupil
Fovea
Optic nerve
Blind spot
Retina
Lens
Nonsensor cells of retina

Retina
- Rods
- Cones

Visual Processing

- Color vision
   Trichromatic theory
   Opponent process theory
- Feature detection

Primary visual area of cerebral cortex
Optic tract
Optic chiasm
Optic nerve
Right visual field
Left visual field

MODULE 12 Hearing and Other Senses

Ear Structure

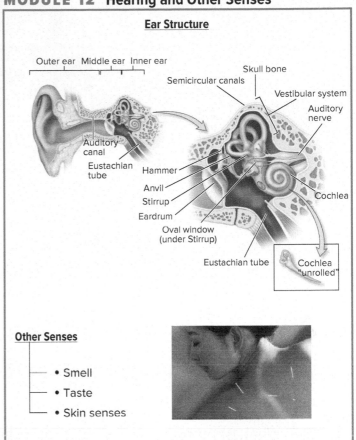

Outer ear Middle ear Inner ear
Skull bone
Semicircular canals
Vestibular system
Auditory nerve
Auditory canal
Eustachian tube
Hammer
Anvil
Stirrup
Eardrum
Oval window (under Stirrup)
Cochlea
Eustachian tube
Cochlea "unrolled"

Other Senses

- Smell
- Taste
- Skin senses

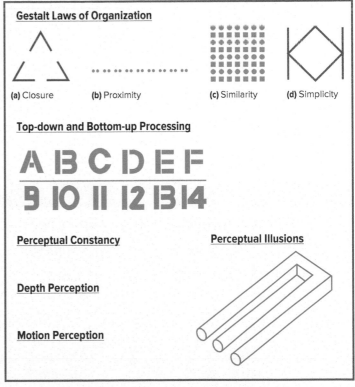

MODULE 13 Perception

Gestalt Laws of Organization

(a) Closure   **(b)** Proximity   **(c)** Similarity   **(d)** Simplicity

Top-down and Bottom-up Processing

A B C D E F
9 10 11 12 13 14

Perceptual Constancy

Depth Perception

Motion Perception

Perceptual Illusions

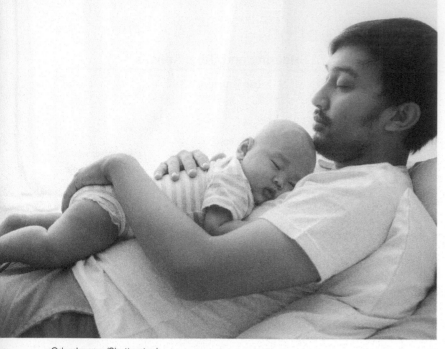

Odua Images/Shutterstock

CHAPTER 5
States of Consciousness

LEARNING OUTCOMES FOR CHAPTER 5

	MODULE 14

LO 14-1 What are the states of consciousness?

LO 14-2 What happens when we sleep, and what are the meaning and function of dreams?

LO 14-3 What are the major sleep disorders, and how can they be treated?

LO 14-4 How much do we daydream?

SLEEP AND DREAMS
The Stages of Sleep
REM Sleep: The Paradox of Sleep
Why Do We Sleep, and How Much Sleep Is Necessary?
Neuroscience in Your Life: Why Are We So Emotional When We Don't Get Enough Sleep?
The Function and Meaning of Dreaming
Applying Psychology in the 21st Century: Is Sleep-Learning Real?
Sleep Disturbances: Slumbering Problems
Circadian Rhythms: Life Cycles
Daydreams: Dreams Without Sleep
Becoming an Informed Consumer of Psychology: Sleeping Better

	MODULE 15

LO 15-1 What is hypnosis, and are hypnotized people in a different state of consciousness?

LO 15-2 What are the effects of meditation?

HYPNOSIS AND MEDITATION
Hypnosis: A Trance-Forming Experience?
Meditation: Regulating Our Own State of Consciousness
Exploring Diversity: Cross-Cultural Routes to Altered States of Consciousness

PROLOGUE *A LIFE CUT SHORT*

Tyler Skaggs seemed to have it all, both professionally and personally. A starting pitcher for the Los Angeles Angels baseball team, Skaggs had recently married. He was known for his energy and dry wit. His teammates found him likable and engaging. At the end of seven years in the major leagues, he held great promise.

But no storybook career or life lay ahead for Skaggs. He was found dead at the age of 27, alone in a hotel room in Texas, just hours before the scheduled start of a game. An autopsy showed that Skaggs had a lethal combination of fentanyl, oxycodone, and alcohol in his system (Draper & Kepner, 2019).

LOOKING *Ahead*

Tyler Skagg's death from opioids and alcohol is far from unique. The United States is experiencing a full-blown opiate epidemic, with nearly 70,000 deaths from drug overdoses in 2018 alone. Drug overdoses are now the most frequent cause of death of those under the age of 50, and nearly 130 Americans die every day from an opioid overdose (Katz, 2017; Hedegaard, Miniño, & Warner, 2018; BBC, 2019).

Opiates such as heroin and fentanyl promise relief from anxiety and stress, as well as physical pain. While we don't know exactly what drove Skaggs to use narcotics, he clearly had a compelling desire to create an altered state of consciousness. Why people seek to alter their consciousness, what conscious experience is, and how and why we can alter it are some of the questions we explore in this chapter.

Consciousness is the awareness of the sensations, thoughts, and feelings we are experiencing at a given moment. Consciousness is our subjective understanding of both the environment around us and our private internal world, unobservable to outsiders.

In *waking consciousness*, we are awake and aware of our thoughts, emotions, and perceptions. All other states of consciousness are considered *altered states of consciousness*. Among these, sleeping and dreaming occur naturally; drug use and hypnosis, in contrast, are methods of deliberately altering one's state of consciousness.

In the past, because consciousness is so personal a phenomenon, some psychologists were reluctant to study it. After all, who can say that your consciousness is similar to or, for that matter, different from anyone else's? Although the earliest psychologists, including William James (1890), saw the study of consciousness as central to the field, later psychologists suggested that it was out of bounds for the discipline. They argued that consciousness could be understood only by relying "unscientifically" on what experimental participants said they were experiencing. In this view, it was philosophers—not psychologists—who should speculate on such knotty issues as whether consciousness is separate from the physical body, how people know they exist, and how the body and mind are related to each other (Barresi, 2007; James, 2015).

Contemporary psychologists reject the view that the study of consciousness is unsuitable for the field of psychology. Instead, they argue that several approaches permit the scientific study of consciousness. For example, behavioral neuroscientists can measure brain-wave patterns under conditions of consciousness ranging from sleep to waking to hypnotic trances. Furthermore, new understanding of the chemistry of drugs such as marijuana and alcohol has provided insights into the way they produce their pleasurable—as well as adverse—effects. And new cross-species insights about the functioning of the brain are helping scientists explore whether consciousness is a uniquely human quality (Malouff & Rooke, 2013; Liechti, Dolder & Schmid, 2017; Mora, Urdaneta, & Chaya, 2019).

Yet precisely how humans experience consciousness remains an open question. Some psychologists believe that the experience of consciousness is produced by a quantitative increase in neuronal activity that occurs throughout the brain. For example, an alarm clock moves us from sleep to waking consciousness by its loud ringing, which stimulates neurons throughout the brain as a whole (Koch & Greenfield, 2007; Ward, 2011; Blackmore, 2018).

In contrast, others believe that states of consciousness are produced by particular sets of neurons and neuronal pathways that are activated in specific ways. In this view, an alarm clock wakes us from sleep into consciousness because specific neurons related to the auditory nerve are activated; the auditory nerve then sends a message to other neurons to release particular neurotransmitters that produce awareness of the alarm (Tononi & Koch, 2008; Saper, 2013; Schurger et al., 2015).

Although we don't know yet which of these views is correct, it is clear that whatever state of consciousness we are in—be it waking, sleeping, hypnotic, or drug-induced—the complexities of consciousness are profound.

consciousness The awareness of the sensations, thoughts, and feelings being experienced at a given moment. (Module 14)

Module 14
Sleep and Dreams

LEARNING OUTCOMES

LO 14-1 What are the states of consciousness?

LO 14-2 What happens when we sleep, and what are the meaning and function of dreams?

LO 14-3 What are the major sleep disorders, and how can they be treated?

LO 14-4 How much do we daydream?

During a 9-day cross-country bike race, 29-year-old Mike Trevino averaged 1 hour of sleep per day. The first 3 days he didn't sleep at all, and over the next 6, he took completely dream-free naps of at most 90 minutes. His waking thoughts became fuzzy, depicting movielike plots starring himself and his crew. The whole experience was like a serial dream in which he remained conscious, if only barely. He finished in second place.

Trevino's case is unusual—in part because he was able to function with so little sleep for so long—and it raises a host of questions about sleep and dreams. Can we live without sleep? What is the meaning of dreams? More generally, what is sleep?

Although sleeping is a state that we all experience, there are still many unanswered questions about sleep that remain, along with a considerable number of myths. Test your knowledge of sleep and dreams by answering the questionnaire in Figure 1.

FIGURE 1 There are many unanswered questions about sleep. Taking this quiz can help you clear up some of the myths.

Sources: Adapted from Maas, J. (2016). Sleep Myths—True or False? American Sleep Association. Retrieved from https://www.sleepassociation.org/blog-post/sleep-myths-true-false, and Palladino, J. J., & Carducci, B. J. (1984). Students' knowledge of sleep and dreams. *Teaching of Psychology*, 11(3), 189–191.

Sleep Quiz

Although sleeping is something we all do for a significant part of our lives, myths and misconceptions about the topic abound. Check your knowledge by reading each statement below and check True or False.

1. It is a proven fact that 8 hours of sleep are needed to remain mentally healthy. ☐ True ☐ False	6. The best long-term cure for sleeplessness is regular use of insomnia medications. ☐ True ☐ False
2. Sleep "turns off" most brain activity to promote brain rest and recovery. ☐ True ☐ False	7. Dreams are most often the result of stomach distress caused by what and when we eat. ☐ True ☐ False
3. Sleep deprivation always causes mental imbalance. ☐ True ☐ False	8. When we are asleep and dreaming, our muscles are the most relaxed they can get. ☐ True ☐ False
4. It is impossible to go more than 48 hours without sleep. ☐ True ☐ False	9. If you can't remember your dreams, it's because you want to forget them. ☐ True ☐ False
5. If we lose sleep we can always make it up another night or on the weekend. ☐ True ☐ False	10. Many people never dream. ☐ True ☐ False

Scoring: It is easy to score this quiz because every statement is false. But don't lose any sleep if you missed a few; these are among the most widely held misconceptions about sleeping and dreaming.

The Stages of Sleep

Most of us consider sleep a time of tranquility when we set aside the tensions of the day and spend the night in uneventful slumber. However, a closer look at sleep shows that a good deal of activity occurs throughout the night.

Measures of electrical activity in the brain show that the brain is quite active during sleep. It produces electrical discharges with systematic, wavelike patterns that change in height (or amplitude) and speed (or frequency) in regular sequences. There is also significant physical activity in muscle and eye movements.

People progress through a series of distinct stages of sleep during a night's rest—known as *stage 1* through *stage 3* and *REM sleep*—moving through the stages in cycles lasting about 90 minutes. Each of these sleep stages is associated with a unique pattern of brain waves, which you can see in Figure 2.

When people first go to sleep, they move from a waking state in which they are relaxed with their eyes closed into **stage 1 sleep,** which is characterized by relatively rapid, low-amplitude brain waves. This is actually a stage of transition between wakefulness and sleep and lasts only a few minutes. During stage 1, images sometimes appear, as if we were viewing still photos, although this is not true dreaming, which occurs later in the night.

As sleep becomes deeper, people enter **stage 2 sleep,** which makes up about half of the total sleep of those in their early 20s and is characterized by a slower, more regular wave pattern. However, there are also momentary interruptions of sharply pointed, spiky waves that are called, because of their configuration, *sleep spindles*. It becomes increasingly difficult to awaken a person from sleep as stage 2 progresses.

As people drift into **stage 3 sleep,** the deepest stage, the brain waves become slower, with higher peaks and lower valleys in the wave pattern. During stage 3, people are least responsive to outside stimulation.

As you can see in Figure 3, stage 3 sleep is most likely to occur during the early part of the night. In the first half of the night, sleep is dominated by stage 3. The second half is characterized by stages 1 and 2—as well as a fourth stage, REM sleep, during which dreams occur.

stage 1 sleep The state of transition between wakefulness and sleep, characterized by relatively rapid, low-amplitude brain waves. (Module 14)

stage 2 sleep A sleep deeper than that of stage 1, characterized by a slower, more regular wave pattern, along with momentary interruptions of "sleep spindles." (Module 14)

stage 3 sleep The deepest stage of sleep, during which we are least responsive to outside stimulation. (Module 14)

FIGURE 2 Brain-wave patterns (measured by an EEG apparatus) vary significantly during the different stages of sleep. As sleep moves from stage 1 through stage 3, brain waves become slower. During REM sleep, however, the fast wave patterns are similar to relaxed wakefulness.
Source: Hobson, J. A. (1989). *Sleep.* New York: W. H. Freeman.

FIGURE 3 During the night, the typical sleeper passes through all three stages of sleep and several REM periods.

Source: Hartmann, E. (1967). *The biology of dreaming*. Springfield, IL: Charles C. Thomas Publisher.

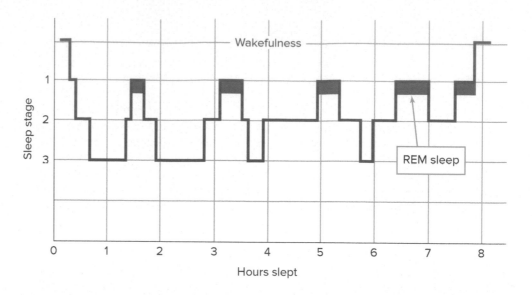

REM Sleep: The Paradox of Sleep

Several times a night, when sleepers have cycled back to a shallower state of sleep, something curious happens. Their heart rate increases and becomes irregular, their blood pressure rises, and their breathing rate increases. Most characteristic of this period is that their eyes move rapidly, as if they were watching an action-filled movie.

This stage of sleep is called rapid eye movement sleep. **Rapid eye movement, or REM, sleep,** is characterized by quick, back-and-forth eye movements, and it contrasts with stages 1 through 3, which are collectively labeled *non-REM* (or *NREM*) sleep. REM sleep occupies a little more than 20% of adults' total sleeping time.

While heart rate, blood pressure, and breathing increase during REM sleep, the major muscles of the body appear to be paralyzed. In addition, and most important, REM sleep is usually accompanied by dreams, which—whether or not people remember them—are experienced by *everyone* during some part of their night's sleep. Although

rapid eye movement (REM) sleep
The period of sleep characterized by quick, back-and-forth eye movements; increased heart rate, blood pressure, and breathing rate; erections in men; and the experience of dreaming. (Module 14)

People progress through three distinct stages of sleep during a night's rest spread over cycles lasting about 90 minutes. REM sleep occupies only 20% of adults' sleeping time. These photos, taken at different times of night, show the synchronized patterns of a couple accustomed to sleeping in the same bed.

Ted Spagna/Science Source

some dreaming occurs in non-REM stages of sleep, dreams are most likely to occur in the REM period, where they are the most vivid and easily remembered (Manni & Terzaghi, 2013; Sikka et al., 2017; Blagrove et al., 2019).

There is good reason to believe that REM sleep plays a critical role in everyday human functioning. People deprived of REM sleep–by being awakened every time they begin to display the physiological signs of that stage–show a *rebound effect* when allowed to rest undisturbed. With this rebound effect, REM-deprived sleepers spend significantly more time in REM sleep than they normally would. In addition, REM sleep may play a role in learning and memory, allowing us to rethink and restore information and emotional experiences that we've had during the day (Walker & van der Helm, 2009; Nielsen et al., 2015; Karabulut et al., 2019).

Study Alert
Differentiate the stages of sleep (stage 1, stage 2, stage 3, and REM sleep), which produce different brain-wave patterns.

From the perspective of...

An Educator How might you use the findings in sleep research to maximize student learning?

Andersen Ross/Blend Images/Getty Images

Why Do We Sleep, and How Much Sleep Is Necessary?

Sleep is a requirement for normal human functioning, although, surprisingly, the reason why has long baffled scientists. It certainly is reasonable to expect that our bodies would require a tranquil "rest and relaxation" period to revitalize themselves, and experiments with rats show that total sleep deprivation results in death. But why?

One explanation, based on an evolutionary perspective, suggests that sleep permitted our ancestors to conserve energy at night, a time when food was relatively hard to come by. Consequently, they were better able to forage for food when the sun was up.

A second explanation for why we sleep is that sleep restores and replenishes our brains and bodies. For instance, the reduced activity of the brain during non-REM sleep may give neurons in the brain a chance to repair themselves. That reduced activity may also weaken connections among particular nerve cells to conserve energy, which has the effect of aiding memory. Furthermore, the onset of REM sleep stops the release of neurotransmitters called *monoamines* and so permits receptor cells to get some necessary rest and to increase their sensitivity during periods of wakefulness (Bub, Buckhalt, & El-Sheikh, 2011; Tononi & Cirelli, 2013; Menon et al., 2019).

Another primary purpose of sleep may be to help us forget. In this view, sleep allows the brain to eliminate unnecessary information that accumulates throughout the day so that it doesn't become burdensome or confusing, a process called *reverse learning* (Heller et al., 2014: Feld & Born, 2017).

Finally, sleep may be essential because it assists physical growth and brain development in children. For example, the release of growth hormones is associated with deep sleep (Peterfi et al., 2010; Grigg-Damberger, 2017).

Still, these explanations remain speculative, and there is no definitive answer as to why sleep is essential. What is increasingly clear is that sleep serves multiple functions and that without sleep, we will eventually die (Stickgold, 2015).

However, scientists have been unable to establish just how much sleep is absolutely required. Most people today sleep between 7 and 8 hours each night, which is 3 hours a night *less* than people slept a hundred years ago (see Figure 4).

In addition, individuals vary widely, with some people needing as little as 3 hours of sleep. Still, survey data shows that for most people, the more sleep they get, the greater their sense of well-being (McCarthy & Brown, 2015; Gariépy et al., 2019).

Men and women sleep differently. Women typically fall asleep more quickly, they sleep for longer periods and more deeply than men do, and they get up fewer times in the night. On the other hand, men have fewer concerns about the amount of sleep they get than women do, even though they get less sleep. Furthermore, sleep requirements vary over the course of a lifetime: As they age, people generally need less and less sleep (Monk et al., 2011; Petersen, 2011).

People who participate in sleep deprivation experiments, in which they are kept awake for stretches as long as 200 hours, show no lasting effects. It's no fun—they feel weary and irritable, can't concentrate, and show a loss of creativity, even after only minor deprivation. They also show a decline in logical reasoning ability. However, after being allowed to sleep normally, they bounce back quickly and are able to perform at predeprivation levels after just a few days (Mograss et al., 2009; Jackson et al., 2013; Maturana et al., 2015).

In short, as far as we know, most people suffer no permanent consequences of such temporary sleep deprivation. But—and this is an important but—a lack of sleep can make us feel edgy, slow our reaction time, and lower our performance on academic and physical tasks. In addition, we put ourselves and others at risk when we carry out routine activities, such as driving, when we're very sleepy (Anderson & Home, 2006; Morad et al., 2009; Simon et al., 2017). (Also see *Neuroscience in Your Life*.)

NEUROSCIENCE IN YOUR LIFE: WHY ARE WE SO EMOTIONAL WHEN WE DON'T GET ENOUGH SLEEP?

After a restless night, many people feel increased stress and overreact to events in their lives the next day. Recent research has now identified the neural basis for these reactions. For example, in one study, participants were kept awake all night and then asked to perform an experiment involving exposure to emotional and neutral images. Participants who were sleep deprived reacted to the neutral images as if they were emotional, and they had less connectivity between the amygdala (a region of the brain that processes emotion) and the anterior cingulate cortex (a region of frontal cortex important for emotional regulation). The green in the scan below shows the area of anterior cingulate that has greater connectivity to the amygdala for sleep-rested than sleep-deprived participants. These findings suggest that sleep loss increases emotional reactivity by interfering with our ability to control our emotions (Simon et al., 2015; Krause et al., 2017).

Left

Source: Adapted from Simon et al. (2015). Losing neutrality: The neural basis of impaired emotional control without sleep. *Journal of Neuroscience, 35*(38), 13194-13205.

The Function and Meaning of Dreaming

I was being chased, and I couldn't get away. My attacker, wearing a mask, was carrying a long knife. He was gaining ground on me. I felt it was hopeless; I knew I was about to be killed.

If you have had dreams like this, you know how utterly convincing they can be. *Nightmares* are unusually frightening dreams. Perhaps surprisingly, they occur fairly often. In one survey, almost half of a group of college students who kept records of their dreams over a 2-week period reported having at least one nightmare. Furthermore, nightmares often are associated with negative experiences during the day, including worry and anxiety (Schredl & Reinhard, 2011; Cranston et al., 2017; Reks, Sheaves, & Freeman, 2017).

However, most of the 150,000 dreams the average person experiences by the age of 70 are much less dramatic. They typically encompass everyday events such as going to the supermarket, working at the office, and preparing a meal. Students dream about going to class; professors dream about lecturing. Dental patients dream of getting their teeth drilled; dentists dream of drilling the wrong tooth. The English have tea with the queen in their dreams; in the United States, people go to a bar with the president (Schredl & Piel, 2005; Taylor & Bryant, 2007; Nosek et al., 2015). Figure 5 shows the most common themes found in people's dreams.

But what, if anything, do all these dreams mean? Whether dreams have a specific significance and function is a question that scientists have considered for many years, and they have developed the three alternative theories we discuss below (and summarize in Figure 6).

Study Alert
Use Figure 6 to learn the differences between the three main explanations of dreaming.

FIGURE 5 Although dreams tend to be subjective to the person having them, common elements frequently occur in everyone's dreams. Why do you think so many common dreams are unpleasant and so few are pleasant? Do you think this tells us anything about the function of dreams?

Source: Schneider, A., & Domhoff, G. W. (2015). The quantitative study of dreams. Retrieved from http://www.dreamresearch.net.

Thematic Event	Percentage of Dreams Reporting at Least One Event	
	Males	Females
Aggression	47%	44%
Friendliness	38	42
Sexuality	12	4
Misfortune	36	33
Success	15	8
Failure	15	10

PSYCHOANALYTIC EXPLANATIONS OF DREAMS: DO THEY REPRESENT UNCONSCIOUS WISH FULFILLMENT?

unconscious wish fulfillment theory Sigmund Freud's theory that dreams represent unconscious wishes that dreamers desire to see fulfilled. (Module 14)

Using psychoanalytic theory, Sigmund Freud viewed dreams as a guide to the unconscious (Freud, 1900). In his **unconscious wish fulfillment theory,** he proposed that dreams represent unconscious wishes that dreamers desire to see fulfilled. To Freud, the *manifest content* of the dream is what we remember and report about the dream–its story line. The manifest content, however, disguises the *latent content*, which includes the actual, underlying wishes that the dream represents. Because the underlying wishes (the latent content) are threatening to the dreamer, they are hidden in the dream's story line (the manifest content).

To Freud, it was important to pierce the armor of a dream's manifest content to understand its true meaning. To do this, Freud tried to get people to discuss their dreams, associating symbols in the dreams with events in the past. He also suggested that certain common symbols with universal meanings appear in dreams. For example, to Freud, dreams in which a person is flying symbolize a wish for sexual intercourse. (See Figure 7 for other common symbols.)

Many psychologists reject Freud's view that dreams typically represent unconscious wishes and that particular objects and events in a dream are symbolic. Rather, they believe that the direct, overt action of a dream is the focal point of its meaning. For example, a dream in which we are walking down a long hallway to take an exam for which we haven't studied does not relate to unconscious, unacceptable wishes. Instead, it simply may mean that we are concerned about an impending test. Even

Theory	Basic Explanation	Meaning of Dreams	Is Meaning of Dream Disguised?
Unconscious wish fulfillment theory (Freud)	Psychoanalytical explanation in which dreams represent unconscious wishes the dreamer wants to fulfill	Latent content reveals unconscious wishes.	Yes, by manifest content of dreams
Dreams-for-survival theory	Evolutionary explanation in which information relevant to daily survival is reconsidered and reprocessed	Clues to everyday concerns about survival	Not necessarily
Activation-synthesis theory	Neuroscience explanation in which dreams are the result of random activation of various memories, which are tied together in a logical story line	Dream scenario that is constructed is related to dreamer's concerns.	Not necessarily

FIGURE 6 Three theories of dreams. As researchers have yet to agree on the fundamental meaning of dreams, several theories about dreaming have emerged.

Symbol (Manifest Content of Dream)	Interpretation (Latent Content)
Climbing up a stairway, crossing a bridge, riding an elevator, flying in an airplane, walking down a long hallway, entering a room, train traveling through a tunnel	Sexual intercourse
Apples, peaches, grapefruits	Breasts
Bullets, fire, snakes, sticks, umbrellas, guns, hoses, knives	Male sex organs
Ovens, boxes, tunnels, closets, caves, bottles, ships	Female sex organs

FIGURE 7 According to Freud, dreams contain common symbols with universal meanings.
Progressman/Shutterstock

more complex dreams can often be interpreted in terms of everyday concerns and stress (Cartwright, Agargum, & Kirkby, 2006; Boag, 2017).

Moreover, some dreams reflect events occurring in the dreamer's environment as he or she is sleeping. For example, sleeping participants in one experiment were sprayed with water while they were dreaming. Those unlucky volunteers reported more dreams involving water than did a comparison group of participants who were left to sleep undisturbed (Dement & Wolpert, 1958). Similarly, it is not unusual to wake up to find that the doorbell that was heard ringing in a dream is actually an alarm clock telling us it is time to get up.

However, PET brain scan research does lend a degree of support for the wish fulfillment view. For instance, the limbic and paralimbic regions of the brain, which are associated with emotion and motivation, are particularly active during REM sleep. At the same time, the association areas of the prefrontal cortex, which control logical analysis and attention, are inactive during REM sleep. The high activation of emotional and motivational centers of the brain during dreaming makes it more plausible that dreams may reflect unconscious wishes and instinctual needs, as Freud suggested (Occhionero, 2004; Wehrle et al., 2007; Perogamvros & Schwartz, 2015).

EVOLUTIONARY EXPLANATIONS OF DREAMS: DREAMS-FOR-SURVIVAL THEORY

According to the **dreams-for-survival theory,** which is based in the evolutionary perspective, dreams permit us to reconsider and reprocess during sleep information that is critical for our daily survival. Dreaming is considered an inheritance from our animal ancestors, whose small brains were unable to sift sufficient information during waking hours. Consequently, dreaming provided a mechanism that permitted the processing of information 24 hours a day.

In the dreams-for-survival theory, dreams represent concerns about our daily lives, illustrating our uncertainties, indecisions, ideas, and desires. Dreams are seen, then, as consistent with everyday living. Rather than being disguised wishes, as Freud suggested, they represent key concerns growing out of our daily experiences (Ross, 2006; Horton, 2011).

Research supports the dreams-for-survival theory, suggesting that certain dreams permit people to focus on and to consolidate memories, particularly dreams that pertain to "how-to-do-it" memories related to motor skills. For example, rats seem to dream about mazes that they learned to run through during the day, at least according to the patterns of brain activity that appear while they are sleeping (Stickgold et al., 2001; Kuriyama, Stickgold, & Walker, 2004; Smith, 2006).

A similar phenomenon appears to work in humans. For instance, in one experiment, participants learned a visual memory task late in the day. They were then sent to bed but awakened at certain times during the night. When they were awakened at times that did not interrupt dreaming, their performance on the memory task typically improved the next day. But when they were awakened during rapid eye movement (REM) sleep—the stage of sleep when people dream—their performance declined. The implication is that dreaming, at least when it is uninterrupted, can play a role in

dreams-for-survival theory The theory suggesting that dreams permit information that is critical for our daily survival to be reconsidered and reprocessed during sleep. (Module 14) helping us remember material to which we have been previously exposed (Marshall & Born, 2007; Nishida et al., 2009; Blechner, 2013; Schoch et al., 2019).

NEUROSCIENCE EXPLANATIONS OF DREAMS: ACTIVATION-SYNTHESIS THEORY

activation-synthesis theory Hobson's theory that the brain produces random electrical energy during REM sleep that stimulates memories stored in the brain. (Module 14)

Using the neuroscience perspective, psychiatrist J. Allan Hobson has proposed the activation-synthesis theory of dreams. The **activation-synthesis theory** focuses on the random electrical energy that the brain produces during REM sleep, possibly as a result of changes in the production of particular neurotransmitters. This electrical energy randomly stimulates memories stored in the brain. (Also see Applying Psychology in the 21st Century feature.) Because we have a need to make sense of our world even while asleep, the brain takes these chaotic memories and weaves them into a logical story line, filling in the gaps to produce a rational scenario (Hobson, 2005; Hangya et al., 2011).

Activation-synthesis theory has been refined by the *activation information modulation (AIM)* theory. According to AIM, dreams are initiated in the brain's pons, which sends random signals to the cortex. Areas of the cortex that are involved in particular waking behaviors are related to the content of dreams. For example, areas of the brain related to vision are involved in the visual aspects of the dream, whereas areas of the brain related to movement are involved in aspects of the dream related to motion (Hobson, 2007).

APPLYING PSYCHOLOGY IN THE 21ST CENTURY

IS SLEEP-LEARNING REAL?

Do you wish you could learn whatever you need to know while you sleep? Perhaps you'd like to be able to record your professors' lectures, play them overnight on an endless loop, and when you awaken in the morning, find you've absorbed it all without any of the drudgery of studying or memorization? If so, you're not alone. The notion of sleep-learning is so tantalizing that we not only find it in science-fiction novels and movies but also as the subject of serious research.

In a recent example, researchers asked participants to turn over cards on a layout of face-down cards on a computer screen until they could correctly identify the locations of matching card pairs at least 60% of the time (much like playing the card game "concentration"). While the participants performed this task, the scent of roses was repeatedly presented to them. A control group performed the task without the associated scent. Then the participants who had been exposed to the scent were allowed to sleep, during which time the rose scent was once again presented to them, but only while an fMRI scan showed that they were engaged in slow-wave (deep) sleep. Memory for the location of the card pairs was significantly better for the participants who were stimulated

Could we use the time we are sleeping to study for an upcoming test?
Andriy Popov/123RF

during sleep with the scent that was associated with the learning task, as compared to control participants who did not experience the scent during sleep and to additional control participants who experienced the scent during sleep but had not experienced it during the learning task. Interestingly, the effect only worked for slow-wave sleep and did not work when the scent was presented during REM sleep, suggesting that deep sleep plays an important role in

consolidating new memories (Rasch et al., 2007; Paller & Oudiette, 2018).

Subsequent research showed that sleep stimulation could improve targeted learning as well as general learning. Participants once again engaged in a location-memory task, but this time, they learned the locations of many everyday objects. Each object had a specific sound associated with it, such as a tea kettle that whistled or a cat that meowed. While participants were later engaged in slow-wave sleep, the sounds of only a subset of the memorized objects were softly played. During a subsequent memory test, participants showed better recall for the locations of the objects whose sounds they heard while they were sleeping than they did for the objects whose sounds were not heard during sleep (Creery et al., 2015).

While the evidence is limited, research at least suggests that learning might be enhanced somewhat during sleep but also can be boosted with associated scent or sound stimulation.

QUESTIONS TO CONSIDER

1. Could you try making use of these research findings to enhance your own learning during sleep? How?
2. Could this research be extended to efforts to unlearn bad habits, such as smoking? How might that work?

Activation-synthesis and AIM theories do not entirely reject the view that dreams reflect unconscious wishes. They suggest that the particular scenario a dreamer produces is not random but instead is a clue to the dreamer's fears, emotions, and concerns. Hence, what starts out as a random process culminates in something meaningful.

Sleep Disturbances: Slumbering Problems

At one time or another, almost all of us have difficulty sleeping—a condition known as insomnia. It could be due to a particular situation, such as the breakup of a relationship, concern about a test score, or the loss of a job. Some cases of insomnia, however, have no obvious cause. Some people are simply unable to fall asleep easily, or they go to sleep readily but wake up frequently during the night. Insomnia is a problem that afflicts as many as one-third of all people. Women and older adults are more likely to suffer from insomnia, as well as people who are unusually thin or are depressed (Karlson et al., 2013; Ong, 2017; Hallit et al., 2019).

Some people who *think* they have sleeping problems actually are mistaken. For example, researchers in sleep laboratories have found that some people who report being up all night actually fall asleep in 30 minutes and stay asleep all night. Furthermore, some people with insomnia accurately recall sounds that they heard while they were asleep, which gives them the impression that they were awake during the night (Semler & Harvey, 2005; Yapko, 2006; Crönlein et al., 2019).

Other sleep problems are less common than insomnia, although they are still widespread. For instance, some 20 million people suffer from sleep apnea. *Sleep apnea* is a condition in which a person has difficulty breathing while sleeping. The result is disturbed, fitful sleep and a significant loss of REM sleep, as the person is constantly reawakened when the lack of oxygen becomes great enough to trigger a waking response. Some people with apnea wake as many as 500 times during the course of a night, although they may not even be aware that they have wakened. Not surprisingly, such disturbed sleep results in extreme fatigue the next day. Sleep apnea also may play a role in *sudden infant death syndrome (SIDS)*, a mysterious killer of seemingly normal infants who die while sleeping (Tippin, Sparks, & Rizzo, 2009; Arimoto et al., 2011; Bjornsdottir et al., 2015).

Night terrors are sudden awakenings from non-REM sleep that are accompanied by extreme fear, panic, and strong physiological arousal. Night terrors may be so frightening that a sleeper awakens screaming. Although night terrors initially produce great agitation, victims usually can get back to sleep fairly quickly. They are far less frequent than nightmares, and, unlike nightmares, they typically occur during stage 3, non-REM sleep. They occur most frequently in children between the ages of 3 and 8 (Lowe, Humphreys, & Williams, 2007; Sasayama, Washizuka, & Honda, 2016).

Narcolepsy is uncontrollable sleeping that occurs for short periods while a person is awake. No matter what the activity—holding a heated conversation, exercising, or driving—a narcoleptic will suddenly fall asleep. People with narcolepsy go directly from wakefulness to REM sleep, skipping the other stages. The causes of narcolepsy are not known, although there could be a genetic component because narcolepsy runs in families (Ervik, Abdelnoor, & Heier, 2006; Nishino, 2007; Billiard, 2008; Zamarian et al., 2015).

We know relatively little about sleeptalking and sleepwalking, two sleep disturbances that are usually harmless. Both occur during stage 3 sleep and are more common in children than in adults. Sleeptalkers and sleepwalkers usually have a vague consciousness of the world around them, and a sleepwalker may be able to walk with agility around obstructions in a crowded room. Unless a sleepwalker wanders into a dangerous environment, sleepwalking typically poses little risk. And the common idea that it's dangerous to wake a sleepwalker? It's just superstition (Licis et al., 2011; Haridi et al., 2017; Drakatos et al., 2019).

PsychTech

Surveys show that use of laptops, tablets, texting, or other technologies in the hour prior to going to bed is associated with sleeping problems.

Many people struggle with insomnia, the most common sleep disorder.

Koldunova Anna/Shutterstock

Bright lights may counter some of the symptoms of seasonal affective disorder, which occur during the winter.
Image Point Fr/Shutterstock

Circadian Rhythms: Life Cycles

circadian rhythms Biological processes that occur regularly on approximately a 24-hour cycle. (Module 14)

The fact that we cycle back and forth between wakefulness and sleep is one example of the body's circadian rhythms. **Circadian rhythms** (from the Latin *circa diem*, or "about a day") are biological processes that occur regularly on approximately a 24-hour cycle. Sleeping and waking, for instance, occur naturally to the beat of an internal pacemaker that works on a cycle of about 24 hours. Several other bodily functions, such as body temperature, hormone production, and blood pressure, also follow circadian rhythms (Beersma & Gordijn, 2007; Blatter & Cajochen, 2007; Labrecque & Cermakian, 2015).

Circadian cycles are complex, and they involve a variety of behaviors. For instance, sleepiness occurs not just in the evening but throughout the day in regular patterns, with most of us getting drowsy in mid-afternoon—regardless of whether or not we have eaten a heavy lunch. By making an afternoon siesta part of their everyday habit, people in several cultures take advantage of the body's natural inclination to sleep at this time (Takahashi et al., 2004; Reilly & Waterhouse, 2007; Egan et al., 2017).

The brain's *suprachiasmatic nucleus (SCN)* controls our circadian rhythms, but there are a number of circadian "clocks" associated with specific parts of the body. For instance, circadian rhythms speed up the heart before dawn to prepare us for the day's challenges. Similarly, the release and retention of various substances in the kidneys are affected by circadian rhythms. Even the processing of information in various areas of the brain may be affected by circadian rhythms and help shape how we perceive the world (Hickok, 2015; Summa & Turek, 2015).

Furthermore, the relative amount of light and darkness, which varies with the seasons of the year, also plays a role in regulating circadian rhythms. In fact, some people experience *seasonal affective disorder*, a form of severe depression in which feelings of despair and hopelessness increase during the winter and lift during the rest of the year. The disorder appears to be a result of the brevity and gloom of winter days. Daily exposure to bright lights is sometimes sufficient to improve the mood of those with this disorder (Monteleone, Martiadis, & Maj, 2011; Patten et al., 2017; Rohan et al., 2019).

People's moods also follow regular patterns. By examining more than 500 million tweets using publicly available Twitter records, a team of psychologists found that words with positive associations (*fantastic, super*) and negative associations (*afraid, mad*) followed regular patterns. Across the globe and among different cultures, people were happier in the morning and less so during the day, with a rebound in the evening. Moods are also happier on certain days of the week: we're happier on weekends and holidays. Finally,

Average Happiness for Twitter

FIGURE 8 A year of tweets shows that Fridays, Saturdays, and Sundays are happier than weekdays. The happiest days are holidays, and the unhappiest days are associated with bad news.

Average Happiness for Twitter. The MITRE Corporation. Reprinted by permission.

positive emotions increase from late December to late June as the days get longer, and negative emotions increase as days get shorter (see Figure 8; Golder & Macy, 2011).

Furthermore, there seem to be optimal times for carrying out various tasks. Most adults are at their peak for carrying out cognitive tasks in the late morning. In contrast, focus and concentration on academic tasks decline throughout the afternoon. On the other hand, some research findings show that creativity increases in the evening when people are tired. It may be that fatigue decreases inhibitions, allowing for more creative thought (Wieth & Zacks, 2011; Shellenbarger, 2012; Barber, 2019).

Finally, health issues are more apt to appear at certain times of the day. For instance, heart attacks and strokes occur most frequently and are most severe between 6:00 a.m. and noon. Asthma attacks and heartburn are more common during the evening hours (Beck, 2015).

Daydreams: Dreams Without Sleep

It is the stuff of magic: Our past mistakes can be wiped out and the future filled with noteworthy accomplishments. Fame, happiness, and wealth can be ours. In the next moment, though, the most horrible tragedies can occur, leaving us devastated, alone, and penniless.

The source of these scenarios is **daydreams,** fantasies people construct while awake. Unlike dreaming that occurs during sleep, daydreams are more under people's control. Therefore, their content is more often related to immediate events in the environment than is the content of the dreams that occur during sleep. Although they may include sexual content, daydreams also pertain to the full gamut of activities or events that are relevant to a person's life. While we are daydreaming, we are still experiencing waking consciousness. However, our awareness of the environment around us declines.

People vary considerably in the amount of daydreaming they do. For example, around 2% to 4% of the population spend at least half their free time fantasizing. Although most people daydream much less frequently, almost everyone fantasizes to some degree. In fact, a study in which experimenters sent texts at random times found that the participants were thinking about something other than what they were doing

daydreams Fantasies that people construct while awake. (Module 14)

Daydreams are fantasies that people construct while they are awake. What are the similarities and differences between daydreams and night dreams?
Drazen Zigic/Shutterstock

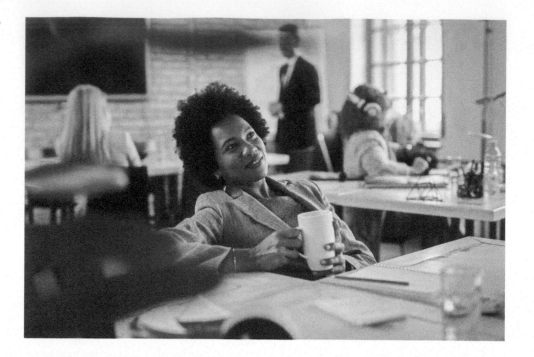

about half the time (Pisarik, Rowell, & Currie, 2013; Reddy, 2016; Ostojic-Aitkens, Brooker, & Miller, 2019).

The brain is surprisingly active during daydreaming. For example, several areas of the brain that are associated with complex problem solving become activated during daydreaming. In fact, daydreaming may be the only time these areas are activated simultaneously, suggesting that daydreaming may lead to insights about problems that we are grappling with. Consistent with that notion, scientists and writers find that creative ideas routinely arise during periods in which the mind wanders (Kounios et al., 2008; Carciofo et al., 2017; Gable, Hopper, & Schooler, 2019).

Furthermore, daydreaming may contain elements of *inner speech*, in which people talk to themselves in their heads. Inner speech may help us to plan, be creative, and regulate our emotions (Ren, Wang, & Jarrold, 2016; Alderson-Day et al., 2017; Fernyhough, 2017).

Some scientists see a link between daydreaming and dreams during sleep. The content of daydreams and dreams show many parallels, and the brain areas and processes involved in daydreaming and dreams during sleep are related (Domhoff, 2011).

BECOMING AN INFORMED CONSUMER
of Psychology

Sleeping Better

Do you have trouble sleeping? You're not alone—70 million people in the United States have sleep problems. Half of Americans aged 19 to 29 report they rarely or never get a good night's sleep on weekdays, and nearly a third of working adults get less than 6 hours of sleep a night (Randall, 2012).

For those of us who spend hours tossing and turning in bed, psychologists studying sleep disturbances have a number of suggestions for overcoming insomnia. Here are some ideas (Buysse et al., 2011; Reddy, 2013; Chung et al., 2018):

- *Exercise during the day (at least 6 hours before bedtime)*. Not surprisingly, it helps to be tired before going to sleep! Moreover, learning systematic relaxation techniques and biofeedback can help you unwind from the day's stresses and tensions.

- *Avoid long naps—but consider taking short ones.* If you have trouble sleeping at night, it's best to avoid long naps. On the other hand, a short nap lasting 10 to 20 minutes may be ideal to boost energy and increase alertness. In fact, research shows that, at least in preschool children, midday naps improve recall of material learned earlier in the day—although we don't yet know if that applies to older individuals (Kurdziel, Duclos, & Spencer, 2013; Weir, 2016).
- *Choose a regular bedtime and stick to it.* Adhering to a habitual schedule helps your internal timing mechanisms regulate your body more effectively.
- *Avoid screen time before bed.* The blue light emitted by computers and smartphones reduces melatonin production and increases alertness, which is certainly not conducive to sleep. So avoid use of electronic devices for 2 or 3 hours before heading to bed (Twenge, Hisler, & Krizan, 2019).
- *Avoid drinks with caffeine after lunch.* The effects of beverages such as coffee, tea, and some soft drinks can linger for as long as 8 to 12 hours after they are consumed.
- *Drink a glass of warm milk at bedtime.* Your grandparents were right when they dispensed this advice: Milk contains the chemical tryptophan, which helps people fall asleep.
- *Avoid sleeping pills.* Even though 25% of U.S. adults report having taken medication for sleep in the previous year and some 60 *million* sleeping aid prescriptions are filled annually, in the long run sleep medications can do more harm than good because they disrupt the normal sleep cycle. Rather than sleeping pills, try behavioral therapy; it's been proven to work better than drugs (DeAngelis, 2016).
- *Try* not *to sleep.* This approach works because people often have difficulty falling asleep because they are trying so hard. A better strategy is to go to bed only when you feel tired. If you don't get to sleep within 10 minutes, leave the bedroom and do something else, returning to bed only when you feel sleepy. Continue this process all night if necessary. But get up at your usual hour in the morning, and don't take any naps during the day. After 3 or 4 weeks, most people become conditioned to associate their beds with sleep—and fall asleep rapidly at night (Smith & Lazarus, 2001).

For long-term problems with sleep, you might consider visiting a sleep disorders center. For information on accredited clinics, consult the American Academy of Sleep Medicine at www.aasmnet.org.

RECAP/EVALUATE/RETHINK

RECAP

LO 14-1 What are the different states of consciousness?

- Consciousness is a person's awareness of the sensations, thoughts, and feelings at a given moment. Waking consciousness can vary from more active to more passive states.
- Altered states of consciousness include naturally occurring sleep and dreaming, as well as hypnotic and drug-induced states.

LO 14-2 What happens when we sleep, and what are the meaning and function of dreams?

- The brain is active throughout the night, and sleep proceeds through stages 1 through 3, which are identified by unique patterns of brain waves.

- REM (rapid eye movement) sleep is characterized by an increase in heart rate, a rise in blood pressure, an increase in the rate of breathing, and, in males, erections. Dreams most often occur during this stage.
- According to Freud's psychoanalytic approach, dreams have both a manifest content (an apparent story line) and a latent content (a true meaning). He suggested that the latent content provides a guide to a dreamer's unconscious, revealing unfulfilled wishes or desires.
- The dreams-for-survival theory, grounded in an evolutionary perspective, suggests that information relevant to daily survival is reconsidered and reprocessed in dreams.
- Taking a neuroscience approach, the activation-synthesis theory proposes that dreams are a result of random electrical energy that stimulates different memories, which then are woven into a coherent story line.

LO 14-3 What are the major sleep disorders, and how can they be treated?

- Insomnia is a sleep disorder characterized by difficulty sleeping. Sleep apnea is a condition in which people have difficulty sleeping and breathing at the same time. People with narcolepsy have an uncontrollable urge to sleep. Sleepwalking and sleeptalking are relatively harmless.

LO 14-4 How much do we daydream?

- Wide individual differences exist in the amount of time devoted to daydreaming. Almost everyone daydreams or fantasizes to some degree.

EVALUATE

1. _____ is the term used to describe our understanding of the world external to us, as well as our own internal world.
2. A great deal of neural activity goes on during sleep. True or false?
3. Dreams most often occur in _____ sleep.
4. _____ _____ are internal bodily processes that occur on a daily cycle.
5. Freud's theory of unconscious _____ _____ states that the actual wishes an individual expresses in dreams are disguised because they are threatening to the person's conscious awareness.

6. Match the theory of dreaming with its definition.
   1. activation-synthesis theory
   2. dreams-for-survival theory
   3. dreams as wish fulfillment

   a. Dreams permit important information to be reprocessed during sleep.
   b. The manifest content of dreams disguises the latent content of the dreams.
   c. Electrical energy stimulates random memories, which are woven together to produce dreams.

RETHINK

1. Suppose that a new "miracle pill" allows a person to function with only 1 hour of sleep per night. However, because a night's sleep is so short, a person who takes the pill will never dream again. Knowing what you do about the functions of sleep and dreaming, what would be some advantages and drawbacks of such a pill from a personal standpoint? Would you take such a pill?
2. How would studying the sleep patterns of nonhuman species potentially help us figure out which of the theories of dreaming provides the best account of the functions of dreaming?

Answers to Evaluate Questions

1. Consciousness; 2. True; 3. REM; 4. Circadian rhythms; 5. wish fulfillment; 6. 1-c, 2-a, 3-b

KEY TERMS

consciousness	stage 3 sleep	unconscious wish	activation-synthesis theory
stage 1 sleep	rapid eye movement	fulfillment theory	circadian rhythms
stage 2 sleep	(REM) sleep	dreams-for-survival theory	daydreams

Module 15
Hypnosis and Meditation

You are feeling relaxed and drowsy. You are getting sleepier. Your body is becoming limp. Your eyelids are feeling heavier. Your eyes are closing; you can't keep them open anymore. You are totally relaxed. Now, place your hands above your head. But you will find they are getting heavier and heavier–so heavy you can barely keep them up. In fact, although you are straining as hard as you can, you will be unable to hold them up any longer.

An observer watching this scene would notice a curious phenomenon. Many of the people listening to the voice are dropping their arms to their sides. The reason for this strange behavior? Those people have been hypnotized.

LEARNING OUTCOMES

LO 15-1 What is hypnosis, and are hypnotized people in a different state of consciousness?

LO 15-2 What are the effects of meditation?

Hypnosis: A Trance-Forming Experience?

People under **hypnosis** are in a trancelike state of heightened susceptibility to the suggestions of others. In some respects, it appears that they are asleep. Yet other aspects of their behavior contradict this notion, for people are attentive to the hypnotist's suggestions and may carry out bizarre or silly suggestions.

How is someone hypnotized? Typically, the process follows a series of four steps. First, a person is made comfortable in a quiet environment. Second, the hypnotist explains what is going to happen, such as telling the person that he or she will experience a pleasant, relaxed state. Third, the hypnotist tells the person to concentrate on a specific object or image, such as the hypnotist's moving finger or an image of a calm lake. The hypnotist may have the person concentrate on relaxing different parts of the body, such as the arms, legs, and chest. Fourth, once the subject is in a highly relaxed state, the hypnotist may make suggestions that the person interprets as being produced by hypnosis, such as "Your arms are getting heavy" and "Your eyelids are more difficult to open." Because the person begins to experience these sensations, he or she believes they are caused by the hypnotist and becomes susceptible to the suggestions of the hypnotist.

Despite their apparent compliance when hypnotized, people do not lose all will of their own. They will not perform antisocial behaviors or self-destructive acts. People will not reveal hidden truths about themselves, and they are capable of lying. Moreover, people cannot be hypnotized against their will–despite popular misconceptions (Raz, 2007; Lynn, Laurence, & Kirsch, 2015).

There are wide variations in people's susceptibility to hypnosis. About 5% to 20% of the population cannot be hypnotized at all, and some 15% are very easily hypnotized. Most people fall somewhere in between. Moreover, the ease with which a person is hypnotized is related to a number of other characteristics. People who are readily hypnotized are also easily absorbed while reading books or listening to music, becoming unaware of what is happening around them, and they often spend an unusual amount of time daydreaming. In sum, then, they show a high ability to concentrate and to become completely absorbed in what they are doing (Parris, 2017; Gurney, Dienes, & Scott, 2019; Palfi et al., 2019).

hypnosis A trancelike state of heightened susceptibility to the suggestions of others. (Module 15)

Despite common misconceptions, people cannot be hypnotized against their will, nor do they lose all will of their own when they are hypnotized.
Pixel-Shot/Shutterstock

A DIFFERENT STATE OF CONSCIOUSNESS?

The question of whether hypnosis is a state of consciousness that differs qualitatively from normal waking consciousness is controversial. Some psychologists believe hypnosis represents a state of consciousness that differs significantly from other states. In this view, high suggestibility, increased ability to recall and construct images, and acceptance of suggestions that clearly contradict reality characterize it as a different state. Moreover, people who are hypnotized show certain kinds of changes in electrical activity in the brain. Such electrical changes support the position that hypnosis is a state of consciousness different from normal waking (Fingelkurts, Fingelkurts, & Kallio, 2007; Hinterberger, Schöner, & Halsband, 2011; Keppler, 2017).

In this view, hypnosis represents a state of *divided consciousness*. According to famed hypnosis researcher Ernest Hilgard, hypnosis brings about a *dissociation*, or division, of consciousness into two simultaneous components. In one stream of consciousness, hypnotized people are following the commands of the hypnotist. Yet on another level of consciousness, they are acting as "hidden observers," aware of what is happening to them. For instance, hypnotic subjects may appear to be following the hypnotist's suggestion about feeling no pain, yet in another stream of consciousness, they may be actually aware of the pain.

On the other side of the controversy are psychologists who reject the notion that hypnosis is a state significantly different from normal waking consciousness. They argue that altered brain-wave patterns are not sufficient to demonstrate a qualitative difference because no other specific physiological changes occur when people are in trances. Furthermore, little support exists for the contention that adults can recall memories of childhood events accurately while hypnotized. That lack of evidence suggests that there is nothing qualitatively special about the hypnotic trance (Hongchun & Ming, 2006; Wagstaff, 2009; Wagstaff, Wheatcroft, & Jones, 2011).

The controversy over the nature of hypnosis has led to extreme positions on both sides of the issue. In contrast, more recent approaches suggest that the hypnotic state may best be viewed as lying along a continuum. In this view, hypnosis is neither a totally different state of consciousness nor totally similar to normal waking consciousness (Kihlstrom, 2005b; Jamieson, 2007; Ranscombe, 2019).

Study Alert
The question of whether hypnosis represents a different state of consciousness or is similar to normal waking consciousness is a key issue.

THE VALUE OF HYPNOSIS

As arguments about the true nature of hypnosis continue, though, one thing is clear: Hypnosis has been used successfully to solve practical human problems. In fact, psychologists working in many different areas have found hypnosis to be a reliable, effective tool. It has been applied to a number of areas, including the following:

- *Controlling pain.* Patients have had chronic pain reduced through hypnotic suggestion. In addition, people can be taught to hypnotize themselves to relieve pain or gain a sense of control over their symptoms. Hypnosis has proved to be particularly useful during childbirth and dental procedures (Accardi & Milling, 2009; Spiegel, 2015; Thompson et al., 2019).

- *Reducing smoking.* Although it hasn't been successful in stopping drug and alcohol abuse, hypnosis more frequently helps people stop smoking through hypnotic suggestions that the taste and smell of cigarettes are unpleasant (Green, Lynn, & Montgomery, 2008; Li et al., 2019).

- *Treating psychological disorders.* Hypnosis sometimes is used during treatment for psychological disorders. For example, it may be employed to heighten relaxation, reduce anxiety, increase expectations of success, or modify self-defeating thoughts (Iglesias, 2005; Golden, 2006; Etzrodt, 2013).

- *Assisting in law enforcement.* Witnesses and victims are sometimes better able to recall the details of a crime when hypnotized. In one case, a witness to the kidnapping of a group of California schoolchildren was placed under hypnosis and was able to recall all but one digit of the license number on the kidnapper's vehicle. On the other hand, hypnotic recollections may also be inaccurate. Consequently, the legal status of hypnosis is unresolved (Kazar, 2006; Knight & Meyer, 2007; Major, 2019).

- *Improving athletic performance.* Athletes sometimes turn to hypnosis to improve their performance. For example, some baseball players have used hypnotism to increase their concentration when batting, with considerable success (Barker & Jones, 2008; Tramontana, 2011; Carlstedt, 2017).

Meditation: Regulating Our Own State of Consciousness

When traditional practitioners of the ancient Eastern religion of Zen Buddhism want to achieve greater spiritual insight, they turn to a technique that has been used for centuries to alter their state of consciousness. This technique is called meditation.

Meditation is a learned technique for refocusing attention that brings about an altered state of consciousness. Meditation typically consists of the repetition of a *mantra*— a sound, word, or syllable—over and over. In some forms of meditation, the focus is on a picture, flame, or specific part of the body. Regardless of the nature of the particular initial stimulus, the key to the procedure is concentrating on it so thoroughly that the meditator becomes unaware of any outside stimulation and reaches a different state of consciousness.

After meditation, people report feeling thoroughly relaxed. They sometimes relate that they have gained new insights into themselves and the problems they are facing. The long-term practice of meditation may even improve health because of the biological changes it produces. For example, during meditation, oxygen usage decreases, heart rate and blood pressure decline, and brain-wave patterns change (Lee, Kleinman, & Kleinman, 2007; Travis et al., 2009; Steinhubl et al., 2015).

meditation A learned technique for refocusing attention that brings about an altered state of consciousness. (Module 15)

Meditation leads to short-term changes in a person's physiological state, as well as to longer-term health benefits.

FatCamera/Getty Images

Anyone can meditate by following a few simple procedures. The fundamentals include sitting in a quiet room with the eyes closed, breathing deeply and rhythmically, and repeating a word or sound—such as the word *one*—over and over. Practiced twice a day for 20 minutes, the technique is effective in bringing about greater relaxation not only during meditation but afterward. Evidence even supports long-term positive effects of some kinds of meditation, such as in the reduction of heart disease (Shaner et al., 2017; Yadav et al., 2017; Voiß et al., 2019).

From the perspective of...

A Human Resources Specialist Would you allow (or even encourage) employees to engage in meditation during the workday? Why or why not?

Dex Image/Getty Images

Many cultures use meditation to alter consciousness, though it can take different forms and serve different purposes, depending on the culture. In fact, one reason psychologists study consciousness is the realization that people in many cultures routinely seek ways to alter their states of consciousness (Walsh & Shapiro, 2006).

Exploring Diversity

Cross-Cultural Routes to Altered States of Consciousness

A group of Native-American Sioux men sit naked in a steaming sweat lodge as a medicine man throws water on sizzling rocks to send billows of scalding steam into the air.

Aztec priests smear themselves with a mixture of crushed poisonous herbs, hairy black worms, scorpions, and lizards. Sometimes they drink the potion.

During the 16th century, a devout Hasidic Jew lies across the tombstone of a celebrated scholar. As he murmurs the name of God repeatedly, he seeks to be possessed by the soul of the dead wise man's spirit. If successful, he will attain a mystical state, and the deceased's words will flow out of his mouth.

Each of these rituals has a common goal: suspension from the bonds of everyday awareness and access to an altered state of consciousness. Although they may seem exotic from the vantage point of many Western cultures, these rituals represent an apparently universal effort to alter consciousness (Bartocci, 2004; Irwin, 2006).

Some scholars suggest that the quest to alter consciousness represents a basic human desire. Whether or not we accept such an extreme view, variations in states of consciousness clearly share some basic characteristics across a variety of cultures. One is an alteration in thinking, which may become shallow, illogical, or otherwise different from normal. In addition, people's sense of time can become disturbed, and their perceptions of the physical world and of themselves may change. They may lose self-control, doing things that they would never otherwise do. Finally, they may feel a sense of *ineffability*—the inability to understand an experience rationally or describe it in words (Finkler, 2004; Travis, 2006).

Of course, realizing that efforts to produce altered states of consciousness are widespread throughout the world's societies does not answer a fundamental question: Is the experience of unaltered states of consciousness similar across different cultures?

Because humans share basic biological commonalities in the ways their brains and bodies are wired, we might assume that the fundamental experience of consciousness is similar across cultures. As a result, we could suppose that consciousness shows some basic similarities across cultures. However, the ways in which certain aspects of consciousness are interpreted and viewed show substantial differences from culture to culture. For example, people in disparate cultures view the experience of the passage of time in varying ways. For instance, Arabs appear to perceive the passage of time more slowly than North Americans do (Alon & Brett, 2007).

> **! Study Alert**
> Remember that although there are alternate techniques used in meditation, they are all designed to bring about an altered state of consciousness in which attention is refocused.

RECAP/EVALUATE/RETHINK

RECAP

LO 15-1 What is hypnosis, and are hypnotized people in a different state of consciousness?

- Hypnosis produces a state of heightened susceptibility to the suggestions of the hypnotist. Under hypnosis, significant behavioral changes occur, including increased concentration and suggestibility, heightened ability to recall and construct images, lack of initiative, and acceptance of suggestions that clearly contradict reality.

LO 15-2 What are the effects of meditation?

- Meditation is a learned technique for refocusing attention that brings about an altered state of consciousness.
- Different cultures have developed their own unique ways to alter states of consciousness.

EVALUATE

1. _____ is a state of heightened susceptibility to the suggestions of others.

2. A friend tells you, "I once heard of a person who was murdered by being hypnotized and then told to jump from the Golden Gate Bridge!" Could such a thing have happened? Why or why not?

3. _____ is a learned technique for refocusing attention to bring about an altered state of consciousness.

4. Leslie repeats a unique sound, known as a _____, when she engages in meditation.

RETHINK

1. Why do you think people in almost every culture seek ways of altering their states of consciousness?

2. Meditation produces several physical and psychological benefits. Does this suggest that we are physically and mentally burdened in our normal state of waking consciousness? Why?

Answers to Evaluate Questions

1. Hypnosis; 2. No; people who are hypnotized cannot be made to perform self-destructive acts; 3. Meditation; 4. mantra

KEY TERMS

hypnosis
meditation

Module 16
Drug Use: The Highs and Lows of Consciousness

Brittany was desperate. As the rest of her family were grieving over the loss of her grandmother, whose funeral they had just attended, she was searching for cash. She finally found a $5 bill in the purse belonging to her 6-year-old cousin. How low was it to steal from a 6-year-old to buy drugs? she wondered. But it didn't matter. Her head was aching, and her mouth was dry, and she would do anything to buy the drugs she needed to get high.

Like many others caught up in the opioid crisis facing the United States, Brittany's descent into addiction started with a legal drug, Percocet, that she was prescribed to deal with pain following the removal of her wisdom teeth. She didn't know that it was highly addictive, and even after the pain was gone, Brittany kept on craving the drug. It turned her from an honors student to an addict desperate for drugs. (Larsen, 2014)

Drugs of one sort or another are a part of almost everyone's life. From infancy on, most people take vitamins, aspirin, cold-relief medicine. However, these drugs rarely produce an altered state of consciousness.

In contrast, some substances, known as psychoactive drugs, lead to an altered state of consciousness. **Psychoactive drugs** influence a person's emotions, perceptions, and behavior. Yet even this category of drugs is common in most of our lives. If you have ever had a cup of coffee or sipped a beer, you have taken a psychoactive drug. A large number of individuals have used more potent—and more dangerous—psychoactive drugs than coffee and beer (see Figure 1); for instance, 49% of high school seniors have used an illegal drug in the past year. In addition, 43% report having been drunk on alcohol. The figures for the adult population are even higher (Meich et al., 2019).

Of course, drugs vary widely in the effects they have on users, in part because they affect the nervous system in very different ways. Some drugs alter the limbic system, and others affect the operation of specific neurotransmitters across the synapses of neurons. For example, some drugs block or enhance the release of neurotransmitters, others block the receipt or the removal of a neurotransmitter, and still others mimic the effects of a particular neurotransmitter (see Figure 2).

Addictive drugs produce a biological or psychological dependence (or both) on a drug in the user. When a drug is addictive, its absence leads leads to a craving for it that may be overpowering and nearly irresistible. In *biological drug dependence*, the body becomes so accustomed to functioning in the presence of a drug that it cannot function without it. In *psychological drug dependence*, people believe that they need the drug to respond to the stresses of daily living. Although we generally associate addiction with drugs such as heroin, everyday sorts of drugs, such as caffeine (found in coffee) and nicotine (found in cigarettes), have addictive aspects as well (Li, Volkow, & Baler, 2007; Falbe et al., 2019).

We know surprisingly little about the underlying causes of addiction. One of the problems in identifying those causes is that different drugs (such as alcohol and cocaine) affect the brain in very different ways—yet they may be equally addicting. Furthermore, it takes longer to become addicted to some drugs than to others, even though the ultimate consequences of addiction may be equally grave (Smart, 2007; Holmes, 2017).

LEARNING OUTCOME

LO 16-1 What are the major classifications of drugs, and what are their effects?

psychoactive drugs Drugs that influence a person's emotions, perceptions, and behavior. (Module 16)

addictive drugs Drugs that produce a biological or psychological dependence in the user so that withdrawal from them leads to a craving for the drug that, in some cases, may be nearly irresistible. (Module 16)

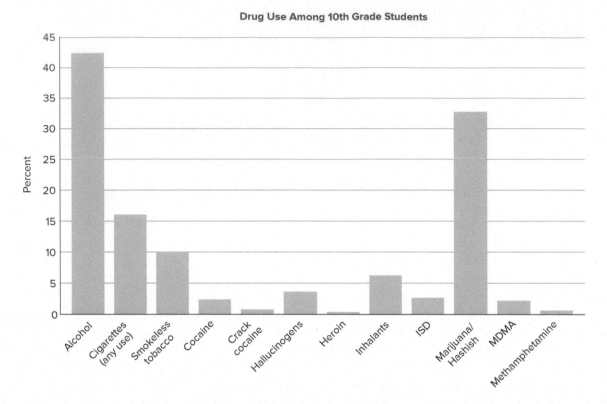

Drug Use Among 10th Grade Students

FIGURE 1 How many teenagers use drugs? The results of the most recent comprehensive survey of adolescent drug use in the United States show the percentage who have used various substances for nonmedical purposes at least once in their lifetime.

Data Source: Miech, R. A., Johnston, L. D., O'Malley, P. M., Bachman, J. G., Schulenberg, J. E., & Patrick, M. E. (2019). Monitoring the Future national survey results on drug use, 1975–2018: Volume I, Secondary school students. Ann Arbor: Institute for Social Research, The University of Michigan.

FIGURE 2 Different drugs affect different parts of the nervous system and brain, and each drug functions in one of these specific ways.

Why do people take drugs in the first place? They do so for many reasons, including the perceived pleasure of the experience. In other words, it simply feels good.

In addition, though, a drug-induced high allows people to escape, at least temporarily, from the everyday pressures of life. And in some cases, people use drugs to attempt to achieve a religious or spiritual state (Korcha et al., 2011; Chapman & Wu, 2015).

In addition, people may be influenced to use drugs by the highly publicized drug use of role models such as movie stars and professional athletes, the easy availability of some illegal drugs, or peer pressure. In some cases, the motive is simply the thrill of trying something new.

Finally, genetic factors may predispose some people to be more susceptible to drugs and to become addicted to them. Regardless of the forces that lead a person to begin using drugs, drug addiction is among the most difficult of all behaviors to modify, even with extensive treatment (Ray & Hutchison, 2007; Vrieze et al., 2013; Reilly et al., 2017).

Because of the difficulty in treating drug problems, most experts believe that the best hope for dealing with the overall societal problem of substance abuse is to prevent people from becoming involved with addictive drugs in the first place. However, there is little accord on how to accomplish this goal.

Even widely employed drug reduction programs—such as D.A.R.E. (Drug Abuse Resistance Education)—are of questionable effectiveness. At one time used in more than 80% of school districts in the United States, D.A.R.E. consists of a 10-week series of lessons on the dangers of drugs, alcohol, and gangs taught to 5th- and 6th-graders by a police officer. The program was highly popular with school officials, parents, and politicians.

The problem with D.A.R.E.? Repeated careful evaluations have been unable to demonstrate that the D.A.R.E. program is effective in reducing drug use over the long term. In fact, one study even showed that D.A.R.E. graduates were more likely to use marijuana than was a comparison group of nongraduates. On the other hand, D.A.R.E. has updated its curriculum, and some preliminary evidence suggests it may be more successful than the previous version. But the jury is still out on its effectiveness (Vincus et al., 2010; Singh et al., 2011; Caputi & McLellan, 2017).

Stimulants: Drug Highs

It's 1:00 A.M., and you still haven't finished reading the last chapter of the text on which you will be tested later in the morning. Feeling exhausted, you turn to the one thing that may help you stay awake for the next 2 hours: a cup of strong black coffee.

If you have ever found yourself in such a position, you have resorted to a major *stimulant*, caffeine, to stay awake. *Caffeine* is one of a number of **stimulants,** drugs whose effect on the central nervous system causes a rise in heart rate, blood pressure, and muscular tension. Caffeine is present not only in coffee; it is an important ingredient in tea, soft drinks, and chocolate as well (see Figure 3).

Caffeine produces several reactions. The major behavioral effects are an increase in attentiveness and a decrease in reaction time. Caffeine can also bring about an improvement in mood, most likely by mimicking the effects of a natural brain chemical, adenosine. Too much caffeine, however, can result in nervousness and insomnia. People can build up a biological dependence on the drug. Regular users who suddenly stop drinking coffee may experience headaches or depression. Many people who drink large amounts of coffee on weekdays have headaches on weekends because of the sudden drop in the amount of caffeine they are consuming (Kennedy & Haskell, 2011; Kamimori et al., 2015; Sweeney et al., 2019).

Nicotine, found in cigarettes, is another common stimulant. The soothing effects of nicotine help explain why cigarette smoking is addictive. Smokers develop a dependence on nicotine, and those who suddenly stop smoking develop a strong craving for the drug. This is not surprising: Nicotine activates neural mechanisms similar to those activated by cocaine, which, as we see in the section on cocaine, is also highly addictive (Haberstick et al., 2005; Ray et al., 2008; Wilcox et al., 2017).

PsychTech
Drugs are not the only source of addiction. Increasing evidence suggests that people can develop psychological dependence on the use of technologies, such as social networking sites such as Facebook or e-mail.

Study Alert
Use Figure 2 to learn the different ways that drugs produce their effects on a neurological level.

stimulants Drugs that have an arousal effect on the central nervous system, causing a rise in heart rate, blood pressure, and muscular tension. (Module 16)

FIGURE 3 How much caffeine do you consume? This chart shows the range of caffeine found in common foods, drinks, and legal drugs.

Source: Center for Science in the Public Interest. (nd). Caffeine Chart. Retrieved from https://cspinet.org/eating-healthy/ingredients-of-concern/caffeine-chart

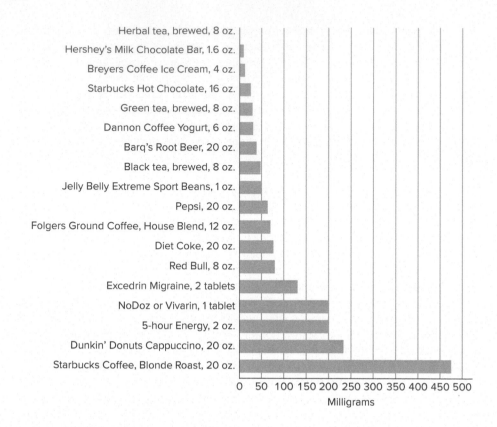

AMPHETAMINES

Amphetamines such as dexedrine and benzedrine, popularly known as speed, are strong stimulants. In small quantities, amphetamines—which stimulate the central nervous system—bring about a sense of energy and alertness, talkativeness, heightened confidence, and a mood "high." They increase concentration and reduce fatigue.

But not all the effects of amphetamines are positive: They also cause a loss of appetite, increased anxiety, and irritability. When taken over long periods of time, amphetamines can cause feelings of being persecuted by others, as well as a general sense of suspiciousness. People taking amphetamines may lose interest in sex. If taken in too large a quantity, amphetamines overstimulate the central nervous system to such an extent that convulsions and death can occur (Carhart-Harris, 2007).

Methamphetamine is a white, crystalline drug that U.S. police now say is the most dangerous street drug. "Meth" is highly addictive and relatively cheap, and it produces a strong, lingering high. It has made addicts of people across the social spectrum, ranging from soccer moms to urban professionals to rural farmers. After becoming addicted, users take it more and more frequently and in increasing doses. Long-term use of the drug can lead to brain damage (Halkitis, 2009; Kish et al., 2009; Rindone, 2015).

More than 1.5 million people in the United States are regular methamphetamine users. Because it can be made from nonprescription cold pills, retailers such as Walmart and Target have removed these medications from the shelves and keep them behind the pharmacy counter. Illicit labs devoted to the manufacture of methamphetamine have sprung up in many locations around the United States.

Adderall is an amphetamine college students often abuse. It was developed to help those who suffer from ADHD, or attention-deficit hyperactivity disorder. However, many college students use the drug illegally, believing that it increases their focus and the ability to study for long hours. Unfortunately, Adderall is addictive, and users need higher and higher doses to achieve the drug's supposed benefits (Diller, 2017; Lueck, Constantini, & Knobloch, 2019).

Figure 4 provides a summary of the effects of amphetamines and other illegal drugs.

Drugs	Street Name	Effects	Withdrawal Symptoms	Adverse/Overdose Reactions
Stimulants				
Amphetamines		Increased confidence, mood elevation, sense of energy and alertness, decreased appetite, anxiety, irritability, insomnia, transient drowsiness, delayed orgasm	Apathy, general fatigue, prolonged sleep, depression, disorientation, suicidal thoughts, agitated motor activity, irritability, bizarre dreams	Elevated blood pressure, increase in body temperature, face picking, suspiciousness, bizarre and repetitious behavior, vivid hallucinations, convulsions, possible death
Benzedrine	Speed			
Dexedrine	Speed			
Cocaine	Coke, blow, snow, lady, crack			
Cathinone	Bath salts			
Depressants				
Alcohol	Booze	Anxiety reduction, impulsiveness, dramatic mood swings, bizarre thoughts, suicidal behavior, slurred speech, disorientation, slowed mental and physical functioning, limited attention span	Weakness, restlessness, nausea and vomiting, headaches, nightmares, irritability, depression, acute anxiety, hallucinations, seizures, possible death	Confusion, decreased response to pain, shallow respiration, dilated pupils, weak and rapid pulse, coma, possible death
Barbiturates				
Nembutal	Yellowjackets			
Seconal	Reds			
Phenobarbital				
Rohypnol	Roofies, rope, "date-rape drug"	Muscle relaxation, amnesia, sleep	Seizures	Seizures, coma, incapacitation, inability to resist sexual assault
Narcotics				
Heroin	H, hombre, junk, smack	Reduction of anxiety and pain, difficulty in concentration, slowed speech, decreased physical activity, euphoria	Anxiety, vomiting, sneezing, diarrhea, lower back pain, watery eyes, runny nose, yawning, irritability, tremors, panic, chills and sweating, cramps	Depressed levels of consciousness, low blood pressure, rapid heart rate, shallow breathing, convulsions, coma, possible death
Morphine	Drugstore dope, cube, first line, mud			
Opioids (synthetic drugs such as Vicodin, Percocet, fentanyl, OxyContin)	Oxy, OC, Percs	Pain reduction, shallow breathing, slow heartbeat, seizure (convulsions); cold, clammy skin; confusion	Sweating, chills, abdominal cramps, insomnia, vomiting, diarrhea	Extreme drowsiness, muscle weakness, confusion, cold and clammy skin, pinpoint pupils, shallow breathing, slow heart rate, fainting, or coma
Hallucinogens				
Cannabis	Bhang, kif, ganja, dope, grass, pot, hemp, joint, weed, bone, Mary Jane, reefer	Euphoria, relaxed inhibitions, increased appetite, disoriented behavior	Hyperactivity, insomnia, decreased appetite, anxiety	Severe reactions rare but include panic, paranoia, fatigue, bizarre and dangerous behavior, decreased testosterone over long-term; immune-system effects
Marijuana				
Hashish				
Hash oil				
MDMA	Ecstasy, Molly	Heightened sense of oneself and insight, feelings of peace, empathy, energy	Depression, anxiety, sleeplessness	Increase in body temperature, memory difficulties
LSD	Acid, quasey, microdot, white lightning	Heightened aesthetic responses; vision and depth distortion; heightened sensitivity to faces and gestures; magnified feelings; paranoia, panic, euphoria	Not reported	Nausea and chills; increased pulse, temperature, and blood pressure; slow, deep breathing; loss of appetite; insomnia; bizarre, dangerous behavior
Steroids				
	Rhoids, juice	Aggression, depression, acne, mood swings, masculine traits in women and feminine traits in men	Symptoms can mimic other medical problems and include weakness, fatigue, decreased appetite, weight loss; women may note menstrual changes.	Long-term, high-dose effects of steroid use are largely unknown but can lead to swelling and weight gain.

FIGURE 4 Drugs and their effects. A comprehensive breakdown of effects of the most commonly used drugs.

Bath salts are an amphetamine-like stimulant containing chemicals related to cathinone. They can produce euphoria and a rise in sociability and sex drive, but the side effects can be severe, including paranoia and agitation (Airuehia, Walker, & Nittler, 2015; Palamar, Rutherford, & Keyes, 2019).

COCAINE

The stimulant *cocaine*, and its derivative *crack*, represent a serious concern, although the scope of the problem has declined in recent years. Cocaine is inhaled or "snorted" through the nose, smoked, or injected directly into the bloodstream. It is rapidly absorbed into the body and takes effect almost immediately.

When used in relatively small quantities, cocaine produces feelings of profound psychological well-being, increased confidence, and alertness. Cocaine produces this "high" through the neurotransmitter dopamine. Dopamine is one of the chemicals that transmit messages between neurons that are related to ordinary feelings of pleasure. Normally, when dopamine is released, excess amounts of the neurotransmitter are reabsorbed by the releasing neuron. However, when cocaine enters the brain, it blocks reabsorption of leftover dopamine. As a result, the brain is flooded with dopamine-produced pleasurable sensations (Redish, 2004; Jarlais, Arasteh, & Perlis, 2007; Singer et al., 2017).

However, there is a steep price to be paid for the pleasurable effects of cocaine. The brain may become permanently rewired, triggering a psychological and physical addiction in which users grow obsessed with obtaining the drug. Over time, users deteriorate mentally and physically. In extreme cases, cocaine can cause hallucinations–a common one is of insects crawling over one's body. Ultimately, an overdose of cocaine can lead to death (Little et al., 2009; Roncero et al., 2013; Li et al., 2015).

Almost 2.5 million people in the United States are occasional cocaine users, and as many as 1.5 million people use the drug regularly. Given the strength of cocaine, withdrawal from the drug is difficult. Although the use of cocaine among high school students has declined in recent years, the drug still represents a major problem (Johnston et al., 2009; National Institute on Drug Abuse, 2018).

> **Study Alert**
> Figure 4, which summarizes the different categories of drugs (stimulants, depressants, narcotics, and hallucinogens), will help you learn the effects of particular drugs.

Depressants: Drug Lows

depressants Drugs that slow down the nervous system. (Module 16)

In contrast to the initial effect of stimulants, which is an increase in arousal of the central nervous system, the effect of **depressants** is to impede the nervous system by causing neurons to fire more slowly. Small doses result in at least temporary feelings of *intoxication*–drunkenness–along with a sense of euphoria and joy. When large amounts are taken, however, speech becomes slurred and muscle control becomes disjointed, making motion difficult. Ultimately, heavy users may lose consciousness entirely.

ALCOHOL

The most common depressant is alcohol, which is used by more people than is any other drug. Based on liquor sales, the average person over the age of 14 drinks 2½ gallons of pure alcohol over the course of a year. This works out to more than 200 drinks per person. Although alcohol consumption has declined steadily over the last decade, surveys show that more than three-fourths of college students indicate that they have had a drink within the last 30 days (Midanik, Tam, & Weisner, 2007; Lui, 2019).

One of the more disturbing trends is the high frequency of binge drinking among college students. For men, *binge drinking* is defined as having five or more drinks in one sitting; for women, who generally weigh less than men and whose bodies absorb alcohol less efficiently, binge drinking is defined as having four or more drinks at one sitting (Mokdad, Brewer, & Naimi, 2007; Rooke & Hine, 2011).

In Figure 5, people of different ages reported binge drinking in the past 30 days. Note that the highest percentage of binge drinkers are young adults.

Who Binge Drinks?

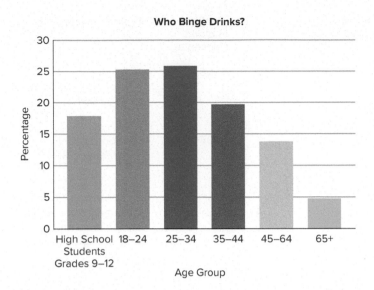

FIGURE 5 Self-reported binge drinking at different ages. For men, binge drinking was defined as consuming five or more drinks in one sitting; for women, the total was four or more.
Source: Adapted from Centers for Disease Control and Prevention. (2015). Youth Risk Behavior Surveillance System—2015 Surveillance Summaries.

Furthermore, in college settings, it turns out that even light drinkers are affected by the high rate of alcohol use by their classmates: Two-thirds of lighter drinkers say they had their studying or sleep disturbed by drunk students, and a quarter of women surveyed say they had been targets of unwanted sexual advances by drunk classmates (Wechsler et al., 2002; CDC, 2010; Greene & Maggs, 2017).

Women are typically somewhat lighter drinkers than men—although the gap between the sexes is narrowing for older women and has closed completely for teenagers. Women are more susceptible to the effects of alcohol, and alcohol abuse may harm the brains of women more than it harms the brains of men (Mancinelli, Binetti, & Ceccanti, 2007; Chavez et al., 2011; Holzhauer, Wemm & Wulfert, 2017)

There are also cultural and ethnic differences in alcohol consumption. For example, teenagers in Europe drink more than teenagers in the United States do. Furthermore, people of East Asian backgrounds who live in the United States tend to drink significantly less than do Caucasians and African Americans, and their incidence of alcohol-related problems is lower. It may be that physical reactions to drinking, which may include sweating, a quickened heartbeat, and flushing, are more unpleasant for East Asians than for other groups (Garlow, Purselle, & Heninger, 2007; Kantrowitz & Underwood, 2007; McCabe, Lee, & Viray, 2019).

Although alcohol is a depressant, most people believe that it increases their sense of sociability and well-being. This belief is caused because initially alcohol may lead to a reduction in tension and stress, feelings of happiness, and loss of inhibitions.

The effects of alcohol vary significantly, depending on who is drinking it and the setting in which people drink. If alcohol were a newly discovered drug, do you think its sale would be legal?
(Left): Dmytro Sidelnikov/123RF; (Right): Jim Arbogast/Getty Images

FIGURE 6 The effects of alcohol. The quantities represent only rough benchmarks; the effects vary significantly depending on an individual's weight, height, recent food intake, genetic factors, and even psychological state.

Number of drinks consumed in 2 hours	Alcohol in blood (percentage)	Typical effects
2	0.05	Judgment, thought, and restraint weakened; tension released, giving carefree sensation
3	0.08	Tensions and inhibitions of everyday life lessened; cheerfulness
4	0.10	Voluntary motor action affected, making hand and arm movements, walk, and speech clumsy
7	0.20	Severe impairment—staggering, loud, incoherent, emotionally unstable, 100 times greater traffic risk; exuberance and aggressive inclinations magnified
9	0.30	Deeper areas of brain affected, with stimulus-response and understanding confused; stuporous; blurred vision
12	0.40	Incapable of voluntary action; sleepy, difficult to arouse; equivalent of surgical anesthesia
15	0.50	Comatose; centers controlling breathing and heartbeat anesthetized; death increasingly probable

However, as the dose of alcohol increases, the depressive effects become more pronounced (see Figure 6). People may feel emotionally and physically unstable. They also show poor judgment and may act aggressively. Moreover, memory is impaired, brain processing of spatial information is diminished, and speech becomes slurred and incoherent. Eventually, they may fall into a stupor and pass out. If they drink enough alcohol in a short time, they may die of alcohol poisoning (Thatcher & Clark, 2006; Wombacher et al., 2019).

Although most people fall into the category of casual users, 14 million people in the United States–1 in every 13 adults–have a drinking problem. *Alcoholics*, people with alcohol-abuse problems, come to rely on alcohol and continue to drink even though it causes serious difficulties. In addition, they become increasingly immune to the effects of alcohol. Consequently, alcoholics must drink progressively more to experience the initial positive feelings that alcohol produces.

In some cases of alcoholism, people must drink constantly in order to feel well enough to function in their daily lives. In other cases, though, people drink inconsistently but occasionally go on binges in which they consume large quantities of alcohol.

It is not clear why certain people become alcoholics and develop a tolerance for alcohol, whereas others do not. There may be a genetic cause, although the question of whether there is a specific inherited gene that produces alcoholism is controversial. What is clear is that the chances of becoming an alcoholic are considerably higher if alcoholics are present in earlier generations of a person's family. However, not all alcoholics have close relatives who are alcoholics. In these cases, environmental stressors are suspected of playing a larger role (Nurnberger & Bierut, 2007; Gizer et al., 2011; Buckner & Shah, 2015).

BARBITURATES

Barbiturates are a form of central nervous system depressant. They include drugs such as Nembutal, Seconal, and phenobarbital. Barbiturates produce a sense of relaxation and are frequently prescribed by physicians to induce sleep or reduce stress. At larger doses, they produce altered thinking, faulty judgment, and sluggishness.

Even legal drugs, when used improperly, lead to addiction.
David Smart/Shutterstock

Barbiturates are psychologically and biologically addictive. When combined with alcohol, they can be deadly because such a combination relaxes the muscles of the diaphragm to such an extent that the user stops breathing.

ROHYPNOL

Rohypnol is sometimes called the "date rape drug" because when it is mixed with alcohol, it can prevent victims from resisting sexual assault. Sometimes people who are unknowingly given the drug are so incapacitated that they have no memory of the assault.

Narcotics, Opiates, and Opioids: Relieving Pain and Anxiety

Narcotics are drugs that increase relaxation and relieve pain and anxiety. Two of the most powerful narcotics, *morphine* and *heroin,* are derived from the poppy seed pod. Although morphine is used medically to control severe pain, heroin is illegal in the United States. This status has not prevented its widespread abuse.

narcotics Drugs that increase relaxation and relieve pain and anxiety. (Module 16)

Heroin users usually inject the drug directly into their veins with a hypodermic needle. The immediate effect has been described as a "rush" of positive feeling, similar in some respects to a sexual orgasm—and just as difficult to describe. After the rush, a heroin user experiences a sense of well-being and peacefulness that lasts 3 to 5 hours.

However, when the effects of heroin wear off, users feel extreme anxiety and a desperate desire to repeat the experience. Moreover, larger amounts of heroin are needed each time to produce the same pleasurable effect. These last two properties are all the ingredients necessary for biological and psychological dependence: The user is constantly either shooting up or attempting to obtain ever-increasing amounts of the drug. Eventually, the life of the addict revolves around heroin.

Heroin is part of a class of drugs called opiates. *Opiates* are narcotics that are derived from natural substances, and they include such drugs as morphine and codeine in addition to heroin. In contrast, *opioids* are synthetic narcotics such as Vicodin, Percocet, fentanyl, and OxyContin, all of which are created in laboratories and are often prescribed to alleviate pain. (The terms *opiates* and *opioids* are often used interchangeably, and when people speak of the "opioid crisis," they typically are referring to both categories.)

Opiate and opioid use has reached epidemic proportions. For example, heroin use more than doubled among young adults 18 to 25 years old from 2002-2004 to 2011-2013. Furthermore, the rate of overdose deaths related to heroin increased almost 400% between 2010 and 2017 (Cook, 2015; Katz, 2017; Levy, 2019).

Although it's not totally clear why use of opioids has increased so rapidly, one reason is that the cost of the drugs has plummeted at the same time the supply has increased substantially Furthermore, some of the newest opioids are 100 times as potent as natural heroin. And that means drugs bought on the street, which could contain virtually anything, are particularly dangerous and can easily lead to overdoses.

Because of the powerful positive feelings opioids produce, addiction to them is particularly difficult to cure. In one treatment that has shown some success, users are given alternative drugs that reduce dependence on heroin and other addictive opiates. For example, *methadone* is a synthetic chemical that satisfies a heroin user's biological cravings for the drug without providing the "high" that accompanies heroin. Similarly, *Suboxone* is a painkiller that reduces the withdrawal symptoms from heroin. Suboxone comes in tablet form as well as small film strips, both of which are put under the tongue to dissolve quickly. Another treatment is *Vivitrol*, an injection that lasts about a month. It prevents withdrawal symptoms, and it prevents heroin from producing the positive effects that users crave if heroin is used (Shah, Young, & Vieira, 2014).

Methadone, Suboxone, and Vivitrol allow heroin users to function relatively normally and without the drug cravings. However, although such drugs remove the psychological dependence on heroin, they replace the biological dependence on heroin with a biological dependence on the alternative drugs. Consequently, researchers are attempting to identify nonaddictive chemical substitutes that do not produce a biological craving (Joe, Flynn, & Broome, 2007; Oviedo-Joekes et al., 2009; Prieto et al, 2019).

Hallucinogens: Psychedelic Drugs

hallucinogens Drugs that are capable of producing alterations in perception, thoughts, and feelings. (Module 16)

Hallucinogens are drugs that alter perceptions, thoughts, and feelings. They can even produce *hallucinations*, the experience of sensing things such as sights, sounds, or smells that seem real but are not.

MARIJUANA

The most common hallucinogen in widespread use today is *marijuana*, whose active ingredient–tetrahydrocannabinol (THC)–is found in a common weed, cannabis. Marijuana is typically smoked in cigarettes or pipes, although it can be cooked and eaten. Close to 40% of high school seniors and around 15% of 8th-graders report having used marijuana in the last year (Johnston et al., 2016; see Figure 7).

FIGURE 7 Although the level of marijuana use has declined slightly in recent years, overall the absolute number of teenagers who have used the drug in the past year remains relatively high.
Source: The Regents of the University of Michigan, "Teen use of any illicit drug other than marijuana at new low, same true for alcohol." https://news.umich.edu/.

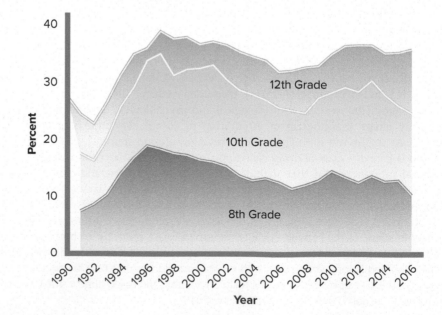

The effects of marijuana vary from person to person, but they typically consist of feelings of euphoria and general well-being. Sensory experiences seem more vivid and intense, and a person's sense of self-importance seems to grow. Memory may be impaired, causing users to feel pleasantly "spaced out."

Is marijuana safe? The scientific evidence is somewhat mixed. On the one hand, marijuana does not seem to produce addiction except in a small number of heavy users. Furthermore, little scientific evidence supports the belief that users "graduate" from marijuana to more dangerous drugs. Overall, most research suggests its use is less harmful than the use of tobacco and alcohol (Barcott & Scherer, 2015; Śledziński et al., 2019).

On the other hand, some research suggests that there are similarities in the way marijuana and drugs such as cocaine and heroin affect the brain, as well as evidence that heavy use may impact negatively on cognitive ability in the long run. Furthermore, heavy use may at least temporarily decrease the production of the male sex hormone testosterone, potentially affecting sexual activity and sperm count (Rossato, Pagano, & Vettor, 2008; Pardini et al., 2015; Berenson, 2019).

In addition, marijuana smoked during pregnancy may have lasting effects on children who are exposed prenatally, although the research results are inconsistent. Heavy use also affects the ability of the immune system to fight off germs and increases stress on the heart, although it is unclear how strong these effects are. Finally, there is one unquestionably negative consequence of smoking marijuana: The smoke damages the lungs much the way cigarette smoke does, producing an increased likelihood of developing cancer and other lung diseases (Reid, MacLeod, & Robertson, 2010; Pinky et al., 2019).

Despite the possible dangers of marijuana, its use is increasingly accepted. It clearly has several medical uses: it can prevent nausea from chemotherapy, treat some AIDS symptoms, and relieve muscle spasms for people with spinal cord injuries. Furthermore, it may be helpful in the treatment of Alzheimer's disease (Barcott & Scherer, 2015; Finn, 2015).

Many states have made the use of the drug legal if it is prescribed by a health care provider—although it remains illegal under U.S. federal law. And a growing number of states are joining the 11 in which the use and sale of marijuana are legal, even for recreational use, with no prescription required (Baumrucker et al., 2011; Roffman, 2013; Bradford & Bradford, 2017).

MDMA (ECSTASY OR MOLLY) AND LSD

MDMA (*Ecstasy* or *Molly*) and *lysergic acid diethylamide* (*LSD* or *acid*) are hallucinogens. Both drugs affect the operation of the neurotransmitter serotonin in the brain, causing an alteration in brain-cell activity and perception (Buchert et al., 2004; Aleksander, 2013).

MDMA produces feelings of increased energy and euphoria, and users report feeling increased empathy and connection with others. Use of forms of MDMA known as *Ecstasy* or *Molly* were initially used primarily at raves and music festivals, but they now affect a broader population. Those who use MDMA may experience declines in memory and performance on intellectual tasks. Such findings suggest that MDMA use may lead to long-term changes in serotonin receptors in the brain (McKinley, 2013; Ebrahimian et al., 2017; Parrott et al., 2017).

LSD, which is structurally similar to serotonin, produces vivid hallucinations and is one of the most powerful mind-altering chemicals. Perceptions of colors, sounds, and shapes are altered so much that even the most mundane experience—such as looking at the knots in a wooden table—can seem moving and exciting. Time perception is distorted, and objects and people may be viewed in a new way, with some users reporting that LSD increases their understanding of the world. For others, however, the experience brought on by LSD can be terrifying, particularly if users have had emotional difficulties in the past. Furthermore, people occasionally experience flashbacks, in which they hallucinate long after they initially used the drug (Yanakieva, 2019; Modak, Bhad, & Rao, 2019).

This drawing, made by someone taking LSD, suggests the effects of hallucinogens on thinking.

Omikron/Science Source/Getty Images

BECOMING AN INFORMED CONSUMER
of Psychology

Identifying Drug and Alcohol Problems

In a society bombarded with commercials for drugs that are guaranteed to cure everything from restless leg syndrome to erectile dysfunction, it is no wonder that drug-related problems are a major social issue. Yet many people with drug and alcohol problems deny that they have them, and even close friends and family members may fail to realize when occasional social use of drugs or alcohol has turned into abuse.

Certain signs, however, indicate when use becomes abuse (National Institute on Drug Abuse, 2019). Among them are the following:

- Always getting high to have a good time
- Being high more often than not
- Getting high to get oneself going
- Going to work or class while high
- Missing or being unprepared for class or work because you were high
- Feeling bad later about something you said or did while high
- Driving a car while high
- Coming in conflict with the law because of drugs
- Doing something while high that you wouldn't do otherwise
- Being high in nonsocial, solitary situations
- Being unable to stop getting high
- Feeling a need for a drink or a drug to get through the day
- Becoming physically unhealthy
- Failing at school or on the job
- Thinking about liquor or drugs all the time
- Avoiding family or friends while using liquor or drugs

Any combination of these symptoms should be sufficient to alert you to the potential of a serious drug problem. Because drug and alcohol dependence are almost impossible to cure on one's own, people who suspect that they have a problem should seek immediate attention from a psychologist, physician, or counselor.

You can also get help from national hotlines. For alcohol difficulties, call the National Council on Alcoholism at (800) 622-2255. For drug problems, call the National Institute on Drug Abuse at (800) 662-4357. You can also search the web for a local listing of Alcoholics Anonymous or Narcotics Anonymous. In addition, you can check out the websites of the National Institute on Alcohol Abuse and Alcoholism (www.niaaa.nih.gov) and the National Institute on Drug Abuse (www.nida.nih.gov).

From the perspective of...

A Substance Abuse Counselor How would you explain why people start using drugs to the family members of someone who was addicted? What types of drug prevention programs would you advocate?

Uppercut/Getty Images

RECAP/EVALUATE/RETHINK

RECAP

LO 16-1 What are the major classifications of drugs, and what are their effects?

- Drugs can produce an altered state of consciousness. However, they vary in how dangerous they are and in whether they are addictive.
- Stimulants cause arousal in the central nervous system. Two common stimulants are caffeine and nicotine. More dangerous are cocaine and amphetamines, which in large quantities can lead to convulsions and death.
- Depressants decrease arousal in the central nervous system. They can cause intoxication along with feelings of euphoria. The most common depressants are alcohol and barbiturates.
- Alcohol is the most frequently used depressant. Its initial effects of released tension and positive feelings yield to depressive effects as the dose of alcohol increases. Both heredity and environmental stressors can lead to alcoholism.
- Morphine and heroin are narcotics, drugs that produce relaxation and relieve pain and anxiety. Because of their addictive qualities, morphine and heroin are particularly dangerous.
- Hallucinogens are drugs that produce hallucinations or other changes in perception. The most frequently used hallucinogen is marijuana, which has several long-term risks. Two other hallucinogens are LSD and Ecstasy.
- A number of signals indicate when drug use becomes drug abuse. A person who suspects that he or she has a drug problem should get professional help. People are almost never capable of solving drug problems on their own.

EVALUATE

1. Drugs that affect a person's consciousness are referred to as _____ .

2. Match the type of drug to an example of that type.
   1. narcotic–a pain reliever
   2. amphetamine–a strong stimulant
   3. hallucinogen–capable of producing hallucinations

   a. LSD
   b. heroin
   c. dexedrine, or speed
3. Classify each drug listed as a stimulant (S), depressant (D), hallucinogen (H), or narcotic (N).
   1. nicotine
   2. cocaine
   3. alcohol
   4. morphine
   5. marijuana
4. The effects of LSD can recur long after the drug has been taken. True or false?
5. _____ is a drug that has been used to treat people with heroin addiction.

RETHINK

1. Why have drug education campaigns largely been ineffective in stemming the use of illegal drugs? Should the use of certain now-illegal drugs be made legal? Would stressing reduction of drug use be more effective than completely prohibiting drug use?
2. People often use the word *addiction* loosely, speaking of an addiction to candy or a television show. Can you explain the difference between this type of "addiction" and a true biological addiction? Is there a difference between this type of "addiction" and a psychological addiction?

Answers to Evaluate Questions

1. psychoactive; 2. 1-b, 2-c, 3-a; 3. 1-S, 2-S, 3-D, 4-N, 5-H; 4. True; 5. Methadone

KEY TERMS

psychoactive drugs   stimulants   narcotics
addictive drugs   depressants   hallucinogens

LOOKING *Back*

EPILOGUE

Our examination of states of consciousness has ranged widely. It focuses both on natural factors, such as sleep, dreaming, and daydreaming, and on more intentional modes of altering consciousness, including hypnosis, meditation, and drugs. As we consider why people seek to alter their consciousness, we need to reflect on the uses and abuses of the various consciousness-altering strategies in which people engage.

Return briefly to the prologue of this chapter about the death of baseball player Tyler Skaggs and the opioid epidemic, and answer the following questions in light of your understanding of addictive drugs:

1. What class of drug are opiates? Why do you think they are usually prescribed to young people? Do you think that's a defensible medical practice? Why or why not?
2. How would you describe the addictive properties of drugs such as opiates to discourage their use?
3. If you suspected a friend or classmate were addicted to painkillers, what symptoms would you watch for? What actions could you take if you wanted to help?
4. What factors might be responsible for the increasing rate of overdoses on prescription painkillers by young people?

VISUAL SUMMARY 5 States of Consciousness

MODULE 14 Sleep and Dreams

Stages of Sleep: Three stages of sleep, plus REM sleep

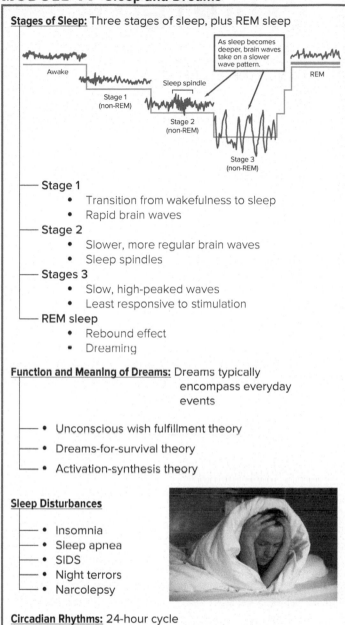

As sleep becomes deeper, brain waves take on a slower wave pattern.

Awake

Stage 1 (non-REM)

Sleep spindle

Stage 2 (non-REM)

Stage 3 (non-REM)

REM

— **Stage 1**
- Transition from wakefulness to sleep
- Rapid brain waves

— **Stage 2**
- Slower, more regular brain waves
- Sleep spindles

— **Stages 3**
- Slow, high-peaked waves
- Least responsive to stimulation

— **REM sleep**
- Rebound effect
- Dreaming

Function and Meaning of Dreams: Dreams typically encompass everyday events

— Unconscious wish fulfillment theory

— Dreams-for-survival theory

— Activation-synthesis theory

Sleep Disturbances

— Insomnia
— Sleep apnea
— SIDS
— Night terrors
— Narcolepsy

Circadian Rhythms: 24-hour cycle

MODULE 15 Hypnosis and Meditation

Hypnosis: A trancelike state of heightened suggestibility

Meditation: Learned technique for refocusing attention

MODULE 16 Drug Use

Stimulants: Increase arousal in the nervous system

- Caffeine
- Cocaine
- Amphetamines

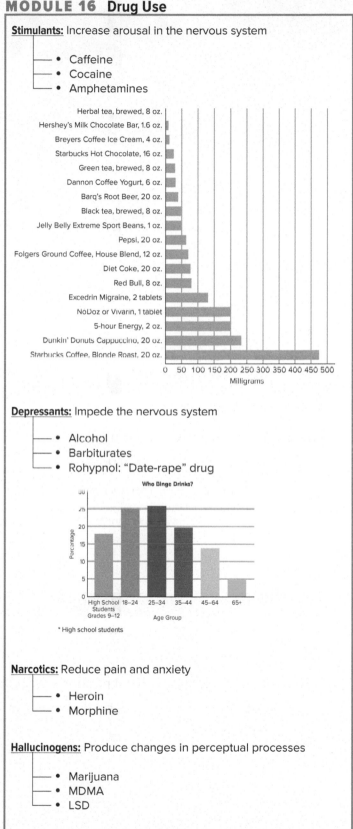

Herbal tea, brewed, 8 oz.
Hershey's Milk Chocolate Bar, 1.6 oz.
Breyers Coffee Ice Cream, 4 oz.
Starbucks Hot Chocolate, 16 oz.
Green tea, brewed, 8 oz.
Dannon Coffee Yogurt, 6 oz.
Barq's Root Beer, 20 oz.
Black tea, brewed, 8 oz.
Jelly Belly Extreme Sport Beans, 1 oz.
Pepsi, 20 oz.
Folgers Ground Coffee, House Blend, 12 oz.
Diet Coke, 20 oz.
Red Bull, 8 oz.
Excedrin Migraine, 2 tablets
NoDoz or Vivarin, 1 tablet
5-hour Energy, 2 oz.
Dunkin' Donuts Cappuccino, 20 oz.
Starbucks Coffee, Blonde Roast, 20 oz.

0 50 100 150 200 250 300 350 400 450 500
Milligrams

Depressants: Impede the nervous system

- Alcohol
- Barbiturates
- Rohypnol: "Date-rape" drug

Who Binge Drinks?

Percentage

High School Students Grades 9-12   18-24   25-34   35-44   45-64   65+

Age Group

* High school students

Narcotics: Reduce pain and anxiety

- Heroin
- Morphine

Hallucinogens: Produce changes in perceptual processes

- Marijuana
- MDMA
- LSD

(Module 14): Source: W. H. Freeman and Company, Sleep.; Koldunova Anna/Shutterstock; (Module 15): Pixel-Shot/Shutterstock; FatCamera/Getty Images; (Module 16): Source: Center for Science in the Public Interest. (nd). Caffeine Chart. Retrieved 6/1/19 from https://cspinet.org/eating-healthy/ingredients-of-concern/caffeine-chart; Source: Adapted from Centers for Disease Control and Prevention. (2015). Youth Risk Behavior Surveillance System—2015 Surveillance Summaries.

MJTH/Shutterstock

CHAPTER 6
Learning

LEARNING OUTCOMES FOR CHAPTER 6

	MODULE 17
LO 17-1 What is learning?	**CLASSICAL CONDITIONING**
LO 17-2 How do we learn to form associations between stimuli and responses?	The Basics of Classical Conditioning
	Applying Conditioning Principles to Human Behavior
	Extinction
	Generalization and Discrimination
	Beyond Traditional Classical Conditioning: Challenging Basic Assumptions

	MODULE 18
LO 18-1 What are the roles of reward and punishment in learning?	**OPERANT CONDITIONING**
	Thorndike's Law of Effect
	The Basics of Operant Conditioning
LO 18-2 What are some practical methods for bringing about behavior change, both in ourselves and in others?	**Applying Psychology in the 21st Century:** Spanking Children Makes Things Worse
	Becoming an Informed Consumer of Psychology: Using Behavior Analysis and Behavior Modification

LO 19-1 What are the roles of cognition and thought in learning?

PROLOGUE *A HELPING HAND*

Thirty-one-year-old Travis Amick is grateful for the help he receives from his roommate, Siggy. Following a tragic accident, Travis lost the use of his legs, has only partial use of his arms, and uses a wheelchair.

Siggy opens doors and drawers for Travis and helps him position his legs on footrests. He opens bottles, operates electronic equipment, fetches objects, and even turns the pages when Travis wants to read a book. Once, Travis needed help when his wheelchair got stuck. He was desperately trying to call his sister when he dropped his cell phone and the battery popped out. Siggy couldn't manage the wheelchair, but he did fix the phone for Travis.

What makes Siggy's efforts so remarkable? He is a 30-year-old capuchin monkey, trained specifically as a full-time aide (Kluger, 2010).

LOOKING *Ahead*

Siggy's astonishing skills did not come naturally to him. Rather, his ability to enhance Travis Amrick's quality of life relies on the fact that service animals like him can be trained and, more important, learn so effectively.

Learning is a fundamental topic for psychologists and plays a central role in almost every specialty area of psychology. For example, a psychologist studying perception might ask, "How do we learn that people who look small from a distance are far away and not simply tiny?" A developmental psychologist might inquire, "How do babies learn to distinguish their mothers from other people?" A clinical psychologist might wonder, "Why do some people learn to be afraid when they see a spider?" A social psychologist might ask, "How do we learn to believe that we've fallen in love?"

Each of these questions, although drawn from very different branches of psychology, can be answered only through an understanding of basic learning processes. In each case, a skill or a behavior is acquired, altered, or refined through experience.

In this chapter, we will explore several ways in which learning occurs, including through classical and operant conditioning approaches, which focus on outward, behavioral processes, as well as through cognitive approaches, which focus on mental processes. We will discuss cultural differences in learning and individual differences in learning styles that influence learning effectiveness, and we will examine practical learning programs, such as behavior modification, which are based on these learning approaches.

Module 17
Classical Conditioning

learning A relatively permanent change in behavior brought about by experience. (Module 17)

Does the mere sight of the golden arches in front of McDonald's make you feel pangs of hunger and think about hamburgers? If it does, you are displaying an elementary form of learning called classical conditioning. *Classical conditioning* helps explain such diverse phenomena as crying at the sight of a bride walking down the aisle, fearing the dark, and falling in love.

Classical conditioning is one of a number of different types of learning that psychologists have identified, but a general definition encompasses them all: **Learning** is a relatively permanent change in behavior that is brought about by experience.

How do we know when a behavior has been influenced by learning–or even is a result of learning? Part of the answer relates to the nature-nurture question, one of the fundamental issues underlying the field of psychology. In the acquisition of behaviors, experience–which is essential to the definition of learning–is the "nurture" part of the nature-nurture question.

However, it's not always easy to identify whether a change in behavior is due to nature or nurture because some changes in behavior or performance come about through maturation alone and don't involve experience. For instance, children become better tennis players as they grow older partly because their strength increases with their size–a maturational phenomenon. To understand when learning has occurred, we must differentiate maturational changes from improvements resulting from practice, which indicate that learning actually has occurred.

Similarly, short-term changes in behavior that are due to factors other than learning, such as declines in performance resulting from fatigue or lack of effort, are different from performance changes that are due to actual learning. If Serena Williams has a bad day on the tennis court because of tension or fatigue, this does not mean that she has not learned to play correctly or has "unlearned" how to play well. Because there is not always a one-to-one correspondence between learning and performance, understanding when true learning has occurred is difficult.

It is clear that we are primed for learning from the beginning of life. Infants exhibit a simple type of learning called habituation. *Habituation* is the decrease in response to a stimulus that occurs after repeated presentations of the same stimulus. For example, young infants may initially show interest in a novel stimulus, such as a brightly colored toy, but they will soon lose interest if they see the same toy over and over. (Adults exhibit habituation, too: Newlyweds soon stop noticing that they are wearing a wedding ring.) Habituation permits us to ignore things that have stopped providing new information.

Most learning is considerably more complex than habituation, and the study of learning has been at the core of the field of psychology. Although philosophers since the time of Aristotle have speculated on the foundations of learning, the first systematic research on learning was done at the beginning of the 20th century, when Ivan Pavlov (does the name ring a bell?) developed the framework for learning called classical conditioning.

The Basics of Classical Conditioning

Ivan Pavlov, a Russian physiologist, never intended to do psychological research. In 1904 he won the Nobel Prize for his work on digestion, testimony to his contribution to that field. Yet Pavlov is remembered not for his physiological research but for his experiments on basic learning processes–work that he began quite accidentally (Marks, 2004; Samoilov & Zayas, 2007; Grant & Wingate, 2011).

Pavlov had been studying the secretion of stomach acids and salivation in dogs in response to eating varying amounts and kinds of food. While doing his research, he observed a curious phenomenon: Sometimes salivation would begin in the dogs when they had not yet eaten any food. Just the sight of the experimenter who normally brought the food or even the sound of the experimenter's footsteps was enough to produce salivation in the dogs.

Pavlov's genius lay in his ability to recognize the implications of this discovery. He saw that the dogs were responding not only on the basis of a biological need (hunger) but also as a result of learning—or, as it came to be called, classical conditioning. **Classical conditioning** is a type of learning in which a neutral stimulus (such as the experimenter's footsteps) comes to elicit a response after being paired with a stimulus (such as food) that naturally brings about that response.

Ivan Pavlov (center) developed the principles of classical conditioning.
Sovfoto/Universal Images Group/Getty Images

To demonstrate classical conditioning, Pavlov (1927) attached a tube to the salivary gland of a dog, allowing him to measure precisely the dog's salivation. He then rang a bell and, just a few seconds later, presented the dog with meat. This pairing occurred repeatedly and was carefully planned so that, each time, exactly the same amount of time elapsed between the presentation of the bell and the meat. At first the dog would salivate only when the meat was presented, but soon it began to salivate at the sound of the bell. In fact, even when Pavlov stopped presenting the meat, the dog still salivated after hearing the sound. The dog had been classically conditioned to salivate to the bell.

As you can see in Figure 1, the basic processes of classical conditioning that underlie Pavlov's discovery are straightforward. However, the terminology he chose is not simple.

First, consider the diagram in Figure 1a. Before conditioning, there are two unrelated stimuli: the ringing of a bell and meat. We know that typically the sound of a bell does not lead to salivation but instead to some other response, such as pricking up the ears or perhaps a startle reaction. The bell is therefore called the neutral stimulus. A **neutral stimulus** is a stimulus that, before conditioning, does not naturally bring about the response in which we are interested.

Prior to conditioning, we also know that meat naturally causes a dog to salivate. Because food placed in a dog's mouth automatically causes salivation to occur, it is known as an unconditioned stimulus. An **unconditioned stimulus (UCS)** is a stimulus that naturally brings about a particular response without having been learned.

The response that the meat elicits (salivation) is called an unconditioned response. An **unconditioned response (UCR)** is a natural, innate response that occurs automatically and needs no training. Unconditioned responses are always brought about by the presence of unconditioned stimuli.

Figure 1b illustrates what happens during conditioning. The bell is rung just before each presentation of the meat. The goal of conditioning is for the dog to associate the bell with the unconditioned stimulus (meat) and therefore to bring about the same sort of response as the unconditioned stimulus.

After a number of pairings of the bell and meat, the bell alone causes the dog to salivate (as in Figure 1c). When conditioning is complete, the bell has changed from a neutral stimulus to what is called a conditioned stimulus. A **conditioned stimulus (CS)** is a once-neutral stimulus that has been paired with an unconditioned stimulus to bring about a response formerly caused only by the unconditioned stimulus. This time, salivation that occurs as a response to the conditioned stimulus (bell) is called a **conditioned response (CR).** After conditioning, then, the conditioned stimulus brings about the conditioned response.

The sequence and timing of the presentation of the unconditioned stimulus and the conditioned stimulus are particularly important. Like a malfunctioning warning

classical conditioning A type of learning in which a neutral stimulus comes to bring about a response after it is paired with a stimulus that naturally brings about that response. (Module 17)

neutral stimulus A stimulus that, before conditioning, does not naturally bring about the response of interest. (Module 17)

unconditioned stimulus (UCS) A stimulus that naturally brings about a particular response without having been learned. (Module 17)

unconditioned response (UCR) A response that is natural and needs no training (e.g., salivation at the smell of food). (Module 17)

conditioned stimulus (CS) A once-neutral stimulus that has been paired with an unconditioned stimulus to bring about a response formerly caused only by the unconditioned stimulus. (Module 17)

conditioned response (CR) A response that, after conditioning, follows a previously neutral stimulus (e.g., salivation at the ringing of a bell). (Module 17)

FIGURE 1 The basic process of classical conditioning. (a) *Before conditioning:* The sound of a bell does *not* produce salivation, meaning that the bell is a neutral stimulus. In contrast, meat naturally brings about salivation, making the meat an unconditioned stimulus (UCS) and salivation an unconditioned response (UCR). (b) *During conditioning:* The bell rings just before the presentation of the meat. (c) *After conditioning:* Eventually, the sound of the bell alone produces salivation. We now can say that conditioning has been accomplished: The previously neutral stimulus of the bell is now considered a conditioned stimulus (CS) that brings about the conditioned response of salivation (CR).

(a) Before conditioning

Neutral stimulus — Sound of bell → Response unrelated to meat — Pricking of ears

Unconditioned stimulus (UCS) — Meat → Unconditioned response (UCR) — Salivation

(b) During conditioning

Neutral stimulus — Sound of bell → Unconditioned response (UCR) — Salivation

Unconditioned stimulus (UCS) — Meat

(c) After conditioning

Conditioned stimulus (CS) — Sound of bell → Conditioned response (CR) — Salivation

Study Alert

Figure 1 can help you to learn and understand the process (and terminology) of classical conditioning, which can be confusing.

light at a railroad crossing that goes on after the train has passed by, a neutral stimulus that *follows* an unconditioned stimulus has little chance of becoming a conditioned stimulus. However, just as a warning light works best if it goes on right before a train passes, a neutral stimulus that is presented *just before* the unconditioned stimulus is most apt to result in successful conditioning. More specifically, conditioning is most effective if the neutral stimulus (which will become a conditioned stimulus) precedes the unconditioned stimulus by between a half second and several seconds, depending on what kind of response is being conditioned (Jennings et al., 2013; Harvie, Moseley, & Hillier, 2017; Vandbakk, Olaff, & Holth, 2019).

Although the terminology Pavlov used to describe classical conditioning may seem confusing, the following summary can help make the relationships between stimuli and responses easier to understand and remember:

- Conditioned = learned
- Unconditioned = not learned

- An *un*conditioned stimulus (UCS) leads to an *un*conditioned response (UCR).

- *Un*conditioned stimulus-*un*conditioned response pairings are *not* learned and *not* trained: They are naturally occurring.

- During conditioning, a previously neutral stimulus is transformed into the conditioned stimulus.

- A conditioned stimulus (CS) leads to a conditioned response (CR), and a conditioned stimulus-conditioned response pairing is a consequence of learning and training.

- An *un*conditioned response and a conditioned response are similar (such as salivation in Pavlov's experiment). But the *un*conditioned response occurs naturally, whereas the conditioned response is learned.

Applying Conditioning Principles to Human Behavior

Although the initial conditioning experiments were carried out with animals, classical conditioning principles were soon found to explain many aspects of everyday human behavior. Recall, for instance, the earlier illustration of how people may experience hunger pangs at the sight of McDonald's golden arches. The cause of this reaction is classical conditioning: The previously neutral arches have become associated with the food inside the restaurant (the unconditioned stimulus), causing the arches to become a conditioned stimulus that brings about the conditioned response of hunger.

Because of a previous, unpleasant experience, a person may expect a similar occurrence when faced with a comparable situation in the future, a process known as stimulus generalization. Can you think of ways that this process occurs in everyday life?
Robert Daly/OJO Images/age fotostock

Many emotional responses are learned through classical conditioning processes. For instance, how do some of us develop fears of mice, spiders, and other creatures that are typically harmless? In a now infamous case study, psychologist John B. Watson and colleague Rosalie Rayner (1920) showed that classical conditioning was at the root of such fears by conditioning an 11-month-old infant named Albert to be afraid of rats. "Little Albert," like most infants, initially was frightened by loud noises but had no fear of rats.

In the study, the experimenters sounded a loud noise whenever Little Albert touched a white, furry rat. The noise (the unconditioned stimulus) evoked fear (the unconditioned response). After just a few pairings of noise and rat, Albert began to show fear of the rat by itself, bursting into tears when he saw it. The rat, then, had become a CS that brought about the CR, fear. Furthermore, the effects of the conditioning lingered: five days later, Albert reacted with some degree of fear not only when shown a rat but also when shown objects that looked similar to the white, furry rat, including a white rabbit, a white sealskin coat, and even a white Santa Claus mask. (By the way, we don't know for certain what happened to Little Albert, and his fate remains a source of considerable speculation. In any case, Watson, the experimenter, has been condemned for using ethically questionable procedures that could never be conducted today [Griggs, 2015; Digdon, 2017; Hermans, Boddez, & Vervliet, 2019].)

Learning by means of classical conditioning also occurs during adulthood. For example, you may not go to a dentist as often as you should because of previous associations of dentists with pain. In more extreme cases, classical conditioning can lead to the development of *phobias*, which are intense, irrational fears. For example, an insect phobia might develop in someone who is stung by a bee. The insect phobia might be so severe that the person refrains from leaving home.

Posttraumatic stress disorder (PTSD), suffered by some war veterans and others who have had traumatic experiences, can also be produced by classical conditioning. Even years after their battlefield experiences, veterans may feel a rush of fear and anxiety at a stimulus such as a loud noise (Schreurs, Smith-Bell, & Burhans, 2011; Rosellini et al., 2015; Allen et al., 2019).

On the other hand, classical conditioning also relates to pleasant experiences. For instance, you may have a particular fondness for the smell of a certain perfume or aftershave lotion because thoughts of an early love come rushing back whenever you encounter it. Or hearing a certain song can bring back happy or bittersweet emotions due to associations that you have developed in the past.

Classical conditioning also explains why drug addictions are so difficult to treat. Drug addicts learn to associate certain stimuli–such as drug paraphernalia such as a syringe or a room where they use drugs–with the pleasant feelings produced by the drugs. So simply seeing a syringe or entering a certain room can produce reactions associated with the drug and continued cravings for it (Saunders, Yager, & Robinson, 2013; Valyear, Villaruel, & Chaudhri, 2017).

From the perspective of...

An Advertising Executive How might knowledge of classical conditioning be useful in creating an advertising campaign? What, if any, ethical issues arise from this use?

Image Source/Getty Images

Extinction

extinction A basic phenomenon of learning that occurs when a previously conditioned response decreases in frequency and eventually disappears. (Module 17)

What do you think would happen if a dog that had become classically conditioned to salivate at the ringing of a bell never again received food when the bell was rung? The answer lies in one of the basic phenomena of learning: extinction. **Extinction** occurs when a previously conditioned response decreases in frequency and eventually disappears.

To produce extinction, one needs to end the association between conditioned stimuli and unconditioned stimuli. For instance, if we had trained a dog to salivate (the conditioned response) at the ringing of a bell (the conditioned stimulus), we could produce extinction by repeatedly ringing the bell but *not* providing meat (the unconditioned stimulus; see Figure 2). At first, the dog would continue to salivate when it heard the bell, but after a few such instances, the amount of salivation would probably decline, and the dog would eventually stop responding to the bell altogether. At that point, we could say that the response had been extinguished. In sum, extinction occurs when the conditioned stimulus is presented repeatedly without the unconditioned stimulus.

We should keep in mind that extinction can be a helpful phenomenon. Consider, for instance, what it would be like if the fear you experienced while watching the shower murder scene in the classic movie *Psycho* never was extinguished. You might well tremble with fright every time you took a shower.

Once a conditioned response has been extinguished, has it vanished forever? Not necessarily. Pavlov discovered this phenomenon when he returned to his dog a few days after the conditioned behavior had seemingly been extinguished. If he rang a bell, the dog once again salivated–an effect known as spontaneous recovery. **Spontaneous recovery** is the reemergence of an extinguished conditioned response after a period of time and with no further conditioning.

spontaneous recovery The reemergence of an extinguished conditioned response after a period of rest and with no further conditioning. (Module 17)

Spontaneous recovery also helps explain why it is so hard to overcome drug addictions. For example, cocaine addicts who are thought to be "cured" can experience

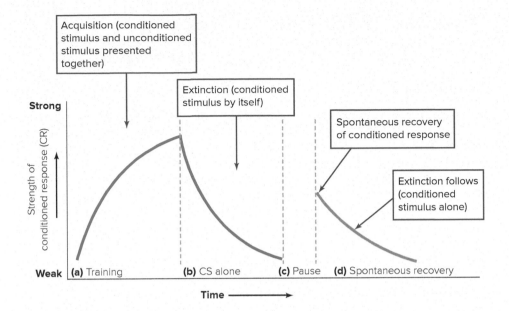

Acquisition (conditioned stimulus and unconditioned stimulus presented together)

Extinction (conditioned stimulus by itself)

Spontaneous recovery of conditioned response

Extinction follows (conditioned stimulus alone)

Strong

Weak

Strength of conditioned response (CR)

(a) Training   **(b)** CS alone   **(c)** Pause   **(d)** Spontaneous recovery

Time ⟶

FIGURE 2 Acquisition, extinction, and spontaneous recovery of a classically conditioned response. (a) A conditioned response (CR) gradually increases in strength during training. (b) However, if the conditioned stimulus (CS) is presented by itself enough times, the conditioned response gradually fades, and extinction occurs. (c) After a pause (d) in which the conditioned stimulus is not presented, spontaneous recovery can occur. However, extinction typically reoccurs soon after.

an irresistible impulse to use the drug again if they are subsequently confronted by a stimulus with strong connections to the drug, such as a white powder (Tunstall, Verendeev, & Kearns, 2013; Santos, Carey, & Carrera, 2017; Steins-Loeber et al., 2019).

Generalization and Discrimination

Despite differences in color and shape, to most of us a rose is a rose is a rose. The pleasure we experience at the beauty, smell, and grace of the flower is similar for different types of roses. Pavlov noticed a similar phenomenon. His dogs often salivated not only at the ringing of the bell that was used during their original conditioning but at the sound of a buzzer as well.

Such behavior is the result of stimulus generalization. **Stimulus generalization** is a process in which after a stimulus has been conditioned to produce a particular response, other stimuli that are similar to the original stimulus produce the same response. The greater the similarity between two stimuli, the greater the likelihood of stimulus generalization. Little Albert, who, as we mentioned earlier, was conditioned to be fearful of white rats, grew afraid of other furry white things as well. However, consistent with the principle of stimulus generalization, it is unlikely that he would have been afraid of a black dog because its color would have differentiated it sufficiently from the original fear-evoking stimulus.

The conditioned response elicited by the new stimulus is usually not as intense as the original conditioned response, although the more similar the new stimulus is to the old one, the more similar the new response will be. It is unlikely, then, that Little Albert's fear of the Santa Claus mask was as great as his learned fear of a rat. Still, stimulus generalization permits us to know, for example, that we ought to brake at all red lights, even if there are minor variations in size, shape, and shade.

In contrast, **stimulus discrimination** occurs if two stimuli are sufficiently distinct from each other such that one evokes a conditioned response but the other does not. Stimulus discrimination provides the ability to differentiate between stimuli. For example, my dog Cleo comes running into the kitchen when she hears the sound of the electric can opener, which she has learned is used to open her dog food when her dinner is about to be served. She does not bound into the kitchen at the sound of the food processor, although it sounds somewhat similar. In other words, she discriminates between the stimuli of can opener and food processor. Similarly, our ability to discriminate between the behavior of a growling dog and that of one whose tail is wagging can lead to adaptive behavior—avoiding the growling dog and petting the friendly one.

Study Alert
Remember that stimulus generalization relates to stimuli that are similar to one another, whereas stimulus discrimination relates to stimuli that are different from one another.

stimulus generalization A process in which after a stimulus has been conditioned to produce a particular response, stimuli that are similar to the original stimulus produce the same response. (Module 17)

stimulus discrimination The process that occurs if two stimuli are sufficiently distinct from one another such that one evokes a conditioned response but the other does not; the ability to differentiate between stimuli. (Module 17)

Beyond Traditional Classical Conditioning: Challenging Basic Assumptions

Although Pavlov hypothesized that all learning is nothing more than long strings of conditioned responses, this notion has not been supported by subsequent research. It turns out that classical conditioning provides us with only a partial explanation of how people and animals learn; indeed, Pavlov was wrong in some of his basic assumptions.

For example, according to Pavlov, the process of linking stimuli and responses occurs in a mechanistic, automatic, and unthinking way. In contrast to this perspective, learning theorists influenced by cognitive psychology have argued that learners actively develop an understanding and expectancy about which particular unconditioned stimuli are matched with specific conditioned stimuli. A ringing bell, for instance, gives a dog something to think about: the impending arrival of food (Kirsch et al., 2004).

Traditional explanations of how classical conditioning operates have also been challenged by John Garcia, a learning psychologist. He found that some organisms—including humans—were *biologically prepared* to quickly learn to avoid foods that smelled or tasted like something that made them sick. For instance, a dog quickly learns to avoid rotting food that in the past made it sick. Similarly, if every time you ate peanuts you had an upset stomach several hours later, eventually you would learn to avoid peanuts. In fact, you might develop a learned *taste aversion*, when the taste of a particular food is associated with unpleasant symptoms such as nausea or vomiting. If you developed a taste aversion to peanuts, merely tasting (or even smelling or in more extreme cases seeing a peanut) could produce such disagreeable symptoms (Garcia, 2003; Lin, Arthurs, & Reilly, 2017; Schier et al., 2019).

The surprising part of Garcia's discovery was his demonstration that conditioning could occur even when the interval between exposure to the conditioned stimulus of tainted food and the response of sickness was as long as 8 hours. Furthermore, the conditioning persisted over very long periods and sometimes occurred after just one exposure.

These findings have had important practical implications. For example, to keep crows from stealing eggs, dairy farmers may lace an egg with a chemical and leave it in a place where crows will find it. The drug temporarily makes the crows ill, but it does not harm them permanently. After exposure to a chemical-laden egg, crows no longer find the eggs appetizing (Baker, Johnson, & Slater, 2007; Bouton et al., 2011; Tobajas et al., 2019).

RECAP/EVALUATE/RETHINK

RECAP

LO 17-1 What is learning?

- Learning is a relatively permanent change in behavior resulting from experience.

LO 17-2 How do we learn to form associations between stimuli and responses?

- One major form of learning is classical conditioning, which occurs when a neutral stimulus—one that normally brings about no relevant response—is repeatedly paired with a stimulus (called an unconditioned stimulus) that brings about a natural, untrained response.
- Conditioning occurs when the neutral stimulus is repeatedly presented just before the unconditioned stimulus. After repeated pairings, the neutral stimulus elicits the same response that the unconditioned stimulus brings about. When this occurs, the neutral stimulus has become a conditioned stimulus, and the response a conditioned response.
- Learning is not always permanent. Extinction occurs when a previously learned response decreases in frequency and eventually disappears.
- Stimulus generalization is the tendency for a conditioned response to follow a stimulus that is similar to, but not the same as, the original conditioned stimulus. The opposite phenomenon, stimulus discrimination, occurs when an organism learns to distinguish between stimuli.

EVALUATE

1. _____ involves changes brought about by experience, whereas maturation describes changes resulting from biological development.

2. _____ is the name of the scientist responsible for discovering the learning phenomenon known as _____ conditioning, whereby an organism learns a response to a stimulus to which it normally would not respond.

Refer to the passage below to answer questions 3 through 5:
The last three times little Theresa visited Dr. Lopez for checkups, he administered a painful preventive immunization shot that left her in tears. Today, when her mother takes her for another checkup, Theresa begins to sob as soon as she comes face to face with Dr. Lopez, even before he has had a chance to say hello.

3. The painful shot that Theresa received during each visit was a(n) _____ _____ that elicited the _____ _____, her tears.

4. Dr. Lopez is upset because his presence has become a _____ _____ for Theresa's crying.

5. Fortunately, Dr. Lopez gave Theresa no more shots for quite some time. Over that period, she gradually stopped crying and even came to like him. _____ had occurred.

RETHINK

1. How likely is it that Little Albert, Watson's experimental subject, might have gone through life afraid of Santa Claus? Describe what could have happened to prevent his continual dread of Santa.

2. Can you think of ways that classical conditioning is used by politicians? Advertisers? Moviemakers? Do ethical issues arise from any of these uses?

Answers to Evaluate Questions

1. Learning; 2. Pavlov, classical; 3. unconditioned stimulus, unconditioned response; 4. conditioned stimulus; 5. Extinction

KEY TERMS

learning	unconditioned stimulus (UCS)	conditioned stimulus (CS)	stimulus generalization
classical conditioning		conditioned response (CR)	stimulus discrimination
neutral stimulus	unconditioned response (UCR)	extinction	
		spontaneous recovery	

Module 18
Operant Conditioning

LEARNING OUTCOMES

LO 18-1 What are the roles of reward and punishment in learning?

LO 18-2 What are some practical methods for bringing about behavior change, both in ourselves and in others?

operant conditioning Learning in which a voluntary response is strengthened or weakened, depending on the response's favorable or unfavorable consequences. (Module 18)

Very good . . . What a clever idea . . . Fantastic . . . I agree . . . Thank you . . . Excellent . . . Super . . . Right on . . . This is the best paper you've ever written; you get an A . . . You are really getting the hang of it . . . I'm impressed . . . You're getting a raise . . . Have a cookie . . . You look great . . . I love you . . . .

Few of us mind being the recipient of any of these comments. But what is especially noteworthy about them is that each of these simple statements can be used, through a process known as operant conditioning, to bring about powerful changes in behavior and to teach the most complex tasks. Operant conditioning is the basis for many of the most important kinds of human and animal learning.

Operant conditioning is learning in which a voluntary response is strengthened or weakened, depending on the response's favorable or unfavorable consequences. When we say that a response has been strengthened or weakened, we mean that it has been made more or less likely to recur regularly.

Unlike classical conditioning, in which the original behaviors are the natural, biological responses to the presence of a stimulus such as food, water, or pain, operant conditioning applies to voluntary responses that an organism performs deliberately to produce a desirable outcome. The term *operant* emphasizes this point: The organism *operates* on its environment to produce a desirable result. Operant conditioning is at work when we learn that toiling industriously can bring about a raise or that studying hard results in good grades.

As with classical conditioning, the basis for understanding operant conditioning was laid by work with animals. We turn now to some of that early research, which began with a simple inquiry into the behavior of cats.

Thorndike's Law of Effect

If you placed a hungry cat in a cage and then put a small piece of food outside the cage, just beyond the cat's reach, chances are that the cat would eagerly search for a way out of the cage. The cat might first claw at the sides or push against an opening. Suppose, though, you had rigged things so that the cat could escape by stepping on a small paddle that released the latch to the door of the cage (see Figure 1).

FIGURE 1 Edward L. Thorndike devised this puzzle box to study the process by which a cat learns to press a paddle to escape from the box and receive food. Do you think Thorndike's work has relevance to the question of why people voluntarily work on puzzles and play games, such as sudoku, Angry Birds, and jigsaw puzzles? Do they receive any rewards?

Eventually, as it moved around the cage, the cat would happen to step on the paddle, the door would open, and the cat would eat the food.

What would happen if you then returned the cat to the box? The next time, it would probably take a little less time for the cat to step on the paddle and escape. After a few trials, the cat would deliberately step on the paddle as soon as it was placed in the cage. What would have occurred, according to Edward L. Thorndike (1932), who studied this situation extensively, was that the cat would have learned that pressing the paddle was associated with the desirable consequence of getting food. To summarize that relationship, Thorndike formulated the *law of effect*, which states that responses that lead to satisfying consequences are more likely to be repeated.

Thorndike believed that the law of effect operates as automatically as leaves fall off a tree in autumn. It was not necessary for an organism to understand that there was a link between a response and a reward. Instead, Thorndike believed, over time and through experience, the organism would make a direct connection between the stimulus and the response without any awareness that the connection existed.

The Basics of Operant Conditioning

Thorndike's early research served as the foundation for the work of one of the 20th century's most influential psychologists, B. F. Skinner (1904–1990). You may have heard of the Skinner box (shown in Figure 2), a chamber with a highly controlled environment that was used to study operant conditioning processes with laboratory animals. Whereas Thorndike's goal was to get his cats to learn to obtain food by leaving the box, animals in a Skinner box learn to obtain food by operating on their environment within the box. Skinner became interested in specifying how behavior varies as a result of alterations in the environment.

Skinner, whose work went far beyond perfecting Thorndike's earlier apparatus, is considered the inspiration for a whole generation of psychologists studying operant conditioning. To illustrate Skinner's contribution, let's consider what happens to a rat in the typical Skinner box (Soorya, Carpenter, & Romanczyk, 2011; Huston et al., 2013; De Meyer et al., 2019).

Suppose you want to teach a hungry rat to press a lever that is in its box. At first, the rat will wander around the box, exploring the environment in a relatively

FIGURE 2 B. F. Skinner with a Skinner box used to study operant conditioning. Laboratory rats learn to press the lever in order to obtain food, which is delivered in the tray.
Nina Leen/The LIFE Picture Collection/Getty Images

random fashion. At some point, however, it will probably press the lever by chance, and when it does, it will receive a food pellet. The first time this happens, the rat will not learn the connection between pressing a lever and receiving food and will continue to explore the box. Sooner or later, the rat will press the lever again and receive a pellet, and in time the frequency of the pressing response will increase. Eventually, the rat will press the lever continually until it satisfies its hunger, thereby demonstrating that it has learned that the receipt of food is contingent on pressing the lever.

REINFORCEMENT: THE CENTRAL CONCEPT OF OPERANT CONDITIONING

Skinner called the process that leads the rat to continue pressing the key "reinforcement." **Reinforcement** is the process by which a stimulus increases the probability that a preceding behavior will be repeated. In other words, pressing the lever is more likely to occur again because of the stimulus of food.

In a situation such as this one, the food is called a reinforcer. A **reinforcer** is any stimulus that increases the probability that a preceding behavior will occur again. Hence, food is a reinforcer because it increases the probability that the behavior of pressing (formally referred to as the *response* of pressing) will take place.

What kind of stimuli can act as reinforcers? Bonuses, toys, and good grades can serve as reinforcers–if they strengthen the probability of the response that occurred before their introduction. What makes something a reinforcer depends on individual preferences. Although a Hershey's bar can act as a reinforcer for one person, an individual who dislikes chocolate may find one dollar more desirable. The only way we can know if a stimulus is a reinforcer for a particular organism is to observe whether the frequency of a previously occurring behavior increases after the presentation of the stimulus.

Of course, we are not born knowing that one dollar can buy us a candy bar. Rather, through experience we learn that money is a valuable commodity because of its association with stimuli, such as food and drink, that are naturally reinforcing. This fact suggests a distinction between primary reinforcers and secondary reinforcers. A *primary reinforcer* satisfies some biological need and works naturally, regardless of a person's previous experience. Examples of primary reinforcers include food for a hungry person, warmth for a cold person, and relief for a person in pain.

In contrast, a *secondary reinforcer* is a stimulus that becomes reinforcing because of its association with a primary reinforcer. For instance, we know that money is valuable because we have learned that it allows us to obtain other desirable objects, including primary reinforcers such as food and shelter. Money thus becomes a secondary reinforcer (Qu, Zhang, & Chen, 2013; Thrailkill & Bouton, 2017; Rosenthal-von der Pütten et al., 2019).

Secondary reinforcers make up the heart of *token systems* sometimes used in the treatment of some psychological disorders for those who are in institutions. In a token system, a patient is rewarded for showing desired behavior with a token such as a poker chip. The token–an example of a secondary reinforcer–can then be redeemed for something desirable, such as snacks, games, or money.

Neuroscientists are beginning to explore the biological underpinnings of reinforcers. For example, we now know that the neurotransmitter *dopamine* plays a key role in the reinforcement of behavior. When we are exposed to certain kinds of stimuli, a flood of dopamine cascades through parts of the brain, leading to feelings of pleasure that are reinforcing (Trujillo-Pisanty et al., 2011; Thompson & Wolpaw, 2015).

POSITIVE REINFORCERS, NEGATIVE REINFORCERS, AND PUNISHMENT

In many respects, reinforcers can be thought of in terms of rewards; both a reinforcer and a reward increase the probability that a preceding response will occur again. But the term *reward* is limited to *positive* occurrences, and this is where it differs from a reinforcer–for it turns out that reinforcers can be positive or negative.

reinforcement The process by which a stimulus increases the probability that a preceding behavior will be repeated. (Module 18)

reinforcer Any stimulus that increases the probability that a preceding behavior will occur again. (Module 18)

! Study Alert
Remember that primary reinforcers satisfy a biological need; secondary reinforcers are effective due to previous association with a primary reinforcer.

A **positive reinforcer** is a stimulus *added* to the environment that brings about an increase in a preceding response. If food, water, money, or praise is provided after a response, it is more likely that that response will occur again in the future. The paychecks that workers get at the end of the week, for example, increase the likelihood that they will return to their jobs the following week.

In contrast, a **negative reinforcer** refers to an unpleasant stimulus whose removal leads to an increase in the probability that a preceding response will be repeated in the future. For example, if you have an itchy rash (an unpleasant stimulus) that is relieved when you apply a certain brand of ointment, you are more likely to use that ointment the next time you have an itchy rash. Using the ointment, then, is negatively reinforcing because it removes the unpleasant itch. Similarly, if your smartphone's volume is so loud that it hurts your ears when you first turn it on, you are likely to reduce the volume level. Lowering the volume is negatively reinforcing, and you are more apt to repeat the action in the future when you first turn it on. Negative reinforcement, then, teaches the individual that taking an action removes a negative condition that exists in the environment. Like positive reinforcers, negative reinforcers increase the likelihood that preceding behaviors will be repeated (Magoon & Critchfield, 2008; DePaolo, Gravina, & Harvey, 2019).

Note that negative reinforcement is not the same as punishment. **Punishment** refers to a stimulus that *decreases* the probability that a prior behavior will occur again. Unlike negative reinforcement, which produces an *increase* in behavior, punishment reduces the likelihood of a prior response. If we receive a shock that is meant to decrease a certain behavior, then we are receiving punishment, but if we are already receiving a shock and do something to stop that shock, the behavior that stops the shock is considered to be negatively reinforced. In the first case, the specific behavior is apt to decrease because of the punishment; in the second, it is likely to increase because of the negative reinforcement.

There are two types of punishment: positive punishment and negative punishment, just as there are positive reinforcement and negative reinforcement. In both cases, "positive" means adding something, and "negative" means removing something. *Positive punishment* weakens a response by applying an unpleasant stimulus. For instance, spanking a child for misbehaving or sending someone to jail for 10 years for committing a crime are examples of positive punishment. (In both cases, an unpleasant stimulus has been applied.)

In contrast, *negative punishment* consists of the removal of something pleasant. For instance, when a teenager is told she can no longer use her cell phone because she stayed out past her curfew or when an employee is informed that he will have a cut in pay because of a poor job evaluation, negative punishment is being administered. (In both cases, something pleasant–cell phone use or more pay–is being removed.)

Both positive and negative punishment result in a decrease in the likelihood that a prior behavior will be repeated. So a jail term is meant to lead to a reduction in criminal behavior, and loss of a teenager's cell phone is meant to reduce the likelihood of staying out past curfew.

The following rules (and the summary in Figure 3) can help you distinguish these concepts from one another:

- Reinforcement *increases* the frequency of the behavior preceding it; punishment *decreases* the frequency of the behavior preceding it.
- The *application* of a *positive* stimulus brings about an increase in the frequency of behavior and is referred to as positive reinforcement; the *application* of a *negative* stimulus decreases or reduces the frequency of behavior and is called positive punishment.
- The *removal* of a *negative* stimulus that results in an increase in the frequency of behavior is negative reinforcement; the *removal* of a *positive* stimulus that decreases the frequency of behavior is negative punishment.

positive reinforcer A stimulus added to the environment that brings about an increase in a preceding response. (Module 18)

negative reinforcer An unpleasant stimulus whose removal leads to an increase in the probability that a preceding response will be repeated in the future. (Module 18)

punishment A stimulus that decreases the probability that a previous behavior will occur again. (Module 18)

! Study Alert
The differences between positive reinforcement, negative reinforcement, positive punishment, and negative punishment are tricky, so pay special attention to Figure 3 and the definitions in the text.

Intended result	When stimulus is added, the result is. . .	When stimulus is removed or terminated, the result is . . .
Increase in behavior (reinforcement)	**Positive reinforcement** Example: Giving a raise for good performance Result: *Increase* in response of good performance	**Negative reinforcement** Example: Applying ointment to relieve an itchy rash leads to a higher future likelihood of applying the ointment Result: *Increase* in response of using ointment
Decrease in behavior (punishment)	**Positive punishment** Example: Yelling at a teenager when she steals a bracelet Result: *Decrease* in frequency of response of stealing	**Negative punishment** Example: Restricting teenager's access to car due to breaking curfew Result: Decrease in response of breaking curfew

FIGURE 3 Types of reinforcement and punishment.

(Top, Left): ©Andrey_Popov/Shutterstock; (Top, Right): Stockbyte/Getty Images; (Bottom, Left): Light Field Studios/123RF; (Bottom, Right): ©Amy Etra/PhotoEdit

THE PROS AND CONS OF PUNISHMENT: WHY REINFORCEMENT BEATS PUNISHMENT

Is punishment an effective way to modify behavior? Punishment often presents the quickest route to changing behavior that, if allowed to continue, might be dangerous to an individual. For instance, a parent may not have a second chance to warn a child not to run into a busy street, and so punishing the first incidence of this behavior may prove to be wise. Moreover, the use of punishment to suppress behavior, even temporarily, provides an opportunity to reinforce a person for subsequently behaving in a more desirable way (Bruno, 2016).

However, punishment has several disadvantages that make its routine use questionable. For one thing, punishment is frequently ineffective, particularly if it is not delivered shortly after the undesired behavior or if the individual is able to leave the setting in which the punishment is being given. An employee who is reprimanded by the boss may quit; a teenager who loses the use of the family car may borrow a friend's car instead. In such instances, the initial behavior that is being punished may be replaced by one that is even less desirable.

Even worse, physical punishment can convey to the recipient the idea that physical aggression is permissible and perhaps even desirable. A father who yells at and hits his son for misbehaving teaches the son that aggression is an appropriate, adult response. The son soon may copy his father's behavior by acting aggressively toward others. In addition, physical punishment is often administered by people who are themselves angry or enraged. It is unlikely that individuals in such an emotional state will be able to think through what they are doing or control carefully the degree of punishment they are inflicting. Ultimately, those who resort to physical punishment run the risk that they will grow to be feared. Punishment can also reduce the self-esteem of recipients unless they can understand the reasons for it (Smith, Springer, & Barrett, 2011; Alampay et al., 2017; Gonzalez et al., 2019).

APPLYING PSYCHOLOGY IN THE 21ST CENTURY

SPANKING CHILDREN MAKES THINGS WORSE

Perhaps you've seen it yourself: a harried parent in a shopping center, a child who is out of control, some embarrassment or frustration thrown into the mix, and the desperate parent resorts to spanking the child. Or perhaps it's more urgent: The child's behavior is putting him or someone else in danger of serious harm, and he must be corrected immediately. Is spanking appropriate in that circumstance? Is it ever appropriate?

Many adults think it is, at least sometimes. One survey found that about two-thirds of American parents agreed with the statement "sometimes a child just needs a good hard spanking" (Clement, 2015).

But a large and growing body of research on this question doesn't concur. For example, a large-scale analysis of five decades of studies showed significant links between spanking and multiple detrimental child outcomes, such as further misbehavior and mental health problems. In fact, some outcomes of spanking are similar to the outcomes of physical abuse (Gershoff & Grogan-Kaylor, 2016).

Still, research on the effects of spanking has been hampered by an important methodological problem: It's not ethical to run a controlled study with random assignment, with some parents assigned to spank their children and others to never spank their children. But a recent study attempts to tackle that problem head-on (Gershoff, 2017).

In the study, researchers examined data from over 12,000 children participating in

Experts concur: spanking is *never* appropriate.

Parinya Agsararattananont/123RF

the national Early Childhood Longitudinal Study. The data included parental reports taken at age 5 of how often they spanked their child in the past week, which the research team used to divide the sample into children who had been spanked at that age and those who had not. The team then matched pairs of spanked and unspanked children on 38 other characteristics of the child and the family reported in the longitudinal study, such as parental age and education, socioeconomic status, parenting style, and general conflict in the home. Pairing in

this fashion created two groups of children who were equal in all these respects, except that one group had been spanked at age 5 and the other had not, as a way of approximating the experimental control provided by random assignment (Gershoff, Sattler, & Ansari, 2018).

The longitudinal study data included teacher reports of how frequently they observed various misbehaviors such as arguing, fighting, angry outbursts, and interrupting ongoing activities at ages 6 and 8. The results were clear: The children who had been spanked at age 5 showed significantly more misbehavior at ages 6 and 8 than children who had not been spanked at that age.

"The fact that knowing whether a child had ever been spanked was enough to predict their levels of behavior problems years later was a bit surprising," said the lead researcher, Elizabeth Gershoff. "It suggests that spanking at any frequency is potentially harmful to children" (Gershoff, 2017).

QUESTIONS TO CONSIDER

- Why do you think a majority of parents advocate spanking if it leads to such negative outcomes?
- Why do you think children respond to being spanked by acting out more? What might be some reasons why spanking doesn't work as an effective form of positive punishment?

Finally, punishment does not convey any information about what an alternative, more appropriate behavior might be. To be useful in bringing about more desirable behavior in the future, punishment must be accompanied by specific information about the behavior that is being punished, along with specific suggestions concerning a more desirable behavior. Punishing a child for staring out the window in school could merely lead her to stare at the floor instead. Unless we teach her appropriate ways to respond, we have merely managed to substitute one undesirable behavior for another. If punishment is not followed up with reinforcement for subsequent behavior that is more appropriate, little will be accomplished. That's why the scientific research is clear: spanking is both ineffective and ultimately harmful to children. Even punishment in the form of yelling is damaging (Wang & Kenny, 2013; Kubanek, Snyder, & Abrams, 2015; also see the *Applying Psychology in the 21st Century* feature).

In short, reinforcing desired behavior is a more appropriate technique for modifying behavior than is using punishment. Both in and out of the scientific arena, then, reinforcement usually beats punishment (Sidman, 2006; Hall et al., 2011; Bruno, 2016).

SCHEDULES OF REINFORCEMENT: TIMING LIFE'S REWARDS

The world would be a different place if poker players never played cards again after the first losing hand, fishermen returned to shore as soon as they missed a catch, or telemarketers never made another phone call after their first hang-up. The fact that such unreinforced behaviors continue, often with great frequency and persistence, illustrates that reinforcement need not be received continually for behavior to be learned and maintained. In fact, behavior that is reinforced only occasionally can ultimately be learned better than can behavior that is always reinforced.

The pattern of the frequency and timing of reinforcement that follow desired behavior is known as the **schedule of reinforcement.** In a **continuous reinforcement schedule,** behavior is reinforced every time it occurs. In contrast, in a **partial (or intermittent) reinforcement schedule**, behavior is reinforced some but not all the time it occurs. Although learning occurs more rapidly under a continuous reinforcement schedule, behavior lasts longer after reinforcement stops when it was learned under a partial reinforcement schedule (Reed, 2007; Holtyn & Lattal, 2013; Mullane et al., 2017).

Why should intermittent reinforcement result in stronger, longer-lasting learning than with continuous reinforcement? We can answer the question by examining how we might behave when using a candy vending machine compared with a Las Vegas slot machine. When we use a vending machine, previous experience has taught us that every time we put in the appropriate amount of money, the reinforcement, a candy bar, ought to be delivered. In other words, the schedule of reinforcement is continuous. In comparison, a slot machine offers intermittent reinforcement. We have learned that after putting in our cash, most of the time we will not receive anything in return. At the same time, though, we know that we will occasionally win something.

Now suppose that, unknown to us, both the candy vending machine and the slot machine are broken, and so neither one is able to dispense anything. It would not be very long before we stopped depositing coins into the broken candy machine. Probably at most we would try only two or three times before leaving the machine in disgust. But the story would be quite different with the broken slot machine. Here, we would drop in money for a considerably longer time, even though there would be no payoff.

In formal terms, we can see the difference between the two reinforcement schedules: Partial reinforcement schedules (such as those provided by slot machines) maintain performance longer than do continuous reinforcement schedules (such as those established in candy vending machines) before *extinction*–the disappearance of the conditioned response–occurs.

Fixed- and Variable-Ratio Schedules   Certain kinds of partial reinforcement schedules produce stronger and lengthier responding before extinction than do others. Some schedules are related to the *number of responses* made before reinforcement is given, and others are related to the *amount of time* that elapses before reinforcement is provided (Miguez, Witnauer, & Miller, 2011; Manzo et al., 2015; Langford, Pitts, & Hughes, 2019).

In a **fixed-ratio schedule,** reinforcement is given only after a specific number of responses. For instance, a rat might receive a food pellet every 10th time it pressed a lever; here, the ratio would be 1:10. Similarly, garment workers are generally paid on fixed-ratio schedules: They receive a specific number of dollars for every blouse they sew. Because a greater rate of production means more reinforcement, people on fixed-ratio schedules are apt to work as quickly as possible (see Figure 4).

In a **variable-ratio schedule,** behaviors are reinforced after an average number of responses, but exactly when reinforcement will occur is unpredictable. A good example of a variable-ratio schedule is a telephone salesperson's job. He might make a sale during the 3rd, 8th, 9th, and 20th calls without being successful during any call in between. Although the number of responses he must make before closing a sale

---

schedule of reinforcement The pattern of frequency and timing of reinforcement following desired behavior. (Module 18)

continuous reinforcement schedule A schedule in which behavior is reinforced every time the behavior occurs. (Module 18)

partial (or intermittent) reinforcement schedule Reinforcing of a behavior some but not all of the time. (Module 18)

fixed-ratio schedule A schedule in which reinforcement is given only after a specific number of responses are made. (Module 18)

variable-ratio schedule A schedule in which reinforcement occurs after an average number of responses, but the reinforcement schedule is unpredictable. (Module 18)

Study Alert

Remember that the different schedules of reinforcement affect the rapidity with which a response is learned and how long it lasts after reinforcement is no longer provided.

(a) Fixed-ratio schedule

Cumulative frequency of responses

There are relatively short pauses in responding after reinforcement is provided.

Time

(b) Variable-ratio schedule

Cumulative frequency of responses

Responding occurs at a high, steady rate.

Time

(c) Fixed-interval schedule

Cumulative frequency of responses

There are typically long pauses in responding after reinforcement is provided.

Time

(d) Variable-interval schedule

Cumulative frequency of responses

Responding occurs at a steady rate.

Time

FIGURE 4 Typical outcomes of different reinforcement schedules. (a) In a fixed-ratio schedule, reinforcement is provided after a specific number of responses are made. Because more responses lead to more reinforcement, fixed-ratio schedules produce a high rate of responding. (b) In a variable-ratio schedule, responding also occurs at a high rate. (c) A fixed-interval schedule produces lower rates of responding, especially just after reinforcement has been presented, because the organism learns that a specified time period must elapse between reinforcements. (d) A variable-interval schedule produces a fairly steady stream of responses.

varies, it averages out to a 20% success rate. Under these circumstances, you might expect that the salesperson would try to make as many calls as possible in as short a time as possible. This is the case with all variable ratio schedules, which lead to a high rate of response and resistance to extinction.

Fixed- and Variable-Interval Schedules: The Passage of Time In contrast to fixed and variable-ratio schedules, in which the crucial factor is the *number* of responses, fixed-interval and variable-interval schedules focus on the *amount of time* that has elapsed since a person or animal was rewarded. One example of a fixed-interval schedule is a weekly paycheck. For people who receive regular, weekly paychecks, it typically makes relatively little difference exactly how much they produce in a given week.

A **fixed-interval schedule** provides reinforcement for a response only if a fixed time period has elapsed. Consequently, overall rates of response are relatively low. This is especially true in the period just after reinforcement, when the time before another reinforcement is relatively great. Students' study habits often exemplify this reality. If the periods between exams are relatively long (meaning that the opportunity for reinforcement for good performance is given fairly infrequently), students often study minimally or not at all until the day of the exam draws near. Just before the exam, however, students begin to cram for it, signaling a rapid increase in the rate of their studying response. As you might expect, immediately after the exam there is a rapid decline in the rate of responding, with few people opening a book the day after a test. Fixed-interval schedules produce the kind of "scalloping" pattern shown in Figure 4 (Saville, 2009; Daniels & Sanabria, 2017).

One way to decrease the delay in responding that occurs just after reinforcement and to maintain the desired behavior more consistently throughout an interval

fixed-interval schedule A schedule in which reinforcement is provided for a response only after a fixed time period has elapsed. (Module 18)

variable-interval schedule A schedule by which the time between reinforcements varies around some average rather than being fixed. (Module 18)

is to use a variable-interval schedule. In a **variable-interval schedule,** the time between reinforcements varies around some average rather than being fixed. For example, a professor who gives surprise quizzes that vary from one every 3 days to one every 3 weeks, averaging one every 2 weeks, is using a variable-interval schedule. Compared to the study habits we observed with a fixed-interval schedule, students' study habits under such a variable-interval schedule would most likely be very different. Students would be apt to study more regularly because they would never know when the next surprise quiz was coming. Variable-interval schedules, in general, are more likely to produce relatively steady rates of responding than are fixed-interval schedules, with responses that take longer to extinguish after reinforcement ends.

From the perspective of...

An Educator How would you use your knowledge of operant conditioning to set up a program to increase the likelihood that students will complete their homework more frequently?

Andersen Ross/Blend Images/Getty Images

DISCRIMINATION AND GENERALIZATION IN OPERANT CONDITIONING

It does not take a child long to learn that a red light at an intersection means stop and a green light indicates that it is permissible to continue, in the same way that a pigeon can learn to peck a key when a green light goes on but not when a red light appears. Just as in classical conditioning, then, operant learning involves the phenomena of discrimination and generalization.

The process by which people learn to discriminate stimuli is known as stimulus control training. In *stimulus control training,* a behavior is reinforced in the presence of a specific stimulus but not in its absence. For example, one of the most difficult discriminations many people face is determining when someone's friendliness is not mere friendliness but a signal of romantic interest. People learn to make the discrimination by observing the presence of certain nonverbal cues–such as increased eye contact and touching–that indicate romantic interest. When such cues are absent, people learn that no romantic interest is indicated. In this case, the nonverbal cue acts as a discriminative stimulus, one to which an organism learns to respond during stimulus control training. A *discriminative stimulus* signals the likelihood that reinforcement will follow a response. For example, if you wait until your roommate is in a good mood before you ask to borrow her favorite sweater, your behavior can be said to be under stimulus control because you can discriminate between her moods.

Just as in classical conditioning, the phenomenon of stimulus generalization, in which an organism learns a response to one stimulus and then exhibits the same response to slightly different stimuli, occurs in operant conditioning. If you have learned that being polite helps you to get your way in a certain situation (reinforcing your politeness), you are likely to generalize your response to other situations. Sometimes, though, generalization can have unfortunate consequences, as when people behave negatively toward all members of a racial group because they have had an unpleasant experience with one member of that group.

PsychTech

Computer-based *adaptive learning* techniques—based on the principles of shaping—present students with new material and then quiz them on it online. Presentation of subsequent material is based on students' previous performance on the quiz, so that the level and difficulty of new material are personalized, leading to great student success.

SHAPING: REINFORCING WHAT DOESN'T COME NATURALLY

Consider the difficulty of using operant conditioning to teach people to repair an automobile transmission. If you had to wait until they chanced to fix a transmission perfectly before you provided them with reinforcement, the Model T Ford might be back in style long before they mastered the repair process.

There are many complex behaviors, ranging from auto repair to zoo management, that we would not expect to occur naturally as part of anyone's spontaneous behavior. For such behaviors, for which there might otherwise be no opportunity to provide reinforcement (because the behavior would never occur in the first place), a procedure known as shaping is used. **Shaping** is the process of teaching a complex behavior by rewarding closer and closer approximations of the desired behavior. In shaping, you start by reinforcing any behavior that is at all similar to the behavior you want the person to learn. Later, you reinforce only responses that are closer to the behavior you ultimately want to teach. Finally, you reinforce only the desired response. Each step in shaping, then, moves only slightly beyond the previously learned behavior, permitting the person to link the new step to the behavior learned earlier (Krueger & Dayan, 2009; Egervari et al., 2017).

shaping The process of teaching a complex behavior by rewarding closer and closer approximations of the desired behavior. (Module 18)

Shaping allows even lower animals to learn complex responses that would never occur naturally, ranging from lions jumping through hoops, dolphins rescuing divers lost at sea, or rodents finding hidden land mines. Shaping also underlies the learning of many complex human skills. For instance, the organization of most textbooks is based on the principles of shaping. Typically, information is presented so that new material builds on previously learned concepts or skills. Thus, the concept of shaping could not be presented until we had discussed the more basic principles of operant learning

BIOLOGICAL CONSTRAINTS ON LEARNING: YOU CAN'T TEACH AN OLD DOG JUST ANY TRICK

Not all behaviors can be trained in all species equally well. Instead, there are *biological constraints*, built-in limitations in the ability of animals to learn particular behaviors. In some cases, an organism has a special predisposition that will aid in its learning a behavior (such as pecking behaviors in pigeons). In other cases, biological constraints act to prevent or inhibit an organism from learning a behavior.

For example, it's impossible to train pigs to pick up a disk because they are genetically programmed to push objects like it along the ground and *not* genetically programmed to pick objects up. Similarly, although a raccoon can be conditioned to drop a single coin into a piggy bank, it will do so only after rubbing the coin against the outside of the bank. The reason? After catching a fish, raccoons instinctively rub them against the ground to remove their outer covering (Breland & Breland, 1966; Thurman & Lu, 2013).

The existence of biological constraints is consistent with evolutionary explanations of behavior. Clearly, there are adaptive benefits that promote survival for organisms that quickly learn—or avoid—certain behaviors. For example, our ability to rapidly learn to avoid touching hot surfaces increases our chances of survival. Additional support for the evolutionary interpretation of biological constraints lies in the fact the associations that animals learn most readily involve stimuli that are most relevant to the specific environment in which they live (Cosmides & Tooby, 2004; Davis, 2007; Behrendt, 2011).

Furthermore, psychologists taking an evolutionary perspective have suggested that we may be genetically predisposed to be fearful of certain stimuli, such as snakes or even threatening

Biological constraints make it nearly impossible for animals to learn certain behaviors. Here, psychologist Marian Breland Bailey attempts to overcome the natural limitations that inhibit the success of conditioning this rooster.

Dr. Marian Breland Bailey

faces. For example, people in experiments learn associations relatively quickly between photos of faces with threatening expressions and neutral stimuli (such as an umbrella). In contrast, they are slower to learn associations between faces that have pleasant expressions and neutral stimuli. Stimuli that pose potential threats, such as snakes or people with hostile facial expressions, posed a potential danger to early humans, and there may be an evolved "fear module" in the brain that is sensitized to such threats (DeLoache & LoBue, 2009; Gerdes, Uhl, & Alpers, 2009; Lester et al., 2017).

COMPARING CLASSICAL AND OPERANT CONDITIONING

We've considered classical conditioning and operant conditioning as two completely different processes. And, as summarized in Figure 5, there are a number of key distinctions between the two forms of learning. For example, the key concept in classical conditioning is the association between stimuli, whereas in operant conditioning it is reinforcement. Furthermore, classical conditioning involves an involuntary, natural, innate behavior, but operant conditioning is based on voluntary responses made by an organism.

Some researchers are asking if, in fact, the two types of learning are so different after all. Some learning psychologists have suggested that classical and operant conditioning might share some underlying processes. Arguing from an evolutionary viewpoint, they contend that it is unlikely that two completely separate basic processes would evolve. Instead, one process—albeit with considerable complexity in the way it operates—might better explain behavior. Although it's too early to know if this point of view will be supported, it is clear that there are a number of processes that operate both in classical and operant conditioning, including extinction, stimulus generalization, and stimulus discrimination (Donahoe & Vegas, 2004; Silva, Gonçalves, & Garcia-Mijares, 2007; Lattal et al., 2017).

Concept	Classical Conditioning	Operant Conditioning
Basic principle	Building associations between a conditioned stimulus and conditioned response	Reinforcement *increases* the frequency of the behavior preceding it; punishment *decreases* the frequency of the behavior preceding it.
Nature of behavior	Based on involuntary, natural, innate behavior. Behavior is elicited by the unconditioned or conditioned stimulus.	Organism voluntarily operates on its environment to produce a desirable result. After behavior occurs, the likelihood of the behavior occurring again is increased or decreased by the behavior's consequences.
Order of events	Before conditioning, an unconditioned stimulus leads to an unconditioned response. After conditioning, a conditioned stimulus leads to a conditioned response.	Reinforcement leads to an increase in behavior; punishment leads to a decrease in behavior.
Example	After a physician gives a child a series of painful injections (an unconditioned stimulus) that produce an emotional reaction (an unconditioned response), the child develops an emotional reaction (a conditioned response) whenever he sees the physician (the conditioned stimulus).	A student who, after studying hard for a test, earns an A (the positive reinforcer), is more likely to study hard in the future. A student who, after going out drinking the night before a test, fails the test (punishment) is less likely to go out drinking the night before the next test.

FIGURE 5 Comparing key concepts in classical conditioning and operant conditioning.
(Left): Jill Braaten/McGraw-Hill; (Right): Antoniodiaz/Shutterstock

BECOMING AN INFORMED CONSUMER
of Psychology

Using Behavior Analysis and Behavior Modification

A couple who had been living together for 3 years began to fight frequently. The issues of disagreement ranged from who was going to do the dishes to the quality of their love life.

Disturbed, the couple went to a *behavior analyst,* a psychologist who specialized in behavior-modification techniques. He asked them to keep a detailed written record of their interactions over the next 2 weeks.

When they returned with the data, he carefully reviewed the records with them. In doing so, he noticed a pattern: Each of their arguments had occurred just after one or the other had left a household chore undone, such as leaving dirty dishes in the sink or draping clothes on the only chair in the bedroom.

Using the data the couple had collected, the behavior analyst asked them to list all the chores that could possibly arise and assign each one a point value depending on how long it took to complete. Then he had them divide the chores equally and agree in a written contract to fulfill the ones assigned to them. If either failed to carry out one of the assigned chores, he or she would have to place $1 per point in a fund for the other to spend. They also agreed to a program of verbal praise, promising to reward each other verbally for completing a chore.

The couple agreed to try it for a month and to keep careful records of the number of arguments they had during that period. To their surprise, the number declined rapidly.

The case just presented provides an illustration of behavior modification. **Behavior modification** is a technique for increasing the frequency of desirable behaviors and decreasing the incidence of unwanted ones.

Using the basic principles of learning theory, behavior-modification techniques have proved to be helpful in a variety of situations. People with severe intellectual disability have been taught to dress and feed themselves for the first time in their lives. Behavior modification has also helped people lose weight, give up smoking, behave more safely, and study more effectively (Geller, 2011; Etienne, 2013; Warmbold-Brann et al., 2017; Hutten-Lenz, 2019).

The techniques used by behavior analysts are as varied as the list of processes that modify behavior. They include reinforcement scheduling, shaping, generalization training, discrimination training, and extinction. Participants in a behavior-change program do, however, typically follow a series of similar basic steps that include the following:

- *Identifying goals and target behaviors.* The first step is to define desired behavior. Is it an increase in time spent studying? A decrease in weight? An increase in the use of language? A reduction in the amount of aggression displayed by a child? The goals must be stated in observable terms and must lead to specific targets. For instance, a goal might be "to increase study time," whereas the target behavior would be "to study at least 2 hours per day on weekdays and an hour on Saturdays."
- *Designing a data-recording system and recording preliminary data.* To determine whether behavior has changed, it is necessary to collect data before any changes are made in the situation. This information provides a baseline against which future changes can be measured.
- *Selecting a behavior-change strategy.* The crucial step is to choose an appropriate strategy. Typically, a variety of treatments is used. This might include the systematic use of positive reinforcement for desired behavior (verbal praise or something more tangible, such as food), as well as a program of extinction for undesirable behavior (ignoring a child who throws a tantrum). Selecting the right reinforcers is critical, and it may be necessary to experiment a bit to find out what is important to a particular individual.

behavior modification A technique whose goal is to increase the frequency of desirable behaviors and decrease the incidence of unwanted ones (Module 18)

- *Implementing the program.* Probably the most important aspect of program implementation is consistency. It is also important to reinforce the intended behavior. For example, suppose a mother wants her son to spend more time on his homework, but as soon as he sits down to study, he asks for a snack. If the mother gets a snack for him, she is likely to be reinforcing her son's delaying tactic, not his studying.
- *Keeping careful records after the program is implemented.* Another crucial task is record keeping. If the target behaviors are not monitored, there is no way of knowing whether the program has actually been successful.
- *Evaluating and altering the ongoing program.* Finally, the results of the program should be compared with baseline, preimplementation data to determine its effectiveness. If the program has been successful, the procedures employed can be phased out gradually. For instance, if the program called for reinforcing every instance of picking up one's clothes from the bedroom floor, the reinforcement schedule could be modified to a fixed-ratio schedule in which every third instance is reinforced. However, if the program has not been successful in bringing about the desired behavior change, consideration of other approaches might be advisable.

Behavior-change techniques based on these general principles have enjoyed wide success and have proved to be one of the most powerful means of modifying behavior. Clearly, it is possible to employ the basic notions of learning theory to improve our lives.

RECAP/EVALUATE/RETHINK

RECAP

LO 18-1 What are the roles of reward and punishment in learning?

- Operant conditioning is a form of learning in which a voluntary behavior is strengthened or weakened. According to B. F. Skinner, the major mechanism underlying learning is reinforcement, the process by which a stimulus increases the probability that a preceding behavior will be repeated.
- Primary reinforcers are rewards that are naturally effective without previous experience because they satisfy a biological need. Secondary reinforcers begin to act as if they were primary reinforcers through association with a primary reinforcer.
- Positive reinforcers are stimuli that are added to the environment and lead to an increase in a preceding response. Negative reinforcers are stimuli that remove something unpleasant from the environment, also leading to an increase in the preceding response.
- Punishment decreases the probability that a prior behavior will occur. Positive punishment weakens a response through the application of an unpleasant stimulus, whereas negative punishment weakens a response by the removal of something positive. In contrast to reinforcement, in which the goal is to increase the incidence of behavior, punishment is meant to decrease or suppress behavior.
- Schedules and patterns of reinforcement affect the strength and duration of learning. Generally, partial reinforcement schedules—in which reinforcers are not delivered on every trial—produce stronger and longer-lasting learning than do continuous reinforcement schedules.
- Among the major categories of reinforcement schedules are fixed- and variable-ratio schedules, which are based on the number of responses made, and fixed- and variable-interval schedules, which are based on the time interval that elapses before reinforcement is provided.
- Stimulus control training (similar to stimulus discrimination in classical conditioning) is reinforcement of a behavior in the presence of a specific stimulus but not in its absence. In stimulus generalization, an organism learns a response to one stimulus and then exhibits the same response to slightly different stimuli.
- Shaping is a process for teaching complex behaviors by rewarding closer and closer approximations of the desired final behavior.
- There are biological constraints, or built-in limitations, on the ability of an organism to learn: Certain behaviors will be relatively easy for individuals of a species to learn, whereas other behaviors will be either difficult or impossible for them to learn.

LO 18-2 What are some practical methods for bringing about behavior change, both in ourselves and in others?

- Behavior modification is a method for formally using the principles of learning theory to promote the frequency of desired behaviors and to decrease or eliminate unwanted ones.

EVALUATE

1. _____ conditioning describes learning that occurs as a result of reinforcement.
2. Match the type of operant learning with its definition:

   1. An unpleasant stimulus is presented to decrease behavior.
   2. An unpleasant stimulus is removed to increase behavior.
   3. A pleasant stimulus is presented to increase behavior.
   4. A pleasant stimulus is removed to decrease behavior.

   a. positive reinforcement
   b. negative reinforcement
   c. positive punishment
   d. negative punishment

3. Sandy had had a rough day, and his son's noisemaking was not helping him relax. Not wanting to resort to scolding, Sandy told his son in a serious manner that he was very tired and would like the boy to play quietly for an hour. This approach worked. For Sandy, the change in his son's behavior was
   a. positively reinforcing.
   b. negatively reinforcing.
4. In a _____ reinforcement schedule, behavior is reinforced some of the time, whereas in a _____ reinforcement schedule, behavior is reinforced all the time.

5. Match the type of reinforcement schedule with its definition.

   1. Reinforcement occurs after a set time period.
   2. Reinforcement occurs after a set number of responses.
   3. Reinforcement occurs after a varying time period.
   4. Reinforcement occurs after a varying number of responses.

   a. fixed-ratio
   b. variable-interval
   c. fixed-interval
   d. variable-ratio

RETHINK

1. Using the scientific literature as a guide, what would you tell parents who want to know if the routine use of physical punishment is a necessary and acceptable form of child rearing?
2. How might operant conditioning be used to address serious personal concerns, such as smoking and unhealthy eating?

Answers to Evaluate Questions

1. Operant; 2. 1-c, 2-b, 3-a, 4-d; 3. b; 4. partial (or intermittent), continuous; 5. 1-c, 2-a, 3-b, 4-d

KEY TERMS

operant conditioning
reinforcement
reinforcer
positive reinforcer
negative reinforcer

punishment
schedule of reinforcement
continuous reinforcement
  schedule

partial (or intermittent)
  reinforcement schedule
fixed-ratio schedule
variable-ratio schedule

fixed-interval schedule
variable-interval schedule
shaping
behavior modification

Module 19
Cognitive Approaches to Learning

LEARNING OUTCOMES

LO 19-1 What are the roles of cognition and thought in learning?

Consider what happens when people learn to drive a car. They don't just get behind the wheel and stumble around until they randomly put the key into the ignition and, later, after many false starts, accidentally manage to get the car to move forward, thereby receiving positive reinforcement. Rather, they already know the basic elements of driving from previous experience as passengers, when they more than likely noticed how the key was inserted into the ignition, the car was put in drive, and the gas pedal was pressed to make the car go forward.

Previous experience as an observant passenger in a car helps people learn to drive themselves.
Garnet Photo/Shutterstock

Study Alert

Remember that the cognitive learning approach focuses on the *internal* thoughts and expectations of learners, whereas classical and operant conditioning approaches focus on *external* stimuli, responses, and reinforcement.

cognitive learning theory An approach to the study of learning that focuses on the thought processes that underlie learning. (Module 19)

Clearly, not all learning is due to operant and classical conditioning. In fact, such activities as learning to drive a car imply that some kinds of learning must involve higher-order processes in which people's thoughts and memories and the way they process information account for their responses. Such situations argue against regarding learning as the unthinking, mechanical, and automatic acquisition of associations between stimuli and responses, as in classical conditioning, or the presentation of reinforcement, as in operant conditioning.

Some psychologists view learning in terms of the thought processes, or cognitions, that underlie it, an approach known as cognitive learning theory. **Cognitive learning theory** focuses on how people think. Psychologists who use the cognitive learning perspective do not deny the importance of classical and operant conditioning; however, they have developed approaches that focus on the unseen mental processes that occur during learning, rather than concentrating solely on external stimuli, responses, and reinforcements.

In its most basic formulation, cognitive learning theory suggests that it is not enough to say that people make responses because there is an assumed link between a stimulus and a response—a link that is the result of a past history of reinforcement for a response. Instead, according to this point of view, people and even lower animals develop an *expectation* that they will receive a reinforcer after making a response. Two types of learning in which no obvious prior reinforcement is present are latent learning and observational learning.

Latent Learning

Evidence for the importance of cognitive processes comes from a series of animal experiments that revealed a type of cognitive learning called latent learning. In **latent learning,** a new behavior is learned but not demonstrated until some incentive is provided for displaying it (Tolman & Honzik, 1930). In short, latent learning occurs without reinforcement.

In the studies demonstrating latent learning, psychologists examined the behavior of rats in a maze such as the one shown in Figure 1a. In one experiment, a group of rats was allowed to wander around the maze once a day for 17 days without ever receiving a reward (called the unrewarded group). Understandably, those rats made many errors and spent a relatively long time reaching the end of the maze. A second group, however, was always given food at the end of the maze (the rewarded group). Not surprisingly, those rats learned to run quickly and directly to the food box, making few errors.

A third group of rats (the experimental group) started out in the same situation as the unrewarded rats but only for the first 10 days. On the 11th day, a critical experimental manipulation was introduced: From that point on, the rats in this group were given food for completing the maze. The results of this manipulation were dramatic, as you can see from the graph in Figure 1b. The previously unrewarded rats, which had earlier seemed to wander about aimlessly, showed such reductions in

latent learning Learning in which a new behavior is acquired but is not demonstrated until some incentive is provided for displaying it. (Module 19)

(a)   **(b)**

FIGURE 1 Latent learning. (a) Rats were allowed to roam through a maze of this sort once a day for 17 days. (b) The rats that were never rewarded (the unrewarded control condition) consistently made the most errors, whereas those that received food at the finish every day (the rewarded control condition) consistently made far fewer errors. But the results also showed latent learning: Rats that were rewarded only after the 10th day (the experimental group) showed an immediate reduction in errors and soon became similar in error rate to the rats that had been rewarded consistently. According to cognitive learning theorists, the reduction in errors indicates that the rats had developed a cognitive map—a mental representation—of the maze. Can you think of other examples of latent learning?

(a and b): Source: Adapted from Tolman, E. C., & Honzik, C. H. (1930). Introduction and removal of reward and maze performance in rats. *University of California Publications in Psychology, 4,* 257–275.

running time and declines in error rates that their performance almost immediately matched that of the group that had received rewards from the start.

To cognitive theorists, it seemed clear that the unrewarded rats had learned the layout of the maze early in their explorations; they just never displayed their latent learning until the reinforcement was offered. Instead, those rats seemed to develop a *cognitive map* of the maze–a mental representation of spatial locations and directions.

People, too, develop cognitive maps of their surroundings. For example, latent learning may permit you to know the location of a kitchenware store at a local mall you've frequently visited, even though you've never entered the store and don't even like to cook.

The possibility that we develop our cognitive maps through latent learning presents something of a problem for strict operant conditioning theorists. If we consider the results of the maze-learning experiment, for instance, it is unclear what reinforcement permitted the rats that initially received no reward to learn the layout of the maze because there was no obvious reinforcer present. Instead, the results support a cognitive view of learning, in which changes occurred in unobservable mental processes (Lin et al., 2011; Malin et al., 2015; Forbus, Liang, & Rabkina, 2017).

Observational Learning: Learning Through Imitation

Let's return for a moment to the case of a person learning to drive. How can we account for instances in which an individual with no direct experience in carrying out a particular behavior learns the behavior and then performs it? To answer this question, psychologists have focused on another aspect of cognitive learning: observational learning.

According to psychologist Albert Bandura and colleagues, a major part of human learning consists of **observational learning,** which is learning by watching the behavior of another person, or *model*. Because of its reliance on observation of others–a social phenomenon–the perspective taken by Bandura is often referred to as a *social cognitive* approach to learning (Bandura, 2009; Waismeyer & Meltzoff, 2017; Carcea & Froemke, 2019).

Bandura dramatically demonstrated the ability of models to stimulate learning in a classic experiment. In the study, young children saw a film of an adult wildly hitting a 5-foot-tall inflatable punching toy called a Bobo doll (Bandura, Ross, & Ross, 1963a, 1963b). Later the children were given the opportunity to play with the Bobo doll themselves, and, sure enough, most displayed the same kind of behavior, in some cases mimicking the aggressive behavior almost identically.

Not only negative behaviors are acquired through observational learning. In one experiment, for example, children who were afraid of dogs were exposed to a model–dubbed the Fearless Peer–playing with a dog (Bandura, Grusec, & Menlove, 1967). After exposure, observers were considerably more likely to approach a strange dog than were children who had not viewed the Fearless Peer.

Observational learning is particularly important in acquiring skills in which the operant conditioning technique of shaping is inappropriate. Piloting an airplane and performing brain surgery, for example, are behaviors that could hardly be learned by using trial-and-error methods without grave cost–literally–to those involved in the learning process.

Observational learning may have a genetic basis. For example, we find observational learning at work with mother animals teaching their young such activities as hunting. In addition, the discovery of *mirror neurons* that fire when we observe another person carrying out a behavior suggests that the capacity to imitate others may be innate (McElreath, Wallin, & Fasolo, 2013; Fernald, 2015; Catmur & Heyes, 2019); also see *Neuroscience in Your Life.*

observational learning Learning by observing the behavior of another person, or model. (Module 19)

Study Alert

A key point of observational learning approaches: Behavior of models who are rewarded for a given behavior is more likely to be imitated than that of models who are punished for the behavior.

NEUROSCIENCE IN YOUR LIFE: LEARNING THROUGH IMITATION

Infants often learn by imitating adults. But what is the neural mechanism for this ability to imitate? Previous research with adults has focused on decreases in *mu activity*, a neural indicator of motor activity in the brain, when subjects are watching and producing actions. But until now this neural marker of imitative behavior has not been tested in infants. A recent study showed that imitation by 7-month-old infants was also related to decreases in mu activity. Specifically, trials in which the infants imitated the experimenter showed a greater decrease in mu activity (shown in green; left image) compared with mu activity on trials in which the infants did not imitate the experimenter (shown in green; image on the right) (Filippi et al., 2016; Debnath et al., 2019).

Source: Adapted from Filippi, C. A., Cannon, E. N., Fox, N. A., Thorpe, S. G., Ferrari, P. F., & Woodward, A. L. (2016). Motor system activation predicts goal imitation in 7-month-old infants. *Psychological Science, 27*(5), 675–684.

Not all behavior that we witness is learned or carried out, of course. One crucial factor that determines whether we later imitate a model is whether the model is rewarded for his or her behavior. If we observe a friend being rewarded for putting more time into his studies by receiving higher grades, we are more likely to imitate his behavior than we would if his behavior resulted only in being stressed and tired. Models who are rewarded for behaving in a particular way are more apt to be mimicked than are models who receive punishment. Observing the punishment of a model, however, does not necessarily stop observers from learning the behavior. Observers can still describe the model's behavior—they are just less apt to perform it (Bandura, 1994).

Observational learning is central to a number of important issues relating to the extent to which people learn simply by watching the behavior of others. For instance, the degree to which observation of media aggression produces subsequent aggression on the part of viewers is a crucial—and controversial—question, as we discuss next.

This young boy is displaying observational learning based on earlier experiences with his father. How does observational learning contribute to learning gender roles?
Oksana Kuzmina/123RF

VIOLENCE IN TELEVISION AND VIDEO GAMES: DO THE MEDIA'S MESSAGES MATTER?

In an episode of *The Sopranos*, the famous television series, fictional mobster Tony Soprano murdered one of his associates. To make identification of the victim's body difficult, Soprano and one of his henchmen dismembered the body and dumped the body parts.

A few months later, in real life, two half brothers in Riverside, California, strangled their mother and then cut her head and hands from her body. Victor Bautista, 20, and Matthew Montejo, 15, were caught by police after a security guard noticed that the bundle they were attempting to throw in a Dumpster had a foot sticking out of it. They told police that the plan to dismember their mother was inspired by the *Sopranos* episode (Martelle, Hanley, & Yoshino, 2003).

PsychTech

Video gaming can also have positive consequences: Playing video games with positive, prosocial themes increases empathy and thoughts about helping others.

Like other "media copycat" killings, the brothers' cold-blooded brutality raises a critical issue: Does observing violent, antisocial acts in the media lead viewers to behave in similar ways? Because research on modeling shows that people frequently learn and imitate the aggression that they observe, this question is among the most important issues being addressed by psychologists.

Certainly, the amount of violence in the mass media is enormous. By the age of 18 years, the average young person has viewed some 200,000 acts of violence on television (American Academy of Pediatrics Council on Communication and Media, 2009).

Most psychologists agree that watching high levels of media violence makes viewers more susceptible to acting aggressively. For example, one survey showed that one-fourth of violent young male offenders incarcerated in Florida had attempted to commit a media-inspired copycat crime. A significant proportion of those teenage offenders noted that they paid close attention to the media (Savage & Yancey, 2008; Boxer et al., 2009; Ferguson, 2015).

Playing violent video games has also been blamed as a source of actual violence. Certainly, after every mass shooting in the United States, some politicians suggest that participation in violent gaming is at the root of the shooter's behavior. Is there any truth to such assertions (Draper, 2019)?

In fact, some evidence supports a link between participating in violent video games and actual aggression. In one of a series of studies by psychologist Craig Anderson and his colleagues, college students who frequently played violent video games, such as *Postal* or *Doom*, were more likely to have been involved in delinquent behavior and aggression. Frequent players also had lower academic achievement (Anderson & Bushman, 2018).

On the other hand, a few contrary research findings exist. For example, one meta-analysis of video game influences finds minimal effects on aggression. Furthermore, some researchers argue that violent video games may produce certain positive results—such as a rise in social networking among players (Ferguson, 2015b; Ferguson & Beresin, 2017; Ferguson & Wang, 2019).

However, most experts agree that the clear preponderance of evidence points to at least moderate negative outcomes from viewing violent video games. In light of this evidence, a task force of the American Psychological Association suggests that violent video game exposure is associated with higher levels of aggressive behavior, increased thoughts about aggression, higher levels of desensitization to violence, and decreased empathy relating to exposure to violence. Furthermore, the American Pediatric Association has urged parents to minimize their children's exposure to violent media of any sort (American Academy of Pediatrics Council on Communications and Media, 2016; Calvert et al., 2017; Anderson et al., 2017; Mather & VanderWheele, 2019)

From the perspective of...

A Social Worker What advice would you give to families about children's exposure to violent media and video games?

Sam Edwards/OJO Images/age fotostock

Several aspects of media violence may contribute to real-life aggressive behavior. First, viewing violent media may lower inhibitions against behaving aggressively. In other words, watching television portrayals of violence or using violence to win a video game makes aggression seem a legitimate response to particular situations.

Second, exposure to media violence may distort our understanding of the meaning of others' behavior, predisposing us to view even nonaggressive acts by others as aggressive. For example, a teenager who watches considerable media violence may be predisposed to think that a person who accidentally bumps into him as he walks down the street is being purposely aggressive, even if the reality is that it is truly an accident.

Third, a continuous diet of media aggression may leave us desensitized to violence, and what previously would have repelled us now produces little emotional response. Our sense of the pain and suffering brought about by aggression consequently may be diminished (Carnagey, Anderson, & Bushman, 2007; Ramos et al., 2013).

What about real-life exposure to *actual* violence? Does it also lead to increases in aggression? The answer is yes. Exposure to actual firearm violence (being shot or being shot at) doubles the probability that an adolescent will commit serious violence over the next 2 years. In short, whether the violence is real or fictionalized, observing violent behavior leads to increases in aggressive behavior (Allwood, 2007; Quinn et al., 2017; Chesworth, Lanier, & Rizo, 2019).

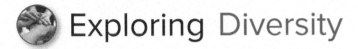 Exploring Diversity

Does Culture Influence How We Learn?

When a member of the Chilcotin Indian tribe teaches her daughter to prepare salmon, at first she allows the daughter only to observe the entire process. A little later, she permits her child to try out some basic parts of the task. Her response to questions is noteworthy. For example, when the daughter asks about how to do "the backbone part," the mother's response is to repeat the entire process with another salmon. The reason? The mother feels that one cannot learn the individual parts of the task apart from the context of preparing the whole fish. (Tharp, 1989)

It should not be surprising that children raised in the Chilcotin tradition, which stresses instruction that starts by communicating the entire task, may have difficulty with traditional Western schooling. In the approach to teaching most characteristic of Western culture, tasks are broken down into their component parts. Only after each small step is learned is it thought possible to master the complete task.

Do the differences in teaching approaches between cultures affect how people learn? Some psychologists, taking a cognitive perspective on learning, suggest that people develop particular *learning styles*, characteristic ways of approaching material, based on their cultural background and unique pattern of abilities (Barmeyer, 2004; Sternberg, 2011; Rogoff et al, 2017).

Learning styles differ along several dimensions. For example, one central dimension is relational versus analytical approaches to learning. As illustrated in Figure 2, people with a *relational learning style* master material best through understanding the "big picture" about something. They need to understand the complete picture of what they're studying before they understand its component parts. For example, students with a relational learning style might learn about the brain by first focusing on the brain as a whole and how it functions. Only after doing that would they then focus on the specific functions of separate areas of the brain.

In contrast, those with an *analytical learning style* do best when they first analyze the the various components underlying an object, phenomenon, or situation. By developing an understanding of the individual parts, they are best able to grasp the full picture. So students with an analytic learning style might learn about the brain most easily by first considering its component parts (neurons, specific areas, lobes) and then by focusing on how they fit together to form the brain.

According to educator Maurianne Adams, certain minority groups in Western societies display characteristic learning styles. For instance, she argues that Caucasian females and

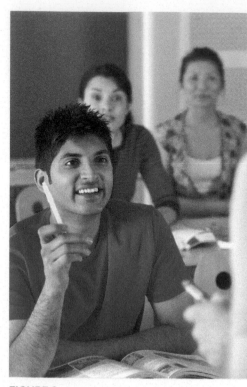

Relational Style	Analytical Style
• Perceive information as part of total picture	• Focus on detail
• Show intuitive thinking	• Show sequential and structured thinking
• More easily learn materials that have a human, social content	• More easily learn materials that are impersonal
• Have a good memory for verbally presented ideas and information	• Have a good memory for abstract ideas
• Are influenced by others' opinions	• Are not greatly affected by the opinions of others
• Style conflicts with the traditional school environment	• Style matches traditional school environments.

FIGURE 2 A comparison of relational versus analytical approaches to learning offers one example of how learning styles differ along several dimensions.

(Photo): ©Fuse/Corbis/Getty Images; Source: Adams, M., Bell, L. A., & Griffin, P. *Teaching for diversity and social justice* (2nd ed.). New York: Routledge/Taylor & Francis Group, 2017.

African-American, Native-American, and Hispanic-American males and females are more apt to use a relational style of learning than are Caucasian and Asian-American males, who are more likely to employ an analytical style (Adams, Bell, & Griffin, 2007; Chin, 2013).

The conclusion that members of particular ethnic and gender groups have similar learning styles is controversial. Because there is so much diversity within each particular racial and ethnic group, critics argue that generalizations about learning styles cannot be used to predict the style of any single individual, regardless of group membership.

Still, values about learning, which are communicated through a person's family and cultural background, clearly have an impact on how successful students are in school. One theory suggests that members of minority groups who were voluntary immigrants are more apt to be successful in school than those who were brought into a majority culture against their will. For example, Korean children in the United States—the sons and daughters of voluntary immigrants—perform quite well, as a group, in school. In contrast, Korean children in Japan, who were often the sons and daughters of people who were forced to immigrate during World War II, essentially as forced laborers, do less well in school. The theory suggests that the motivation to succeed is lower for children in forced immigration groups (Ogbu, 2003; Foster, 2005).

RECAP/EVALUATE/RETHINK

RECAP

LO 19-1 What are the roles of cognition and thought in learning?

- Cognitive approaches to learning consider learning in terms of thought processes, or cognition. Phenomena

such as latent learning—in which a new behavior is learned but not performed until some incentive is provided for its performance—and the apparent development of cognitive maps support cognitive approaches.

- Learning also occurs from observing the behavior of others. The major factor that determines whether an observed behavior will actually be performed is the nature of the reinforcement or punishment a model receives.

- Observation of violence is linked to a greater likelihood of subsequently acting aggressively.
- Learning styles are characteristic ways of approaching learning, based on a person's cultural background and unique pattern of abilities. Whether an individual has an analytical or a relational style of learning, for example, may reflect family background or culture.

EVALUATE

1. Cognitive learning theorists are concerned only with overt behavior, not with its internal causes. True or false?
2. In cognitive learning theory, it is assumed that people develop a(n) _____ about receiving a reinforcer when they behave a certain way.
3. In _____ learning, a new behavior is learned but is not shown until appropriate reinforcement is presented.

4. Bandura's _____ theory of learning states that people learn through watching a(n) _____ (another person displaying the behavior of interest).

RETHINK

1. The relational style of learning sometimes conflicts with the traditional school environment. Could a school be created that takes advantage of the characteristics of the relational style? How? Are there types of learning for which the analytical style is clearly superior?
2. What is the relationship between a model (in Bandura's sense) and a role model (as the term is used popularly)? Celebrities often complain that their actions should not be scrutinized closely because they do not want to be role models. How would you respond?

Answers to Evaluate Questions

1. False; cognitive learning theorists are primarily concerned with mental processes; 2. expectation; 3. latent; 4. observational, model

---

KEY TERMS

cognitive learning theory   latent learning   observational learning

---

LOOKING *Back*

EPILOGUE

In this chapter, we discussed several kinds of learning, ranging from classical conditioning, which depends on the existence of natural stimulus–response pairings, to operant conditioning, in which reinforcement is used to increase desired behavior. These approaches to learning focus on outward, behavioral learning processes. Cognitive approaches to learning focus on mental processes that enable learning.

We have also noted that learning is affected by culture and individual differences, with individual learning styles potentially affecting the ways in which people learn most effectively. And we saw some ways in which our learning about learning can be put to practical use through such means as behavior-modification programs designed to decrease negative behaviors and increase positive ones.

Return to the prologue of this chapter and consider the following questions about Travis Amick, who lost normal use of his arms and legs, and his helper monkey, Siggy:

1. What operant conditioning principles were likely used in training Siggy to perform his tasks?
2. How might Siggy's trainers have made use of shaping and chaining principles? Of schedules of reinforcement?
3. Siggy was not specifically trained to reinsert a dislocated cell phone battery, but he knew what to do anyway. What learning principles might explain this phenomenon?

VISUAL SUMMARY 6 Learning

MODULE 17 Classical Conditioning

Ivan Pavlov: Basic principles of classical conditioning

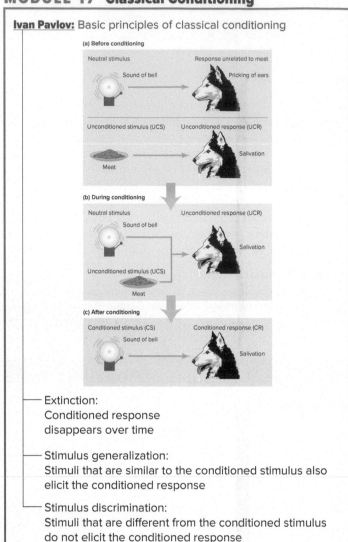

(a) Before conditioning

Neutral stimulus — Sound of bell → Response unrelated to meat — Pricking of ears

Unconditioned stimulus (UCS) — Meat → Unconditioned response (UCR) — Salivation

(b) During conditioning

Neutral stimulus — Sound of bell → Unconditioned response (UCR) — Salivation

Unconditioned stimulus (UCS) — Meat

(c) After conditioning

Conditioned stimulus (CS) — Sound of bell → Conditioned response (CR) — Salivation

— Extinction:
Conditioned response
disappears over time

— Stimulus generalization:
Stimuli that are similar to the conditioned stimulus also
elicit the conditioned response

— Stimulus discrimination:
Stimuli that are different from the conditioned stimulus
do not elicit the conditioned response

MODULE 18 Operant Conditioning

Basic Principle: Behavior changes in frequency according
to its consequences

— Reinforcement: A stimulus that increases the
probability that a preceding behavior will be repeated

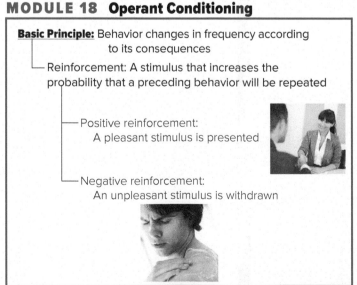

— Positive reinforcement:
A pleasant stimulus is presented

— Negative reinforcement:
An unpleasant stimulus is withdrawn

Basic Principle: Behavior changes in frequency according
to its consequences *(continued)*

— Punishment : A stimulus that decreases the probability
that a preceding behavior will be repeated

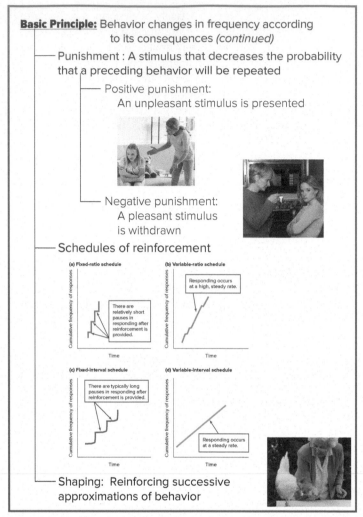

— Positive punishment:
An unpleasant stimulus is presented

— Negative punishment:
A pleasant stimulus
is withdrawn

— Schedules of reinforcement

(a) Fixed-ratio schedule
There are relatively short pauses in responding after reinforcement is provided.

(b) Variable-ratio schedule
Responding occurs at a high, steady rate.

(c) Fixed-interval schedule
There are typically long pauses in responding after reinforcement is provided.

(d) Variable-interval schedule
Responding occurs at a steady rate.

— Shaping: Reinforcing successive
approximations of behavior

MODULE 19 Cognitive Approaches to Learning

Cognitive Learning Theory: Focuses on the internal
thoughts and expectations

— Latent learning: A new behavior is learned but is not
demonstrated until it is reinforced

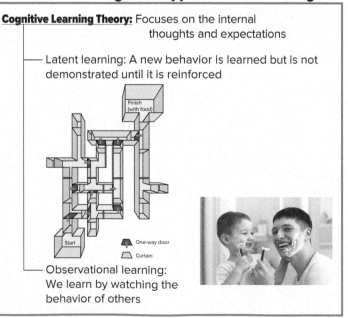

Finish (with food)

Start

▲ One-way door
△ Curtain

— Observational learning:
We learn by watching the
behavior of others

(Module 18): (Interview): Andrey Popov/Shutterstock; (young man shoulder): Stockbyte/Getty Images; (Mother holding keys): Amy Etra/PhotoEdit; (Angry mother yelling): Light Field Studios/123RF; (Dr. Marian): Dr. Marian Breland Bailey; (bottom): (Latent learning): Source: University of California Publications in Psychology, "Introduction and removal of reward and maze performance in rats."; (Photo): Oksana Kuzmina/123RF

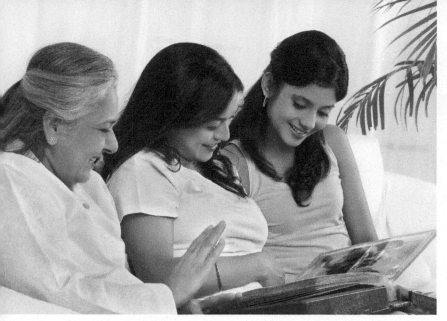

India Picture/Shutterstock

CHAPTER 7
Memory

LEARNING OUTCOMES FOR CHAPTER 7

MODULE 20

LO 20-1 What is memory?

LO 20-2 Are there different kinds of memory?

LO 20-3 What are the biological bases of memory?

THE FOUNDATIONS OF MEMORY

Sensory Memory

Short-Term Memory

Working Memory

Long-Term Memory

Neuroscience in Your Life: Superior Memory

MODULE 21

LO 21-1 What causes difficulties and failures in remembering?

RECALLING LONG-TERM MEMORIES

Retrieval Cues

Levels of Processing

Explicit and Implicit Memory

Flashbulb Memories

Constructive Processes in Memory: Rebuilding the Past

Exploring Diversity: Are There Cross-Cultural Differences in Memory?

LO 22-1   Why do we forget information?

LO 22-2   What are the major memory impairments?

PROLOGUE *NOT FORGETTING A THING*

Ten years later, Markie Pasternak can tell you exactly where she was and what she was doing on December 11, 2009. "I chaperoned a middle school dance as a volunteer through my high school. And then I went shopping with my boyfriend for Christmas stuff," she reports matter-of-factly, as if it were yesterday. She can even recall that it was a Friday.

But nothing is particularly special about December 11, 2009. Pasternak can do the same for practically any random date after she turned 11.

Pasternak is one of fewer than 100 people in the world identified with the very rare ability to remember the details of their day-to-day personal experiences with great precision—dates, times, locations, events, people they were with, even what they wore, and what they ate—years later (Runevitch, 2019).

LOOKING *Ahead*

Markie Pasternak's condition, known as *highly superior autobiographical memory (HSAM)*, affects the part of memory that stores experiences related to life events. Researchers

have discovered that people with HSAM process short-term memories the same way most of us do. The difference is that the accuracy and detail of their memories actually *improve* over time (McGaugh & LePort, 2014; Morris, 2017; Wolk et al., 2017; Mazzoni et al., 2019.)

Pasternak's extraordinary memory illustrates the complexity and the mystery of the phenomenon we call memory. Memory allows us to retrieve a vast amount of information—from the name of a friend we haven't talked with for years to the details of a picture that hung in our childhood bedroom. At the same time, though, memory failures are common. We forget where we left the keys to the car and are unable to answer an exam question about material we studied only a few hours earlier. Why?

We turn now to the nature of memory, considering the ways in which information is stored and retrieved. We examine the problems of retrieving information from memory, the accuracy of memories, and the reasons we sometimes forget information. We also consider the biological foundations of memory and discuss some practical means of increasing memory capacity.

Module 20
The Foundations of Memory

You are playing a game of Trivial Pursuit, and winning the game comes down to one question: On what body of water is Mumbai located? As you rack your brain for the answer, several fundamental processes relating to memory come into play. You may never, for instance, have been exposed to information regarding Mumbai's location. Or if you have been exposed to it, it may simply not have registered in a meaningful way. In other words, the information might not have been recorded properly in your memory. The initial process of recording information in a form usable to memory, a process called *encoding*, is the first stage in remembering something.

Even if you had been exposed to the information and originally knew the name of the body of water, you may still be unable to recall it during the game because of a failure to retain it. Memory specialists speak of *storage*, the maintenance of material saved in memory. If the material is not stored adequately, it cannot be recalled later.

Memory also depends on one last process–*retrieval*: Material in memory storage has to be located and brought into awareness to be useful. Your failure to recall Mumbai's location, then, may rest on your inability to retrieve information that you learned earlier.

In sum, psychologists consider **memory** to be the process by which we encode, store, and retrieve information (see Figure 1). Each of the three parts of this definition–encoding, storage, and retrieval–represents a different process. You can think of these processes as being analogous to a computer's keyboard (encoding), hard drive (storage), and software that accesses the information for display on the screen (retrieval). Only if all three processes have operated will you experience success and be able to recall the body of water on which Mumbai is located: the Arabian Sea.

Recognizing that memory involves encoding, storage, and retrieval gives us a start in understanding the concept. But how does memory actually function? How do we explain what information is initially encoded, what gets stored, and how it is retrieved?

According to the *three-system approach to memory* that dominated memory research for several decades, there are different memory storage systems or stages through which information must travel if it is to be remembered (Atkinson & Shiffrin, 1968). Historically, the approach has been extremely influential in the development of our understanding of memory, and–although new theories have augmented it–it still provides a useful framework for understanding how information is recalled.

LEARNING OUTCOMES

LO 20-1 What is memory?

LO 20-2 Are there different kinds of memory?

LO 20-3 What are the biological bases of memory?

memory The process by which we encode, store, and retrieve information. (Module 20)

Encoding
(Initial recording of information)

Storage
(Information saved for future use)

Retrieval
(Recovery of stored information)

loading from/drive a

FIGURE 1 Memory is built on three basic processes—encoding, storage, and retrieval—that are analogous to a computer's keyboard, hard drive, and software to access the information for display on the screen. The analogy is not perfect, however, because human memory is less precise than a computer. How might you modify the analogy to make it more accurate?

FIGURE 2 In this three-stage model of memory, information initially recorded by the person's sensory system enters sensory memory, which momentarily holds the information. The information then moves to short-term memory, which stores it for 15 to 25 seconds. Finally, the information can move into long-term memory, which is relatively permanent. Whether the information moves from short-term to long-term memory depends on the kind and amount of rehearsal of the material that is performed.
C Squared Studios/Getty Images

The three-system memory theory proposes the existence of the three separate memory stores shown in Figure 2. *Sensory memory* refers to the initial, momentary storage of information that lasts only an instant. Here, an exact replica of the stimulus recorded by a person's sensory system is stored very briefly. In a second stage, *short-term memory* holds information for 15 to 25 seconds and stores it according to its meaning, rather than as mere sensory stimulation. The third type of storage system is *long-term memory*. Information is stored in long-term memory on a relatively permanent basis, although it may be difficult to retrieve.

Sensory Memory

A momentary flash of lightning, the sound of a twig snapping, and the sting of a pinprick all represent stimulation of exceedingly brief duration, but they may nonetheless provide important information that can require a response. Such stimuli are initially—and fleetingly—stored in sensory memory.

Sensory memory is the first storehouse of the information the world presents to us. Actually, we have several types of sensory memories, each related to a different kind of sensory information. For instance, *iconic memory* reflects information from the visual system. *Echoic memory* stores auditory information coming from the ears. In addition, there are corresponding memories for each of the other senses.

Sensory memory can store information for only a very short time. If information does not pass into short-term memory, it is lost for good. For instance, iconic memory seems to last less than a second, and echoic memory typically fades within 2 or 3 seconds. However, despite the brief duration of sensory memory, its precision is high: Sensory memory can store an almost exact replica of each stimulus to which it is exposed (Vlassova & Pearson, 2013; Rimmele, Sussman, & Poeppel, 2015).

Psychologist George Sperling (1960) demonstrated the existence of sensory memory in a series of clever and now-classic studies. He briefly exposed people to a series of 12 letters arranged in the following pattern:

sensory memory The initial, momentary storage of information, lasting only an instant. (Module 20)

A momentary flash of lightning leaves a sensory visual memory, a fleeting but exact replica of the stimulus, which then fades away.
Steve Allen/Brand X Pictures/Getty Images

```
F    T    Y    C

K    D    N    L

Y    W    B    M
```

When exposed to this pattern of letters for just one twentieth of a second, most people could recall only four or five of the letters accurately. Although they knew that they had seen more, the memory of those letters had faded by the time they reported the first few letters. It was possible, then, that the information had initially been accurately stored in sensory memory. But during the time it took to verbalize the first four or five letters, the memory of the other letters faded.

To test that possibility, Sperling conducted an experiment in which a high, medium, or low tone sounded just after a person had been exposed to the full pattern of letters. People were told to report the letters in the highest line if a high tone was sounded, the middle line if the medium tone occurred, or the lowest line at the sound of the low tone. Because the tone occurred after the exposure, people had to rely on their memories to report the correct row.

The results of the study clearly showed that people had been storing the complete pattern in memory. They accurately recalled the letters in the line that had been indicated by the tone regardless of whether it was the top, middle, or bottom line. Obviously, *all* the lines they had seen had been stored in sensory memory. Despite its rapid loss, then, the information in sensory memory was an accurate representation of what people had seen.

By gradually lengthening the time between the presentation of the visual pattern and the tone, Sperling was able to determine with some accuracy the length of time that information was stored in sensory memory. The ability to recall a particular row of the pattern when a tone was sounded declined progressively as the period between the visual exposure and the tone increased. This decline continued until the period reached about 1 second in duration, at which point the row could not be recalled accurately at all. Sperling concluded that the entire visual image was stored in sensory memory for less than a second.

In sum, sensory memory operates as a kind of snapshot that stores information—which may be of a visual, auditory, or other sensory nature—for a brief moment in time. But it is as if each snapshot, immediately after being taken, is destroyed and replaced with a new one. Unless the information in the snapshot is transferred to some other type of memory, it is lost.

> **Study Alert**
> Although the three types of memory are discussed as separate memory stores, these are not mini-warehouses located in specific areas of the brain. Instead, they represent three different types of memory systems with different characteristics.

Short-Term Memory

Because the information that is stored briefly in sensory memory consists of representations of raw sensory stimuli, it is not meaningful to us. If we are to make sense of it and possibly retain it, the information must be transferred to the next stage of memory: short-term memory. **Short-term memory** is the memory store in which information first has meaning, although the maximum length of retention there is relatively short (Hamilton & Martin, 2007; Cao, Nosofsky, & Shiffrin, 2017).

short-term memory Memory that holds information for 15 to 25 seconds. (Module 20)

The specific process by which sensory memories are transformed into short-term memories is not clear. Some theorists suggest that the information is first translated into graphical representations or images, and others hypothesize that the transfer occurs when the sensory stimuli are changed to words (Baddeley & Wilson, 1985). What is clear, however, is that unlike sensory memory, which holds a relatively full and detailed—if short-lived—representation of the world, short-term memory has incomplete representational capabilities.

In fact, researchers have identified the specific amount of information we can hold in short-term memory: 7 items, or "chunks," of information, with variations up to plus or minus 2 chunks (remember it this way: 7 ± 2). A **chunk** is a group of separate pieces of information stored as a single unit in short-term memory. For example, telephone numbers are typically depicted in three chunks of information in order to make them easier to remember: (201) 226-4610, rather than a string of the separate numbers 2012264610.

chunk A group of separate pieces of information stored as a single unit in short-term memory. (Module 20)

Chunks also may consist of categories as words or other meaningful units. For example, consider the following list of 21 letters:

P B S F O X C N N A B C C B S M T V N B C

Because the list of individual letters exceeds seven items, it is difficult to recall the letters after one exposure. But suppose they were presented as follows:

PBS   FOX   CNN   ABC   CBS   MTV   NBC

In this case, even though there are still 21 letters, you'd be able to store them in short-term memory since they represent only seven chunks.

Chunks can vary in size from single letters or numbers to categories that are far more complicated. The specific nature of what constitutes a chunk varies according to one's past experience. You can see this for yourself by trying an experiment that was first carried out as a comparison between expert and inexperienced chess players and is illustrated in Figure 3 (deGroot, 1978; Schneider & Logan, 2015; Tanida, Nakayama, & Saito, 2019).

The chunks of information in short-term memory do not last very long. Just how brief is short-term memory? If you've ever looked up a telephone number, repeated the number to yourself, and then forgotten the number after you've tapped the first three numbers into your phone, you know that information does not remain in short-term memory very long. Most psychologists believe that information in short-term memory is lost after 15 to 25 seconds–unless it is transferred to long-term memory.

REHEARSAL

rehearsal The repetition of information that has entered short-term memory. (Module 20)

The transfer of material from short- to long-term memory proceeds largely on the basis of rehearsal. **Rehearsal** is the repetition of information that has entered short-term memory. Rehearsal accomplishes two things. First, as long as we repeat the information, we lengthen the time it is maintained in short-term memory. More important, however,

FIGURE 3 Examine the chessboard on the left for about 5 seconds. Then cover up the board and draw the position of the pieces on the blank chessboard. (You could also use your own chessboard and place the pieces in the same positions.) Unless you are an experienced chess player, you are likely to have great difficulty carrying out such a task. Yet chess masters—those who win tournaments—do this quite well (deGroot, 1966; Villanfaina et al., 2019). They are able to reproduce correctly 90% of the pieces on the board. In comparison, inexperienced chess players are typically able to reproduce only 40% of the board properly. The chess masters generally test normally on other measures of memory. What they can do better than others is see the board in terms of chunks or meaningful units and reproduce the position of the chess pieces by using those units.

rehearsal allows us to transfer the information into long-term memory (Jarrold & Tam, 2011; Grenfell-Essam, Ward, & Tan, 2013; Festini & Reuter-Lorenz, 2017).

Whether the transfer is made from short- to long-term memory seems to depend largely on the kind of rehearsal that is carried out. If the information is simply repeated over and over again—as we might do with a telephone number someone tells us as we rush to store it in our phone—it is kept current in short-term memory, but it will not necessarily be placed in long-term memory. Instead, as soon as we stop punching in the phone numbers, the number is likely to be replaced by other information and will be completely forgotten.

In contrast, if the information in short-term memory is rehearsed using a process called elaborative rehearsal, it is much more likely to be transferred into long-term memory. *Elaborative rehearsal* occurs when the information is considered and organized in some fashion. The organization might include expanding the information to make it fit into a logical framework, linking it to another memory, turning it into an image, or transforming it in some other way. For example, a list of vegetables to be purchased at a store could be woven together in memory as items being used to prepare an elaborate salad, could be linked to the items bought on an earlier shopping trip, or could be thought of in terms of the image of a farm with rows of each item.

We can vastly improve our retention of information using such organizational strategies, which are known as mnemonics. *Mnemonics* (pronounced "neh MON ix") are strategies for organizing information in a way that makes the information more likely to be remembered. For instance, when a beginning musician learns that the spaces on the music staff spell the word *FACE*, or when we learn the rhyme "Thirty days hath September, April, June, and November . . . ," we are using mnemonics (Stålhammar, Nordlund, & Wallin, 2015; Choi, Kensinger, & Rajaram, 2017).

Working Memory

Rather than seeing short-term memory as an independent way station into which memories arrive, either to fade or to be passed on to long-term memory, most contemporary memory theorists conceive of short-term memory as far more active. In this view, short-term memory is like an information-processing system that manages both new material gathered from sensory memory and older material that has been pulled from long-term storage. In this increasingly influential view, short-term memory is referred to as working memory.

Working memory is the memory system that holds information temporarily while actively manipulating and rehearsing that information. If you use the analogy of a computer, working memory is the processing that occurs in an open window on your desktop, as compared with the long-term storage of information in the computer's hard drive (Vandierendonck & Szmalec, 2011; Adami, Alilou, & Nazari, 2019).

Researchers now assume that working memory is made up of several parts. First, it contains a *central executive* processor that is involved in reasoning, decision making, and planning. The central executive integrates and coordinates information from three distinct subsystems, and it determines what we pay attention to and what we ignore.

The three subsystems of working memory serve as storage-and-rehearsal systems: the visual store, the verbal store, and the episodic buffer. The *visual store* specializes in visual and spatial information. In contrast, the *verbal store* holds and manipulates material relating to language, including speech, words, and numbers. Finally, the *episodic buffer* contains information that represents events and occurrences—things that happen to us (see Figure 4; Baddeley, Allen, & Hitch, 2011; Kuncel & Beatty, 2013; Hilbert et al., 2017).

Working memory permits us to keep information in an active state briefly so that we can do something with the information. For instance, we use working memory when we're doing a multistep arithmetic problem in our heads, storing the result of

working memory A memory system that holds information temporarily while actively manipulating and rehearsing that information. (Module 20)

FIGURE 4 Working memory is an active "workspace" in which information is retrieved and manipulated and in which information is held through rehearsal. Working memory includes a central executive processor that coordinates the visual store, verbal store, and episodic buffer.
Source: Adapted from Lexcellent, C. (2019). *Human memory and material memory.* Cham, Switzerland: Springer Nature.

one calculation while getting ready to move to the next stage. (I make use of my working memory when I figure a 20% tip in a restaurant by first calculating 10% of the total bill and then doubling it.)

As working memory processes information, it uses a significant amount of cognitive resources during its operation. Furthermore, the amount of information that can be held and processed in working memory seems to be just three to four chunks, depending on the nature of the chunks (Cowan, 2001; Beam, 2014; Heathcoate et al., 2015).

The cognitive effort in the processing of information in working memory also can make us less aware of our surroundings–something that has implications for why it's unsafe to use cell phones while driving. If a phone conversation requires thinking, it will burden working memory and leave drivers less aware of their surroundings, an obviously dangerous state of affairs (Sifrit, 2006; Strayer & Drews, 2007).

Furthermore, stress can reduce the effectiveness of working memory by reducing its capacity. In fact, one study found that students with the highest working memory capacity and greatest math ability were the ones who were most vulnerable to pressure to perform well. Those who should have performed best, then, were the ones most apt to choke on the test because their working memory capacities were reduced by the stress (Edwards et al., 2015; Banks & Boals, 2017; Bosquet Enlow et al., 2019).

long-term memory Memory that stores information on a relatively permanent basis, although it may be difficult to retrieve. (Module 20)

PsychTech
Research shows that when we are faced with complicated questions and material, we are primed to think of computers and search engines such as Google. In what is called the *Google effect,* we are then less likely to store the information in short-term memory and less likely to recall it—but have a better memory for where we can find it on the web (Sparrow, Liu, & Wegner, 2011; Danovitch, 2019).

Long-Term Memory

Material that makes its way from short-term memory enters a storehouse of almost unlimited capacity, called long-term memory. **Long-term memory** stores information on a relatively permanent basis. Like a new file we save on a hard drive, the information in long-term memory is filed and coded so that we can retrieve it when we need it.

Evidence of the existence of long-term memory, as distinct from short-term memory, comes from a number of sources. For example, people with certain kinds of brain damage have no lasting recall of new information received after the damage occurred, although people and events stored in memory before the injury remain intact (Milner, 1966). Because information that was encoded and stored before the injury can be recalled and because short-term memory after the injury appears to be operational—new material can be recalled for a very brief period—we can infer that there are two distinct types of memory: one for short-term and one for long-term storage.

Results from laboratory experiments are also consistent with the notion of separate short-term and long-term memory. For example, in one set of studies, people were asked to recall a relatively small amount of information (such as a set of three letters). Then, to prevent practice of the initial information, participants were required to recite some extraneous material aloud, such as counting backward by threes (Brown, 1958; Peterson & Peterson, 1959). By varying the amount of time between the presentation of the initial material and the need for its recall, investigators found that recall was quite good when the interval was very short, but recall declined rapidly thereafter. After 15 seconds had gone by, recall hovered at around 10% of the material initially presented.

Apparently, the distraction of counting backward prevented almost all the initial material from reaching long-term memory. Initial recall was good because it was coming from short-term memory, but those memories were lost at a rapid rate. Eventually, all that could be recalled was the small amount of material that had made its way into long-term storage despite the distraction of counting backward.

The distinction between short- and long-term memory is also demonstrated by the fact that ability to recall information in a list depends on where in the list an item appears. For instance, in some cases, a *primacy effect* occurs, in which items presented early in a list are remembered better. In other cases, a *recency effect* is seen, in which items presented late in a list are remembered best (Jacoby & Wahlheim, 2013; Tam, Bonardi, & Robinson, 2015; Osth & Farrell, 2019).

LONG-TERM MEMORY MODULES

Just as short-term memory is often conceptualized in terms of working memory, many contemporary researchers now regard long-term memory as having several components, or *memory modules*. Each of these modules represents a separate memory system in the brain.

One major distinction within long-term memory is that between declarative and procedural memory. **Declarative memory** is memory for factual information: names, faces, dates, and facts, such as "a bike has two wheels." The information stored in declarative memory can be verbally communicated to others and is sometimes called "explicit memory."

In contrast, **procedural memory** (sometimes called *nondeclarative memory* or *implicit memory*) refers to memory for skills and habits, such as how to ride a bike or hit a baseball. For example, procedural memory allows us to ice skate, even if we haven't done it for a long time. (Try to explain how you know how to balance on a bike or catch a ball; it's nearly impossible. Yet you're able to do so because the information is stored in procedural memory.)

You can remember the difference between declarative and procedural memory this way: Information about *things* is stored in declarative memory; information about *how to do things* (procedures) is stored in procedural memory (Freedberg, 2011; Gade et al., 2017; Xie et al., 2019).

Declarative memory can be subdivided into semantic memory and episodic memory. **Semantic memory** is memory for general knowledge and facts about the world, as well as memory for the rules of logic that are used to deduce other facts. Because of semantic memory, we remember that the ZIP code for Beverly Hills is 90210, that Mumbai is on the Arabian Sea, and that *memoree* is the incorrect spelling of *memory*. Thus, semantic memory is somewhat like a mental almanac of facts (McNamara, 2013; Grady, St-Laurent, & Burianová, 2015; Weidemann et al., 2019).

In contrast, **episodic memory** is memory for events that occur in a particular time, place, or context. For example, recall of learning to hit a baseball, our first kiss, or arranging a surprise 21st birthday party for our brother is based on episodic memories. Episodic memories relate to particular contexts. For example, remembering *when* and *how* we learned that $2 \times 2 = 4$ would be an episodic memory; the fact itself (that $2 \times 2 = 4$) is a semantic memory. (Also see Figure 5.)

declarative memory Memory for factual information: names, faces, dates, and the like. (Module 20)

procedural memory Memory for skills and habits, such as riding a bike or hitting a baseball; sometimes referred to as *nondeclarative memory or implicit memory*. (Module 20)

semantic memory Memory for general knowledge and facts about the world, as well as memory for the rules of logic that are used to deduce other facts. (Module 20)

episodic memory Memory for events that occur in a particular time, place, or context. (Module 20)

FIGURE 5 Long-term memory can be subdivided into several types. What type of long-term memory is involved in your recollection of the moment you first arrived on your campus at the start of college? What type of long-term memory is involved in remembering the lyrics to a song, compared with the tune of a song?

Study Alert
Use Figure 5 to help clarify the distinctions between the different types of long-term memory.

Episodic memories can be surprisingly detailed. Consider, for instance, how you'd respond if you were asked to identify what you were doing on a specific day 2 years ago. Impossible? You may think otherwise as you read the following exchange between a researcher and a participant in a study who was asked, in a memory experiment, what he was doing "on Monday afternoon in the third week of September two years ago."

PARTICIPANT: Come on. How should I know?

EXPERIMENTER: Just try it anyhow.

PARTICIPANT: OK. Let's see: Two years ago . . . I would be in high school in Pittsburgh. . . . That would be my senior year. Third week in September–that's just after summer–that would be the fall term. . . . Let me see. I think I had chemistry lab on Mondays. I don't know. I was probably in chemistry lab. Wait a minute–that would be the second week of school. I remember he started off with the atomic table–a big fancy chart. I thought he was crazy trying to make us memorize that thing. You know, I think I can remember sitting . . . . (Lindsay & Norman, 1977)

Episodic memory, then, can provide information about events that happened long in the past. But semantic memory is no less impressive, permitting us to dredge up tens of thousands of facts ranging from the date of our birthday to the knowledge that $1 is less than $5.

SEMANTIC NETWORKS

Try to recall, for a moment, as many things as you can think of that are the color red. Now pull from your memory the names of as many fruits as you can recall.

Did the same item appear when you did both tasks? For many people, an apple comes to mind in both cases since it fits equally well in each category. And the fact that you might have thought of an apple when doing the first task makes it even more likely that you'll think of it when doing the second task.

It's actually quite amazing that we're able to retrieve specific material from the vast store of information in our long-term memories. One key organizational tool that allows us to recall detailed information from long-term memory is the associations that we build between pieces of information. In this view, knowledge is stored in **semantic networks,** mental representations of clusters of interconnected information (Cummings, Ceponiene, & Koyama, 2006; Poirier et al., 2015).

semantic networks Mental representations of clusters of interconnected information. (Module 20)

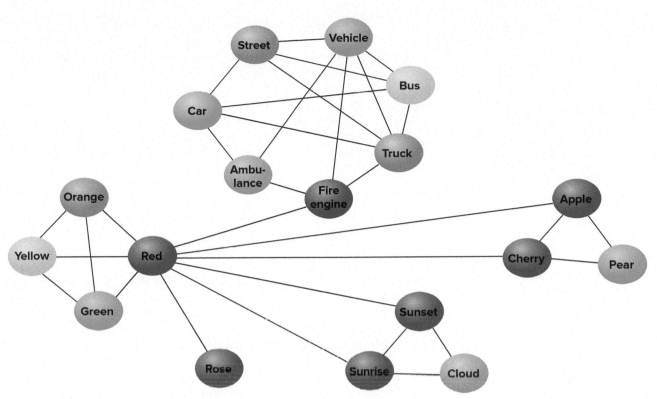

FIGURE 6 Semantic networks in memory consist of relationships between pieces of information, such as those relating to the concept of a fire engine. The lines suggest the connections that indicate how the information is organized within memory. The closer together two concepts are, the greater the strength of the association.

Adapted from: Lexcellent, C. (2019). *Human memory and material memory*. Cham, Switzerland: Springer Nature.

Consider, for example, Figure 6, which shows some of the relationships in memory relating to fire engines, the color red, and a variety of other semantic concepts. Thinking about a particular concept leads to recall of related concepts. For example, seeing a fire engine may activate our recollections of other kinds of emergency vehicles, such as an ambulance, which in turn may activate recall of the related concept of a vehicle. And thinking of a vehicle may lead us to think about a bus that we've seen in the past. Activating one memory triggers the activation of related memories in a process known as *spreading activation* (Kreher et al., 2008; Nelson et al., 2013; Kenett et al., 2017).

From the perspective of...

A Marketing Specialist How might advertisers use ways of enhancing memory to promote their products? What ethical principles are involved?

Eclipse Studios/McGraw-Hill

THE NEUROSCIENCE OF MEMORY

Can we pinpoint a location in the brain where long-term memories reside? Is there a single site that corresponds to a particular memory, or is memory distributed in different regions across the brain? Do memories leave an actual physical trace that scientists can view?

Amygdala

Hippocampus

FIGURE 7 The hippocampus and amygdala, parts of the brain's limbic system, play a central role in the consolidation of memories.

Source: Adapted from Van De Graaff, K. (2000). *Human anatomy* (5th ed.). Boston: McGraw-Hill.

The *engram* is the term for the physical memory trace in the brain that corresponds to a memory. Locating the engram has proved to be a major challenge to psychologists and neuroscientists interested in memory. But by using advanced brain scanning procedures, investigators have learned that certain brain areas and structures specialize in different types of memory-related activities.

The *hippocampus*, a part of the brain's limbic system (see Figure 7), helps to consolidate memories, stabilizing them after they are initially acquired. The hippocampus acts as a kind of neurological e-mail system. That information is subsequently passed along to the cerebral cortex of the brain, where it is actually stored (Lavenex & Lavenex, 2009; Dudai, 2011; Wilmot, Puhger, & Wiltgen, 2019).

The significance of the hippocampus is exemplified by studies of individuals who have particularly good, yet specialized, types of memories. For instance, taxi drivers in London, England, must have accurate, complete recall of the location of the maze of streets and alleys within a 6-mile radius of the center of the city. It takes years of study to memorize the material.

It turns out that MRI brain scans of taxi drivers show differences in the shape of the hippocampus compared to non-taxi drivers. The differences are consistent with the idea that particular areas of the hippocampus are involved in the consolidation of spatial memories (Woollett & Maguire, 2009; Jiang, Miao, & Chen, 2017).

The *amygdala*, another part of the limbic system, also plays an important role in memory. The amygdala is especially involved with memories involving emotion. For example, if you are frightened by a large, growling pit bull dog, you're likely to remember the event vividly—an outcome related to the functioning of the amygdala. Encountering the pit bull or any large dog in the future is likely to reactivate the amygdala and bring back the unpleasant memory (Pendyam et al., 2013; Kochli et al., 2015; Ressler & Maren, 2019).

Memory at the Level of Neurons Although it is clear that the hippocampus and amygdala play a central role in memory formation, how is the transformation of information into a memory reflected at the level of neurons?

One answer is *long-term potentiation*, which shows that certain neural pathways become easily excited while a new response is being learned. At the same time, the number of synapses between neurons increases as the dendrites branch out to receive messages. These changes reflect a process called *consolidation*, in which memories become fixed and stable in long-term memory. Long-term memories take some time to stabilize; this explains why events and other stimuli are not suddenly fixed in memory. Instead, consolidation may continue for days and even years (Kawashima, Izaki, & Grace, 2006; Hwang et al., 2017; Park et al., 2019).

Because a stimulus may contain different sensory aspects, visual, auditory, and other areas of the brain may be simultaneously processing information about that stimulus. Information storage appears to be linked to the sites where this processing occurs, and it is therefore located in the particular areas that initially processed the information in terms of its visual, auditory, and other sensory stimuli. For this reason, memory traces are distributed throughout the brain. For example, when you recall a beautiful beach sunset, your recollection draws on memory stores located in visual areas of the brain (the view of the sunset), auditory areas (the sounds of the ocean), and tactile areas (the feel of the wind) (Squire, Clark, & Bayley, 2004; Murayama & Kitagami, 2013).

In short, the physical stuff of memory—the engram—is produced by a complex of biochemical and neural processes. Scientists are just beginning to understand how the brain compiles the individual neural components into a single, coherent memory. It may be that the same neurons that fire when we are initially exposed to material are reactivated during efforts to recall that information.

As researchers increasingly understand the biology of memory, they open the door to treatments for people with memory disorders. For example, new research shows that a brain implant that works like a pacemaker helps improve memory. In the research, a method called *transcranial alternating current stimulation (tACS)* stimulates the brain and in turn improves memory in experimental settings (Kucewicz et al., 2018; Nguyen, Deng, & Reinhart, 2019).

In addition to increasingly understanding the biological basis of how memories are formed and recalled, memory specialists are also beginning to understand how to help people *forget* information through biological treatment. Specifically, they are seeking to understand how to help people forget traumatic events, persistent fears, or even annoying habits. And they are making advances in that direction, learning how to reliably alter memories in mice through a combination of a drug called HDAC inhibitor and training. In humans, such drugs might be used to disrupt the initial encoding of memories, such as treating rape victims soon after the rape to reduce the long-term trauma of the event (Johnson, 2014; Lu, 2015; Takamiya et al., 2019).

Still, although memory researchers have made considerable strides in understanding the neuroscience behind memory, more remains to be learned–and remembered (Gelbard-Sagiv et al., 2008; Brown & Banks, 2015). (For more on the biological basis of memory, see *Neuroscience in Your Life*.)

NEUROSCIENCE IN YOUR LIFE: SUPERIOR MEMORY

Some people have astounding memory and can memorize as many as 100 words in just 5 minutes. But can anyone have superior memory with the appropriate training? Apparently, the answer is yes, for recent research has shown that people's memory can be trained to show significant changes in capacity, and these changes are reflected in changes in the brain. For example, participants in one study spent 30 minutes a day for 6 weeks practicing to improve their memory. Following training, participants were given 10 minutes to remember as many words as they could, and their memory capacity increased from 26 words to 62 words. This improvement was paralleled by increased connectivity between areas of the *medial temporal lobe*, including the hippocampus, and the frontal cortex, similar to what is found in those with strongly superior memories (memory athletes).

In the view of the brain below, the lines show the difference between nonathletes and athletes, with the blue lines showing more connectivity for nonathletes and the red lines showing more connectivity for athletes. The balls indicate major hubs for these connections, with the largest hubs in the frontal cortex. This research demonstrates that even after our ability to remember information is established, practice can enhance it, and that practice results in lasting effects on the way our brains are wired (Dresler et al., 2017).

Source: Adapted from Dresler, M., Shirer, W. R., Konrad, B. N., Muller, N. C., Wagner, I. C., Fernandez, G., et al. (2017). Mnemonic training reshapes brain networks to support superior memory. *Neuron, 93*(5), 1227-1235 e1226. doi: 10.1016/j.neuron.2017.02.003.

RECAP/EVALUATE/RETHINK

RECAP

LO 20-1 What is memory?

- Memory is the process by which we encode, store, and retrieve information.

LO 20-2 Are there different kinds of memory?

- Sensory memory, corresponding to each of the sensory systems, is the first place where information is saved. Sensory memories are very brief, but they are precise, storing a nearly exact replica of a stimulus.
- Roughly 7 (plus or minus 2) chunks of information can be transferred and held in short-term memory. Information in short-term memory is held from 15 to 25 seconds and then, if not transferred to long-term memory, is lost.
- Memories are transferred into long-term storage through rehearsal. If memories are transferred into long-term memory, they become relatively permanent.
- Some theorists view short-term memory as a working memory in which information is retrieved, manipulated, and held through rehearsal. In this view, it is a central executive processor involved in reasoning and decision making; it coordinates a visual store, a verbal store, and an episodic buffer.
- Long-term memory can be viewed in terms of memory modules, each of which is related to separate memory systems in the brain. For instance, we can distinguish between declarative memory and procedural memory. Declarative memory is further divided into episodic memory and semantic memory.
- Semantic networks suggest that knowledge is stored in long-term memory as mental representations of clusters of interconnected information.

LO 20-3 What are the biological bases of memory?

- The hippocampus and amygdala are especially important in the establishment of memory.

- Memories are distributed across the brain, relating to the different sensory information-processing systems involved during the initial exposure to a stimulus.

EVALUATE

1. Match the type of memory with its definition:
   1. Long-term memory
   2. Short-term memory
   3. Sensory memory

   a. Holds information 15 to 25 seconds
   b. Stores information on a relatively permanent basis
   c. Direct representation of a stimulus

2. A(n) _____ is a meaningful group of stimuli that can be stored together in short-term memory.
3. There appear to be two types of declarative memory: _____ memory for knowledge and facts and _____ memory for personal experiences.
4. Some memory researchers believe that long-term memory is stored as associations between pieces of information in _____ networks.

RETHINK

1. It is a truism that "you never forget how to ride a bicycle." Why might this be so? In what type of memory is information about bicycle riding stored?
2. The ability to remember specific skills and the order in which they are used is known as procedural memory. Because driving involves procedural memory, why is it so unsafe to use a cell phone while driving?

Answers to Evaluate Questions

1. 1-b, 2-a, 3-c; 2. chunk; 3. semantic, episodic; 4. semantic

KEY TERMS

memory	**long-term memory**	**working memory**	**semantic memory**
sensory memory	**chunk**	**declarative memory**	**episodic memory**
short-term memory	**rehearsal**	**procedural memory**	**semantic networks**

Module 21
Recalling Long-Term Memories

An hour after his job interview, Ricardo was sitting in a coffee shop, telling his friend Laura how well it had gone, when the woman who had interviewed him walked in. "Well, hello, Ricardo. How are you doing?" Trying to make a good impression, Ricardo began to make introductions but suddenly realized he could not remember the interviewer's name. Stammering, he desperately searched his memory but to no avail. "I *know* her name," he thought to himself, "but here I am, looking like a fool. I can kiss this job good-bye."

Have you ever tried to remember someone's name, convinced that you knew it but unable to recall it no matter how hard you tried? This common occurrence—known as the **tip-of-the-tongue phenomenon**—exemplifies how difficult it can be to retrieve information stored in long-term memory (Schwartz, 2008; Schwartz & Metcalfe, 2011; Cleary, 2019).

Retrieval Cues

Perhaps recall of names and other memories is not perfect because there is so much information stored in long-term memory. Because the material that makes its way to long-term memory is relatively permanent, the capacity of long-term memory is vast. For instance, if you are like the average college student, your vocabulary includes some 50,000 words, you know hundreds of mathematical "facts," and you are able to conjure up images—such as the way your childhood home looked—with no trouble at all. In fact, simply cataloging all your memories would probably take years of work.

How do we sort through this vast array of material and retrieve specific information at the appropriate time? One way is through retrieval cues. A *retrieval cue* is a stimulus that allows us to recall more easily information that is in long-term memory. It may be a word, an emotion, or a sound; whatever the specific cue, a memory will suddenly come to mind when the retrieval cue is present. For example, the smell of roasting turkey may evoke memories of Thanksgiving or family gatherings.

Retrieval cues guide people through the information stored in long-term memory in much the same way that a search engine such as Google guides people through the Internet. They are particularly important when we are making an effort to *recall* information, as opposed to being asked to *recognize* material stored in memory. In **recall,** a specific piece of information must be retrieved—such as that needed to answer a fill-in-the-blank question or to write an essay on a test. In contrast, **recognition** occurs when people are presented with a stimulus and asked whether they have been exposed to it previously or are asked to identify it from a list of alternatives.

As you might guess, recognition is generally a much easier task than recall (see Figures 1 and 2). Recall is more difficult because it consists of a series of processes: a search through memory, retrieval of potentially relevant information, and then a decision regarding whether the information you have found is accurate. If the information appears to be correct, the search is over, but if it is not, the search must continue. In contrast, recognition is simpler because it involves fewer steps (Leigh, Zinkhan, & Swaminathan, 2006; Moen, Miller, & Lloyd, 2017).

LEARNING OUTCOMES

LO 21-1 What causes difficulties and failures in remembering?

tip-of-the-tongue phenomenon The inability to recall information that one realizes one knows—a result of the difficulty of retrieving information from long-term memory. (Module 21)

recall Memory task in which specific information must be retrieved. (Module 21)

recognition Memory task in which individuals are presented with a stimulus and asked whether they have been exposed to it in the past or to identify it from a list of alternatives. (Module 21)

! Study Alert
Remember the distinction between recall (in which specific information must be retrieved) and recognition (in which information is presented and must be identified or distinguished from other material).

FIGURE 1 Try to recall the names of the Seven Dwarfs in the Disney movie. Because this is a recall task, it is relatively difficult.
Walt Disney Productions/Album/Newscom

FIGURE 2 Naming the characters in Figure 1 (a recall task) is more difficult than solving the recognition problem posed in this list.

levels-of-processing theory The theory of memory that emphasizes the degree to which new material is mentally analyzed. (Module 21)

| Answer this recognition question: |
| Which of the following are the names of the seven dwarfs in the Disney movie *Snow White and the Seven Dwarfs?* |

Goofy	Bashful
Sleepy	Meanie
Smarty	Doc
Scaredy	Happy
Dopey	Angry
Grumpy	Sneezy
Wheezy	Crazy

(The correct answers are Bashful, Doc, Dopey, Grumpy, Happy, Sleepy, and Sneezy.)

Levels of Processing

One determinant of how well memories are recalled is the way in which material is first perceived, processed, and understood. The **levels-of-processing theory** emphasizes the degree to which new material is mentally analyzed. It suggests that the amount of information processing that occurs when material is initially encountered is central in determining how much of the information is ultimately remembered. According to this approach, the depth of information processing during exposure to material—meaning the degree to which it is analyzed and considered—is critical; the greater the intensity of its initial processing, the more likely we are to remember it (Craik & Lockhart, 2008; Mungan, Peynircioğlu, & Halpern, 2011; Catrysse, Gijbels, & Donche, 2019).

Because we do not pay close attention to much of the information to which we are exposed, very little mental processing typically takes place, and we forget new material almost immediately. However, information to which we pay greater attention is processed more thoroughly. Therefore, it enters memory at a deeper level—and is less apt to be forgotten than is information processed at shallower levels.

The theory goes on to suggest that there are considerable differences in the ways in which information is processed at various levels of memory. At shallow levels, information is processed merely in terms of its physical and sensory aspects. For example, we may pay attention only to the shapes that make up the letters in the word *dog*. At an intermediate level of processing, the shapes are translated into meaningful units—in this case, letters of the alphabet. Those letters are considered in the context of words, and specific phonetic sounds may be attached to the letters.

At the deepest level of processing, information is analyzed in terms of its meaning. We may see it in a wider context and draw associations between the meaning of the information and broader networks of knowledge. For instance, we may think of dogs not merely as animals with four legs and a tail but also in terms of their relationship to cats and other mammals. We may form an image of our own dog, thereby relating the concept to our own lives. According to the levels-of-processing approach, the deeper the initial level of processing of specific information, the longer the information will be retained.

There are considerable practical implications to the notion that recall depends on the degree to which information is initially processed. For example, the depth of information processing is critical when learning and studying course material. Rote memorization of a list of key terms for a test is unlikely to produce long-term recollection of information because processing occurs at a shallow level. In contrast, thinking about the meaning of the terms and reflecting on how they relate to information that one currently knows results in far more effective long-term retention (Conway, 2002; Wenzel, Zetocha, & Ferraro, 2007; Albanese & Case, 2015).

Explicit and Implicit Memory

If you've ever had surgery, you probably hoped that the surgeons were focused completely on the surgery and gave you their undivided attention while slicing into your body. The reality in most operating rooms is quite different, though. Surgeons may be chatting with nurses about a new restaurant as soon as they sew you up.

If you are like most patients, you are left with no recollection of the conversation that occurred while you were under anesthesia. However, although you had no conscious memories of the discussions about the merits of the restaurant, on some level you probably did recall at least some information. In fact, people who are anesthetized during surgery can sometimes recall snippets of conversations they heard during surgery—even though they have no conscious recollection of the information (Sleigh et al., 2019).

The discovery that people have memories about which they are unaware has been an important one. It has led to speculation that two forms of memory, explicit and implicit, may exist side by side. **Explicit memory** refers to intentional or conscious recollection of information. When we try to remember a name or date we have encountered or learned about previously, we are searching our explicit memory.

In contrast, **implicit memory** refers to memories of which people are not consciously aware but that can affect subsequent performance and behavior. Skills that operate automatically and without thinking, such as jumping out of the path of an automobile coming toward us as we walk down the side of a road, are stored in implicit memory. Similarly, a feeling of vague dislike for an acquaintance, without knowing why we have that feeling, may be a reflection of implicit memories. Perhaps the person reminds us of someone else in our past that we didn't like, even though we are not aware of the memory of that other individual (Gopie, Craik, & Hasher, 2011; Wu, 2013; Vöhringer et al., 2017).

Implicit memory is closely related to the prejudice and discrimination people exhibit toward members of minority groups. Although people may say and even believe they harbor no prejudice, assessment of their implicit memories may reveal that they have negative associations about members of minority groups. Such associations can influence people's behavior without their being aware of their underlying beliefs (Hofmann et al., 2008; Enge, Lupo, & Zárate, 2015; Lucas et al., 2019).

One way that memory specialists study implicit memory is through experiments that use priming. **Priming** occurs when exposure to a word or concept (called a *prime*) later makes it easier to recall information related to the prime. Priming allows us to remember new information better and faster because of material we already have stored in memory. Priming effects occur even when people have no conscious memory of the original word or concept (Geyer, Gokce, & Müller, 2011; Akhtar & Howe, 2019).

The typical experiment designed to illustrate priming helps clarify the phenomenon. In priming experiments, participants are rapidly exposed to a stimulus such as a word, an object, or perhaps a drawing of a face. The second phase of the experiment is done after an interval ranging from several seconds to several months. At that point, participants are exposed to incomplete perceptual information that is related to the first stimulus, and they are asked whether they recognize it. For example, the new material may consist of the first letter of a word that had been presented earlier or a part of a face that had been shown earlier. If participants are able to identify the stimulus more readily than they identify stimuli that have not been presented earlier, priming has taken place. Clearly, the earlier stimulus has been remembered—although the material resides in implicit memory, not explicit memory.

The same thing happens to us in our everyday lives. Suppose several months ago you watched a documentary on the planets, and the narrator described the moons of Mars, focusing on its moon named Phobos. You promptly forget the name of the moon, at least consciously. Then, several months later, you're completing a crossword puzzle that you have partially filled in, and it includes the letters *obos*. As soon as you look

explicit memory Intentional or conscious recollection of information. (Module 21)

implicit memory Memories of which people are not consciously aware but that can affect subsequent performance and behavior. (Module 21)

priming A phenomenon that occurs when exposure to a word or concept (called a prime) later makes it easier to recall information related to the prime. (Module 21) at the set of letters, you think of Phobos, and suddenly you recall for the first time since your initial exposure to the information that it is one of the moons of Mars. The sudden recollection occurred because your memory was primed by the letters *obos*.

In short, when information that we are unable to consciously recall affects our behavior, implicit memory is at work. Our behavior may be influenced by experiences of which we are unaware—an example of what has been called "retention without remembering" (Horton et al., 2005; White, 2013; Rossi-Arnaud et al, 2017).

Flashbulb Memories

Ask anyone old enough to recall the day terrorist attacks brought down the Twin Towers in New York City on September 11, 2001. They will likely recall exactly where they were when they heard the news, even though the incident happened years ago.

flashbulb memories Memories of a specific, important, or surprising emotionally significant event that are recalled easily and with vivid imagery. (Module 21)

Their ability to remember details about this fatal event illustrates a phenomenon known as flashbulb memory. **Flashbulb memories** are memories related to a specific, important, or surprising event that are so vivid they represent a virtual snapshot of the event. Several types of flashbulb memories are common among college students. For example, involvement in a car accident, meeting one's roommate for the first time, and the night of high school graduation are all typical flashbulb memories (see Figure 3; Talarico, 2009; Lanciano et al., 2013; Talarico, Bohn, & Wessel, 2019).

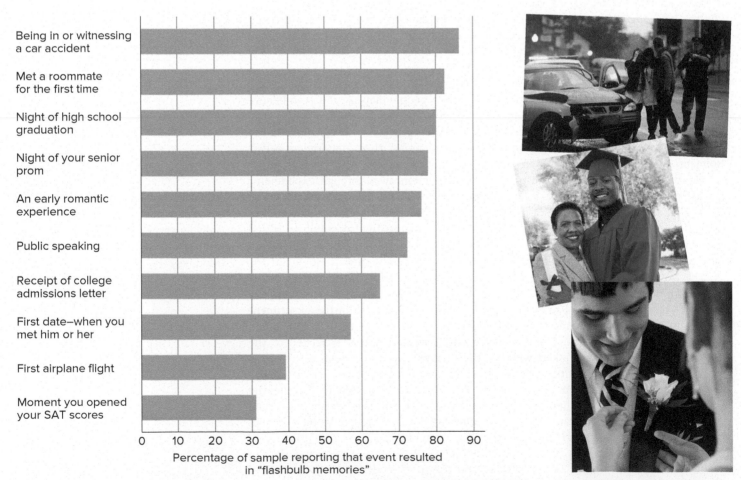

FIGURE 3 These are the most common flashbulb memory events, based on a survey of college students. What are some of your flashbulb memories?

(first): Image Source/Getty Images; (second): Digital Vision/SuperStock; (third): DreamPictures/VStock/Getty Images; (Graph): Source: Adapted from Rubin, D. C. (1986, September). The subtle deceiver: Recalling our past. *Psychology Today*, pp. 39–46.

Of course, flashbulb memories do not contain every detail of an original scene. I remember vividly that decades ago I was sitting in Mr. Sharp's 10th-grade geometry class when I heard that President John Kennedy had been shot. However, although I recall where I was sitting and how my classmates reacted to the news, I do not recollect what I was wearing or what I had for lunch that day.

Furthermore, the details recalled in flashbulb memories are often inaccurate, particularly when they involve highly emotional events. For example, those old enough to remember the day when the World Trade Center in New York was attacked by terrorists typically remember watching television that morning and seeing images of the first plane and then the second plane striking the towers. However, that recollection is wrong: In fact, television broadcasts showed images only of the second plane on September 11. No video of the first plane was available until early the following morning, September 12, when it was shown on television (Schaefer, Halldorson, & Dizon-Reynante, 2011; Hirst et al., 2015).

Flashbulb memories illustrate a more general phenomenon about memory: Memories that are exceptional are more easily retrieved (although not necessarily accurately) than are those relating to events that are commonplace. The more distinctive a stimulus is and the more personal relevance the event has, the more likely we are to recall it later (Talarico & Rubin, 2007; Schaefer, Halldorson, & Dizon-Reynante, 2011; Gandolphe & El Haj, 2017).

Even with a distinctive stimulus, however, we may not remember where the information came from. *Source amnesia* occurs when an individual has a memory for some material but cannot recall where he or she encountered it. For example, source amnesia can explain situations in which you meet someone you know but can't remember where you met that person initially.

Similarly, our motivation to remember material when we are exposed to it initially affects how well we can later recall it. If we know we are going to need to recall material later, we are going to be more attentive to it. In contrast, if we don't expect to need to recall material later, then we are less likely to remember it (Kassam et al., 2009; Phukhachee et al., 2019).

Constructive Processes in Memory: Rebuilding the Past

As we have seen, although it is clear that we can have detailed recollections of significant and distinctive events, it is difficult to gauge the accuracy of such memories. In fact, it is apparent that our memories reflect, at least in part, **constructive processes,** processes in which memories are influenced by the meaning we give to events. When we retrieve information, then, the memory that is produced is affected not just by the direct prior experience we have had with the stimulus but also by our guesses and inferences about its meaning.

The notion that memory is based on constructive processes was first put forward by Frederic Bartlett, a British psychologist. He suggested that people tend to remember information in terms of **schemas,** organized bodies of information stored in memory that bias the way new information is interpreted, stored, and recalled (Bartlett, 1932). Because we use schemas to organize information, our memories often consist of a reconstruction of previous experience. Consequently, schemas are based not only on the actual material to which people are exposed but also on their understanding of the situation, their expectations about the situation, and their awareness of the motivations underlying the behavior of others.

One of the earliest demonstrations of schemas came from a classic study that involved a procedure similar to the children's game of "telephone," in which information from memory is passed sequentially from one person to another. In the study, a participant viewed a drawing in which there were a variety of people of differing racial and ethnic backgrounds on a subway car, one of whom—a white person—was shown

constructive processes Processes in which memories are influenced by the meaning we give to events. (Module 21)

schemas Organized bodies of information stored in memory that bias the way new information is interpreted, stored, and recalled. (Modules 21, 52)

Study Alert
A key fact about memory is that it is a constructive process in which memories are influenced by the meaning given to what is being recalled.

FIGURE 4 Yankee and Red Sox fans were more accurate recalling details of a championship game their team won than they were of a championship game that their team lost.

Source: Adapted from Breslin, C. W., & Safer, M. A. (2011). Effects of event valence on long-term memory for two baseball championship games. *Psychological Science, 20*, 1–5.

with a razor in his hand (Allport & Postman, 1958). The first participant was asked to describe the drawing to someone else without looking back at it. Then that person was asked to describe it to another person (without looking at the drawing), and then the process was repeated with still one more participant.

The report of the last person differed in significant, yet systematic, ways from the initial drawing. Specifically, many people described the drawing as depicting an African American with a knife—an incorrect recollection, given that the drawing showed a razor in the hand of a Caucasian person. The transformation of the Caucasian's razor into an African American's knife clearly indicates that the participants held a schema that included the unwarranted prejudice that African Americans are more violent than Caucasians and thus more apt to be holding a knife. In short, our expectations and knowledge—and prejudices—affect the reliability of our memories (McDonald & Hirt, 1997; Newby-Clark & Ross, 2003; De Brigard et al., 2017).

Although the constructive nature of memory can result in memories that are partially or completely false, they also may be beneficial in some ways. For example, false memories may allow us to keep hold of positive self-images. In addition, they may help us maintain positive relationships with others as we construct overly positive views of them (Howe, 2011).

Similarly, memory is affected by the emotional meaning of experiences. For example, in one experiment, researchers asked devoted Yankee or Red Sox fans about details of two decisive baseball championship games between the teams, one won by the Yankees and the other won by the Red Sox. Fans recalled details of the game their team won significantly more accurately than the game their team lost (see Figure 4; Breslin & Safer, 2011; Guida et al., 2013; Tassone, Reed, & Carstensen, 2019).

MEMORY IN THE COURTROOM: THE EYEWITNESS ON TRIAL

For Calvin Willis, the inadequate memories of two people cost him more than two decades of his life. Willis was the victim of mistaken identity when a young rape victim picked out his photo as the perpetrator of the rape. On that basis, he was tried, convicted, and sentenced to life in prison. Twenty-one years later, DNA testing showed that Willis was innocent and the victim's identification wrong. (Corsello, 2005)

Unfortunately, Willis is not the only victim to whom apologies have had to be made; many cases of mistaken identity have led to unjustified legal actions. Research on eyewitness identification of suspects, as well as on memory for other details of crimes, has shown that eyewitnesses are apt to make significant errors when they try to recall details of criminal activity—even if they are highly confident about their recollections. Because more than 75,000 prosecutions a year are totally based on eyewitness recollections, the problem is significant (Paterson, Kemp, & Ng, 2011; Lehrer, 2012; McCann et al., 2015).

One reason eyewitnesses tend to make significant errors is the impact of the weapons used in crimes. When a criminal perpetrator displays a gun or knife, it acts like a perceptual magnet, attracting the eyes of the witnesses. As a consequence, witnesses pay less attention to other details of the crime and are less able to recall what actually occurred (Zaitsu, 2007; Pickel, 2009; Sheahan et al., 2017).

The specific wording of questions posed to eyewitnesses by police officers or attorneys also can lead to memory errors. For example, in one experiment, the participants were shown a film of two cars crashing into each other. Some were then asked the question, "About how fast were the cars going when they *smashed* into each other?" On average, they estimated the speed to be 40.8 miles per hour. In contrast, when another group of participants was asked, "About how fast were the cars going when they *contacted* each other?" the average estimated speed was only 31.8 miles per hour (see Figure 5; Loftus & Palmer, 1974; Dobbins & Kanter, 2019).

Although eyewitnesses are often confident in their recollections, in many cases, their confidence is misplaced. In fact, the relationship between confidence and accuracy is often small and sometimes even negative; in some cases, the more confident a witness, the less

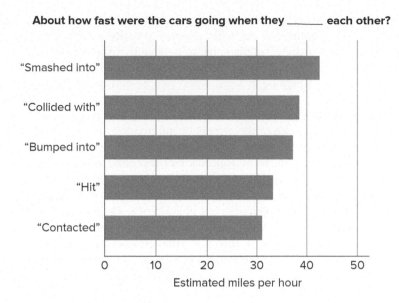

About how fast were the cars going when they _____ each other?

"Smashed into"

"Collided with"

"Bumped into"

"Hit"

"Contacted"

Estimated miles per hour

FIGURE 5 After viewing an accident involving two cars, the participants in a study were asked to estimate the speed of the two cars involved in the collision. Estimates varied substantially, depending on the way the question was worded.

Source: Adapted from Loftus, E. F., & Palmer, J. C. (1974). Reconstruction of automobile destruction: An example of the interface between language and memory. *Journal of Verbal Learning and Verbal Behavior, 13,* 585–589.

accurate are their recollections. On the other hand, several conditions affect the relationship between eyewitness confidence and better accuracy. Specifically, accuracy improves when witnesses see only one suspect at a time; when the suspects don't look conspicuous in the lineup due to their clothing or ethnicity or race; and when the witness is told the offender is not necessarily in the lineup (Wixted & Wells, 2017; Sauer, Palmer, & Brewer, 2019).

Children's Reliability The problem of memory reliability becomes even more acute when children are witnesses because increasing evidence suggests that children's memories are highly vulnerable to the influence of others. For instance, in one experiment, 5- to 7-year-old girls who had just had routine physical examinations were shown an anatomically explicit doll. The girls were shown the doll's genital area and asked, "Did the doctor touch you here?" Three of the girls who did not have a vaginal or anal exam said that the doctor had in fact touched them in the genital area, and one of those three made up the detail "The doctor did it with a stick" (Brown, Goldstein, & Bjorklund, 2000).

Children's memories are especially susceptible to influence when the situation is highly emotional or stressful. For example, in trials in which there is significant pretrial publicity or in which alleged victims are questioned repeatedly, often by untrained interviewers, the memories of the alleged victims may be influenced by the types of questions they are asked (Goodman & Quas, 2008; Wright, Nash, & Wade, 2015; Saywitz et al., 2019).

Repressed and False Memories: Separating Truth from Fiction Consider the case of Paul Shanley, a Catholic priest. He was convicted and jailed for 12 years for sexual abuse of a victim who claimed he had no memory until adulthood of being abused as a child over a 6-year period. It was not until adulthood that he claimed his repressed memories gradually moved into consciousness. At that point, he reported clearly recalling his years of abuse, and on the basis of those previously repressed memories, the priest was convicted (Wolf, Guyer, & Sharpe, 2010; Otgaar, Howe, & Muris, 2017; Goodman, Gonzalves, & Wolpe, 2019).

Repressed memories are apparent recollections of events that are initially so shocking that the mind responds by pushing them into the unconscious. Supporters of the notion of repressed memory (based on Freud's psychoanalytic theory) suggest that traumatic memories may remain hidden, possibly throughout a person's lifetime, unless they are triggered by some current circumstance, such as the probing that occurs during psychological therapy.

However, many memory researchers maintain that there is little evidence for the phenomenon of repressed memories. They assert that so-called repressed memories may well be inaccurate or even wholly false, a phenomenon *false memory*, in which a person remembers information that did not happen or remembers it in an inaccurate way.

Children's memories may show considerable unreliability when they are called as witnesses during trials.

Rob Crandall/SCPhotos/Alamy Stock Photo

For example, when recalling an event based on an unclear or ambiguous memory, people may become confused about whether they actually experienced the event or instead imagined it. Ultimately, people come to believe that the event actually occurred (Bernstein & Loftus, 2009a; Choi, Kensinger, & Rajaram, 2013; Lynn et al., 2015).

False memories also may be at work when people embrace what has come to be called "fake news." That is, a person hears or reads news from an unreliable source, such as a biased website or a conversation overheard at the grocery store. Later, they may may not recall the source of the erroneous information, and they eventually come to believe in its accuracy (Bronstein et al., 2019).

Great controversy surrounds the legitimacy of repressed memories and false memories. Many therapists give great weight to authenticity of repressed memories, and their views are supported by research showing that there are specific regions of the brain that help keep unwanted memories out of awareness. On the other side of the issue are researchers who maintain that there is insufficient scientific support for the existence of such memories. There is also a middle ground: memory researchers who suggest that false memories are a result of normal information processing. The challenge for those on all sides of the issue is to distinguish truth from fiction (Strange, Clifasefi, & Garry, 2007; Bernstein & Loftus, 2009b;).

Autobiographical Memory: Where Past Meets Present Your memory of experiences in your own past may well be, in part, a fiction–or at least a distortion of what actually occurred. The same constructive processes that make us inaccurately recall the behavior of others also reduce the accuracy of autobiographical memories. **Autobiographical memory** is our recollections of our own life experiences. Autobiographical memories encompass the episodic memories we hold about ourselves (Sutin & Robins, 2007; Nalbantian, 2011; Bauer et al., 2019).

For example, we tend to forget information about our past that is incompatible with the way in which we currently see ourselves. One study found that adults who were well adjusted but who had been treated for emotional problems during the early years of their lives tended to forget important but troubling childhood events, such as being in foster care. College students misremember their bad grades–but remember their good ones (see Figure 6; Walker, Skowronski, & Thompson, 2003; Kemps & Tiggemann, 2007; Stanley et al., 2017).

Similarly, when a group of 48-year-olds was asked to recall how they had responded on a questionnaire they had completed when they were high school freshmen, their accuracy was no better than chance. For example, although 61% of the questionnaire respondents said that playing sports and other physical activities was their favorite pastime, only 23% of the adults recalled it accurately (Offer et al., 2000).

It is not just certain kinds of events that are distorted; particular periods of life are remembered more easily than others. For example, when people reach late adulthood, they remember periods of life in which they experienced major transitions, such as attending college and working at their first jobs, better than they remember their middle-age years. Similarly, although most adults' earliest memories of their own lives are of events that occurred when they were toddlers, toddlers show evidence of recall of events that occurred when they were as young as 6 months old (Mace, Bernas, & Clevinger, 2015; Wang et al., 2019).

autobiographical memory Our recollections of our own life experiences. (Module 21)

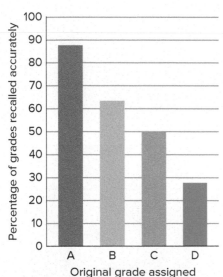

FIGURE 6 We tend to distort memories of unpleasant events. For example, college students are much more likely to accurately recall their good grades while inaccurately recalling their poor ones. Now that you know this, how well do you think you can recall your high school grades?

Source: Adapted from Bahrick, H. P., Hall, L. K., & Berger, S. A. (1996). Accuracy and distortion in memory for high school grades. *Psychological Science, 7,* 265–269.

Exploring Diversity

Are There Cross-Cultural Differences in Memory?

Explorers who have visited parts of the world in which there is no written language sometimes return with tales of individuals with phenomenal memories. For instance, storytellers in some preliterate cultures recount long chronicles that include the names and activities of people over multiple generations.

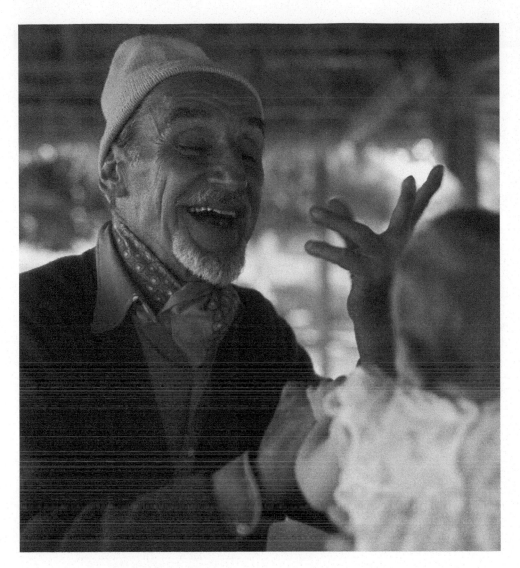

Storytellers in many cultures can recount hundreds of years of history in vivid detail. Research has found that this amazing ability is due less to basic memory processes than to the ways in which they acquire and retain information.
Albert Moldvay/National Geographic/Getty Images

Such feats of memory initially led experts to believe that people in preliterate societies develop a different, and perhaps better, type of memory than do those in cultures that employ a written language. They suggested that in a society that lacks writing, people are motivated to recall information with accuracy, especially information relating to tribal histories and traditions that would be lost if they were not passed down orally from one generation to another (Daftary & Meri, 2002; Berntsen & Rubin, 2004).

Today, however, memory researchers dismiss that view. For one thing, preliterate peoples don't have an exclusive claim to amazing memory feats. Some Hebrew scholars memorize thousands of pages of text and can recall the locations of particular words on the page. Similarly, poetry singers in the Balkans can recall thousands of lines of poetry. Even in cultures in which written language exists, then, astounding feats of memory are possible (Strathern & Stewart, 2003; Rubin et al., 2007).

Memory researchers now believe that there are both similarities and differences in memory across cultures. Basic memory processes seem to be similar. For example, short-term memory capacity, working memory, and the structure of long-term memory—the "hardware"—are universal and operate similarly in people in all cultures.

In contrast, the way information is acquired and the degree to which it is rehearsed—the "software" of memory—do differ from culture to culture. Culture determines how people frame information initially, how much they practice learning it, and which strategies they use to recall it (Mack, 2003; Wang & Conway, 2006; Rubin et al., 2007; Goyal et al., 2019).

RECAP/EVALUATE/RETHINK

RECAP

LO 21-1 What causes difficulties and failures in remembering?

- The tip-of-the-tongue phenomenon is the temporary inability to remember information that one is certain one knows. Retrieval cues are a major strategy for recalling information successfully.
- The levels-of-processing approach to memory suggests that the way in which information is initially perceived and analyzed determines the success with which it is recalled. The deeper the initial processing, the greater the recall.
- Explicit memory refers to intentional or conscious recollection of information. In contrast, implicit memory refers to memories of which people are not consciously aware but that can affect subsequent performance and behavior.
- Flashbulb memories are memories centered on a specific, emotionally significant event. The more distinctive a memory is, the more easily it can be retrieved.
- Memory is a constructive process: We relate memories to the meaning, guesses, and expectations we give to events. Specific information is recalled in terms of schemas, organized bodies of information stored in memory that bias the way new information is interpreted, stored, and recalled.
- Eyewitnesses are apt to make substantial errors when they try to recall the details of crimes. The problem of memory reliability becomes even more acute when the witnesses are children.
- Autobiographical memory is influenced by constructive processes.

EVALUATE

1. While with a group of friends at a dance, Eva bumps into a man she dated last month. But when she tries to introduce him to her friends, she cannot remember his name. What is the term for this occurrence?
2. _____ is the process of retrieving a specific item from memory.
3. A friend tells you, "I know exactly where I was and what I was doing when I heard that Prince died." What is this type of memory phenomenon called?
4. _____ _____ _____ theory states that the more a person analyzes a statement, the more likely he or she is to remember it later.

RETHINK

1. Research shows that an eyewitness's memory for details of crimes can contain significant errors. How might a lawyer use this information when evaluating an eyewitness's testimony? Should eyewitness accounts be permissible in a court of law?
2. How do schemas help people process information during encoding, storage, and retrieval? In what ways are they helpful? How can they contribute to inaccurate autobiographical memories?

Answers to Evaluate Questions

1. tip-of-the-tongue phenomenon; 2. Recall; 3. flashbulb memory; 4. Levels-of-processing

KEY TERMS

tip-of-the-tongue phenomenon	recognition	implicit memory	constructive processes
recall	levels-of-processing theory	priming	schemas
	explicit memory	flashbulb memories	autobiographical memory

Module 22
Forgetting: When Memory Fails

He could not remember his childhood friends, the house he grew up in, or what he had eaten for breakfast that morning. H. M., as he is referred to in the scientific literature, had lost his ability to remember anything beyond a few minutes, the result of experimental surgery intended to minimize his epileptic seizures. But the removal of his brain's hippocampus and the loss of his temporal lobes quite literally erased H. M.'s past. He had enjoyed a normal memory until he underwent the operation at age 27. After that, H. M. said, every moment felt like waking from a dream. He never knew where he was or the identities of the people around him (Milner, 2005; MacKay, 2019).

As the case of H. M. illustrates, a person without a normal memory faces severe difficulties. All of us who have experienced even routine instances of forgetting–such as not remembering an acquaintance's name or a fact on a test–understand the very real consequences of memory failure.

Of course, memory failure is also essential to remembering important information. The ability to forget inconsequential details about experiences, people, and objects helps us avoid being burdened and distracted by trivial stores of meaningless data. Forgetting helps keep unwanted and unnecessary information from interfering with retrieving information that is wanted and necessary (Schooler & Hertwig, 2012).

Forgetting also permits us to form general impressions and recollections. For example, the reason our friends consistently look familiar to us is because we're able to forget their clothing, facial blemishes, and other transient features that change from one occasion to the next. Instead, our memories are based on a summary of various critical features–a far more economical use of our memory capabilities.

Finally, forgetting provides a practical educational benefit: When we have forgotten something and then are forced to relearn it, we're more likely to remember it better in the future (Bjork, 2015; Boser, 2017).

The first attempts to study forgetting were made by German psychologist Hermann Ebbinghaus about 100 years ago. Using himself as the only participant in his study, Ebbinghaus memorized lists of three-letter nonsense syllables–meaningless sets of two consonants with a vowel in between, such as FIW and BOZ. By measuring how easy it was to relearn a given list of words after varying periods of time had passed since the initial learning, he found that forgetting occurred systematically, as shown in Figure 1. As the figure indicates, the most rapid forgetting occurs in the first 9 hours, particularly in the first hour. After 9 hours, the rate of forgetting slows and declines little, even after the passage of many days.

Despite his primitive methods, Ebbinghaus's study had an important influence on subsequent research, and his basic conclusions have been upheld. There is almost always a strong initial decline in memory, followed by a more gradual drop over time. Furthermore, relearning of previously mastered material is almost always faster than starting from scratch, whether the material is academic information or a motor skill such as serving a tennis ball (Wixted & Carpenter, 2007; Radvansky, Pettijohn, & Kim, 2015).

Why We Forget

Why do we forget? One reason is that we may not have paid attention to the material in the first place–a failure of *encoding*. For example, if you live in the United States, you probably have been exposed to thousands of pennies during your life. Despite this experience, you probably don't have a clear sense of the details of the coin. (See this

FIGURE 1 In his classic work, Ebbinghaus found that the most rapid forgetting occurs in the first 9 hours after exposure to new material. However, the rate of forgetting then slows down and declines very little even after many days have passed. Check your own memory: What were you doing exactly 2 hours ago? What were you doing last Tuesday at 5 p.m.? Which information is easier to retrieve?

Source: Adapted from Ebbinghaus, H. (1885/1913). *Memory: A contribution to experimental psychology* (H. A. Roger & C. E. Bussenius, Trans.). New York: Columbia University Press.

for yourself by looking at Figure 2.) Consequently, the reason for your memory failure is that you probably never encoded the information into long-term memory initially. Obviously, if information was not placed in memory to start with, there is no way the information can be recalled.

But what about material that has been encoded into memory and that can't later be remembered? Several processes account for memory failures, including decay, interference, and cue-dependent forgetting.

decay The loss of information in memory through its nonuse. (Module 22)

Decay is the loss of information in memory through nonuse. This explanation for forgetting assumes that *memory traces,* the physical changes that take place in the brain when new material is learned, simply fade away or disintegrate over time (Grann, 2007; Ricker et al., 2019).

Although there is evidence that decay does occur, this does not seem to be the complete explanation for forgetting. Often there is no relationship between how long ago a

FIGURE 2 One of these pennies is the real thing. Can you find it? Why is this task harder than it seems at first?

Source: Adapted from Nickerson, R. S., & Adams, M. J. (1979). Long-term memory for a common object. *Cognitive Psychology, 11,* 297.

person was exposed to information and how well that information is recalled. If decay explained all forgetting, we would expect that the more time that has elapsed between the initial learning of information and our attempt to recall it, the harder it would be to remember it because there would be more time for the memory trace to decay. Yet people who take several consecutive tests on the same material often recall more of the initial information when taking later tests than they did on earlier tests. If decay were operating, we would expect the opposite to occur (Hardt, Nader, & Nadel, 2013; Sachser et al., 2017).

Because decay does not fully account for forgetting, memory specialists have proposed an additional mechanism: interference. In **interference**, information stored in memory disrupts the recall of other information stored in memory. For example, if I'm trying to recall my college classmate Jake's name and all I can remember is the name of another classmate, James, interference may be at work (Solesio-Jofre et al., 2011; Ecker, Tay, & Brown, 2015).

To distinguish between decay and interference, think of the two processes in terms of a row of books on a library shelf. In decay, the old books are constantly crumbling and rotting away, leaving room for new arrivals. Interference processes suggest that new books knock the old ones off the shelf, where they become hard to find or even totally inaccessible.

Finally, forgetting may occur because of **cue-dependent forgetting,** forgetting that occurs when there are insufficient retrieval cues to rekindle information that is in memory. For example, you may not be able to remember where you lost a set of keys until you mentally walk through your day, thinking of each place you visited. When you think of the place where you lost the keys—say, the library—the retrieval cue of the library may be sufficient to help you recall that you left them on the desk in the library. Without that retrieval cue, you may be unable to recall the location of the keys (Weller et al., 2013).

Most research suggests that interference and cue-dependent forgetting are key processes in forgetting. We forget things mainly because new memories interfere with the retrieval of old ones or because appropriate retrieval cues are unavailable, not because the memory trace has decayed (Radvansky, 2010; also see *Applying Psychology in the 21st Century.*)

interference The phenomenon by which information in memory disrupts the recall of other information. (Module 22)

cue-dependent forgetting Forgetting that occurs when there are insufficient retrieval cues to rekindle information that is in memory. (Module 22)

Study Alert
Memory loss through decay comes from nonuse of the memory; memory loss through interference is due to the presence of other information in memory.

Proactive and Retroactive Interference: The Before and After of Forgetting

There are actually two sorts of interference that influence forgetting. One is proactive interference, and the other is retroactive interference (Oberauer, Awh, & Sutterer, 2017; Redick, Wiemers, & Engle, 2019).

In **proactive interference,** information learned earlier disrupts the recall of newer material. Suppose, as a student of foreign languages, you first learned French in the 10th grade, and then in the 11th grade you took Spanish. When in the 12th grade you take a college subject achievement test in Spanish, you may find you have difficulty recalling the Spanish translation of a word because all you can think of is its French equivalent.

In contrast, **retroactive interference** occurs when material that was learned later disrupts the retrieval of information that was learned earlier. If, for example, you have difficulty on a French subject achievement test because of your more recent exposure to Spanish, retroactive interference is the culprit (see Figure 3). Similarly, retroactive interference can account for the lack of accuracy of eyewitness memories, as newer information about a crime obtained from newspaper accounts may disrupt the initial memory of the observation of the crime.

One way to remember the difference between proactive and retroactive interference is to keep in mind that *pro*active interference progresses in time—the past interferes with the present. In contrast, *retro*active interference retrogresses in time, working backward as the present interferes with the past.

proactive interference Interference in which information learned earlier disrupts the recall of material learned later. (Module 22)

retroactive interference Interference in which material that was learned later disrupts the retrieval of information that was learned earlier. (Module 22)

APPLYING PSYCHOLOGY IN THE 21ST CENTURY

THE UPSIDE OF FORGETTING

Do you have trouble remembering names and facts, or the date of your mom's birthday so you can be sure to call her? Do you worry that your forgetfulness is a sign of mental weakness? Or do you envy friends who seem to have an effortless ability to retrieve details from memory? If so, you're not alone. We all have memory failures from time to time, and that's not necessarily a bad thing. In fact, research suggests that forgetting serves an important purpose in keeping our thoughts uncluttered and manageable. The phenomenon is known as retrieval-induced forgetting.

The prefrontal cortex of the brain manages access to information stored in memory, enhancing access to information we use most frequently while also inhibiting access to conflicting information. Rather than remembering everything, the brain prioritizes information, giving more emphasis to the big ideas and less to the niggling details. By reducing competing memories, our brains allow us to more easily work with important information so that we can, for example, draw uncomplicated conclusions or detect important underlying patterns. Sometimes learning even requires forgetting. In one research example, mice were well trained to find a specific location within a maze. When they were then being trained to run instead to a different

Forgetting can have an upside, although it may not always be apparent.
Baru Cameragirl/Shutterstock

location in the same maze—that is, to forget their old response and acquire a new one—they were better able to do so when the researchers induced growth of new neurons. Forgetting, then, can sometimes indicate the growth of new pathways in the course of learning new material (Wimber et al., 2015; Santoro, Frankland, & Richards, 2016; Schlichting, & Frankland, 2017).

You might think that having access to more, or even all, of the information stored in your brain is better, but that's not always

true. Forgetting reduces the occurrence of other kinds of memory problems, such as interference. You'll be very happy if you can remember where you parked your car on campus last so that you can find it again. But if you had equally accessible memories of the location of your car for every single time you ever parked it on campus, you would likely have difficulty pulling up just the one that will lead you to where your car is today. In fact, one study found that trying to intentionally forget some things allowed participants to better remember others (Popov et al., 2019).

Forgetting also serves another purpose: it disrupts old patterns of responding, clearing the way for new and potentially more creative or more effective responses. Sometimes our habits can keep us from seeing new solutions, and forgetting can force us to take a fresh perspective on an old problem. So the next time you can't recall your wi-fi password, take heart: rather than an annoyance, your forgetfulness may offer an opportunity to come up with a more memorable password!

RETHINK

- Can you think of additional situations in which learning a new task might entail the need to forget an old one?
- Can you think of other kinds of memories that might be more helpful to forget than to retain?

Although the concepts of proactive and retroactive interference illustrate how material may be forgotten, they still do not explain whether forgetting is caused by the actual loss or modification of information or by problems in the retrieval of information. Most research suggests that material that has apparently been lost because of interference can eventually be recalled if appropriate stimuli are presented, but the question has not been fully answered (Radvansky, 2010).

Memory Dysfunctions: Afflictions of Forgetting

PsychTech

Having trouble remembering something on your computer screen? According to research by Connor Diemand-Yauman (2010) and colleagues, changing the font into something *harder* to read may make it easier to remember. The explanation is that the unusual font forces us to concentrate more intently on the information, making it more memorable.

Memory loss creeps up on its victims. It starts with little things such as misplacing keys or glasses. Then, you forget the names of common household items, and you miss appointments. Next, you can't drive in traffic without becoming confused and anxious. You try to hide what's happening, but others notice. Finally, your lapses become more

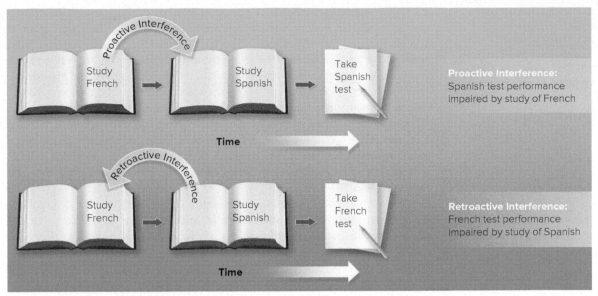

FIGURE 3 Proactive interference occurs when material learned earlier interferes with the recall of newer material. In this example, studying French before studying Spanish interferes with performance on a Spanish test. In contrast, retroactive interference exists when material learned after initial exposure to other material interferes with the recall of the first material. In this case, retroactive interference occurs when recall of French is impaired because of later exposure to Spanish.

consequential: You nearly get run over; you have a traffic accident. You no longer can manage the routines of everyday living, such as getting dressed.

These memory problems are symptomatic of **Alzheimer's disease,** a progressive brain disorder that leads to a gradual and irreversible decline in cognitive abilities. Alzheimer's is the fourth-leading cause of death among adults in the United States, affecting an estimated 5.8 million people.

In the beginning, Alzheimer's symptoms appear as simple forgetfulness of things such as appointments and birthdays. As the disease progresses, memory loss becomes more profound, and even the simplest tasks–such as using a phone–are forgotten. Ultimately, victims may lose their ability to speak or comprehend language, and physical deterioration sets in, leading to death.

The causes of Alzheimer's disease are not fully understood. Increasing evidence suggests that Alzheimer's results from an inherited susceptibility to a defect in the production of the protein beta amyloid, which is necessary for the maintenance of nerve cell connections. When the synthesis of beta amyloid goes awry, large clumps of cells form, triggering inflammation and the deterioration of nerve cells in the brain (Hyman, 2011; Tan, Yu, & Tan, 2015; Reddy et al., 2019).

Alzheimer's disease A progressive brain disorder that leads to a gradual and irreversible decline in cognitive abilities (Modules 22, 39)

From the perspective of...

A Health-Care Provider What sorts of activities might health-care providers offer their patients to help them combat the memory loss of Alzheimer's disease?

Rubberball/Getty Images

amnesia Memory loss that occurs without other mental difficulties. (Module 22)

retrograde amnesia Amnesia in which memory is lost for occurrences prior to a certain event but not for new events. (Module 22)

anterograde amnesia Amnesia in which memory is lost for events that follow an injury. (Module 22)

Korsakoff's syndrome A disease that afflicts long-term alcoholics, leaving some abilities intact but including hallucinations and a tendency to repeat the same story. (Module 22)

! **Study Alert**
Except for Alzheimer's disease, memory disorders are relatively rare.

Alzheimer's disease is one of a number of memory dysfunctions. Another is **amnesia,** memory loss that occurs without other mental difficulties. The type of amnesia immortalized in countless Hollywood films involves a victim who receives a blow to the head and is unable to remember anything from their past. In reality, amnesia of this type, known as retrograde amnesia, is quite rare. In **retrograde amnesia,** memory is lost for occurrences prior to a certain event but not for new events. Usually, lost memories gradually reappear, although full restoration may take as long as several years. In certain cases, some memories are lost forever. But even in cases of severe memory loss, the loss is generally selective. For example, although people suffering from retrograde amnesia may be unable to recall friends and family members, they still may be able to play complicated card games or knit a sweater quite well (Lee, McDonald, & Sutherland, 2019).

A second type of amnesia is exemplified by people who remember nothing of their current activities. In **anterograde amnesia,** loss of memory occurs for events that follow an injury. Information cannot be transferred from short-term to long-term memory, resulting in the inability to remember anything other than what was in long-term storage before the injury (Gilboa, Winocur, & Rosenbaum, 2006; Stöllberger al., 2019).

Amnesia is also a result of **Korsakoff's syndrome,** a disease that afflicts long-term alcoholics. Although many of their intellectual abilities may be intact, Korsakoff's sufferers display a strange array of symptoms, including hallucinations and a tendency to repeat the same story over and over (Wester et al., 2013; Scalzo, Bowden, & Hillborn, 2015).

Fortunately, most of us have intact memory, and the occasional failures we suffer may actually be preferable to having a perfect memory. Consider, for instance, the case of a man who had total recall. After reading passages of Dante's *The Divine Comedy* in Italian–a language he did not speak–he was able to repeat them from memory some 15 years later. He could memorize lists of 50 unrelated words and recall them at will more than a decade later. He could even repeat the same list of words backward, if asked (Luria, 1968).

Such a skill at first may seem to be enviable, but it actually presented quite a problem. The man's memory became a jumble of lists of words, numbers, and names; when he tried to relax, his mind was filled with images. Even reading was difficult because every word evoked a flood of thoughts from the past that interfered with his ability to understand the meaning of what he was reading. Partially as a consequence of the man's unusual memory, psychologist A. R. Luria, who studied his case, found him to be a "disorganized and rather dull-witted person" (Luria, 1968). We might be grateful, then, that forgetfulness plays a role in our lives.

BECOMING AN INFORMED CONSUMER
of Psychology

Improving Your Memory

Apart from the advantages of forgetting, say, a bad date, most of us would like to find ways to improve our memories. Among the effective strategies for studying and remembering course material are:

- *Rely on organization cues.* Recall material you read in textbooks or online by organizing the material in memory the first time you read it. For example, use cues such as chapter outlines or learning objectives. If you take advantage of these "advance organizers," you can make connections, see relationships among the various facts, and process the material at a deeper level, which in turn will later aid recall (Korur, Toker, & Eryilmaz, 2016).

- *Take effective notes.* "Less is more" is perhaps the best advice for taking lecture notes that facilitate recall. Rather than trying to jot down every detail of a lecture, it is better to listen and think about the material, and take down the main points. In effective note taking, thinking about the material when you first hear it is more important than writing it down. This is one reason that borrowing someone else's notes is a bad idea; you will have no framework in memory that you can use to understand them (Feldman, 2017).

- *Practice, practice, practice.* Although practice does not necessarily make perfect, it helps. Use *overlearning,* the process of studying and rehearsing material well beyond your initial mastery of it. Lots of research shows that people demonstrate better long-term recall when they overlearn rather than when they stop practicing just after they initially learn the material (Shibata et al., 2017).

- *Use the keyword technique.* If you are studying a foreign language, try pairing a foreign word with a common English word that has a similar sound. This English word is known as the *keyword.* For example, to learn the Spanish word for duck (*pato,* pronounced *pot-o*), you might choose the keyword *pot.* Once you have thought of a keyword, think of an image in which the the Spanish word *pato* is interacting with the English keyword. For example, you might envision a duck being cooked in a pot to remember the word *pato* (Wyra, Lawson, & Hungi, 2007; Miyatsu & McDaniel, 2019).

- *Test yourself.* If you have trouble remembering names of people you have recently met, one way to help yourself is to say their names out loud when you are first introduced. And just a little later, test yourself by trying to recall the name (Shellenbarger, 2019).

- *Be skeptical about claims that certain drugs improve memory.* Advertisements for vitamins with ginkgo biloba or a "Mental Sharpness Product" would have you believe that taking a drug or supplement can improve your memory. Not so, according to the results of numerous studies. No research has shown that commercial memory enhancers are effective (McDaniel, Maier, & Einstein, 2002; Burns, Bryan, & Nettelbeck, 2006).

RECAP/EVALUATE/RETHINK

RECAP

LO 22-1 Why do we forget information?

- Several processes account for memory failure, including decay, interference (both proactive and retroactive), and cue-dependent forgetting.

LO 22-2 What are the major memory impairments?

- Among the memory dysfunctions are Alzheimer's disease, which leads to a progressive loss of memory, and amnesia, a memory loss that occurs without other mental difficulties and can take the forms of retrograde amnesia and anterograde amnesia. Korsakoff's syndrome is a disease that afflicts long-term alcoholics, resulting in memory impairment.

- Techniques for improving memory include the keyword technique to memorize foreign language vocabulary; organizing text material and lecture notes; talking to yourself; and practice and rehearsal, leading to overlearning.

EVALUATE

1. If, after learning the history of the Middle East for a class 2 years ago, you now find yourself unable to recall what you learned, you are experiencing memory _____, caused by nonuse.

2. Difficulty in accessing a memory because of the presence of other information is known as _____.

3. _____ interference occurs when material is difficult to retrieve because of subsequent exposure to other material; _____ interference refers to difficulty in retrieving material as a result of the interference of previously learned material.

4. Match the following memory disorders with the correct information:

1. Affects alcoholics; may result in hallucinations
2. Memory loss occurring without other mental problems
3. Beta amyloid defect; progressive forgetting and physical deterioration

   a. Alzheimer's disease
   b. Korsakoff's syndrome
   c. Amnesia

RETHINK

1. What are the implications of proactive and retroactive interference for learning multiple foreign languages? Would earlier language training in a different language help or hinder learning a new language?
2. Does the phenomenon of interference help to explain the unreliability of autobiographical memory? Why?

Answers to Evaluate Questions

1. decay; 2. interference; 3. Retroactive, proactive; 4. 1-b, 2-c, 3-a

KEY TERMS

decay	proactive interference	Alzheimer's disease	anterograde amnesia
interference	retroactive	amnesia	Korsakoff's syndrome
cue-dependent forgetting	interference	retrograde amnesia	

LOOKING *Back*

EPILOGUE

Our examination of memory has highlighted the processes of encoding, storage, and retrieval, and theories about how these processes occur. We also encountered several phenomena relating to memory, including the tip-of-the-tongue phenomenon and flashbulb memories. Above all, we observed that memory is a constructive process by which interpretations, expectations, and guesses contribute to the nature of our memories.

Before moving on to chapter 8, return to the prologue of this chapter on Markie Pasternack's perfect memory of the events in her life. Consider the following questions in light of what you now know about memory.

1. Despite her extraordinary memory, Pasternak can only recall the events of a given day in history if she can tie them to a personal experience. Why do you think this is?
2. Do you think that having highly superior autobiographical memory is more of a benefit or a curse? Why do you think so? What might be some drawbacks of this ability?
3. What kinds of questions about memory and forgetting might researchers be able to answer by studying people such as Pasternak?

VISUAL SUMMARY 7 Memory

MODULE 20 The Foundations of Memory

Memory: Encoding, storing, and retrieving information

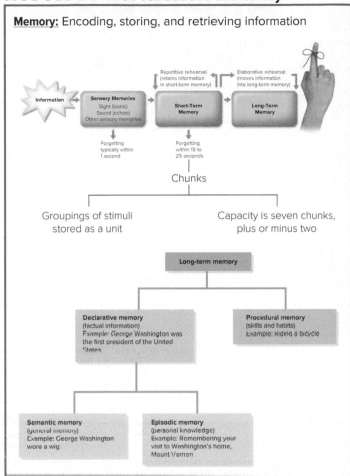

Chunks

Groupings of stimuli stored as a unit

Capacity is seven chunks, plus or minus two

Long-term memory

Declarative memory
(factual information)
Example: George Washington was the first president of the United States

Procedural memory
(skills and habits)
Example: Riding a bicycle

Semantic memory
(general memory)
Example: George Washington wore a wig

Episodic memory
(personal knowledge)
Example: Remembering your visit to Washington's home, Mount Vernon

MODULE 21 Recalling Long-Term Memories

Retrieval Cues: Stimuli that allow recall of information stored in long-term memory
- Recall: Remembering specific information
- Recognition: Knowing whether one has been previously exposed to given information

Levels of Processing Theory: Recall depends on how much the information was processed when it was first encountered

Explicit Memories: Conscious recall of information

Implicit Memories: Memories of which people are not consciously aware

Flashbulb Memories:
Memories of a specific, important, or surprising emotionally significant event that are recalled easily and with vivid imagery

Constructive Processes: Processes in which memories are influenced by the meaning we give to events

Schemas: Organized bodies of stored information that bias the way we interpret, store, and recall new information

Autobiographical memory: Our recollections of our own life experiences

MODULE 22 Forgetting: When Memory Fails

Decay: Loss of information through nonuse

Cue-dependent forgetting: Forgetting that occurs when insufficient retrieval cues are available

Interference: Information in memory disrupts the recall of other information

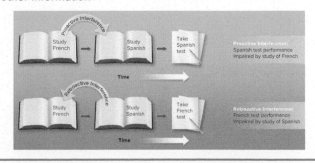

(Module 20) (Art) Sources: Journal of Experimental Psychology: General, "Working memory and the control of action: Evidence from task switching."; Springer Nature, "Human Memory and Material Memory."; (Photo): C Squared Studios/Getty Images; (Module 21) (Photo): Digital Vision/SuperStock; (Art): Source: Psychological Science, "Effects of event valence on long-term memory for two baseball championship games."; (Module 22, Decay) Source: Columbia University Press, "Memory: A contribution to experimental psychology."

Andersen Ross Photography Inc/DigitalVision/Getty Images

CHAPTER 8
Cognition and Language

LEARNING OUTCOMES FOR CHAPTER 8

LO 25-1 How do people use language?

LO 25-2 How does language develop?

PROLOGUE *CHESS-MASTER MACHINES*

Stockfish is a fearsome chess master, able to vanquish one opponent after another.

But Stockfish is not a person. It is a computer program that uses brute computing force to play the game of chess. Stockfish wins by applying the rules of chess to compute all the various potential next moves it can make, and then all the various potential moves that could result from each of those, and so on, until it whittles down the possibilities to the move that offers it the best advantage. It employs no strategy and has no insight into the nuances of the game, yet it plays phenomenally well, beating the best of its human competitors.

Still, Stockfish is a chess dunce compared to AlphaZero. AlphaZero is a new kind of chess-playing computer program. Rather than using a brute-force strategy, it was programmed to learn from its own mistakes and formulate its own rules for game play. It was given only the basic rules of the game, and then it was allowed to play against itself millions of times. Within hours, it became the best chess player in history—human or machine.

AlphaZero trounces Stockfish by playing smarter rather than harder or faster. Even when Stockfish is given ten times more time to make its moves, AlphaZero beats it because AlphaZero is using nuanced chess strategies of its own devising, including unusual risks and gambits—strategies no human understands because AlphaZero cannot communicate them, except to show that they work (Strogatz, 2018; Knight, 2019).

LOOKING *Ahead*

Although AlphaZero cannot communicate its strategies, psychologists can still learn a great deal by studying its decisions and moves. Certain types of games, including chess, can improve reaction times, decision making under pressure, fine-motor control, task switching, spatial sense, and, especially, attention-focusing. Results such these have led researchers to consider developing games for therapeutic uses to address certain types of cognitive deficits induced by aging or trauma (Granic, Lobel, & Engels, 2014; Gabbiandini & Greitemeyer, 2017; Lillo-Crespo et al., 2019).

Adapting to new experiences and honing new or existing cognitive skills are just two of the many tasks that our own amazing human computer—the brain—can accomplish in the course of our daily lives, even though we may have little or no idea how it does so. The mystery of how the brain processes language and all its nuances—as well as how it uses information to solve problems and make decisions—is the subject to which we now turn.

Cognitive psychology is the branch of psychology that focuses on the study of higher mental processes, including thinking, language, memory, problem solving, knowing, reasoning, judging, and decision making. Although the realm of cognitive psychology is broad, we will focus on three major topics. The first topic we consider in this chapter is thinking and reasoning. Then we examine different strategies for approaching problems, means of generating solutions, and ways of making judgments about the usefulness and accuracy of solutions. Finally, we discuss how language is developed and acquired, its basic characteristics, and the relationship between language and thought.

cognitive psychology The branch of psychology that focuses on the study of higher mental processes, including thinking, language, memory, problem solving, knowing, reasoning, judging, and decision making. (Module 23)

Module 23
Thinking and Reasoning

LEARNING OUTCOMES

LO 23-1 What is thinking?

LO 23-2 What processes underlie reasoning and decision making?

thinking Brain activity in which people mentally manipulate information, including words, visual images, sounds, or other data. (Module 23)

mental images Representations in the mind of an object or event. (Module 23)

PsychTech

Researcher Adam Wilson has developed a method of tweeting by thinking. The process involves being outfitted with electrodes that react to changes in brain activity. It's slow going, though: the fastest tweeters by thinking are able to create tweets at only 8 characters per minute.

Professional musicians often use mental imagery to focus on their performance, a process they call "getting in the zone." What are some other occupations that require the use of strong mental imagery?
Phuttharak/Shutterstock

What are you thinking about at this moment?

The mere ability to pose such a question underscores the distinctive nature of the human ability to think. No other species contemplates, analyzes, recollects, or plans the way humans do. Understanding what thinking is, however, goes beyond knowing that we think. Philosophers, for example, have argued for generations about the meaning of thinking, with some placing it at the core of human beings' understanding of their own existence.

Psychologists define **thinking** as brain activity in which we mentally manipulate information, including words, visual images, sounds, or other data. Thinking transforms information into new and different forms, allowing us to answer questions, make decisions, solve problems, or make plans.

Although a clear sense of what specifically occurs when we think remains elusive, our understanding of the nature of the fundamental elements involved in thinking is growing. We begin by considering our use of mental images and concepts, the building blocks of thought.

Mental Images: Examining the Mind's Eye

Think of your best friend.

Chances are that you "see" some kind of visual image when asked to think of her or him, or any other person or object, for that matter. To some cognitive psychologists, such mental images constitute a major part of thinking.

Mental images are representations in the mind of an object or event. They are not just visual representations; our ability to "hear" a tune in our heads also relies on a mental image. In fact, every sensory modality may produce corresponding mental images (Gardini et al., 2009; Koçak et al., 2011; Senden et al., 2019).

Research has found that our mental images have many of the properties of the actual stimuli they represent. For example, it takes the mind longer to scan mental images of large objects than small ones, just as the eye takes longer to scan an actual large object than to scan an actual small one. Similarly, we are able to manipulate and rotate mental images of objects, just as we are able to manipulate and rotate them in the real world (Mast & Kosslyn, 2002; Zacks, 2008; Reisberg, 2013; see Figure 1).

Some experts see the production of mental images as a way to improve various skills. For instance, many athletes use mental imagery in their training. Basketball players may try to produce vivid and detailed images of the court, the basket, the ball, and the noisy crowd. They may visualize themselves taking a foul shot, watching the ball, and hearing the swish as it goes through the net. And it works: The use of mental imagery can lead to improved performance in sports (Velentzas, Heinen, & Schack, 2011; Wimmer et al., 2017; Lauer, Martin, & Zakrajsek, 2019).

Mental imagery may improve other types of skills as well. For example, piano players who simply mentally rehearse an exercise show brain activity that is virtually identical to that of the people who actually practice the exercise manually. Apparently, carrying out the task involved the same network of brain cells as the network used in mentally rehearsing it (Sanders et al., 2008; Davidson-Kelly et al., 2015). (Also see *Applying Psychology in the 21st Century.*)

FIGURE 1 Try to mentally rotate one of each pair of patterns to see if it is the same as the other member of that pair. It's likely that the farther you have to mentally rotate a pattern, the longer it will take to decide if the patterns match one another. Does this mean that it will take you longer to visualize a map of the world than a map of the United States? Why or why not?

Source: Adapted from Shepard, R. N., & Metzler, J. (1971). Mental rotation of three-dimensional objects. *Science, 171*(3972), 701–703.

APPLYING PSYCHOLOGY IN THE 21ST CENTURY

NAVIGATING WITH COGNITIVE MAPS

If you were walking across your college campus one day and a stranger asked you for directions to the campus library, how would you answer?

If you had never traversed the route to the library from that particular location, you would probably respond as most people do by creating a cognitive map in your mind. A *cognitive map* is a layout you create in your mind of a given region, with landmarks, pathways, relative distances, and other environmental details–at least as you understand them to be. So, to answer the lost stranger, you could refer to this cognitive map to work out where the library is in relation to your present location and what the optimal path to get there would be.

On the other hand, you're more likely to suggest that the stranger pull out her smartphone, fire up a GPS app, and get real-time, turn-by-turn directions that will take her directly to the library. Many of us now carry GPS-enabled devices in our pockets and cars that make the idea of working out directions from a cognitive map seem old-fashioned.

But recent research suggests that there's value in solving directional problems using our own mental representation of the environment, and we may not be doing ourselves

Cognitive maps allow people to navigate the physical world.
Twinsterphoto/123RF

any favors by taking the easy way with GPS. The brain's hippocampus is where cognitive maps are generated and manipulated, and creating such maps involves practice. In one study, researchers asked participants to find their way around a simulated virtual neighborhood that included forced detours. Some used guided directions from a GPS-like device, while others worked out where they were going in their minds, using visual cues and engaging in spatial problem solving. The participants who were letting a device

do the work showed less brain engagement than did those who had to figure it out on their own. Specifically, the hippocampus, the part of the brain involved in memory skills, showed less activity in those who used the GPS to provide the route.

Researchers don't know whether relying on GPS will have long-term effects on the brain and cognitive ability, but findings such as these raise concern. The hippocampus responds to use, developing over time when it's used more and atrophying when it's used less. And navigational skills peak in young adulthood, after which time people start relying more on habits than on problem solving to find their way around. Getting lost and having to find your way home using attention to the environment and to spatial cues exercises your navigational skill–and research suggests that it helps develop the hippocampus as well. Taken together, these findings suggest that using your cognitive maps now and then, rather than always relying on GPS, might be a wise strategy (Maguire & Spiers, 2006; Konishi & Bohbot, 2013; Coutrot et al., 2018).

> **QUESTIONS TO CONSIDER**
> - In what ways are navigational problems unlike other kinds of problems?
> - Why wouldn't following GPS directions stimulate the hippocampus the way navigating by visual cues does?

From the perspective of...

A Human Resources Specialist How might you use the research on mental imagery to improve employees' performance?

Dex Image/Getty Images

Concepts: Categorizing the World

If someone asks you what is in your kitchen cabinet, you might answer with a detailed list of items (a jar of peanut butter, three boxes of macaroni and cheese, six unmatched dinner plates, and so forth). More likely, though, you would respond by naming some broader categories, such as "food" and "dishes."

concepts Mental groupings of similar objects, events, or people. (Module 23)

Using such categories reflects the operation of concepts. **Concepts** are mental groupings of similar objects, events, or people. Concepts enable us to organize complex phenomena into cognitive categories that are easier to understand and remember (Connolly, 2007; Kreppner et al., 2011; Mack, Love, & Preston, 2016).

Concepts help us classify newly encountered objects on the basis of our past experience. For example, we can surmise that someone tapping a handheld screen is probably using some kind of computer or tablet, even if we have never encountered that specific model before. Ultimately, concepts influence behavior. We would assume, for instance, that it might be appropriate to pet an animal after determining that it is a dog, whereas we would behave differently after classifying the animal as a wolf.

When cognitive psychologists first studied concepts, they focused on those that were clearly defined by a unique set of properties or features. For example, an equilateral triangle is a closed shape that has three sides of equal length. If an object has these characteristics, it is an equilateral triangle; if it does not, it is not an equilateral triangle.

Other concepts–often those with the most relevance to our everyday lives–are more ambiguous and difficult to define. For instance, broader concepts such as "table" and "bird" have a set of general, relatively loose characteristic features, rather than unique, clearly defined properties, that distinguish an example of the concept from a nonexample.

prototypes Typical, highly representative examples of a concept. (Module 23)

When we consider these more ambiguous concepts, we usually think in terms of examples called prototypes. **Prototypes** are typical, highly representative examples of a concept that correspond to our mental image or best example of the concept. For instance, for most people, the prototype of a dog is something like the common beagle, rather than the relatively rare shih tzu, Finnish spitz, otterhound, or mudi (breeds you've probably never heard of). Similarly, although a robin and an ostrich are both examples of birds, the robin is an example that comes to most people's minds far more readily. Consequently, robin is a prototype of the concept "bird."

Study Alert

Figure 2 will help you remember that prototypes represent "best" or most common examples of a particular concept. For example, a Prius might be a prototype of the concept of "hybrid car."

Relatively high agreement exists among people in particular cultures about which examples of a concept are prototypes as well as which examples are not. For instance, most people in Western cultures consider cars and trucks good examples of vehicles, whereas elevators and wheelbarrows are not considered very good examples. Consequently, cars and trucks are prototypes of the concept of a vehicle (see Figure 2).

Concepts enable us to think about and understand more readily the complex world in which we live. For example, the suppositions we make about the reasons for other people's behavior are based on the ways in which we classify behavior. Hence, our conclusion about a person who washes her hands 20 times a day could vary, depending on whether we place her behavior within the conceptual framework of a health-care worker or a mental patient. Similarly, physicians make diagnoses by

Ranking of Prototype	Furniture	Vehicle	Weapon	Vegetable
1—Most Typical	Chair	Car	Gun	Peas
2	Sofa	Truck	Knife	Carrots
3	Table	Bus	Sword	String beans
4	Dresser	Motorcycle	Bomb	Spinach
5	Desk	Train	Hand grenade	Broccoli
6	Bed	Trolley car	Spear	Asparagus
7	Bookcase	Bicycle	Cannon	Corn
8	Footstool	Airplane	Bow and arrow	Cauliflower
9	Lamp	Boat	Club	Brussels sprouts
10	Piano	Tractor	Tank	Lettuce
11	Cushion	Cart	Tear gas	Beets
12	Mirror	Wheelchair	Whip	Tomato
13	Rug	Tank	Ice pick	Lima beans
14	Radio	Raft	Fists	Eggplant
15—Least Typical	Stove	Sled	Rocket	Onion

(Concept Category heading above the table)

FIGURE 2 Prototypes are typical, highly representative examples of a concept. For instance, a highly typical prototype of the concept "furniture" is a chair, whereas a stove is not a good prototype. High agreement exists within a culture about which examples of a concept are prototypes.

(chair): Stockbyte/Getty Images; (car): Gary He/McGraw-Hill; (gun): Suradin (Pinkblue) Suradingura/123RF; (peas): Isabelle Rozenbaum/Frederic Cirou/PhotoAlto/PunchStock/Getty Images; Source: Adapted from Rosch, E., & Mervis, C. B. (1975). Family resemblances: Studies in the internal structure of categories. *Cognitive Psychology, 7,* 573–605.

drawing on concepts and prototypes of symptoms that they learned about in medical school. Finally, concepts and prototypes facilitate our efforts to draw suitable conclusions through the cognitive process we turn to next: reasoning.

Reasoning: Making Up Your Mind

Professors deciding when students' assignments are due

An employer determining whom to hire out of a pool of job applicants

The president concluding that it is necessary to send troops to a foreign nation

What do these three situations have in common? Each requires *reasoning*, the process by which information is used to draw conclusions and make decisions.

Although philosophers and logicians have considered the foundations of reasoning for centuries, it is only relatively recently that cognitive psychologists have begun to investigate how people reason and make decisions. Their efforts have contributed to our understanding of formal reasoning processes as well as the cognitive shortcuts we routinely use—shortcuts that sometimes may lead our reasoning capabilities astray (Johnson-Laird, 2006; Brownlee, 2019).

FORMAL REASONING

When (the fictitious) Sherlock Holmes sought to solve a crime, he carefully observed the scene of the crime and then made informed guesses about what those observations meant. For example, in one story, the ever-observant Holmes noted that cuts on the side of a shoe suggested that a potential criminal must have had mud on his shoes that needed to be scraped off.

The type of reasoning that Holmes used is known as deductive reasoning. **Deductive reasoning** is reasoning from the general to the specific. Psychologists, like all scientists, use deductive reasoning when they start with a general, broad theory, then derive a hypothesis from the theory, and ultimately test the hypothesis by collecting data to arrive at a conclusion.

deductive reasoning Reasoning from the general to the specific. (Module 23)

inductive reasoning Reasoning from the specific to the general. (Module 23)

The other major class of reasoning is inductive reasoning. **Inductive reasoning** is reasoning from the specific to the general. Inductive reasoning is data driven, in that we accumulate pieces of information and put them together to form a conclusion. That's what psychologists do when they study a sample of participants (for instance, 20 color-blind college students), and then they use the information they observe to form a conclusion about the broader population from which the sample is drawn (all color-blind college students).

If we consistently used deductive and inductive reasoning, we would make decisions and solve problems quite logically. However, as we'll see next, that often doesn't happen, leading to less-than-optimal results.

ALGORITHMS AND HEURISTICS

algorithm A rule that, if applied appropriately, guarantees a solution to a problem. (Module 23)

When faced with making a decision, we often turn to various kinds of cognitive shortcuts, known as algorithms and heuristics, to help us. An **algorithm** is a rule that, if applied appropriately, guarantees a solution to a problem. We can use an algorithm even if we cannot understand why it works. For example, you may know that you can find the length of the third side of a right triangle by using the formula $a^2 + b^2 = c^2$, although you may not have the foggiest notion of the mathematical principles behind the formula.

heuristic A thinking strategy that may lead us to a solution to a problem or decision but–unlike algorithms–may sometimes lead to errors. (Module 23)

For many problems and decisions, however, no algorithm is available. In those instances, we may be able to use heuristics to help us. A **heuristic** is a thinking strategy that may lead us to a solution to a problem or decision but–unlike algorithms– may sometimes lead to errors. Heuristics increase the likelihood of success in coming to a solution, but, unlike algorithms, they cannot ensure it.

For example, when I play tic-tac-toe, I follow the heuristic of placing an X in the center square when I start the game. This tactic doesn't guarantee that I will win, but experience has taught me that it will increase my chances of success. Similarly, some students follow the heuristic of preparing for a test by ignoring the assigned textbook reading and only studying their lecture notes–a strategy that may or may not pay off.

Study Alert

Remember that algorithms are rules that *always* provide a solution, whereas heuristics are shortcuts that *may* provide a solution.

Although heuristics often help people solve problems and make decisions, certain kinds of heuristics may lead to inaccurate conclusions. For example, when we rely on the *availability heuristic*, we judge the likelihood of an event occurring on the basis of how easily we can bring to mind examples of the event. That is, we assume that events we remember easily are likely to have occurred more frequently in the past–and are more likely to occur in the future–than events that are harder to remember.

For instance, the availability heuristic makes us more afraid of dying in a plane crash than in an auto accident, despite statistics clearly showing that airplane travel is much safer than auto travel. Similarly, although 10 times as many people die from falling out of bed than from lightning strikes, we're more afraid of being hit by lightning. The reason is that plane crashes and lightning strikes receive far more publicity, and they are therefore more easily remembered (Caruso, 2008; Geurten et al., 2015; Blake & Castel, 2019).

We also make use of a familiarity heuristic. The *familiarity heuristic* leads us to prefer familiar objects, people, and things to those that that are unfamiliar or strange to us. For example, we might purchase a book written by a familiar author rather than one written by an author we never heard of, even if the topic of the book by the unfamiliar author sounds more appealing.

The familiarity heuristic typically saves us a great deal of time when we are making decisions, since we often just go with what seems most familiar. On the other hand, it's not so good if you are an emergency room physician susceptible to the familiarity heuristic. If you simply settle on the first, most obvious diagnosis for a patient presenting particular symptoms (the ones that are most familiar to you), you may miss making a more accurate diagnosis (Herbert, 2011).

Another common heuristic is the *present bias*, which is the tendency to more heavily weight options that are closer to the present than ones further away. For example, suppose you were given the choice between receiving $150 today or $180 a month from now. If you're like most people, you'll probably choose the $150 today. It's actually a bad move: you're giving up a 20 percent return on investment.

But suppose the question you were faced with was to choose between taking $150 in 12 months versus $180 in 13 months. When it's put that way, most people will take the $180, which is definitely the better choice. Bottom line: the present bias is a heuristic that keeps us from thinking logically (Wang & Sloan, 2018; Yagoda, 2018).

Are algorithms and heuristics confined to human thinking, or can we program computers to mimic human thinking and problem solving? As we discuss next, scientists are certainly trying.

Computers and Problem Solving: Searching for Artificial Intelligence

To the music experts, there was no mistaking who had written the piano piece: Johann Sebastian Bach, the prolific German composer who was born in the 17th century.

But the experts were wrong. The piece they all thought was a Bach composition was actually created by a computer named "EMI" by David Cope of the University of California. After a variety of Bach pieces had been scanned into its memory, EMI was able to produce music that was so similar to Bach's actual music that it fooled knowledgeable listeners (Cope, 2001; Vincent, 2019).

Such computer mimicry is possible because composers have a particular "signature" that reflects patterns, sequences, and combinations of notes. By employing those "signatures," computers can create compositions that have the full scope and emotional appeal of actual works—and show just as much creativity as those written by the actual composer (Cope, 2001, 2003).

Computers are making significant inroads in terms of the ability to solve problems and carry out some forms of intellectual activities. *Artificial intelligence* is the field that examines how to use technology to imitate human thinking, problem solving, and creative activities.

A computer using artificial intelligence software was able to mimic compositions by Johann Sebastian Bach so successfully it fooled expert musicologists.
Photos.com/Getty Images

Initially, attempts to mimic human problem-solving with artificial intelligence proved inadequate because programmers couldn't come up with the range of possibilities a computer might encounter. Today, artificial intelligence uses machine learning, which processes immense amounts of data and makes probabilistic guesses. Experts argue that current artificial intelligence programs have the ability to come close to, and may ultimately go beyond, human thinking abilities (Ghahramani, 2015; Hernández-Orallo, 2017; Greenwald, 2018).

Computers using artificial intelligence are particularly good at tasks that require speed, persistence, and a huge memory, as you might realize if you've used Apple's Siri or Amazon's Alexa. For example, artificial intelligence is used today to inform decisions about whether a bank should loan money to a customer, which involve synthesizing vast amounts of information (including loan-repayment history) to determine how likely the customer is to repay the loan. And this is just the start; thousands of job categories, ranging from radiology to truck driving, will likely use artificial intelligence in the future. Still, it remains to be seen whether the quality of thinking produced by artificial intelligence will match that of humans (Gopnik, 2017; Lee, 2017; Topol, 2019).

Does Playing Video Games Improve Your Thinking—but Reduce Your Attention Span?

People who love video games spend a great many hours engaged in their pastime. Some rationalize the time spent by claiming that video games sharpen their cognitive skills—that is, they help them become better at solving challenges and problems, or they improve their memory, or they sharpen their attention. And a large number of studies back up those claims, studies showing that gamers perform better than nongamers on a number of tests of cognitive and perceptual abilities, ranging from hand-eye coordination to working memory to control of attention (Powers et al., 2013; Granic, Lobel, & Engels, 2014; Gong et al., 2019).

But this research has its critics, who suggest the benefits of gaming may be overstated. A recent study addressed some of these criticisms, and it found surprising results. Instead of categorizing participants into just two groups, as most studies do (frequent players versus nonplayers), the new study considered the full range of playing frequency, from nonplayers to low-frequency, moderate-frequency, and high-frequency players. When looked at this way, the previous findings that gamers outperformed nongamers on cognitive abilities simply vanished. The researchers concluded that previous studies used methods that had the unintended effect of inflating the apparent influence of video-game play on cognitive measures (Unsworth et al., 2015; Redick et al., 2017).

Other research findings hint that participation in gaming and use of technology may reduce attention span. Although the evidence is far from definitive, software giant Microsoft conducted research involving surveys and brain scans of 2,000 Canadians. The findings showed that attention span, which was defined as the duration of concentrated effort on a task without becoming distracted, had fallen from an average of 12 seconds in 2000 (around the time when mobile devices were taking off) to 8 seconds 15 years later. Attention was worst for participants who were heavier consumers of media, particularly social media, and who were early adopters of new technology or frequently used multiple media devices, such as using a tablet or smartphone while watching television (McSpadden, 2015).

At this point, the research on the effects of involvement in video games and more broadly technology is far from definitive. More work needs to be done before we can draw clear conclusions.

RECAP/EVALUATE/RETHINK

RECAP

LO 23-1 What is thinking?

- Cognitive psychology encompasses the higher mental processes, including the way people know and understand the world, process information, make decisions and judgments, and describe their knowledge and understanding to others.
- Thinking is brain activity in which we purposefully manipulate mental representations of information. Thinking transforms such representations into novel and different forms, permitting people to answer questions, solve problems, and reach goals.
- Mental images are representations in the mind of an object or event.
- Concepts are categorizations of objects, events, or people that share common properties.
- Prototypes are representative examples of concepts.

LO 23-2 What processes underlie reasoning and decision making?

- Deductive reasoning is reasoning from the general to the specific, whereas inductive reasoning is reasoning from the specific to the general.

- Decisions sometimes (but not always) may be improved through the use of algorithms and heuristics. An algorithm is a rule that, if applied appropriately, guarantees a solution; a heuristic is a cognitive shortcut that may lead to a solution but is not guaranteed to do so.

EVALUATE

1. _____ _____ are representations in the mind of an object or event.
2. _____ are categorizations of objects that share common properties.
3. When you think of the concept "chair," you immediately think of a comfortable easy chair. A chair of this type could be thought of as a _____ of the category "chair."
4. When you ask your friend how best to study for your psychology final, he tells you, "I've always found it best to skim over the notes once, then read the book, then go over the notes again." What decision-making tool might this be an example of?

RETHINK

1. How might the availability heuristic contribute to prejudices based on race, age, and gender? Can awareness of this heuristic prevent prejudices from arising?

2. In what ways might prototypes for the category of "vehicle" differ between members of a tribe living in a rural African village compared with people living in a Western city?

Answers to Evaluate Questions

1. Mental images; 2. Concepts; 3. prototype; 4. heuristic

KEY TERMS

cognitive psychology	concepts	deductive reasoning	algorithm
thinking	prototypes	inductive reasoning	heuristic
mental images			

Module 24
Problem Solving

LEARNING OUTCOMES

LO 24-1 How do people approach and solve problems?

LO 24-2 What are the major obstacles to problem solving?

LO 24-3 What is creativity?

According to an old legend, a group of Vietnamese monks guard three towers on which sit 64 golden rings. The monks believe that if they succeed in moving the rings from the first tower to the third according to a series of rigid rules, the world as we know it will come to an end. (Should you prefer that the world remain in its present state, there's no need for immediate concern: The puzzle is so complex that it will take the monks about a trillion years to solve it.)

In the Tower of Hanoi puzzle, a simpler version of the task facing the monks, three disks are placed on three posts in the order shown in Figure 1. The goal of the puzzle is to move all three disks to the third post, arranged in the same order, by using as few moves as possible. There are two restrictions: Only one disk can be moved at a time, and no disk can ever cover a smaller one during a move.

Why are cognitive psychologists interested in the Tower of Hanoi problem? Because the way people go about solving such puzzles helps illuminate how people solve complex, real-life problems. Psychologists have found that problem solving typically involves the three steps illustrated in Figure 2: preparing to create solutions, producing solutions, and evaluating the solutions that have been generated.

Preparation: Understanding and Diagnosing Problems

When approaching a problem like the Tower of Hanoi, most people begin by trying to understand the problem thoroughly. If the problem is a novel one, they probably will pay particular attention to any restrictions placed on coming up with a solution—such as the rule for moving only one disk at a time in the Tower of Hanoi problem. If, by contrast, the problem is a familiar one, they are apt to spend considerably less time in this preparation stage.

Problems vary from well defined to ill defined. In a *well-defined problem*—such as a mathematical equation or the solution to a jigsaw puzzle—both the nature of the problem itself and the information needed to solve it are available and clear. Thus, we can make straightforward judgments about whether a potential solution is appropriate. With an *ill-defined problem*, such as how to increase morale on an assembly line or to bring peace to the Middle East, not only may the specific nature of the problem be

> **Study Alert**
> Use the three steps of problem solving to organize your studying: Preparation, Production, and Judgment (PPJ).

	Start				Finish	

FIGURE 1 The goal of the Tower of Hanoi puzzle is to move all three disks from the first post to the third and still preserve the original order of the disks, using the fewest number of moves possible while following the rules that only one disk at a time can be moved and no disk can cover a smaller one during a move. Try it yourself before you look at the solution, which provides the sequence of moves.

Solution: Move C to 3, B to 2, C to 2, A to 3, C to 1, B to 3, C to 3, and C to 3.

unclear, the information required to solve the problem may be even less obvious (Newman, Willoughby, & Pruce, 2011; Mayer, 2013; Tschentscher & Hauk, 2017).

KINDS OF PROBLEMS

Typically, a problem falls into one of the three categories shown in Figure 3: arrangement, inducing structure, and transformation. Solving each type requires somewhat different kinds of psychological skills and knowledge. (See Figure 4 for solutions to these problems.)

Arrangement problems require the problem solver to rearrange or recombine elements of the problem in a way that will satisfy specific criteria. Usually, several different arrangements can be made, but only one or a few of the arrangements will produce a solution. Anagram problems and jigsaw puzzles are examples of arrangement problems (Reed, 2017; Tillema, 2019).

In *problems of inducing structure,* a person must identify the existing relationships among the elements presented in the problem and then construct a new relationship among them. In such a problem, the problem solver must determine not only the relationships among the elements but also the structure and size of the elements involved. In the example shown in Figure 3b, a person must first determine that the solution requires the numbers to be considered in pairs (14-24-34-44-54-64). Only after identifying that part of the problem can a person determine the solution rule (the first number of each pair increases by one, while the second number remains the same).

The Tower of Hanoi puzzle represents the third kind of problem–*transformation problems*–that consist of an initial state, a goal state, and a method for changing the initial state into the goal state. In the Tower of Hanoi problem, the initial state is the original configuration, the goal state is to have the three disks on the third peg, and the method is the rules for moving the disks (Majeres, 2007; Van Belle et al., 2011; Schiff & Vakil, 2015).

Whether the problem is one of arrangement, inducing structure, or transformation, the preparation stage of understanding and diagnosing is critical in problem solving because it allows us to develop our own cognitive representation of the problem and to place it within a personal framework. We may divide the problem into subparts or ignore some information as we try to simplify the task. Winnowing out nonessential information is often a critical step in the preparation stage of problem solving.

REPRESENTING AND ORGANIZING THE PROBLEM

A crucial aspect of the initial encounter with a problem is the way in which we represent, characterize, and organize the information presented to us. Consider the following problem:

> A man climbs a mountain on Saturday, leaving at daybreak and arriving at the top near sundown. He spends the night at the top. The next day, Sunday, he leaves at daybreak and heads down the mountain, following the same path that he climbed the day before. The question is this: Will there be any time during the 2nd day when he will be at exactly the same point on the mountain as he was at exactly that time on the 1st day?

If you try to solve this problem by using algebraic or verbal representations, you will have a good deal of trouble. However, if you represent the problem with the kind of simple diagram shown in Figure 5, the solution will become apparent.

The way in which we represent a problem–and the solution we eventually come to–depends on the way a problem is initially framed for us. Imagine that you were a cancer patient having to choose between either the option of surgery or of radiation, as shown in Figure 6, and you were given some statistical information about the options. What would you choose?

It turns out that participants in a study made very different choices depending on how the problem was framed. When their choices were framed in terms of the likelihood of *survival,* only 18% of participants chose radiation over surgery. However, when the choice was framed in terms of the likelihood of *dying,* 44% chose radiation over surgery–even though the outcomes are similar with either treatment option (Tversky & Kahneman, 1987; Krauth-Gruber & Bonnot, 2019).

FIGURE 2 Steps in problem solving.

FIGURE 3 The three major categories of problems: (a) arrangement, (b) inducing structure, and (c) transformation. Solutions appear in Figure 4.

Source: Adapted from Bourne, L. E., Dominowski, R. L., Loftus, E. F., & Healy, A. F. (1986). *Cognitive processes* (2nd ed.). Englewood Cliffs, NJ: Prentice Hall.

a. Arrangement problems

1. Anagrams: Rearrange the letters in each set to make an English word:

2. Two strings hang from a ceiling but are too far apart to allow a person to hold one and walk to the other. On the floor are a book of matches, a screwdriver, and a few pieces of cotton. How could the strings be tied together?

b. Problems of inducing structure

1. What number comes next in the series?
   1 4 2 4 3 4 4 4 5 4 6 4

2. Complete these analogies:
   baseball is to bat as tennis is to _____

   merchant is to sell as customer is to _____

c. Transformation problems

1. Water jars: A person has three jars with the following capacities:

   Jar A: 28 ounces   Jar B: 7 ounces   Jar C: 5 ounces

   How can the person measure exactly 11 ounces of water?

2. Ten coins are arranged in the following way. By moving only two of the coins make two rows that each contains six coins.

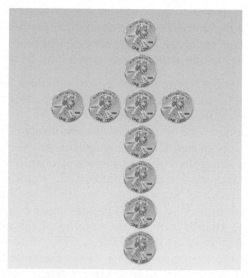

a. **Arrangement problems**

  1. FACET, DOUBT, THICK, NAIVE, ANVIL

  2. The screwdriver is tied to one of the strings. This makes a pendulum that can be swung to reach the other string.

b. **Problems of inducing structure**

  1. 7

  2. racket; buy

c. **Transformation problems**

  1. Fill jar A; empty into jar B once and into jar C twice. What remains in jar A is 11 ounces.

  2.

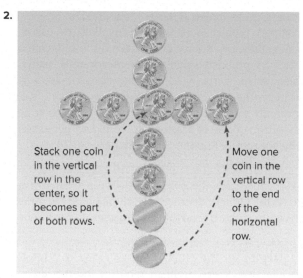

Stack one coin in the vertical row in the center, so it becomes part of both rows.

Move one coin in the vertical row to the end of the horizontal row.

FIGURE 4 Solutions to the problems in Figure 3.

Source: Adapted from Bourne, L. E., Dominowski, R. L., Loftus, E. F., & Healy, A. F. (1986). *Cognitive processes* (2nd ed.). Englewood Cliffs, NJ: Prentice Hall.

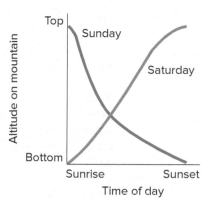

FIGURE 5 You can solve the mountain-climbing problem by using a graph. Keep in mind that the goal is not to determine the time but just to indicate whether an exact time exists. Consequently, the speed at which the traveler is moving is unimportant. Can you think of other approaches that might lead to a solution?

Source: Anderson, B. F. (1980). *The complete thinker: A handbook of techniques for creative and critical problem solving.* Englewood Cliffs, NJ: Prentice Hall.

Problem: Surgery or radiation?

Survival Frame	**Mortality Frame**
Surgery: Of 100 people having surgery, 90 live through the post-operative period, 68 are alive at the end of the 1st year, and 34 are alive at the end of 5 years.	**Surgery:** Of 100 people having surgery, 10 die during surgery, 32 die by the end of the 1st year, and 66 die by the end of 5 years.
Radiation: Of 100 people having radiation therapy, all live through the treatment, 77 are alive at the end of 1 year, and 22 are alive at the end of 5 years.	**Radiation:** Of 100 people having radiation therapy, none die during the treatment, 23 die by the end of 1 year, and 78 die by the end of 5 years.
Far more patients choose surgery	Far more patients choose radiation

FIGURE 6 A decision often is affected by the way a problem is framed. In this case, most would choose radiation over surgery, despite similar results.

(left): Hoby Finn/Getty Images; (right): Stockbyte/Punch-Stock/Getty Images

Production: Generating Solutions

After preparation, the next stage in problem solving is the production of possible solutions. If a problem is relatively simple, we may already have a direct solution stored in long-term memory, and all we need to do is retrieve the appropriate information. If we cannot retrieve or do not know the solution, we must generate possible solutions and compare them with information in long- and short-term memory.

At the most basic level, we can solve problems through trial and error. Thomas Edison invented the lightbulb only because he tried thousands of different kinds of materials for a filament before he found one that worked (carbon). The difficulty with trial and error, of course, is that some problems are so complicated that it would take a lifetime to try out every possibility. For example, according to some estimates, there are some 10^{120} possible sequences of chess moves (Fine & Fine, 2003).

In place of trial and error, complex problem solving often involves the use of heuristics, cognitive shortcuts that can generate solutions, as we have discussed. One of the most frequently applied heuristics in problem solving is a means-ends analysis. In a **means-ends analysis**, a problem solver starts by considering the ultimate goal (the end) and determining the best strategy (the means) for attaining the goal. Using a means-end analysis, problem solvers repeatedly test for differences between what their desired goal is and where they currently are in terms of reaching it, trying to get closer and closer to the desired outcome (Bieberstein & Roosen, 2015; Abascal, 2019).

Consider this simple example of a means-ends analysis:

I want to take my son to preschool. What's the difference between what I have and what I want? One of distance. What changes distance? My automobile. My automobile won't work. What is needed to make it work? A new battery. What has new batteries? An auto repair shop. . . .

In a means-end analysis, each step brings the problem solver closer to a resolution. Although this approach is often effective, if the problem requires indirect steps that temporarily *increase* the discrepancy between a current state and the solution, means-ends analysis can be counterproductive. For example, sometimes the fastest route to the summit of a mountain requires a mountain climber to backtrack temporarily; a means-end approach–which implies that the mountain climber should always forge ahead and upward–will be ineffective in such instances.

For other problems, the best approach is to work backward by focusing on the goal, rather than the starting point, of the problem. Consider, for example, the water lily problem:

Water lilies are growing on Blue Lake. The water lilies grow rapidly, so that the amount of water surface covered by lilies doubles every 24 hours. On the first day of summer, there was just one water lily. On the 90th day of the summer, the lake was entirely covered. On what day was the lake half covered? (Reisberg, 1997)

If you start searching for a solution to the problem by thinking about the initial state on day 1 (one water lily) and move forward from there, you're facing a daunting task of trial-and-error estimation. But try taking a different approach: Start with day 90, when the entire lake was covered with lilies. Given that the lilies double their coverage daily, on the prior day only half the lake was covered. The answer, then, is day 89, a solution found by working backward (Bourne et al., 1986; Hunt, 1994; Shogren & Wehrmeyer, 2017).

FORMING SUBGOALS: DIVIDING PROBLEMS INTO THEIR PARTS

Another heuristic commonly used to generate solutions is to divide a problem into intermediate steps, or *subgoals*, and solve each of those steps. For instance, in our modified Tower of Hanoi problem, we could choose several obvious subgoals, such as moving the largest disk to the third post.

If solving a subgoal is a step toward the ultimate solution to a problem, identifying subgoals is an appropriate strategy. In some cases, however, forming subgoals is not all that

means-ends analysis A strategy in which a problem-solver considers the ultimate goal (the end) and determines the best strategy for attaining the goal. (Module 24)

PsychTech

Research comparing people working together to solve problems face-to-face versus communicating via e-mail finds that those using e-mail are more satisfied with the process and believe they find better solutions.

helpful and may actually increase the time needed to find a solution. For example, some problems cannot be subdivided. Others–like some complicated mathematical problems–are so complex that it takes longer to identify the appropriate subdivisions than to solve the problem by other means (Fishbach, Dhar, & Zhang, 2006; Ribas-Fernandes et al., 2019).

INSIGHT: SUDDEN AWARENESS

Have you ever had this experience? You're working on a difficult problem, mulling over possible answers, but you can't seem to come up with a viable solution. And then, seemingly out of nowhere, a solution comes to you.

If this has happened to you, you experienced a process known as insight. **Insight** is a sudden awareness of the relationships among various elements that had previously appeared to be unrelated. The phenomenon of insight was demonstrated in a classic study by German psychologist Wolfgang Köhler, who examined learning and problem-solving processes in chimpanzees (Köhler, 1927). In his studies, Köhler exposed chimps to challenging situations in which the elements of the solution were all present; all the chimps needed to do was put them together.

In one of Köhler's studies, chimps were kept in a cage in which boxes and sticks were strewn about, and a bunch of tantalizing bananas was hung from the ceiling, out of reach. Initially, the chimps made trial-and-error attempts to get to the bananas: They would throw the sticks at the bananas, jump from one of the boxes, or leap wildly from the ground. Frequently, they would seem to give up in frustration, leaving the bananas dangling temptingly overhead. But then, in what seemed like a sudden revelation, they would stop whatever they were doing and stand on a box to reach the bananas with a stick (Figure 7). Köhler used the term *insight* to label the cognitive process underlying the chimps' new behavior.

Although Köhler emphasized the apparent suddenness of insightful solutions, subsequent research has shown that prior experience and trial-and-error practice in problem solving must precede "insight." Consequently, the chimps' behavior may simply represent the chaining together of previously learned responses, no different from the way a pigeon learns, by trial and error, to peck a key (Kizilirmak et al., 2015).

insight A sudden awareness of the relationships among various elements that had previously appeared to be independent of one another. (Module 24)

(a)

(b)

(c)

FIGURE 7 (a) In an impressive display of insight, Sultan, one of the chimpanzees in Köhler's experiments in problem solving, sees a bunch of bananas that is out of reach. (b) He then carries over several crates, stacks them, and (c) stands on them to reach the bananas. (all): 3LH/SuperStock

Can we help people achieve insight when they are seeking to solve problems? The answer is yes. One way is to directly train them, giving them practice in generating solutions that require out-of-the-box thinking. Another way is to provide cross-cultural experiences that show people that their traditional ways of thinking may be inadequate when applied to the problems faced by those living in other cultures (Leung & Chiu, 2010; Wen, Butler, & Koutstaal, 2013).

Judgment: Evaluating Solutions

The final stage in problem solving is judging the adequacy of a solution. Often this is a simple matter: If the solution is clear—as in the Tower of Hanoi problem—we will know immediately whether we have been successful (Varma, 2007).

If the solution is less concrete or if there is no single correct solution, evaluating solutions becomes more difficult. In such instances, we must decide which alternative solution is best. Unfortunately, we often quite inaccurately estimate the quality of our own ideas. For instance, a team of drug researchers working for a particular company may consider their remedy for an illness to be superior to all others, overestimating the likelihood of their success and downplaying the approaches of competing drug companies (Eizenberg & Zaslavsky, 2004; Mihalca, Mengelkamp, & Schnotz, 2017).

Theoretically, if we rely on appropriate heuristics and valid information, we can make accurate choices among alternative solutions. However, several kinds of obstacles to problem solving act to bias the decisions and judgments we make. In fact, a wide range of behaviors are affected by these biases, ranging from the judgments we form of others to the choices we make about financial investments. Examining biases in decision making has influenced the development of an influential new field known as *behavioral economics*, which examines how psychological factors can explain economic decision making (Cox, Green, & Hennig-Schmidt, 2016; Peters et al., 2017; Jacobsen et al., 2019).

Impediments to Solutions: Why Is Problem Solving Such a Problem?

Consider the following problem-solving test illustrated in Figure 8 (Duncker, 1945):

> You are given a set of tacks, candles, and matches, each in a small box, and told your goal is to place three candles at eye level on a nearby door so that wax will not drip on the floor as the candles burn. How would you approach this challenge?

If you have difficulty solving the problem, you are not alone. Most people cannot solve it when it is presented in the manner illustrated in the figure, in which the objects are *inside* the boxes. However, if the objects were presented *beside* the boxes, just resting on the table, chances are that you would solve the problem much more readily—which, in case you are wondering, requires tacking the boxes to the door and then placing the candles inside them (see Figure 9).

The difficulty you probably encountered in solving this problem stems from its presentation, which misled you at the initial preparation stage. Actually, significant obstacles

FIGURE 8 The problem here is to place three candles at eye level on a nearby door so that the wax will not drip on the floor as the candles burn—using only material in the figure. For a solution, see Figure 9.

Source: Adapted from Duncker, K. (1945). On problem solving. *Psychological Monographs, 58* (5, whole no. 270).

to problem solving can exist at each of the three major stages. Although cognitive approaches to problem solving suggest that thinking proceeds along fairly rational, logical lines as a person confronts a problem and considers various solutions, several factors can hinder the development of creative, appropriate, and accurate solutions.

FUNCTIONAL FIXEDNESS

The impediment to solving the candle problem is functional fixedness. **Functional fixedness** is the tendency to think of an object only in terms of the way it is most frequently or typically used. For instance, functional fixedness probably leads you to think of a book as something to read instead of its potential use as a doorstop or as kindling for a fire. In the candle problem, because the objects are first presented inside the boxes, functional fixedness leads most people to see the boxes simply as containers for the objects they hold rather than as a potential part of the solution. They cannot envision another function for the boxes.

A classic experiment (Luchins, 1946) demonstrates functional fixedness. As you can see in Figure 10, the object of the task is to use the jars in each row to measure out the designated amount of liquid. (Try it yourself to get a sense of the power of functional fixedness before moving on.)

If you have tried to solve the problem, you know that the first five rows are all solved in the same way: First fill the largest jar (B) and then from it fill the middle-size jar (A) once and the smallest jar (C) two times. What is left in B is the designated amount. (Stated as a formula, the designated amount is B-A-2C.) The demonstration of functional fixedness comes in the sixth row of the problem, a point at which you probably encountered some difficulty. If you are like most people, you tried the formula and were perplexed when it failed. Chances are, in fact, that you missed the simple (but different) solution to the problem, which involves merely subtracting C from A. Interestingly, people who were given the problem in row 6 *first* had no difficulty with it at all.

Functional fixedness is related to the concept of mental set. *Mental set* is the tendency to solve problems in a certain way, based on past experience, thereby hindering one's ability to come up with other solutions. For example, mental set can prevent us from seeing beyond the apparent constraints of a problem. For example, try to draw four straight lines so that they pass through all nine dots in the grid below—without lifting your pencil from the page.

FIGURE 9 A solution to the problem in Figure 8 involves tacking the boxes to the door and placing the candles in the boxes.

Source: Adapted from Duncker, K. (1945). On problem solving. *Psychological Monographs, 58* (5, whole no. 270).

functional fixedness The tendency to think of an object only in terms of the way it is most frequently or typically used. (Module 24)

Given jars with these capacities (in ounces):			
A	B	C	Obtain:
1.	21	127	3	100
2.	14	163	25	99
3.	18	43	10	5
4.	9	42	6	21
5.	20	59	4	31
6.	28	76	3	25

FIGURE 10 Try this classic demonstration, which illustrates the importance of functional fixedness in problem solving. The object is to use the jars in each row to obtain the designated amount of liquid.

FIGURE 11 A solution to the nine-dot problem requires the use of lines drawn beyond the boundaries of the figure—something that our mental set may prevent us from seeing easily.

confirmation bias The tendency to seek out and weight more heavily information that supports one's initial hypothesis and to ignore contradictory information that supports alternative hypotheses or solutions. (Module 24)

If you had difficulty with the problem, it was probably because you felt compelled to keep your lines within the grid. If you had gone outside the boundaries, however, you would have succeeded by using the solution shown in Figure 11. (The phrase "thinking outside the box"–a commonly used term to encourage creativity–stems from research on overcoming the constraining effects of functional fixedness and mental set.)

INACCURATE EVALUATION OF SOLUTIONS

When the United States invaded Iraq in 2003, it did so because governmental leaders believed that the country secretly had weapons of mass destruction that posed a danger to the United States. But later evidence showed that the belief was false. Still, government leaders had made up their minds early on that there were such weapons, and they ignored contradictory evidence and focused more on information that supported their view (U.S. Senate Select Committee on Intelligence, 2004).

The mistake made by governmental leaders exemplifies **confirmation bias** in which problem solvers prefer their first hypothesis and ignore contradictory information that supports alternative hypotheses or solutions. Even when we find evidence that contradicts a solution we have chosen, we are apt to stick with our original hypothesis.

Confirmation bias occurs for several reasons. For one thing, because rethinking a problem that appears to be solved already takes extra cognitive effort, we are apt to stick with our first solution. For another, we give greater weight to subsequent information that supports our initial position than to information that is not supportive of it (Rajsic, Wilson, & Pratt, 2015; Mercier, 2017; Pearson & Knobloch-Westerwick, 2019).

EVALUATING OTHERS' CONCLUSIONS: THE SCIENCE OF FAKE NEWS

Sometimes we draw erroneous conclusions because others have actively attempted to mislead us. One example is in the rise of *fake news*, fabricated information that is made to look and sound like legitimate news, with the intent of persuading readers to accept false information. The spread of fake news, and claims about it, have provided considerable discussion among politicians and citizens alike, particularly because it's impossible to identify unless it is compared with additional sources of information (Lazer et al., 2018).

Psychologists and other scholars are just beginning to study fake news and how it is spread and influences us. In one pioneering study, researchers investigated all verified true and false news stories that were distributed on Twitter from 2006 to 2017–some 126,00 of them. They found that false stores (such as rumors of terror attacks) were distributed significantly farther, faster, and more broadly than true news. One reason for this seems to be that the fake news was more novel than true news, thus contributing to its faster distribution (Vosoughi, Roy, & Aral, 2018; Grinberg et al., 2019).

The science of fake news is just developing. More research clearly needs to be done to understand and address this significant social issue.

creativity The ability to generate original ideas or solve problems in novel ways. (Module 24)

Creativity and Problem Solving

Despite obstacles to problem solving, many people adeptly discover creative solutions to problems. One enduring question that cognitive psychologists have sought to answer is what factors underlie **creativity**, the ability to generate original ideas or solve problems in novel ways.

Understanding the stages people go through as they approach and solve problems still leaves us with the question: Why are some people better at finding good solutions than other people are? Even the simplest situations reveal a wide range of abilities in problem solving. To explore this for yourself, make a list of all the uses you can think of for a glass jar. When you feel you have run out of possibilities, compare your list to this one compiled by a 12-year-old girl:

> You can keep seashells from your vacation in it to decorate your room. You can put sand on the bottom of it and pour melted wax over the sand and stick a wick in it to make a candle. You can use it as a drinking glass. You can keep rubber bands or paper clips or colored marbles in it. You can make a granola mix and store it for months if the jar has a tight lid. You can put water in the bottom and start an avocado tree from a pit. You can store bacon grease in a jar or fill it with hand soaps and place it by the bathroom sink. You can use it as a flower vase or a "candy dish" for wrapped candies. If you punch holes in the lid, a jar can be a salt or sugar shaker. You can layer pudding and berries and whipped cream in it for a fancy dessert. You can keep your loose change in a jar or use it as a cocktail shaker. You can keep your goldfish in it while you clean the tank. You can organize shelves in the garage or basement by putting small things like nails and screws and bolts with others of the same size, each in their own jar. You can organize your pantry, too: a jar for white rice, one for wild rice, another for black beans, and so on. You can measure rainfall for a month with a jar. Or place it beneath a leaky sink pipe.

This list shows extraordinary creativity. Unfortunately, it is much easier to identify *examples* of creativity than to determine its causes. Similarly, it's not clear that the kind of creativity shown by highly creative people in the arts, such as Lin-Manuel Miranda, is the same kind of creativity shown by highly creative people in the sciences, such as Steven Hawking (Simonton, 2009; Lavazza & Manzotti, 2013; Yi, Plucker, & Guo, 2015).

However, we do know that several characteristics are associated with creativity. For one thing, highly creative individuals show divergent thinking. **Divergent thinking** generates multiple and novel, although potentially appropriate, responses to problems or questions. When we use "out-of-the-box" thinking, we're showing divergent thinking.

Divergent thinking contrasts with convergent thinking. **Convergent thinking** is thinking in which a problem is viewed as having a single answer and which produces a solution that is based primarily on knowledge and logic. For instance, someone relying on convergent thinking would answer "You read it" to the query "What can you do with a newspaper?" In contrast, "You can use it as a dustpan" is a more divergent—and creative—response (Schepers & van den Berg, 2007; Zeng, Proctor, & Salvendy, 2011; Haas, 2017).

Creative people also show cognitive complexity in their thinking. *Cognitive complexity* is the preference for elaborate, intricate, and complex thoughts and solutions to problems. For instance, creative people often have a wider range of interests and are more independent and more interested in philosophical or abstract problems than are less creative individuals (Barron, 1990; Richards, 2006; Kaufman & Plucker, 2011).

Brilliant artists such as Lin-Manuel Miranda, who created the Broadway show *Hamilton*, are typically divergent thinkers.
Roy Rochlin/Getty Images

divergent thinking Thinking that generates multiple and novel, although potentially appropriate, responses to problems or questions. (Module 24)

convergent thinking Thinking in which a problem is viewed as having a single answer and which produces a solution that is based primarily on knowledge and logic. (Module 24)

From the perspective of...

A Manufacturer How might you encourage your employees to develop creative ways to improve the products you produce?

Kali Nine LLC/Getty Images

! Study Alert
Remember *d*ivergent thinking produces *d*ifferent and *d*iverse kinds of responses, whereas convergent thinking produces more commonsense kinds of responses.

One factor that is *not* closely related to creativity is intelligence. Traditional intelligence tests, which ask focused questions that have only one acceptable answer, tap convergent thinking skills. Highly creative people may therefore find that such tests penalize their divergent thinking. This may explain why researchers consistently find that creativity is only slightly related to school grades and intelligence when intelligence is measured using traditional intelligence tests (Norton, Heath, & Ventura, 2013; Jung & Chang, 2017).

Does creativity change as we age? Research suggests that we actually become *less* creative the older we get. One reason may be that as we get older, we know more. Although this increased knowledge is generally advantageous, it may hinder creativity because we are more apt to ignore evidence that contradicts what we believe to be true. In a sense, we get stuck in our ways. Furthermore, when we get older, we already have developed a set of solutions to common problems, and we are more likely to turn to them and avoid exploring more creative ideas. In short, getting older is not helpful in finding creative solutions to problems (Gopnik, Griffiths, & Lucas, 2015; Gopnik & Griffiths, 2017; Hui, He, & Wong, 2019).

BECOMING AN INFORMED CONSUMER
of Psychology

Thinking Critically and Creatively

Can we learn to be better and more creative thinkers?

Cognitive researchers have found that people can learn the abstract rules of logic and reasoning and that such knowledge can improve our reasoning about the underlying causes of everyday events in our lives. Research suggests that critical and creative thinkers are made, not born. Consider, for instance, the following suggestions for increasing critical thinking and creativity (Burbach, Matkin, & Fritz, 2004; Kaufman & Baer, 2006).

- *Redefine problems*. We can modify boundaries and assumptions by rephrasing a problem at either a more abstract or a more concrete level.

The Disney Concert Hall in Los Angeles, designed by legendary architect Frank Gehry, is known as a masterpiece of visionary architecture. What processes might account for Gehry's creativity?
Frank Gehry/Marek Slusarczyk/Tupungato/123RF

- *Use subgoals.* By developing subgoals, we can divide a problem into intermediate steps. This process, known as *fractionation*, allows us to examine each part for new possibilities and approaches, leading to a novel solution for the problem as a whole.
- *Adopt a critical perspective.* Rather than passively accepting assumptions or arguments, we can evaluate material critically, consider its implications, and think about possible exceptions and contradictions.
- *Consider the opposite.* By considering the opposite of a concept we're seeking to understand, we can sometimes make progress. For example, to define "good mental health," it may be useful to consider what "poor mental health" means.
- *Use analogies.* Analogies provide alternative frameworks for the interpretation of facts and help us uncover new understanding. One effective means of coming up with analogies is to look for examples in the animal world. For instance, architects discovered how to construct the earliest skyscrapers by noting how lily pads on a pond could support the weight of a person (Gertner & Holyoak, 1997; Bearman, Ball, & Ormerod, 2007; Cho, Holyoak, & Cannon, 2007).
- *Think divergently.* Instead of the most logical or common use for an object, consider how you might use the object if you were forbidden to use it in the usual way.
- *Think convergently.* Although it sounds counterintuitive, researchers have found that a combination of divergent *and* convergent thinking can lead to greater creativity. Programs that attempt to teach children to be more creative train participants to alternate periods of divergent thinking with intense convergent thinking (Beghetto & Kaufman, 2010).
- *Use heuristics.* Heuristics are cognitive shortcuts that can help bring about a solution to a problem. If the problem has a single correct answer and you can use or construct a heuristic, you can often find the solution more rapidly and effectively.
- *Experiment with various solutions.* Don't be afraid to use different routes to find solutions for problems (verbal, mathematical, graphic, even dramatic). For instance, try to come up with every conceivable idea you can, no matter how wild or bizarre it may seem at first. After you've come up with a list of solutions, review each one and try to think of ways to make what at first appeared impractical seem more feasible.
- *Remember that good enough is good enough.* You may never come up with the perfect solution to a problem. And that's fine. Accept that sometimes an OK solution, even if it's not perfect, is perfectly acceptable (Shain, 2019).
- *Walk away.* Sometimes just taking a step back from a problem you're trying to solve and doing something routine and even thoughtless can help bring about creativity. Watching TV, taking a shower, or having a snack may free our minds to come up with innovative solutions (Wiley & Jarosz, 2012; Shellenbarger, 2013).

RECAP/EVALUATE/RETHINK

RECAP

LO 24-1 How do people approach and solve problems?

- Problem solving typically involves three major stages: preparation, production of solutions, and evaluation of solutions that have been generated.
- Preparation involves placing the problem in one of three categories. In arrangement problems, a group of elements must be rearranged or recombined in a way that will satisfy a certain criterion. In problems of inducing structure, a person first must identify the existing relationships among the elements presented and then construct a new relationship among them. Finally, transformation problems consist of an initial state, a goal state, and a method for changing the initial state into the goal state.
- A crucial aspect of the preparation stage is the representation and organization of the problem.
- In the production stage, people try to generate solutions. They may find solutions to some problems in long-term memory. Alternatively, they may solve some problems through simple trial and error and use algorithms and heuristics to solve more complex problems.
- Using the heuristic of a means-ends analysis, a person will repeatedly test for differences between the desired outcome and what currently exists, trying each time to come closer to the goal.

- Köhler's research with chimpanzees illustrates insight, a sudden awareness of the relationships among elements that had previously seemed unrelated.

LO 24-2 What are the major obstacles to problem solving?

- Several factors hinder effective problem solving. Functional fixedness is the cognitive bias in which we think of an object only in terms of the way it is most frequently or typically used. Inappropriate use of algorithms and heuristics can also act as an obstacle to the production of solutions. Confirmation bias, in which initial hypotheses are favored, can hinder the accurate evaluation of solutions to problems.

LO 24-3 What is creativity?

- Creativity is the ability to combine responses or ideas in novel ways. Creativity is related to divergent thinking (the ability to generate unusual, but still appropriate, responses to problems or questions) and cognitive complexity.

EVALUATE

1. Solving a problem by trying to reduce the difference between the current state and the goal state is known as a _____.

2. _____ is the term used to describe the sudden "flash" of revelation that often accompanies the solution to a problem.
3. Thinking of an object only in terms of its typical use is known as _____ _____.
4. _____ _____ describes the phenomenon of favoring an initial hypothesis and ignoring subsequent competing hypotheses.
5. Generating unusual but appropriate approaches to a question is known as _____ _____.

RETHINK

1. Why do you think people use algorithms and heuristics? How can we avoid coming to poor solutions based on their use?
2. Are divergent thinking and convergent thinking mutually exclusive or complementary? Why? Are there situations in which one way of thinking is clearly superior? Can the two ways of thinking be combined? How?

Answers to Evaluate Questions

1. transformation; 2. Insight; 3. functional fixedness; 4. Confirmation bias; 5. divergent thinking

KEY TERMS

means-ends analysis	functional fixedness	creativity	convergent thinking
insight	confirmation bias	divergent thinking	

Module 25
Language

'Twas brillig, and the slithy toves
Did gyre and gimble in the wabe:
All mimsy were the borogoves,
And the mome raths outgrabe.

Although few of us have ever come face to face with a tove, we have little difficulty in discerning that in Lewis Carroll's (1872) poem "Jabberwocky," the expression *slithy toves* contains an adjective, *slithy*, and the noun it modifies, *toves*.

Our ability to make sense out of nonsense, if the nonsense follows typical rules of language, illustrates the complexity of both human language and the cognitive processes that underlie its development and use. The use of **language**—the communication of information through symbols arranged according to systematic rules—is a central cognitive ability, one that is indispensable for us to communicate with one another. Not only is language central to communication, but it is also closely tied to the very way in which we think about and understand the world. Without language, our ability to transmit information, acquire knowledge, and cooperate with others would be tremendously hindered. No wonder psychologists have devoted considerable attention to studying language (Reisberg, 2009; LaPointe, 2013; Carnevale, Luna, & Lerman, 2017).

Grammar: Language's Language

To understand how language develops and relates to thought, we first need to review some of the formal elements of language. The basic structure of language rests on **grammar,** the system of rules that determine how our thoughts can be expressed.

Grammar deals with three major components of language: phonology, syntax, and semantics. **Phonology** is the study of **phonemes,** the smallest basic units of speech that affect meaning, and of the way we use those sounds to form words and produce meaning. For instance, the *a* sound in *fat* and the *a* sound in *fate* represent two different phonemes in English (Creel & Bregman, 2011; Monaghan & Fletcher, 2019).

Linguists have identified 869 different phonemes among all the world's languages. Although English speakers use just 52 phonemes to produce words, other languages use as few as 15 to as many as 141. Differences in phonemes are one reason people have difficulty learning other languages. For example, for a Japanese speaker, whose native language does not have an *r* phoneme, pronouncing such English words as *roar* presents some difficulty (Gibbs, 2002; Iverson et al., 2003; Redford, 2017).

Syntax refers to the rules that indicate how words and phrases can be combined to form sentences. Every language has intricate rules that guide the order in which words may be strung together to communicate meaning. English speakers have no difficulty recognizing that "TV down the turn" is not a meaningful sequence, whereas "Turn down the TV" is. To understand the effect of syntax in English, consider the changes in meaning caused by the different word orders in the following three utterances: "John kidnapped the boy," "John, the kidnapped boy," and "The boy kidnapped John" (Frank, Goldwater, & Keller, 2013; Hu, 2019).

Semantics is the third major component of language. **Semantics** refers to the meaning of words and sentences. Every word has particular semantic features. For example, *boy* and *man* share certain semantic features (both refer to males), but they also differ semantically (in terms of age).

language The communication of information through symbols arranged according to systematic rules. (Module 25)

grammar The system of rules that determine how our thoughts can be expressed. (Module 25)

phonology The study of the smallest units of speech, called phonemes. (Module 25)

phonemes The smallest units of speech. (Module 25)

syntax Ways in which words and phrases can be combined to form sentences. (Module 25)

semantics The aspect of language referring to the meaning of words and sentences. (Module 25)

Semantic rules allow us to use words to convey the subtle nuances in meaning. For instance, we can use slightly different wording–semantics–about an event to convey subtle differences in meaning. If we had just seen a girl named Laura get hit by a truck, we might say, "A truck hit Laura." But if we were answering a question about why Laura was not at a party the night before, we might say, "Laura was hit by a truck" (Paciorek & Williams, 2015; Srinivasan et al., 2017).

Despite the complexities of language, most of us acquire the basics of grammar without even being aware that we have learned its rules. Moreover, even though we may have difficulty explicitly stating the rules of grammar, our linguistic abilities are so sophisticated that we can utter an infinite number of different statements. How do we acquire such abilities?

Language Development: Developing a Way with Words

To parents, the sounds of their infant babbling and cooing are music to their ears (except, perhaps, at 3 o'clock in the morning). These sounds also serve an important function. They mark the first step on the road to the development of language.

BABBLING

babble Meaningless, speechlike sounds made by children from around the age of 3 months through 1 year. (Module 25)

Children **babble**–make speechlike but meaningless sounds–from around the age of 3 months through 1 year. While babbling, they may produce, at one time or another, any of the sounds found in all languages, not just the language to which they are exposed. Even deaf children display their own form of babbling because infants who are unable to hear yet who are exposed to sign language from birth "babble" with their hands (Shehata-Dieler et al., 2013; Elmlinger, Schwade, & Goldstein, 2019).

An infant's babbling increasingly reflects the specific language being spoken in the infant's environment, initially in terms of pitch and tone and eventually in terms of specific sounds. Young infants can distinguish among all 869 phonemes that have been identified across the world's languages. However, after the age of 6 to 8 months, that ability begins to decline. Infants begin to "specialize" in the language to which they are exposed as neurons in their brains reorganize to respond to the particular phonemes infants routinely hear.

Some theorists argue that a *critical period* exists for language development early in life in which a child is particularly sensitive to language cues and most easily acquires language. In fact, if children are not exposed to language during this critical period, later they will have great difficulty overcoming this deficit (Bates, 2005; Shafer & Garrido-Nag, 2007; Choubsaz & Gheitury, 2017).

Cases in which abused children have been isolated from contact with others support the theory of such critical periods. In one case, for example, a girl named Genie was exposed to virtually no language from the age of 20 months until she was rescued at age 13. She was unable to speak at all. Despite intensive instruction, she learned only some words and was never able to master the complexities of language (Rymer, 1994; Veltman & Browne, 2001).

PRODUCTION OF LANGUAGE

By the time children are approximately 1 year old, they stop producing sounds that are not in the language to which they have been exposed. It is then a short step to the production of actual words. In English, these are typically short words that start with a consonant sound such as b, d, m, p, and t–this helps explain why *mama* and *dada* are so often among babies' first words. Of course, even before they produce their first words, children can understand a fair amount of the language they hear. Language comprehension precedes language production.

A syllable in signed language, similar to the ones seen in the manual babbling of deaf infants and in the spoken babbling of hearing infants. The similarities in language structure suggest that language has biological roots.

Courtesy, Dr. Laura Ann Petitto @1991. Photo by Robert LaMarche

After the age of 1 year, children begin to learn more complicated forms of language. They produce two-word combinations, the building blocks of sentences, and sharply increase the number of different words they are able to use.

By age 2, the average child has a vocabulary of more than 50 words. Just 6 months later, at $2\frac{1}{2}$ years of age, that vocabulary has grown to several hundred words.

Also around the age of 2, children begin to produce short, two-word sentences. However, the sentences children first produce are characterized as telegraphic speech. **Telegraphic speech** consists of sentences in which only essential words are used, usually nouns and verbs only. Rather than saying, "I showed you the book," a child using telegraphic speech may say, "I show book," and "I am drawing a dog" may become "Drawing dog." As children get older, of course, they use less telegraphic speech and produce increasingly complex sentences (Volterra et al., 2003; Pérez-Leroux, Pirvulescu, & Roberge, 2011).

By age 3, children learn to make plurals by adding -s to nouns and to form the past tense by adding -ed to verbs. However, these skills also lead to speech errors, since children tend to apply rules inflexibly, a process known as overgeneralization. In **overgeneralization,** children employ language rules they have learned, even when doing so results in an error. Thus, although it is correct to say "he walked" for the past tense of *walk*, the -ed rule doesn't work quite so well when children say "he runned" for the past tense of *run* (Gershkoff-Stowe, Connell, & Smith, 2006; Kidd & Lum, 2008; Pozzan & Valian, 2017).

By age 5, children have acquired the basic rules of language. However, they do not attain a full vocabulary and the ability to comprehend and use subtle grammatical rules until later. For example, a 5-year-old boy who sees a blindfolded doll and is asked, "Is the doll easy or hard to see?" would have great trouble answering the question. In fact, if he were asked to make the doll easier to see, he would probably try to remove the doll's blindfold. By the time they are 8 years old, however, children have little difficulty understanding this question because they realize that the doll's blindfold has nothing to do with an observer's ability to see the doll (Hoff, 2003; Dockrell & Marshall, 2015).

UNDERSTANDING LANGUAGE ACQUISITION: IDENTIFYING THE ROOTS OF LANGUAGE

Anyone who spends even a little time with children will notice the enormous strides that they make in language development throughout childhood. However, the reasons for this rapid growth are far from obvious. Psychologists have offered three major explanations: one based on learning theory, one based on innate processes, and one that involves something of a combination of the two.

Learning-Theory Approaches: Language as a Learned Skill The **learning-theory approach** suggests that language acquisition follows the principles of reinforcement and conditioning discovered by psychologists who study learning. For example, a child who says "mama" receives hugs and praise from her mother, which reinforce the behavior of saying "mama" and make its repetition more likely. This view suggests that children first learn to speak by being rewarded for making sounds that approximate speech. Ultimately, through a process of shaping, language becomes more and more like adult speech (Skinner, 1957; Ornat & Gallo, 2004).

In support of the learning-theory approach to language acquisition, the more that parents speak to their young children, the more proficient the children become in language use. In addition, by the time they are 3 years old, children who hear higher levels of linguistic sophistication in their parents' speech show a greater rate of vocabulary growth, vocabulary use, and even general intellectual achievement than do children whose parents' speech is simpler (Hart & Risley, 1997; Ferjan Ramírez et al., 2019).

The learning-theory approach is less successful in explaining how children acquire language rules. Children are reinforced not only when they use language correctly but also when they use it incorrectly. For example, parents answer a child's query of "Why the dog won't eat?" as readily as they do the correctly phrased question, "Why won't

telegraphic speech Sentences in which only essential words are used, typically including only nouns and verbs. (Module 25)

overgeneralization The phenomenon by which children over-apply a language rule, thereby making a linguistic error. (Module 25)

learning-theory approach (to language development) The theory that language acquisition follows the principles of reinforcement and conditioning. (Module 25) the dog eat?" Listeners understand both sentences equally well. Learning theory, then, has difficulty fully explaining language acquisition.

Nativist Approaches: Language as an Innate Skill Pointing to such problems with learning-theory approaches to language acquisition, linguist Noam Chomsky (1978, 1991) provided a groundbreaking alternative. He argued that humans are born with an innate linguistic capability that emerges primarily as a function of maturation.

According to Chomsky's **nativist approach**, humans are genetically prewired to learn language at certain periods in their lives and in a particular way. Furthermore, he suggests that all the world's languages share a common underlying structure that is prewired, genetically determined, and universal across all people.

The nativist approach argues that the human brain contains an inherited neural system, which Chomsky calls *universal grammar*, that lets us understand the structure language provides. These inborn capabilities give us strategies and techniques for learning the unique characteristics of our own native language (McGilvray, 2004; White, 2007; Yang et al., 2017).

Some evidence collected by neuroscientists directly supports Chomsky's view. This research suggests that the ability to use language, which was a significant evolutionary advance in human beings, is tied to specific neurological developments. For example, scientists have discovered a gene related to the development of language abilities that may have emerged as recently—in evolutionary terms—as 100,000 years ago.

Furthermore, the brain clearly has specific sites that are closely tied to language, and the shape of the human mouth and throat are clearly tailored to the production of speech. And evidence indicates that features of specific types of languages are tied to particular genes, such as in "tonal" languages in which pitch is used to convey meaning (Grigorenko, 2009; Perovic & Radenovic, 2011; Lieberman, 2015).

However, Chomsky's nativist view is contradicted by some researchers. For instance, learning theorists contend that the apparent ability of certain animals, such as chimpanzees, to learn the fundamentals of human language (as we discuss later in this module) contradicts the innate linguistic capability view. Furthermore, some cognitive psychologists believe that what underlies children's language learning is their use of general cognitive abilities, not abilities tied directly to language processing in the brain.

nativist approach (to language development) The theory that humans are genetically prewired to learn language at certain times and in particular ways. (Module 25)

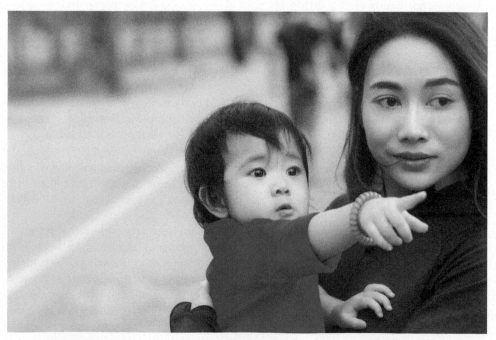

According to Chomsky and other proponents of the nativist view, the development of language is genetically wired into the brain.
Surachet1969/Shutterstock

Furthermore, language development also seems to reflect skills attained through social interaction with others, such as learning to read others' intentions, in contradiction to Chomsky's view (Ibbotson & Tomasello, 2016; Tomasello, 2019).

Interactionist Approaches To reconcile the differing views of the learning-theory and nativist approaches, many theorists hold a compromise view, known as the interactionist approach to language development. The **interactionist approach** suggests that language development is determined by both genetic and social factors, produced through a combination of genetically determined predispositions *and* the social world in which one is raised.

Specifically, proponents of the interactionist approach suggest that the brain is hardwired for our acquisition of language, in essence providing the "hardware" that allows us to develop language. However, it is the exposure to language from social interactions with others that allows us to develop the appropriate "software" to understand and produce language.

The interactionist approach has many proponents. Still, the issue of how language is acquired remains hotly contested (Pinker & Jackendoff, 2005; Hoff, 2008; Waxman, 2009).

From the perspective of...

A Child-Care Provider How would you encourage children's language abilities at the different stages of development?

Nicole Hill/Rubberball/Getty Images

interactionist approach (to language development) The view that language development is determined by genetic and social factors, produced through a combination of genetically determined predispositions and the social world in which one is raised. (Module 25)

The Influence of Language on Thinking: Do Eskimos Have More Words for Snow Than Texans Do?

Do Eskimos living in the frigid Arctic have a more expansive vocabulary for discussing snow than people living in warmer climates do?

It makes sense, and arguments that the Eskimo language has many more words than English does for snow have been made since the early 1900s. At that time, linguist Benjamin Lee Whorf contended that because snow is so relevant to Eskimos' lives, their language provides a particularly rich vocabulary to describe it–considerably larger than what we find in other languages, such as English (Martin & Pullum, 1991; Pinker, 1994).

The contention that the Eskimo language is especially abundant in snow-related terms led to the linguistic-relativity hypothesis. According to the **linguistic-relativity hypothesis**, language shapes and helps determine the way people perceive and understand the world. That is, language provides us with categories we use to construct our view of others and events in the world around us. In this way, language shapes and produces thought (Whorf, 1956; Bylund & Athanasopoulos, 2017; Lowry & Bryant, 2019).

Let's consider another possibility, however. Suppose that instead of language being the *cause* of certain ways of thinking, thought *produces* language. The only reason to expect that Eskimo language might have more words for snow than English does is that snow is considerably more relevant to Eskimos than it is to people in other cultures.

Which view is correct? Most current research refutes the linguistic-relativity hypothesis and suggests, instead, that thinking produces language. In fact, new analyses

linguistic-relativity hypothesis The hypothesis that language shapes and helps determine the way people perceive and understand the world. (Module 25) of the Eskimo language suggest that Eskimos have no more words for snow than English speakers do. If one examines the English language closely, one sees that it is hardly impoverished when it comes to describing snow (consider, for example, *sleet, slush, blizzard, dusting,* and *avalanche*).

Still, the linguistic-relativity hypothesis has not been entirely discarded. A newer version of the hypothesis suggests that speech patterns may influence certain aspects of thinking. For example, English speakers distinguish between nouns that can be counted (such as "five chairs") and nouns that require a measurement unit to be quantified (such as "a liter of water"). However, in some other languages, such as the Mayan language called Yucatec, all nouns require a measurement unit. In such cultures, people appear to think more closely about what things are made of than do people in cultures in which languages such as English are spoken (Gentner, Goldin, & Goldin-Meadow, 2003; Tsukasaki & Ishii, 2004; Stam, 2015).

Similarly, Russian speakers have more words for light and dark blues and are better able to discriminate shades of blue visually than English speakers. The Icelandic language contains 24 words for types of waves. Furthermore, speakers of Kuuk Thaayorre, a language spoken by a native tribe in northeastern Australia, use north, south, east, and west to describe spatial orientation rather than left and right. And the Piraha language uses terms such as *few* and *many*, rather than specific numbers, and speakers are unable to keep track of exact quantities (Boroditsky, 2010; Fuhrman et al., 2011).

Finally, language seems to foster and support certain kinds of reasoning. In essence, language makes us better able to think in more sophisticated ways, helping us to understand such concepts as cause and effect (Gentner, 2016).

In short, although research does not support the linguistic-relativity hypothesis that language *causes* thought, it is clear that language influences how we think. And, of course, it certainly is the case that thought influences language, suggesting that language and thinking interact in complex ways (Ross, 2004; Thorkildsen, 2006; Proudfoot, 2009).

Do Animals Use Language?

One question that has long puzzled psychologists is whether language is uniquely human or if other animals are able to acquire it as well. Many animals communicate with one another in rudimentary forms. For instance, fiddler crabs wave their claws to signal, bees dance to indicate the direction in which food will be found, and certain birds call "*zick, zick*" during courtship and "*kia*" when they are about to fly away. However, researchers have yet to demonstrate conclusively that these animals use true language, which is characterized in part by the ability to produce and communicate new and unique meanings by following a formal grammar.

Psychologists, however, have been able to teach chimps to communicate at surprisingly high levels. For instance, after 4 years of training, a chimp named Washoe learned to make signs for 132 words and combine those signs into simple sentences. Even more impressively, Kanzi, a bonobo (a kind of small chimpanzee), has linguistic skills that some psychologists claim are close to those of a 2-year-old human being. Kanzi's trainers suggest that he can create grammatically sophisticated sentences and can even invent new rules of syntax (Savage-Rumbaugh, Toth, & Schick, 2007; Slocombe, Waller, & Liebal, 2011).

More generally, researchers have found evidence that nonhuman primates use several basic components of human language. For example, they use vocalizations that they modify based on social and other environmental influences, and they take turns communicating about food resources. Furthermore, they have physical structures that allow them to produce vowel sounds similar to human language (Snowdon, 2017).

Despite the languagelike capabilities of primates such as Kanzi, critics contend that the language such animals use still lacks the grammar and the complex and novel constructions of human language. Instead, they maintain that the chimps are displaying a skill no different from that of a dog that learns to lie down on command to get a

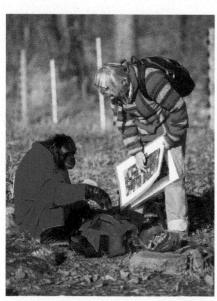

Psychologist and primatologist Sue Savage-Rumbaugh with a primate friend, Kanzi. Does the use of sign language by primates indicate true mastery of language?

Laurentiu Garofeanu/Barcroft USA/Barcroft Media/ Getty Images reward. Furthermore, we lack firm evidence that animals can recognize and respond to the mental states of others of their species, an important aspect of human communication. Consequently, the issue of whether other animals can use language in a way that humans do remains controversial (Beran, Smith, & Perdue, 2013; Crockford, Wittig, & Zuberbühler, 2015; ten Cate, 2017).

 # Exploring Diversity

Teaching with Linguistic Variety: Bilingual Education

In New York City, nearly half of the students speak a language other than English in their homes, with more than 180 languages represented. Furthermore, 1 in 6 of the city's 1.1 million students is enrolled in some form of bilingual or English as a Second Language instruction.

And New York City is far from the only school district with a significant population of nonnative English speakers. From the biggest cities to the most rural areas, the face—and voice—of education in the United States is changing. More and more schoolchildren today have last names like Kim, Valdez, and Karachnicoff. In seven states, including Texas and Colorado, more than one-quarter of the students are not native English speakers. For some 55 million Americans, English is their second language (see Figure 1; Holloway, 2000; Shin & Kominski, 2010).

How to appropriately and effectively teach the increasing number of children who do not speak English is not always clear. Many educators maintain that *bilingual education* is best. With a bilingual approach, students learn some subjects in their native language while simultaneously learning English. Proponents of bilingualism believe that students must develop a sound footing in basic subject areas and that, initially at least, teaching those subjects in their native language is the only way to provide them with that foundation. During the same period, they learn English, with the eventual goal of shifting all instruction into English.

In contrast, other educators insist that all instruction ought to be in English from the moment students, including those who speak no English at all, enroll in school. In *immersion programs*, students are immediately plunged into English instruction in all subjects. The reasoning—endorsed by voters in California in a referendum designed to end bilingual education—is that teaching students in a language other than English simply hinders nonnative English speakers' integration into society and ultimately does them a disservice. Proponents of English immersion programs point as evidence to improvements in standardized test scores that followed the end of bilingual education programs (Wildavsky, 2000).

French Creole 1.17%
Portuguese 1.22%
Italian 1.33%
Arabic 1.33%
Russian 1.48%
German 1.94%
Korean 1.94%
French 2.24%
Vietnamese 2.24%
Tagalog 2.70%
Chinese 2.96%
Other 17.32%
Spanish 62.13%

FIGURE 1 The language of diversity. One-fifth of the people in the United States speak a language other than English at home. Spanish is most prevalent; the rest of non-English speakers use an astounding variety of languages.

Source: Adapted from MLA. (2010). MLA Language Map; all languages other than English combined. Retrieved from http://www.mla.org/census_map&source=county (based on 2000 U.S. Census Bureau figures).

Although the controversial issue of bilingual education versus immersion has strong political undercurrents, evidence shows that the ability to speak two languages provides significant cognitive benefits over speaking only one language. For example, bilingual speakers show more cognitive flexibility and may understand concepts more easily than do those who speak only one language. They have more linguistic tools for thinking because of their multiple-language abilities. In turn, this makes them more creative and flexible in solving problems (Yim & Rudoy, 2013; Christoffels et al., 2015; Hartanto & Yang, 2019; Hartanto, Toh, & Yang, 2019).

In addition, the advantages of bilingualism start early: by the time bilingual children are 3 or 4 years old, their cognitive development is superior to that of children who speak only one language. This advantage may last into old age. In fact, bilingualism may provide protection from the cognitive declines that often occur in late adulthood (Bialystok & Craik, 2011; Bialystok, 2011; Heim et al., 2019).

Furthermore, speaking several languages changes the organization of the brain. For example, bilingual speakers who learn their second language as adults show different areas of brain activation compared with those who learn their second language in childhood. And those who are immersed in intensive language instruction show growth in the hippocampus. In addition, brain scans show that people who speak multiple languages have distinct patterns of brain activity according to the language that they are using, and bilingualism produces more efficient processing on some cognitive tasks (Bialystok et al., 2010; Kluger, 2013; Legault et al., 2019). (Also see *Neuroscience in Your Life*.)

Related to questions about bilingual education is the matter of *biculturalism*—that is, being a member of two cultures and its psychological impact. Some psychologists argue that society should promote an *alternation model* of bicultural competence. Such a model supports members of a culture in their efforts to maintain their original cultural identity as well as in their integration into the adopted culture. In this view, a person can belong to two cultures and have two cultural identities without having to choose between them. In any case, research suggests that a bicultural identity produces mental health benefits and increases feelings of well-being (Benet-Martínez, Lee, & Leu, 2006; Tadmor, 2007; Schwartz et al., 2019).

NEUROSCIENCE IN YOUR LIFE: BEING BILINGUAL AFFECTS THE BRAIN

Because it appears increasingly clear that people who are bilingual have certain cognitive advantages, such as greater cognitive flexibility, researchers are now exploring whether being bilingual affects the structure and functioning of the brain. And they have found, for example, that Spanish-English bilingual adults have more grey matter volume in frontal and parietal brain regions than English monolinguals. This can be seen in the two images of the brain below, where the red indicates the areas that have more grey matter volume for bilinguals. The findings suggest that managing the use of two separate languages affects the structure of the brain, potentially affecting its functioning (Olulade et al., 2016).

Left side of brain   **Right side of brain**

Source: Adapted from Olulade, O. A., Jamal, N. I., Koo, D. S., Perfetti, C. A., LaSasso, C., & Eden, G. F. (2016). Neuroanatomical evidence in support of the bilingual advantage theory. *Cerebral Cortex, 26*(7), 3196-3204. doi: 10.1093/cercor/bhv152.

RECAP/EVALUATE/RETHINK

RECAP

LO 25-1 How do people use language?

- Language is the communication of information through symbols arranged according to systematic rules. All languages have a grammar—a system of rules that determines how thoughts can be expressed—that encompasses the three major components of language: phonology, syntax, and semantics.

LO 25-2 How does language develop?

- Language production, which follows language comprehension, develops out of babbling, which then leads to the production of actual words. After 1 year of age, children use two-word combinations, increase their vocabulary, and use telegraphic speech, which drops words not critical to the message. By age 5, acquisition of language rules is relatively complete.
- Learning theorists suggest that language is acquired through reinforcement and conditioning. In contrast, the nativist approach suggests that an innate language-acquisition device guides the development of language. The interactionist approach argues that language development is produced through a combination of genetically determined predispositions and environmental circumstances that help teach language.
- The linguistic-relativity hypothesis suggests that language shapes and may determine the way people think about the world. Most evidence suggests that although language does not determine thought, it does influence it.
- The degree to which language is a uniquely human skill remains an open question. Some psychologists contend that even though certain primates communicate at a high level, those animals do not use language. Other psychologists suggest that those primates truly understand and produce language in much the same way as humans.
- People who speak more than one language may have a cognitive advantage over those who speak only one.

EVALUATE

1. Match the component of grammar with its definition:
   1. Syntax
   2. Phonology
   3. Semantics
   a. Rules showing how words can be combined into sentences
   b. Rules governing the meaning of words and sentences
   c. The study of the sound units that affect speech
2. Language production and language comprehension develop in infants about the same time. True or false?
3. _____ _____ refers to the phenomenon in which young children omit nonessential portions of sentences.
4. A child knows that adding *-ed* to certain words puts them in the past tense. As a result, instead of saying "He came," the child says "He comed." This is an example of _____.
5. _____ theory assumes that language acquisition is based on principles of operant conditioning and shaping.
6. In his theory of language acquisition, Chomsky argues that language acquisition is an innate ability tied to the structure of the brain. True or false?

RETHINK

1. Do people who use two languages, one at home and one at school, automatically have two cultures? Why might people who speak two languages have cognitive advantages over those who speak only one?
2. Why is overgeneralization seen as an argument against a strict learning-theory approach to explaining language acquisition?

Answers to Evaluate Questions

1. 1-a, 2-c, 3-b; 2. False; language comprehension precedes language; 3. Telegraphic speech; 4. overgeneralization; 5. Learning; 6. True

KEY TERMS

language	babble	nativist approach (to language development)	linguistic-relativity hypothesis
grammar	telegraphic speech	interactionist approach (to language development)	
phonology	overgeneralization		
phonemes	learning-theory approach (to language development)		
syntax			
semantics			

LOOKING *Back*

EPILOGUE

The study of cognition occupies a central place in the field of psychology and encompasses a variety of areas—including thinking, problem solving, decision making, creativity, language, memory, and intelligence. Specialists in cognitive psychology have made significant advances in the last decade that have influenced the entire field of psychology.

Before proceeding, turn back to the prologue of this chapter about the master chess-players, Stockfish and the more sophisticated AlphaZero. Answer the following questions in light of what you have learned about thinking, problem solving, and creativity:

1. In what ways is AlphaZero's strategizing similar to the use of an algorithm? In what ways does it differ?
2. Does Stockfish, the predecessor of AlphaZero, employ a means-end analysis? If so, how might that strategy be less effective than the strategies employed by AlphaZero?
3. Is it fair to say that AlphaZero shows creativity? Why or why not?
4. Would you characterize AlphaZero's approach as convergent thinking or divergent thinking? Why do you think so?

VISUAL SUMMARY 8 Cognition and Language

MODULES 23 and 24 Thinking, Reasoning, and Problem Solving

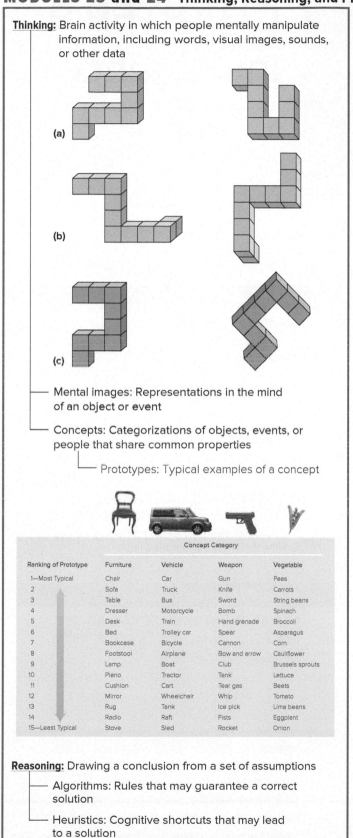

Thinking: Brain activity in which people mentally manipulate information, including words, visual images, sounds, or other data

(a)

(b)

(c)

Mental images: Representations in the mind of an object or event

Concepts: Categorizations of objects, events, or people that share common properties

Prototypes: Typical examples of a concept

	Concept Category			
Ranking of Prototype	Furniture	Vehicle	Weapon	Vegetable
1—Most Typical	Chair	Car	Gun	Peas
2	Sofa	Truck	Knife	Carrots
3	Table	Bus	Sword	String beans
4	Dresser	Motorcycle	Bomb	Spinach
5	Desk	Train	Hand grenade	Broccoli
6	Bed	Trolley car	Spear	Asparagus
7	Bookcase	Bicycle	Cannon	Corn
8	Footstool	Airplane	Bow and arrow	Cauliflower
9	Lamp	Boat	Club	Brussels sprouts
10	Piano	Tractor	Tank	Lettuce
11	Cushion	Cart	Tear gas	Beets
12	Mirror	Wheelchair	Whip	Tomato
13	Rug	Tank	Ice pick	Lima beans
14	Radio	Raft	Fists	Eggplant
15—Least Typical	Stove	Sled	Rocket	Onion

Reasoning: Drawing a conclusion from a set of assumptions

Algorithms: Rules that may guarantee a correct solution

Heuristics: Cognitive shortcuts that may lead to a solution

Problem Solving: Well-defined and ill-defined problems

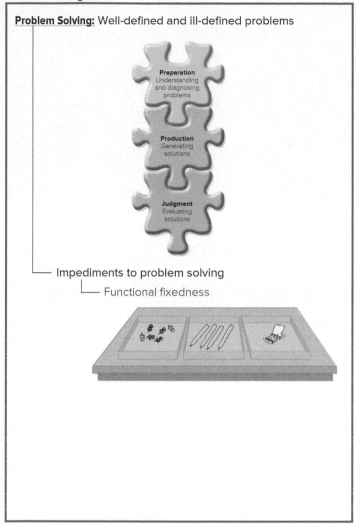

Preparation
Understanding and diagnosing problems

Production
Generating solutions

Judgment
Evaluating solutions

Impediments to problem solving

Functional fixedness

MODULE 25 Language

Language Development: Acquiring language

Babbling: Speechlike sounds that are meaningless

Telegraphic speech: Sentences in which only essential words are used

Overgeneralization: The phenomenon in which children over-apply a language rule, thereby making a linguistic error

Approaches to learning language

Learning-theory approach

Nativist approach

Interactionist approach

Linguistic-Relativity Hypothesis: The hypothesis that language shapes and may determine the way people perceive and understand the world

(MODULES 23 and 24) (Art) Source: Science. "Mental rotation of three-dimensional objects."; Courtesy, Dr. Laura Ann Petitto @1991. Photo by Robert LaMarche; Source: The American psychological association, inc., "On problem-solving, Volume 58." (MODULES 23 and 24) (Photo) Chair: Stockbyte/Getty Images; Car: Gary He/McGraw-Hill; Gun: Suradin (Pinkblue) Suradingura/123RF; Peas: Isabelle Rozenbaum/Frederic Cirou/PhotoAlto/PunchStock/Getty Images; Source: Cognitive Psychology, "Family resemblances: Studies in the internal structure of categories." (MODULES 25) (Photo) Laurentiu Garofeanu/Barcroft USA/Barcroft Media/Getty Images

Laurence Griffiths/Getty Images

CHAPTER 9
Intelligence

LEARNING OUTCOMES FOR CHAPTER 9

PROLOGUE *A TYPICAL CHILD?*

Aayush Sen is in many ways a typical kid. He likes to to read and sing. And he loves playing basketball and soccer.

But Aayush has another side. He has mastered all the basic math functions and can solve complex math problems. Moreover, in his spare time, he has been reading the works of Nobel prize winners and can recite portions of their speeches from memory.

This fall, Aayush hopes to start kindergarten. He is only 5 years old (Smith, 2019).

LOOKING *Ahead*

By most people's standards, Aayush is a genius. But what is genius exactly, and how can it be measured?

In the following modules, we consider questions such as these as we look at intelligence in all its many varieties. We begin by considering the challenges involved in defining and measuring intelligence. If you are like most people, you have probably wondered how smart you are compared with others. Psychologists, too, have pondered the nature of intelligence. We examine some of their conceptions of intelligence as well as efforts to develop and use standardized tests as a means of measuring intelligence.

We also consider the two extremes of individual differences in intelligence: intellectual disability and giftedness. Finally, we explore what are probably the two most controversial issues surrounding intelligence: the degree to which intelligence is influenced by heredity and by the environment, and whether traditional tests of intelligence are biased toward the dominant cultural groups in society—difficult issues that have both psychological and social significance.

Module 26
What Is Intelligence?

Native sailors in the Marshall Islands in the South Pacific are capable of traveling 100 miles in open ocean waters. Although their destination may be just a small dot of land less than a mile wide, the sailors are able to navigate precisely toward it without the aid of a compass, chronometer, sextant, or any of the other sailing tools that are used by Western navigators. They are able to sail accurately even when the winds do not allow a direct approach to the island and they must take a zigzag course. (Tingley, 2016)

How are the Marshall Islands sailors able to navigate so effectively? If you asked them, they could not explain it. They might tell you that they use a process that takes into account the rising and setting of the stars and the appearance, sound, and feel of the waves against the side of the boat. But at any given moment as they are sailing along, they could not identify their position or say why they are doing what they are doing. Nor could they explain the navigational theory underlying their sailing technique.

Some people might say that the inability of the Marshall Islands sailors to explain in Western terms how their sailing technique works is a sign of primitive or even unintelligent behavior. In fact, if we gave these sailors a Western standardized test of navigational knowledge and theory or, for that matter, a traditional test of intelligence, they might do poorly on it. Yet, as a practical matter, it is not possible to accuse the sailors of being unintelligent: Despite their inability to explain how they do it, they are able to navigate successfully through the open ocean waters.

The navigation used by Marshall Island natives points out the difficulty in coming to grips with what is meant by intelligence. To a Westerner, traveling in a straight line along the most direct and quickest route by using a sextant and other navigational tools is likely to represent the most "intelligent" kind of behavior; in contrast, a zigzag course, based on the "feel" of the waves, would not seem very reasonable. To the Marshall Island sailors, who are used to their own system of navigation, however, the use of complicated navigational tools might seem so overly complex and unnecessary that they might think of Western navigators as lacking in intelligence.

It is clear from this example that the term *intelligence* can take on many different meanings. If, for instance, you lived in a remote part of the Australian outback, the way you would differentiate between more intelligent and less intelligent people might have to do with successfully mastering hunting skills, whereas to someone living in the heart of urban Miami, intelligence might be exemplified by being "streetwise" or by achieving success in business.

Each of these conceptions of intelligence is reasonable. Each represents an instance in which more intelligent people are better able to use the resources of their environment than are less-intelligent people, a distinction that is presumably basic to any definition of intelligence. Yet it is also clear that these conceptions represent very different views of intelligence.

That two such different sets of behavior can exemplify the same psychological concept has long posed a challenge to psychologists. For years, they have grappled with the issue of

Some South Pacific islanders are able to navigate with great accuracy across open seas without the standard navigation tools used by sailors in Western cultures. Their abilities illustrate that there are multiple ways to attain our goals and that there is no single route to success.

Danita Delimont/Gallo Images/Getty Images

devising a general definition of intelligence. Ironically, laypersons have fairly clear ideas of what intelligence is, although the nature of their ideas is related to their culture. Westerners view intelligence as the ability to establish categories and debate rationally. In contrast, people in Eastern cultures and some African communities view intelligence more in terms of understanding and relating to one another (Crowne, 2013; Blackwell, Rodriguez, & Guerra-Carrillo, 2015; Chao, Takeuchi, & Farh, 2017).

The definition of intelligence that psychologists employ contains some of the same elements found in the layperson's conception. To psychologists, **intelligence** is the capacity to understand the world, think rationally, and use resources effectively when faced with challenges.

intelligence The capacity to understand the world, think rationally, and use resources effectively when faced with challenges. (Module 26)

This definition does not lay to rest a key question asked by psychologists: Is intelligence a unitary attribute, or are there different kinds of intelligence? We turn now to various theories of intelligence that address the issue.

Theories of Intelligence: Are There Different Kinds of Intelligence?

Perhaps you see yourself as a good writer but as someone who lacks ability in math. Or maybe you view yourself as a "science" person who easily masters physics but has few strengths in interpreting literature. Perhaps you view yourself as generally fairly smart with intelligence that permits you to excel across domains.

The ways in which people view their own talents mirror a question that psychologists have grappled with: Is intelligence a single, general ability, or is it multifaceted and related to specific abilities? Early psychologists assumed that intelligence could be embodied in a concept they called *g*. In this view, ***g*, or the *g*-factor,** was the single, general factor that produced intelligence. This assumption was based on the fact that different measures of intelligence, whether they focused on, say, mathematical expertise, verbal competency, or spatial visualization skills, all ranked test-takers in roughly the same order. People who were good on one test generally were good on others; those who did poorly on one test tended to do poorly on others.

***g* or *g*-factor** The single, general factor for mental ability assumed to underlie intelligence in some early theories of intelligence. (Module 26)

Given this association between performance on different types of tests, the assumption was that a general, global intellectual ability was at work—the *g-factor*. This *g*-factor was assumed to underlie performance in every aspect of intelligence, and it was the *g*-factor that was presumably being measured on tests of intelligence (Major, Johnson, & Bouchard, 2011; Das, 2015; Debatin, 2019).

More recent theories explain intelligence in a different light. Rather than viewing intelligence as a unitary entity, some psychologists consider it to be a multidimensional concept that includes different types of intelligence (Stankov, 2003; Sternberg & Pretz, 2005; Tutwiler, Lin, & Chang, 2013).

FLUID AND CRYSTALLIZED INTELLIGENCE

Some psychologists suggest that there are two kinds of intelligence: fluid intelligence and crystallized intelligence. **Fluid intelligence** is the ability to think logically, reason abstractly, solve problems, and find patterns. We use fluid intelligence when we are solving a personal problem or grappling with a political issue (Di Fabio & Palazzeschi, 2009; Euler et al., 2015; Kyllonen & Kell, 2017).

fluid intelligence Intelligence that reflects the ability to think logically, reason abstractly, solve problems, and find patterns. (Module 26)

In contrast, **crystallized intelligence** is the accumulation of information, knowledge, and skills that people have learned through experience and education. It reflects the facts we have learned and the information that resides in our long-term memory. When we learn a new language, we use crystallized intelligence as we acquire new vocabulary words.

crystallized intelligence The accumulation of information, knowledge, and skills that people have learned through experience and education, reflecting the facts that we have learned. (Module 26)

Piloting a helicopter requires the use of both fluid intelligence and crystallized intelligence. Which of the two kinds of intelligence do you believe is more important for such a task?
Benedetta Barbanti/Benny Marty/bennymarty/123RF

theory of multiple intelligences
Gardner's intelligence theory that proposes that there are eight distinct spheres of intelligence. (Module 26)

!**Study Alert**
Remember, Gardner's theory suggests that each individual has every kind of intelligence but in different degrees.

The differences between fluid intelligence and crystallized intelligence become especially evident in late adulthood. At that point in the life span, people show declines in fluid, but not crystallized, intelligence (Ackerman, 2011; Pezoulas et al., 2017; Taylor & Bisson, 2019).

GARDNER'S MULTIPLE INTELLIGENCES: THE MANY WAYS OF SHOWING INTELLIGENCE

Psychologist Howard Gardner has taken an approach very different from traditional thinking about intelligence. Gardner argues that rather than asking "How smart are you?" we should be asking a different question: "How are you smart?" In answering the latter question, Gardner has developed a **theory of multiple intelligences** that has become quite influential (Gardner, 2000; Kaufman, Kaufman, & Plucker, 2013; Jung & Chang, 2017).

Gardner argues that we have a minimum of eight different forms of intelligence, each relatively independent of the others: musical, bodily kinesthetic, logical-mathematical, linguistic, spatial, interpersonal, intrapersonal, and naturalist. (Figure 1 describes the eight types of intelligence, with examples of people who excel in each type.) In Gardner's view, each of the multiple intelligences is linked to an independent system in the brain. Furthermore, he suggests that there may be even more types of intelligence, such as *existential intelligence*, which involves identifying and thinking about the fundamental questions of human existence. For example, in addition to his intrapersonal intelligence (see Figure 1), the Dalai Lama might exemplify this type of intelligence (Gardner, 1999, 2000).

Although Gardner illustrates his conception of the specific types of intelligence with descriptions of well-known people, each person has the same eight kinds of intelligence—in different degrees. Moreover, although the eight basic types of intelligence are presented individually, Gardner suggests that these separate intelligences do not operate in isolation. Normally, any activity encompasses several kinds of intelligence working together.

The concept of multiple intelligences has led to the development of intelligence tests that include questions in which more than one answer can be correct; these provide an opportunity for test-takers to demonstrate creative thinking. In addition, many educators, embracing the concept of multiple intelligences, have designed classroom curricula that are meant to draw on different aspects of intelligence (Davis et al., 2011; Sternberg, 2015; Islam, 2019).

The Biological Basis of Intelligence

Using brain-scanning methods, researchers have identified several areas of the brain that relate to intelligence. For example, the brains of people completing intelligence test questions in both verbal and spatial domains show activation in a similar location: the lateral prefrontal cortex. That area is above the outer edge of the eyebrow about where people rest their heads in the palms of their hands if they are thinking hard about a problem. This area of the brain is critical to juggling many pieces of information simultaneously and solving new problems. In addition, higher intelligence is related to the thickness of the cerebral cortex (Brant et al., 2013; MacLennan, 2017; Goriounova & Mansvelder, 2019).

Similarly, tasks requiring different types of intelligence involve different areas of the brain. For instance, when tasks require more general global intelligence, more areas of the brain are involved than in tasks requiring more specific sorts of intelligence (such as fluid and crystallized intelligence) (Colom et al., 2009; Haier, 2011; Zappasodi et al., 2019).

1. Musical intelligence (skills in tasks involving music). Example:

When he was 3, Yehudi Menuhin was smuggled into San Francisco Orchestra concerts by his parents. By the time he was 10 years old, Menuhin was an international performer.

2. Bodily kinesthetic intelligence (skills in using the whole body or various portions of it in the solution of problems or in the construction of products or displays, exemplified by dancers, athletes, actors, and surgeons). Example:

Known for his athleticism, former New York Yankees baseball captain Derek Jeter played baseball and basketball, and he also ran track in high school.

3. Logical-mathematical intelligence (skills in problem solving and scientific thinking). Example:

Katherine Johnson was an African-American NASA space scientist, mathematician, and physicist who calculated the orbits of astronauts during the early days of human space exploration.

4. Linguistic intelligence (skills involved in the production and use of language). Example:

Writer Toni Morrison, who died in 2019, won Pulitzer and Nobel Prizes. She began writing as a college student at Howard University. She wrote her first novel while working at a full-time job and raising two children as a single mother, getting up at 4 A.M. each day to work on the book.

5. Spatial intelligence (skills involving spatial configurations, such as those used by artists and architects). Example:

Natives of the Truk Islands navigate at sea without instruments. During the actual trip, the navigator must envision mentally a reference island as it passes under a particular star, and from that he computes the number of segments completed, the proportion of the trip remaining, and any corrections in heading.

6. Interpersonal intelligence (skills in interacting with others, such as sensitivity to the moods, temperaments, motivations, and intentions of others). Example:

Rescue workers who provide help following disasters and in emergency situations often demonstrate particularly high levels of interpersonal intelligence in dealing with survivors.

7. Intrapersonal intelligence (knowledge of the internal aspects of oneself; access to one's own feelings and emotions). Example:

The Dalai Lama, the spiritual leader of the Tibetan people, is viewed as having extraordinary compassion and understanding of the inner mind and body.

8. Naturalist intelligence (ability to identify and classify patterns in nature). Example:

Naturalist David Attenborough helped create interest in the natural world through his deep knowledge of plant and animal life, and through numerous media broadcasts that sparked the curiosity of millions.

FIGURE 1 Howard Gardner describes eight major kinds of intelligences, corresponding to abilities in different domains. In what area does your greatest intelligence reside, and why do you think you have particular strengths in that area?

(1) Erich Auerbach/Hulton Archive/Getty Images; (2) Rena Schild/Shutterstock; (3) Donaldson Collection/Michael Ochs Archives/Getty Images; (4) John Blanding/The Boston Globe/Getty Images; (5) Danita Delimont/Gallo Images/Getty Images; (6) Anne Chaon/AFP/Getty Images; (7) Salvacampillo/Shutterstock; (8) Daniel Berehulak/Getty Images

NEUROSCIENCE IN YOUR LIFE: WHAT MAKES SOMEONE INTELLIGENT?

In their efforts to understand the neural basis of intelligence, neuroscientists have recently found that individual differences in general intelligence are associated with differences in both structure and function of the brain. For example, a review of 16 studies showed that general intelligence, as measured by standard intelligence tests, was related to brain activity in eight clusters in the frontal, parietal, and temporal cortices.

The images below show five views of the brain and indicate regions related to intelligence that were active across experiments in the review, with red indicating more studies showing effects in this region. These results suggest that a network of frontal and parietal brain regions may be the main neural basis of intelligence (Basten, Hilger, & Fiebach, 2015; Hilger et al., 2017).

Left   Right

Source: Adapted from Basten, U., Hilger, K., & Fiebach, C. J. (2015). Where smart brains are different: A quantitative meta-analysis of functional and structural brain imaging studies on intelligence. *Intelligence*, 51, 10–17.

These findings suggest that there is a global "workspace" in the brain that organizes and coordinates information, helping to transfer material to other parts of the brain. In this view, the activity in the workspace represents general intelligence (Gray, Chabris, & Braver, 2003).

Research using nonhumans has also begun to help us better understand the biological underpinnings of intelligence. For example, rats raised in enriched environments (meaning an environment containing more toys, tunnels, and so on) develop more complex connections between neurons along with more rapid learning and better memory. Other studies show differences in metabolism (the rate at which food is converted to energy and expended by the body) that seem to be related to intelligence (Haier, 2003; Yang et al., 2007; Santarnecchi, Rossi, & Rossi, 2015).

Ultimately, the search for the biological underpinnings of intelligence will not lead in a single direction. Rather, the most plausible scenario is that multiple areas of the brain, as well as multiple kinds of functioning, are related to intelligent behavior (also see *Neuroscience in Your Life*).

Practical and Emotional Intelligence: Toward a More Intelligent View of Intelligence

Consider the following situation:

> An employee who reports to one of your subordinates has asked to talk with you about waste, poor management practices, and possible violations of both company policy and the law on the part of your subordinate. You have been in your present position only a year, but in that time, you have had no indications of trouble about the subordinate in question. Neither you nor your company has an "open door" policy, so it is expected that employees should take their concerns to their immediate supervisors before bringing a matter to the attention of anyone else. The employee who wishes to meet with you has not discussed this matter with her supervisors because of its delicate nature. (Sternberg, 1998)

Your response to this situation has a lot to do with your future success in a business career, according to psychologist Robert Sternberg. The question is one of a series designed to help give an indication of your intelligence. However, it is not traditional intelligence that the question is designed to tap but rather intelligence of a specific kind: practical intelligence. **Practical intelligence** is intelligence related to overall success in living (Wagner, 2011; Baczyńska & Thornton, 2017; Griffith, Sawyer, Poole, 2019).

Noting that traditional tests were designed to relate to academic success, Sternberg points to evidence showing that most traditional measures of intelligence do not relate especially well to *career* success. Specifically, although successful business executives usually score at least moderately well on intelligence tests, the rate at which they advance and their ultimate business achievements are only minimally associated with traditional measures of their intelligence.

Sternberg argues that career success requires a very different type of intelligence from that required for academic success. Whereas academic success is based on knowledge of a specific information base obtained from reading and listening, practical intelligence is learned mainly through observation of others' behavior. People who are high in practical intelligence are able to learn general norms and principles and apply them appropriately. Consequently, practical intelligence tests, such as the one shown in Figure 2, measure the ability to employ broad principles in solving everyday problems (Stemler & Sternberg, 2006; Stemler et al., 2009; Sternberg, 2013).

In addition to practical intelligence, Sternberg argues there are two other basic, interrelated types of intelligence related to life success: analytical intelligence and creative intelligence. *Analytical intelligence* focuses on traditional types of problems measured on IQ tests, whereas *creative intelligence* involves the generation of novel ideas and products (Sternberg, Kaufman, & Pretz, 2004; Sternberg, Grigorenko, & Kidd, 2005; Sternberg, Kaufman, & Roberts, 2019).

Some psychologists broaden the concept of intelligence even further beyond the intellectual realm to include emotions. **Emotional intelligence** is the set of skills that underlie the accurate assessment, evaluation, expression, and regulation of emotions (Mayer, Salovey, & Caruso, 2008; Humphrey, Curran, & Morris, 2007; Anderson, Paul, & Brown, 2017).

Emotional intelligence is the basis of empathy for others, self-awareness, and social skills. It encompasses the ability to get along well with others. It provides us with an understanding of what other people are feeling and experiencing, which permits us to respond appropriately to others' needs. These abilities may help explain why people with only modest scores on traditional intelligence tests can be quite successful: The basis of their success may be a high emotional intelligence, which allows them to respond appropriately and quickly to others' feelings.

Although the notion of emotional intelligence makes sense, it has yet to be quantified in a rigorous manner. Furthermore, the view that emotional intelligence is so important that skills related to it should be taught in school has raised concerns among

practical intelligence According to Sternberg, intelligence related to overall success in living. (Module 26)

emotional intelligence The set of skills that underlie the accurate assessment, evaluation, expression, and regulation of emotions. (Module 26)

Study Alert

Traditional intelligence relates to academic performance; practical intelligence relates to success in life; emotional intelligence relates to emotional skills.

FIGURE 2 Most standard tests of intelligence primarily measure analytical skills; more comprehensive tests measure creative and practical abilities as well.

Source: Adapted from Sternberg, R. J. (2000). Intelligence and wisdom. In R. J. Sternberg (Ed.), *Handbook of intelligence*. New York: Cambridge University Press.

You are given a map of an entertainment park.
You walk from the lemonade stand to the computer games arcade.
Your friend walks from the shooting gallery to the roller coaster.
Which of these are you BOTH most likely to pass?

A the merry-go-round   B the music hall
C the pizza stand   D the dog show

some educators. They suggest that the nurturance of emotional intelligence is best left to students' families, especially because there is no well-specified set of criteria for what constitutes emotional intelligence (Becker, 2003; Vesely, Saklofske, & Leschied, 2013).

Still, the notion of emotional intelligence reminds us that there are many ways to demonstrate intelligent behavior–just as there are multiple views of the nature of intelligence (Fox & Spector, 2000; Barrett & Salovey, 2002; Parke, Seo, & Sherf, 2015). Figure 3 presents a summary of the different approaches used by psychologists. (Also see *Applying Psychology in the 21st Century*).

FIGURE 3 Just as there are many views of the nature of intelligence, there are also numerous ways to demonstrate intelligent behavior. This summary provides an overview of the various approaches used by psychologists.

Major Approaches to Intelligence	
Approach	**Characteristics**
Fluid and crystallized intelligence	Fluid intelligence relates to the ability to think logically, reason abstractly, and solve problems; crystallized intelligence relates to information, skills, and strategies learned through experience
Gardner's multiple intelligences	Eight independent forms of intelligence
Practical intelligence	Intelligence in terms of nonacademic, career, and personal success
Emotional intelligence	Intelligence that provides an understanding of what other people are feeling and experiencing and permits us to respond appropriately to others' needs

APPLYING PSYCHOLOGY IN THE 21ST CENTURY

CAN TECHNOLOGY MAKE US SMARTER?

Will technology improve on human intelligence in the future?

In some ways, it seems the answer already is "yes." Technological advances are allowing computers to work on nuanced perceptual and decision-making tasks—ones that increasingly entail analyzing human behaviors and emotions. Some achieve this by analyzing vocal tone and inflections, others by scrutinizing the briefest of facial expressions, and still others by examining both speech and appearance.

One example comes from the field of mental health. A mobile system known as Companion assists with the treatment of patients. The patients download a smartphone app and use it to record regular audio diary entries. The Companion system then analyzes the patient's vocal patterns, as well as certain behavioral patterns such as how and when they are using their smartphones, for indicators of unusual changes in mood or behavior. If Companion detects evidence of trouble, it alerts human caregivers to check in on the patient. Thus, it functions as an early warning system that can catch a potential worsening of a patient's condition before it can progress very far (Ahern & Faust, 2012; Luxton, 2016; Liebelt et al., 2017).

Technology is also emerging that can be used in the fight against heart disease, one

Emerging technology can help keep drivers alert and focused on the road.
Belchonock/123RF

of the leading killers of Americans. Researchers at the Mayo Clinic are trying to train computers to spot subtle indicators of heart disease early in its progression. In one study, researchers used inexpensive echocardiograms to analyze disorders that are normally very difficult to detect without expensive and intrusive methods. In another study, computers analyzed the vocal patterns of patients to determine if they gave any indication of coronary heart disease. The software was then able to use these vocal biomarkers to predict which

patients about to undergo a diagnostic procedure would show evidence of coronary artery disease (Attia et al., 2019)

Another emerging technology is being used to alert drivers who may be at risk of falling asleep at the wheel. The technology uses cameras built into the car's steering column to watch the driver's posture, head position, and facial expressions as well as microphones that listen for vocal inflections consistent with fatigue—and also for simple yawning. If the system detects signs of fatigue, it can use speech synthesis to suggest that the driver take a break or to keep them alert by engaging in conversation.

Other technologies currently under development help call center operators develop better emotional intelligence, help companies select the most compatible candidates for hiring, flag insurance claims for potential fraud, and even help determine the physical appearance of criminals from the sound of their voices. Although we're certainly not at the point where human intelligence will be deemed unnecessary, we are certainly moving in surprising directions (McCormick, 2019).

RETHINK

- Why do you think computers are often better than humans at detecting patterns in complex data?
- What might be some ethical concerns regarding the use of technology to assist with decisions that were previously entirely human-based?

Assessing Intelligence

Given the variety of approaches to the components of intelligence, it is not surprising that measuring intelligence has proved challenging. Psychologists who study intelligence have focused much of their attention on the development of **intelligence tests** that quantify a person's level of intelligence. These tests have proved to be of great benefit in identifying students in need of special attention in school, diagnosing specific learning difficulties, and helping people make the best educational and vocational choices. At the same time, their use has proved controversial, raising important social and educational issues.

Historically, the first effort at intelligence testing was based on an uncomplicated but completely wrong assumption: that the size and shape of a person's head could be used as an objective measure of intelligence. The idea was put forward by Sir Francis Galton (1822-1911), an eminent English scientist whose ideas in other domains proved to be considerably better than his notions about intelligence.

intelligence tests Tests devised to quantify a person's level of intelligence. (Module 26)

Galton's motivation to identify people of high intelligence stemmed from personal prejudices. He sought to demonstrate the natural superiority of people of high social class (including himself) by showing that intelligence is inherited. He hypothesized that head configuration, which is genetically determined, is related to brain size and therefore is related to intelligence.

Galton's theories were proved wrong on virtually every count. Head size and shape are not related to intellectual performance. However, Galton's work did have at least one desirable result: He was the first person to suggest that intelligence could be quantified and measured in an objective manner. Furthermore, the advent of advanced brain-scanning techniques has found that brain size–*not* head size–does show some association with intelligence, although the results are preliminary at this point (Lee et al., 2019).

BINET AND THE DEVELOPMENT OF IQ TESTS

French psychologist Alfred Binet (1857–1911) developed the first real intelligence test. His tests followed from a simple premise: If performance on certain tasks or test items improved with *chronological*, or physical, age, performance could be used to distinguish more intelligent people from less intelligent ones within a particular age group. On the basis of this principle, Binet devised the first formal intelligence test, which was designed to identify the "dullest" students in the Paris school system in order to provide them with remedial aid.

Binet began by presenting tasks to same-age students who had been labeled "bright" or "dull" by their teachers. If a task could be completed by the bright students but not by the dull ones, he retained that task as a proper test item; otherwise, it was discarded. In the end, he came up with a test that distinguished between the bright and dull groups, and–with further work–one that distinguished among children in different age groups (Binet & Simon, 1916; Sternberg & Jarvin, 2003; Wasserman, 2018).

On the basis of the Binet test, children were assigned a score relating to their **mental age,** the age for which a given level of performance is average or typical. For example, if the average 8-year-old answered, say, 45 items correctly on a test, anyone who answered 45 items correctly would be assigned a mental age of 8 years. Consequently, whether the person taking the test was 20 years old or 5 years old, he or she would have the same mental age of 8 years (Cornell, 2006).

Assigning a mental age to students provided an indication of their general level of performance. However, it did not allow for adequate comparisons among people of different chronological ages. By using mental age alone, for instance, we might assume that an 18-year-old responding at a 20-year-old's level would be demonstrating the same degree of intelligence as a 5-year-old answering at a 7-year-old's level, when actually the 5-year-old would be displaying a much greater *relative* degree of intelligence.

A solution to the problem came in the form of the intelligence quotient, or IQ. The **intelligence quotient (IQ)** is a measure of intelligence that takes into account an individual's mental *and* chronological (physical) age. Historically, the first IQ scores employed the following formula in which *MA* stands for mental age and *CA* for chronological age:

$$\text{IQ score} = \frac{\text{MA}}{\text{CA}} \times 100$$

Using this formula, we can return to the earlier example of an 18-year-old performing at a mental age of 20 and calculate an IQ score of $(20/18) \times 100 = 111$. In contrast, the 5-year-old performing at a mental age of 7 comes out with a considerably higher IQ score: $(7/5) \times 100 = 140$.

As a bit of trial and error with the formula will show you, anyone who has a mental age equal to his or her chronological age will have an IQ equal to 100. Moreover, people with a mental age that is lower than their chronological age will have IQs that are lower than 100.

Although the basic principles behind the calculation of an IQ score still hold, today IQ scores are determined in a different manner and are known as *deviation IQ scores*. First, the average test score for everyone of the same age who takes the test is determined,

Alfred Binet
Photo 12/Universal Images Group/Getty Images

mental age The age for which a given level of performance is average or typical. (Module 26)

intelligence quotient (IQ) A score that takes into account an individual's mental and chronological ages. (Module 26)

Study Alert

It's important to know the traditional formula for IQ scores in which IQ is the ratio of mental age divided by chronological age, multiplied by 100. Remember, though, that today, the actual calculation of IQ scores is done in a more sophisticated manner.

The average IQ score is 100, and 68% of people score between 85 and 115.

68%

95%

0.1%   2%   14%   34%   34%   14%   2%   0.1%

Number of scores →

0   55   70   85   100   115   130   145   160

Intelligence test score

FIGURE 4 The average and most common IQ score is 100, and 68% of all people are within a 30-point range centered on 100. Some 95% of the population have scores that are within 30 points above or below 100, and 99.8% have scores that are between 55 and 145.

and that average score is assigned an IQ of 100. Then, with the aid of statistical techniques that calculate the differences (or "deviations") between each score and the average, IQ scores are assigned.

As you can see in Figure 4, when IQ scores from large numbers of people are plotted on a graph, they form a *bell-shaped distribution* (called "bell-shaped" because it looks like a bell when plotted). Approximately two-thirds of all individuals fall within 15 IQ points of the average score of 100. As scores increase or fall beyond that range, the percentage of people in a category falls considerably.

Contemporary IQ Tests: Gauging Intelligence

Remnants of Binet's original intelligence test are still with us, although the test has been revised in significant ways. Now in its fifth edition and called the *Stanford-Binet Intelligence Scale*, the test consists of a series of items that vary according to the age of the person being tested (Roid, Nellis, & McLellan, 2003). For example, young children are asked to copy figures or answer questions about everyday activities. Older people are asked to solve analogies, explain proverbs, and describe similarities that underlie sets of words.

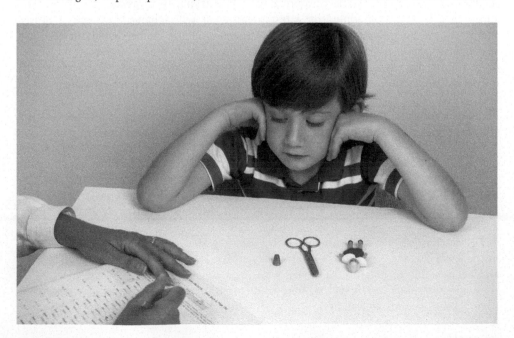

Now in its fifth edition, the Stanford-Binet test consists of a series of items that vary in nature according to the age of the person being tested. What can we learn about a person from a test of this type?
Lewis J. Merrim/Science Source

The test is administered orally and includes both verbal and nonverbal assessments. An examiner begins by finding a mental age level at which a person is able to answer all the questions correctly and then moves on to successively more difficult problems. When a mental age level is reached at which no items can be answered, the test is over. By studying the pattern of correct and incorrect responses, the examiner is able to compute an IQ score for the person being tested. In addition, the Stanford-Binet test yields separate subscores that provide clues to a test-taker's particular strengths and weaknesses.

The IQ tests most frequently used in the United States were devised by psychologist David Wechsler and are known as the *Wechsler Adult Intelligence Scale-IV*, or, more commonly, the *WAIS-IV* (for adults) and a children's version, the *Wechsler Intelligence Scale for Children-V*, or *WISC-V*. Both the WAIS-IV and the WISC-V measure verbal comprehension, perceptual reasoning, working memory, and processing speed (see sample WAIS-IV items in Figure 5).

Because the Stanford-Binet, WAIS-IV, and WISC-V all require individualized, one-on-one administration, they are relatively difficult to administer and score on a large-scale basis. Consequently, there are now a number of IQ tests that allow group administration. Rather than having one examiner ask one person at a time to respond to individual items, group IQ tests are strictly paper-and-pencil tests. The primary advantage of group tests is their ease of administration (Anastasi & Urbina, 1997; Danner et al., 2011).

However, sacrifices are made in group testing that, in some cases, may outweigh the benefits. For instance, group tests generally offer fewer kinds of questions than do tests administered individually. Furthermore, people may be more motivated to perform at their highest ability level when working on a one-to-one basis with a test administrator than they are in a group. Finally, in some cases, it is simply impossible to employ group tests, particularly with young children or people with unusually low IQs (Brown-Chidsey & Andren, 2015).

RELIABILITY AND VALIDITY: TAKING THE MEASURE OF TESTS

When we use a ruler, we expect to find that it measures an inch in the same way it did the last time we used it. When we weigh ourselves on the bathroom scale, we hope that the variations we see on the scale are due to changes in our weight and not to errors on the part of the scale (unless the change in weight is in an unwanted direction!).

In the same way, we hope that psychological tests have reliability. **Reliability** refers to the consistency of a test in measuring what it is trying to measure. We need to be sure that each time we administer a test, a test-taker will achieve the same or nearly similar results, assuming that nothing about the person has changed relevant to what is being measured.

Suppose, for instance, that when you first took the SAT exams, you scored 400 on the verbal section of the test. Then, after taking the test again a few months later, you scored 700. On receiving your new score, you might well stop celebrating for a moment to question whether the test is reliable because the score is so different. Your abilities could not likely have changed enough to raise your score by 300 points.

But suppose your score changed hardly at all, and both times you received a score of about 400. You couldn't complain about a lack of reliability. However, if you knew your verbal skills were above average, you might be concerned that the test did not adequately measure what it was supposed to measure. In sum, the question has now become one of validity rather than reliability. A test has **validity** when it actually measures what it is supposed to measure.

Knowing that a test is reliable is no guarantee that it is also valid. For instance, in the 19th century, Sir Francis Galton believed that skull size is related to intelligence, and he was able to measure skull size with great reliability. However, the measure of skull size was not valid—it had nothing to do with intelligence. In this case, then, we have reliability without validity.

reliability The consistency of a test in measuring what it is trying to measure. (Module 26)

validity The degree to which a test actually measures what it is supposed to measure. (Module 26)

Types of Items on WAIS-IV		
Name	**Goal of Item**	**Example**
Information	Assess general information	Who wrote *Tom Sawyer?*
Comprehension	Assess understanding and evaluation of social norms and past experience	Why is copper often used for electrical wires?
Arithmetic	Assess math reasoning through verbal problems	Three women divided 18 golf balls equally among themselves. How many golf balls did each person receive?
Similarities	Test understanding of how objects or concepts are alike, tapping abstract reasoning	In what way are a circle and a triangle alike?
Figure weights	Test perceptual reasoning	Problems require test-taker to determine which possibility balances the final scale.
Matrix reasoning	Test spatial reasoning	Test-taker must decide which of the five possibilities replaces the question mark and completes the sequence.
Block design item	Test understanding of relationship of parts to whole	Problems require test-takers to reproduce a design in fixed amount of time.

FIGURE 5 Typical kinds of items similar to those found on the Wechsler Adult Intelligence Scales (WAIS-IV). (Simulated items are similar to those in the *Wechsler Adult Intelligence Scale, Fourth Edition [WAIS-IV].*)

Source: Adapted from *Wechsler Adult Intelligence Scale-Fourth Edition* (WAIS-IV). (2008). Pearson Education, Inc.

However, if a test is unreliable, it cannot be valid. Assuming that all other factors—motivation to score well, knowledge of the material, health, and so forth—are similar, if a person scores high the first time he or she takes a specific test and low the second time, the test cannot be measuring what it is supposed to measure. Therefore, the test is both unreliable and not valid.

Test validity and reliability are prerequisites for accurate assessment of intelligence, as well as for any other measurement task psychologists carry out. Consequently, the measures of personality carried out by personality psychologists, clinical psychologists' assessments of psychological disorders, and social psychologists' measures of attitudes must meet the tests of validity and reliability for the results to be meaningful (Markus & Borsboom, 2013; Deng & Georgiou, 2015; Gignac, Bartulovich, & Salleo, 2019).

Assuming that a test is both valid and reliable, one further step is necessary in order to interpret the meaning of a particular test-taker's score: the establishment of norms. **Norms** are standards of test performance that permit the comparison of one person's score on a test to the scores of others who have taken the same test. For example, a norm permits test-takers to know that they have scored, say, in the top 15% of those who have taken the test previously. Tests for which norms have been developed are known as *standardized tests*.

Test designers develop norms by calculating the average score achieved by a specific group of people for whom the test has been designed. Then the test designers can determine the extent to which each person's score differs from the scores of the other individuals who have taken the test in the past and provide future test-takers with a qualitative sense of their performance.

Obviously, the samples of test-takers who are employed in the establishment of norms are critical to the norming process. The people used to determine norms must be representative of the individuals to whom the test is directed.

norms Standards of test performance that permit the comparison of one person's score on a test with the scores of other individuals who have taken the same test. (Module 26)

Dex Image/Getty Images

From the perspective of...

A Human Resource Specialist Job interviews are really a kind of test, but they rely on interviewers' judgments and have no formal validity or reliability. Do you think job interviews can be made to have greater validity and reliability?

ADAPTIVE TESTING: USING COMPUTERS TO ASSESS PERFORMANCE

Ensuring that tests are reliable, valid, and based on appropriate norms has become more critical with computer-administered testing. In computerized versions of tests such as the Graduate Record Exam, a test used to determine entrance to graduate school, not only are test questions viewed and answered on a computer, but the test itself is individualized. With adaptive testing, every test-taker receives a different set of test questions. With *adaptive testing*, not every test-taker receives identical sets of questions. Or every test-taker receives different sets of test questions. Instead, the computer first presents a randomly selected question of moderate difficulty. If the test-taker answers it correctly, the computer then presents a randomly chosen item of slightly greater difficulty. If the test-taker answers it incorrectly, the computer presents a slightly easier item. Each question becomes slightly harder or easier than the question preceding it, depending on whether the previous response is correct. Ultimately, the greater the number of difficult questions answered correctly, the higher the score (see Figure 6) (Barrada, Abad, & Olea, 2011; Liu, Ying, & Zhang, 2015; Cheng, Diao, & Behrens, 2017).

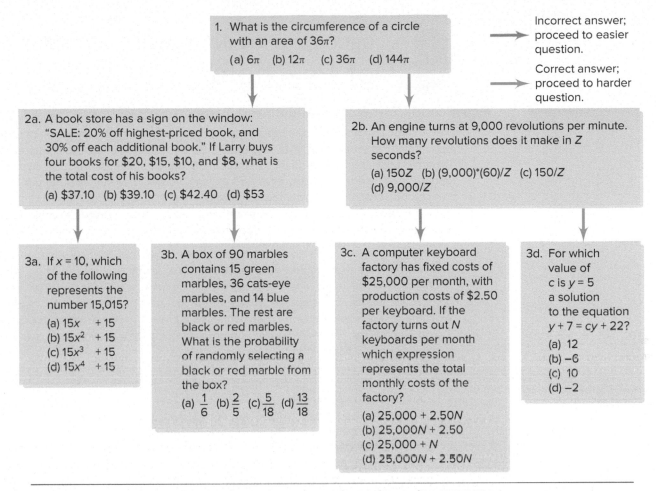

1. What is the circumference of a circle with an area of 36π?

   (a) 6π   (b) 12π   (c) 36π   (d) 144π

→ Incorrect answer; proceed to easier question.

→ Correct answer; proceed to harder question.

2a. A book store has a sign on the window: "SALE: 20% off highest-priced book, and 30% off each additional book." If Larry buys four books for $20, $15, $10, and $8, what is the total cost of his books?

   (a) $37.10   (b) $39.10   (c) $42.40   (d) $53

2b. An engine turns at 9,000 revolutions per minute. How many revolutions does it make in Z seconds?

   (a) 150Z (b) (9,000)*(60)/Z (c) 150/Z (d) 9,000/Z

3a. If $x = 10$, which of the following represents the number 15,015?

   (a) $15x + 15$
   (b) $15x^2 + 15$
   (c) $15x^3 + 15$
   (d) $15x^4 + 15$

3b. A box of 90 marbles contains 15 green marbles, 36 cats-eye marbles, and 14 blue marbles. The rest are black or red marbles. What is the probability of randomly selecting a black or red marble from the box?

   (a) $\frac{1}{6}$ (b) $\frac{2}{5}$ (c) $\frac{5}{18}$ (d) $\frac{13}{18}$

3c. A computer keyboard factory has fixed costs of $25,000 per month, with production costs of $2.50 per keyboard. If the factory turns out N keyboards per month which expression represents the total monthly costs of the factory?

   (a) $25,000 + 2.50N$
   (b) $25,000N + 2.50$
   (c) $25,000 + N$
   (d) $25,000N + 2.50N$

3d. For which value of c is $y = 5$ a solution to the equation $y + 7 = cy + 22$?

   (a) 12
   (b) −6
   (c) 10
   (d) −2

Answers: 1. b, 2a. b, 2b. a, 3a. c, 3b. c, 3c. a, 3d. d

FIGURE 6 Adaptive testing. In computer adaptive testing, a computer randomly selects a first question of medium difficulty. When the test-taker answers correctly, the computer selects a harder question. When the test-taker answers incorrectly, the computer "backs off," selecting a question at the next-lower level of difficulty, as shown in the example. Scores are based on the difficulty level of the questions that have been answered correctly, meaning that test-takers who answer the same number of questions correctly may end up with very different scores. What do you think are the drawbacks of adaptive testing of this sort? Do you think such tests may discriminate against test-takers who have less access to computers compared with those who have greater access to them?

Source: Adapted from Winerip, M. (1993, November 15). A new approach in testing. *The New York Times*, B9.

Because computerized adaptive testing pinpoints a test-taker's level of proficiency fairly quickly, the total time spent taking the exam is shorter than it is with a traditional exam. Test-takers are not forced to spend a great deal of time answering questions that are either much easier or much harder than they can handle.

On the other hand, adaptive testing has its drawbacks. For example, a large number of test items must be created and carefully calibrated in terms of their difficulty. Moreover, high-ability test-takers who make an early mistake and find the items getting easier may begin to feel anxious, leading to a downward spiral in their performance. Still, most research suggests that adaptive testing provides scores equivalent to those of traditional paper-and-pencil measures for most types of testing (Tonidandel, Quinones, & Adams, 2002; Passos, Berger, & Tan, 2007; Rulison & Loken, 2009).

PsychTech

Critics of adaptive testing suggest that it may discriminate against lower socioeconomic test-takers who have less access to computers and thus may have less practice with them, thereby increasing the "digital divide."

BECOMING AN INFORMED CONSUMER
of Psychology

Scoring Better on Standardized Tests

Even though psychologists disagree about the nature of intelligence, intelligence tests—as well as many other kinds of tests—are widely used in a variety of situations. For example, if you are thinking about becoming a physician, a lawyer, or almost any other kind of professional in a field that requires advanced training, you will have to take a formal exam in order to be accepted for postgraduate training.

If you do have to take such an exam, you can do several things to maximize your score, including the following (Lurie, Robinson, & Pecsenye, 2005; Feldman, 2013):

- *Learn as much as you can about the test before you take it.* Know what sections will be on the test and how much each section is worth.
- *Practice, practice, practice.* Try as many practice tests as you can find. The more practice you have, the easier it will be when you actually take the test.
- *If the test is administered on a computer, as it probably will be, take practice tests on a computer.* The more familiar you are with computers, the more at ease you will feel when you sit down to take the test.
- *Time yourself carefully.* Don't spend too much time on early items at the expense of later ones. Your goal should be not perfection but maximization of the number of correct responses you get.
- *Be aware of the scoring policy.* If you are not penalized for wrong answers, guess. If there are penalties, be more conservative about guessing.
- *If it is a paper-and-pencil test, complete answer sheets accurately.* Check and check again. If the test is on a computer, check your answer thoroughly before going on to the next question because you won't be able to go back and change your answer once you've submitted it.
- *Reduce text anxiety by eating right and getting enough sleep.* You also should take a realistic view of the test, remembering that your future does not hinge on your performance on a single test.

RECAP/EVALUATE/RETHINK

RECAP

LO 26-1 What are the different definitions and conceptions of intelligence?

- Because intelligence can take many forms, defining it is challenging. One commonly accepted view is that intelligence is the capacity to understand the world, think rationally, and use resources effectively when faced with challenges.
- The earliest psychologists assumed that there is a general factor for mental ability called *g*. However, later psychologists disputed the view that intelligence is unidimensional.
- Some researchers suggest that intelligence can be broken down into fluid intelligence and crystallized intelligence. Gardner's theory of multiple intelligences proposes that there are eight spheres of intelligence.

- Practical intelligence is intelligence related to overall success in living; emotional intelligence is the set of skills that underlie the accurate assessment, evaluation, expression, and regulation of emotions.

LO 26-2 What are the major approaches to measuring intelligence, and what do intelligence tests measure?

- Intelligence tests have traditionally compared a person's mental age and chronological age to yield an IQ, or intelligence quotient, score.
- Specific tests of intelligence include the Stanford-Binet test, the Wechsler Adult Intelligence Scale-IV (WAIS-IV), and the Wechsler Intelligence Scale for Children-V (WISC-V).
- Tests are expected to be both reliable and valid. Reliability refers to the consistency with which a test measures what it is trying to measure. A test has

validity when it actually measures what it is supposed to measure.

- Norms are standards of test performance that permit the comparison of one person's score on a test to the scores of others who have taken the same test.

EVALUATE

1. _____ is a measure of intelligence that takes into account a person's chronological and mental ages.
2. Some psychologists make the distinction between _____ intelligence, which reflects the ability to think logically, reason abstractly, and solve problems, and _____ intelligence, which is the accumulation of information, knowledge, and skills that people have learned through experience and education.

RETHINK

1. What is the role of emotional intelligence in the classroom? How might emotional intelligence be tested? Should emotional intelligence be a factor in determining academic promotion to the next grade?
2. If such concepts as fluid and crystallized intelligence do exist, how might they be tested? What applications would each of these types of intelligence have?

Answers to Evaluate Questions

1. IQ. 2. fluid, crystallized.

KEY TERMS

intelligence
g or g-factor
fluid intelligence
crystallized intelligence

theory of multiple intelligences
practical intelligence
emotional intelligence

intelligence tests
mental age
intelligence quotient (IQ)

reliability
validity
norms

Module 27
Variations in Intellectual Ability

LEARNING OUTCOMES

LO 27-1 How are the extremes of intelligence characterized?

LO 27-2 How can we help people reach their full potential?

"Hey, hey, hey, Fact Track!" The 11-year-old speaker chose one of his favorite programs. . . .

"What is your name?" appeared on the monitor.

"Daniel Skandera," he typed. A menu scrolled up listing the program's possibilities. Daniel chose multiplication facts, Level 1. . . .

Randomly generated multiplication facts flashed on the screen: "4 × 6," "2 × 9," "3 × 3," "7 × 6." Daniel responded, deftly punching in his answers on the computer's numeric keypad. . . .

The computer tallied the results. "You completed 20 problems in 66 seconds. You beat your goal. Problems correct = 20. Congratulations Daniel!" And with that the 11-year-old retreated hastily to the TV room. The Lakers and 76ers were about to tip off for an NBA championship game. (Heward & Orlansky, 1988)

If you consider people with intellectual disabilities as inept and dull, it is time to revise your view. As in the case of Daniel Skandera, individuals with deficits of intellectual abilities can lead full, rounded lives and in some cases perform well in certain kinds of academic endeavors.

More than 7 million people in the United States, including around 11 per 1,000 children, have been identified as far enough below average in intelligence that they can be regarded as having serious deficits (they don't all have the same deficit). Individuals with low IQs (people with intellectual disabilities) as well as those with unusually high IQs (the intellectually gifted) require special attention if they are to reach their full potential.

Intellectual Disabilities

Although sometimes thought of as a rare phenomenon, intellectual disabilities occur in 1% to 3% of the population. There is wide variation among those labeled intellectually disabled (formerly known as *mentally retarded*), in large part because of the inclusiveness of the definition developed by the American Association on Intellectual and Developmental Disabilities. The association suggests that **intellectual disability** is a disability characterized by significant limitations in both intellectual functioning and in adaptive behavior, which covers many everyday social and practical skills, and originates before the age of 18 (American Association of Intellectual and Developmental Disabilities, 2015).

Although below-average intellectual functioning can be measured in a relatively straightforward manner–using standard IQ tests–it is more difficult to determine how to gauge limitations in adaptive behavior. Consequently, there is a lack of uniformity in how experts apply the term *intellectual disabilities*. People labeled intellectually disabled vary from those who can be taught to work and function with little special attention to those who cannot be trained and are institutionalized throughout their lives (Greenspan, 2006; American Association of Intellectual and Developmental Disabilities, 2015).

Most people with intellectual disabilities have relatively minor deficits and are classified as having *mild intellectual disability*. These individuals, who have IQ scores ranging from 55 to 69, constitute some 90% of all people with intellectual disabilities.

intellectual disability A disability characterized by significant limitations in both intellectual functioning and in adaptive behavior, which covers many everyday social and practical skills. (Module 27)

Although their development is typically slower than that of their peers, they can function quite independently by adulthood and are able to hold jobs and have families of their own (Smith, 2006; van Nieuwenhuijzen et al., 2011; Nouwens et al., 2017).

With greater degrees of intellectual deficit, the difficulties are more pronounced. For people with *moderate intellectual disability* (IQs of 40 to 54), deficits are obvious early, with language and motor skills lagging behind those of peers. Although these individuals can hold simple jobs, they need to have a some degree of supervision throughout their lives. Individuals with *severe intellectual disability* (IQs of 25 to 39) and *profound intellectual disability* (IQs below 25) are generally unable to function independently and typically require care for their entire lives (Garwick, 2007; Bertelli et al., 2019).

IDENTIFYING THE ROOTS OF INTELLECTUAL DISABILITIES

What produces intellectual disabilities? In nearly one-third of the cases, there is an identifiable cause related to biological or environmental factors. The most common preventable cause of intellectual disabilities is **fetal alcohol syndrome,** produced by a mother's use of alcohol while pregnant. Increasing evidence shows that even small amounts of alcohol intake can produce intellectual deficits. One in every 750 infants is born with fetal alcohol syndrome in the United States (Murthy et al., 2009; Jacobson et al., 2011; Lewis et al., 2015).

fetal alcohol syndrome The most common cause of intellectual disability in newborns, occurring when the mother uses alcohol during pregnancy. (Module 27)

Down syndrome represents another major cause of intellectual disabilities. *Down syndrome* results when a person is born with 47 chromosomes instead of the usual 46. In most cases, there is an extra copy of the 21st chromosome, which leads to problems in how the brain and body develop (Sherman et al., 2007; Vicari, Pontillo, & Armando, 2013).

In other cases of intellectual disabilities, an abnormality occurs in the structure of particular chromosomes. Birth complications, such as a temporary lack of oxygen, may also cause intellectual disability. In some cases, intellectual disabilities begin after birth following a head injury, a stroke, or infections such as meningitis (Plomin, 2005; Bittles, Bower, & Hussain, 2007; Fevang et al., 2017).

However, the majority of cases of intellectual disabilities are classified as familial intellectual disability. **Familial intellectual disability** is intellectual disability in which no apparent biological or genetic problems exist, but there is a history of intellectual disability among family members. Whether the family background of intellectual disabilities is caused by environmental factors, such as extreme continuous poverty leading to malnutrition, or by some underlying genetic factor is usually impossible to determine (Zigler et al., 2002; Franklin & Mansuy, 2011).

familial intellectual disability Intellectual disability in which no apparent biological or genetic problems exist, but there is a history of intellectual disability among family members. (Module 27)

INTEGRATING INDIVIDUALS WITH INTELLECTUAL DISABILITIES

Important advances in the care and treatment of those with intellectual disabilities have been made since the Education for All Handicapped Children Act (Public Law 94-142) was passed by Congress in the mid-1970s. In this federal law, Congress stipulated that people with intellectual disabilities are entitled to a full education and that they must be educated and trained in the least restrictive environment—a process known as mainstreaming. *Mainstreaming* is the practice of educating students with intellectual deficits and other special needs in regular classes during specific time periods (Aussilloux & Bagdadli, 2006; Gibb et al., 2007; De Bruin, 2019).

The philosophy behind mainstreaming suggests that the interaction of students with and without intellectual disabilities in regular classrooms will improve educational opportunities for those with intellectual disabilities, increase their social acceptance, and facilitate their integration into society as a whole. In mainstreaming, special education classes still exist; some individuals with intellectual disabilities function at too low of a level to benefit from placement in regular classrooms. Moreover, children with intellectual disabilities who are mainstreamed into regular classes typically attend special classes for at least part of the day (Hastings & Oakford, 2003; Williamson, McLeskey, & Hoppey, 2006; Benitez et al., 2017).

Some educators argue that an alternative to mainstreaming, called full inclusion, is a better strategy for educating students with intellectual disabilities. *Full inclusion* is the total integration of all students, even those with the most severe intellectual disabilities, into regular classes.

Schools with full inclusion programs have no separate special education classes. Instead, teacher aides are assigned to help children with special needs progress in the classrooms they share with non-special-needs students (Hassouneh, Alcala-Moss, & McNeff, 2011; Stainton & Clare, 2012; Nepi et al., 2015).

Full inclusion is a controversial practice. Although proponents of full inclusion—who essentially want to abolish special-needs classes—argue that it is the legal and moral right of all students to be educated together, parents of students without special needs sometimes assert that the presence of special-needs students will be disruptive. Furthermore, the use of classroom aides is expensive. Consequently, full inclusion is not widely used (Spence-Cochran & Pearl, 2006; Begeny & Martens, 2007; Rooney, 2019).

From the perspective of...

An Educator What advantages and disadvantages do you think full inclusion programs would present for students with intellectual disability? For students without it?

Andersen Ross/Blend Images/Getty Images

The Intellectually Gifted

intellectually gifted The 2%-4% segment of the population who have IQ scores greater than 130. (Module 27)

Another group of people—the intellectually gifted—differ from those with average intelligence as much as individuals with intellectual disability do, although in a different manner. Accounting for 2% to 4% of the population, the **intellectually gifted** have IQ scores greater than 130.

Although stereotypes about the gifted suggests that they are awkward, shy social misfits who don't get along well with peers, most research indicates just the opposite: The intellectually gifted do well across almost every domain. They are most often outgoing, well-adjusted, healthy, popular people who are able to do most things better than the average person can (Mueller, 2009; Sternberg, Jarvin, & Grigorenko, 2011; Strenze, 2015).

For example, in a famous study by psychologist Lewis Terman that started in the early 1920s and continued for decades, 1,500 children who had IQ scores above 140 were followed for the rest of their lives. From the start, the members of this group were more physically, academically, and socially capable than their nongifted peers. In addition to doing better in school, they also showed better social adjustment than average. All these advantages paid off in terms of career success: As a group, the gifted received more awards and distinctions, earned higher incomes, and made more contributions in art and literature than typical individuals. Perhaps most important, they reported greater satisfaction in life than did the nongifted (Hegarty, 2007; Warne & Liu, 2017; Warne, 2019).

Of course, not every member of the group Terman studied was successful. Furthermore, high intelligence is not a homogeneous quality; a person with a high overall IQ is not necessarily gifted in every academic subject but may excel in just one or two. A high IQ is not a universal guarantee of success (Shurkin, 1992; Winner, 2003; Clemons, 2006).

Although special programs attempting to overcome the deficits of people with intellectual disability are common, programs targeted at the intellectually gifted are rarer. One reason for this lack of attention is that although there are as many gifted individuals as there are those with intellectual disability, the definition of *gifted* is vague, especially compared with definitions of intellectual disability. Furthermore, there is a persistent view that the gifted ought to be able to "make it on their own"; if they can't, they really weren't gifted in the first place (Parke, 2003; Robinson, 2003; Sparks, 2007).

More enlightened approaches, however, have acknowledged that without some form of special attention, the gifted become bored and frustrated with the pace of their schooling and may never reach their potential. Consequently, programs for the gifted are designed to provide enrichment that allows participants' talents to flourish (Adams-Byers, Squilkr, & Moon, 2004; Delcourt, Cornell, & Goldberg, 2007; Freeman, 2013).

RECAP/EVALUATE/RETHINK

RECAP

LO 27-1 How are the extremes of intelligence characterized?

- The levels of intellectual disability include mild, moderate, severe, and profound intellectual disability.
- About one-third of the cases of intellectual disability have a known biological cause; fetal alcohol syndrome is the most common. Most cases, however, are classified as familial intellectual disability, for which there is no known biological cause.
- The intellectually gifted are people with IQ scores greater than 130. Intellectually gifted people tend to be healthier and more successful than the nongifted.

LO 27-2 How can we help people reach their full potential?

- Advances in the treatment of people with intellectual disability include mainstreaming, the integration of individuals with intellectual disability into regular education classrooms as much as possible (along with some participation in segregated special education classes); and full inclusion, in which all students, even those with the most severe educational disabilities, are fully integrated into regular classes (and separate classes are avoided).

EVALUATE

1. The term *intellectual disability* is applied specifically to people with an IQ below 60. True or false?

2. _____ _____ is a disorder caused by an extra chromosome that is responsible for some cases of intellectual disability.

3. _____ is the process by which students with intellectual disability are placed in normal classrooms to facilitate learning and reduce isolation.

4. Most forms of intellectual disability have no identifiable biological cause. True or false?

5. People with high intelligence are generally shy and socially withdrawn. True or false?

RETHINK

1. Why do you think negative stereotypes of gifted individuals and people with intellectual disabilities persist, even in the face of contrary evidence? How can these stereotypes be changed?

2. Do you think it's appropriate for parents of students without special needs to assert that their children will be somehow put at a disadvantage by the presence of special-needs students in classes in which full inclusion is used?

Answers to Evaluate Questions

1. False; the term is used to describe a wide range of people with various degrees of mental impairment.; 2. Down syndrome; 3. Mainstreaming; 4. True; 5. False; the gifted are generally more socially adept than those with a lower IQ.

KEY TERMS

intellectual disability
fetal alcohol syndrome

familial intellectual disability

intellectually gifted

Module 28

Group Differences in Intelligence: Genetic and Environmental Determinants

LEARNING OUTCOMES

LO 28-1 Are traditional IQ tests culturally biased?

LO 28-2 Are there racial differences in intelligence?

LO 28-3 To what degree is intelligence influenced by the environment and to what degree by heredity?

Kwang is often washed with a pleck tied to a:

(a) rundel   (c) pove

(b) flink   (d) quirj

If you found this kind of item on an intelligence test, you would probably complain that the test was totally absurd and had nothing to do with your intelligence or anyone else's—and rightly so. How could anyone be expected to respond to items presented in a language that was so unfamiliar?

Yet to some people, even more reasonable questions may appear just as nonsensical. Consider the example of a child raised in a city who is asked about procedures for milking cows or someone raised in a rural area who is asked about subway ticketing procedures. Obviously, the previous experience of the test-takers would affect their ability to answer correctly. And if such types of questions were included on an IQ test, a critic could rightly contend that the test had more to do with prior experience than with intelligence.

Although IQ tests do not include questions that are so clearly dependent on prior knowledge as questions about cows and subways, the background and experiences of test-takers do have the potential to affect results. In fact, the issue of devising fair intelligence tests that measure knowledge unrelated to culture and family background and experience is central to explaining an important and persistent finding: Members of certain racial and cultural groups consistently score lower on traditional intelligence tests than do members of other groups.

For example, as a group, blacks tend to average 10 to 15 IQ points lower than whites. Does this variation reflect a true difference in intelligence, or are the questions biased with regard to the kinds of knowledge they test? Clearly, if whites perform better because of their greater familiarity with the kind of information that is being tested, their higher IQ scores are not an indication that they are more intelligent than members of other groups (Morgan, Marsiske, & Whitfield, 2008; Suzuki, Short, & Lee, 2011; Loehlin et al., 2015).

There is good reason to believe that some standardized IQ tests contain elements that discriminate against minority-group members whose experiences differ from those of the white majority. As we discuss in *Exploring Diversity*, these issues have led to the development of what are known as *culture-fair IQ tests*.

 # Exploring Diversity

Can We Develop Culture-Fair IQ Tests?

Consider this question: "What should you do if another child grabs your hat and runs off with it?" Most white middle-class children answer that they would tell an adult, and this response is scored as correct on a common IQ test. However, a reasonable response might be to chase the person and fight to get the hat back, the answer that many urban black children choose—but one that is scored as incorrect (Reynolds & Ramsay, 2003).

In an attempt to produce a **culture-fair IQ test,** one that does not discriminate against the members of any minority group, psychologists have tried to devise test items that assess experiences common to all cultures or emphasize questions that do not require language usage. However, test makers have found this difficult to do because past experiences, attitudes, and values almost always have an impact on respondents' answers (Fagan & Holland, 2009; Rizzi & Posthuma, 2013).

For example, children raised in Western cultures group things on the basis of what they are (such as putting *dog* and *fish* into the category of *animal*). In contrast, members of the Kpelle tribe in Africa group things according to what they *do* (grouping *fish* with *swim*). Similarly, when asked to memorize the positions on a chessboard of objects typical to a U.S. household, children in the United States performed better than did children living in remote African villages. But if rocks are used instead of household objects, the African children do better (Serpell, 2000; Valencia & Suzuki, 2003; Barnett et al., 2011).

Finally, tests may include even subtler forms of bias against minority groups. For example, assessments of cognitive ability developed in the United States may favor responses that implicitly reflect North American or European values, customs, or traditions, such as the "rugged individualism" of Western cultures. At the same time, such tests may be biased against African and other cultural value systems that place a greater emphasis on the importance of social groups and embody a more communal worldview.

Statewide high school tests have also been proven to show bias. For example, a study by Stanford University researchers recently found racial bias in a writing test that all high school students in Massachusetts were required to pass in order to graduate. Specifically, the researchers found that the test included an essay question that some African-American students found racist and which led to systematic declines in their test performance. Consequently, education officials adjusted their scores in an effort to remove the bias from their test scores (Vanis, 2019).

In short, producing a truly culture-fair test is difficult but not impossible; some cross-cultural test comparisons show relatively minor differences in scores regardless of racial and ethnic group membership. Still, creating a truly culture-fair IQ test has remained an elusive goal (Byrne & Watkins, 2003; Teovanović, Knežević, & Stankov, 2015; Haggman vanArx, Lemola, & Grob, 2018).

culture-fair IQ test A test that does not discriminate against the members of any minority group. (Module 28)

IQ and Heritability: The Relative Influence of Genetics and Environment

The efforts of psychologists to produce culture-fair measures of intelligence relate to a lingering controversy over whether members of different racial and ethnic groups differ in intelligence. In attempting to identify whether such differences do indeed exist, psychologists have had to confront a broader issue: what is the relative contribution to intelligence of genetic factors (heredity) versus experience (environment)–the nature–nurture issue that is so basic in psychology.

Richard Herrnstein, a psychologist, and Charles Murray, a sociologist, fanned the flames of the debate with the publication of their book *The Bell Curve* in the mid-1990s (Herrnstein & Murray, 1994). They argued that an analysis of IQ differences between whites and blacks demonstrated that although environmental factors played a role, basic genetic differences also existed between the two races.

They based their argument on a number of findings. For instance, on average, whites score 15 points higher than blacks on traditional IQ tests even when socioeconomic status (SES) is taken into account. According to Herrnstein and Murray, middle- and upper-SES blacks score lower than middle- and upper-SES whites, just as lower-SES blacks score lower on average than lower-SES whites. Intelligence differences between blacks and whites, they concluded, could not be attributed to environmental differences alone.

heritability The degree to which a characteristic is related to inherited genetic factors. (Module 28)

Intelligence clearly shows high heritability. **Heritability** is the degree to which a characteristic is related to inherited genetic factors. That is, a trait with high heritability is strongly related to genetic factors. In contrast, low-heritability traits are weakly related to genetic factors and thus more influenced by the environment in which a person is raised (e.g., Plomin, 2009; van Soelen et al., 2011; Tosto et al., 2017; Toto et al., 2019).

As can be seen in Figure 1, the closer the genetic link between two related people, the greater the correspondence of IQ scores. Using data such as these, Herrnstein and Murray argued that differences between races in IQ scores were largely caused by genetically based differences in intelligence.

However, many psychologists reacted strongly against the arguments laid out in *The Bell Curve*, refuting several of the book's basic conclusions. One criticism is that even within similar socioeconomic groups, wide variations in IQ remain among individual households. Furthermore, the living conditions of blacks and whites are likely different even when their socioeconomic status is similar. In addition, as we discussed earlier, there is reason to believe that traditional IQ tests may discriminate against lower-SES urban blacks by asking for information pertaining to experiences they are unlikely to have had (Nisbett, 2007; Levine, 2011).

Moreover, blacks who are raised in economically enriched environments have IQ scores similar to whites in comparable environments. For example, in a study of black children who had been adopted at an early age by white middle-class families of above-average intelligence, the IQ scores of those children averaged 106—about 15 points above the average IQ scores of unadopted black children in the study. Other research shows that the racial gap in IQ narrows considerably after a college education, and cross-cultural data demonstrate that when racial gaps exist in other cultures, the economically disadvantaged groups typically have lower scores. In short, the evidence that genetic factors play the major role in determining racial differences in IQ is not compelling (Scarr & Weinberg, 1976; Fagan & Holland, 2007; Nisbett, 2009; Thaler et al., 2015).

Furthermore, drawing comparisons between races on any dimension, including IQ scores, is an imprecise, potentially misleading, and often fruitless venture. By far, the greatest discrepancies in IQ scores occur when comparing *individuals*, not when

Relationship	Genetic overlap	Rearing	Correlation
Monozygotic (identical) twins	100%	Together	.86
Dizygotic (fraternal) twins	50%	Together	.62
Siblings	50%	Together	.41
Siblings	50%	Apart	.24
Parent-child	50%	Together	.35
Parent-child	50%	Apart	.31
Adoptive parent-child	0%	Together	.16
Unrelated children	0%	Together	.25
Spouses	0%	Apart	.29

The difference between these two correlations shows the impact of the environment

The relatively low correlation for unrelated children raised together shows the importance of genetic factors

FIGURE 1 The relationship between IQ and closeness of genetic relationship. In general, the more similar the genetic and environmental background of two people, the greater the correlation is. Note, for example, that the correlation for spouses, who are genetically unrelated and have been reared apart, is relatively low, whereas the correlation for identical twins reared together is substantial.

Source: Adapted from Henderson, N. D. (1982). Correlations in IQ for pairs of people with varying degrees of genetic relatedness and shared environment. *Annual Review of Psychology, 33,* 219–243.

Social and economic inequality are associated with differences in performance on IQ tests. Those who have greater educational opportunities and who suffer fewer economic constraints score higher on measures of intelligence.
Tom Werner/DigitalVision/Getty Images

comparing mean IQ scores of different *groups*. Some blacks score high on IQ tests and some whites score low, just as some whites score high and some blacks score low. For the concept of intelligence to aid in the betterment of society, we must examine how *individuals* perform and not the groups to which they belong (Fagan & Holland, 2002, 2007).

ARE WE GETTING SMARTER?: WHY IQ SCORES ARE RISING

IQ tests are normed, which means that individual scores indicate performance on the test relative to the average score, which is set to 100. However, over the course of the roughly 100-year history of IQ tests, the test designers have noticed something peculiar: They have had to repeatedly renorm the test as the average score kept creeping up, gradually making it more and more challenging. The phenomenon has become known as the *Flynn effect*, named for a researcher who brought early attention to it (Flynn, 2009; Rindermann, Becker, & Coyle, 2017; O'Keefe & Rodgers, 2019).

The change in IQ scores amounts to roughly a 3-point increase every decade. That may not sound like much, but it means that test-takers today score a staggering 30 points higher on average than test-takers did a century ago. It's unclear why this change is happening, but many theories have been offered, including improvements in education, nutrition, technology, and even in test-taking behavior.

A recent meta-analysis, combining the results of 271 studies going back to the start of intelligence testing, helps us to make better sense of the Flynn effect. The study confirmed the existence and the extent of the growth of IQ scores. The gains were strong between the two world wars but weakened during World War II. Scores grew steadily after the war until about 1970, when the gains slowed down again, although they have continued to increase to the present (Williams, 2013; Pietschnig & Voracek, 2015).

Why is this happening? Some of the study's findings are informative. The gains are stronger for adults than for children, which points to improvements in education as a possible cause (although the gains were in fluid intelligence rather than crystallized intelligence, and children showed gains too, so education cannot be the entire cause). Gains in IQ were associated with increases in gross domestic product, an indicator of economic prosperity, suggesting that perhaps better nutrition or access to technology are contributing factors.

But the answer may not be something direct and simple. One complex explanation is that even small initial environmental changes, such as improved health, become magnified by a feedback loop wherein cognitive function improves, which produces even better health, which produces even more improvement in cognitive function, and so on. Another complex explanation is that better living conditions favor a longer childhood, whereas stressful living conditions favor a short childhood (given that delaying the responsibilities of adulthood is in many ways a luxury). Longer childhood in turn leads to better learning.

Finally, researchers caution against reading too much into the changes over time. For example, rather than all of us being geniuses compared to the early 20th-century population, it's more likely that we are simply smarter in different ways–the ways that the test happens to measure most accurately (Pietschnig & Voracek, 2015).

From the perspective of...

A College Admissions Officer Imagine you notice that students who are members of minority groups systematically receive lower scores on standardized college entrance exams. What suggestions do you have for helping these students improve their scores?

Flying Colours Ltd/Getty Images

PLACING THE HEREDITY–ENVIRONMENT QUESTION IN PERSPECTIVE

Ultimately, we have no final answer to the question of how much intelligence is influenced by heredity as compared with the environment. No definitive experiments can be devised to unambiguously determine cause and effect. And given that we can't come to a precise answer, the more critical question to ask may be this: *What can we do to maximize the intellectual development of every individual?*

By focusing on how to improve each person's intellectual performance, we can focus on how to make changes in the environment, which may take the form of enriched home environments and better schooling. Such changes may lead each person to reach his or her potential.

RECAP/EVALUATE/RETHINK

RECAP

LO 28-1 Are traditional IQ tests culturally biased?

- Traditional intelligence tests have frequently been criticized for being biased in favor of the white middle-class population. This controversy has led to attempts to devise culture-fair tests, IQ measures that avoid questions that depend on a particular cultural background.

LO 28-2 Are there racial differences in intelligence?

- Issues of racial differences in intelligence are very controversial in part because disagreement over what con-stitutes unbiased measures of racial differences and because there are confounding factors such as socioeconomic status differences related to race. Consequently, evidence that genetic factors play the major role in determining racial differences in IQ is not compelling.

LO 28-3 To what degree is intelligence influenced by the environment and to what degree by heredity?

- Attempting to distinguish environmental from hereditary factors in intelligence is probably futile and certainly misguided. Because individual IQ scores vary far more than group IQ scores do, it is more critical to ask what can be done to maximize the intellectual development of each individual.

EVALUATE

1. Intelligence tests may be biased toward the prevailing culture in such a way that minorities are put at a disadvantage when taking these tests. True or false?
2. A(n) _____ test tries to use only questions appropriate to all the people taking the test.
3. IQ tests can accurately determine the intelligence of entire groups of people. True or false?
4. Intelligence can be seen as a combination of _____ and _____ factors.

RETHINK

1. There's been a steady rise in average IQ scores in the United States over the last several decades. Why might this be the case? Do you think it represents an actual increase in intelligence?
2. Why might a test that identifies a disproportionate number of minority group members for special educational services and remedial assistance be considered potentially biased? Isn't the purpose of the test to help persons at risk of falling behind academically? How can a test created for a good purpose be biased?

Answers to Evaluate Questions

1. True; 2. culture-fair; 3. False; IQ tests are used to measure individual intelligence; within any group, there are wide variations in individual intelligence. 4. hereditary, environmental

culture-fair IQ test   heritability

LOOKING *Back*

EPILOGUE

We've just examined one of the most controversial areas of psychology—intelligence. Some of the most heated discussions in all of psychology focus on this topic, engaging educators, policymakers, politicians, and psychologists. The issues include the very meaning of intelligence, its measurement, individual extremes of intelligence, and, finally, the heredity–environment question. We saw that the quest to partition intelligence into hereditary factors versus environmental factors is generally pointless. In the area of intelligence, the focus of our efforts should be on making sure that every individual has the opportunity to achieve their potential.

Before we leave the topic of intelligence, return to the prologue of this chapter about 5-year-old Aayush Sen. Consider the following questions on the basis of what you have learned about intelligence.

1. If Aayush is typical of intellectually gifted children, what advantages can he reasonably expect to enjoy throughout life?
2. How would you explain to Aayush's parents what his IQ score means?
3. Aayush's parents believe that his high IQ was influenced in part by their habit of reading books to him since his birth. Does their hypothesis have merit? Why or why not?

VISUAL SUMMARY 9 Intelligence

MODULE 26 What Is Intelligence?

Theories of Intelligence

Major Approaches to Intelligence	
Approach	**Characteristics**
Fluid and crystallized intelligence	Fluid intelligence relates to the ability to think logically, reason abstractly, and solve problems; crystallized intelligence relates to information, skills, and strategies learned through experience
Gardner's multiple intelligences	Eight independent forms of intelligence
Practical intelligence	Intelligence in terms of nonacademic, career, and personal success
Emotional intelligence	Intelligence that provides an understanding of what other people are feeling and experiencing and permits us to respond appropriately to others' needs

— *g*-factor: Single factor underlying mental ability

— Fluid intelligence: ability to think logically, reason abstractly, and solve problems

— Crystallized intelligence: accumulation of information, knowledge, and skills learned through experience and education

— Gardner's multiple intelligences

— Practical intelligence: Intelligence related to overall success in living

— Emotional intelligence: Skills that underlie the accurate assessment, evaluation, expression, and regulation of emotions

Assessing Intelligence: Intelligence tests

— Binet developed IQ tests

— Mental age: the average age of individuals who achieve a particular level of performance on a test

— IQ: a score based on an individual's mental and chronological ages

$$\text{IQ score} = \frac{MA}{CA} \times 100$$

The average IQ score is 100, and 68% of people score between 85 and 115.

— Contemporary IQ tests

— Wechsler Adult Intelligence Scale–III

— Wechsler Intelligence Scale for Children–V

MODULE 27 Variations in Intellectual Ability

Intellectual Disability

— A disability characterized by significant limitations both in intellectual functioning and in conceptual, social, and practical adaptive skills

— Fetal alcohol syndrome and familial intellectual disability

Intellectually Gifted

— IQ scores greater than 130

— Most often outgoing, well adjusted, healthy, popular

MODULE 28 Group Differences in Intelligence: Genetic and Environmental Determinants

Culture-fair IQ Test

IQ and Heritability

Relationship	Genetic overlap	Rearing	Correlation
Monozygotic (identical) twins	100%	Together	.86
Dizygotic (fraternal) twins	50%	Together	.62
Siblings	50%	Together	.41
Siblings	50%	Apart	.24
Parent-child	50%	Together	.35
Parent-child	50%	Apart	.31
Adoptive parent-child	0%	Together	.16
Unrelated children	0%	Together	.25
Spouses	0%	Apart	.29

The difference between these two correlations shows the impact of the environment

The relatively low correlation for unrelated children raised together shows the importance of genetic factors

(Module 26, photo), Pilot: Benedetta Barbanti/Benny Marty/bennymarty/123RF; Baseball: Rena Schild/Shutterstock; Source: Annual Review of Psychology, "Correlations in IQ for pairs of people with varying degrees of genetic relatedness and shared environment."

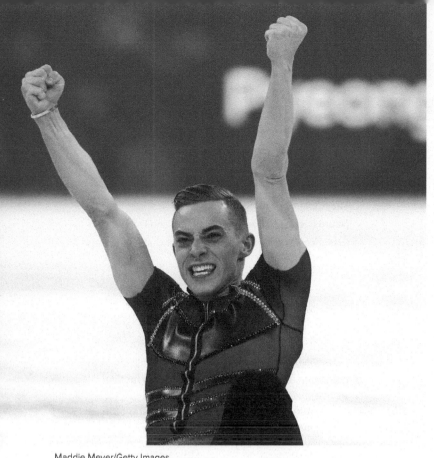

Maddie Meyer/Getty Images

CHAPTER 10
Motivation and Emotion

LEARNING OUTCOMES FOR CHAPTER 10

LO 31-1 What are emotions, and how do we experience them?

LO 31-2 What are the functions of emotions?

LO 31-3 What are the explanations for emotions?

LO 31-4 How does nonverbal behavior relate to the expression of emotions?

PROLOGUE *NEVER THIN ENOUGH*

At 5-foot-7 and 150 pounds, Olympic figure skater Adam Rippon is already small. But when he was in training for the 2016 U.S. Championships, small just wasn't small enough for him.

Rippon compared himself to his competitors, who tended not only to be several years younger but also genetically slight in stature, and he felt he didn't measure up. It didn't help that his own coaches had critiqued him for his thick, muscular legs and buttocks. He wanted his figure to be as lean and lithe as possible, the better to impress the skating judges.

Despite his rigorous workouts, Rippon's daily diet at that time consisted of little more than three slices of lightly buttered wheat bread and three cups of artificially sweetened coffee. He was basically starving himself (Krouse, 2018).

LOOKING *Ahead*

How did Adam Rippon's desire to be thin lead him to a diet that was beyond inadequate?

That's a question psychologists who study the topics of motivation and emotion would like to answer. Psychologists who study motivation seek to discover the particular desired goals— the motives—that underlie behavior. Behaviors as basic as drinking to satisfy thirst and as inconsequential as taking a stroll to get exercise exemplify motives. Psychologists specializing in the study of motivation assume that such underlying motives steer our choices of activities.

While motivation concerns the forces that direct future behavior, emotion pertains to the feelings we experience throughout our lives. The study of emotions focuses on our internal experiences at any given moment. All of us feel a variety of emotions: happiness at succeeding at a difficult task, sadness over the death of a loved one, anger at being treated unfairly. Because emotions not only play a role in motivating our behavior but also act as a reflection of our underlying motivation, they play an important role in our lives.

We begin this set of modules by focusing on the major conceptions of motivation, discussing how different motives and needs jointly affect behavior. We consider motives that are biologically based and universal in the animal kingdom, such as hunger, as well as motives that are unique to humans, such as the need for achievement.

We then turn to emotions. We consider the roles and functions that emotions play in people's lives and discuss several approaches that explain how people understand their emotions. Finally, we look at how nonverbal behavior communicates emotions.

Module 29
Explaining Motivation

In just a moment, 27-year-old Aron Ralston's life changed. An 800-pound boulder dislodged where Ralston was hiking in a narrow, isolated Utah canyon, pinning his lower arm to the ground.

For the next 5 days, Ralston lay trapped, unable to escape. An experienced climber who had search-and-rescue training, he had ample time to consider his options. He tried unsuccessfully to chip away at the rock, and he rigged up ropes and pulleys around the boulder in a vain effort to move it.

Finally, out of water and nearly dehydrated, Ralston reasoned there was only one option left short of dying. In acts of incredible bravery, Ralston broke two bones in his wrist, applied a tourniquet, and used a dull pen knife to amputate his arm beneath the elbow.

Freed from his entrapment, Ralston climbed out from where he had been pinned and then hiked 5 miles to safety. (Cox, 2003; Lofholm, 2003)

What factors lay behind Ralston's resolve?

To answer this question, psychologists employ the concept of **motivation,** the factors that direct and energize the behavior of humans and other organisms. Motivation has biological, cognitive, and social aspects, and the complexity of the concept has led psychologists to develop a variety of approaches. All seek to explain the energy that guides people's behavior in specific directions.

LEARNING OUTCOMES

LO 29-1 How does motivation direct and energize behavior?

motivation The factors that direct and energize the behavior of humans and other organisms. (Module 29)

What was the motivation behind Aron Ralston's heroic efforts to free himself from the rock that had pinned his arm to the ground?
Aron Ralston/ZUMA Press/Newscom

Instinct Approaches: Born to Be Motivated

instincts Inborn patterns of behavior that are genetically determined rather than learned. (Module 29)

instinct approaches to motivation The explanation of motivation that suggests people and animals are born preprogrammed with sets of behaviors essential to their survival. (Module 29)

When psychologists first tried to explain motivation, they turned to instincts. **Instincts** are inborn patterns of behavior that are genetically determined rather than learned. According to **instinct approaches to motivation,** people and animals are born preprogrammed with sets of behaviors essential to their survival. Those instincts provide the energy that channels behavior in appropriate directions. Hence, sexual behavior may be a response to an instinct to reproduce, and exploratory behavior may be motivated by an instinct to examine one's territory.

This instinct approach presents several difficulties, however. For one thing, psychologists do not agree on what, or even how many, primary instincts exist. One early psychologist, William McDougall (1908), suggested that there are 18 instincts. Other theorists came up with even more–with one sociologist (Bernard, 1924) claiming that there are exactly 5,759 distinct instincts!

Furthermore, instinct approaches are unable to explain why certain patterns of behavior and not others have evolved in a given species. In addition, although it is clear that a great deal of animal behavior is based on instincts, much of the variety and complexity of human behavior is learned and thus cannot be seen as instinctual.

As a result of these shortcomings, newer explanations have replaced conceptions of motivation based on instincts. However, instinct approaches still play a role in certain theories, especially those based on evolutionary approaches that focus on our genetic inheritance. Furthermore, Freud's work suggests that instinctual drives of sex and aggression motivate behavior (Katz, 2001).

Drive-Reduction Approaches: Satisfying Our Needs

drive-reduction approaches to motivation Theories suggesting that a lack of some basic biological need produces a drive to push an organism to satisfy that need. (Module 29)

drive Motivational tension, or arousal, that energizes behavior to fulfill a need. (Module 29)

After rejecting instinct theory, psychologists first proposed simple drive-reduction theories of motivation to take its place (Hull, 1943). **Drive-reduction approaches to motivation** suggest that a lack of some basic biological need (such as a lack of water) produces a drive to push an organism to satisfy that need (in this case, seeking water).

To understand this approach, we begin with the concept of drive. A **drive** is motivational tension, or arousal, that energizes behavior to fulfill a need. Many basic drives, such as hunger, thirst, sleep, and sex, are related to biological needs of the body or of the species as a whole. These are called *primary drives*. Primary drives contrast with secondary drives in which behavior fulfills no obvious biological need. In *secondary drives*, prior experience and learning bring about needs. For instance, some people have strong needs to achieve academically and professionally. We can say that their achievement need is reflected in a secondary drive that motivates their behavior (Huang, Etkin, & Jin, 2017; Tellis et al., 2019).

We usually try to satisfy a primary drive by reducing the need underlying it. For example, we become hungry after not eating for a few hours and may raid the refrigerator, especially if the next scheduled meal is not imminent. If the weather turns cold, we put on extra clothing or raise the setting on the thermostat to keep warm. If our bodies need liquids to function properly, we experience thirst and seek out water.

HOMEOSTASIS

homeostasis The body's tendency to maintain a steady internal state. (Module 29)

Homeostasis, the body's tendency to maintain a steady internal state, underlies primary drives. Using feedback loops, homeostasis brings deviations in body functioning back to an optimal state, similar to the way a thermostat and a furnace work in a home heating system to maintain a steady temperature (see Figure 1). Receptor cells

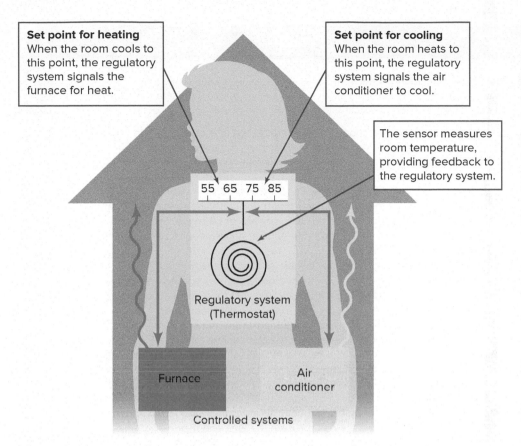

Set point for heating
When the room cools to this point, the regulatory system signals the furnace for heat.

Set point for cooling
When the room heats to this point, the regulatory system signals the air conditioner to cool.

The sensor measures room temperature, providing feedback to the regulatory system.

55 65 75 85

Regulatory system (Thermostat)

Furnace

Air conditioner

Controlled systems

FIGURE 1 With homeostasis, a series of feedback loops regulates body functions, similar to the way a thermostat turns on the furnace when a room's air temperature becomes too cool and turns it off when the air temperature becomes too warm. Similarly, when body temperature becomes too low, the blood vessels constrict, and we shiver and seek warmth. When body temperature becomes too high, the blood vessels expand, and we sweat as our bodies try to lower the temperature. Can you think of other internal systems that operate via homeostasis?

throughout the body constantly monitor such factors as temperature and nutrient levels. When deviations from the ideal state occur, the body adjusts in an effort to return to an optimal state. Many fundamental needs, including the needs for food, water, stable body temperature, and sleep, operate via homeostasis (Porkka-Heiskanen, 2013; Betley et al., 2015; Williams et al., 2019).

Although drive reduction theories provide a good explanation of how primary drives motivate behavior, they cannot fully explain a behavior in which the goal is not to reduce a drive but rather to maintain or even increase the level of excitement or arousal. For instance, some behaviors seem to be motivated by nothing more than curiosity, such as constantly checking our phones for new messages. Similarly, many people pursue thrilling activities such as riding a roller coaster or steering a raft down the rapids of a river. Such behaviors certainly don't suggest that people seek to reduce all drives as drive-reduction approaches would indicate (Begg & Langley, 2001; Rosenbloom & Wolf, 2002; Wishart, Somoray, & Rowland, 2017).

Both curiosity and thrill-seeking behavior, then, shed doubt on drive-reduction approaches as a complete explanation for motivation. In both cases, rather than seeking to reduce an underlying drive, people and animals appear to be motivated to increase their overall level of stimulation and activity. To explain this phenomenon, psychologists have devised an alternative: arousal approaches to motivation.

Arousal Approaches: Beyond Drive Reduction

Arousal approaches seek to explain behavior in which the goal is to maintain or increase excitement. According to **arousal approaches to motivation,** people try to maintain a steady level of stimulation and activity. As with the drive-reduction model, this approach suggests that if our stimulation and activity levels become too high, we try to reduce them. But, in contrast to the drive-reduction perspective, the arousal approach

Study Alert
To remember the concept of homeostasis, keep in mind the analogy of a thermostat that regulates the temperature in a house.

arousal approaches to motivation
The belief that people try to maintain a steady level of stimulation and activity. (Module 29)

FIGURE 2 Some people seek high levels of arousal, while others are more easygoing. You can get a sense of your own preferred level of stimulation by completing this questionnaire.

Source: Adapted from Zuckerman, M. (1978, February). The search for high sensation. *Psychology Today*, pp. 30–46.

Are You a Sensation Seeker?

How much do you crave stimulation in your everyday life? Complete the following questionnaire to find out. Circle either A or B in each pair or statements.

1. A My definition of the good life is to be at peace and comfortable in my skin.
   B My definition of the good life is to grab every experience possible.
2. A When I see an unfamiliar ride at an amusement park, I get right in line.
   B When I see a new ride, I need to watch how it works a few times before trying it.
3. A My ideal job would involve travel and a wealth of new experiences.
   B My ideal job would be to do something I like and keep getting better at it.
4. A I am a big fan of a lazy summer day, a beach or backyard, and a good book.
   B I love winter with its brisk days and outdoor activities such as skiing and snowboarding.
5. A I look forward to meeting new people and trying new things.
   B I like hanging out with my friends and doing things we know we enjoy.
6. A I think it's foolish to take unnecessary risks just for a sense of adventure.
   B I am attracted to challenges, even if they're a bit dangerous.
7. A I like movies that are funny or where I know the good guys are going to win.
   B I like edgy movies that are unpredictable or explore new ideas.
8. A The best art makes you think or shakes up your old ideas and preconceptions.
   B Good art is beautiful and makes you feel serene.
9. A For vacations, I prefer to go places I like and eat at restaurants I know.
   B My ideal vacation is to go somewhere new where I can try different things.
10. A If I lived in frontier days, I would head West to pursue potential opportunities.
    B If I lived in frontier days, I would stay in the East and make a good life there.
11. A The people I'm drawn to are unusual and have kind of wild ideas.
    B I like people who are like me and know who they are.
12. A I would never allow myself to be hypnotized, especially in public.
    B I would probably volunteer to be hypnotized, just to give it a try.
13. A I would love to try things like parachuting, bungee jumping, and hang gliding.
    B It makes no sense to jump out of a perfectly good airplane or off a bridge.

Scoring: Give yourself a point for each of these responses: 1B, 2A, 3A, 4B, 5A, 6B, 7B, 8A, 9B, 10A, 11A, 12B, 13A. Add up the points, and then use the following key to find your sensation-seeking score.

12–13 Very high sensation seeking
10–11 High sensation seeking
6–9 Average sensation seeking
4–5 Low sensation seeking
1–3 Very low sensation seeking

Your results can give you a rough idea of your sensation-seeking tendencies. Understand that this is a short questionnaire based on the responses of a small sample of college students, giving at best an imprecise picture. Understand, too, that as people age, their sensation scores tend to become lower.

also suggests that if levels of stimulation and activity are too low, we will try to increase them by seeking stimulation.

People vary widely in the optimal level of arousal they seek out, with some people looking for especially high levels of arousal. For example, people who participate in daredevil sports, high-stakes gamblers, and criminals who pull off high-risk robberies may be exhibiting a particularly high need for arousal (see Figure 2; Lang & Bradley, 2013; Stevens et al., 2015; Hayes & Wedell, 2020).

Incentive Approaches: Motivation's Pull

When a luscious dessert appears on the table after a filling meal, its appeal has little or nothing to do with internal drives or the maintenance of arousal. Rather, if we choose to eat the dessert, such behavior is motivated by the external stimulus of the dessert itself, which acts as an anticipated reward. This reward, in motivational terms, is an *incentive*.

Incentive approaches to motivation suggest that motivation stems from the desire to attain rewards, known as *incentives*. In this view, the desirable properties of external stimuli—whether grades, money, affection, recognition, food, or sex—account for a person's motivation (Festinger et al., 2009; Bruni et al., 2019).

Although the theory explains why we may succumb to an incentive (such as a mouth-watering dessert) even though we lack internal cues (such as hunger), it does not provide a complete explanation of motivation because organisms sometimes seek to fulfill needs even when incentives are not apparent. Consequently, many psychologists believe that the internal drives proposed by drive-reduction theory work in tandem with the external incentives of incentive theory to "push" and "pull" behavior, respectively. Thus, at the same time that we seek to satisfy our underlying hunger needs (the push of drive-reduction theory), we are drawn to food that appears very appetizing (the pull of incentive theory). Rather than contradicting each other, then, drives and incentives may work together in motivating behavior (Berridge, 2004; Belasen & Fortunato, 2013; Goswami & Urminsky, 2017).

incentive approaches to motivation Theories suggesting that motivation stems from the desire to attain external rewards, known as incentives. (Module 29)

Cognitive Approaches: The Thoughts Behind Motivation

Cognitive approaches to motivation suggest that motivation is the outcome of people's thoughts, beliefs, expectations, and goals. For instance, the degree to which people are motivated to study for a test is based on their expectation of how well studying will pay off in terms of a good grade.

Cognitive theories of motivation draw a key distinction between intrinsic and extrinsic motivation. *Intrinsic motivation* causes us to participate in an activity for our own enjoyment rather than for any actual or concrete reward that it will bring us. In contrast, *extrinsic motivation* causes us to do something for money, a grade, or some other actual, concrete reward (Finkelstein, 2009; Hofeditz et al., 2017; Maresh et al., 2019).

For example, when a physician works long hours because she loves medicine, intrinsic motivation is prompting her; if she works hard to make a lot of money, extrinsic motivation underlies her efforts. Similarly, if we study a lot because we love the subject matter, we are being guided by intrinsic motivation. On the other hand,

cognitive approaches to motivation Theories suggesting that motivation is the outcomes of people's thoughts, beliefs, expectations, and goals. (Module 29)

From the perspective of...

An Educator Do you think that giving students grades serves as an external reward that may decrease intrinsic motivation for learning about the subject matter? Why or why not?

Andersen Ross/Blend Images/Getty Images

if all we care about is the grade we get in the course, that studying is due to extrinsic motivation (Emmett & McGee, 2013).

We are more apt to persevere, work harder, and produce work of higher quality when motivation for a task is intrinsic rather than extrinsic. In fact, in some cases, providing rewards for desirable behavior (thereby increasing extrinsic motivation) actually may decrease intrinsic motivation (Grant, 2008; Nishimura, Kawamura, & Sakurai, 2011; Bolkan, 2015).

Maslow's Hierarchy: Ordering Motivational Needs

What do Eleanor Roosevelt, Abraham Lincoln, and Albert Einstein have in common? The common thread, according to a model of motivation devised by psychologist Abraham Maslow, is that each of them fulfilled the highest levels of motivational needs underlying human behavior.

Maslow's model places motivational needs in a hierarchy and suggests that before more sophisticated, higher-order needs can be met, certain primary needs must be satisfied (Maslow, 1970, 1987). A pyramid can represent the model with the more basic needs at the bottom and the higher-level needs at the top (see Figure 3). To activate a specific higher-order need, thereby guiding behavior, a person must first fulfill the more basic needs in the hierarchy.

The basic needs are primary drives: needs for water, food, sleep, sex, and the like. To move up the hierarchy, a person must first meet these basic physiological needs. Safety needs come next in the hierarchy; Maslow suggests that people need a safe, secure environment in order to function effectively. Physiological and safety needs compose the lower-order needs.

Only after meeting the basic lower-order needs can a person consider fulfilling higher-order needs, such as the needs for love and a sense of belonging, esteem, and

FIGURE 3 Maslow's hierarchy shows how our motivation progresses up the pyramid from the broadest, most fundamental biological needs to higher-order ones. Do you agree that lower-order needs must be satisfied before higher-order needs? Do hermits and monks who attempt to fulfill spiritual needs while denying basic physical needs contradict Maslow's hierarchy?

Source: Maslow, A. H. (1970). *Motivation and personality*. New York: Harper & Row.

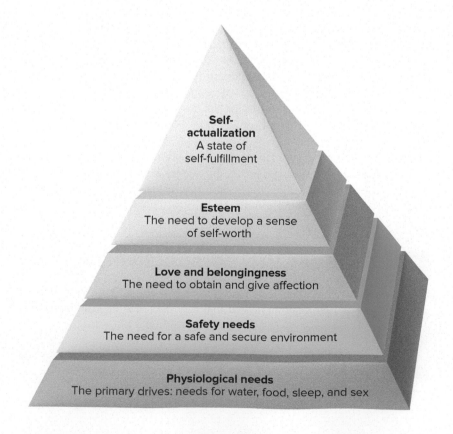

Self-actualization
A state of self-fulfillment

Esteem
The need to develop a sense of self-worth

Love and belongingness
The need to obtain and give affection

Safety needs
The need for a safe and secure environment

Physiological needs
The primary drives: needs for water, food, sleep, and sex

self-actualization. Love and belongingness needs include the needs to obtain and give affection and to be a contributing member of some group or society. After fulfilling these needs, a person strives for esteem. Esteem is the recognition that others value your competence and worth, and that they admire you for your qualities.

After these four sets of needs (physiological needs, safety needs, love and belonging-ness, and esteem) are fulfilled—no easy task—a person is able to strive for the highest-level need, self-actualization. **Self-actualization** is a state of self-fulfillment in which people realize their highest potentials in their own unique way. Although Maslow first suggested that self-actualization occurred in only a few famous individuals, he later expanded the concept to encompass everyday people. For example, a parent with excellent nurturing skills who raises a family, a teacher who year after year creates an environment that maximizes students' opportunities for success, and an artist who realizes his creative potential all may be self-actualized. The important thing is that people feel at ease with themselves and satisfied that they are using their talents to the fullest. In a sense, achiev-ing self-actualization reduces the striving and yearning for greater fulfillment that mark most people's lives and instead provides a sense of satisfaction with their current state of affairs (Ivtzan et al., 2013; Winston, Maher, & Easvaradoss, 2017; Fabian, 2019).

Although research has been unable to validate the specific ordering of Maslow's stages and it is difficult to measure self-actualization objectively, Maslow's hierarchy of needs is important for two reasons: First, it highlights the complexity of human needs, and it emphasizes the idea that until more basic biological needs are met, people will be rela-tively unconcerned with higher-order needs. For example, if people are hungry, their first interest will be in obtaining food, they will not be concerned with needs such as love and self-esteem (Ojha & Pramanick, 2009; LaLumiere & Kalivas, 2013; Beitel et al., 2015).

A second reason for the importance of Maslow's hierarchy of needs is that not only has it been influential in multiple disciplines outside psychology (among them business, nursing, and several sciences), it has also spawned other theories of motivation. For example, Richard Ryan and Edward Deci have considered human needs in terms of psychological well-being. They suggest in their *self-determination theory* that people have the need for these three basics: (1) competence, (2) autonomy, and (3) relatedness. Competence is the need to produce desirable outcomes, whereas autonomy is the need to feel control over our own lives. Finally, relatedness is the need to be involved in close, warm relationships with others. In the view of self-determination theory, these three psychological needs are genetically determined and universal across cultures, and they are as essential as basic biological needs (Ryan & Deci, 2011; Ryan & Deci, 2017; Bridgman, Cummings, & Ballard, 2019).

Applying the Different Approaches to Motivation

The various theories of motivation (summarized in Figure 4) give several perspectives on it. Which provides the fullest account of motivation? Actually, many of the approaches are complementary rather than contradictory. In fact, employing more than one approach can help us understand motivation in a particular instance.

Consider, for example, Aron Ralston's accident while hiking (described earlier). His interest in climbing in an isolated and potentially dangerous area may be explained by arousal approaches to motivation. From the perspective of instinct approaches, we realize that Aron had an overwhelming instinct to preserve his life at all costs. From a cognitive perspective, we see his careful consideration of various strategies to extri-cate himself from the boulder.

In short, applying multiple approaches to motivation in a given situation provides a broader understanding than we might obtain by employing only a single approach. We'll see this again when we consider specific motives—such as the needs for food, achievement, affiliation, and power—and draw on several of the theories for the fullest account of what motivates our behavior.

self-actualization A state of self-fulfillment in which people realize their highest potential in their own unique way. (Modules 29, 41)

Study Alert
Use Figure 4 to learn the distinctions among the different explanations for motivation (instinct, drive reduction, arousal, incentive, cognitive, and Maslow's hierarchy of needs).

Instinct

People and animals are born with preprogrammed sets of behaviors essential to their survival.

Drive reduction

When some basic biological requirement is lacking, a drive is produced.

Arousal

People seek an optimal level of stimulation. If the level of stimulation is too high, they act to reduce it; if it is too low, they act to increase it.

Incentive

External rewards direct and energize behavior.

Cognitive

Thoughts, beliefs, expectations, and goals direct motivation.

Hierarchy of needs

Needs form a hierarchy; before higher-order needs are met, lower-order needs must be fulfilled.

FIGURE 4 The major approaches to motivation.

(top, left): Westend61/Getty Images; (top, middle): Digital Vision/Getty Images; (top, right): wavebreakmedia/Shutterstock; (bottom, left): Source: LCPL Casey N. Thurston, USMC/DoD Media; (bottom, right): Corbis/VCG/Getty Images

RECAP/EVALUATE/RETHINK

RECAP

LO 29-1 How does motivation direct and energize behavior?

- Motivation relates to the factors that direct and energize behavior.
- Drive is the motivational tension that energizes behavior to fulfill a need.
- Homeostasis, the maintenance of a steady internal state, often underlies motivational drives.
- Arousal approaches suggest that we try to maintain a particular level of stimulation and activity.
- Incentive approaches focus on the positive aspects of the environment that direct and energize behavior.
- Cognitive approaches focus on the role of thoughts, expectations, and understanding of the world in producing motivation.

- Maslow's hierarchy suggests that there are five basic needs: physiological, safety, love and belongingness, esteem, and self-actualization. Only after the more basic needs are fulfilled can a person move toward meeting higher-order needs.

EVALUATE

1. _____are forces that guide a person's behavior in a certain direction.
2. Biologically determined, inborn patterns of behavior are known as _____.
3. Your psychology professor tells you, "Explaining behavior is easy! When we lack something, we are motivated to get it." Which approach to motivation does your professor subscribe to?

4. By drinking water after running a marathon, a runner tries to keep his or her body at an optimal level of functioning. This process is called _____.

5. I help an elderly person cross the street because doing a good deed makes me feel good. What type of motivation is at work here? What type of motivation would be at work if I were to help an elderly man across the street because he paid me $20?

6. According to Maslow, a person with no job, no home, and no friends can become self-actualized. True or false?

RETHINK

1. Which approaches to motivation are more commonly used in the workplace? How might each approach be used to design employment policies that can sustain or increase motivation?

2. A writer who works all day composing copy for an advertising firm has a hard time keeping her mind on her work and continually watches the clock. After work, she turns to a collection of stories she is creating and writes long into the night, completely forgetful of the clock. What ideas from your reading on motivation help to explain this phenomenon?

Answers to Evaluate Questions

1. Motives 2. instincts 3. drive reduction 4. homeostasis 5. intrinsic, extrinsic 6. False; lower-order needs must be fulfilled before self-actualization can occur.

KEY TERMS

motivation
instincts
instinct approaches
  to motivation

drive-reduction approaches
  to motivation
drive
homeostasis

arousal approaches
  to motivation
incentive approaches
  to motivation

cognitive approaches
  to motivation
self-actualization

Module 30
Human Needs and Motivation: Eat, Drink, and Be Daring

LEARNING OUTCOMES

LO 30-1 What biological and social factors underlie hunger?

LO 30-2 How are needs relating to achievement, affiliation, and power motivation exhibited?

As a sophomore at the University of California, Santa Cruz, Lisa Arndt followed a menu of her own making: For breakfast, she ate cereal or fruit with 10 diet pills and 50 chocolate-flavored laxatives. Lunch was a salad or sandwich; dinner, chicken and rice. But it was the feast that followed that Arndt relished most. Almost every night at about 9 P.M., she would retreat to her room and eat an entire small pizza and a whole batch of cookies. Then she'd wait for the day's laxatives to take effect. "It was extremely painful," says Arndt of those days. . . . "But I was that desperate to make up for my bingeing. I was terrified of fat the way other people are afraid of lions or guns." (Hubbard, O'Neill, & Cheakalos, 1999)

Lisa was one of the estimated 10 million women and 1 million men who suffer from eating disorders. These disorders, which usually appear during adolescence, can bring about extraordinary weight loss and other forms of physical deterioration. Extremely dangerous, they sometimes result in death.

Why are Lisa and others like her subject to such disordered eating, which revolves around the motivation to avoid weight gain at all costs? And why do so many other people engage in overeating, which leads to obesity?

To answer these questions, we must consider some of the specific needs that underlie behavior. In this module, we examine several of the most important human needs. We begin with hunger, the primary drive that has received the most attention from researchers, and then we turn to secondary drives–those uniquely human endeavors based on learned needs and past experience that help explain why people strive to achieve, to affiliate with others, and to seek power over others.

The Motivation Behind Hunger and Eating

obesity Body weight that is more than 20% above the average weight for a person of a particular height. (Module 30)

Nearly 40% of adults and 18% of children in the United States suffer from **obesity**, body weight that is more than 20% above the average weight for a person of a particular height. Many others are considered *overweight*, above average weight that doesn't reach the threshold for obesity (Ogden et al., 2014; Hales et al., 2017).

And the rest of the world is not far behind: A billion people around the globe are overweight or obese. With average weight rising in most countries, the World Health Organization has said that worldwide obesity has reached epidemic proportions, producing increases in heart disease, diabetes, cancer, and premature deaths. Obesity rates have doubled in 73 countries, and that has led to 4 million premature deaths (Datar, 2017; Jacobs & Richtel, 2017; McConkey et al., 2019).

The most widely used measure of obesity is *body mass index (BMI)*, which is based on a ratio of weight to height. People with a BMI greater than 30 are considered obese, whereas those with a BMI between 25 and 30 are overweight. (Use the formula in Figure 1 to determine your own BMI.)

Although the definition of obesity is clear from a scientific point of view, people's perceptions of what an ideal body looks like vary significantly across different cultures and within Western cultures from one time period to another. For instance, many

FIGURE 1 Use this process to find your body mass index.

To calculate your body mass index, follow these steps:

1. Indicate your weight in pounds: _____ pounds
2. Indicate your height in inches: _____ inches
3. Divide your weight (item 1) by your height (item 2), and write the outcome here:
   _____.
4. Divide the result above (item 3) by your height (item 2), and write the outcome here: _____.
5. Multiply the number above by 703, and write the product here: _____. This is your body mass index.

Example:
   For a person who weights 210 pounds and who is 6 feet tall, divide 210 pounds by 72 inches, which equals 2.917. Then divide 2.917 by 72 inches (item 3), which yields .041. Multiplying .041 (from item 4) by 703 yields a BMI of 28.5.

Interpretation:
• Underweight = less than 18.5
• Normal weight = 18.5–24.9
• Overweight = 25–29.9
• Obesity = BMI of 30 or greater

Keep in mind that a BMI greater than 25 may or may not be due to excess body fat. For example, professional athletes may have little fat but weigh more than the average person because they have greater muscle mass.

contemporary Western cultures stress the importance of slimness in women—a relatively recent view. In 19th-century Hawaii, the most attractive women were those who were the heaviest. Furthermore, for most of the 20th century—except for periods in the 1920s and the most recent decades—the ideal female figure was relatively full. Even today, weight standards differ among different cultural groups. For instance, in some traditional Arab cultures, obese women are so prized as wives that parents force-feed their female children to make them more desirable (Marsh, Hau, & Sung, 2007; Franko & Roehrig, 2011; Lin et al., 2015).

Regardless of cultural standards for appearance and weight, no one doubts that being overweight represents a major health risk. However, controlling weight is complicated because eating behavior involves a variety of mechanisms. In our discussion of what motivates people to eat, we'll start with the biological aspects of eating.

BIOLOGICAL FACTORS IN THE REGULATION OF HUNGER

In contrast to human beings, other species are unlikely to become obese. Internal mechanisms regulate not only the quantity of food they take in but also the kind of food they desire. For example, rats that have been deprived of particular foods seek out alternatives that contain the specific nutrients their diet is lacking, and many species, given the choice of a wide variety of foods, select a well-balanced diet (Woods et al., 2000; Jones & Corp, 2003; Adler, 2013).

Complex biological mechanisms tell organisms whether they require food or should stop eating. It's not just a matter of an empty stomach causing hunger pangs and a full one alleviating those pangs. (Even individuals who have had their stomachs removed still experience the sensation of hunger.) One important factor is changes in the chemical composition of the blood. For instance, changes in levels of *glucose,* a kind of sugar, regulate feelings of hunger. In addition, the hormone *insulin* leads the body to store excess

FIGURE 2 The hypothalamus acts as the brain's "feeding center" and is primarily responsible for monitoring food intake.
(Photo) Ryan McVay/Getty Images

sugar in the blood as fats and carbohydrates. Finally, the hormone *ghrelin* communicates to the brain feelings of hunger. The production of ghrelin increases according to meal schedules as well as the sight or smell of food, producing the feeling that tells us we're hungry and should eat (Kojima & Kangawa, 2008; Langlois et al., 2011; Massadi et al., 2017).

The brain's *hypothalamus* monitors glucose levels (see Figure 2). Increasing evidence suggests that the hypothalamus carries the primary responsibility for monitoring food intake. Injury to the hypothalamus has radical consequences for eating behavior, depending on the site of the injury. For example, rats whose *lateral hypothalamus* is damaged may literally starve to death. They refuse food when it is offered; unless they are force-fed, they eventually die. Rats with an injury to the *ventromedial hypothalamus* display the opposite problem: extreme overeating. Rats with this injury can increase in weight by as much as 400%. Similar phenomena occur in humans who have tumors of the hypothalamus (Barson, Morganstern, & Leibowitz, 2011; Nakhate, Subhedar, & Kokare, 2019; Arrigoni, Chee, & Fuller, 2019).

Although the important role the hypothalamus plays in regulating food intake is clear, the exact way this organ operates is still unclear. One hypothesis suggests that injury to the hypothalamus affects the **weight set point,** or the particular level of weight that the body strives to maintain, which in turn regulates food intake. Acting as a kind of internal weight thermostat, the hypothalamus calls for either greater or less food intake (Berthoud, 2002; Cornier, 2011; Alboni et al., 2017).

In most cases, the hypothalamus does a good job. Even people who are not deliberately monitoring their weight show only minor weight fluctuations in spite of substantial day-to-day variations in how much they eat and exercise. However, injury to the hypothalamus can alter the weight set point, and a person then struggles to meet the internal goal by increasing or decreasing food consumption. Even temporary exposure to certain drugs can alter the weight set point (Khazaal et al., 2008; Sternson, Betley, & Cao, 2013; Palmiter, 2015).

Genetic factors determine the weight set point, at least in part. People seem destined, through heredity, to have a particular **metabolism,** the rate at which food is converted to energy and expended by the body. People with a high metabolic rate can eat virtually as much as they want without gaining weight, whereas others with low metabolism may eat literally half as much yet gain weight readily (Westerterp, 2006; Krause et al., 2019).

weight set point The particular level of weight that the body strives to maintain. (Module 30)

metabolism The rate at which food is converted to energy and expended by the body. (Module 30)

SOCIAL FACTORS IN EATING

You've just finished a full meal and feel completely stuffed. Suddenly your host announces with great fanfare that he will be serving his "house specialty" dessert, bananas flambé, and that he has spent the better part of the afternoon preparing it. Even though you are full and don't even like bananas, you accept a serving of his dessert and eat it all.

Clearly, internal biological factors do not fully explain our eating behavior. External social factors, based on societal rules and on what we have learned about appropriate eating behavior, also play an important role. Take, for example, the simple fact that people customarily eat breakfast, lunch, and dinner at approximately the same times every day. Because we tend to eat on schedule every day, we feel hungry as the usual hour approaches, sometimes quite independently of what our internal cues are telling us.

Similarly, we put roughly the same amount of food on our plates every day, even though the amount of exercise we may have had (and consequently our need for energy replenishment) varies from day to day. We also tend to prefer particular foods over others. Rats and dogs may be a delicacy in certain Asian cultures, but few people in Western cultures find them appealing, despite their potentially high nutritional value. Even the amount of food we eat varies according to cultural norms. For instance, people in the United States eat bigger portions than do people in France. In sum, cultural influences and our individual habits play important roles in determining when, what, and how much we eat (Rozin et al., 2003; Leeman, Fischler, & Rozin, 2011; Gu et al., 2017).

Other social factors relate to our eating behavior as well. Some of us head toward the refrigerator after a difficult day, seeking solace in a pint of Heath Bar Crunch ice cream. Why? Perhaps when we were children, our parents gave us food when we were upset. Eventually, we may have learned through the basic mechanisms of classical and operant conditioning to associate food with comfort and consolation. Similarly, we may learn that eating, which focuses our attention on immediate pleasures, provides an escape from unpleasant thoughts. Consequently, we may eat when we feel distressed (Tsenkova, Boylan, & Ryff, 2013; Higgs, 2015; Lee et al., 2019).

! Study Alert
A key point: Eating and hunger are influenced both by biological and social factors.

THE ROOTS OF OBESITY

Given that both biological and social factors influence eating behavior, determining the causes of obesity has proved to be a challenging task. Researchers have followed several paths.

Some psychologists suggest that oversensitivity to external eating cues based on social factors, coupled with insensitivity to internal hunger cues, produces obesity.

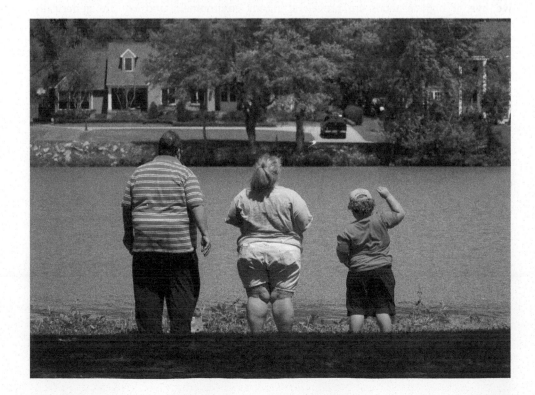

Although obesity is reaching epidemic proportions in the United States, its exact causes remain unclear.
Roberto Michel/Shutterstock

Others argue that overweight people have higher weight set points than other people do. Because their set points are unusually high, their attempts to lose weight by eating less may make them especially sensitive to external, food-related cues and therefore more apt to overeat and perpetuate their obesity (Tremblay, 2004; West, Harvey-Berino, & Raczynski, 2004; Kanoski et al., 2011).

But why might some people's weight set points be higher than those of others? One explanation is genetics: Some people have a clear genetic risk of obesity, and multiple genes appear to be involved (Khera et al., 2019).

Furthermore, obese individuals have higher levels of the hormone *leptin*, which appears to be designed, from an evolutionary standpoint, to "protect" the body against weight loss. The body's weight-regulation system thus appears to be designed more to protect against losing weight than to protect against gaining it. Therefore, it's easier to gain weight than to lose it (Wabitsch et al., 2015; Pontzer, 2017; Clawson et al., 2019).

Another biologically based explanation for obesity relates to fat cells in the body. Starting at birth, the body stores fat either by increasing the number of fat cells or by increasing the size of existing fat cells. Furthermore, any loss of weight past infancy does not decrease the number of fat cells; it only affects their size. Consequently, people are stuck with the number of fat cells they inherit from an early age, and the rate of weight gain during the first 4 months of life is related to being overweight during later childhood (Stettler et al., 2005; Moore, Wilkie, & Desrochers, 2017).

According to the *weight-set-point hypothesis*, the presence of too many fat cells from earlier weight gain may result in the set point's becoming "stuck" at a higher level than desirable. In such circumstances, losing weight becomes a difficult proposition because one is constantly at odds with one's own internal set point when dieting (Müller, Bosy-Wesphal, & Heymsfield, 2010).

Not everyone agrees with the set-point explanation for obesity. For example, it's hard to see how the set-point explanation could explain the rapid rise in obesity that has occurred over the past several decades in the United States. Why would so many people's weight set points simultaneously increase?

Consequently, some researchers argue that the body does not try to maintain a fixed weight set point. Instead, they suggest, the body has a *settling point*, determined by a combination of our genetic heritage and the nature of the environment in which we live. If high-fat foods are prevalent in our environment and we are genetically predisposed to obesity, we settle into an equilibrium that maintains relatively high weight. In contrast, if our environment is nutritionally healthier, a genetic predisposition to obesity will not be triggered, and we will settle into an equilibrium in which our weight is lower (Pi-Sunyer, 2003; Sullivan, Smith, & Grove, 2011; also see *Applying Psychology in the 21st Century*).

Eating Disorders

Eating disorders are among the 10 most frequent causes of disability in young women. One devastating weight-related disorder is **anorexia nervosa**. In this severe eating disorder, people may refuse to eat while denying that their behavior and appearance—which can become skeleton-like—are unusual. Some 10% of people with anorexia literally starve themselves to death (Striegel-Moore & Bulik, 2007; Arcelus et al., 2011).

Anorexia nervosa most often afflicts females between the ages of 12 and 40, although both men and women of any age may develop it. While the disorder has sometimes been thought of as particularly affecting women who are successful, attractive, and affluent, we now know it afflicts those at all socioeconomic levels (National Eating Disorders Association, 2019).

The disorder often begins after serious dieting, which somehow gets out of control. Life begins to revolve around food: Although people with the disorder eat little, they may cook for others, go shopping for food frequently, or collect cookbooks (Polivy, Herman, & Boivin, 2005; Myers, 2007; Jacobs et al., 2009).

anorexia nervosa A severe eating disorder in which people may refuse to eat while denying that their behavior and appearance—which can become skeleton-like—are unusual. (Module 30)

APPLYING PSYCHOLOGY IN THE 21ST CENTURY

MIND OVER GUT: WEIGHT LOSS INVOLVES THE BRAIN AS WELL AS THE BODY

For the past several decades, bariatric surgery has been the option of last resort for people whose obesity threatens their health and who have tried and failed at more conventional weight-loss strategies. Under this procedure, the size of the stomach is surgically reduced, with the result that a patient feels full faster and eats less. At least this has always been the theory behind the procedure. But newer research shows that the surgery has other surprising effects that contribute to its effectiveness—and reveals new insights into the complexities of hunger and satiety and the interconnectedness of the mind and the gut.

One important finding is that after recovering from bariatric surgery, many patients have reduced cravings for sweet, fatty, and salty foods, such that in addition to eating much less food, they are also eating different foods—often ones that are less calorically dense. A study of rats showed that bariatric surgery caused them to lose their preference for a high-fat diet, and a study of human patients showed that they lost their cravings for sweets and fast foods after the surgery. One reason this seems to happen is that a particular neural pathway in the brain becomes more active after the surgery, and activation in this pathway is associated with reduced appetite and other changes in food preferences (Leahey et al, 2012; Shin et al, 2013; Stetka, 2019).

Another new and surprising explanation for bariatric surgery's effectiveness involves the microbiota—the system of trillions of bacteria and other unicellular organisms that inhabit our large intestines. In one study, mice were given gastric bypass surgery, and then samples of their microbiota were extracted from their digestive systems and implanted in the digestive systems of mice that had not been given surgery. The mice that received this bacterial transplant proceeded to lose about 5 percent of their body weight, suggesting that an alteration of the microbiota is part of the reason for bariatric surgery's effectiveness. Possible reasons for the post-surgery change in the microbiota include a change in diet, a change in the acidity of the environment, and a change in how far undigested food travels down the digestive tract.

Researchers don't yet understand why a change in the microbiota would lead to weight loss. One possible explanation is

Many unhealthy foods are also among the most tempting.
beats1/Shutterstock

that most of the body's supply of the neurotransmitter serotonin is manufactured in the gut in a process that involves the microbiota, and serotonin plays a role in the regulation of appetite. These early research findings suggest exciting new possibilities for the treatment of obesity—ones that focus less on the size of the stomach and more on the complex relationships between the brain, the body's bacterial ecosystems, and the properties of various kinds of foods (Liou et al., 2013; Tremaroli et al., 2015; Yano et al., 2015; Mumphrey et al., 2016).

> **RETHINK**
> - How would you explain these research findings to a friend who is considering bariatric surgery for weight loss?
> - Does knowing that bariatric surgery affects the brain as well as the gut influence your opinion of it as a weight-loss solution? Explain.

A related problem, **bulimia,** from which Lisa Arndt (described at the start of this module) suffered, is a disorder in which people binge on large quantities of food. For instance, they may consume an entire gallon of ice cream and a whole pie in a single sitting. After such a binge, sufferers feel guilt and depression and often induce vomiting or take laxatives to rid themselves of the food—behavior known as purging. Constant bingeing-and-purging cycles and the use of drugs to induce vomiting or diarrhea can lead to heart failure. Often, though, the weight of a person with bulimia remains normal (Mora-Giral et al., 2004; Couturier & Lock, 2006; Lampard et al., 2011).

Eating disorders represent a significant problem: Estimates show that between 1% and 4% of high school-age and college-age women have either anorexia nervosa or

bulimia A disorder in which a person binges on large quantities of food, followed by efforts to purge the food through vomiting or other means. (Module 30)

Despite looking skeleton-like to others, people with the eating disorder anorexia nervosa see themselves as overweight.

Denis Putilov/Alamy Stock Photo

bulimia. As many as 10% of women suffer from bulimia at some point in their lives. Furthermore, an increasing amount of research shows that almost as many men suffer from binge eating as do women (Park, 2007; Striegel et al., 2011; Douglas et al., 2019).

What are the causes of anorexia nervosa and bulimia? Some researchers suspect a biological cause, such as a chemical imbalance in the hypothalamus or pituitary gland. Furthermore, the *orbitofrontal cortex*, which is involved in signaling when we should stop eating, functions differently in those with eating disorders. Furthermore, brain scans of people with eating disorders show that they process information about food differently from healthy individuals (Mohr & Messina, 2015; Weir, 2016; deAbreu & Filho, 2017).

In addition, eating disorders also may have genetic roots; both anorexia and bulemia are highly heritable. For example, people with anorexia nervosa are genetically driven to high levels of physical activity. They are also likely to have other conditions with genetic roots, including depression and anxiety (Huckins et al., 2018).

Others believe that the cause has roots in society's valuation of slenderness and the parallel notion that obesity is undesirable. These researchers maintain that people with anorexia nervosa and bulimia become preoccupied with their weight and take to heart the cliché that one can never be too thin. This may explain why eating disorders increase as countries become more developed and Westernized, and dieting becomes more popular. Finally, some psychologists suggest that the disorders result from overly demanding parents or other family problems (Kluck, 2008; Cook-Cottone & Smith, 2013; Milos et al., 2017).

The complete explanations for anorexia nervosa and bulimia remain elusive. These disorders most likely stem from both biological and social causes, and successful treatment probably encompasses several strategies, including therapy and dietary changes (Wilson, Grilo, & Vitousek, 2007; Cooper & Shafran, 2008; Murray et al., 2019).

If you or a family member needs advice or help with an eating problem, contact the National Eating Disorders Association at www.nationaleatingdisorders.org or call (800) 931-2237. You can get more information at www.nlm.nih.gov/medlineplus/eatingdisorders.html.

BECOMING AN INFORMED CONSUMER
of Psychology

Dieting and Losing Weight Successfully

Although 60% of the people in the United States say they want to lose weight, it's a losing battle for most of them. Most people who diet eventually regain the weight they lost, so they try again and get caught in a seemingly endless cycle of weight loss and gain.

To increase the chances of successfully losing weight, aim to keep several things in mind (Freedman & Waldrop, 2011; Varkevisser et al., 2019):

- *There is no easy route to weight control.* You will have to make permanent changes in your life to lose weight without gaining it back. The most obvious strategy—cutting down on the amount of food you eat—is just the first step toward a lifetime commitment to changing your eating habits.
- *Keep track of what you eat and what you weigh.* Unless you keep careful records, you won't really know how much you are eating and whether any diet is working.
- *Eat "big" foods.* Eat fiber and foods that are bulky and heavy but low in calories, such as grapes and soup. Such foods trick your body into thinking you've eaten more and thus decrease hunger.
- *Cut down on screen time.* One reason for the epidemic of obesity is the number of hours people in the United States spend viewing entertainment on their devices. Not only does screen time preclude activities that burn calories (even walking around the house is helpful), it is also associated with gorging on junk food (Robinson et al, 2017).

PsychTech

Wireless monitoring systems that track what dieters eat and how much they exercise help them to increase self-monitoring, one of the keys to effective weight loss.

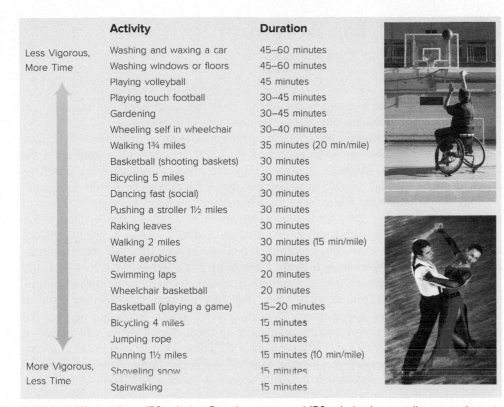

	Activity	Duration
Less Vigorous, More Time	Washing and waxing a car	45–60 minutes
	Washing windows or floors	45–60 minutes
	Playing volleyball	45 minutes
	Playing touch football	30–45 minutes
	Gardening	30–45 minutes
	Wheeling self in wheelchair	30–40 minutes
	Walking 1¾ miles	35 minutes (20 min/mile)
	Basketball (shooting baskets)	30 minutes
	Bicycling 5 miles	30 minutes
	Dancing fast (social)	30 minutes
	Pushing a stroller 1½ miles	30 minutes
	Raking leaves	30 minutes
	Walking 2 miles	30 minutes (15 min/mile)
	Water aerobics	30 minutes
	Swimming laps	20 minutes
	Wheelchair basketball	20 minutes
	Basketball (playing a game)	15–20 minutes
	Bicycling 4 miles	15 minutes
	Jumping rope	15 minutes
	Running 1½ miles	15 minutes (10 min/mile)
More Vigorous, Less Time	Shoveling snow	15 minutes
	Stairwalking	15 minutes

FIGURE 3 Ways to burn 150 calories: People can expend 150 calories by spending more time at a less vigorous activity or spending less time at a more vigorous activity.

Source: U.S. Department of Health and Human Services. (1996). *Physical Activity and Health: A Report of the Surgeon General.* Atlanta, GA: U.S. Department of Health and Human Services, Centers for Disease Control and Prevention, National Center for Chronic Disease Prevention and Health Promotion; (photos): (top) Image Source/Getty Images; (bottom) Oleg66/E+/Getty Images

- *Exercise.* Exercise at least 30 consecutive minutes three times each week. When you exercise, you use up fat stored in your body as fuel for muscles, which is measured in calories. As you use up this fat, you will probably lose weight. Almost any activity helps burn calories (see Figure 3).
- *Decrease the influence of external social stimuli on your eating behavior.* Serve yourself smaller portions of food, and leave the table before you see what is being served for dessert. Don't even buy snack foods such as nachos and potato chips; if they're not readily available in the kitchen cupboard, you're not apt to eat them. Wrap refrigerated foods in aluminum foil so that you cannot see the contents and be tempted every time you open the refrigerator.
- *Avoid fad diets.* No matter how popular they are at a particular time, extreme diets, including liquid diets, usually don't work in the long run and can be dangerous to your health.
- *Avoid taking any of the numerous diet pills advertised on television that promise quick and easy results.* They don't work.
- *Lose weight with others by joining a support group.* Being part of a group that is working to lose weight will encourage you to keep to your diet.
- *Maintain good eating habits.* When you have reached your desired weight, maintain the new habits you learned while dieting to avoid gaining back the weight you have lost.
- *Set reasonable goals.* Know how much weight you want to lose before you start to diet. Don't try to lose too much weight too quickly, or you may doom yourself to failure. Even small changes in behavior—such as walking 15 minutes a day or eating a few less bites at each meal—can prevent weight gain (Kirk et al., 2003; Freedman & Waldrop, 2011).

The Need for Achievement: Striving for Success

Although hunger may be one of the more potent primary drives in our day-to-day lives, powerful secondary drives that have no clear biological basis also motivate us. Among the more prominent of these is the need for achievement.

need for achievement A person's desire to strive for and achieve challenging accomplishments. (Module 30)

The **need for achievement** refers to a person's desire to strive for and achieve challenging accomplishments (McClelland et al., 1953). People with a high need for achievement seek out situations in which they can compete against some objective standard—such as grades, money, or winning a game—and prove themselves successful.

But people who have a high need for achievement are selective when it comes to picking their challenges: They tend to avoid situations in which success will come too easily (which would be unchallenging) or situations in which success is highly unlikely. Instead, people high in achievement motivation generally choose tasks that are of intermediate difficulty (Speirs-Neumeister & Finch, 2006; Mills, 2011; Staniewski & Awruk, 2019).

In contrast, people with low achievement motivation tend to be motivated primarily by a desire to avoid failure. As a result, they seek out easy tasks so they are sure to avoid failure, or they seek out very difficult tasks for which failure has no negative implications because almost anyone would fail at them. People with a high fear of failure will stay away from tasks of intermediate difficulty because they may fail where others have been successful (Puca, 2005; Morrone & Pintrich, 2006; Pekrun, 2017).

> ⚠ **Study Alert**
> A key feature of people with a high need for achievement is that they prefer tasks of *moderate* difficulty.

A high need for achievement generally produces positive outcomes, at least in a success-oriented culture such as Western society. For instance, people motivated by a high need for achievement are more likely to attend college than are their low-achievement counterparts; once they are in college, they tend to receive higher grades in classes that are related to their future careers. Furthermore, high achievement motivation indicates future economic and occupational success (McClelland, 1985; Thrash & Elliot, 2002; Liem, 2015).

MEASURING ACHIEVEMENT MOTIVATION

How can we measure a person's need for achievement? The measuring instrument used most frequently is the *Thematic Apperception Test (TAT)*.

In the TAT, participants are shown a series of ambiguous pictures, such as the one in Figure 4. They are then asked to write a story that describes what is happening, who the people are, what led to the situation, what the people are thinking or wanting, and what will happen next.

Researchers then use a standard scoring system to determine the amount of achievement imagery in people's stories. For example, someone who writes a story in which the main character strives to beat an opponent, studies hard in order to do well at some task, or puts in a lot of effort in order to get a promotion shows clear signs of an achievement orientation. The inclusion of such achievement-related imagery in the participants' stories is assumed to indicate an unusually high degree of concern with—and therefore a relatively strong need for—achievement (Verdon, 2011; McCreadie & Morey, 2019; Joo & Park, 2019).

GROWTH MINDSET AND ACHIEVEMENT

Do you believe that some people are born smart, talented, and destined to be high achievers, while others simply don't have enough intelligence and talent to ever do well in school and life?

If so, consider the work of psychologist Carol Dweck. In her view—and a considerable amount of supportive research—intelligence and other human capabilities are fluid and flexible, and through hard work and effort, people can increase their achievement. In fact, Dweck likens the brain to any muscle: The more you use it, the stronger it becomes (Dweck & Yager, 2018; Dweck & Yeager, 2019).

FIGURE 4 This ambiguous picture is similar to those used in the Thematic Apperception Test to determine people's underlying motivation. What do you see? Do you think your response is related to your motivation?
Science Source

People who believe in this fluidity and flexibility are said to hold a **growth mindset,** which provides them with grit. *Grit* is the perseverance and passion for long-term goals. They challenge themselves to increase their success, even if at first they fail. They are more persistent in the face of obstacles, and they try harder. They think about the goals they want to accomplish, and they are passionate about achieving them (Duckworth, 2016; Crede, 2018; Hagger & Hamilton, 2019).

In contrast, those with a **fixed mindset** inappropriately believe that individual characteristics such as intelligence, talent, and motivation are set at birth and vary little throughout the lifespan. Students with fixed mindsets may label themselves as "not smart" or "incompetent" rather than believing that with effort they can do better. As a result, they do not work as hard as others, which has the self-defeating effect of leading to failure.

Can one develop a growth mindset and avoid a fixed mindset? The answer seems to be yes. Those who tell themselves that success is the result of effort, not of how smart one is, are more likely to succeed.

The Need for Affiliation: Striving for Friendship

Few of us choose to lead our lives as hermits. Why?

One main reason is that most people have a **need for affiliation,** an interest in establishing and maintaining relationships with other people. Individuals with a high need for affiliation write TAT stories that emphasize the desire to maintain or reinstate friendships and show concern over being rejected by friends.

People who have higher affiliation needs are particularly sensitive to relationships with others. They desire to be with their friends more of the time and alone less often, compared with people who are lower in the need for affiliation. However, gender is a greater determinant of how much time is actually spent with friends: Regardless of their affiliative orientation, female students spend significantly more time with their friends and less time alone than male students do (Johnson, 2004; Semykina & Linz, 2007; Hofer et al., 2017).

The Need for Power: Striving for Impact on Others

If your fantasies include becoming president of the United States or running Microsoft, your dreams may reflect a high need for power. The **need for power,** a tendency to seek impact, control, or influence over others and to be seen as a powerful individual, is an additional type of motivation (Winter, 2007; Pratto et al., 2011; Winter, 2016).

As you might expect, people with strong needs for power are more apt to belong to organizations and seek office than are those low in the need for power. They also tend to work in professions in which their power needs may be fulfilled, such as business management and—you may or may not be surprised—teaching (Jenkins, 1994). In addition, they seek to display the trappings of power. Even in college, they are more likely to collect prestigious possessions, such as electronic equipment and sports cars.

Some significant gender differences exist in the display of need for power. Men with high power needs tend to show unusually high levels of aggression, drink heavily, act in a sexually exploitative manner, and participate more frequently in competitive sports—behaviors that collectively represent somewhat extravagant, flamboyant behavior. In contrast, women display their power needs with more restraint; this is congruent with traditional societal constraints on women's behavior. Women with high power needs are more apt than men to channel those needs in a socially responsible manner, such as by showing concern for others or displaying highly nurturing behavior (Schultheiss & Schiepe-Tiska, 2013; Sibunruang, Capezio, & Restubog, 2015; Hofer & Busch, 2019).

growth mindset The belief that individual characteristics, such as intelligence, talent, and motivation, can be developed through hard work. (Module 30)

fixed mindset The erroneous belief that individual characteristics, such as intelligence, talent, and motivation, are set at birth and vary little throughout the life span. (Module 30)

need for affiliation An interest in establishing and maintaining relationships with other people. (Module 30)

need for power A tendency to seek impact, control, or influence over others and to be seen as a powerful individual. (Module 30)

From the perspective of...

A Human Resources Specialist How might you use characteristics such as need for achievement, need for affiliation, and need for power to select workers for jobs?

Dex Image/Getty Images

RECAP/EVALUATE/RETHINK

RECAP

LO 30-1 What biological and social factors underlie hunger?

- Eating behavior is subject to homeostasis, as most people's weight stays within a relatively stable range. The hypothalamus in the brain is central to the regulation of food intake.
- Social factors, such as mealtimes, cultural food preferences, and other learned habits, also play a role in the regulation of eating by determining when, what, and how much one eats. An oversensitivity to social cues and an insensitivity to internal cues may also be related to obesity. In addition, obesity may be caused by an unusually high weight set point–the weight the body attempts to maintain–and genetic factors.

LO 30-2 How are needs relating to achievement, affiliation, and power motivation exhibited?

- Need for achievement refers to a person's desire to strive for and achieve challenging accomplishments. Need for achievement is usually measured through the Thematic Apperception Test (TAT), a series of pictures about which a person writes a story.
- The need for affiliation is a concern with establishing and maintaining relationships with others, whereas the need for power is a tendency to seek to exert an impact on others.

EVALUATE

1. Match the following terms with their definitions:
   1. Hypothalamus
   2. Lateral hypothalamic damage
   3. Ventromedial hypothalamic damage

   a. Leads to refusal of food and starvation
   b. Responsible for monitoring food intake
   c. Causes extreme overeating

2. The _____ _____ _____ is the specific level of weight the body strives to maintain.
3. _____ is the rate at which the body produces and expends energy.
4. Julio is the type of person who constantly strives for excellence. He feels intense satisfaction when he is able to master a new task. Julio most likely has a high need for _____.
5. Debbie's Thematic Apperception Test (TAT) story depicts a young girl who is rejected by one of her peers and seeks to regain her friendship. What major type of motivation is Debbie displaying in her story?
   a. Need for achievement
   b. Need for motivation
   c. Need for affiliation
   d. Need for power

RETHINK

1. In what ways do societal expectations, expressed by television shows and commercials, contribute to both obesity and excessive concern about weight loss? How could television contribute to better eating habits and attitudes toward weight? Should it be required to do so?
2. Considering need for achievement, need for affiliation, and need for power, which of these motivational traits are most predominant in you? Why do you think that, and how do they affect your everyday behavior?

Answers to Evaluate Questions

1. 1-b, 2-a, 3-c 2. weight set point 3. Metabolism 4. achievement 5. c

KEY TERMS

obesity	anorexia nervosa	growth mindset	need for affiliation
weight set point	bulimia	fixed mindset	need for power
metabolism	need for achievement		

Module 31
Understanding Emotional Experiences

Karl Andrews held in his hands the envelope he had been waiting for. It could be the ticket to his future: an offer of admission to his first-choice college. But what was it going to say? He knew it could go either way. His grades were pretty good, and he had been involved in some extracurricular activities, but his SAT scores had not been terrific. He felt so nervous that his hands shook as he opened the thin envelope (not a good sign, he thought). Here it comes. "Dear Mr. Andrews," it read. "The Trustees of the University are pleased to admit you. . . ." That was all he needed to see. With a whoop of excitement, Karl found himself jumping up and down gleefully. A rush of emotion overcame him as it sank in that he had, in fact, been accepted. He was on his way.

At one time or another, all of us have experienced the strong feelings that accompany both very pleasant and very negative experiences. Perhaps we have felt the thrill of getting a sought-after job, the joy of being in love, the sorrow over someone's death, or the anguish of inadvertently hurting someone. Moreover, we experience such reactions on a less intense level throughout our daily lives with such things as the pleasure of a friendship, the enjoyment of a movie, and the embarrassment of breaking a borrowed item.

Despite the varied nature of these feelings, they all represent emotions. Although everyone has an idea of what an emotion is, formally defining the concept has proved to be an elusive task. Here, we'll use a general definition: **Emotions** are feelings that generally have both physiological and cognitive elements and that influence behavior.

Think, for example, about how it feels to be happy. First, we obviously experience a feeling that we can differentiate from other emotions. It is likely that we also experience some identifiable physical changes in our bodies: Perhaps the heart rate increases, or—as in the example of Karl Andrews—we find ourselves "jumping for joy." Finally, the emotion probably encompasses cognitive elements: Our understanding and evaluation of the meaning of what is happening prompt our feelings of happiness.

It is also possible, however, to experience an emotion without the presence of cognitive elements. For instance, we may react with fear to an unusual or novel situation (such as coming into contact with an erratic, unpredictable individual), or we may experience pleasure over sexual excitation without having cognitive awareness or understanding of just what makes the situation exciting.

Some psychologists argue that one system governs emotional responses to a given situation and another governs cognitive reactions to it. Assuming there are two systems, does one predominate over the other? Some theorists suggest that we first respond to a situation with an emotional reaction and later try to make sense of it cognitively. For example, we may enjoy a complex modern symphony without at first understanding it or knowing why we like it. In contrast, other theorists propose that people first develop cognitions about a situation and then react emotionally. This school of thought suggests that we must think about and understand a stimulus or situation, relating it to what we already know, before we can react on an emotional level (Lazarus, 1995; Martin & Kerns, 2011).

Because proponents of both sides of this debate can cite research to support their viewpoints, the question is far from resolved. Perhaps the sequence varies from situation

LEARNING OUTCOMES

LO 31-1 What are emotions, and how do we experience them?

LO 31-2 What are the functions of emotions?

LO 31-3 What are the explanations for emotions?

LO 31-4 How does nonverbal behavior relate to the expression of emotions?

emotions Feelings that generally have both physiological and cognitive elements and that influence behavior. (Module 31) to situation, with emotions predominating in some instances and cognitive processes occurring first in others. Both sides agree that we can experience emotions that involve little or no conscious thought. We may not know why we're afraid of mice because we understand objectively that they represent no danger, but we may still be frightened when we see them. Neuroimaging studies of the brain may help resolve this debate as well as others about the nature of emotions (Niedenthal, 2007; Karaszewski, 2008; López-Pérez, 2015).

The Functions of Emotions

Imagine what it would be like if we didn't experience emotion. We would have no depths of despair, no depression, and no remorse, but at the same time, we would also have no happiness, joy, or love. Obviously, life would be considerably less satisfying and even dull if we lacked the capacity to sense and express emotion.

But do emotions serve any purpose beyond making life interesting? Indeed they do. Psychologists have identified several important functions that emotions play in our daily lives (Gross, 2006; Siemer, Mauss, & Gross, 2007; Rolls, 2011). Among the most important of those functions are the following:

- *Preparing us for action.* Emotions act as a link between events in our environment and our responses to them. For example, if you saw an angry dog charging toward you, your emotional reaction (fear) would be associated with physiological arousal of the sympathetic division of the autonomic nervous system, the activation of the "fight-or-flight" response.

- *Shaping our future behavior.* Emotions promote learning that will help us make appropriate responses in the future. For instance, your emotional response to unpleasant events teaches you to avoid similar circumstances in the future.

- *Helping us interact more effectively with others.* We often communicate the emotions we experience through our verbal and nonverbal behaviors, making our emotions obvious to observers. These behaviors can act as signals to observers, allowing them to understand better what we are experiencing and to help them predict our future behavior.

Determining the Range of Emotions: Labeling Our Feelings

If we were to list the words in the English language that have been used to describe emotions, we would end up with at least 500 examples (Averill, 1975). The list would range from such obvious emotions as *happiness* and *fear* to less common ones, such as *adventurousness* and *pensiveness*.

One challenge for psychologists has been to sort through this list to identify the most important, fundamental emotions. Theorists have hotly contested the issue of cataloging emotions and have come up with different lists, depending on how they define the concept of emotion. In fact, some reject the question entirely, saying that *no* set of emotions should be singled out as most basic and that emotions are best understood by breaking them down into their component parts. Other researchers argue for looking at emotions in terms of a hierarchy, dividing them into positive and negative categories and then organizing them into increasingly narrower subcategories (see Figure 1; Dillard & Shen, 2007; Livingstone et al., 2011; Cowen & Keltner, 2019).

Still, most researchers suggest that a list of basic emotions would include, at a minimum, happiness, anger, fear, sadness, and disgust. Other lists are broader, including emotions such as surprise, contempt, guilt, and joy (Shweder, 1994; Tracy & Robins, 2004; Greenberg, 2015).

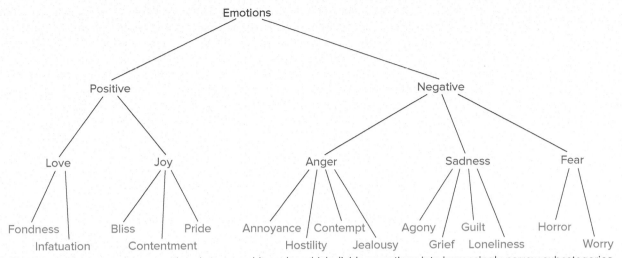

FIGURE 1 One approach to organizing emotions is to use a hierarchy, which divides emotions into increasingly narrow subcategories.
Source: Adapted from Fischer, K. W., Shaver, P. R., & Carnochan, P. (1990). How emotions develop and how they organize development. *Cognition and Emotion, 4*, 81–127.

One difficulty in defining a basic set of emotions is that substantial differences exist in descriptions of emotions among various cultures. For instance, Germans report experiencing *schadenfreude,* a feeling of pleasure over another person's difficulties, and the Japanese experience *hagaii,* a mood of vulnerable heartache colored by frustration. In Tahiti, people experience *musu,* a feeling of reluctance to yield to unreasonable demands made by one's parents.

Finding *schadenfreude, hagaii,* or *musu* in a particular culture doesn't mean that the members of other cultures are incapable of experiencing such emotions, of course. It suggests, though, that fitting a particular emotion into a linguistic category to describe that emotion may make it easier to discuss, contemplate, and perhaps experience (van Dijk et al., 2011; Dasborough & Harvey, 2017; Lange & Boecker, 2019).

The Roots of Emotions

I've never been so angry before; I feel my heart pounding, and I'm trembling all over. . . . I don't know how I'll get through the performance. I feel like my stomach is filled with butterflies. . . . That was quite a mistake I made! My face must be incredibly red. . . . When I heard the footsteps in the night, I was so frightened that I couldn't catch my breath.

English offers multiple ways to describe how we feel when we experience an emotion. However, the language we use to describe emotions is, for the most part, based on the physical symptoms that are associated with a particular emotional experience (Manstead & Wagner, 2004; Spackman, Fujiki, & Brinton, 2006; Sun et al., 2019).

Consider, for instance, the experience of fear. Imagine that it is late on New Year's Eve. You are walking down a dark street, and you hear a stranger approaching behind you. He is clearly not trying to hurry by but is getting closer and closer to you. You think about what you will do if the stranger attempts to hurt you.

While these thoughts are running through your head, something dramatic will be happening to your body. The most likely reactions, which are associated with activation of the autonomic nervous system, include an increase in your rate of breathing, an acceleration of your heart rate, a widening of your pupils (to increase visual sensitivity), and a dryness in your mouth as the functioning of your salivary glands and, in fact, of your entire digestive system ceases. At the same time, though, your sweat glands probably will increase their activity because increased sweating will help you rid yourself of the excess heat developed by any emergency activity in which you engage.

Of course, all these physiological changes are likely to occur without your awareness. At the same time, though, the emotional experience accompanying them will be obvious to you: You most surely would report being fearful.

Although it is easy to describe the general physical reactions that accompany emotions, defining the specific role that those physiological responses play in the experience of emotions has proved to be a major puzzle for psychologists. As we shall see, some theorists suggest that specific physiological reactions *cause* us to experience a particular emotion. For example, when the heart is pounding and we are breathing deeply, we then experience fear. In contrast, other theorists suggest the opposite sequence–that is, we experience an emotion, and that causes us to have a physiological reaction. In this view, then, as a result of experiencing the emotion of fear, our heart pounds and our breathing deepens.

THE JAMES-LANGE THEORY: DO GUT REACTIONS EQUAL EMOTIONS?

William James and Carl Lange were among the first researchers to explore the nature of emotions. To them, emotional experience is, very simply, our body's reactions that instinctively occur as a result of some situation or event in the environment. This view is summarized in James's statement, "We feel sorry because we cry, angry because we strike, afraid because we tremble" (James, 1890).

James and Lange took the view that the instinctive response of crying at a loss leads us to feel sorrow, that striking out at someone who frustrates us results in our feeling anger, that trembling at a menacing threat causes us to feel fear. They suggested that every major emotion has an accompanying physiological or "gut" reaction of internal organs–called a *visceral experience,* or arousal of the autonomic nervous system. It is this specific pattern of visceral response that leads us to label the emotional experience.

James-Lange theory of emotion The belief that emotional experience is a reaction to bodily events occurring as a result of an external situation ("I feel sad because I am crying"). (Module 31)

In sum, James and Lange proposed that we experience emotions as a result of physiological changes that produce specific sensations. The brain interprets these sensations as specific kinds of emotional experiences (see the first part of Figure 2). This view has come to be called the **James-Lange theory of emotion** (Cobos et al., 2002; Stolorow & Stolorow, 2013; Šolcová & Lačev, 2017).

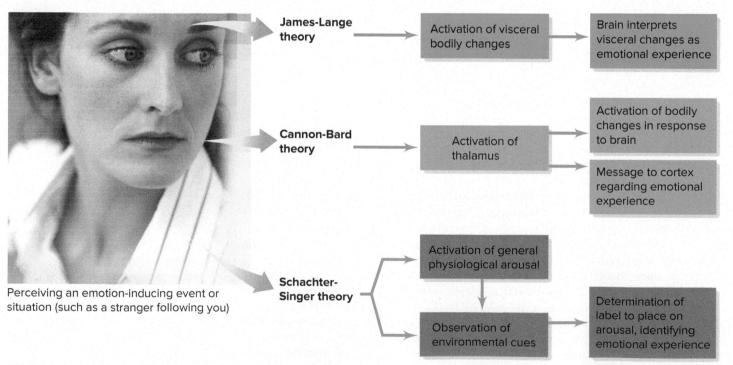

Perceiving an emotion-inducing event or situation (such as a stranger following you)

James-Lange theory → Activation of visceral bodily changes → Brain interprets visceral changes as emotional experience

Cannon-Bard theory → Activation of thalamus → Activation of bodily changes in response to brain / Message to cortex regarding emotional experience

Schachter-Singer theory → Activation of general physiological arousal / Observation of environmental cues → Determination of label to place on arousal, identifying emotional experience

FIGURE 2 A comparison of three theories of emotion.
Stockbyte/Getty Images

However, the James-Lange theory has some serious shortcomings. For the theory to be valid, visceral changes would have to occur rapidly because we experience some emotions—such as fear upon hearing a stranger rapidly approaching on a dark night—almost instantaneously. Yet certain kinds of visceral changes occur slowly. Therefore, it's hard to see how they could be the source of an immediate emotional experience.

The James-Lange theory poses another difficulty: Physiological arousal does not invariably produce emotional experience. For example, a person who is jogging has an increased heartbeat and respiration rate, as well as many of the other physiological changes associated with certain emotions. Yet joggers typically do not think of such changes in terms of emotion. Thus, visceral changes by themselves are not always sufficient to produce emotion.

Finally, our internal organs produce a relatively limited range of sensations. Although some types of physiological changes are associated with specific emotional experiences, it is difficult to imagine how each of the many emotions that people are capable of experiencing could be the result of a unique visceral change. Many emotions actually are associated with relatively similar sorts of visceral changes, a fact that contradicts the James-Lange theory (Cameron, 2002; Rinaman, Banihashemi, & Koehnle, 2011).

THE CANNON-BARD THEORY: PHYSIOLOGICAL REACTIONS AS THE RESULT OF EMOTIONS

In response to the difficulties inherent in the James-Lange theory, Walter Cannon and later Philip Bard suggested an alternative view. In what has come to be known as the **Cannon-Bard theory of emotion,** they proposed the model illustrated in the second part of Figure 2 (Cannon, 1929). This theory rejects the view that physiological arousal alone leads to the perception of emotion. Instead, the theory assumes that both physiological arousal *and* the emotional experience are produced simultaneously by the same nerve stimulus, which Cannon and Bard suggested emanates from the *thalamus* in the brain.

The theory states that after we perceive an emotion-producing stimulus, the thalamus is the initial site of the emotional response. Next, the thalamus sends a signal to the autonomic nervous system, thereby producing a visceral response. At the same time, the thalamus also communicates a message to the cerebral cortex regarding the nature of the emotion being experienced. Hence, it is not necessary for different emotions to have unique physiological patterns associated with them—as long as the message sent to the cerebral cortex differs according to the specific emotion.

The Cannon-Bard theory seems to have been accurate in rejecting the view that physiological arousal alone accounts for emotions. However, more recent research has led to some important modifications of the theory. For one thing, we now understand that the hypothalamus and the limbic system, not the thalamus, play a major role in emotional experience. In addition, the simultaneous occurrence of the physiological and emotional responses, which is a fundamental assumption of the Cannon-Bard theory, has yet to be demonstrated conclusively. This ambiguity has allowed room for yet another theory of emotions: the Schachter-Singer theory.

THE SCHACHTER-SINGER THEORY: EMOTIONS AS LABELS

Suppose that as you are being followed down that dark street on New Year's Eve, you notice a man being followed by another shady figure on the other side of the street. Now assume that instead of reacting with fear, the man begins to laugh and act gleeful. Would the reactions of this other individual be sufficient to lay your fears to rest? Might you, in fact, decide there is nothing to fear and get into the spirit of the evening by beginning to feel happiness and glee yourself?

According to an explanation that focuses on the role of cognition, the **Schachter-Singer theory of emotion,** this might very well happen. This approach to explaining emotions emphasizes that we identify the emotion we are experiencing by observing

Cannon-Bard theory of emotion
The belief that both physiological arousal and emotional experience are produced simultaneously by the same nerve stimulus. (Module 31)

Study Alert
Use Figure 2 to distinguish the three classic theories of emotion (James-Lange, Cannon-Bard, and Schachter-Singer).

Schachter-Singer theory of emotion
The belief that emotions are determined jointly by a nonspecific kind of physiological arousal and its interpretation, based on environmental cues. (Module 31)

our environment and comparing ourselves with others (Schachter & Singer, 1962; Schachter & Singer, 2001; Shaked & Clore, 2017).

Schachter and Singer's classic experiment found evidence for this hypothesis. In the study, participants were told that they would receive an injection of a vitamin. In reality, they were given epinephrine, a drug that causes responses that typically occur during strong emotional reactions, such as an increase in physiological arousal, including higher heart and respiration rates and a reddening of the face. The members of both groups were then placed individually in a situation in which a confederate of the experimenter acted in one of two ways. In one condition, he acted angry and hostile; in the other condition, he behaved as if he were exuberantly happy.

The purpose of the experiment was to determine whether participants' emotions would be influenced by the confederate's behavior. And they were: When participants were asked to describe their own emotional state at the end of the experiment, those participants exposed to the angry confederate reported that they felt angry, whereas those participants exposed to the happy confederate reported feeling happy. In sum, the results suggest that participants used the behavior of the confederate to explain the physiological arousal they were experiencing.

The results of the Schachter-Singer experiment, then, supported a cognitive view of emotions in which emotions are determined jointly by a relatively nonspecific kind of physiological arousal *and* the labeling of that arousal on the basis of cues from the environment (refer to the third part of Figure 2). Although later research has found that arousal is more specific than Schachter and Singer believed, they were right in assuming that when the source of physiological arousal is unclear, we may look to our surroundings to determine what we are experiencing.

From the perspective of...

An Advertising Executive How might you use Schachter and Singer's findings on the labeling of arousal to create interest in a product?

Image Source/Getty Images

CONTEMPORARY PERSPECTIVES ON THE NEUROSCIENCE OF EMOTIONS

When Schachter and Singer carried out their groundbreaking experiment on the cognitive influences of emotions in the early 1960s, the ways in which they could evaluate the physiological changes that accompany emotion were limited. However, advances in the measurement of the nervous system and other parts of the body have allowed researchers to examine more closely the biological responses involved in individual emotions. As a result, evidence is growing that specific patterns of biological arousal are associated with specific emotions (Woodson, 2006; Stifter, Dollar, & Cipriano, 2011; Christensen et al., 2017).

For instance, researchers have found that different emotions produce activation of different portions of the brain. In one study, participants undergoing positron emission tomography (PET) brain scans were asked to recall events that made them sad, such as deaths and funerals, or events that made them feel happy, such as weddings and births. They also looked at photos of faces that appeared to be happy or sad. The results of the PET scans were clear: Happiness was related to a decrease in activity in certain areas of the cerebral cortex, whereas sadness was associated with increases in activity in particular portions of the cortex (Prohovnik et al., 2004; Johnston & Olson, 2015; Kanel et al., 2019).

FIGURE 3 Connections from the amygdala allow it to mediate many of the autonomic expressions of emotional states through the hippocampus and visual cortex.

(photo): Image Source/Getty Images; Source: Adapted from Dolan, R. J. (2002). Emotion, cognition, and behavior. *Science, 298*, 1191–1194.

In addition, new research shows that the *amygdala,* in the brain's temporal lobe, plays an important role in the experience of emotions. The amygdala provides a link between the perception of an emotion-producing stimulus and the recall of that stimulus later. For example, if we've once been attacked by a vicious pit bull, the amygdala processes that information and leads us to react with fear when we see a pit bull at future times (LaBar, 2007; Pessoa, 2011; Christensen et al., 2017; Ressler & Maren, 2019).

Because neural pathways connect the amygdala, the visual cortex, and the *hippocampus* (which plays an important role in the consolidation of memories), some scientists speculate that emotion-related stimuli can be processed and responded to almost instantaneously (see Figure 3). This immediate response occurs so rapidly that higher-order, more rational thinking, which takes more time, seems not to be involved initially. In a slower but more thoughtful response to emotion-evoking stimuli, emotion-related sensory information is first evaluated and then sent on to the amygdala. It appears that the quicker system offers an immediate response to emotion-evoking stimuli, whereas the slower system helps confirm a threat and prepare a more thoughtful response (Dolan, 2002). And for further insight into the neurological aspects of emotions, read the *Neuroscience in Your Life* feature.

Study Alert

It is important to understand the basic neuroscience of emotional experience.

NEUROSCIENCE IN YOUR LIFE: EMOTION AND THE BRAIN

Our emotions may seem very personal, but neuroscientists are now discovering that they have a distinct neurological basis that is similar across individuals. In an innovative approach to studying the brain, researchers measured brain activity while participants watched movies or imagined six basic emotions (disgust, fear, happiness, sadness, anger, and surprise). The researchers then identified a distributed pattern of activity across the brain for each basic emotion (see images below). Based on the activity pattern for each emotion, the researchers accurately predicted which emotion the participants were experiencing (Saarimaki et al., 2016).

Movies   **Imagery**

■ Anger
■ Disgust
■ Fear
■ Happiness
■ Sadness
■ Surprise
■ Neutral

Source: Adapted from Saarimaki, H., Gotsopoulos, A., Jaaskelainen, I. P., Lampinen, J., Vuilleumier, P., Hari, R., et al. (2016). Discrete neural signatures of basic emotions. *Cerebral Cortex, 26*(6), 2563–2573. doi: 10.1093/cercor/bhv086.

MAKING SENSE OF THE MULTIPLE PERSPECTIVES ON EMOTION

As new approaches to emotion continue to develop, it is reasonable to ask why so many theories of emotion exist and, perhaps more important, which one provides the most complete explanation. Actually, we have only scratched the surface. There are almost as many explanatory theories of emotion as there are individual emotions (e.g., Frijda, 2005; Prinz, 2007; Herzberg, 2009; Ford & Gross, 2019).

Why are theories of emotion so plentiful? For one thing, emotions are not a simple phenomenon but are intertwined closely with motivation, cognition, neuroscience, and a host of related branches of psychology. For example, evidence from brain imaging studies shows that even when people come to supposedly rational, nonemotional decisions—such as making moral, philosophical judgments—emotions come into play.

In short, emotions are such complex phenomena, encompassing both biological and cognitive aspects, that no single theory has been able to explain fully all the facets of emotional experience. Furthermore, contradictory evidence of one sort or another challenges each approach, and therefore, no theory has proved invariably accurate in its predictions.

This abundance of perspectives on emotion is not a cause for despair—or unhappiness, fear, or any other negative emotion. It simply reflects the fact that psychology is an evolving, developing science. As we gather more evidence, the specific answers to questions about the nature of emotions will become clearer.

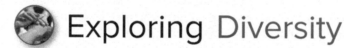

Exploring Diversity

Do People in All Cultures Express Emotion Similarly?

Consider, for a moment, the six photos displayed in Figure 4. Can you identify the emotions being expressed by the person in each of the photos?

If you are a good judge of facial expressions, you will conclude that these expressions display six of the basic emotions: happiness, anger, sadness, surprise, disgust, and fear. Hundreds of studies of nonverbal behavior show that these emotions are consistently distinct and identifiable even by untrained observers (Ekman, 2007).

Interestingly, these six emotions are not unique to members of Western cultures; rather, they constitute the basic emotions expressed universally by members of the human race, regardless of where individuals have been raised and what learning experiences they have had. Psychologist Paul Ekman convincingly demonstrated this point when he studied members of an isolated New Guinea jungle tribe who had had almost no contact with Westerners (Ekman, 1972). The people of the tribe did not speak or understand English, had never seen a movie, and had very limited experience with Caucasians before Ekman's arrival. Yet their nonverbal responses to emotion-evoking stories, as well as their ability to identify basic emotions, were quite similar to those of Westerners.

Being so isolated, the New Guineans could not have learned from Westerners to recognize or produce similar facial expressions. Instead, their similar abilities and manner of responding emotionally appear to have been present innately. Although one could argue that similar experiences in both cultures led the members of each one to learn similar types of nonverbal behavior, this appears unlikely because the two cultures are so very different. The expression of basic emotions, thus, seems to be universal (Ekman, 1994b; Izard, 1994; Matsumoto, 2002).

Why do people across cultures express emotions similarly? A hypothesis known as the **facial-affect program** offers one explanation. The facial-affect program—which is assumed to be universally present at birth—is analogous to a computer software program that is activated when a particular emotion is experienced. When set in motion, the "program" produces a set of nerve impulses that make the face display an appropriate expression. Each primary emotion is related to a unique set of muscular movements, forming the kinds of expressions shown in Figure 4. For example, the emotion of happiness is universally displayed by movement of the zygomatic major, a muscle that raises the corners of the mouth and forms what we would call a smile (Ekman, 2003; Kendler et al., 2008; Krumhuber & Scherer, 2011).

PsychTech

Because human facial expressions of emotions involve using dozens of muscles, it is only recently that researchers, such as Rana el-Kaliouby at MIT Media Lab, have been able to develop software to read them reasonably accurately.

---

facial-affect program The theory that a set of nerve impulses produce a facial display reflecting an emotion that is universal across cultures. (Module 31)

FIGURE 4 These photos demonstrate six of the primary emotions: happiness, sadness, disgust, anger, surprise, and fear.
(all, photos): 1988 Matsumoto Photos

However, the link between facial expressions and emotion is not as clear-cut and universal as once thought. According to a recent review of more than 1,000 studies, a group of eminent psychologists found that people communicate the typically expected facial expression—such as smiling when happy—only 20 to 30% of the time. The remainder of the time, they express emotions in ways that relate to the specific situation, the context, and/or the culture. Personality factors also play a critical role (Barrett et al., 2019).

Still, facial expressions remain a fundamental way in which we communicate not only with others but also apparently with ourselves, according to an intriguing notion known as the **facial-feedback hypothesis.** According to this hypothesis, facial expressions not only *reflect* emotional experience, but they also help *determine* how people experience and label emotions. Basically, "wearing" an emotional expression provides muscular feedback to the brain that helps produce an emotion congruent with that expression (Balconi, Bortolotti, & Crivelli, 2013; Damjanovic, Meyer, & Sepulveda, 2017; Carpenter & Niedenthal, 2019).

For instance, the muscles activated when we smile may send a message to the brain indicating the experience of happiness—even if there is nothing in the environment that would produce that particular emotion. Some theoreticians have gone further by suggesting that facial expressions are *necessary* for an emotion to be experienced (Rinn, 1991). In this view, if no facial expression is present, the emotion cannot be felt.

Support for this facial-feedback hypothesis comes from a classic experiment carried out by psychologist Paul Ekman and colleagues (Ekman, Levenson, & Friesen, 1983). In the study, professional actors were asked to follow very explicit instructions regarding the movements of muscles in their faces. You might try this example yourself:

- Raise your brows and pull them together.
- Raise your upper eyelids.
- Now stretch your lips horizontally back toward your ears.

After carrying out these directions—which, as you may have guessed, are meant to produce an expression of fear—the actors' heart rates rose and their body temperatures

facial-feedback hypothesis The hypothesis that facial expressions not only reflect emotional experience but also help determine how people experience and label emotions. (Module 31) declined, physiological reactions that characterize fear. Overall, facial expressions representing the primary emotions produced physiological effects similar to those accompanying the genuine emotions in other circumstances (Keillor et al., 2002; Soussignan, 2002).

RECAP/EVALUATE/RETHINK

RECAP

LO 31-1 What are emotions, and how do we experience them?

- Emotions are broadly defined as feelings that may affect behavior and generally have both a physiological component and a cognitive component. Debate continues over whether separate systems govern cognitive and emotional responses and whether one has primacy over the other.

LO 31-2 What are the functions of emotions?

- Emotions prepare us for action, shape future behavior through learning, and help us interact more effectively with others.

LO 31-3 What are the explanations for emotions?

- Several theories explain emotions. The James-Lange theory suggests that emotional experience is a reaction to bodily, or visceral, changes that occur as a response to an environmental event and are interpreted as an emotional response.
- In contrast, the Cannon-Bard theory contends that both physiological arousal and an emotional experience are produced simultaneously by the same nerve stimulus and that the visceral experience does not necessarily differ among differing emotions.
- The Schachter-Singer theory suggests that emotions are determined jointly by a relatively nonspecific physiological arousal and the subsequent labeling of that arousal, using cues from the environment to determine how others are behaving in the same situation.
- The most recent approaches to emotions focus on their biological origins. For instance, it now seems that specific patterns of biological arousal are associated with individual emotions. Furthermore, new scanning techniques have identified the specific parts of the brain that are activated during the experience of particular emotions.

LO 31-4 How does nonverbal behavior relate to the expression of emotions?

- A person's facial expressions can reveal emotions. In fact, members of different cultures understand others'

emotional expressions in similar ways. One explanation for this similarity is that an innate facial-affect program activates a set of muscle movements representing the emotion being experienced.
- The facial-feedback hypothesis suggests that facial expressions not only reflect but also produce emotional experiences.

EVALUATE

1. Emotions are always accompanied by a cognitive response. True or false?
2. The _____ theory of emotion states that emotions are a response to instinctive bodily events.
3. According to the _____ theory of emotion, both an emotional response and physiological arousal are produced simultaneously by the same nerve stimulus.
4. Your friend—a psychology major—tells you, "I was at a party last night. During the course of the evening, my general level of arousal increased. Since I was at a party where people were enjoying themselves, I assume I must have felt happy." What theory of emotion does your friend subscribe to?
5. What are the six primary emotions that can be identified from facial expressions?

RETHINK

1. If researchers learned how to control emotional responses so that targeted emotions could be caused or prevented, what ethical concerns might arise? Under what circumstances, if any, should such techniques be used?
2. Many people enjoy watching movies, sporting events, and music performances in crowded theaters and arenas more than they like watching them at home alone. Which theory of emotions may help explain this? How?

Answers to Evaluate Questions

1. False; emotions may occur without a cognitive response. 2. James-Lange 3. Cannon-Bard 4. Schachter-Singer 5. surprise, sadness, happiness, anger, disgust, and fear

KEY TERMS

emotions	Cannon-Bard theory	Schachter-Singer theory	facial-affect program
James-Lange theory	of emotion	of emotion	facial-feedback hypothesis
of emotion			

LOOKING *Back*

EPILOGUE

Motivation and emotions are two interrelated aspects of psychology. In these modules, we first considered the topic of motivation, which has spawned a great deal of theory and research examining primary and secondary drives. We then turned to a discussion of emotions, beginning with their functions and proceeding to a review of three major theories that seek to explain what emotions are and how they, and their associated physiological symptoms, emerge in the individual. Finally, we looked at cultural differences in the expression and display of emotions, and discussed the facial-affect program, which seems to be innate and to regulate the nonverbal expression of the basic emotions.

Return to the prologue of this group of modules, which describes skater Adam Rippon's unhealthy desire to lose weight. Using your knowledge of motivation and emotion, consider the following questions:

1. Does Rippon fit the description of a person with an eating disorder? If so, what disorder specifically?
2. Why do you think men are generally less willing to discuss their body image issues than are women?
3. What approaches to understanding motivation might best explain his competitiveness in figure skating? Would those approaches also help explain his disordered eating? Explain.
4. If you were Rippon's skating coach, how would you advise him to adopt healthier eating habits?
5. Where would you place Rippon on Maslow's hierarchy of needs? Explain your reasoning.

VISUAL SUMMARY 10 Motivation and Emotion

MODULE 29 Explaining Motivation

Motivation: The factors that direct and energize the behavior of humans and other organisms

— The major approaches to motivation

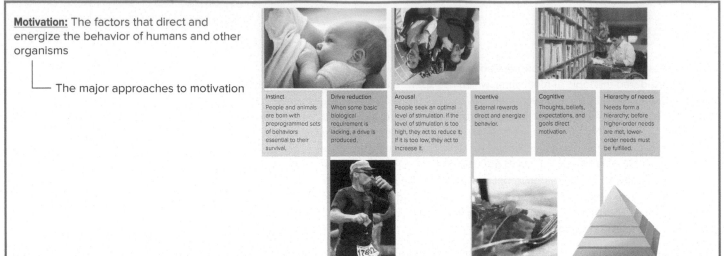

Instinct
People and animals are born with preprogrammed sets of behaviors essential to their survival.

Drive reduction
When some basic biological requirement is lacking, a drive is produced.

Arousal
People seek an optimal level of stimulation. If the level of stimulation is too high, they act to reduce it; if it is too low, they act to increase it.

Incentive
External rewards direct and energize behavior.

Cognitive
Thoughts, beliefs, expectations, and goals direct motivation.

Hierarchy of needs
Needs form a hierarchy; before higher-order needs are met, lower-order needs must be fulfilled.

MODULE 30 Human Needs and Motivation

Motivation Behind Hunger and Eating: Obesity has reached epidemic proportions

Factors that affect eating
- Biological factors

Hypothalamus

Pituitary gland

- Social factors and learned eating behaviors

Eating disorders
- Anorexia nervosa

- Bulimia

Need for Achievement: Striving for and attaining a level of excellence

Need for Affiliation: Establishing and maintaining relationships with other people

Need for Power: Impacting, controlling, or influencing others

MODULE 31 Understanding Emotional Experiences

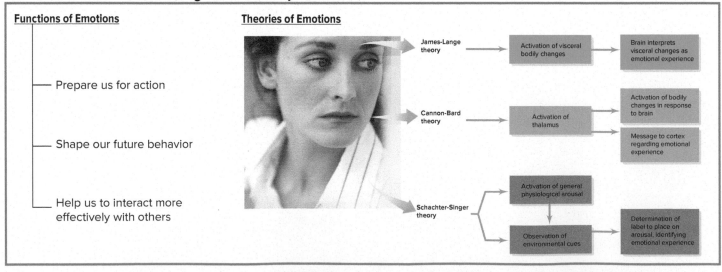

Functions of Emotions

— Prepare us for action

— Shape our future behavior

— Help us to interact more effectively with others

Theories of Emotions

James-Lange theory → Activation of visceral bodily changes → Brain interprets visceral changes as emotional experience

Cannon-Bard theory → Activation of thalamus → Activation of bodily changes in response to brain / Message to cortex regarding emotional experience

Schachter-Singer theory → Activation of general physiological arousal / Observation of environmental cues → Determination of label to place on arousal, identifying emotional experience

Gpointstudio/Cultura/age fotostock

CHAPTER 11
Sexuality and Gender

LEARNING OUTCOMES FOR CHAPTER 11

LO 34-1 What is "normal" sexual behavior?

LO 34-2 How do most people behave sexually?

LO 34-3 How prevalent are rape and other forms of nonconsensual sex, and what are their causes?

LO 34-4 What are the major sexually transmitted infections?

LO 34-5 What sexual difficulties do people most frequently encounter?

PROLOGUE *SHE WAS AN EAGLE SCOUT*

Sophie Kozub enjoyed a happy childhood. She grew up in a two-parent household, attended a private high school, and was an enthusiastic Boy Scout. A Boy Scout because Sophie was assigned male at birth and lived her childhood as a boy.

But at the age of 21, Sophie felt an emptiness that she couldn't seem to fill, despite graduating as her college's valedictorian and successfully starting her career. The difficulty: Although she had come to understand that she identified as a female, she was living as a man, and she wanted to bring her gender presentation in line with her identity.

But it wasn't an easy decision. Just a few years previously, she had achieved the rank of Eagle Scout, an accomplishment that she had long worked for and that was deeply meaningful to her. She worried that transitioning to female would negate that and other male-typical endeavors she still cherished. Ultimately, Sophie decided that becoming a transgender woman would give new meaning to her prior life and accomplishments rather than diminishing them (Norman & Randle, 2019).

LOOKING *Ahead*

Sophie Kozub represents a small but growing number of people who are searching for an identity they believe accurately describes who they are. Lesbian, gay, pansexual, transgender, gender fluid, asexual, aromantic, bisexual, agender, and genderqueer are just a few of the identity labels millennials are adopting—and inventing in

some cases—to express what they view as the wide spectrum of possibilities within the human experience (DeBord et al., 2017).

Kozub's story illustrates the emotion and confusion that often characterize sexual and gender identity. Exemplifying major personal as well as societal concerns, sex and the interrelated topic of gender are also key subjects for psychologists in a variety of specialties.

For instance, psychologists interested in motivation view sexuality in terms of sexual needs, drives, and gratification. Neuroscientists consider sexuality from the perspective of the relationship of the brain and nervous system to the functioning of the sexual organs. Social psychologists and psychologists who specialize in the study of women focus on society's rules of sexual conduct and the role sexual behavior plays in interpersonal behavior.

In this set of modules, we consider human sexuality from several of these vantage points. We begin by examining gender and discussing differences in societal expectations about how men and women should behave and the impact of those expectations on behavior and attitudes. Next, we turn to sexual behavior. We describe the biological aspects of sexual excitement and arousal, and then examine the variety of sexual activities in which people engage. We conclude with a discussion of nonconsenting sex, sexually transmitted infections, and the psychological aspects of sexual difficulties.

Module 32
Gender and Sex

"It's a girl!" "It's a boy!"

A variant of one of these exclamations is typically the first sentence uttered upon the birth of a child. However, the consequences of whether we are born with male or female sex organs extend well beyond the moment of birth. Throughout our lives, the ways that others think of us and even the ways we view ourselves are based to a large extent on whether society labels us as a male or a female–our gender.

Gender is the perception of being male or female. Although there is a good deal of overlap (and sometimes confusion) between the concepts of sex and gender, they are not the same: *Sex* typically refers to sexual anatomy and sexual behavior, whereas *gender* refers to one's sense of being a male or female. Sex is biological; gender is psychological.

Although most people think of their own gender identity in terms of the two categories of female or male, a minority of individuals reject those designations as inappropriate or too rigid (as we first discussed in the chapter prologue). The range of gender labels now includes lesbian, gay, bisexual, transgender, cisgender, pansexual, asexual, queer, genderqueer, and more. This broader view of gender has moved toward mainstream acceptance: Facebook, for example, offers its 1 billion users 60 options for identifying their gender, and more than 200 recurring characters with nontraditional gender identities now appear on cable television and streaming media. Furthermore, Canada now allows "X" as a third sex category on its passports (Steinmetz, 2017).

LEARNING OUTCOME

LO 32-1 What are the major differences between male and female gender roles?

gender The perception of being male or female. (Module 32)

Study Alert
The distinction between gender and sex is subtle. Keep in mind that *sex* relates to anatomy and *gender* relates to perception.

Gender Roles: Society's Expectations for Women and Men

Gender roles are the set of expectations, defined by a particular society, that indicate what is appropriate behavior for men and women. Our beliefs about what is or is not "appropriate" behavior for others and ourselves are based on gender roles.

Beliefs about gender roles may result in favoritism toward members of one of the sexes. Gender roles also may produce *stereotyping*, judgments about individual members of a group on the basis of their membership in that group. Stereotypes about gender roles can result in sexism. **Sexism** refers to negative attitudes and behavior toward a person that are based on that person's gender.

Regardless of their age, economic status, and social and educational background, people in Western societies often hold stereotypes about men and women. Specifically, men are more apt to be viewed as having personality traits involving competence, such as independence, objectivity, and competitiveness. In contrast, women tend to be seen as having personality traits involving warmth and expressiveness, such as gentleness and awareness of others' feelings. However, Western society traditionally values competence (attributed more to men than women) more than it values warmth and expressiveness (attributed more to women than men), which means that the perceived differences between men and women are biased in favor of men (González-Torres & Fernandez-Rivas, 2015; Bian, Leslie, & Cimpian, 2017; Kromer & Parry, 2019).

In addition, cross-cultural research finds remarkable similarity in the content of gender stereotypes in societies across the world (see Figure 1). For example, a 25-nation study identified a core set of descriptors that were consistently used across cultures to describe men and women. Women were seen as sentimental, submissive, and superstitious, whereas men were seen as adventurous, forceful, and independent. These stereotypical similarities

gender roles The set of expectations, defined by a particular society, that indicate what is appropriate behavior for men and women. (Module 32)

sexism Negative attitudes and behavior toward a person based on that person's gender. (Module 32)

Words Used to Describe Males		Words Used to Describe Females
Active	Initiative	Affected
Adventurous	Inventive	Affectionate
Aggressive	Lazy	Attractive
Ambitious	Logical	Charming
Arrogant	Loud	Curious
Assertive	Masculine	Dependent
Autocratic	Opportunistic	Dreamy
Clear-thinking	Progressive	Emotional
Coarse	Rational	Fearful
Courageous	Realistic	Feminine
Cruel	Reckless	Gentle
Daring	Robust	Mild
Determined	Rude	Sensitive
Disorderly	Self-confident	Sentimental
Dominant	Serious	Sexy
Egotistical	Severe	Softhearted
Energetic	Stern	Submissive
Enterprising	Stolid	Superstitious
Forceful	Strong	Talkative
Hardheaded	Unemotional	Weak
Hardhearted	Wise	
Independent		

across cultures may be due to similarities in status between men and women across the cultures; in most, men typically attain higher status than women do (Williams & Best, 1990; Ghavami & Peplau, 2013; Safdar & Kosakowska-Berezecka, 2015).

Such stereotypes matter. By shaping beliefs about how men and women should behave, these stereotypes potentially keep inequalities between the genders alive. Stereotypes put pressure on people to fulfill the stereotypes, and they may lead people to perform in accordance with the stereotypes rather than in accordance with their own abilities. Attaining gender equality remains a significant challenge throughout the world (see Figure 2; Lips, 2003; Verhaeghen, Aikman, & Van Gulick, 2011; Li, Bagger, & Cropanzano, 2017).

Sexism on the Job

Differences still exist regarding which occupations are deemed appropriate for men and which for women. Women continue to be viewed as best suited for traditionally female jobs–that is, pink-collar jobs such as secretary, nurse, cashier, and jobs in other female-dominated professions that often feature low pay and low status. Men and women alike still report that they expect greater success when they enter a profession viewed as appropriate for their gender. Furthermore, women hold lower expectations than men do about the size of their starting salaries and how high their peak salaries will be (Casad, 2007; Ragins & Winkel, 2011; Heilman & Kusev, 2017).

Consistent with these expectations, women, on average, earn less than men do. Although the gap has been decreasing, women overall earn an average of 82¢ for every dollar that men earn. Women who are members of minority groups fare worse: Black women earn 63¢ for every dollar white, non-Hispanic men make, and Hispanic and Latino women earn just 59¢ for every dollar white men earn. Furthermore, even when they are in the same professions as men, women generally earn less than men in similar jobs (see Figure 3; Bureau of Labor Statistics, 2017; Graf, Brown, & Patten, 2019).

The pay gap starts early. For example, unequal pay is evident in adolescence: Research finds that daughters, age 15 to 19, spend more time doing chores than sons of the same age, but they earn lower allowances (Miller, 2018).

Country	Rank	Country	Rank
Iceland	1	Moldova	26
Finland	2	Cuba	27
Norway	3	Barbados	28
Sweden	4	Spain	29
Rwanda	5	Belarus	30
Ireland	6	Portugal	31
Philippines	7	Costa Rica	32
Slovenia	8	Argentina	33
New Zealand	9	Luxembourg	34
Nicaragua	10	Canada	35
Switzerland	11	Cape Verde	36
Burundi	12	Bahamas	37
Germany	13	Poland	38
Namibia	14	Colombia	39
South Africa	15	Ecuador	40
Netherlands	16	Bulgaria	41
France	17	Jamaica	42
Latvia	18	Lao PDR	43
Denmark	19	Trinidad and Tobago	44
United Kingdom	20	United States	45
Mozambique	21	Australia	46
Estonia	22	Panama	47
Bolivia	23	Serbia	48
Belgium	24	Israel	49
Lithuania	25	Italy	50

FIGURE 2 Gender discrepancies throughout the world. The World Economic Forum ranks countries on the basis of gender equality, considering educational attainment, economic participation and opportunity, political empowerment, and health and survival. Out of 149 countries, the United States ranks 51st worldwide.

Source: World Economic Forum. (2018). *The global gender gap report 2018.* Geneva: World Economic Forum. Retrieved from http://reports.weforum.org/global-gender-gap-report-2018/data-explorer/.

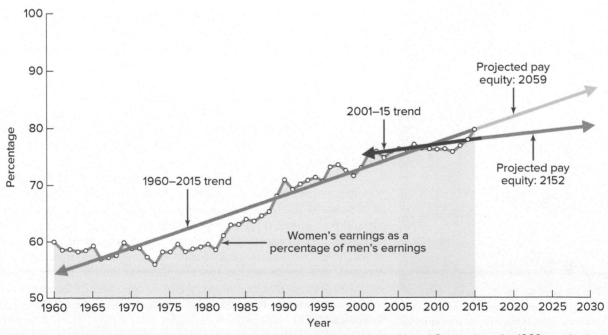

FIGURE 3 Although the disparity between women's and men's wages has improved in the United States since the 1960s, projections show that some sort of disparity will remain for many years. What factors account for the continuing gap between men's and women's wages?

Source: American Association of University Women. (2016). *The simple truth about the gender pay gap,* Washington, DC: AAUW.

The good news is that most people would like to see gender equality in the workplace (as well as the home). Furthermore, they believe that women should be given the same opportunities as men.

For example, just about as many men as women endorse the idea that jobs should offer flexible work schedules in order to be family friendly. In addition, polls today find that most men no longer believe that a woman's most appropriate role is to care for her home and children while men should be earning money—a shift from the 1970s, when the majority of men endorsed that traditional view (Barnett, 2004; Stam, Verbakel, & Graaf, 2013; Sørensen, 2017).

Still, even when women are successful on the job and are promoted into upper-level, high-status positions, they may face significant hurdles in their efforts to move up the corporate ladder. Such obstacles are especially true for professional women who become mothers; they tend to be newly perceived as warm but less competent than they were prior to motherhood. The same thing doesn't happen to men who become fathers; they are most likely to be viewed as warm *and* competent (Cuddy, Fiske, & Glick, 2004; Hagelskamp et al., 2011; Moen, 2015).

Because of such stereotypical views, many women eventually hit what has come to be called the glass ceiling. The *glass ceiling* is the term for unstated but real barriers within an organization that prevent women from being promoted beyond a certain level because of gender discrimination. The glass ceiling is even found in colleges and universities. For example, although women hold 29% of science and engineering jobs at U.S. educational institutions, they occupy only 15% of those positions at the top 50 research universities (Hoobler, Lemmon, & Wayne, 2011; Faniko et al., 2017; Lewellyn & Muller-Kahle, 2019).

As phenomena such as the glass ceiling make clear, gender stereotypes about males are typically more positive than are stereotypes about females. And such stereotypes matter because people often act as if they were real and modify their behavior to conform to the stereotypes. As a result, gender stereotypes determine both women's and men's behavior and ultimately lead to the unfortunate consequence of preferential treatment of men.

SEXUAL HARASSMENT

In addition to pay inequity and limited job advancement, women—even those in high-status professions—may face workplace sexism in the form of sexual harassment. *Sexual harassment* is unwanted sexual attention, the creation of a hostile or abusive environment, or explicit coercion to engage in unwanted sexual activity.

Sexual harassment is not a minor problem. Twenty percent of women say they have been sexually harassed at work, and some surveys find that one-third of women report being sexually harassed at some point in their career. And it is not just women who encounter harassment: Some 10% of men report experiencing sexual harassment on the job (Stockdale & Sagrestano, 2011; Vagianos, 2015; Cassino & Bessen, 2019).

Sexual harassment is not only a workplace issue. Thirty percent of the female graduates of one large California university reported receiving some form of harassment. Such harassment begins early in life. In one survey, 81% of middle and high school students reported receiving some form of sexual harassment in school; 6 in 10 experienced physical sexual harassment at some point in their school lives (see Figure 4). One-third of students are afraid of being sexually harassed; girls are more than twice as likely as boys to report concern. Overall, estimates suggest that one of every two women will be harassed at some point during her academic or working life (Klein, Apple, & Kahn, 2011; AAUW, 2012; Gialopsos, 2017).

Sexual harassment often has more to do with men's desire to demonstrate power over females than with sexual motivations. In this view, higher-status

Billionaire Jeffrey Epstein, who committed suicide in prison, was convicted of having sex with multiple underaged women.

Rick Friedman Photography/Corbis News/Getty Images

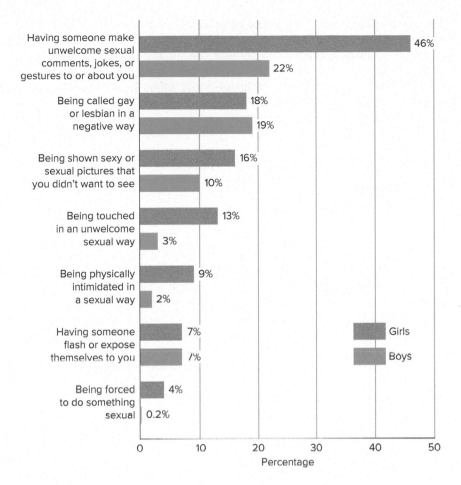

FIGURE 4 Sexual harassment in school. The number of students who report experiencing unwelcomed sexual attention often or occasionally at school is significant.

Source: Adapted from American Association of University Women. (2012). *Hostile hallways: Bullying, teasing, and sexual harassment in school*. Washington, DC: Author.

persons who engage in harassment seek to exert power over their victims (Huerta, Cortina, & Pang, 2006).

In some cases, harassment stems from *benevolent sexism*, attitudes relating to gender that appear on the surface to be beneficial to women but are, in reality, harmful. For example, a male employer may compliment a woman on her physical attractiveness or offer her an easy job so that she'll have more time with her children. The reality, however, is that such comments may undermine the employee's sense of competence, and she may feel that she is not being taken seriously (Delacollette et al., 2013; Reilly, Rackley, & Awad, 2017; Hopkins-Doyle et al., 2019).

From the perspective of...

A Business Executive If you wanted to end sexism in business settings, how might you narrow the gap between men and women in terms of occupations and salary?

Regardless of the motivation that lies behind sexual harassment, the consequences for the victim are clear. Feelings of shame and embarrassment are typical and may be compounded by a sense of helplessness and powerlessness because targets of harassment are typically in lower-status positions. People who experience harassment often suffer emotional and physical consequences, and the quality of their work may decline. Furthermore, they have lower aspirations, believing they are unlikely to attain better positions (Magley, 2002; Miner-Rubino & Cortina, 2007; Chiodo et al., 2009).

Gender Differences: More Similar Than Dissimilar

Not surprisingly, gender stereotyping, combined with other factors, results in actual behavior differences between men and women. Before we consider the nature of gender differences, however, it is important to keep in mind men and women are more similar to one another in most respects than they are different. Furthermore, the differences that have been found reflect *average* male and female differences; this finding tells us little or nothing about any *individual* male or female.

For example, even if we find that males are generally more talkative than females—as research shows they are, despite the stereotype that women talk more—an individual man can be less talkative than most women. Similarly, an individual woman may be more talkative than most men. When we consider any single person, our focus should be on the individual rather than on his or her gender group. It is important to take this into account as we examine the findings on gender differences (Mehl et al., 2007; Halpern, 2010). (Also see *Applying Psychology in the 21st Century.*)

PERSONALITY FACTORS

One of the most pronounced differences between men and women lies in their degree of aggressive behavior. By the time they are 2 years old, boys tend to display more aggression than girls do, and this higher level of aggression persists throughout the life span. Furthermore, compared with men, women experience greater anxiety and guilt about their aggressiveness and are more concerned about its effects on their victims (Hyde, Mezulis, & Abramson, 2008; Cross & Campbell, 2011; Helgeson, 2015).

Men generally have higher self-esteem than women do, although the difference is not large. Furthermore, women's self-esteem is influenced primarily by their perception of their sense of interdependence and connection with others. In contrast, men's self-esteem stems more from their assessment of their unique characteristics and abilities, traits that help them distinguish themselves from other people (Hasnain, Ansari, & Sethi, 2011; Stapleton et al., 2017; Magee & Upenieks, 2019).

Men and women also view their relationships in terms of self-esteem, although they view them differently. Men tend to view relationships in terms of the social status they provide, and women tend to view them in terms of the companionship they provide (Kwang et al., 2013).

Men and women differ in how positively they view their own abilities and how they estimate the probability of their future success. In general, women evaluate themselves more harshly than men do. Such self-perceptions matter because they influence motivation as well as academic and career choices, and even may affect performance (Keller, 2007; Carr & Steele, 2009; Tao & Gloria, 2019).

Boys from age 2 tend to be more aggressive than girls, a pattern that continues throughout the lifespan.
Nirut Saelim/123RF

APPLYING PSYCHOLOGY IN THE 21ST CENTURY

WHY IS ALEXA A GIRL?

"Hey, Siri, call Mom."

"Alexa, shuffle my party playlist."

"Hey, Google, turn on the coffee maker."

Virtual assistants increasingly live in our computers, smartphones, cars, and dedicated devices, always alert and ready to execute our next verbal command. But have you noticed that they're almost always female? Microsoft's Cortana, Apple's Siri, Amazon's Alexa, and even Google's unnamed Google Assistant all are programmed to speak with female voices, either by default or with no other option, and to express other stereotypically feminine characterizations. They're cheerful, deferential, and above all, subservient. They answer your commands promptly with an audible smile, and they never talk back or get sassy—even when you insult them or call them vulgar names.

None of this is coincidence, according to a 2019 report from the United Nations Educational, Scientific, and Cultural Organization (UNESCO). Technology providers claim that users generally prefer a female voice over a male one, although research suggests that many people actually prefer an opposite-gender voice, and that they tend to prefer authoritative statements from a male voice but helpful statements from a female voice. UNESCO claims that sexism is therefore built into the virtual assistant from the start: It defaults to a male preference, and it reinforces a stereotype of women playing the role of helper (Nass & Brave, 2005; Mitchell et al., 2011; Anderson & Klofstad, 2012; UNESCO, 2019).

Seewhatmitchsee/Shutterstock

UNESCO argues, however, that the ubiquitous feminization of virtual assistants is even more insidious than that. The practice of barking commands without any of the usual niceties at an always-female assistant that you summon with a "hey" or an "OK" conditions people, perhaps especially children, that women are to be bossed around. Industry research shows that the virtual assistants receive quite a lot of sexually explicit questions and even verbal abuse, to which they often respond in an evasive or even playful manner, thereby failing to model appropriate responses to sexual harassment. And it doesn't help that the virtual voices are rapidly becoming increasingly humanlike, perhaps encouraging generalization of communication habits established with them to living women. Finally, virtual assistants make mistakes—often seemingly dumb ones—when they fail to correctly understand or execute spoken requests, which is not uncommon. They are also programmed to give brief and uncomplicated answers to queries whenever possible. Those "dumb" mistakes and oversimplifications then get associated in the minds of users with a female character (UNESCO, 2019; Lai & Banaji, 2020).

While research hasn't yet been conducted to confirm the worst of UNESCO's fears, a solution doesn't have to wait. Some technology providers have already rolled out male voice options for their virtual assistants, giving users the final say as to the voice they want to hear.

RETHINK

- If you use virtual assistant technology, do you prefer that it have a female voice or a male one? Why do you think you have that preference?
- What other solutions to these concerns could technology providers implement, even without altering the gender of the virtual assistant's voice?

The content of men's and women's speech also differs. For example, women's speech patterns lead others to view them as more tentative and less assertive. Women more often raise their pitch at the end of a sentence and add qualifiers at the end of an opinion rather than stating the opinion outright. For example, instead of saying, "It's awfully warm today," a female speaker might say, "It's awfully warm today, *isn't it?*"—which makes her appear less certain of her opinion. When women use such tentative language, they are judged to be less competent and knowledgeable than they are when they speak assertively (Popp, Donovan, & Crawford, 2003; Leaper & Ayres, 2007; Munson & Babel, 2019).

Women's and men's nonverbal behavior differs as well in several significant respects. In conversations with people of the other sex, women look at their partners significantly

PsychTech

According to a survey by the Pew Research Center, men engage in Internet activities more intensively than women, and men are more likely to try new technologies earlier than women—although these differences may be diminishing.

more while listening than while speaking (thereby communicating cooperation). In contrast, men look at their partners about the same length of time while listening and speaking, which is typically interpreted as a sign of power. Furthermore, women are generally better than men at reading the meaning of others' facial expressions, providing them with greater sensitivity, compared with men, regarding the communications of others (Coats & Feldman, 1996; LaFrance & Harris, 2004; Grebelsky-Lichtman & Katz, 2019).

COGNITIVE ABILITIES

Research is clear in showing that no general differences exist between men and women in average IQ scores, learning, memory, problem solving, and concept-formation tasks. Although a few differences in more specific cognitive subareas have been identified in some studies, other research has called into question the true nature of those differences—and even their existence (Halpern, 2011).

This was not always the accepted wisdom about sex differences. When Eleanor Maccoby and Carol Jacklin carried out a pioneering study of sex differences almost 50 years ago (Maccoby & Jacklin, 1974), they concluded that girls outperformed boys in verbal abilities and that boys had superior quantitative and spatial abilities. Psychologists— and the public—widely accepted that conclusion as true, and it was widely believed for decades.

However, more sophisticated analyses have questioned these earlier findings. In a ground-breaking study, psychologist Janet Hyde and colleagues examined the mathematical performance of 7 million U.S. students in grades 2 through 11—a huge sample of students. Contrary to traditional wisdom, the average mathematical performance of males and females did not differ. Even when they looked at only the most gifted students, they found no gender difference (Hyde et al., 2008).

Similarly, cross-cultural data also show no difference between genders in math performance. For example, Japanese boys and girls perform quite similarly on math tests except for the single math area of probability; Japanese girls routinely outperform both boys and girls in the United States on comparable tests of mathematical ability. In addition, cross-cultural data show that on international science test results, girls often outperform boys—except in the United States. In short, no consistent nor meaningful differences appear to exist between males and females in math performance (Hyde & Mertz, 2009; Fairfield, 2012; Bench et al., 2015).

Psychologists have drawn a similar conclusion about the extent of gender differences in verbal skills. Despite the earlier view that women show superior verbal abilities compared with men, a more careful analysis of 165 studies of gender differences in verbal ability, which represents the testing of close to 1.5 million subjects, has led to the conclusion that verbal gender differences are insignificant. Furthermore, verbal SAT scores are quite similar for boys and girls (Hyde, 2005; Pahlke, Hyde, & Mertz, 2013).

In short, current evidence suggests that gender differences in cognitive skills are minimal. On the other hand, particular tests of mathematical and verbal skills do elicit differences in performance, as in the example of the mathematics part of the SAT in which most of the very high scorers are male (Hyde, 2005; Ripley, 2005; Zell, Krizan, & Teeter, 2015).

Furthermore, even when no differences are found in men's and women's performance on specific tasks, there may be underlying differences in how the brain processes information. For example, one study found that when men and women named particular objects, such as tools and plants, their brains were activated in different ways, depending on their experience with the objects (see *Neuroscience in Your Life*). In short, gender differences are complex, and we still do not have the full story on differences between men and women when it comes to their cognitive abilities (Hugdahl, Thomsen, & Ersland, 2006).

NEUROSCIENCE IN YOUR LIFE: DO WOMEN'S BRAINS DIFFER FROM MEN'S?

A continuing controversy in neuroscience research is the role of the brain's structure and function in determining differences in behavior between men and women. Because research has found that nonhuman males show a larger amygdala than nonhuman females, investigators recently examined the structure in humans. However, in a review of 46 studies comparing the volume of the amygdala in men and women, researchers found no difference when correcting for overall brain size. These findings suggest that the neurobiology of men and women may be more similar than different (Marwha, Halari, & Eliot, 2017).

The amygdala is highlighted in red.

Cliparea | Custom media/Shutterstock

Sources of Gender Differences: Where Biology and Society Meet

If the identification of gender differences has presented a difficult challenge for researchers, the search for their causes has proved even more daunting. Given the indisputable fact that sex is a biological variable, it would seem reasonable to look at factors involving biological differences between men and women. It is also true that people are treated differently on the basis of their sex from the time they are born. Consequently, we must take into account both biological and social factors when we try to understand the source of gender differences.

Although we'll consider biological and environmental variables separately, neither alone can provide a full explanation for gender differences. Some combination of the two, interacting with each other, will ultimately provide us with an understanding of why men and women may behave differently.

BIOLOGICAL AND EVOLUTIONARY FACTORS

Do differences between male and female brains cause sex and gender differences? This intriguing hypothesis has been put forward by psychologists studying brain structure and functioning. For instance, in one study, scientists studied a group of girls whose mothers had accidentally taken drugs containing high levels of *androgen,* a male hormone, prior to their birth. Girls exposed to androgens were more likely to play with toys that boys stereotypically prefer (such as cars) and less likely to play with toys that girls stereotypically prefer (such as dolls). Perhaps exposure to particular hormones prior to birth affected the children's brain development, making children favor toys that involve certain kinds of skills, such as those related to spatial abilities (Fink, Manning, & Williams, 2007; Hines & Alexander, 2008; Moskowitz et al., 2015).

Similarly, research studies have found that women perform better on tasks involving verbal skill and muscular coordination during periods when their production of the female sex hormone *estrogen* is relatively high. In contrast, they perform better on tasks involving spatial relationships when their estrogen level is relatively low (Rosenberg & Park, 2002; Abraham et al., 2013).

Some psychologists argue that evolutionary forces lead to certain differences between men's and women's behavior. For example, David Buss and colleagues point to differences in the nature of jealousy between men and women. Men are more jealous in cases of sexual infidelity than in cases of emotional infidelity; women are more jealous in cases of emotional infidelity than in cases of sexual infidelity (Buss, 2003; Salmon, 2017; de Visser et al., 2019).

According to Buss's controversial explanation, the root cause for the differences in jealousy lies in the evolutionary implications of sexual infidelity versus emotional infidelity for men and women. (*Sexual infidelity* occurs when a partner has sex with another individual outside of a relationship. *Emotional infidelity* occurs when a partner develops an emotional attachment to someone outside of a relationship.)

Buss argues that for males, sexual infidelity represents a threat to their ability to ensure that their children are actually their own (and are the ones who have inherited their genes). In contrast, females have no doubt that a child they carry through pregnancy is their own. However, their major concern is ensuring the male's protection and support during child rearing. Thus, to females, maintaining males' emotional attachment is crucial.

Psychologists using the evolutionary approach also argue that similarities in the division of labor between men and women across different cultures suggest that sex differences are due to evolutionary factors. In a controversial argument, they point to evidence that even in very different types of cultures, men tend to be more aggressive, competitive, and prone to taking risks than women. Such traits are assumed to hold an evolutionary advantage (Buss, 2003; Chang & Geary, 2007; Frank & Hou, 2015).

However, many critics question the assumptions of the evolutionary approach. Rather than assuming that the differences are due to evolutionary forces, some psychologists suggest that differences in males' and females' beliefs about the meaning of infidelity are the actual cause of their jealousy differences. For instance, men may believe that women have sex only when they are in love. Consequently, sexual infidelity may be seen as a sign that a woman is in love with another man and may produce more jealousy than emotional infidelity alone would. In contrast, women may believe that men are capable of having sex without being in love; consequently, they may find a man's sexual infidelity less bothersome because it does not necessarily mean that he is in love with someone else (Fine, 2010; Jordan-Young, 2010; Lalasz & Weigel, 2011).

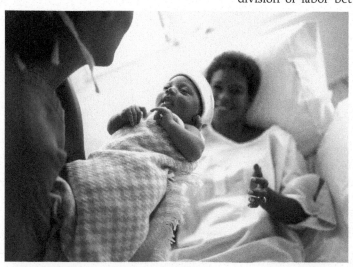

From the moment of birth, gender differences are defined by outside influences. Is it possible for a family to block these influences completely? Would it be desirable to do so?

Stockbyte/Getty Images

Psychologists Alice Eagly and Wendy Wood criticize evolutionary explanations for gender differences on different grounds. In their *biosocial explanation of gender differences*, they argue that one important source of gender differences lies in the differing physical capabilities of men and women. Consistently across cultures, men carry out tasks that are based on their greater size, strength, and speed. In contrast, women carry out tasks that are related to their capacity for pregnancy and caring for children.

For example, women may be more caring and sensitive not because they are genetically so. Instead, it is their physical attributes (the ability to give birth to children) that lead them to be more caring and sensitive during child rearing. Hence, a combination of biological and social factors leads to their behavior (Wood & Eagly, 2002, 2015; Eagly & Wood, 2013; Eagly, 2016).

The extent to which biological and evolutionary factors may underlie gender differences is an unanswered and highly controversial question. One thing is clear, however: Biological factors and evolutionary factors alone do not explain the complete range of differences between male and female behavior. To fully understand the source of gender differences, we also must consider the social environment, which we do next.

> **! Study Alert**
> Remember that gender differences are caused by a combination of biological, evolutionary, and social factors.

THE SOCIAL ENVIRONMENT

From the moment of birth, with blue blankets for boys and pink ones for girls, most parents and other adults provide environments that differ in important respects according to gender. For example, boys and girls are given different kinds of toys, and—until protests brought the practice to an end—items in the largest toy store chain in the United States were laid out according to the gender appropriateness of particular toys (Dender & Stagnitti, 2011; Endendijk et al., 2017; MacPhee & Prendergast, 2019).

Parents interact with their children differently, depending on their sex. Fathers play more roughly with their infant sons than they do with their infant daughters. Middle-class mothers tend to talk more to their daughters than to their sons. It is clear that adults in general frequently treat children differently on the basis of gender (Tenenbaum & Leaper, 2002; Kwon et al., 2013).

Such differences in behavior (and there are many more) produce different socialization experiences for men and women. *Socialization* is the process by which individuals learn the rules and norms of appropriate behavior in a given society or culture. In this case, socialization refers to learning the different rules about behavior for men versus women. According to social learning theory, boys are taught and rewarded for performing the socially perceived appropriate behaviors for men, while girls are taught what society says is appropriate for women (Liben & Bigler, 2002; Leaper & Friedman, 2007; Lee & Troop-Gordon, 2011).

It is not just parents, of course, who provide socialization experiences for children. Society as a whole communicates clear messages to children as they are growing up. Children's story books traditionally have portrayed girls in stereotypically nurturing roles, whereas boys have been given more physical and action-oriented roles. The media, too, act as a particularly influential source of socialization. For example, men outnumber women on television, and women are often cast in such stereotypical roles as housewife, secretary, and mother. The potency of television as an agent of socialization is underscored by data indicating that the more television children watch, the more sexist they become (Abelman, 2007; Dill & Thill, 2007; Lee & Chin, 2019).

Our educational system also treats boys and girls differently. For example, in elementary school, boys are five times more likely than girls to receive attention from classroom teachers. Boys receive significantly more praise, criticism, and remedial help than girls do. They are also more likely to be praised for the intelligence shown in their work, whereas girls are more apt to be commended for their neatness. Even in college classes, male students receive more eye contact from their professors than female students do, men are called upon more frequently in class, and men are more apt to receive extra help from their professors (Einarsson & Granstroem, 2002; Koch, 2003).

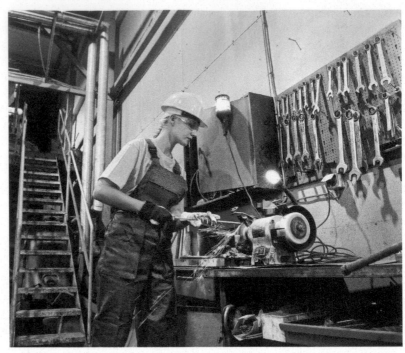

Despite many entrenched stereotypes, gender schemas have now expanded to include a greater range of possibilities, and ideas of appropriate and inappropriate are shifting.

(left): Purestock/Getty Images; (right): Nejron Photo/Shutterstock

gender schema A mental framework that organizes and guides a child's understanding of information relevant to gender. (Module 32)

Socialization produces a **gender schema,** a mental framework that organizes and guides a child's understanding of information relevant to gender. On the basis of their schemas for appropriate and inappropriate behavior for males and females, children begin to behave in ways that reflect society's gender roles. Hence, children who are offered the opportunity to sew a costume for a school play may evaluate the activity not in terms of the intrinsic components of the process (such as the mechanics of using a needle and thread) but in terms of whether the activity is compatible with their gender schema. Such evaluation may potentially limit the range of experiences to which children are exposed (Le Maner-Idrissi & Renault, 2006; Frawley, 2008; Clément-Guillotin & Fontayne, 2011).

RECAP/EVALUATE/RETHINK

RECAP

LO 32-1 What are the major differences between male and female gender roles?

- Gender is the perception of being male or female. Gender roles are the expectations, defined by society, of what is appropriate behavior for men and women. When gender roles reflect favoritism toward one sex, they lead to stereotyping and produce sexism.
- The gender-role stereotype for men suggests that they are endowed with competence-related traits, whereas women are seen in terms of their capacity for warmth and expressiveness. Actual sex differences are much less clear and of smaller magnitude than the stereotypes

would suggest. The differences that do exist are produced by a combination of biological and environmental factors.
- Biological causes of sex difference are reflected by evidence suggesting a possible difference in brain structure and functioning between men and women and may be associated with differential exposure to hormones before birth.
- An evolutionary approach explains gender differences in terms of different male-female concerns regarding the inheritance of genes and the need for child rearing, but this approach is highly controversial.
- Socialization experiences produce gender schemas, mental frameworks that organize and guide a child's understanding of information relevant to gender.

EVALUATE

1. _____ _____ are sets of societal expectations about what is appropriate behavior for men and women.
2. Gender stereotypes have generally disappeared today. True or false?
3. Which of the following statements about male-female differences in aggression is true?
   a. Males are physically more aggressive than females only during childhood.
   b. Male-female differences in aggression first become evident during adolescence.
   c. Males are more aggressive than females throughout the life span.
   d. Females and males feel equally anxious about their aggressive acts.
4. _____ _____ are frameworks that organize understanding of gender-specific information.

RETHINK

1. Until recently, U.S. law prohibited women from directly participating in front-line combat positions, in the interest of keeping women safe. Do you think such laws were protective or sexist? How might this be an example of "benevolent sexism"?
2. If you wanted to raise a child in as androgynous a manner as possible, how would you do it? What problems might the child encounter in the everyday world? Do you think this is the best way to raise a child in today's society?

Answers to Evaluate Questions

1. Gender roles; 2. False; they are still prevalent; 3. c; 4. Gender schemas

KEY TERMS

gender   gender roles   sexism   gender schema

Module 33

Understanding Human Sexual Response: The Facts of Life

LEARNING OUTCOMES

LO 33-1 Why, and under what circumstances, do we become sexually aroused?

When I started "tuning out," teachers thought I was sick–physically sick, that is. They kept sending me to the school nurse to have my temperature taken. If I'd told them I was carrying on with Jennifer Lopez in their classes while supposedly learning my Caesar and my Latin vocabulary, they'd have thought I was–well, delirious. I was! (based on Coles & Stokes, 1985)

Not everyone's sexual fantasies are as consuming as those reported by this teenage boy. Yet sex is an important consideration in most people's lives; although the physical aspects of human sex are not all that different from those of other species, the meaning, values, and feelings that humans place on sexual behavior elevate it to a special plane. To fully appreciate this difference, however, it is necessary to understand the basic biology underlying sexual responses.

The Basic Biology of Sexual Behavior

Anyone who has seen two dogs mating knows that sexual behavior has a biological basis. Their sexual behavior appears to occur naturally without much prompting on the part of others. A number of genetically controlled factors influence the sexual behavior of nonhuman animals. For instance, animal behavior is affected by the presence of certain hormones in the blood. Moreover, female animals are receptive to sexual advances only during certain relatively limited periods of the year.

Human sexual behavior, by comparison, is more complicated, although the underlying biology is not all that different from that of related species. In males, for example, the *testes* begin to secrete **androgens,** male sex hormones, at puberty. (See Figure 1 for the basic anatomy of the male and female **genitals,** or sex organs.) Not only do androgens produce secondary sex characteristics, such as the growth of body hair and a deepening of the voice, they also increase the sex drive. Because the level of androgen production by the testes is fairly constant, men are capable of (and interested in) sexual activities without any regard to biological cycles. Given the proper stimuli leading to arousal, male sexual behavior can occur at any time (Goldstein, 2000).

Women show a different pattern. When they reach maturity at puberty, the two *ovaries* begin to produce **estrogens,** female sex hormones. However, those hormones are not produced consistently; instead, their production follows a cyclical pattern. The greatest output occurs during **ovulation,** when an egg is released from the ovaries, making the chances of fertilization by a sperm cell highest. While in nonhumans the period around ovulation is the only time the female is receptive to sex, people are different. Although there are variations in reported sex drive, women are receptive to sex throughout their cycles (Leiblum & Chivers, 2007).

In addition, some evidence suggests that males have a stronger sex drive than females do or at least spend more time than women do thinking about it. For instance, while 54% of men report thinking about sex every day, only 19% of women report thinking about it on a daily basis (Baumeister & Stillman, 2006; Carvalho & Nobre, 2011).

Though biological factors "prime" people for sex, it takes more than hormones to motivate and produce sexual behavior. In animals, the presence of a partner who provides arousing stimuli leads to sexual activity. Humans are considerably more versatile;

androgens Male sex hormones secreted by the testes. (Module 33)

genitals The male and female sex organs. (Module 33)

estrogens Class of female sex hormones. (Module 33)

ovulation The point at which an egg is released from the ovaries. (Module 33)

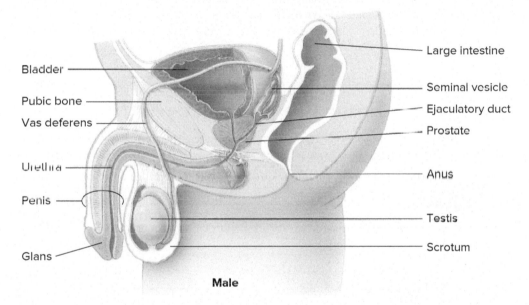

FIGURE 1 Cutaway side views of the female and male sex organs.

not only other people but nearly any object, sight, smell, sound, or other stimulus can lead to sexual excitement. Because of prior associations, then, people may be turned on sexually by the smell of perfume or the sound of a favorite song hummed softly in their ears. The reaction to a specific, potentially arousing stimulus, as we shall see, is highly individual—what turns one person on may do just the opposite for another (Benson, 2003; Schäfer et al., 2019).

Physiological Aspects of Sexual Excitement: What Turns People On?

If you were to argue that the major human sex organ is the brain, in a sense you would be right. Much of what is considered sexually arousing in our society has little or nothing to do with our genitals; instead, it is related to external stimuli that, through a process of learning, have come to be labeled as erotic, or sexually stimulating.

For example, there are no areas of the body that *automatically* produce sexual arousal when touched. Areas of the body, called **erogenous zones,** that have an unusually rich array of nerve receptors are particularly sensitive not just to sexual touch but to any kind of touch. When a physician touches a breast or a penis, the

erogenous zones Areas of the body that are particularly sensitive because of the presence of an unusually rich array of nerve receptors. (Module 33) information sent to the brain by the nerve cells is essentially the same as that sent when a sexual partner touches that spot. What differs is the interpretation given to the touch. Sexual arousal is likely only when a certain part of the body is touched in what people define as a sexual manner and when a person is receptive to sexual activity (Goldstein, 2000; Wiederman, 2011).

Although people can learn to respond sexually to almost any stimulus, there is a good deal of agreement within a society or culture about what usually represents an erotic stimulus. In many Western societies, breast size is often the standard by which female appeal is measured, but in many other cultures, breast size is irrelevant (Furnham & Swami, 2007; Dawson, Fretz, & Chivers, 2017).

Sexual fantasies also play an important role in people's lives. People often have fantasies of a sexual nature during their everyday, nonsexual activities. Furthermore, most people fantasize about sex during sexual intercourse–and they often fantasize about people other than their current partner (Critelli & Bivona, 2008; Goldey & van Anders, 2011; Bogaert, Visser, & Pozzebon, 2015).

Men's and women's fantasies differ little from each other in terms of content or quantity, although men seem to fantasize about sex more than women do. But both men and women wish they kissed more, engaged in more oral sex, and had vaginal intercourse more frequently than they actually do (Shulman & Horne, 2006; Santtila et al., 2008; Wehrum et al., 2013).

From the perspective of...

A Sex Counselor How do people learn to be aroused by the stimuli that their society considers erotic? When do they learn this, and where does the message come from?

Chris Ryan/OJO Images/age fotostock

The Phases of Sexual Response: The Ups and Downs of Sex

Although the kinds of stimuli that produce sexual arousal are to some degree unique to each individual, we all share some basic aspects of sexual responsiveness. According to pioneering work done by William Masters and Virginia Johnson (1966), who studied sexual behavior in carefully controlled laboratory settings, sexual responses follow a regular pattern consisting of four phases: excitement, plateau, orgasm, and resolution. Although other researchers argue that sexual responses proceed somewhat differently (e.g., Zilbergeld & Ellison, 1980), Masters and Johnson's research is the most widely accepted account of what happens when people become sexually excited.

In the **excitement phase,** which can last from just a few minutes to more than an hour, an arousing stimulus begins a sequence that prepares the genitals for sexual intercourse. In the male, the *penis* becomes erect when blood flows into it. In the female, the *clitoris* swells because of an increase in the blood supply to that area, and the *vagina* becomes lubricated. Women may also experience a "sex flush," a red rash that typically spreads over the chest and throat.

Next comes the **plateau phase,** the body's preparation for orgasm. During this stage, the maximum level of sexual arousal is attained as the penis and clitoris swell with blood. Women's breasts and vaginas expand, heartbeat and blood pressure rise, and breathing rate increases. Muscle tension becomes greater as the body prepares

excitement phase The period in which an arousing stimulus begins a sequence that prepares the genitals for sexual intercourse. (Module 33)

plateau phase The period in which the maximum level of arousal is attained, the penis and clitoris swell with blood, and the body prepares for orgasm. (Module 33)

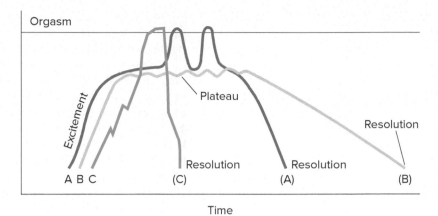

(a) Male pattern   **(b) Female patterns**

FIGURE 2 A four-stage model of the sexual response cycle for males and females based on the findings of Masters and Johnson (1966). Note how the male pattern (a) includes a refractory period. Part (b) shows three possible female patterns. In A, the pattern is closest to the male cycle except that the woman has two orgasms in a row. In B, there is no orgasm, whereas in C, orgasm is reached quickly and the woman rapidly returns to an unaroused state.

Source: Adapted from Masters, W. H., & Johnson, V. E. (1966). *Human sexual response*. Boston: Little, Brown.

itself for the next stage, orgasm. Although it is difficult to explain the sensation of **orgasm** beyond saying that it is an intense, highly pleasurable experience, the biological events that accompany the feeling are fairly straightforward. When the orgasm stage is reached, rhythmic muscular contractions occur in the genitals every eight-tenths of a second. In the male, the contractions expel *semen*, a fluid containing sperm, from the penis—a process known as *ejaculation*. For women and men, breathing and heart rates reach their maximum.

After orgasm, people move into the last stage of sexual arousal, the **resolution stage.** The body returns to its resting state, reversing the changes brought about by arousal. The genitals resume their unaroused size and shape; blood pressure, breathing, and heart rate return to normal.

Male and female responses differ significantly during the resolution stage; these differences are depicted in Figure 2. Women are able to cycle back to the orgasm phase and experience repeated orgasms. Ultimately, of course, females enter the final resolution stage, and then they return to their prestimulation state. In contrast, it generally is thought that men enter a refractory period during the resolution stage. During the **refractory period,** men are unable to develop an erection. Therefore, men are unable to have another orgasm and ejaculate. The refractory period may last from a few minutes to several hours; in the elderly, it may continue for several days (Goldstein, 2000).

orgasm The peak of sexual excitement, during which rhythmic muscular contractions occur in the genitals. (Module 33)

resolution stage The interval after orgasm in which the body returns to its unaroused state, reversing the changes brought about by arousal. (Module 33)

refractory period A temporary period that follows the resolution stage and during which the male cannot develop an erection again. (Module 33)

 # Exploring Diversity

Female Circumcision: A Celebration of Culture—or Genital Mutilation?

Waris Dirie was only 5 when her mother agreed to the operation that would cleanse her of her inborn "filth" and make her worthy of marriage. Waris, a normal Somali girl who just wanted a husband some day, was innocently eager to be circumcised.

A few months later, her mother blindfolded her and held her down while a woman performed the operation with a dull, dirty razor and no anesthetic, using a thorn and thread to sew up the incision. "It's not a pain you forget," Waris recalls. Neither can she escape intense pain every time she urinates or menstruates—pain to the point of fainting. (Dirie, 2011; London, 2013)

The operation in question—female circumcision—represents one of the most controversial procedures relating to sex throughout the world. In such an operation, the clitoris is removed, resulting in permanent inability to experience sexual pleasure.

Some 200 million women and children around the globe have undergone female circumcision. Most of them live in Africa and Asia, but this number includes around 500,000 women and girls in the United States who underwent the procedure or are at risk for it in the future. More than 90% of women in countries such as Somalia, Guinea, and Egypt have been circumcised during childhood, with most cutting occurring between the ages of 5 and 14 years. Furthermore, in some cases, more extensive surgery is carried out in which additional parts of the female genitals are removed or are sewn together with catgut or thorns (Davidson, 2016; Kandala et al., 2018).

Those who practice female circumcision say it upholds an ancient societal tradition and is no different from other cultural customs. Its purpose, they say, is to preserve virginity before marriage, keep women faithful to their husbands after marriage, and enhance a woman's beauty. Furthermore, proponents believe that it differs little from the common Western practice of male circumcision in which the foreskin of the penis is surgically removed soon after birth.

In contrast, critics argue that female circumcision is nothing less than female mutilation. Not only does the practice permanently eliminate sexual pleasure, but it can also lead to constant pain, infection, and, in some cases, death. Furthermore, because the procedure is traditionally conducted in a ritualistic fashion using a razor blade, sawtooth knife, or glass and without an anesthetic, the circumcision itself can be physically traumatic (Renshaw, 2006; Buggio et al., 2019).

The procedure raises some difficult issues that have been brought to light in various court cases. For instance, a Nigerian immigrant, living temporarily in the United States, went to court to argue that she should be allowed to remain permanently. Her plea: If she and her young daughters were sent back to Nigeria, her daughters would face circumcision upon their return. The court agreed and permitted her to stay indefinitely (Gregory, 1994; Dugger, 1996).

In reaction to the controversy about female circumcision, Congress made the practice illegal in the United States. Still, some critics argue that female circumcision is a valued cultural custom and that no one, particularly someone judging from the perspective of another culture, should prevent people from carrying out the customs they think are important. In addition, they point out that the practice of male circumcision is an accepted practice in the United States, based largely on religious, social, and cultural traditions (Boyle et al., 2002; Johnsdotter & Essén, 2005; Renshaw, 2006).

In any case, the practice of female circumcision is showing a gradual, although significant, decline in Africa and the Middle East. In Egypt, for example, 81% of 15- to 19-year-old girls have been circumcised, compared to 96% of women in their late 40s. Moreover, attitudes are changing: just one-third of teenage girls in Egypt thought the practice should continue, whereas two-thirds of older women approved of it (Dugger, 2013).

RECAP/EVALUATE/RETHINK

RECAP

LO 33-1 Why, and under what circumstances, do we become sexually aroused?

- Biological factors, such as the presence of androgens (male sex hormones) and estrogens (female sex hormones), prime people for sex. But almost any kind of stimulus can produce sexual arousal, depending on a person's prior experience.

- People's sexual responses follow a regular pattern consisting of four phases: excitement, plateau, orgasm, and resolution.

EVALUATE

1. Match the phase of sexual arousal with its characteristics.
   1. Excitement phase
   2. Plateau phase
   3. Orgasm phase
   4. Resolution phase

   a. Maximum level of sexual arousal
   b. Erection and lubrication
   c. Rhythmic muscular contractions and ejaculation
   d. Return of body to resting state

2. Men are generally thought to enter a _____ period after sex, in which orgasm is impossible for a varying period of time.

3. Whereas men are interested in sexual activity regardless of their biological cycles, women are truly receptive to sex only during ovulation, when the production of their sex hormones is greatest. True or false?

RETHINK

1. Why do you think humans differ from other species in their year-round receptivity to sex and in the number and variety of stimuli they perceive as sexual? What evolutionary purpose might this difference serve in humans?

2. Why do discussions of sexual behavior, which is such a necessary part of human life, have so many negative connotations in Western society?

Answers to Evaluate Questions

1. 1-b, 2-a, 3-c, 4-d; 2. refractory; 3. False; women are receptive throughout their cycle.

KEY TERMS

androgens	ovulation	plateau phase	resolution stage
genitals	erogenous zones	orgasm	refractory period
estrogens	excitement phase		

Module 34
The Diversity of Sexual Behavior

A boy who practices this habit can never be the best that Nature intended him to be. His wits are not so sharp. His memory is not so good. His power of fixing his attention on whatever he is doing is lessened. . . . A boy like this is a poor thing to look at. . . . [He is] untrustworthy, unreliable, untruthful, and probably even dishonest. (Schofield & Vaughan-Jackson, 1913)

The cause of this condition: masturbation—at least according to the authors of the early 1900s sex manual *What Every Boy Should Know.* The consequences of masturbation for women were considered no less severe. In the words of one 19th-century physician, "There is hardly an end to the diseases caused by masturbation: dyspepsia, spinal disease, headache, epilepsy, various kinds of fits...impaired eyesight, palpitation of the heart, pain in the side and bleeding at the lungs, spasm of the heart, and sometimes sudden death" (Gregory, 1856).

Such views may seem as bizarre and far-fetched to you as they do to contemporary experts on human sexual behavior. However, at one time they were considered perfectly sound by quite reasonable people. Indeed, trivia buffs might be interested to learn that corn flakes owe their invention to a 19th-century physician, J. W. Kellogg, who believed that the enjoyment of tasty food provoked sexual excitation so an alternative of "unstimulating" grains was needed.

Clearly, sex and sex-related behavior are influenced by expectations, attitudes, beliefs, and the state of medical and biological knowledge in a given period. Today we know that sexual behavior may take diverse forms, and much of what was once seen as "unnatural" and "lewd" is often more likely to be accepted in contemporary society. Similarly, sexual behavior that is commonplace in one culture is seen as appalling in others. For instance, seven societies are known in which kissing never occurs (Mason, 1995). In sum, distinctions between normal and abnormal sexual behavior are not easy to draw. This reality certainly hasn't prevented people from trying to draw them, however.

Times change: The veiled sexuality of Victorian-era paintings has given way to a more frank acknowledgment of sexual behavior.
(left): leminuit/iStock/Getty Images; (right): Christian Mueller/Shutterstock

Approaches to Sexual Normality

One approach to sexual normality is to behavior in terms of deviation from the average, or typical, behavior. To determine abnormality, we simply observe what behaviors are rare and uncommon in a society and label those deviations from the norm as abnormal.

The difficulty with such an approach, however, is that some behaviors that are statistically unusual hardly seem worthy of concern. Even though most people have sexual intercourse in the bedroom, does the fact that someone prefers sex in the dining room imply abnormality? If some people prefer portly sexual partners, are they abnormal in a society that holds slimness in high regard? Since the answer to both of these questions is clearly no, an approach that defines sexual abnormality in terms of deviation from the average is inappropriate. (The same difficulties are encountered in considering definitions of psychological abnormality.)

An alternative approach would be to compare sexual behavior against some standard or ideal. But here, again, there is a problem: What standard should we use? Some of us might suggest philosophy, some might turn to the Bible, and some might even consider psychology the ultimate determinant. The trouble is that none of these potential sources of standards is universally acceptable. Furthermore, since standards change radically with shifts in societal attitudes and new knowledge, such an approach is undesirable. For instance, at one point, the American Psychiatric Association labeled homosexuality a mental illness. However, as evidence to the contrary accumulated, in 1973 the organization determined that homosexuality should no longer be considered a mental disorder. Obviously, the behavior had not changed. Only the label the psychiatric profession gave it had been modified.

In light of the difficulties with other approaches, probably the most reasonable definition of sexual normality is one that considers the psychological consequences of the behavior. In this approach, sexual behavior is considered abnormal if it produces a sense of distress, anxiety, or guilt—or if it is harmful to some other person. According to this view, then, sexual behaviors can be seen as abnormal only when they have a negative impact on a person's own sense of well-being or if they hurt someone else.

Although same-sex marriage is legal throughout the United States, it remains a divisive social issue. However, it is becoming an increasingly accepted part of American society, representing a major change in attitudes.
Rawpixel.com/Shutterstock

It is important to recognize that societal values dictate what is seen as normal or abnormal sexual behavior, and dramatic shifts have occurred from one generation to another in such definitions. People can and should make their own personal value judgments about what is appropriate in their own sex lives, but there are few universally accepted absolute rights and wrongs.

Surveying Sexual Behavior: What's Happening Behind Closed Doors?

For most of recorded history, the vast variety of sexual practices remained shrouded in ignorance. However, in the late 1930s, biologist Alfred Kinsey launched a series of surveys on the sexual behavior of people in the United States. The result was the first comprehensive attempt to see what people were actually doing sexually and was highlighted by the publication of Kinsey's landmark volumes, *Sexual Behavior in the Human Male* (Kinsey, Pomeroy, & Martin, 1948) and *Sexual Behavior in the Human Female* (Kinsey et al., 1953).

Kinsey's research was the first major systematic effort in learning about human sexual behavior. Kinsey and his colleagues interviewed tens of thousands of people. The interview techniques they devised are still regarded as a model for other sex researchers because of their ability to prompt sensitive information without causing embarrassment.

On the other hand, Kinsey's samples reflected an overrepresentation of college students, young people, well-educated individuals, urban dwellers, and people living in Indiana and the Northeast. Furthermore, as with all surveys involving volunteer participants, it is unclear how representative his data are of people who refused to participate in the study. Similarly, because no survey observes behavior directly, it is difficult to assess how accurately people's descriptions of what they do in private match their actual sexual practices.

Kinsey's work set the stage for later surveys. But due to political reasons (the use of government funding for sex surveys is controversial), surprisingly few comprehensive, large-scale, representative surveys–either in the United States or in other countries–have been carried out since Kinsey did his initial work. However, by examining the common results gleaned from different samples of subjects, we now have a reasonably complete picture of contemporary sexual practices–to which we turn next.

MASTURBATION: SOLITARY SEX

masturbation Sexual self-stimulation. (Module 34)

If you listened to physicians 100 years ago, you would have been told that **masturbation,** sexual self-stimulation often using the hand to rub the genitals, would lead to a wide variety of physical and mental disorders, ranging from hairy palms to insanity. If those physicians had been correct, however, most of us would be wearing gloves to hide the sight of our hair-covered palms because masturbation is one of the most frequently practiced sexual activities. Some 94% of all males and 63% of all females have masturbated at least once; among college students, the frequency ranges from "never" to "several times a day" (Hunt, 1974; Michael et al., 1994; Polonsky, 2006; Buerkle, 2011).

Men and women typically begin to masturbate for the first time at different ages, as you can see in Figure 1. Furthermore, men masturbate considerably more often than women do, although there are differences in frequency according to age. Male masturbation is most common in the early teens and then declines; females both begin and reach a maximum frequency later. There are also some racial differences: African American men and women masturbate less than whites do (Oliver & Hyde, 1993; Pinkerton et al., 2002; Das, Parish, & Laumann, 2009).

Although masturbation is often considered an activity to engage in only if no other sexual outlets are available, this view bears little relationship to reality. Close to three-fourths

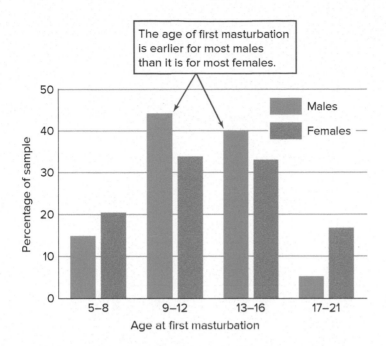

The age of first masturbation is earlier for most males than it is for most females.

FIGURE 1 The age at which a sample of college students first masturbated. The percentages are based on only those people who had experience with masturbation.

Source: Adapted from Arafat, I., & Cotton, W. L. (1974). Masturbation practices of males and females. *Journal of Sex Research, 10,* 293–307.

of married men ages 20 to 40 report masturbating an average of 24 times a year, and 68% of the married women in the same age group masturbate an average of 10 times a year (Michael et al., 1994; Das, 2007; Regnerus, Price, & Gordon, 2017).

Despite the high incidence of masturbation, attitudes toward it still reflect some of the negative views of yesteryear. For instance, one survey found that around 10% of people who masturbated experienced feelings of guilt; 5% of the males and 1% of the females considered their behavior perverted. Despite these negative attitudes, however, most experts on sex view masturbation as a healthy and legitimate—and harmless—sexual activity. In addition, masturbation is seen as providing a means of learning about one's own sexuality and a way of discovering changes in one's body, such as the emergence of precancerous lumps (Arafat & Cotton, 1974; Levin, 2007; Herbenick et al., 2009).

Heterosexuality

For heterosexuals, engaging in sexual intercourse often is perceived as achieving one of life's major milestones. However, **heterosexuality,** sexual attraction and behavior directed to the other sex, consists of far more than male-female intercourse. Kissing, petting, caressing, massaging, and other forms of sex play are all components of heterosexual behavior. Still, sex researchers' focus has been on the act of intercourse, especially in terms of its first occurrence and its frequency.

heterosexuality Sexual attraction and behavior directed to the other sex. (Module 34)

PREMARITAL SEX

Before the start of the 21st century, premarital sexual intercourse, at least for women, was considered one of the major taboos in our society. Traditionally, women were warned by society that "nice girls don't do it"; at the same time, men were told that premarital sex was okay for them, but they should marry virgins. This view that premarital sex is permissible for males but not for females is called the **double standard** (Lyons et al., 2011; Penhollow, Young, & Nnaka, 2017; Guo, 2019).

In fact, 40 years ago, the majority of adult Americans believed that premarital sex was always wrong. But public opinion has shifted dramatically since then. For example, as you can see in Figure 2, the percentage of people who believe that premarital sex is "not wrong at all" has increased from just over 25% in the early 1970s to more than 55% in 2012. More than half say that living together before marriage is morally

double standard The view that premarital sex is permissible for males but not for females. (Module 34)

FIGURE 2 Percentage of people who believe premarital sex is "not wrong at all." Attitudes toward premarital sex have become considerably more positive over the past decades.
Source: Adapted from Smith, T. W., & Son, J. (2013). *Trends in public attitudes about sexual morality.* Chicago: NORC at the University of Chicago.

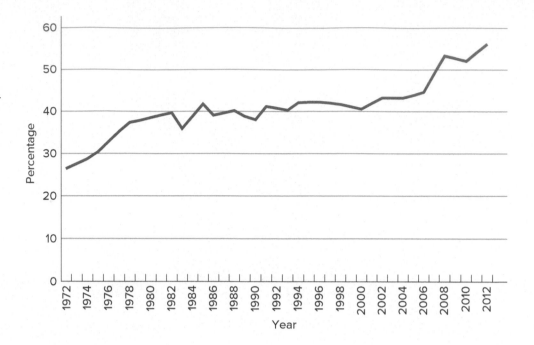

acceptable (Thornton & Young-DeMarco, 2001; Harding & Jencks, 2003; Smith & Son, 2013).

Actual rates of premarital sexual activity have matched changes in attitude. For instance, more than one-half of women between the ages of 15 and 19 have had premarital sexual intercourse. These figures are close to double the number of women in the same age range who reported having intercourse in 1970. Clearly, the trend over the last 50 years has been toward more women engaging in premarital sexual activity (Jones, Darroch, & Singh, 2005; Sprecher, Treger, & Sakaluk, 2013; Elias, Fullerton, & Simpson, 2015).

Males, too, have shown an increase in the incidence of premarital sexual intercourse, although the increase has not been as dramatic as it has been for females—probably because the rates for males were higher to begin with. For instance, the first surveys of premarital intercourse carried out in the 1940s showed an incidence of 84% across males of all ages; recent figures are closer to 95%. Moreover, the average age of males' first sexual experience has been declining steadily. Almost half of males have had sexual intercourse by the age of 18; by the time they reach age 20, 88% have had intercourse. Overall, 70% of all teens have had intercourse by their 19th birthday (Guttmacher Institute, 2012; Lindberg, Maddow-Zimet, & Marcell, 2019).

What may be most interesting about the patterns of premarital sex is that they show a convergence of male and female attitudes and behavior. But is the change sufficient to signal an end to the double standard?

Probably. For many people, particularly younger individuals, the double standard has been succeeded by a new view: *permissiveness with affection.* According to those holding this view, premarital intercourse is permissible for both men and women if it occurs within a long-term, committed, or loving relationship (DeGaton, Weed, & Jensen, 1996; Hyde, Mezulis, & Abramson, 2008).

Still, the double standard has not disappeared completely. Where differing standards remain, the attitudes are almost always more lenient toward the male than toward the female (Sprecher & Hatfield, 1996).

Furthermore, there are substantial cultural differences regarding the incidence and acceptability of premarital intercourse. For instance, the proportions of male teenagers who have intercourse before their 17th birthday in Jamaica, the United States, and Brazil are about 10 times the level reported in the Philippines. And in some cultures, such as those in sub-Saharan Africa, women become sexually active at an earlier age than men—although this may be due to the fact that they marry at a younger age than men (Singh et al., 2000).

MARITAL SEX

To judge by the number of articles about sex in heterosexual marriages, one would think that sexual behavior was the number one standard by which marital bliss is measured. Married couples are often concerned that they are having too little sex, too much sex, or the wrong kind of sex (Harvey, Wenzel, & Sprecher, 2004).

Although sex in marriage is measured along many dimensions, one is certainly the frequency of heterosexual intercourse. What is typical? As with most other types of sexual activities, there is no easy answer to the question because there are such wide variations in patterns between individuals. We do know that 43% of married hetero-sexual couples have sexual intercourse a few times a month and 36% of couples have it two or three times a week. With increasing age and length of marriage, the frequency of intercourse declines. Still, sex continues into late adulthood, with almost half of people reporting that they engage in high-quality sexual activity at least once a month (Powell, 2006; Grøntvedt, Kennair, & Bendixen, 2019).

According to the most recent trends in sexual activity, the number of adults reporting no sex at all in the past year has reached an all-time high. The numbers seem to be driven by an increase in numbers of people entering older adulthood, when sex is less frequent. But interestingly, younger people are also having less sex. The proportion of 18- to 29-year-olds reporting no sex in the past year more than doubled between 2008 and 2018, to 23 percent. The reason for this increase in abstinence may be that people in that age group are less likely to have live-in partners or are living with their parents for extended periods, although these explanations remains speculative (Ingraham, 2019; see Figure 3).

When it does occur, sexual activity provides benefits beyond the immediate pleasure. Sexual activity generates a kind of sexual afterglow that cements relationships and increases marital satisfaction. Moreover, the frequency of sexual intercourse may be related to relationship satisfaction (Brody & Costa, 2017; Meltzer et al., 2017).

Although early research found **extramarital sex** to be widespread, the current reality appears to be otherwise. According to surveys, 85% of married women and more than 75% of married men report having no sexual partners other than their spouses. Furthermore, the median number of sex partners inside and outside of marriage since the age of 18 was six for men and two for women. Accompanying these numbers is a high, consistent degree of disapproval of extramarital sex, with 9 of 10 people saying that it is "always" or "almost always" wrong (Whisman & Snyder, 2007; DeMaris, 2013; Labrecque & Whisman, 2017).

extramarital sex Sexual activity between a married person and someone who is not his or her spouse. (Module 34)

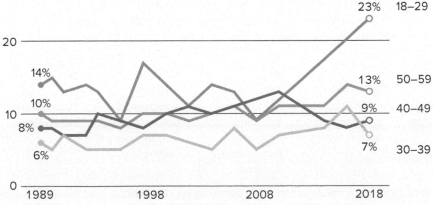

Note: Rates of no sex among adults over age 60 have consistently hovered around 50 percent and are not shown here.

FIGURE 3 Proportion of people stating that they had no sex in the prior year. The proportion of 18- to 29-year-olds reporting that they have had no sex in the past year more than doubled between 2008 and 2018. Why do you think this might be true?

Source: Adapted from Ingraham, C. (2019, March 29). The share of Americans not having sex has reached a record high. *Washington Post.* Retrieved from https://www.washingtonpost.com/business/2019/03/29/share-americans-not-having-sex-has-reached-record-high/; and the General Social Survey, https://gssdataexplorer.norc.org/variables/5057/vshow.

Homosexuality and Bisexuality

homosexuals Persons who are sexually attracted to members of their own sex. (Module 34)

bisexuals Persons who are sexually attracted to people of the same gender as well as other genders. (Module 34)

Homosexuals are sexually attracted to members of their own sex, whereas **bisexuals** are sexually attracted to people of the same gender as well as other genders. Most people now use the terms *gay* and *lesbian* to refer to male and female homosexuals, respectively, in part because the terms *gay* and *lesbian* refer to a broader array of attitudes and lifestyles than the term *homosexual*, which focuses on the sexual act.

The number of people who have had same-sex sexual partners at one point in their lives is considerable. Estimates suggest that around 20–25% of males and about 15% of females have had at least one gay or lesbian experience during adulthood. The exact number of people who identify themselves as exclusively homosexual has proved difficult to gauge; some estimates are as low as 1.1% and some as high as 10%. Some experts suggest that around 3.5% of adults in the United States identify as lesbian, gay, or bisexual, and 5–10% of both men and women are exclusively gay or lesbian during extended periods of their lives (Chandra, Mosher, & Copen, 2011; Gates, 2017).

Although people often view homosexuality and heterosexuality as two completely distinct sexual orientations, the issue is not that simple. Pioneering sex researcher Alfred Kinsey acknowledged this when he considered sexual orientation along a scale or continuum with "exclusively homosexual" at one end and "exclusively heterosexual" at the other. In the middle were people who showed both homosexual and heterosexual behavior (see Figure 4). Kinsey's approach suggests that sexual orientation is dependent on a person's sexual feelings and behaviors and romantic feelings (Weinberg, Williams, & Pryor, 1991; Jeffery, 2015).

DETERMINING THE CAUSES OF SEXUAL ORIENTATION

What determines people's sexual orientation? Although a number of theories exist, none has proved completely satisfactory.

Considerable research suggests that biological and genetic factors underlie sexual orientation. For example, in one of the largest and most comprehensive studies, a group of researchers examined DNA from almost half a million men and women and found five genes associated with same-sex sexual behavior. These genes don't act alone, but in conjunction with other genes, they may account for as much as a third of the influence in determining whether an individual engages in same-sex behavior (Ganna et al., 2019; Mills, 2019).

Studies of identical twins provide evidence for a genetic cause of sexual orientation. For example, when one twin identified himself or herself as homosexual, the occurrence of homosexuality in the other twin was higher than it was in the general population. Such results occur even for twins who have been separated early in life and who therefore are not necessarily raised in similar social environments. Furthermore, some research suggests there is an area on the X chromosome associated with homosexuality (Gooren, 2006; LeVay, 2011; Servick, 2014).

Hormones also may play a role in determining sexual orientation. For example, research shows that women exposed before birth to DES (diethylstilbestrol), a drug

0	1	2	3	4	5	6
Exclusive heterosexual behavior	Primarily heterosexual, but incidents of homosexual behavior	Primarily heterosexual, but more than incidental homosexual behavior	Equal amounts of heterosexual and homo-sexual behavior	Primarily homosexual, but more than incidental heterosexual behavior	Primarily homosexual, but incidents of heterosexual behavior	Exclusively homosexual behavior

FIGURE 4 The Kinsey scale is designed to define the degree to which sexual orientation is heterosexual, homosexual, or bisexual. Although Kinsey saw people as falling along a continuum, most people believe that they belong to a specific category.
Source: Kinsey, A. C., Pomeroy, W. B., & Martin, C. E. (1948). *Sexual behavior in the human male.* Philadelphia: Saunders.

their mothers took to avoid miscarriage, were more likely to be gay or bisexual (Reinisch, Mortensen, & Sanders, 2017).

Further evidence suggests that differences in brain structures may be related to sexual orientation. For instance, the structure of the anterior hypothalamus, an area of the brain that governs sexual behavior, differs in male homosexuals and heterosexuals. Similarly, other research shows that, compared with heterosexual men or women, gay men have a larger anterior commissure, which is a bundle of neurons connecting the right and left hemispheres of the brain (Rahman & Yusuf, 2015; Niebergal, Swanson, & Sánchez, 2019).

In short, considerable research suggests the importance of biological and genetic factors at the roots of homosexuality, but the research is not conclusive in pinpointing the specific cause. Nevertheless, it seems likely that some inherited or biological factor predisposes people toward homosexuality (Rahman, Kumari, & Wilson, 2003; Burri, Spector, & Qazi, 2015).

In contrast, little evidence suggests that sexual orientation is brought about by child-rearing practices or family dynamics. Although proponents of psychoanalytic theories once argued that the nature of the parent-child relationship can produce homosexuality (e.g., Freud, 1922/1959), research evidence does not support such explanations (Roughton, 2002).

Another early explanation for sexual orientation rests on learning theory (Masters & Johnson, 1979). According to this view, sexual orientation is learned through rewards and punishments in much the same way we may learn to prefer swimming over tennis. For example, a young adolescent who had an unpleasant heterosexual experience might develop disagreeable associations with the other sex. If the same person had a rewarding, pleasant gay or lesbian experience, the adolescent might incorporate homosexuality into his or her sexual fantasies, which might later lead to homosexual behavior.

However, learning-theory explanations seem inadequate as a sole determinant of sexual orientation. Because our society has traditionally held homosexuality in low esteem, one ought to expect that the negative treatment of homosexual behavior would outweigh the rewards attached to it. Furthermore, children growing up with a gay or lesbian parent are statistically unlikely to become homosexual, which contradicts the notion that homosexual behavior may be learned from others (Tasker, 2005; Frias-Navarro et al., 2018).

In short, at this point we have no definitive explanation of what determines sexual orientation, and no single factor can likely be viewed as the basis. Instead, it seems reasonable to assume that a combination of biological, genetic, and environmental factors is involved (Hyde, Mezulis, & Abramson, 2008; Bailey et al, 2016; Ganna et al., 2019).

Although we don't know exactly why people develop a certain sexual orientation, one thing is clear: Despite increasingly positive attitudes toward homosexuality, many gays and lesbians face antigay attitudes and discrimination, and it can take a toll. Lesbians and gays have higher rates of depression and suicide than do their straight counterparts. There are even physical health disparities due to prejudice that gays and lesbians may experience. Because of this, the American Psychological Association and other major mental health organizations have endorsed efforts to eliminate discrimination against gays and lesbians (Lick, Durso, & Johnson, 2013; Moody et al., 2017; Goldhammer, Krinsky, & Keuroghlian, 2019).

Transgender Individuals

An increasing number of individuals consider themselves transgender. **Transgender** is a general term encompassing people whose gender identity, gender expression, or behavior is not consistent with the sex to which they were assigned at birth.

Transgender people may have male bodies but view their gender identity as female or may have female bodies and have a male gender identity. In other cases, transgender

transgender A general term for persons whose gender identity, gender expression, or behavior is not consistent with that typically associated with the sex to which they were assigned at birth. (Module 34) individuals may view themselves as a third gender (neither male nor female). They also may wish to be referred to not as "she" or "he" but rather some other, more neutral pronoun, such as "ze" or "they" (Prince, 2005; Hyde, Mezulis, & Abramson, 2008; Scelfo, 2015).

In some cases, transgender individuals may seek gender-confirmation surgery in which the goal is to create the physical appearance and functional abilities of the gender that transgender individuals consider themselves to be. Several steps, including intensive counseling, hormone injections, and living as a member of the desired sex for several years, precede surgery, which is, not surprisingly, highly complicated. The outcome, though, can be quite positive (Lobato, Koff, & Manenti, 2006; Richards, 2011; Gorton & Erickson-Schroth, 2017).

Transgender issues have become increasingly prominent in recent years. For instance, college campuses have struggled with how to best provide restrooms that address the needs of the transgender community. Do individuals who have the genitals of a male but identify as females use traditional men's rooms or women's rooms? One solution has been the establishment of unisex or all-gender restrooms (Steinmetz, 2015; Callahan & Zukowski, 2019).

Whereas the term *transgender* centers on gender identity concerns, the term *intersex person* refers to the small number of people born with genitals that make their sexual identity ambiguous. An *intersex person* has an atypical combination of sexual organs or chromosomal or gene patterns, making their sexual identity unclear. In some cases, they are born with both male and female sexual organs, or the organs appear ambiguous in their physical configuration. It is a rare condition, found in 1 in 4,500 births. Intersexism involves a complex mix of physiological and psychological issues (Lehrman, 2007; Diamond, 2009; Roen, 2019).

TheChoperPilot/Shutterstock

Sexual Difficulties and Issues

When sex—an activity that should be pleasurable, joyful, and intimate—is forced on someone, it becomes one of the ultimate acts of aggression and brutality, and few crimes produce such profound and long-lasting consequences. But sexual crimes are not the only category of serious problems related to sex. Few personal difficulties produce as much anxiety, embarrassment, and even shame as sexually transmitted infections and sexual dysfunctions. We now turn to the major types of problems related to sex.

RAPE

rape The act by which one person forces another person to submit to sexual activity. (Module 34)

Rape occurs when one person forces another person to submit to sexual activity such as intercourse or oral-genital sex. Although it usually applies to a male forcing a female, rape can occur when members of either sex are forced into sexual activities without their consent.

Most people think of rape as a rare crime committed by strangers. Unfortunately, they are wrong on both counts. In fact, rape occurs far more frequently than is commonly thought, and rapists are typically acquaintances of their victims. A survey by the Centers for Disease Control and Prevention found that 20% of women report that they have been the victim of a rape or attempted rape during their lifetimes. Furthermore, more than 200,000 sexual assaults directed against women are reported to police in the United States each year. Because only about one-third of rapes and sexual assaults are reported to police, the actual figure is probably much higher (Catalano, 2006; CDC, 2011).

In fact, a national survey of nearly 100,000 college students found that 26% of women and 7% of men say they experienced some form of nonconsensual sexual contact while enrolled in college. The rate of unwanted sexual contact was also high for gender nonconforming students, standing at 20%. Another survey conducted at 35 universities revealed that 1 out of 8 female college students reported having been raped. Among the women who had been raped, about half said the rapists were first dates, casual dates, or romantic acquaintances—a phenomenon called **date rape** (Koss, 2011; DiJulio et al., 2015; Cantor et al., 2019).

Girls in high school also suffer both sexual and physical abuse: In one survey, 9% of 14- to 18-year-old girls said they had been forced into sexual activity by a date, and in more than half of those cases, the incident had been accompanied by hitting, slapping, or shoving (Koss, 1993; Ackard & Neumark-Sztainer, 2002; Aiello, 2006; Koss, 2011).

Women in some segments of society are more at risk for rape than are others. Although the likelihood of sexual assault is considerably lower among Latino women in comparison to non-Latino white women, the rate for black women is slightly higher in comparison to white women. Such racial differences may stem from differing cultural views of women and male dominance (Koss, 1993; Black & Weisz, 2004).

Although on the surface it might appear that rape is primarily a sex crime, in many cases, sex is not the primary motivation. For example, some rapists use sex as a means of demonstrating power and control over the victim. In such cases, little is sexually satisfying about rape to the rapist; instead, the pleasure comes from forcing someone else to be submissive (Yamawaki, Darby, & Queiroz, 2007; Hipp et al., 2017).

In other cases of rape, anger is the primary motivation. Sexual behavior is used to show the rapist's rage at women in general, usually because of some perceived rejection or hurt that he has suffered in the past. Such rapes are likely to include physical violence and degrading acts against the victim.

Still, some rapes are based primarily on a desire for sexual gratification. Some men hold the attitude that it is appropriate and desirable for them to actively seek out sex. To them, sexual encounters represent a form of "war" between the sexes—with winners and losers—and violence is sometimes considered an appropriate way to obtain what they want. According to their reasoning, using force to obtain sexual gratification is permissible (Malamuth et al., 1995; Hall, 1996; Mann & Hollin, 2007).

Finally, there is a common, although unfounded, societal belief that many women offer token resistance to sex, saying no to sex when they mean yes. If a man holds such a view, he feels he may ignore a woman's protestations that she doesn't want sex (Anderson, Cooper, & Okamura, 1997; Yost & Zurbriggen, 2006; Sarmiento, 2011).

Consequences of Rape The repercussions of rape are devastating for the victims. During a rape, women experience fear, terror, and physical pain. The prefrontal cortex shuts down due to a surge of chemicals that significantly impairs thinking. Later, victims report shock, disbelief, panic, extreme anxiety, and suspiciousness—reactions that are sometimes intensified by implications that somehow the victim was to blame because of her style of dress, her presence in the wrong neighborhood, or because she did not fight back (Hopper & Lisak, 2014).

It doesn't matter whether a rape involves a date or a stranger; the psychological reactions are just as bad. The negative feelings may continue for years, even though the victim outwardly appears to have recovered. However, immediate psychological intervention, such as that provided by rape crisis centers, may help diminish the long-term reactions to rape (Ullman & Townsend, 2007; Campbell, 2008; Westmarland & Alderson, 2013).

Although men are the victim of rape less frequently than women, the consequences are no less devastating. In fact, men may face additional challenges due to societal conceptions of masculinity, which may make them think they should have been strong enough to fight off a perpetrator. Furthermore, men may sometimes experience involuntary erections during a sexual assault, which may lead to confusion over their sexual identity, and they are apt to feel at fault (Javaid, 2017; Levy & Adams, 2018).

CHILDHOOD SEXUAL ABUSE

One form of sexual behavior that is surprisingly common yet little understood is the sexual abuse of children. Although it is difficult to make accurate estimates of the true

date rape Rape in which the rapist is either a date or a romantic acquaintance. (Module 34)

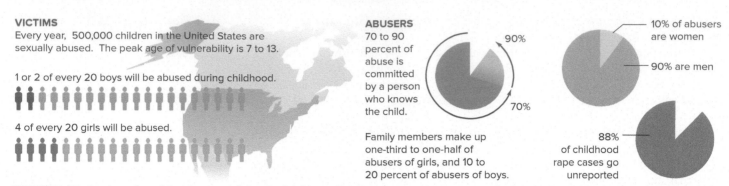

VICTIMS
Every year, 500,000 children in the United States are sexually abused. The peak age of vulnerability is 7 to 13.

1 or 2 of every 20 boys will be abused during childhood.

4 of every 20 girls will be abused.

ABUSERS
70 to 90 percent of abuse is committed by a person who knows the child.

90%

70%

Family members make up one-third to one-half of abusers of girls, and 10 to 20 percent of abusers of boys.

10% of abusers are women

90% are men

88% of childhood rape cases go unreported

FIGURE 5 Studies have found that the sexual abuse of children often is committed by a person who knows the child, with almost a third of the abusers being family members.
Source: Adapted from Finkelhor, D. (2002). *Sexual abuse in the United States*. Durham, NH: University of New Hampshire.

incidence of child sexual abuse because most cases go unreported, experts estimate that each year a half million children are sexually abused. Between 5% and 10% of boys and 20% of girls will be abused at some point (see Figure 5; Villarosa, 2002; Finkelhor & Jones, 2004).

Who commits child sexual abuse? In most cases, it is a relative or acquaintance; in only about one-quarter of the cases is the abuse carried out by a stranger. The most vulnerable age for being molested is between the ages of 7 and 13; the abusers tend to be about 20 years older than their victims. In most instances, the abuser is a male heterosexual; overall, in 88% of substantiated cases of abuse, the perpetrator is male. Furthermore, increasingly, child predators are using the web to make contact with potential victims (Alaggia, Collin-Vézina, & Lateef, 2019; National Sexual Violence Resource Center, 2019).

The short- and long-term consequences of childhood sexual abuse can be extremely damaging. In terms of initial effects, victims report fear, anxiety, depression, anger, and hostility. Long-term effects may include depression, self-destructive behavior, feelings of isolation, poor self-esteem, and substance abuse. Although they may experience sexual difficulties later in life, the victims are not more likely to become sexual abusers themselves. Ultimately, the consequences of childhood sexual abuse are related to the specific nature of the abuse. Experiences involving fathers, genital contact, and the use of force are the most damaging (Buzi, Weinman, & Smith, 2007; Malloy, Brubacher, & Lamb, 2011; Turner et al., 2017).

SEXUALLY TRANSMITTED INFECTIONS

sexually transmitted infection (STI)
A disease acquired through sexual contact. (Module 34)

Millions of people suffer the discomfort—not to mention the psychological distress—of a **sexually transmitted infection (STI),** a disease acquired through sexual contact. Estimates suggest that in the United States, 1 person in 5 is infected with some form of STI and at least 1 person in 4 will probably contract an STI during his or her lifetime. Some 19 million new infections occur every year, nearly half in people ages 15 to 24 (National Prevention Information Network, 2011).

The United States has the highest rate of sexually transmitted infections of all the economically developed countries in the world, in part because people in the United States don't talk about sex as frankly or receive as much sex education as people in other developed nations (see Figure 6; CDC, 2013; CDC, 2018).

These are the major STIs:

- *Human papilloma virus (HPV).* HPV is the most common sexually transmitted infection, with more than 14 million new cases each year. Spread through vaginal, anal, or oral sex, it is usually not harmful, although it can lead to serious health problems such as genital warts and cervical cancer. HPV vaccines are now available that protect against some of the most harmful types of HPV.

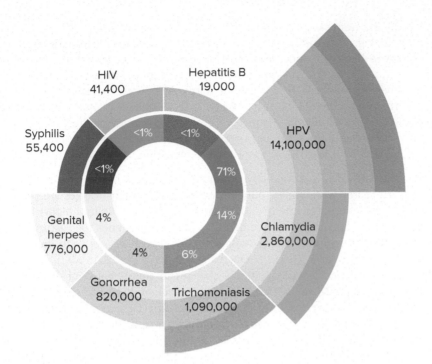

FIGURE 6 Estimates of the numbers of new cases annually of sexually transmitted infections in the United States. Each year, new cases of HPV greatly outnumber any other sexually transmitted infection.
Source: Adapted from Centers for Disease Control and Prevention. (2013). *STD surveillance tables.* Atlanta: Author.

- *Chlamydia.* Another widespread STI is *chlamydia,* a disease that in women initially produces no symptoms and in men causes a burning sensation during urination and a discharge from the penis. If it is left untreated, chlamydia can lead to pelvic inflammation, urethral damage, arthritis, and even sterility. There are almost 3 million new cases each year in the United States. Because it usually produces no symptoms in females, the Centers for Disease Control and Prevention recommends that sexually active women under age 26 should be tested for the disease every year. Once diagnosed, chlamydia can be cured with antibiotics, most often azithromycin or doxycycline.

- *Genital herpes.* *Genital herpes* is a virus related to the cold sores that sometimes appear around the mouth. Herpes first appears as small blisters or sores around the genitals that later break open, causing severe pain. These sores heal after a few weeks, but the disease usually reappears typically four or five times in the year following infection. Later outbreaks are less frequent, but the infection, which cannot be cured, often causes psychological distress for those who know they are infected. During the active phases of the disease, it can be transmitted to sexual partners. Genital herpes is common among college-age students: About 17% of 20- to 29-year-olds have the infection.

- *Trichomoniasis.* *Trichomoniasis* is an infection in the vagina or penis. Caused by a parasite, it is often without symptoms, especially in men. Eventually, it can cause painful urination and intercourse, a discharge from the vagina, itching, and an unpleasant odor. The 5 million cases reported each year can be treated with antibiotics.

- *Gonorrhea.* *Gonorrhea* often has no symptoms but can produce a burning sensation during urination or a discharge from the penis or vagina. The infection can lead to fertility problems and, in women, pelvic inflammatory disease. Although antibiotics usually can cure gonorrhea, the number of drug-resistant strains of the disease is growing, making treatment more difficult.

- *Syphilis.* If untreated, *syphilis* may affect the brain, the heart, and a developing fetus. It can even be fatal. Syphilis first reveals itself through a small sore at the point of sexual contact. In its secondary stage, it may include a rash. Syphilis can be treated successfully with antibiotics if it is diagnosed early enough.

acquired immune deficiency syndrome (AIDS) A sexually transmitted infection caused by a virus that destroys the body's immune system. (Module 34)

- *AIDS.* In the near past, no sexually transmitted infection has had a greater impact on sexual behavior—and society as a whole—than **acquired immune deficiency syndrome (AIDS).** Although in the United States, AIDS at first was found primarily in gay men, it soon spread to other populations, such as intravenous drug users and heterosexuals. In the United States, AIDS is the seventh leading cause of death among men 25-44 years of age, and 1.8 million people are living with the disease. The worldwide figures are even more daunting: Already, 39 million people have died from AIDS, and people living with the disease number 35 million worldwide (UNAIDS, 2013; Kaiser Family Foundation, 2014).

The spread of AIDS is particularly pronounced among women, who now make up almost half the cases worldwide. Younger women and women of color are particularly vulnerable. For instance, the rate of AIDS diagnosis is around 25 times higher for African American women than for white women and four times higher for Hispanic women. In the United States, young African American men who have sex with men are most seriously affected by AIDS (Quinn & Overbaugh, 2005; CDC, 2013).

The AIDS epidemic led to significant changes in sexual behavior. People are less likely to engage in casual sex with new acquaintances, and the use of condoms during sexual intercourse has increased. Nonetheless, the only foolproof method of avoiding AIDS is total abstinence—an alternative that many people find unrealistic. However, there are several ways to reduce the risk of contracting AIDS as well as other sexually transmitted infections; these methods have come to be called "safer sex" practices:

- *Know your sexual partner—well.* Before having sex with someone, learn about his or her sexual history.

- *Use condoms.* For those in sexual relationships, condoms are the most reliable means of preventing transmission of the AIDS virus.

- *Avoid the exchange of bodily fluids, particularly semen.* In particular, avoid anal intercourse. The AIDS virus can spread through small tears in the rectum, making anal intercourse without condoms particularly dangerous. Oral sex, once thought relatively safe, is now viewed as potentially dangerous.

- *Stay sober.* Using alcohol and drugs impairs judgment and can lead to poor decisions—and it makes using a condom correctly more difficult.

- *Consider the benefits of monogamy.* People in long-term, monogamous relationships with partners who have been faithful are at a lower risk of contracting AIDS.

> ! **Study Alert**
> Use Figure 6 to learn the major types of sexually transmitted infections and their prevalence.

From the perspective of...

A Politician What responsibilities do people who learn they have a sexually transmitted infection have to their sexual partners, and what responsibilities do public health officials have? Should legislation be designed to restrict sexual behavior for those who have sexually transmitted infections?

Exactostock/SuperStock

SEXUAL PROBLEMS

Few people would feel embarrassed by a sprained ankle or broken arm. In contrast, sexual difficulties are often a source of concern and self-consciousness because of the importance that society places on "desirable" sexual conduct. And such difficulties are surprisingly common, with more than 40% of women and about one-third of men experiencing problems associated with sexual performance. Among the most widespread are the disorders we discuss here (Goldstein, 2000; Rosner, 2001).

Erectile disorder is a male's inability to achieve or maintain an erection. The rare case is a male who has never been able to have an erection, and the more common case is a male who, though now unable to have an erection, has had one at least once in the past. Erectile dysfunction is not an uncommon problem, even among younger men—about 5% to 10% of men under 50 have erection problems. It is the rare man who has never experienced it at least once during his lifetime. This is hardly surprising because the ability to achieve and hold an erection is sensitive to alcohol, drugs, performance fears, anxiety, and a host of other factors. Erectile dysfunction becomes a more serious problem when it occurs more than occasionally (Jacob, 2011; Brody & Weiss, 2015; Balon, 2017).

Drugs such as Viagra have brought about significant advances in the treatment of erectile dysfunction and have brought the disorder into the open through a constant barrage of ads on television and in magazines. Viagra treats erectile dysfunction by increasing the flow of blood through a man's penis and producing an erection relatively quickly.

In **premature (early) ejaculation,** a male is unable to delay orgasm as long as he wishes. Because "as long as he wishes" is dependent on a man's—and his partner's—attitudes and opinions about how long is appropriate, this is a difficult disorder to diagnose. Sometimes the problem can be resolved simply by having a male redefine how long he wants to delay ejaculation. Premature ejaculation is most often a psychological problem since there are rarely physical reasons for it. One cause may be early sexual learning: Because sexual experiences during adolescence are often accompanied by a fear of being caught, some men learn early in their lives to reach orgasm as quickly as possible (Sadeghi-Nejad & Watson, 2008; Jannini, McMahon, & Waldinger, 2013; Rastrelli et al., 2019).

Delayed ejaculation disorder occurs when it takes an extended period of sexual stimulation for a male to ejaculate. Delayed ejaculation disorder is only a problem if it causes stress for the male or his partner. Sometimes, learning general relaxation techniques allows men to overcome this difficulty.

In **female orgasmic disorder,** women do not experience orgasm, or the orgasm is delayed or of reduced intensity. In *primary orgasmic dysfunction,* a woman has never experienced orgasm during her lifetime. In *secondary orgasmic dysfunction,* a woman has had an orgasm at some point in her life but no longer does, or she is able to have orgasms only under certain conditions—such as during masturbation—but not during sexual intercourse.

In fact, the lack of orgasm during sexual intercourse is common (despite Hollywood film depictions to the contrary). By far the majority of women report they do not receive sufficient stimulation to reach orgasm during sexual intercourse. Consequently, most scientists today believe that the lack of orgasm during sexual intercourse is not dysfunctional at all but is merely a normal variation of female sexuality (McCabe, 2009; Wallen & Lloyd, 2011).

Finally, **sexual interest/arousal disorder** occurs when the motivation for sexual activity is restrained or lacking entirely. When people with inhibited sexual desire find themselves in circumstances that typically would evoke sexual feelings, they begin to turn off sexually and may even experience a kind of "sexual anesthesia." Ultimately, they may begin to avoid situations of a sexual nature, thereby forgoing intimacy with others (Meston, 2003; Hertlein, Weeks, & Gambescia, 2007; Rosen et al., 2019).

It is important to realize that many of the problems we have discussed turn up at one time or another in most people's sex lives. It is only when these problems persist, cause undue anxiety, and turn sex from play into work that they are cause for concern. Furthermore, treatments for common sexual problems have a good rate of success.

erectile disorder A male's inability to achieve or maintain an erection. (Module 34)

premature (early) ejaculation A male's inability to delay orgasm as long as he wishes. (Module 34)

delayed ejaculation disorder A disorder in which it takes an extended period of sexual stimulation for a male to be able to ejaculate (Module 34)

female orgasmic disorder A female's lack of orgasm. (Module 34)

sexual interest/arousal disorder A sexual dysfunction in which the motivation for sexual activity is restrained or lacking entirely. (Module 34)

BECOMING AN INFORMED CONSUMER
of Psychology

Lowering the Risks of Date Rape

As we have seen, surveys of college students make clear that the greatest danger of rape comes not from unknown assailants but from fellow students. How can one, then, reduce the likelihood of date rape? The following suggestions provide some guidance for women and men (American College Health Association, 2006; Watkins, 2007; Smith et al., 2018):

- Believe in your right to set limits, and communicate those limits clearly, firmly, and early on.
- Say no when you mean no—and if you hear your partner saying no, respect his or her wishes without question.
- Be assertive in refusing to engage in any activity that makes you uncomfortable. Keep in mind that your partner may interpret passivity as permission.
- Be aware of situations in which you may be at risk.
- Keep in mind that others interpret certain kinds of dress as sexually provocative and that not everyone subscribes to the same standards of sexual behavior as you do.
- Keep close tabs on what you are given to drink in social situations; victims of date rape have sometimes been given mind-altering "date-rape" drugs.
- Understand that, in general, alcohol and drugs cloud judgment and hinder communication with your partner.

RECAP/EVALUATE/RETHINK

RECAP

LO 34-1 What is "normal" sexual behavior?

- There are a number of approaches to determining normality: deviation from the average, comparison of sexual behavior with some standard or ideal, and consideration of the psychological and physical consequences of the behavior to the person and to others.

LO 34-2 How do most people behave sexually?

- The frequency of masturbation is high, particularly for males. Although attitudes toward masturbation are increasingly liberal, they have traditionally been negative even though no negative consequences have been detected.
- Heterosexuality, or sexual attraction to members of the other sex, is the most common sexual orientation.
- The double standard by which premarital sex is thought to be more permissible for men than for women has declined, particularly among young people. For many people, the double standard has been

replaced by endorsement of "permissiveness with affection," the view that premarital intercourse is permissible if it occurs in the context of a loving and committed relationship.

- The frequency of marital sex varies widely. However, younger couples tend to have sexual intercourse more frequently than older ones. In addition, most married men and women do not engage in extramarital sex.
- Homosexuals are sexually attracted to members of their own sex; bisexuals are sexually attracted to people of the same sex and the other sex. No explanation for why people become homosexual has been confirmed; among the possibilities are genetic or biological factors, childhood and family influences, and prior learning experiences and conditioning. However, no relationship exists between sexual orientation and psychological adjustment.
- Transgender is a broad term encompassing people whose gender identity, gender expression, or behavior does not conform to the sex to which they were assigned at birth

LO 34-3 How prevalent are rape and other forms of nonconsensual sex, and what are their causes?

- Rape occurs when one person forces another person to submit to sexual activity. Often the victim is acquainted with the rapist. Sexual gratification is sometimes the motivation for rape. More frequently, however, it is power, aggression, or anger.
- Childhood sexual abuse is surprisingly widespread. Most often the perpetrator is an acquaintance or a family member.

LO 34-4 What are the major sexually transmitted infections?

- Acquired immune deficiency syndrome, or AIDS, is bringing about profound changes in people's sexual practices. Other sexually transmitted infections include chlamydia, genital herpes, trichomoniasis, gonorrhea, syphilis, and genital warts.

LO 34-5 What sexual difficulties do people most frequently encounter?

- Among the major sexual problems are erectile disorder, premature (early) ejaculation, delayed ejaculation disorder, female orgasmic disorder, and sexual interest/arousal disorder.

EVALUATE

1. The work carried out by _____ in the late 1930s was the first systematic study of sexual behavior ever undertaken.
2. Although the incidence of masturbation among young adults is high, once men and women become involved in intimate relationships, they typically cease masturbating. True or false?

3. The increase in premarital sex in recent years has been greater for women than for men. True or false?
4. _____ _____ _____ refers to the view that premarital sex is acceptable within a loving, long-term relationship.
5. Research comparing homosexuals and heterosexuals clearly demonstrates that there is no difference in the level of adjustment or psychological functioning between the two groups. True or false?
6. Which of the following is unlikely to be a motivation for the act of rape?
   a. Need for power
   b. Desire for sexual intimacy
   c. Desire for sexual gratification
   d. Anger against women in general
7. Which of the following STIs is the most widespread?
   a. Genital herpes
   b. Gonorrhea
   c. Chlamydia
   d. Syphilis

RETHINK

1. What societal factors have led to a reduction in the double standard by which sexuality in men and women is regarded differently? Do you think the double standard has completely vanished?
2. In what ways might a sample of respondents to a survey about sexual practices be biased? How might bias in such a survey be reduced?

Answers to Evaluate Questions

1. Kinsey; 2. False; even people in married relationships show a continued incidence of masturbation; 3. True; 4. Permissiveness with affection; 5. True; 6. b; 7. c

---

KEY TERMS

masturbation	transgender	acquired immune deficiency syndrome (AIDS)	delayed ejaculation disorder
heterosexuality	rape		
double standard	date rape		female orgasmic disorder
extramarital sex	sexually transmitted infection (STI)	erectile disorder	sexual interest/arousal disorder
homosexuals		premature (early) ejaculation	
bisexuals			

LOOKING *Back*

EPILOGUE

We have seen how psychologists are dealing with the topics of gender and sex, first with regard to gender roles, gender stereotyping, gender schemas, and sexism. Society's expectations regarding male and female characteristics and behaviors lead to inequities in the treatment of men and women in school, the workplace, and the rest of society—inequities that largely favor men.

With regard to sexuality, we discussed the nature of the physical processes that surround sexuality and addressed the controversial issue of "normality" in sexual behavior. We saw the broad diversity of sexual behavior, and we discussed premarital sex and marital sex, as well as heterosexuality, homosexuality, and bisexuality. We also examined rape and other forms of nonconsensual sex, including childhood sexual abuse.

Finally, we looked at the sexual problems that people may have, including STIs and sexual dysfunctions. We explored the nature of these problems and discussed ways to treat and deal with them.

Before we move on to the next chapter, return to the prologue about Sophie Kozub, who transitioned from male to female. Using your knowledge of identity and gender, consider the following questions.

1. What challenges might Kozub experience in living as a transgender woman?
2. What does Kozub's difficulty in integrating her male-typical achievements with her female gender identity say about the experience of gender? Did she have to choose one gender over the other?
3. Can you make assumptions about whether Kozub is sexually attracted to males or to females (or to both, to neither, or to people with blended or ambiguous gender characteristics) from her transition to a transgender woman? Why or why not?

VISUAL SUMMARY 11 Sexuality and Gender

MODULE 32 Gender and Sex

Distinction between gender and sex

Gender: The perception of being male or female

Sex: Refers to sexual anatomy and sexual behavior

Gender Differences: More similar than different

- Large difference in aggressive behavior
- Men view their own abilities and estimates of future success more positively than women do
- No general differences in cognitive abilities

Sources of Gender Differences

- Biological causes suggest a difference in brain structure and functioning

- Socialization experiences produce gender schemas

MODULE 33 Understanding Human Sexual Response: The Facts of Life

Basic Biology of Sexual Behavior

- Puberty
  - Boys: Testes begin to secrete androgens
  - Girls: Ovaries begin to produce estrogen and progesterone

- Men and women differ in hormone production and perhaps differ in sex drive
- Sexual responsiveness includes excitement, plateau, orgasm, resolution, refractory period

(a) Male pattern   (b) Female patterns

MODULE 34 The Diversity of Sexual Behavior

Approaches to Sexual Normality

- Sexual behaviors may be abnormal when they negatively impact a person's well-being or hurt someone else

Sexual Behavior

- Masturbation: widely viewed as healthy, legitimate, and harmless
- Heterosexuality: sexual attraction to the other sex
- Premarital sex: permissible for men but not for women, which is a double standard
- Homosexuality: sexual attraction to one's own sex

0	1	2	3	4	5	6
Exclusive heterosexual behavior	Primarily heterosexual, but incidents of homosexual behavior	Primarily heterosexual, but more than incidental homosexual behavior	Equal amounts of heterosexual and homosexual behavior	Primarily homosexual, but more than incidental heterosexual behavior	Primarily homosexual, but incidents of heterosexual behavior	Exclusively homosexual behavior

- Bisexuality: sexual attraction to one's own gender as well as other genders
- Transgender: refers to persons whose gender identity, gender expression, or behavior does not conform to that associated with the sex to which they were assigned at birth

Sexual Difficulties

- Rape: forced sexual activities without consent
- Childhood sexual abuse: often committed by relative or acquaintance
- One in five people in the United States: infected with an STI

Sexual disorders

- Erectile dysfunction
- Premature ejaculation
- Delayed ejaculation disorder
- Female orgasmic disorder
- Inhibited sexual desire

(Module 32, photo) Nirut Saelim/123RF; Stockbyte/Getty Images (Module 33) Source: Masters, William H., Virginia E. Johnson. Human sexual response. Boston: Little, Brown, 1966. (Module 34) Source: Kinsey, Alfred Charles, Wardell Baxter Pomeroy, and Clyde Eugene Martin. Sexual behavior in the human male. Philadelphia: Saunders, 1948.; Source: Centers for Disease Control and Prevention. "Incidence, Prevalence, and Cost of Sexually Transmitted Infections in the United States." https://www.cdc.gov/.

Nancy Mao Smith/Shutterstock

CHAPTER 12
Development

LEARNING OUTCOMES FOR CHAPTER 12

LO 39-1 What are the principal kinds of physical, social, and intellectual changes that occur in early and middle adulthood, and what are their causes?

LO 39-2 How does the reality of late adulthood differ from the stereotypes about that period?

LO 39-3 How can we adjust to death?

PROLOGUE *TEST TUBE PIONEERS*

When Elizabeth Carr and Louise Brown first met on stage at the Midwest Reproductive Symposium International in Chicago, the two women already shared a powerful bond. Both were celebrities of sorts at the conference they were attending, and both had been famous from the moment of their birth. In 1981, Elizabeth was the first person in the United States born via in-vitro fertilization, and in 1978, Louise was the first one in the entire world.

Both women had life experiences that only the other could really understand. They were media sensations as babies, infantile pioneers in an entirely new high-tech method of human reproduction. Conceived from eggs and sperm cells in a laboratory and implanted in their mothers' uteruses as embryos, their very existence inspired curiosity and controversy.

Physicians studied them closely for the slightest indication of any abnormality to verify that the procedure was truly viable, while strangers debated whether their scientifically assisted contraception was even ethical. After all, the very idea was unheard of at the time, and people knew next to nothing about it.

Today, both women are mothers of their own children and lead normal lives—except on rare occasions when they are stars at reproductive health conferences (Schencker, 2017).

LOOKING *Ahead*

It used to be simpler. People came into the world in one basic way: a man's sperm fertilized a woman's egg, and the resulting embryo developed over the course of 9 months into an infant. Today, scientists, motivated by the desire to help people for whom the basics aren't working, have developed a range of techniques to give the fertilization and birth process a helping hand.

Developmental psychology is the branch of psychology that studies the patterns of growth and change that occur throughout life. It deals with issues ranging from new ways of conceiving children, to learning how to raise children most sensibly, to understanding the milestones of life that we all face.

Developmental psychologists study the interaction between the unfolding of biologically predetermined patterns of behavior and a constantly changing, dynamic environment. They ask how our genetic background affects our behavior throughout our lives and whether heredity limits our potential. Similarly, they seek to understand the ways in which the environment works with—or against—our genetic capabilities, how the world we live in affects our development, and how we can be encouraged to reach our full potential.

We begin by examining the approaches psychologists use to study development change across the life span. Then we consider the very start of development, beginning with conception and the 9 months of life before birth. We look at both genetic and environmental influences on the unborn individual and the way they can affect behavior throughout the remainder of the life cycle.

Next, we examine development that occurs after birth: the enormous and rapid growth that takes place during the early stages of life and the physical, social, and cognitive change throughout infancy, toddlerhood, and middle childhood. We then move on to development from adolescence through adulthood and end with a discussion of the ways in which people prepare themselves for death.

Module 35
Nature and Nurture: The Enduring Developmental Issue

LEARNING OUTCOMES

LO 35-1 How do psychologists study the degree to which development is an interaction of hereditary and environmental factors?

How many bald, 6-foot-6, 250-pound volunteer firefighters in New Jersey wear droopy mustaches, aviator-style eyeglasses, and a key ring on the right side of the belt? The answer is two: Gerald Levey and Mark Newman. They are twins who were separated at birth. Neither twin even knew the other existed until they were reunited–in a fire station–by a fellow firefighter who knew Newman and was startled to see his double, Levey, at a firefighters' convention.

The lives of the twins, although separate, took remarkably similar paths. Levey went to college and studied forestry; Newman planned to study forestry in college but instead took a job trimming trees. Both had jobs in supermarkets. One had a job installing sprinkler systems; the other installed fire alarms.

Both men are unmarried and find the same kind of woman–"tall, slender, long hair"–attractive. They share similar hobbies and enjoy hunting, fishing, going to the beach, and watching old John Wayne movies and professional wrestling. Both like Chinese food and drink the same brand of beer. Their mannerisms are also similar–for example, each one throws his head back when he laughs. And, of course, there is one more thing: They share a passion for fighting fires.

The similarities we see in twins Gerald Levey and Mark Newman vividly raise one of the fundamental questions posed by **developmental psychology,** the study of the patterns of growth and change that occur throughout life. The question is this: How can we distinguish between the *environmental* causes of behavior (the influence of parents, siblings, family, friends, schooling, nutrition, and all the other experiences to which a child is exposed) and *hereditary* causes (those based on an individual's genetic

developmental psychology The branch of psychology that studies the patterns of growth and change that occur throughout life. (Module 35)

Identical twins Mark Newman (left) and Gerald Levey (right), who were separated at birth and reunited 31 years later. They are shown with researcher Dr. Nancy Segal, co-director of the Twins Reared Apart study.

AP Images

makeup that influence growth and development throughout life)? This question embodies the **nature-nurture issue.** In this context, nature refers to hereditary factors, and nurture refers to environmental influences.

Although the question was first posed as a nature-*versus*-nurture issue, developmental psychologists today agree that *both* nature and nurture interact to produce specific developmental patterns and outcomes. Consequently, the question has evolved into this: *How and to what degree* do environment and heredity both produce their effects? No one develops free of environmental influences or without being affected by his or her inherited *genetic makeup*. However, the debate over the comparative influence of the two factors remains active; different approaches and different theories of development emphasize the environment or heredity to a greater or lesser degree (Perovic & Radenovic, 2011; Gruber, 2013; Limberg, 2015).

For example, some developmental theories rely on basic psychological principles of learning and stress the role learning plays in producing changes in a developing child's behavior. Such theories emphasize the role of the environment in development. In contrast, other developmental theories emphasize the influence of one's physiological makeup and functioning on development. Such theories stress the role of heredity and *maturation*–the unfolding of biologically predetermined patterns of behavior–in producing developmental change. Maturation can be seen, for instance, in the development of sex characteristics (such as breasts and body hair) that occurs at the start of adolescence.

Furthermore, the work of *behavioral geneticists*, who study the effects of heredity on behavior, and the theories of evolutionary psychologists, who identify behavior patterns that result from our genetic inheritance, have influenced developmental psychologists. Behavioral geneticists are finding increasing evidence that cognitive abilities, personality traits, sexual orientation, and psychological disorders are determined to some extent by genetic factors (Schermer et al., 2011; Krüger, Korsten, & Hoffman, 2017; Burt, Plaisance, & Hambrick, 2019).

Behavioral genetics lies at the heart of the nature-nurture question. Although no one would argue that our behavior is determined *solely* by inherited factors, evidence collected by behavioral geneticists does suggest that our genetic inheritance predisposes us to respond in particular ways to our environment and even to seek out particular kinds of environments (Bienvenu, Davydow, & Kendler, 2011; Barnes & Jacobs, 2013; Majlesi et al., 2019).

Despite their differences over theory, developmental psychologists concur on some points. They agree that genetic factors not only provide the potential for specific behaviors or traits to emerge but also place limitations on the emergence of such behavior or traits. For instance, heredity defines people's general level of intelligence and sets an upper limit that–regardless of the quality of the environment–people cannot exceed. Heredity also places limits on physical abilities; humans simply cannot run at a speed of 60 miles an hour or grow as tall as 10 feet, no matter the quality of their environment (Dodge, 2004; Pinker, 2004; Loehlin et al., 2015).

Figure 1 lists some of the characteristics most affected by heredity. As you consider these items, keep in mind that these characteristics are not *entirely* determined by heredity because environmental factors also play a role.

Developmental psychologists also agree that in most instances, environmental factors play a critical role in enabling people to reach the potential capabilities that their genetic background makes possible. If Albert Einstein had received no intellectual stimulation as a child and had not been sent to school, it is unlikely that he would have reached his genetic potential. Similarly, a great athlete such as baseball star Derek Jeter would have been unlikely to display much physical skill if he had not been raised in an environment that nurtured his innate talent and gave him the opportunity to train and perfect his natural abilities.

Clearly, the relationship between heredity and environment is complex. Therefore, developmental psychologists typically take an *interactionist* position on the nature-nurture issue by suggesting that a combination of hereditary and environmental factors influences development. Developmental psychologists face the challenge of identifying

nature-nurture issue The issue of the degree to which environment and heredity influence behavior. (Module 35)

Study Alert

The nature–nurture issue is a key question that is pervasive throughout the field of psychology. It explores how and to what degree environment and heredity produce their joint effects.

FIGURE 1 Characteristics influenced significantly by genetic factors. Although these characteristics have strong genetic components, they are also affected by environmental factors.

Physical Characteristics	Intellectual Characteristics	Emotional Characteristics and Disorders
Height	Memory	Shyness
Weight	Intelligence	Extraversion
Obesity	Age of	Emotionality
Tone of voice	language	Neuroticism
Blood pressure	acquisition	Schizophrenia
Tooth decay	Reading	Anxiety
Athletic ability	disability	Alcoholism
Firmness of	Intellectual	
handshake	disabilities	
Age of death		
Activity level		

the relative strength of each of these influences on the individual as well as that of identifying the specific changes that occur over the course of development (McGregor & Capone, 2004; Moffitt, Caspi, & Rutter, 2006; Steinbeis et al., 2017).

Determining the Relative Influence of Nature and Nurture

Developmental psychologists use several approaches to determine the relative influence of genetic and environmental factors on behavior. In one approach, researchers can experimentally control the genetic makeup of laboratory animals by carefully breeding them for specific traits. For instance, by observing animals with identical genetic backgrounds placed in varied environments, researchers can learn the effects of specific kinds of environmental stimulation. Although researchers must be careful when generalizing the findings of nonhuman research to a human population, findings from animal research provide important information that cannot be obtained for ethical reasons by using human participants.

Human twins serve as another important source of information about the relative effects of genetic and environmental factors. **Identical twins** are genetically identical; they share the same genes and look alike. If identical twins display different patterns of development, those differences have to be attributed to variations in the environment in which the twins were raised. The most useful data come from identical twins (such as Gerald Levey and Mark Newman) who are adopted at birth by different sets of adoptive parents and raised apart in differing environments. Studies of nontwin siblings who are raised in totally different environments also shed some light on the issue. Because they have relatively similar genetic backgrounds, siblings who show similarities as adults provide strong evidence for the importance of heredity (Farnsworth, 2015; Wertz et al., 2019).

Researchers can also take the opposite tack. Instead of concentrating on people with similar genetic backgrounds who are raised in different environments, they may consider people raised in similar environments who have totally dissimilar genetic backgrounds. For example, if they find similar courses of development in two adopted children who have different genetic backgrounds and have been raised in the same family, they have evidence for the importance of environmental influences on development. Moreover, psychologists can carry out research involving animals with dissimilar genetic backgrounds; by experimentally varying the environment in which the animals are raised, they can determine the influence of environmental factors (independent of heredity) on development (Petrill & Deater-Deckard, 2004; Beam & Turkheimer, 2013; Tosto et al., 2017).

identical twins Twins who are genetically identical. (Module 35)

Developmental Research Techniques

Because of the demands of measuring behavioral change across different ages, developmental researchers use several unique methods. The most frequently used, **cross-sectional research,** compares people of different ages at the same point in time. Cross-sectional studies provide information about differences in development between different age groups (Card, 2017; Damian et al., 2019).

Suppose, for instance, we were interested in the development of intellectual ability in adulthood. To carry out a cross-sectional study, we might compare a sample of 25-, 45-, and 65-year-olds who all take the same IQ test. We then can determine whether average IQ test scores differ in each age group.

Cross-sectional research has limitations, however. For instance, we cannot be sure that the differences in IQ scores we might find in our example are due to age differences alone. Instead, the scores may reflect differences in the educational attainment of the cohorts represented. A *cohort* is a group of people who grow up at similar times, in similar places, and in similar conditions. In the case of IQ differences, any age differences we find in a cross-sectional study may reflect educational differences among the cohorts studied: People in the older age group may belong to a cohort that was less likely to attend college than were the people in the younger groups.

A longitudinal study, the second major research strategy developmental psychologists use, provides one way around this problem. **Longitudinal research** assesses the behavior of one or more participants as the participants get older. Longitudinal studies assess *change* in behavior over time, whereas cross-sectional studies assess *differences* among groups of people.

For instance, consider how we might investigate intellectual development during adulthood by using a longitudinal research strategy. First, we might give an IQ test to a group of 25-year-olds. We'd then come back to the same people 20 years later and retest them at age 45. Finally, we'd return to them once more when they were 65 years old and test them again.

By examining changes at several points in time, we can see how individuals develop. Clearly, though, longitudinal research has some drawbacks. First, it requires a significant expenditure of time as the researcher waits for the participants to get older. In addition, participants who begin a study at an early age may drop out, move away, or die as the research continues. Moreover, participants who take the same test at several points in time may become "test-wise" and perform better each time they take it just because they have become more familiar with the test. Still, longitudinal research is an important technique of developmental researchers.

cross-sectional research A research method that compares people of different ages at the same point in time. (Module 35)

longitudinal research A research method that investigates behavior as participants get older. (Module 35)

Study Alert
Be sure to be able to distinguish the two different types of developmental research: cross-sectional (comparing people of different ages at the same time) and longitudinal (studying participants as they age).

RECAP/EVALUATE/RETHINK

RECAP

LO 35-1 How do psychologists study the degree to which development is an interaction of hereditary and environmental factors?

- Developmental psychology studies growth and change throughout life. One fundamental question is how much developmental change is due to heredity and how much is due to environment—the nature–nurture issue. Heredity seems to define the upper limits of our growth and change, whereas the environment affects the degree to which the upper limits are reached.

- Cross-sectional research compares people of different ages with one another at the same point in time. In contrast, longitudinal research traces the behavior of one or more participants as the participants become older.

EVALUATE

1. Developmental psychologists are interested in the effects of both _____ and _____ on development.
2. Environment and heredity both influence development, with genetic potentials generally establishing limits on environmental influences. True or false?

3. By observing genetically similar animals in differing environments, we can increase our understanding of the influences of hereditary and environmental factors in humans. True or false?

4. _____ research studies the same individuals over a period of time, whereas _____ _____ research studies people of different ages at the same time.

RETHINK

1. When researchers find similarities in development between very different cultures, what implications might such findings have for the nature–nurture issue?

2. Consider the factors that might determine when a child learns to walk. What kinds of environmental influences might be involved? What kinds of genetic influences might be involved?

Answers to Evaluate Questions

1. heredity (or nature), environment (or nurture); 2. True; 3. True; 4. Longitudinal, cross-sectional

KEY TERMS

developmental psychology   nature–nurture issue   cross-sectional research   longitudinal research

Module 36
Prenatal Development: Conception to Birth

Leah and John Howard's joy at learning Leah was pregnant turned to anxiety when Leah's doctor discovered that her brother had died from Duchenne muscular dystrophy (DMD) at age 12. The disease, the doctor explained, was an X-linked inherited disorder. If Leah turned out to be a carrier, there was a 50% chance that the baby would inherit the disease if it were male. The doctor advised them to have an ultrasound to determine the baby's sex. It turned out to be a boy.

The Howards faced two options. The doctor could take a chorion villus sampling now or wait a month and perform an amniocentesis. Both carried a very low risk for miscarriage. Leah chose amniocentesis, but the results were inconclusive. The doctor then suggested a fetal muscle biopsy to confirm the presence or lack of the muscle protein dystrophin. The absence of dystrophin would signal DMD. The risk of miscarriage, however, was not inconsiderable.

Four months pregnant at this point and tired of the worries and tears, Leah and John decided to take their chances and look forward to their baby's birth.

The Howards' case shows the difficult choices that parents may encounter due to our increasing understanding of life spent inside a mother's womb.

Yet, our knowledge of the biology of *conception*—when a male's sperm cell penetrates a female's egg cell—and its aftermath makes the start of life no less of a miracle. Let's consider how an individual is created by looking first at the genetic endowment that a child receives at the moment of conception.

The Basics of Genetics

The one-cell entity established at conception contains 23 pairs of **chromosomes,** rod-shaped structures that contain all basic hereditary information. One member of each pair is from the mother, and the other is from the father.

Each chromosome contains thousands of **genes**—smaller units through which genetic information is transmitted. Either individually or in combination, genes produce each person's particular characteristics. Composed of sequences of *DNA (deoxyribonucleic acid)* molecules, genes are the biological equivalent of "software" that programs the future development of all parts of the body's hardware. Humans have some 25,000 different genes (see Figure 1).

Some genes control the development of systems common to all members of the human species—the heart, circulatory system, brain, lungs, and so forth; others shape the characteristics that make each human unique, such as facial configuration, height, and eye color. The child's sex is also determined by a particular combination of genes. Specifically, a child inherits an X chromosome from its mother and either an X or a Y chromosome from its father. When it receives an XX combination, it is a female; with an XY combination, it develops as a male. Male development is triggered by a single gene on the Y chromosome; without the presence of that specific gene, the individual will develop as a female (see Figure 2).

As behavioral geneticists have discovered, genes are also at least partially responsible for a wide variety of personal characteristics, including cognitive abilities, personality

LEARNING OUTCOMES

LO 36-1 What is the nature of development before birth?

LO 36-2 What factors can affect a child during the mother's pregnancy?

chromosomes Rod-shaped structures that contain all basic hereditary information. (Module 36)

genes The parts of the chromosomes through which genetic information is transmitted. (Module 36)

Study Alert

It's important to understand the basic building blocks of genetics: chromosomes, which contain genes, which in turn are composed of sequences of DNA.

(a) Conception   (b) 23 pairs of chromosomes   (c) DNA sequence   (d) Genes

FIGURE 1 One's characteristics are determined by specific genetic information. (a) At the moment of conception, (b) humans receive 23 pairs of chromosomes, half from the mother and half from the father. (c) These chromosomes are made up of sequences of DNA. (d) Each chromosome contains thousands of genes that "program" the future development of the body.

(a): MedicalRF.com; (b): L. Willatt/East Anglian Regional Genetics Service/Science Source; (c): Double Brain/Shutterstock; (d): Biophoto Associates/Science Source

traits, and psychological disorders. Of course, few of these characteristics are determined by a single gene. Instead, most traits result from a combination of multiple genes that operate together with environmental influences (Armbruster et al., 2011; Kazantseva et al., 2015; Weinschenk et al., 2019).

THE HUMAN GENOME PROJECT

Our understanding of genetics took a giant leap forward in 2001, when scientists were able to map the specific location and sequence of every human gene as part of the massive *Human Genome Project*. The accomplishment was one of the most important

FIGURE 2 When an egg and a sperm meet at the moment of fertilization, the egg provides an X chromosome, and the sperm provides either an X or a Y chromosome. If the sperm contributes an X chromosome, the child will have an XX pairing on the 23rd chromosome and will be a girl. If the sperm contributes a Y chromosome, the result will be an XY pairing—a boy.

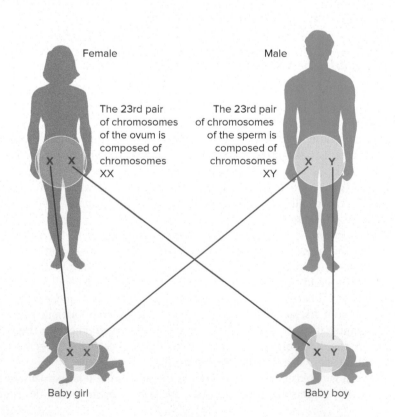

in the history of biology (International Human Genome Sequencing Consortium, 2003; Grigorenko & Dozier, 2013; Özdemir et al., 2017).

The success of the Human Genome Project started a revolution in health care because scientists can identify the particular genes responsible for genetically caused disorders. It is already leading not only to the identification of risk factors in children but also to the development of new treatments for physical and psychological disorders.

The Earliest Development

When an egg becomes fertilized by the sperm, the resulting one-celled entity, called a **zygote,** immediately begins to develop. The zygote starts out as a microscopic speck. Three days after fertilization, though, the zygote increases to around 32 cells; within a week, it has grown to 100-150 cells. These first 2 weeks are known as the *germinal period.*

Two weeks after conception, the developing individual enters the *embryonic period,* which lasts from week 2 through week 8; he or she is now called an **embryo.** As an embryo develops through an intricate, preprogrammed process of cell division, it grows 10,000 times larger by 4 weeks of age and attains a length of about one-fifth of an inch. At this point, it has developed a rudimentary beating heart, a brain, an intestinal tract, and a number of other organs. Although all these organs are at a primitive stage of development, they are clearly recognizable. Moreover, by week 8, the embryo is about an inch long and has discernible arms, legs, and a face.

From week 8 and continuing until birth, the developing individual enters the *fetal period* and is called a **fetus.** At the start of this period, it begins to respond to touch; it bends its fingers when touched on the hand. At 16 to 18 weeks, its movements become strong enough for the mother to sense them. At the same time, hair may begin to grow on its head, and the facial features become similar to those the child will display at birth. The major organs begin functioning, although the fetus could not be kept alive outside the mother. In addition, a lifetime's worth of brain neurons are produced—although it is unclear whether the brain is capable of thinking at this early stage.

Within the womb, the fetus continues to develop before birth. It begins to grow fatty deposits under the skin, and it gains weight. The fetus reaches the **age of viability,** the point at which it can survive if born prematurely, at about prenatal age 22 weeks. By week 24, a fetus has many of the characteristics it will display as a newborn. In fact, when an infant is born prematurely at this age, it can open and close its eyes; suck; cry; look up, down, and around; and even grasp objects placed in its hands.

zygote The new cell formed by the union of an egg and sperm. (Module 36)

embryo A developed zygote that has a heart, a brain, and other organs. (Module 36)

fetus A developing individual from 8 weeks after conception until birth. (Module 36)

age of viability The point at which a fetus can survive if born prematurely. (Module 36)

These remarkable photos of live fetuses display the degree of physical development at prenatal ages 5 and 15 weeks.
(left): Steve Allen/Science Source; (right): Claude Edelmann/Science Source

At prenatal age 28 weeks, the fetus weighs less than 3 pounds and is about 16 inches long. It may be capable of learning: One study found that the infants of mothers who had repeatedly read aloud *The Cat in the Hat* by Dr. Seuss before the infants' birth preferred the sound of that particular story to other stories after they were born (Spence & DeCasper, 1982; Del Giudice, 2011; Moon, Lagercrantz, & Kuhl, 2013).

Before birth, a fetus passes through several *sensitive periods*. A sensitive period is the time when organisms are particularly susceptible to certain kinds of stimuli. For example, fetuses are especially affected by their mothers' use of drugs during certain sensitive periods before birth. If they are exposed to a particular drug before or after the sensitive period, it may have relatively little impact; if exposure comes during a sensitive period, the impact will be significant (Werker & Tees, 2005; Uylings, 2006; Sandman, 2015).

Sensitive periods can also occur after birth. Some language specialists suggest, for instance, that there is a period in which children are particularly receptive to developing language. If children are not exposed to appropriate linguistic stimuli, their language development may be impaired (Sohr-Preston & Scaramella, 2006; Opendak, Gould, & Sullivan, 2017; Dunn et al., 2019).

From the perspective of...

An Educator How would you use your knowledge of sensitive periods in language development to improve students' learning? Would you want to teach children more than one language during this time?

Andersen Ross/Blend Images/Getty Images

In the final weeks of pregnancy, the fetus continues to gain weight and grow. At the end of the normal 38 weeks of pregnancy, the fetus typically weighs 7 pounds and is about 20 inches in length. However, the story is different for *preterm infants,* who are born before week 38. Because they have not been able to develop fully, they are at higher risk for illness, future problems, and even death. For infants who have been in the womb for more than 30 weeks, the prospects are relatively good. However, for those born before week 30, the story is often less positive. Such newborns, who may weigh as little as 2 pounds at birth, are in grave danger because they have immature organs; they have less than a 50-50 chance of survival. If they do survive—and it takes extraordinarily heroic (and expensive) medical intervention to ensure this—they may later experience significant developmental delays.

GENETIC INFLUENCES ON THE FETUS

The process of fetal growth that we have just described reflects normal development, which occurs in 95–98% of all pregnancies. Some individuals are less fortunate; in the remaining 2–5% of cases, children are born with serious birth defects. A major cause of such defects is faulty genes or chromosomes. Here are some of the more common genetic and chromosomal difficulties.

- *Phenylketonuria (PKU).* A child born with the inherited disease phenylketonuria cannot produce an enzyme that is required for normal development. This deficiency results in an accumulation of poisons that eventually cause profound intellectual disability. The disease is treatable, however, if it is caught early. Most infants today are routinely tested for PKU, and children with the disorder can be placed on a special diet that allows them to develop normally (Widaman, 2009; Romani et al., 2017; Canton et al., 2019).

- *Sickle-cell anemia.* About 10% of the African American population has the possibility of passing on sickle-cell anemia, a disease that gets its name from the abnormally shaped red blood cells it causes. Children with the disease may have episodes of pain, yellowish eyes, stunted growth, and vision problems (Selove, 2007; Wills, 2013).

- *Tay-Sachs disease.* Children born with Tay-Sachs disease, a disorder most often found in Jews of Eastern European ancestry, usually die by age 3 or 4 because of the body's inability to break down fat. If both parents carry the genetic defect that produces the fatal illness, their child has a 1 in 4 chance of being born with the disease (Weinstein, 2007; Zhang et al., 2019).

- *Down syndrome.* Down syndrome, one of the causes of intellectual disability, occurs when the zygote receives an extra chromosome at the moment of conception. Down syndrome is often related to the mother's age; mothers over 35 stand a higher risk than do other women of having a child with the syndrome (Sherman et al., 2007; Nærland et al., 2017).

PRENATAL ENVIRONMENTAL INFLUENCES

Genetic factors are not the only causes of difficulties in fetal development. Environmental influences—the *nurture* part of the nature-nurture equation—also affect the fetus. Some of the more profound consequences are brought about by **teratogens,** environmental agents such as a drug, chemical, virus, or other factor that produce a birth defect. Among the major prenatal environmental influences on the fetus are the following:

teratogens Environmental agents such as a drug, chemical, virus, or other factor that produce a birth defect. (Module 36)

- *Mother's nutrition.* What a mother eats during her pregnancy can have important implications for the health of her baby. Seriously undernourished mothers cannot provide adequate nutrition to a growing fetus, and they are likely to give birth to underweight babies. Poorly nourished babies are also more susceptible to disease, and a lack of nourishment may have an adverse impact on their mental development (Nyaradi et al., 2013; Carmichael et al., 2019).

- *Mother's illness.* Even minor illnesses that a mother catches during the early months of pregnancy can have devastating consequences for a developing fetus. For example, contracting rubella (German measles), syphilis, diabetes, and high blood pressure may produce permanent, lifelong effects on the fetus (Magoni et al., 2005; Mirambo et al., 2019).

- *Mother's emotional state.* A mother's emotional state affects her baby. Mothers who are anxious and tense during the last months of their pregnancies are more apt to have irritable infants who sleep and eat poorly. The reason? The autonomic nervous system of the fetus becomes especially sensitive as a result of chemical changes produced by the mother's emotional state (Hollins, 2007; Kumari & Joshi, 2013).

- *Mother's use of drugs.* Mothers who take illegal, physically addictive drugs such as cocaine run the risk of giving birth to babies who are similarly addicted. Their newborns suffer painful withdrawal symptoms and sometimes show permanent physical and mental impairment. Even legal drugs taken by a pregnant woman (who may not know that she has become pregnant) can have a tragic effect (Singer & Richardson, 2011; Nygaard et al., 2017).

- *Alcohol.* Alcohol is extremely dangerous to fetal development. For example, as many as 1.5 out of every 1,000 infants are born with *fetal alcohol syndrome disorder (FASD),* a condition resulting in below-average intelligence, growth delays, and facial deformities. FASD is now the primary preventable cause of intellectual disability. Even mothers who use small amounts of alcohol during pregnancy place their child at risk (Niccols, 2007; Murthy et al., 2009; Lewis et al., 2015).

FIGURE 3 A variety of environmental factors can play a role in prenatal development.

Environmental Factor	Possible Effect on Prenatal Development
Rubella (German measles)	Blindness, deafness, heart abnormalities, stillbirth
Syphilis	Intellectual disability, physical deformities, maternal miscarriage
Addictive drugs	Low birth weight, addiction of infant to drug, with possible death after birth from withdrawal
Nicotine	Premature birth, low birth weight and length
Alcohol	Intellectual disability, lower-than-average birth weight, small head, limb deformities
Radiation from X-rays	Physical deformities, intellectual disability
Inadequate diet	Reduction in growth of brain, smaller-than-average weight and length at birth
Mother's age—younger than 18 at birth of child	Premature birth, increased incidence of Down syndrome
Mother's age—older than 35 at birth of child	Increased incidence of Down syndrome
DES (diethylstilbestrol)	Reproductive difficulties and increased incidence of genital cancer in children of mothers who were given DES during pregnancy to prevent miscarriage
AIDS	Possible spread of AIDS virus to infant; facial deformities; growth failure
Accutane	Intellectual disability and physical deformities

- *Nicotine use.* Pregnant mothers who smoke put their children at considerable risk. Smoking while pregnant can lead to miscarriage and infant death. For children who do survive, the negative consequences of mother's tobacco use can last a lifetime (Rogers, 2009; Magee et al., 2013; Zambrano-Sánchez et al., 2019).

Several other environmental factors have an impact on the child before and during birth (see Figure 3). Keep in mind, however, that although we have been discussing the influences of genetics and environment separately, neither factor works alone. Furthermore, despite the emphasis here on some of the ways in which development can go wrong, the vast majority of births occur without difficulty. And in most instances, subsequent development also proceeds normally.

ALTERNATIVE PATHS TO CONCEPTION

For most couples, conception is routine, and pregnancy unfolds without incident. In other cases, though, conception represents a major challenge. Sometimes infertility, the inability to become pregnant, results because the male produces too few sperm. In other cases, it is due to the advanced age of the parents, use of drugs, or previous cases of sexually transmitted infection.

Scientists have devised several remedies to overcome infertility. One option is *in vitro fertilization (IVF)*. IVF is a procedure in which a woman's eggs are removed from her ovaries, and a man's sperm is used to fertilize the eggs in a laboratory. A fertilized egg is then implanted in a woman's uterus. Similarly, *gamete intrafallopian transfer (GIFT)* and *zygote intrafallopian transfer (ZIFT)* are procedures in which an egg and sperm or fertilized egg are implanted in a woman's fallopian tubes. In IVF, GIFT, and ZIFT, the fertilized egg typically is implanted in the woman who provided the eggs. In some cases, eggs are implanted in a *surrogate mother,* a woman who agrees to carry the child to term.

RECAP/EVALUATE/RETHINK

RECAP

LO 36-1 What is the nature of development before birth?

- Each chromosome contains genes through which genetic information is transmitted. Genes, which are composed of DNA sequences, are the "software" that programs the future development of the body's hardware.
- Genes affect not only physical attributes but also a wide array of personal characteristics such as cognitive abilities, personality traits, and psychological disorders.
- At the moment of conception, a male's sperm cell and a female's egg cell unite; each contributes to the new individual's genetic makeup. The union of sperm and egg produces a zygote, which contains 23 pairs of chromosomes; one member of each pair comes from the father, and the other comes from the mother.
- After 2 weeks, the zygote becomes an embryo. By week 8, the embryo is called a fetus and is responsive to touch and other stimulation. At about week 22, it reaches the age of viability, which means it may survive if born prematurely. A fetus is normally born after 38 weeks of pregnancy; it weighs around 7 pounds and measures about 20 inches.

LO 36-2 What factors can affect a child during the mother's pregnancy?

- Genetic abnormalities produce birth defects such as phenylketonuria (PKU), sickle-cell anemia, Tay-Sachs disease, and Down syndrome.
- Among the environmental influences on fetal growth are the mother's nutrition, illnesses, and drug intake.

EVALUATE

1. Match each of the following terms with its definition:

   1. Zygote
   2. Gene
   3. Chromosome

   a. Smallest unit through which genetic information is passed
   b. Fertilized egg
   c. Rod-shaped structure containing genetic information

2. Specific kinds of growth must take place during a _____ period if the embryo is to develop normally.

3. A _____ is an environmental agent such as a drug, chemical, virus, or other factor that produces a birth defect.

RETHINK

1. Given the possible effects of the environment on a developing fetus, do you think pregnant women should be prosecuted for the use of alcohol and other drugs that may do serious harm to their unborn children? Defend your position.

2. What sort of policy might you create to deal with the notification of persons who have genetically based disorders that can be identified by genetic testing? Would your policy treat potentially fatal disorders differently from less serious ones? Would it make a distinction between treatable and nontreatable disorders?

Answers to Evaluate Questions

1. 1-b, 2-a, 3-c; 2. critical; 3. teratogen

KEY TERMS

chromosomes	zygote	fetus	teratogens
genes	embryo	age of viability	

Module 37
Infancy and Childhood

neonate A newborn child. (Module 37)

His head was molded into a long melon shape and came to a point at the back. . . . He was covered with a thick greasy white material known as "vernix," which made him slippery to hold and also allowed him to slip easily through the birth canal. In addition to a shock of black hair on his head, his body was covered with dark, fine hair known as "lanugo." His ears, his back, his shoulders, and even his cheeks were furry. . . . His skin was wrinkled and quite loose, ready to scale in creased places such as his feet and hands. . . . His ears were pressed to his head in unusual positions—one ear was matted firmly forward on his cheek. His nose was flattened and pushed to one side by the squeeze as he came through the pelvis. (Brazelton, 1969)

What kind of creature is this? Although the description hardly fits that of the adorable babies seen in advertisements for baby food, we are in fact talking about a normal, completely developed child just after the moment of birth. Called a **neonate,** a newborn arrives in the world in a form that hardly meets the standards of beauty against which we typically measure babies. Yet ask any parents: Nothing is more beautiful or exciting than the first glimpse of their newborn.

The Extraordinary Newborn

Several factors cause a neonate's strange appearance. The trip through the mother's birth canal may have squeezed the incompletely formed bones of the skull together and squashed the nose into the head. Also, the skin of newborns may be slippery because it secretes *vernix*, a white, greasy covering, for protection before birth. In addition, the baby may have *lanugo*, a soft fuzz, over the entire body for a similar purpose. And the infant's eyelids may be puffy with an accumulation of fluids because of the upside-down position during birth.

All these features change during the first 2 weeks of life as the neonate takes on a more familiar appearance. Even more impressive are the capabilities a neonate begins to display from the moment of birth—capabilities that grow at an astounding rate over the ensuing months.

reflexes Unlearned, involuntary responses that occur automatically in the presence of certain stimuli. (Module 37)

REFLEXES

A neonate is born with a number of **reflexes**—unlearned, involuntary responses that occur automatically in the presence of certain stimuli. Critical for survival, many of those reflexes unfold naturally as part of an infant's ongoing maturation. The *rooting reflex*, for instance, causes neonates to turn their heads toward things that touch their cheeks—such as the mother's nipple or a bottle. Similarly, a *sucking reflex* prompts infants to suck at things that touch their lips. Among other reflexes are a *gag reflex* (to clear the throat), the *startle reflex* (a series of movements in which an infant flings out the arms, fans the fingers, and arches the back in response to a sudden noise), and the *Babinski reflex* (a baby's toes fan out when the outer edge of the sole of the foot is stroked).

Infants lose these primitive reflexes after the first few months of life and replace them with more complex and organized

Many of the reflexes that a neonate is born with are critical for survival and unfold naturally as a part of the infant's ongoing maturation. Do you think humans have more or fewer reflexes than other animals?
Emma Kim/Cultura/Getty Images

| 3.2 months: rolling over | 3.3 months: grasping rattle | 5.9 months: sitting without support | 7.2 months: standing while holding on | 8.2 months: grasping with thumb and finger |

| 11.5 months: standing alone well | 12.3 months: walking well | 14.8 months: building tower of two cubes | 16.6 months: walking up steps | 23.8 months: jumping in place |

FIGURE 1 Although at birth a neonate can make only jerky, limited voluntary movements, during the first year of life, the ability to move independently grows enormously. The ages indicate the time when 50% of children are able to perform each skill. Remember, however, that the time when each skill appears can vary considerably. For example, 25% of children are able to walk well at age 11 months; by 15 months, 90% of children are walking well.

Source: Adapted from Frankenburg, W. K., Dodds, J. Archer, P., Shapiro, H. & Bresnick, B. (1992). The Denver II: A major revision and restandardization of the Denver developmental screening test. *Pediatrics, 89*, 91–97.

behaviors. Although at birth a neonate is capable of only jerky, limited voluntary movements, the ability to move independently grows enormously during the first year of life. The typical baby rolls over by the age of about 3 months, sits without support at about 6 months, stands alone at about 11 months, and walks at just over a year old. Not only does the ability to make large-scale movements improve during this time but fine-muscle movements also become increasingly sophisticated (see Figure 1).

> **Study Alert**
> The basic reflexes—unlearned, involuntary responses—include the rooting reflex, the sucking reflex, the gag reflex, the startle reflex, and the Babinski reflex.

DEVELOPMENT OF THE SENSES: TAKING IN THE WORLD

When proud parents peer into the eyes of their neonate, is the child able to return their gaze? Although it was thought for some time that newborns can only see a hazy blur, most current findings indicate that neonates' capabilities are far more impressive. Newborns can see objects reasonably well that are within 7- to 8-inches of their eyes, although they have a limited capacity to see beyond that distance, and can follow moving objects within their field of vision. They also show the beginnings of depth perception as they react by raising their hands when an object appears to be moving rapidly toward the face (Maurer et al., 1999; Craighero et al., 2011).

You might think that it would be hard to figure out just how well neonates can see because their lack of both language and reading ability clearly prevents them from saying what direction the E on a vision chart is facing. However, researchers have devised a number of ingenious methods that rely on the newborn's biological responses and innate reflexes to test perceptual skills.

For instance, infants who see a novel stimulus typically pay close attention to it; as a consequence, their heart rates increase. But if they repeatedly see the same stimulus, their attention to it decreases, as indicated by a return to a slower heart rate. This phenomenon is known as **habituation,** the decrease in the response to a stimulus that occurs after repeated presentations of the same stimulus. By studying habituation, developmental psychologists can tell when a child who is too young to speak

habituation The decrease in the response to a stimulus that occurs after repeated presentations of the same stimulus. (Module 37) can detect and discriminate a stimulus (del Rosal, Alonso, & Moreno, 2006; Molina et al., 2015).

Researchers have developed many other methods for measuring neonate and infant perception. One technique, for instance, involves babies sucking on a nipple attached to a computer. A change in the rate and vigor with which the babies suck helps researchers infer that babies can perceive variations in stimuli. Other approaches include examining babies' eye movements and observing which way babies move their heads in response to a visual stimulus (Franklin, Pilling, & Davies, 2005; Bulf, Johnson, & Valenza, 2011).

Through the use of such research techniques, we now know that infants' visual perception is remarkably sophisticated from the start of life. At birth, babies prefer patterns with contours and edges over less distinct patterns, indicating that they can respond to the configuration of stimuli. Furthermore, even newborns are aware of size constancy because they are apparently sensitive to the phenomenon by which objects stay the same size even though the image on the retina may change size as the distance between the object and the retina varies (Norcia et al., 2005; Moore, Goodwin, & George, 2007; Hadad, Maurer, & Lewis, 2017).

In fact, neonates can discriminate facial expressions—and even imitate them. As you can see in Figure 2, newborns can produce a good imitation of an adult's expressions. Even very young infants, then, can respond to the emotions and moods that their caregivers' facial expressions reveal. This capability provides the foundation for social interaction skills in children (Meltzoff, 1996; Bahrick, Lickliter, & Castellanos, 2013; de Klerk et al., 2019).

Other visual abilities grow rapidly after birth. By the end of their first month, babies can distinguish some colors from others; after 4 months, they can focus on near or far objects. By the age of 4 or 5 months, they are able to recognize two- and three-dimensional objects, and they can perceive the Gestalt organizing principles discovered by psychologists who study perception. By the age of 7 months, neural systems related to the processing of information about facial expressions are highly sophisticated and cause babies to respond differently to specific facial expressions (see *Neuroscience in Your Life*). Overall, their perceptual abilities rapidly improve: Sensitivity to visual stimuli, for instance, becomes three to four times greater at 1 year of age than it was at birth (Striano & Vaish, 2006; Leppänen et al., 2007; Xiao et al., 2015).

FIGURE 2 This newborn infant is clearly imitating the expressions of the adult model in this photo. How does this ability contribute to social development?
Allen Donikowski/Getty Images

NEUROSCIENCE IN YOUR LIFE: EMOTIONAL RESPONSES IN INFANCY

Particular emotions elicit particular neural responses, even in early infancy. Furthermore, infants differ significantly in their neural responses to different emotions. Are these differences in brain response related to temperament? To answer this question, researchers measured neural activity while 7-month-old infants looked at pictures of happy faces. Compared with those who scored high on negative emotionality, the infants who scored low on negative emotionality—that is, those who had a propensity toward more positive thinking—had a greater neural response to happy faces in the left frontal cortex. The results suggest that neural responses to emotional stimuli are related to an infant's temperament (Ravicz et al, 2015).

In the image, you can see when brain activity occurred (*x*-axis) and how much hemoglobin levels changed (*y*-axis) as blood went to active brain areas.

Source: Adapted from Ravicz, M. M., Perdue, K. L., Westerlund, A., Vanderwert, R. E., & Nelson, C. A. (2016). Infants' neural responses to facial emotion in the prefrontal cortex are correlated with temperament: a functional near-infrared spectroscopy study. *Frontiers in Psychology, 6,* 922

In addition to vision, infants display other impressive sensory capabilities. Newborns can distinguish different sounds to the point of being able to recognize their own mothers' voices at the age of 3 days. They can also make the subtle perceptual distinctions that underlie language abilities. For example, at 2 days of age, infants can distinguish between their native tongue and foreign languages, and they can discriminate between such closely related sounds as *ba* and *pa* when they are 4 days old. By 6 months of age, they can discriminate virtually any difference in sound that is relevant to the production of language. Moreover, they can recognize different tastes and smells at a very early age. There even seems to be something of a built-in sweet tooth: Neonates prefer liquids that have been sweetened with sugar over their unsweetened counterparts (Purdy et al., 2013; Smith et al., 2017; Nicklaus & Schwartz, 2019).

Infancy Through Childhood

Three-year-old Lisa Palermo always had Cheerios on her breath. Mindy Crowell, Lisa's day care teacher, thought little of it until she noticed that the classroom Cheerios stash was steadily dwindling.

The Cheerios were stored in a plastic bin in the clothes closet. Keeping an eye on the closet, Mindy soon saw Lisa enter it, manipulate the fastener of the bin, reach in, withdraw a hand laden with Cheerios, and let the bin refasten itself, as it was designed to do. Mindy was amazed: Somehow, Lisa, barely able to navigate a crayon, had learned how to undo the supposedly child-proof fastener—a task that Mindy herself found difficult.

Mindy waited to see what would happen next. What she found was that Lisa was an excellent teacher. In the next few days, Paul, Olivia, and Kelly began to frequent the bin and do exactly what Lisa had done.

At 3 years old, Lisa asserted her personality, illustrating the tremendous growth that occurs in a variety of domains during the first year of life. Throughout the remainder of childhood, moving from infancy into middle childhood and the start of adolescence around age 11 or 12, children develop physically, socially, and cognitively in extraordinary ways. In the remainder of this module, we'll consider this development.

PHYSICAL DEVELOPMENT

Children's physical growth provides the most obvious sign of development. During the first year of life, children typically triple their birthweight, and their height increases by about half. This rapid growth slows down as the child gets older—think how gigantic adults would be if that rate of growth was constant. From age 3 to the beginning of adolescence at around age 13, growth averages a gain of about 5 pounds and 3 inches a year (see Figure 3).

The physical changes that occur as children develop are not just a matter of increasing growth; the relationship of the size of the various body parts to one another changes dramatically as children age. As you can see in Figure 4, the head of a fetus (and a newborn) is disproportionately large. However, the head soon becomes more proportional in size to the rest of the body as growth occurs mainly in the trunk and legs (Adolph & Berger, 2011).

DEVELOPMENT OF SOCIAL BEHAVIOR: TAKING ON THE WORLD

As anyone who has seen infants smiling at the sight of their mothers can guess, at the same time that infants grow physically and hone their perceptual abilities, they also

FIGURE 3 The average heights and weights of males and females in the United States from age 2 through age 20. At what ages are girls typically heavier and taller than boys?

Source: Adapted from National Center for Health Statistics. (2000). *Health United States, 2000 with adolescent health chartbook*. Hyattsville, MD: National Center for Health Statistics.

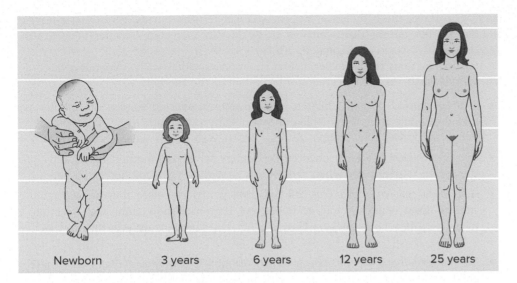

FIGURE 4 As development progresses, the size of the head relative to the rest of the body decreases until the individual reaches adulthood. Why do you think the head starts out so large?
Source: Adapted from Robbins, W. J. (1929). *Growth*. New Haven, CT: Yale University Press.

Newborn   3 years   6 years   12 years   25 years

develop socially. The nature of a child's early social development provides the foundation for social relationships that will last a lifetime.

Attachment is the positive emotional bond that develops between a child and a particular individual. Attachment is the most important form of social development that occurs during infancy. The earliest studies of attachment were carried out by animal ethologist Konrad Lorenz (1966). Lorenz focused on newborn goslings, which under normal circumstances instinctively follow their mother, the first moving object they perceive after birth. Lorenz found that goslings whose eggs were raised in an incubator and which viewed him immediately after hatching would follow his every movement as if he were their mother. He labeled this process *imprinting*, behavior that takes place during a critical period and involves attachment to the first moving object that is observed.

Our understanding of attachment progressed when psychologist Harry Harlow, in a classic study, gave infant monkeys the choice of cuddling a wire "monkey" that provided milk or a soft, terry-cloth "monkey" that was warm but did not provide milk. Their choice was clear: They spent most of their time clinging to the warm cloth "monkey," although they made occasional forays to the wire monkey to nurse. Obviously, the cloth monkey provided greater comfort to the infants; milk alone was insufficient to create attachment (see Figure 5; Harlow & Zimmerman, 1959; Blum, 2002; Levine & Munsch, 2011).

Building on this pioneering work, developmental psychologists have suggested that human attachment grows through the responsiveness of infants' caregivers to signals, such as crying, smiling, reaching, and clinging. The more that caregivers respond to signals that children give off regarding their emotions, the more likely it is that the child will become securely attached to the caregiver.

Full attachment eventually develops as a result of the complex series of interactions between caregiver and child. In the course of these interactions, the infant plays as critical and active of a role as the caregiver in the formation of the bond between them. Infants who respond positively to a caregiver produce more positive behavior on the caregiver's part, which, in turn, produces an even stronger degree of attachment in the child.

Assessing Attachment Developmental psychologists have devised a quick and direct way to measure attachment. Developed by Mary Ainsworth, the *Ainsworth strange situation* consists of a sequence of events involving a child and (typically) his or her mother. Initially, the mother and baby enter an unfamiliar room, and the mother permits the baby to explore while she sits down. An adult stranger then enters the room; after this, the mother leaves. The mother returns, and the stranger leaves. The mother

attachment The positive emotional bond that develops between a child and a particular individual. (Module 37)

FIGURE 5 Although the wire "mother" dispensed milk to the hungry infant monkey, the infant preferred the soft, terry-cloth "mother." Do you think human babies would react the same way? What does this experiment tell us about attachment?
Nina Leen/The LIFE Picture Collection/Getty Images

Study Alert
Attachment—the positive emotional bond that develops between a child and a particular individual—is a key concept in understanding the social development of children.

once again leaves the baby alone, and the stranger returns. Finally, the stranger leaves, and the mother returns (Ainsworth et al., 1978; Van Rosmalen, Van der Veer, & Van der Horst, 2015; Posada & Trumbell, 2017).

Babies' reactions to the experimental situation vary drastically, depending, according to Ainsworth, on their degree of attachment to the mother:

- *Securely attached children.* Children who are *securely attached* employ the mother as a kind of home base; they explore independently but return to her occasionally. When she leaves, they exhibit distress, and they go to her when she returns.

- *Avoidant children. Avoidant* children do not cry when the mother leaves, and they seem to avoid her when she returns as if they were indifferent to her.

- *Ambivalent children. Ambivalent* children display anxiety before they are separated and are upset when the mother leaves, but they may show ambivalent reactions to her return, such as seeking close contact but simultaneously hitting and kicking her.

- *Disorganized-disoriented children.* A fourth reaction is *disorganized-disoriented;* these children show inconsistent and often contradictory behavior. For example, they may approach their mother but do so avoiding eye contact or otherwise acting in an inappropriate way.

The nature of attachment between children and their mothers has far-reaching consequences for later development. For example, children who are securely attached to their mothers tend to be more socially and emotionally competent than are their less securely attached peers, and others find them more cooperative, capable, and playful. Furthermore, children who are securely attached at age 1 show fewer psychological difficulties when they grow older compared with avoidant and ambivalent youngsters. Children who are securely attached tend, as adults, to have more successful romantic relationships. On the other hand, being securely attached at an early age does not guarantee good adjustment later; conversely, children who lack secure attachment do not always have difficulties later in life (Hardy, 2007; Redshaw & Martin, 2013; Hennessy & Shair, 2017).

The Father's Role Although early developmental research focused largely on the mother-child relationship, more recent research has highlighted the father's role in parenting—and with good reason: The number of fathers who are primary caregivers for their children has grown significantly, and fathers play an increasingly important role in their children's lives. For example, in almost 13% of families with children, the father is the parent who stays at home to care for preschoolers (Day & Lamb, 2004; Halford, 2006; Kulik & Sadeh, 2015).

When fathers interact with their children, their play often differs from mothers' play. Fathers engage in more physical, rough-and-tumble sorts of activities, whereas mothers play more verbal and traditional games, such as peekaboo. Despite such behavioral differences, the nature of attachment between fathers and children compared with that between mothers and children can be similar. In fact, children can form multiple attachments simultaneously (Diener et al., 2008; Bureau et al., 2017; Lin, Xie, & Li, 2019).

Social Relationships with Peers By the time they are 2 years old, children become less dependent on their parents. They are more self-reliant and increasingly prefer to play with friends. Initially, they engage in what is known as *parallel play*—meaning that they play physically near each other, but they don't try to influence each other's behavior. Thus, even though they may be playing side by side, 2-year-olds pay more attention to their toys than to one another. Later, however, as they play, children actively interact, modify one another's behavior, and exchange roles (Whitney & Green, 2011; Stone, 2015).

Cultural factors also affect children's styles of play. For example, Korean American children engage in less pretend play than do their Anglo American counterparts (Drewes, 2005; Suizzo & Bornstein, 2006; Rentzou et al., 2019).

As children reach school age, their social interactions become more frequent, and they begin to follow set patterns of behavior. For example, they may engage in elaborate games involving teams and rigid rules. In addition to providing enjoyment, such play allows children to become increasingly competent in their interactions with others. For instance, during play, they learn to take the perspective of other people. Children also learn to infer others' thoughts and feelings, even when those thoughts and feelings are not directly expressed (Royzman, Cassidy, & Baron, 2003; Yang et al., 2013).

In short, social interaction helps children interpret the meaning of others' behavior and develop the capacity to respond appropriately. Furthermore, children learn physical and emotional self-control: They learn to avoid hitting a playmate who beats them at a game. They learn to be polite and to control their emotional displays and facial expressions (e.g., smiling even when receiving a disappointing gift). Situations that provide children with opportunities for social interaction, then, may enhance their social development (Talukdar & Shastri, 2006; Whitebread et al., 2009).

Screen Time: Monitoring Children's Use of Media Another way children learn about their social world is through the media. In many households, children as young as one are exposed to significant amounts of screen time, sometimes from traditional television and sometimes from computers and other devices.

It's very much an open question as to how screen time affects development, but the World Health Organization (WHO) recently issued strict guidelines. According to WHO, children in the first year of life should *never* be exposed to screen time, and children 2 to 4 should spend no more than an hour a day watching a screen (World Health Organization, 2019).

The WHO guidelines are roughly consistent with recommendations from the American Academy of Pediatrics. That group recommends that children under 18 months should never get screen time and that those between 2 and 5 should be limited to an hour a day. Moreover, they recommend that any screen time should involve "co-watching" with an engaged adult (American Academy of Pediatrics, 2016).

Although the jury is still out on how or whether screen time affects child development, it seems reasonable to restrict children's exposure to media and to maximize face-to-face interaction and physical activity.

The Consequences of Child Care Outside the Home Research on the importance of social interaction is corroborated by work that examines the benefits of child care out of the home, which is an important part of an increasing number of children's lives. For instance, almost 30% of preschool children whose mothers work outside the home spend their days in child-care centers. By the age of 6 months, almost two-thirds of infants are cared for by people other than their mothers for part of the day. Most of these infants begin child care before the age of 4 months and are cared for by people other than their mothers almost 30 hours per week (see Figure 6; National Research Council, 2001; NICHD Early Child Care Research Network, 2006).

Do child-care arrangements outside the home benefit children's development? If the programs are of high quality, they can. According to the results of a large study supported by the U.S. National Institute of Child Health and Development, children who attend high-quality child-care centers may not only do as well as children who stay at home with their parents but in some respects they may actually do better. Children in child care are generally more considerate and sociable than other children, and they interact more positively with teachers. They may also be more compliant and regulate their own behavior more effectively (NICHD Early Child Care Research Network, 2001).

In addition, especially for children from poor or disadvantaged homes, child care in specially enriched environments—those with many toys, books, a variety of children, and high-quality providers—may be more intellectually stimulating than the home environment. Such child care can lead to increased intellectual achievement, demonstrated in higher IQ scores, and better language development. In fact, children in care centers sometimes are found to score higher on tests of cognitive abilities than those who are cared for by their mothers or by sitters or home day-care providers—effects that last into adulthood (Burchinal, Roberts, & Riggins, 2000; Dearing, McCartney, & Taylor, 2009; Reid, Martin, & Brooks-Gunn, 2017).

FIGURE 6 According to a study by the National Institute of Child Health and Human Development, children were more likely to spend time in some kind of child care outside the home or family as they got older.

Source: Adapted from National Institute of Child Health and Human Development (NICHD) Early Child Care Research Network. (2006). Child-care effect sizes for the NICHD study of early child care and youth development. *American Psychologist, 61,* 99–116.

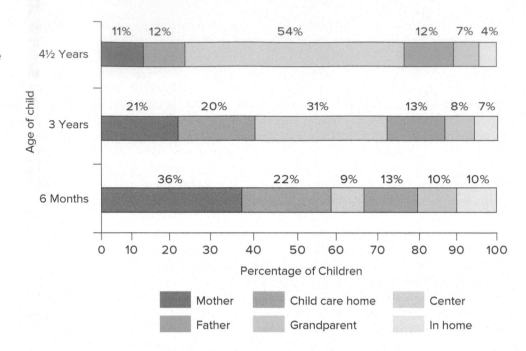

However, child care outside the home does not have universally positive outcomes. Children may feel insecure after placement in low-quality child care or in multiple child-care settings. Furthermore, some research suggests that infants who are involved in outside care more than 20 hours a week in the first year show less secure attachment to their mothers than do those who have not been in child care outside the home. Finally, children who spent long hours in child care as infants and preschoolers may have a reduced ability to work independently and to manage their time effectively when they reach elementary school (NICHD Early Child Care Research Network, 2001; Vandell et al., 2005; Pluess & Belsky, 2009).

The key to the success of nonparental child care is its quality. High-quality child care produces benefits; low-quality child care provides little or no gain and may even hinder children's development. In short, significant benefits result from the social interaction and intellectual stimulation provided by high-quality child-care centers—especially for children from impoverished environments (Landry et al., 2013; Araujo, Dormal, & Schady, 2019).

Parenting Styles and Social Development Parents' child-rearing practices are critical in shaping their children's social competence. According to classic research by developmental psychologist Diana Baumrind, four main categories describe different parenting styles (see Figure 7).

authoritarian parents Parents who are rigid and punitive and value unquestioning obedience from their children. (Module 37)

permissive parents Parents who give their children relaxed or inconsistent direction and, although they are warm, require little of them. (Module 37)

authoritative parents Parents who are firm, set clear limits, reason with their children, and explain things to them. (Module 37)

uninvolved parents Parents who show little interest in their children and are emotionally detached. (Module 37)

- **Authoritarian parents** are rigid and punitive, and they value unquestioning obedience from their children. They have strict standards and discourage expressions of disagreement.

- **Permissive parents** give their children relaxed or inconsistent direction and, although they are warm, require little of them.

- **Authoritative parents** are firm and set limits for their children. As the children get older, these parents try to reason and explain things to them. They also set clear goals and encourage their children's independence.

- **Uninvolved parents** show little interest in their children. Emotionally detached, they view parenting as nothing more than providing food, clothing, and shelter for children. At their most extreme, uninvolved parents are guilty of neglect, a form of child abuse (Baumrind, 2005; Lagacé-Séguin & d'Entremont, 2006; Lewis & Lamb, 2011).

	Parenting Style	Parent Behavior	Type of Behavior Produced in Child
	Authoritarian	Rigid, punitive, strict standards (example: "If you don't clean your room, I'm going to take away your iPhone for good and ground you.")	Unsociable, unfriendly, withdrawn
	Permissive	Lax, inconsistent, undemanding (example: "It might be good to clean your room, but I guess it can wait.")	Immature, moody, dependent, low self-control
	Authoritative	Firm, sets limits and goals, uses reasoning, encourages independence (example: "You'll need to clean your room before we can go out to the restaurant. As soon as you finish, we'll leave.")	Good social skills, likable, self-reliant, independent
	Uninvolved	Detached emotionally, sees role only as providing food, clothing, and shelter (example: "I couldn't care less if your room is a pigsty.")	Indifferent, rejecting behavior

FIGURE 7 According to developmental psychologist Diana Baumrind (1971), four main parenting styles characterize child rearing.

Source: National Institute of Child Health and Human Development (NICHD) Early Child Care Research Network. (2006). Child-care effect sizes for the NICHD study of early child care and youth development. *American Psychologist, 61,* 99–116; (photo): Gary John Norman/Digital Vision/Getty Images

As you might expect, the four kinds of child-rearing styles seem to produce very different kinds of behavior in children (with many exceptions, of course). Children of authoritarian parents tend to be unsociable, unfriendly, and relatively withdrawn. In contrast, permissive parents' children show immaturity, moodiness, dependence, and low self-control. The children of authoritative parents fare best: With high social skills, they are likable, self-reliant, independent, and cooperative. Worst off are the children of uninvolved parents; they feel unloved and emotionally detached, and their physical and cognitive development are impeded (Berk, 2005; Snyder, Cramer, & Afrank, 2005; Llorca-Mestre et al., 2017).

Before we rush to congratulate authoritative parents and condemn authoritarian, permissive, and uninvolved ones, it is important to note that in many cases, nonauthoritative parents also produce perfectly well-adjusted children. Moreover, children are born with a particular **temperament**–a basic, inborn characteristic way of responding and behavioral style. Some children are naturally easygoing and cheerful, whereas others are irritable and fussy or pensive and quiet. The kind of temperament a baby is born with may in part bring about specific kinds of parental child-rearing styles (Coplan, Reichel, & Rowan, 2009; Costa & Figueiredo, 2011; Wittig & Rodriguez, 2019).

In addition, children vary considerably in their degree of *resilience*, the ability to overcome circumstances that place them at high risk for psychological or even physical harm. Highly resilient children have temperaments that evoke positive responses from caregivers and others in their lives. Such children display unusual social skills: outgoingness, intelligence, and a feeling that they have control over their lives. In a sense, resilient children try to shape their own environment rather than being victimized by it. In fact, as adults, they see their struggles as something from which they drew strength (Deater-Deckard, Ivy, & Smith, 2005; Vellacott, 2007; Naglieri, LeBuffe, & Ross, 2013; Jay, 2017).

We also need to keep in mind that these findings regarding child-rearing styles apply primarily to U.S. society, which highly values children's growing independence and diminishing reliance on their parents. In contrast, Japanese parents encourage dependence to promote the values of cooperation and community life. These differences in cultural values result in very different philosophies of child rearing. For example,

Study Alert
Know the four major types of child-rearing practices—authoritarian, permissive, authoritative, and uninvolved—and their effects.

temperament A basic, inborn characteristic way of responding and behavioral style. (Module 37)

Japanese mothers believe it is a punishment to make a young child sleep alone; thus, many children sleep next to their mothers throughout infancy and toddlerhood (Jones, 2007; Pinquart & Kauser, 2017).

Furthermore, those who have come to the United States from other countries and cultures may use child-rearing techniques learned in their original home culture, and these may differ considerably from those found in the typical U.S. home. Still, as parents integrate into U.S. society, children of immigrants generally do quite well, showing levels of adjustment and achievement similar to, and sometimes better, than that of children of nonimmigrant parents (OECD, 2018; Suárez-Orozco & Suárez-Orozco, 2018).

In sum, a child's upbringing results from the child-rearing philosophy parents hold, the specific practices they use, and the nature of their own and their child's personalities. As is the case with other aspects of development, then, behavior is a function of a complex interaction of environmental and genetic factors.

Erikson's Theory of Psychosocial Development In tracing the course of social development, some theorists have considered how the challenges of society and culture change as an individual matures. Following this path, psychoanalyst Erik Erikson developed one of the more comprehensive theories of social development. Erikson (1963) viewed the developmental changes that occur throughout life as a series of eight stages of psychosocial development; of these, four occur during childhood. **Psychosocial development** involves changes in our interactions and understanding of one another as well as in our knowledge and understanding of ourselves as members of society.

Erikson suggests that passage through each of the stages necessitates the resolution of a crisis or conflict. Accordingly, Erikson represents each stage as a pairing of the most positive and most negative aspects of the crisis of that period. Although each crisis is never resolved entirely—life becomes increasingly complicated as we grow older—it has to be resolved sufficiently to equip us to deal with demands made during the following stage of development.

The first stage of psychosocial development is the **trust-versus-mistrust stage** (ages birth to 1½ years). During this period, infants develop feelings of trust or mistrust, primarily depending on how well their caregivers meet their needs. If their physical requirements and psychological needs for attachment are consistently met and their interactions with the world are generally positive, they will develop a sense of trust. In contrast, inconsistent care and unpleasant interactions with others can lead to mistrust and a view of the world as a harsh and unfriendly place.

In the second stage, the **autonomy-versus-shame-and-doubt stage** (ages 1½–3 years), toddlers develop independence and autonomy if caregivers encourage exploration and freedom. On the other hand, they experience shame, self-doubt, and unhappiness if they are overly restricted and protected. According to Erikson, the key to the development of a sense of independence during this period is for the child's caregivers to provide a reasonable amount of control. If parents are overly controlling, children cannot assert themselves nor develop their own sense of control over their world; if parents provide too little control, children can become demanding and dictatorial.

Next, children face the crises of the **initiative-versus-guilt stage** (ages 3-6 years). In this stage, children's desire to act independently conflicts with the guilt that comes from the unintended and unexpected consequences of such behavior. Children in this period come to understand that they are persons in their own right, and they begin to make decisions about their behavior. If parents react positively to children's attempts at independence, their children will develop skills in accomplishing tasks and overcoming challenges.

The fourth and last stage of childhood is the **industry-versus-inferiority stage** (ages 6-12 years), which is focused on efforts to meet the challenges presented by parents, peers, school, and other societal institutions. During this period, increasing competency in all areas, whether social interactions or academic skills, characterizes successful psychosocial development. In contrast, difficulties in this stage lead to feelings of failure and inadequacy.

psychosocial development Development of individuals' interactions and understanding of each other and of their knowledge and understanding of themselves as members of society. (Module 37)

trust-versus-mistrust stage According to Erikson, the first stage of psychosocial development, occurring from birth to age 1½ years, during which time infants develop feelings of trust or lack of trust. (Module 37)

autonomy-versus-shame-and-doubt stage The period during which, according to Erikson, toddlers (ages 1½ to 3 years) develop independence and autonomy if exploration and freedom are encouraged or shame and self-doubt if they are restricted and overprotected. (Module 37)

initiative-versus-guilt stage According to Erikson, the period during which children ages 3 to 6 years experience conflict between independence of action and the sometimes negative results of that action. (Module 37)

industry-versus-inferiority stage According to Erikson, the last stage of childhood, during which children ages 6 to 12 years may develop positive social interactions with others or may feel inadequate and become less sociable. (Module 37)

Erikson's theory suggests that psychosocial development continues throughout life, and he proposes four more crises that are faced after childhood (described in module 38). Although his theory has been criticized on several grounds—such as the imprecision of the concepts he employs and his greater emphasis on male development than female development—it remains influential and is one of the few theories that encompass the entire life span.

COGNITIVE DEVELOPMENT: CHILDREN'S THINKING ABOUT THE WORLD

Suppose you had two drinking glasses of different shapes—one short and broad, and one tall and thin. Now imagine that you filled the short, broad one with soda about halfway and then poured the liquid from that glass into the tall one. The soda would appear to fill about three-quarters of the second glass. If someone asked you whether there was more soda in the second glass than there had been in the first, what would you say?

You might think that such a simple question hardly deserves an answer; of course, there is no difference in the amount of soda in the two glasses. However, most 4-year-olds would be likely to say that there is more soda in the second glass. If you then poured the soda back into the short glass, they would say there is now less soda than there was in the taller glass.

Why are young children confused by this problem? The reason is not immediately obvious. Anyone who has observed preschoolers must be impressed by how far they have progressed from the early stages of development. They speak with ease, know the alphabet, count, play complex games, use computers, tell stories, and communicate ably. Yet despite this seeming sophistication, there are deep gaps in children's understanding of the world. The gaps in children's understanding relate to their level of cognitive development.

Cognitive development is the process by which a child's understanding of the world changes due to their age and experience. In contrast to the theories of physical and social development discussed earlier (such as those of Erikson), theories of cognitive development seek to explain the quantitative and qualitative intellectual advances that occur during development.

Piaget's Theory of Cognitive Development No theory of cognitive development has had more impact than that of Swiss psychologist Jean Piaget. Piaget (1970) suggested that children around the world proceed through a series of four stages in a fixed order. He maintained that these stages differ not only in the *quantity* of information acquired at each stage but in the *quality* of knowledge and understanding as well. Taking an interactionist point of view, he suggested that movement from one stage to the next occurs when a child reaches an appropriate level of maturation *and* is exposed to relevant types of experiences. Piaget assumed that, without having such experiences, children cannot reach their highest level of cognitive growth.

Piaget's Four Stages of Cognitive Development Piaget proposed four stages: the sensorimotor, preoperational, concrete operational, and formal operational (see Figure 8). Let's examine each of them and the approximate ages that they span.

Sensorimotor Stage: Birth to 2 Years. During the **sensorimotor stage,** children base their understanding of the world primarily on touching, sucking, chewing, shaking, and manipulating objects. In the initial part of the stage, children have relatively little competence in representing the environment by using images, language, or other kinds of symbols. Consequently, infants lack what Piaget calls object permanence. **Object permanence** is the awareness that objects—and people—continue to exist even if they are out of sight.

How can we know that children lack object permanence? Although we cannot ask infants, we can observe their reactions when a toy they are playing with is hidden

Cognitive Stage	Approximate Age Range	Major Characteristics
Sensorimotor	Birth–2 years	Development of object permanence, development of motor skills, little or no capacity for symbolic representation
Preoperational	2–7 years	Development of language and symbolic thinking, egocentric thinking
Concrete operational	7–12 years	Development of conservation, mastery of the concept of reversibility
Formal operational	12 years–adulthood	Development of logical and abstract thinking

FIGURE 8 According to Piaget, all children pass through four stages of cognitive development.
(photo): Patrick Grehan/Corbis Historical/Getty Images

Children who have not mastered the principle of conservation assume that the volume of liquid increases when it is poured from a short, wide container to a tall, thin one. What other tasks might a child under age 7 have difficulty comprehending?
Tony Freeman/PhotoEdit

preoperational stage According to Piaget, the period from 2 to 7 years of age that is characterized by language development. (Module 37)

egocentric thought A way of thinking in which a child views the world entirely from his or her own perspective. (Module 37)

principle of conservation The understanding that quantity is unrelated to the arrangement and physical appearance of objects. (Module 37)

under a blanket. Until the age of about 9 months, children will make no attempt to locate the hidden toy. However, soon after that age, they will begin an active search for the missing object, indicating that they have developed a mental representation of the toy. Object permanence, then, is a critical development during the sensorimotor stage.

Preoperational Stage: 2-7 Years. During the the **preoperational stage,** children develop the use of language. The internal representational systems they develop allow them to describe people, events, and feelings. They even use symbols in play, pretending, for example, that a book pushed across the floor is a car.

Although children use more advanced thinking in this stage than they did in the earlier sensorimotor stage, their thinking is still qualitatively inferior to that of adults. We see this when we observe a preoperational child using **egocentric thought,** a way of thinking in which the child views the world entirely from his or her own perspective. Preoperational children think that everyone shares their perspective and knowledge. Thus, children's stories and explanations to adults can be maddeningly uninformative because they are delivered without any context. For example, a preoperational child may start a story with, "He wouldn't let me go," neglecting to mention who "he" is or where the storyteller wanted to go. We also see egocentric thinking when children at the preoperational stage play hiding games. For instance, 3-year-olds frequently hide with their faces against a wall and covering their eyes–although they are still in plain view. It seems to them that if *they* cannot see, then no one else will be able to see them because they assume that others share their view.

In addition, preoperational children have not yet developed the ability to comprehend the **principle of conservation,** which is the understanding that quantity is unrelated to the arrangement and physical appearance of objects. Children who can use the principle of conservation have awareness that important attributes of objects (such as amount or volume) do not change despite superficial changes. In contrast, children who have not mastered conservation do not understand that the overall amount or volume of an object does not change when its shape or configuration changes.

The question about the two glasses–one short and broad, and the other tall and thin–with which we began our discussion of cognitive development illustrates this point clearly. Children who do not understand the principle of conservation believe that the amount of liquid changes as it is poured back and forth between glasses of different sizes. They simply are unable to comprehend that a change in appearance does not mean there is a change in amount. Instead, they truly believe that quantity changes as appearance changes (see Figure 9).

Conservation of ...	Modality	Change in physical appearance	Average age at full mastery
Number	Number of elements in a collection	Rearranging or dislocating elements	6–7 years
Substance (mass)	Amount of a malleable substance (e.g., clay or liquid)	Altering shape	7–8 years
Length	Length of a line or object	Altering shape or configuration	7–8 years
Area	Amount of surface covered by a set of plane figures	Rearranging the figures	8–9 years
Weight	Weight of an object	Altering shape	9–10 years
Volume	Volume of an object (in terms of water displacement)	Altering shape	14–15 years

FIGURE 9 These tests are frequently used to assess whether children have learned the principle of conservation across a variety of dimensions. Do you think children in the preoperational stage can be taught to avoid conservation mistakes before the typical age of mastery?

Source: Adapted from Schickedanz, J. A., Schickedanz, D. I., Forsyth, P. D., & Forsyth, G. A. (2001). *Understanding Children and Adolescents* (4th ed.). Upper Saddle River, NJ: Pearson Education.

Concrete Operational Stage: 7-12 Years. Mastery of the principle of conservation marks the beginning of the **concrete operational stage.** However, children do not fully understand some aspects of conservation–such as conservation of weight and volume–for a number of years.

During the concrete operational stage, children develop the ability to think in a more logical manner and begin to overcome some of the egocentrism characteristic of the preoperational period. One of the major principles children learn during this stage is reversibility, the idea that some changes can be undone by reversing an earlier action. For example, they can understand that when someone rolls a ball of clay into a long sausage shape, that person can recreate the original ball by reversing the action. Children can even conceptualize this principle in their heads without having to see the action performed before them.

Although children make important advances in their logical capabilities during the concrete operational stage, their thinking still displays one major limitation: They are largely bound to the concrete, physical reality of the world. For the most part, they have difficulty understanding questions of an abstract or hypothetical nature.

Formal Operational Stage: 12 Years to Adulthood. The **formal operational stage** produces a new kind of thinking that is abstract, formal, and logical. Thinking is no

concrete operational stage According to Piaget, the period from 7 to 12 years of age that is characterized by logical thought and a loss of egocentrism. (Module 37)

formal operational stage According to Piaget, the period from age 12 to adulthood that is characterized by abstract thought. (Module 37) longer tied to events that individuals observe in the environment but makes use of logical techniques to resolve problems.

The way in which children approach the "pendulum problem" devised by Piaget (Piaget & Inhelder, 1958) illustrates the emergence of formal operational thinking. The problem solver is asked to figure out what determines how fast a pendulum swings. Is it the length of the string, the weight of the pendulum, or the force with which the pendulum is pushed? (For the record, the answer is the length of the string.)

Children in the concrete operational stage approach the problem haphazardly without a logical or rational plan of action. For example, they may simultaneously change the length of the string, the weight on the string, and the force with which they push the pendulum. Because they are varying all the factors at once, they cannot tell which factor is the critical one. In contrast, people in the formal operational stage approach the problem systematically. Acting as if they were scientists conducting an experiment, they examine the effects of changes in one variable at a time. This ability to rule out competing possibilities characterizes formal operational thought.

Although formal operational thought emerges during the teenage years, some individuals use this type of thinking only infrequently. Moreover, it appears that many individuals never reach this stage at all; most studies show that only 40-60% of college students and adults fully reach it, with some estimates running as low as 25% of the general population. In addition, in certain cultures—particularly those that are less technically oriented than Western societies—almost no one reaches the formal operational stage (Keating & Clark, 1980; Super, 1980; Genovese, 2006).

Stages Versus Continuous Development: Is Piaget Right? No other theorist has given us as comprehensive a theory of cognitive development as Piaget has. Still, many contemporary theorists suggest that a better explanation of how children develop cognitively can be provided by theories that do not involve a stage approach. For instance, children are not always consistent in their performance of tasks that—if Piaget's theory is accurate—ought to be performed equally well at a particular stage (Feldman, 2003, 2004; Bjorkland, 2018).

Furthermore, some developmental psychologists suggest that cognitive development proceeds in a more continuous fashion than Piaget's stage theory implies. In other words, rather than moving from one stage to another in a relatively abrupt manner, later findings suggest that cognitive development advances smoothly, in smaller, steadier increments.

Moreover, critics of Piaget propose that cognitive development is primarily quantitative rather than qualitative. They argue that although there are differences in when, how, and to what extent a child can use specific cognitive abilities—reflecting quantitative changes—the underlying cognitive processes change relatively little with age (Chen, 2014).

Piaget also underestimated the age at which infants and children can understand specific concepts and principles; in fact, they seem to be more sophisticated in their cognitive abilities than Piaget believed. For instance, some evidence suggests that infants as young as 5 months have rudimentary mathematical skills (Wynn, Bloom, & Chiang, 2002; McCrink & Wynn, 2007; van Marle & Wynn, 2009).

Despite such criticisms, most developmental psychologists agree that although the processes that underlie changes in cognitive abilities may not unfold in the manner Piaget's theory suggests, he has generally provided us with an accurate account of age-related changes in cognitive development. Moreover, his theory has had an enormous influence in education. For example, Piaget suggests that individuals cannot increase their cognitive performance unless both cognitive readiness brought about by maturation and appropriate environmental stimulation are present. This view has inspired the nature and structure of educational curricula and teaching methods. Researchers have also used Piaget's theory and methods to investigate issues surrounding animal cognition, such as whether primates show object permanence (they seem to) (Egan, 2005; Cunningham, 2006; Jablonka, 2017).

Information-Processing Approaches: Charting Children's Mental Programs If cognitive development does not proceed as a series of stages as Piaget suggested, what does underlie the enormous growth in children's cognitive abilities that even the most untutored eye can observe? To many developmental psychologists, changes in information-processing capabilities account for cognitive development. **Information processing** refers to the way in which people take in, use, and store information (Casasola, 2011; Lillard & Woolley, 2015).

According to the information-processing approach, quantitative changes occur in children's ability to organize and manipulate information. From this perspective, children become increasingly adept at information processing, much as a computer program may become more sophisticated as a programmer modifies it on the basis of experience. Information-processing approaches consider the kinds of "mental programs" that children invoke when approaching problems.

Several significant changes occur in children's information-processing capabilities. For one thing, speed of processing increases with age as some abilities become more automatic. The speed at which children can scan, recognize, and compare stimuli increases with age. As they grow older, children can pay attention to stimuli longer and discriminate between different stimuli more readily, and they are less easily distracted (Van den Wildenberg & Van der Molen, 2004; Diaz & Bell, 2011; Marchman et al., 2019).

Memory also improves dramatically with age. Preschoolers can hold only two or three chunks of information in short-term memory, 5-year-olds can hold four, and 7-year-olds can hold five. (Adults are able to keep seven, plus or minus two, chunks in short-term memory.) The size of the chunks also grows with age, as does the sophistication and organization of knowledge stored in memory (see Figure 10). Still, memory capabilities are impressive at a very early age: Even before they can speak, infants can remember for months events in which they actively participated (Bayliss et al., 2005; Slusarczyk & Niedzwienska, 2013).

Finally, improvement in information processing relates to advances in **metacognition,** an awareness and understanding of one's own cognitive processes. Metacognition involves the planning, monitoring, and revising of cognitive strategies. Younger children, who lack an awareness of their own cognitive processes, often do not realize their incapabilities. Thus, when they misunderstand others, they may fail to recognize their own errors. It is only later, when metacognitive abilities become more sophisticated, that children are able to know when they *don't* understand. Such increasing sophistication reflects a change in children's *theory of mind*, their knowledge and beliefs about the way the mind operates (Sodian, 2011; O'Leary & Sloutsky, 2017; Pennequin et al., 2019).

Vygotsky's View of Cognitive Development: Considering Culture According to Russian developmental psychologist Lev Vygotsky, the culture in which we are raised significantly affects the nature of our cognitive development. In an increasingly influential view, Vygotsky suggested that the focus on individual performance of both Piagetian and information-processing approaches is misplaced. Instead, he held that we cannot understand cognitive development without taking into account the social and cultural aspects of learning (Vygotsky, 1926/1997; Maynard & Martini, 2005; Rieber & Robinson, 2006).

Vygotsky argued that cognitive development occurs as a consequence of social interactions in which children work with others to jointly solve problems. Through such interactions, children's cognitive skills increase, and they gain the ability to function intellectually on their own. More specifically, he suggested that children's cognitive abilities increase when they encounter information that falls within their zone of proximal development. The **zone of proximal development (ZPD)** is the gap between what children already are able to accomplish on their own and what they are not quite ready to do by themselves. When children receive information that falls within the ZPD, they

information processing The way in which people take in, use, and store information. (Module 37)

metacognition An awareness and understanding of one's own cognitive processes. (Module 37)

zone of proximal development (ZPD) According to Vygotsky, the gap between what children already are able to accomplish on their own and what they are not quite ready to do by themselves. (Module 37)

PsychTech

A quarter of parents with children between the ages of 0–5 report that their children use the Internet.

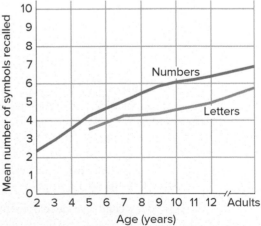

FIGURE 10 Memory span increases with age for both numbers and letters.

Source: Adapted from Dempster, F. N. (1981). Memory span: Sources for individual and developmental differences. *Psychological Bulletin, 89*, 63–100.

can increase their understanding or master a new task. In contrast, if the information lies outside children's ZPD, they will not be able to master it.

In short, cognitive development occurs when parents, teachers, or skilled peers assist a child by presenting new information that resides within the child's ZPD, a process Vygotsky called scaffolding. *Scaffolding* is support for learning and problem solving that encourages independence and growth. Vygotsky claimed that scaffolding not only helps children to solve specific problems but also aids in the development of overall cognitive abilities (Schaller & Crandall, 2004; Coulson & Harvey, 2013).

More than other approaches to cognitive development, Vygotsky's theory considers how an individual's specific cultural and social context affects intellectual growth. The way in which children understand the world grows out of interactions with parents, peers, and other members of a specific culture (John-Steiner & Mahn, 2003; Kozulin et al., 2003).

RECAP/EVALUATE/RETHINK

RECAP

LO 37-1 What are the major competencies of newborns?

- Newborns, or neonates, have reflexes–unlearned, involuntary responses that occur automatically in the presence of certain stimuli.
- Sensory abilities develop rapidly; infants can distinguish color, depth, sound, tastes, and smells relatively soon after birth.
- After birth, physical development also is rapid; children typically triple their birthweight in a year.

LO 37-2 What are the milestones of physical and social development during childhood?

- Attachment–the positive emotional bond between a child and a particular individual–marks social development in infancy. Measured in the laboratory by means of the Ainsworth strange situation, attachment relates to later social and emotional adjustment.
- As children become older, the nature of their social interactions with peers changes. Initially play occurs relatively independently, but it becomes increasingly cooperative.
- The different child-rearing styles include authoritarian, permissive, authoritative, and uninvolved.
- According to Erikson, eight stages of psychosocial development involve people's changing interactions and understanding of themselves and others. During childhood, the four stages are trust-versus-mistrust (birth to 1½ years), autonomy-versus-shame-and-doubt (1½–3 years), initiative-versus-guilt (3–6 years), and industry-versus-inferiority (6–12 years).

LO 37-3 How does cognitive development proceed during childhood?

- Piaget's theory suggests that cognitive development proceeds through four stages in which qualitative

changes occur in thinking: the sensorimotor stage (birth to 2 years), the preoperational stage (2–7 years), the concrete operational stage (7–12 years), and the formal operational stage (12 years to adulthood).

- Information-processing approaches suggest that quantitative changes occur in children's ability to organize and manipulate information about the world, such as significant increases in speed of processing, attention span, and memory. In addition, children advance in metacognition, the awareness and understanding of one's own cognitive processes.
- Vygotsky argued that children's cognitive development occurs as a consequence of social interactions in which children and others work together to solve problems.

EVALUATE

1. Researchers studying newborns use _____, or the decrease in the response to a stimulus that occurs after repeated presentations of the same stimulus, as an indicator of a baby's interest.
2. The emotional bond that develops between a child and its caregiver is known as _____.
3. Match the parenting style with its definition:
   1. Permissive
   2. Authoritative
   3. Authoritarian
   4. Uninvolved

   a. Rigid; highly punitive; demanding obedience
   b. Gives little direction; lax on obedience
   c. Firm but fair; tries to explain parental decisions
   d. Emotionally detached and unloving
4. Erikson's theory of _____ development involves a series of eight stages, each of which must be resolved for a person to develop optimally.

5. Match the stage of development with the thinking style characteristic of that stage:

1. Egocentric thought	**a.** Sensorimotor
2. Object permanence	**b.** Formal operational
3. Abstract reasoning	**c.** Preoperational
4. Conservation; reversibility	**d.** Concrete operational

6. _____ theories of development suggest that the way in which a child handles information is critical to his or her development.

7. According to Vygotsky, information that is within a child's _____ _____ _____ _____ is most likely to result in cognitive development.

RETHINK

1. Do you think the widespread use of IQ testing in the United States contributes to parents' views that their children's academic success is due largely to the children's innate intelligence? Why? Would it be possible (or desirable) to change this view?

2. In what ways might the infant's major reflexes–the rooting, sucking, gagging, and Babinski reflexes–have had survival value from an evolutionary perspective? Does the infant's ability to mimic the facial expressions of adults have a similar value?

Answers to Evaluate Questions

1. habituation; **2.** attachment; **3.** 1-b, 2-c, 3-a, 4-d; **4.** psychosocial; **5.** 1-c, 2-a, 3-b, 4-d; **6.** Information-processing; **7.** zone of proximal development

KEY TERMS

neonate	temperament	industry-versus-inferiority stage	concrete operational stage
reflexes	psychosocial development	cognitive development	formal operational stage
habituation	trust-versus-mistrust stage	sensorimotor stage	information processing
attachment	autonomy-versus-shame-and-doubt stage	object permanence	metacognition
authoritarian parents		preoperational stage	zone of proximal development (ZPD)
permissive parents	initiative-versus-guilt stage	egocentric thought	
authoritative parents		principle of conservation	
uninvolved parents			

Module 38
Adolescence: Becoming an Adult

adolescence The developmental stage between childhood and adulthood. (Module 38)

Joseph Charles, age 13: "Being 13 is very hard at school. I have to be bad in order to be considered cool. I sometimes do things that aren't good. I have talked back to my teachers and been disrespectful to them. I do want to be good, but it's just too hard." (Gibbs, 2005)

Marco Colson, age 15: "Trevor Kelson" says the sign on Marco's door. Inside, the floor is cluttered with dirty clothes, candy wrappers, and other debris. What color is the carpet on the floor? "I don't think I remember," says Marco with a smile.

Alissa Cruz, age 17: "I was invited to join the National Honor Society because of my grades. But at the induction, the parents just stared at me. It was like they couldn't believe that someone with a nose stud and pink streaks in her hair could be smart enough to be in the National Honor Society. I'm hoping to be a teacher in the public schools, but do you think they'd hire someone who looks like me?"

Although Joseph, Marco, and Alissa have never met, they share anxieties that are common to adolescence—concerns about friends, parents, appearance, independence, and their futures. **Adolescence** is the developmental stage between childhood and adulthood, and it is a crucial period. It is a time of profound changes and, occasionally, turmoil. Considerable biological change occurs as adolescents attain sexual and physical maturity. At the same time and rivaling these physiological changes, important social, emotional, and cognitive changes occur as adolescents strive for independence and move toward adulthood.

Because many years of schooling precede most people's entry into the workforce in Western societies, the stage of adolescence is fairly long; it begins just before the teenage years and ends just after them. Adolescents are no longer children, yet society doesn't quite consider them adults. They face a period of rapid physical, cognitive, and social change that affects them for the rest of their lives.

Dramatic changes in society also affect adolescents' development. More than half of all children in the United States will spend all or some of their childhood and adolescence in single-parent families. Furthermore, adolescents spend considerably less time with their parents and more with their peers than they did several decades ago. Finally, the ethnic and cultural diversity of adolescents as a group is increasing dramatically. A third of all adolescents today are of non-European descent; by the year 2045, the number of adolescents of Hispanic, African American, Native American, and Asian origin collectively will surpass that of whites (Frey, 2018).

Physical Development: The Changing Adolescent

If you think back to the start of your own adolescence, the most dramatic changes you probably remember are physical. A spurt in height, the growth of breasts in girls, deepening voices in boys, the development of body hair, and intense sexual feelings cause curiosity, interest, and sometimes embarrassment for individuals entering adolescence.

Not since infancy has development been so dramatic. Beginning around age 10 for girls and age 12 for boys, a growth spurt leads to rapid increases in weight and height. Adolescents may grow as much as 5 inches in 1 year. The physical changes that occur at the start of adolescence result largely from a surge in levels of growth hormone, and they affect virtually every aspect of an adolescent's life.

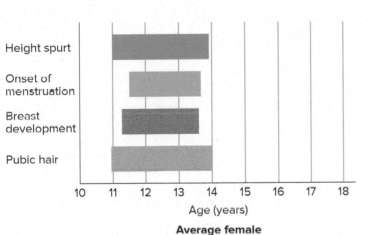

FIGURE 1 The range of ages during which major sexual changes occur during adolescence is shown by the colored bars.

Source: Adapted from Tanner, J. M. (1978). *Education and physical growth* (2nd ed.). New York: International Universities Press.

Puberty is the period at which maturation of the sexual organs occurs. Over the past century in Western cultures, the average age at which adolescents reach sexual maturity has been steadily decreasing, most likely as a result of improved nutrition and medical care.

For girls, puberty typically begins at about age 11 or 12, when menstruation starts. However, there are wide variations (see Figure 1). For example, some girls begin to menstruate as early as age 8 or 9 or as late as age 16. Furthermore, sexual attraction to others begins even before the maturation of the sexual organs at around age 10 (Finlay, Jones, & Coleman, 2002; Shanahan et al., 2013; Herting & Sowell, 2017).

For boys, their first ejaculation, formally known as *spermarche*, typically happens at the beginning of puberty. Spermarche usually occurs around the age of 13 (see Figure 1). At first, relatively few sperm are produced during an ejaculation, but the amount increases significantly within a few years.

The age at which puberty begins has significant implications for the way adolescents feel about themselves—as well as the way others treat them. Preadolescents who start puberty considerably earlier than their peers may feel isolated and different, and they are at risk for mental health issues (Mendle et al., 2016; Weir, 2016; Park, Yun, & Walsh, 2017; Sadeh, Bounoua, & Javdani, 2019).

In some cases, early maturation is favorable for boys. For example, early-maturing boys do better in athletics, are generally more popular with peers, and have more positive self-concepts. However, the picture differs for girls. Although early-maturing girls are more sought after as dates and have better self-esteem than later-maturing girls do, some consequences of early physical

puberty The period at which maturation of the sexual organs occurs, beginning at about age 11 or 12 for girls and 13 or 14 for boys. (Module 38)

Although puberty begins around 11 or 12 for girls and 13 or 14 for boys, there are wide variations. What are some of the advantages and disadvantages of early puberty?
Purestock/SuperStock

maturation may be less positive. For example, early breast development may set them apart from their peers and be a source of ridicule (Blumenthal et al., 2011; Mensah et al., 2013; Natsuaki, Samuels, & Leve, 2015; Copeland et al., 2019).

Late physical maturation may produce certain psychological difficulties for both boys and girls. Boys who are smaller and less coordinated than their more mature peers tend to feel ridiculed and less attractive. Similarly, late-maturing girls are at a disadvantage in middle school and early high school. They hold relatively low social status and may be overlooked in dating (Lanza & Collins, 2002).

Clearly, the rate at which physical changes occur during adolescence can affect the way in which people are viewed by others and the way they view themselves. Just as important as physical changes, however, are the psychological and social changes that unfold during adolescence.

Moral and Cognitive Development: Distinguishing Right from Wrong

In a European country, a woman is near death from a special kind of cancer. The one drug that the doctors think might save her is a medicine that a medical researcher has recently discovered. The drug is expensive to make, and the researcher is charging 10 times the cost, or $5,000, for a small dose. The sick woman's husband, Henry, approaches everyone he knows in hope of borrowing money, but he can get together only about $2,500. He tells the researcher that his wife is dying and asks him to lower the price of the drug or let him pay later. The researcher says, "No, I discovered the drug, and I'm going to make money from it." Henry is desperate and considers stealing the drug for his wife.

What would you tell Henry to do?

KOHLBERG'S THEORY OF MORAL DEVELOPMENT

In the view of psychologist Lawrence Kohlberg, the advice you give Henry reflects your level of moral development. According to Kohlberg, people pass through a series of stages in the evolution of their sense of justice and in the kind of reasoning they use to make moral judgments (Kohlberg, 1984).

Specifically, Kohlberg suggests that changes in moral reasoning can be understood best as the three-level sequence described in Figure 2. Because of their cognitive limitations, preadolescent children who reason at Level 1 morality tend to think in terms of concrete, unvarying rules ("It is always wrong to steal" or "I'll be punished if I steal"). At Level 2 morality, older children tend to focus on the broad rules of society ("Good people don't steal" or "What if everyone stole?"). Those at Level 2 consider moral questions in terms of their own position as good and responsible members of society.

Adolescents, however, however, can reason on a higher plane and potentially have the ability to reason at Level 3. At Level 3, adolescents consider moral issues in terms of principles that are broader than the rules of individual societies. Because they can comprehend broad, universal moral principles, they understand that morality is not always black and white and that conflict can exist between two sets of socially accepted standards.

Kohlberg's theory assumes that people move through the levels in a fixed order and that they cannot reach the highest level until about age 13—primarily because of limitations in cognitive development before that age. However, many people never reach the highest level of moral reasoning. In fact, Kohlberg found that only a relatively small percentage of adults rise above the second level of his model (Kohlberg & Ryncarz, 1990; Gibbs, 2013; Vera-Estay, Dooley, & Beauchamp, 2015).

Although Kohlberg's theory has had a substantial influence on our understanding of moral development, the research support is mixed. One difficulty with the theory is that it pertains to moral *judgments*, not moral *behavior*. Knowing right from wrong

	Sample Moral Reasoning	
Level	**In Favor of Stealing the Drug**	**Against Stealing the Drug**
Level 1 Preconventional morality: The main considerations at this level are the avoidance of punishment and the desire for rewards.	"You shouldn't just let your wife die. People will blame you for not doing enough, and they'll blame the scientist for not selling you the drug for less money."	"You can't steal the drug because you'll be arrested and go to jail. Even if you aren't caught, you'll feel guilty, and you'll always worry that the police may figure out what you did."
Level 2 Conventional morality: Membership in society becomes important at this level. People behave in ways that will win the approval of others.	"Who will blame you if you steal a life-saving drug? But if you just let your wife die, you won't be able to hold your head up in front of your family or neighbors."	"If you steal the drug, everyone will treat you like a criminal. They will wonder why you couldn't have found some other way to save your wife."
Level 3 Postconventional morality: People accept that there are certain broad principles of morality that should govern our actions. These principles are more critical than the particular laws in a society.	"If you simply follow the law, you will violate the underlying principle of saving your wife's life. If you do steal the drug, society will understand your actions and respect them. You can't let an inadequate, outdated law prevent you from doing the right thing."	"You can't change your standards of honesty whenever it suits your needs. Others may not blame you for stealing the drug, but your conscience will blame you for betraying your own moral code."

FIGURE 2 Developmental psychologist Lawrence Kohlberg theorized that people move through a three-level sequence of moral reasoning in a fixed order. However, he contended that few people ever reach the highest level of moral reasoning.

Source: Adapted from Kohlberg, L. (1969). Stage and sequence: The cognitive-developmental approach to socialization. In D. Goslin (Ed.), *Handbook of socialization theory and research* (pp. 381–382). Chicago: Rand McNally; (photo): Steven Puetzer/Photographer's Choice/Getty Images

does not mean that we will always act in accordance with our judgments. In addition, the theory applies primarily to Western society and its moral code; cross-cultural research conducted in cultures with different moral systems suggests that Kohlberg's theory is not necessarily applicable (Stey, Lapsley, & McKeever, 2013; Buon, Habib, & Frey, 2017; Mathes, 2019).

MORAL DEVELOPMENT IN WOMEN

One glaring shortcoming of Kohlberg's research is that he primarily used male participants. Furthermore, psychologist Carol Gilligan (1996) argues that because of men's and women's distinctive socialization experiences, a fundamental difference exists in the way each gender views moral behavior. According to Gilligan, men view morality primarily in terms of broad principles, such as justice and fairness. In contrast, women see it in terms of responsibility toward individuals and willingness to make sacrifices to help a specific individual within the context of a particular relationship. Compassion for individuals is a more salient factor in moral behavior for women than it is for men.

Because Kohlberg's model defines moral behavior largely in terms of abstract principles such as justice, Gilligan finds that it inadequately describes females' moral development. She suggests that women's morality centers on individual well-being and social relationships—a morality of *caring*. In her view, compassionate concern for the welfare of others represents the highest level of morality.

The fact that Gilligan's conception of morality differs greatly from Kohlberg's suggests that gender plays an important role in determining what a person sees as moral. Although the research evidence is not definitive, it seems plausible that their differing conceptions of what constitutes moral behavior may lead men and women to regard the morality of a specific behavior in different ways (Sherblom, 2008; Walker & Frimer, 2009; Capraro & Sippel, 2017).

Study Alert
The difference between the Kohlberg and Gilligan approaches to moral development is significant. Kohlberg's theory focuses on stages, and Gilligan's rests on gender differences.

Social Development: Finding One's Self in a Social World

"Who am I?" "How do I fit into the world?" "What is life all about?"

Questions such as these assume special significance during the teenage years as adolescents seek to find their place in the broader social world. As we will see, this quest takes adolescents along several routes.

ERIKSON'S THEORY OF PSYCHOSOCIAL DEVELOPMENT: THE SEARCH FOR IDENTITY

Erikson's theory of psychosocial development emphasizes the search for identity during the adolescent years. As noted earlier, psychosocial development encompasses the way people's understanding of themselves, one another, and the world around them changes during the course of development (Erikson, 1963).

The fifth stage of Erikson's theory (summarized, with the other stages, in Figure 3), the **identity-versus-role-confusion stage,** encompasses adolescence. During this stage, a time of major testing, people try to determine what is unique about themselves. They attempt to discover who they are, what their strengths are, and what kinds of roles they are best suited to play for the rest of their lives–in short, their **identity.** A person confused about the most appropriate role to play in life may lack a stable identity, adopt an unacceptable role such as that of a social deviant, or have difficulty maintaining close personal relationships later in life (Vleioras & Bosma, 2005; Goldstein, 2006; Wicks, Berger, Camic, 2019).

During the identity-versus-role-confusion period, an adolescent feels pressure to identify what to do with his or her life. Because these pressures come at a time of major physical changes as well as important changes in what society expects of them, adolescents can find the period an especially difficult one. The identity-versus-role-confusion stage has another important characteristic: declining reliance on adults for information with a shift toward using the peer group as a source of social judgments.

identity-versus-role-confusion stage According to Erikson, a time in adolescence of major testing to determine one's unique qualities. (Module 38)

identity The distinguishing character of the individual: who each of us is, what our roles are, and what we are capable of. (Module 38)

Erik Erikson

Stage	Approximate Age	Positive Outcomes	Negative Outcomes
1. Trust-vs.-mistrust	Birth–1½ years	Feelings of trust from environmental support	Fear and concern regarding others
2. Autonomy-vs.-shame-and-doubt	1½–3 years	Self-sufficiency if exploration is encouraged	Doubts about self, lack of independence
3. Initiative-vs.-guilt	3–6 years	Discovery of ways to initiate actions	Guilt from actions and thoughts
4. Industry-vs.-inferiority	6–12 years	Development of sense of competence	Feelings of inferiority, no sense of mastery
5. Identity-vs.-role-confusion	Adolescence	Awareness of uniqueness of self, knowledge of role to be followed	Inability to identify appropriate roles in life
6. Intimacy-vs.-isolation	Early adulthood	Development of loving, sexual relationships and close friendships	Fear of relationships with others
7. Generativity-vs.-stagnation	Middle adulthood	Sense of contribution to continuity of life	Trivialization of one's activities
8. Ego-integrity-vs.-despair	Late adulthood	Sense of unity in life's accomplishments	Regret over lost opportunities of life

FIGURE 3 Erikson's stages of psychosocial development. According to Erikson, people proceed through eight stages of psychosocial development across their lives. He suggested that each stage requires the resolution of a crisis or conflict and may produce both positive and negative outcomes.

(photo): Jon Erikson/Science Source

APPLYING PSYCHOLOGY IN THE 21ST CENTURY

SCREEN TIME BEATS FACE TIME FOR ADOLESCENT FRIENDSHIPS

How do you spend time with your friends? Do you talk with them on the phone? Hang out with them face-to-face? Or do you prefer to interact with them online, via social media?

If you do prefer to interact with them virtually, you're not alone. According to the results of a recent comprehensive study of teenagers' relationships, most are taking their friendships from the real world into the virtual one. The study surveyed over a thousand teenagers, 13–17 years old, about their use of digital media, following up on a similar survey conducted 6 years earlier to give researchers a window into the changes that have occurred during that time.

And significant changes did occur: Whereas about half of the 2012 respondents said their preferred way of talking to friends was face-to-face, that proportion dropped to just about a third in 2018. To researchers, this finding indicates an ongoing shift in how people communicate, and they suggest that the trend may continue into the future (Morris, 2018; Rideout, 2018).

Additional survey findings fill in the reasons behind this trend. The percentage of teens who reported owning a smartphone more than doubled, from 41% in 2012 to 89% in 2018. A similar doubling occurred in the percentage of teens who reported using social media more than once per day, from 34% in 2012 to 70% in 2018. In fact, "daily" isn't fine-grained enough to capture the change in teens' frequency of social media use: 38% of the 2018 respondents

Many adolescents prefer virtual to face-to-face interaction.
Syda Productions/Shutterstock

said they use it multiple times an hour, and 16% reported almost constant use.

The researchers expressed concerns about how the upswing in social media use might affect teens' lives. For example, 57% reported that social media use frequently distracts them from doing their homework. Emotionally troubled teens were more likely than others to say they had been harmed by social media, but also more of them reported being helped by it in 2018 than in 2012, suggesting that it exerts both good and bad influences. In any case, teen-

agers are very attached to their devices: more than a third of them wake up in the middle of the night to check their smartphones (Robb, 2019).

It remains to be seen whether these trends will continue. Furthermore, we don't know the extent to which social media use may have an influence beyond mere communication patterns—for example, whether it will affect how young people think about themselves and relate to others. But it seems clear that important shifts have and will continue to occur.

RETHINK

- What might be some reasons why teens are increasingly preferring to communicate online rather than face-to-face?
- What kinds of negative effects might heavy social media use have on emotionally vulnerable teens? What kinds of positive effects might it have?

The peer group becomes increasingly important, enabling adolescents to form close, adultlike relationships and helping them clarify their personal identities. According to Erikson, the identity-versus-role-confusion stage marks a pivotal point in psychosocial development, paving the way for continued growth and the future development of personal relationships (also see the Applying Psychology in the 21st Century box).

During early adulthood, people enter the **intimacy-versus-isolation stage.** Spanning the period of early adulthood (from postadolescence to the early 30s), this stage focuses on developing close relationships with others. Difficulties during this stage result in feelings of loneliness and a fear of such relationships; successful resolution of

intimacy-versus-isolation stage
According to Erikson, a period during early adulthood that focuses on developing close relationships. (Module 38)

the crises of this stage results in the possibility of forming relationships that are intimate on a physical, intellectual, and emotional level.

Development continues during middle adulthood as people enter the **generativity-versus-stagnation stage.** Generativity is the ability to contribute to one's family, community, work, and society, and to assist the development of the younger generation. Success in this stage results in a people feeling positive and optimistic about the continuity of life and their contribution to humanity. On the other hand, difficulties in this stage lead people to feel that their activities are trivial and unimportant and that their lives are stagnant. They may feel they have made poor choices.

Finally, the last stage of psychosocial development, the **ego-integrity-versus-despair stage,** spans later adulthood and continues until death. People in this stage ask themselves if they have lived a meaningful life. If they see their lives positively, they feel a sense of accomplishment; if not, they feel regret over a misspent life.

Notably, Erikson's theory suggests that development does not stop at adolescence but continues throughout adulthood. A substantial amount of research now confirms this view. For instance, a 22-year study by psychologist Susan Whitbourne found considerable support for the fundamentals of Erikson's theory; the study determined that psychosocial development continues through adolescence and adulthood. In sum, adolescence is not an end point but rather a way station on the path of psychosocial development (Whitbourne et al., 1992; McAdams et al., 1997; Filip, Lukavská, & Šolcová, 2019).

Although Erikson's theory provides a broad outline of identity development, critics have pointed out that his approach is anchored in male-oriented concepts of individuality and competitiveness. In an alternative conception, psychologist Carol Gilligan suggests that women may develop identity through the establishment of relationships. In her view, a primary component of women's identity is the construction of caring networks among themselves and others (Gilligan, 2004).

STORMY ADOLESCENCE: MYTH OR REALITY?

Does puberty invariably foreshadow a stormy, rebellious period of adolescence?

At one time, psychologists thought that adolescence was a period filled with stress and unhappiness. Today, however, research shows that this characterization is largely a myth. The reality is that most young people pass through adolescence without great turmoil in their lives and that they get along with their parents reasonably well (Granic, Hollenstein, & Dishion, 2003; Steinberg, 2016).

Not that adolescence is completely calm! In most families with adolescents, the amount of arguing and bickering clearly rises. Most young teenagers, as part of their search for identity, experience tension between their attempts to become independent from their parents and their actual dependence on them. They may experiment with a range of behaviors and flirt with a variety of activities that their parents, and even society as a whole, find objectionable. Happily, though, for most families, such tensions stabilize during middle adolescence—around age 15 or 16—and eventually decline around age 18 (Smetana, Daddis, & Chuang, 2003; Smetana, 2005; Hadiwijaya et al., 2017).

One reason for the increase in discord during adolescence appears to be the protracted period in which children stay at home with their parents. In prior historical periods—and in some non-Western cultures today—children leave home immediately after puberty and are considered adults. Today, however, sexually mature adolescents may spend as many as 7 or 8 years with their parents. Current social trends even hint at an extension of the conflicts of adolescence beyond the teenage years because a significant number of young adults—known as *boomerang children*—return to live with their parents, typically for economic reasons, after leaving home for some period. Although some parents welcome the return of their children, others are less sympathetic, which opens the way to conflict (Lewin, 2003; Otters & Hollander, 2015; Kreiczer-Levy, 2019).

---

generativity-versus-stagnation stage According to Erikson, a period in middle adulthood during which we take stock of our contributions to family and society. (Module 38)

ego-integrity-versus-despair stage According to Erikson, a period from late adulthood until death during which we review life's accomplishments and failures. (Module 38)

❗ Study Alert
The characterization of adolescence as stormy is a myth for most adolescents.

PsychTech
Adolescent use of social media such as Facebook is growing rapidly: 94% of teenagers use Facebook, and a quarter of them access their Facebook pages continuously throughout the day.

Another source of strife with parents lies in the way adolescents think. Adolescence fosters *adolescent egocentrism,* a state of self-absorption in which a teenager views the world from his or her own point of view. Egocentrism leads adolescents to be highly critical of authority figures, unwilling to accept criticism, and quick to fault others. It also makes them believe that they are the center of everyone else's attention, which leads to self-consciousness.

Furthermore, adolescents develop *personal fables*–the belief that one's experience and beliefs are unique, exceptional, and shared by no one else. Such personal fables may make adolescents feel invulnerable to the risks that threaten others (Schwartz, Maynard, & Uzelac, 2008; Boeve-de Pauw, Donche, & Van Petegem, 2011; Zheng, Ni, & Luo, 2019).

Finally, parent-adolescent discord occurs because adolescents are much more apt to engage in risky behavior than they are later in life. In part, their riskiness is due to the immaturity of brain systems that regulate impulse control, some of which do not fully develop until people are in their mid-20s. Furthermore, adolescents have a greater tolerance for ambiguity and uncertainty, leading them to tolerate risks that adults would be less likely to accept (Steinberg, 2007; Steinberg, 2016).

ADOLESCENT SUICIDE

Although the vast majority of teenagers pass through adolescence without major psychological difficulties, some experience unusually severe psychological problems. Sometimes those problems become so extreme that adolescents take their own lives.

Suicide is the second leading cause of death among individuals between the ages of 10 and 17 (after accidents) in the United States, and the rate of suicide increased 26% between 2007 and 2017. More teenagers and young adults die from suicide than from cancer, heart disease, birth defects, stroke, pneumonia and influenza, and chronic lung disease combined. The increase in adolescent suicide is consistent with the increase in other age groups (NIMH, 2019; Lovett, 2019).

The reported rate may actually be understated because medical personnel hesitate to report suicide as a cause of death. Instead, they frequently label a death as an accident in an effort to protect the survivors. Overall, as many as 200 adolescents may attempt suicide for every one who actually takes his or her own life. And consistent with the growing number of actual suicides, the occurrence of suicidal thoughts and attempts at suicide by adolescents nearly doubled from 2008 to 2015 (CDC, 2000; Brausch & Gutierrez, 2009; Plemmons et al., 2019).

Male adolescents are five times more likely to commit suicide than females are, although females *attempt* suicide more often than males do. The rate of adolescent suicide is significantly greater among whites than among nonwhites. On the other hand, Native Americans have the highest suicide rate of any ethnic group in the United States, and Asian Americans have the lowest rate (Boden, Fergusson, & Horwood, 2007; Bossarte & Swahn, 2011; Yildiz et al., 2019).

What accounts for the increase in suicide rate among adolescents? Some psychologists suggest that the sharp rise in stress that teenagers experience–in terms of academic and social pressure, alcoholism, drug abuse, and family difficulties–provokes the most troubled adolescents to take their own lives. Easy access to weapons also tends to increase the chance of suicide (Valois, Zullig, & Hunter, 2013; Sood & Linker, 2017; McGinty, 2019).

Although the question of why adolescent suicide rates are so high remains unanswered, several factors put adolescents at risk. One factor is depression, characterized by unhappiness, extreme fatigue, and–a variable that seems especially important–a profound sense of hopelessness. In other cases, adolescents who commit suicide are perfectionists who are inhibited socially and prone to extreme anxiety when they face any social or academic challenge. Furthermore, in some cases, bullying, both in person and cyberbullying, may result in suicide (see Figure 4; Caelian, 2006; Barzilay et al., 2015; Young et al., 2017).

These young people are mourning the death of a peer who committed suicide. Why do you think the suicide rate among teenagers has risen significantly over the past few decades?

RichLegg/Getty Images

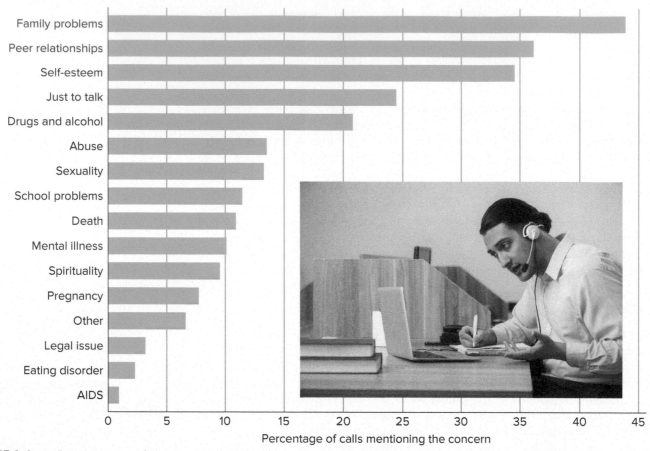

FIGURE 4 According to a review of phone calls to one telephone help line, adolescents who were considering suicide most often mentioned family, peer relationships, and self-esteem problems.

Source: Adapted from Boehm, K. E., & Campbell, N. B. (1995). Suicide: A review of calls to an adolescent peer listening phone service. *Child Psychiatry and Human Development, 26,* 61–66; (photo): Elnur Amikishiyev/123RF

Family background and adjustment difficulties are also related to suicide. A long-standing history of conflicts between parents and children may lead to adolescent behavior problems, such as delinquency, dropping out of school, and aggressive tendencies. In addition, teenage alcoholics and abusers of other drugs have a relatively high rate of suicide. Finally, suicides sometimes come in clusters, meaning that the suicide of one adolescent can trigger the suicide of others (Bagge & Sher, 2008; Hardt et al., 2008; Lovett, 2019).

Several warning signs indicate when a teenager's problems may be severe enough to warrant concern about the possibility of a suicide attempt. They include the following:

- School problems, such as missing classes, truancy, and a sudden change in grades

- Frequent incidents of self-destructive behavior, such as careless accidents

- Loss of appetite or excessive eating

- Withdrawal from friends and peers

- Sleeping problems

- Signs of depression, tearfulness, or overt indications of psychological difficulties, such as hallucinations

- A preoccupation with death, an afterlife, or what would happen "if I died"

- Putting affairs in order, such as giving away prized possessions or making arrangements for the care of a pet

- An explicit announcement of thoughts of suicide

If you know someone who shows signs that he or she is suicidal, urge that person to seek professional help. You may need to take assertive action, such as enlisting the assistance of family members, friends, or campus administrators such as Student Affairs personnel. Talk of suicide is a serious signal for help and not a confidence to be kept.

For immediate help with a suicide-related problem, call (800) 273-8255, a national hotline staffed with trained counselors, or access www.suicidepreventionlifeline.org. You can also text 741741 to reach help.

From the perspective of...

A Social Worker How might you determine if an adolescent is at risk for suicide? What strategies would you use to prevent the teen from committing suicide? Would you use different strategies depending on the teenager's gender?

Sam Edwards/OJO Images/age fotostock

 # Exploring Diversity

Rites of Passage: Coming of Age Around the World

It is not easy for male members of the Awa tribe in New Guinea to make the transition from childhood to adulthood. First come whippings with sticks and prickly branches both for the boys' own past misdeeds and in honor of those tribesmen who were killed in warfare. In the next phase of the ritual, adults jab sharpened sticks into the boys' nostrils. Then they force a 5-foot length of vine into the boys' throats until they gag and vomit. Finally, tribesmen cut the boys' genitals, causing severe bleeding.

Although the rites that mark the coming of age of boys in the Awa tribe sound horrifying to Westerners, they are comparable to those in other cultures. In some, youths must kneel on hot coals without displaying pain. In others, girls must toss wads of burning cotton from hand to hand and allow themselves to be bitten by hundreds of ants (Selsky, 1997).

Other cultures have less fearsome, although equally important, ceremonies that mark the passage from childhood to adulthood. For instance, when a girl first menstruates in traditional Apache tribes, the event is marked by dawn-to-dusk chanting. Western religions, too, have several types of celebrations, including bar mitzvahs and bat mitzvahs at age 13 for Jewish boys and girls, respectively, and confirmation ceremonies for children in many Christian denominations (Magida, 2006).

In most societies, males are the focus of coming-of-age ceremonies. The reason for this gender distinction may be that in most cultures, men traditionally have higher status than women, and therefore, those cultures regard boys' transition into adulthood as more important to celebrate.

However, another fact may explain why most cultures place greater emphasis on male rather than female rites: For females, the transition from childhood is marked by a definite biological event: menstruation. For males, in contrast, no single event can be used to pinpoint entry into adulthood. Thus, men are forced to rely on culturally determined rituals to acknowledge their arrival into adulthood.

RECAP/EVALUATE/RETHINK

RECAP

LO 38-1 What major physical, social, and cognitive transitions characterize adolescence?

- Adolescence, the developmental stage between childhood and adulthood, is marked by the onset of puberty, the point at which sexual maturity occurs. The age at which puberty begins has implications for the way people view themselves and the way others see them.
- Moral judgments during adolescence increase in sophistication, according to Kohlberg's three-level model. Although Kohlberg's levels provide an adequate description of males' moral judgments, Gilligan suggests that women view morality in terms of caring for individuals rather than in terms of broad general principles of justice.
- According to Erikson's model of psychosocial development, adolescence may be accompanied by an identity crisis. Adolescence is followed by three more stages of psychosocial development that cover the remainder of the life span.
- Suicide is the third leading cause of death in adolescents.

EVALUATE

1. _____ is the period during which the sexual organs begin to mature.

2. Delayed maturation typically provides both males and females with a social advantage. True or false?

3. _____ proposed a set of three levels of moral development ranging from reasoning based on rewards and punishments to abstract thinking involving concepts of justice.

4. Erikson believed that during adolescence, people must search for _____, whereas during the early adulthood, the major task is _____.

RETHINK

1. In what ways do school environments help or hurt teenage students who are going through adolescence? What school policies might benefit early-maturing girls and late-maturing boys? Explain how same-sex schools could help students going through adolescence, as some have argued.

2. Many cultures have rites of passage through which young people are officially recognized as adults. Do you think such rites can be beneficial? Does the United States have any such rites? Would setting up an official designation that one has achieved "adult" status have benefits?

Answers to Evaluate Questions

1. Puberty; 2. False; both male and female adolescents suffer if they mature late; 3. Kohlberg; 4. identity, intimacy

KEY TERMS

adolescence
puberty
identity-versus-role-
    confusion stage

identity
intimacy-versus-isolation
    stage

generativity-versus-
    stagnation stage

ego-integrity-versus-
    despair stage

Module 39
Adulthood

LEARNING OUTCOMES

LO 39-1 What are the principal kinds of physical, social, and intellectual changes that occur in early and middle adulthood, and what are their causes?

LO 39-2 How does the reality of late adulthood differ from the stereotypes about that period?

LO 39-3 How can we adjust to death?

emerging adulthood The period beginning in the late teenage years and extending into the mid-20s. (Module 39)

I thought I got better as I got older. I found out that wasn't the case in a real hurry last year. After going 12 years in professional football and 12 years before that in amateur football without ever having surgery performed on me, the last two seasons of my career I went under the knife three times. It happened very quickly and without warning, and I began to ask myself, "Is this age? Is this what's happening?" Because up until that moment, I'd never realized that I was getting older. (Kotre & Hall, 1990)

As a former professional football player, Brian Sipe intensely felt the changes in his body brought about by aging. But the challenges he experienced are part of a normal process that affects all people as they move through adulthood.

Psychologists generally agree that early adulthood begins around age 20 and lasts until about age 40 to 45, when middle adulthood begins and continues until around age 65. Despite the enormous importance of these periods of life in terms of both the accomplishments that occur in them and their overall length (together they span some 44 years), they have been studied less than has any other stage. For one reason, the physical changes that occur during these periods are less apparent and more gradual than those at other times during the life span. In addition, the diverse social changes that arise during this period defy simple categorization.

The variety of changes that occur in early adulthood have led many developmental psychologists to view the start of the period as a transitional phase called emerging adulthood. **Emerging adulthood** is the period beginning in the late teenage years and extending into the mid-20s.

During emerging adulthood, people are no longer adolescents, although the brain is still growing and modifying its neural pathways. It is typically a period of uncertainty in which postadolescents haven't fully taken on the responsibilities of adulthood. Instead, they are still engaged in determining who they are and what their life and career paths should be. It is a time of uncertainty and instability, as well as self-discovery (Lamborn & Groh, 2009; Schwartz et al., 2013; Pratt & Matsuba, 2019).

The view that adulthood is preceded by an extended period of emerging adulthood reflects the reality of the economies of industrialized countries. These economies have shifted away from manufacturing to a focus on technology and information, thus requiring increasing time spent in educational training. Furthermore, the age at which most people marry and have children has risen significantly (Arnett, 2007, 2011).

There's also an increasing ambivalence about reaching adulthood. When people in their late teens and early 20s are asked if they feel they have reached adulthood, most say "yes and no" (see Figure 1). In short, emerging adulthood is an age of identity exploration in which individuals are more self-focused and uncertain than they will be later in early adulthood (Arnett, 2006; Verschueren et al., 2017; Mannerström, Muotka, & Salmela-Aro, 2019).

As we discuss the changes that occur through emerging adulthood, early adulthood, middle adulthood, and ultimately late adulthood, keep in mind the demarcations between the periods are fuzzy. However, the changes are certainly no less profound than they were in earlier periods of development.

FIGURE 1 Evidence of a period of emerging adulthood is provided by the responses to a questionnaire asking, "Do you feel that you have reached adulthood?" Most people between the ages of 18 and 25 were ambivalent, responding "yes and no." Later, this ambivalence disappeared, with most people 26–35 saying "yes."

Source: Adapted from Arnett, J. J. (2006). *Emerging adulthood: The winding road from the late teens through the twenties.* New York: Oxford University Press.

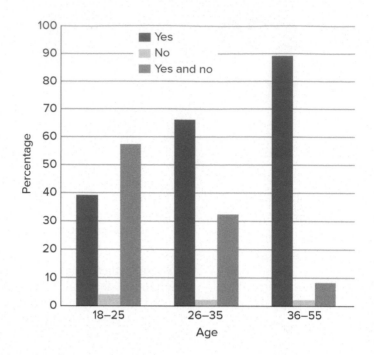

menopause The period during which women stop menstruating and are no longer fertile. (Module 39)

Physical Development: The Peak of Health

For most people, early adulthood marks the peak of physical health. From about 18 to 25 years of age, people's strength is greatest, their reflexes are quickest, and their chances of dying from disease are quite slim. Moreover, reproductive capabilities are at their highest level.

Around age 25, the body becomes slightly less efficient and more susceptible to disease. Overall, however, ill health remains the exception; most people stay remarkably healthy during early adulthood. (Can you think of any machine other than the body that can operate without pause for so long a period?)

During middle adulthood, people gradually become aware of changes in their bodies. They often experience weight gain (although they can avoid such increases through diet and exercise). Furthermore, the sense organs gradually become less sensitive, and reactions to stimuli are slower. But generally, the physical declines that occur during middle adulthood are minor and often unnoticeable (Kekäläinen et al., 2019).

The major biological change that does occur during middle adulthood pertains to reproductive capabilities. On average, during their late 40s or early 50s, women begin **menopause,** during which they stop menstruating and are no longer fertile. Because menopause is accompanied by a significant reduction in the production of estrogen, a female hormone, women sometimes experience hot flashes, sudden sensations of heat. Some doctors treat these with *hormone therapy (HT)* in which menopausal women take the hormones estrogen and progesterone.

However, hormone therapy poses several dangers, such as an increase in the risk of breast cancer, blood clots, and coronary heart disease. These uncertainties make the routine use of HT controversial. Currently, the medical consensus seems to be that younger women with severe menopausal symptoms ought to consider HT on a short-term basis. On the other hand, HT is less appropriate for older women after menopause (MacLennan, 2009; McCarrey & Resnick, 2015; Shifren, Crandall, & Manson, 2019).

Menopause was once blamed for a variety of psychological symptoms, including depression and memory loss. However, if such difficulties occur, they may be caused

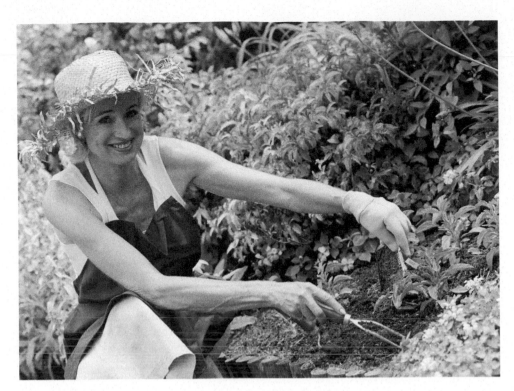

Women's reactions to menopause vary significantly across cultures. According to one study, the more a society values old age, the less difficulty its women have during menopause. Why do you think this would be the case?
BananaStock/Alamy Stock Photo

by women's expectations about reaching an "old" age in a society that highly values youth. For example, women's reactions to menopause vary significantly across cultures. The more a society values old age, the less difficulty its women have during menopause (Beyene, Gilliss, & Lee, 2007; Espinola, DeVinney & Steinberg, 2017).

For men, the aging process during middle adulthood is more subtle. Men have no physiological signals of increasing age equivalent to the end of menstruation in women; that is, no male menopause exists. In fact, men remain fertile and capable of fathering children until well into late adulthood.

However, some gradual physical decline occurs. Men typically become less physically fit, especially after the age of 45. Sperm production decreases, and the frequency of orgasm declines. As is the case for women, though, psychological difficulties associated with these changes are usually brought about more by aging men's inability to meet the exaggerated standards of youthfulness than by men's physical deterioration (Jackson et al., 2009; Kuosmanen et al., 2016).

Social Development: Working at Life

Whereas physical changes during adulthood reflect development of a quantitative nature, social developmental transitions are qualitative and more profound. During this period, people typically launch themselves into careers, marriage, and families.

The entry into early adulthood is usually marked by leaving one's childhood home and entering the world of work. People envision life goals and make career choices. Their lives often center on their careers, which form an important part of their identity (Vaillant & Vaillant, 1990; Levinson, 1992; Fadjukoff et al., 2019).

In their early 40s, however, people may begin to question their lives as they enter a period called the *midlife transition*. The idea that life will end at some point can become more influential in their thinking, which leads them to question their past accomplishments (Boylan & Ryff, 2015; Kurther & Burnell, 2019).

Although some psychologists—and popular opinion—suggest that physical aging and dissatisfaction with one's life mark a so-called "midlife crisis," there is little evidence for such a "crisis." In fact, the passage into middle age is relatively calm for most people.

Most 40-year-olds view their lives and accomplishments positively enough to proceed relatively smoothly through midlife, and the 40s and 50s are often a particularly rewarding period. Rather than looking to the future, people concentrate on the present; their involvement with their families, friends, and other social groups takes on new importance. A major developmental thrust of this period is coming to terms with one's circumstances (Whitbourne, 2010; Dare, 2011; Wojciechowska, 2017).

Finally, during the last stages of adulthood, people become more accepting of others and of their own lives and are less concerned about issues or problems that once bothered them. They come to accept the fact that death is inevitable, and they try to understand their accomplishments in terms of the broader meaning of life. Although people may begin for the first time to label themselves as "old," many also develop a sense of wisdom and feel freer to enjoy life (Miner-Rubino, Winter, & Stewart, 2004; Ward-Baker, 2007; Galambos et al., 2015).

Marriage, Children, and Divorce: Family Ties

In the typical fairy tale, a dashing young man and a beautiful young woman marry, have children, and live happily ever after. However, that scenario does not match the realities of love and marriage in the 21st century. Today, it is just as likely that the man and woman would first live together, then get married and have children, but ultimately get divorced.

The percentage of U.S. households made up of unmarried couples has increased dramatically over the last two decades. At the same time, the average age at which marriage takes place is higher than at any time since the turn of the last century. These changes have been dramatic, and they suggest that the institution of marriage has changed considerably from earlier historical periods.

When people do marry, the possibility of divorce is not trivial. Many marriages end in divorce, though divorce rates have been declining since they peaked in 1979. Today, the rate is 16.1 divorces for every 1,000 marriages, which works out to 39% of first marriages ending in divorce (Luscomb, 2018; McGinty, 2019).

Furthermore, divorce is not only a U.S. phenomenon, and in many countries, such as Russia, the divorce rate is even higher than that in the United States. Overall, the divorce rate has accelerated across the globe over the past several decades, particularly in industrialized countries (Park & Raymo, 2013; Olson & DeFrain, 2014; Zahl-Olsen, Thuen, & Espehaug, 2019).

In addition, 27% of all family households are now headed by one parent, compared with 13% in 1970. If present trends continue, almost three-fourths of American children will spend some portion of their lives in a single-parent family before they turn 18. For children in minority households, the numbers are even higher. Almost 60% of all African American children and more than a third of all Hispanic children live in homes with only one parent. Furthermore, in most single-parent families, the children live with the mother rather than the father—a phenomenon that is consistent across racial and ethnic groups throughout the industrialized world (Sarsour et al., 2011; U.S. Bureau of the Census, 2016).

What are the economic and emotional consequences for children living in homes with only one parent? Single-parent families are often economically less well off, and this economic disadvantage has an impact on children's opportunities. More than a third of single-mother families with children have incomes below the poverty line. In addition, good child care at an affordable price is often hard to find. Furthermore, for children of divorce, the parents' separation is often a painful experience that may result in obstacles to establishing close relationships later in life. Children may blame themselves for the breakup or feel pressure to take sides (Liu, He, & Wu, 2007; Carr et al., 2019).

Most evidence suggests, however, that children from single-parent families are no less well adjusted than are those from two-parent families. In fact, children may be more successful growing up in a harmonious single-parent family than in a two-parent family that engages in continuous conflict (Kelly, 2000; Olson & DeFrain, 2005; Koh et al., 2017).

Changing Roles of Men and Women

One of the major changes in family life in the last four decades has been the evolution of men's and women's roles. More women than ever before act simultaneously as wives, mothers, and wage earners—in contrast to women in traditional marriages in which the husband is the sole wage earner and the wife assumes primary responsibility for care of the home and children.

Almost three-fourths of all women with children under the age of 18 are employed outside the home, and 65% of mothers with children under age 6 are working. In the mid-1960s, only 17% of mothers of 1-year-olds worked full-time; now, more than half are in the labor force (Bureau of Labor Statistics, 2013).

Most married working women are not free of household responsibilities. Even in marriages in which the spouses hold jobs that have similar status and require similar hours, the distribution of household tasks between husbands and wives has not changed substantially. Working wives are still more likely than husbands to feel responsible for traditional homemaking tasks such as cooking and cleaning. In contrast, husbands still view themselves as responsible primarily for household tasks such as repairing broken appliances and doing yardwork (Damaske, 2011; Hwang, Lee, & Lee, 2019).

WOMEN'S "SECOND SHIFT"

Working mothers can put in a staggering number of hours. One survey, for instance, found that if we add the number of hours worked on the job and in the home, employed mothers of children under 3 years of age put in an average of 90 hours per week! The additional work women perform is sometimes called the "second shift." National surveys show women who are both employed and mothers put in an extra month of 24-hour days during the course of a year. Researchers see similar patterns in many developing societies throughout the world, with women working at full-time jobs and having primary responsibilities for child care (Hochschild, 2001; Jacobs & Gerson, 2004; U.S. Bureau of Labor Statistics, 2007).

Consequently, rather than careers being a substitute for what women do at home, they are often an addition to the role of homemaker. It is not surprising that some wives feel resentment toward husbands who spend less time on child care and house-work than the wives had expected before the birth of their children (Gerstel, 2005; Fagan & Press, 2008; Brailey & Slatton, 2019).

Later Years of Life: Growing Old

I've always enjoyed doing things in the mountains—hiking or, more recently, active cliff-climbing. The more difficult the climb, the more absorbing it is. The climbs I really remember are the ones I had to work on. Maybe a particular section where it took two or three tries before I found the right combination of moves that got me up easily—and, preferably, elegantly. It's a wonderful exhilaration to get to the top and sit down and perhaps have lunch and look out over the landscape and be so grateful that it's still possible for me to do that sort of thing. (Lyman Spitzer, age 74, quoted in Kotre & Hall, 1990)

If you can't quite picture a 74-year-old rock-climbing, some rethinking of your view of late adulthood may be in order. In spite of the societal stereotype of "old age" as a time of inactivity and physical and mental decline, gerontologists, specialists who study aging, are beginning to paint a very different portrait of late adulthood.

FIGURE 2 Projections suggest that by the year 2050, more than 20% of the U.S. population will be over age 65. What implications does this statistic have for U.S. society?

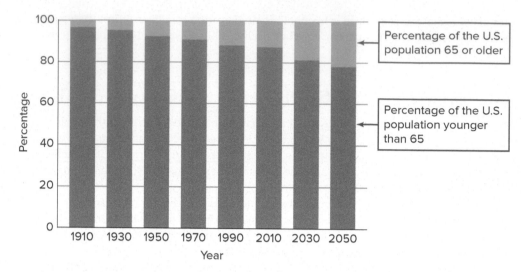

Percentage of the U.S. population 65 or older

Percentage of the U.S. population younger than 65

By focusing on the period of life that starts at around age 65, gerontologists are making important contributions to clarifying the capabilities of older adults. Their work is demonstrating that significant developmental processes continue even during old age. And as people live longer, the absolute numbers of people within older adulthood will continue to increase (see Figure 2). Consequently, developing an understanding of late adulthood has become a critical priority for psychologists (Schaie, 2005b; Jia, Zack, & Thompson, 2011).

Physical Changes in Late Adulthood: The Aging Body

Napping, eating, walking, conversing. It probably doesn't surprise you that these relatively nonstrenuous activities represent the typical pastimes of late adulthood. But it is striking that these activities are identical to the most common leisure activities reported in a survey of college students (Harper, 1978). Although the students cited more active pursuits—such as sailing and playing basketball—as their favorite activities, in actuality they engaged in such sports relatively infrequently and spent most of their free time napping, eating, walking, and conversing.

Although the leisure activities in which older adults engage may not differ all that much from the ones that younger people pursue, many physical changes are, of course, brought about by the aging process. The most obvious are those of appearance—hair thinning and turning gray, skin wrinkling and folding, and sometimes a slight loss of height as the thickness of the disks between vertebrae in the spine decreases. But subtler changes also occur in the body's biological functioning. For example, sensory capabilities decrease as a result of aging: Vision, hearing, smell, and taste become less sensitive. Reaction time slows, and physical stamina changes (Madden, 2007; Schilling & Diehl, 2015; Tucker-Drob, Brandmaier, & Lindenberger, 2019).

genetic programming theories of aging Theories that suggest that our DNA genetic code includes a built-in time limit to the reproduction of human cells and that they are no longer able to divide after a certain time. (Module 39)

wear-and-tear theories of aging Theories that suggest that the mechanical functions of the body simply stop working efficiently. (Module 39)

What are the reasons for these physical declines? **Genetic programming theories of aging** suggest that the DNA genetic code includes a built-in time limit for the reproduction of human cells. These theories suggest that after a certain time cells stop dividing or become harmful to the body—as if a kind of automatic self-destruct button had been pushed. In contrast, **wear-and-tear theories of aging** suggest that the mechanical functions of the body simply work less efficiently as people age. Waste by-products of energy production eventually accumulate, and mistakes are made when cells divide. Eventually, the body in effect wears out like an old automobile (Miquel, 2006; Hayflick, 2007; Helgeson & Zajdel, 2017).

Evidence supports both the genetic programming and the wear-and-tear views, and it may be that both processes contribute to natural aging. It is clear, however, that physical aging is not a disease but a natural biological process. Many physical functions do not decline with age. For example, sex remains pleasurable well into old age (although the frequency of sexual activity decreases), and some people report that the pleasure they derive from sex increases during late adulthood (Gelfand, 2000; DeLamater & Sill, 2005; Wilkin & Haddock, 2011).

Cognitive Changes: Thinking About—and During—Late Adulthood

At one time, many gerontologists would have agreed with the popular view that older adults are forgetful and confused. Today, however, most research indicates that this assessment is far from an accurate one of older people's capabilities.

One reason for the change in view is that more sophisticated research techniques exist for studying the cognitive changes that occur in late adulthood. For example, if we were to give a group of older adults an IQ test, we might find that the average score was lower than the score achieved by a group of younger people. We might conclude that this signifies a decline in intelligence. Yet, if we looked a little more closely at the specific test, we might find that the conclusion was unwarranted. For instance, many IQ tests include portions based on physical performance (such as arranging a group of blocks) or on speed. In such cases, poorer performance on the IQ test may be due to gradual decreases in reaction time—a physical decline that accompanies late adulthood and has little or nothing to do with older adults' intellectual capabilities.

Other difficulties hamper research into cognitive functioning during late adulthood. For example, older people are often less healthy than younger ones; when only *healthy* older adults are compared to healthy younger adults, intellectual differences are far less evident. Furthermore, the average number of years in school is often lower in older adults (for historical reasons) than in younger ones, and older adults may be less motivated to perform well on intelligence tests than younger people are. Finally, traditional IQ tests may be inappropriate measures of intelligence in late adulthood. Older adults sometimes perform better on tests of practical intelligence than younger individuals do (Dixon & Cohen, 2003; Johnson & Deary, 2011).

Still, some declines in intellectual functioning during late adulthood do occur, although the pattern of age differences is not uniform for different types of cognitive abilities (see Figure 3). In general, skills relating to *fluid intelligence* (which involves information-processing skills such as memory, calculations, and analogy solving) show declines in late adulthood. In contrast, skills relating to *crystallized intelligence* (intelligence based on the accumulation of information, skills, and strategies learned through experience) remain steady and in some cases actually improve (Kaufman, Johnson, & Liu, 2008; Dixon et al., 2013; Wettstein et al., 2019).

Although fluid intelligence declines in late adulthood, skills relating to crystallized intelligence remain steady and may actually improve.
icsnaps/Shutterstock

FIGURE 3 Age-related changes in intellectual skills vary according to the specific cognitive ability in question.

Source: Adapted from Schaie, K. W. (2005). Longitudinal studies. In Schaie, K. W., *Developmental influences on adult intelligence: The Seattle Longitudinal Study.* New York: Oxford University Press.

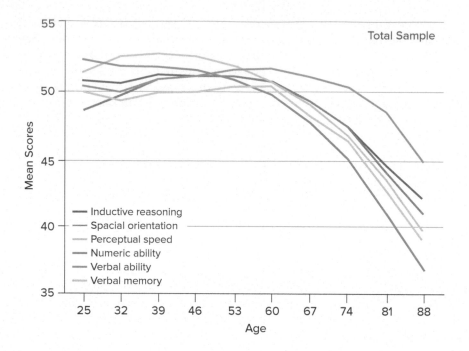

Even when changes in intellectual functioning occur during later adulthood, people often are able to compensate for any decline. They can still learn what they want to learn; it may just take more time. Furthermore, teaching older adults strategies for dealing with new problems can prevent declines in performance (Cavallini, Pagnin, & Vecchi, 2003; Peters et al., 2007; Finke, Howe, & Huston, 2017).

MEMORY CHANGES IN LATE ADULTHOOD: ARE OLDER ADULTS FORGETFUL?

One of the characteristics most frequently attributed to late adulthood is forgetfulness. How accurate is this assumption?

Most evidence suggests that memory change is not an inevitable part of the aging process. For instance, older people in cultures in which older adults are held in high esteem, such as China, are less likely to show memory losses than are those living in cultures in which the expectation is that memory will decline. Similarly, when older people in Western societies are reminded of the advantages of age (for example, "age brings wisdom"), they tend to do better on tests of memory (Levy, 1996; Dixon, Rust, & Feltmate, 2007; Pinal, Zurrón, & Díaz, 2015).

Even when people show memory declines during late adulthood, their deficits are limited to certain types of memory. For instance, losses tend to be limited to episodic memories that relate to specific experiences in people's lives. Other types of memories, such as semantic memories (those that refer to general knowledge and facts) and implicit memories (memories of which we are not consciously aware), are largely unaffected by age (Blumen, Rajaram, & Henkel, 2013; Gurven, 2017; Sejunaite, Lanza, & Riepe, 2019).

Declines in episodic memories can often be traced to changes in older adults' lives. For instance, it is not surprising that a retired person, who may no longer face the same kind of consistent intellectual challenges encountered on the job, may have less practice in using memory or even be less motivated to remember things, which leads to an apparent decline in memory. Even in cases in which long-term memory declines, older adults can profit from training that targets memory skills (West, Bagwell, & Dark-Freudeman, 2007; Morcom & Friston, 2011; Després et al., 2017).

In the past, older adults with severe cases of memory decline accompanied by other cognitive difficulties were said to suffer from *senility*. Now, most gerontologists view senility as an imprecise label that has outlived its usefulness. Instead, gerontologists explain symptoms of mental deterioration using more precise factors.

For example, rather than use *senility* to describe memory loss in general, gerontologists now recognize **Alzheimer's disease** as a progressive brain disorder that leads to a gradual and irreversible decline in cognitive abilities. More than 5.5 million Americans have the disease, and 1 in 10 people age 65 and older are afflicted. Unless a cure is found, some 11 million people are expected to have Alzheimer's in 2050 (Rogers, 2007; Alzheimer's Association, 2017).

Alzheimer's occurs when production of the *beta amyloid precursor protein* goes awry, producing large clumps of cells that trigger inflammation and deterioration of nerve cells. The brain shrinks, neurons die, and several areas of the hippocampus and frontal and temporal lobes deteriorate. So far, there is no effective treatment, although preliminary research suggests that diet, exercise, and an active social life can slow the decline in cognitive capabilities brought on by Alzheimer's (Behrens, Lendon, & Roe, 2009; Kivipelto & Hakansson, 2017; Milne et al., 2019).

In other cases, cognitive declines may be caused by temporary anxiety and depression, which can be treated successfully, or may even be due to overmedication. The danger is that people with such symptoms may be left untreated, thereby continuing their decline (Sachs-Ericsson et al., 2005; Diniz et al., 2013).

In sum, declines in cognitive functioning in late adulthood are, for the most part, not inevitable. The key to maintaining cognitive skills may lie in intellectual stimulation. Like the rest of us, older adults need a stimulating environment in order to hone and maintain their skills (Glisky, 2007; Hertzog et al., 2008; Hartshorne & Germine, 2015).

THE SOCIAL WORLD OF LATE ADULTHOOD: OLD BUT NOT ALONE

Just as the view that old age predictably means mental decline has proved to be wrong, so has the view that late adulthood inevitably brings loneliness. People in late adulthood most often see themselves as functioning members of society; only a small number of them report that loneliness is a serious problem (Berkman, Ertel, & Glymour, 2011; Luong, Rauers & Fingerman, 2015; Domènech-Abella et al., 2019).

Certainly, late adulthood brings significant challenges. People who have spent their adult lives working and then enter retirement bring about a major shift in the roles they play. Moreover, many people must face the death of their spouse. Especially if the marriage has been a long and good one, the death of a partner means the loss of a companion, confidante, and lover. It can also bring about changes in economic well-being.

There is no single way to age successfully, and several theories have been developed to describe the process. According to the **disengagement theory of aging,** aging is characterized by a gradual withdrawal from the world. In this view, as people get older, they separate themselves from others on physical, psychological, and social levels. In this view, such disengagement is appropriate and even beneficial. The reason is that disengagement serves the purpose of providing an opportunity for increased reflectiveness and decreased emotional investment in others at a time of life when social relationships will inevitably be ended by death (Adams, 2004; Wrosch, Bauer, & Scheier, 2005).

However, only a little research supports the disengagement theory of aging, and alternative theories have been suggested. The major alternative is the activity theory of aging. According to the **activity theory of aging,** people who age most successfully are those who maintain

Alzheimer's disease A progressive brain disorder that leads to a gradual and irreversible decline in cognitive abilities. (Modules 22, 39)

! **Study Alert**
It's important to be able to describe the nature of intellectual changes during late adulthood.

disengagement theory of aging The theory that suggests that successful aging is characterized by a gradual withdrawal from the world on physical, psychological, and social levels. (Module 39)

activity theory of aging The theory that suggests that successful aging is characterized by maintaining the interests and activities of earlier stages of life. (Module 39)

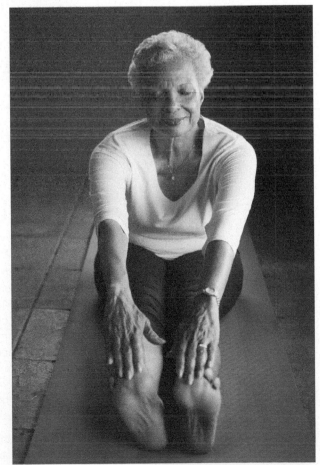

Maintaining interests and activities one had during middle age can contribute to a more successful late adulthood, according to the activity theory of aging.
Jupiterimages/Getty Images

life review The process by which people examine and evaluate their lives. (Module 39)

the interests, activities, and level of social interaction they experienced during their earlier periods of adulthood. Activity theory argues that people who are aging effectively show a continuation of the activities in which they participated during the earlier part of their lives (Crosnoe & Elder, 2002; Nimrod & Kleiber, 2007; Roos & Zaaiman, 2017).

Most research supports the activity theory of aging. On the other hand, not all people in late adulthood need a life filled with activities and social interaction to be happy. As in every stage of life, some older adults are just as satisfied leading a relatively inactive, solitary existence. What may be more important is how people view the aging process: Evidence shows that positive self-perceptions of aging are associated with increased longevity (Levy & Myers, 2004; Amesberger et al., 2019).

Regardless of how people age, most engage in a process of **life review** in which they examine and evaluate their lives. Remembering and reconsidering what has occurred in the past, people in late adulthood often come to a better understanding of themselves. They sometimes resolve lingering problems and conflicts, and face their lives with greater wisdom and serenity.

Clearly, people in late adulthood are not just marking time until death. Rather, old age is a time of continued growth and development as important as any other period of life.

From the perspective of...

A Health-Care Provider What sorts of recommendations would you make to your older patients about how to deal with aging? How would you handle someone who believed that getting older had only negative consequences?

Tetra Images/Getty Images

BECOMING AN INFORMED CONSUMER
of Psychology

Adjusting to Death

At some time in our lives, we all face death—certainly our own as well as the deaths of friends, loved ones, and even strangers. Although death is inevitable, it remains a frightening, emotion-laden topic. Little is more stressful than the death of a loved one or the contemplation of our own imminent death, and preparing for death is one of our most crucial developmental tasks (Aiken, 2000).

A few generations ago, talk of death was taboo. The topic was never mentioned to dying people, and gerontologists had little to say about it. That changed, however, with the pioneering work of Elisabeth Kübler-Ross (1969), who brought the subject of death into the open with her observation that those facing impending death tend to move through five broad stages:

- *Denial.* In this stage, people resist the idea that they are dying. Even if told that their chances for survival are small, they refuse to admit that they are facing death.
- *Anger.* After moving beyond the denial stage, dying people become angry—angry at people around them who are in good health, angry at medical professionals for being ineffective, angry at God.

- *Bargaining*. Anger leads to bargaining in which the dying try to think of ways to postpone death. They may decide to dedicate their lives to religion if God saves them. They may say, "If only I can live to see my son married, I will accept death then."
- *Depression*. When dying people come to feel that bargaining is no use, they move to the next stage: depression. They realize that their lives really are coming to an end, which leads to what Kübler-Ross calls "preparatory grief" for their own deaths.
- *Acceptance*. In this stage, people accept impending death. Usually they are unemotional and uncommunicative; it is as if they have made peace with themselves and are expecting death with no bitterness.

Keep in mind that not everyone experiences each of these stages in the same way. In fact, Kübler-Ross's stages pertain only to people who are fully aware that they are dying and have the time to evaluate their impending death. Furthermore, vast differences occur in the way individuals react to impending death. The specific cause and duration of dying, as well as the person's sex, age, personality, and the type of support received from family and friends, all have an impact on how people respond to death (Carver & Scheier, 2002; Coyle, 2006).

Few of us enjoy the contemplation of death. Yet awareness of its psychological aspects and consequences can make its inevitable arrival less anxiety producing and perhaps more understandable.

RECAP/EVALUATE/RETHINK

RECAP

LO 39-1 What are the principal kinds of physical, social, and intellectual changes that occur in early and middle adulthood, and what are their causes?

- Early adulthood marks the peak of physical health. Physical changes occur relatively gradually in men and women during adulthood.
- One major physical change occurs at the end of middle adulthood for women: They begin menopause, after which they are no longer fertile.
- During middle adulthood, people typically experience a midlife transition in which the notion that life will end becomes more important. Despite the common view that there is a midlife crisis, typically the passage into middle age is relatively calm.
- As aging continues during middle adulthood, people realize in their 50s that their lives and accomplishments are fairly well set, and they try to come to terms with them.
- Among the important developmental milestones during adulthood are marriage, family changes, and divorce. Another important determinant of adult development is work.

LO 39-2 How does the reality of late adulthood differ from the stereotypes about that period?

- Old age may bring marked physical declines caused by genetic programming or physical wear and tear. Although the activities of people in late adulthood are not all that different from those of younger people, older adults experience declines in reaction time, sensory abilities, and physical stamina.

- Intellectual declines are not an inevitable part of aging. Fluid intelligence does decline with age, and long-term memory abilities are sometimes impaired. In contrast, crystallized intelligence shows slight increases with age, and short-term memory remains at about the same level.
- Although disengagement theory sees successful aging as a process of gradual withdrawal from the physical, psychological, and social worlds, there is little research supporting this view. Instead, activity theory, which suggests that the maintenance of interests and activities from earlier years leads to successful aging, is a more accurate explanation.

LO 39-3 How can we adjust to death?

- According to Kübler-Ross, dying people move through five stages as they face death: denial, anger, bargaining, depression, and acceptance.

EVALUATE

1. Rob recently turned 40 and surveyed his goals and accomplishments to date. Although he has accomplished a lot, he realized that many of his goals will not be met in his lifetime. This stage is called a _____ _____

2. In households in which both partners have similar jobs, the division of labor that generally occurs is the same as in "traditional" households in which the husband works and the wife stays at home. True or false?

3. _____ _____ theories suggest that there is a maximum time span in which cells are able to reproduce. This time limit explains the eventual breakdown of the body.

4. Lower IQ test scores during late adulthood do not necessarily mean a decrease in intelligence. True or false?

5. During old age, a person's _____ intelligence continues to increase, whereas _____ intelligence may decline.

6. In Kübler-Ross's _____ stage, people resist the idea of death. In the _____ stage, they attempt to make deals to avoid death, and in the _____ stage, they passively await death.

RETHINK

1. Is the possibility that life may be extended for several decades a mixed blessing? What societal consequences might an extended life span bring about?

2. Does the finding that people in late adulthood require intellectual stimulation have implications for the societies in which older people live? In what way might stereotypes about older individuals contribute to their isolation and lack of intellectual stimulation?

Answers to Evaluate Questions

1. midlife transition; 2. True; 3. Genetic programming; 4. True; 5. crystallized, fluid; 6. denial, bargaining, acceptance

KEY TERMS

emerging adulthood	wear-and-tear theories of	disengagement theory of	life review
menopause	aging	aging	
genetic programming	Alzheimer's disease	activity theory of aging	
theories of aging			

LOOKING *Back*

EPILOGUE

We have traced major events in the development of physical, social, and cognitive growth throughout the life span. Clearly, people change throughout their lives.

As we explored each area of development, we encountered anew the nature–nurture issue, concluding in every significant instance that both nature and nurture contribute to a person's development of skills, personality, and interactions. Specifically, our genetic inheritance—nature—lays down general boundaries within which we can advance and grow; our environment—nurture—helps determine the extent to which we take advantage of our potential.

Before proceeding to the next set of modules, turn to the prologue of this chapter that discussed Elizabeth Carr and Louise Brown, who were born using in-vitro fertilization (IVF). Using your knowledge of human development, consider the following questions.

1. At one time, IVF commonly involved the implantation of multiple embryos at once in order to maximize the likelihood that at least one would develop. Sometimes that strategy resulted in multiple births. Would such newborns likely be identical twins? Why or why not?

2. Which kinds of abnormalities might Elizabeth Carr and Louise Brown have been tested for as newborns?

3. If you were Elizabeth Carr's or Louise Brown's parents, how would you explain the IVF process to a curious friend?

4. What are some modern alternatives to IVF, and how do they differ from it?

VISUAL SUMMARY 12 Development

MODULES 35 and 36
Nature and Nurture; Prenatal Development

Developmental Research Techniques
- Cross-sectional, longitudinal, sequential

Basics of Genetics: Chromosomes and genes

Earliest Development

- Zygote: a fertilized egg

- Embryo: between 2 and 8 weeks old after conception

- Fetus: between 8 weeks and birth

- Age of viability: about 22 weeks from conception

Nature and Nurture

- Nature: Refers to hereditary factors

- Nurture: Refers to environmental influences

MODULE 37 Infancy and Childhood

The Extraordinary Newborn

- Reflexes: Rooting, sucking, gag, Babinski

- Development of the senses

Infancy through Middle Childhood, about age 12

- Physical development: rapid growth

- Social development
  - Attachment: positive emotional bond between child and caregiver
  - Ainsworth strange situation
  - Social relationships with peers
- Child care outside the home
- Four parenting styles
- Erikson's theory of psychosocial development
  - Trust-versus-mistrust stage: birth to age 1½
  - Autonomy-versus-shame-and-doubt stage: ages 1½ to 3
  - Initiative-versus-guilt stage: ages 3 to 6
  - Industry-versus-inferiority stage: ages 6 to 12
- Cognitive development
  - Piaget's theory of cognitive development

Cognitive Stage	Approximate Age Range	Major Characteristics
Sensorimotor	Birth–2 years	Development of object permanence, development of motor skills, little or no capacity for symbolic representation
Preoperational thinking	2–7 years	Development of language and symbolic thinking, egocentric thinking
Concrete operational mastery	7–12 years	Development of conservation, of concept of reversibility
Formal operational	12 years–adulthood	Development of logical and abstract thinking

  - Information processing approaches

MODULE 38 Adolescence: Becoming an Adult

Physical Development: Rapid weight and height gains; onset of puberty

Moral Development: Changes in moral reasoning

Sample Moral Reasoning

Level	In Favor of Stealing the Drug	Against Stealing the Drug
Level 1 Preconventional morality: The main considerations at this level are the avoidance of punishment and the desire for rewards.	"You shouldn't just let your wife die. People will blame you for not doing enough, and they'll blame the scientist for not selling you the drug for less money."	"You can't steal the drug because you'll be arrested and go to jail. Even if you aren't caught, you'll feel guilty and you'll always worry that the police may figure out what you did."
Level 2 Conventional morality: Membership in society becomes important at this level. People behave in ways that will win the approval of others.	"Who will blame you if you steal a life-saving drug? But if you just let your wife die, you won't be able to hold your head up in front of your family or neighbors."	"If you steal the drug, everyone will treat you like a criminal. They will wonder why you couldn't have found some other way to save your wife."
Level 3 Postconventional morality: People accept that there are certain broad principles of morality that should govern our actions. These principles are more critical than the particular laws in a society.	"If you simply follow the law, you will violate the underlying principle of saving your wife's life. If you do steal the drug, society will understand your actions and respect them. You can't let an inadequate, outdated law prevent you from doing the right thing."	"You can't change your standards of honesty whenever it suits your needs. Others may not blame you for stealing the drug, but your conscience will blame you for betraying your own moral code."

Social Development: Erikson's theory of psychosocial development

Stage	Approximate Age	Positive Outcomes	Negative Outcomes
1. Trust-vs-mistrust	Birth–1½ years	Feelings of trust from environmental support	Fear and concern regarding others
2. Autonomy-vs-shame-and-doubt	1½–3 years	Self-sufficiency if exploration is encouraged	Doubts about self, lack of independence
3. Initiative-vs-guilt	3–6 years	Discovery of ways to initiate actions	Guilt from actions and thoughts
4. Industry-vs-inferiority	6–12 years	Development of sense of competence	Feelings of inferiority, no sense of mastery
5. Identity-vs-role-confusion	Adolescence	Awareness of uniqueness of self, knowledge of role to be followed	Inability to identify appropriate roles in life
6. Intimacy-vs-isolation	Early adulthood	Development of loving, sexual relationships and close friendships	Fear of relationships with others others
7. Generativity-vs-stagnation	Middle adulthood	Sense of contribution to continuity of life	Trivialization of one's activities
8. Ego-integrity-vs-despair	Late adulthood	Sense of unity in life's accomplishments	Regret over lost opportunities of life

MODULE 39 Adulthood

Physical Development

- Early adulthood: peak of health
- Middle adulthood: menopause for women

Social Development

- Early adulthood: Focus on career, marriage, family
- Midlife transition: Relatively calm, come to terms with one's circumstances
- Late adulthood: Acceptance of others and one's circumstances

Marriage, Children, and Divorce

- People marry later in life than ever before; about half of all first marriages end in divorce
- Many single-parent households

Growing Old: Late adulthood

- Physical changes
  - Genetic preprogramming aging theory
  - Wear-and-tear aging theory
- Cognitive changes
  - Fluid intelligence declines; crystallized intelligence remains steady
  - Memory change not inevitable
    - Alzheimer's disease: Gradual, irreversible brain disorder that leads to a decline in cognitive abilities
- Social world
  - Disengagement theory of aging
  - Activity theory of aging

Santypan/Shutterstock

CHAPTER 13
Personality

LEARNING OUTCOMES FOR CHAPTER 13

LO 42-1 How can we most accurately assess personality?

LO 42-2 What are the major types of personality measures?

PROLOGUE *GOOD GUY OR GOOD FELLA?*

By most accounts, Charlie and Carol Gasko were an unremarkable couple—typical retirees living a comfortable quiet life in an apartment building near the beach in Santa Monica, California. Neighbors found them polite enough, if a bit secretive. They had friends in the community but largely kept to themselves, enjoying the 16 years they spent there.

No one who knew the couple would have guessed that Charlie was actually notorious Boston gangster James "Whitey" Bulger, and Carol was his long-time girlfriend, Catherine Greig. For many years, Bulger was number one on the FBI's most wanted criminal list. Among the many crimes he stood accused of were the brutal executions of multiple rival mobsters and the murder of the girlfriend of Bulger's own business partner. After he was identified and arrested, the FBI and many witnesses who testified against him portrayed Bulger as a viciously cruel man (Simon, 2018; Murphy, 2019).

LOOKING *Ahead*

Many people, like Bulger, have more than one side to their personalities, appearing one way to some people and quite differently to others. Still, you also probably know people who are so consistent in their behavior that you can easily predict what they are going to do, no matter what the situation. Determining who a person truly is falls to a branch of psychology that seeks to understand the characteristic ways people behave—personality psychology.

Personality is the pattern of enduring characteristics that produce consistency and individuality in a given person. Personality encompasses the behaviors that make each of us unique and that differentiate us from others. Personality also leads us to act consistently in different situations and over extended periods of time.

We will consider a number of approaches to personality. For historical reasons, we begin with psychodynamic theories of personality, which emphasize the importance of the unconscious. Next, we consider approaches that concentrate on identifying the most fundamental personality traits; theories that view personality as a set of learned behaviors; biological and evolutionary perspectives on personality; and approaches, known as humanistic theories, that highlight the uniquely human aspects of personality. We end our discussion by focusing on how personality is measured and how personality tests can be used.

personality The pattern of enduring characteristics that produce consistency and individuality in a given person. (Module 40)

Module 40
Psychodynamic Approaches to Personality

LEARNING OUTCOMES

LO 40-1 How do psychologists define and use the concept of personality?

LO 40-2 What do the theories of Freud and his successors tell us about the structure and development of personality?

psychodynamic approaches to personality Approaches that assume that personality is primarily unconscious and motivated by inner forces and conflicts about which people have little awareness. (Module 40)

The college student was intent on making a good first impression on an attractive woman he had spotted across a crowded room at a party. As he walked toward her, he mulled over a line he had heard in an old movie the night before: "I don't believe we've been properly introduced yet." To his horror, what came out was a bit different. After threading his way through the crowded room, he finally reached the woman and blurted out, "I don't believe we've been properly seduced yet."

Although this student's error may seem to be merely an embarrassing slip of the tongue, according to some personality theorists, such a mistake is not an error at all (Motley, 1987). Instead, *psychodynamic personality theorists* might argue that the error illustrates one way in which behavior is triggered by inner forces that are beyond our awareness. These hidden drives, shaped by childhood experiences, play an important role in energizing and directing everyday behavior.

Psychodynamic approaches to personality are based on the idea that personality is primarily unconscious and motivated by inner forces and conflicts about which people have little awareness. The most important pioneer of the psychodynamic approach was Sigmund Freud. A number of Freud's followers, including Carl Jung, Karen Horney, and Alfred Adler, refined Freud's theory and developed their own psychodynamic approaches.

Freud's Psychoanalytic Theory: Mapping the Unconscious Mind

psychoanalytic theory Freud's theory that unconscious forces act as determinants of personality. (Module 40)

unconscious A part of the personality that contains the memories, knowledge, beliefs, feelings, urges, drives, and instincts of which the individual is not aware. (Module 40)

Sigmund Freud, an Austrian physician, developed psychoanalytic theory in the early 1900s. **Psychoanalytic theory** assumes that much of our behavior is driven by unconscious determinants. According to Freud's theory, conscious experience is only a small part of our psychological makeup and experience. He argued that much of our behavior is motivated by the **unconscious,** a part of the personality that contains the memories, knowledge, beliefs, feelings, urges, drives, and instincts of which the individual is not aware.

Like the unseen mass of a floating iceberg, the contents of the unconscious far surpass in quantity the information in our conscious awareness. Freud maintained that to understand personality, it is necessary to expose what is in the unconscious. But because the unconscious disguises the meaning of the material it holds, the content of the unconscious cannot be observed directly. It is therefore necessary to interpret clues to the unconscious–slips of the tongue, fantasies, and dreams–to understand the unconscious processes that direct behavior. A slip of the tongue such as the one quoted earlier (sometimes termed a *Freudian slip*) may be interpreted as revealing the speaker's unconscious sexual desires.

To Freud, much of our personality is determined by our unconscious. Some of the unconscious is made up of the *preconscious,* which contains material that is not threatening and is easily brought to mind, such as the knowledge that 2 + 2 = 4. But deeper in the unconscious are instinctual drives–the wishes, desires, demands, and needs that are hidden from conscious awareness because of the conflicts and pain they would cause if they were part of our everyday lives. The unconscious provides a "safe haven" for our recollections of threatening events.

STRUCTURING PERSONALITY: ID, EGO, AND SUPEREGO

To describe the structure of personality, Freud developed a comprehensive theory that held that personality consists of three separate but interacting components: the id, the ego, and the superego. Freud suggested that the three structures can be diagrammed to show how they relate to the conscious and the unconscious (see Figure 1).

Although the three components of personality Freud described may appear to be actual physical structures in the nervous system, they are not. Instead, they represent abstract conceptions of a general *model* of personality that describes the interaction of forces that motivate behavior.

If personality consisted only of primitive, instinctual cravings and longings, it would have just one component: the id. The **id** is the instinctual and unorganized part of personality. From the time of birth, the id attempts to reduce tension created by primitive drives related to hunger, sex, aggression, and irrational impulses. Those drives are fueled by "psychic energy," which we can think of as a limitless energy source constantly putting pressure on the various parts of the personality.

The id operates according to the *pleasure principle* in which the goal is the immediate reduction of tension and the maximization of satisfaction. However, in most cases, reality prevents the fulfillment of the demands of the pleasure principle: We cannot always eat when we are hungry, and we can discharge our sexual drives only when the time and place are appropriate. To account for this fact of life, Freud suggested a second component of personality, which he called the ego.

The **ego** is the rational and logical part of personality. The ego attempts to balance the desires of the id and the realities of the objective, outside world. It starts to develop soon after birth.

In contrast to the pleasure-seeking id, the ego operates according to the *reality principle* in which instinctual energy is restrained to maintain the individual's safety and to help integrate the person into society. In a sense, then, the ego is the "executive" of personality: It makes decisions, controls actions, and allows thinking and problem solving of a higher order than the id's capabilities permit.

The superego is the final personality structure to develop in childhood. According to Freud, the **superego** is the part of personality that harshly judges the morality of our behavior. It represents the rights and wrong of society as taught and modeled by a person's parents, teachers, and other significant individuals.

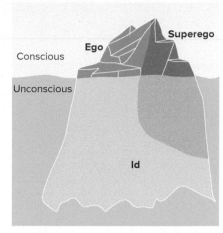

FIGURE 1 In Freud's personality model, there are three major components: the id, the ego, and the superego. As the iceberg analogy shows, only a small portion of personality is conscious. Why do you think that only the ego and superego have conscious components?

id The instinctual and unorganized part of personality whose sole purpose is to reduce tension created by primitive drives related to hunger, sex, aggression, and irrational impulses. (Module 40)

ego The rational, logical part of personality that attempts to balance the desires of the id and the realities of the objective, outside world. (Module 40)

superego The part of personality that harshly judges the morality of our behavior. (Module 40)

! Study Alert
Remember that the three parts of personality in Freud's theory—the id, the ego, and the superego—are abstract conceptions that don't exist as physical structures in the brain.

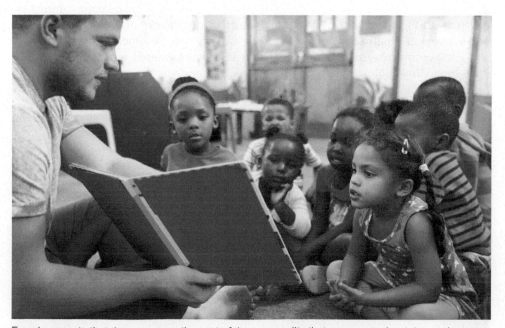

Freud suggests that the superego, the part of the personality that represents the rights and wrongs of society, develops from direct teaching by parents, teachers, and other significant individuals.
Monkey Business Images/Shutterstock

The superego includes the *conscience*, which prevents us from behaving in a morally improper way by making us feel guilty if we do wrong. The superego helps us control impulses coming from the id, making our behavior less selfish and more virtuous.

Neither the id nor superego parts of personality are realistic, practical, or logical in that they do not consider the realities society imposes. For example, the superego, if left to operate by itself and without restraint, would create perfectionists unable to make the moral compromises that life sometimes requires. On the other hand, an unrestrained id would produce primitive, pleasure-seeking, thoughtless individuals on a mission to fulfill every desire without delay. Consequently, the ego must constrain and negotiate between the conflicting demands of the superego and id.

DEVELOPING PERSONALITY: PSYCHOSEXUAL STAGES

Freud also provided us with a view of how personality develops. He suggests personality development proceeds through a series of five **psychosexual stages** during which children encounter conflicts between the demands of society and their own sexual urges (in which sexuality is more about experiencing pleasure and less about lust).

According to Freud, if we are not able to resolve the conflicts that occur at a particular psychosexual stage, we may become locked in that conflict throughout life—something he called fixation. **Fixations** are conflicts or concerns that persist beyond the developmental period in which they first occur. Such conflicts may be due to having needs ignored, such as ending breast feeding too early or being treated too strictly during toilet training. Alternatively, fixation may occur if children are overindulged during an earlier period, such as when parents are overly attentive to a child or provide lavish rewards during toilet training.

The sequence Freud proposed is noteworthy because it explains how experiences and difficulties during a particular childhood stage may predict specific characteristics in the adult personality. This theory is also unique in associating each stage with a major biological function, which Freud assumed to be the focus of pleasure in a given period. (See Figure 2 for a summary of the stages.)

In the first psychosexual stage of development, called the **oral stage,** the baby's mouth is the focal point of pleasure. During the first 12 to 18 months of life, children suck, eat, mouth, and bite anything they can put into their mouths. To Freud, this behavior suggested that the mouth is the primary site of a kind of sexual pleasure and that weaning (withdrawing the breast or bottle) represents the main conflict during the oral stage. If infants are either overindulged (perhaps by being fed every time they cry) or frustrated in their search for oral gratification, they may become fixated at this stage.

For example, fixation might occur if an infant's oral needs were constantly gratified immediately at the first sign of hunger rather than if the infant learned that feeding takes place on a schedule because eating whenever an infant wants to eat is

psychosexual stages Developmental periods that children pass through during which they encounter conflicts between the demands of society and their own sexual urges. (Module 40)

fixations Conflicts or concerns that persist beyond the developmental period in which they first occur. (Module 40)

oral stage According to Freud, a stage from birth to age 12-18 months in which an infant's center of pleasure is the mouth. (Module 40)

! **Study Alert**
The five psychosexual stages of personality development in Freud's theory—oral, anal, phallic, latency, and genital—indicate how personality develops as people age.

FIGURE 2 Freud's theory of personality development suggests several distinct stages.

Stage	Age	Major Characteristics
Oral	Birth to 12–18 months	Interest in oral gratification from sucking, eating, mouthing, biting
Anal	12–18 months to 3 years	Gratification from expelling and withholding feces; coming to terms with society's controls relating to toilet training
Phallic	3 to 5–6 years	Interest in the genitals, coming to terms with Oedipal conflict leading to identification with same-sex parent
Latency	5–6 years to adolescence	Sexual concerns largely unimportant
Genital	Adolescence to adulthood	Reemergence of sexual interests and establishment of mature sexual relationships

not always realistic. Fixation at the oral stage might produce an adult who was unusually interested in oral activities–eating, talking, smoking–or who showed symbolic sorts of oral interests such as being "bitingly" sarcastic or very gullible ("swallowing" anything).

From around age 12–18 months until 3 years of age–a period in which the emphasis in Western cultures is on toilet training–a child enters the **anal stage.** At this point, the major source of pleasure changes from the mouth to the anal region, and children obtain considerable pleasure from both retention and expulsion of feces. If toilet training is particularly demanding, fixation might occur. Fixation during the anal stage might result in unusual rigidity, orderliness, punctuality–or extreme disorderliness or sloppiness–in adulthood.

At about age 3, the **phallic stage** begins. At this point, there is another major shift in the child's primary source of pleasure. Now interest focuses on the genitals and the pleasures derived from fondling them. During this stage, the child must also negotiate one of the most important hurdles of personality development: the Oedipal conflict.

The **Oedipal conflict** is a child's intense, sexual interest in his or her opposite-sex parent. According to Freudian theory, the Oedipal conflict plays out as children focus attention on their genitals and the differences between male and female anatomy become more salient.

According to Freud, a male child unconsciously begins to develop a sexual interest in his mother, starts to see his father as a powerful rival, and harbors a wish to replace his father and enjoy the affections of his mother. (The situation mirrors a tragic Greek play in which the son Oedipus kills his father and marries his mother, hence the term *Oedipal conflict*.) But because a son views his father as too powerful, he develops a fear that his father may retaliate drastically by removing the source of the threat: his penis.

Also according to Freud, the fear of losing his penis leads to *castration anxiety,* which ultimately becomes so powerful that the child represses his desires for his mother and identifies with his father. **Identification** is the process of wanting to be like another person as much as possible, imitating that person's behavior and adopting similar beliefs, attitudes, and values. By identifying with his father, a son seeks to obtain a woman like his unattainable mother.

Freud argued that the process is different for girls. He suggested that they experience sexual arousal related to their fathers and begin to have penis envy. They wish they had the anatomical part that seems most clearly "missing" from their bodies–that is, girls realize they lack a penis.

Blaming their mothers for this missing piece of anatomy, girls come to believe that their mothers are responsible for their "castration." Like males, though, they find that they can resolve such unacceptable feelings by identifying with the same-sex parent, behaving like her, and adopting her attitudes and values. In this way, a girl's identification with her mother is completed. (We should note that these ideas about the identification process in girls led to considerable criticism that Freud was sexist, favoring males over females.)

Through these complicated–and to many critics, far-fetched–sequences of events, Freud argued that the Oedipal conflict is resolved and that both males and females move on to the next stage of development. If difficulties arise during the resolution of the Oedipal conflict, however, all sorts of problems are thought to occur, including improper sex-role behavior and the failure to develop a conscience.

After the resolution of the Oedipal conflict, typically around age 5 or 6, children move into the **latency period,** which lasts until puberty. During this period, sexual interests become dormant, even in the unconscious. Then, during adolescence, sexual feelings re-emerge, which marks the start of the final period, the **genital stage,** which extends until death. The focus during the genital stage is on mature, adult sexuality, which Freud defined as sexual intercourse.

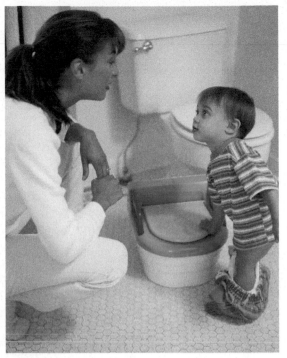

According to Freud, a child goes through the anal stage from age 12–18 months until 3 years of age. Toilet training is a crucial event at this stage—one that psychoanalytic theory claims directly influences the formation of an individual's personality.
Exactostock/SuperStock

anal stage According to Freud, a stage from age 12–18 months to 3 years of age in which a child's pleasure is centered on the anus. (Module 40)

phallic stage According to Freud, a period beginning around age 3 during which a child's pleasure focuses on the genitals. (Module 40)

Oedipal conflict A child's intense, sexual interest in his or her opposite-sex parent. (Module 40)

identification The process of wanting to be like another person as much as possible, imitating that person's behavior and adopting similar beliefs and values. (Module 40)

latency period According to Freud, the period between the phallic stage and puberty during which children's sexual concerns are temporarily put aside. (Module 40)

genital stage According to Freud, the period from puberty until death, marked by mature sexual behavior (that is, sexual intercourse). (Module 40)

DEFENSE MECHANISMS

Freud's efforts to describe and theorize about the underlying dynamics of personality and its development were motivated by very practical problems that his patients faced in dealing with *anxiety,* an intense, negative emotional experience. According to Freud, anxiety is a danger signal to the ego. Although anxiety can arise from realistic fears—such as seeing a poisonous snake about to strike—it can also occur in the form of *neurotic anxiety* in which irrational impulses emanating from the id threaten to burst through and become uncontrollable.

Because anxiety is obviously unpleasant, Freud believed that people develop a range of ways to deal with it, which he called defense mechanisms. **Defense mechanisms** are unconscious strategies that people use to reduce anxiety by distorting reality and concealing the source of the anxiety from themselves.

The primary defense mechanism is repression. **Repression** occurs when the ego pushes unacceptable or unpleasant thoughts and impulses out of consciousness but maintains them in the unconscious.

Repression is the most direct method of dealing with anxiety; instead of handling an anxiety-producing impulse on a conscious level, we simply ignore it. For example, a college student who feels hatred for his mother may repress those personally and socially unacceptable feelings. The feelings remain lodged within the unconscious because acknowledging them would provoke anxiety. Similarly, memories of childhood abuse may be repressed. Although such memories may not be consciously recalled, according to Freud they can affect later behavior, and they may be revealed through dreams or slips of the tongue or symbolically in some other fashion.

If repression is ineffective in keeping anxiety at bay, we might use other defense mechanisms. Freud and later his daughter, Anna Freud (who became a well-known psychoanalyst), formulated an extensive list of potential defense mechanisms. The major defense mechanisms are summarized in Figure 3 (Boag, 2015; Zhang & Guo, 2017; Kupfersmid, 2019).

defense mechanisms In Freudian theory, unconscious strategies that people use to reduce anxiety by distorting reality and concealing the source of the anxiety from themselves. (Module 40)

repression The defense mechanism in which the ego pushes unacceptable or unpleasant thoughts and impulses out of consciousness but maintains them in the unconscious. (Module 40)

! Study Alert
Use Figure 3 to remember the most common defense mechanisms (unconscious strategies used to reduce anxiety by concealing its source from ourselves and others).

Freud's Defense Mechanisms		
Defense Mechanism	**Explanation**	**Example**
Repression	Unacceptable or unpleasant impulses are pushed out of awareness and back into the unconscious.	A woman is unable to consciously recall that she was raped.
Regression	People behave as if they were at an earlier stage of development.	A boss has a temper tantrum when an employee makes a mistake.
Displacement	The expression of an unwanted feeling or thought is redirected from a more threatening powerful person to a weaker one.	A brother yells at his younger sister after a teacher gives him a bad grade.
Rationalization	People provide self-justifying explanations in place of the actual, but threatening, reason for their behavior.	A student who goes out drinking the night before a big test rationalizes his behavior by saying the test isn't all that important.
Denial	People refuse to accept or acknowledge an anxiety-producing piece of information.	A student refuses to believe that he has flunked a course.
Projection	People attribute unwanted impulses and feelings to someone else.	A man who is unfaithful to his wife and feels guilty suspects that his wife is unfaithful.
Sublimation	People divert unwanted impulses into socially approved thoughts, feelings, or behaviors.	A person with strong feelings of aggression becomes a soldier.
Reaction formation	Unconscious impulses are expressed as their opposite in consciousness.	A mother who unconsciously resents her child acts in an overly loving way toward the child.

FIGURE 3 According to Freud, people use a wide range of defense mechanisms to cope with anxieties.

All of us employ defense mechanisms to some degree, according to Freudian theory, and they can serve a useful purpose by protecting us from unpleasant information. Yet some people fall prey to them to such an extent that they must constantly direct a large amount of psychic energy toward hiding and rechanneling unacceptable impulses. When this occurs, everyday living becomes difficult. In such cases, the result is a mental disorder produced by anxiety—what Freud called "neurosis." (Psychologists rarely use this term today, although it endures in everyday conversation.)

EVALUATING FREUD'S LEGACY

Freud's theory has had a significant impact on the field of psychology—and even more broadly on Western philosophy and literature. The general ideas that we have unconscious thoughts that influence behavior, that we employ defense mechanisms, and that some adult psychological problems have their roots in childhood difficulties are widely accepted (Boag, Brakel, & Tavitie, 2016; Zhang et al., 2016; Rehan et al., 2019).

However, contemporary personality psychologists have leveled significant criticisms against many foundational explanations of personality development in psychoanalytic theory. Among the most important is the lack of compelling scientific data to support the process of personality development that Freud laid out. Although individual case studies *seem* supportive, we lack conclusive evidence that shows the personality is structured and operates along the lines Freud laid out (Tummala-Nara, 2016).

The lack of research evidence is due, in part, to the fact that Freud's conception of personality is built on unobservable abstract concepts. Moreover, the stages of personality Freud laid out may not provide an accurate description of personality development. For example, we know now that important changes in personality can occur in adolescence and adulthood—something that Freud did not believe happened. Instead, he argued that personality largely is set by the time we reach adolescence.

The vague nature of Freud's theory also makes it difficult to predict how an adult will display certain developmental difficulties. For instance, if a person is fixated at the anal stage, according to Freud, he or she may be unusually messy or unusually neat. Freud's theory offers no way to predict how the difficulty will be exhibited. Furthermore, Freud can be faulted for seeming to view women as inferior to men because he argued that women have weaker superegos than men do and in some ways unconsciously yearn to be men (the concept of penis envy).

Finally, Freud made his observations and derived his theory from a limited population. His theory was based almost entirely on upper-class Austrian women living

Freud developed his theory on observations of upper-class Austrian women, but critics have suggested his conclusions may not apply to people living in cultures that are very different.
Ariel Skelley/Blend Images LLC

in the strict, puritanical era of the early 1900s who had come to him seeking treatment for psychological and physical problems. How far one can generalize beyond this population is a matter of considerable debate. For instance, in some Pacific Island societies, the mother's oldest brother and not the father plays the role of disciplinarian. In such a culture, one cannot reasonably argue that the Oedipal conflict will progress in the same way it did in Austrian society, where the father typically was the major disciplinarian. In short, a cross-cultural perspective raises questions about the universality of Freud's view of personality development (Doi, 1990; Grünbaum, 2015; Shapira-Berman, 2019).

Still, Freud generated an important method of treating psychological disturbances called *psychoanalysis*. As we will see when we discuss treatment approaches to psychological disorders, psychoanalysis remains in use today (Frosch, 2011; Altman & Stile, 2015).

Moreover, Freud's emphasis on the unconscious has been partially supported by current research on dreams and implicit memory. As first noted when we discussed dreaming, advances in neuroscience are consistent with some of Freud's arguments. For example, the fact that some behavior is motivated by occurrences that apparently have been forgotten, as well as the discovery of neural pathways relating to emotional memories, supports the notion of repression.

Furthermore, cognitive and social psychologists have found increasing evidence that unconscious processes help us think about and evaluate our world, set goals, and choose a course of action. Unconscious processes also help determine how we form attitudes toward others (Teague, 2013; Bargh, 2014; Fayek, 2017).

The Neo-Freudian Psychoanalysts: Building on Freud

Freud laid the foundation for important work done by a series of successors who were trained in traditional Freudian theory but later rejected some of its major points. These theorists are known as **neo-Freudian psychoanalysts.**

neo-Freudian psychoanalysts Psychoanalysts who were trained in traditional Freudian theory but who later rejected some of its major points. (Module 40)

The neo-Freudians placed greater emphasis than Freud did on the functions of the ego by suggesting that it has more control than the id does over day-to-day activities. They focused more on the social environment and minimized the importance of sex as a driving force in people's lives. They also paid greater attention to the effects of society and culture on personality development.

JUNG'S COLLECTIVE UNCONSCIOUS

Carl Jung (pronounced "yoong"), one of the most influential neo-Freudians, rejected Freud's view of the primary importance of unconscious sexual urges. Instead, he looked at the primitive urges of the unconscious more positively. He argued that they represented a more general and positive life force that goes back to the dawn of the existence of life, motivating creativity and positive conflict resolution (Cassells, 2007; Wilde, 2011; Addison, 2017).

collective unconscious According to Jung, an inherited set of ideas, feelings, images, and symbols that are shared with all humans because of our common ancestral past. (Module 40)

Jung suggested that we have a universal **collective unconscious**—an inherited set of ideas, feelings, images, and symbols that are shared with all humans because of our common ancestral past. This collective unconscious, which is in the deepest layer of the unconscious, is similar in everyone and is displayed in behavior that is common across diverse cultures—such as love of mother, belief in a supreme being, and even behavior as specific as fear of snakes (Hauke, 2006; Finn, 2011).

archetypes According to Jung, universal symbolic representations of particular types of people, objects, ideas, or experiences. (Module 40)

Jung went on to propose that the collective unconscious contains **archetypes,** universal symbolic representations of particular types of people, objects, ideas, or experiences. For instance, a *mother archetype*, which contains reflections of our ancestors' relationships with mother figures, is suggested by the prevalence of mothers in art,

In terms of Jung's theory, Luke Skywalker and Kylo Ren from the *Star Wars* movies represent the archetypes, or universally recognizable symbols, of good and evil.
(left): AF Archive/Alamy Stock Photo; (right): Lucasfilm/Photo 12/Alamy Stock Photo

religion, literature, and mythology. (Think of the Virgin Mary, Earth Mother, wicked stepmothers in fairy tales, Mother's Day, and so forth!) Jung also suggested that men possess an unconscious *feminine archetype* that affects how they behave and women have an unconscious *male archetype* that colors their behavior (Jung, 1961; Potash, 2015; Vaughn Becker & Neuberg, 2019).

To Jung, archetypes play an important role in determining our day-to-day reactions, attitudes, and values. For example, Jung might explain the popularity of the *Star Wars* movies as being due to their use of broad archetypes of good (Luke Skywalker) and evil (Kylo Ren).

Although no reliable research evidence confirms the existence of the collective unconscious—and even Jung acknowledged that such evidence would be difficult to produce—Jung's theory has had significant influence in areas beyond psychology. For example, personality types derived from Jung's personality approach form the basis for the Myers-Briggs personality test, which is widely used in business and industry to provide insights into how employees make decisions and perform on the job (Wilde, 2011; Mills, 2013; Wang et al., 2017).

From the perspective of...

An Advertising Executive How might you use Jung's concept of archetypes in designing your advertisements? Which of the archetypes would you use?

Image Source/Getty Images

HORNEY'S NEO-FREUDIAN PERSPECTIVE

Karen Horney (pronounced "HORN-eye") was one of the earliest psychologists to champion women's issues and is sometimes called the first feminist psychologist. Horney suggested that personality develops in the context of social relationships and depends particularly on the relationship between parents and child and how well the child's needs are met. She rejected Freud's suggestion that women have penis envy; she asserted that what women envy most in men is not their anatomy but the independence, success, and freedom women often are denied (Horney, 1937; Coolidge et al., 2011; Forsythe, 2019).

Horney was also one of the first to stress the importance of cultural factors in the determination of personality. For example, she suggested that society's rigid gender roles for women lead them to experience ambivalence about success because they fear

Psychologist Karen Horney was one of the earliest proponents of women's issues.

Bettmann/Getty Images

they will make enemies if they are too successful. Her conceptualizations, developed in the 1930s and 1940s, laid the groundwork for many of the central ideas of feminism that emerged decades later (Eckardt, 2005; Jones, 2006).

ADLER AND THE OTHER NEO-FREUDIANS

Alfred Adler, another important neo-Freudian psychoanalyst, also considered Freudian theory's emphasis on sexual needs misplaced. Instead, Adler proposed that the primary human motivation is a striving for superiority, not in terms of superiority over others but in a quest for self-improvement and perfection.

Adler used the term *inferiority complex* to describe adults who have not been able to overcome feelings of inadequacy they developed as children. An *inferiority complex* is a lack of self-worth, a feeling that one is not as good as others. Early social relationships with parents have an important effect on children's ability to outgrow feelings of personal inferiority. If children have positive experiences, they can orient themselves toward attaining socially useful goals.

Other neo-Freudians included Erik Erikson, whose theory of psychosocial development we discussed in other modules, and Freud's daughter, Anna Freud. Like Adler and Horney, they focused less than Freud did on inborn sexual and aggressive drives and more on the social and cultural factors behind personality.

RECAP/EVALUATE/RETHINK

RECAP

LO 40-1 How do psychologists define and use the concept of personality?

- Personality is the pattern of enduring, distinctive characteristics that produce consistency and individuality in a given person.

LO 40-2 What do the theories of Freud and his successors tell us about the structure and development of personality?

- According to psychodynamic approaches to personality, much behavior is caused by parts of personality that are found in the unconscious and of which we are unaware.
- Freud's psychoanalytic theory, one of the psychodynamic approaches, suggests that personality is composed of the id, the ego, and the superego. The id is the unorganized, inborn part of personality whose purpose is to immediately reduce tensions relating to hunger, sex, aggression, and other primitive impulses. The ego restrains instinctual energy to maintain the individual's safety and to help the person be a member of society. The superego represents society's rights and wrongs and includes the conscience.

- Freud's psychoanalytic theory suggests that personality develops through a series of psychosexual stages (oral, anal, phallic, latency, and genital), each of which is associated with a primary biological function.
- Defense mechanisms, according to Freudian theory, are unconscious strategies that people use to reduce anxiety by distorting reality and concealing the true source of the anxiety from themselves.
- Freud's psychoanalytic theory has provoked a number of criticisms, including a lack of supportive scientific data, the theory's inadequacy in making predictions, and its reliance on a highly restricted population. On the other hand, recent neuroscience research has offered some support for the concept of the unconscious.
- Neo-Freudian psychoanalytic theorists built on Freud's work, although they placed greater emphasis on the role of the ego and paid more attention to the role of social factors in determining behavior.

EVALUATE

1. _____ approaches state that behavior is motivated primarily by unconscious forces.

2. Match each section of the personality (according to Freud) with its description:

1. Ego
2. Id
3. Superego

a. Determines right from wrong on the basis of cultural standards

b. Operates according to the "reality principle"; energy is redirected to integrate the person into society

c. Seeks to reduce tension brought on by primitive drives

3. Which of the following represents the proper order of personality development, according to Freud?

a. Oral, phallic, latency, anal, genital
b. Anal, oral, phallic, genital, latency
c. Oral, anal, phallic, latency, genital
d. Latency, phallic, anal, genital, oral

4. _____ _____ is the term Freud used to describe unconscious strategies used to reduce anxiety by distorting reality and concealing the source of the anxiety from themselves.

RETHINK

1. Can you think of ways in which Freud's theories of unconscious motivations are commonly used in popular culture? How accurately do you think such popular uses of Freudian theories reflect Freud's ideas?

2. What are some examples of archetypes in addition to those mentioned in this module? In what ways are archetypes similar to and different from stereotypes?

Answers to Evaluate Questions

1. Psychodynamic; 2. 1-b, 2-c, 3-a; 3. c; 4. Defense mechanisms

KEY TERMS

personality	id	anal stage	defense mechanisms
psychodynamic approaches to personality	ego	phallic stage	repression
	superego	Oedipal conflict	neo-Freudian psychoanalysts
	psychosexual stages	identification	
psychoanalytic theory	fixations	latency period	collective unconscious
unconscious	oral stage	genital stage	archetypes

Module 41

Trait, Learning, Biological and Evolutionary, and Humanistic Approaches to Personality

LEARNING OUTCOMES

LO 41-1 What are the major aspects of trait, learning, biological and evolutionary, and humanistic approaches to personality?

"Tell me about Nelson," said Johnetta.

"Oh, he's just terrific. He's the friendliest guy I know–goes out of his way to be nice to everyone. He hardly ever gets mad. He's just so even-tempered, no matter what's happening. And he's really smart, too. About the only thing I don't like is that he's always in such a hurry to get things done. He seems to have boundless energy, much more than I have."

"He sounds great to me, especially in comparison to Rico," replied Johnetta. "He is so self-centered and arrogant that it drives me crazy. I sometimes wonder why I ever started going out with him."

Friendly. Even-tempered. Smart. Energetic. Self-centered. Arrogant.

The above exchange is made up of a series of trait characterizations of the speakers' friends. In fact, much of our own understanding of others' behavior is based on the premise that people possess certain traits that are consistent across different situations. For example, we generally assume that if someone is outgoing and sociable in one situation, he or she is outgoing and sociable in other situations (Mischel, 2004; Leising et al., 2014).

Dissatisfaction with the emphasis in psychoanalytic theory on unconscious–and difficult-to-demonstrate–processes in explaining a person's behavior led to the development of alternative approaches to personality, including a number of trait-based approaches. Other theories reflect established psychological perspectives, such as learning theory, biological and evolutionary approaches, and the humanistic approach.

Trait Approaches: Placing Labels on Personality

traits Consistent, habitual personality characteristics and behaviors that are displayed across different situations. (Module 41)

trait theory A model of personality that seeks to identify the basic traits necessary to describe personality. (Module 41)

If someone asked you to characterize another person, as Johnetta did of her friend, you probably would come up with a list of traits. **Traits** are consistent, habitual personality characteristics and behaviors that are displayed across different situations.

Trait theory is the personality approach that seeks to identify the basic traits necessary to describe personality. Trait theorists do not assume that some people have a particular trait while others do not. Instead, they propose that all people possess a set of traits, but the degree to which a particular trait applies to a specific person varies and can be quantified.

For instance, they might assume that all people have the trait of "friendliness" but in different degrees. You may be relatively friendly, whereas I may be relatively unfriendly. But we both have a "friendliness" trait, although your degree of "friendliness" is higher than mine.

The major challenge for trait theorists taking this approach has been to identify the specific basic traits necessary to describe personality. As we shall see, different theorists have come up with surprisingly different sets of traits. (Also see *Applying Psychology in the 21st Century*.)

APPLYING PSYCHOLOGY IN THE 21ST CENTURY

OVERESTIMATING AND UNDERESTIMATING OURSELVES

How good a driver do you think you are? If you're like most people, you probably consider yourself a better-than-average driver. The problem, of course, is that it's mathematically impossible for most people to be better than average; that would violate the definition of *average*. So, the point is that many people overestimate their own driving ability. Research has long established this tendency toward overconfidence in one's own traits and skills (Dunning, 2019).

New research, however, paints a somewhat more charitable picture, revealing that although people do sometimes overestimate themselves, at other times they underestimate themselves, depending on the domain of behavior in question. For example, in addition to driving, people tend to be overconfident about their kissing skills, their ability to use a computer, and their ability to have an interesting conversation. On the other hand, people consistently are underconfident in their ability to dance, drive a race car, paint a portrait, or recite the alphabet backward (Greenberg & Stephens-Davidowitz, 2019).

In their research, scientists sought to understand what factors determined whether people tended to be over- or underconfident in a given domain. To do so, they asked participants to rate themselves along multiple dimensions on traits

Most people rate themselves as better-than-average drivers, overestimating their own abilities.
Michael Simons/123RF

for which people tend toward overconfidence, and certain key commonalities emerged. First, people tend to be overconfident with regard to traits that are diagnostic of their character—that is, ones that make them "good people," such as their ethics or their reliability as a friend. Second, people tend to be overconfident in traits they perceive as affirming their gender identity. So for men, that means being better than others in science and playing poker, while women were underconfident

in those same domains. Women, on the other hand, tended to see themselves as better than others at cooking and child-rearing—domains where men tended to be underconfident.

Ambiguity of the domain emerged as the third factor predicting overconfidence. Specifically, compared with more easily quantifiable traits, if it's hard or somewhat subjective to judge ability in a particular domain, then people were more likely to be overconfident. A fourth factor was the easiness of the task: People tended to be overconfident about simple tasks and much less confident about hard ones.

Finally, a fifth factor was the familiarity of the task; it's easier to be overconfident in one's ability to drive or use a computer than in one's ability to drive a race car or paint a portrait—tasks with which most people have far less experience. The researchers did report one amusing domain that was an exception to this rule: men (but not women) tended to think they would be better than average at surviving a zombie apocalypse! Hopefully, that's one hypothesis that won't be put to the test.

> **QUESTIONS TO CONSIDER**
>
> - Why do you think people would be overconfident in tasks that are stereotypical for their gender?
> - What might be some positive and negative consequences of overestimating (or underestimating) yourself?

ALLPORT'S TRAIT THEORY: IDENTIFYING BASIC CHARACTERISTICS

When personality psychologist Gordon Allport systematically pored over an unabridged dictionary in the 1930s, he came up with some 18,000 separate terms that could be used to describe personality. Although he was able to pare down the list to 4,500 descriptors after eliminating words with similar meanings, he was left with a problem crucial to all trait approaches: Which traits are the most important in characterizing personality?

Allport eventually answered this question by suggesting that there are three fundamental categories of traits: cardinal, central, and secondary (Allport, 1966):

- **Cardinal traits.** A *cardinal trait* is a single, overriding characteristic that motivates most of a person's behavior. For example, a totally selfless woman may direct all her energy toward humanitarian activities; an intensely power-hungry person may be driven by an all-consuming need for control.

Extraversion
• Sociable
• Lively
• Active
• Assertive
• Sensation-seeking

Neuroticism
• Anxious
• Depressed
• Guilt feelings
• Low self-esteem
• Tense

Psychoticism
• Aggressive
• Cold
• Egocentric
• Impersonal
• Impulsive

FIGURE 1 Eysenck described personality in terms of three major dimensions: extraversion, neuroticism, and psychoticism. Using these dimensions, he could predict people's behavior in many types of situations.

Source: Eysenck, H. J. (1991). Biological dimensions of personality. In L. A. Pervin (Ed.), *Handbook of personality: Theory and research*. New York: Guilford Press.

Study Alert

You can remember the Big Five set of personality traits by using the acronym OCEAN (openness to experience, conscientiousness, extraversion, *a*greeableness, and *n*euroticism).

• **Central traits.** Few people have a single, comprehensive cardinal trait. Instead, they possess 5-10 central traits that make up the core of personality. *Central traits*, such as warmth or honesty, describe an individual's major characteristics. Each central trait is assumed to imply the presence of other traits. For example, people who have a central trait of warmth also are likely to be sociable and friendly.

• **Secondary traits.** Finally, *secondary traits* are characteristics that affect behavior in fewer situations and are less influential than central or cardinal traits. For instance, a reluctance to eat meat and a love of modern art would be considered secondary traits (Smrtnik-Vitulić & Zupančič, 2011; Kahn et al., 2013; Zhao & Smillie, 2015).

CATTELL AND EYSENCK: FACTORING OUT PERSONALITY

Later attempts to identify primary personality traits centered on a statistical technique known as factor analysis. *Factor analysis* is a statistical method of identifying patterns among a large number of variables and combining them into more fundamental groupings. For example, a personality researcher might ask a large group of people to rate themselves on a number of specific traits. By using factor analysis and statistically computing which traits are associated with one another, a researcher can identify the fundamental patterns of traits—called *factors*—that cluster together in the same person.

Using factor analysis, personality psychologist Raymond Cattell suggested that 16 pairs of *traits* represent the basic dimensions of personality. Using that set of traits, he developed the Sixteen Personality Factor Questionnaire, or 16 PF, a personality scale that is still in use today (Cattell, Cattell, & Cattell, 2000; Djapo et al., 2011; Wright, 2017).

Another trait theorist, psychologist Hans Eysenck (1995), also used factor analysis to identify patterns of traits, but he came to a very different conclusion about the nature of personality. He found that personality could best be described in terms of just three major dimensions: extraversion, neuroticism, and psychoticism. The *extraversion* dimension describes a person's level of sociability, whereas the *neuroticism* dimension encompasses an individual's emotional stability. Finally, *psychoticism* is the degree to which reality is distorted. By evaluating people along these three dimensions, Eysenck was able to predict behavior accurately in a variety of situations. Figure 1 lists specific traits associated with each of the dimensions.

THE BIG FIVE PERSONALITY TRAITS

For the last two decades, the most influential trait approach contends that five traits or factors—called the "Big Five"—lie at the core of personality. Using factor analytic statistical techniques, a consistent body of research has identified a similar set of five factors that underlie personality. The specific five factors are *openness to experience, conscientiousness, extraversion, agreeableness,* and *neuroticism* (emotional stability). They are described in Figure 2.

The Big Five emerge consistently across a number of domains. For example, factor analyses of major personality inventories, self-report measures made by observers of others' personality traits, and checklists of self-descriptions yield similar factors. In addition, the Big Five emerge consistently in different populations of individuals, including children, college students, older adults, and speakers of different languages. Cross-cultural research conducted in areas ranging from Europe to the Middle East to Africa also has been supportive. Finally, studies of brain functioning show that Big Five personality traits are related to the way the brain processes information (Saucier & Srivastava, 2015; Bouvard & Roulin, 2017; Hall et al., 2019).

In short, a growing consensus exists that the Big Five represent the best description of personality traits we have today. Still, the debate over the specific number and kinds of traits—and even the usefulness of trait approaches in general—remains a lively one.

The Big Five Personality Factors and Dimensions of Sample Traits	
Openness to experience	**Agreeableness**
Independent—Conforming	Sympathetic—Fault-finding
Imaginative—Practical	Kind—Cold
Preference for variety—Preference for routine	Appreciative—Unfriendly
Conscientiousness	**Neuroticism (Emotional stability)**
Careful—Careless	Stable—Tense
Disciplined—Impulsive	Calm—Anxious
Organized—Disorganized	Secure—Insecure
Extraversion	
Talkative—Quiet	
Fun-loving—Sober	
Sociable—Retiring	

FIGURE 2 Five broad trait factors, referred to as the "Big Five," are considered to be the core of personality.

Sources: Adapted from John, O. P., Robins, R. W., & Pervin, L. A. (2010). *Handbook of Personality*. (3rd ed.). New York: Guilford Press.

EVALUATING TRAIT APPROACHES TO PERSONALITY

Trait approaches have several virtues. They provide a clear, straightforward explanation of people's behavioral consistencies. Furthermore, traits allow us to readily compare one person with another. Because of these advantages, trait approaches to personality have had an important influence on the development of several useful personality measures (Larsen & Buss, 2006; Cook, 2013; Boyle, 2019).

However, trait approaches also have some drawbacks. For example, we have seen that various trait theories describing personality come to different conclusions about which traits are the most fundamental and descriptive. The difficulty in determining which of the theories is the most accurate has led some personality psychologists to question the validity of trait conceptions of personality in general.

Trait approaches suffer from an even more fundamental difficulty: Even if we identify a set of primary traits, all we have done is provide a set of labels for personality. But labeling personality traits is not an *explanation* of how those traits developed in a person nor of how they function to determine behavior. For example, if we say that someone who donates money to charity has the trait of generosity, we still do not know *why* that person became generous in the first place or why the person displays generosity in a specific situation. In the view of some critics, then, traits do not provide explanations for behavior; they merely label it.

Learning Approaches: We Are What We've Learned

The psychodynamic and trait approaches we've been discussing concentrate on the "inner" person–the fury of a powerful id or a critical set of traits that describes the core of an individual. In contrast, learning approaches to personality focus on the external world in which a person lives and how external influences determine and affect personality.

SKINNER'S BEHAVIORIST APPROACH

According to the most influential learning theorist, B. F. Skinner (who carried out pioneering work on operant conditioning), personality is a collection of learned behavior patterns (Skinner, 1975). Similarities in responses across different situations are caused by similar patterns of reinforcement that have been received in such situations in the past. If I am sociable both at parties and at meetings, it is because I have been reinforced for displaying social behaviors—not because I am fulfilling an unconscious wish based on experiences during my childhood or because I have an internal trait of sociability.

Learning theorists such as Skinner are less interested in the consistencies in behavior across situations than in ways of modifying behavior. To a learning theorist who subscribes to Skinner's view, humans are infinitely changeable through the process of learning new behavior patterns. If we are able to control and modify the patterns of reinforcers in a situation, behavior that other theorists would view as stable and unyielding can be changed and ultimately improved. Learning theorists are optimistic in their attitudes about the potential for resolving personal and societal problems through treatment strategies based on learning theory.

SOCIAL COGNITIVE APPROACHES TO PERSONALITY

Not all learning theories of personality take such a rigid view in rejecting the importance of what is "inside" a person by focusing solely on the "outside." Unlike other learning approaches to personality, **social cognitive approaches to personality** emphasize the influence of cognition—thoughts, feelings, expectations, and values—as well as observation of others' behavior, on personality. According to Albert Bandura, one of the main proponents of this point of view, people can foresee the possible outcomes of certain behaviors in a specific setting without actually having to carry them out. This understanding comes primarily through *observational learning*—viewing the actions of others and observing the consequences (Bandura, 1999).

For instance, children who view a model behaving in, say, an aggressive manner tend to copy the behavior if the consequences of the model's behavior are seen as positive. If, in contrast, the model's aggressive behavior has resulted in no consequences or negative consequences, children are considerably less likely to act aggressively. According to social cognitive approaches, then, personality develops through repeated observation of others' behavior.

Bandura places particular emphasis on the role played by self-efficacy. **Self-efficacy** is the belief that we can master a situation and produce positive outcomes. Self-efficacy underlies people's faith in their ability to successfully carry out a particular task or to produce a desired outcome. People with high self-efficacy have higher aspirations and greater persistence in working to attain goals than those with lower self-efficacy. Furthermore, they ultimately achieve greater success (Bandura & Locke, 2003; Sezgin & Erdogan, 2015; Tazouti & Jarlégan, 2019).

How do we develop self-efficacy? One way is by paying close attention to our prior successes and failures. If we try snowboarding and experience little success, we'll be less likely to try it again. However, if our initial efforts appear promising, we'll be more likely to attempt it again. Direct reinforcement and encouragement from others also play a role in developing self-efficacy (Buchanan & Selmon, 2008; Artistico et al., 2013; Wright, 2017).

Compared with other learning theories of personality, social cognitive approaches are distinctive in their emphasis on the reciprocity between individuals and their environment. Not only is the environment assumed to affect personality, but people's behavior and personalities are also assumed to "feed back" and modify the environment (Bandura, 1999, 2000).

HOW MUCH CONSISTENCY EXISTS IN PERSONALITY?

Another social cognitive theorist, Walter Mischel, takes a different approach to personality from that of Albert Bandura. He rejects the view that personality consists of broad traits that lead to substantial consistencies in behavior across different situations. Instead, he sees personality as considerably more variable from one situation to another (Mischel, 2009).

In this view, particular situations give rise to particular kinds of behavior. Some situations are especially influential (think of a movie theater, where everyone displays

social cognitive approaches to personality Theories that emphasize the influence of a person's cognitions—thoughts, feelings, expectations, and values—as well as observation of others' behavior, in determining personality. (Module 41)

self-efficacy The belief that we can master a situation and produce positive outcomes. (Module 41)

PsychTech

Researchers have been investigating differences in self-efficacy between people in their use of technology. One difference is age: younger adults appear to have more confidence in their technological expertise than older adults do.

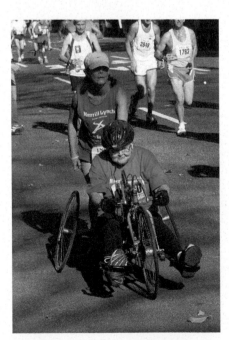

Self-efficacy, the belief in one's own capabilities, leads to higher aspirations and greater persistence.

Lars A. Niki

pretty much the same behavior by sitting quietly and watching the film). Other situations permit much variability in behavior (such as a party, for example, where some people may be dancing, while others are eating and drinking).

From this perspective, personality cannot be considered without taking the particular context of the situation into account—a view known as *situationism*. In his *cognitive-affective processing system (CAPS)* theory, Mischel argues that people's thoughts and emotions about themselves and the world determine how they view, and then react, in particular situations. Personality is thus seen as a reflection of how people's prior experiences in different situations, as well as the specifics of the situation they are in at the moment, interact and determine their behavior (Mischel & Shoda, 2008; McCrae et al., 2011; Huprich & Nelson, 2015).

SELF-ESTEEM

Our behavior also reflects the view we have of ourselves and the way we value the various parts of our personalities. **Self-esteem** is the component of personality that encompasses our positive and negative evaluations of ourselves. Unlike self-efficacy, which focuses on our views of whether we are able to carry out a task, self-esteem relates to how we feel about ourselves.

self-esteem The component of personality that encompasses our positive and negative self-evaluations. (Module 41)

Although people have a general level of self-esteem, it is not unidimensional. We may see ourselves positively in one domain but negatively in others. For example, a good student may have high self-esteem in academic domains but lower self-esteem in athletics (Gadbois & Sturgeon, 2011; Mirzairad et al., 2017; Musetti & Corsano, 2019).

The development of self-esteem is strongly affected by cultural factors. For example, consider the characteristic of *relationship harmony*, which is a sense of success in forming close bonds with others. For people living in Asian cultures, having high relationship harmony is a more important component of self-esteem than it is for those living in more individualistic Western societies (Lun & Bond, 2006; Cheng & Kwan, 2008; Chin, 2015).

Although almost all of us go through periods in which our self-esteem is challenged and temporarily reduced (for instance, after an undeniable failure), some people are chronically low in self-esteem. For them, failure seems to be an inevitable part of life. In fact, low self-esteem may lead to a cycle of failure in which past failure breeds future failure.

For example, consider students with low self-esteem who are studying for a test. Because of their low self-esteem, they expect to do poorly on the test. In turn, this belief raises their anxiety level, which makes it increasingly difficult to study and perhaps even leads them not to work as hard. Because of these attitudes, they do, in fact, perform badly on the test. Ultimately, the failure reinforces their low self-esteem, and the cycle is perpetuated, as illustrated in Figure 3. In short, low self-esteem can lead to a self-destructive cycle of failure.

On the other hand, high levels of self-esteem can also be troublesome if they are unwarranted. According to a growing body of data, an increasing number of college-age students have high levels of *narcissism*, in which people show self-absorption and hold inflated views of themselves. For example, over the past three decades, thousands of American college students participating in a variety of psychological research studies were asked to take the Narcissism Personality Inventory (NPI), a test of narcissistic tendencies. A summary of more than 100 such studies conducted over a 25-year period

FIGURE 3 The cycle of low self-esteem begins with an individual already having low self-esteem. As a consequence, the person will have low performance expectations and expect to fail a test, thereby producing anxiety and reduced effort. As a result, the person will actually fail, and failure in turn reinforces low self-esteem.

Research suggests that narcissism, the degree to which people show self-absorption and hold inflated views of themselves, has increased over the past three decades.

William Perugini/Image Source/Getty Images

showed a significant increase in participants' narcissism scores (Dingfelder, 2011; Twenge & Kasser, 2013; Barry et al., 2017).

What might produce the increase in narcissism in young Americans? Research points to social networking media. In recent years, it has become typical for young people to self-promote in carefully edited online profiles. The most mundane aspects of their daily lives are viewed as worthy of broadcasting to the world, whether in Twitter tweets, Instagram photos, Facebook postings, or YouTube videos. Another explanation is that parents may increasingly be inflating their children's sense of self-importance by shielding them from situations in which they might fail (Twenge, 2013; Kauten et al., 2015; Wang, 2019).

From the perspective of...

An Educator How might you encourage your students' development of self-esteem and self-efficacy? What steps would you take to ensure that their self-esteem did not become overinflated?

Andersen Ross/Blend Images/Getty Images

EVALUATING LEARNING APPROACHES TO PERSONALITY

Because they ignore the internal processes, such as thoughts and emotions, traditional learning theorists such as Skinner have been accused of oversimplifying personality far too much. Their critics think that reducing behavior to a series of stimuli and responses and excluding thoughts and feelings from the realm of personality leaves behaviorists practicing an unrealistic and inadequate form of science.

Of course, some of these criticisms are blunted by social cognitive approaches, which explicitly consider the role of cognitive processes in personality. Still, learning approaches tend to share a highly *deterministic* view of human behavior, which maintains that behavior is shaped primarily by forces beyond the individual's control. As in psychoanalytic theory (which suggests that personality is determined by the unconscious forces) and trait approaches (which view personality in part as a mixture of genetically determined traits), learning theory's reliance on deterministic principles de-emphasizes people's ability to pilot their own course through life.

Nonetheless, learning approaches have had a major impact on the study of personality. For one thing, they have helped make personality psychology an objective, scientific venture by focusing on observable behavior and the effects of the environments. In addition, they have produced important, successful means of treating a variety of psychological disorders. The degree of success of these treatments is a testimony to the merits of learning theory approaches to personality.

Biological and Evolutionary Approaches: Are We Born with Personality?

Approaching the question of what determines personality from a different direction, **biological and evolutionary approaches to personality** suggest that important components of personality are inherited. Building on the work of behavioral geneticists, researchers using biological and evolutionary approaches argue that personality is determined at least in part by our genes in much the same way that our height is largely a result of genetic contributions from our ancestors. The evolutionary perspective assumes that personality traits that led to our ancestors' survival and reproductive success are more likely to be preserved and passed on to subsequent generations (Buss, 2011; Yarkoni, 2015; Mõttus et al., 2019).

The results of research studies conducted on twins who are genetically identical but raised apart from one another by different caretakers illustrate the importance of genetic factors in personality. Personality tests indicate that in major respects, genetically identical twins raised apart are quite similar in personality, even if they were separated at an early age.

Moreover, certain traits are more heavily influenced by heredity than are others. For example, *social potency* (the degree to which a person assumes mastery and leadership roles in social situations) and *traditionalism* (the tendency to follow authority)

biological and evolutionary approaches to personality Theories that suggest that important components of personality are inherited. (Module 41)

Biological and evolutionary approaches to personality seek to explain the consistencies in personality that are found in some families.
Photo and Co/The Image Bank/Getty Images

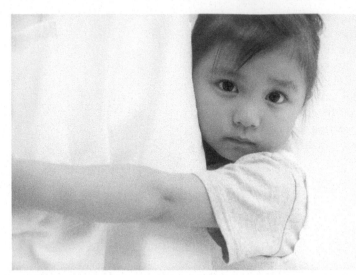

Infants are born with particular temperaments—dispositions that are consistent throughout childhood.
Isadora Getty Buyou/Image Source

temperament An individual's behavioral style and characteristic way of responding that emerges early in life. (Module 41)

had particularly strong genetic components, whereas achievement and social closeness had relatively weak genetic components (see Figure 4; Bouchard et al., 2004).

Furthermore, it is increasingly clear that the roots of adult personality emerge early in life. Infants are born with a specific **temperament,** an individual's behavioral style and characteristic way of responding. Temperament encompasses several dimensions, including general activity level and mood. For instance, some babies are quite active, whereas others are relatively calm. Similarly, some are relatively easygoing, whereas others are irritable, easily upset, and difficult to soothe. Temperament is quite consistent, with significant stability from infancy well into adolescence (Hori et al., 2011; Bates & Pettit, 2015; Planalp & Goldsmith, 2019.

Some researchers contend that specific genes are related to personality. For example, people with a longer dopamine-4 receptor gene are more likely to be thrill-seekers than are those without such a gene. These thrill-seekers tend to be extroverted, impulsive, quick-tempered, and always in search of excitement and novel situations. Furthermore, the structure of their brains may reflect their thrill-seeking tendencies (Golimbet et al., 2007; Ray et al., 2009; Wishart, Somoray, & Rowland, 2017; also see *Neuroscience in Your Life*).

NEUROSCIENCE IN YOUR LIFE: THE NEUROLOGICAL UNDERPINNINGS OF PERSONALITY

A large part of what makes us who we are is personality. Although the five-factor model has been influential in describing personality traits, its neurobiological basis has been largely unknown. However, in a recent study with over 500 participants, neuroscientists looked at how the shape of the brain relates to the five basic personality traits of openness to experience, conscientiousness, extraversion, agreeableness, and neuroticism. They found that the shape of certain brain areas relates to each of the five personality traits. For example, high levels of conscientiousness related to thicker cortex in two brain areas (shown in blue in three views of the brain below) (Riccelli et al., 2017).

Caudal middle frontal   Precuneus

Source: Adapted from Riccelli, R., Toschi, N., Nigro, S., Terracciano, A., & Passamonti, L. (2017). Surface-based morphometry reveals the neuroanatomical basis of the five-factor model of personality. *Social Cognitive and Affective Neuroscience, 12*(4), 671–684. doi: 10.1093/scan/nsw175.

Does the identification of specific genes linked to personality, coupled with the existence of temperaments from the time of birth, mean that we are destined to have certain types of personalities? Hardly. First, it is unlikely that any single gene is linked to a specific trait. For instance, the dopamine-4 receptor accounts for only around 10% of the variation in novelty seeking between different individuals. The rest of the variation is attributable to other genes and environmental factors (Keltikangas-Järvinen et al., 2004; Lahti et al., 2005; Kandler, Riemann, & Angleitner, 2013).

More important, genes interact with the environment. As we see in discussions of the heritability of intelligence and the nature–nurture issue, it is impossible to completely divorce genetic factors from environmental factors. Although studies of identical twins raised in different environments are helpful, they are not definitive because it is impossible to assess and control environmental factors fully. Furthermore, estimates of the influence of genetics are just that–estimates–and apply to groups, not individuals. Consequently, findings such as those shown in Figure 4 must be regarded as approximations.

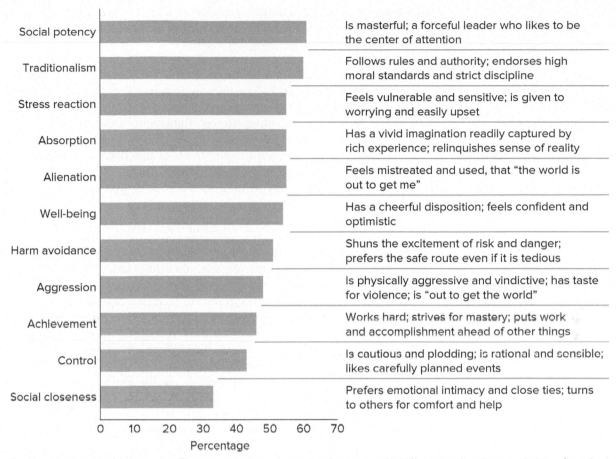

FIGURE 4 The inherited roots of personality. The percentages indicate the degree to which 11 personality characteristics reflect the influence of heredity.

Source: Adapted from Tellegen, A., Lykken, D. T., Bouchard, T. J., Jr., Wilcox, K. J., Segal, N. L., & Rich, S. (1998). Personality similarity in twins reared apart and together. *Journal of Personality and Social Psychology, 54*, 1031–1039.

Finally, even if more genes are found to be linked to specific personality characteristics, genes still cannot be viewed as the sole cause of personality. For one thing, genetically determined characteristics may not be expressed if they are not "turned on" by particular environmental experiences. Furthermore, behaviors produced by genes may help to create a specific environment. For instance, a cheerful, smiley baby may lead the parents to smile more and be more responsive, thereby creating a supportive, pleasant environment. In contrast, the parents of a cranky, fussy baby may be less inclined to smile at the child; in turn, the environment in which that child is raised will be less supportive and pleasant. In a sense, then, genes not only influence a person's behavior—they also help produce the environment in which a person develops (Kim-Cohen, Caspi, & Moffitt, 2003; Kendler et al., 2017; Azeredo et al., 2019).

Although an increasing number of personality theorists are taking biological and evolutionary factors into account, no comprehensive, unified theory that considers biological and evolutionary factors is widely accepted. Still, it is clear that certain personality traits have substantial genetic components and that heredity and environment interact to determine personality (Bouchard, 2004; South & Krueger, 2008; South et al., 2013).

Humanistic Approaches: The Uniqueness of You

In all the approaches to personality that we have discussed, where is an explanation for the saintliness of a Mother Teresa, the creativity of a Michelangelo, and the brilliance and perseverance of an Einstein? An understanding of such unique individuals—as well as more ordinary sorts of people who have some of the same attributes—comes from humanistic theory.

According to humanistic theorists, all the approaches to personality we have discussed share a fundamental misperception in their views of human nature. Instead of seeing people as controlled by unconscious, unseen forces (psychodynamic approaches), a set of stable traits (trait approaches), situational reinforcements and punishments (learning theory), or inherited factors (biological and evolutionary approaches), **humanistic approaches to personality** emphasize people's inherent goodness and their tendency to move toward higher levels of functioning. It is this conscious, self-motivated ability to change and improve, along with people's unique creative impulses, that humanistic theorists argue make up the core of personality.

ROGERS AND THE NEED FOR SELF-ACTUALIZATION

The major proponent of the humanistic point of view is Carl Rogers (1971). Along with other humanistic theorists, such as Abraham Maslow, Rogers maintains that all people have a fundamental need for **self-actualization,** a state of self-fulfillment in which people realize their highest potential, each in a unique way. He further suggests that people develop a need for positive regard that reflects the desire to be loved and respected. Because others provide this positive regard, we grow dependent on them. We begin to see and judge ourselves through the eyes of other people, relying on their values and being preoccupied with what they think of us.

According to Rogers, one outgrowth of placing importance on others' opinions is that a conflict may grow between people's actual life experiences and their self-concept. *Self-concept* is the set of beliefs people hold about their own abilities, behavior, and personality. If the discrepancies between people's self-concepts and what they actually experience in their lives are minor, the consequences are minor. But if the discrepancies between one's experience and one's self-concept are great, they will lead to psychological disturbances in daily functioning. For instance, people with large discrepancies may experience frequent anxiety.

Rogers suggests that one way of overcoming the discrepancy between experience and self-concept is through the receipt of unconditional positive regard from another person—a parent, friend, spouse, or even a therapist. **Unconditional positive regard** refers to an attitude of acceptance and respect on the observer's part, no matter what a person says or does. This acceptance, says Rogers, gives people the opportunity to evolve and grow both cognitively and emotionally and to develop more realistic self-concepts. You may have experienced the power of unconditional positive regard when you confided in someone, revealing embarrassing secrets because you knew the listener would still love and respect you even after hearing the worst about you (Marshall, 2007; Patterson & Joseph, 2013; Jayne, Purswell, & Stulmaker, 2019).

In contrast, *conditional positive regard* depends on your behavior. In such cases, others withdraw their love and acceptance if you do something of which they don't approve. The result is a discrepancy between your true self and what others wish you would be, which leads to anxiety and frustration (see Figure 5).

EVALUATING HUMANISTIC APPROACHES

Although humanistic theories suggest the value of providing unconditional positive regard toward people, unconditional positive regard toward humanistic theories has been less forthcoming. The criticisms have centered on the difficulty of verifying the basic assumptions of the approach as well as on the question of whether unconditional positive regard does, in fact, lead to greater personality adjustment.

Humanistic approaches have also been criticized for making the assumption that people are basically "good"—a notion that is unverifiable—and, equally important, for using nonscientific values to build supposedly scientific theories. Still, humanistic theories

humanistic approaches to personality Theories that emphasize people's innate goodness and desire to achieve higher levels of functioning. (Module 41)

self-actualization A state of self-fulfillment in which people realize their highest potential in their own unique way. (Modules 29, 41)

unconditional positive regard An attitude of acceptance and respect on the part of an observer, no matter what a person says or does. (Module 41)

FIGURE 5 According to the humanistic view of Carl Rogers, people have a basic need to be loved and respected. If you receive unconditional positive regard from others, you will develop a more realistic self-concept and ultimately can reach self-actualization. But if the response from others is conditional, it may lead to anxiety and frustration.

have been important in highlighting the uniqueness of human beings and guiding the development of a significant form of therapy designed to alleviate psychological difficulties (Elkins, 2009; Kogstad, Ekeland, & Hummelvoll, 2011; Hounkatin et al., 2015).

Comparing Approaches to Personality

In light of the multiple approaches we have discussed, you may be wondering which of the theories provides the most accurate description of personality. That question cannot be answered precisely. Each theory is built on different assumptions and focuses on somewhat different aspects of personality (see Figure 6).

Furthermore, there is no clear way to scientifically test the various approaches and their assumptions against one another. Given the complexity of every individual, it seems reasonable that personality can be viewed from a number of perspectives simultaneously (Pervin, 2003).

Theoretical Approach and Major Theorists	Conscious Versus Unconscious Determinants of Personality	Nature (Hereditary Factors) Versus Nurture (Environmental Factors)	Free Will Versus Determinism	Stability Versus Modifiability
Psychodynamic (Freud, Jung, Horney, Adler)	Emphasizes the unconscious	Stresses innate, inherited structure of personality while emphasizing importance of childhood experience	Stresses determinism, the view that behavior is directed and caused by factors outside one's control	Emphasizes the stability of characteristics throughout a person's life
Trait (Allport, Cattell, Eysenck)	Disregards both conscious and unconscious	Approaches vary	Stresses determinism, the view that behavior is directed and caused by factors outside one's control	Emphasizes the stability of characteristics throughout a person's life
Learning (Skinner, Bandura)	Disregards both conscious and unconscious	Focuses on the environment	Stresses determinism, the view that behavior is directed and caused by factors outside one's control	Stresses that personality remains flexible and resilient throughout one's life
Biological and evolutionary (Tellegen)	Disregards both conscious and unconscious	Stresses the innate, inherited determinants of personality	Stresses determinism, the view that behavior is directed and caused by factors outside one's control	Emphasizes the stability of characteristics throughout a person's life
Humanistic (Rogers, Maslow)	Stresses the conscious more than the unconscious	Stresses the interaction between nature and nurture	Stresses the freedom of individuals to make their own choices	Stresses that personality remains flexible and resilient throughout one's life

FIGURE 6 The multiple perspectives on personality.

RECAP/EVALUATE/RETHINK

RECAP

LO 41-1 What are the major aspects of trait, learning, biological and evolutionary, and humanistic approaches to personality?

- Trait approaches have been used to identify relatively enduring dimensions along which people differ from one another—dimensions known as traits.
- Learning approaches to personality concentrate on observable behavior. To a strict learning theorist, personality is the sum of learned responses to the external environment.
- Social cognitive approaches concentrate on the role of cognition in determining personality. Those approaches pay particular attention to self-efficacy and self-esteem in determining behavior.
- Biological and evolutionary approaches to personality focus on the way in which personality characteristics are inherited.
- Humanistic approaches emphasize people's inherent goodness. They consider the core of personality in terms of a person's ability to change and improve.
- The major personality approaches differ substantially from one another; the differences may reflect both their focus on different aspects of personality and the overall complexity of personality.

EVALUATE

1. Carl's determination to succeed is the dominant force in all his activities and relationships. According to Allport's theory, this is an example of a _____ trait. In contrast, Cindy's fondness for old western movies is an example of a _____ trait.

2. Eysenck might describe a person who enjoys activities such as parties and hang gliding as high on what trait?
3. Proponents of which approach to personality would be most likely to agree with the statement, "Personality can be thought of as learned responses to a person's upbringing and environment"?
   a. Humanistic
   b. Biological and evolutionary
   c. Learning
   d. Trait
4. Bandura would rate a person who would make the statement, "I know I can't do it" as low on _____ _____ .
5. Which approach to personality emphasizes the innate goodness of people and their desire to grow?
   a. Humanistic
   b. Psychodynamic
   c. Learning
   d. Biological and evolutionary

RETHINK

1. If personality traits are merely descriptive and not explanatory, what use are they? Can assigning a trait to a person be harmful—or helpful? Why or why not?
2. In what ways are Cattell's 16 source traits, Eysenck's three dimensions, and the Big Five factors similar, and in what ways are they different? Which traits seem to appear in all three schemes (under one name or another), and which are unique to one scheme? Why is this significant?

Answers to Evaluate Questions

1. cardinal, secondary; 2. extraversion; 3. c; 4. self-efficacy; 5. a

KEY TERMS

traits	self-efficacy	temperament	self-actualization
trait theory	self-esteem	humanistic approaches to	unconditional positive
social cognitive	biological and	personality	regard
approaches to	evolutionary approaches		
personality	to personality		

Module 42

Assessing Personality: Determining What Makes Us Distinctive

You have a need for other people to like and admire you.

You have a tendency to be critical of yourself.

You have a great deal of unused potential that you have not turned to your advantage.

Although you have some personality weaknesses, you generally are able to compensate for them.

Relating to members of the opposite sex has presented problems for you.

Although you appear to be disciplined and self-controlled to others, you tend to be anxious and insecure inside.

At times you have serious doubts about whether you have made the right decision or done the right thing.

You prefer a certain amount of change and variety and become dissatisfied when hemmed in by restrictions and limitations.

You do not accept others' statements without satisfactory proof.

You have found it unwise to be too frank in revealing yourself to others.

If you think these statements provide a surprisingly accurate account of your personality, you are not alone: Most college students think that these descriptions are tailored just to them. In fact, the statements were designed intentionally to be so vague that they apply to just about anyone (Forer, 1949; Russo, 1981).

The ease with which we can agree with such imprecise statements underscores the difficulty in coming up with accurate and meaningful assessments of people's personalities. Psychologists interested in assessing personality must be able to define the most meaningful ways of discriminating between one person's personality and another's. To do this, they use **psychological tests,** standard measures devised to assess behavior objectively. With the results of such tests, psychologists can help people better understand themselves and make decisions about their lives. Researchers interested in the causes and consequences of personality also employ psychological tests (Hambleton, 2006; Miller, McIntire, & Lovler, 2011; Hambleton & Zenisky, 2013).

Like the assessments that seek to measure intelligence, all psychological tests must have reliability and validity. *Reliability* refers to a test's measurement consistency. If a test is reliable, it yields the same result each time it is administered to a specific person or group. In contrast, unreliable tests give different results each time they are administered.

For meaningful conclusions to be drawn, tests also must be valid. Tests have *validity* when they actually measure what they are designed to measure. If a test is constructed to measure sociability, for instance, we need to know that it actually measures sociability and not some other trait.

Finally, psychological tests are based on *test norms,* the distribution of test scores for a large sample of individuals who have taken a test. Test norms allow us to compare one person's score on a test with the scores of others who have taken the same test. For example, knowing the norms of a test permits test-takers who have received

LO 42-1 How can we most accurately assess personality?

LO 42-2 What are the major types of personality measures?

psychological tests Standard measures devised to assess behavior objectively; used by psychologists to help people make decisions about their lives and understand more about themselves. (Module 42)

Study Alert
The distinction between reliability and validity is important. For instance, a test that measures trustfulness is reliable if it yields the same results each time it is administered, whereas it is valid if it measures trustfulness accurately.

451

a certain score to know that they have scored in the top 10% of all those who have taken the test.

Test norms are established by administering a specific test to a large number of people and determining the typical scores. It is then possible to compare a single person's score with the scores of the group, which provides a comparative measure of test performance against the performance of others who have taken the test.

The establishment of appropriate test norms is not a simple endeavor. For instance, the specific group that is employed to determine test norms has a profound effect on the way an individual's performance is evaluated. In fact, as we discuss in *Exploring Diversity*, the process of establishing test norms can take on political overtones.

 # Exploring Diversity

Should Race and Ethnicity Be Used to Establish Test Norms?

The passions of politics may confront the objectivity of science when test norms are established, at least in the realm of standardized tests that are meant to predict future job performance. In fact, a national controversy has developed around the question of whether different test norms should be established for members of various racial and ethnic groups (Manly & Echemendia, 2007; Pedraza & Mungas, 2008; Nettles, 2019).

The test that sparked the controversy was the U.S. government's General Aptitude Test Battery, a test that measures a broad range of abilities from eye-hand coordination to reading proficiency. The problem was that African Americans and Hispanics tend to score lower on the test, on average, than do members of other groups. The lower scores often are due to a lack of prior relevant experience and job opportunities, which in turn has been due to prejudice and discrimination.

To promote the employment of minority racial groups, the government developed a separate set of test norms for African Americans and Hispanics. Rather than using the pool of all people who took the tests, the scores of African American and Hispanic applicants were compared only with the scores of other African Americans and Hispanics. Consequently, a Hispanic who scored in the top 20% of the Hispanics taking the test was considered to have performed equivalently to a white job applicant who scored in the top 20% of the whites who took the test, even though the absolute score of the Hispanic might be lower than that of the white.

Critics of the adjusted test norming system suggested that such a procedure discriminates in favor of certain racial and ethnic groups at the expense of others, thereby fanning the flames of racial bigotry. The practice was challenged legally; with the passage of the Civil Rights Act in 1991, race-based test norming on the General Aptitude Test Battery was discontinued (Galef, 2001).

However, proponents of race-based test norming continue to argue that test norming procedures that take race into account are an affirmative action tool that simply permits minority job-seekers to be placed on an equal footing with white job-seekers. Furthermore, a panel of the National Academy of Sciences supported the practice of adjusting test norms. It suggested that the unadjusted test norms are not very useful in predicting job performance and that they would tend to screen out otherwise qualified minority group members (Fleming, 2000).

Job testing is not the only area in which issues arise regarding test norms and the meaning of test scores. The issue of how to treat racial differences in IQ scores is also controversial and divisive. Clearly, race-based test norming raises profound and intense feelings that may come into conflict with scientific objectivity (Rushton & Jensen, 2006; Davis, 2009; Hutchinson & Mitchell, 2019).

The issue of establishing test norms is further complicated by the existence of a wide array of personality measures and approaches to assessment. We next consider some of these measures.

From the perspective of...

A Politician Imagine that you had to vote on a law that would require institutions and organizations to perform race-based test norming procedures on standardized tests. Would you support such a law? Why or why not? In addition to race, should test norming procedures take other factors into account? Which ones and why?

Exactostock/SuperStock

Self-Report Measures of Personality

If someone wanted to assess your personality, one possible approach would be to carry out an extensive interview with you to determine the most important events in your childhood, your social relationships, and your successes and failures. Obviously, though, such a technique would take extraordinary time and effort.

It is also unnecessary. Just as physicians draw only a small sample of your blood to test, psychologists can use self report measures. In a **self-report measure,** people are asked questions about their own behavior and traits. This sampling of self-report data is then used to infer the presence of particular personality characteristics. For example, a researcher who was interested in assessing a person's orientation to life might administer the questionnaire shown in Figure 1. Although the questionnaire consists of only a few questions, the answers can be used to generalize about personality characteristics. (Try it yourself!)

self-report measure A method of gathering data about people by asking them questions about their own behavior and traits. (Module 42)

MINNESOTA MULTIPHASIC PERSONALITY INVENTORY (MMPI)

One of the best examples of a self-report measure, and one of the most frequently used personality tests, is the **Minnesota Multiphasic Personality Inventory-2-Restructured Form (MMPI-2-RF).** Although the original purpose of this measure was to identify people with specific sorts of psychological difficulties, it has been found to predict a variety of other behaviors. For instance, MMPI-2-RF scores have been shown to be good predictors of whether college students will marry within 10 years of graduating and whether they will get advanced degrees. Police departments use the test to measure whether police officers are likely to use their weapons. Psychologists in Russia administer a modified form of the MMPI-2-RF to the country's astronauts and Olympic athletes (Butcher, 2011; Zahn et al., 2017; Lee et al., 2019).

The test consists of a series of 338 items to which a person responds "true," "false," or "cannot say." The questions cover a variety of issues ranging from mood ("I feel useless at times") to opinions ("People should try to understand their dreams") to physical and psychological health ("I am bothered by an upset stomach several times a week" and "I have strange and peculiar thoughts").

There are no right or wrong answers. Instead, interpretation of the results rests on the pattern of responses. The test yields scores on 51 separate scales, including several scales meant to measure the validity of the respondent's answers. For example, there is a "lie scale" that indicates when people are falsifying their responses in order to present themselves more favorably (through items such as, "I can't remember

Minnesota Multiphasic Personality Inventory-2-Restructured Form (MMPI-2-RF) A widely used self-report test that identifies people with psychological difficulties and is employed to predict some everyday behaviors. (Module 42)

The Life Orientation Test

Use the following scale to answer the items below:

0	1	2	3	4
Strongly Disagree	Disagree	Neutral	Agree	Strongly agree

1. In uncertain times, I usually expect the best.
2. It's easy for me to relax.
3. If something can go wrong for me, it will.
4. I'm always optimistic about my future.
5. I enjoy my friends a lot.
6. It's important for me to keep busy.
7. I hardly ever expect things to go my way.
8. I don't get upset too easily.
9. I rarely count on good things happening to me.
10. Overall, I expect more good things to happen to me than bad.

Scoring: First, reverse your answers to questions 3, 7, and 9. Do this by changing a 0 to a 4, a 1 to a 3, a 3 to a 1, and a 4 to a 0 (answers of 2 stay as 2). Then sum the reversed scores, and add them to the scores you gave to questions 1, 4, and 10. (Ignore questions 2, 5, 6, and 8, which are filler items.)

    The total score you get is a measure of a particular orientation to life: your degree of optimism. The higher your scores, the more positive and hopeful you generally are about life. For comparison purposes the average score for college students is 14.3, according to the results of a study by Scheier, Carver, and Bridges (1994). People with a higher degree of optimism generally deal with stress better than do those with lower scores.

FIGURE 1 The Life Orientation Test. Complete this test by indicating the degree to which you agree with each of the 10 statements, using the scale from 0 to 4 for each item. Try to be as accurate as possible. There are no right or wrong answers.

Source: Adapted from Scheier, M. F., Carver, C. S., & Bridges, M. W. (1994). Distinguishing optimism from neuroticism (and trait anxiety, self-mastery, and self-esteem): A reevaluation of the Life Orientation Test. *Journal of Personality and Social Psychology, 67,* 1063–1078.

test standardization A technique used to validate questions on personality tests by analyzing the responses of people who have completed the same set of questions, under the same circumstances. The responses can then be used to compare the responses and determine individuals' personality characteristics. (Module 42)

ever having a bad night's sleep") (Stein & Graham, 2005; Bacchiochi, 2006; Anderson et al., 2015).

How did the authors of the MMPI-2-RF determine what specific patterns of responses indicate? The procedure they used is typical of personality test construction—a process known as test standardization. **Test standardization** is a technique used to validate questions on personality tests by analyzing the responses of people who have completed the same set of questions, under the same circumstances. The responses then can be used to determine an individual's key personality characteristics.

To create and standardize the MMPI-2-RF, the test authors asked groups of psychiatric patients with a specific diagnosis, such as depression or schizophrenia, to complete a large number of items. They then determined which items best differentiated members of those groups from a comparison group of normal participants and included those specific items in the final version of the test. By systematically carrying out this procedure on groups with different diagnoses, the test authors were able to devise a number of subscales that identified forms of abnormal behavior (see Figure 2).

When the MMPI-2-RF is used for the purpose for which it was devised—identification of personality disorders—it does a good job. However, like other personality tests, it presents an opportunity for abuse. For instance, employers who use it as a screening

Clinical scales

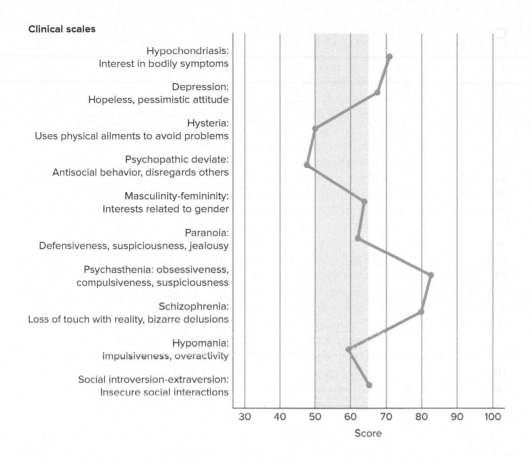

Hypochondriasis:
Interest in bodily symptoms

Depression:
Hopeless, pessimistic attitude

Hysteria:
Uses physical ailments to avoid problems

Psychopathic deviate:
Antisocial behavior, disregards others

Masculinity-femininity:
Interests related to gender

Paranoia:
Defensiveness, suspiciousness, jealousy

Psychasthenia: obsessiveness,
compulsiveness, suspiciousness

Schizophrenia:
Loss of touch with reality, bizarre delusions

Hypomania:
Impulsiveness, overactivity

Social introversion-extraversion:
Insecure social interactions

30   40   50   60   70   80   90   100

Score

FIGURE 2 An MMPI-2-RF profile of a person who suffers from obsessional anxiety, social withdrawal, and delusional thinking.

tool for job applicants may interpret the results improperly by relying too heavily on the results of individual scales instead of taking into account the overall patterns of results, which requires skilled interpretation. Furthermore, critics point out that the individual scales overlap, which makes their interpretation difficult. In sum, although the MMPI-2-RF remains the most widely used personality test and has been translated into more than 100 languages, it must be used with caution (Williams & Butcher, 2011; Ben-Porath, Corey, & Tarescavage, 2017).

OTHER SELF-REPORT MEASURES

The MMPI is not the only self-report questionnaire. For example, a commonly used one is the *Kuder Career Interest Assessment--Likert (KCIA-L),* which measures the relative level of interest a person has in six broad areas. These results are used to identify career pathways and occupations that match those interests. The Kuder test has been carefully validated, and research has supported its use (Suen, 2015).

Another self-report measure that is widely used in business settings is the *Myers-Briggs Type Indicator,* which aims to place people along four dimensions: (1) introverts versus extraverts; (2) intuitors versus sensors; (3) thinkers versus feelers; and (4) perceivers versus judgers. Originators of the test argue that employees work best in situations where others share or complement their types and where their personality type is well suited to the tasks on which they must work (Myers and Briggs Foundation, 2019).

Despite its widespread use—some 2 million people a year take the test, at a cost of billions of dollars—many critics believe that objective scientific validation for the test is lacking. They argue that researchers have failed to find that the test predicts much of interest, including professional job-related success. The disconnect between its widespread use and the lack of scientific support is puzzling (Emre, 2019; Lake et al., 2019; Stein & Swan, 2019).

Projective Methods

If you were shown the shape presented in Figure 3 and asked what it represented to you, you might not think that your impressions would mean very much. But to a psychodynamic theoretician, your responses to such an ambiguous figure would provide valuable clues to the state of your unconscious and ultimately to your general personality characteristics.

The shape in the figure is representative of inkblots used in projective personality tests. In **projective personality tests,** people are shown an ambiguous, vague stimulus and asked to describe it or to tell a story about it in order to infer information about their personality. Responses are considered to be "projections" of the test-taker's personality, and they are scored and interpreted using a standardized scoring method.

The best-known projective test is the **Rorschach test.** Devised by Swiss psychiatrist Hermann Rorschach (1924), the test involves showing a series of symmetrical stimuli similar to the one in Figure 3 to people who are then asked what the figures represent to them. Their responses are recorded, and people are classified into personality types requiring a complex set of judgments on the part of the examiner. For instance, individuals who see a bear in one particular Rorschach inkblot are thought to have a strong degree of emotional control, according to the scoring guidelines Rorschach developed (Silverstein, 2007; Searls, 2017).

The **Thematic Apperception Test (TAT)** is another well-known projective test. The TAT consists of a series of pictures about which a person is asked to write a story. The stories are then used to draw inferences about the writer's personality characteristics. For example, the TAT is used to assess need for achievement and other motivational needs (Langan-Fox & Grant, 2006; Manjhi & Purty, 2017).

Tests with stimuli as ambiguous as those used in the Rorschach and TAT require a high degree of training, skill, and care in their interpretation–so much so that many psychologists question the validity of projective test results. The Rorschach in particular has been criticized for requiring examiners to make many broad inferences that lack an objective basis, at least in the view of critics. Furthermore, attempts to standardize the scoring of the Rorschach have frequently failed.

projective personality test A test in which a person is shown an ambiguous stimulus and asked to describe it or tell a story about it in order to infer information about their personality. (Module 42)

Rorschach test A test that involves showing a series of symmetrical visual stimuli to people who then are asked what the figures represent to them. (Module 42)

Thematic Apperception Test (TAT) A test consisting of a series of pictures about which a person is asked to write a story. (Module 42)

FIGURE 3 This inkblot is similar to the type used in the Rorschach personality test. What do you see in it?
Spencer Grant/Science Source

Despite such problems, both the Rorschach and the TAT are widely used, especially in clinical settings, and their proponents suggest that their reliability and validity are great enough to provide useful inferences about personality (Campos, 2011; Husain, 2015; Miura et al., 2019).

Behavioral Assessment

If you were a psychologist subscribing to a learning approach to personality, you would be likely to object to the indirect nature of projective tests. Instead, you would be more apt to use **behavioral assessment**–direct measures of an individual's behavior designed to describe characteristics indicative of personality. As with observational research, behavioral assessment may be carried out naturalistically by observing people in their own settings: in the workplace, at home, or in school. In other cases, behavioral assessment occurs in the laboratory under controlled conditions in which a psychologist sets up a situation and observes an individual's behavior (Miller & Leffard, 2007; O'Brien & Young, 2013; Wannez et al., 2017).

behavioral assessment Direct measures of an individual's behavior used to describe personality characteristics. (Module 42)

Regardless of the setting in which behavior is observed, an effort is made to ensure that behavioral assessment is carried out objectively and quantifies behavior as much as possible. For example, an observer may record the number of social contacts a person initiates, the number of questions asked, or the number of aggressive acts. Another method is to measure the duration of events: the duration of a child's temper tantrum, the length of a conversation, the amount of time spent working, or the time spent in cooperative behavior.

Behavioral assessment is particularly appropriate for observing–and eventually remedying–specific behavioral difficulties, such as shyness in children. It provides a means of assessing the specific nature and incidence of a problem and subsequently allows psychologists to determine whether intervention techniques have been successful.

Behavioral assessment techniques based on learning theories of personality have also made important contributions to the treatment of certain kinds of psychological difficulties. In addition, they are also used to make hiring and personnel decisions in the workplace.

BECOMING AN INFORMED CONSUMER
of Psychology

Assessing Personality Assessments

Many companies, ranging from General Motors to Microsoft, employ personality tests to help determine who gets hired. In fact, workplace personality testing has become a big business, with companies spending $500 million a year to help identify the best employees (Weber & Dwoskin, 2014; Lundgren, Kroon, & Poell, 2019).

What kinds of questions are potential workers asked? In one example, potential Microsoft employees have been asked brainteasers such as "If you had to remove one of the 50 U.S. states, which would it be?" (Hint: First define *remove*. If you mean the death of everyone in the state, suggest a low-population state. If you mean quitting the country, then go for an outlying state such as Alaska or Hawaii.) Other employers ask questions that are even more vague ("Describe November"). With such questions, it's not always clear that the tests are reliable or valid (McGinn, 2003).

Before relying too heavily on the results of such personality testing as a potential employee, employer, or consumer of testing services, you should keep several points in mind:

- *Understand what the test claims to measure.* Standard personality measures are accompanied by information that discusses how the test was developed, to whom it is most applicable, and how the results should be interpreted. Read any explanations of the test; they will help you understand the results.

- *Do not base a decision only on the results of any one test.* Test results should be interpreted in the context of other information, such as academic records, social interests, and home and community activities.
- *Remember that test results are not always accurate.* The results may be in error; the test may be unreliable or invalid. For example, you may have had a "bad day" when you took the test, or the person scoring and interpreting the test may have made a mistake. You should not place too much significance on the results of a single administration of any test.

In sum, it is important to keep in mind the complexity of human behavior—particularly your own. No single test can provide an understanding of the intricacies of someone's personality without considering a good deal more information than can be provided in a single testing session (Gladwell, 2004; Paul, 2004; Hogan, Davies, & Hogan, 2007).

RECAP/EVALUATE/RETHINK

RECAP

LO 42-1 How can we most accurately assess personality?

- Psychological tests such as the MMPI-2-RF are standard assessment tools that measure behavior objectively. They must be reliable (measuring what they are trying to measure consistently) and valid (measuring what they are supposed to measure).

LO 42-2 What are the major types of personality measures?

- Self-report measures ask people about a sample range of their behaviors. These reports are used to infer the presence of particular personality characteristics.
- Projective personality tests (such as the Rorschach and the TAT) present an ambiguous stimulus; the test administrator infers information about the test-taker from his or her responses.
- Behavioral assessment is based on the principles of learning theory. It employs direct measurement of an individual's behavior to determine characteristics related to personality.

EVALUATE

1. _____ is the consistency of a personality test; _____ is the ability of a test to actually measure what it is designed to measure.

2. _____ _____ are standards used to compare scores of different people taking the same test.
3. Tests such as the MMPI-2-RF, in which a small sample of behavior is assessed to determine larger patterns, are examples of which of the following?
   a. Cross-sectional tests
   b. Projective tests
   c. Achievement tests
   d. Self-report tests
4. A person shown a picture and asked to make up a story about it would be taking a _____ personality test.

RETHINK

1. Should personality tests be used for personnel decisions? Should they be used for other social purposes, such as identifying individuals at risk for certain types of personality disorders?
2. What do you think are some of the problems that developers and interpreters of self-report personality tests must deal with in their effort to provide useful information about test-takers? Why is a "lie scale" included on such measures?

Answers to Evaluate Questions

1. Reliability, validity; 2. Test norms; 3. d; 4. projective

psychological tests
self-report measures
Minnesota Multiphasic
 Personality Inventory-2-
 Restructured Form
 (MMPI-2-RF)

test standardization
projective personality test
Rorschach test
Thematic Apperception
 Test (TAT)
behavioral assessment

LOOKING *Back*

EPILOGUE

We have discussed the ways in which psychologists have interpreted the development and structure of personality. The perspectives we examined ranged from Freud's analysis of personality based primarily on internal, unconscious factors to the externally based view championed by learning theorists of personality as a learned set of traits and actions. We also noted that there are many ways to interpret personality; by no means does a consensus exist on a set of key traits central to personality.

Return to the prologue of this chapter and consider the case of James Bulger and Catherine Greig. Use your understanding of personality to consider the following questions.

1. From what you know about him, would you say that James Bulger was id-dominated, superego-dominated, or ego balanced? Why do you think so?
2. What defense mechanisms might Bulger have used to restrain his aggressive impulses while living as Charlie Gasko?
3. Did Bulger seem to have a cardinal trait? If so, what was it?
4. Did Bulger seem to be particularly high or particularly low on any of the Big Five personality traits? If so, which ones and why do you think so?
5. Which approach to personality do you think best captures a person such as Bulger? Explain.

VISUAL SUMMARY 13 Personality

MODULE 40 Psychodynamic Approaches

Freud's Psychoanalytic Theory

— Conscious experience: only part of our psychological experience

— Unconscious: part of the personality of which we are not aware

— Structure of personality

 • Id: Represents the raw, unorganized, inborn part of personality

 • Ego: Strives to balance desires of the id and realities of the outside world

 • Superego: Harshly judges the morality of our behavior

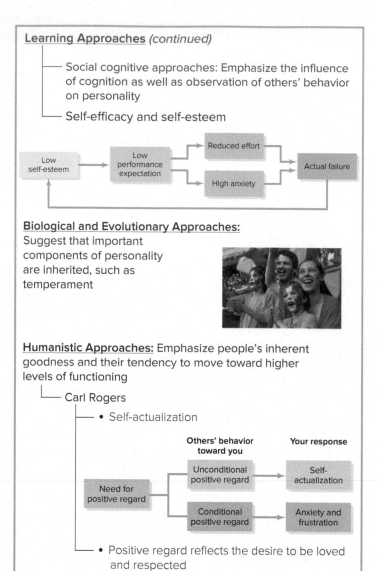

— Psychosexual stages

Stage	Age	Major Characteristics
Oral	Birth to 12–18 months	Interest in oral gratification from sucking, eating, mouthing, biting
Anal	12–18 months to 3 years	Gratification from expelling and withholding feces; coming to terms with society's controls relating to toilet training
Phallic	3 to 5–6 years	Interest in the genitals, coming to terms with Oedipal conflict leading to identification with same-sex parent
Latency	5–6 years to adolescence	Sexual concerns largely unimportant
Genital	Adolescence to adulthood	Reemergence of sexual interests and establishment of mature sexual relationships

— Defense mechanisms: Unconscious strategies people use to reduce anxiety

Neo-Freudian Psychoanalysts: Emphasize the ego more than Freud: Carl Jung, Karen Horney, Alfred Adler

MODULE 41 Trait, Learning, Biological and Evolutionary, and Humanistic Approaches

Trait Approaches: Emphasize consistent personality characteristics and behaviors called traits

— Eysenck: Extraversion, neuroticism, and psychoticism

— The big five personality traits: Openness to experience, conscientiousness, extraversion, agreeableness, neuroticism

Learning Approaches: Emphasize that personality is the sum of learned responses to the external environment

— B. F. Skinner: Personality is a collection of learned behavior patterns that are a result of reinforcement

Learning Approaches (continued)

— Social cognitive approaches: Emphasize the influence of cognition as well as observation of others' behavior on personality

— Self-efficacy and self-esteem

Low self-esteem → Low performance expectation → Reduced effort / High anxiety → Actual failure

Biological and Evolutionary Approaches: Suggest that important components of personality are inherited, such as temperament

Humanistic Approaches: Emphasize people's inherent goodness and their tendency to move toward higher levels of functioning

— Carl Rogers

 • Self-actualization

Others' behavior toward you / Your response

Need for positive regard → Unconditional positive regard → Self-actualization

Need for positive regard → Conditional positive regard → Anxiety and frustration

 • Positive regard reflects the desire to be loved and respected

MODULE 42 Assessing Personality

Psychological Tests: Standard measures that assess behavior objectively

 • Reliability
 • Validity
 • Norms

Self-report Measures: A method of gathering data by asking people questions about their own behavior and traits

Projective Methods: People are shown an ambiguous stimulus and asked to describe it or tell a story about it

— Rorschach test

— Thematic Apperception Test (TAT)

Behavioral Assessment: Measures of a person's behavior designed to describe characteristics indicative of personality

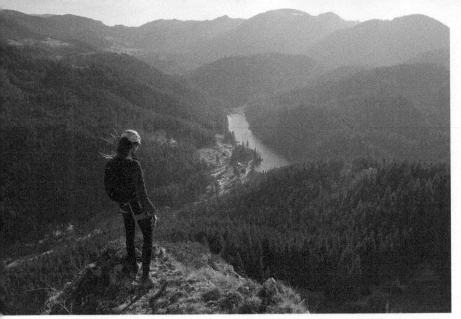

Alxcrs/Shutterstock

CHAPTER 14

Health Psychology: Stress, Coping, and Well-Being

LEARNING OUTCOMES FOR CHAPTER 14

Matt Murphy was easy-going and well liked at his high school, and he always stayed away from drugs and alcohol. So it was just a lark when Murphy agreed to try puffing on a Juul, a brand of electronic cigarette that delivers nicotine in a puff of flavored water vapor, while clowning around with friends at a party. But he took an immediate and unexpected liking to the instant head-rush.

In the days to come, he continued to bum puffs of Juul from his friends. Just a few weeks later, on a vacation with his family, Murphy found he couldn't bear going without a vape any longer; he slipped away and hired an Uber to take him to the nearest vendor where he could buy his fix—an act of desperation that set him back a cool $100.

Before Murphy knew it, most of his pocket money was going toward his Juul habit. He was going through a pod a day or more and couldn't stop, even though it was interfering with his school and his social life. He got winded during athletic activities and was having an increasingly difficult time hiding his habit from his parents. No longer enjoying the experience, Murphy kept puffing Juul just to keep the gut-wrenching anxiety of withdrawal at bay.

Murphy became a vocal anti-Juul advocate, urging friends not to get started on it lest they suffer his fate, even as he was unable to stop vaping himself. He was just one of hundreds of thousands of individuals addicted to vaping (Hoffman, 2018).

LOOKING *Ahead*

For Matt Murphy, it was love at first puff. It took him years to kick the habit and give up the rush that the nicotine in Juul gave him, despite knowing the toll it was taking on him.

Why did Murphy fall into a habit that he knew held some dangers? More broadly, why do people engage in behaviors that hold clear potential risks to their wellness?

Psychologists interested in health and wellness seek to answer questions such as these, and they belong to a branch of psychology known as health psychology. **Health psychology** investigates the psychological factors related to wellness and illness, including the prevention, diagnosis, and treatment of medical problems. Health psychologists investigate the effects of psychological factors such as stress on illness. They examine the psychological principles underlying treatments for disease and illness.

Healthy psychologists also study prevention and behavior change. For example, during the coronavirus pandemic, health psychologists helped to craft messages that would lead people to self-quarantine and to socially distance themselves from others.

Health psychologists take a decisive stand on the enduring mind–body issue that philosophers and, later, psychologists have debated since the time of the ancient Greeks. In their view, the mind and the body are clearly linked rather than representing two distinct systems (Sternberg, 2000; Dalal & Misra, 2006; Grosso, 2015).

Health psychologists recognize that good health and the ability to cope with illness are affected by psychological factors such as thoughts, emotions, and the ability to manage stress. They have paid particular attention to the *immune system,* the complex system of organs, glands, and cells that constitutes our bodies' natural line of defense in fighting disease.

In fact, health psychologists are among the primary investigators in a growing field called **psychoneuroimmunology, *or* PNI,** the study of the relationship among psychological factors, the immune system, and the brain. PNI has led to discoveries such as the existence of an association between a person's emotional state and the success of the immune system in fighting disease (Mathews & Janusek, 2011; Sperner-Unterweger & Fuchs, 2015; Ayling et al., 2017).

In sum, health psychologists view the mind and the body as two parts of a whole human being that cannot be considered independently. This more recent view marks a sharp departure from earlier thinking. Previously, disease was seen as a purely biological phenomenon, and psychological factors were of little interest to most health-care workers. In the early 20th century, the primary causes of death were short-term infections from which one either rapidly recovered—or died. Now, however, the major causes of death, such as heart disease, cancer, and diabetes, are chronic illnesses that pose significant psychological issues because they often cannot be cured and may linger for years (Rotan & Ospina-Kammerer, 2007; Berecki-Gisolf et al., 2013; Chen et al., 2017).

Advances in health psychology have had an impact across a variety of disciplines and professions. For instance, health-care professionals such as physicians and nurses, social workers, dietitians, pharmacists, occupational therapists, and even clergy are increasingly likely to receive training in health psychology.

In the following modules, we discuss the ways in which psychological factors affect health. We first focus on the causes and consequences of stress as well as on the means of coping with it. Next, we explore the psychological aspects of several major health problems, including heart disease, cancer, and ailments resulting from smoking. Finally, we examine the ways in which patient–physician interactions influence our health and offer suggestions for increasing people's compliance with recommendations about behavior that will improve their well-being.

health psychology The branch of psychology that investigates the psychological factors related to wellness and illness, including the prevention, diagnosis, and treatment of medical problems. (Module 43)

psychoneuroimmunology (PNI) The study of the relationship among psychological factors, the immune system, and the brain. (Module 43)

Module 43
Stress and Coping

Sheila Gray remembers the worst moment of her life: The day she heard about the mass shootings at Sandy Hook Elementary School in Connecticut. Though Gray lives in Michigan, she immediately jumped in the car and drove to her 7-year-old daughter's school. She brought the girl home. "My heart was pounding. I started crying, and I just couldn't stop," Gray says. Then and there, she decided that her daughter, Merilee, would never return to her school. She began homeschooling the girl. Friends could come over, but Gray found she couldn't let Merilee out of her sight. "So much can happen when you walk away from your child," Gray says. "I was terrified by that loss of control."

Most of us need little introduction to the phenomenon of **stress,** people's response to events that threaten or challenge them. Whether the result of a school shooting, or-more likely-a paper deadline, exam, or work or family problem, life is full of circumstances and events known as *stressors* that produce threats to our well-being. Even pleasant events-such as planning a party or beginning a sought-after job-can produce stress, although negative events result in greater detrimental consequences than positive ones do.

Stress: Reacting to Threat and Challenge

All of us face stress in our lives. Some health psychologists believe that daily life actually involves a series of repeated sequences of perceiving a threat, considering ways to cope with it, and ultimately adapting to the threat with greater or lesser success. Although adaptation is often minor and occurs without our awareness, adaptation requires a major effort when stress is more severe or long-lasting. Ultimately, our attempts to overcome stress may produce biological and psychological responses that result in health problems (Finan, Zautra, & Wershba, 2011; Dierolf et al., 2017; Furuyashiki & Kitaoka, 2019).

THE NATURE OF STRESSORS: MY STRESS IS YOUR PLEASURE

Stress is a very personal thing. Although certain kinds of events, such as the death of a loved one or participation in military combat, are universally stressful, other situations may or may not be stressful to a specific person.

Consider, for instance, bungee jumping. Some people would find jumping off a bridge while attached to a slender rubber tether extremely stressful. However, there are individuals who see such an activity as challenging and fun-filled. Whether bungee jumping is stressful depends in part, then, on a person's perception of the activity.

For people to consider an event stressful, they must perceive it as threatening or challenging and must lack all the resources to deal with it effectively. Consequently, the same event may at some times be stressful and at other times provoke no stressful reaction at all. A young man experiences stress when he is turned down for a date-if he attributes the refusal to his unattractiveness or unworthiness. But if he attributes it to some factor unrelated to his self-esteem, such as a previous commitment of the woman he

LEARNING OUTCOMES

LO 43-1 How is health psychology a union between medicine and psychology?

LO 43-2 What is stress, how does it affect us, and how can we best cope with it?

stress A person's response to events that are threatening or challenging (Module 43)

Study Alert
Remember the distinction between stressors and stress, which can be tricky: Stressors (such as an exam) cause stress (the physiological and psychological reaction that comes from the exam).

Even positive events can produce significant stress.
Beijing Eastphoto stockimages Co.,Ltd/Alamy Stock Photo

asked, the experience of being refused may create no stress at all. Hence, a person's interpretation of events plays an important role in the determination of what is stressful (Giacobbi et al., 2004; Friborg, Hjemdal, & Rosenvinge, 2006; Tuckey et al., 2015).

CATEGORIZING STRESSORS

What kinds of events tend to be seen as stressful? There are three general types of stressors: cataclysmic events, personal stressors, and background stressors.

cataclysmic events Strong stressors that occur suddenly and typically affect many people at once (e.g., natural disasters). (Module 43)

Cataclysmic events **Cataclysmic events** are strong stressors that occur suddenly and typically affect many people simultaneously. Disasters such as wildfires and plane crashes as well as terrorist attacks are examples of cataclysmic events that can affect hundreds or thousands of people simultaneously.

Although it might seem that cataclysmic events would produce potent, lingering stress, in many cases they do not. In fact, cataclysmic events involving natural disasters may produce less stress in the long run than events that initially are not as devastating. One reason is that natural disasters have a clear start and ending. Once they are over, people can look to the future and work toward recovery. Moreover, others who also experienced the disaster share the stress induced by cataclysmic events. Such sharing permits people to offer one another social support and a firsthand understanding of the difficulties others are going through (Yesilyaprak, Kisac, & Sanlier, 2007; Schwarzer & Luszczynska, 2013).

In contrast, terrorist attacks such as the one on the World Trade Center in 2001, the Boston Marathon bombings in 2013, or the coronavirus pandemic are cataclysmic events that produce considerable stress. Terrorist attacks are deliberate, and victims (and observers) suspect that future attacks are likely. Furthermore, exposure to repeated events, whether experienced directly or through the media, may lead to increased sensitivity to stress. Thus, the coronavirus pandemic, which lasted for months and disrupted everyday life in unprecedented ways, was clearly a cataclysmic event that produced considerable stress; see Figure 1 (Watson, Brymer, & Bonanno, 2011; Garfin, Holman, & Silver, 2015; Idås, Backholm, & Korhonen, 2019).

personal stressors Major life events, such as the death of a family member, that have immediate negative consequences that generally fade with time. (Module 43)

posttraumatic stress disorder (PTSD) A phenomenon in which victims of major catastrophes or strong personal stressors feel long-lasting effects that may include re-experiencing the event in vivid flashbacks or dreams. (Module 43)

Personal Stressors The second major category of stressor is the personal stressor. **Personal stressors** include major life events such as the death of a parent or spouse, the loss of one's job, a major personal failure, or even something positive such as getting married. Typically, personal stressors produce an immediate major reaction that soon tapers off. For example, stress arising from the death of a loved one tends to be greatest just after the time of death, but people begin to feel less stress and are better able to cope with the loss after the passage of time.

Some victims of major catastrophes, cataclysmic events, and severe personal stressors experience **posttraumatic stress disorder, or PTSD,** in which a person has experienced a significantly stressful event that has long-lasting effects that may include

FIGURE 1 The coronavirus pandemic caused considerable stress and anxiety, as the results of this survey of college students clearly showed.
Source: Active Minds, 2020.

re-experiencing the event in vivid flashbacks or dreams. An episode of PTSD may be triggered by an otherwise innocent stimulus, such as the sound of a honking horn, that leads a person to re-experience a past event that produced considerable stress.

Symptoms of posttraumatic stress disorder also include emotional numbing, sleep difficulties, interpersonal problems, alcohol and drug abuse, and in some cases suicide. For instance, the suicide rate for military veterans, many of whom participated in the Iraq and Afghanistan wars, is twice as high as for nonveterans (Magruder & Yeager, 2009; Munjiza et al., 2017; Coleman, Ingram, & Sheerin, 2019).

Between 10–18% of soldiers returning from Iraq and Afghanistan show symptoms of PTSD, and the United States spends $3 billion a year on treating the disorder in military veterans. Furthermore, people who have experienced child abuse or rape, rescue workers facing overwhelming situations, and victims of sudden natural disasters or accidents that produce feelings of helplessness and shock may suffer from the same disorder (Horesh et al., 2011; Huang & Kashubeck-West, 2015; Thompson, 2015).

In addition to traditional forms of PTSD, soldiers who have faced multiple tours of duty and who may have actually thrived during years of combat face their own kind of PTSD. After they return home, they may have to unlearn the skills that helped them survive in combat, such as constant vigilance, an intolerance for carelessness, and extreme decisiveness (Carey, 2016).

Terrorist attacks produce high incidences of PTSD. For example, 11% of people in New York City had some form of PTSD in the months after the September 11 terrorist attacks. But the responses varied significantly with a resident's proximity to the attacks; the closer someone lived to the World Trade Center, the greater the likelihood of PTSD. Furthermore, for many people, the effects of PTSD were still evident a decade after the attacks (Lee, Isaac, & Janca, 2007; Marshall et al., 2007; Neria, DiGrande, & Adams, 2011).

One personal stressor that became an increasing part of everyday life—that is, before the pandemic changed so much about our lives—was the prospect of being injured or killed in a mass shooting. Over 1,300 U.S. citizens have been killed in mass shootings since 1966, and the number keeps rising. In 2019 alone, over 400 mass shootings occurred (Gun Violence Archive, 2019).

The stress produced by the fear of being involved in a mass shootings was considerable. Surveys showed that one-third of Americans avoided certain places or certain events because they feared being shot. In some urban neighborhoods, the threat of violence is an everyday concern (FBI, 2019).

Furthermore, members of racial and ethnic minority groups often experience particularly high levels of personal stressors. Not only do they face the potential of discrimination and prejudice, but they must contend with objective threats to health, safety, and financial insecurity. The coronavirus pandemic made racial and ethnic disparities particularly clear: blacks and Hispanics were hospitalized and died from the virus at disproportionate levels (APA Working Group on Stress and Health Disparities, 2017; Aubrey, 2020).

Background Stressors **Background stressors** or, more informally, *daily hassles*, are the third major category of stressors. Exemplified by standing in a long line at a supermarket checkout and getting stuck in a traffic jam, daily hassles are the minor irritations of life that we all face time and time again. Another type of background stressor is a long-term, chronic problem, such as being dissatisfied with school or a job, being in an unhappy relationship, or living in crowded quarters without privacy (Weinstein et al., 2004; McIntyre, Korn, & Matsuo, 2008; Barke, 2011; Aoued et al., 2019).

By themselves, daily hassles do not require much coping or even a response on the individual's part, although they certainly produce unpleasant emotions and moods. Yet, daily hassles add up—and ultimately, they may take as great of a toll as a single, more stressful incident. In fact, the *number* of daily hassles people face is associated with psychological symptoms and health problems such as flu, sore throat, and backaches.

The flip side of hassles is *uplifts*, the minor positive events that make us feel good—even if only temporarily. As indicated in Figure 2, uplifts range from relating well to a companion to finding one's surroundings pleasing. What is especially intriguing

background stressors ("daily hassles") Everyday annoyances, such as being stuck in traffic, that cause minor irritations and may have long-term ill effects if they continue or are compounded by other stressful events. (Module 43)

For these subway riders in Tokyo, the everyday commute was a stressful ordeal.
Rafael Macia/mauritius images GmbH/Alamy Stock Photo

FIGURE 2 The most common every-day hassles and uplifts. How many of these are part of your life, and how do you cope with the hassles?

Sources: Adapted from (hassles) Chamberlain, K., & Zika, S. (1990). The minor events approach to stress: Support for the use of daily hassles. *British Journal of Psychology, 81*(4), 469-481; (uplifts) Kanner, A. D., Coyne, J. C., Schaefer, C., & Lazarus, R. S. (1981). Comparison of two modes of stress measurement: Daily hassles and uplifts versus major life events. *Journal of Behavioral Medicine, 4*(1), 1–39.

PsychTech

An analysis of the emotional content of words sent in text messages during the hours following the 9/11 terrorist attack showed that over the course of the day, sadness and anxiety-related words remained steady but anger-related words increased steadily.

Study Alert

Remember the three categories of stressors—cataclysmic events, personal stressors, and background stressors—and that they produce different levels of stress.

about uplifts is that they are associated with people's psychological health in just the opposite way that hassles are: The greater the number of uplifts we experience, the fewer the psychological symptoms we report later (Chamberlain & Zika, 1990; Hurley & Kwon, 2013; Schmidt et al., 2017).

The High Cost of Stress

Stress has both biological and psychological consequences. Some of those consequences begin almost instantaneously, whereas others unfold over time.

Often the most immediate reaction to stress is biological. Specifically, exposure to stressors generates a rise in hormone secretions by the adrenal glands, an increase in heart rate and blood pressure, and changes in how well the skin conducts electrical impulses. On a short-term basis, these responses may be adaptive because they produce an "emergency reaction" in which the body prepares to defend itself through activation of the sympathetic nervous system. Those responses may allow more effective coping with the stressful situation (Berger et al., 2019).

However, continued exposure to stress results in a decline in the body's overall level of biological functioning because of the constant secretion of stress-related hormones. Over time, stressful reactions can promote deterioration of body tissues such as blood vessels and the heart. Ultimately, we become more susceptible to disease as our ability to fight off infection is lowered (Ellins et al., 2008; Miller, Chen, & Parker, 2011; Farrell et al., 2017).

Furthermore, stress can produce or worsen physical problems. Specifically, **psychophysiological disorders** are medical problems that are influenced by an interaction of psychological, emotional, and physical difficulties. Common psychophysiological disorders include high blood pressure, headaches, backaches, skin rashes, indigestion, fatigue, and constipation. Stress has even been linked to the common cold (Andrasik, 2006; Gupta, 2013; Gianaros & Wager, 2015).

On a psychological level, high levels of stress prevent people from adequately coping with life. Their view of the environment can become clouded (for example, a minor criticism made by a friend is blown out of proportion). Moreover, at the highest levels of stress, emotional responses may be so extreme that people are unable to act at all. People under a lot of stress also become less able to deal with new stressors.

In short, stress affects us in multiple ways. It may increase the risk that we will become ill, it may directly cause illness, it may make us less able to recover from a disease, and it may reduce our ability to cope with future stress. (See Figure 3 to get a measure of your own level of stress.)

psychophysiological disorders
Medical problems influenced by an interaction of psychological, emotional, and physical difficulties. (Module 43)

How Stressed Are You?

Find out how stressed you are by responding to the following statements in terms of the last month only. Add up the score from each box. The rough scoring guide below will help you get a sense of your stress level.

1. I was convinced that the big things in my life were beyond my control.
   - [ ] 0=never, 1=infrequently, 2=sometimes, 3=fairly often, 4=very often

2. I felt that I could at least control the minor irritations in my life.
   - [ ] 4=never, 3=infrequently, 2=sometimes, 1=fairly often, 0=very often

3. I became upset at something that I didn't expect to happen.
   - [ ] 4=never, 3=infrequently, 2=sometimes, 1=fairly often, 0=very often

4. I felt confident that I could handle my personal problems.
   - [ ] 4=never, 3=infrequently, 2=sometimes, 1=fairly often, 0=very often

5. I felt nervous, anxious, and under stress.
   - [ ] 0=never, 1=infrequently, 2=sometimes, 3=fairly often, 4=very often

6. I felt myself to be the master of my life.
   - [ ] 4=never, 3=infrequently, 2=sometimes, 1=fairly often, 0=very often

7. I realized that I simply couldn't manage or cope with everything I had to do.
   - [ ] 0=never, 1=infrequently, 2=sometimes, 3=fairly often, 4=very often

8. I felt that troubles and worries were mounting so high I couldn't get past them.
   - [ ] 0=never, 1=infrequently, 2=sometimes, 3=fairly often, 4=very often

9. I felt that, overall, things were heading in the right direction.
   - [ ] 4=never, 3=infrequently, 2=sometimes, 1=fairly often, 0=very often

10. I lost my temper because of something that I couldn't control.
    - [ ] 0=never, 1=infrequently, 2=sometimes, 3=fairly often, 4=very often

Here's a rough scoring guide:

0–10 low stress
11–20 moderately low stress
21–30 moderately high stress
31–40 high stress

FIGURE 3 To get a sense of the level of stress in your life, complete this questionnaire.

Source: Adapted from Cohen, S., Kamarck, T., & Mermelstein, R. (1983). A global measure of perceived stress. *Journal of Health and Social Behavior, 24,* 385–396.

THE GENERAL ADAPTATION SYNDROME MODEL: THE COURSE OF STRESS

The effects of long-term stress are illustrated in a series of stages proposed by Hans Selye (pronounced "sell-yay"), a pioneering stress theorist (Selye, 1993). Selye called this model the general adaptation syndrome. The **general adaptation syndrome (GAS)** suggests that the physiological response to stress follows the same set pattern regardless of the cause of stress.

As shown in Figure 4, the GAS has three phases. The first stage—*alarm and mobilization*—occurs when people become aware of the presence of a stressor. On a biological level, the sympathetic nervous system becomes energized, which helps a person cope initially with the stressor.

However, if the stressor persists, people move into the second response stage: *resistance*. During this stage, the body is actively fighting the stressor on a biological level. During resistance, people use a variety of means to cope with the stressor—sometimes successfully but at a cost of some degree of physical or psychological well-being. For example, a student who faces the stress of failing several courses might spend long hours studying, seeking to cope with the stress.

If resistance is inadequate, people enter the last stage of the GAS: *exhaustion*. During the exhaustion stage, a person's ability to fight the stressor declines to the point where negative consequences of stress appear: physical illness and psychological symptoms in the form of an inability to concentrate, heightened irritability, or, in severe cases, disorientation and a loss of touch with reality. In a sense, people wear out, and their physiological resources to fight the stressor are used up.

How do people move out of the third stage after they have entered it? In some cases, exhaustion allows people to escape a stressor. For example, people who become ill from overwork may be excused from their duties for a time, which gives them a temporary respite from their responsibilities. At least for a time, then, the immediate stress is reduced.

general adaptation syndrome (GAS)
A theory developed by Selye that suggests that a person's response to a stressor consists of three stages: alarm and mobilization, resistance, and exhaustion. (Module 43)

! Study Alert
Remember the three stages of the general adaptation syndrome with the acronym *ARE* (*A*larm and mobilization; *R*esistance; and *E*xhaustion).

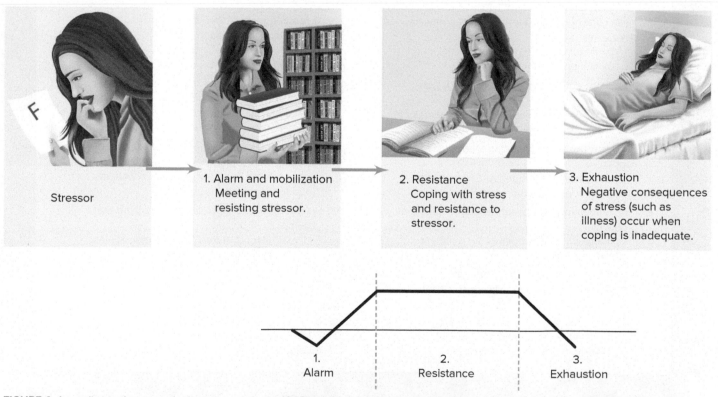

Stressor

1. Alarm and mobilization
Meeting and resisting stressor.

2. Resistance
Coping with stress and resistance to stressor.

3. Exhaustion
Negative consequences of stress (such as illness) occur when coping is inadequate.

1.
Alarm

2.
Resistance

3.
Exhaustion

FIGURE 4 According to the general adaptation syndrome (GAS) model, there are three major stages to stress responses: alarm and mobilization; resistance; and exhaustion. The graph below the illustration shows the degree of effort expended to cope with stressors at each of the three stages.

Although the GAS has had a substantial impact on our understanding of stress, critics have challenged Selye's theory. Specifically, the theory suggests that one's biological reaction to stress is similar regardless of the stressor. However, some health psychologists disagree, asserting instead that people's biological responses are specific to the way they appraise a stressful event. Research supporting this perspective has led to an increased focus on psychoneuroimmunology, as we consider next (Gaab et al., 2005; Irwin, 2008; Taylor, 2015).

PSYCHONEUROIMMUNOLOGY AND STRESS

Contemporary health psychologists specializing in **psychoneuroimmunology (PNI)** have taken a broader approach to stress. Focusing on the outcomes of stress, they have identified three main consequences of it (see Figure 5).

First, stress has direct physiological results, including an increase in blood pressure, an increase in hormonal activity, and an overall decline in the functioning of the immune system. Second, stress leads people to engage in behaviors that are harmful to their health, including increased nicotine, drug, and alcohol use; poor eating habits; and decreased sleep. Third, stress produces some indirect consequences that ultimately result in declines in health. For example, high levels of stress reduce the likelihood a person will seek health care. In addition, stress may result in less compliance with medical advice when it is sought. Both the reductions in seeking medical care and decreased compliance can indirectly lead to declines in health (Lindblad, Lindahl, & Theorell, 2006; Stowell, Robles, & Kane, 2013; Douthit & Russotti, 2017).

Why is stress so damaging to the immune system? One reason is that stress likely decreases the ability of the immune system to respond to disease, permitting germs that produce colds to reproduce more easily or allowing cancer cells to spread more rapidly. In normal circumstances, our bodies produce disease-fighting white blood cells called *lymphocytes*. Our bodies normally produce them at an extraordinary rate—some 10 million every few seconds. Stress may decrease this level of production (Zhou et al., 2017).

Another way that stress affects the immune system is by overstimulating it. Rather than fighting invading bacteria, viruses, and other foreign invaders, the immune system

The ability to fight off disease is related to psychological factors. Here a cell from the body's immune system engulfs and destroys disease-producing bacteria.
Science Source

psychoneuroimmunology (PNI)
The study of the relationship among psychological factors, the immune system, and the brain. (Module 43)

FIGURE 5 Three major types of consequences result from stress: direct physiological effects, harmful behaviors, and indirect health-related behaviors.
Source: Adapted from Baum, A. (1994). Behavioral, biological, and environmental interactions in disease processes. In S. Blumenthal, K. Matthews, & S. Weiss (Eds.), *New research frontiers in behavioral medicine: Proceedings of the National Conference.* Washington, DC: NIH Publications.

may begin to attack the body itself and damage healthy tissue. When that happens, it can lead to disorders such as arthritis and allergic reactions (Baum, Lorduy, & Jenkins, 2011; Marques et al., 2015; Buscemi et al., 2019).

Coping with Stress

Stress is a normal part of life—and not necessarily a completely bad part. For example, without stress, we might not be sufficiently motivated to complete the activities we need to accomplish.

However, it is also clear that too much stress can take a toll on physical and psychological health. How do people deal with stress? Is there a way to reduce its negative effects?

coping The efforts to control, reduce, or learn to tolerate the threats that lead to stress. (Module 43)

Efforts to control, reduce, or learn to tolerate the threats that lead to stress are known as **coping.** We habitually use certain coping responses to deal with stress. Most of the time, we're not aware of these responses—just as we may be unaware of the minor stressors of life until they build up to harmful levels (Wrzesniewski & Chylinska, 2007; Chao, 2011).

We also have other, more direct, and potentially more positive ways of coping with stress, which fall into two main categories (Folkman & Moskowitz, 2004; Baker & Berenbaum, 2007; Pow & Cashwell, 2017).

- **Emotion-focused coping.** In *emotion-focused coping,* people try to manage their emotions in the face of stress by seeking to change the way they feel about or perceive a problem. Examples of emotion-focused coping include strategies such as accepting sympathy from others and looking at the bright side of a situation.

- **Problem-focused coping.** *Problem-focused coping* attempts to modify the stressful problem or source of stress. Problem-focused strategies lead to changes in behavior or to the development of a plan of action to deal with stress. Starting a study group to improve poor classroom performance is an example of problem-focused coping. In addition, one might take a time-out from stress by creating positive events. For example, taking a day off from caring for a relative with a serious, chronic illness to go a health club or spa can bring significant relief from stress.

People often employ both emotion-focused and problem-solving coping strategies simultaneously to deal with stress. In other cases, the type of strategy differs according to the situation. For example, they tend to use emotion-focused strategies more frequently when they perceive circumstances as being unchangeable, and they use problem-focused strategies more often in situations they see as relatively modifiable (Penley, Tomaka, & Wiebe, 2002; Tamannaeifar & Shahmirzaei, 2019).

Some forms of coping are less successful. One of the least effective forms of coping is avoidant coping. In *avoidant coping,* a person may use wishful thinking to reduce stress or use more direct escape routes, such as drug use, alcohol use, and overeating. An example of wishful thinking to avoid a test would be to say to oneself, "Maybe it will snow so hard tomorrow that the test will be canceled." Alternatively, a person might get drunk to avoid a problem. Either way, avoidant coping usually results in a postponement of dealing with a stressful situation, and this often makes the problem even worse (Glass et al., 2009; Sikkema et al., 2013; Dunkley et al., 2017).

Another way of dealing with stress occurs unconsciously through the use of defense mechanisms. *Defense mechanisms* are unconscious strategies that people use to reduce anxiety by concealing the source from themselves and others. Defense mechanisms permit people to avoid stress by acting as if the stress were not even there. For example, one study examined California college students who lived in dormitories close to a geological fault (Lehman & Taylor, 1988). Those who lived in dorms that were known to be unlikely to withstand an earthquake were significantly *more* likely to doubt experts' predictions of an impending earthquake than were those who lived in safer structures.

Another defense mechanism used to cope with stress is *emotional insulation* in which a person stops experiencing any emotions at all and thereby remains unaffected and unmoved by both positive and negative experiences. The problem with defense mechanisms, of course, is that they merely hide the problem and do not deal with reality.

LEARNED HELPLESSNESS

Have you ever faced an intolerable situation that you just couldn't resolve, and you finally simply gave up and accepted things the way they were? This example illustrates one of the possible consequences of being in an environment in which control over a situation is not possible–a state that produces learned helplessness. **Learned helplessness** occurs when people conclude that unpleasant or aversive stimuli cannot be controlled. They develop a view of the world that becomes so ingrained that they cease trying to remedy the aversive circumstances even if they actually can exert some influence on the situation. For example, students who decide they are simply "no good in math" may not work very hard in math classes because they believe that no matter how hard they try, they'll never succeed. Their learned helplessness virtually ensures that they won't do well in math classes (Seligman, 2007; Filippello et al., 2015; Burland et al., 2019).

Victims of learned helplessness have concluded that there is no link between the responses they make and the outcomes that occur. People experience more physical symptoms and depression when they perceive that they have little or no control than they do when they feel a sense of control over a situation (Chou, 2005; Bjornstad, 2006; Figen, 2011).

learned helplessness A state in which people conclude that unpleasant or aversive stimuli cannot be controlled– a view of the world that becomes so ingrained that they cease trying to remedy the aversive circumstances even if they actually can exert some influence on the situation. (Module 43)

COPING STYLES: HARDINESS AND RESILIENCE

Most of us characteristically cope with stress by employing a *coping style* that represents our general tendency to deal with stress in a specific way. For example, you may know people who habitually react to even the smallest amount of stress with hysteria and others who calmly confront even the greatest stress in an unflappable manner. These kinds of people clearly have very different coping styles.

Hardiness Among those who cope with stress most successfully are people who exhibit a personality trait known as hardiness. **Hardiness** is a personality trait characterized by a sense of commitment to one's goals, viewing problems as challenges, and having a sense of control over one's life and environment. People with the hardiness trait have a lower rate of stress-related illness (Maddi, 2007; Maddi et al., 2011; Abdollahi et al., 2019).

Specifically, the three components of hardiness operate in different ways:

hardiness A personality trait characterized by a sense of commitment, viewing problems as challenges, and having a sense of control over one's life and environment. (Module 43)

- *Commitment.* People with a strong level of commitment tend to throw themselves into whatever they are doing. They have a sense that their activities are important and meaningful.

- *Challenge.* Hardy people believe that change, rather than stability, is the standard condition of life. To them, the anticipation of change is something positive, rather than change being seen as a threat to their security.

- *Control.* Hardiness is marked by a sense of control–the perception that people can influence the events in their lives.

Hardy individuals approach stress optimistically and take direct action to learn about and deal with stressors; they thereby change stressful events into less threatening ones. As a consequence, hardiness acts as a defense against stress-related illness (Bartone et al., 2008; Vogt et al., 2008; Stoppelbein, McRae & Greening, 2017).

Resilience For those who confront the most profound difficulties, such as the death of a loved one or a permanent injury such as paralysis after an accident, a key ingredient in their psychological recovery is their degree of resilience. **Resilience** is the ability to withstand, overcome, and actually thrive after profound adversity (Bonanno, 2004; Norlander, Von Schedvin, & Archer, 2005; Jackson, 2006.) (Also see *Neuroscience in Your Life.*)

resilience The ability to withstand, overcome, and actually thrive after profound adversity. (Module 43)

NEUROSCIENCE IN YOUR LIFE: THE NEUROSCIENCE OF RESILIENCE

Those who have experienced extreme stress, such as soldiers in combat, may develop psychological disorders such as posttraumatic stress disorder (PTSD). But not everyone who has lived through trauma develops these psychological disorders.

What are the neurobiological differences between those who develop such disorders and those who are resilient to stress? Recent evidence suggests that resilience to stress is related to structural differences in certain parts of the brain involved in executive control and emotional arousal (shown in the images below). These brain differences may thus be important markers for understanding who is and is not predisposed to psychological disorders when exposed to high levels of stress (Gupta et al., 2017).

Source: Adapted from Gupta, A., Love, A., Kilpatrick, L. A., Labus, J. S., Bhatt, R., Chang, L., et al. (2017). Morphological brain measures of cortico-limbic inhibition related to resilience. *Journal of Neuroscience Research, 95*(9), 1760–1775. doi: 10.1002/jnr.24007.

Resilient people are generally optimistic, good-natured, and have good social skills. They are usually independent, and they have a sense of control over their own destiny—even if fate has dealt them a devastating blow. In short, they work with what they have and make the best of whatever situation they find themselves in (Friborg et al., 2005; Deshields et al., 2006; Sinclair et al., 2013).

Resilience may have its origins in a complex series of biological reactions that occur when people confront devastating situations. These reactions involve the release of the hormone cortisol. Although cortisol is helpful in responding to challenges, too much can produce damage. Other chemicals, however, can moderate the effects of cortisol, and it may be that drugs or therapy can stimulate the production of these moderating chemicals. Furthermore, some people may be genetically predisposed to produce these chemicals, making them more resilient (Cole et al., 2010; Stix, 2011; Choi et al., 2019).

Resilience sometimes gives rise to *posttraumatic growth,* positive change that people experience as a result of a traumatic event. Rather than bouncing back to the psychological state they were in before the traumatic event, they actually see new opportunities emerge in their lives. Some people form closer connections with others who have also suffered. Finally, they may develop a sense of self-efficacy, the feeling that because they survived a highly stressful, life-altering event, they can live through anything life throws their way. In a sense, then, resilient people may find that a highly traumatic event leads to personal growth (Tedeschi et al., 2017; Wlodarczyk et al., 2017).

SOCIAL SUPPORT: WE'RE ALL IN THIS TOGETHER

social support A mutual network of caring, interested others. (Module 43)

Our relationships with others also help us cope with stress. Researchers have found that having **social support,** being part of a mutual network of caring, interested others, enables us to experience lower levels of stress, better cope with the stress we do undergo, and generally experience better health in general (García-Herrero et al., 2013; Pietromonaco & Collins, 2017; Braasch, Buchwald, & Hobfoll, 2019).

During the Coronavirus pandemic, the importance of social support was embodied in the frequently repeated phrase, "We're all in this together." Even while isolated, people craved the company of others and sought social engagement through Zoom calls and other social media. These online connections made the negative, socially isolating aspects of the pandemic more tolerable (Pfefferbaum & North, 2020).

The social and emotional support people provide each other helps in dealing with stress in several ways. For instance, such support demonstrates that a person is an important and valued member of a social network. Similarly, other people can provide information and advice about appropriate ways of dealing with stress (Day & Livingstone, 2003; Lindorff, 2005; Li et al., 2015).

Finally, people who are part of a social support network can provide actual, physical aid to help others in stressful situations. For instance, they can supply temporary living quarters to a person whose house has burned down, or they can offer study help to a student who is experiencing stress because of poor academic performance (Takizawa, Kondo, & Sakihara, 2007).

Even casual acquaintances who are part of our social networks can help reduce stress and provide health benefits: People with whom we trade greetings at the gym, the person we see regularly behind the counter at the dining commons, even strangers who we repeatedly say hello to while waiting for a bus. The greater one's social integration, the greater the benefits (Cohen, Murphy, & Prather, 2019).

Recent research is also beginning to identify ways in which social support affects brain processing. For instance, one experiment found that activation of the brain areas reflecting stress was reduced when social support—simply being able to hold the hand of another person—was available (Coan, Schaefer, & Davidson, 2006; Graff, Luke, & Birmingham, 2019).

From the perspective of...

A Social Worker How would you help people deal with and avoid stress in their everyday lives? How might you encourage people to create social support networks?

Sam Edwards/OJO Images/age fotostock

BECOMING AN INFORMED CONSUMER
of Psychology

Effective Coping Strategies

How can we deal with the stress in our lives? Although there is no universal solution because effective coping depends on the nature of the stressor and the degree to which it can be controlled, here are some general guidelines (Folkman & Moskowitz, 2000):

- *Turn a threat into a challenge.* When a stressful situation might be controllable, the best coping strategy is to treat the situation as a challenge and focus on ways to control it. For instance, if you experience stress because your car is always breaking down, you might take a course in auto mechanics and learn to deal directly with the car's problems.

- *Make a threatening situation less threatening.* When a stressful situation seems to be uncontrollable, you need to take a different approach. It is possible to change your appraisal of the situation, view it in a different light, and modify your attitude toward it. Research supports the old truism "Look for the silver lining in every cloud" (Smith & Lazarus, 2001; Cheng & Cheung, 2005).
- *Change your goals.* If you are faced with an uncontrollable situation, a reasonable strategy is to adopt new goals that are practical in view of the particular situation. For example, a dancer who has been in an automobile accident and has lost full use of her legs may no longer aspire to a career in dance but might modify her goals and try to become a choreographer.
- *Modify your physiological reactions to stress.* Many people don't know that they can directly change their physiological reactions to stress, which can help with coping. For example, biofeedback (in which a person learns to control internal physiological processes through conscious thought) can alter basic physiological reactions to stress and permit the person to reduce blood pressure, heart rate, and other consequences of heightened stress. Exercise can also be effective in reducing stress (Langreth, 2000; Spencer et al., 2003; Hamer, Taylor, & Steptoe, 2006).
- *Change the situations that are likely to cause stress.* In *proactive coping*, you anticipate and try to head off stress *before* you encounter it. For example, if you know your upcoming week is going to be grueling because you must take a number of major tests, rearrange your schedule so you have more time to study or take direct steps to improve your chances for success by attending test review sessions (Bode et al., 2007; Kalka, 2017).

RECAP/EVALUATE/RETHINK

RECAP

LO 43-1 How is health psychology a union between medicine and psychology?

- The field of health psychology considers how psychology can be applied to the prevention, diagnosis, and treatment of medical problems.

LO 43-2 What is stress, how does it affect us, and how can we best cope with it?

- Stress is a response to threatening or challenging environmental conditions. People encounter stressors–the circumstances that produce stress–of both a positive and a negative nature.
- The way an environmental circumstance is interpreted affects whether it will be considered stressful. Still, there are general classes of events that provoke stress: cataclysmic events, personal stressors, and background stressors (daily hassles).
- Stress produces immediate physiological reactions. In the short term, those reactions may be adaptive, but in the long term, they may have negative consequences, including the development of psychophysiological disorders.

- The consequences of stress can be explained in part by Selye's general adaptation syndrome (GAS), which suggests that there are three stages in stress responses: alarm and mobilization, resistance, and exhaustion.
- Coping with stress can take a number of forms, including the unconscious use of defense mechanisms and the use of emotion-focused or problem-focused coping strategies.
- Stress can be reduced by developing a sense of control over one's circumstances. In some cases, however, people develop a state of learned helplessness.

EVALUATE

1. _____ is defined as a response to challenging or threatening events.
2. Match each portion of the GAS with its definition.

   1. Alarm and mobilization
   2. Exhaustion Resistance

   a. Ability to adapt to stress diminishes; symptoms appear
   b. Activation of sympathetic nervous system
   c. Use of various strategies to cope with a stressor

3. Stressors that affect a single person and produce an immediate major reaction are known as
   a. Personal stressors
   b. Psychic stressors
   c. Cataclysmic stressors
   d. Daily stressors
4. People with the personality characteristic of _____ seem to be better able to successfully combat stressors.

RETHINK

1. Why are cataclysmic stressors less stressful in the long run than other types of stressors? Does the reason relate to the coping phenomenon known as social support? How?
2. Given what you know about coping strategies, how would you train people to avoid stress in their everyday lives? How would you use this information with a group of veterans from the war in Afghanistan suffering from posttraumatic stress disorder?

KEY TERMS

health psychology
stress
cataclysmic events
personal stressors
posttraumatic stress
  disorder (PTSD)

background stressors
  ("daily hassles")
psychophysiological
  disorders
general adaptation
  syndrome (GAS)

psychoneuroimmunology
  (PNI)
coping
learned helplessness
hardiness
resilience

social support

Module 44
Psychological Aspects of Illness and Well-Being

Can simply talking with others about your experiences as a patient fighting cancer extend your life?

As recently as three decades ago, most psychologists and health-care providers would have scoffed at the notion that participating in a discussion group could improve a cancer patient's chances of survival. Today, however, such methods have gained increasing acceptance.

Growing evidence suggests that psychological factors have a substantial impact both on major health problems that were once seen in purely physiological terms and on our everyday sense of health, well-being, and happiness. We'll consider the psychological components of three major health problems–heart disease, cancer, and smoking–and then consider the nature of people's well-being and happiness.

The As, Bs, and Ds of Coronary Heart Disease

Tim knew it wasn't going to be his day when he got stuck in traffic behind a slow-moving farm truck. How could the driver dawdle like that? Didn't he have anything of any importance to do? Things didn't get any better when Tim arrived on campus and discovered the library didn't have the books he needed. He could almost feel the tension rising.

"I need that material to finish my paper," he thought to himself.

He knew that meant he wouldn't be able to get his paper done early, and that meant he wouldn't have the time he wanted to revise the paper. He wanted it to be a first-class paper. This time, Tim wanted to get a better grade than his roommate, Luis. Although Luis didn't know it, Tim felt that they were in competition and that Luis was always trying to better him, whether academically or just playing cards.

"In fact," Tim mused to himself, "I feel like I'm in competition with everyone, no matter what I'm doing."

Have you, like Tim, ever seethed impatiently at being caught behind a slow-moving vehicle, felt anger and frustration at not finding material you needed at the library, or experienced a sense of competitiveness with your classmates?

Many of us experience these sorts of feelings at one time or another, but for some people, they represent a pervasive, characteristic set of personality traits known as the Type A behavior pattern. The **Type A behavior pattern** is a cluster of behaviors involving hostility, competitiveness, time urgency, and feeling driven. In contrast, the **Type B behavior pattern** is characterized by a patient, cooperative, noncompetitive, and nonaggressive manner. It's important to keep in mind that Type A and Type B represent the ends of a continuum and most people fall somewhere in between the two endpoints. Few people are purely a Type A or a Type B.

The importance of the Type A behavior pattern lies in its links to coronary heart disease. Men who display the Type A pattern develop coronary heart disease twice as

Type A behavior pattern A cluster of behaviors involving hostility, competitiveness, time urgency, and feeling driven. (Module 44)

Type B behavior pattern A cluster of behaviors characterized by a patient, cooperative, noncompetitive, and non-aggressive manner. (Module 44)

often and suffer significantly more fatal heart attacks than do those classified as having the Type B pattern. Moreover, the Type A pattern predicts who is going to develop heart disease at least as well as–and independently of–any other single factor, including age, blood pressure, smoking habits, and cholesterol levels in the body (Korotkov et al., 2011; Schneiderman, McIntosh, & Antoni, 2019).

Hostility is the key component of the Type A behavior pattern that is related to heart disease. Although competition, time urgency, and feelings of being driven may produce stress and potentially other health and emotional problems, they aren't linked to coronary heart disease the way that hostility is (Williams et al., 2000; Boyle et al., 2005; Ohira et al., 2007).

Why is hostility so toxic? The key reason is that hostility produces excessive physiological arousal in stressful situations. That arousal, in turn, results in increased production of the hormones epinephrine and norepinephrine as well as increases in heart rate and blood pressure. Such an exaggerated physiological response ultimately produces an increased incidence of coronary heart disease (Demaree & Everhart, 2004; Eaker et al., 2004; Myrtek, 2007).

Keep in mind that not everyone who displays Type A behaviors is destined to have coronary heart disease. For one thing, a firm association between Type A behaviors and coronary heart disease has not been established for women; most findings pertain to males partly because, until recently, most research was done on men. In addition, other types of negative emotions besides the hostility found in Type A behavior appear to be related to heart attacks. For example, psychologist Johan Denollet has found evidence that what he calls *Type D*–for "distressed"–behavior is linked to coronary heart disease. In this view, insecurity, anxiety, and the negative outlook Type Ds display put them at risk for repeated heart attacks (Šmigelskas et al., 2015; Lin et al., 2017; Aluja et al., 2019).

! **Study Alert**
It's important to distinguish among Type A (hostility, competitiveness), Type B (patience, cooperativeness), and Type D (distressed) behaviors.

From the perspective of...

A Health-Care Provider What advice would you give to your patients about the connections between personality and disease? For example, would you encourage Type A people to become "less Type A" to decrease their risk of heart disease?

Rubberball/Getty Images

Psychological Aspects of Cancer

Hardly any disease is feared more than cancer. Most people think of cancer in terms of lingering pain, and being diagnosed with the disease is typically viewed as receiving a death sentence.

Although a diagnosis of cancer is not as grim as it once was–several kinds of cancer have a high cure rate if detected early enough–cancer remains the second leading cause of death after coronary heart disease. The precise trigger for the disease is not well understood, but the process by which cancer spreads is straightforward. Certain cells in the body become altered and multiply rapidly in an uncontrolled fashion. As those cells grow, they form tumors; if left unchecked, the tumors suck nutrients from healthy cells and body tissue and ultimately destroy the body's ability to function properly.

Although the processes involved in the spread of cancer are basically physiological, some research suggests that the emotional responses of cancer patients to their disease may affect its course. For example, some findings show that a "fighting spirit" leads to better coping. On the other hand, there is little evidence that long-term survival rates are better than for patients with less-positive attitudes (Rom, Miller, & Peluso, 2009; Heitzmann et al., 2011; Brandao et al., 2015).

Despite conflicting evidence, health psychologists believe that patients' emotions may at least partially determine the course of their disease. In the case of cancer, it is possible that positive emotional responses may help generate specialized "killer" cells that help control the size and spread of cancerous tumors. Conversely, negative emotions may suppress the ability of those cells to fight tumors (Mosher et al., 2015; Lutgendorf & Andersen, 2015; Cheng et al., 2019).

Is a particular personality type linked to cancer? Some researchers suggest that cancer patients are less emotionally reactive, suppress anger, and lack outlets for emotional release. However, the data are too tentative and inconsistent to suggest firm conclusions about a link between personality characteristics and cancer. Certainly no conclusive evidence suggests that people who develop cancer would not have done so if their personality had been of a different sort or if their attitudes had been more positive (Holland & Lewis, 2001; Porcerelli et al., 2015).

What is increasingly clear, however, is that certain types of psychological therapy have the potential for improving quality of life and even extending the lives of cancer patients by slowing the progression of the disease. For example, the results of one study showed that women with breast cancer who received psychological treatment lived at least a year and a half longer and experienced less anxiety and pain than did women who did not participate in therapy. Research on patients with other health problems, such as heart disease, also has found that therapy can be both psychologically and medically beneficial (Lemogne et al., 2013; Spiegel, 2014; Perrier & Ginis, 2017).

Smoking

Would you walk into a convenience store and buy an item with a label warning you that its use could kill you? Although most people would probably answer no, millions make such a purchase everyday: a pack of cigarettes. Furthermore, they do this despite clear, well-publicized evidence that smoking is linked to cancer, heart attacks, strokes, bronchitis, emphysema, and a host of other serious illnesses. Smoking is the leading preventable cause of death in the United States; worldwide, 8 million people die each year from the effects of smoking (World Health Organization, 2019a).

WHY PEOPLE SMOKE

Why do people smoke despite all the evidence showing that it is bad for their health? It is not that they are somehow unaware of the link between smoking and disease; surveys show that most *smokers* agree with the statement "Cigarette smoking frequently causes disease and death." And almost three-quarters of the 45 million smokers in the United States say they would like to quit (Price, 2008; CDC, 2013, 2019).

Genetics seems to determine, in part, whether people will become smokers, how much they will smoke, and how easily they can quit. Genetics also influences how susceptible people are to the harmful effects of smoking. For instance, although African Americans smoke fewer cigarettes than whites, they are more likely to die from smoking-related illnesses than whites. This difference may be due to genetically produced variations in how efficiently enzymes can reduce the effects of the cancer-causing chemicals in tobacco smoke (Li et al., 2008; Minică, 2017; Erzurumluoglu et al., 2019).

Although genetics plays a role in smoking, social factors are the primary cause of the habit. Smoking at first may be seen as "cool" or sophisticated, as a rebellious act, or as facilitating calm performance in stressful situations. Exposure to smoking in media

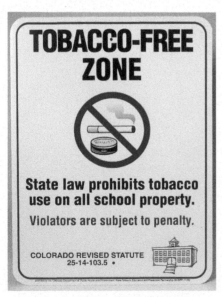

Although smoking is prohibited in an increasing number of places, it remains a substantial social problem.

Jack Holtel/McGraw-Hill

such as film also leads to a higher risk of becoming an established smoker. In addition, smoking is sometimes viewed as a "rite of passage" for adolescents, undertaken at the urging of friends and seen as a sign of growing up (Wills et al., 2008; Heatherton & Sargent, 2009; Mayer et al., 2015).

Ultimately, smoking becomes a habit. And it's an easy habit to pick up: Smoking even a single cigarette can lead to a smoker finding that *not* smoking requires an effort or involves discomfort. Subsequently, people begin to label themselves smokers, and smoking becomes part of how they view themselves. Moreover, they become dependent physiologically because nicotine, a primary ingredient of tobacco, is highly addictive.

When people become addicted to smoking, a complex relationship develops among smoking, nicotine levels, and a smoker's emotions. When this happens, a certain nicotine level becomes associated with a positive emotional state brought about by smoking. As a result, people smoke in an effort to regulate *both* their emotional states and the nicotine levels in the blood (Kassel et al., 2007; Ursprung, Sanouri, & DiFranza, 2009; Dennis, 2011).

Vaping and E-cigarettes The newest trend in smoking is *vaping*, the inhalation of vapors created by electronic cigarettes. *Electronic cigarettes*, or *e-cigarettes*, are battery-powered, cigarette shaped devices that deliver nicotine that is vaporized to form a mist. Some e-cigarettes, such as those manufactured by Juul, contain replaceable pods, while some newer versions of vaping products consist of one-time use disposables. All provide the experience of smoking tobacco.

E-cigarette use has grown exponentially, and it is increasingly concerning to medical experts. For example, the use among high school students is considerable: More than a third have tried e-cigarettes at least once, and the numbers continue to rise. Data from the Centers for Disease Control and Prevention show that e-cigarette use among middle- and high-school age youth rose 900% between 2011 and 2015, surpassing use of every other form of tobacco among those age groups. A quarter of 12th-grade students report using e-cigarettes in the prior month (CDC, 2015; Tavernise, 2015; U.S. Department of Health & Human Services, 2016; see Figure 1).

The trend is worrisome for several reasons. Although e-cigarettes do not contain the tar and other toxic chemicals found in cigarette smoke, the nicotine itself is harmful to developing adolescent brains. Also, in an increasing number of cases, contaminants in e-cigarettes have led to serious health consequences, lung damage, and, in some cases, even the deaths of users. Some municipalities have banned the sale of vaping equipment (Sun, 2019).

Moreover, the nicotine in e-cigarettes such as Juul is an addictive substance that can become a long-term habit, as we discussed in the case in the Prologue to the chapter. Furthermore, some research suggests that young users may be more prone to smoke regular cigarettes in the future, although the research findings are mixed on this point. Such concerns have led to laws restricting advertising targeted at teenagers and banning flavor additives (CDC, 2015; CDC, 2019).

FIGURE 1. The percentage of teenagers who reported using nicotine vaping products in the past month soared from 2017 to 2019.

Source: Miech, R., Johnston, L., O'Malley, P. M., Bachman, J. G., & Patrick, M. E. (2019). Trends in adolescent vaping, 2017-2019. *New England Journal of Medicine, 381(15)*, 1490–1491.

The risks of vaping are becoming more apparent as increasing research shows its dangers.
Pixinoo/Shutterstock

Because they are so new, little is known about the long-term effects of using e-cigarettes. Teenagers who have a clear understanding of the risks of cigarette smoking are often unsure about the risks of using e-cigarettes, and instead, they point to benefits such as looking cool and being trendy, as well as enjoying the flavorings of the e-cigarettes.

Not surprisingly, teens who perceive e-cigarettes as being less harmful than are other forms of tobacco are more likely to use them, even if they have never tried any form of tobacco before. Although some research finds that e-cigarette use may make it easier to give up smoking of regular cigarettes, the rise in e-cigarette use remains of deep concern (Giovenco & Delnevo, 2018).

QUITTING SMOKING

Because smoking has both psychological and biological components, few habits are as difficult to break. Long-term successful treatment typically occurs in just 15% of those who try to stop smoking; once smoking becomes a habit, it is as hard to stop as an addiction to cocaine or heroin. In fact, some of the biochemical reactions to nicotine are similar to those to cocaine, amphetamines, and morphine. Furthermore, changes in brain chemistry brought about by smoking may make smokers more resistant to antismoking messages (Foulds et al., 2006; Dani & Montague, 2007).

Many people try to quit smoking but fail. The average smoker tries to quit 8–10 times before being successful, and even then, many relapse. Even long-time quitters can fall off the wagon: About 10% relapse after more than a year of avoiding cigarettes (Grady & Altman, 2008).

Among the most effective tools for ending the smoking habit are drugs that replace the nicotine found in cigarettes. Whether in the form of gum, patches, nasal sprays, or inhalers, these products provide a dose of nicotine that reduces dependence on cigarettes. In addition, one study found that e-cigarettes containing nicotine were more effective than other nicotine substitutes in helping smokers quit, although for some people, the risk of vaping may outweigh the benefits of smoking cessation (Hajek et al., 2019).

Another approach is exemplified by the drugs Zyban and Chantix. Rather than replacing nicotine, they reduce the pleasure from smoking and suppress withdrawal symptoms that smokers experience when they try to stop (Brody, 2008; Dohnke, Weiss-Gerlach, & Spies, 2011; Dawkins et al., 2019).

Behavioral strategies, which view smoking as a learned habit and concentrate on changing the smoking response, can also be effective. Initial "cure" rates of 60% have been reported, and 1 year after treatment, more than half of those who quit have not resumed smoking. Individual or group counseling also increases the rate of success in breaking the habit. The best treatment seems to be a combination of nicotine replacement and counseling. What doesn't work? Going it alone: Only 5% of smokers who quit cold turkey on their own are successful (Woodruff, Conway, & Edwards, 2007; Green & Lynn, 2019; World Health Organization, 2019b).

In the long term, the most effective means of reducing smoking may be changes in societal norms and attitudes toward the habit. For instance, many cities and towns have made smoking in public places illegal; legislation based on strong popular sentiment that bans smoking in places such as college classrooms and buildings is being passed with increasing frequency. In addition, smokers are more likely to quit when their friends are quitting, so the social support of others quitting is helpful (Christakis & Fowler, 2008; McDermott et al., 2013; Mollen et al., 2017).

The long-term effect of the barrage of information regarding the negative consequences of smoking on people's health has been substantial; overall, smoking has declined over the last 2 decades, particularly among males. Still, more than one-fourth

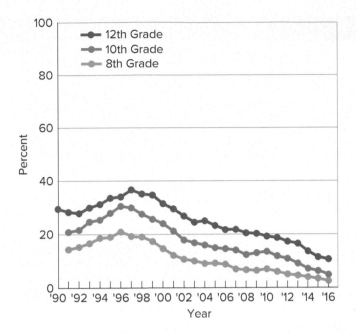

FIGURE 2 Although smoking among teenagers has declined considerably over the past several decades, a significant number still report smoking regularly. What factors might account for the continued high use of tobacco by teenagers despite the increase in antismoking advertising?

Source: Adapted from Johnston, L. D., O'Malley, P. M., Miech, R. A., Bachman, J. G., & Schulenberg, J. E. (2017). *Monitoring the Future national survey results on drug use, 1975–2016: Overview, key findings on adolescent drug use.* Ann Arbor, MI: Institute for Social Research.

of students enrolled in high school are active smokers by the time they graduate, and there is evidence that the decline in smoking is leveling off. Among these students, around 10% become active smokers as early as the 8th grade (see Figure 2; Fichtenberg & Glantz, 2006; Johnston et al., 2017).

 # Exploring Diversity

Hucksters of Death: Promoting Smoking Throughout the World

> A Jeep decorated with the Camel logo pulls up to a high school in Buenos Aires. A woman begins handing out free cigarettes to 15- and 16-year-olds during their lunch recess. At a video arcade in Taipei, free American cigarettes are strewn atop each game. At a disco filled with high school students, free packs of Salems are on each table. (Ecenbarger, 1993)

Because the number of smokers has steadily declined in the United States, cigarette manufacturers have turned their sights to other parts of the world, where they see a fertile market for their product. Although they must often sell cigarettes more cheaply than they do in the United States, the huge number of potential smokers still makes it financially worthwhile for the tobacco companies. The United States is now the world's largest exporter of cigarettes (Brown, 2001).

Clearly, the push into worldwide markets has been successful. In some Latin American cities, as many as 50% of teenagers smoke. Children as young as age 7 smoke in Hong Kong; 30% of children smoked their first whole cigarette before the age of 10 in India, Ghana, Jamaica, and Poland. The World Health Organization predicts that smoking will prematurely kill some 200 million of the world's children and that ultimately 10% of the world's population will die as a result of smoking. Of everyone alive today, 500 million will eventually die from tobacco use (Mackay & Eriksen, 2002).

One reason for the increase in smoking in developing countries is that their governments make little effort to discourage it. In fact, many governments are in the tobacco business themselves and rely on revenues from tobacco. For example, the world's largest manufacturer of cigarettes is the China National Tobacco Corporation, which is owned by the Chinese government (Marsh, 2008; World Health Organization, 2019b).

In some countries, children as young as age 6 smoke regularly.

jan_ta_r/Shutterstock

RECAP/EVALUATE/RETHINK

RECAP

LO 44-1 How do psychological factors affect health-related problems such as coronary heart disease, cancer, and smoking?

- Hostility, a key component of the Type A behavior pattern, is linked to coronary heart disease. The Type A behavior pattern is a cluster of behaviors involving hostility, competitiveness, time urgency, and feeling driven.
- People's attitudes and emotional responses may affect the course of cancer through links to the immune system.
- Smoking, the leading preventable cause of health problems, has proved to be difficult to quit, even though most smokers are aware of the dangerous consequences of the behavior.

EVALUATE

1. Type _____ behavior is characterized by cooperativeness and by being easygoing; Type _____ behavior is characterized by hostility and competitiveness.

2. The Type A behavior pattern is known to directly cause heart attacks. True or false?
3. A cancer patient's attitude and emotions may affect their _____ system and thus help or hinder their fight against the disease.
4. Smoking is used to regulate both nicotine levels and emotional states in smokers. True or false?

RETHINK

1. Is there a danger of "blaming the victim" when we argue that the course of cancer can be improved if a person with the disease holds positive attitudes or beliefs, particularly when we consider people with cancer who are not recovering? Explain your answer.
2. Do you think Type A or Type B behavior is more widely encouraged in the United States? Why?

Answers to Evaluate Questions

1. B, A; 2. False; Type A behavior is related to a higher incidence of coronary heart disease but does not necessarily cause it directly; 3. immune; 4. True

KEY TERMS

Type A behavior pattern   **Type B behavior pattern**

Module 45
Promoting Health and Wellness

When Stuart Grinspoon first noticed the small lump in his arm, he assumed it was just a bruise from the touch football game he had played the previous week. But as he thought about it more, he considered more serious possibilities and decided that he'd better get it checked out at the university health service. But the visit was less than satisfactory. A shy person, Stuart felt embarrassed talking about his medical condition. Even worse, after answering a string of questions, he couldn't even understand the physician's diagnosis and was too embarrassed to ask for clarification.

Many of us share Stuart Grinspoon's attitudes toward health care. We approach physicians the same way we approach auto mechanics. When something goes wrong with the car, we want the mechanic to figure out the problem and then fix it. In the same way, when something isn't working right with our bodies, we want a diagnosis of the problem and then a (we hope, quick) repair.

Yet such an approach ignores the fact that—unlike auto repair—good health care requires taking psychological factors into account. Health psychologists have sought to determine the factors involved in the promotion of good health and, more broadly, a sense of well-being and happiness. Let's take a closer look at two areas they have tackled: increasing compliance with health-related advice and identifying the determinants of well-being and happiness.

LEARNING OUTCOMES

LO 45-1 How do our interactions with physicians affect our health and compliance with medical treatment?

LO 45-2 How does a sense of well-being develop?

Following Medical Advice

We're not very good at following medical advice. Consider these figures:

- As many as 85% of patients do not fully comply with their physician's recommendations.
- Some 10% of adolescent pregnancies result from noncompliance with birth control practices.
- Thirty-one percent of patients don't fill their drug prescriptions.
- Forty-nine percent of patients forget to take prescribed medications.
- Thirteen percent take someone else's medicine.
- Sixty percent of all patients cannot identify their own medicines.
- From 30-50% of all patients ignore instructions or make errors in taking medication

Some of these errors are deliberate: Patients sometimes practice *creative nonadherence*, in which they alter a treatment prescribed by a physician by substituting their own medical judgment. Not surprisingly, patients' lack of medical knowledge may be harmful (Hamani et al., 2007).

For example, even during the height of the coronavirus pandemic, some people minimized its severity. Others chose go to bars and restaurants, claiming they had the "right" to go out or saying they wanted to support local businesses (Montgomery, 2020).

Noncompliance also can be a result of misunderstanding medical directions. For example, patients with low literacy skills may find complex instructions difficult to understand. In one study, only 34% of patients were able to understand that the direction "take two tablets by mouth twice daily" meant that they should take a total of 4 pills a day (Landro, 2011).

APPLYING PSYCHOLOGY IN THE 21ST CENTURY

ANTI-VAX ADVOCATES KNOW LESS THAN THEY THINK

One of the greatest public health success stories of the 20th century has been vaccination. Vaccines have totally eradicated smallpox, eliminated polio in the United States, and prevented countless millions of cases of other potentially crippling or deadly diseases such as measles, mumps, rubella, tetanus, and influenza. Through systematic research, vaccines have been thoroughly established as both safe and effective (Institute of Medicine Immunization Safety Review Committee, 2004).

Yet, none of these facts has stopped certain groups of citizens and politicians from challenging the scientific consensus on vaccine safety and advocating for a parent's right to refuse to vaccinate their children on religious or philosophical grounds. They claim, without evidence, that vaccines are dangerous or deadly—all based on a single study that purported to show a link between the measles, mumps, and rubella (MMR) vaccine and autism, which has since been discredited and retracted. Furthermore, social media has enabled widespread conspiracy theories and other misinformation to influence the public discourse on vaccine safety, despite the fact that absolutely no scientific evidence supports a link between vaccines and autism (Eggertson, 2010; Hviid et al., 2019).

This all might not be a concern if parents were putting only their own health at risk by refusing vaccines. But in many cases, they are risking the health of their children, who have no voice in the decision. Moreover, their refusal increases the number of unvaccinated children in schools and in the community, thus increasing the number of children who can potentially contract and spread diseases. In turn, then, these parents are also risking the health of other people who cannot be vaccinated for medical reasons or because they are still too young (Kluger, 2019).

Researchers wondered about the source of the disconnect between the clear message from the scientific community on the safety of vaccines and the persistent skepticism from those involved in the anti-vaccine ("anti-vax") movement. Past research on a phenomenon known as the Dunning-Kruger effect shows that people can be so ignorant about a body of knowledge that they lack even the understanding necessary to appreciate the depth of their own ignorance; as a result, they tend to overestimate and express overconfidence in their understanding. The researchers hypothesized that the Dunning-Kruger effect is causing anti-vax supporters to value their own opinions over those of scientists (Motta, Callaghan, & Sylvester, 2018).

To test this hypothesis, researchers asked over 1,300 adult participants to assess their own knowledge about the causes of autism relative to that of physicians and scientists and to complete a test of their actual knowledge about autism. Overall, 34% of participants indicated that they knew as much or more about the causes of autism than scientists do, and 36% indicated that they knew as much or more than physi-

Refusing to vaccinate one's children can have deadly consequences.
CHBD/E+/Getty Images

cians do. Of participants who actually knew the least about autism (who performed the worse on the test), 62% believed they knew as much or more about it than both physicians and scientists. By contrast, of those who actually knew the most about autism (who performed the best on the test), only 15% believed their knowledge exceeded that of physicians and scientists.

This research provides compelling evidence that people who think they know better than medical experts about the causes of autism tend to overestimate their knowledge and to support public policy decisions that align with their limited but overly certain understanding of the issue. With these findings in mind, the researchers recommend using nonexpert sources to help disseminate accurate information about the causes of autism and the safety of vaccines (Motta, Callaghan, & Sylvester, 2018).

QUESTIONS TO CONSIDER

- Why do you think so many people distrust the opinions of medical experts on the issue of vaccine safety?
- What other measures could be taken to persuade skeptics of the medical evidence that vaccines are safe and effective?

Whatever their causes, noncompliance and medical errors committed by patients and health-care providers are the third-leading cause of death in the United States. Nearly 125,000 Americans die annually from medical mistakes (Hobson, 2011; DeAngelis, 2016; Sunshine et al., 2019). (Also see *Applying Psychology in the 21st Century.*)

COMMUNICATING EFFECTIVELY WITH HEALTH-CARE PROVIDERS

Teresa Logan lay in the surgical ward as a her doctor drew incision lines on her chest with a felt-tipped pen. The operation would be grueling: 6 hours of surgery to use muscle tissue from her back to reconstruct her breasts, which had been removed months earlier to combat her cancer.

Teresa knew the operation wasn't the worst part; the extended recovery time would be even more grueling. She dreaded the damper it would put on her life as the mother of three young children and a serious runner and swimmer. As the doctor decorated her chest with marker ink, her husband asked a question that no one had asked before. "Is this operation really necessary?"

The answer was mind-blowing: No, it wasn't. If she left her chest as it was, she would recover in half the time with less pain and no adverse effects. The doctor had simply assumed that Teresa would want the reconstructive surgery for cosmetic reasons. Teresa and her husband looked at each other and reached a silent decision. "Get me up off this gurney, please," said Teresa.

Lack of communication between medical care providers and patients can be a major obstacle to good medical care. Such communication failures occur for several reasons. One is that physicians make assumptions about what patients prefer, or they push a specific treatment that they prefer without consulting patients.

Furthermore, the relatively high prestige of physicians may intimidate patients. Patients may also be reluctant to volunteer information that might cast them in a bad light, and physicians may have difficulties encouraging their patients to provide information. In many cases, physicians dominate an interview with questions of a technical nature, whereas patients attempt to communicate a personal sense of their illness and the impact it is having on their lives (Wallace et al., 2013; Xiang & Stanley, 2017; Houwen et al., 2019).

Furthermore, the view many patients hold that physicians are "all knowing" can result in serious communication problems. Many patients do not understand their treatments yet fail to ask their physicians for clear explanations of a prescribed course of action. About half of all patients are unable to report accurately how long they are to continue taking a medication prescribed for them, and about a quarter do not even know the purpose of the drug. In fact, some patients are not even sure, as they are about to be rolled into the operating room, why they are having surgery (Atkinson, 1997; Halpert, 2003)!

Sometimes patient–physician communication difficulties occur because the material that must be communicated is too technical for patients, who may lack fundamental knowledge about the body and basic medical practices. In an overreaction to this problem, some health-care providers use baby talk (calling patients "honey" or telling them to go "night-night") and assume that patients cannot understand even simple information. In other cases, physicians are uncomfortable breaking bad news to patients, so they use medical jargon to avoid being direct (Mika et al., 2007; Feng et al., 2011).

To address such problems, medical schools increasingly include training to improve the communication skills of health-care providers. For example, they teach physicians to allow patients to speak first and ask questions, and how to convey empathy and honesty through their speech (Reddy, 2015).

The amount and quality of physician–patient communication also are related to the gender of a physician and patient. Overall, female primary-care physicians provide more patient-centered communications than do male primary-care physicians. Furthermore, patients often prefer same-sex physicians (Bertakis, 2009; Bertakis, Franks, & Epstein, 2009; Shin et al., 2015).

Cultural values and expectations also contribute to communication barriers between patients and their physicians. Providing medical advice to a patient whose native language is not English may be problematic. Furthermore, medical practices differ between cultures, and medical practitioners need to be familiar with a patient's culture in order to produce compliance with medical recommendations (Ho et al., 2004; Culhane-Pera, Borkan, & Patten, 2007).

Finally, the newest approaches to improving communication between health-care providers and patients is *e-health communication*, which uses technology to convey information. For example, patients may be virtually reminded using smartphone technology to take their prescribed medicines. Similarly, some health-care providers offer virtual office hours in which patients can communicate with them via Skype or Facetime (Reynolds & Maughan, 2015; Celi et al., 2017; Chang et al., 2019).

What can patients do to improve communication with health-care providers? Here are some tips (National Institutes of Health, 2015):

- Make a list of your medical questions and concerns before your visit.

- To prepare for a visit, write down the names and dosages of every drug you currently take.

- Take notes during your visit so you can remember what your health-care provider tells you.

- Ask how to access your medical records online and whether you can communicate with your health-care provider via e-mail and phone.

- Consider bringing a friend or relative with you. They can ask questions and in general advocate for you.

INCREASING COMPLIANCE WITH MEDICAL ADVICE

Although compliance with medical advice does not guarantee that a patient's medical problems will go away, it does optimize the possibility that the patient's condition will improve. What, then, can health-care providers do to produce greater compliance on the part of their patients? One strategy is to provide clear instructions to patients regarding drug regimens. Maintaining good, warm relations with patients also leads to increased compliance (Arbuthnott & Sharpe, 2009).

In addition, honesty helps. Patients generally prefer to be well informed—even if the news is bad; their degree of satisfaction with their medical care is linked to how well and how accurately physicians are able to convey the nature of their medical problems and treatments (Zuger, 2005).

The way in which a message is framed also can result in more positive responses to health-related information. *Positively framed messages* suggest that a change in behavior will lead to a gain and thus emphasize the benefits of carrying out a health-related behavior. For instance, suggesting that skin cancer is curable if it is detected early and

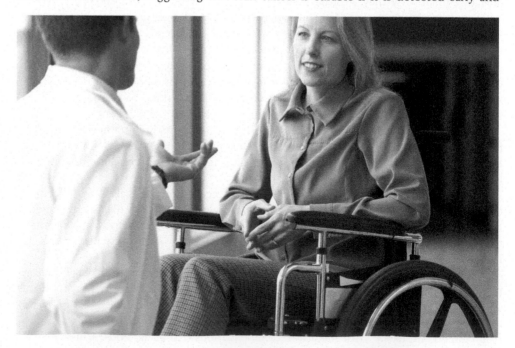

Positively framed messages suggest that a change in behavior will lead to a health-related gain.

UpperCut Images/SuperStock

that you can reduce your chances of getting the disease by using a sunscreen places information in a positive frame. In contrast, *negatively framed messages* highlight what you can lose by not performing a behavior. For instance, a physician might say that if you don't use sunscreen, you're more likely to get skin cancer, which can kill you if it's not detected early.

What type of message is more effective? It depends on the type of health behavior the health-care provider is trying to bring about. Positively framed messages are best for motivating *preventive* behavior. However, negatively framed messages are most effective in producing behavior that will lead to the detection of a disease (McCaul, Johnson, & Rothman, 2002; Apanovich, McCarthy, & Salovey, 2003; Lee & Aaker, 2004).

From the perspective of...

A Health-Care Provider How would you try to better communicate with your patients? How might your techniques vary depending on the patient's background, gender, age, and culture?

Tetra Images/Getty Images

Well-Being and Happiness

What makes for a good life?

This is a question that philosophers and theologians have pondered for centuries. Now health psychologists are turning their spotlight on the question by investigating **subjective well-being,** people's sense of their happiness and satisfaction with their lives (Kesebir & Diener, 2008; Giannopoulos & Vella-Brodrick, 2011; Vally & D'Souza, 2019).

subjective well-being People's sense of their happiness and satisfaction with their lives. (Module 45)

WHAT ARE THE CHARACTERISTICS OF HAPPY PEOPLE?

Research on the subject of well being shows that happy people share several characteristics (Nisbet, Zelenski, & Murphy, 2011; Burns, 2017; Orúzar et al., 2019):

- *Happy people have high self-esteem.* People who are happy like themselves. This is particularly true in Western cultures, which emphasize the importance of individuality. Furthermore, people who are happy see themselves as more intelligent and better able to get along with others than the average person is. In fact, they may hold *positive illusions* in which they hold moderately inflated views of themselves, believing that they are good, competent, and desirable (Taylor et al., 2000; Boyd-Wilson, McClure, & Walkey, 2004; McLeod, 2015).

- *Happy people have a strong sense of control over their environment and themselves.* They feel more in control of events in their lives, unlike those who feel they are the pawns of others and who experience learned helplessness.

- *Happy individuals are optimistic.* Their optimism permits them to persevere at tasks and ultimately to achieve more. In addition, their health is better (Peterson, 2000; Efklides & Moraitou, 2013).

- *Men and women generally are made happy by the same sorts of activities–but not always.* Most of the time, adult men and women achieve the same level of happiness from the same things, such as hanging out with friends. But there are some differences: For example, women get less pleasure from being with their parents than men do. The explanation? For women, time spent with their parents more closely resembles work, such as helping them cook or pay the bills. For men, it's more likely to involve recreational activities, such as watching a football game with their fathers. The result is that men report being slightly happier than women (Kreuger, 2007).

- *Happy people like to be around other people.* They tend to be extroverted and have a supportive network of close relationships.

Perhaps most important, most people living in a wide variety of circumstances report being at least moderately happy most of the time. Furthermore, life-altering events that one might expect would produce long-term spikes in happiness, such as winning the lottery, probably won't make you much happier than you already are, as we discuss next.

DOES MONEY BUY HAPPINESS?

If you were to win the lottery, would you be happier?

Probably not, at least in the long run. That's the implication of health psychologists' research on subjective well-being. That research shows that although winning the lottery brings an initial surge in happiness, a year later, winners' level of happiness returns to what it was before they won.

A similar pattern, although in reverse, occurs for people who have had extremely serious injuries in accidents, such as losing a limb or becoming paralyzed: Initially, they decline in happiness after the accident. But in the long run, most victims return to their prior levels of happiness after the passage of time (Priester & Petty, 2011; Weimann, Knabe, & Schöb, 2015; Wang et al., 2017).

Why is the level of subjective well-being so stable? One explanation is that people have a general *set point* for happiness, a marker that establishes the tone for one's life. Although specific events may temporarily elevate or depress one's mood (a surprise promotion or a job loss, for example), people ultimately return to their general level of happiness.

Although it is not certain how people's happiness set points are initially established, some evidence suggests that the set point is determined at least in part by genetic factors. Specifically, identical twins who grow up in widely different circumstances turn out to have very similar levels of happiness (Diener, Lucas, & Scollon, 2006; Weiss, Bates, & Luciano, 2008; Sheldon & Lucas, 2014).

Most people's well-being set point is relatively high. For example, some 30% of people in the United States rate themselves as "very happy," and only 10% rate themselves "not too happy." Most people declare themselves to be "pretty happy." Such feelings are graphically confirmed by people who are asked to place themselves on the measure of happiness illustrated in Figure 1. The scale clearly illustrates that most people view their lives quite positively.

Similar results are found when people are asked to compare themselves with others. For example, when asked "Who of the following people do you think is the happiest?" survey respondents answered "Oprah Winfrey" (23%), "Bill Gates" (7%), "the Pope" (12%), and "yourself" (49%), with 6% saying they didn't know (Black & McCafferty, 1998; Rosenthal, 2003).

> **! Study Alert**
>
> Remember the concept that individuals have a set point (a general, consistent level) relating to subjective well-being.

Faces Scale: "Which face comes closest to expressing how you feel about your life as a whole?"

| 20% | 46% | 27% | 4% | 2% | 1% | 0% |

FIGURE 1 Most people in the United States rate themselves as happy, while only a small minority indicate they are "not too happy."

Source: Adapted from Andrews, F. M., & Withey, S. B. (1976). *Social indicators of well-being: Americans' perceptions of life quality.* New York: Plenum.

Few differences exist between members of different demographic groups. Men and women report being equally happy, and African Americans are only slightly less likely than European Americans to rate themselves as "very happy." Furthermore, happiness is hardly unique to U.S. culture. Even countries that are not economically prosperous have, on the whole, happy residents (Suh, 2002; Suhail & Chaudhry, 2004; Cummings, 2019).

The bottom line: Money does *not* seem to buy happiness. Of course, one needs some minimal level of income; research shows that people living in extreme poverty are sadder than those with higher incomes. Furthermore, income used to purchase services that allow us more free time (someone to clean the house or bring us groceries) produces greater happiness than income spent on objects such as clothing (Kushlev, Dunn, & Lucas, 2015; Whillans et al., 2017; Whillans & Dunn, 2019).

Despite the ups and downs of life, then, most people tend to be reasonably happy, and they adapt to the trials and tribulations–and joys and delights–of life by returning to a steady-state level of happiness. That habitual level of happiness can have profound–and even life-prolonging–consequences (Diener & Seligman, 2004; Hecht, 2007; Grover & Helliwell, 2019).

RECAP/EVALUATE/RETHINK

RECAP

LO 45-1 How do our interactions with physicians affect our health and compliance with medical treatment?

- Although patients would often like physicians to base a diagnosis only on a physical examination, communicating one's problem to the physician is equally important.
- Patients may find it difficult to communicate openly with their physicians because of physicians' high social prestige and the technical nature of medical information.

LO 45-2 How does a sense of well-being develop?

- Subjective well-being, the measure of how happy people are, is highest in people with high self-esteem, a sense of control, optimism, and a supportive network of close relationships.

EVALUATE

1. Health psychologists are most likely to focus on which of the following problems with health care?
   a. Incompetent health-care providers
   b. Rising health-care costs
   c. Ineffective communication between physician and patient
   d. Scarcity of medical research funding

2. If you want people to floss more to prevent gum disease, the best approach is to
   a. Use a negatively framed message.
   b. Use a positively framed message.
   c. Have a dentist deliver an encouraging message on the pleasures of flossing.
   d. Provide people with free dental floss.

3. Winning the lottery is likely to
   a. Produce an immediate and long term increase in the level of well-being.
   b. Produce an immediate but not lingering increase in the level of well-being.
   c. Produce a decline in well-being over the long run.
   d. Lead to an increase in greed over the long run.

RETHINK

1. Do you think stress plays a role in making communication between physicians and patients difficult? Why?
2. If money doesn't buy happiness, what *can* you do to make yourself happier? As you answer, consider the research findings on stress and coping, as well as on emotions.

Answers to Evaluate Questions

1. c; 2. b; 3. b

KEY TERMS

subjective well-being

EPILOGUE

In this set of modules, we have explored the intersection of psychology and biology. We have seen how the emotional and psychological experience of stress can lead to physical symptoms of illness, how personality factors may be related to major health problems, and how psychological factors can interfere with effective communication between physician and patient. We have also looked at the other side of the coin, noting that some relatively simple strategies can help us control stress, affect illness, and improve our interactions with physicians.

Turn back to the prologue of this set of modules, about Matt Murphy's experience vaping.

1. What factors might have influenced Murphy to start using Juul e-cigarettes?
2. Why was it so difficult for Murphy to stop using Juul, even though he clearly wanted to?
3. If you were Murphy's friend, what cessation strategies would you suggest to him?
4. If Murphy's physician were advising him on quitting Juul, what factors might be most effective in gaining his compliance?
5. Could using Juul been one of Murphy's strategies for coping with stress? What healthier alternative strategies might he have used to cope with his stress?

VISUAL SUMMARY 14 Health Psychology

MODULE 43 Stress and Coping

Stress: People's response to events that threaten or challenge them

— Interpretation of events is important in determining what is stressful

- Cataclysmic events
- Personal stressors
- Background stressors (daily stressors)

— Posttraumatic Stress Disorder (PTSD)

The Cost of Stress

— Psychophysiological disorders: An interaction of psychological, emotional, and physical difficulties

Stress

Direct physiological effects
- Elevated blood pressure
- Decrease in immune system functioning
- Increased hormonal activity
- Psychophysiological conditions

Harmful behaviors
- Increased smoking, alcohol use
- Decreased nutrition
- Decreased sleep
- Increased drug use

Indirect health-related behaviors
- Decreased compliance with medical advice
- Increase in delays in seeking medical advice
- Decrease in likelihood of seeking medical advice

— General Adaptation Syndrome (GAS) Model: The physiological response to stress follows the same pattern regardless of the cause of stress

— Psychoneuroimmunology: Relationship among psychological factors, the immune system, and the brain

Coping with Stress: Emotion-focused or problem-focused coping

MODULE 44 Psychological Aspects of Illness and Well-Being

Coronary Heart Disease

— Type A behavior: A cluster of behaviors involving hostility, competitiveness, time urgency, and feeling driven

— Type B behavior: Characterized by a patient, cooperative, noncompetitive and nonaggressive manner

— Type D behavior: Insecure, anxious, and negative outlook

Cancer: Psychological therapy may improve quality of life

Smoking

— Over 5 million people die each year from smoking

— Heredity, in part, determines whether people will become smokers and are susceptible to harmful effects of smoking

— Few habits are as difficult to break

MODULE 45 Promoting Health and Wellness

Following Medical Advice: Noncompliance with medical advice takes many forms

— Communicating with health-care providers

- Lack of communication can be a major obstacle

— Increasing compliance with medical advice

- Patients prefer to be well informed even if the news is bad
- Positively framed messages: most likely to motivate preventive behavior

- Negatively framed messages: most likely to lead to the detection of a disease

Well-Being and Happiness

— Subjective well-being: People's own evaluation of their lives in terms of their thoughts and their emotions

— Characteristics of happy people: high self-esteem, sense of control, optimism, enjoy being with others

— Most people are moderately happy most of the time

Faces Scale: "Which face comes closest to expressing how you feel about your life as a whole?"

20% 46% 27% 4% 2% 1% 0%

(Module 43) (Art): Source: NIH Publications, "Behavioral, biological, and environmental interactions in disease processes." In New research frontiers in behavioral medicine: Proceedings of the National Conference.; (Module 44): (Photo): Pixinoo/Shutterstock; (Module 45): (Photo): UpperCut Images/SuperStock; (Art): Source: Adapted from Andrews, F. M., & Withey, S. B. (1976). *Social indicators of well-being: Americans' perceptions of life quality.* New York: Plenum.

Andrey_Popov/Shutterstock

CHAPTER 15
Psychological Disorders

LEARNING OUTCOMES FOR CHAPTER 15

LO 48-1 How prevalent are psychological disorders?

LO 48-2 What indicators signal a need for the help of a mental health practitioner?

PSYCHOLOGICAL DISORDERS IN PERSPECTIVE

The Social and Cultural Context of Psychological Disorders

Exploring Diversity: DSM and Culture—and the Culture of DSM

Becoming an Informed Consumer of Psychology: Deciding When You Need Help

PROLOGUE *HEARING VOICES AND SEEING VISIONS*

The first time Chris Coles heard the voice, it spoke to him after midnight. In a gentle tone, it instructed him to meet his friend at a beach cove, right then, and apologize: Chris, the voice told him, had been planning to date the friend's girlfriend. Although Coles was planning no such thing, he did as instructed, arriving at the cove at 2 a.m. It was deserted.

He dismissed the incident; imagination, after all, can play tricks in the twilight between waking and dreaming. But the voices kept intruding.

Coles saw visions, too. At the beach near his California home, he often saw a profusion of whales and dolphins swimming onto the beach and a golden Buddha glowing from the bushes by the dunes.

"I also had delusions of grandeur," says Coles, now 47. "I felt that I had power over things in nature, influence over the whales and dolphins and waves. I thought I could make things happen magically in the water" (Begley, 2019).

LOOKING *Ahead*

Chris Coles was losing his grip on reality. He was suffering from schizophrenia, one of the more severe psychological disorders. Although drug treatments eventually stilled the voices that ran through his head, his experience raises many questions. What caused his disorder? Were genetic factors involved, or were stressors in his life primarily responsible? Were there signs that family and friends should have noticed earlier? Could his schizophrenia have been prevented? And, more generally, how do we distinguish normal from abnormal behavior?

We address the issues raised by Coles's case in this chapter. We begin by discussing the difference between normal and abnormal behavior, which can be surprisingly indistinct. We then turn to a consideration of the most significant kinds of psychological disorders. Finally, we'll consider ways of evaluating behavior—one's own and that of others—to determine whether seeking help from a mental health professional is warranted.

Module 46
Normal Versus Abnormal: Making the Distinction

LEARNING OUTCOMES

LO 46-1 How can we distinguish normal from abnormal behavior?

LO 46-2 What are the major perspectives on psychological disorders used by mental health professionals?

LO 46-3 What are the major categories of psychological disorders?

Universally that person's acumen is esteemed very little perceptive concerning whatsoever matters are being held as most profitable by mortals with sapience endowed to be studied who is ignorant of that which the most in doctrine erudite and certainly by reason of that in them high mind's ornament deserving of veneration constantly maintain when by general consent they affirm that other circumstances being equal by no exterior splendour is the prosperity of a nation. . . .

It would be easy to conclude that these words are the musings of a madman. To most people, the passage does not seem to make any sense at all. But literary scholars would disagree. Actually, this passage is from James Joyce's classic *Ulysses*, hailed as one of the major works of 20th-century literature (Joyce, 1934).

As this example illustrates, casually examining a person's writing is insufficient to determine the degree to which that person is "normal." But even when we consider more extensive samples of a person's behavior, we will find that there may be only a fine line between behavior that is considered normal and behavior that is considered abnormal.

Defining Abnormality

Because of the difficulty in distinguishing normal from abnormal behavior, psychologists have struggled to devise a precise, scientific definition of "abnormal behavior." For instance, consider the following definitions, each of which has advantages and disadvantages:

- *Abnormality as a deviation from average behavior.* According to this definition, behaviors that are unusual or rare in a society or culture are considered abnormal. It is basically a statistical definition: If most people behave in a certain way, it is viewed as normal; if only a few people do it, it is considered abnormal.

  The difficulty with this definition is that some statistically unusual behaviors hardly seem abnormal. If most people eat meat but you are a vegetarian, this deviation from the average hardly makes your behavior abnormal. Similarly, a concept of abnormality that depends on what is unusual would unreasonably label a person who has an unusually high IQ as abnormal simply because a high IQ is statistically rare. In short, a definition of abnormality that rests on deviation from the average is insufficient.

- *Abnormality as a deviation from an ideal.* An alternative definition of abnormality considers behavior in relation to some kind of ideal or morally appropriate standard toward which most people are striving.

  This sort of definition considers behavior abnormal if it is different from what society considers ideal behavior or from some moral standard. However, society has few ideals on which people universally agree. (For example, it would be hard to find agreement on whether the New Testament, the Koran, the Talmud, or the Book of Mormon provides the most appropriate ideal behavior.) Furthermore, standards that do arise change over time and vary across cultures. Thus, the deviation-from-the-ideal approach is also inadequate.

- *Abnormality as producing a sense of personal discomfort.* A more useful definition concentrates on the psychological consequences of behavior for the individual. In this

Study Alert

Remember the definitions of abnormality: deviation from average behavior, deviation from ideal behavior, a sense of personal discomfort, an inability to function effectively, and abnormality as a legal concept.

approach, behavior is considered abnormal if it produces a sense of personal distress, anxiety, or guilt in an individual–or if it is harmful to others in some way.

However, even a definition that relies on personal discomfort has drawbacks. For example, in some especially severe forms of mental disturbance, people report feeling wonderful, even though their behavior seems bizarre to others. In such cases, a person feels fine, although most people would consider the behavior abnormal. Similarly, most of us would think that a woman who says she hears uplifting messages from Martians would be displaying abnormal behavior even though she may say that the messages bring her great satisfaction.

- *Abnormality as the inability to function effectively.* Most people are able to feed themselves, hold a job, get along with others, and in general live as productive members of society. Yet there are those who are unable to adjust to the demands of society or function effectively.

  According to this view of abnormality, people who are unable to function effectively and to adapt to the demands of society are considered abnormal. For example, an unemployed, homeless woman living on the street may be considered unable to function effectively. Therefore, her behavior can be viewed as abnormal even if she has chosen to live this way. Her inability to adapt to the requirements of society is what makes her "abnormal," according to this approach.

- *Abnormality as a legal concept.* According to the jury that first heard her case, Andrea Yates, a woman who drowned her five children in a bathtub, was sane. She was sentenced to life in prison for her act (Chan, 2016).

  Although you might question this view (and an appeals court jury overturned the conviction), the initial verdict reflected the way in which the law defines abnormal behavior. To the judicial system, the distinction between normal and abnormal behavior rests on the definition of *insanity*, which is a legal but not a psychological term.

  In fact, the definition of *insanity* varies from one jurisdiction to another. In some states, *insanity* simply means that defendants cannot understand the difference between right and wrong at the time they commit a criminal act. Other states consider whether defendants are substantially incapable of understanding the criminality of their behavior or unable to control themselves. And in some jurisdictions, pleas of insanity are not allowed at all (Reisner, Piel, & Makey, 2013; Yelderman & Miller, 2017; Gilligan, 2019).

Clearly, none of the previous definitions is broad enough to cover all instances of abnormal behavior, and the distinction between normal and abnormal behavior often remains ambiguous even to trained professionals. Furthermore, to a large extent, cultural expectations for "normal" behavior in a particular society influence the understanding of "abnormal behavior."

Given the difficulties in precisely defining the construct, psychologists typically use a broad definition of abnormal behavior. Specifically, **abnormal behavior** is generally defined as behavior that causes people to experience distress and hinders them from functioning in their daily lives (Nolen-Hoeksema, 2007; Bassett & Baker, 2015).

Andrea Yates, who initially was found sane by a jury despite having drowned her five children in a bathtub, was later found innocent due to insanity.
Brett Coomer/Pool Houston Chronicle/AP Images

abnormal behavior Behavior that causes people to experience distress and prevents them from functioning in their daily lives. (Module 46)

From the perspective of...

An Employer Imagine that you learned that a well-paid employee was arrested for shoplifting a sweater that cost only $15. Would you fire the employee if you thought the behavior was caused by a psychological disorder?

Sam Edwards/OJO Images/age fotostock

Because this definition is imprecise, it's best to view abnormal behavior and normal behavior as marking two ends of a continuum rather than as absolute, precise conditions. Behavior should be evaluated in terms of gradations that range from fully normal functioning to extremely abnormal behavior. Behavior typically falls somewhere between those extremes.

Perspectives on Abnormality: From Superstition to Science

Throughout much of human history, people linked abnormal behavior to superstition, magic, and spells. Individuals who displayed abnormal behavior were accused of being possessed by the devil or some sort of demonic god. Authorities felt justified in "treating" abnormal behavior by attempting to drive out the source of the problem. This often involved whipping, immersion in hot water, starvation, or other forms of torture in which the cure was worse than the affliction (Scull, 2016).

Contemporary approaches take a more enlightened view. Today, six major perspectives are used to understand psychological disorders. These perspectives, which are discussed next, suggest not only different causes of abnormal behavior but different treatment approaches as well. Furthermore, some perspectives are more applicable to specific disorders than are others.

MEDICAL PERSPECTIVE

medical perspective The perspective that suggests that when an individual displays symptoms of abnormal behavior, the root cause will be found in a physical examination of the individual, which may reveal a hormonal imbalance, a chemical deficiency, or a brain injury. (Module 46)

When people display the symptoms of tuberculosis, medical professionals can generally find tubercular bacteria in their body tissue. Similarly, the **medical perspective** suggests that when an individual displays symptoms of a psychological disorder, the fundamental cause will be found through a physical examination of the individual, which may reveal a hormonal imbalance, a chemical deficiency, or a brain injury. Indeed, when we speak of mental "illness," "symptoms" of psychological disorders, and mental "hospitals," we are using terminology associated with the medical perspective.

Because a growing body of research shows that many forms of abnormal behavior are linked to biological causes, the medical perspective provides at least part of the explanation for psychological disorders. Yet serious criticisms have been leveled against it. For one thing, some types of abnormal behavior have no apparent biological cause. In addition, some critics have argued that the use of the term *mental illness* implies that people who display abnormal behavior have no responsibility for or control over their actions (Yang et al., 2013; Prior & Bond, 2017).

Still, recent advances in our understanding of the neurological bases of behavior underscore the importance of considering physiological factors in abnormal behavior. For instance, some of the more severe forms of psychological disorders, such as major depression and schizophrenia, clearly are influenced in important ways by genetic factors and malfunctions in neurotransmitter signals (Hariri, 2015; Pillai et al., 2018; Borgmann-Winter et al., 2019).

PSYCHOANALYTIC PERSPECTIVE

psychoanalytic perspective The perspective that suggests that abnormal behavior stems from childhood conflicts over opposing wishes regarding sex and aggression. (Module 46)

Whereas the medical perspective suggests that biological causes are at the root of abnormal behavior, the **psychoanalytic perspective** holds that abnormal behavior stems from childhood conflicts over opposing wishes regarding sex and aggression. According to Freud, children pass through a series of stages in which sexual and aggressive impulses take different forms and produce conflicts that require resolution. If these childhood conflicts are not dealt with successfully, they remain unresolved in the unconscious and eventually bring about abnormal behavior during adulthood.

To uncover the roots of people's disordered behavior, the psychoanalytic perspective scrutinizes their early life history. However, there is no sure way to link what happens to people during childhood to abnormal behavior that they display as adults. Consequently, we can never be sure that specific childhood experiences can be linked to specific adult abnormal behaviors.

In addition, psychoanalytic theory paints a picture of people as having relatively little control over their behavior. Instead, the theory assumes that behavior is largely guided by unconscious impulses over which people have neither control nor awareness. Consequently, in the eyes of some critics, this perspective suggests that people have little responsibility for their own behavior.

On the other hand, the contributions of psychoanalytic theory have been significant. More than any other approach to abnormal behavior, this perspective highlights the fact that people can have a rich, involved inner life. Furthermore, it underscores that experiences that occurred long ago in the past can have a profound effect on current psychological functioning (Bornstein, 2003; Rangell, 2007).

BEHAVIORAL PERSPECTIVE

Both the medical and psychoanalytic perspectives look at abnormal behaviors as *symptoms* of an underlying problem. In contrast, the **behavioral perspective** looks at the rewards and punishments in the environment that determine abnormal behavior. It views the disordered behavior itself as the problem. Using the basic principles of learning, behavioral theorists see both normal and abnormal behaviors as responses to various stimuli—responses that have been learned through past experience and are guided in the present by stimuli in the individual's environment. To explain why abnormal behavior occurs, we must analyze how an individual has learned it and observe the circumstances in which it is displayed.

The emphasis on observable behavior represents both the greatest strength and the greatest weakness of the behavioral approach to abnormal behavior. This perspective provides the most precise and objective approach for examining behavioral symptoms of specific disorders, such as attention-deficit hyperactivity disorder (ADHD), which we discuss in module 47. At the same time, though, critics charge that the perspective ignores the rich inner world of thoughts, attitudes, and emotions that may contribute to abnormal behavior.

behavioral perspective The perspective that looks at the rewards and punishments in the environment that determine abnormal behavior. (Module 46)

COGNITIVE PERSPECTIVE

The medical, psychoanalytic, and behavioral perspectives view people's behavior as the result of factors largely beyond their control. To many critics of these views, however, people's thoughts cannot be ignored.

In response to such concerns, some psychologists employ a **cognitive perspective.** Rather than considering only external behavior, as in traditional behavioral approaches, the cognitive approach assumes that *cognitions* (people's thoughts and beliefs) are central to a person's abnormal behavior. A primary goal of treatment using the cognitive perspective is to explicitly teach new, more adaptive ways of thinking.

For instance, suppose that you develop the erroneous belief that "doing well on this exam is crucial to my entire future" whenever you take an exam. Through therapy, you might learn to hold the more realistic and less anxiety-producing thought, "my entire future is not dependent on this one exam." By changing cognitions in this way, psychologists working within a cognitive framework help people free themselves from thoughts and behaviors that are potentially maladaptive (Everly & Lating, 2007; Ray et al.,2015; Robbins et al., 2019).

The cognitive perspective has its critics. For example, they argue that rather than maladaptive cognitions being the *cause* of a psychological disorder, they could be just another *symptom* of the disorder. Furthermore, under certain circumstances, negative beliefs may not be irrational at all but simply reflect accurately the realities of people's lives. (For example, feeling depressed because you've been found guilty of a crime may be entirely rational because you are, in fact, likely to go to jail.) Still, cognitive theorists would argue that there are adaptive ways of framing beliefs even in the most negative circumstances.

cognitive perspective The perspective that suggests that people's thoughts and beliefs are central components of abnormal behavior. (Module 46)

HUMANISTIC PERSPECTIVE

humanistic perspective The perspective that emphasizes the responsibility people have for their own behavior, even when such behavior is abnormal. (Module 46)

The **humanistic perspective** emphasizes the responsibility people have for their own behavior, even when such behavior is abnormal. The humanistic perspective–growing out of the work of Carl Rogers and Abraham Maslow–concentrates on what is uniquely human–that is, it views people as basically rational, oriented toward a social world, and motivated to seek self-actualization (Rogers, 1995; DeRobertis & Bland, 2019).

Humanistic approaches focus on the relationship of the individual to society; they consider the ways in which people view themselves in relation to others and see their place in the world. The humanistic perspective views people as having an awareness of life and of themselves that leads them to search for meaning and self-worth. Rather than assuming that individuals require a "cure," the humanistic perspective suggests that they can, by and large, set their own limits of what is acceptable behavior. As long as they are not hurting others and do not feel personal distress, people should be free to choose the behaviors in which they engage.

Although the humanistic perspective has been criticized for its reliance on unscientific, unverifiable information and its vague, almost philosophical formulations, it offers a distinctive view of abnormal behavior. It stresses the unique aspects of being human and provides a number of important suggestions for helping those with psychological problems.

SOCIOCULTURAL PERSPECTIVE

sociocultural perspective The perspective that assumes that society and culture shape abnormal behavior (Module 46)

The **sociocultural perspective** assumes that society and culture shape abnormal behavior. According to this view, societal and cultural factors such as poverty and prejudice may be at the root of abnormal behavior. Specifically, the kinds of stresses and conflicts people experience in their daily lives can promote and maintain abnormal behavior.

Consistent with the sociocultural perspective, some kinds of psychological disorders are far more prevalent among particular social classes, races, and ethnicities than they are in others. For instance, diagnoses of schizophrenia tend to be higher among members of lower socioeconomic groups than among members of more affluent groups. Proportionally more African American individuals are hospitalized involuntarily for psychological disorders than are whites.

Furthermore, poor economic times seem to be linked to general declines in psychological functioning, and social problems such as homelessness are associated with psychological disorders and deeply intertwined with socioeconomic factors. Homelessness, in particular, is linked with high levels of psychological disorder: between 20-25% of homeless people in the United States suffer from serious psychological disorders (Treatment Advocacy Center, 2016).

Also consistent with the sociocultural perspective, the coronavirus pandemic, which massively disrupted people's daily lives, including their health and economic security, led to a significant increase in reports of psychological disorders. For example, one poll two months into the pandemic found that almost half the people surveyed said that the pandemic was harming their mental health (see Figure 1). Moreover, an emergency hotline run by the U.S. federal government showed a 1,000 percent increase in calls and texts over the previous year (Kirzinger et al., 2020; Solomon, 2020).

Of course, social factors alone do not account for cases of psychological disorder, and there are plausible alternative explanations for the association between psychological difficulties and social factors. For example, people from lower socioeconomic levels may be less likely than those from higher levels to seek help or to have access to it. Similarly, in the case of the pandemic, it may be that the unprecedented disruption and isolation of quarantine intensified problems from which people already suffered. Still, the sociocultural perspective provides important insights into our understanding of the causes of psychological disorders (White et al., 2017).

Figure 2 summarizes the main perspectives on psychological disorders. In addition, it applies each of them to the case of Chris Coles, discussed in the chapter prologue.

! Study Alert
Use Figure 2 to review the six major perspectives on abnormality and consider how they relate to the major perspectives on the field of psychology.

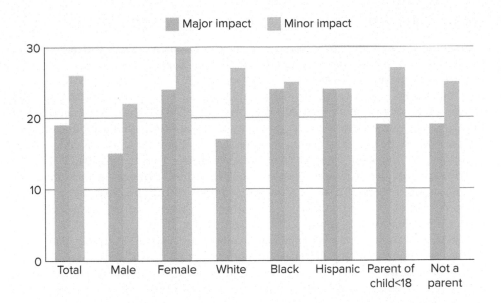

FIGURE 1 The impact of the Coronavirus pandemic on perceptions of mental health. The graph shows the percentage of people who said they felt that worry or stress related to coronavirus had a negative impact on their mental health.
Source: Kirzinger, A, Kearney, A., Hamel, L., & Brodie, M. (2020, April 2). KFF Health tracking poll—early April 2020: The impact of coronavirus on life in America. KFF Health Tracking Poll. Kaiser Family Foundation.

Perspectives on Psychological Disorders

Perspective	Description	Application of Perspective to Chris Coles Case, Discussed in Chapter Prologue
Medical	Assumes that physiological causes are at the root of psychological disorders	Examine Coles for medical problems, such as brain tumor, chemical imbalance in the brain, or disease.
Psychoanalytic	Argues that psychological disorders stem from childhood conflicts	Seek out information about Coles's past, considering possible childhood conflicts.
Behavioral	Assumes that abnormal behaviors are learned responses	Concentrate on rewards and punishments for Coles's behavior, and identify environmental stimuli that reinforce his behavior.
Cognitive	Assumes that cognitions (people's thoughts and beliefs) are central to psychological disorders	Focus on Coles's perceptions of himself and his environment.
Humanistic	Emphasizes people's responsibility for their own behavior and the need to self-actualize	Consider Coles's behavior in terms of his choices and efforts to reach his potential.
Sociocultural	Assumes that behavior is shaped by family, society, and culture	Focus on how societal demands contributed to Cole's disorder.

FIGURE 2 In considering the case of Chris Coles, discussed in the prologue, we can employ each of the perspectives on abnormal behavior. Note that because of the nature of his psychological disorder, some of the perspectives are more applicable than others.

Classifying Abnormal Behavior: The ABCs of DSM

Crazy. Nuts. Mental. Loony. Insane. Neurotic. Psycho. Strange. Demented. Odd. Possessed.

Society has long placed labels on people who display abnormal behavior. Unfortunately, most of the time, these labels have reflected intolerance and have been used with little thought as to what each signifies.

Providing appropriate and specific names and classifications for abnormal behavior has presented a major challenge to psychologists. It is not hard to understand why, given the difficulties discussed earlier in simply distinguishing normal from abnormal behavior. Yet psychologists and other careproviders need to classify abnormal behavior in order to diagnose it and ultimately treat it.

Diagnostic and Statistical Manual of Mental Disorders, Fifth Edition (DSM-5) A system, devised by the American Psychiatric Association, used by most professionals to classify and define psychological disorders. (Module 46)

DSM-5: DETERMINING DIAGNOSTIC DISTINCTIONS

The ***Diagnostic and Statistical Manual of Mental Disorders,*** **Fifth Edition (DSM-5)** is the most widely used system to classify and define psychological disorders (American Psychiatric Association, 2013).

The DSM-5, most recently revised in 2013, provides comprehensive and relatively precise definitions for more than 200 disorders. By following the criteria presented in the DSM-5 classification system, diagnosticians use clients' reported symptoms to identify the specific problem the clients are experiencing. Figure 3 provides a brief outline of the major diagnostic categories (American Psychiatric Association, 2013).

The authors of the newest update of DSM suggest that the manual should be viewed as the "DSM-5.0." The "5.0" name emphasizes that the DSM-5 is a work in progress, subject to revision based on users' feedback. (The next revision will be called DSM-5.1; Kupfer, Kuhl, & Regier, 2013; Wakefield, 2013).

DSM-5 takes an *atheoretical* approach to identifying psychological disorders, meaning it does not rely on any particular theoretical perspective. Consequently, it is primarily descriptive and attempts to avoid suggesting an underlying cause for an individual's behavior and problems. Instead, it seeks to paint a picture of the behavior that is being displayed.

For example, DSM does not use the term *neurotic*—a label commonly used by people in their everyday descriptions of abnormal behavior—as a category. Because the term *neurosis* refers to problems associated with a specific cause based in Freud's theory of personality, it is not included in DSM-5.

H.S. Photos/Alamy Stock Photo

Categories of Disorders	Examples
Anxiety (problems in which anxiety impedes daily functioning)	Generalized anxiety disorder, panic disorder, phobic disorder
Somatic symptom and related disorders (psychological difficulties displayed through physical problems)	Illness anxiety disorder, conversion disorder
Dissociative (the splitting apart of crucial parts of personality that are usually integrated)	Dissociative identity disorder (multiple personality), dissociative amnesia, dissociative fugue
Mood (emotions of depression or euphoria that are so strong they intrude on everyday living)	Major depressive disorders, bipolar disorder
Schizophrenia spectrum and other psychotic disorders (declines in functioning, thought and language disturbances, perception disorders, emotional disturbances, and withdrawal from others)	Delusional disorder
Personality (problems that create little personal distress but that lead to an inability to function as a normal member of society)	Antisocial (sociopathic) personality disorder, narcissistic personality disorder
Sexual (problems related to sexual arousal from unusual objects or problems related to functioning)	Paraphilic disorders, sexual dysfunction
Substance-related (problems related to drug dependence and abuse)	Alcohol, cocaine, hallucinogens, marijuana
Neurocognitive disorders	Alzheimer's

FIGURE 3 This list of disorders represents the major categories from the DSM-5. It is only a partial list of the scores of disorders included in the diagnostic manual.

Source: Adapted from American Psychiatric Association. (2013). *Diagnostic and statistical manual of mental disorders* (5th ed.). Washington, DC: Author.

Why is this atheoretical, descriptive approach be important? For one thing, it allows communication between mental health professionals of diverse backgrounds and theoretical approaches. In addition, precise classification enables researchers to explore the causes of a problem. Without reliable descriptions of abnormal behavior, researchers would be hard pressed to find ways to investigate the disorder. Finally, DSM-5 provides a kind of conceptual shorthand through which professionals can describe the behaviors that tend to occur together in an individual (Widiger, 2015; Busch, Morey, & Hopwood, 2017).

CONNING THE CLASSIFIERS: THE SHORTCOMINGS OF DSM

When clinical psychologist David Rosenhan and eight colleagues sought admission to separate mental hospitals across the United States in the 1970s, each stated that he or she was hearing voices—"unclear voices" that said "empty," "hollow," and "thud"—and each was immediately admitted to the hospital. However, the truth was that they actually were conducting a study, and none of them was really hearing voices. Aside from these misrepresentations, *everything* else they did and said represented their true behavior, including the responses they gave during extensive admission interviews and their answers to the battery of tests they were asked to complete. In fact, as soon as they were admitted, they said they no longer heard any voices. In short, each of the pseudo-patients acted in a "normal" way (Rosenhan, 1973).

We might assume that Rosenhan and his colleagues would have been quickly discovered as the impostors they were, but this was not the case. Instead, each of them was diagnosed as severely abnormal on the basis of observed behavior. Mental health professionals labeled most as suffering from schizophrenia and kept them in the hospital 3 to 52 days, with the average stay of 19 days. Even when they were discharged, most of the "patients" left with the label *schizophrenia—in remission*, implying that the abnormal behavior had only temporarily subsided and could recur at any time. Most disturbing, no one on the hospital staff identified any of the pseudo-patients as impostors—although some of the actual patients figured out the ruse.

THE STIGMA OF LABELING

The results of Rosenhan's classic study illustrate that placing labels on individuals powerfully influences the way mental health workers perceive and interpret their actions. It also points out that determining who is psychologically disordered is not always a clear-cut or accurate process.

Gender dysphoria (in which one's gender identity is in conflict with one's biological sex) provides a modern illustration of the dilemma between the pros of a formal diagnosis and the cons of patient labeling. For example, most medical insurance providers require a formal, specific diagnosis in order to provide health-care coverage for procedures such as a sex change operation. Many individuals who experience a conflict between their gender identity and their biological sex object theoretically to the idea that their desire to be the other sex should be labeled a "disorder." Yet without a formal diagnosis, those same individuals may be forced to pay out of pocket for an expensive medical procedure.

This diagnosis-based system of insurance coverage often creates a Catch-22 for mental health-care professionals: They must decide between potentially stigmatizing their clients by providing a formal diagnosis, implying some type of disorder, or leaving patients undiagnosed and potentially without the financial support necessary to receive important procedures that will significantly improve the clients' quality of life (Kamens, 2011; Kleinplatz, Moser, & Lev, 2013).

Critics of the DSM argue that labeling an individual as abnormal provides a dehumanizing, lifelong stigma. (Think, for example, of political contenders whose candidacies have been terminated by the disclosure that they received treatment for severe psychological disorders.) Furthermore, after an initial diagnosis has been made, mental health professionals, who may concentrate on the initial diagnostic category, could overlook other diagnostic possibilities (Frances, 2013; Kim et al., 2017; Parrish et al., 2019).

Although the DSM-5 was developed to provide more accurate and consistent diagnoses of psychological disorders, it isn't always successful. For instance, critics charge that because it was drawn up by psychiatrists, who are trained as physicians, psychologically disordered behavior is viewed as a symptom of an underlying medical problem. Moreover, critics suggest that DSM-5 compartmentalizes people into inflexible, all-or-none categories rather than considering the degree to which a person displays psychologically disordered behavior (Ferranti, 2015; Lasalvia, 2015).

Still, despite the drawbacks inherent in any labeling system, the DSM-5 has had an important influence on the way in which mental health professionals view psychological disorders. It has increased both the reliability and the validity of diagnostic categorization. In addition, it offers a logical way to organize examination of the major types of mental disturbances.

Study Alert

It is important to understand the advantages and weaknesses of the DSM classification system.

RECAP/EVALUATE/RETHINK

RECAP

LO 46-1 How can we distinguish normal from abnormal behavior?

- Definitions of abnormality include deviation from average behavior, deviation from ideal behavior, a sense of personal discomfort, the inability to function effectively, and legal conceptions.
- Although no single definition is adequate, abnormal behavior can be considered to be behavior that causes people to experience distress and prevents them from functioning in their daily lives. Most psychologists believe that abnormal and normal behavior should be considered in terms of a continuum.

LO 46-2 What are the major perspectives on psychological disorders used by mental health professionals?

- The medical perspective views abnormality as a symptom of an underlying disease.
- Psychoanalytic perspectives suggest that abnormal behavior stems from childhood conflicts in the unconscious.
- Behavioral approaches focus on the rewards and punishments in the environment that determine abnormal behavior.
- The cognitive approach suggests that abnormal behavior is the result of faulty cognitions (thoughts and beliefs). In this view, abnormal behavior can be remedied by changing one's flawed thoughts and beliefs.
- Humanistic approaches emphasize the responsibility people have for their own behavior even when such behavior is seen as abnormal.
- Sociocultural approaches view abnormal behavior in terms of difficulties arising from family and other social relationships.

LO 46-3 What are the major categories of psychological disorders?

- The most widely used system for classifying psychological disorders is DSM-5–*Diagnostic and Statistical Manual of Mental Disorders*, Fifth Edition.

EVALUATE

1. One problem in defining abnormal behavior is that
   a. Statistically rare behavior may not be abnormal.
   b. Not all abnormalities are accompanied by feelings of discomfort.
   c. Cultural standards are too general to use as a measuring tool.
   d. All of the above are correct.
2. If abnormality is defined as behavior that causes personal discomfort or harms others, which of the following people is most likely to need treatment?
   a. An executive is afraid to accept a promotion because it would require moving from his ground-floor office to the top floor of a tall office building.
   b. A woman decides to quit her job and chooses to live on the street in order to live a "simpler life."
   c. A man believes that friendly spacemen visit his house every Thursday.
   d. A photographer lives with 19 cats in a small apartment, lovingly caring for them.
3. Virginia's mother thinks that her daughter's behavior is clearly abnormal because, despite being offered admission to medical school, Virginia decides to become a waitress. What approach is Virginia's mother using to define abnormal behavior?

4. Which of the following is a strong argument against the medical perspective on abnormality?
   a. Physiological abnormalities are almost always impossible to identify.
   b. There is no conclusive way to link past experience and behavior.
   c. The medical perspective rests too heavily on the effects of nutrition.
   d. Assigning behavior to a physical problem takes responsibility away from the individual for changing his or her behavior.
5. Cheryl is painfully shy. According to the behavioral perspective, the best way to deal with her "abnormal" behavior is to
   a. Treat the underlying physical problem.
   b. Use the principles of learning theory to modify her shy behavior.
   c. Express a great deal of caring.
   d. Uncover her negative past experiences through hypnosis.

RETHINK

1. Do you agree or disagree that DSM should be updated every several years? Why? What makes abnormal behavior so variable?
2. Imagine that an acquaintance of yours was recently arrested for shoplifting a $15 necktie. Write an explanation for this behavior from *each* perspective on abnormality: the medical perspective, the psychoanalytic perspective, the behavioral perspective, the cognitive perspective, the humanistic perspective, and the sociocultural perspective.

Answers to Evaluate Questions

1. d; 2. a; 3. deviation from the ideal; 4. d; 5. b

KEY TERMS

abnormal behavior	behavioral perspective	*Diagnostic and Statistical*
medical perspective	cognitive perspective	*Manual of Mental Disorders,*
psychoanalytic perspective	humanistic perspective	Fifth Edition (DSM-5)
	sociocultural perspective	

Module 47
The Major Psychological Disorders

Sally's first panic attack was a surprise. Visiting her parents after college, she suddenly felt dizzy, broke into a cold sweat, and began hyperventilating. Her father clocked her pulse at 180 and rushed her to the hospital, where all symptoms vanished. She laughed it off and returned to her apartment.

But the panic attacks continued. At the gym, at work, in restaurants and movie theaters, Sally was never safe from them. Not just frightening, they were downright embarrassing. She quit her job to work at home. She avoided crowds and turned down invitations to dinners, parties, and movies. The only way to escape humiliation was to wall herself inside her apartment with a blanket and a pillow.

Sally suffered from panic disorder, one of the specific psychological disorders we'll consider in this module. Keep in mind that although we'll be discussing these disorders objectively, each represents a very human set of difficulties that influence and in some cases considerably disrupt people's lives.

Anxiety Disorders

All of us at one time or another experience *anxiety*, a feeling of apprehension or tension, in reaction to stressful situations. There is nothing "wrong" with such anxiety. It is a normal reaction to stress that often helps rather than hinders our daily functioning. Without some anxiety, for instance, most of us probably would not have much motivation to study hard, undergo physical exams, or spend long hours at our jobs (see Applying Psychology in the 21st Century).

But some people experience anxiety in situations in which there is no apparent reason or cause for such distress. **Anxiety disorders** occur when anxiety arises without external justification and begins to affect people's daily functioning. We'll discuss three major types of anxiety disorders: phobic disorder, panic disorder, and generalized anxiety disorder.

anxiety disorder The occurrence of anxiety without an obvious external cause that affects daily functioning. (Module 47)

PHOBIC DISORDER

Forty-five-year-old Donna is terrified of electricity. She's unable to change a light bulb for fear of getting electrocuted. The thought of static electricity on clothing sends her into a panic. She can't even open a refrigerator door without being terrified a short circuit will send electricity through her body. And thunderstorms? Forget it: She is beside herself with fear of getting electrocuted by lightning (Kluger, 2001).

specific phobia Intense, irrational fear of specific objects or situations. (Module 47)

Donna suffers from a **specific phobia,** an intense, irrational fear of a specific object or situation. For example, claustrophobia is a fear of enclosed places, acrophobia is a fear of high places, xenophobia is a fear of strangers, social phobia is the fear of being judged or embarrassed by others, and—as in Donna's case—electrophobia is a fear of electricity.

The actual danger posed by an anxiety-producing stimulus (which can be just about anything, as you can see in Figure 1) is typically small or nonexistent. However, to someone suffering from the phobia, the danger is great, and a full-blown panic attack may follow exposure to the stimulus. Phobic disorders differ from generalized anxiety disorders and panic disorders in that there is a specific, identifiable stimulus that sets off the anxiety reaction.

Phobias may have only a minor impact on people's lives if those who suffer from them can avoid the stimuli that trigger fear. For example, a fear of heights may have

APPLYING PSYCHOLOGY IN THE 21ST CENTURY

STRESS, CORONAVIRUS, AND YOUNG AMERICANS' MENTAL HEALTH

Are you feeling stressed out, perhaps more than some of the adults around you seem to feel? How did the coronavirus pandemic affect your level of stress? Significantly? If so, you're not alone. Many others of the current generation of college students report feeling the same way, and the stress is taking a toll on their mental health.

Even before the pandemic, a report by the American Psychological Association (2018) detailed the findings of an online survey of over 3,500 adults (plus an additional 300 teens between 15 and 17 years old) investigating their perceived stress levels and mental health. Sixty-four percent of adults reported feeling stressed over money and work. Among Americans aged 15 to 21 (known as Generation Z), 30% reported feeling significantly stressed by housing insecurity, while fully a third were stressed by personal debt. Alarmingly, 28% reported hunger or food insecurity as ongoing sources of stress in their lives.

Current events seem to be a major source of stress for Generation Z, in some cases impacting them more than older generations. During the pandemic, many college students said that their mental health worsened significantly, as they saw

Many people experience significant amounts of stress in their lives, potentially impacting their mental health.
g-stockstudio/Shutterstock

their college plans disrupted and future job opportunities disappear. Self-reports of anxiety, depression, and other mental conditions rose. To make matters worse, at the same time many college mental health facilities shut down along with their college campuses (Jones, 2020; Kerr, 2020).

Moreover, ongoing sources of stress did not disappear during the pandemic. Three-quarters of Generation Z reported that mass shootings were a significant source of

stress for them (compared to 62% of adults overall). Sixty-two percent of Generation Z feel stressed by a rise in suicide rates (compared to 44% of adults). Climate change stresses 58% of Generation Z (and 51% of adults).

What, precisely, is the effect of all this stress on young Americans' mental health? While the nature of the relationship is murky, Generation Z is clearly expressing more mental health concerns than other generations. Significantly more of them, 27%, reported having only fair or poor mental health compare with the millennial generation (15%) or Generation X (13%). And their stress is turning into distress: More than 90% reported feeling at least one physical or emotional symptom of stress; 58% reported feeling depressed or sad; and 55% reported lacking interest, motivation, or energy. Finally, following the onset of the Coronavirus pandemic, more than half of college students reported the need for mental health services since their schools closed.

QUESTIONS TO CONSIDER

- Why do you think Generation Z feels more distress over current events than older generations do?
- If younger Americans are more inclined than older generations to seek out therapy, does that necessarily mean they have worse mental health? Explain.

---

little impact on people's everyday lives (although it may prevent them from living in an apartment on a high floor). On the other hand, a *social phobia*, or a fear of strangers, presents a more serious problem. For example, in one extreme case, a Washington woman left her home just three times in 30 years—once to visit her family, once for an operation, and once to purchase ice cream for a dying companion (Kimbrel, 2007; Wong, Sarver, & Beidel, 2011; Stopa et al., 2013).

PANIC DISORDER

In another type of anxiety disorder, **panic disorder,** *panic attacks* occur that last from a few seconds to several hours. Panic disorders do not have any identifiable, specific triggers (unlike phobias, which are triggered by specific objects or situations). Instead, during an attack such as those Sally experienced in the case described earlier, anxiety suddenly—and often without warning—rises, and an individual feels a sense of impending, unavoidable doom.

Although the physical symptoms of a panic attack differ from person to person, they may include heart palpitations, shortness of breath, unusual amounts of sweating, faintness and dizziness, gastric sensations, and sometimes a sense of imminent death.

panic disorder Anxiety disorder that takes the form of panic attacks lasting from a few seconds to several hours. (Module 47)

Phobic Disorder	Description	Example
Agoraphobia	Fear of places, such as unfamiliar or crowded spaces, where help might not be available in case of emergency	Person becomes housebound because any place other than the person's home arouses extreme anxiety symptoms.
Specific phobias	Fear of specific objects, places, or situations	
Animal type	Specific animals or insects	Person has extreme fear of dogs, cats, or spiders.
Natural environment type	Events or situations in the natural environment	Person has extreme fear of storms, heights, or water.
Situational type	Public transportation, tunnels, bridges, elevators, flying, driving	Person becomes extremely claustrophobic in elevators.
Blood injection injury type	Blood, injury, injections	Person panics when viewing a child's scraped knee.
Social phobia	Fear of being judged or embarrassed by others	Person avoids all social situations and becomes a recluse for fear of encountering others' judgment.

FIGURE 1 Phobic disorders differ from generalized anxiety and panic disorders because with phobic disorders, a specific stimulus can be identified. Listed here are a number of types of phobias and their triggers.

Source: Adapted from Nolen-Hoeksema, S. (2013). *Abnormal psychology* (6th ed.). New York: McGraw-Hill.

(spider) Pets in Frames/Shutterstock; (needle) Photodisc Collection/Getty Images; (woman) Maridav/123RF; (man) JohnnyGreig/E+/Getty Images

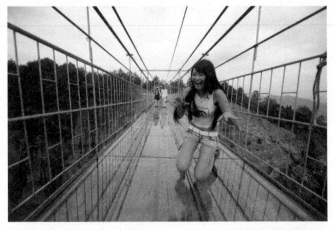

Acrophobia, the fear of heights, is not an uncommon phobia. What sort of behavior-modification approaches might be used to deal with acrophobia?

Imagine China/Newscom

After such an attack, it is no wonder that people tend to feel exhausted (Laederach-Hofmann Messerli-Buergy, 2007; Montgomery, 2011; Carleton et al., 2014).

Panic attacks seemingly come out of nowhere and are unconnected to any specific stimulus. Because they don't know what triggers their feelings of panic, victims of panic attacks may become fearful of going places. In fact, some people with panic disorder develop a complication called *agoraphobia,* the fear of being in a situation in which escape is difficult and in which help for a possible panic attack would not be available. In extreme cases, people with agoraphobia never leave their homes (McTeague et al., 2011; Kim & Yoon, 2017; Stech et al., 2019).

In addition to the physical symptoms, panic disorder affects how the brain processes information. For instance, people with panic disorder have reduced reactions in the anterior cingulate cortex to stimuli (such as viewing a fearful face) that normally produce a strong reaction in those without the disorder. It may be that recurring high levels of emotional arousal that patients with panic disorder experience desensitize them to emotional stimuli (Pillay et al., 2007; Maddock et al., 2013; Lai, 2019).

GENERALIZED ANXIETY DISORDER

generalized anxiety disorder The experience of long-term, persistent anxiety and worry. (Module 47)

People with **generalized anxiety disorder** experience long-term, persistent anxiety and uncontrollable worry. Sometimes their concerns are about identifiable issues involving family, money, work, or health. In other cases, though, people with the disorder feel that something dreadful is about to happen but can't identify the reason and thus experience "free-floating" anxiety.

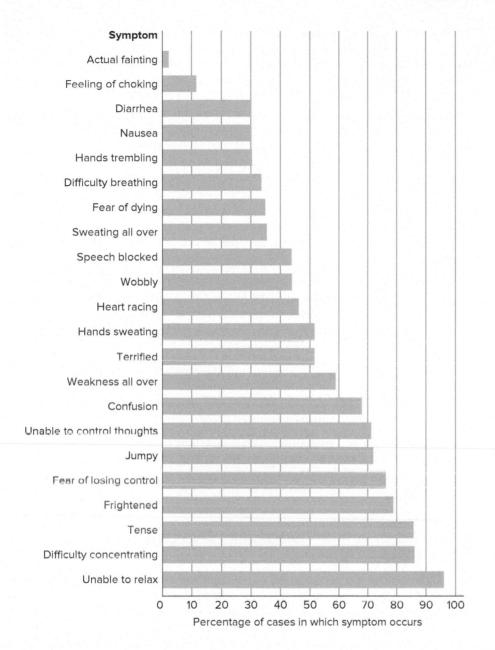

FIGURE 2 Frequency of symptoms in cases of generalized anxiety disorder.

Source: Adapted from Beck, A. T., & Emery, G., with Greenberg, R. L. (1985). *Anxiety disorders and phobias: A cognitive perspective*. New York: Basic Books.

Symptom
Actual fainting, Feeling of choking, Diarrhea, Nausea, Hands trembling, Difficulty breathing, Fear of dying, Sweating all over, Speech blocked, Wobbly, Heart racing, Hands sweating, Terrified, Weakness all over, Confusion, Unable to control thoughts, Jumpy, Fear of losing control, Frightened, Tense, Difficulty concentrating, Unable to relax

Percentage of cases in which symptom occurs

Because of persistent anxiety, people with generalized anxiety disorder cannot concentrate or set their worry and fears aside; their lives become centered on their worry. Furthermore, their anxiety is often accompanied by physiological symptoms, such as muscle tension, headaches, dizziness, heart palpitations, or insomnia (Starcevic et al., 2007). Figure 2 shows the most common symptoms of generalized anxiety disorder.

Obsessive-Compulsive Disorder

In **obsessive-compulsive disorder (OCD),** people are plagued by unwanted thoughts, called *obsessions*, or feel that they must carry out behaviors, termed *compulsions*, that they feel driven to perform.

An **obsession** is a persistent, unwanted thought or idea that keeps recurring. For example, a student may be unable to stop thinking that she has neglected to put her name on a test and may think about it constantly for the 2 weeks it takes to get the paper back. A man may go on vacation and wonder the whole time whether he locked his house. A woman may hear the same tune running through her head over and over.

obsessive-compulsive disorder (OCD) A disorder characterized by obsessions or compulsions. (Module 47)

obsession A persistent, unwanted thought or idea that keeps recurring. (Module 47)

In each case, the thought or idea is unwanted and difficult to put out of mind. Of course, many people suffer from mild obsessions from time to time, but usually such thoughts persist only for a short period. For people with serious obsessions, however, the thoughts persist for days or months and may consist of bizarre, troubling images (Rassin & Muris, 2007; Wenzel, 2011; Iliceto et al., 2017).

As the name suggests, as part of an obsessive-compulsive disorder, people may also experience compulsions. **Compulsions** are irresistible urges to repeatedly carry out some behavior that seems strange and unreasonable even to them. Whatever the compulsive behavior is, people experience extreme anxiety if they cannot do it, even if it is something they want to stop. The acts may be relatively trivial, such as repeatedly checking the stove to make sure all the burners are turned off, or more unusual, such as washing one's hands so much that they bleed (Moretz & McKay, 2009; Gillan & Sahakian, 2015; Robbins, Vaghi, & Banca, 2019).

For example, consider this passage from the autobiography of a person with obsessive-compulsive disorder:

> I thought my parents would die if I didn't do everything in exactly the right way. When I took my glasses off at night I'd have to place them on the dresser at a particular angle. Sometimes I'd turn on the light and get out of bed seven times until I felt comfortable with the angle. If the angle wasn't right, I felt that my parents would die. The feeling ate up my insides.
>
> If I didn't grab the molding on the wall just the right way as I entered or exited my room; if I didn't hang a shirt in the closet perfectly; if I didn't read a paragraph a certain way; if my hands and nails weren't perfectly clean, I thought my incorrect behavior would kill my parents. (Summers, 2000)

Although carrying out compulsive rituals may lead to some immediate reduction of anxiety, in the long run the anxiety returns. In fact, people with severe cases lead lives filled with unrelenting tension (Dittrich, Johansen, & Fineberg, 2011; Kalanthroff et al., 2013).

compulsion An irresistible urge to repeatedly carry out some behavior that seems strange and unreasonable. (Module 47)

PsychTech

Although some people seem to use the Internet compulsively, psychologists have yet to agree on whether it represents a true psychological disorder.

THE CAUSES OF ANXIETY DISORDERS AND OBSESSIVE-COMPULSIVE DISORDER

We've considered several of the major types of anxiety disorders and obsessive-compulsive disorder, but there are many other related disorders. The variety of anxiety disorders means that no single explanation fits all cases.

Genetic factors clearly are part of the picture. For example, if one member of a pair of identical twins has panic disorder, there is a 30% chance that the other twin will have it also. Furthermore, a person's characteristic level of anxiety is related to a specific gene involved in the production of the neurotransmitter serotonin. This is consistent with findings indicating that certain chemical deficiencies in the brain appear to produce some kinds of anxiety disorder (Beidel & Turner, 2007; Chamberlain et al., 2008; Yagi et al., 2017).

Some researchers believe that an overactive autonomic nervous system may be at the root of panic attacks. Specifically, they suggest that poor regulation of the brain's *locus coeruleus* may lead to panic attacks, which cause the limbic system to become overstimulated. In turn, the overstimulated limbic system produces chronic anxiety, which ultimately leads the locus ceruleus to generate still more panic attacks (Davies et al., 2008; Dresler et al., 2013; Wyrofsky et al., 2019).

There are also biological causes involved in obsessive-compulsive disorder. For example, researchers have found specific differences in the brains of those with the disorder compared to those without it (Christian et al., 2008; Okada et al., 2015; Ravindran et al., 2019).

Psychologists who employ the behavioral perspective have taken a different approach to explaining anxiety disorders that emphasizes environmental factors. They consider anxiety to be a learned response to stress. For instance, suppose a dog bites a young girl. When the girl next sees a dog, she is frightened and runs away—a behavior that relieves her anxiety and thereby reinforces her avoidance behavior. After repeated encounters with dogs in which she is reinforced for her avoidance behavior, she may develop a full-fledged phobia regarding dogs.

Finally, the cognitive perspective suggests that anxiety disorders grow out of inappropriate and inaccurate thoughts and beliefs about circumstances in a person's world. For example, people with anxiety disorders may view a friendly puppy as a ferocious and savage pit bull, or they may see an air disaster looming every moment they are in the vicinity of an airplane. According to the cognitive perspective, people's maladaptive thoughts about the world are at the root of an anxiety disorder (Wang & Clark, 2002; Ouimet, Gawronski, & Dozois, 2009; Bouvard et al., 2017).

Somatic Symptom Disorders

Somatic symptom disorders are psychological difficulties that take on a physical (somatic) form for which there is no medical cause. Even though an individual with a somatic symptom disorder reports physical symptoms, no biological cause exists, or if there is a medical problem, the person's reaction is greatly exaggerated.

One relatively common type of somatic symptom disorder is illness anxiety disorder. Those with **illness anxiety disorder** have a constant fear of illness and a preoccupation with their health. These individuals may believe that everyday aches and pains are symptoms of a dread disease. The "symptoms" are not faked; the individuals actually experience something. However, they misinterpret those aches and pains as evidence of some serious illness, often in the face of clear medical evidence to the contrary (Olatunji, 2008; Weck et al., 2011; Scarella, Boland, & Barsky, 2019).

Conversion disorder is another somatic symptom disorder. Unlike illness anxiety disorder, in which there is no physical problem, **conversion disorders** involve an apparent physical disturbance, such as the inability to see or hear or to move an arm or leg. However, *the cause* of the physical disturbance is purely psychological; there is no biological reason for the problem. Some of Freud's classic cases involved conversion disorders. For instance, one of Freud's patients suddenly became unable to use her arm without any apparent physiological cause. Later, just as abruptly, the problem disappeared.

Conversion disorders often begin suddenly. Previously normal people wake up one day blind or deaf, or they experience numbness that is restricted to a certain part of the body. A hand, for example, may become entirely numb, while an area above the wrist, controlled by the same nerves, remains sensitive to touch—something that is physiologically implausible. Mental health professionals refer to such a condition as "glove anesthesia" because the numb area is the part of the hand covered by a glove and not a region related to pathways of the nervous system (see Figure 3).

Surprisingly, people who experience conversion disorders frequently remain unconcerned about symptoms that most of us would expect to be highly anxiety producing. For instance, a person in good health who wakes up blind may react in a bland, matter-of-fact way. Considering how most of us would feel if we woke up unable to see, this unemotional reaction hardly seems appropriate (Brasic, 2002; Loriedo & Leone, 2017).

somatic symptom disorders Psychological difficulties that take on a physical (somatic) form for which there is no medical cause. (Module 47)

illness anxiety disorder A somatic symptom disorder in which people have a constant fear of illness and a preoccupation with their health. (Module 47)

conversion disorder A major somatic symptom disorder that involves an actual physical disturbance, such as the inability to use a sensory organ or the complete or partial inability to move an arm or leg. (Module 47)

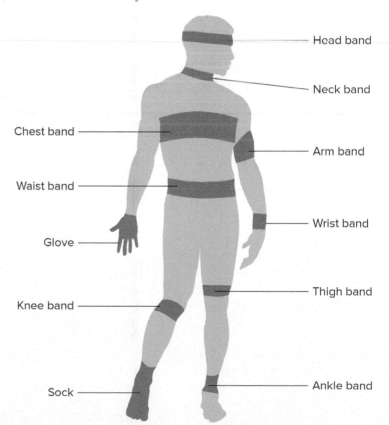

FIGURE 3 Conversion disorders sometimes produce numbness in specific and isolated areas of the body (indicated by the shaded areas in the figure). For instance, in glove anesthesia, the area of the body covered by a glove feels numb. However, the condition is biologically implausible because of the nerves involved, which suggests that the problem results from a psychological disorder rather than from actual nerve damage.

Dissociative Disorders

The classic movie *The Three Faces of Eve* (about a woman with three wildly different personalities) and the book *Sybil* (about a girl who allegedly had 16 personalities) represent a highly dramatic, rare, and controversial class of disorders: dissociative disorders. **Dissociative disorders** are characterized by the separation (or dissociation) of different facets of a person's personality that are normally integrated and work together. By dissociating key parts of who they are, people are able to keep disturbing memories or perceptions from reaching conscious awareness and thereby reduce their anxiety (Houghtalen & Talbot, 2007; Laddis, Dell, & Korzekwa, 2017).

dissociative disorders Psychological dysfunctions characterized by the separation of different facets of a person's personality that are normally integrated. (Module 47)

Several dissociative disorders exist, although all of them are rare. A person with a **dissociative identity disorder (DID)** (once called *multiple personality disorder*) displays characteristics of two or more distinct personalities, identities, or personality fragments. Individual personalities often have a unique set of likes and dislikes and their own reactions to situations. Some people with multiple personalities even carry several pairs of glasses because their vision changes with each personality. Moreover, each individual personality can be well adjusted when considered on its own (Stickley & Nickeas, 2006; Howell, 2011; Hartmann & Benum, 2019).

dissociative identity disorder (DID) A disorder in which a person displays characteristics of two or more distinct personalities. (Module 47)

The diagnosis of dissociative identity disorder is controversial. It was rarely diagnosed before 1980, when it was added as a category in the third edition of DSM for the first time. At that point, the number of cases increased significantly. Some clinicians suggest the increase was due to more precise identification of the disorder. On the other hand, critics suggest that widespread publicity about cases of DID may have influenced patients to report symptoms of more common personality disorders in ways that made it more likely they would receive a diagnosis of DID (Kihlstrom, 2005a; Xiao et al., 2006; Ross, 2015).

Dissociative amnesia is another dissociative disorder in which a significant, selective memory loss occurs. Dissociative amnesia is unlike simple amnesia, which involves an actual loss of information from memory and typically results from a physiological cause. In contrast, in cases of dissociative amnesia, the "forgotten" material is still present in memory—it simply cannot be recalled. The term *repressed memories* is sometimes used to describe the lost memories of people with dissociative amnesia.

dissociative amnesia A disorder in which a significant, selective memory loss occurs. (Module 47)

In the most severe form of dissociative amnesia, individuals cannot recall their names, are unable to recognize parents and other relatives, and do not know their addresses. In other respects, though, they may appear quite normal. Apart from an inability to remember certain facts about themselves, they may be able to recall skills and abilities that they developed earlier. For instance, even though a chef may not remember where he grew up and received training, he may still be able to prepare gourmet meals.

In some cases of dissociative amnesia, the memory loss is profound. For example, in one dramatic case, Raymond Power Jr., an attorney, husband, father of two, and Boy Scout leader, left home to go to work one morning. Two days later, he was homeless, living a new life a thousand miles away, and had no memory of who he was or how he got there. He was found 6 months later but still had no recollection of his previous life, including any knowledge of his wife of 30 years or even that he had children (Foderaro, 2006; Dell, 2013).

dissociative fugue A form of amnesia in which a person leaves home and assumes a new identity. (Module 47)

Dissociative fugue is a form of amnesia in which a person leaves home suddenly and assumes a new identity. In this unusual and rare state, people take sudden, impulsive trips and adopt a new identity. After a period of time—days, months, or sometimes even years—they suddenly realize that they are in a strange place and completely forget the time they have spent wandering. Their last memories are those from the time just before they entered the fugue state (Hennig-Fast et al., 2008).

The common thread among dissociative disorders is that they allow people to escape from some anxiety-producing situation. Either the person produces a new personality to deal with stress, or the individual forgets or leaves behind the situation that caused the stress as he or she journeys to some new—and perhaps less anxiety-ridden—environment (Brown, 2006; Lynn et al., 2019).

Mood Disorders

From the time I woke up in the morning until the time I went to bed at night, I was unbearably miserable and seemingly incapable of any kind of joy or enthusiasm. Everything–every thought, word, movement–was an effort. Everything that once was sparkling now was flat. I seemed to myself to be dull, boring, inadequate, thick brained, unlit, unresponsive, chill skinned, bloodless, and sparrow drab. I doubted, completely, my ability to do anything well. It seemed as though my mind had slowed down and burned out to the point of being virtually useless. (Jamison, 1995)

We all experience mood swings. Sometimes we are happy, perhaps even euphoric; at other times, we feel upset, saddened, or depressed. Such changes in mood are a normal part of everyday life.

In some people, however, moods are so pronounced and lingering–like the feelings described above by writer (and psychiatrist) Kay Jamison–that they interfere with the ability to function effectively. **Mood disorders** are disturbances in emotional experience that are strong enough to interfere with everyday living. In extreme cases, a mood may become life threatening; in other cases, it may cause the person to lose touch with reality.

mood disorder A disturbance in emotional experience that is strong enough to interfere with everyday living. (Module 47)

MAJOR DEPRESSIVE DISORDER

President Abraham Lincoln. Queen Victoria. Lady Gaga.

The common link among these people? Each suffered from periodic attacks of major depressive disorder. **Major depressive disorder** is a severe form of depression that interferes with concentration, decision making, and sociability.

Major depressive disorder is one of the more common forms of mood disorders. Nearly 18 million people in the United States suffer from major depression, and at any one time, 6-10% of the U.S. population is clinically depressed. Almost 1 in 5 people in the United States experiences major depression at some point in life, and 15% of college students have received a diagnosis of depression. The cost of depression is more than $200 billion a year in lost productivity and other costs (Edoka, Petrou, & Ramchandani, 2011; Greenberg, 2015; Substance Abuse and Mental Health Services Administration, 2019).

major depressive disorder A severe form of depression that interferes with concentration, decision making, and sociability (Module 47)

Women are twice as likely to experience major depression as men are, with one-fourth of all females apt to encounter it at some point during their lives. Furthermore, although no one is sure why, the rate of depression is going up throughout the world. Results of in-depth interviews conducted in the United States, Puerto Rico, Taiwan, Lebanon, Canada, Italy, Germany, and France indicate that the incidence of depression has increased significantly over previous rates in every area. In fact, in some countries, the likelihood that individuals will have major depression at some point in their lives is three times higher than it was for earlier generations. Worldwide, over 300 million people suffer from major depressive disorder (Pratt & Brody, 2014; Sarubin et al., 2017; Ojagbemi et al., 2018).

When psychologists speak of major depressive disorder, they do not mean the sadness that accompanies one of life's disappointments, which we all have experienced. Some depression is normal after the breakup of a long-term relationship, the death of a loved one, or the loss of a job. It is normal even after less serious problems, such as doing badly on a test or having a romantic partner forget one's birthday.

People who suffer from major depressive disorder experience similar feelings, but the severity tends to be considerably greater. They may feel useless, worthless, and lonely, and they may think the future is hopeless and no one can help them. They may lose their appetite and have no energy. Moreover, they may experience such feelings for months or even years. They may cry uncontrollably, have sleep disturbances, and be at risk for suicide. The depth and duration of such behavior

Study Alert
Major depression differs from the normal depression that occasionally occurs during most people's lives; major depression is more intense, lasts longer, and may have no clear trigger.

A Test for Major Depression

To complete the questionnaire, count the number of statements with which you agree:

1. I feel sad, anxious, or empty.
2. I feel hopeless or pessimistic.
3. I feel guilty, worthless, or helpless.
4. I feel irritable or restless.
5. I have lost interest in activities or hobbies that were once pleasurable, including sex.
6. I feel tired and have decreased energy.
7. I have difficulty concentrating, remembering details, and making decisions.
8. I have insomnia, early-morning wakefulness, or sleep too much.
9. I overeat or have appetite loss.
10. I have thoughts of suicide or have attempted suicide.
11. I have aches or pains, headaches, cramps, or digestive problems that do not ease even with treatment.

Scoring: If you agree with at least five of the statements, including either 1 or 2, and if you have had these symptoms for at least 2 weeks, help from a professional is strongly recommended. If you answer yes to number 10, seek immediate help. And remember: These are only general guidelines. If you feel you may need help, seek it.

are the hallmarks of major depressive disorder. (Figure 4 provides a self-assessment of depression.)

MANIA AND BIPOLAR DISORDER

mania An extended state of intense, wild elation. (Module 47)

While depression leads to the depths of despair, mania leads to emotional heights. **Mania** is an extended state of intense, wild elation. People experiencing mania feel intense happiness, power, invulnerability, and energy. Believing they will succeed at anything they attempt, they may become involved in wild schemes. Consider, for example, the following description of an individual who experienced a manic episode:

> Mr. O'Reilly took a leave of absence from his civil service job. He purchased a large number of cuckoo clocks and then an expensive car, which he planned to use as a mobile showroom for his wares, anticipating that he would make a great deal of money. He proceeded to "tear around town" buying and selling clocks and other merchandise, and when he was not out, he was continuously on the phone making "deals." . . . He was $3,000 in debt and had driven his family to exhaustion with his excessive activity and talkativeness. He said, however, that he felt "on top of the world." (Spitzer et al., 1983)

bipolar disorder A disorder in which a person alternates between periods of euphoric feelings of mania and periods of depression. (Module 47)

Some people sequentially experience periods of mania and depression. This alternation of mania and depression is called **bipolar disorder** (a condition previously known as *manic-depressive disorder*). The swings between highs and lows may occur a few days apart or may alternate over a period of years. In addition, in bipolar disorder, periods of depression are usually longer than periods of mania.

Ironically, some of society's most creative individuals may have suffered from bipolar disorder. The imagination, drive, excitement, and energy that they display during manic stages allow them to make unusually creative contributions. For instance, historical analysis of the composer Robert Schumann's music shows that he was most prolific during periods of mania. In contrast, his output dropped off drastically during periods of depression (see Figure 5). On the other hand, the high output associated with mania does not necessarily lead to higher quality: Some of Schumann's greatest works were created outside his periods of mania (Szegedy Maszak, 2003; Kyaga et al., 2013).

Although creativity may be increased when someone is experiencing mania, persons who experience this disorder often show a recklessness that produces emotional and sometimes physical self-injury. They may alienate people with their talkativeness, inflated self-esteem, and indifference to the needs of others (Simonton, 2014; Miller, Perich, & Meade, 2019).

CAUSES OF MOOD DISORDERS

Because they represent a major mental health problem, mood disorders—and, in particular, depression—have received a good deal of study. Several approaches have been used to explain the disorders.

Genetic and biological causes of mood disorders. Some mood disorders have clear genetic and biological roots. In fact, most evidence suggests that bipolar disorders are caused primarily by biological factors. For instance, bipolar disorder (and some forms of major depression) clearly runs in some families, pointing to a genetic cause. Furthermore, researchers have found that several neurotransmitters play a role in depression. For example, alterations in the functioning of serotonin and norepinephrine in the brain are related to the disorder.

In addition, research on neuroimaging suggests that a brain structure called *area 25* is related to depression: When area 25 is smaller than normal, it is associated with a higher risk of depression. Furthermore, the right anterior insula, a region of the brain related to self-awareness and interpersonal experience, also appears to be related to depression (Cisler et al., 2013; Serretti, 2017; Coenen et al., 2019).

FIGURE 5 The number of pieces written by composer Robert Schumann in a given year was related to his periods of depression and mania. Why do you think mania might be associated with creative productivity in some people?

Source: Slater, E., & Meyer, A. (1959). Contributions to a pathography of the musicians: Robert Schumann. *Confinia Psychiatrica.* Reprinted in K. R. Jamison, *Touched with fire: Manic-depressive illness and the artistic temperament.* New York: Free Press; reprinted in Jamison, K. R. (1995). *An unquiet mind: A memoir of moods and madness.* New York: Knopf..

Internal, unconscious conflicts as causes of mood disorders. Supporters of psychoanalytic perspectives see depression as the result of feelings of loss (real or potential) or of anger directed inwardly at oneself. However, little research supports this explanation (Vanheule et al., 2006; Sa, 2015).

Environmental causes of mood disorders. Some explanations of depression take a behavioral approach, looking to influences outside the person. For example, behavioral theories of depression argue that the stresses of life produce a reduction in positive reinforcers. As a result, people begin to withdraw, which only reduces positive reinforcers further. In addition, people receive attention for their depressive behavior, which further reinforces the depression (Lewinsohn et al., 2003; Domschke, 2013; Kwong et al., 2019).

Cognitive and emotional causes of mood disorders. Some explanations for mood disorders attribute them to cognitive factors. For example, psychologist Martin Seligman suggests that depression is largely a response to learned helplessness. *Learned helplessness* is a learned expectation that events in one's life are uncontrollable and that one cannot escape from the situation. As a consequence, people simply give up fighting aversive events and submit to them, which thereby produces depression. Other theorists go a step further and suggest that depression results from hopelessness, a combination of learned helplessness and an expectation that negative outcomes in one's life are inevitable (Bjornstad, 2006; Li et al., 2011; Shirayama & Hashimoto, 2017).

Clinical psychologist Aaron Beck has proposed that faulty cognitions underlie people's depressed feelings. Specifically, his cognitive theory of depression suggests that depressed individuals typically view themselves as life's losers and blame themselves whenever anything goes wrong. By focusing on the negative side of situations, they feel inept and unable to act constructively to change their environment. In sum, their negative cognitions lead to feelings of depression (Newman et al., 2002).

Brain imaging studies suggest that people with depression experience a general blunting of emotional reactions. For example, one study found that the brains of people with depression showed significantly less activation when they viewed photos of human faces displaying strong emotions than did those without the disorder (Gotlib et al., 2004).

DEPRESSION IN WOMEN

The various theories of depression have not provided a complete answer to an elusive question that has dogged researchers: Why does depression occur in approximately twice as many women as men—a pattern that is similar across a variety of cultures?

One explanation suggests that the stress women experience may be greater than the stress men experience at certain points in their lives—such as when a woman must simultaneously earn a living and be the primary caregiver for her children. In addition, women have a higher risk for physical and sexual abuse, typically earn lower wages than men, report greater unhappiness with their marriages, and generally experience chronic negative circumstances. Furthermore, women and men may respond to stress with different coping mechanisms. For instance, men may abuse drugs, whereas women respond with depression (Hyde, Mezulis, & Abramson, 2008; Komarovskaya et al., 2011; Sun et al., 2017).

Biological factors may also explain some women's depression. For example, the rate of female depression begins to rise during puberty, so some psychologists believe that hormones make women more vulnerable to the disorder. In addition, 25-50% of women who take oral contraceptives report symptoms of depression, and depression that occurs after the birth of a child is linked to hormonal changes. Finally, structural differences in men's and women's brains may be related to gender differences in depression (Jones et al., 2017; Yang et al., 2017; Post & Leuner, 2019).

Ultimately, it is clear that researchers have discovered no definitive solutions to the puzzle of depression, and there are many alternative explanations. Most likely, a complex interaction of several factors causes mood disorders.

Schizophrenia

Things that relate, the town of Antelope, Oregon, Jonestown, Charlie Manson, the Hillside Strangler, the Zodiac Killer, Watergate, King's trial in L.A., and many more. In the last 7 years alone, over 23 Star Wars scientists committed suicide for no apparent reason. The AIDS cover-up, the conference in South America in 87 had over 1,000 doctors claim that insects can transmit it. To be able to read one's thoughts and place thoughts in one's mind without the person knowing it's being done. Realization is a reality of bioelectromagnetic control, which is thought transfer and emotional control, recording individual brainwave frequencies of thought, sensation, and emotions. (Nolen-Hoeksema, 2007)

This excerpt illustrates the efforts of a person with schizophrenia, one of the more severe forms of mental disturbance, to communicate. People with schizophrenia account for by far the largest percentage of those hospitalized for psychological disorders. They are also in many respects the least likely to recover from their difficulties.

Schizophrenia refers to a class of disorders in which severe distortion of reality occurs. Thinking, perception, and emotion may deteriorate; the individual may withdraw from social interaction; and the person may display bizarre behavior. The symptoms displayed by persons with schizophrenia may vary considerably over time. Nonetheless, a number of characteristics reliably distinguish schizophrenia from other disorders. They include the following:

schizophrenia A class of disorders in which severe distortion of reality occurs. (Module 47)

- *Decline from a previous level of functioning.* An individual can no longer carry out activities he or she was once able to do.
- *Disturbances of thought and speech.* People with schizophrenia use logic and language in a peculiar way. Their thinking often does not make sense, and their logic is frequently faulty, which is referred to as a *formal thought disorder.* They also do not follow conventional linguistic rules (Penn et al., 1997). Consider, for example, the following response to the question "Why do you think people believe in God?"

  > Uh, let's, I don't know why, let's see, balloon travel. He holds it up for you, the balloon. He don't let you fall out, your little legs sticking down through the clouds. He's down to the smokestack, looking through the smoke trying to get the balloon gassed up you know. Way they're flying on top that way, legs sticking out. I don't know, looking down on the ground, heck, that'd make you so dizzy you just stay and sleep you know, hold down and sleep there. I used to be sleep outdoors, you know, sleep outdoors instead of going home. (Chapman & Chapman, 1973)

As this selection illustrates, although the basic grammatical structure may be intact, the substance of thinking that is characteristic of schizophrenia is often illogical, garbled, and lacking in meaningful content (Holden, 2003; Heinrichs, 2005).

- *Delusions.* People with schizophrenia often have delusions—firmly held, unshakable beliefs with no basis in reality. Among the common delusions people with schizophrenia experience are the beliefs that they are being controlled by someone else, they are being persecuted by others, and their thoughts are being broadcast so that others know what they are thinking (Coltheart, Langdon, & McKay, 2007; Startup, Bucci, & Langdon, 2009; Phalen et al., 2017).
- *Hallucinations and perceptual problems.* People with schizophrenia sometimes do not perceive the world as most other people do. For example, they may have *hallucinations,* the experience of perceiving things that do not actually exist. Furthermore, they may see, hear, or smell things differently from others (see Figure 6). In fact, they may not even have a sense of their bodies in the way that others do, having difficulty determining where their bodies stop and the rest of the world begins (Bauer, Schwab, & McAdams, 2011; Phadke, Karia, & DeSousa, 2015; Siemerkus, Tomiello, & Stephan, 2019).

FIGURE 6 This unusual art was created by an individual suffering from a severe psychological disorder.

Wellcome Images/Science Source

- *Inappropriate emotions.* People with schizophrenia sometimes show a lack of emotion, with even the most dramatic events producing little or no emotional response. Alternately, they may display strong bursts of emotion that are inappropriate to a situation. For example, a person with schizophrenia may laugh uproariously at a funeral or react with rage when being helped by someone.

- *Withdrawal.* People with schizophrenia tend to have little interest in others. They tend not to socialize or hold real conversations with others, although they may talk at another person. In the most extreme cases, they do not even acknowledge the presence of other people and appear to be in their own isolated worlds.

Usually, the onset of schizophrenia occurs in early adulthood, and the symptoms follow one of two primary courses. In *process schizophrenia*, the symptoms develop slowly and subtly. There may be a gradual withdrawal from the world, excessive daydreaming, and a blunting of emotion until eventually the disorder reaches the point where others cannot overlook it. In other cases, known as *reactive schizophrenia*, the onset of symptoms is sudden and conspicuous. The treatment outlook for reactive schizophrenia is relatively favorable, but process schizophrenia has proved more difficult to treat.

DSM-5 classifies the symptoms of schizophrenia into two types. *Positive-symptom schizophrenia* is indicated by the presence of disordered behavior such as hallucinations, delusions, and emotional extremes. Those with positive-symptom schizophrenia clearly lose touch with reality.

In contrast, those with *negative-symptom schizophrenia* show disruptions to normal emotions and behaviors. For example, there may be an absence or loss of normal functioning, such as social withdrawal or blunted emotions (Levine & Rabinowitz, 2007; Tandon et al., 2013; Lauriello & Rahman, 2015).

The distinction between positive and negative symptoms of schizophrenia is important because it suggests that two different kinds of causes might trigger schizophrenia. Furthermore, it has implications for predicting treatment outcomes.

SOLVING THE PUZZLE OF SCHIZOPHRENIA: BIOLOGICAL CAUSES

Although schizophrenic behavior clearly departs radically from normal behavior, its causes are less apparent. It does appear, however, that schizophrenia has both biological and environmental origins (Sawa & Snyder, 2002; Pavão, Tort, & Amaral, 2015; Torrey & Yolken, 2019).

Let's first consider the evidence pointing to a biological cause. Because schizophrenia is more common in some families than in others, genetic factors seem to be involved in producing at least a susceptibility to or readiness for developing schizophrenia. For example, the closer the genetic link between a person with schizophrenia and another individual, the greater the likelihood that the other person will experience the disorder (see Figure 7; Plomin & McGuffin, 2003; Gottesman & Hanson, 2005; Rodrigues-Amorim et al., 2017).

However, if genetics alone were responsible for schizophrenia, the chance of both of two identical twins having schizophrenia would be 100% instead of just under 50% because identical twins have the same genetic makeup. Moreover, attempts to find a link between schizophrenia and a particular gene have been only partly successful. Apparently, genetic factors alone do not produce schizophrenia (Lenzenweger & Dworkin, 1998; Abel & Nicki-Jochschat, 2016).

Some researchers suggest that epigenetics are involved in schizophrenia. *Epigenetics* looks at the way in which genes are expressed and influenced by the environment. In this view, genes by themselves do not invariably lead a person to display schizophrenia. Instead, they are affected by the environment. Furthermore, genes can be altered in a way that then passes on the behavior to future generations. An epigenetic

Risk of Developing Schizophrenia, Based on Genetic Relatedness to a Person with Schizophrenia		
Relationship	**Genetic Relatedness, %**	**Risk of Developing Schizophrenia, %**
Identical twin	100	48
Child of two schizophrenic parents	100	46
Fraternal twin	50	17
Offspring of one schizophrenic parent	50	17
Sibling	50	9
Nephew or niece	25	4
Spouse	0	2
Unrelated person	0	1

FIGURE 7 The closer the genetic links between two people, the greater the likelihood that if one experiences schizophrenia, so will the other sometime during his or her lifetime. However, genetics is not the full story; if it were, the risk of identical twins having schizophrenia would be 100% and not the 48% shown in this figure.

Source: Adapted from Gottesman, I. I. (1991). *Schizophrenia genesis: The origins of madness.* New York: Freeman.

explanation of schizophrenia, then, suggests that changes in gene expression may produce the disorder and that subsequently it can be passed on genetically (Alelú-Paz et al., 2017; Whitton et al., 2017; Föcking et al., 2019).

Despite advances in our understanding of genetic and epigenetic causes of schizophrenia, most researchers agree that no single gene is responsible for the disorder. Consequently, scientists have looked to other possible biological causes (Balter, 2017).

Another biological explanation suggests that the brains of people with schizophrenia may have a biochemical imbalance. For example, the *dopamine hypothesis* suggests that schizophrenia results from excess activity in the areas of the brain that use dopamine as a neurotransmitter. This explanation came to light after the discovery that drugs that block dopamine action in brain pathways can be effective in reducing the symptoms of schizophrenia. Other research suggests that glutamate, another neurotransmitter, may contribute to the disorder, and drugs that reduce the release of glutamate in the brain show promise in alleviating symptoms of schizophrenia (Kendler & Schaffner, 2011; Beck, Javitt, & Howes, 2016; Howes et al., 2017).

Another biological explanation relates to structural abnormalities in the brains of people with schizophrenia. For example, researchers have found abnormalities in the neural circuits of the cortex and limbic systems, as well as reduced amounts of gray matter, in the brains of those with schizophrenia. Furthermore, differences exist in the way the brain functions (see *Neuroscience in Your Life;* Reichenberg & Harvey, 2007; Reichenberg et al., 2009; Bustillo et al., 2017).

Further evidence for the importance of biological factors shows that when people with schizophrenia hear voices during hallucinations, the parts of the brain responsible for hearing and language processing become active. When they have visual hallucinations, the parts of the brain involved in movement and color are active. At the same time, people with schizophrenia often have unusually low activity in the brain's frontal lobes—the parts of the brain involved with emotional regulation, insight, and the evaluation of sensory stimuli (Stern & Silbersweig, 2001; Lavigne et al., 2015).

SITUATIONAL CAUSES OF SCHIZOPHRENIA

Biological factors provide important pieces of the puzzle of schizophrenia. However, we also need to consider past and current experiences of people who develop the disturbance.

For instance, psychoanalytic explanations suggest that schizophrenia occurs when people experience regression to earlier stages of life. Specifically, Freud believed that people with schizophrenia lack egos that are strong enough to cope with their unacceptable impulses. They regress to the oral stage—a time when the id and ego are not

NEUROSCIENCE IN YOUR LIFE: BRAIN NETWORKS RELATED TO MEMORY DEFICITS IN SCHIZOPHRENIA

Psychological disorders are well known for their psychological symptoms, but they are also marked by significant cognitive declines. For example, patients with schizophrenia suffer from hallucinations, but they also suffer from memory deficits that can greatly impact their lives. In a recent study, neuroscientists scanned the brains of patients with schizophrenia and healthy control participants while each group attempted to memorize and later recall pictures. As you can see from the images below, healthy control participants (left) showed more activity in certain brain regions of the prefrontal cortex (indicated by more yellow) than patients with schizophrenia (right) in both the left hemisphere (top) and the right hemisphere (bottom) (Ragland et al., 2015).

Source: Adapted from Ragland, J. D., Ranganath, C., Harms, M. P., Barch, D. M., Gold, J. M., Layher, E., et al. (2015). Functional and neuroanatomic specificity of episodic memory dysfunction in schizophrenia: A functional magnetic resonance imaging study of the relational and item-specific encoding task. *JAMA Psychiatry, 72*(9), 909-916. doi: 10.1001/jamapsychiatry.2015.0276.

yet separated. Therefore, individuals with schizophrenia essentially are presumed to act out impulses without concern for reality.

However, little research evidence supports psychoanalytic explanations. More plausible theories suggest that the emotional and communication patterns of the families of people with schizophrenia are to blame for the disorder. For instance, some researchers suggest that schizophrenia is related to a family interaction style known as expressed emotion.

Expressed emotion is an interaction style characterized by high levels of criticism, hostility, and emotional intrusiveness within a family. Other researchers suggest that faulty communication patterns lie at the heart of schizophrenia (Lobban, Barrowclough, & Jones, 2006; Nader et al., 2013).

Psychologists who take a cognitive perspective on schizophrenia suggest that the problems in thinking that people with the disorder experience point to a cognitive cause. Some suggest that schizophrenia results from *overattention* to stimuli in the environment. Rather than being able to screen out unimportant or inconsequential stimuli and focus on the most important things in the environment, people with schizophrenia may be excessively receptive to virtually everything in their environment. As a consequence of their inability to screen out noncritical information, their information-processing capabilities become overloaded and eventually break down.

Other cognitive experts argue that schizophrenia results from *underattention* to certain stimuli. According to this explanation, people with schizophrenia fail to focus sufficiently on important stimuli and pay attention to other, less important information in their surroundings (Cadenhead & Braff, 1995; Remington et al., 2014).

Although it is plausible that overattention and underattention are related to different forms of schizophrenia, these phenomena do not explain the origins of such information-processing disorders. Consequently, cognitive approaches–like other environmental explanations–do not provide a full explanation of the disorder.

THE MULTIPLE CAUSES OF SCHIZOPHRENIA: THE PREDISPOSITION EXPLANATION

Most scientists now believe that schizophrenia is caused by a combination of biological and situational factors. Specifically, *predisposition explanations of schizophrenia* suggests that individuals may inherit a predisposition or an inborn sensitivity to develop schizophrenia. This genetic predisposition makes them particularly vulnerable to stressors in their lives, such as social rejection, dysfunctional family communication patterns, or severe economic stress.

The stressors in people's lives may vary, but if they are strong enough and are coupled with a genetic predisposition, they result in the appearance of schizophrenia. Furthermore, a strong genetic predisposition may lead to the onset of schizophrenia even when the environmental stressors are relatively weak. On the other hand, someone with a genetic predisposition to develop schizophrenia may avoid developing the disorder if that person experiences relatively few life stressors.

In short, schizophrenia is related to several kinds of biological and situational factors. It is increasingly clear, then, that no single factor but rather a combination of interrelated variables produces schizophrenia (Opler et al., 2008; Balter, 2017; Aas et al., 2018).

> **Study Alert**
> Remember that the multiple causes of schizophrenia include biological and environmental factors.

Personality Disorders

I had always wanted lots of things; as a child I can remember wanting a bullet that a friend of mine had brought in to show the class. I took it and put it into my school bag and when my friend noticed it was missing, I was the one who stayed after school with him and searched the room, and I was the one who sat with him and bitched about the other kids and how one of them took his bullet. I even went home with him to help him break the news to his uncle, who had brought it home from the war for him.

But that was petty compared with the stuff I did later. I wanted a Ph.D. very badly, but I didn't want to work very hard–just enough to get by. I never did the experiments I reported; hell, I was smart enough to make up the results. I knew enough about statistics to make anything look plausible. I got my master's degree without even spending one hour in a laboratory. I mean, the professors believed anything. I'd stay out all night drinking and being with my friends, and the next day I'd get in just before them and tell 'em I'd been in the lab all night. They'd actually feel sorry for me. (Duke & Nowicki, 1979)

This excerpt provides a graphic first-person account of a person with a personality disorder. A **personality disorder** is characterized by a set of inflexible, maladaptive behavior patterns that keep a person from functioning appropriately in society.

Unlike the other disorders we have discussed, people with personality disorders typically have little sense of personal distress. Moreover, people with personality disorders frequently lead seemingly normal lives. However, just below the surface lies a set of inflexible, maladaptive personality traits that prevent them from functioning effectively as members of society (Clarkin & Lenzenweger, 2004; Friedman, Oltmanns, & Turkheimer, 2007; Anderson et al., 2015).

The best-known type of personality disorder, illustrated by the case above, is the **antisocial personality disorder** (sometimes referred to as a sociopathic personality). Individuals with this disturbance show no regard for the moral and ethical rules of society or the rights of others. Although they can appear quite intelligent and likable (at least at first), upon closer examination they turn out to be manipulative and

personality disorder A disorder characterized by a set of inflexible, maladaptive behavior patterns that keep a person from functioning appropriately in society. (Module 47)

antisocial personality disorder A disorder in which individuals show no regard for the moral and ethical rules of society or the rights of others. (Module 47) deceptive. Moreover, they lack any guilt or anxiety about their wrongdoing. When those with antisocial personality disorder behave in a way that injures someone else, they understand intellectually that they have caused harm but feel no remorse (Bateman, 2011; Rosenström et al., 2017; Velotti et al., 2019).

People with antisocial personality disorder are often impulsive and lack the ability to withstand frustration. They can be extremely manipulative. They also may have excellent social skills; they can be charming, engaging, and highly persuasive. Some of the best con artists have antisocial personalities.

What causes such an unusual constellation of problem behaviors? A variety of factors have been suggested ranging from an inability to experience emotions appropriately to problems in family relationships. For example, in many cases of antisocial behavior, the individual has come from a home in which a parent has died or left or one in which there is a lack of affection, a lack of consistency in discipline, or outright rejection. Other explanations concentrate on sociocultural factors because an unusually high proportion of people with antisocial personalities come from lower socioeconomic groups. Still, no one has been able to pinpoint the specific causes of antisocial personalities, and it is likely that some combination of factors is responsible (Rosenstein & Horowitz, 1996; Costa & Widiger, 2002; Chen et al., 2011).

People with **borderline personality disorder** have problems regulating emotions and thoughts, display impulsive and reckless behavior, and have unstable relationships with others. They also have difficulty in developing a clear understanding of who they are. As a consequence, they tend to rely on relationships with others to define their identity. The problem with this strategy is that even minor rejection by others is devastating to those with borderline personality disorder. Furthermore, they generally distrust others and have difficulty controlling their anger. Their emotional volatility leads to impulsive and self-destructive behavior.

Individuals with borderline personality disorder often feel empty and alone, and they have difficulty cooperating with others. They may form intense, sudden, one-sided relationships in which they demand the attention of another person and then feel angry when they don't receive it. One reason for this behavior is that they may have a background in which others discounted or criticized their emotional reactions, and they may not have learned to regulate their emotions effectively (King-Casas et al., 2008; Hopwood et al., 2009; Samuel et al., 2013).

The narcissistic personality disorder is another type of personality disorder. The **narcissistic personality disorder** is characterized by an exaggerated sense of self-importance. Those with the disorder expect special treatment from others while also disregarding others' feelings, showing little or no sense of empathy for them.

There are several other categories of personality disorder that range in severity from individuals who may simply be regarded by others as eccentric, obnoxious, or difficult to people who act in a manner that is criminal and dangerous to others. Although they are not out of touch with reality like people with schizophrenia, people with personality disorders often lead lives that put them on the fringes of society (Trull & Widiger, 2003; Wright et al., 2016).

> ## Study Alert
> Unlike most psychological disorders, personality disorders produce little or no personal distress.

borderline personality disorder
A disorder characterized by problems regulating emotions and thoughts, displaying impulsive and reckless behavior, and having unstable relationships with others. (Module 47)

narcissistic personality disorder A personality disturbance characterized by an exaggerated sense of self-importance. (Module 47)

From the perspective of...

A Social Worker Because people with personality disorders often appear from the outside to function well in society, should you try to address their problems?

Sam Edwards/OJO Images/age fotostock

Disorders That Impact Childhood

We typically view childhood as a time of innocence and relative freedom from stress. In reality, though, almost 20% of children and 40% of adolescents experience significant emotional or behavioral disorders (Kafali et al., 2019; Nolen-Hoeksema, 2020).

For example, although major depression is more prevalent in adults, around 2.5% of children and more than 8% of adolescents suffer from the disorder. In fact, by the time they reach age 20, 15–20% of children and adolescents will experience an episode of major depression. Among adolescents, 14.4% will have had an episode of major depression in the previous year. Other disorders change in prevalence with increasing age; see Figure 8 (Frodl et al., 2017; Substance Abuse and Mental Health Services Administration, 2019).

Children do not always display depression in the same way adults do. Rather than showing the expression of profound sadness or hopelessness, childhood depression may produce the expression of exaggerated fears, clinginess, or avoidance of everyday activities. In older children, the symptoms may be sulking, school problems, and even acts of delinquency (Seroczynski, Jacquez, & Cole, 2003; Blain-Arcaro & Vaillancourt, 2019).

A considerably more common childhood disorder is **attention-deficit hyperactivity disorder, or ADHD,** a disorder marked by inattention, impulsiveness, a low tolerance for frustration, and generally a great deal of inappropriate activity. Although all children show such behavior some of the time, it is so common in children diagnosed with ADHD that it interferes with their everyday functioning (Barkley, Knouse, & Murphy, 2011; Walton, Murphy, & Bartram, 2017).

ADHD is surprisingly widespread, with estimates ranging between 3–5% of the school-age population—or some 3.5 million children under the age of 18 in the United States. Children diagnosed with the disorder are often exhausting to parents and teachers, and even their peers find them difficult to deal with.

The cause of ADHD is not known, although most experts feel that it is produced by dysfunctions in the nervous system. For example, one theory suggests that unusually low levels of arousal in the central nervous system cause ADHD. To compensate, children with ADHD seek out stimulation to increase arousal. Still, such theories are speculative. Furthermore, because many children occasionally show behaviors characteristic of ADHD, it often is misdiagnosed or in some cases overdiagnosed. Only the

attention-deficit hyperactivity disorder (ADHD) A disorder marked by inattention, impulsiveness, a low tolerance for frustration, and a great deal of inappropriate activity. (Module 47)

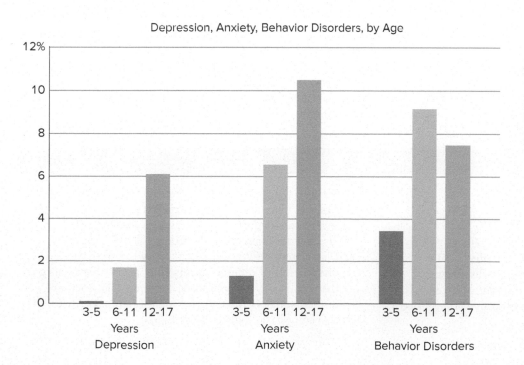

FIGURE 8. Various disorders change in prevalence with increasing age.

Sources: Centers for Disease Control and Prevention. (2019). Facts about mental disorders in U.S. children. Downloaded from https://www.cdc.gov/childrensmentalhealth/data.html; U.S. Department of Health and Human Services (2019, April 19). Data and Statistics on Children's Mental Health. https://www.cdc.gov/childrensmentalhealth/data.html, September 11, 2019.

frequency and persistence of the symptoms of ADHD allow for a correct diagnosis, which only a trained professional can do (Barkley, 2000; Sciutto & Eisenberg, 2007; Ketisch & Jones, 2013).

autism spectrum disorder A severe developmental disability that impairs children's ability to communicate and relate to others. (Module 47)

Autism spectrum disorder, a severe developmental disability that impairs one's ability to communicate and relate to others, is another disorder that usually appears in the first 3 years and typically continues throughout life. Children with autism have difficulties in both verbal and nonverbal communication, and they may avoid social contact. About 1 in 88 children are now thought to have the disorder, and its prevalence has risen significantly in the last decade. Whether the increase is the result of an actual rise in the incidence of autism or is due to better reporting is a question of intense debate among researchers (Rice, 2009; Neal, Matson, & Belva, 2013).

One variant of autism spectrum disorder is *Asperger's syndrome.* People who experience Aspberger's syndrome often function at a high level, though they may experience emotions atypically and may have difficulty with everyday social interactions. One example of someone with Asperger's syndrome is climate activist Greta Thunberg.

In the most severe cases of autism spectrum disorder, children display self-injurious behavior and must wear protective head gear.
Tony Freeman/PhotoEdit

Other Disorders

It's important to keep in mind that the various forms of psychological disorders described in DSM-5 cover much more ground than we have been able to discuss in this module. Some relate to topics considered in other chapters. For example, *psychoactive substance use disorder* relates to problems that arise from the use and abuse of drugs. Furthermore, *alcohol use disorders* are among the most serious and widespread problems. Both psychoactive substance use disorder and alcohol use disorder co-occur with many other psychological disorders, such as mood disorders, trauma- and stress-or-related disorders, and schizophrenia, which complicate treatment considerably (Salgado, Quinlan, & Zlotnick, 2007).

Another widespread problem is *eating disorders.* They include such disorders as *anorexia nervosa* and *bulimia,* which we considered in the chapter on motivation and emotion, as well as *binge-eating disorder,* characterized by binge eating without behaviors designed to prevent weight gain. Finally, *sexual disorders,* in which one's sexual activity is unsatisfactory, are another important class of problems. They include *sexual desire disorders, sexual arousal disorders,* and *paraphilic disorders,* atypical sexual activities that may include nonhuman objects or nonconsenting partners.

Another important class of disorders is *neurocognitive disorders,* problems with a biological cause that affect thinking and behavior. We considered some of them earlier, such as Alzheimer's disease and some types of developmental disabilities that are fully the consequence of biological issues. Furthermore, there are many other disorders that we have not mentioned at all, and each of the categories of disorder we have discussed can be divided into several subcategories (Pratt et al., 2003; Reijonen et al., 2003; American Psychiatric Association, 2013).

RECAP/EVALUATE/RETHINK

RECAP

LO 47-1 What are the major psychological disorders?

- Anxiety disorders are present when a person experiences so much anxiety that it affects daily functioning. Specific types of anxiety disorders include phobic disorder, panic disorder, and generalized anxiety disorder. Also related is obsessive-compulsive disorder.

- Somatic symptom disorders are psychological difficulties that take in a physical (somatic) form but for which there is no medical cause. Examples are illness anxiety disorder and conversion disorders.

- Dissociative disorders are marked by the separation, or dissociation, of different facets of a person's personality that are usually integrated. Major kinds of dissociative disorders include dissociative identity disorder, dissociative amnesia, and dissociative fugue.

- Mood disorders are characterized by emotional states of depression or euphoria so strong that they intrude on everyday living. They include major depression and bipolar disorder.
- Schizophrenia is one of the more severe forms of mental illness. Symptoms of schizophrenia include declines in functioning, thought and language disturbances, perceptual disorders, emotional disturbance, and withdrawal from others.
- Strong evidence links schizophrenia to genetic, biochemical, and environmental factors. According to the predisposition explanation of schizophrenia, an interaction among various factors produces the disorder.
- People with personality disorders experience little or no personal distress, but they do suffer from an inability to function as normal members of society. These disorders include antisocial personality disorder, borderline personality disorder, and narcissistic personality disorder.
- Childhood disorders include major depression, attention-deficit hyperactivity disorder (ADHD), and autism spectrum disorder.

EVALUATE

1. Kathy is terrified of elevators. She could be suffering from a(n)
   a. Obsessive-compulsive disorder
   b. Phobic disorder
   c. Panic disorder
   d. Generalized anxiety disorder
2. Carmen described an incident in which her anxiety suddenly rose to a peak and she felt a sense of impending doom. Carmen experienced a(n) _____ _____

3. Troubling thoughts that persist for weeks or months are known as
   a. Obsessions
   b. Compulsions
   c. Rituals
   d. Panic attacks
4. An overpowering urge to carry out a strange ritual is called a(n) _____
5. The separation of the personality, which provides escape from stressful situations, is the key factor in _____ disorders.
6. States of extreme euphoria and energy paired with severe depression characterize _____ disorder.
7. _____ schizophrenia is characterized by symptoms that are sudden and of easily identifiable onset; _____ schizophrenia develops gradually over a person's life span.
8. The _____ states that schizophrenia may be caused by an excess of certain neurotransmitters in the brain

RETHINK

1. What cultural factors might contribute to the rate of anxiety disorders found in a culture? How might the experience of anxiety differ among people of different cultures?
2. Personality disorders are often not apparent to others, and many people with these problems seem to live basically normal lives and are not a threat to others. Because these people can function well in society, why should they be considered psychologically disordered?

Answers to Evaluate Questions

1. b; 2. panic attack; 3. a; 4. compulsion; 5. dissociative; 6. bipolar; 7. Reactive, process; 8. dopamine hypothesis

KEY TERMS

anxiety disorder	somatic symptom disorders	mood disorder	borderline personality disorder
specific phobias	illness anxiety disorder	major depressive disorder	narcissistic personality disorder
panic disorder	conversion disorder	mania	attention-deficit
generalized anxiety disorder	dissociative disorders	bipolar disorder	hyperactivity disorder (ADHD)
obsessive-compulsive disorder (OCD)	dissociative identity disorder (DID)	schizophrenia	autism spectrum disorder
obsession	dissociative amnesia	personality disorder	
compulsion	dissociative fugue	antisocial personality disorder	

Module 48
Psychological Disorders in Perspective

LEARNING OUTCOMES

LO 48-1 How prevalent are psychological disorders?

LO 48-2 What indicators signal a need for the help of a mental health practitioner?

How common are the kinds of psychological disorders we've been discussing? Here's one answer: One out of two people in the United States is likely to experience a psychological disorder at some point in their lives.

That's the conclusion drawn from the most comprehensive study on the prevalence of psychological disorders conducted. In that study, researchers conducted face-to-face interviews with more than 8,000 men and women between the ages of 15 and 54. The sample was designed to be representative of the population of the United States.

According to results of the study, 48% of those interviewed had experienced a disorder at some point in their lives. In addition, 30% experienced a disorder in any particular year. Furthermore, many people experience comorbidity. *Cormorbidity* is the appearance of multiple, simultaneous psychological disorders in the same person (Welkowitz et al., 2000; Merikangas et al., 2007; Kessler & Wang, 2008).

The most common disorder reported in the study was depression. Some 17% of those surveyed reported at least one major episode. Ten percent had suffered from depression during the current year. The next most common disorder was alcohol dependence, which occurred at a lifetime incidence rate of 14%. In addition, 7% of those interviewed had experienced alcohol dependence in the previous year. Other frequently occurring psychological disorders were drug dependence, disorders involving panic (such as an overwhelming fear of talking to strangers or terror of heights), and posttraumatic stress disorder.

Although some researchers think the estimates of severe disorders may be too high (Narrow et al., 2002), the national findings are consistent with studies of college students and their psychological difficulties. For example, in one study of the students who visited college mental health centers, almost a quarter had anxiety, and around 20% were depressed (see Figure 1) (Center for Collegiate Mental Health, 2019).

! **Study Alert**
Remember that the incidence of various psychological disorders in the general population is surprisingly high, particularly in terms of depression and alcohol dependence.

From the perspective of...

A College Counselor What indicators might be most important in determining whether a college student is experiencing a psychological disorder?

Chris Ryan/OJO Images/age fotostock

The significant level of psychological disorders is a problem not only in the United States; according to the World Health Organization, mental health difficulties are a global concern. Globally, 970 million people have some sort of psychological or substance use disorder, which amounts to 13% of the world's population (see Figure 2; Ritchie & Roser, 2018).

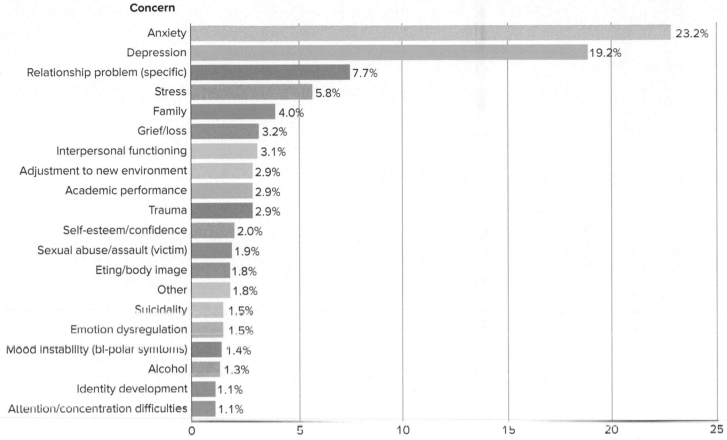

Concern

Concern	Percentage
Anxiety	23.2%
Depression	19.2%
Relationship problem (specific)	7.7%
Stress	5.8%
Family	4.0%
Grief/loss	3.2%
Interpersonal functioning	3.1%
Adjustment to new environment	2.9%
Academic performance	2.9%
Trauma	2.9%
Self-esteem/confidence	2.0%
Sexual abuse/assault (victim)	1.9%
Eting/body image	1.8%
Other	1.8%
Suicidality	1.5%
Emotion dysregulation	1.5%
Mood Instability (bi-polar symtoms)	1.4%
Alcohol	1.3%
Identity development	1.1%
Attention/concentration difficulties	1.1%

FIGURE 1 These are the top problems of students visiting college counseling center.s Would you have predicted this pattern of psychological difficulties?

Source: Adapted from Center for Collegiate Mental Health. (2019, January). 2018 Annual Report (Publication no. STA 19-180), p. 17.

Furthermore, economic disparities affect treatment; more affluent people with mild disorders receive more and better treatment than do poor people who have more severe disorders. In fact, psychological disorders make up 14% of global illness, but 90% of people in developing countries receive no care at all for their disorders (Jacob et al., 2007; Wang et al., 2007; Scott et al., 2018).

Also, keep in mind that the incidence of specific disorders varies significantly in other cultures. For instance, cross-cultural surveys show that the incidence of major depression varies significantly from one culture to another. The probability of having at least one episode of depression is only 1.5% in Taiwan and 2.9% in Korea, compared with 11.6% in New Zealand and 16.4% in France. Such notable differences underscore the importance of considering the cultural context of psychological disorders (Weissman et al., 1997; Tseng, 2003; De Los Reyes et al., 2019).

The Social and Cultural Context of Psychological Disorders

In considering the nature of the psychological disorders described in DSM-5, it's important to keep in mind that the disorders that were included in the manual are a reflection of Western culture at the start of the 21st century. The classification system provides a snapshot of how its authors viewed mental disorder when it was published. In fact, the development of the most recent version of the DSM was a source of great debate, which in part reflects issues that divide society.

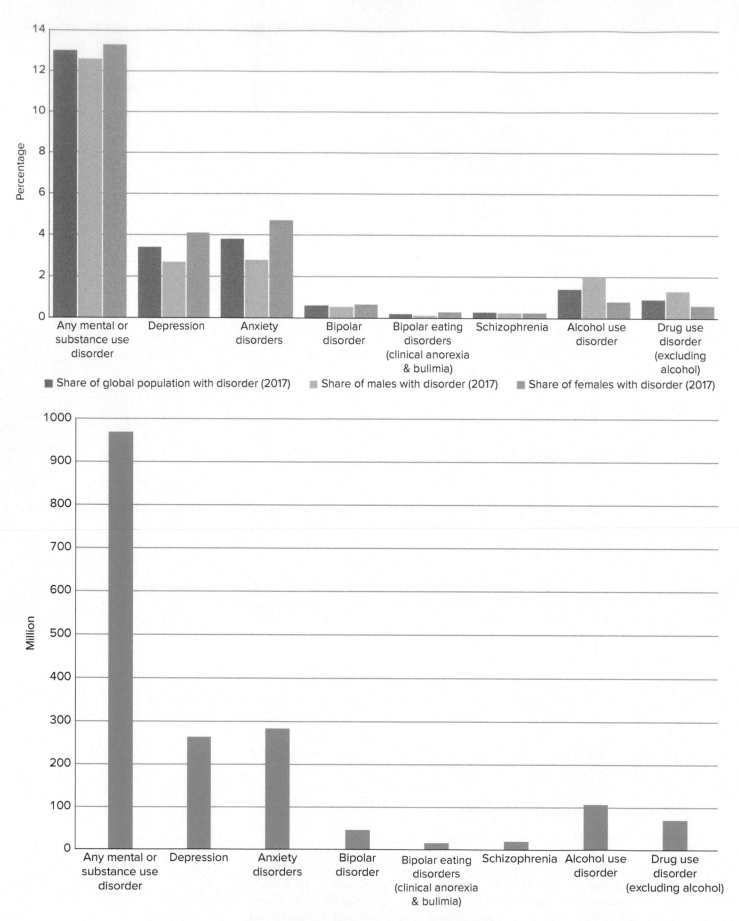

FIGURE 2 This summary shows the distribution of psychological and substance use disorders across the globe.

One specific, newly classified disorder that was added to DSM-5 and that has caused controversy is known as disruptive mood dysregulation disorder. This particular diagnosis is characterized by temperamental outbursts grossly out of proportion to the situation, both verbally and physically, in children between the ages of 6 and 18. Some practitioners argue these symptoms simply define a child having a temper tantrum rather than a disorder (Frances, 2013; Bruno et al., 2019; Moore et al., 2019).

Similarly, someone who overeats 12 times in 3 months can be considered to be suffering from the new classification of binge-eating disorder, which seems to some critics to be overly inclusive. Finally, hoarding behavior is now placed in its own category of psychological disorder. Some critics, however, suggest that the inclusion of hoarding as a category is more a reflection of the rise of reality television shows focusing on hoarding rather than a distinct category of psychological disturbance (Hudson et al., 2012; Racine et al., 2017; Moulding et al., 2017).

The social and cultural environment may also play a role in the mass shootings that plague the United States. According to some politicians, mass murderers are severely psychologically disordered, while others claim that the easy availability of guns is the root of the problem.

The scientific data are clear, though: While a small percentage of mass murderers do have some diagnosable disorder, the majority have no such history. Instead, they are likely to feel disgruntled, aggrieved, and humiliated about circumstances in their lives. They ultimately turn to violence when triggered by some threatening event rather than by a mental disorder, and easy access to weapons permits a violent response. In support of this reasoning, we can look to the rates of psychological disturbance across the world and the rates of gun violence. What we find is that although rates of psychological disturbance are similar globally, in countries where access to guns is more restricted, we don't find the same level of violence as we do in the United States. Such conclusions are politically controversial, however, and debates about the source of mass violence will likely continue (Budenz et al., 2018; Leander et al., 2019; Yelderman et al., 2019).

Such controversies underline the fact that our understanding of abnormal behavior reflects the society and culture in which we live. Future revisions of DSM may include a different catalog of disorders. Even now, other cultures might include a list of disorders that differ significantly from the list that appears in the current DSM, as we discuss next.

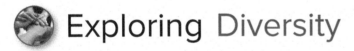 Exploring Diversity

DSM and Culture—and the Culture of DSM

To most people raised in the United States, a person who hears voices of the recently deceased is probably a victim of a psychological disturbance. Yet some Plains Indians routinely hear the voices of the dead calling to them from the afterlife, and in their culture, that's considered perfectly normal.

The voices Plains Indians hear are only one example of the role of culture in determining what behavior should be labeled as "abnormal." In fact, among all the major adult disorders included in the DSM categorization, just a minority are found across all cultures of the world. Most others only are prevalent in North America and Western Europe (Jacob, 2014; Allen & Becker, 2019; Langa & Gone, 2019).

For instance, take anorexia nervosa, the disorder in which people become obsessed with their weight and sometimes stop eating, ultimately starving to death in the process. It turns out that anorexia nervosa occurs most frequently in cultures that hold the societal standard that slender female bodies are the most desirable. In most of the world, where such a standard does not exist, anorexia nervosa is rare. Furthermore, the disorder may appear in specific ways in a particular culture. For instance, in Hong Kong, symptoms of one form of anorexia relate to complaints of bloated stomachs, rather than fears of becoming fat (Watters, 2010; Munro, Randell, & Lawrie, 2017; Fadus et al., 2019).

Similarly, dissociative identity (multiple personality) disorder makes sense as a problem only in societies in which a sense of self is fairly concrete. In India, the self is based more on external factors that are relatively independent of the person. There, when an individual displays symptoms of what people in a Western society would call dissociative identity disorder, Indians assume that that person is possessed either by demons (which they view as a malady) or by gods (which does not require treatment).

Furthermore, even though disorders such as schizophrenia are found throughout the world, cultural factors influence the specific symptoms of the disorder. Hence, catatonic schizophrenia, in which unmoving patients appear to be frozen in the same position (sometimes for days), is rare in North America and Western Europe. In contrast, in India, 80% of those with schizophrenia are catatonic.

Other cultures have disorders that do not appear in the West. For example, in Malaysia, a behavior called *amok* is characterized by a wild outburst in which a usually quiet and withdrawn person kills or severely injures another. *Koro* is a condition found in Southeast Asian males who develop an intense panic that their penis is about to withdraw irretrievably into their abdomens. Finally, *ataque de nervios* is a disorder found most often among Latinos from the Caribbean. It is characterized by trembling, crying, uncontrollable screams, and incidents of verbal or physical aggression (Cohen, Slomkowski, & Robins, 1999; Adams & Dzokoto, 2007; Ebigbo, Lekwas, & Chukwunenyem, 2015).

Explanations for and experiences of psychological disorders also differ among cultures. For example, in China, psychological disorders are commonly viewed as weaknesses of the heart, a concept that derives from thousands of years of traditional Chinese medicine. Chinese people are more likely than people in Western cultures to express their emotional anguish in terms of physical symptoms such as heart pain, "heart panic," or "heart vexed." Similarly, Nigerians' acute anxiety may be accompanied by the sensation of insects crawling under their skin, a condition known as *odi ori* (Lee, Kleinman, & Kleinman, 2007; Watters, 2010; McRobbie, 2018).

In sum, we should not assume that the DSM provides the final word on psychological disorders. The disorders it includes are very much a creation and function of Western cultures at a particular moment in time, and its categories should not be seen as universally applicable (Tseng, 2003).

BECOMING AN INFORMED CONSUMER
of Psychology

Deciding When You Need Help

After you've considered the range and variety of psychological disturbances that can afflict people, you may begin to feel that you suffer from one (or more) of the problems we have discussed. In fact, this perception has a name: *medical student's disease*. Although in this case it might more aptly be labeled *psychology student's disease,* the basic symptoms are the same: feeling that you suffer from the same sorts of problems you are studying.

Most often, of course, your concerns will be unwarranted. As we have discussed, the differences between normal and abnormal behavior are often so fuzzy that it is easy to jump to the conclusion that you might have the same symptoms that are involved in serious forms of mental disturbance.

Before coming to such a conclusion, though, keep in mind that from time to time, we all experience a wide range of emotions, and it is not unusual to feel deeply unhappy, fantasize about bizarre situations, or feel anxiety about life's circumstances. It is the persistence, depth, and consistency of such behavior that set normal reactions apart from abnormal ones. If you have not previously had serious doubts about the normality of your behavior, it is unlikely that reading about others' psychological disorders will prompt you to re-evaluate your earlier conclusion.

On the other hand, many people do have problems that merit concern, and in such cases, it is important to consider the possibility that professional help is warranted. The following list of symptoms can serve as a guideline to help you determine whether outside intervention might be useful (American Psychiatric Association, 2018; American Psychological Association, 2019).

- Long-term feelings of distress that interfere with your sense of well-being, competence, and ability to function effectively in daily activities
- Occasions in which you experience overwhelmingly high stress accompanied by feelings of inability to cope with the situation
- Prolonged depression or feelings of hopelessness, especially when they do not have any clear cause
- Withdrawal from others
- Thoughts of inflicting harm on oneself or suicide
- A chronic physical problem for which no physical cause can be determined
- A fear or phobia that prevents you from engaging in everyday activities
- Feelings that other people are out to get you or are talking about and plotting against you
- Inability to interact effectively with others, preventing the development of friendships and loving relationships
- Alcohol or drug abuse
- Changes in sleeping, eating, and personal hygiene habits.

This list offers a rough set of guidelines for determining when the normal problems of everyday living have escalated beyond your ability to deal with them by yourself. In such situations, the *least* reasonable approach would be to pore over the psychological disorders we have discussed in an attempt at self-diagnosis. A more reasonable strategy is to consider seeking professional help.

RECAP/EVALUATE/RETHINK

RECAP

LO 48-1 How prevalent are psychological disorders?

- About half the people in the United States are likely to experience a psychological disorder at some point in their lives; 30% experience a disorder in any specific year.

LO 48-2 What indicators signal a need for the help of a mental health practitioner?

- The signals that indicate a need for professional help include long-term feelings of psychological distress, feelings of inability to cope with stress, withdrawal from other people, thoughts of inflicting harm on oneself or suicide, prolonged feelings of hopelessness, chronic physical problems with no apparent causes, phobias and compulsions, paranoia, and an inability to interact with others.

EVALUATE

1. The latest version of DSM is considered to be the definitive guide to defining psychological disorders. True or false?
2. Match the disorder with the culture in which it is most common:

   1. *Amok*   a. India
   2. Anorexia nervosa   b. Malaysia
   3. *Ataque de nervios*   c. United States
   4. Catatonic schizophrenia   d. Caribbean

RETHINK

1. Why is inclusion in DSM-5 of disorders such as hoarding behavior so controversial and political? What disadvantages does inclusion bring? Does inclusion bring any benefits?

2. What societal changes would have to occur for psychological disorders to be regarded as the equivalent of appendicitis or another treatable physical disorder?

Do you think a person who has been treated for a psychological disorder could become president of the United States? Should such a person become president?

Answers to Evaluate Questions

1. False; the development of the latest version of DSM was a source of great controversy, in part reflecting issues that divide society; 2. 1-b, 2-c, 3-d, 4-a

LOOKING *Back*

EPILOGUE

We've discussed some of the many types of psychological disorders to which people are prone, noted the difficulty psychologists and physicians have in clearly differentiating normal from abnormal behavior, and looked at some of the approaches mental health professionals have taken to explain and treat psychological disorders. We considered today's most commonly used classification scheme, categorized in DSM-5, and examined some of the more prevalent forms of psychological disorders. To gain a perspective on the topic of psychological disorders, we discussed the surprisingly broad incidence of psychological disorders in U.S. society and the cultural nature of such disorders.

Turn back to the prologue, which described the case of Chris Coles. Using the knowledge you've gained about psychological disorders, consider the following questions.

1. How can we tell that Chris Coles's behavior is abnormal?
2. In what ways does his behavior fit the definition of schizophrenia? If you were his physician, what other symptoms would you watch for?
3. How would each perspective on abnormality explain Coles's condition?
4. Which perspective on abnormality do you think gives the best insight into the origin of Coles's condition? Why do you think so?

VISUAL SUMMARY 15 Psychological Disorders

MODULE 46 Normal Versus Abnormal: Making the Distinction

Defining Abnormality

- Deviation from average behavior
- Deviation from ideal behavior
- Sense of personal discomfort
- Inability to function effectively
- Legal concept

Perspectives on Abnormality

Perspectives on Psychological Disorders

Perspective	Description	Possible Application of Perspective to Chris' Case
Medical	Assumes that physiological causes are at the root of psychological disorders	Examine Chris for medical problems, such as brain tumor, chemical imbalance in the brain, or disease
Psychoanalytic	Argues that psychological disorders stem from childhood conflicts	Seek out information about Chris' past, considering possible childhood conflicts
Behavioral	Assumes that abnormal behaviors are learned responses	Concentrate on rewards and punishments for Chris' behavior, and identify environmental stimuli that reinforce his behavior
Cognitive	Assumes that cognitions (people's thoughts and beliefs) are central to psychological disorders	Focus on Chris' perceptions of self and his environment
Humanistic	Emphasizes people's responsibility for their own behavior and the need to self-actualize	Consider Chris' behavior in terms of his choices and efforts to reach his potential
Sociocultural	Assumes that behavior is shaped by family, society, and culture	Focus on how societal demands contributed to Chris' disorder

Classifying Abnormal Behavior: DSM 5 attempts to provide comprehensive and relatively precise definitions for more than 200 disorders

MODULE 47 Major Psychological Disorders

Anxiety Disorders: Anxiety without external justification

- Phobic disorder
- Panic disorder
- Generalized anxiety disorder
- Causes of anxiety disorders

Obsessive-Compulsive Disorder

Somatic Symptom Disorders: Psychological difficulties that take on a physical form with no medical cause

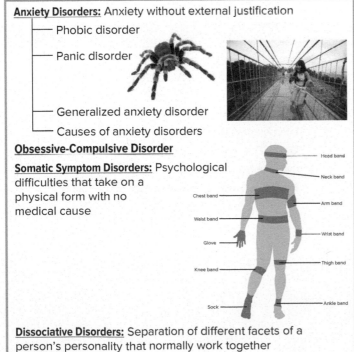

Dissociative Disorders: Separation of different facets of a person's personality that normally work together

Mood Disorders: Disturbances in emotional experience

- Major depressive disorder
- Mania and bipolar disorder
- Causes of mood disorders
    - Genetics
    - Psychological: feelings of loss or anger
    - Behavioral: stress
    - Cognitive: learned helplessness and no hope

Schizophrenia Spectrum: A class of disorders in which distortion of reality occurs

- Decline from a previous level of functioning
- Disturbances of thought and language
- Delusions
- Hallucinations and perceptual disorders
- Emotional disturbances

Personality Disorders: A set of inflexible, maladaptive behavior patterns

- Antisocial personality disorder
- Borderline personality disorder
- Narcissistic personality disorder

Childhood Disorders: Start during childhood or adolescence

- Attention-deficit hyperactivity disorder
- Autism spectrum disorder

MODULE 48 Psychological Disorders in Perspective

Social and Cultural Context: The significant level of psychological disorders is a problem not only in the United States; according to the World Health Organization, mental health difficulties are a global concern.

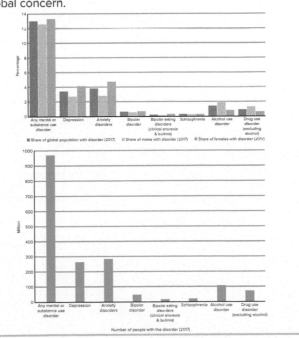

(Module 46) top: Brett Coomer/Pool Houston Chronicle/AP Images; bottom: H.S. Photos/Alamy Stock Photo; (Module 47) Imagine China/Newscom; (Module 48) Source: Ritchie, H., & Roser, M. (2018, April). Mental health. Our World in Data.

SeventyFour/Shutterstock

CHAPTER 16
Treatment of Psychological Disorders

LEARNING OUTCOMES FOR CHAPTER 16

LO 51-1 How are drug, electroconvulsive, and psychosurgical techniques used today in the treatment of psychological disorders?

PROLOGUE *PSYCHEDELIC THERAPY*

Michael knew this would not be any ordinary therapy session. He knew this in part because of preparation sessions. At these sessions, his therapist had told him what to expect and had asked him to specify an intention—that is, what he wanted to accomplish. Michael wanted to quit smoking. The therapist also encouraged Michael to put his full trust in the therapy process and to let it take him wherever it might lead.

"Even if you feel like you might be losing your mind, going crazy, dissolving into nothingness, or dying—just go with it. Go with it. Let it happen. Trust the experience," advised his therapist.

At the main session, Michael discovered a treatment room that was inviting and comforting—designed to give him a sense of safety and security. He sat quietly with his eyes closed, as instructed, while his therapist recited a traditional Native American prayer.

And here's where Michael's therapy departed radically from traditional therapy: The therapist handed him a psilocybin mushroom, designed to produce an altered state of consciousness. Michael swallowed it.

For the next several hours, Michael's therapist observed him carefully, acting as a guide and keeping him safe during his psychedelic experience. The hope was that Michael's session would break down his well-ingrained worldview, giving him new perspectives on the world and himself, and making the way for new behavioral patterns—ones that didn't include smoking.

The next day, after he had a chance to rest and recover, Michael and his therapist would meet again for a debriefing session. At that meeting, they would review Michael's experience, and they would work together to find the enduring meaning in it (Pollan, 2018).

LOOKING *Ahead*

Psychedelic therapy is one of the newest—and most controversial—ways in which people experiencing psychological disorders receive treatment. Although particularly radical, this treatment shares a common objective with more traditional forms of therapy: to enable individuals to achieve richer, more meaningful, and more fulfilling lives.

Approaches to treating psychological disorders fall into two main categories: psychologically based and biologically based therapies. **Psychotherapy** is psychologically based treatment in which a trained professional—a therapist—uses psychological techniques to help someone overcome psychological difficulties and disorders, resolve problems in living, or bring about personal growth. The goal of psychotherapy is to produce lasting psychological change in a person (called a *client* or *patient*) through discussions and interactions with the therapist. In contrast, **biomedical therapy** is biologically based and relies on drugs and medical procedures to improve psychological functioning.

As we describe the various approaches to therapy, keep in mind that although the distinctions may seem clear-cut, the classifications and procedures overlap a good deal. In fact, many therapists today take an *eclectic approach* to therapy, which means they use a variety of methods with an individual patient. Assuming that psychological as well as biological processes often produce psychological disorders, eclectic therapists may draw from several perspectives simultaneously to address the psychological as well as the biological aspects of a person's problems.

psychotherapy Psychologically based treatment in which a trained professional—a therapist—uses psychological techniques to help a person overcome psychological difficulties and disorders, resolve problems in living, or bring about personal growth. (Module 49)

biomedical therapy Biologically based therapy that relies on drugs and other medical procedures to improve psychological functioning. (Module 49)

Module 49
Psychotherapy: Psychodynamic, Behavioral, and Cognitive Approaches to Treatment

LEARNING OUTCOMES

LO 49-1 What are the goals of psychologically based and biologically based treatment approaches?

LO 49-2 What are the psychodynamic, behavioral, and cognitive approaches to treatment?

There are are hundreds of varieties of psychotherapy. They range from the truly experimental (such as the guided use of psychedelic drugs described in the prologue) to tried-and-true methods that have a long and proven history of use and effectiveness.

Although the methods are diverse, all psychological approaches have a common perspective: They seek to solve psychological problems by modifying people's behavior and helping them obtain a better understanding of themselves and their past, present, and future.

In light of the variety of psychological approaches, it is not surprising that the people who provide therapy vary considerably in educational background and training (see Figure 1). Many have doctoral degrees in psychology, having attended graduate school, learned clinical and research techniques, and held an internship in a facility that treats people with psychological disorders. But therapy is also provided by people in fields allied with psychology, such as psychiatrists (who have a medical degree with a specialization in psychological disorders) and social workers (who have a master's degree and have specialized in psychological disorders).

Depending on the kind of problem a person is experiencing, certain types of therapists may be more appropriate than others. For example, a person who is suffering

FIGURE 1 A variety of professionals provide therapy and counseling. Each could be expected to give helpful advice and direction. However, the nature of the problem a person is experiencing may make one or another therapist more appropriate.

Getting Help from the Right Person
Clinical Psychologists Psychologists with a PhD or PsyD with about 5 years of training and who have also completed a postgraduate internship. They specialize in assessment and treatment of psychological difficulties, providing psychotherapy and, in some U.S. states, can prescribe drugs.
Counseling Psychologists Psychologists with a PhD or EdD who typically treat day-to-day adjustment problems, often in a university mental health clinic
Psychiatrists MDs with postgraduate training in psychological disorders. Because they can prescribe medication, they often treat the most severe disorders.
Psychoanalysts Either MDs or psychologists who specialize in psychoanalysis, the treatment technique first developed by Freud
Licensed Professional Counselors or Clinical Mental Health Counselors Professionals with a master's degree who provide therapy to individuals, couples, and families and who hold a national or state certification
Clinical or Psychiatric Social Workers Professionals with a master's degree and specialized training who may provide therapy, usually regarding common family and personal problems

from a severe disturbance and who has lost touch with reality may typically require some sort of biologically based drug therapy. In that case, a psychiatrist—who has trained as a physician—might be the professional of choice. In contrast, those suffering from milder disorders, such as difficulty adjusting to the death of a family member, have a broader array of choices, including other types listed in Figure 1.

Regardless of their specific training, all psychotherapists employ one of four major approaches to therapy that we'll consider next: psychodynamic, behavioral, cognitive, and humanistic treatment approaches. These approaches grow out of the perspectives of personality and psychological disorders developed by psychologists.

Psychodynamic Approaches to Therapy

Psychodynamic therapy seeks to bring unresolved past conflicts and unacceptable impulses from the unconscious into the conscious, where patients may deal with the problems more effectively. Although psychodynamic approaches originally derived from Freud's psychoanalytic theories of personality, today they encompass a wider range of therapies. The common assumptions behind psychodynamic therapies are that unconscious forces affect our behavior and that the goal of therapy is to try to identify and control them.

Psychodynamic approaches hold that people employ *defense mechanisms*, psychological strategies to protect themselves from unacceptable unconscious impulses. The most common defense mechanism is *repression*, which pushes threatening and unpleasant thoughts and impulses back into the unconscious. However, because people cannot completely bury their unacceptable thoughts and impulses, anxiety associated with them can produce abnormal behavior.

How do we rid ourselves of the anxiety produced by unconscious, unwanted thoughts and impulses? To Freud, the answer was to confront the conflicts and impulses by bringing them out of the unconscious part of the mind and into the conscious part. Freud assumed that this technique would reduce anxiety stemming from past conflicts and that the patient could then participate in his or her daily life more effectively.

A psychodynamic therapist, then, faces the challenge of finding a way to assist patients' attempts to explore and understand the unconscious. The technique that has evolved has a number of components, but basically it consists of guiding patients to consider and discuss their past experiences in explicit detail from the time of their first memories. This process assumes that patients will eventually stumble upon long-hidden crises, traumas, and conflicts that are producing anxiety in their adult lives. They will then be able to "work through"—understand and rectify—those difficulties.

PSYCHOANALYSIS: FREUD'S THERAPY

Psychoanalysis is Freud's specific version of psychodynamic therapy. The goal of psychoanalysis is to release hidden thoughts and feelings from the unconscious part of our mind in order to reduce their power in controlling behavior.

In traditional psychoanalysis, which tends to be a lengthy and expensive process, patients may meet with a therapist with considerable frequency, sometimes as much as 50 minutes a session, 4 to 5 days a week, for several years. In their sessions, therapists and patients typically use a technique developed by Freud called *free association*. Patients using free association say aloud whatever comes to mind, regardless of its apparent irrelevance or senselessness. The psychoanalyst then attempts to recognize and label the connections between what a patient says and the patient's unconscious.

Therapists also use *dream interpretation*, examining dreams to find clues to unconscious conflicts and problems. Moving beyond the surface description of a dream (called

psychodynamic therapy Therapy that seeks to bring unresolved past conflicts and unacceptable impulses from the unconscious into the conscious, where patients may deal with the problems more effectively. (Module 49)

psychoanalysis Freud's form of psychotherapy in which the goal is to release hidden thoughts and feelings from the unconscious part of our minds in order to reduce their power in controlling behavior. (Module 49)

 Study Alert
To better understand how psychodynamic therapy works, review Freud's psychoanalytic theory discussed in the chapter on personality.

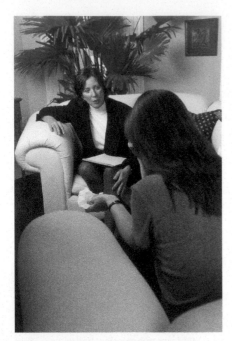

The close and intense relationship between therapist and patient often becomes highly complex.
David Buffington/Photodisc/Getty Images

transference The transfer of feelings to a psychoanalyst of love or anger that had been originally directed to a patient's parents or other authority figures. (Module 49)

the *manifest content*), therapists seek its underlying meaning (the *latent content*), which supposedly reveals the true unconscious meaning of the dream (Blum, 2011; Hill et al., 2013; Sandford, 2017).

The processes of free association and dream interpretation do not always move forward easily. The same unconscious forces that initially produced repression may keep past difficulties out of the conscious mind, which produces resistance. *Resistance* is an inability or unwillingness to discuss or reveal particular memories, thoughts, or motivations.

Patients can show resistance in many ways. For instance, they may be discussing a childhood memory and suddenly forget what they were saying, or they may abruptly change the subject completely. It is the therapist's job to discern instances of resistance and interpret their meaning. The therapists also need to try to make patients return to the subject they are trying to avoid—which is likely to hold difficult or painful memories for the patients.

Because of the close, almost intimate interaction between patient and psychoanalyst, the relationship between the two often becomes emotionally charged and takes on a complexity unlike most other relationships. Patients may eventually think of the analyst as a symbol of a significant other in their past, perhaps a parent or a lover, and apply some of their feelings for that person to the analyst—a phenomenon known as transference. **Transference** is the transfer of feelings to a psychoanalyst of love or anger that had been originally directed to a patient's parents or other authority figures (Høglend et al., 2011; Turri, 2015; McCluskey & O'Toole, 2019).

A therapist can use transference to help a patient recreate past relationships that were psychologically difficult. For instance, if a patient undergoing transference views her therapist as a symbol of her father with whom she had a difficult relationship, the patient and therapist may "redo" an earlier interaction, this time including more positive aspects. Through this process, the patient may resolve conflicts regarding her real father—something that is beginning to happen in the following therapy session:

Sandy: My father . . . never took any interest in any of us. . . . It was my mother–rest her soul–who loved us, not our father. He worked her to death. Lord, I miss her. . . . I must sound angry at my father. Don't you think I have a right to be angry?

Therapist: Do you think you have a right to be angry?

Sandy: Of course, I do! Why are you questioning me? You don't believe me, do you?

Therapist: You want me to believe you.

Sandy: I don't care whether you believe me or not. . . . I know what you're thinking–you think I'm crazy–you must be laughing at me–I'll probably be a case in your next book! You're just sitting there–smirking–making me feel like a bad person–thinking I'm wrong for being mad, that I have no right to be mad.

Therapist: Just like your father.

Sandy: Yes, you're just like my father.–Oh my God! Just now–I–I–thought I was talking to him. (Sue & Sue, 1990)

CONTEMPORARY PSYCHODYNAMIC APPROACHES

Few people have the time, money, or patience to participate in years of traditional psychoanalysis. Even more important, no conclusive evidence shows that psychoanalysis, as Freud originally conceived it in the 19th century, works better than other, more recent forms of psychodynamic therapy.

Today, psychodynamic therapy tends to be of shorter duration, usually lasting no longer than 3 months or 20 sessions. Psychodynamic therapists take a more active role than Freud would have prescribed, and they prod and advise the patient with considerable directness. Finally, contemporary psychodynamic therapists put less emphasis on a patient's past history and childhood. Instead, they concentrate on an individual's current relationships and specific concerns (Brafman, 2011; Dreissen et al., 2017).

EVALUATING PSYCHODYNAMIC THERAPY

Even with its current modifications, psychodynamic therapy has its critics. In its longer versions, it can be time-consuming and expensive, especially in comparison with other forms of psychotherapy, such as behavioral and cognitive approaches. Furthermore, less articulate patients may not do as well as more articulate ones.

Ultimately, the most important concern about psychodynamic treatment is whether it actually works, and there is no simple answer to this question. Psychodynamic treatment techniques have been controversial since Freud introduced them. Part of the problem is the difficulty in establishing whether patients have improved after psycho-dynamic therapy. Determining effectiveness depends on reports from the therapist or the patients themselves—reports that are obviously open to bias and subjective inter-pretation.

Furthermore, critics have questioned the entire theoretical basis of psychodynamic theory; they maintain that constructs such as the unconscious have not been scientif-ically confirmed. Despite the criticism, though, the psychodynamic treatment approach has remained viable. For some people, it provides solutions to difficult psychological issues, provides effective treatment for psychological disturbance, and permits the potential development of an unusual degree of insight into one's life (Anestis, Anestis, & Lilienfeld, 2011; Thase, 2013; Sell, Möller, & Taubner, 2017).

Behavioral Approaches to Therapy

Perhaps, when you were a child, your parents rewarded you with an ice cream cone when you were especially good . . . or sent you to your room if you misbehaved. Sound principles back up such a child-rearing strategy: Good behavior is maintained by reinforcement, and unwanted behavior can be eliminated by punishment.

These principles represent the basic underpinnings of behavioral treatment approaches. **Behavioral treatment approaches** use the principles of learning, such as reinforcement and extinction, to reduce or eliminate maladaptive behav-ior. These approaches are built on a fundamental assumption: Both abnormal behavior and normal behavior are *learned*.

In this view, people who act abnormally either have failed to learn the skills they need to cope with problems of living, or they have acquired faulty skills and patterns that are being maintained through some form of reinforce-ment. To modify abnormal behavior, then, proponents of these approaches propose that people must learn new behavior to replace the faulty skills they have developed, and they need to unlearn their maladaptive behavior patterns (Norton & Price, 2007; Kowalik et al., 2011; Kivlighan et al., 2015).

Behavioral psychologists do not need to delve into people's pasts or their psyches. Rather than viewing abnormal behavior as a symptom of an underlying problem, they consider the abnormal behavior as the problem in need of modifi-cation. The goal of therapy is to change people's behavior to allow them to function more effectively. In this view, then, there is no problem other than the maladaptive behavior itself; if you can change that behavior, treatment is successful.

CLASSICAL CONDITIONING TREATMENTS

Suppose you bite into your favorite candy bar and find that not only is it infested with ants, but you've also swallowed a bunch of them. You immediately become sick to your stomach and throw up. Your long-term reaction? You never eat that kind of candy bar again, and it may be months before you eat any type of candy. You have learned through the basic process of classical conditioning to avoid candy so that you will not get sick and throw up.

behavioral treatment approaches
Treatment approaches that make use of the basic principles of learning, such as reinforcement and extinction, to reduce or eliminate maladaptive behavior. (Module 49)

Behavioral approaches to treatment would seek to modify the behavior of this couple rather than to focus on the underlying causes of the behavior.
Metinkiyak/Getty Images

aversive conditioning A form of therapy that reduces the frequency of undesired behavior by pairing an aversive, unpleasant stimulus with undesired behavior. (Module 49)

Aversive Conditioning This simple example illustrates how a person can be classically conditioned to modify behavior. Behavior therapists use this principle in **aversive conditioning,** which aims to reduce the frequency of undesired behavior by pairing an unpleasant stimulus with undesired behavior. For example, behavior therapists might use aversive conditioning by pairing alcohol with a drug that causes severe nausea and vomiting. After the two have been paired a few times, the person associates the alcohol alone with vomiting and finds alcohol less appealing.

Aversion therapy works reasonably well with some specific kinds of disorders, including substance-abuse problems such as alcoholism and certain kinds of sexual disorders. On the other hand, critics question the long-term effectiveness of aversion therapy because rates of relapse are significant (Waters et al., 2017).

In addition, important ethical concerns surround aversion techniques such as electric shock, even though therapists use such potent stimuli only in the most extreme cases, such as with patients who harm themselves. Clearly, though, aversion therapy offers an important procedure for eliminating maladaptive responses for some period of time—a respite that provides, even if only temporarily, an opportunity to encourage more adaptive behavior patterns (Twining et al., 2015; Surya, Bishnoi, & Shashank, 2019).

systematic desensitization A behavioral technique based on classical conditioning in which exposure to an anxiety-producing stimulus is paired with deep relaxation to reduce or eliminate anxiety. (Module 49)

Systematic Desensitization Another treatment that grew out of the classical conditioning is systematic desensitization. **Systematic desensitization** is a behavioral technique in which exposure to an anxiety-producing stimulus is paired with deep relaxation in order to reduce an anxiety response. The idea is to learn to associate relaxation with a stimulus that previously produced anxiety (Triscari et al., 2011; Ijeoma & Oladipo, 2019).

Suppose, for instance, you were extremely afraid of flying. The very thought of being in an airplane would make you begin to sweat and shake, and you couldn't get yourself near enough to an airport to know how you'd react if you actually had to fly somewhere. Using systematic desensitization to treat your problem, you would first be trained in relaxation techniques by a behavior therapist and learn to relax your body fully—a highly pleasant state, as you might imagine (see Figure 2).

Picturenet/Blend Images

To achieve a state of relaxation, follow these steps once or twice a day.

Step 1. Choose a word or phrase that you can repeat to achieve calm. This might be a yoga mantra (*Om* or *Om mani padme hum,* for instance), a word such as *peace* or *shalom,* or any word or phrase that sounds soft and resonant to you (such as *Peace to my heart*).

Step 2. Find a quiet and comfortable place and sit down.

Step 3. Close your eyes and try to see and feel the darkness.

Step 4. Relax your muscles one by one, starting from your toes and moving slowly up to your scalp.

Step 5. Keep your breathing steady and natural, neither deep nor shallow, and repeat your word or phrase continuously.

Step 6. Do not monitor yourself, but become passive and accepting. If outside thoughts arrive, dismiss them lightly with a smile and return to your repeated word or phrase.

Step 7. Keep this up for 15 minutes. Do not set an alarm; just open your eyes when you feel it is right. If you fall asleep, that is fine.

Step 8. When you have finished, sit quietly, eyes closed, for a minute or two, then stand up.

FIGURE 2 Following these basic steps will help you achieve a sense of calmness by employing the relaxation response.

Source: Adapted from Benson, H., Kornhaber, A., Kornhaber, C., LeChanu, M. N., Zuttermeister, P. C., Myers, P., et al. (1994). Increases in positive psychological characteristics with a new relaxation-response curriculum in high school students. *Journal of Research and Development in Education, 27,* 226–231.

The next step would involve constructing a *hierarchy of fears*–a list in order of increasing severity of the things you associate with your fears. For instance, your hierarchy might resemble this one:

1. Watching a plane fly overhead
2. Going to an airport
3. Buying a ticket
4. Stepping into the plane
5. Seeing the plane door close
6. Having the plane taxi down the runway
7. Taking off
8. Being in the air

From the perspective of...

A Child-Care Provider How might you use systematic desensitization to help children overcome their fears?

Nicole Hill/Rubberball/Getty Images

Once you had developed this hierarchy and learned relaxation techniques, you would learn to associate the two sets of responses. To do this, your therapist might ask you to put yourself into a relaxed state and then imagine yourself in the first situation identified in your hierarchy. Once you could consider that first step while remaining relaxed, you would move on to the next situation. Eventually, you would move up the hierarchy in gradual stages until you could imagine yourself being in the air without experiencing anxiety. Ultimately, you would be asked to make a visit to an airport and later to take a flight.

flooding A behavioral treatment for anxiety in which people are suddenly confronted with a stimulus that they fear. (Module 49)

The newest form of exposure therapy makes use of virtual reality technology. In *virtual reality exposure therapy*, clients wear virtual reality goggles that provide highly realistic depictions of stimuli that trigger anxiety. For example, someone who fears heights might be taken virtually to the top of a skyscraper. Or a person who has developed anxiety about driving after a car crash could be taken virtually to the intersection where the crash occurred. Once at the (virtual) site of the source of their anxiety, clients can be treated with traditional systematic desensitization techniques.

The extreme realism of virtual reality ensures that clients face their fears in a highly impactful manner, yet one that can be controlled more precisely than traditional means permit. The treatment is promising, although it is so new that the long-term effectiveness is not yet clear (Metz, 2017; McClay et al., 2017; North & North, 2017).

Flooding Treatments Although systematic desensitization has proven to be a successful treatment, today it is often replaced with a less-complicated form of therapy called flooding. **Flooding** is a behavioral treatment for anxiety in which people are suddenly confronted with a stimulus that they fear. However, unlike systematic desensitization, relaxation training is not included. The goal behind

Virtual reality exposure therapy immerses clients in highly realistic depictions of stimuli that trigger anxiety.

Monika Wisniewska/Alamy Stock Photo

flooding is to allow the maladaptive response of anxiety or avoidance to become extinct (Havermans et al., 2007; Hofmann, 2007; Bush, 2008).

For example, a patient who has a deep fear of germs may be made to soil her hands in dirt and to keep them dirty for hours. For a person with a fear of germs, initially this is a highly anxiety-producing situation. After a few hours, however, the anxiety will decline, leading to extinction of the anxiety.

Flooding has proved to be an effective treatment for a number of problems, including phobias, anxiety disorders, and even impotence and fear of sexual contact. Through this technique, people can learn to enjoy the things they once feared (Tuerk et al., 2011; de Jong et al., 2019).

OPERANT CONDITIONING TECHNIQUES

Some behavioral approaches make use of the operant conditioning principles that we discussed in the chapter on learning. These approaches are based on the notion that we should reward people for carrying out desirable behavior and extinguish undesirable behavior by either ignoring it or punishing it.

One example of the systematic application of operant conditioning principles is the *token system*, which rewards a person for desired behavior with a token such as a poker chip or some kind of play money. The person can later exchange the chip or play money for an actual reward, such as real money or food.

Token systems are most frequently used in institutions for people with relatively serious problems and sometimes with children as a classroom-management technique. The system resembles what parents do when they give children money for being well behaved–money that the children can later exchange for something they want. The desired behavior may range from simple things such as keeping one's room neat to personal grooming and interacting with other people. In institutions, patients can exchange tokens for some object or activity, such as snacks, new clothes, or, in extreme cases, sleeping in one's own bed rather than in a sleeping bag on the floor.

Contingency contracting is a variant of the token system that has proved quite effective in modifying behavior. In *contingency contracting*, the therapist and client prepare a written agreement, known as a contract. The contract states a series of behavioral goals the client hopes to achieve. It also specifies positive consequences for the client if she or he reaches those goals–usually an explicit reward such as money or privileges.

Contingency contracts also may state negative consequences if clients do not meet their goals. For example, clients who are trying to quit smoking might write out a check to a cause they have no interest in supporting (for instance, the National Rifle Association if they are strong supporters of gun control). If the client smokes on a given day, the therapist will mail the check.

Behavior therapists also use observational learning to systematically teach people new skills and ways of handling their fears and anxieties. *Observational learning* occurs through observing the behavior of others. For example, for clients who are socially fearful, a therapist may model and teach basic social skills, such as maintaining eye contact during conversation and acting assertively. Similarly, children with dog phobias have been able to overcome their fears by watching another child–called the "Fearless Peer"–repeatedly walk up to a dog, touch it, pet it, and finally play with it. Observational learning, then, can play a role in resolving some kinds of behavior difficulties, especially if the person being observed receives a reward for his or her behavior (Bandura, Grusec, & Menlove, 1967; Waismeyer & Meltzoff, 2017; Bruton, Shearer, & Mellalieu, 2019).

EVALUATING BEHAVIOR THERAPY

Behavior therapy works especially well for eliminating anxiety disorders, treating phobias and compulsions, establishing control over impulses, and learning complex social skills to replace maladaptive behavior. More than any of the other therapeutic techniques, it provides methods that nonprofessionals can use to change their own behavior. Moreover, it is efficient because it focuses on solving carefully defined problems (Richard & Lauterbach, 2006; Barlow, 2007; Kertz et al., 2015).

Critics of behavior therapy believe that because it emphasizes changing external behavior, it ignores people's inner life—their thoughts and anxieties. Consequently, people do not necessarily gain insight into thoughts and expectations that may be fostering their maladaptive behavior.

On the other hand, neuroscientific evidence shows that behavioral treatments can produce actual changes in brain functioning, which suggests that behavioral treatments can produce changes beyond external behavior. For example, one experiment looked at the neurological reactions of patients with borderline personality disorder who participated in a 12-week behavioral therapy program. Compared with a control group composed of people who did not have the disorder, the patients showed significant changes in their reactions to highly arousing, emotion-evoking stimuli. Following therapy, the patients' neurological functioning was more similar to those without the disorder than it was prior to therapy (Schnell & Herpertz, 2007).

Cognitive Approaches to Therapy

If you assumed that illogical thoughts and beliefs lie at the heart of psychological disorders, wouldn't the most direct treatment route be to teach people new, more adaptive modes of thinking? The answer is yes, according to psychologists who take a cognitive approach to treatment.

Cognitive treatment approaches teach people to think in more adaptive ways by changing their dysfunctional cognitions about the world and themselves. In contrast to behavior therapists, who primarily focus on modifying external behavior, cognitive therapists focus on changing the way people think. Because they often use basic principles of learning, the methods they employ are sometimes referred to as the **cognitive-behavioral approach** (Kalodner, 2011; Sivec et al., 2017; Gros et al., 2019).

Although cognitive treatment approaches take many forms, they all share the assumption that anxiety, depression, and negative emotions develop from maladaptive thinking. Accordingly, cognitive treatments seek to change the thought patterns that lead to getting "stuck" in dysfunctional ways of thinking. Therapists systematically teach clients to challenge their assumptions and adopt new approaches to old problems.

Cognitive therapy is relatively short-term and usually lasts a maximum of 20 sessions. Therapy tends to be highly structured and focused on concrete problems. Therapists often begin by teaching the theory behind the approach and then continue to take an active role throughout the course of therapy by acting as a combination of teacher, coach, and partner.

One example of cognitive therapy is rational-emotive behavior therapy. **Rational-emotive behavior therapy** attempts to restructure a person's belief system into a more realistic, rational, and logical set of views. By adopting more accurate thought patterns, it is assumed that people will lead more psychologically healthy lives.

Building on these views, psychologist Albert Ellis (**2004**) suggests that many people lead unhappy lives and suffer from psychological disorders because they harbor irrational, unrealistic ideas such as these:

- We need the love or approval of virtually every significant other person for everything we do.

- We should be thoroughly competent, adequate, and successful in all possible respects in order to consider ourselves worthwhile.

- It is horrible when things don't turn out the way we want them to.

cognitive treatment approaches Treatment approaches that teach people to think in more adaptive ways by changing their dysfunctional cognitions about the world and themselves. (Module 49)

cognitive-behavioral approach A treatment approach that incorporates basic principles of learning to change the way people think. (Module 49)

rational-emotive behavior therapy A form of therapy that attempts to restructure a person's belief system into a more realistic, rational, and logical set of views by challenging dysfunctional beliefs that maintain irrational behavior. (Module 49)

FIGURE 3 In the A-B-C model of rational-emotive behavior therapy, negative activating conditions (A) lead to the activation of an irrational belief system (B), which leads to emotional consequences (C). Those emotional consequences then feed back and support the belief system. At what steps in the model could change occur as a result of rational-emotive behavior therapy?

Source: Ellis, A. (1974). *Growth through reason.* Hollywood, CA: Wilshire Books.

Such irrational beliefs trigger negative emotions, which in turn support the irrational beliefs and lead to a self-defeating cycle. Ellis calls it the A-B-C model in which negative activating conditions (A) lead to the activation of an irrational belief system (B), which in turn leads to emotional consequences (C). For example, if a person experiences the breakup of a close relationship (A) and holds the irrational belief (B) that "I'll never be loved again," this triggers negative emotions (C) that in turn feed back into support of the irrational belief (see Figure 3).

The goal of rational-emotive therapy is to help clients eliminate maladaptive thoughts and beliefs and adopt more effective thinking. To accomplish this goal, therapists take an active, directive role during therapy and openly challenge patterns of thought that appear to be dysfunctional. Consider this example:

> Martha: The basic problem is that I'm worried about my family. I'm worried about money. And I never seem to be able to relax.
> Therapist: Why are you worried about your family? . . . What's to be concerned about? They have certain demands which you don't want to adhere to.
> Martha: I was brought up to think that I mustn't be selfish.
> Therapist: Oh, we'll have to knock that out of your head!
> Martha: My mother feels that I shouldn't have left home—that my place is with them. There are nagging doubts about what I should—
> Therapist: Why are there doubts? Why should you?
> Martha: I think it's a feeling I was brought up with that you always have to give of yourself. If you think of yourself, you're wrong.
> Therapist: That's a belief. Why do you have to keep believing that—at your age? You believed a lot of superstitions when you were younger. Why do you have to retain them? Your parents indoctrinated you with this nonsense, because that's their belief. . . . Who needs that philosophy? All it's gotten you, so far, is guilt. (Ellis, 1974)

By poking holes in Martha's reasoning, the therapist is attempting to help her adopt a more realistic view of herself and her circumstances (Ellis, 2002; Dryden & David, 2008).

Another influential form of therapy that builds on a cognitive perspective is that of Aaron Beck (Beck, 2004; Beck, Davis, & Freeman, 2015). Like rational-emotive behavior therapy, Beck's *cognitive behavior therapy* aims to change people's illogical thoughts about themselves and the world.

However, cognitive behavior therapy is considerably less confrontational and challenging than rational-emotive behavior therapy is. Instead of the therapist actively arguing with clients about their dysfunctional cognitions, cognitive behavior therapists more often play the role of teacher. Therapists urge clients to obtain information on their own that will lead them to discard their inaccurate thinking through a process of cognitive appraisal.

In *cognitive appraisal*, clients are asked to evaluate situations, themselves, and others in terms of their memories, values, beliefs, thoughts, and expectations. During the course of treatment, therapists help clients discover ways of thinking more appropriately about themselves and others (Leaper, Brown, & Ayres, 2013; Simães, Gomes, Costa, 2019; also see *Neuroscience in Your Life*).

Cognitive appraisal can also be used to help change students' attributions about the causes of their academic success or failure. For example, rather than attributing academic failure to a lack of intelligence, students can be helped to see that their performance is related to the amount of hard work and perseverance they invest in academic tasks (Elliot, Dweck, & Yeager, 2017),

NEUROSCIENCE IN YOUR LIFE: HOW COGNITIVE BEHAVIORAL THERAPY CHANGES YOUR BRAIN

Psychotherapy has been shown to be effective for multiple psychological disorders. But does it show measurable changes in the brain?

Recent research examining the effects of psychotherapy on brain structure and function suggests that it does. Specifically, neuroscientists compared the structure and function of the amygdala, the brain area involved in fear and anxiety, in patients with social anxiety disorder before and after 9 weeks of online cognitive behavioral therapy (CBT). Compared to those who had alternative treatments, the patients who had CBT were less anxious and showed changes in brain volume and activity (see images). These results highlight the fact that psychological therapies have an impact on the brain related to the reduction of symptoms of psychological disorders (Mansson et al., 2016; Neufang et al., 2019).

The images show that the CBT group had smaller left amygdala (shown in blue in the left image) and less active right amygdala (shown in blue in the right image) after CBT than the alternative treatment group.

Source: Adapted from Mansson, K. N., Salami, A., Frick, A., Carlbring, P., Andersson, G., Furmark, T., & Boraxbekk, C. J. (2016). Neuroplasticity in response to cognitive behavior therapy for social anxiety disorder. *Translational Psychiatry, 6*, e727. doi: 10.1038/tp.2015.218.

EVALUATING COGNITIVE APPROACHES TO THERAPY

Cognitive approaches to therapy have proved successful in dealing with a broad range of disorders, including anxiety disorders, depression, substance abuse, and eating disorders. Furthermore, the willingness of cognitive therapists to incorporate additional treatment approaches (e.g., combining cognitive and behavioral techniques in cognitive behavior therapy) has made this approach a particularly effective form of treatment (Mitte, 2005; Ishikawa et al., 2007; Bhar et al., 2008).

At the same time, critics have pointed out that the focus on helping people to think more rationally ignores the fact that life is in reality sometimes irrational. Changing one's assumptions to make them more reasonable and logical thus may not always be helpful—even assuming it is possible to bring about true cognitive change. Still, the success of cognitive approaches has made them some of the most frequently employed therapies (Beck & Rector, 2005; Fresco, 2013). (Also see *Applying Psychology in the 21st Century*.)

PsychTech

Psychologist David Mohr found that an Internet-based treatment for depression in which patients logged into a website and also received e-mail and telephone support was effective in reducing depressive episodes.

APPLYING PSYCHOLOGY IN THE 21ST CENTURY

"BOOT CAMP" THERAPY

In Houston, adolescents with obsessive-compulsive disorder can participate in a treatment program that runs during the week-long spring school break. And in Atlanta, Chicago, and Boston, combat veterans are getting relief from their symptoms of post-traumatic stress disorder in programs lasting just 2 weeks.

Therapy is commonly a 1-hour-per-week commitment over a period of many weeks or even months or years. But a newer and more concentrated approach is being developed, with substantial potential benefits for clients as well as therapists. Called concentrated or intensive therapy, or simply "boot camp," it condenses those hour-long sessions over many weeks into intensive 1- or 2-week periods of multiple sessions per day, sometimes including group meetings and various guided and solo behavioral practice assignments (Peterson, 2018).

Intensive treatments work best for clients with certain kinds of anxiety disorders. Sessions with a therapist are mixed with many hours of exposure therapy in which clients are required to confront repeatedly the objects or situations that give them anxiety, both with their individual therapists and on their own, and to do so without using any strategies to reduce the anxiety they feel. Experiencing exposure in a variety of contexts, including many real-life ones, improves the effectiveness of the therapy.

Research shows that these concentrated therapy programs are often just as effective as the more traditional once-a-week approach. One large-scale meta-analysis

"Boot camp" therapy offers an intense, short-term experience that can produce positive results for certain kinds of psychological disorders.
Wavebreak Media Ltd/123RF

found that remission rates for the two approaches did not differ significantly and that the rate at which clients dropped out of treatment was actually lower for the concentrated approach (Öst & Ollendick, 2017).

Why might clients prefer "boot camp" therapy? The advantages are many. Most obviously, intensive therapy can offer quicker relief; fast relief is important in its own right, of course, but it can also be vital to clients whose symptoms are preventing them from attending school or work. Also,

clients often find it easier to devote a single school break or vacation week to a concentrated therapy effort than to find time in their schedules for weekly sessions—especially clients living in remote areas who would have to travel some distance to each weekly appointment. And some people may benefit from being removed from the distractions of their daily lives to focus all their attention on their therapy in a sustained fashion (Jónsson, Kristensen, & Arendt, 2015).

The approach does have some drawbacks, too. It typically comes with a large price tag—one that many insurers don't cover. It also requires a certain degree of motivation and willingness to be immersed in the intensive experience. But for those with the means and the motivation, intensive therapy appears to be a promising option for treating various anxiety disorders.

> **RETHINK**
> _____
>
> • Do you think a college student with a psychological disorder might be particularly open to trying an intensive program? Why might some object to it?
> • Besides the ones mentioned above, what might be some other advantages or drawbacks to intensive therapy programs?

RECAP/EVALUATE/RETHINK

RECAP

LO 49-1 What are the goals of psychologically based and biologically based treatment approaches?

• Psychotherapy (psychologically based therapy) and biomedical therapy (biologically based therapy) share the goal of resolving psychological problems by modifying people's thoughts, feelings, expectations, evaluations, and ultimately behavior.

LO 49-2 What are the psychodynamic, behavioral, and cognitive approaches to treatment?

• Psychoanalytic approaches seek to bring unresolved past conflicts and unacceptable impulses from the unconscious into the conscious, where patients may deal with the problems more effectively. To do this, therapists use techniques such as free association and dream interpretation.

- Behavioral approaches to treatment view abnormal behavior as the problem rather than viewing that behavior as a symptom of some underlying cause. To bring about a "cure," this view suggests that the outward behavior must be changed by using methods such as aversive conditioning, systematic desensitization, observational learning, token systems, and contingency contracting.
- Cognitive approaches to treatment consider that the goal of therapy is to help a person restructure his or her faulty belief system into a more realistic, rational, and logical view of the world. Two examples of cognitive treatments are the rational-emotive behavior therapy and cognitive behavior therapy.

EVALUATE

1. Match the following mental health practitioners with the appropriate description.

1. Psychiatrist	a. PhD specializing in the treatment of psychological disorders
2. Clinical psychologist	b. Professional specializing in Freudian therapy techniques
3. Counseling psychologist	c. MD trained in abnormal behavior
4. Psychoanalyst	d. PhD specializing in the adjustment of day-to-day problems

2. According to Freud, people use _____ _____ as a means of preventing unwanted impulses from intruding on conscious thought.
3. In dream interpretation, a psychoanalyst must learn to distinguish between the _____ content of a dream, which is what appears on the surface, and the _____ content, its underlying meaning.
4. Which of the following treatments deals with phobias by gradual exposure to the item producing the fear?
    a. Systematic desensitization
    b. Partial reinforcement
    c. Behavioral self-management
    d. Aversion therapy

RETHINK

1. In what ways are psychoanalysis and cognitive therapy similar, and how do they differ?
2. How might you examine the reliability of dream interpretation?

Answers to Evaluate Questions

1. 1 c, 2 a, 3 d, 1-b; **2.** defense mechanisms; **3.** manifest, latent; **4.** a

KEY TERMS

psychotherapy
biomedical therapy
psychodynamic therapy
psychoanalysis

transference
behavioral treatment
    approaches
aversive conditioning

systematic desensitization
flooding
cognitive treatment
    approaches

cognitive-behavioral
    approach
rational-emotive behavior
    therapy

Module 50
Psychotherapy: Humanistic, Interpersonal, and Group Approaches to Treatment

humanistic therapy Therapy in which the underlying rationale is that people have control of their behavior, can make choices about their lives, and are essentially responsible for solving their own problems. (Module 50)

Humanistic therapy focuses on self-responsibility.

Don Hammond/DesignPics/Getty Images

Humanistic Therapy

As you know from your own experience, a student cannot master the material covered in a course without some hard work, no matter how good the teacher and the textbook are. *You must* take the time to study, memorize the vocabulary, and learn the concepts. Nobody else can do it for you. If you choose to put in the effort, you'll succeed; if you don't, you'll fail. The responsibility is primarily yours.

Humanistic therapy reflects this philosophy. **Humanistic therapy** is the approach that assumes people have control of their behavior, can make choices about their lives, and are essentially responsible for solving their own problems.

Humanistic therapists believe that people naturally are motivated to strive for self-actualization. As we discussed in the chapter on motivation, *self-actualization* is the term that clinical psychologist Abraham Maslow used to describe the state of self-fulfillment in which people realize their highest potentials in their own unique way.

Instead of acting in the more directive manner of some psychodynamic and behavioral approaches, humanistic therapists view themselves as guides or facilitators. Therapists using humanistic techniques seek to help people understand themselves and find ways to come closer to the ideal they hold for themselves. In this view, psychological disorders result from the inability to find meaning in life, from feelings of loneliness, and from a lack of connection to others (Watson, Goldman, & Greenberg, 2011; Lewis & Umbreit, 2015; Van Deurzen et al., 2019).

Humanistic approaches have produced many therapeutic techniques. Among the most important is person-centered therapy.

PERSON-CENTERED THERAPY

Consider the following therapy session excerpt:

> Alice: I was thinking about this business of standards. I somehow developed a sort of a knack, I guess, of–well–habit–of trying to make people feel at ease around me, or to make things go along smoothly. . . .
>
> Therapist: In other words, what you did was always in the direction of trying to keep things smooth and to make other people feel better and to smooth the situation.
>
> Alice: Yes. I think that's what it was. Now the reason why I did it probably was–I mean, not that I was a good little Samaritan going around making other people happy, but that was probably the role that felt easiest for me to play. . . .
>
> Therapist: You feel that for a long time you've been playing the role of kind of smoothing out the frictions or differences or what not. . . .
>
> Alice: M-hm.
>
> Therapist: Rather than having any opinion or reaction of your own in the situation. Is that it? (Rogers, 1951)

The therapist does not interpret or answer the questions the client has raised. Instead, the therapist clarifies or reflects back what the client has said (e.g., "In other words, what you did. . . ."; "You feel that. . . ."; "Is that it?"). This therapeutic technique, known as *nondirective counseling,* is at the heart of person-centered therapy, which was first practiced by Carl Rogers in the mid-20th century (Raskin & Rogers, 1989; Joseph, 2019).

Person-centered therapy (also called *client-centered therapy*) aims to enable people to reach their potential for self-actualization. By providing a warm and accepting environment, therapists hope to motivate clients to air their problems and feelings. In turn, this enables clients to make realistic and constructive choices and decisions about the things that bother them in their current lives (Cooper & McLeod, 2011; McLean et al., 2017; Knutson & Koch, 2019).

Instead of directing the choices clients make, therapists provide what Rogers calls unconditional positive regard. *Unconditional positive regard* involves providing whole-hearted acceptance, support, and understanding, and no disapproval, no matter what feelings and attitudes a client expresses. By doing this, therapists hope to create an atmosphere that enables clients to come to decisions that can improve their lives (Vieira & Freire, 2006; Patterson & Joseph, 2013).

Furnishing unconditional positive regard does not mean that therapists must approve of everything their clients say or do. Rather, therapists need to communicate that they are caring, nonjudgmental, and *empathetic*—that is, understanding of a client's emotional experiences (Fearing & Clark, 2000).

Today, therapists using person-centered therapy techniques are more directive with their clients. Rather than merely reflecting back their clients' statements, therapists actively nudge clients toward insights. However, therapists still view their clients' insights as central to the therapeutic process.

person-centered therapy Therapy in which the goal is to reach one's potential for self-actualization. (Module 50)

> **Study Alert**
>
> To better remember the concept of unconditional positive regard, try offering it to a friend during a conversation by showing your support, acceptance, and understanding no matter what thought or attitude your friend expresses.

EVALUATING HUMANISTIC APPROACHES TO THERAPY

The notion that psychological disorders result from restricted growth potential appeals philosophically to many people. Furthermore, when humanistic therapists acknowledge that the freedom we possess can lead to psychological difficulties, clients find an unusually supportive environment for therapy. In turn, this atmosphere can help clients discover solutions to difficult psychological problems (Cooper, 2007).

However, humanistic treatments lack specificity, a problem that has troubled their critics. Humanistic approaches are not very precise and are probably the least scientifically and theoretically developed type of treatment. Moreover, this form of treatment works best for the same type of highly verbal client who profits most from psychoanalytic treatment.

Interpersonal Therapy

Interpersonal therapy (IPT) is short-term therapy designed to help patients control their moods and emotions by focusing on the context of their current social relationships. Although its roots stem from psychodynamic approaches, interpersonal therapy concentrates more on the here and now with the goal of improving a client's existing relationships. It typically focuses on interpersonal issues such as conflicts with others, social skills issues, role transitions (such as divorce), or grief (Weissman, Markowitz, & Klerman, 2007; Stangier et al., 2011; Dimaggio et al., 2015).

Interpersonal therapy is more active and directive than are traditional psychodynamic approaches, and sessions are more structured. The approach makes no assumptions about the underlying causes of psychological disorders but focuses on the interpersonal context in which a disorder is developed and maintained. It also tends to be shorter than traditional psychodynamic approaches and typically lasts only 12-16 weeks. During those sessions, therapists make concrete suggestions on improving relations with others and actively offer recommendations and advice.

interpersonal therapy (IPT) Short-term therapy designed to help patients control their moods and emotions by focusing on the context of their current social relationships. (Module 50)

Considerable research supports the effectiveness of interpersonal therapy. It is especially effective in dealing with depression, anxiety, addictions, and eating disorders (Bohn et al., 2013; Dimaggio et al., 2017; Lee & Mason, 2019;).

Group Therapies

group therapy Therapy in which people meet in a group with a therapist to discuss problems. (Module 50)

Although most treatment takes place between a single individual and a therapist, some forms of therapy involve groups of people seeking treatment. In **group therapy,** several unrelated people meet with a therapist to discuss some aspect of their psychological functioning.

People typically discuss with the group their problems, which often center on a common difficulty, such as alcoholism or a lack of social skills. The other members of the group provide emotional support and dispense advice on ways they have coped effectively with similar problems (Scaturo, 2004; Rigby & Waite, 2007; Schachter, 2011).

Groups vary greatly in terms of the particular model they employ; there are psychoanalytic groups, humanistic groups, and groups corresponding to the other therapeutic approaches. Furthermore, groups also differ with regard to the degree of guidance the therapist provides. In some, the therapist is quite directive; in others, the members of the group set their own agenda and determine how the group will proceed (Beck & Lewis, 2000; Stockton, Morran, & Krieger, 2004; Arlo, 2017).

Because several people are treated simultaneously in group therapy, it is a much more economical means of treatment than individual psychotherapy is. On the other hand, critics argue that group settings lack the individual attention inherent in one-to-one therapy and that especially shy and withdrawn individuals may not receive the attention they need in a group setting.

family therapy An approach that focuses on the family and its dynamics. (Module 50)

FAMILY THERAPY

One specialized form of group therapy is family therapy. As the name implies, **family therapy** involves two or more family members, one (or more) of whose problems led to treatment. But rather than focusing simply on the members of the family who present the initial problem, family therapists consider the family as a unit to which each member contributes. By meeting with the entire family simultaneously, family therapists try to understand how the family members interact with one another (Strong & Tomm, 2007; Bischoff et al., 2011).

Family therapists view the family as a system, and they assume that individuals cannot improve without understanding the conflicts that exist among family members. Thus, therapists expect each member of a family to contribute to the resolution of the problem being addressed (Wretman, 2016; Scarborough, 2019).

Family therapists believe that family members often fall into rigid roles or patterns of behavior. For example, one person may act as the victim, another as a bully, and so forth. In their view, that system of roles supports and perpetuates family disturbances. One goal of family therapy, then, is to get family members to adopt new, more constructive patterns of behavior and to get members of the family to view others in new ways (Sori, 2006; Conoley et al., 2015).

SELF-HELP THERAPY

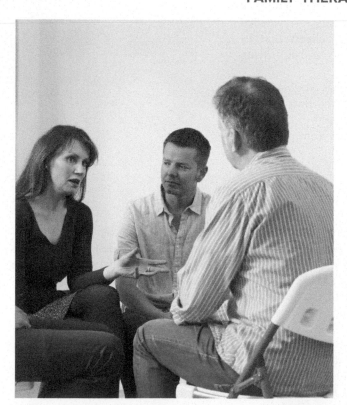

In group therapy, people with psychological difficulties meet with a therapist to discuss their problems.
highwaystarz/123RF

In self-help therapy, people with similar problems get together to discuss their shared feelings and experiences, sometimes without any formal therapist participating. For example, people who have recently experienced the death of a spouse might meet in a *bereavement support group*, or college students may get together to discuss their adjustment to college.

One of the best-known self-help groups is Alcoholics Anonymous (AA), a type of treatment program designed to help members deal with alcohol-related problems. AA prescribes 12 steps that alcoholics must pass through on their road to recovery. Alcoholics begin by admitting that they are alcoholics and powerless over alcohol and move through additional steps in the process of recovery by attending frequent AA meetings. Proponents of AA believe that no one is fully cured of alcoholism and that members should permanently think of themselves as recovering alcoholics (Greenfield & Tonigan, 2013; Best, 2017; Williams & Mee-Lee, 2019).

Alcoholics Anonymous does not work for everyone. For one thing, the program has a strong spiritual component, and it emphasizes the need for a higher power, which does not appeal to some people. More important, some critics say that AA's requirement of total abstinence from alcohol may not be an effective or realistic approach. Finally, despite its popularity, the scientific evidence about the effectiveness of AA is mixed, with some studies showing it is effective and others finding less support for the program (Humphreys et al., 2014; Dodes, 2015; Glaser, 2015).

Still, AA provides more treatment for alcoholics than does any other therapy. Furthermore, research studies show that AA and other 12-step programs (such as Narcotics Anonymous) can be as successful in treating alcohol and other substance-abuse problems as traditional types of therapy (Gossop, Stewart, & Marsden, 2008; Pagano et al., 2013; Galanter, 2018).

Online Therapy: A Lifeline During the Coronavirus Pandemic

At the height of the coronavirus pandemic, almost 45% of those polled said that their mental health had been affected by the global health and economic crisis. For them, and for most quarantined people, online therapy, whether via Zoom, FaceTime, or some other medium, was the only way of getting access to psychotherapy (Hoffman, 2020; Meraji & Hodges, 2020).

Actually, online psychotherapy was available even before the onset of the pandemic because its potential benefits were and are considerable. First, online sessions can be scheduled with ease for convenient times, and transportation isn't an issue. Furthermore, some clients may lack the emotional strength to get themselves to a real-world therapy session, in which case online therapy brings the therapist to them. Furthermore, sessions can be conducted in real-time teleconferencing style, by text-based chat, or even asynchronously--that is, not in real time, but more like an exchange of e-mails (American Psychological Association, 2019; Kecmanovic, 2020).

However, online therapy has limitations. For one thing, it's probably not the best channel for treating clients with serious mental disorders. Furthermore, some clients find it cold and impersonal, and therapists may find it difficult to assess clients accurately without direct face-to-face contact. Finally, legal and ethical concerns exist about conducting therapy via telecommunications companies that may not fully comply with privacy laws and other codes of conduct for therapists (Novotney, 2017; Drerup & Ahmed-Jauregui, 2019; Rolles-Abraham, 2020).

Evaluating Psychotherapy: Does Therapy Work?

Your best friend, Ben, comes to you because he just hasn't been feeling right about things lately. He's upset because he and his girlfriend aren't getting along, but his difficulties go beyond that. He can't concentrate on his studies, has a lot of trouble getting to sleep, and–this is what really bothers him–has begun to think that people are ganging up on him, talking about him behind his back. He feels that no one really cares about or understands him or makes any effort to see why he's become so miserable.

Ben knows that he ought to get *some* kind of help, but he is not sure where to turn. He is fairly skeptical of psychologists and thinks that a lot of what they say is just mumbo-jumbo, but he's willing to put his doubts aside and try anything to feel better. He also knows that many types of therapy are available, but he doesn't have a clue about which would be best for him. He turns to you for advice because he knows you are taking a psychology course. He asks, "Which kind of therapy works best?"

IS THERAPY EFFECTIVE?

This question requires a complex response. In fact, identifying the single most appropriate form of treatment is a controversial and still unresolved task for psychologists specializing in psychological disorders. In fact, even before considering whether one form of therapy works better than another, we need to determine whether therapy in any form effectively alleviates psychological disturbances.

Until the 1950s, most people simply assumed that therapy was effective. But in 1952, psychologist Hans Eysenck published an historically important study challenging that assumption. He claimed that people who received psychodynamic treatment and related therapies were no better off at the end of treatment than were people who were placed on a waiting list for treatment but never received it. Eysenck concluded that people would go into **spontaneous remission,** recovery without formal treatment, if they were simply left alone–certainly a cheaper and simpler process.

Although other psychologists quickly challenged Eysenck's conclusions, his review stimulated a continuing stream of better controlled, more carefully crafted studies on the effectiveness of psychotherapy. Today most psychologists agree: Therapy does work. Several comprehensive reviews indicate that therapy brings about greater improvement than no treatment at all, with the rate of spontaneous remission being fairly low. In most cases, then, the symptoms of abnormal behavior do not go away by themselves if left untreated–although the issue continues to be hotly debated (Gaudiano & Miller, 2013; Abbass et al., 2017; Cuijpers et al., 2019).

WHICH KIND OF THERAPY WORKS BEST?

Almost all psychologists agree that psychotherapeutic treatment *in general* is more effective than no treatment at all. However, the question of what specific *kind* of treatment is superior to others has not been answered definitively (Westen, Novotny, & Thompson-Brenner, 2004; Abboud, 2005; Tryer et al., 2015).

For instance, one classic study comparing the effectiveness of various approaches found that although success rates vary somewhat by treatment form, most treatments show fairly equal success rates. As Figure 1 indicates, the rates ranged from about 75-80% greater success for treated compared with untreated individuals. Behavioral and cognitive approaches tended to be slightly more successful, but that result may have been due to differences in the severity of the cases treated (Smith, Glass, & Miller, 1980; Orwin & Condray, 1984).

Other research, which relies on *meta-analysis* in which data from a large number of studies are statistically combined, yields similar general conclusions. Furthermore, a large survey of 186,000 individuals found that respondents felt they had benefited substantially from psychotherapy. However, there was little difference in "consumer satisfaction" on the basis of the specific type of treatment they had received (Seligman, 1995; Cuijpers et al., 2008; Dakin & Areán, 2013).

Study Alert

Pay special attention to the discussion of (1) whether therapy is effective in general and (2) what specific types of therapy are effective because these are key issues for therapists.

spontaneous remission Recovery without formal treatment. (Module 50)

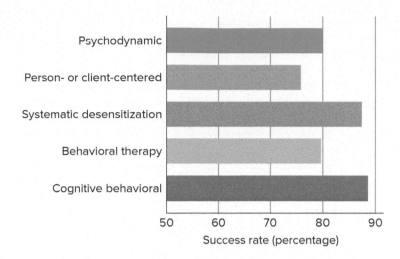

Success rate (percentage)

FIGURE 1 Estimates of the effectiveness of types of treatment, in comparison to control groups of untreated people. The percentage scores show how much more effective a specific type of treatment is for the average patient compared with those who have had no treatment. For example, people given psychodynamic treatment score, on average, more positively on outcome measures than do about 80% of untreated people.

Source: Adapted from Smith, M. L., Glass, G. V., & Miller, T. I. (1980). *The benefits of psychotherapy.* Baltimore: The Johns Hopkins University Press.

In short, converging evidence allows us to draw several conclusions about the effectiveness of psychotherapy:

- *For most people, psy*chotherapy is effective. This conclusion holds over different lengths of treatment, specific kinds of psychological disorders, and various types of treatment. Thus, the question, "Does psychotherapy work?" appears to have been answered convincingly: It does (Westen, Novotny, & Thompson-Brenner, 2004; Payne & Marcus, 2008; Gaudiano & Miller, 2013; Leszcz et al., 2015).

- On the other hand, psychotherapy doesn't work for everyone. As many as 10% of people treated show no improvement—or actually deteriorated (Lilienfeld, 2007; Wendt, Gone, & Nagata, 2015; Duffy, Sharpe, & Schwannauer, 2019).

- No single form of therapy works best for every problem, and certain specific types of treatment are better, although not invariably, for specific types of problems. For example, cognitive therapy works especially well for panic disorders, and flooding therapy relieves specific phobias effectively. However, there are exceptions to these generalizations, and often the differences in success rates for different types of treatment are not substantial (Westen, Novotny, & Thompson-Brenner, 2004; McAleavey et al., 2019; Duffy, Sharpe, & Schwannauer, 2019).

- Most therapies share several basic similar elements. Despite the fact that the specific methods used in different therapies are very different from one another, there are several common themes that lead them to be effective. These elements include the opportunity for a client to develop a positive relationship with a therapist, an explanation or interpretation of a client's symptoms, and confrontation of negative emotions. The fact that these common elements exist in most therapies makes it difficult to compare one treatment against another (Norcross, 2002; Norcross, Beutler, & Levant, 2006; Wampold, 2019).

Consequently, there is no single, definitive answer to the broad question, "Which therapy works best?" because of the complexity in sorting out the various factors that enter into successful therapy. Recently, however, clinicians and researchers have reframed the question by focusing on evidence-based psychotherapy practice. *Evidence-based psychotherapy practice* seeks to use research findings to determine the best practices for treating a specific disorder. To determine best practices, researchers use clinical interviews, client self-reports of improvement in quality of life, reductions in symptoms, observations of behavior, and other outcomes to compare different therapies. By using objective research findings, clinicians are increasingly able to determine the most effective treatment for a specific disorder (Kazdin, 2008; Gaudiano & Miller, 2013; Maguen et al., 2019).

Because no single type of psychotherapy is invariably effective for every individual, some therapists use an eclectic approach to therapy. In an *eclectic approach to therapy*, therapists use a variety of techniques, thus integrating several perspectives, to treat a person's problems. By employing more than one approach, therapists can choose the appropriate mix of evidence-based treatments to match the individual's specific needs. Furthermore, therapists with certain personal characteristics may work better with particular individuals and types of treatments, and—as we consider next—even racial and ethnic factors may be related to the success of treatment (Hays, 2008; Kertz et al., 2015; Wampold, 2019).

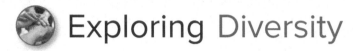 # Exploring Diversity

Racial and Ethnic Factors in Treatment: Should Therapists Be Color-Blind?

Consider the following case report written by a school counselor about Jimmy Jones, a 12-year-old student who was referred to a counselor because of his lack of interest in schoolwork:

> Jimmy does not pay attention, daydreams often, and frequently falls asleep during class. There is a strong possibility that Jimmy is harboring repressed rage that needs to be ventilated and dealt with. His inability to directly express his anger had led him to adopt passive-aggressive means of expressing hostility, i.e., inattentiveness, daydreaming, falling asleep. It is recommended that Jimmy be seen for intensive counseling to discover the basis of the anger. (Sue & Sue, 1990)

The counselor was wrong, however. Rather than suffering from "repressed rage," Jimmy lived in a poverty-stricken and disorganized home. Because of overcrowding at his house, he did not get enough sleep and consequently was tired the next day. Frequently, he was also hungry. In short, the stresses arising from his environment and not any deep-seated psychological disturbances caused his problems.

This incident underscores the importance of taking people's environmental and cultural backgrounds into account during treatment for psychological disorders. In particular, members of racial and ethnic minority groups, especially those who are also poor, may behave in ways that help them deal with a society that discriminates against them. As a consequence, behavior that may signal psychological disorder in middle-class and upper-class whites may simply be adaptive in people from other racial and socioeconomic groups. For instance, characteristically suspicious and distrustful people may be displaying a survival strategy to protect themselves from psychological and physical injury rather than suffering from a psychological disturbance (Paniagua, 2000; Tseng, 2003; Pottick et al., 2007).

In fact, therapists must question some basic assumptions of psychotherapy when dealing with racial, ethnic, and cultural minority group members. For example, compared with the dominant culture, Asian and Latino cultures typically place much greater emphasis on the group, family, and society. When an Asian or Latino faces a critical decision, the family helps make it—a cultural practice suggesting that family members should also play a role in psychological treatment. Similarly, the traditional Chinese recommendation for dealing with depression or anxiety is to urge people who experience such problems to avoid thinking about whatever is upsetting them. Consider how this advice contrasts with treatment approaches that emphasize the value of insight (McCarthy, 2005; Leitner, 2007; Tanaka-Matsumi, 2019).

Therapists' interpretation of their clients' behavior is influenced by racial, ethnic, cultural, and social class backgrounds of the clients. For example, this man could be seen as lazy, drunk, or merely exhausted, depending on the context.

Arts Illustrated Studios/Shutterstock

Clearly, therapists *cannot* be "color-blind." Instead, they must take into account the racial, ethnic, cultural, and social class backgrounds of their clients in determining the nature of a psychological disorder and the course of treatment (Pedersen et al., 2002; Hays, 2008; Moodley, Gielen, & Wu, 2013).

From the perspective of...

A Social Worker How might the types of therapies you employ vary depending on a client's cultural and socioeconomic background?

Sam Edwards/OJO Images/age fotostock

RECAP/EVALUATE/RETHINK

RECAP

LO 50-1 What are humanistic approaches to treatment?

- Humanistic therapy is based on the premise that people have control of their behavior, that they can make choices about their lives, and that it is up to them to solve their own problems. Humanistic therapies, which take a nondirective approach, include person-centered therapy.

LO 50-2 What is interpersonal therapy?

- Interpersonal therapy focuses on interpersonal relationships and strives for immediate improvement during short-term therapy.

LO 50-3 How does group therapy differ from individual types of therapy?

- In group therapy, several unrelated people meet with a therapist to discuss some aspect of their psychological functioning and often center on a common problem.

LO 50-4 How effective is psychotherapy, and which kind of psychotherapy works best in a given situation?

- Most research suggests that, in general, therapy is more effective than no therapy, although how much more effective is not known.
- The more difficult question of which therapy works best is harder to answer, but it is clear particular kinds of therapy are more appropriate for some problems than for others.
- Because no single type of psychotherapy is invariably effective, eclectic approaches in which a therapist uses a variety of techniques and thus integrates several perspectives are sometimes used.

EVALUATE

1. Match each of the following treatment strategies with the statement you might expect to hear from a therapist using that strategy.

   1. Group therapy
   2. Unconditional positive regard
   3. Behavioral therapy
   4. Nondirective counseling

   a. "In other words, you don't get along with your mother because she hates your girlfriend, is that right?"
   b. "I want you all to take turns talking about why you decided to come and what you hope to gain from therapy."
   c. "I can understand why you wanted to wreck your friend's car after she hurt your feelings. Now tell me more about the accident."
   d. "That's not appropriate behavior. Let's work on replacing it with something else."

2. _____ therapies assume that people should take responsibility for their lives and the decisions they make.

3. One of the major criticisms of humanistic therapies is that
   a. They are too imprecise and unstructured.
   b. They treat only the symptom of the problem.
   c. The therapist dominates the patient-therapist interaction.
   d. They work well only on clients of lower socioeconomic status.

4. In a controversial study, Eysenck found that some people go into _____ _____, or recovery without treatment, if they are simply left alone instead of treated.

RETHINK

1. How can people be successfully treated in group therapy when individuals with the "same" problem are so different? What advantages might group therapy offer over individual therapy?
2. List some examples of behavior that might be considered abnormal among members of one cultural or economic group and normal by members of a different cultural or economic group. Suppose that most therapies had been developed by psychologists from minority culture groups and lower socioeconomic status; how might they differ from current therapies?

Answers to Evaluate Questions

1. 1-b, 2-c, 3-d, 4-a; **2.** Humanistic; **3.** a; **4.** spontaneous remission

KEY TERMS

humanistic therapy
person-centered therapy

interpersonal therapy (IPT)

group therapy
family therapy

spontaneous remission

Module 51

Biomedical Therapy: Biological Approaches to Treatment

If you get a kidney infection, your doctor gives you an antibiotic; with luck, your kidneys should be as good as new about a week later. If your appendix becomes inflamed, a surgeon removes it, and your body functions normally once more. Could a comparable approach that focuses on the body's physiology be effective for psychological disturbances?

According to biological approaches to treatment, the answer is yes. Therapists routinely use biomedical therapies that rely on drugs and medical procedures to improve psychological functioning.

The biomedical approach focuses treatment directly on altering brain chemistry or other neurological factors rather than concentrating on a patient's psychological conflicts, past traumas, or other issues of daily life that may produce psychological disorder. To do this, therapists provide treatment with drugs, electric shock, or surgery, as we will discuss.

LEARNING OUTCOMES

LO 51-1 How are drug, electro-convulsive, and psychosurgical techniques used today in the treatment of psychological disorders?

Drug Therapy

Drug therapy is the treatment of psychological disorders using medication. Drug therapy works by altering the operation of neurons and neurotransmitters in the brain.

Some drugs operate by *inhibiting* neurotransmitters or receptor neurons, which reduces activity at particular synapses. (Recall from our discussion of neurons in the neuroscience chapter that synapses are the gaps where nerve impulses travel from one neuron to another.) Thus, particular neurons are inhibited from firing.

Other drugs do just the opposite: They *increase* the activity of certain neurotransmitters or neurons, which allows particular neurons to fire more frequently (see Figure 1).

drug therapy Treatment of psychological disorders through the use of medication that alters the operation of neurons and neurotransmitters in the brain and body. (Module 51)

ANTIPSYCHOTIC DRUGS

Probably no greater change has occurred in mental hospitals than the successful introduction in the mid-1950s of **antipsychotic drugs**—drugs used to reduce severe symptoms of disturbance, such as loss of touch with reality and agitation. Previously, the typical mental hospital wasn't very different from the stereotypical 19th-century insane asylum; it gave mainly custodial care to screaming, moaning, clawing patients who displayed bizarre behaviors. However, in just a matter of days after hospital staff members administered antipsychotic drugs, the wards became considerably calmer environments in which professionals could do more than just try to get patients through the day without causing serious harm to themselves or others.

antipsychotic drugs Drugs that temporarily reduce psychotic symptoms such as agitation, hallucinations, and delusions. (Module 51)

This dramatic change came about through the introduction of the drug *chlorpromazine*. Along with other similar drugs, chlorpromazine rapidly became the most popular and successful treatment for schizophrenia. Today, drug therapy is typically the preferred treatment for most cases of severely abnormal behavior and is used for most patients hospitalized with psychological disorders. The newest generation of antipsychotics, referred to as *atypical antipsychotics*, have fewer side effects; they include *risperidone, olanzapine,* and *paliperidone* (Hattori et al.,2017; Henshall et al., 2019).

How do antipsychotic drugs work? Most block dopamine receptors at the brain's synapses, the space between pairs of neurons that communicate via chemical messengers.

Drug Treatments			
Class of Drug	**Effects of Drug**	**Primary Action of Drug**	**Examples**
Antipsychotic Drugs	Reduction in loss of touch with reality, agitation	Block dopamine receptors	Antipsychotic: chlorpromazine (Thorazine), clozapine (Clozaril), haloperidol (Haldol) Atypical antipsychotic: risperidone, olanzapine
Antidepressant Drugs			
Tricyclic antidepressants	Reduction in depression	Permit rise in neurotransmitters such as norepinepherine	Trazodone (Desyrel), amitriptyline (Elavil), desipramine (Norpamin)
MAO inhibitors	Reduction in depression	Prevent MAO from breaking down neurotransmitters	Phenelzine (Nardil), tranylcypromine (Parnate)
Selective serotonin reuptake inhibitors (SSRIs)	Reduction in depression	Inhibit reuptake of serotonin	Fluoxetine (Prozac), Luvox, Paxil, Celexa, Zoloft, nefazodone (Serzone)
Mood Stabilizers			
Lithium	Mood stabilization	Can alter transmission of impulses within neurons	Lithium (Lithonate), Depakote, Tegretol
Antianxiety Drugs	Reduction in anxiety	Increase activity of neurotransmitter GABA	Benzodiazepines (Valium, Xanax)

FIGURE 1 The major classes of drugs used to treat psychological disorders have different effects on the brain and nervous system.

Atypical antipsychotics affect both serotonin and dopamine levels in the brain, particularly those related to planning and goal-directed activity (Sawa & Snyder, 2002; Advokat, 2005; Mizrahi et al., 2011).

Despite the effectiveness of antipsychotic drugs, they do not produce a "cure" in the same way that, say, penicillin cures an infection. Most of the time, the symptoms reappear when the drug is withdrawn. Furthermore, such drugs can have long-term side effects, such as dryness of the mouth and throat, dizziness, and sometimes tremors and loss of muscle control, which may continue after drug treatments are stopped (Voruganti et al., 2007; Pijnenborg et al., 2015).

ANTIDEPRESSANT DRUGS

antidepressant drugs Medications that improve a severely depressed patient's mood and feeling of well-being. (Module 51)

As their name suggests, **antidepressant drugs** are a class of medications used in cases of severe depression to improve a patient's mood and feeling of well-being. They are also sometimes used for other disorders, such as anxiety disorders and bulimia (Hedges et al., 2007; Deacon & Spielmans, 2017; McElroy et al., 2019).

Most antidepressant drugs work by changing the concentration of specific neurotransmitters in the brain. For example, *tricyclic drugs* increase the availability of norepinephrine at the synapses of neurons, whereas *MAO inhibitors* prevent the enzyme monoamine oxidase (MAO) from breaking down neurotransmitters. Newer antidepressants—such as Lexapro—are *selective serotonin reuptake inhibitors (SSRIs)*. SSRIs target the neurotransmitter serotonin and permit it to linger at the synapse. Some antidepressants produce a combination of effects. For instance, nefazodone (Serzone) blocks serotonin at some receptor sites but not others, whereas bupropion (Wellbutrin and Zyban) affects the norepinephrine and dopamine systems (see Figure 2; Dhillon, Yang, & Curran, 2008; Harmer, Duman, & Cowen, 2017).

Finally, there are some newer drugs on the horizon. For instance, scientists have found that the anesthetic *ketamine* blocks the neural receptor NMDA, which affects the neurotransmitter *glutamate*. Glutamate plays an important role in mood regulation and the ability to experience pleasure, and researchers believe that ketamine blockers may prove to be useful in the treatment of depression (Skolnick, Popik, & Trullas, 2009; Schwartzmant, Alexander, & Grothusen, 2011).

Study Alert

To help organize your study of different drugs used in therapy, review Figure 1, which classifies them according to the categories of antipsychotic, antidepressant, mood-stabilizing, and antianxiety drugs.

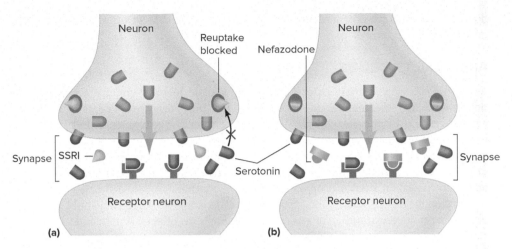

FIGURE 2 In (a), selective serotonin reuptake inhibitors (SSRIs) reduce depression by permitting the neurotransmitter serotonin to remain in the synapse. In (b), a newer antidepressant, nefazodone (Serzone), operates more selectively to block serotonin at some sites but not others, which helps to reduce the side effects of the drug.
Source: Adapted from Mischoulon, D. (2000, June). Anti-depressants: Choices and controversy. *HealthNews,* 4.

Overall, the success rates of antidepressant drugs are quite good. In fact, antidepressants can produce lasting, long-term recovery from depression. In many cases, even after patients stop taking the drugs, their depression does not return. On the other hand, antidepressant drugs may produce side effects such as drowsiness and cognitive deficits such as memory loss. Evidence also suggests that SSRI antidepressants can increase the risk of suicide in children and adolescents—clearly a significant concern (Prus et al., 2015; Shehab, Brent, & Maalouf, 2016; Forsman et al., 2019).

Consumers spend billions of dollars each year on antidepressant drugs. Ten percent of Americans now take antidepressants, and for women in their 40s and 50s, the figure is 25%. In particular, the antidepressant *fluoxetine,* sold under the trade name *Prozac,* has been highlighted on magazine covers and has been the topic of best-selling books (Rabin, 2013).

Does Prozac deserve its acclaim? In some respects, yes. It is effective and has relatively few side effects. Furthermore, many people who do not respond to other types of antidepressants do well on Prozac. On the other hand, 20–30% of users report experiencing nausea and diarrhea, and a smaller number report sexual dysfunctions (Brambilla et al., 2005; Fenter, 2006).

Another substance that has received a great deal of publicity is *St. John's wort,* an herb that some have called a "natural" antidepressant. Although it is widely used in Europe for the treatment of depression, the U.S. Food and Drug Administration considers it a dietary supplement, and therefore, the substance is available here without a prescription.

Despite the popularity of St. John's wort, definitive clinical tests have found that the herb is ineffective in the treatment of depression. However, because some research shows that the herb successfully reduces certain psychological symptoms, some proponents argue that using it is reasonable. In any case, people should not use St. John's wort to medicate themselves without consulting a mental health-care professional (Rapaport et al., 2011; Ng, Venkatanarayanan, & Ho, 2017; Forsdike & Pirotta, 2019).

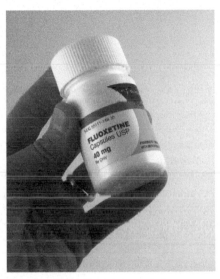

The drug fluoxetine, commonly known as Prozac, is a widely prescribed antidepressant.
Jill Braaten/McGraw-Hill

MOOD STABILIZERS

Mood stabilizers are used to treat mood disorders characterized by intense mood swings, especially manic episodes in bipolar disorder. For example, the drug *lithium,* a form of mineral salts, has been used very successfully in patients with bipolar disorders. Although no one knows definitely why, lithium and other mood stabilizers such as divalproex sodium (*Depakote*) and carbamazepine (*Tegretol*) effectively reduce manic episodes. However, they do not effectively treat depressive phases of bipolar disorder, so antidepressants are usually prescribed during those phases (Smith et al., 2007; Salvi et al., 2008; Inoue et al., 2011).

Lithium and similar drugs have a quality that sets them apart from other drug treatments: They can be a *preventive* treatment that blocks future episodes of manic depression. Often, people who have had episodes of bipolar disorder can take a daily

mood stabilizers Drugs used to treat mood disorders characterized by intense mood swings, especially manic episodes in bipolar disorder. (Module 51) dose of lithium to prevent a recurrence of their symptoms. Most other drugs are useful only when symptoms of psychological disturbance occur.

ANTIANXIETY DRUGS

antianxiety drugs Drugs that reduce the level of anxiety a person experiences and increase feelings of well-being. (Module 51)

As the name implies, **antianxiety drugs** reduce the level of anxiety a person experiences and increase feelings of well-being. They are prescribed not only to reduce general tension in people who are experiencing temporary difficulties but also to aid in the treatment of more serious anxiety disorders.

Antianxiety drugs such as alprazolam and Valium are among the medications physicians most frequently prescribe. In fact, more than half of all U.S. families have someone who has taken such a drug at one time or another.

Although the popularity of antianxiety drugs suggests that they hold few risks, they can produce a number of potentially serious side effects. For instance, they can cause fatigue, and long-term use can lead to dependence. Moreover, when taken in combination with alcohol, some antianxiety drugs can be lethal. But a more important issue concerns their use to suppress anxiety. Almost every therapeutic approach to psychological disturbance views continuing anxiety as a signal of some other sort of problem. Thus, drugs that mask anxiety may simply be hiding other difficulties. Consequently, rather than confronting their underlying problems, people may be hiding from them through the use of antianxiety drugs.

Electroconvulsive Therapy (ECT)

electroconvulsive therapy (ECT)
A procedure used in the treatment of severe depression in which an electric current of 70–150 volts is briefly administered to a patient's head. (Module 51)

First introduced in the 1930s, **electroconvulsive therapy (ECT)** is a procedure in which an electric current of 70–150 volts is briefly administered to a patient's head, which causes a loss of consciousness and often causes seizures. It is used most frequently to treat severe major depression that has not responded to other treatments.

Typically, health-care professionals sedate patients and give them muscle relaxants before administering the current; such preparations help reduce the intensity of muscle contractions produced during ECT. The typical patient receives about 10 ECT treatments in the course of a month, but some patients continue with maintenance treatments for months afterward (Glass, Forester, & Hermida, 2017; Martin et al., 2019).

ECT is a controversial technique. Apart from the obvious distastefulness of a treatment that evokes images of electrocution, side effects occur frequently. For instance, after treatment patients often experience disorientation, confusion, and sometimes memory loss that may remain for months. Furthermore, ECT often does not produce long-term improvement; one study found that without follow-up medication, depression returned in most patients who had undergone ECT treatments. Finally, even when ECT does work, we do not know why, and some critics believe it may cause permanent brain damage (Gardner & O'Connor, 2008; Kato, 2009; Weiner & Falcone, 2011).

In light of the drawbacks to ECT, why do therapists use it at all? Basically, because in many severe cases of major depression, it offers the only quickly effective treatment. For instance, it may prevent depressed, suicidal individuals from committing suicide, and it can act more quickly than antidepressive medications.

The use of ECT has increased in the past decade, with more than 100,000 people undergoing it each year. Advances in the procedure have reduced its side effects, and practitioners are trying to reduce the stigma that surrounds it. In fact, research shows that ECT may be useful in reducing the symptoms of dementia. Still, ECT tends to be used only when other treatments have proved ineffective, and researchers continue to search for alternative treatments (Tokutsu et al., 2013; Izuhara et al., 2019; Reddy, 2019).

transcranial magnetic stimulation (TMS) A depression treatment in which a precise magnetic pulse is directed to a specific area of the brain. (Module 51)

One new and promising alternative to ECT is **transcranial magnetic stimulation (TMS)**. TMS creates a precise magnetic pulse in a specific area of the brain. By activating particular neurons, TMS has been effective in relieving the symptoms of major depression in a number of controlled experiments. However, the therapy can produce side effects, such as seizures and convulsions, and it is still considered experimental (Kim, Pesiridou, & O'Reardon, 2009; Bentwich et al., 2011).

Another promising therapy, still in the early stages of development, is the use of implants placed deep inside the brain to provide short jolts of electricity, a method called *deep brain stimulation (DBS)*. Unlike ECT, which affects the entire brain, DBS pinpoints specific, tiny regions of the brain. It has been shown to provide relief from major depression (Lozano & Mayberg, 2015; Sun et al., 2015; Ng et al., 2019).

Because DBS treatment is so new, researchers are still trying the stimulation in different regions of the brain and fine-tuning the exact placement within given regions to get the best results. The location may vary depending on the specific symptoms the patient is experiencing. Furthermore, the optimal level, frequency, and duration of stimulation are also being explored, as are the long-term effects. Still, initial results are promising (deGusmao, Pollak, & Sharma, 2017).

Psychosurgery

If ECT strikes you as a questionable procedure, the use of **psychosurgery**—brain surgery in which the object is to reduce symptoms of mental disorder—probably appears even more dubious. A technique used exceedingly rarely today, psychosurgery was introduced as a "treatment of last resort" in the 1930s.

psychosurgery Brain surgery once used to reduce the symptoms of mental disorder but rarely used today. (Module 51)

The first form of psychosurgery to be developed was the prefrontal lobotomy. *Prefrontal lobotomy* consists of surgically destroying or removing parts of a patient's frontal brain lobes, which surgeons thought controlled emotionality. In the 1930s and 1940s, surgeons performed the procedure on thousands of patients, often with little precision. For example, in one common technique, surgeons jabbed an ice pick under a patient's eyeball and swiveled it back and forth; in other cases, they drilled into the patient's skull (Phillips, 2013; Chodakiewitz et al., 2015; Carroll, 2017).

Psychosurgery sometimes did improve a patient's behavior but not without drastic side effects. Along with remission of the symptoms of the mental disorder, patients sometimes experienced personality changes and became bland, colorless, and unemotional. In other cases, patients became aggressive and unable to control their impulses. In the worst cases, treatment resulted in the patient's death.

With the introduction of effective drug treatments—and the obvious ethical questions regarding the appropriateness of forever altering someone's personality—psychosurgery became nearly obsolete. However, it is still used in very rare cases when all other procedures have failed and the patient's behavior presents a high risk to the patient and others. For example, surgeons sometimes use a more precise form of psychosurgery called a *cingulotomy* in rare cases of obsessive-compulsive disorder in which they destroy tissue in the *anterior cingulate* area of the brain. In another technique, *gamma knife surgery*, beams of radiation are used to destroy areas of the brain related to obsessive-compulsive disorder (Wilkinson, 2009; Eljamel, 2015; Staudt et al., 2019).

Occasionally, dying patients with severe, uncontrollable pain also receive psychosurgery. Still, even these cases raise important ethical issues, and psychosurgery remains a highly controversial treatment (Mashour, Walker, & Martuza, 2005; Steele et al., 2007; Garfield, 2014).

From the perspective of...

A Politician How would you go about regulating the use of electroconvulsive therapy and psychosurgery?

Exactostock/SuperStock

Biomedical Therapies in Perspective

In some respects, no greater revolution has occurred in the field of mental health than biological approaches to treatment. As previously violent, uncontrollable patients have been calmed by the use of drugs, mental hospitals have been able to concentrate more on actually helping patients and less on custodial functions. Similarly, patients whose lives have been disrupted by depression or bipolar episodes have been able to function normally, and other forms of drug therapy have also shown remarkable results.

Furthermore, new forms of biomedical therapy are promising. For example, the newest treatment possibility—which remains experimental at this point—is gene therapy. Specific genes may be introduced to particular regions of the brain. These genes then have the potential to reverse or even prevent biochemical events that give rise to psychological disorders (Tuszynski, 2007; Valenzuela et al., 2016; Anguela & High, 2019).

Another new treatment, now in its infancy, addresses disorders such as depression and anxiety using brain scan neurofeedback. In *brain scan neurofeedback*, patients are exposed to real-time brain scans showing brain activity as they recall emotion-laden memories or triggers for anxiety. By attempting to modify their brain activity, they seem to better cope with their symptoms (McDonald et al., 2017; Young et al., 2017).

Despite their current usefulness and future promise, biomedical therapies do not represent a complete and lasting cure for psychological disorders. For example, biomedical therapies typically provide only temporary relief of symptoms, and in most cases, symptoms return as soon as the drugs are withdrawn. Consequently, biomedical treatment may not solve the underlying problems that led a patient to therapy in the first place.

Second, critics note that drugs may produce side effects that range from minor to serious physical reactions. In the worst case, biomedical therapies may lead to the development of new symptoms of a psychological disorder.

Finally, an overreliance on biomedical therapies may lead therapists to overlook alternative forms of treatment, such as psychotherapy, that may be helpful. In fact, new research demonstrates that adding psychotherapy involving talk sessions with a therapist to drug treatments is preferable in even severe psychological disorders such as schizophrenia (Carey, 2015; Kane et al., 2016; Browne et al., 2017).

Thus, biomedical therapies—sometimes alone and more often in conjunction with psychotherapy—have permitted millions of people to function more effectively. Furthermore, although biomedical therapy and psychotherapy appear distinct, research shows that biomedical therapies ultimately may not be as different from talk therapies as one might imagine, at least in terms of their consequences.

Specifically, measures of brain functioning as a result of drug therapy compared with psychotherapy show little difference in outcomes. For example, one study compared the reactions of patients with major depression who received either an antidepressant drug or psychotherapy. After 6 weeks of either therapy, activity in the portion of the brain related to the disorder—the basal ganglia—had changed in similar ways, and that area appeared to function more normally. Although such research is not definitive, it does suggest that at least for some disorders, psychotherapy may be just as effective as biomedical interventions—and vice versa. Research also makes it clear that no single treatment is effective universally and that each type of treatment has advantages as well as disadvantages (Greenberg & Goldman, 2009; Gaudiano & Miller, 2013).

> **!** **Study Alert**
>
> Remember that biomedical treatments have benefits as well as drawbacks.

Community Psychology: Focus on Prevention

community psychology A branch of psychology that focuses on the prevention and minimization of psychological disorders in the community. (Module 51)

Each of the treatments we have reviewed has a common element: It is a "restorative" treatment aimed at alleviating psychological difficulties that already exist. However, an approach known as **community psychology** has a different aim: to prevent or minimize the incidence of psychological disorders.

Community psychology came of age in the 1960s, when mental health professionals developed plans for a nationwide network of community mental health centers. The hope was that those centers would provide low-cost mental health services, including short-term therapy and community educational programs. In another development, the population of mental hospitals has plunged as drug treatments made physical restraint of patients unnecessary.

The community psychology movement encouraged deinstitutionalization. **Deinstitutionalization** is the process of transferring patients who have been hospitalized for long periods into less-isolated community mental health settings. Proponents of deinstitutionalization wanted to ensure not only that deinstitutionalized patients received proper treatment but also that their civil rights were maintained (Henckes, 2011; Pow et al., 2015; Hudson, 2019).

Unfortunately, the promise of deinstitutionalization has not been met. One important reason is that deinstitutionalized patients rarely receive sufficient resources. What started as a worthy attempt to move people out of mental institutions ended, in many cases, with former patients being dumped into the community without any real support. Many became homeless—around 25% of all homeless adults are thought to have a major psychological disorder—and some become involved in illegal acts caused by their disorders (Whitaker, 2009; Searight, 2013; Durbin et al., 2019).

In short, many people who need treatment do not get it, and in some cases, care for people with psychological disorders has simply shifted from one type of treatment site to another. In fact, for many people, the only form of mental health treatment comes in emergency rooms of hospitals, with little or no follow-up care (Tsemberis & Macnaughton, 2017).

On the other hand, the community psychology movement has had some positive outcomes. Its emphasis on prevention has led to new approaches to psychological disorders. Furthermore, hotlines, available through phone calls or texts, are now common. At any time of the day or night, people experiencing acute stress can call a trained, sympathetic listener who can provide immediate—although obviously limited—treatment (Cauce, 2007; Nelson & MacLeod, 2017; Ramchand, 2017).

College and high school crisis centers are another innovation that grew out of the community psychology movement. Modeled after suicide prevention hot-line centers, crisis centers give callers an opportunity to discuss life crises with a sympathetic listener, who is often a volunteer.

While deinstitutionalization has had many successes, it has also contributed to the release of mental patients into the community with little or no support. As a result, many have become homeless.
Gary He/McGraw-Hill

deinstitutionalization The process of transferring patients who have been hospitalized for long periods into less-isolated community mental health settings. (Module 51)

BECOMING AN INFORMED CONSUMER
of Psychology

Choosing the Right Therapist

If you decide to seek therapy, you're faced with a daunting task. Choosing a therapist is not a simple matter. One place to begin the process of identifying a therapist is at the "Help Center" of the American Psychological Association at http://www.apa.org/helpcenter. And if you start therapy, several general guidelines can help you determine whether you've made the right choice:

You and your therapist should agree on the goals for treatment. They should be clear, specific, and attainable.

- *You should feel comfortable with your therapist.* You should not be intimidated by or in awe of a therapist. Rather, you should trust the therapist and feel free to discuss the most personal issues without fearing a negative reaction. In sum, the "personal chemistry" should be right.
- *Therapists should have appropriate training and credentials and should be licensed by appropriate state and local agencies.* Check therapists' membership in national

and state professional associations. In addition, the cost of therapy, billing practices, and other business matters should be clear. It is not a breach of etiquette to put these matters on the table during an initial consultation.

- *You should feel that you are making progress after therapy has begun, despite occasional setbacks.* If you have no sense of improvement after repeated visits, you and your therapist should discuss this issue frankly. Although there is no set timetable, the most obvious changes resulting from therapy tend to occur relatively early in the course of treatment. For instance, half of patients in psychotherapy improve by the 8th session and three-fourths by the 26th session. The average number of sessions with college students is just five (Lazarus, 1997; Taibbi, 2018).

Be aware that you will have to put in a great deal of effort in therapy. Although our culture promises quick cures for any problem, in reality, solving difficult problems is not easy. You must be committed to making therapy work and should know that it is you, not the therapist, who must do most of the work to resolve your problems. The effort has the potential to pay off handsomely—as you experience a more positive, fulfilling, and meaningful life.

RECAP/EVALUATE/RETHINK

RECAP

LO 51-1 How are drug, electroconvulsive, and psychosurgical techniques used today in the treatment of psychological disorders?

- Biomedical treatment approaches suggest that therapy should focus on the physiological causes of abnormal behavior rather than considering psychological factors. Drug therapy, the best example of biomedical treatments, has brought about dramatic reductions in the symptoms of mental disturbance.
- Antipsychotic drugs such as chlorpromazine very effectively reduce psychotic symptoms. Antidepressant drugs such as Prozac reduce depression so successfully that they are used very widely. Antianxiety drugs, or minor tranquilizers, are among the most frequently prescribed medications of any sort.
- In electroconvulsive therapy (ECT), used in severe cases of depression, a patient receives a brief electric current of 70-150 volts.
- Psychosurgery typically consists of surgically destroying or removing certain parts of a patient's brain.
- The community psychology approach encouraged deinstitutionalization in which previously hospitalized mental patients were released into the community.

EVALUATE

1. Antipsychotic drugs have provided effective, long-term, and complete cures for schizophrenia. True or false?

2. One highly effective biomedical treatment for a psychological disorder that is used mainly to arrest and prevent manic-depressive episodes is
   a. Chlorpromazine
   b. Lithium
   c. Librium
   d. Valium

3. Psychosurgery has grown in popularity as a method of treatment as surgical techniques have become more precise. True or false?

4. The trend toward releasing more patients from mental hospitals and into the community is known as _____.

RETHINK

1. One of the main criticisms of biological therapies is that they treat the symptoms of mental disorder without uncovering and treating the underlying problems from which people are suffering. Do you agree with this criticism? Why?

2. If a dangerously violent person could be "cured" of violence through a new psychosurgical technique, would you approve the use of this technique? Suppose the person agreed to—or requested—the technique? What sort of policy would you develop for the use of psychosurgery?

Answers to Evaluate Questions

1. False; schizophrenia can be controlled but not cured by medication; 2. b; 3. False; psychosurgery is now used only as a treatment of last resort; 4. deinstitutionalization

KEY TERMS

drug therapy	antianxiety drugs	transcranial magnetic	community
antipsychotic drugs	electroconvulsive therapy	stimulation (TMS)	psychology
antidepressant drugs	(ECT)	psychosurgery	deinstitutionalization
mood stabilizers			

LOOKING *Back*

EPILOGUE

We have examined how psychological professionals treat people with psychological disorders. We have considered a range of approaches that include both psychologically based and biologically based therapies. Clearly, the field has made substantial progress in recent years both in treating the symptoms of mental disorders and in understanding their underlying causes.

Before we leave the topic of treating psychological disorders, turn back to the prologue describing Michael's psychedelic therapy. On the basis of your understanding of the treatment of psychological disorders, consider the following questions.

1. Do you think that undergoing a worldview-altering psychedelic experience is an appropriate approach for someone who wants to quit smoking? Why or why not?
2. What traditional approach to therapy is most consistent with the psychedelic approach?
3. What traditional approach to therapy would most likely be enhanced by adding a psychedelic component? What traditional approach would least likely be enhanced by such an addition?
4. What other therapy options does Michael have for his problem? Which do you think would be the most effective for him, and why do you think so?

VISUAL SUMMARY 16 Treatment of Psychological Disorders

MODULE 49 Psychotherapy: Psychodynamic, Behavioral, and Cognitive Approaches

Psychodynamic Therapy

- Psychoanalysis
  - Free association: say aloud whatever comes to mind
  - Dream interpretation: looking for clues to unconscious conflicts and problems in dreams
  - Frequent sessions for a long time
- Contemporary psychodynamic approaches
  - Sessions are of shorter duration
  - Therapist takes more active role: focus is more in the present

Behavioral Treatment Approaches: Help modify behavior rather than find underlying causes

- Classical conditioning treatments
  - Aversive conditioning
  - Systematic desensitization
  - Flooding
- Operant conditioning techniques
  - Token system
  - Contingency contracting
  - Observational learning

Cognitive Approaches: Teach people to think in adaptive ways

- Rational-emotive behavior therapy

A	B	C
Negative Activating condition	**Irrational Belief system**	**Emotional Consequences**
(Close relationship breaks up)	("I'll never be loved again")	(Anxiety, loneliness, sadness, depression)

MODULE 50 Psychotherapy: Humanistic, Interpersonal, and Group Approaches

Humanistic Therapy: Focuses on self-responsibility in treatment techniques

- Person-centered therapy: helps people to reach their potential for self-actualization using unconditional positive regard

Interpersonal Therapy: Focuses on interpersonal relationships and improvement through short-term therapy

Group Therapy: Several people meet with a therapist to discuss psychological functioning

- Family therapy
- Self-help therapy

Does Psychotherapy Work?

Success rate (percentage)

- More effective than no treatment for most people
- Certain types of therapy work better for particular problems
- Most therapy approaches share basic elements

MODULE 51 Biomedical Therapy: Biological Approaches to Treatment

Drug Therapy: Controlling psychological disorders with drugs

Drug Treatments			
Class of Drug	Effects of Drug	Primary Action of Drug	Examples
Antipsychotic Drugs, Atypical Antidepressant Drugs	Reduction in loss of touch with reality, agitation	Block dopamine receptors	Antipsychotic: chlorpromazine (Thorazine), clozapine (Clozaril), haloperidol (Haldol)
			Atypical antipsychotic: risperidone, olanzapine
Antipsychotic Drugs Tricyclic antidepressants	Reduction in depression	Permit rise in neurotransmitters such as norepinepherine	Trazodone (Desyrel), amitriptyline (Elavil), desipramine (Norpamin)
MAO inhibitors	Reduction in depression	Prevent MAO from breaking down neurotransmitters	Phenelzine (Nardil), tranylcypromine (Parnate)
Selective serotonin reuptake inhibitors (SSRIs)	Reduction in depression	Inhibit reuptake of serotonin	Fluoxetine (Prozac), Luvox, Paxil, Celexa, Zoloft, nefazodone (Serzone)
Mood Stabilizers Lithium	Mood stabilization	Can alter transmission of impulses within neurons	Lithium (Lithonate), Depakote, Tegretol
Antianxiety Drugs	Reduction in anxiety	Increase activity of neurotransmitter GABA	Benzodiazepines (Valium, Xanax)

Electroconvulsive Therapy: Used as the only quickly effective treatment for severe depression

Psychosurgery: Brain surgery to reduce symptoms of mental disorders

Community Psychology: Prevention of the incidence of psychological disorders

- Deinstitutionalization: transfer of mental patients into the community where they may not receive necessary treatment

(Module 49): Source: Ellis, A. (1974). *Growth through reason*. Hollywood, CA: Wilshire Books; (Module 50): highwaystarz/123RF; Source: Adapted from Smith, M. L., Glass, G. V., & Miller, T. I. (1980). *The benefits of psychotherapy*. Baltimore: The Johns Hopkins University Press; (Module 51): Gary He/McGraw-Hill

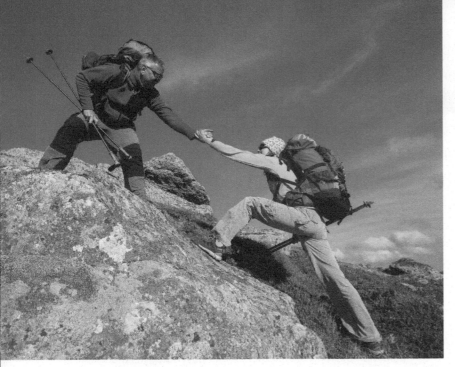

Vitalii Nesterchuk/123RF

CHAPTER 17
Social Psychology

LEARNING OUTCOMES FOR CHAPTER 17

LO 55-1 Why are we attracted to certain people, and what progression do social relationships follow?

LO 55-2 What factors underlie aggression and prosocial behavior?

PROLOGUE *A FRIEND IN NEED*

Jim McGee, a 69-year-old former Air Force pilot and Vietnam War veteran, was hesitant to attend an upcoming reunion of his old military buddies. It wasn't the cross-country trip that gave him pause; it was the dialysis. Jim's kidneys had failed, and he desperately needed a kidney donor. Without one, his chances of living much longer were poor. Taking a long trip might be a strain on his body, but he decided it was worth it to see his friends again. He had no idea how good a decision that would be.

At the reunion, Jim ran into fellow aviator Doug Coffman, whom Jim hadn't seen in nearly 50 years. The two men had together taken an intensive course in Vietnamese before they went off to war. When he learned of Jim's predicament, Doug immediately wanted to help. Although he himself was 70 years old, he knew he was in excellent health and that he had two healthy kidneys. Medical tests soon proved him right and showed that he was a good match for Jim. Doug wasted no time scheduling the earliest surgery date available for him to become Jim's kidney donor.

Just a couple months after that chance encounter at the reunion, Jim and Doug woke up side-by-side in a surgical recovery room, with Doug's kidney now functioning normally inside Jim's body. "There's nothing finer than knowing I've helped another person live a better life," Doug later said (McCaffery, 2019).

LOOKING *Ahead*

We can assume that hundreds of individuals knew about Jim McGee's condition since its onset. Yet none of them offered a kidney. What drove Doug Coffman to act so selflessly, particularly for someone he had not seen for 50 years?

We can answer this and similar questions only by taking into account findings from the field of social psychology, the branch that focuses on the aspects of human behavior that unite—and separate—us from one another. **Social psychology** is the scientific study of how people's thoughts, feelings, and actions are affected by others. Social psychologists consider the kinds and causes of the individual's behavior in social situations. They examine how the nature of situations in which we find ourselves influences our behavior in important ways.

The broad scope of social psychology is conveyed by the kinds of questions social psychologists ask, such as: How can we convince people to change their attitudes or adopt new ideas and values? In what ways do we come to understand what others are like? How are we influenced by what others do and think? Why do some people display so much violence, aggression, and cruelty toward others that people throughout the world live in fear of annihilation at their hands? And why, in comparison, do some people place their own lives at risk to help others? In exploring these and other questions, we also discuss strategies for confronting and solving a variety of problems and issues that all of us face, ranging from achieving a better understanding of persuasive tactics to forming more accurate impressions of others.

We begin with a look at how our attitudes shape our behavior and how we form judgments about others. We'll discuss how we are influenced by others, and we will consider prejudice and discrimination by focusing on their roots and the ways we can reduce them. After examining what social psychologists have learned about the ways people form friendships and relationships, we'll conclude with a look at the determinants of aggression and helping—two opposing sides of human behavior.

social psychology The scientific study of how people's thoughts, feelings, and actions are affected by others. (Module 52)

Module 52
Attitudes and Social Cognition

What do Jennifer Aniston and Tom Brady have in common? Both have appeared in advertisements designed to mold or change our attitudes. Such commercials are part of the barrage of messages we receive each day from sources as varied as politicians, sales staff in stores, and celebrities–all of which are meant to influence us.

Persuasion: Changing Attitudes

Attitudes are one of the central concepts of social psychology. **Attitudes** are evaluations of people, objects, ideas, and behavior. We have all sorts of attitudes, ranging from those about others ("I think the president is great"), to attitudes about behavior ("I hate it when people are late for appointments"), to attitudes toward more abstract concepts ("I support affirmative action") (Hegarty & Massey, 2007; Simon & Hoyt, 2008).

Persuasion involves changing attitudes. The ease with which attitudes can be changed depends on a number of factors, including:

- *Message source.* The characteristics of a person who delivers a persuasive message, known as an *attitude communicator,* have a major impact on the effectiveness of that message. Communicators who are physically and socially attractive produce greater attitude change than do those who are less attractive. Moreover, the communicator's expertise and trustworthiness are related to the impact of a message–except in situations in which the audience believes the communicator has an ulterior motive (Messner, Reinhard, & Sporer, 2008; Bebermeier et al., 2015).

- *Characteristics of the message.* It is not just *who* delivers a message but what the message is like that affects attitudes. Generally, two-sided messages–which include both the communicator's position and the one he or she is arguing against–are more effective than one-sided messages, given the assumption that the arguments for the other side can be effectively refuted and the audience is knowledgeable about the topic. In addition, fear-producing messages ("If you don't practice safer sex, you'll get AIDS") are generally effective when they provide the audience with a means for reducing the fear. However, if the fear that is aroused is too strong, messages may evoke people's defense mechanisms and be ignored (Keer et al., 2013; Bigsby, Monahan, & Ewoldsen, 2017; Cornelis, Heuvinck, & Majmundar, 2019).

- *Characteristics of the target.* Once a communicator has delivered a message, characteristics of the *target* of the message may determine whether the message will be accepted. For example, intelligent people are more resistant to persuasion than are those who are less intelligent. Gender differences in persuadability also seem to exist. In public settings, women are somewhat more easily persuaded than men, particularly when women have less knowledge about the message's topic. However, they are as likely as men to change their private attitudes. In fact, the magnitude of the differences in resistance to persuasion between men and women is not large (Guadagno & Cialdini, 2002; Shang, Kallmann, & Arif, 2019).

ROUTES TO PERSUASION

Recipients' receptiveness to persuasive messages relates to the type of information-processing they use. Social psychologists have discovered two primary information-processing routes

LEARNING OUTCOMES

LO 52-1 What are attitudes, and how are they formed, maintained, and changed?

LO 52-2 How do people form impressions of what others are like and the causes of their behavior?

LO 52-3 What are the biases that influence the ways in which people view others' behavior?

attitudes Evaluations of people, objects, ideas, and behavior. (Module 52)

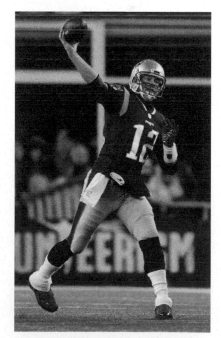

Do celebrities such as former Patriot quarterback Tom Brady influence attitudes? Advertisers certainly believe this is true, investing millions of dollars in endorsement fees.

John Cetrino/EPA-EFE/Shutterstock

central route processing The type of mental processing that occurs when a persuasive message is evaluated by thoughtful consideration of the issues and arguments used to persuade. (Module 52)

peripheral route processing The type of mental processing that occurs when a persuasive message is evaluated on the basis of irrelevant or extraneous factors. (Module 52)

Study Alert

Central route processing involves the content of the message; peripheral route processing involves how the message is provided.

to persuasion: central route and peripheral route processing. **Central route processing** occurs when the recipient thoughtfully considers the issues and arguments involved in persuasion. In central route processing, people are swayed in their judgments by the logic, merit, and strength of arguments.

In contrast, **peripheral route processing** occurs when people are persuaded on the basis of factors unrelated to the nature or quality of the content of a persuasive message. Instead, factors that are irrelevant or extraneous to the issue, such as who is providing the message, how long the arguments are, or the emotional appeal of the arguments, influence them (Kao, 2011; Xie & Johnson, 2015; Manca et al., 2019).

In general, people who are highly involved and motivated use central route processing to comprehend a message. However, if a person is disinterested, unmotivated, bored, or distracted, the characteristics of the message become less important, and peripheral factors become more influential (see Figure 1). Although both central route and peripheral route processing lead to attitude change, central route processing generally leads to stronger, more lasting attitude change.

Are some people more likely than others to habitually use central route processing rather than peripheral route processing? The answer is yes. *Need for cognition* is someone's typical level of thoughtfulness and cognitive activity. People who have a high need for cognition are more likely to employ central route processing. In contrast, people with a low need for cognition are more likely to use peripheral route processing. See Figure 2 to get a sense of your own need for cognition (Dai & Wang, 2007; Hill et al., 2013; Luttrell, Petty, & Xu, 2017).

People who have a high need for cognition enjoy thinking, philosophizing, and reflecting on the world. Because they are more likely to reflect on persuasive messages by using central route processing, they are persuaded by complex, logical, and detailed messages. In contrast, those who have a low need for cognition become impatient when forced to spend too much time thinking about an issue. Consequently, they usually use peripheral route processing and are persuaded by factors other than the quality and detail of messages (Dollinger, 2003; Van Overwalle & Siebler, 2005; Sohlberg, 2019).

From the perspective of...

A Sales Specialist Suppose you were selling an automobile to a customer who walked in the door. What strategies might you use to be persuasive?

Amos Morgan/Photodisc/Getty Images

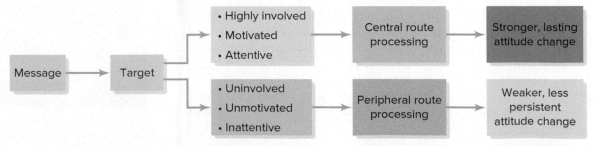

FIGURE 1 Routes to persuasion. Targets who are highly involved, motivated, and attentive use central route processing when they consider a persuasive message, which leads to a more lasting attitude change. In contrast, uninvolved, unmotivated, and inattentive targets are more likely to use peripheral route processing, and attitude change is likely to be less enduring. Can you think of specific advertisements that try to produce central route processing?

The Need for Cognition

Which of the following statements apply to you?

1. I really enjoy a task that involves coming up with new solutions to problems.

2. I would prefer a task that is intellectual, difficult, and important to one that is somewhat important but does not require much thought.

3. Learning new ways to think doesn't excite me very much.

4. The idea of relying on thought to make my way to the top does not appeal to me.

5. I think only as hard as I have to.

6. I like tasks that require little thought once I've learned them.

7. I prefer to think about small, daily projects rather than long-term ones.

8. I would rather do something that requires little thought than something that is sure to challenge my thinking abilities.

9. I find little satisfaction in deliberating hard and for long hours.

10. I don't like to be responsible for a situation that requires a lot of thinking.

Scoring: The more you agree with statements 1 and 2, and disagree with the rest, the greater the likelihood that you have a high need for cognition.

FIGURE 2 This simple questionnaire will give you a general idea of the level of your need for cognition.

Source: Adapted from Cacioppo, J. T., Berntson, G. G., & Crites, S. L., Jr. (1996). Social neuroscience: Principles of psychophysiological arousal and response. In E. T. Higgins & A. W. Kruglanski (Eds.), *Social psychology: Handbook of basic principles.* New York: Guilford.

THE LINK BETWEEN ATTITUDES AND BEHAVIOR

Attitudes influence behavior. The strength of the link between particular attitudes and behavior varies, of course, but generally, people strive for consistency between their attitudes and their behavior. Furthermore, people hold fairly consistent attitudes. For instance, you would probably not hold the attitude that eating meat is immoral and still have a positive attitude toward hamburgers (Levi, Chan, & Pence, 2006; Elen et al., 2013; Rodrigues & Girandola, 2017).

Ironically, the consistency that leads attitudes to influence behavior sometimes works the other way around; in some cases, our behavior shapes our attitudes. Consider, for instance, the following incident:

> You've just spent what you feel is the most boring hour of your life turning pegs for a psychology experiment. Just as you finally finish and are about to leave, the experimenter asks you to do him a favor. He tells you that he needs a helper for future experimental sessions to introduce subsequent participants to the peg-turning task. Your specific job will be to tell them that turning the pegs is an interesting, fascinating experience. Each time you tell this tale to another participant, you'll be paid $1.

If you agree to help the experimenter, you may be setting yourself up for a state of psychological tension called cognitive dissonance. **Cognitive dissonance** is the mental conflict that occurs when a person holds two contradictory thoughts, beliefs, or attitudes (Festinger, 1957).

If you participate in the situation just described, you are likely to experience two contradictory thoughts: (1) I believe the task is boring, but (2) I said it was interesting with little justification ($1). Given the contradiction between them, these two thoughts should arouse cognitive dissonance.

How can you reduce the cognitive dissonance? You cannot deny having said that the task is interesting because you just said it. On the other hand, it is relatively easy to change your attitude toward the task—and thus, the theory predicts that participants

cognitive dissonance The mental conflict that occurs when a person holds two contradictory thoughts, beliefs, or attitudes . (Module 52)

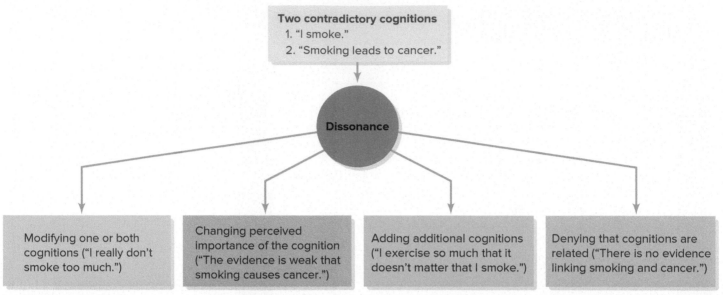

FIGURE 3 Cognitive dissonance. The simultaneous presence of two contradictory cognitions ("I smoke." and "Smoking leads to cancer.") produces dissonance, which can be reduced through several methods. What are additional ways in which dissonance can be reduced?

will reduce dissonance by adopting more positive attitudes toward the task (Dickinson & Oxoby, 2011; Harmon-Jones, Harmon-Jones, & Levy, 2015; Cooper, 2019).

A classic experiment (Festinger & Carlsmith, 1959) confirmed this prediction. The experiment followed essentially the same procedure outlined earlier in which a participant was offered $1 to describe a boring task as interesting. In addition, in a comparison condition, some participants were offered $20 to say that the task was interesting. The reasoning behind this condition was that $20 was so much money that participants in this condition had a good reason to be conveying incorrect information; dissonance would not be aroused, and less attitude change would be expected. The results supported this notion. More of the participants who were paid $1 changed their attitudes (becoming more positive toward the peg-turning task) than did participants who were paid $20.

Cognitive dissonance explains many everyday events involving attitudes and behavior. For example, smokers who know that smoking leads to lung cancer hold contradictory cognitions: (1) I smoke, and (2) smoking leads to lung cancer. The theory predicts that these two thoughts will lead to a state of cognitive dissonance. More important, it predicts that smokers will be motivated to reduce their dissonance.

There are four ways to reduce the dissonance in this case:

- Modifying one or both of the cognitions (e.g., "I really don't smoke that much.")
- Changing the perceived importance of one cognition ("The link between cancer and smoking is weak.")
- Adding cognitions ("I exercise so much that I'm really a healthy person.")
- Denying that the two cognitions are related to each other ("There's no compelling evidence linking smoking and cancer.")

Whichever strategy the smoker uses results in reduced dissonance (see Figure 3).

Social Cognition: Understanding Others

Regardless of Bill Clinton's personal transgressions and impeachment trial in the late 1990s, many Americans continued to find him extremely likable throughout his presidency, and even today he is among the most popular U.S. politicians. Cases like this illustrate the power of our impressions and attest to the importance of determining how people develop an understanding of others. One of the dominant areas in social psychology during the last few years has focused on learning how we come to understand what others are like and how we explain the reasons underlying others' behavior.

UNDERSTANDING WHAT OTHERS ARE LIKE

Consider for a moment the enormous amount of information about other people to which we are exposed. How can we decide what is important and what is not and make judgments about the characteristics of others? Social psychologists interested in this question study **social cognition**—the way people understand and make sense of others and themselves. Those psychologists have learned that individuals have highly developed **schemas,** sets of cognitions about people and social experiences. Those schemas organize information stored in memory; represent in our minds the way the social world operates; and give us a framework to recognize, categorize, and recall information relating to social stimuli such as people and groups (Amodio & Ratner, 2011; Leahy, 2015; Kitayama, 2017).

We typically hold schemas for specific types of people. Our schema for "teacher," for instance, generally consists of a number of characteristics: knowledge of the subject matter he or she is teaching, a desire to impart that knowledge, and an awareness of the student's need to understand what is being said. Or we may hold a schema for "mother" that includes the characteristics of warmth, nurturance, and caring. Regardless of their accuracy, schemas are important because they organize the way in which we recall, recognize, and categorize information about others. Moreover, they help us predict what others are like on the basis of relatively little information because we tend to fit people into schemas even when we do not have much concrete evidence to go on (Yamada & Itsukushima, 2013; McArthur et al., 2019).

FORMING IMPRESSIONS OF OTHERS

How do we decide that Sayreeta is a flirt, Jacob is obnoxious, or Hector is a really nice guy? The earliest work on social cognition examined *impression formation*, the process by which an individual organizes information about another person to form an overall impression of that person. In a classic study, for instance, students learned that they were about to hear a guest lecturer (Kelley, 1950). Researchers told one group of students that the lecturer was "a rather warm person, industrious, critical, practical, and determined" and told a second group that he was "a rather cold person, industrious, critical, practical, and determined."

The simple substitution of "cold" for "warm" caused drastic differences in the way the students in each group perceived the lecturer even though he gave the same talk in the same style in each condition. Students who had been told he was "warm" rated him considerably more positively overall than did students who had been told he was "cold."

The findings from this experiment led to additional research on impression formation that focused on the way in which people pay particular attention to certain unusually important traits—known as **central traits**—to help them form an overall impression of others. According to this work, the presence of a central trait alters the meaning of other traits. Hence, the description of the lecturer as "industrious" presumably meant something different when it was associated with the central trait "warm" than it meant when it was associated with "cold" (Glicksohn & Nahari, 2007; McCarthy & Skowronski, 2011; Huang, Sacchi, & Sherman, 2017).

Some researchers have used information-processing approaches to develop mathematical models of how we combine individual personality traits to develop an overall impression of others. Generally, we calculate a kind of psychological "average" of the individual traits we see in a person to form an overall judgment, just as we would find the mathematical average of several numbers (Mignon & Mollaret, 2002).

We also form impressions remarkably quickly. In just a few seconds, using what have been called "thin slices of behavior," we are able to make judgments of people. Interestingly, these quick impressions are surprisingly accurate and typically match

social cognition The cognitive processes by which people understand and make sense of others and themselves. (Module 52)

schemas Organized bodies of information stored in memory that bias the way new information is interpreted, stored, and recalled. (Modules 21, 52)

central traits The major traits considered in forming impressions of others. (Module 52) those of people who make judgments based on longer samples of behavior (Holleran, Mehl, & Levitt, 2009; Pretsch et al., 2013; Murphy et al., 2019).

Of course, as we gain more experience with people and see them exhibiting behavior in a variety of situations, our impressions of them become more complex. However, because our knowledge of others usually has gaps, we still tend to fit individuals into personality schemas that represent particular "types" of people. For instance, we may hold a "gregarious person" schema made up of the traits of friendliness, aggressiveness, and openness. The presence of just one or two of those traits may be sufficient to make us assign a person to a particular schema.

However, our schemas are susceptible to error. For example, mood affects how we perceive others. Happy people form more favorable impressions and make more positive judgments than do people who are in a bad mood (Forgas & Laham, 2005; Human & Biesanz, 2011).

Even when schemas are not entirely accurate, they serve an important function: They allow us to develop expectations about how others will behave. Those expectations permit us to plan our interactions with others more easily and serve to simplify a complex social world.

ATTRIBUTION PROCESSES: UNDERSTANDING THE CAUSES OF BEHAVIOR

When Barbara Washington, a new employee at the Ablex Computer Company, completed a major staffing project 2 weeks early, her boss, Yolanda, was delighted. At the next staff meeting, she announced how pleased she was with Barbara and explained that *this* was an example of the kind of performance she was looking for in her staff. The other staff members looked on resentfully, trying to figure out why Barbara had worked night and day to finish the project not just on time but 2 weeks early. She must be an awfully compulsive person, they decided.

attribution theory The theory that considers how we decide, on the basis of samples of a person's behavior, what the specific causes of that behavior are. (Module 52)

At one time or another, most of us have puzzled over the reasons behind someone's behavior. Perhaps it was in a situation similar to the one above, or it may have been in more formal circumstances, such as being a judge on a student judiciary board in a cheating case. **Attribution theory** considers how we decide, on the basis of samples of a person's behavior, what the specific causes of that behavior are. Unlike impression formation, which focuses on how people develop an overall impression of others' personality traits, attribution theory asks the "why" question: Why is someone acting in a particular way?

situational causes (of behavior) Causes of behavior that are external to a person. (Module 52)

In seeking an explanation for behavior, we must answer one central question: Is the cause situational or dispositional? **Situational causes** are causes of behavior that are external to a person. For instance, someone who knocks over a quart of milk and then cleans it up probably does the cleaning not because he or she is necessarily a neat person but because the *situation* requires it. In contrast, a person who spends hours shining the kitchen floor probably does so because he or she is an unusually neat person. Hence, the behavior has a dispositional cause. **Dispositional causes** are causes of behavior brought about by a person's traits or personality characteristics.

dispositional causes (of behavior) Perceived causes of behavior brought about by a person's traits or personality characteristics. (Module 52)

In our example involving Barbara Washington, her fellow employees attributed her behavior to her disposition rather than to the situation. But from a logical standpoint, it is equally plausible that something about the situation caused the behavior. If asked, Barbara might attribute her accomplishment to situational factors and explain that she had so much other work to do she just had to get the project out of the way or that the project was not all that difficult and was easy to complete ahead of schedule. To her, then, the reason for her behavior might not be dispositional at all; it could be situational.

ATTRIBUTION BIASES: TO ERR IS HUMAN

! Study Alert
The central question in making an attribution is whether the cause of behavior is due to situational or dispositional factors.

If we always processed information in the rational manner that attribution theory suggests, the world might run a lot more smoothly. Unfortunately, although attribution theory generally makes accurate predictions, people do not always process information about others as logically as the theory seems to suggest. In fact, research reveals consistent biases in the ways people make attributions. Typical biases include the following:

- *The halo effect.* Harry is intelligent, kind, and loving. Is he also conscientious? If you were to guess, your most likely response probably would be yes. Your guess reflects the **halo effect,** a phenomenon in which an initial understanding that a person has positive traits is used to infer other uniformly positive characteristics. The opposite would also hold true. Learning that Harry was unsociable and argumentative would probably lead you to assume that he was lazy as well. However, few people have either uniformly positive or uniformly negative traits, so the halo effect leads to misperceptions of others (Park, Park, & Dubinsky, 2011; Forgas & Laham, 2017; Austin & Halvorson, 2019).

- *Assumed-similarity bias.* How similar to you—in terms of attitudes, opinions, likes, and dislikes—are your friends and acquaintances? Most people believe that their friends and acquaintances are fairly similar to themselves. This belief exemplifies the **assumed-similarity bias,** which is the tendency to think of people as being similar to oneself. Given the diversity of people in the world, this assumption often impairs our ability to make accurate judgments (Lemay, Clark, & Feeney, 2007; Lemay & Clark, 2008; Kouros & Papp, 2019).

- *The self-serving bias.* When their teams win, coaches usually feel that the success is due to their coaching. But when their teams lose, coaches may think it's due to their players' poor skills. Similarly, if you get an A on a test, you may think it's due to your hard work, but if you get a poor grade, it's due to the professor's inadequacies. The reason is the **self-serving bias,** the tendency to attribute success to personal factors (skill, ability, or effort) and attribute failure to factors outside oneself (Shepperd, Malone, & Sweeny, 2008; Ferring, Tournier, & Mancini, 2015; Warach, Josephs, & Gorman, 2019).

- *The fundamental attribution error.* One of the more common attribution biases is the **fundamental attribution error,** which is the tendency to overattribute others' behavior to dispositional causes and the corresponding failure to recognize the importance of situational causes. The fundamental attribution error is prevalent in Western cultures. We tend to exaggerate the importance of personality characteristics (dispositional causes) in producing others' behavior and minimize the influence of the environment (situational factors). For example, we are more likely to jump to the conclusion that someone who is often late to work

halo effect A phenomenon in which an initial understanding that a person has positive or negative traits is used to infer other uniformly positive or negative characteristics. (Module 52)

assumed-similarity bias The tendency to think of people as being similar to oneself even when meeting them for the first time. (Module 52)

self-serving bias The tendency to attribute personal success to personal factors (skill, ability, or effort) and to attribute failure to factors outside oneself. (Module 52)

fundamental attribution error A tendency to overattribute others' behavior to dispositional causes and minimize the importance of situational causes. (Module 52)

The assumed-similarity bias leads us to believe that others hold similar attitudes, opinions, and likes and dislikes.
James Hardy/PhotoAlto/SuperStock

is lazy or a routinely tardy person (dispositional causes) than to assume that, perhaps, the subway they take to work frequently runs behind schedule, causing them to be late (a situational cause).

Why is the fundamental attribution error so common? One reason pertains to the nature of information available to the people making an attribution. When we view another person's behavior in a particular setting, the most conspicuous information is the person's behavior. Because the individual's immediate surroundings remain relatively unchanged and less attention grabbing, we center our attention on the person whose behavior we're considering. Consequently, we are more likely to make attributions based on personal dispositional factors and less likely to make attributions relating to the situation (Langdridge & Butt, 2004; Tal-Or & Papirman, 2007; Weber, 2019).

Social psychologists' awareness of attribution biases has led, in part, to the development of a new branch of economics called behavioral economics. *Behavioral economics* is concerned with how economic conditions are affected by individuals' biases and irrationality. Rather than viewing people as rational, thoughtful decision makers who are impartially weighing choices to draw conclusions, behavioral economists focus on the irrationality of judgments (Ariely & Norton, 2009).

 # Exploring Diversity

Attribution Biases in a Cultural Context: How Fundamental Is the Fundamental Attribution Error?

Attribution biases do not affect all of us in the same way. The culture in which we are raised clearly plays a role in the way we attribute others' behavior.

Take, for example, the fundamental attribution error: the tendency to overestimate the importance of personal, dispositional factors and underattribute situational factors in determining the causes of others' behavior. The error is pervasive in Western cultures and not in Eastern societies. For instance, adults in India were more likely to use situational attributions than to use dispositional ones in explaining events. These findings are the opposite of those for the United States, and they contradict the fundamental attribution error (Lien et al., 2006; Mahesh, 2019).

One reason for the difference may lie in the values of Eastern society, which emphasize social responsibility and societal obligations to a greater extent than Western societies do. In addition, the language spoken in a culture may lead to different sorts of attributions. For instance, a tardy person using English may say, "I am late"; this suggests a personal, dispositional cause ("I am a tardy person"). In contrast, speakers of Spanish who are late say, "The clock caused me to be late." Clearly, the statement in Spanish implies that the cause is situational (Macduff, 2006; Alon & Brett, 2007).

Cultural differences in attributions affect subsequent behavior. For example, parents in Asia tend to attribute good academic performance to effort and hard work (situational factors). In contrast, parents in Western cultures tend to de-emphasize the role of effort and attribute school success to innate ability (a dispositional factor). As a result, Asian students in general may strive harder to achieve and ultimately outperform U.S. students in school (Stevenson, Lee, & Mu, 2000; Lien et al., 2006).

The difference in thinking between people in Asian and Western cultures is a reflection of a broader difference in the way the world is perceived. Asian societies generally have a *collectivistic orientation,* a worldview that promotes the notion of interdependence. People with a collectivistic orientation generally see themselves as parts of a larger, interconnected social network and as responsible to others. In contrast, people in Western cultures are more likely to hold an *individualist orientation* that emphasizes personal identity and the uniqueness of the individual. They focus more on what sets them apart from others and what makes them special (Wang, 2004; Markus, 2007; Dean & Koenig, 2019).

RECAP/EVALUATE/RETHINK

RECAP

LO 52-1 What are attitudes, and how are they formed, maintained, and changed?

- Social psychology is the scientific study of the ways in which people's thoughts, feelings, and actions are affected by others and the nature and causes of individual behavior in social situations.
- Attitudes are evaluations of a particular person, behavior, belief, or concept.
- Cognitive dissonance occurs when an individual simultaneously holds two cognitions–attitudes or thoughts–that contradict each other. To resolve the contradiction, the person may modify one cognition, change its importance, add a cognition, or deny a link between the two cognitions–thus bringing about a reduction in dissonance.

LO 52-2 How do people form impressions of what others are like and the causes of their behavior?

- Social cognition involves the way people understand and make sense of others and themselves. People develop schemas that organize information about people and social experiences in memory and allow them to interpret and categorize information about others.
- People form impressions of others in part through the use of central traits–personality characteristics that receive unusually heavy emphasis when we form an impression.
- Information-processing approaches have found that we tend to average together sets of traits to form an overall impression.
- Attribution theory tries to explain how we understand the causes of behavior, particularly with respect to situational or dispositional factors.

LO 52-3 What are the biases that influence the ways in which people view others' behavior?

- Even though logical processes are involved, attribution is prone to error. For instance, people are susceptible to the halo effect, assumed-similarity bias, self-serving bias, and fundamental attribution error (the tendency to overattribute others' behavior to dispositional causes

and the corresponding failure to recognize the importance of situational causes).

EVALUATE

1. An evaluation of a particular person, behavior, belief, or concept is called a(n) _____.
2. One brand of peanut butter advertises its product by describing its taste and nutritional value. It is hoping to persuade customers through _____ route processing. In ads for a competing brand, a popular actor happily eats the product–but does not describe it. This approach hopes to persuade customers through _____ route processing.
3. Cognitive dissonance theory suggests that we commonly change our behavior to keep it consistent with our attitudes. True or false?
4. Sopan was happy to lend his textbook to a fellow student who seemed bright and friendly. He was surprised when his classmate did not return it. His assumption that the bright and friendly student would also be responsible reflects the _____ effect.

RETHINK

1. Joan sees Annette, a new coworker, acting in a way that seems abrupt and curt. Joan concludes that Annette is unkind and unsociable. The next day, Joan sees Annette acting kindly toward another worker. Is Joan likely to change her impression of Annette? Why or why not? Finally, Joan sees several friends of hers laughing and joking with Annette, treating her in a very friendly fashion. Is Joan likely to change her impression of Annette? Why or why not?
2. Suppose you were assigned to develop a full advertising campaign for a product, including television, radio, and print ads. How might the theories in this chapter guide your strategy to suit the different media?

Answers to Evaluate Questions

1. attitude; 2. central, peripheral; 3. False: we typically change our attitudes and not our behavior to reduce cognitive dissonance; 4. halo

KEY TERMS

social psychology	cognitive dissonance	situational causes (of behavior)	assumed-similarity bias
attitudes	social cognition	dispositional causes (of behavior)	self-serving bias
central route processing	schemas		fundamental attribution error
peripheral route processing	central traits	halo effect	
	attribution theory		

Module 53
Social Influence and Groups

LEARNING OUTCOMES

LO 53-1 What are the major sources and tactics of social influence?

social influence The process by which social groups and individuals exert pressure on an individual, either deliberately or unintentionally. (Module 53)

group Two or more people who interact with one another, perceive themselves as part of a group, and are interdependent. (Module 53)

You have just transferred to a new college and are attending your first class. When the professor enters, your fellow classmates instantly rise, bow to the professor, and then stand quietly with their hands behind their backs. You've never encountered such behavior, and it makes no sense to you. Is it more likely that you will (1) jump up to join the rest of the class or (2) remain seated?

Most people would probably choose the first option. As you undoubtedly know from your own experience, pressures to conform to others' behavior can be painfully strong and can bring about changes in behavior that otherwise never would have occurred.

Conformity pressures are just one type of social influence. **Social influence** is the process by which social groups and individuals exert pressure on an individual, either deliberately or unintentionally.

Social influence is so powerful in part because groups and other people generally play a central role in our lives. As defined by social psychologists, **groups** consist of two or more people who (1) interact with one another; (2) perceive themselves as part of a group; and (3) are interdependent—that is, the events that affect one group member affect other members, and the behavior of members has significant consequences for the success of the group in meeting its goals.

Groups develop and hold *norms*, informal beliefs, expectations, and standards about what is appropriate behavior for group members. Norms not only tell us how people in a group should behave ("wearing pink is fashionable this year") but also what members shouldn't do ("under no circumstances wear black"). Group members understand that not adhering to group norms can result in retaliation from other group members, ranging from being ignored to being overtly derided or even being rejected or excluded by the group. Thus, people conform to meet the beliefs and expectations of the group (Miles, Schaufeli, & van den Bos, 2011; Becker, Brackbill, & Centola, 2017).

Groups exert considerable social pressure over individuals. We'll consider three types of social pressure: conformity, compliance, and obedience.

Conformity: Following What Others Do

conformity A change in behavior or attitudes brought about by a desire to follow the beliefs or standards of other people. (Module 53)

Conformity is a change in behavior or attitudes brought about by a desire to follow the beliefs or standards of other people. Subtle or even unspoken social pressure results in conformity.

The classic demonstration of pressure to conform comes from a series of studies carried out in the 1950s by Solomon Asch (1951). In the experiments, the participants thought they were taking part in a test of perceptual skills with six other people. The experimenter showed the participants one card with three lines of varying length and a second card that had a fourth line that matched one of the first three (see Figure 1). The task was seemingly straightforward: Each of the participants had to announce aloud which of the first three lines was identical in length to the "standard" line on the second card. Because the correct answer was always obvious, the task seemed easy to the participants.

Indeed, because the participants all agreed on the first few trials, the procedure appeared to be simple. But then something odd began to happen. From the perspective of the participant in the group who answered last on each trial, all the answers of the first six participants seemed to be wrong—in fact, unanimously wrong. And this pattern persisted. Over and over again, the first six participants provided answers that contradicted what the last participant believed to be correct. The last participant faced the dilemma of whether to follow his or her own perceptions or follow the group by repeating the answer everyone else was giving.

As you might have guessed, there was more to this experiment than it first appeared. The first six participants were actually confederates (paid employees of the experimenter) who had been instructed to give unanimously erroneous answers on many of the trials. And the study had nothing to do with perceptual skills. Instead, the issue under investigation was conformity.

Asch found that in about one-third of the trials, the participants conformed to the erroneous group answer; about 75% of all participants conformed at least once. However, he found strong individual differences. Some participants conformed nearly all the time, whereas others never did.

Standard line   Comparison lines

FIGURE 1 Which of the three comparison lines is the same length as the "standard" line?

CONFORMITY CONCLUSIONS

Since Asch's pioneering work, literally hundreds of studies have examined conformity, and we now know a great deal about the phenomenon. Significant findings focus on:

- *The characteristics of the group.* The more attractive a group appears to its members, the greater its ability to produce conformity. Furthermore, a person's relative **status,** the social standing of someone within a group, is critical: The lower a person's status in the group, the greater groups' power over that person's behavior (Abrams & Hogg, 2017).

- *The situation in which the individual is responding.* Conformity is considerably higher when people must respond publicly than it is when they can do so privately, as the founders of the United States noted when they authorized secret ballots in voting.

- *The kind of task.* People working on ambiguous tasks and questions (those with no clear answer) are more susceptible to social pressure. When asked to give an opinion on something, such as what type of clothing is fashionable, a person will more likely yield to conformist pressures than he or she will if asked a question of fact. In addition, tasks at which an individual is less competent than others in the group make conformity more likely. For example, a person who is an infrequent computer user may feel pressure to conform to an opinion about computer brands when in a group of experienced computer users.

- *Unanimity of the group.* Groups that unanimously support a position show the most pronounced conformity pressures. But what about the case in which people with dissenting views have an ally in the group, known as a **social supporter,** who agrees with them? Having just one person present who shares the minority point of view is sufficient to reduce conformity pressures (Goodwin, Costa, & Adonu, 2004; Levine & Moreland, 2006).

status The social standing of someone in a group. (Module 53)

social supporter A group member whose dissenting views make nonconformity to the group easier. (Module 53)

GROUPTHINK: CAVING IN TO CONFORMITY

Although we usually think of conformity in terms of our individual relations with others, in some instances, conformity pressures in organizations can lead to disastrous effects with long-term consequences. One classic example from 2003 concerns the space shuttle *Columbia* and the engineers who had to consider whether insulation that slammed into the space shuttle during takeoff would pose danger during landing. In fact, despite misgivings on the part of some engineers, a strong consensus emerged among them that the insulation would not impair the landing. Ultimately, that consensus proved wrong: The shuttle came apart as it attempted to land, killing all the astronauts on board (Schwartz & Wald, 2003; Mintz & Wayne, 2014).

Groupthink may explain the poor decision making of NASA engineers that led to the destruction of the space shuttle *Columbia*.

Jim Sugar/Corbis Documentary/Getty Images

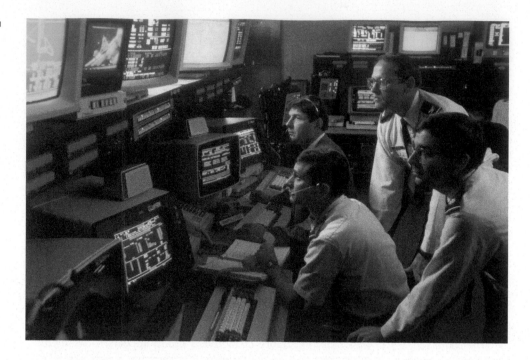

groupthink A type of thinking in which group members share such a strong motivation to achieve consensus that they lose the ability to critically evaluate alternative points of view. (Module 53)

PsychTech

Through the use of Facebook, Twitter, and other social media, social norms can develop and be rapidly communicated to others.

compliance Behavior that occurs in response to direct social pressure. (Module 53)

How could they have made such a poor decision?

A phenomenon known as groupthink may provide an explanation. **Groupthink** is a type of thinking in which group members share such a strong motivation to achieve consensus that they lose the ability to critically evaluate alternative points of view. Groupthink is most likely to occur when a popular or powerful leader is surrounded by people of lower status—which is obviously the case with any U.S. president and his advisers but is also true for leaders in a variety of other organizations.

Groupthink may have been a partial cause of numerous questionable decisions and conclusions in the political and business worlds. For example, the United States invading Iraq or the consensus among media experts that Hillary Clinton would beat Donald Trump in the 2016 presidential election can be seen at least in part as a result of groupthink (Henningsen, Henningsen, & Eden, 2006; Baumeister, Ainsworth, & Vohs, 2015; Levine, 2019).

Groupthink typically leads to poor decisions. Groups limit the list of possible solutions to just a few, and they spend relatively little time considering any alternatives once the leader seems to be leaning toward a particular solution. In addition, groups may fall prey to *entrapment*, a circumstance in which commitments to a failing point of view or course of action are increased to justify investments in time and energy that have already been made (Turner, Pratkanis, & Struckman, 2007; Willis, 2017).

Ultimately, group members may completely ignore information that challenges a developing consensus. Because historical research suggests that many disastrous decisions reflect groupthink, it is important for groups to be on guard (Chapman, 2006; Packer, 2009).

Compliance: Submitting to Direct Social Pressure

When we refer to conformity, we usually mean a phenomenon in which the social pressure is subtle or indirect. But in some situations, social pressure is much more obvious with direct, explicit pressure to endorse a particular point of view or behave in a certain way. **Compliance** is behavior that occurs in response to direct social pressure.

Several specific techniques represent attempts to gain compliance. Those frequently employed include:

- *Foot-in-the-door technique.* The use of the *foot-in-the-door technique* begins when someone asks a target to comply with a small, trivial request. Because such a request is easy to fulfill, the likelihood that the target of the request will comply is high. Later, though, the target is asked to comply with a significantly larger request related to the first one. It turns out that compliance with the second request increases substantially when the target has first agreed to the initial, smaller request.

    Researchers first demonstrated the foot-in-the-door phenomenon in a study in which experimenters went door to door asking residents to sign a petition in favor of safe driving (Freedman & Fraser, 1966). Almost everyone complied with that small, easy-to-agree-to request. However, a few weeks later, different experimenters contacted the residents and made a request that took considerably more effort, asking residents to erect a huge sign on their front lawns that read, "Drive Carefully." The results were clear: 55% of those who had initially signed the petition to the request to put up a sign, whereas only 17% of those in a control group who initially had not been asked to sign the petition agreed to put up a sign.

    Why does the foot-in-the-door technique work? For one reason, consideration of the small request may lead to an interest in the topic of the request or issue; taking an action—any action—makes the individual more committed to the issue, thereby increasing the likelihood of future compliance. Another explanation revolves around people's self-perceptions. By complying with the initial request, individuals may come to see themselves as people who provide help when asked. Then, when confronted with the larger request, they agree in order to maintain the kind of consistency in attitudes and behavior that we described earlier. Although we don't know which of these two explanations is more accurate, it is clear that the foot-in-the-door strategy is effective (Bloom, McBride, & Pollak, 2006; Guéguen et al., 2008; Lee & Liang, 2019).

- *Door-in-the-face technique.* A fund raiser asks for a $1,000 contribution. You laughingly refuse and tell her that the amount is way out of your league. She then asks for a $10 contribution. How would you react? If you are like most people, you'll probably be a lot more generous than you would be if she hadn't asked for the huge contribution first. In this tactic, called the *door-in-the-face technique,* someone makes a large request, expects it to be refused, and follows it with a smaller one. This strategy, which is the opposite of the foot-in-the-door approach, has proven to be effective (Dolinski, 2011; Cantarero, Gamian-Wilk, & Dolinski, 2017; Howard, 2019).

    In a research study that demonstrates the success of this approach, experimenters stopped college students on the street and asked them to agree to a substantial favor—acting as unpaid counselors for juvenile delinquents 2 hours a week for 2 years (Cialdini et al., 1975). Unsurprisingly, no one agreed to make such an enormous commitment. But when they were later asked the considerably smaller favor of taking a group of delinquents on a 2-hour trip to the zoo, 50% of the people complied. In comparison, only 17% of a control group of participants who had not first received the larger request agreed.

    The use of this technique is widespread. You may have tried it at some point yourself by perhaps by asking your parents for a large increase in your allowance and later settling for less. Similarly, television writers, by sometimes sprinkling their scripts with obscenities that they know network censors will cut out, hope to keep other key phrases intact (Cialdini & Sagarin, 2005).

- *That's-not-all technique.* In this technique, a salesperson offers you a deal at an inflated price. But immediately after the initial offer, the salesperson offers an incentive, discount, or bonus to clinch the deal.

The persuasive techniques identified by social psychologists can be seen in practice at auto dealerships.
Anton Estrada/123RF

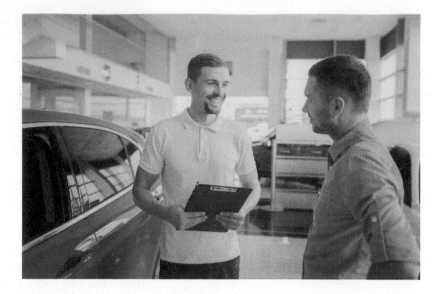

Although it sounds transparent, this practice can be quite effective. In one study, the experimenters set up a booth and sold cupcakes for 75¢ each. In one condition, the experimenters directly told customers that the price was 75¢. In another condition, they told customers that the price was originally $1 but had been reduced to 75¢. As we might predict, more people bought cupcakes at the "reduced" price—even though it was identical to the price in the other experimental condition (Pratkanis, 2007; Lee, Moon, & Feeley, 2019).

- *Not-so-free sample.* If you ever receive a free sample, keep in mind that it comes with a psychological cost. Although they may not couch it in these terms, salespeople who provide samples to potential customers do so to bring the norm of reciprocity into play. The *norm of reciprocity* is the social standard that we should treat other people as they treat us. (It's a variant of the Golden Rule we learn as kids: "Do unto others as they will do unto you.") It's a strong cultural standard: When someone does something nice for us, we tend to feel obligated to return the favor. In the case of the *not-so-free sample,* receiving a free sample activates the norm of reciprocity and makes us feel that we should return the favor—in the form of a purchase (Park & Antonioni, 2007; Burger, 2009; Chernyak et al., 2019).

Companies seeking to sell their products to consumers often use the techniques identified by social psychologists for promoting compliance. Employers also use them to bring about compliance and raise employees' productivity in the workplace. In fact, **industrial-organizational (I/O) psychology,** a close cousin to social psychology, considers issues such as worker motivation, satisfaction, safety, and productivity. I/O psychologists also focus on the operation and design of organizations; they ask questions such as how decision making can be improved in large organizations and how the fit between workers and their jobs can be maximized.

industrial-organizational (I/O) psychology The branch of psychology focusing on work- and job-related issues, including worker motivation, satisfaction, safety, and productivity. (Module 53)

Obedience: Following Direct Orders

The compliance techniques that we've been discussing share a common thread: They are used to gently lead people toward agreement with a request. In some cases, however, requests are made in a strong manner. In fact, they're hardly requests at all but rather commands, aimed at producing obedience. **Obedience** is a change in behavior in response to the commands of others. Although obedience is considerably less common than conformity and compliance, it does occur in several specific kinds of relationships. For example, we may show obedience to our bosses, teachers, or parents merely because of the power they hold to reward or punish us.

obedience A change in behavior in response to the commands of others. (Module 53)

To acquire an understanding of obedience, consider for a moment how you might respond if a stranger said to you:

> I've devised a new way of improving memory. All I need is for you to teach people a list of words and then give them a test. The test procedure requires only that you give learners a shock each time they make a mistake on the test. To administer the shocks, you will use a "shock generator" that gives shocks ranging from 15 to 450 volts. You can see that the switches are labeled from "slight shock" through "danger: severe shock" at the top level, where there are three red Xs. But don't worry; although the shocks may be painful, they will cause no permanent damage.

Presented with this situation, you would be likely to think that neither you nor anyone else would go along with the stranger's unusual request. Clearly, it lies outside the bounds of what we consider good sense.

Or does it? Suppose the stranger asking for your help was a psychologist conducting an experiment. Or suppose the request came from your teacher, your employer, or your military commander—all people in authority with a seemingly legitimate reason for the request.

If you still believe you would not comply, think again. The situation presented above describes a classic experiment conducted by social psychologist Stanley Milgram in the 1960s. In the study, an experimenter told participants to give increasingly stronger shocks to another person as part of a study on learning (see Figure 2). In reality, the experiment had nothing to do with learning; the real issue under consideration was the degree to which participants would comply with the experimenter's requests. In fact, the "learner" supposedly receiving the shocks was a confederate who never really received any punishment (Milgram, 2005; Maher, 2015; Griggs, 2017).

Most people who hear a description of Milgram's experiment feel it is unlikely that *any* participant would give the maximum level of shock—or, for that matter, any shock at all. Even a group of psychiatrists to whom the situation was described predicted that fewer than 2% of the participants would fully comply and administer the strongest shocks.

However, the results contradicted both experts' and nonexperts' predictions. Some 65% of the participants eventually used the highest setting on the shock generator—450 volts—to shock the learner. This obedience occurred even though the learner, who had mentioned at the start of the experiment that he had a heart condition, demanded to be released, screaming, "Let me out of here! Let me out of here! My heart's bothering me.

! Study Alert

The distinction between the three types of social pressure—conformity, compliance, and obedience—depends on the nature and strength of the social pressure brought to bear on a person.

FIGURE 2 This fearsome "shock generator" led participants to believe they were administering electric shocks to another person, who was connected to the generator by electrodes attached to the skin.

(Both): From the film OBEDIENCE © 1968 by Stanley Milgram, © renewed 1993 by Alexandra Milgram. Permission granted by Alexandra Milgram

Let me out of here!" Despite the learner's pleas, most participants continued to administer the shocks.

Why did so many individuals comply with the experimenter's demands? The participants, who were extensively interviewed after the experiment, said they obeyed primarily because they believed that the experimenter would be responsible for any potential ill effects that befell the learner. The participants accepted the experimenter's orders, then, because they thought that they personally could not be held accountable for their actions—they could always blame the experimenter (Blass, 2004; Kaposi, 2017).

From the perspective of...

An Educator Student obedience in the elementary and secondary classroom is a major issue for many teachers. How might you promote student obedience in the classroom?

Amos Morgan/Photodisc/Getty Images

Most participants in the Milgram experiment said later they felt the knowledge gained from the study outweighed the discomfort they may have felt. However, the experiment has been criticized for creating an extremely trying set of circumstances for the participants, thereby raising serious ethical concerns. Undoubtedly, the same experiment could not be conducted today because of ethical considerations (Perry, 2013).

Other critics have suggested that Milgram's methods were ineffective in creating a situation that actually mirrored real-world obedience. For example, how often are people placed in a situation in which someone orders them to continue hurting a victim while the victim's protests are ignored (Blass, 2004; Werhane et al., 2013)?

Despite these concerns, Milgram's research remains the strongest laboratory demonstration of obedience. And partial replications of Milgram's work, conducted in an ethically defensible way, find similar results, which adds credence to the original work (Blass, 2009; Burger, 2009; Gibson, 2013).

Furthermore, we need only consider actual instances of obedience to authority to witness some frightening real-life parallels. For instance, after World War II, the major defense that Nazi officers gave to excuse their participation in atrocities during the war was that they were "only following orders." Milgram's experiment, which was motivated in part by his desire to explain the behavior of everyday Germans during World War II, forces us to ask ourselves this question: Would we be able to withstand the intense power of authority?

Study Alert

Because of its graphic demonstration of obedience to authority, the Milgram experiment is one of the most famous and influential studies in social psychology.

RECAP/EVALUATE/RETHINK

RECAP

LO 53-1 What are the major sources and tactics of social influence?

- Social influence is the area of social psychology concerned with situations in which the actions of an individual or group affect the behavior of others.
- Conformity refers to changes in behavior or attitudes that result from a desire to follow the beliefs or standards of others.

- Compliance is behavior that results from direct social pressure. Among the ways of eliciting compliance are the foot-in-the-door, door-in-the-face, that's-not-all, and not-so-free sample techniques.
- Obedience is a change in behavior in response to the commands of others.

EVALUATE

1. A _____ _____, or person who agrees with the dissenting viewpoint, is likely to reduce conformity.
2. Who pioneered the study of conformity?
   a. Skinner
   b. Asch
   c. Milgram
   d. Fiala
3. Which of the following techniques asks a person to comply with a small initial request to enhance the likelihood that the person will later comply with a larger request?
   a. Door-in-the-face
   b. Foot-in-the-door
   c. That's-not-all
   d. Not-so-free sample
4. The _____ _____ _____ technique begins with an outrageous request that makes a subsequent, smaller request seem reasonable.
5. _____ is a change in behavior that is due to another person's orders.

RETHINK

1. Why do you think the Milgram experiment is so controversial? What sorts of effects might the experiment have had on participants? Do you think the experiment would have had similar results if it had not been conducted in a laboratory setting but among members of a social group (such as a fraternity or sorority) with strong pressures to conform?
2. Imagine that you have been trained to use the various compliance techniques described in this section. Because these compliance techniques are so powerful, should the use of certain such techniques be forbidden? Should consumers be taught defenses against such techniques? Is the use of such techniques ethically and morally defensible? Why?

Answers to Evaluate Questions

1. social supporter; 2. b; 3. b; 4. door-in-the-face; 5. Obedience

KEY TERMS

social influence	status	compliance	obedience
group	social supporter	industrial-organizational	
conformity	groupthink	(I/O) psychology	

Module 54
Prejudice and Discrimination

LEARNING OUTCOMES

LO 54-1 How do stereotypes, prejudice, and discrimination differ?

LO 54-2 How can we reduce prejudice and discrimination?

stereotype A set of generalized beliefs and expectations about a particular group and its members. (Module 54)

prejudice A negative (or positive) evaluation of a particular group and its members. (Module 54)

discrimination Behavior directed toward individuals on the basis of their membership in a particular group. (Module 54)

> **! Study Alert**
> Remember that *prejudice* relates to *attitudes* about a group and its members, whereas *discrimination* relates to *behavior* directed to a group and its members.

What do you think when someone says, "He's African American," "She's Chinese," or "That's a woman driver"?

If you're like most people, you'll probably automatically form some sort of impression of what each person is like. Most likely your impression is based on a **stereotype,** a set of generalized beliefs and expectations about a specific group and its members. Stereotypes grow out of our tendency to categorize and organize the vast amount of information we encounter in our everyday lives. All stereotypes share the common feature of oversimplifying the world: We view individuals not in terms of their unique, personal characteristics but also in terms of characteristics we attribute to all the members of a particular group.

Stereotypes can lead to **prejudice,** a negative (or positive) evaluation of a group and its members. For instance, racial prejudice occurs when a member of a racial group is evaluated in terms of race and not because of his or her own characteristics or abilities. Although prejudice can be positive ("I love the Irish"), social psychologists have focused on understanding the roots of negative prejudice ("I hate immigrants").

Common stereotypes and forms of prejudice involve race, religion, ethnicity, and gender. Over the years, various groups have been called "lazy" or "shrewd" or "cruel" with varying degrees of regularity by those who are not members of that group. Even today, despite major progress toward reducing legally sanctioned forms of prejudice, such as school segregation, stereotypes remain (Hunt, Seifert, & Armenta, 2006; Devos, 2011; Bhatia, 2017).

Even people who on the surface appear to be unprejudiced may harbor hidden prejudice. For example, when white participants in experiments are shown faces on a computer screen so rapidly that they cannot consciously perceive the faces, they react more negatively to black than to white faces–an example of what has been called *modern racism* (Pearson, Dovidio, & Pratto, 2007; Blanton, Jaccard, & Burrows, 2015).

Stereotypes can have harmful consequences because acting on stereotypes results in discrimination. **Discrimination** is behavior directed toward individuals on the basis of their membership in a particular group. Discrimination can lead to exclusion from jobs, neighborhoods, and educational opportunities, and it may result in lower salaries and benefits for members of specific groups. Discrimination can also result in more favorable treatment to favored groups–for example, when an employer hires a job applicant of his or her own racial group because of the applicant's race (Pager & Shepherd, 2008; Leskinen, Rabelo, & Cortina, 2015).

Stereotyping not only leads to overt discrimination but also can cause members of stereotyped groups to behave in ways that reflect the stereotype through a phenomenon known as the *self-fulfilling prophecy*. Self-fulfilling prophecies are expectations about the occurrence of a future event or behavior that act to increase the likelihood the event or behavior will occur. For example, if people think that members of a specific group lack ambition, they may treat them in a way that actually brings about a lack of ambition (Tappin, McKay, & Abrams, 2017; Peters et al., 2019).

Ultimately, the consequences of prejudice and discrimination can be profound, not only in terms of lost opportunities for victims but also in regard to their psychological functioning. Thus, discrimination may lead targets to feel hurt, inadequate, and anxious, and it can even negatively impact their cognitive functioning, such as their planning, decision-making, and problem-solving capabilities (Ozier, Taylor, & Murphy, 2019).

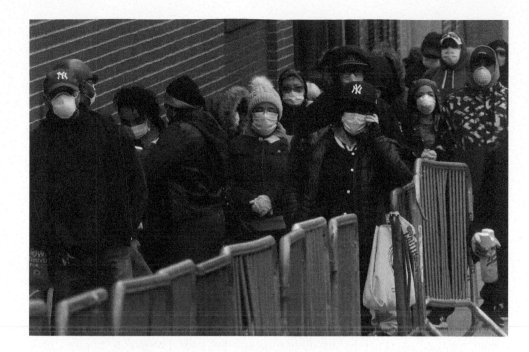

Members of racial and ethnic groups that have long faced discrimination suffered disproportionately from the coronavirus pandemic. Here people line up for testing during the early stages of the pandemic.
Timothy A. Clary/Getty Images

An unquestionably profound and troubling consequence of prejudice and discrimination can be seen in the way the 2020 coronavirus pandemic spread across the United States. Specifically, members of groups who have been traditionally discriminated against suffered from higher rates of infection and death. For instance, African-American and Latino residents of New York City died at twice the rate of white residents during the worst points of the pandemic. The disparity was a reflection of persistent economic inequities and unequal levels of access to health care (Dwyer, 2020; Mays & Newman, 2020).

The Foundations of Prejudice

No one is born disliking a specific racial, religious, or ethnic group. People learn to hate in much the same way that they learn the alphabet.

According to *observational learning approaches* to stereotyping and prejudice, the behavior of parents, other adults, and peers shapes children's feelings about members of various groups. For instance, bigoted parents may commend their children for expressing prejudiced attitudes. Likewise, young children learn prejudice by imitating the behavior of adult models. Such learning starts at an early age: Infants as young as 3 months old who have been exposed primarily to faces of their own race prefer same-race faces to faces of those of other races (Ponterotto, Utsey, & Pedersen, 2006; Bronson & Merryman, 2009; Quinn, Lee, & Pascalis, 2018).

Moreover, the bias people encounter does not need to be overt. Even subtle and ambiguous forms of discriminatory behavior--such as someone avoiding sitting next to a person of color on a bus or providing poor service at a restaurant--can send a message of discrimination (Ozier, Taylor, & Murphy, 2019).

The mass media also provide information about stereotypes not just for children but for adults as well. Even today, some media portray Italians as Mafia-like mobsters, Jews as greedy bankers, and African Americans as promiscuous or lazy. When such inaccurate portrayals are the primary source of information about minority groups, they can lead to the development and maintenance of unfavorable stereotypes (Do, 2006; Scharrer & Ramasubramanian, 2015; Jin, Pei, & Ma, 2019).

Other explanations of prejudice and discrimination focus on how being a member of a specific group helps to magnify one's sense of self-esteem. According to *social identity theory,* we use group membership as a source of pride and self-worth. Social identity theory suggests that people tend to be ethnocentric, viewing the world from their own perspective and judging others in terms of their group membership. Slogans such as "gay pride" and "Black is beautiful" illustrate that the groups to which we belong give us a sense of self-respect (Hogg, 2006; Kahn et al., 2017; Edwards et al., 2019).

However, the use of group membership to provide social respect produces an unfortunate outcome. In an effort to maximize our sense of self-esteem, we may come to think that our own group (our *ingroup*) is better than groups to which we don't belong (our *outgroups*). Consequently, we inflate the positive aspects of our ingroup—and, at the same time, devalue outgroups. Ultimately, we come to view members of outgroups as inferior to members of our ingroup (Tajfel & Turner, 2004). The end result is prejudice toward members of groups of which we are not a part.

Neither the observational learning approach nor the social identity approach provides a full explanation for stereotyping and prejudice. For instance, some psychologists argue that prejudice results when there is perceived competition for scarce societal resources. Thus, when competition exists for jobs or housing, members of majority groups may believe (however unjustly or inaccurately) that minority group members are hindering their efforts to attain their goals; this belief can lead to prejudice. In addition, other explanations for prejudice emphasize human cognitive limitations that lead us to categorize people on the basis of visually conspicuous physical features such as race, sex, and ethnic group. Such categorization can lead to the development of stereotypes and, ultimately, to discriminatory behavior (Weeks & Lupfer, 2004; Hugenberg & Sacco, 2008; Yoo & Pituc, 2013).

The most recent approach to understanding prejudice comes from an increasingly important area in social psychology: social neuroscience. **Social neuroscience** seeks to identify the neurological basis of social behavior. It looks at how we can illuminate our understanding of groups, interpersonal relations, and emotions by understanding their neuroscientific underpinnings (Todorov, Fiske, & Prentice, 2011; Kasemsap, 2017; Kavaliers, Ossenkopp, & Choleris, 2019).

In one example of the value of social neuroscience approaches, researchers examined activation of the *amygdala*, the structure in the brain that relates to emotion-evoking stimuli and situations, while people viewed white and black faces. Because the amygdala is especially responsive to threatening, unusual, or highly arousing stimuli, the researchers hypothesized greater activation of the amygdala during exposure to black faces due to negative cultural associations with racial minorities (Lieberman, 2007; Nelson, 2013).

social neuroscience The subfield of social psychology that seeks to identify the neurological basis of social behavior. (Module 54)

Like father, like son: Social learning approaches to stereotyping and prejudice suggest that attitudes and behaviors toward members of minority groups are learned through the observation of parents and other individuals. How can this cycle be broken?
Barbara Burnes/Science Source

As you can see in *Neuroscience in Your Life,* the hypothesis was confirmed: The amygdala showed more activation when participants saw a black face than when they saw a white one. Because both blacks and whites were participants in the study, it is unlikely that the amygdala activation was simply the result of the novelty of viewing members of a racial minority. Instead, the findings suggest that culturally learned societal messages about race led to the brain activation.

NEUROSCIENCE IN YOUR LIFE: THE PREJUDICED BRAIN

Problems related to racial prejudice are ongoing in the United States. To provide insight into these problems, social neuroscientists have begun to examine how we process social information in the brain and how that processing relates to stereotypes and prejudice.

To examine a potential relationship between racial differences and threat detection, social neuroscientists scanned participants' brains while asking them to look at photos of black or white individuals, determine whether the person in the photo had a weapon, and respond by "shooting" the person in the photo if they thought a gun was present. Participants, who were white, Asian, Hispanic, and of unknown races, more quickly decided to shoot and showed greater brain activity in the parietal and visual cortexes for armed blacks than for armed whites.

In addition, as shown in the images below, greater connectivity occurred (shown in purple) between the amygdala, parietal cortex, visual cortex, and other areas when participants viewed armed blacks than when they viewed armed whites. These results demonstrate possible neural correlates contributing to the greater likelihood of treating blacks as more dangerous than whites (Senholzi et al., 2015; Senholzi & Kubota, 2016; Mattan et al., 2018).

Source: Adapted from Senholzi, K. B., Depue, B. E., Correll, J., Banich, M. T., & Ito, T. A. (2015). Brain activation underlying threat detection to targets of different races. *Social Neuroscience, 10,* 651–662.

Measuring Prejudice and Discrimination: The Implicit Association Test

Could you be prejudiced and not even know it? Probably yes, according to the researchers who developed a test that reveals hidden prejudice.

The *Implicit Association Test,* or *IAT,* is an ingenious measure of prejudice that permits a more accurate assessment of people's discrimination between members of different groups.

The IAT uses the fact that people's automatic, instant reactions often provide the most valid indicator of what they actually believe. The test asks people questions that assess the degree to which they associate members of target groups (say, African Americans versus whites) with positive stimuli (such as a puppy) versus negative stimuli (such as a funeral). The test is based on the fact that growing up in a particular culture teaches us to unconsciously associate members of particular groups with positive or

Study Alert
Remember that the IAT allows measurement of attitudes about which people might not be consciously aware as well as attitudes they wish to keep hidden from others.

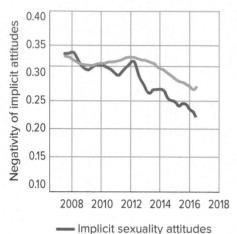

FIGURE 1. Implicit Bias on the Decline?
Implicit bias favoring straight and white people declined from 2007 to 2016.

Source: Charlesworth, T. E. S., & Banaji, M. R. (2019). Patterns of implicit and explicit attitudes: Long-term change and stability from 2007 to 2016. *Psychological Science, 30*(2), 174–192.

negative qualities, and we tend to absorb associations about those groups that reflect the culture without even being aware of it (Blanton, Jaccard, & Burrows, 2015; Roberts, Neate, & Gierasch, 2017; McConnell & Rydell, 2019).

The results of the IAT show that almost 90% of test-takers have an implicit pro-white bias, and more than two-thirds of non-Arab, non-Muslim volunteers display implicit biases against Arab Muslims. Moreover, more than 80% of heterosexuals display an implicit bias against gays and lesbians (Lane et al., 2007).

So, of course, having an implicit bias does not mean that people will overtly discriminate, which is a criticism that has been made of the test. Yet it does mean that the cultural lessons to which we are exposed have a considerable unconscious influence on us. (If you would like to try a version of the IAT yourself, there is a sample test at https://implicit.harvard.edu/implicit. You may well be surprised at the results.)

The good news is that certain types of implicit bias are on the decline. Using responses from 4.4 million online implicit bias test-takers, researchers found that implicit bias declined from 2007 through 2017 in several domains, including a reduction in preferences for white, straight, and light-skinned individuals (see Figure 1). On the other hand, implicit bias regarding older people and those with disabilities remained fairly stable during that period, and it actually increased for overweight people. The reductions in implicit bias suggest changes in societal prejudice that are reflected in individuals' attitudes (Charlesworth & Mahzarin, 2019).

Reducing the Consequences of Prejudice and Discrimination

How can we diminish the effects of prejudice and discrimination? Psychologists have developed several strategies that have proved effective.

- *Increasing contact between the target of stereotyping and the holder of the stereotype.* Research consistently shows that increasing the amount of interaction between people can reduce negative stereotyping. But only certain kinds of contact are likely to reduce prejudice and discrimination. Situations in which contact is relatively intimate, the individuals are of equal status, or participants must cooperate with one another or are dependent on one another are more likely to reduce stereotyping. On the other hand, even virtual contact via social media may be sufficient to improve intergroup relations (Pettigrew & Tropp, 2006; White, Harvey, & Abu-Rayya, 2015; Stone et al., 2019).

- *Making values and norms against prejudice more conspicuous.* Sometimes just reminding people about the values they already hold regarding equality and fair treatment of others is enough to reduce discrimination. Similarly, people who hear others making strong, vehement antiracist statements are subsequently more likely to strongly condemn racism. Furthermore, one study found that even a short, 10-minute conversation with voters asking them to recall a time when they were judged negatively and unfairly was sufficient to reduce prejudice toward transgender people that lasted 3 months (Tropp & Bianchi, 2006; Rutland & Killen, 2015; Broockman & Kalla, 2016).

- *Providing information about the targets of stereotyping.* Probably the most direct means of changing stereotypical and discriminatory attitudes is education: teaching people to be more aware of the positive characteristics of targets of stereotyping. For instance, when the meaning of puzzling behavior is explained to people who hold stereotypes, they may come to appreciate the actual significance of the behavior (Isbell & Tyler, 2003; Banks, 2006; Nagda, Tropp, & Paluck, 2006).

- *Reducing stereotype threat.* Social psychologist Claude Steele suggests that many African Americans suffer from *stereotype vulnerability*, obstacles to performance that stem from their awareness of society's stereotypes regarding minority group members. He argues that African American students too often receive instruction from teachers who doubt their students' abilities and who set up remedial programs to assist their students. As a result of their teachers' (as well as society's) low expectations for their performance, African American students may come to accept society's stereotypes and come to believe that they are likely to fail (Nussbaum & Steele, 2007; Aronson & Dee, 2012; Zhao et al., 2019).

Such beliefs can have devastating effects. When confronted with an academic task, African American students may fear that their performance will simply confirm society's negative stereotypes. The immediate consequence of this fear is anxiety that hampers performance. But the long-term consequences may be even worse: Doubting their ability to perform successfully in academic environments, African Americans may decide that the risks of failure are so great it is not worth the effort even to attempt to do well. Ultimately, they may "disidentify" with academic success by minimizing the importance of academic endeavors (Stone, 2002; Lombaard & Naudé, 2017).

However, Steele's analysis suggests that African Americans may be able to overcome their predicament. Specifically, schools can design intervention programs to train minority group members about their vulnerability to stereotypes and provide them with self-affirmation that reinforces their confidence in their abilities and thereby inoculates them against the fear and doubt triggered by negative stereotypes (Cohen et al., 2006; Wilson, 2006; Shnabel et al., 2013).

- *Increasing the sense of social belonging of ethnic minority students.* Although almost every college student faces feelings of inadequacy and uncertainty about belonging at the start of college, such feelings are especially strong for members of groups who are underrepresented and have been the targets of prejudice and discrimination. However, research shows that a simple intervention in which members of minority groups are made to understand that feelings of inadequacy are not unique to them—and that such feelings usually diminish with time—can help minority students increase their sense of social belonging (Walton & Cohen, 2011; Mullangi & Jagsi, 2019).

From the perspective of...

A Corrections Officer How might overt forms of prejudice and discrimination toward disadvantaged groups (such as African Americans) be reduced in a state or federal prison?

Hill Street Studios/Blend Images

RECAP/EVALUATE/RETHINK

RECAP

LO 54-1 How do stereotypes, prejudice, and discrimination differ?

- Stereotypes are generalized beliefs and expectations about a specific group and its members. Stereotyping can lead to prejudice and self-fulfilling prophecies.
- Prejudice is the negative (or positive) evaluation of a particular group and its members.

- Stereotyping and prejudice can lead to discrimination, behavior directed toward individuals on the basis of their membership in a particular group.
- According to observational learning approaches, children learn stereotyping and prejudice by observing the behavior of parents, other adults, and peers. Social identity theory suggests that group membership is used as a source of pride and self worth, and this may lead people to think of their own group as better than others.

- Social neuroscientific approaches to prejudice examine the functioning of the brain and nervous system to understand the basis of prejudice.

LO 54-2 How can we reduce prejudice and discrimination?

- Among the ways of reducing prejudice and discrimination are increasing contact, demonstrating positive values against prejudice, and education.

EVALUATE

1. Any expectation—positive or negative—about an individual solely on the basis of that person's membership in a group can be a stereotype. True or false?
2. The negative (or positive) evaluation of a group and its members is called
   a. Stereotyping
   b. Prejudice
   c. Self-fulfilling prophecy
   d. Discrimination

3. Paul is a store manager who does not expect women to succeed in business. He therefore offers important, high-profile responsibilities only to men. If the female employees fail to move up in the company, it could be an example of a _____ _____ prophecy.

RETHINK

1. Do you think women can be victims of stereotype vulnerability? In what topical areas might this occur? Can men be victims of stereotype vulnerability? Why?
2. How are stereotypes, prejudice, and discrimination related? In a society committed to equality, which of the three should be changed first? Why?

Answers to Evaluate Questions

1. True; 2. b; 3. self-fulfilling

KEY TERMS

| stereotype | prejudice | discrimination | social neuroscience |

Module 55
Positive and Negative Social Behavior

Like philosophers and theologians, social psychologists have pondered the basic nature of humanity. Is it represented mainly by the violence and cruelty we see throughout the world, or does something special about human nature permit loving, considerate, unselfish, and even noble behavior as well?

We turn to two routes that social psychologists have followed in seeking answers to these questions. We first consider what they have learned about the sources of our attraction to others; we end with a look at two opposite sides of human behavior: aggression and helping.

LEARNING OUTCOMES

LO 55-1 Why are we attracted to certain people, and what progression do social relationships follow?

LO 55-2 What factors underlie aggression and prosocial behavior?

Liking and Loving: Interpersonal Attraction and the Development of Relationships

Nothing is more important in most people's lives than their feelings for others. Consequently, it is not surprising that liking and loving have become a major focus of interest for social psychologists. Known more formally as the study of **interpersonal attraction or close relationships,** this area addresses the factors that lead to positive feelings for others.

interpersonal attraction (or close relationship) Positive feelings for others; liking and loving. (Module 55)

HOW DO I LIKE THEE? LET ME COUNT THE WAYS

By far, the greatest amount of research has focused on liking, probably because it is easier for investigators conducting short-term experiments to produce states of liking in strangers who have just met than to instigate and observe loving relationships over long periods. Consequently, research has given us a good deal of knowledge about the factors that initially attract two people to each other. The important factors social psychologists consider are the following:

- *Proximity.* If you live in a residence hall or an apartment, consider the friends you made when you first moved in. Chances are that you became friendliest with those who lived geographically nearest to you. In fact, this is one of the more firmly established findings in the research on interpersonal attraction: Proximity leads to liking (Smith & Weber, 2005; Semin & Garrido, 2013; Shin et al., 2019).

- *Mere exposure.* Repeated exposure to a person is often sufficient to produce attraction. Interestingly, repeated exposure to *any* stimulus—a person, picture, tweet, or virtually anything—usually makes us like the stimulus more. Becoming familiar with a person can evoke positive feelings; we then transfer the positive feelings stemming from familiarity to the person him- or herself. Of course, there are exceptions: In cases of strongly negative initial encounters, repeated exposure is unlikely to cause us to like a person more. Instead, the more we are exposed to the person, the more we are likely to dislike the individual (Zajonc, 2001; Butler & Berry, 2004).

reciprocity-of-liking effect A tendency to like those who like us. (Module 55)

- *Similarity.* Folk wisdom tells us that birds of a feather flock together. However, folk wisdom also maintains that opposites attract. Which is right? Social psychologists have come up with a clear verdict regarding which of the two statements is correct: We tend to like those who are similar to us. Discovering that others have similar attitudes, values, or traits promotes our liking for them. Furthermore, the more similar others are, the more we like them. One reason similarity increases the likelihood of interpersonal attraction is that we assume people with similar attitudes will evaluate us positively. Because we experience a strong **reciprocity-of-liking effect,** a tendency to like those who like us, knowing that someone evaluates us positively promotes our attraction to that person. In addition, if *we* like someone else, we tend to assume that person likes us in return (Heffernan & Fraley, 2015; Wróbel & Królewiak, 2017).

- *Physical attractiveness.* For most people, the equation *beautiful = good* is quite true. As a result, physically attractive people are more popular than are physically unattractive ones, if all other factors are equal. This finding, which contradicts the values that most people say they hold, is apparent even in childhood (preschoolers' popularity is related to their attractiveness) and continues into adulthood. Indeed, physical attractiveness may be the single most important element promoting initial liking in college dating situations, although its influence eventually decreases when people get to know each other better (Luo & Zhang, 2009; Zhang et al., 2019).

These factors alone, of course, do not account for liking. For example, in one experiment that examined the desired qualities in a friendship, the top-rated qualities in a same-sex friend included sense of humor, warmth and kindness, expressiveness and openness, an exciting personality, and similarity of interests and leisure activities. In addition, our friendships and social networks may be related to neurological factors (Sprecher & Regan, 2002).

Friendship and Social Networking The newest forms of friendship are found on social network sites. Two-thirds of people in the United States and 1 out of 10 people *worldwide* belong to Facebook, and the concentration of college students using the social network site is more than 90%. In addition, other social network sites such as Instagram, SnapChat, and Twitter play an increasingly important role in people's lives. Not only do social media sites provide social networking opportunities, they also provide many people with their understanding of the news and current events (Brandwatch, 2019; Perrin & Anderson, 2019).

For college students, the primary motivation in using social network sites is to keep in touch with their friends. In addition, younger college students may use social media sites to explore their developing identities. Because users can control how they present themselves to the world on a social network profile, they can easily "try on" identities by posting selected photos of themselves, revealing specific tastes and interests, or otherwise shaping their images in new and different ways. The feedback they get from others may help them decide which identities and forms of self-presentation suit them best (Subrahmanyam et al., 2008; Pempek, Yermolayeva, & Calvert, 2009; Phua, Jin, & Kim, 2017).

But how do social network sites affect users' nonvirtual social lives? Maintaining social connections that might otherwise have withered and died seems like a good thing. But it may be detrimental to those who spend so much time engaged in online distant or superficial friendships that they devote little to intimate, face-to-face interactions (Steinfeld, Ellison, & Lampe, 2008; Sharifian & Zahodne, 2019; Yuen et al., 2019).

Furthermore, use of social media has other potential downsides. For example, because posts of others tend to be skewed to positive events, social media often presents a sanitized version of others' lives. Constant exposure to others' apparently positive lives can lead observers to feel that their lives, in comparison, are deficient. Unsurprisingly, then, some research shows that high users of social media experience greater anxiety, loneliness, depression, and even body image problems (de Vries & Kühne, 2015; Shakya & Christakis, 2017; Hogue & Mills, 2019).

PsychTech

Research on Facebook and other social media sites indicates that social networking provides a less-intimidating social outlet for students who otherwise have trouble making and keeping friendships, such as those who are introverted or have low self-esteem.

HOW DO I LOVE THEE? LET ME COUNT THE WAYS

Whereas our knowledge of what makes people like one another is extensive, our understanding of love is more limited in scope and recently acquired. For some time, many social psychologists believed that love was too difficult to observe and study in a controlled, scientific way. However, love is such a central issue in most people's lives that eventually social psychologists could not resist its allure.

As a first step, researchers tried to identify the characteristics that distinguish between mere liking and full-blown love. They discovered that love is not simply a greater quantity of liking but a qualitatively different psychological state. For instance, at least in its early stages, love includes relatively intense physiological arousal, an all-encompassing interest in the other individual, fantasizing about the other, and relatively rapid swings of emotion. Similarly, love, unlike liking, includes elements of passion, closeness, fascination, exclusiveness, sexual desire, and intense caring. We idealize partners by exaggerating their good qualities and minimizing their imperfections (Tamini, Bojhd, & Yazdani, 2011; Gignac & Zajenkowski, 2019).

Other researchers have theorized that there are two main types of love: passionate love and companionate love. **Passionate (or romantic) love** represents a state of intense absorption in someone. It includes intense physiological arousal, psychological interest, and caring for the needs of another. In contrast, **companionate love** is the strong affection we have for those with whom our lives are deeply involved. The love we feel for parents, other family members, and even some close friends falls into the category of companionate love (Loving, Crockett, & Paxson, 2009; Yildirim & Barnett, 2017; Cannas Aghedu et al., 2019).

Psychologist Robert Sternberg makes an even finer differentiation between types of love. He proposes that love consists of three parts (see Figure 1):

- *Decision/commitment*, the initial thoughts that one loves someone and the longer-term feelings of commitment to maintain love

- *Intimacy component*, feelings of closeness and connectedness

- *Passion component*, the motivational drives relating to sex, physical closeness, and romance

According to Sternberg, these three components combine to produce the different types of love. He suggests that different combinations of the three components vary over the course of relationships. For example, in strong, loving relationships, the level of commitment peaks and then remains stable. Passion, on the other hand, peaks quickly and then declines and levels off relatively early in most relationships. In addition, relationships are happiest in which the strength of the various components are similar between the two partners (Sternberg, Hojjat, & Barnes, 2001; Sternberg, 2004, 2006).

Is love a necessary ingredient in a good marriage? Yes, if you live in the United States. In contrast, it's considerably less important in other cultures. Although mutual attraction (love) is the most important characteristic men and women in the United States desire in a mate, men in China rated good health as most important, and women there rated emotional stability and maturity as most important. Among the Zulu in South Africa, men rated emotional stability first and women rated dependable character first (see Figure 2; Buss, Abbott, & Angleitner, 1990).

passionate (or romantic) love
A state of intense absorption in someone that includes intense physiological arousal, psychological interest, and caring for the needs of another. (Module 55)

companionate love The strong affection we have for those with whom our lives are deeply involved. (Module 55)

FIGURE 1 According to Sternberg, love has three main components: intimacy, passion, and decision/commitment. Different combinations of these components can create other types of love. Nonlove contains none of the three components.
Source: Adapted from Sternberg, R. J. (1986). A triangular theory of love. *Psychological Review*, 93(2), 119–135.

	Rank Ordering of Five Desired Characteristics in a Mate					
	United States		China		South Africa Zulu	
	Females	Males	Females	Males	Females	Males
Mutual attraction—love	1	1		4	5	
Emotional stability and maturity	2	2	1	5	2	1
Dependable character	3	3			1	3
Pleasing disposition	4	4			3	4
Education and intelligence	5	5	4			
Good health			3	1	4	5
Desire for home and children			2	2		
Ambition and industriousness			5			
Good cook and housekeeper						2
Chastity (no prior sexual intercourse)				3		

FIGURE 2 Although love may be an important factor in choosing a marriage partner if you live in the United States, other cultures place less importance on it.

Source: Adapted from Buss, D. M., Abbott, M., & Angleitner, A. (1990). International preferences in selecting mates: A study of 37 cultures. *Journal of Cross-Cultural Psychology, 21*, 5–47.

How we meet our romantic partners and spouses has changed drastically over the years. In the 1940s, heterosexual Americans met their future partners most often through family. Now friends and the Internet are much more frequent matchmakers (see Figure 3). The likelihood of meeting online is even greater for same-sex couples today; some 70% of gay couples report meeting online (Rosenfeld & Thomas, 2012).

FIGURE 3 Couples are considerably more likely to meet online today than were couples in earlier generations, a change that holds true for heterosexual as well as same-sex couples.

Source: Rosenfeld, M. J., & Thomas, R. J. (2012). Searching for a mate: The rise of the Internet as a social intermediary. *American Sociological Review, 77*, 523–547.

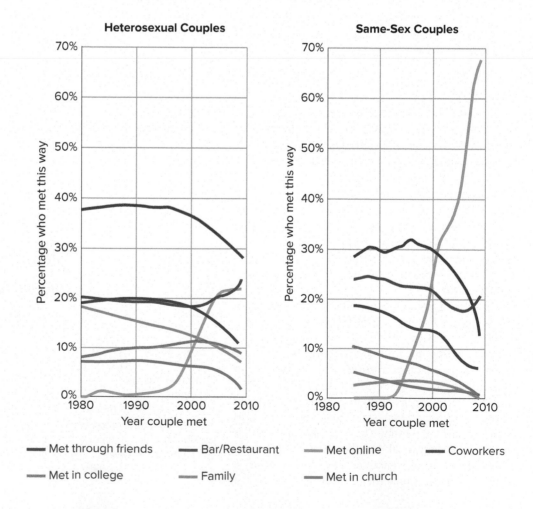

Liking and loving clearly show a positive side of human social behavior. Now we turn to behaviors that are just as much a part of social behavior: aggression and helping behavior.

Aggression and Prosocial Behavior: Hurting and Helping Others

Drive-by shootings, carjackings, and abductions are just a few examples of the violence that seems all too common today. Yet we also find examples of generous, unselfish, thoughtful behavior that suggest a more optimistic view of humankind. Consider, for instance, people such as Mother Teresa, who ministered to the poor in India. Or contemplate the simple kindnesses of life: lending class lecture notes, stopping to help a child who has fallen off a bicycle, or merely sharing a candy bar with a friend. Such instances of helping are no less characteristic of human behavior than are the distasteful examples of aggression.

HURTING OTHERS: AGGRESSION

We need look no further than the daily news cycle to be bombarded with examples of aggression on both a societal level (war, invasion, assassination) and an individual level (crime, child abuse, and the many petty cruelties humans are capable of inflicting on one another). Is such aggression an inevitable part of the human condition? Or is aggression primarily a product of particular circumstances that, if changed, could lead to its reduction?

The difficulty of answering such knotty questions becomes apparent as soon as we consider how best to define the term *aggression*. Depending on the way we define the word, many examples of inflicted pain or injury may or may not qualify as aggression (see Figure 4). For instance, a rapist is clearly acting with aggression toward his victim. On the other hand, it is less certain that a physician carrying out an emergency medical procedure without an anesthetic, thereby causing incredible pain to the patient, should be considered aggressive.

Most social psychologists define aggression in terms of the intent and the purpose behind the behavior. **Aggression** is intentional injury of or harm to another person. By this definition, the rapist is clearly acting aggressively, whereas the physician causing pain during a medical procedure is not (Berkowitz, 2001).

aggression The intentional injury of, or harm to, another person. (Module 55)

Also, the aggression we encounter in our daily lives can take many forms. Not only do we hurt others through direct physical or verbal attacks, but we also can hurt people indirectly by doing such things as spreading rumors or purposely ignoring someone. In fact, some research finds that *microaggressions*—small, daily slights, putdowns, and insults, often perpetrated against members of marginalized groups based on race, gender, and sexual orientation—may be more harmful in the long run than are highly visible acts of aggression. However, the research findings on mircoaggressions are mixed, and more research needs to be done to understand how the daily experience of small acts of prejudice impacts recipients (Lilienfeld, 2017, 2019; Sue, 2017; Williams, 2019).

We turn now to several approaches to understanding aggressive behavior developed by social psychologists.

INSTINCT APPROACHES: AGGRESSION AS A RELEASE

If you have ever punched an adversary in the nose, you may have experienced a certain satisfaction despite your better judgment. Instinct theories, which note the prevalence of aggression not only in humans but in animals as well, propose that aggression is primarily the outcome of innate—or inborn—urges.

FIGURE 4 What is aggression? It depends on how the word is defined and in what context it is used.

Source: Adapted from Benjamin, L. T., Jr. (1985). Defining aggression: An exercise for classroom discussion. *Teaching of Psychology, 12*(1), 40–42.

Is This Aggression?

Defining aggression can be difficult. To see the challenges it raises, read each of the following scenarios and consider whether it describes an aggressive act—according to your own definition of aggressive behavior.

1. A dog chases a rabbit and kills it. Yes _____ No _____

2. A man places a live lobster into boiling water to prepare it for dinner. Yes _____ No _____

3. A war pilot bombs a village, killing both enemy soldiers and civilians. Yes _____ No _____

4. A man repairing a roof accidentally drops a hammer. The hammer hits a child in the yard below, causing permanent brain damage. Yes _____ No _____

5. A boy repeatedly yanks the leash sharply as he walks his dog, ignoring the dog's cries of pain. Yes _____ No _____

6. Mrs. X, hoping to get her son's teacher fired, spreads nasty rumors about the teacher to other parents. Yes _____ No _____

7. A woman continually threatens to spank her toddler for "acting up" while they are shopping for groceries. Yes _____ No _____

8. A man does nothing to help a drowning person at the beach, even though he is an excellent swimmer. Yes _____ No _____

9. A rock star trashes his hotel room while celebrating the success of his latest CD. Yes _____ No _____

10. A woman throws herself under a train. Yes _____ No _____

catharsis The process of discharging built-up aggressive energy. (Module 55)

Sigmund Freud was one of the first to suggest, as part of his theory of personality, that aggression is a primary instinctual drive. Konrad Lorenz, an ethologist (a scientist who studies animal behavior), expanded Freud's notions by arguing that humans, along with members of other species, have a fighting instinct, which in earlier times ensured protection of food supplies and weeded out the weaker of the species (Lorenz, 1974). Lorenz's instinct approach led to the controversial notion that aggressive energy constantly builds up in an individual until the person finally discharges it in a process called **catharsis.** The longer the energy builds up, said Lorenz, the greater the amount of the aggression displayed when it is discharged.

Lorenz believed that society should offer people acceptable ways of experiencing catharsis. For example, he suggested that participation in aggressive sports and games would prevent the discharge of aggression in less socially desirable ways. However, little research has found evidence for the existence of a pent-up reservoir of aggression that needs to be released. In fact, some studies flatly contradict the notion of catharsis, which leads psychologists to look for other explanations for aggression (Verona & Sullivan, 2008; Richardson & Hammock, 2011; Tonnaer, Cima, & Arntz, 2019).

Although little research supports Lorenz's ideas about the need to release pent-up aggression, work on the neural circuitry of the brain does suggest that particular parts of the brain may be involved in aggressive behavior. For example, the amygdala responds to emotionally charged occurrences and is related to threat detection and fear (Fields, 2016; daCunha-Bang et al., 2019).

FRUSTRATION-AGGRESSION APPROACHES: AGGRESSION AS A REACTION TO FRUSTRATION

Suppose you've been working on a paper that is due for a class early the next morning, and your computer printer runs out of ink just before you can print out the paper.

You rush to the store to buy more ink only to find the sales clerk locking the door for the day. Even though the clerk can see you gesturing and begging him to open the door, he refuses, shrugs his shoulders, and points to a sign that indicates when the store will open the next day. At that moment, the feelings you experience toward the sales clerk probably place you on the verge of real aggression, and you are undoubtedly seething inside.

Frustration-aggression approaches explain how the frustration one might feel standing at that closed door could lead to aggression. According to these approaches, frustration (the experience of having one's goals thwarted or blocked) produces anger, which in turn produces a readiness to act aggressively.

But anger doesn't always lead to aggression. Whether actual aggression occurs depends on the presence of aggressive cues. *Aggressive cues* are stimuli that have been associated in the past with actual aggression or violence and that may trigger aggression again (Berkowitz, 2001; Burton et al., 2013).

What kinds of stimuli act as aggressive cues? They can range from the most explicit, such as the presence of weapons, to more subtle cues, such as the mere mention of the name of an individual who behaved violently in the past. For example, angered participants in experiments behave significantly more aggressively when in the presence of a gun than in a comparable situation in which no guns are present. Similarly, frustrated participants who view a violent movie are more physically aggressive toward a confederate with the same name as the star of the movie than they are toward a confederate with a different name (Berkowitz, 2001; Jovanović, Stanojević, & Stanojević, 2011; Wang & Zhong, 2015).

It appears, then, that frustration does lead to aggression—at least when aggressive cues are present. However, psychologists have come to realize that frustration is not the only trigger of aggression. For example, physical pain, verbal insults, and unpleasant experiences in general can also lead to aggression. Similarly, violent behavior increases when the temperature rises—suggesting that one consequence of global warming may be an increase in aggression and intergroup conflict (Van Damme et al., 2017; Plante & Anderson, 2017; Bradshaw, 2019).

Is road rage a result of frustration? According to frustration-aggression approaches, frustration is a likely cause.
Chris Ryan/OJO Images/age fotostock

OBSERVATIONAL LEARNING APPROACHES: LEARNING TO HURT OTHERS

Do we learn to be aggressive? The *observational learning* (sometimes called *social learning*) approach to aggression says that we do. Taking an almost opposite view from instinct theories, which focus on innate explanations of aggression, observational learning theory emphasizes that social and environmental conditions can teach individuals to be aggressive. The theory sees aggression not as inevitable but rather as a learned response that can be understood in terms of rewards and punishments.

Observational learning theory pays attention to the direct rewards and punishments that people receive for acting aggressively. For example, a father may tell his son how glad he was that he "stood up for himself" after getting into a fight, thereby rewarding aggressive behavior.

More frequently, though, people learn aggression through watching others' behavior. According to the *observational learning approach*, we learn to be aggressive by viewing the rewards and punishments that models provide. *Models* are individuals who provide a guide to appropriate behavior through their own behavior. According to observational learning theory, people observe the behavior of models and the subsequent consequences of that behavior. If the consequences are positive, the behavior is likely to be imitated when observers find themselves in a similar situation.

Suppose, for instance, a girl hits her younger brother when he damages one of her new toys. Whereas instinct theory would suggest that the aggression had been pent up and was now being discharged, and frustration-aggression theory would examine the girl's frustration at no longer being able to use her new toy, observational learning theory would look to previous situations in which the girl had viewed others being rewarded for their aggression. For example, perhaps she had watched a friend get to play with a toy after he painfully twisted it out of the hand of another child.

Observational learning theory has received wide research support. For example, children of nursery school age who have watched an adult model behave aggressively and then receive reinforcement for it later display similar behavior themselves if they have been angered, insulted, or frustrated after exposure. Furthermore, a significant amount of research links watching television shows containing violence with subsequent viewer aggression (Greer, Dudek-Singer, & Gautreaux, 2006; Carnagey, Anderson, & Bartholow, 2007).

From the perspective of...

A Criminal Justice Worker How would proponents of the three main approaches to the study of aggression—instinct approaches, frustration-aggression approaches, and observational learning approaches—interpret the aggression of the killer in the Sandy Hook Elementary School shooting, in which 26 children and adults were killed?

DMITRI MARUTA/
Deposit Photos/Glow
Images

Helping Others: The Brighter Side of Human Nature

Turning away from aggression, we move now to the opposite—and brighter—side of human nature: how we provide aid to others. **Prosocial behavior,** which is the term that psychologists use for helping behavior, has been considered under many different conditions. However, the question that psychologists have looked at most closely relates to bystander intervention in emergency situations. What are the factors that lead someone to help a person in need?

One critical factor related to helping in emergency situations is the number of other individuals present. When multiple people witness an emergency situation, a sense of diffusion of responsibility can arise among the bystanders. **Diffusion of responsibility** is the belief that responsibility for taking action is shared, or diffused, among those present. The more people present in an emergency, the less personally responsible each individual feels—and therefore the less help he or she provides (Gray, 2006; Martin & North, 2015; Christensen, 2019).

For example, think back to the classic case of Kitty Genovese that we described when discussing the topic of research. Genovese was stabbed multiple times, and—according to some accounts of the event—no one offered help, despite the fact that allegedly close to 40 people who lived in nearby apartments heard her screams for help. The lack of help has been attributed to diffusion of responsibility: The fact that there were so many potential helpers led each individual to feel diminished personal responsibility (Fischer et al., 2011; Gallo, 2015; Griggs, 2015).

Although most research on helping behavior supports the diffusion-of-responsibility explanation, other factors are clearly involved in helping behavior. The decision to give aid involves four basic steps (see Figure 5; Latané & Darley, 1970; Garcia et al., 2002; López-Pérez et al., 2017):

- *Noticing a person, event, or situation that may require help.* If we are to provide help, we first have to perceive that a situation is one that potentially requires our help and intervention.

prosocial behavior Helping behavior. (Module 55)

diffusion of responsibility The belief that responsibility for taking action is shared, or diffused, among those present. (Module 55)

- *Interpreting the event as one that requires help.* Even if we notice an event, it may be sufficiently ambiguous for us to interpret it as a nonemergency situation that requires no help. Thus, we make an interpretation as to whether or not the event requires help.

- *Assuming responsibility for helping.* It is at this key point that diffusion of responsibility is likely to occur if others are present. Moreover, a bystander's particular expertise is likely to play a role in determining whether he or she helps. For instance, if people with training in medical aid or lifesaving techniques are present, untrained bystanders are less likely to intervene because they feel they have less expertise.

- *Deciding on and implementing the form of helping.* After we assume responsibility for helping, we must decide how to provide assistance. Helping can range from very indirect forms of intervention, such as calling the police, to more direct forms, such as giving first aid or taking the victim to a hospital. Most social psychologists use a *rewards-costs approach* for helping to predict the nature of the assistance a bystander will choose to provide. The general notion is that the bystander's perceived rewards for helping must outweigh the costs if helping is to occur, and most research tends to support this notion (Koper & Jaasma, 2001; Bartlett & DeSteno, 2006; Lin & Lin, 2007).

After determining the nature of the assistance needed, the actual help must be implemented. A rewards-costs analysis suggests that we are most likely to use the least costly form of implementation. However, this is not always the case: In some situations, the help that is provided shows altruism. **Altruism** is behavior meant to help another without regard for self-interest. It is putting the welfare of others above oneself. For example, we can see altruism in soldiers who risk their own lives to save another soldier who is wounded or in a woman who jumps into an icy pond to save a drowning stranger. We saw altruism in the everyday people who put themselves at mortal risk to help strangers escape from the burning World Trade Center towers during the 9/11 terrorist attack or in the behavior of Doug Collman, discussed in the chapter prologue, who gave a kidney to a friend in need (Manor & Gailliot, 2007; Marshall, 2011; Xi, et al., 2017).

People who intervene in emergency situations tend to possess certain personality characteristics that differentiate them from nonhelpers. For example, helpers are more self-assured, sympathetic, emotionally understanding, and empathetic (empathy is a personality trait in which someone observing another person experiences the emotions of that person) than are nonhelpers (Stocks, Lishner, & Decker, 2009; Batson, 2011; Li et al., 2019).

Still, most social psychologists agree that no single set of attributes differentiates helpers from nonhelpers. For the most part, temporary situational factors (such as the mood we're in) determine whether we will intervene in a situation requiring aid (Dovidio et al., 2006; Sallquist et al., 2009; Snyder & Dwyer, 2013).

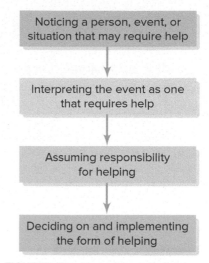

FIGURE 5 The basic steps of helping.
Source: Adapted from Latané, B., & Darley, J. M. (1970). *The unresponsive bystander: Why doesn't he help?* New York: Appleton-Century-Crofts.

altruism Behavior meant to help another person without regard for self-interest. (Module 55)

Altruism is often the only bright side of a natural disaster.
John Glaser/CSM/Shutterstock

APPLYING PSYCHOLOGY IN THE 21ST CENTURY

PEOPLE ARE MORE LIKELY TO RETURN A LOST WALLET WITH CASH

If you found a lost wallet with some ID cards and a key in it but no cash, would you try to track down the owner to return it? What if it also contained a few dollars? What if it contained a lot of cash? Would that make a difference to you?

That's the question researchers set out to answer with a large global study conducted in 355 cities across every inhabited continent. In each locale, research assistants entered police stations, museums, banks, and similar establishments and turned in wallets that they claimed they'd found lying on a nearby street.

The wallets–over 17,000 in all–were transparent business-card cases containing a key, a short grocery list, and a few business cards with a male name and an e-mail address. Some of the wallets contained nothing else, while others also contained $13.45 worth of local currency. The research assistants recorded the gender, age, and friendliness of the person to whom they gave the wallet, along with how busy that person was, whether any coworkers witnessed the event, and whether the person had a computer readily available (Cohn et al., 2019).

If you found a wallet, what would you do?
Happy Nati/Shutterstock

Overall, only 40 percent of the cashless wallets were reported to the owner, compared to 51 percent of those with cash. Across all countries, the wallets containing cash were more likely to be returned than the cashless ones (or the researchers found no significant difference).

In a follow-up study conducted in Poland, the United Kingdom, and the United States, a new condition was added: a wallet containing a lot more cash–nearly $100. Whereas only 46% of the cashless

wallets were reported to the owner, 61% of those with $13.45 and 72% of the "big cash" wallets were. So the more money in the wallet, the more likely it was the wallet would be returned.

Further research suggested a reason for this surprising finding (which neither economics experts nor nonexperts expected): The presence of cash was more likely to activate people's moral concerns. Specifically, when they reported a wallet with cash, they felt they were helping someone; when they failed to report a wallet with cash, they felt they were stealing. That feeling of being a thief gets worse when the amount of cash is higher.

These findings may help us develop strategies that will encourage people to be more honest. For example, prompting people to focus on the morality of their decisions and making them more aware of the negative impact their behavior may have on someone else may lead them to greater honesty (Belluck, 2019).

RETHINK

- What other reasons might people have had for failing to return the cashless wallets beyond the lack of activation of moral concerns?
- Why do you think people's altruistic concerns seemingly outweighed their own self-interest in this study?

More generally, what leads people to make moral decisions? Clearly, situational factors make a difference. For example, one study asked people to judge the morality of plane crash survivors cannibalizing an injured boy to avoid starvation. Participants in the study were more likely to condemn the behavior if they were placed in an emotional state than if they were less emotional (Schnall et al., 2008; Broeders et al., 2011).

Other psychologists, using a neuroscience perspective, believe that there's a kind of tug-of-war between emotion and rational thinking in the brain. If the rational side wins out, we're more likely to take a logical view of moral situations (if you're at risk for starving, go ahead and eat the injured boy). On the other hand, if the emotional side prevails, we're more likely to condemn the cannibalism, even if it means we may be harmed. In support of such reasoning, researchers have found that different areas of the brain are involved in moral decisions (Miller, 2008; Greene & Paxton, 2009; Beauchamp et al., 2019).

Evidence also exists that our brains are hardwired to help us feel empathy for others. In this view, helping others in some ways is just as natural as other, more negative behaviors. The question becomes, then, how we balance the positive and negative behaviors that are equally the result of the functioning of the brain (Pfaff, 2014; de Waal, 2014; Fedyk, 2017). (Also see *Applying Psychology in the 21st Century.*)

BECOMING AN INFORMED CONSUMER
of Psychology

Dealing Effectively with Anger

At one time or another, almost everyone feels angry. The anger may result from a frustrating situation, or it may be due to another individual's behavior. The way we deal with anger may determine the difference between a promotion and a lost job or a broken relationship and one that mends itself.

Social psychologists who have studied the topic suggest several good strategies to deal with anger that maximize the potential for positive consequences (Nelson & Finch, 2000; Bernstein, 2011; Faupel, Herrick, & Sharp, 2018). Among the most useful strategies are the following:

- *Calm down.* Take a walk or engage in some other physical activity in order to cool down your emotional arousal.
- *Look again at the anger-provoking situation from the perspective of others.* By taking others' points of view, you may be able to understand the situation better, and with increased understanding, you may become more tolerant of the apparent shortcomings of others.
- *Minimize the importance of the situation.* Does it really matter that someone is driving too slowly and that you'll be late to an appointment as a result? Reinterpret the situation in a way that is less bothersome.
- *Use language effectively by saying "I," not "you."* Don't say *"You did _____ wrong."* Instead, say *"I felt hurt when you did _____."* When you accuse people of being wrong, they are likely to feel the need to fight back.
- *Fantasize about getting even—but don't act on it.* Fantasy provides a safety valve. In your fantasies, you can yell at that unfair professor all you want and suffer no consequences at all. However, don't spend too much time brooding: Fantasize, but then move on.
- *Relax.* By teaching yourself the relaxation techniques used in systematic desensitization (discussed in the chapter on treatment of psychological disorders), you can help reduce your reactions to anger. In turn, your anger may dissipate.

No matter which of these strategies you try, above all, don't ignore your anger. People who always try to suppress their anger may experience a variety of consequences, such as self-condemnation, frustration, and even physical illness (Quartana & Burns, 2007; Gardner & Moore, 2008).

RECAP/EVALUATE/RETHINK

RECAP

LO 55-1 Why are we attracted to certain people, and what progression do social relationships follow?

- The primary determinants of liking include proximity, exposure, similarity, and physical attractiveness.
- Loving is distinguished from liking by the presence of intense physiological arousal, an all-encompassing interest in another, fantasies about the other, rapid swings of emotion, fascination, sexual desire, exclusiveness, and strong feelings of caring.

- Love can be categorized as passionate or companionate. In addition, love has several components: intimacy, passion, and decision/commitment.

LO 55-2 What factors underlie aggression and prosocial behavior?

- Aggression is intentional injury of or harm to another person.
- Explanations of aggression include instinct approaches, frustration-aggression theory, and observational learning.

- Helping behavior in emergencies is determined in part by the phenomenon of diffusion of responsibility, which results in a lower likelihood of helping when more people are present.
- Deciding to help is the outcome of a four-stage process that consists of noticing a possible need for help, interpreting the situation as requiring aid, assuming responsibility for taking action, and deciding on and implementing a form of assistance.

EVALUATE

1. We tend to like people who are similar to us. True or false?
2. Which of the following sets are the three components of love proposed by Sternberg?
   a. Passion, closeness, sexuality
   b. Attraction, desire, complementarity
   c. Passion, intimacy, decision/commitment
   d. Commitment, caring, sexuality
3. Based on research evidence, which of the following might be the best way to reduce the amount of fighting a young boy does?
   a. Take him to the gym and let him work out on the boxing equipment.
   b. Make him repeatedly watch violent scenes from the film *The Matrix Reloaded* in the hope that it will provide catharsis.
   c. Reward him if he doesn't fight during a certain period.
   d. Ignore it and let it die out naturally.
4. If a person in a crowd does not help in an apparent emergency situation because many other people are present, that person is falling victim to the phenomenon of _____ _____ _____.

RETHINK

1. Can love be studied scientifically? Is there an elusive quality to love that makes it at least partially unknowable? How would you define "falling in love"? How would you study it?
2. How would the aggression of the Boston Marathon bombers be interpreted by the three main approaches to the study of aggression: instinct approaches, frustration-aggression approaches, and observational learning approaches? Do you think one of these approaches fits the bombers' case more closely than the others?

Answers to Evaluate Questions

1. true; 2. c; 3. c; 4. diffusion of responsibility

KEY TERMS

interpersonal attraction (or close relationship)	passionate (or romantic) love	aggression	diffusion of responsibility
reciprocity-of-liking effect	companionate love	catharsis	altruism
		prosocial behavior	

LOOKING *Back*

EPILOGUE

We have touched on some of the major ideas, research topics, and experimental findings of social psychology. We examined how people form, maintain, and change attitudes and how they form impressions of others and assign attributions to them. We also saw how groups, through conformity and tactics of compliance, can influence individuals' actions and attitudes. Finally, we discussed interpersonal relationships, including both liking and loving, and looked at aggression and prosocial behavior, the two sides of a coin that represent the extremes of social behavior.

Turn back to the prologue to this set of modules, which describes Doug Coffman's decision to donate a kidney to Jim McGee. Use your understanding of social psychology to consider the following questions.

1. How would a social psychologist explain Coffman's sacrifice to help a man he hadn't seen in 50 years?
2. What attribution would a casual observer of Coffman's sacrifice be likely to make for his behavior? How would that explanation likely differ from that of a social psychologist?
3. Might the context of meeting McGee again at an Air Force reunion have influenced Coffman's altruism? How so?
4. How might their shared experience of living a highly regimented and mutually dependent life in the military have influenced Coffman's desire to help McGhee?

VISUAL SUMMARY 17 Social Psychology

MODULE 52 Attitudes and Social Cognition

Persuasion and Attitudes

Attitudes: Evaluations of a particular person, behavior, belief, or concept

— Routes to persuasion

— Attitude-behavior link

Social Cognition: How people understand what others and themselves are like

— Forming impressions of others: Central traits help us form impressions of others

— Attribution theory: How we decide the specific causes of a person's behavior

- • Situational causes: of behavior that are external to a person

- • Dispositional causes: of behavior brought about by a person's traits or internal personality characteristics

- • Attribution biases

MODULE 53 Social Influence and Groups

Conformity: A desire to follow the beliefs or standards of other people

— Groupthink: Group members want to achieve consensus and lose the ability to evaluate alternative points of view

— Social roles: Behaviors associated with people in a given position

Compliance: Social pressure to behave in a certain way

— Foot-in-the-door technique

— Door-in-the-face technique

— That's-not-all technique

— Not-so-free sample

Obedience: Behavior change in response to the commands of others

MODULE 54 Prejudice and Discrimination

Prejudice: A negative or positive evaluation of a group

Discrimination: Behavior directed toward individuals on the basis of their membership in a particular group

Stereotype: Generalized beliefs and expectations about a specific group that arise when we categorize information

Reducing Prejudice and Discrimination

— Increase contact between the target of stereotyping and the holder of the stereotype

— Make values and norms against prejudice more conspicuous

— Provide information about the targets of stereotyping

— Reduce stereotype threat

— Increase a sense of belonging

MODULE 55 Positive and Negative Social Behavior

Liking and Loving

— Determinants of liking

- • Proximity

- • Mere exposure

- • Similarity

- • Physical attractiveness

— What is love?

- • Qualitatively different from liking

- • Three components of love

Aggression: Intentional injury of or harm to another person

— Instinct approaches

— Frustration-aggression approach

— Observational learning approaches

Helping (Prosocial) Behavior: Actions intended to provide aid to others

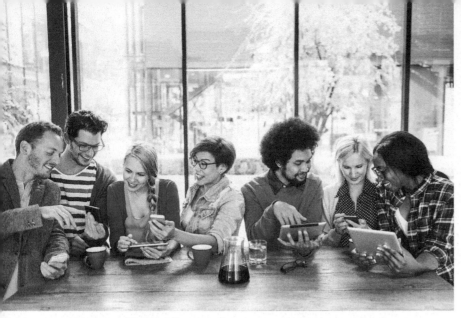
Rawpixel.com/Shutterstock

EPILOGUE
Diversity, Culture, Conflict, and Cooperation

LEARNING OUTCOMES FOR EPILOGUE

LO 1 What are the basic elements of diversity and culture?

DIVERSITY AND CULTURE

The Language of Diversity

Culture

Collectivism and Individualism: The Group Versus the Individual

Our View of Ourselves: Looking Inward

Exploring Diversity: The Culture of Aggression

Immigrants: The Newest Americans

LO 2 What are the roots of conflict?

CONFLICT AND COOPERATION: STRIVING FOR A JUST AND PEACEFUL WORLD

The Roots of Conflict

Misperceiving Our Enemies

Genocidal Violence and Mass Killing: Explaining the Inexplicable

LO 3 How can we reduce the risk of war and increase the chances for peace?

BECOMING AN INFORMED CONSUMER OF PSYCHOLOGY

Reducing War, Promoting Peace, and Creating a Just World

BRIDGING THE DIVIDE OF DIFFERENCE

Haifa Staiti made a friend beside a lake at a summer camp in Maine. Sitting under a canopy of trees, she spoke to another camper who, it turned out, shared many of her dreams and basic values. "I felt I was being heard, and I felt comfortable about sharing my experiences," she said (Epatko, 2018).

What made the exchange unusual was that Staiti was a Palestinian and her fellow camper was an Israeli. Although the two came from cultures that are in a perpetual state of undeclared war, they found they had much in common.

The interchange was possible due to a program called Seeds of Peace, designed to bring Israelis and Palestinians together in a neutral and supportive environment. Staiti's childhood had been difficult, with curfews and repeated imprisonment of her politically active father by the Israeli government.

Initially, the camp experience was not easy for Staiti, who was a shy 14-year-old when she began the program. But by the time her stay at the camp was over, both Staiti and her Israeli acquaintance realized that they had much in common, and they remain friends today (Epatko, 2018).

LOOKING *Ahead*

What is it about racial, ethnic, and cultural differences that evoke strong, and sometimes even deadly, responses? Why do such differences lead to prejudice, discrimination, and violence, both in the United States and across the world? And can programs such as Seeds of Peace bridge the differences that divide the diverse world in which we all live?

No principle of psychology leads us to expect that we are destined to live in constant discord. Indeed, in some communities, minorities and majorities live in tranquility, building societies that both acknowledge and welcome the differences between people.

In this module, we examine issues that shed light on psychology's role in understanding diversity and fostering a better world. In the first section, we look at how diversity and culture affect thinking and behavior in fundamental ways. In the second section, we explore issues of conflict, war, and peace. We consider why conflicts occur between people, groups, and nations. We then look at factors that sustain conflicts, such as the views people develop of enemies, and we explore some of the most extreme forms conflict can take: genocide and nuclear war. We end this epilogue on an optimistic note, considering psychological techniques for promoting peace.

Diversity and Culture

No matter where we live, we are increasingly likely to encounter people who differ from us racially, ethnically, and culturally. Technology is bringing people from across the globe into our homes, as close to us as the phone in our hand or the computer on our desk. Businesses now operate globally, so coworkers are likely to come from many countries and cultures. Being comfortable with people whose backgrounds and beliefs differ from our own is not only a social necessity but also a requirement for career success.

Moreover, by the mid-21st century, the percentage of people in the United States of African, Latin American, Asian, and Arabic ancestry will be greater than the percentage of those of Western European ancestry—a profound statistical, and social, shift. College enrollments will mirror these changes, as populations that were minority become the majority (Alba & Barbosa, 2016; Cohn & Caumont, 2016; Pappano, 2019).

More specifically, consider the following population trends (Cohn & Caumont, 2016; U.S. Census Bureau, 2017, 2019).

- By 2055, the United States will not have any single racial or ethnic majority. Put another way, we will all be members of minority groups.
- Almost 60 million immigrants have come to the United States since 1970.
- Most population growth in the United States is projected to be related to Hispanic and Asian immigration.
- Around 14% of the U.S. population is foreign-born.
- Twenty percent of U.S. residents speak a language other than English at home.

Furthermore, diversity is not just based in racial, ethnic, and cultural characteristics. The world's population is also diverse in terms of sex, gender identity, sexual orientation, age, and mental and physical abilities. Then, layer on factors such as education, religion, and income level, and you can see that each person is a complex mix of identities. The way those diverse identities overlap or interact is known as *intersectionality*. One can be, for instance, a hearing-impaired lesbian African-American woman and evoke responses from others that reflect any, all, or none of those identities (DeBlaere, Watsonk, & Langrehr, 2018; Mays & Ghavami, 2018).

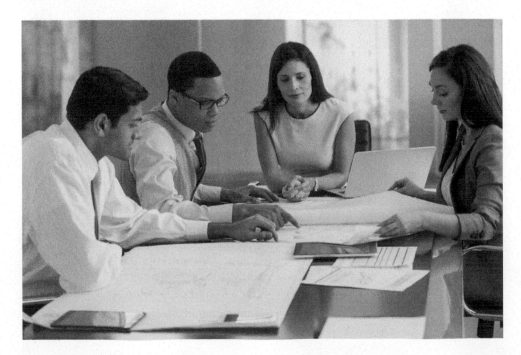

Increasingly, many workplaces will include staff from a wide variety of countries and cultures, and with a wide range of customs and beliefs. What are your experiences with people who differ from you culturally?
Jose Luis Pelaez Inc/Blend Images

The Language of Diversity

The language we use to describe others and their diversity is important, and social-cultural norms often determine what labels are appropriate. For example, should one say African American or black? Caucasian, white, or Euro-American? Hispanic or Latino? American Indian or Native American? Gay, lesbian, straight, or queer? Transgender, cisgender, male, or female? Physically challenged, differently abled, or disabled? The choice of labels matters. The subtleties of language affect how people think about members of particular groups and how they think about themselves (Forson, 2018).

One difficulty in understanding diversity is that many of the terms we use are ill-defined and often overlapping. For example, the term **race** generally refers to obvious physical differences that set one group apart from others. But depending on how race is defined, there are between 3 and 300 races, with no race genetically distinct. And the reality is that 99.9% of our genetic makeup is similar across all human beings. Because of this, race is generally thought of as a *social construction*, something that is defined by people's attitudes and beliefs (Zuberi, Patterson, & Stewart, 2015; Gross & Weiss, 2018).

Ethnicity refers to shared national origins or cultural patterns. In the United States, for example, Puerto Rican, Irish, and Italian American typically are categorized as ethnic groups. However, ethnicity–like race–is very much in the eye of the beholder. For instance, a Cuban American who is a third-generation citizen of the United States may feel few ties or associations to Cuba or Cuban culture. Yet whites may view her as "Hispanic," and blacks may view her as "white."

Race and ethnicity shape each of us to an enormous degree, profoundly influencing our view of others as well as ourselves. They affect how others treat us and how we

race Generally refers to obvious physical differences that set one group apart from others.

ethnicity Shared national origins or cultural patterns.

The term *race* is generally used to refer to obvious physical differences between groups of people. However, as you can see from these images, skin tone, hair texture, and facial features come in many varieties and combinations, so the lines between groups can't be clearly drawn.
Rawpixel.com/Shutterstock

treat them in turn. They can also determine a broad range of behaviors, ranging from whether we look people in the eye when we meet them (in some cultures, direct eye contact is viewed as disrespectful, so it is avoided) or how much food we eat when we're invited to dinner at a friend's house (in some cultures, it is considered impolite to leave food on one's plate) (Mannarini, Talò, & Rochira, 2017; Park et al., 2018).

Even the words we use to describe others reflect our beliefs and values. For instance, the term *African American* is a label that has historical, geographical, and sociological implications. On the other hand, *black* focuses primarily on skin color.

Similarly, we do not yet have clear rules about the language to use for the varieties of gender identities and sexualities individuals may hold. For example, *transgender* refers to individuals whose sense of whether they are male or female (their *gender identity*) does not match the sex they were assigned at birth. Transgender people may refer to themselves as trans, transexual, agender, demigender, or genderqueer, and some prefer the use of gender-neutral pronouns, such as *ze*, *zir*, or *they*.

Furthermore, gender identity is not the same as *sexual orientation*, which describes a person's physical and emotional attraction to another person. For example, people may consider themselves straight, lesbian, gay, bisexual–or something else–depending on who they are attracted to sexually.

Culture

As a graduate student from Korea, Jung felt she was adjusting well to her psychology program in the United States. She got along well with her professors, and her officemates seemed cordial and friendly. But she felt uneasy in one area. Every Friday afternoon, other graduate students would gather at a local bar for what they called "Happy Hour," which–although Jung didn't know it was a long-standing tradition among students in the psychology program. No one extended a personal invitation to Jung, and although she wished she could go with the other students, she felt it would be presumptuous to attend without an invitation. Since they never invited her to go along, she wondered if she had somehow insulted them.

How would you respond to Jung about her concerns? Most people familiar with the social customs of the United States would probably tell her that she needs no invitation to join her fellow students at the bar. Such gatherings are informal, and U.S. natives would neither expect nor routinely offer personal invitations to them.

Jung's confusion over the customs of public gatherings is just one example of the way in which habits differ from one culture to another. Although this problem appears to be relatively trivial, variations in such everyday behaviors indicate fundamental differences between people of diverse cultures. Furthermore, such misunderstandings may lead to stereotyping and prejudice. For example, Jung's classmates might think she was standoffish or unfriendly, and they might generalize such a view to something about Koreans. Learning about culture is essential to understanding the differences between people.

Culture comprises the learned behaviors, beliefs, and attitudes that are characteristic of an individual society or population. Culture is transmitted from one generation to another in both written and spoken form. Culture also encompasses people's creations, such as art, music, literature, and architecture. In sum, culture both shapes and reflects a society's behavior, understanding of the world, attitudes, and values (Wan & Chiu, 2011; Han & Ma, 2015; Bornstein & Lansford, 2019).

Despite their broad impact on people, cultural factors have traditionally received little attention from psychologists. One reason is that many psychologists have instead focused on broad universal principles of human behavior. Presumably, the thinking went, such principles should apply to all people, regardless of their culture.

Today, however, psychologists increasingly appreciate the importance of culture. Rather than considering it an obstacle to finding universal psychological principles, psychologists now view culture as a major factor in shaping our behavior. In fact,

culture The learned behaviors, beliefs, and attitudes that characterize an individual society or population.

Cultures vary in multiple ways, including their funeral ceremonies. In this traditional New Orleans funeral procession, jazz musicians provide a send-off to a loved one on the way to the cemetery. What is the funeral tradition in your culture or religion?

RSBPhoto/Alamy Stock Photo

explanations for many central aspects of behavior remain elusive without an understanding of the consequences of culture. Indeed, psychologists can identify broad, universal principles of behavior only by determining which ones apply across cultures and which are specific to particular cultures. For example, a psychologist studying grief as a universal emotion would want to determine what a festive New Orleans jazz funeral has in common with a more conventional funeral at a graveside (Triandis, 2011; Rosenblatt, 2013; Gercama & Jones, 2020).

Understanding the role of culture has also become increasingly important due to the growing diversity of U.S. society. The fabric of society is changing to reflect the contributions of people of diverse ethnic, racial, and religious backgrounds. We can understand the similarities and differences around us only when we consider culture. Furthermore, when we are aware of the effects of cultural differences, we may overcome our prejudices and better understand the roots of discrimination.

multiculturalism The view that members of all cultures deserve equal respect and that their contributions to society should be recognized.

Furthering interest in culture is the concept of multiculturalism, which has both psychological and political implications for how members of racial, ethnic, religious, and other demographic groups are perceived. **Multiculturalism** is the view that members of all cultures deserve equal respect and that their contributions to society should be recognized. This concept not only acknowledges differences among subcultural groups, it also furthers the argument that society is stronger due to the presence of multiple groups and cultures.

Let's examine some primary psychological considerations related to culture, including differing cultural orientations and how people in different cultures vary in their view of themselves.

Collectivism and Individualism: The Group Versus the Individual

Do you think teenagers should take their parents' views into account when choosing a career? Do you think you ought to help a neighbor who is in financial distress? Do you have an obligation to lend your class notes to a fellow student who missed a class?

If you answer yes to these questions, your responses represent values similar to those found in many Eastern cultures. On the other hand, if you reply no to these questions, your value orientation is more like that fostered in Western cultures.

These two orientations are known as *collectivism* and *individualism*. Cultures that support **collectivism** promote the idea that the well-being of the group or society is more important than that of the individual. People in collectivistic societies place the welfare of the group above their own personal well-being (Nguyen, Le, & Boles, 2010; Arpaci, Baloğlu, & Kesici, 2018).

In contrast, societies that encourage **individualism** hold as a primary value the personal identity, uniqueness, freedom, and worth of the individual person. In individualistic cultures, personal goals are viewed as more important than goals relating to society in general.

The individualistic and collectivistic tendencies of these cultures influence the way people interpret and understand behavior. For example, students and teachers in the United States tend to attribute their scholastic success to stable, internal characteristics. Consequently, a student who does well is seen as being smart, which is a stable, internal trait and is an outgrowth of an individualistic view of the world. In contrast, in China and Japan, both countries that have a more collectivistic culture than the United States, people see scholastic performance in terms of temporary, situational factors, such as how hard a student works.

The varying cultural perceptions that underlie academic success lead to different levels of scholastic motivation. Because Chinese and Japanese students are more apt to assume that academic success results from hard work, they are likely to put greater effort into their studies. U.S. students may exert less effort because they believe that their stable, unvarying level of ability underlies their school performance. After all, students who assume that their internal ability is the primary cause of their performance may not understand that studying harder may bring better results. In other words, they may feel they can't do much to change the outcome (Chen & Zhang, 2011; Fetvadjiev et al., 2018; Wu et al., 2018).

Whether a culture is collectivistic or individualistic also influences people's willingness to share scarce resources with others. For instance, people living in collectivistic cultures primarily employ the *norm of equality* to determine how rewards should be granted. The norm of equality suggests that all people ought to be rewarded equally, regardless of who they are or how competent or successful they are. In this case, an equality norm would mean that all students working on a project together as a group would receive the same grade.

collectivism The concept that the well-being of the group or society is more important than that of the individual.

individualism The concept that holds as a primary value the personal identity, uniqueness, freedom, and worth of the individual person.

In Eastern collectivist cultures, students are more likely to view academic achievement as tied to situational factors, such as how hard they work. In contrast, those in Western individualistic cultures tie achievement to more stable characteristics, such as how smart they think they are. How do you view academic success?
Paul Burns/Blend Images

In contrast, people living in individualistic societies tend to distribute resources according to a *norm of equity*, in which rewards are based on the size of the contribution people make or the quality of their performance. Those who receive the most are the ones who have made the greatest contribution, whereas those who receive the least have made the smallest contribution. In an individualistic society, then, workers are paid according to their perceived merit. As a consequence, great discrepancies exist in the amount of rewards people receive (Boarini, Laslier, & Robin, 2009; Okely, Weiss, & Gale, 2018).

Our View of Ourselves: Looking Inward

In Western cultures, "the squeaky wheel gets the grease." In Asian cultures, "the nail that stands out gets pounded down."

The differences in these two sayings reflect profound cultural variations between the West and East in how people see themselves. In the Western perspective, people tend to differentiate themselves, making their voices heard and letting others know what their individual needs are in a situation. The Asian perspective suggests that the best approach is to blend in, to avoid being noticed (Krassner et al., 2017).

These divergent points-of-view exemplify how people in Eastern and Western cultures view the **self,** the way in which we look inward and define ourselves as individuals. Research suggests that people raised in Asian societies have an **interdependent** view of themselves, in part reflective of their collectivistic orientation. They think of themselves as members of a larger society, working together with others to achieve social harmony. In this view, people strive to fit in, to behave in a way that coincides with how others think, feel, and act (Markus & Kitayama, 2003, 2010; Levine et al., 2016).

People in Western societies, however, see themselves as **independent** of others, reflecting in part their individualistic orientation. Rather than striving to fit in, they may compete rather than cooperate with others. In many cases, they pride themselves on their uniqueness, distinctiveness, and above all, individuality.

These distinct views of the self are revealed on many levels and in all aspects of individualistic cultures. Even the languages people speak reflect the differences. For instance, the English language has more words for emotions focused on oneself, such as jealousy and anger, than the Japanese language. In contrast, the Japanese language contains many more terms for emotions involving others, such as sympathy, than the English language. In fact, the Japanese language contains words for some emotions that do not have similar words in English. *Oime*, for instance, refers to being indebted to another individual—a word for which English has nothing comparable (Markus & Kitayama, 2010; Andersen, 2017).

People in Eastern cultures also view achievement very differently than people in Western cultures. For example, Westerners assess achievement in terms of personal gains. They look at how well they are doing relative to others, comparing whether they are better or worse off. Grades, salaries, and the size of one's home or office are things that people may use to compare and measure achievements. Thus, the value they place on their success is relative to what others achieve.

In contrast, people in interdependent societies tend to measure success in terms of group achievement. Rewards are thought to be appropriate in terms of how well one's group does, rather than how one does as an individual. For example, a student's success on a group project would be measured in terms of how well the overall project turns out, rather than in terms of each student's individual contribution. Similarly, salary raises in a business might be based on the performance of the company as a whole.

Most aspects of a culture, such as the degree of its individualism and collectivism, are neither inherently good nor bad. In an absolute sense, neither individualism nor collectivism is preferable to the other. But elements in some cultures are clearly harmful. One such element is the aggressiveness of a given society, which we consider next.

self A person's essential being distinguishing themselves from others; how we define ourselves as individuals.

interdependent (view of self) To view oneself as a member of a larger society, working together with others to achieve social harmony.

independent (view of self) To view oneself as behaving independently, competing rather than cooperating with others.

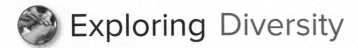 Exploring Diversity

The Culture of Aggression

Violence is as American as apple pie. At least that's the conclusion of some observers of society in the United States, who point to the grim quantity of violence that occurs. For example, the homicide rate in the United States is four times greater than in comparable countries such as France and the United Kingdom. Even within the United States, certain segments of the population are at extraordinary risk: African Americans account for nearly half of all murder victims, yet make up only about 13% of the population. And big-city homicides rose substantially in both 2015 and 2016 (Lepore, 2009; Associated Press, 2011; Rosenfeld et al., 2017).

The United States is also an outlier when it comes to the magnitude of school violence. Since the Columbine High School shooting in 1999, 131 children, educators, and others have been killed in shootings in 217 schools. Furthermore, 215,000 children have witnessed school shootings. In the first 46 weeks of 2019, 45 school shootings occurred—basically, one per week (Cox et al., 2018).; Wolfe & Walker, 2019).

Do these figures imply that U.S. society is uniquely violent compared to other societies? Before we can answer such a question, we need to consider several factors because comparing levels of aggression across cultures is no easy matter.

Take, for instance, the difficulty in defining the term *aggression*. Most researchers suggest that for an act to be considered aggressive, it must involve intentional injury or harm to another person; others use broader definitions. The particular definition of aggression becomes critical when comparing statistics collected from a variety of settings in very different cultures.

In addition, even when a specific definition of aggression can be agreed on, labeling a particular behavior as aggressive may prove problematic. Consider this example of observing children: One boy shoves another from behind and knocks him over; both boys laugh about the incident. Should this behavior be labeled as aggressive or as spirited play?

Finally, cultures are not necessarily homogeneous, which adds to why differences exist in the incidence of aggression. For example, there are regional differences in the United States: The rate of murder in the Texas panhandle is four times higher than the murder rate in Nebraska. Generalizing across an entire country or culture, then, may obscure important differences among subgroups (Nisbett & Cohen, 1996; Anwar, Fry, & Grigaitytė, 2018; Hornsveld et al, 2018).

Despite such critical difficulties in comparing rates of violence across cultures, several researchers have attempted to identify differences between cultures in the levels of aggression. As a result, several findings have emerged.

One finding is that cultures have very different views of aggression. For instance, people in some cultures hold extremely positive attitudes about aggression. Among the Simbu of New Guinea, the most admired people are the most aggressive. The more violent a male is, the more followers he is likely to have and the higher his status. These higher-status males often seek fights and urge others to join in fighting. As a consequence, warfare is frequent (Brown, 1986; Dernbach & Marshall, 2001).

In contrast, some cultures are notably nonviolent. For instance, the Semai, who live in the Malaysian rain forest, traditionally hold negative attitudes about aggression (Bonta, 1997). They tend to deride people who are violent and hold nurturance in high esteem. Perhaps because they live in an area rich in natural resources, they generally see less practical value in antagonistic or adversarial behavior.

Other studies have focused on more direct comparisons. In one classic study, cross-cultural psychologist William Lambert (1971) examined aggression in Kenya, India, Mexico, Okinawa, the Philippines, and the United States. He looked at how mothers, the primary child-care providers in each of the cultures, reacted to their own children's aggression toward other children. The results showed that Mexican mothers were the strictest, whereas mothers in the United States showed the greatest leniency toward aggressive behavior. In contrast, mothers responded differently to acts of aggression by their children toward adults. Children who were aggressive toward adults received the greatest punishment in Kenya, the Philippines, and Mexico and the least punishment in India. U.S. children received a relatively moderate degree of punishment (Stacks et al., 2009; Lansford et al., 2014).

How mothers react to aggression is ultimately reflected in overall rates of societal aggression, although the display of aggression depends on the children's activity level and opportunities for social interaction. For instance, active children who frequently interact with other children seem to learn their culture's lessons about aggression most readily. Thus, active Mexican children are relatively less aggressive than U.S. children because mothers in Mexico tend to react strongly against displays of aggressive behavior. In contrast, active children in the United States show more aggression since their aggression typically earns only a mild rebuke from their mothers.

These findings clearly demonstrate that culture plays a role in providing children with experiences that ultimately result in different levels of social aggression. How a culture trains its children, then, affects their degree of aggressiveness.

Although people in various cultures differ in levels of aggression, at least one common factor bridges across cultures: Males are more aggressive than females. In no culture do females commit more aggressive acts than males, a finding that holds for adults as well as children (Segall, 1988; Slotboom, Hendriks, & Verbruggen, 2011; Bass et al., 2018).

Why should this be true? Although we might attribute the finding to heredity—the idea that males are born with a predisposition to be more aggressive than females—this is not the only possibility. For instance, across cultures, societies may hold similar expectations about the behaviors boys and girls are taught, and it is these expectations that lead to the differences in aggression. In many cultures, boys are explicitly taught to be aggressive, whereas aggression in girls is discouraged. Related explanations suggest that boys act aggressively to accentuate their masculine identity, most likely because their societies value "strong," aggressive males (Whiting, 1965; Pellegrini et al., 2010; Bosson & Vandello, 2011; Aimé et al., 2018).

Although the universal differences in male and female aggression levels are striking, the fact that psychologists find substantial differences in levels of aggression from culture to culture is also noteworthy (Felson & Tedeschi, 1993). It suggests that aggression is not an inevitable aspect of human behavior, and it implies that people may learn to control and reduce violence in the world. In turn, it may be possible to diminish global aggression and to enhance the potential for peace in our time.

Across cultures, males tend to be more aggressive than females. Why might this be true?

Odilon Dimier/PhotoAlto/Getty Images

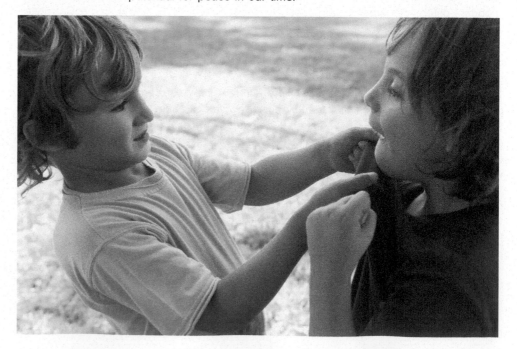

Immigrants: The Newest Americans

Anti-immigrant rhetoric in the United States today describes immigrants as rapists, murders, and worse who are straining the prison system, stealing jobs, living on welfare, and contributing little to society. However, the reality, as embodied by statistical evidence, is quite different.

For instance, consider the following points (Lazear, 2017):

- The majority of legal and illegal immigrants ultimately become financially successful. Although initially they have higher rates of poverty than native-born Americans, most immigrants eventually have higher average family incomes than native-born citizens. They have a higher rate of business startups.

- Most of the projected increase in immigration comes from increases in legal immigration, not illegal immigration.

- Few immigrants come to the United States to receive welfare. Instead, most say they come because of opportunities to work and prosper in the United States. Many come to escape political oppression and crippling poverty, and their goal is to work and earn a living. In fact, the unemployment rate for immigrants is about 10% lower than for the native-born population.

- Although they are initially more costly to the government, immigrants become increasingly productive as they get older, paying taxes that outweigh their cost to government.

Why do immigrants so often end up financially successful? One hypothesis is that those immigrants who voluntarily leave their native countries are unusually motivated to become successful, more so than immigrants who choose not to immigrate. Whatever the reason, the evidence suggests that most immigrants eventually become part of the fabric of U.S. life (López & Bialik, 2017; Houri & Sullivan, 2019; Radford, 2019).

Conflict and Cooperation: Striving for a Just and Peaceful World

Despite their broad cultural differences, the vast majority of the peoples of the world share some fundamental aspirations: They wish to live in peace and harmony with their neighbors and to seek a better life for themselves and their families. Unfortunately, efforts at resolving conflict often fall short of such aspirations, and we inhabit a globe where aggression and war are all too often seen as the solution to problems.

Yet, we can improve our lot. Let's consider why conflicts arise and how we can achieve cooperation and peace.

The Roots of Conflict

Conflict occurs when individuals, groups, or nations perceive that their behavior, goals, or beliefs are incompatible with those of others. What one person—or group or nation—desires, others may see as being potentially damaging. Consider these examples: Community business leaders want to erect a parking garage on land next to a residence for the elderly; the elderly fear that the increased traffic will compromise their safety, the exhaust fumes will harm their health, and the diminished green space will detract from their quality of life. On another scale, Palestinians want to establish an independent country on land currently controlled by Israelis; the Israelis fear this country will threaten their security. In the first example, the conflict may lead to a war of words, petitions, and hurt feelings; in the other, the potential for a war with lethal weapons increases.

realistic conflict theory The theory that conflict arises from direct competition over valued, but limited, resources.

In some cases, conflict may arise from competition over scarce resources. **Realistic conflict theory** argues that conflict is the outcome of direct competition over valued, but limited, resources. According to this perspective, the qualities we most desire, such as security, health, a good job, a safe and comfortable environment, and an adequate

In many places in the world, political refugees live in crowded, unsafe, and unsanitary conditions.
Lexie Harrison-Cripps/Alamy Stock Photo

standard of living, are limited. Consequently, we compete with others to acquire our fair share (Moghaddam, 2008; Tajfel & Turner, 2010; Densley & Peterson, 2018).

But how do we determine what's a fair share? For many people, a fair share is more than just a minimum level of resources. In reckoning how much more than a minimum level they should have, they consider what others have. According to this view, then, people consider their own level of relative deprivation to determine their level of satisfaction. **Relative deprivation** is the sense that one group lacks a desired amount of resources in comparison to another group, which the first group perceives as having more. For example, even relatively well-paid factory workers may feel underpaid when they compare their compensation to the huge salary the chief executive of the company receives (Raviallion & Lokshin, 2010; Greitemeyer & Sagioglou, 2017, 2019).

relative deprivation The sense that one lacks a desired resource in comparison to another group, which is perceived to have more.

In some cases, *perceived* conflict fuels hostility among individuals and groups. Because we use group membership as a source of pride and self-worth, threats to group identity may provoke conflict. For example, the conflict between the Hutu and Tutsi clans in Rwanda in 1994 was based primarily on ethnic rivalries. Tragically, the focus on group membership in this situation resulted in the death or displacement of more than 2 million people (Tajfel & Turner, 2004; Staub, 2011, 2018).

Finally, conflict may occur inadvertently, with individuals pursuing a course of action that benefits them as individuals but has quite negative consequences for society as a whole. In such cases, people fall into *social traps*, situations in which individual rewards come into conflict with the optimal outcome for the group. Consider what happened to the people who fished the waters of the Georges Banks off the coast of Massachusetts in the late 1980s. Each individual sought to catch as many fish as possible—a reasonable strategy for a person seeking to maximize each day's profits. Besides, people thought that no one person could catch so many fish that the overall stock of fish would be threatened. When considered collectively, however, the behavior of the many individuals seeking to maximize their catch resulted in such rapid overfishing that the overall supply was devastated. As a consequence, Massachusetts was forced to pass laws to restrict fishing, and many fishermen went bankrupt. Ironically, their pursuit of individual goals ultimately damaged the long-term interests of all parties involved (Urlacher, 2008; Abel, 2015).

Misperceiving Our Enemies

During a war of words between U.S. President Donald Trump and North Korean leader Kim Jong-un, Trump disparaged Kim by calling him "Rocket Man." In return, the North Korean leader called Trump a "mentally deranged U.S. dotard." The extraordinary public display of name-calling between world leaders illustrated how antagonism can escalate and dehumanize others. In fact, in many situations, our view of our enemies is so distorted that it causes serious strategic miscalculations. For example, psychologists suggest that several distortions in thinking influenced decision-making during the course of the war in Vietnam (White, 2004; Sang-hun, 2017):

- *An image of the enemy as diabolical.* Americans viewed the communist Vietnamese as inscrutable and deceptive, as people who were capable of horrible atrocities and fiendish aggression.
- *A virile self-image.* Americans saw themselves and their military policy as determined, correct, and strong.
- *An overconfident military.* Having never "lost" a war, Americans believed they could win any confrontation in which they participated. It always seemed that just one more battle would bring a final victory.
- *Lack of empathy for the enemy.* Political and military leaders had no clear understanding of what the enemy felt, how it perceived the situation, or even why it was fighting.

- *Selective inattention.* The U.S. government consistently ignored facts and events that might have led it to change its position on or understanding of the war. For example, widespread corruption in the South Vietnamese army, the United States' ally, was ignored, as were South Vietnam's undemocratic government policies.

- *A moral self-image.* The United States viewed itself as superior not only militarily but morally as well.

Such misperceptions of enemies are not restricted to the war in Vietnam. Citizens and powerful world leaders still tend to mischaracterize the pronouncements of their enemies, and they base their views of other nations on stereotypes regarding national personality traits and other characteristics. Many of the mistakes in perception regarding Vietnam also apply to some degree to the U.S. military interventions in Iraq, Afghanistan, and Syria (Jost, Kay, & Thorisdotter, 2009).

Ironically, a nation's enemies are susceptible to similar misperceptions and stereotyping. Consequently, nations often hold *mirror-image perceptions*, views that duplicate those their opponents hold of them. In other words, each side sees itself as virtuous and morally just, and its enemy as evil and ruthless. Moreover, as conflicts escalate, perceptions of one's enemies grow increasingly simplistic. For example, the complexity of the images that both Israelis and Arabs use to describe each other declined as the level of conflict between them increased (Hirschberger, Pyszczynski, & Ein-Dor, 2010; Fischer, 2011; Fisher & Kelman, 2011).

Genocidal Violence and Mass Killing: Explaining the Inexplicable

The genocide of the Armenians in Turkey during World War I. The Holocaust during World War II. The massacres in Rwanda in 1994. The attacks on hundreds of thousands of Rohingya in Myanmar in 2017. The ethnic cleansing of Kurds by Turkey after its invasion of Syria in 2019 (Cockburn, 2019).

All these events, in which collectively *millions* of people were displaced and killed because of their religion, ethnicity, or race, represent the worst of humanity: an extinguishing of the caring and altruistic spark in human beings. How do psychologists explain such horrific behavior?

According to Ervin Staub (2018), *genocides*, in which particular demographic groups are targeted for mass killing, share certain features. They typically occur when difficult life conditions stand in the way of fulfilling some basic human needs, such as physical security and a positive social identity. When these difficult conditions occur, one group of people may blame another group of people in an effort to solve their problems, which may unleash several other processes. For example, people may elevate their own group by belittling others. Moreover, one group may identify another group as the source of the problems—the process called scapegoating. Finally, one group may develop an ideology that holds the promise of an improved future and, at the same time, accuses a particular group of blocking the success of the ideology (Staub, 2019).

Once those in power identify a group as the scapegoat, those in the more powerful group may tolerate minor acts of discrimination against them. Subsequently, these minor acts may escalate into more violent behavior, as bystanders use "just world" reasoning to conclude that the victims are merely getting the treatment they deserve because the bystanders see the world as a just and fair place. As such thinking evolves, people increasingly devalue the victims to the point that they view them as having less moral worth than the perpetrators. At the same time, perpetrators become increasingly committed to their ideology and commit higher levels of violence. Because most bystanders do not intervene, perpetrators reason that they have the tacit approval of the bystanders. Eventually, the level of violence intensifies, and societal norms change. Ultimately, full-blown genocide occurs.

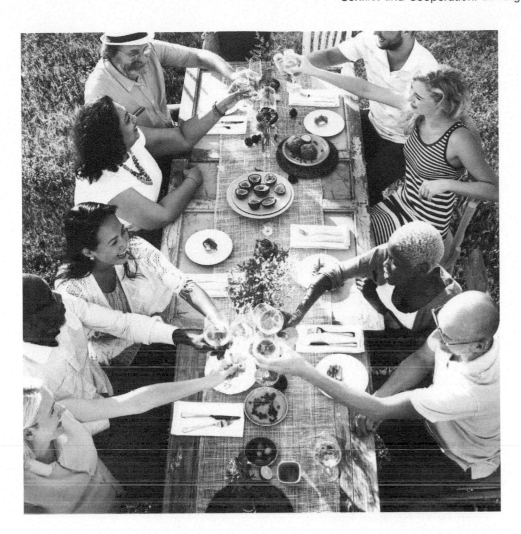

When people come together to promote caring and positive relations, they offer hope for a more peaceful world.
Rawpixel.com/Shutterstock

Although difficult life conditions do not lead inevitably to genocide, some cultures have traditions that may increase its likelihood. These cultures have a history of devaluing other groups. Furthermore, conditions are ripe for genocide in cultures with a particularly strong respect for authority, a fairly homogeneous population, a history of aggression, and a dominant culture that sees itself as superior to other cultures.

Staub's analysis, which suggests that situational conditions combine with cultural factors to permit the development of genocide, is sobering. At the same time, though, it suggests two avenues to prevent its development. One is to deal directly with difficult life conditions by striving to help people economically and socially. The other avenue is to change cultural norms from those that permit the devaluation of others to norms that promote caring and positive relations among groups of people (Staub, Pearlman, & Bilali, 2010; Staub, 2011, 2018).

BECOMING AN INFORMED CONSUMER
of Psychology

Reducing War, Promoting Peace, and Creating a Just World

As the violence in Syria, Afghanistan, Gaza, and many other hot spots shows, the world remains a dangerous place. Although the threat of a major, all-out nuclear war has diminished, the danger remains high for smaller, more limited wars. Furthermore, other problems of the world continue unabated, such as environmental degradation, overpopulation, disease, and famine.

Yet, the world's citizens are not powerless. Several strategies, developed as a result of work conducted by psychologists, can help create a world that is safer and more just in the future. Here are some of the most promising possibilities:

cross-cutting relations The links between groups in the areas of work, education, and recreation.

- *Increase cross-cutting relations between people.* **Cross-cutting relations** are the links between groups in the areas of work, education, and recreation. By arranging opportunities for people to interact with one another, as does the Seeds of Peace program we discussed in the prologue of the chapter, cross-cutting relations can allow people to understand the underlying similarities among all the world's peoples. Ultimately, such relationships can lead to feelings of connectedness and the awareness that we all share basic needs and aspirations (Deutsch, 1994; Nowak et al., 2010; Adler & Aycan, 2018).

- *Use education to overcome attitudes that devalue outgroups.* One method to reduce violence against members of minority groups and other outgroups is to extend the boundaries that delineate the people who are considered "us" to include those who are considered "them." When people become more accepting of other cultures and better understand their own, they learn that their own culture may not be the standard against which to judge all others (Staub, Pearlman, & Bilali, 2010; Staub, 2011, 2018).

- *Create a robust multicultural society.* Demographic trends show that the white majority in the United States is shrinking. Over the coming decades, the rise in the Hispanic population will be particularly dramatic. Experts estimate that by 2050, nearly one in every three Americans will be Hispanic. Whether or not the United States is prepared, it is about to become an even more deeply multicultural society with direct links to countries throughout the world. Indeed, as international travel becomes increasingly affordable and social networking tools such as Facebook and Twitter become steadily more prominent, people all over the globe will have increasing opportunities to interact (Shrestha & Heisler, 2011; Herskovits, 2018).

Increased intercultural interaction can bring several benefits. For one thing, it can reduce ingroup–outgroup bias, in which people hold more favorable opinions about members of ingroups and less favorable opinions about outgroups. By reducing this bias, people can become more flexible in their thinking and better understand the subtleties of others' behavior (Brewer, 2007; Giannakakis, & Fritsche, 2011; Jacoby-Senghor, Sinclair, & Smith, 2015).

Perhaps more important, direct interaction with people from varied racial, cultural, ethnic, and religious backgrounds, and of various sexual orientations, gender identities, and physical abilities may allow us to see the basic similarities that underlie all human behavior. Throughout this book, we discussed the broad principles that psychologists use to explain behavior. The understanding provided by this knowledge can encourage citizens to become keenly interested in the prospects for a more peaceful and just world for all the globe's inhabitants.

RECAP/EVALUATE/RETHINK

RECAP

LO 1 What are the basic elements of diversity and culture?

- Culture comprises the learned behaviors, beliefs, and attitudes that are characteristic of an individual society or population. Culture both shapes and reflects a society's behavior, understanding of the world, attitudes, and values.

- Societies that encourage individualism hold as a primary value the personal identity, uniqueness, freedom, and worth of the individual. In contrast, cultures that support collectivism promote the idea that the well-being of the group or society is more important than that of the individual.

- Culture has an impact on people's view of themselves, meaning the way in which they look inward and define themselves as individuals. People in Eastern societies tend to have an interdependent view, perceiving themselves as members of a larger society and working together with others to achieve social harmony. In comparison, people in Western societies generally see themselves as independent. The emphasis in such societies is on competing rather than cooperating with others.

- Societies and cultures vary significantly in the degree of aggression their members display. However, at least one universal principle crosses cultures: Males are more aggressive than females.
- Despite political rhetoric to the contrary, research shows that most immigrants to the United States are productive and ultimately successful.

LO 2 What are the roots of conflict?

- Conflicts occur when individuals, groups, or nations perceive that their behavior, goals, or beliefs are incompatible with those of others. Realistic conflict theory holds that conflict stems from competition over valued, but limited, resources. The notion of relative deprivation—the perception that one group lacks a desired amount of resources in comparison to the amount held by others—adds to the idea that the sense of resource scarcity may be related to a perception of fairness.
- In some cases, perceived conflict can fuel hostility between groups. If the perception exists that group identity is threatened, conflict may occur. Conflict can also result when people fall into social traps, situations in which individual goals conflict with the optimal outcome for the group.

LO 3 How can we reduce the risk of war and increase the chances for peace?

- Psychologists have studied how people's misperceptions about their enemies act as hindrances to peace. Possible distortions include an image of the enemy as diabolical, a virile self-image, an overconfident military, lack of empathy for the enemy, selective inattention to facts, and a moralistic self-image.

- Genocide is a form of collective murder in which particular demographic groups are targeted for killing. Genocides may occur when people's basic needs are unmet because of difficult life conditions and a particular group is first belittled, then singled out as the scapegoat for those difficult conditions. Genocides are often supported by an ideology that promises a bright future and identifies the targeted group as the main obstacle to achieving that future.
- Among the ways to enhance the chances for future peace are to increase cross-cutting relations between people, to use education to overcome attitudes that devalue outgroups, and to create a robust multicultural society.

EVALUATE

1. _____ comprises the learned behaviors, beliefs, and attitudes that characterize an individual society or population.
2. In _____ cultures, personal goals are viewed as more important than goals relating to society in general.
3. Studies have shown that males are universally more aggressive than females. True or false?
4. Increasing _____ _____ relations between people can be a first step toward creating a more just, secure, and safer world in the future.

RETHINK

1. Does the global spread of Western media contribute to a sense of relative deprivation among people of less developed societies? What effect might this have?
2. Do you consider yourself an aggressive person? Are you more or less aggressive than other members of your family? In what ways and compared to which family members? Do you think you learned to be more or less aggressive from your family or the broader culture, or do you believe you were born more or less aggressive?

Answers to Evaluate Questions

1. Culture; 2. individualistic; 3. True; 4. cross-cutting

KEY TERMS

race	individualism	interdependent (view of self)	realistic conflict theory
ethnicity	collectivism	independent (view of self)	relative deprivation
culture	self		cross-cutting relations
multiculturalism			

Glossary

abnormal behavior Behavior that causes people to experience distress and prevents them from functioning in their daily lives. (Module 46)

absolute threshold The lowest intensity of a stimulus that an organism can detect. (Module 10)

acquired immune deficiency syndrome (AIDS) A sexually transmitted infection caused by a virus that destroys the body's immune system. (Module 34)

action potential An electric nerve impulse that travels through a neuron's axon when it is set off by a "trigger," changing the neuron's charge from negative to positive. (Module 7)

activation-synthesis theory Hobson's theory that the brain produces random electrical energy during REM sleep that stimulates memories stored in the brain. (Module 14)

activity theory of aging The theory that suggests that successful aging is characterized by maintaining the interests and activities of earlier stages of life. (Module 39)

adaptation An adjustment in sensory capacity after prolonged exposure to unchanging stimuli. (Module 10)

addictive drugs Drugs that produce a biological or psychological dependence in the user so that withdrawal from them leads to a craving for the drug that, in some cases, may be nearly irresistible. (Module 16)

adolescence The developmental stage between childhood and adulthood. (Module 38)

age of viability The point at which a fetus can survive if born prematurely. (Module 36)

aggression The intentional injury of, or harm to, another person. (Module 55)

algorithm A rule that, if applied appropriately, guarantees a solution to a problem. (Module 23)

all-or-none law The rule that neurons are either on or off. (Module 7)

altruism Behavior meant to help another person without regard for self-interest. (Module 55)

Alzheimer's disease A progressive brain disorder that leads to a gradual and irreversible decline in cognitive abilities. (Modules 22, 39)

amnesia Memory loss that occurs without other mental difficulties. (Module 22)

anal stage According to Freud, a stage from age 12-18 months to 3 years of age in which a child's pleasure is centered on the anus. (Module 40)

androgens Male sex hormones secreted by the testes. (Module 33)

anorexia nervosa A severe eating disorder in which people may refuse to eat while denying that their behavior and appearance–which can become skeleton-like–are unusual. (Module 30)

anterograde amnesia Amnesia in which memory is lost for events that follow an injury. (Module 22)

antianxiety drugs Drugs that reduce the level of anxiety a person experiences and increase feelings of well-being. (Module 51)

antidepressant drugs Medications that improve a severely depressed patient's mood and feeling of well-being. (Module 51)

antipsychotic drugs Drugs that temporarily reduce psychotic symptoms such as agitation, hallucinations, and delusions. (Module 51)

antisocial personality disorder A disorder in which individuals show no regard for the moral and ethical rules of society or the rights of others. (Module 47)

anxiety disorder The occurrence of anxiety without an obvious external cause that affects daily functioning. (Module 47)

archetypes According to Jung, universal symbolic representations of particular types of people, objects, ideas, or experiences. (Module 40)

archival research Research in which existing data, such as census documents, college records, and newspaper clippings, are examined to test a hypothesis. (Module 5)

arousal approaches to motivation The belief that people try to maintain a steady level of stimulation and activity. (Module 29)

association areas One of the major regions of the cerebral cortex; the site of the higher mental processes, such as thought, language, memory, and speech. (Module 9)

assumed-similarity bias The tendency to think of people as being similar to oneself even when meeting them for the first time. (Module 52)

attachment The positive emotional bond that develops between a child and a particular individual. (Module 37)

attention-deficit hyperactivity disorder (ADHD) A disorder marked by inattention, impulsiveness, a low tolerance for frustration, and a great deal of inappropriate activity. (Module 47)

attitudes Evaluations of people, objects, ideas, and behavior. (Module 52)

attribution theory The theory that considers how we decide, on the basis of samples of a person's behavior, what the specific causes of that behavior are. (Module 52)

authoritarian parents Parents who are rigid and punitive and value unquestioning obedience from their children. (Module 37)

authoritative parents Parents who are firm, set clear limits, reason with their children, and explain things to them. (Module 37)

autism spectrum disorder A severe developmental disability that impairs children's ability to communicate and relate to others. (Module 47)

autobiographical memory Our recollections of our own life experiences. (Module 21)

autonomic division The part of the peripheral nervous system that controls involuntary movement of the heart, glands, lungs, and other organs. (Module 8)

autonomy-versus-shame-and-doubt stage The period during which, according to Erikson, toddlers (ages 1½ to 3 years) develop independence and autonomy if exploration and freedom are encouraged or shame and self-doubt if they are restricted and overprotected. (Module 37)

aversive conditioning A form of therapy that reduces the frequency of undesired behavior by pairing an aversive, unpleasant stimulus with undesired behavior. (Module 49)

axon The part of the neuron that carries messages to other neurons. (Module 7)

babble Meaningless, speechlike sounds made by children from around the age of 3 months through 1 year. (Module 25)

background stressors ("daily hassles") Everyday annoyances, such as being stuck in traffic, that cause minor irritations and may have long-term ill effects if they continue or are compounded by other stressful events. (Module 43)

basilar membrane A vibrating structure that runs through the center of the cochlea, dividing it into an upper chamber and a lower chamber and containing sense receptors for sound. (Module 12)

behavior modification A technique whose goal is to increase the frequency of desirable behaviors and decrease the incidence of unwanted ones. (Module 18)

behavioral assessment Direct measures of an individual's behavior used to describe personality characteristics. (Module 42)

behavioral genetics The study of the effects of heredity on behavior. (Module 8)

behavioral neuroscientists (or biopsychologists) Psychologists who specialize in considering the ways in which the biological structures and functions of the body affect behavior. (Module 7)

behavioral perspective The approach that suggests that observable, external behavior, which can be objectively measured and observed, should be the focus of study. (Module 2)

behavioral perspective The perspective that looks at the rewards and punishments in the environment that determine abnormal behavior. (Module 46)

behavioral treatment approaches Treatment approaches that make use of the basic principles of learning, such as reinforcement and extinction, to reduce or eliminate maladaptive behavior. (Module 49)

biofeedback A procedure in which a person learns to control through conscious thought internal physiological processes such as blood pressure, heart and respiration rate, skin temperature, sweating, and the constriction of particular muscles. (Module 9)

biological and evolutionary approaches to personality Theories that suggest that important components of personality are inherited. (Module 41)

biomedical therapy Biologically based therapy that relies on drugs and other medical procedures to improve psychological functioning. (Module 49)

bipolar disorder A disorder in which a person alternates between periods of euphoric feelings of mania and periods of depression. (Module 47)

bisexuals Persons who are sexually attracted to people of the same gender as well as other genders. (Module 34)

borderline personality disorder A disorder characterized by problems regulating emotions and thoughts, displaying impulsive and reckless behavior, and having unstable relationships with others. (Module 47)

bottom-up processing Perception that consists of the progression of recognizing and processing information from individual components of a stimuli and moving to the perception of the whole. (Module 13)

bulimia A disorder in which a person binges on large quantities of food, followed by efforts to purge the food through vomiting or other means. (Module 30)

Cannon-Bard theory of emotion The belief that both physiological arousal and emotional experience are produced simultaneously by the same nerve stimulus. (Module 31)

case study An in-depth, intensive investigation of an individual or small group of people. (Module 5)

cataclysmic events Strong stressors that occur suddenly and typically affect many people at once (e.g., natural disasters). (Module 43)

catharsis The process of discharging built-up aggressive energy. (Module 55)

central core The "old brain," which controls basic functions such as eating and sleeping and is common to all vertebrates. (Module 9)

central nervous system (CNS) The part of the nervous system that includes the brain and spinal cord. (Module 8)

central route processing The type of mental processing that occurs when a persuasive message is evaluated by thoughtful consideration of the issues and arguments used to persuade. (Module 52)

central tendency An index of the central location within a distribution of scores; the most representative score in a distribution of scores (the mean, median, and mode are measures of central tendency). (Module 56)

central traits The major traits considered in forming impressions of others. (Module 52)

cerebellum (ser-uh-BELL-um) The part of the brain that controls bodily balance. (Module 9)

cerebral cortex The "new brain," responsible for the most sophisticated information processing in the brain; contains four lobes. (Module 9)

chromosomes Rod-shaped structures that contain all basic hereditary information. (Module 36)

chunk A group of separate pieces of information stored as a single unit in short-term memory. (Module 20)

circadian rhythms Biological processes that occur regularly on approximately a 24-hour cycle. (Module 14)

classical conditioning A type of learning in which a neutral stimulus comes to bring about a response after it is paired with a stimulus that naturally brings about that response. (Module 17)

cochlea (KOKE-lee-uh) A coiled tube in the ear filled with fluid that vibrates in response to sound. (Module 12)

cognitive approaches to motivation Theories suggesting that motivation is the outcomes of people's thoughts, beliefs, expectations, and goals. (Module 29)

cognitive development The process by which a child's understanding of the world changes due to the child's age and experience. (Module 37)

cognitive dissonance The mental conflict that occurs when a person holds two contradictory thoughts, beliefs, or attitudes. (Module 52)

cognitive learning theory An approach to the study of learning that focuses on the thought processes that underlie learning. (Module 19)

cognitive perspective The approach that focuses on how people think, understand, and know about the world. (Module 2)

cognitive perspective The perspective that suggests that people's thoughts and beliefs are central components of abnormal behavior. (Module 46)

cognitive psychology The branch of psychology that focuses on the study of higher mental processes, including thinking, language, memory, problem solving, knowing, reasoning, judging, and decision making. (Module 23)

cognitive treatment approaches Treatment approaches that teach people to think in more adaptive ways by changing their dysfunctional cognitions about the world and themselves. (Module 49)

cognitive-behavioral approach A treatment approach that incorporates basic principles of learning to change the way people think. (Module 49)

collective unconscious According to Jung, an inherited set of ideas, feelings, images, and symbols that are shared with all humans because of our common ancestral past. (Module 40)

collectivism The concept that the well-being of the group or society is more important than that of the individual.

community psychology A branch of psychology that focuses on the prevention and minimization of psychological disorders in the community. (Module 51)

companionate love The strong affection we have for those with whom our lives are deeply involved. (Module 55)

compliance Behavior that occurs in response to direct social pressure. (Module 53)

compulsion An irresistible urge to repeatedly carry out some behavior that seems strange and unreasonable. (Module 47)

concepts Mental groupings of similar objects, events, or people. (Module 23)

concrete operational stage According to Piaget, the period from 7 to 12 years of age that is characterized by logical thought and a loss of egocentrism. (Module 37)

conditioned response (CR) A response that, after conditioning, follows a previously neutral stimulus (e.g., salivation at the ringing of a bell). (Module 17)

conditioned stimulus (CS) A once-neutral stimulus that has been paired with an unconditioned stimulus to bring about a response formerly caused only by the unconditioned stimulus. (Module 17)

cones Cone-shaped, light-sensitive receptor cells in the retina that are responsible for sharp focus and color perception, particularly in bright light. (Module 11)

confirmation bias The tendency to seek out and weight more heavily information that supports one's initial hypothesis and to ignore contradictory information that supports alternative hypotheses or solutions. (Module 24)

conformity A change in behavior or attitudes brought about by a desire to follow the beliefs or standards of other people. (Module 53)

consciousness The awareness of the sensations, thoughts, and feelings being experienced at a given moment. (Module 14)

constructive processes Processes in which memories are influenced by the meaning we give to events. (Module 21)

continuous reinforcement schedule A schedule in which behavior is reinforced every time the behavior occurs. (Module 18)

control group A group participating in an experiment that receives no treatment. (Module 5)

convergent thinking Thinking in which a problem is viewed as having a single answer and which produces a solution that is based primarily on knowledge and logic. (Module 24)

conversion disorder A major somatic symptom disorder that involves an actual physical disturbance, such as the inability to use a sensory organ or the complete or partial inability to move an arm or leg. (Module 47)

coping The efforts to control, reduce, or learn to tolerate the threats that lead to stress. (Module 43)

correlation coefficient A numerical measure that indicates the extent of the relationship between two variables. (Module 58)

correlational research Research in which the relationship between two sets of variables is examined to determine whether they are associated, or "correlated." (Module 5)

creativity The ability to generate original ideas or solve problems in novel ways. (Module 24)

cross-cutting relations The links between groups in the areas of work, education, and recreation.

cross-sectional research A research method that compares people of different ages at the same point in time. (Module 35)

crystallized intelligence The accumulation of information, knowledge, and skills that people have learned through experience and education, reflecting the facts that we have learned. (Module 26)

cue-dependent forgetting Forgetting that occurs when there are insufficient retrieval cues to rekindle information that is in memory. (Module 22)

culture The learned behaviors, beliefs, and attitudes that characterize an individual society or population.

culture-fair IQ test A test that does not discriminate against the members of any minority group. (Module 28)

date rape Rape in which the rapist is either a date or a romantic acquaintance. (Module 34)

daydreams Fantasies that people construct while awake. (Module 14)

decay The loss of information in memory through its nonuse. (Module 22)

declarative memory Memory for factual information: names, faces, dates, and the like. (Module 20)

deductive reasoning Reasoning from the general to the specific. (Module 23)

defense mechanisms In Freudian theory, unconscious strategies that people use to reduce anxiety by distorting reality and concealing the source of the anxiety from themselves. (Module 40)

deinstitutionalization The process of transferring patients who have been hospitalized for long periods into less-isolated community mental health settings. (Module 51)

delayed ejaculation disorder A disorder in which it takes an extended period of sexual stimulation for a male to be able to ejaculate (Module 34)

dendrite A cluster of fibers at one end of a neuron that receive messages from other neurons. (Module 7)

dependent variable The variable that is measured in an experiment. It is expected to change as a result of the experimenter's manipulation of the independent variable. (Module 5)

depressants Drugs that slow down the nervous system. (Module 16)

depth perception The ability to view the world in three dimensions and to perceive distance. (Module 13)

descriptive statistics The branch of statistics that provides a means of summarizing data. (Module 56)

determinism The idea that people's behavior is produced primarily by factors outside of their willful control. (Module 3)

developmental psychology The branch of psychology that studies the patterns of growth and change that occur throughout life. (Module 35)

Diagnostic and Statistical Manual of Mental Disorders, Fifth Edition (DSM-5) A system, devised by the American Psychiatric Association, used by most professionals to classify and define psychological disorders. (Module 46)

difference threshold (just noticeable difference) The smallest level of added or reduced stimulation required to sense that a change in stimulation has occurred. (Module 10)

diffusion of responsibility The belief that responsibility for taking action is shared, or diffused, among those present. (Module 55)

discrimination Behavior directed toward individuals on the basis of their membership in a particular group. (Module 54)

disengagement theory of aging The theory that suggests that successful aging is characterized by a gradual withdrawal from the world on physical, psychological, and social levels. (Module 39)

dispositional causes (of behavior) Perceived causes of behavior brought about by a person's traits or personality characteristics. (Module 52)

dissociative amnesia A disorder in which a significant, selective memory loss occurs. (Module 47)

dissociative disorders Psychological dysfunctions characterized by the separation of different facets of a person's personality that are normally integrated. (Module 47)

dissociative fugue A form of amnesia in which a person leaves home and assumes a new identity. (Module 47)

dissociative identity disorder (DID) A disorder in which a person displays characteristics of two or more distinct personalities. (Module 47)

divergent thinking Thinking that generates multiple and novel, although potentially appropriate, responses to problems or questions. (Module 24)

double standard The view that premarital sex is permissible for males but not for females. (Module 34)

dreams-for-survival theory The theory suggesting that dreams permit information that is critical for our daily survival to be reconsidered and reprocessed during sleep. (Module 14)

drive Motivational tension, or arousal, that energizes behavior to fulfill a need. (Module 29)

drive-reduction approaches to motivation Theories suggesting that a lack of some basic biological need produces a drive to push an organism to satisfy that need. (Module 29)

drug therapy Treatment of psychological disorders through the use of medication that alters the operation of neurons and neurotransmitters in the brain and body. (Module 51)

eardrum The part of the ear that vibrates when sound waves hit it. (Module 12)

ego The rational, logical part of personality that attempts to balance the desires of the id and the realities of the objective, outside world. (Module 40)

ego-integrity-versus-despair stage According to Erikson, a period from late adulthood until death during which we review life's accomplishments and failures. (Module 38)

egocentric thought A way of thinking in which a child views the world entirely from his or her own perspective. (Module 37)

electroconvulsive therapy (ECT) A procedure used in the treatment of severe depression in which an electric current of 70–150 volts is briefly administered to a patient's head. (Module 51)

embryo A developed zygote that has a heart, a brain, and other organs. (Module 36)

emerging adulthood The period beginning in the late teenage years and extending into the mid-20s. (Module 39)

emotional intelligence The set of skills that underlie the accurate assessment, evaluation, expression, and regulation of emotions. (Module 26)

emotions Feelings that generally have both physiological and cognitive elements and that influence behavior. (Module 31)

endocrine system A chemical communication network that sends messages throughout the body via the bloodstream. (Module 8)

episodic memory Memory for events that occur in a particular time, place, or context. (Module 20)

erectile disorder A male's inability to achieve or maintain an erection. (Module 34)

erogenous zones Areas of the body that are particularly sensitive because of the presence of an unusually rich array of nerve receptors. (Module 33)

estrogens Class of female sex hormones. (Module 33)

ethnicity Shared national origins or cultural patterns.

evolutionary psychology The branch of psychology that seeks to identify behavior patterns that are a result of our genetic inheritance from our ancestors. (Module 8)

excitatory message A chemical message that makes it more likely that a receiving neuron will fire and an action potential will travel down its axon. (Module 7)

excitement phase The period in which an arousing stimulus begins a sequence that prepares the genitals for sexual intercourse. (Module 33)

experiment The investigation of the relationship between two (or more) variables by deliberately producing a change in one variable in a situation and observing the effects of that change on other aspects of the situation. (Module 5)

experimental bias Factors that distort how the independent variable affects the dependent variable in an experiment. (Module 6)

experimental group Any group participating in an experiment that receives a treatment. (Module 5)

experimental manipulation The change that an experimenter deliberately produces in a situation. (Module 5)

explicit memory Intentional or conscious recollection of information. (Module 21)

extinction A basic phenomenon of learning that occurs when a previously conditioned response decreases in frequency and eventually disappears. (Module 17)

extramarital sex Sexual activity between a married person and someone who is not his or her spouse. (Module 34)

facial-affect program The theory that a set of nerve impulses produce a facial display reflecting an emotion that is universal across cultures. (Module 31)

facial-feedback hypothesis The hypothesis that facial expressions not only reflect emotional experience but also help determine how people experience and label emotions. (Module 31)

familial intellectual disability Intellectual disability in which no apparent biological or genetic problems exist, but there is a history of intellectual disability among family members. (Module 27)

family therapy An approach that focuses on the family and its dynamics. (Module 50)

feature detectors Specialized neurons that are activated only by visual stimuli having specific features, such as a particular shape or pattern. (Module 11)

female orgasmic disorder A female's lack of orgasm. (Module 34)

fetal alcohol syndrome The most common cause of intellectual disability in newborns, occurring when the mother uses alcohol during pregnancy. (Module 27)

fetus A developing individual from 8 weeks after conception until birth. (Module 36)

fixations Conflicts or concerns that persist beyond the developmental period in which they first occur. (Module 40)

fixed-interval schedule A schedule in which reinforcement is provided for a response only after a fixed time period has elapsed. (Module 18)

fixed-ratio schedule A schedule in which reinforcement is given only after a specific number of responses are made. (Module 18)

flashbulb memories Memories of a specific, important, or surprising emotionally significant event that are recalled easily and with vivid imagery. (Module 21)

flooding A behavioral treatment for anxiety in which people are suddenly confronted with a stimulus that they fear. (Module 49)

fluid intelligence Intelligence that reflects the ability to think logically, reason abstractly, solve problems, and find patterns. (Module 26)

formal operational stage According to Piaget, the period from age 12 to adulthood that is characterized by abstract thought. (Module 37)

free will The idea that behavior is caused primarily by choices that are made freely by the individual. (Module 3)

frequency distribution An arrangement of scores from a sample that indicates how often a particular score is present. (Module 56)

frequency theory of hearing The theory that the entire basilar membrane acts like a microphone, vibrating as a whole in response to a sound. (Module 12)

functional fixedness The tendency to think of an object only in terms of the way it is most frequently or typically used. (Module 24)

functionalism An early approach to psychology that concentrated on what the mind does—the functions of mental activity—and the role of behavior in allowing people to adapt to their environments. (Module 2)

fundamental attribution error A tendency to overattribute others' behavior to dispositional causes and minimize the importance of situational causes. (Module 52)

g or g-factor The single, general factor for mental ability assumed to underlie intelligence in some early theories of intelligence. (Module 26)

gate-control theory of pain The theory that particular nerve receptors in the spinal cord lead to specific areas of the brain related to pain. (Module 12)

gender The perception of being male or female. (Module 32)

gender roles The set of expectations, defined by a particular society, that indicate what is appropriate behavior for men and women. (Module 32)

gender schema A mental framework that organizes and guides a child's understanding of information relevant to gender. (Module 32)

general adaptation syndrome (GAS) A theory developed by Selye that suggests that a person's response to a stressor consists of three stages: alarm and mobilization, resistance, and exhaustion. (Module 43)

generalized anxiety disorder The experience of long-term, persistent anxiety and worry. (Module 47)

generativity-versus-stagnation stage According to Erikson, a period in middle adulthood during which we take stock of our contributions to family and society. (Module 38)

genes The parts of the chromosomes through which genetic information is transmitted. (Module 36)

genetic programming theories of aging Theories that suggest that our DNA genetic code includes a built-in time limit to the reproduction of human cells and that they are no longer able to divide after a certain time. (Module 39)

genital stage According to Freud, the period from puberty until death, marked by mature sexual behavior (that is, sexual intercourse). (Module 40)

genitals The male and female sex organs. (Module 33)

Gestalt (geh-SHTALLT) laws of organization A series of principles that describe how we organize bits and pieces of information into meaningful wholes. (Module 13)

Gestalt psychology An approach to psychology that focuses on the organization of perception and thinking in a "whole" sense rather than on the individual elements of perception. (Module 2)

grammar The system of rules that determine how our thoughts can be expressed. (Module 25)

group Two or more people who interact with one another, perceive themselves as part of a group, and are interdependent. (Module 53)

group therapy Therapy in which people meet in a group with a therapist to discuss problems. (Module 50)

groupthink A type of thinking in which group members share such a strong motivation to achieve consensus that they lose the ability to critically evaluate alternative points of view. (Module 53)

habituation The decrease in the response to a stimulus that occurs after repeated presentations of the same stimulus. (Module 37)

hair cells Tiny cells covering the basilar membrane that, when bent by vibrations entering the cochlea, transmit neural messages to the brain. (Module 12)

hallucinogens Drugs that are capable of producing alterations in perception, thoughts, and feelings. (Module 16)

halo effect A phenomenon in which an initial understanding that a person has positive or negative traits is used to infer other uniformly positive or negative characteristics. (Module 52)

hardiness A personality trait characterized by a sense of commitment, viewing problems as challenges, and having a sense of control. (Module 43)

health psychology The branch of psychology that investigates the psychological factors related to wellness and illness, including the prevention, diagnosis, and treatment of medical problems. (Module 43)

hemispheres Symmetrical left and right halves of the brain that control the side of the body opposite to their location. (Module 9)

heritability The degree to which a characteristic is related to inherited genetic factors. (Module 28)

heterosexuality Sexual attraction and behavior directed to the other sex. (Module 34)

heuristic A thinking strategy that may lead us to a solution to a problem or decision but—unlike algorithms—may sometimes lead to errors. (Module 23)

histogram Bar graph. (Module 56)

homeostasis The body's tendency to maintain a steady internal state. (Module 29)

homosexuals Persons who are sexually attracted to members of their own sex. (Module 34)

hormones Chemicals that circulate through the blood and regulate the functioning or growth of the body. (Module 8)

humanistic approaches to personality Theories that emphasize people's innate goodness and desire to achieve higher levels of functioning. (Module 41)

humanistic perspective The approach that suggests that all individuals naturally strive to grow, develop, and be in control of their lives and behavior. (Module 2)

humanistic perspective The perspective that emphasizes the responsibility people have for their own behavior, even when such behavior is abnormal. (Module 46)

humanistic therapy Therapy in which the underlying rationale is that people have control of their behavior, can make

choices about their lives, and are essentially responsible for solving their own problems. (Module 50)

hypnosis A trancelike state of heightened susceptibility to the suggestions of others. (Module 15)

hypothalamus A tiny part of the brain, located below the thalamus, that maintains homeostasis and produces and regulates vital behavior, such as eating, drinking, and sexual behavior. (Module 9)

hypothesis A prediction, stemming from a theory, stated in a way that allows it to be tested. (Module 4)

id The instinctual and unorganized part of personality whose sole purpose is to reduce tension created by primitive drives related to hunger, sex, aggression, and irrational impulses. (Module 40)

identical twins Twins who are genetically identical. (Module 35)

identification The process of wanting to be like another person as much as possible, imitating that person's behavior and adopting similar beliefs and values. (Module 40)

identity The distinguishing character of the individual: who each of us is, what our roles are, and what we are capable of. (Module 38)

identity-versus-role-confusion stage According to Erikson, a time in adolescence of major testing to determine one's unique qualities. (Module 38)

illness anxiety disorder A somatic symptom disorder in which people have a constant fear of illness and a preoccupation with their health. (Module 47)

implicit memory Memories of which people are not consciously aware but that can affect subsequent performance and behavior. (Module 21)

incentive approaches to motivation Theories suggesting that motivation stems from the desire to attain external rewards, known as incentives. (Module 29)

independent (view of self) To view oneself as behaving independently, competing rather than cooperating with others.

independent variable The variable that is manipulated by an experimenter. (Module 5)

individualism The concept that holds as a primary value the personal identity, uniqueness, freedom, and worth of the individual person.

inductive reasoning Reasoning from the specific to the general. (Module 23)

industrial-organizational (I/O) psychology The branch of psychology focusing on work- and job-related issues, including worker motivation, satisfaction, safety, and productivity. (Module 53)

industry-versus-inferiority stage According to Erikson, the last stage of childhood, during which children ages 6 to 12 years may develop positive social interactions with others or may feel inadequate and become less sociable. (Module 37)

inferential statistics The branch of statistics that uses data from samples to make predictions about the larger population from which the sample is drawn. (Module 58)

information processing The way in which people take in, use, and store information. (Module 37)

informed consent A document signed by participants affirming that they have been told the basic outlines of the study and are aware of what their participation will involve. (Module 6)

inhibitory message A chemical message that prevents or decreases the likelihood that a receiving neuron will fire. (Module 7)

initiative-versus-guilt stage According to Erikson, the period during which children ages 3 to 6 years experience conflict between independence of action and the sometimes negative results of that action. (Module 37)

insight A sudden awareness of the relationships among various elements that had previously appeared to be independent of one another. (Module 24)

instinct approaches to motivation The explanation of motivation that suggests people and animals are born preprogrammed with sets of behaviors essential to their survival. (Module 29)

instincts Inborn patterns of behavior that are genetically determined rather than learned. (Module 29)

intellectual disability A disability characterized by significant limitations in both intellectual functioning and in adaptive behavior, which covers many everyday social and practical skills. (Module 27)

intellectually gifted The 2%-4% segment of the population who have IQ scores greater than 130. (Module 27)

intelligence The capacity to understand the world, think rationally, and use resources effectively when faced with challenges. (Module 26)

intelligence quotient (IQ) A score that takes into account an individual's mental and chronological ages. (Module 26)

intelligence tests Tests devised to quantify a person's level of intelligence. (Module 26)

interactionist approach (to language development) The view that language development is determined by genetic and social factors, produced through a combination of genetically determined predispositions and the social world in which one is raised. (Module 25)

interdependent (view of self) To view oneself as a member of a larger society, working together with others to achieve social harmony.

interference The phenomenon by which information in memory disrupts the recall of other information. (Module 22)

interpersonal attraction (or close relationship) Positive feelings for others; liking and loving. (Module 55)

interpersonal therapy (IPT) Short-term therapy designed to help patients control their moods and emotions by focusing on the context of their current social relationships. (Module 50)

intimacy-versus-isolation stage According to Erikson, a period during early adulthood that focuses on developing close relationships. (Module 38)

introspection A procedure used to study the structure of the mind in which a person is asked to describe in detail what they are experiencing when they are exposed to a stimulus. (Module 2)

James-Lange theory of emotion The belief that emotional experience is a reaction to bodily events occurring as a result of an external situation ("I feel sad because I am crying"). (Module 31)

Korsakoff's syndrome A disease that afflicts long-term alcoholics, leaving some abilities intact but including hallucinations and a tendency to repeat the same story. (Module 22)

language The communication of information through symbols arranged according to systematic rules. (Module 25)

latency period According to Freud, the period between the phallic stage and puberty during which children's sexual concerns are temporarily put aside. (Module 40)

latent learning Learning in which a new behavior is acquired but is not demonstrated until some incentive is provided for displaying it. (Module 19)

lateralization The dominance of one hemisphere of the brain in specific functions, such as language. (Module 9)

learned helplessness A state in which people conclude that unpleasant or aversive stimuli cannot be controlled—a view of the world that becomes so ingrained that they cease trying to remedy the aversive circumstances even if they actually can exert some influence on the situation. (Module 43)

learning A relatively permanent change in behavior brought about by experience. (Module 17)

learning-theory approach (to language development) The theory that language acquisition follows the principles of reinforcement and conditioning. (Module 25)

levels-of-processing theory The theory of memory that emphasizes the degree to which new material is mentally analyzed. (Module 21)

life review The process by which people examine and evaluate their lives. (Module 39)

limbic system The part of the brain that controls eating, aggression, and reproduction. (Module 9)

linguistic-relativity hypothesis The hypothesis that language shapes and helps determine the way people perceive and understand the world. (Module 25)

lobes The four major sections of the cerebral cortex: frontal, parietal, temporal, and occipital. (Module 9)

long-term memory Memory that stores information on a relatively permanent basis, although it may be difficult to retrieve. (Module 20)

longitudinal research A research method that investigates behavior as participants get older. (Module 35)

major depressive disorder A severe form of depression that interferes with concentration, decision making, and sociability. (Module 47)

mania An extended state of intense, wild elation. (Module 47)

masturbation Sexual self-stimulation. (Module 34)

mean The average of all scores, arrived at by adding scores together and dividing by the number of scores. (Module 56)

means-ends analysis A strategy in which a problem-solver considers the ultimate goal (the end) and determines the best strategy for attaining the goal. (Module 24)

median The point in a distribution of scores that divides the distribution exactly in half when the scores are listed in numerical order. (Module 56)

medical perspective The perspective that suggests that when an individual displays symptoms of abnormal behavior, the root cause will be found in a physical examination of the individual, which may reveal a hormonal imbalance, a chemical deficiency, or a brain injury. (Module 46)

meditation A learned technique for refocusing attention that brings about an altered state of consciousness. (Module 15)

memory The process by which we encode, store, and retrieve information. (Module 20)

menopause The period during which women stop menstruating and are no longer fertile. (Module 39)

mental age The age for which a given level of performance is average or typical. (Module 26)

mental images Representations in the mind of an object or event. (Module 23)

metabolism The rate at which food is converted to energy and expended by the body. (Module 30)

metacognition An awareness and understanding of one's own cognitive processes. (Module 37)

Minnesota Multiphasic Personality Inventory-2-Restructured Form (MMPI-2-RF) A widely used self-report test that identifies people with psychological difficulties and is employed to predict some everyday behaviors. (Module 42)

mirror neurons Specialized neurons that fire not only when a person enacts a particular behavior but also when a person simply observes *another* individual carrying out the same behavior. (Module 7)

mode The most frequently occurring score in a set of scores. (Module 56)

mood disorder A disturbance in emotional experience that is strong enough to interfere with everyday living. (Module 47)

mood stabilizers Drugs used to treat mood disorders characterized by intense mood swings, especially manic episodes in bipolar disorder. (Module 51)

motivation The factors that direct and energize the behavior of humans and other organisms. (Module 29)

motor area The part of the cortex that is largely responsible for the body's voluntary movement. (Module 9)

motor (efferent) neurons Neurons that communicate information from the brain and nervous system to muscles and glands. (Module 8)

multiculturalism The view that members of all cultures deserve equal respect and that their contributions to society should be recognized.

myelin sheath A protective coat of fat and protein that wraps around the axon. (Module 7)

narcissistic personality disorder A personality disturbance characterized by an exaggerated sense of self-importance. (Module 47)

narcotics Drugs that increase relaxation and relieve pain and anxiety. (Module 16)

nativist approach (to language development) The theory that humans are genetically prewired to learn language at certain times and in particular ways. (Module 25)

naturalistic observation Research in which an investigator simply observes some naturally occurring behavior and does not make a change in the situation. (Module 5)

nature–nurture issue The issue of the degree to which environment and heredity influence behavior. (Module 35)

need for achievement A person's desire to strive for and achieve challenging accomplishments. (Module 30)

need for affiliation An interest in establishing and maintaining relationships with other people. (Module 30)

need for power A tendency to seek impact, control, or influence over others and to be seen as a powerful individual. (Module 30)

negative reinforcer An unpleasant stimulus whose removal leads to an increase in the probability that a preceding response will be repeated in the future. (Module 18)

negative relationship A relationship established by data that shows high values of one variable corresponding with low values of the other. (Module 58)

neo-Freudian psychoanalysts Psychoanalysts who were trained in traditional Freudian theory but who later rejected some of its major points. (Module 40)

neonate A newborn child. (Module 37)

neurons Nerve cells, the basic components of the nervous system. (Module 7)

neuroplasticity The brain's ability to change throughout the life span through the addition of new neurons, new interconnections between neurons, and the reorganization of information-processing areas. (Module 9)

neuroscience perspective The approach that views behavior from the perspective of the brain, the nervous system, and other biological functions. (Module 2)

neurotransmitters Chemicals that communicate messages from one neuron to another neuron across the synapse. (Module 7)

neutral stimulus A stimulus that, before conditioning, does not naturally bring about the response of interest. (Module 17)

normal distribution A distribution of scores that produces a symmetrical, bell-shaped curve in which the right half mirrors the left half and in which the mean, median, and mode all have the same value. (Module 56)

norms Standards of test performance that permit the comparison of one person's score on a test with the scores of other individuals who have taken the same test. (Module 26)

obedience A change in behavior in response to the commands of others. (Module 53)

obesity Body weight that is more than 20% above the average weight for a person of a particular height. (Module 30)

object permanence The awareness that objects–and people–continue to exist even if they are out of sight. (Module 37)

observational learning Learning by observing the behavior of another person, or model. (Module 19)

obsession A persistent, unwanted thought or idea that keeps recurring. (Module 47)

obsessive-compulsive disorder (OCD) A disorder characterized by obsessions or compulsions. (Module 47)

Oedipal conflict A child's intense, sexual interest in his or her opposite-sex parent. (Module 40)

operant conditioning Learning in which a voluntary response is strengthened or weakened, depending on the response's favorable or unfavorable consequences. (Module 18)

operational definition The translation of a hypothesis into specific, testable procedures that can be measured and observed in an experiment. (Module 4)

opponent-process theory of color vision The theory that receptor cells for color are linked in pairs, working in opposition to each other. (Module 11)

optic nerve A bundle of ganglion axons that carry visual information to the brain. (Module 11)

oral stage According to Freud, a stage from birth to age 12-18 months in which an infant's center of pleasure is the mouth. (Module 40)

orgasm The peak of sexual excitement, during which rhythmic muscular contractions occur in the genitals. (Module 33)

overgeneralization The phenomenon by which children over-apply a language rule, thereby making a linguistic error. (Module 25)

ovulation The point at which an egg is released from the ovaries. (Module 33)

panic disorder Anxiety disorder that takes the form of panic attacks lasting from a few seconds to several hours. (Module 47)

parasympathetic division The part of the autonomic division of the nervous system that acts to calm the body after an emergency has ended. (Module 8)

partial (or intermittent) reinforcement schedule Reinforcing of a behavior some but not all of the time. (Module 18)

passionate (or romantic) love A state of intense absorption in someone that includes intense physiological arousal, psychological interest, and caring for the needs of another. (Module 55)

perception The sorting out, interpretation, analysis, and integration of stimuli by the sense organs and brain. (Module 10)

perceptual constancy Our understanding that physical objects are consistent and do not vary, even though sensory input about them may vary. (Module 13)

peripheral nervous system The part of the nervous system that includes the autonomic and somatic subdivisions; made up of neurons with long axons and dendrites, it branches out from the spinal cord and brain and reaches the extremities of the body. (Module 8)

peripheral route processing The type of mental processing that occurs when a persuasive message is evaluated on the basis of irrelevant or extraneous factors. (Module 52)

permissive parents Parents who give their children relaxed or inconsistent direction and, although they are warm, require little of them. (Module 37)

person-centered therapy Therapy in which the goal is to reach one's potential for self-actualization. (Module 50)

personal stressors Major life events, such as the death of a family member, that have immediate negative consequences that generally fade with time. (Module 43)

personality The pattern of enduring characteristics that produce consistency and individuality in a given person. (Module 40)

personality disorder A disorder characterized by a set of inflexible, maladaptive behavior patterns that keep a person from functioning appropriately in society. (Module 47)

phallic stage According to Freud, a period beginning around age 3 during which a child's pleasure focuses on the genitals. (Module 40)

phonemes The smallest units of speech. (Module 25)

phonology The study of the smallest units of speech, called phonemes. (Module 25)

pituitary gland The major component of the endocrine system, or "master gland," that secretes hormones that control growth and other parts of the endocrine system. (Module 8)

place theory of hearing The theory that different areas of the basilar membrane respond to different frequencies. (Module 12)

placebo A false treatment, such as a pill, "drug," or other substance, without any significant chemical properties or active ingredient. (Module 6)

plateau phase The period in which the maximum level of arousal is attained, the penis and clitoris swell with blood, and the body prepares for orgasm. (Module 33)

population All the members of a group of interest. (Module 58)

positive reinforcer A stimulus added to the environment that brings about an increase in a preceding response. (Module 18)

positive relationship A relationship established by data that shows high values of one variable corresponding with high values of another and low values of the first variable corresponding with low values of the other. (Module 58)

posttraumatic stress disorder (PTSD) A phenomenon in which victims of major catastrophes or strong personal stressors feel long-lasting effects that may include re-experiencing the event in vivid flashbacks or dreams. (Module 43)

practical intelligence According to Sternberg, intelligence related to overall success in living. (Module 26)

prejudice A negative (or positive) evaluation of a particular group and its members. (Module 54)

premature (early) ejaculation A male's inability to delay orgasm as long as he wishes. (Module 34)

preoperational stage According to Piaget, the period from 2 to 7 years of age that is characterized by language development. (Module 37)

priming A phenomenon that occurs when exposure to a word or concept (called a *prime*) later makes it easier to recall information related to the prime. (Module 21)

principle of conservation The understanding that quantity is unrelated to the arrangement and physical appearance of objects. (Module 37)

proactive interference Interference in which information learned earlier disrupts the recall of material learned later. (Module 22)

procedural memory Memory for skills and habits, such as riding a bike or hitting a baseball; sometimes referred to as *nondeclarative memory* or *implicit memory*. (Module 20)

projective personality test A test in which a person is shown an ambiguous stimulus and asked to describe it or tell a story about it in order to infer information about their personality. (Module 42)

prosocial behavior Helping behavior. (Module 55)

prototypes Typical, highly representative examples of a concept. (Module 23)

psychoactive drugs Drugs that influence a person's emotions, perceptions, and behavior. (Module 16)

psychoanalysis Freud's form of psychotherapy in which the goal is to release hidden thoughts and feelings from the unconscious part of our minds in order to reduce their power in controlling behavior. (Module 49)

psychoanalytic perspective The perspective that suggests that abnormal behavior stems from childhood conflicts over opposing wishes regarding sex and aggression. (Module 46)

psychoanalytic theory Freud's theory that unconscious forces act as determinants of personality. (Module 40)

psychodynamic approaches to personality Approaches that assume that personality is primarily unconscious and motivated by inner forces and conflicts about which people have little awareness. (Module 40)

psychodynamic perspective The approach based on the view that behavior is motivated by unconscious inner forces over which the individual has little control. (Module 2)

psychodynamic therapy Therapy that seeks to bring unresolved past conflicts and unacceptable impulses from the unconscious into the conscious, where patients may deal with the problems more effectively. (Module 49)

psychological tests Standard measures devised to assess behavior objectively; used by psychologists to help people make decisions about their lives and understand more about themselves. (Module 42)

psychology The scientific study of behavior and mental processes. (Module 1)

psychoneuroimmunology (PNI) The study of the relationship among psychological factors, the immune system, and the brain. (Module 43)

psychophysics The study of the relationship between the physical aspects of a stimulus and people's psychological experience of the stimulus. (Module 10)

psychophysiological disorders Medical problems influenced by an interaction of psychological, emotional, and physical difficulties. (Module 43)

psychosexual stages Developmental periods that children pass through during which they encounter conflicts between the demands of society and their own sexual urges. (Module 40)

psychosocial development Development of individuals' interactions and understanding of each other and of their knowledge and understanding of themselves as members of society. (Module 37)

psychosurgery Brain surgery once used to reduce the symptoms of mental disorder but rarely used today. (Module 51)

psychotherapy Psychologically based treatment in which a trained professional—a therapist—uses psychological techniques to help a person overcome psychological difficulties and disorders, resolve problems in living, or bring about personal growth. (Module 49)

puberty The period at which maturation of the sexual organs occurs, beginning at about age 11 or 12 for girls and 13 or 14 for boys. (Module 38)

punishment A stimulus that decreases the probability that a previous behavior will occur again. (Module 18)

race Generally refers to obvious physical differences that set one group apart from others.

random assignment to condition A procedure in which participants are assigned to different experimental groups or "conditions" on the basis of chance and chance alone. (Module 5)

range The difference between the highest score and the lowest score in a distribution. (Module 57)

rape The act by which one person forces another person to submit to sexual activity. (Module 34)

rapid eye movement (REM) sleep The period of sleep characterized by quick, back and forth eye movements; increased heart rate, blood pressure, and breathing rate; erections; and the experience of dreaming. (Module 14)

rational-emotive behavior therapy A form of therapy that attempts to restructure a person's belief system into a more realistic, rational, and logical set of views by challenging dysfunctional beliefs that maintain irrational behavior. (Module 49)

realistic conflict theory The theory that conflict arises from direct competition over valued, but limited, resources.

recall Memory task in which specific information must be retrieved. (Module 21)

reciprocity-of-liking effect A tendency to like those who like us. (Module 55)

recognition Memory task in which individuals are presented with a stimulus and asked whether they have been exposed to it in the past or to identify it from a list of alternatives. (Module 21)

reflex An automatic, involuntary response to an incoming stimulus. (Module 8)

reflexes Unlearned, involuntary responses that occur automatically in the presence of certain stimuli. (Module 37)

refractory period A temporary period that follows the resolution stage and during which the male cannot develop an erection again. (Module 33)

rehearsal The repetition of information that has entered short-term memory. (Module 20)

reinforcement The process by which a stimulus increases the probability that a preceding behavior will be repeated. (Module 18)

reinforcer Any stimulus that increases the probability that a preceding behavior will occur again. (Module 18)

relative deprivation The sense that one lacks a desired resource in comparison to another group, which is perceived to have more.

reliability The consistency of a test in measuring what it is trying to measure. (Module 26)

replicated research Research that is repeated, sometimes using other procedures, settings, and groups of participants, to increase confidence in prior findings. (Module 5)

repression The defense mechanism in which the ego pushes unacceptable or unpleasant thoughts and impulses out of consciousness but maintains them in the unconscious. (Module 40)

resilience The ability to withstand, overcome, and actually thrive after profound adversity. (Module 43)

resolution stage The interval after orgasm in which the body returns to its unaroused state, reversing the changes brought about by arousal. (Module 33)

resting state The state in which there is a negative electrical charge of about -70 millivolts within a neuron. (Module 7)

reticular formation The part of the brain extending from the medulla through the pons; it is related to changes in the level of arousal of the body. (Module 9)

retina The part of the eye that converts the electromagnetic energy of light to electrical impulses for transmission to the brain. (Module 11)

retroactive interference Interference in which material that was learned later disrupts the retrieval of information that was learned earlier. (Module 22)

retrograde amnesia Amnesia in which memory is lost for occurrences prior to a certain event but not for new events. (Module 22)

reuptake The reabsorption of neurotransmitters by a terminal button. (Module 7)

rods Thin, cylindrical receptor cells in the retina that are highly sensitive to light. (Module 11)

Rorschach test A test that involves showing a series of symmetrical visual stimuli to people who then are asked what the figures represent to them. (Module 42)

sample A representative subgroup of a population of interest. (Module 58)

Schachter-Singer theory of emotion The belief that emotions are determined jointly by a nonspecific kind of physiological arousal and its interpretation, based on environmental cues. (Module 31)

schedule of reinforcement The pattern of frequency and timing of reinforcement following desired behavior. (Module 18)

schemas Organized bodies of information stored in memory that bias the way new information is interpreted, stored, and recalled. (Modules 21, 52)

schizophrenia A class of disorders in which severe distortion of reality occurs. (Module 47)

scientific method The approach through which psychologists systematically acquire knowledge and understanding about behavior and other phenomena of interest. (Module 4)

self A person's essential being distinguishing themselves from others, how we define ourselves as individuals.

self-actualization A state of self-fulfillment in which people realize their highest potential in their own unique way. (Modules 29, 41)

self-efficacy The belief that we can master a situation and produce positive outcomes. (Module 41)

self-esteem The component of personality that encompasses our positive and negative self-evaluations. (Module 41)

self-report measures A method of gathering data about people by asking them questions about their own behavior and traits. (Module 42)

self-serving bias The tendency to attribute personal success to personal factors (skill, ability, or effort) and to attribute failure to factors outside oneself. (Module 52)

semantic memory Memory for general knowledge and facts about the world, as well as memory for the rules of logic that are used to deduce other facts. (Module 20)

semantic networks Mental representations of clusters of interconnected information. (Module 20)

semantics The aspect of language referring to the meaning of words and sentences. (Module 25)

semicircular canals Three tube-like structures of the inner ear containing fluid that sloshes through them when the head moves, signaling rotational or angular movement to the brain. (Module 12)

sensation The activation of the sense organs by a source of physical energy. (Module 10)

sensorimotor stage According to Piaget, the stage from birth to 2 years, during which a child has little competence in representing the environment by using images, language, or other symbols. (Module 37)

sensory (afferent) neurons Neurons that transmit information from the perimeter of the body to the nervous system and brain. (Module 8)

sensory area The site in the brain of the tissue that corresponds to each of the senses, with the degree of sensitivity related to the amount of tissue. (Module 9)

sensory memory The initial, momentary storage of information, lasting only an instant. (Module 20)

sexism Negative attitudes and behavior toward a person based on that person's gender. (Module 32)

sexual interest/arousal disorder A sexual dysfunction in which the motivation for sexual activity is restrained or lacking entirely. (Module 34)

sexually transmitted infection (STI) A disease acquired through sexual contact. (Module 34)

shaping The process of teaching a complex behavior by rewarding closer and closer approximations of the desired behavior. (Module 18)

short-term memory Memory that holds information for 15 to 25 seconds. (Module 20)

significant outcome An outcome of a research study in which the observed results are statistically meaningful. (Module 58)

situational causes (of behavior) Causes of behavior that are external to a person. (Module 52)

skin senses The senses of touch, pressure, temperature, and pain. (Module 12)

social cognition The cognitive processes by which people understand and make sense of others and themselves. (Module 52)

social cognitive approaches to personality Theories that emphasize the influence of a person's cognitions–thoughts, feelings, expectations, and values–as well as observation of others' behavior, in determining personality. (Module 41)

social influence The process by which social groups and individuals exert pressure on an individual, either deliberately or unintentionally. (Module 53)

social neuroscience The subfield of social psychology that seeks to identify the neurological basis of social behavior. (Module 54)

social psychology The scientific study of how people's thoughts, feelings, and actions are affected by others. (Module 52)

social support A mutual network of caring, interested others. (Module 43)

social supporter A group member whose dissenting views make nonconformity to the group easier. (Module 53)

sociocultural perspective The perspective that assumes that society and culture shape abnormal behavior (Module 46)

somatic division The part of the peripheral nervous system that specializes in the control of voluntary movements and the communication of information to and from the sense organs. (Module 8)

somatic symptom disorders Psychological difficulties that take on a physical (somatic) form for which there is no medical cause. (Module 47)

sound The movement of air molecules brought about by a source of vibration. (Module 12)

specific phobia Intense, irrational fear of specific objects or situations. (Module 47)

spinal cord A bundle of neurons that leaves the brain and runs down the length of the back and is the main means for transmitting messages between the brain and the body. (Module 8)

spontaneous recovery The reemergence of an extinguished conditioned response after a period of rest and with no further conditioning. (Module 17)

spontaneous remission Recovery without formal treatment. (Module 50)

stage 1 sleep The state of transition between wakefulness and sleep, characterized by relatively rapid, low-amplitude brain waves. (Module 14)

stage 2 sleep A sleep deeper than that of stage 1, characterized by a slower, more regular wave pattern, along with momentary interruptions of "sleep spindles." (Module 14)

standard deviation An index of the average deviation of a set of scores from the center of the distribution. (Module 57)

statistics The branch of mathematics concerned with collecting, organizing, analyzing, and drawing conclusions from numerical data. (Module 56)

stage 3 sleep The deepest stage of sleep, during which we are least responsive to outside stimulation. (Module 14)

status The social standing of someone in a group. (Module 53)

stereotype A set of generalized beliefs and expectations about a particular group and its members. (Module 54)

stimulants Drugs that have an arousal effect on the central nervous system, causing a rise in heart rate, blood pressure, and muscular tension. (Module 16)

stimulus Energy that produces a response in a sense organ. (Module 10)

stimulus discrimination The process that occurs if two stimuli are sufficiently distinct from one another such that one evokes a conditioned response but the other does not; the ability to differentiate between stimuli. (Module 17)

stimulus generalization A process in which after a stimulus has been conditioned to produce a particular response, stimuli that are similar to the original stimulus produce the same response. (Module 17)

stress A person's response to events that are threatening or challenging. (Module 43)

structuralism Wundt's approach, which focuses on understanding the fundamental mental components of consciousness, thinking, and other kinds of mental states and activities. (Module 2)

subjective well-being People's sense of their happiness and satisfaction with their lives. (Module 45)

superego The part of personality that harshly judges the morality of our behavior. (Module 40)

survey research Research in which people chosen to represent a larger population are asked a series of questions about their behavior, thoughts, or attitudes. (Module 5)

sympathetic division The part of the autonomic division of the nervous system that acts to prepare the body for action in stressful situations, engaging all the organism's resources to respond to a threat. (Module 8)

synapse The space between two neurons where the axon of a sending neuron communicates with the dendrites of a receiving neuron by using chemical messages. (Module 7)

syntax Ways in which words and phrases can be combined to form sentences. (Module 25)

systematic desensitization A behavioral technique based on classical conditioning in which exposure to an anxiety-producing stimulus is paired with deep relaxation to reduce or eliminate anxiety. (Module 49)

telegraphic speech Sentences in which only essential words are used, typically including only nouns and verbs. (Module 25)

temperament A basic, inborn characteristic way of responding and behavioral style. (Module 37)

temperament An individual's behavioral style and characteristic way of responding that emerges early in life. (Module 41)

teratogens Environmental agents such as a drug, chemical, virus, or other factor that produce a birth defect. (Module 36)

terminal buttons The part of the axon that sends messages to other neurons. They look like a small bulge at the end of the axon. (Module 7)

test standardization A technique used to validate questions on personality tests by analyzing the responses of people who have completed the same set of questions, under the same circumstances. The responses can then be used to compare the responses and determine individuals' personality characteristics. (Module 42)

thalamus The part of the brain located in the middle of the central core that acts primarily to relay information about the senses. (Module 9)

Thematic Apperception Test (TAT) A test consisting of a series of pictures about which a person is asked to write a story. (Module 42)

theories Broad explanations and predictions concerning phenomena of interest. (Module 4)

theory of multiple intelligences Gardner's intelligence theory that proposes that there are eight distinct spheres of intelligence. (Module 26)

thinking Brain activity in which people mentally manipulate information, including words, visual images, sounds, or other data. (Module 23)

tip-of-the-tongue phenomenon The inability to recall information that one realizes one knows—a result of the difficulty of retrieving information from long-term memory. (Module 21)

top-down processing Perception that is guided by higher-level knowledge, experience, expectations, and motivations. (Module 13)

trait theory A model of personality that seeks to identify the basic traits necessary to describe personality. (Module 41)

traits Consistent, habitual personality characteristics and behaviors that are displayed across different situations. (Module 41)

transcranial magnetic stimulation (TMS) A depression treatment in which a precise magnetic pulse is directed to a specific area of the brain. (Module 51)

transference The transfer of feelings to a psychoanalyst of love or anger that had been originally directed to a patient's parents or other authority figures. (Module 49)

transgender A general term for persons whose gender identity, gender expression, or behavior is not consistent with that typically associated with the sex to which they were assigned at birth. (Module 34)

treatment The manipulation implemented by the experimenter. (Module 5)

trichromatic theory of color vision The theory that there are three kinds of cones in the retina, each of which responds primarily to a specific range of wavelengths. (Module 11)

trust-versus-mistrust stage According to Erikson, the first stage of psychosocial development, occurring from birth to age 1½ years, during which time infants develop feelings of trust or lack of trust. (Module 37)

Type A behavior pattern A cluster of behaviors involving hostility, competitiveness, time urgency, and feeling driven. (Module 44)

Type B behavior pattern A cluster of behaviors characterized by a patient, cooperative, noncompetitive, and nonaggressive manner. (Module 44)

unconditional positive regard An attitude of acceptance and respect on the part of an observer, no matter what a person says or does. (Module 41)

unconditioned response (UCR) A response that is natural and needs no training (e.g., salivation at the smell of food). (Module 17)

unconditioned stimulus (UCS) A stimulus that naturally brings about a particular response without having been learned. (Module 17)

unconscious A part of the personality that contains the memories, knowledge, beliefs, feelings, urges, drives, and instincts of which the individual is not aware. (Module 40)

unconscious wish fulfillment theory Sigmund Freud's theory that dreams represent unconscious wishes that dreamers desire to see fulfilled. (Module 14)

uninvolved parents Parents who show little interest in their children and are emotionally detached. (Module 37)

validity The degree to which a test actually measures what it is supposed to measure. (Module 26)

variability The spread, or dispersion, of scores in a distribution. (Module 57)

variable-interval schedule A schedule by which the time between reinforcements varies around some average rather than being fixed. (Module 18)

variable-ratio schedule A schedule in which reinforcement occurs after an average number of responses, but the reinforcement schedule is unpredictable. (Module 18)

variables Behaviors, events, or other characteristics that can change, or vary, in some way. (Module 5)

visual illusions Physical stimuli that consistently produce errors in perception. (Module 13)

wear-and-tear theories of aging Theories that suggest that the mechanical functions of the body simply stop working efficiently. (Module 39)

Weber's law A basic law of psychophysics stating that a just noticeable difference is a constant proportion to the intensity of an initial stimulus (rather than a constant amount). (Module 10)

weight set point The particular level of weight that the body strives to maintain. (Module 30)

working memory A memory system that holds information temporarily while actively manipulating and rehearsing that information. (Module 20)

zone of proximal development (ZPD) According to Vygotsky, the gap between what children already are able to accomplish on their own and what they are not quite ready to do by themselves. (Module 37)

zygote The new cell formed by the union of an egg and sperm. (Module 36)

References

Aas, M., Melle, I., Bettella, F., Djurovic, S., Le Hellard, S., Bjella, T., et al. (2018). Psychotic patients who used cannabis frequently before illness onset have higher genetic predisposition to schizophrenia than those who did not. *Psychological Medicine, 48*(1), 43-49.

Aazh, H., & Moore, B. C. J. (2007). Dead regions in the cochlea at 4 kHz in elderly adults: Relation to absolute threshold, steepness of audiogram, and pure-tone average. *Journal of the American Academy of Audiology, 18*, 97-106.

Abascal, T. E. (2019). Indigenous tourism in Australia: Understanding the link between cultural heritage and intention to participate using the means-end chain theory. *Journal of Heritage Tourism, 14*(3), 263-281.

Abbass, A., Town, J., Ogrodniczuk, J., Joffres, M., & Lilliengren, P. (2017). Intensive short-term dynamic psychotherapy trial therapy: Effectiveness and role of "unlocking the unconscious." *Journal of Nervous and Mental Disease, 205*, 453-457.

Abboud, L. (2005, July 27). The next phase in psychiatry. *Wall Street Journal*, pp. D1, D5.

Abdollahi, A., Panahipour, H., Hosseinian, S., & Allen, K. A. (2019). The effects of perceived stress on hope in women with breast cancer and the role of psychological hardiness. *Psycho-Oncology.* https://doi.org/10.1002/pon.5102.

Abel, D. (2015, June 16.) Panel votes to reopen Georges Bank. *Boston Globe.*Retrieved from https://www.bostonglobe.com/metro/2015/06/16/fishing-industry-body-votes-open-parts-georges-bank/c8UBRJ6zsDJbdps19Gu6VN/story.html.

Abel, T., & Nickl-Jockschat, T. (2016). *The neurobiology of schizophrenia.* San Diego, CA, US: Elsevier Academic Press.

Abeles, A. T., Howe, L. C., Krosnick, J. A., & MacInnis, B. (2019). Perception of public opinion on global warming and the role of opinion deviance. *Journal of Environmental Psychology, 63*, 118-129.

Abelman, R. (2007). Fighting the war on indecency: Mediating TV, Internet, and video-game usage among achieving and underachieving gifted children. *Roeper Review, 29*, 100-112.

Abraham, A., Thybusch, K., Pieritz, K., & Hermann, C. (2013). Gender differences in creative thinking: Behavioral and fMRI findings. *Brain Imaging and Behavior, 8*(1), 39-51.

Abrams, D., & Hogg, M. A. (2017). Twenty years of group processes and intergroup relations research: A review of past progress and future prospects. *Group Processes & Intergroup Relations, 20*(5), 561-569.

Accardi, M., & Milling, L. (2009). The effectiveness of hypnosis for reducing procedure-related pain in children and adolescents: A comprehensive methodological review. *Journal of Behavioral Medicine, 32*, 328-339.

Ackard, D. M., & Neumark-Sztainer, D. (2002). Date violence and date rape among adolescents: Associations with disordered eating behaviors and psychological health. *Child Abuse and Neglect, 26*, 455-473.

Ackerman, P. L. (2011). Intelligence and expertise. In R. J. Sternberg & S. Kaufman (Eds.), *The Cambridge handbook of intelligence.* New York: Cambridge University Press.

Acuna, D. E., Berniker, M., Fernandes, H. L., & Kording, K. P. (2015). Using psychophysics to ask if the brain samples or maximizes. *Journal of Vision, 15*, 7-18.

Adami, Z., Alilou, M. M., & Nazari, M. A. (2019). The comparison of emotional working memory capacity in patients with social anxiety disorder and normal subjects. *Advances in Cognitive Science, 20*(4), 35-45.

Adams, G., & Dzokoto, V. A. (2007). Genital-shrinking panic in Ghana: A cultural psychological analysis. *Culture & Psychology, 13*, 83-104.

Adams, K. B. (2004). Changing investment in activities and interests in elders' lives: Theory and measurement. *International Journal of Aging and Human Development, 58*, 87-108.

Adams, M., Bell, L. A., & Griffin, P. (2007). *Teaching for diversity and social justice* (2nd ed.). New York: Routledge/Taylor & Francis Group.

Adams-Byers, J., Squilkr, S., & Moon, S. M. (2004). Gifted students' perceptions of the academic and social/emotional effects of homogeneous and heterogeneous grouping. *Gifted Child Quarterly, 48*, 7-20.

Addison, A. (2017). Jung's psychoid concept: An hermeneutic understanding. *International Journal of Jungian Studies, 9*, 1-16.

Adler, M. (2013). Hunger and longing: A developmental regulation model for exploring core relational needs. In S. P. Gantt & B. Badenoch (Eds.), *The interpersonal neurobiology of group psychotherapy and group process.* London: Karnac Books.

Adler, N. J., & Aycan, Z. (2018). Cross-cultural interaction: What we know and what we need to know. *Annual Review of Organizational Psychology and Organizational Behavior, 5*, 307-333.

Adolph, K. E., & Berger, S. E. (2011). Physical and motor development. In M. H. Bornstein & M. E. Lamb (Eds.), *Cognitive development: An advanced textbook.* New York: Psychology Press.

Advokat, C. (2005). Differential effects of clozapine versus other antipsychotics on clinical outcome and dopamine release in the brain. *Essential Psychopharmacology, 6*, 73-90.

Ahern, D. C., & Faust, D. (2012). Challenging computerized testing and computer-based test interpretations. In D. Faust (Ed.), *Coping with psychiatric and psychological testimony: Based on the original work by Jay Ziskin* (6th ed.), (pp. 470-487). New York: Oxford University Press.

Ahmadi Forooshani, S., Murray, K., Izadikhah, Z., & Khawaja, N. (2020). Identifying the most effective strategies for improving autobiographical memory specificity and its implications for mental health problems: A meta-analysis. *Cognitive Therapy and Research, 44*(2), 258-274.

Aiello, R. J. (2006). Hypermasculinity and psychosocial development as predictors of potential date-rape perpetration on campus. *Dissertation Abstracts International: Section B: The Sciences and Engineering, 67*(2-B), 1178.

Aiken, L. (2000). *Dying, death, and bereavement* (4th ed.). Mahwah, NJ: Erlbaum.

Aimé, C., Paquette, D., Déry, M., & Verlaan, P. (2018). Predictors of childhood trajectories of overt and indirect aggression: An interdisciplinary approach. *Aggressive Behavior,* doi:10.1002/ab.21759.

Ainsworth, M. D. S., Blehar, M. C., Waters, E., & Wall, S. (1978). *Patterns of attachment: A psychological study of the strange situation.* Hillsdale, NJ: Erlbaum.

Airuehia, E., Walker, L. Y., & Nittler, J. (2015). A review of "bath salts": Evolving designer drugs of abuse. *Journal of Child & Adolescent Substance Abuse, 24*, 186-190.

Akhtar, S., & Howe, M. L. (2019). Priming older adults and people with Alzheimer's disease analogical problem-solving with true and false memories. *Journal of Clinical and Experimental Neuropsychology, 41*(7), 704-714.

Al-Shawaf, L., Lewis, D. M. G., & Buss, D. M. (2018). Sex differences in disgust: Why are women more easily disgusted than men? *Emotion Review, 10*(2), 149-160.

Alaggia, R., Collin-Vézina, D., & Lateef, R. (2019). Facilitators and barriers to child sexual abuse (CSA) disclosures: A research update (2000-2016). *Trauma, Violence, & Abuse, 20*(2), 260-283.

Alampay, L. P., Godwin, J., Lansford, J. E., Bombi, A. S., Bornstein, M. H., Chang, L., et al. (2017). Severity and justness do not moderate the relation between corporal punishment and negative child outcomes: A multicultural and longitudinal study. *International Journal of Behavioral Development, 41*, 491-502.

Alba, R., & Barbosa, G. Y. (2016). Room at the top? Minority mobility and the transition to demographic diversity in the USA. *Ethnic and Racial Studies, 39*(6), 917-938. doi:10.1080/0 1419870.2015.1081966.

Albanese, M., & Case, S. M. (2015). Progress testing: Critical analysis and suggested practices. *Advances in Health Sciences Education, 21*, 221-234.

Alboni, S., Di Bonaventura, M. M., Benatti, C., Giusepponi, M. E., Brunello, N., & Cifani, C. (2017). Hypothalamic expression of inflammatory mediators in an animal model of binge eating. *Behavioural Brain Research, 320*, 420-430.

Alderson-Day, B., Weis, S., McCarthy-Jones, S., Moseley, P., Smailes, D., & Fernyhough, C. (2016). The brain's conversation with itself: Neural substrates of dialogic inner speech. *Social Cognitive and Affective Neuroscience, 11*(1), 110-120.

Aleksander, I. (2013, June 23). Molly: Pure, but not so simple. *The New York Times*, p. ST1.

Alelú-Paz, R., Carmona, F. J., Sanchez-Mut, J. V., Cariaga-Martínez, A., González-Corpas, A., Ashour, N., et al. (2016). Epigenetics in schizophrenia: A pilot study of global DNA methylation in different brain regions associated with higher cognitive functions. *Frontiers In Psychology, 7*, 1496.

Alexandersen, P., Karsdal, M. A., & Christiansen, C. (2009). Long-term prevention with hormone-replacement therapy after the menopause: Which women should be targeted? *Women's Health, 5*, 637-647.

Alfaro, A., Bernabeu, Á., Agulló, C., Parra, J., & Fernández, E. (2015). Hearing colors: An example of brain plasticity. *Frontiers in Systems Neuroscience, 9*, 42-50.

Alho, K., Vorobyev, V. A., Medvedev, S. V., Pakhomov, S. V., Starchenko, M. G., Terganiemi, M., et al. (2006). Selective attention to human voice enhances brain activity bilaterally in the superior temporal sulcus. *Brain Research, 1075*, 142-150.

Allakhverdov, V. M. (2019). Consciousness and the problem of free will. *Neuroscience and Behavioral Physiology.* doi:10.1007/s11055-019-00780-6.

Allen, D. N., & Becker, M. L. (2019). Clinical interviewing. In G. Goldstein, D. N. Allen, &

J. DeLuca (Eds.), *Handbook of psychological assessment* (4th ed.). San Diego, CA: Elsevier Academic Press.

Allen, M. T., Handy, J. D., Miller, D. P., & Servatius, R. J. (2019). Avoidance learning and classical eyeblink conditioning as model systems to explore a learning diathesis model of PTSD. *Neuroscience & Biobehavioral Reviews, 100*, 370-386.

Allport, G. W. (1966). Traits revisited. *American Psychologist, 21*, 1-10.

Allport, G. W., & Postman, L. J. (1958). The basic psychology of rumor. In E. D. Maccoby, T. M. Newcomb, & E. L. Hartley (Eds.), *Readings in social psychology* (3rd ed.). New York: Holt, Rinehart and Winston.

Allwood, M. A. (2007). The relations of violence exposure, trauma symptoms and aggressive cognitions to youth violent behavior. *Dissertation Abstracts International: Section B: The Sciences and Engineering, 67*, 5387.

Alon, I., & Brett, J. M. (2007). Perceptions of time and their impact on negotiations in the Arabic-speaking Islamic world. *Negotiation Journal, 23*, 55-73.

Alper, S., & Yilmaz, O. (2019). How is the Big Five related to moral and political convictions: The moderating role of the WEIRDness of the culture. *Personality and Individual Differences, 145*, 32-38.

Altman, N., & Stile, J. (2015). Staying alive: Freud for a new generation. *PsycCRITIQUES, 60*, 25-32.

Aluja, A., Malas, O., Lucas, I., Worner, F., & Bascompte, R. (2019). Assessment of the Type D personality distress in coronary heart disease patients and healthy subjects in Spain. *Personality and Individual Differences, 142*, 301-309.

Alzheimer's Association. (2017). *2017 Alzheimer's disease: Facts and figures.* Chicago: Author.

American Academy of Pediatrics Council on Communication and Media. (2009). Media violence. *Pediatrics, 124*, 1495-1503.

American Academy of Pediatrics Council on Communications and Media. (2016). Virtual violence. *Pediatrics. 138*, e20161298.

American Academy of Pediatrics. (2016). Media and young minds. *Pediatrics, 138*, 1-6.

American Association of Intellectual and Developmental Disabilities. (2015). Frequently asked questions on intellectual disability and the AAIDD definition. Retrieved from http://aaidd.org/docs/default-source/sis-docs/aaiddfaqonid template.pdf?sfvrsn=2.

American Association of University Women (AAUW). (2012). *Hostile hallways: Bullying, teasing and sexual harassment in school.* Washington, DC: Author.

American College Health Association. (2006). *Acquaintance and date rape: What everyone should know.* Baltimore, MD: Author.

American Psychiatric Association. (2013). *Diagnostic and statistical manual of mental disorders* (5th ed.). Washington, DC: Author.

American Psychiatric Association. (2013). *Diagnostic and Statistical Manual of Mental Disorders* (5th ed.). Washington, DC: Author.

American Psychiatric Association. (2018). Warning signs of mental illness. Downloaded from https://www.psychiatry.org/patients-families/warning-signs-of-mental-illness.

American Psychological Association. (2002). *APA ethics code, 2002.* Washington, DC: Author.

American Psychological Association. (2011). *Careers in psychology.* Washington DC: Author.

American Psychological Association. (2013). *APA guidelines for the undergraduate psychology major. Version 2.0.* Washington, DC: American Psychological Association.

American Psychological Association. (2016, June). What do people do with their psychology degrees? *Monitor on Psychology*, p. 12.

American Psychological Association. (2017). Ethical principles of psychologists and code of conduct. https://www.apa.org/ethics/code/.

American Psychological Association. (2018). *Demographics of the U.S. psychology workforce: Findings from the 2007 16 American Community Survey.* Washington, DC: Author.

American Psychological Association (2018). Stress in America: Generation Z. Stress in America™ Survey. Retrieved from https://www.apa.org/news/press/releases/stress/2018/stress-gen-z.pdf.

American Psychological Association. (2019). Guidelines for the practice of telepsychology. Downloaded from https://www.apa.org/practice/guidelines/telepsychology.

American Psychological Association. (2019). Supporting a family member with serious mental illness. Downloaded from https://www.apa.org/helpcenter/improving-care.

American Psychological Association. (2019, August 15). One-third of US adults say fear of mass shootings prevents them from going to certain places or events. Downloaded from https://www.apa.org/news/press/releases/2019/08/fear-mass-shooting.

Amesberger, G., Finkenzeller, T., Müller, E., & Würth, S. (2019). Aging-related changes in the relationship between the physical self-concept and the physical fitness in elderly individuals. *Scandinavian Journal of Medicine & Science in Sports, 29*, 26-34.

Amid, P. K., & Chen, D. C. (2011). Surgical treatment of chronic groin and testicular pain after laparoscopic and open preperitoneal inguinal hernia repair. *Journal of the American College of Surgeons, 213*, 531-536.

Amodio, D. M., & Ratner, K. G. (2011). A memory systems model of implicit social cognition. *Current Directions in Psychological Science, 20*, 143-148.

Anastasi, A., & Urbina, S. (1997). *Psychologicaltesting* (7th ed.). Englewood Cliffs, NJ: Prentice Hall.

Andersen, B. (2017). Careful words: Nursing, language, and emotion in Papua New Guinea. *Medical Anthropology, 36*(8), 758-771. doi:10.1080/01459740.2017.1317771.

Andersen, R. (2019, April). The intention machine. *Scientific American*, 25-31.

Andersen, R., & Buneo, C. (2002). Intentional maps in posterior parietal cortex. *Annual Review of Neuroscience, 25*, 189-220.

Anderson, C., & Home, J. A. (2006). Sleepiness enhances distraction during monotonous task. *Sleep: Journal of Sleep and Sleep Disorders Research, 29*, 573-576.

Anderson, C. A., & Bushman, B. J. (2018). Media violence and the general aggression model. *Journal of Social Issues, 74*(2), 386-413.

Anderson, C. A., Bushman, B. J., Bartholow, B. D., Cantor, J., Christakis, D., Coyne, S. M., . . . Ybarra, M. (2017). Screen violence and youth behavior. *Pediatrics, 140*(5, Supp 2), S142-S147.

Anderson, C. A., Lazard, D. S., & Hartley, D. H. (2017). Plasticity in bilateral superior temporal cortex: Effects of deafness and cochlear implantation on auditory and visual speech processing. *Hearing Research, 343*, 138-149.

Anderson, J. L., Sellbom, M., Pymont, C., Smid, W., De Saeger, H., & Kamphuis, J. H. (2015). Measurement of DSM-5 section II personality disorder constructs using the MMPI-2-RF in clinical and forensic samples. *Psychological Assessment, 27*, 786-800.

Anderson, J. L., Sellbom, M., Pymont, C., Smid, W., De Saeger, H., & Kamphuis, J. H. (2015). Measurement of DSM-5 section II personality disorder constructs using the MMPI-2-RF in clinical and forensic samples. *Psychological Assessment, 27*, 786-800.

Anderson, K. B., Cooper, H., & Okamura, L. (1997). Individual differences and attitudes toward rape: A meta-analytic review. *Personality and Social Psychology Bulletin, 23*, 295-315.

Anderson, L. B., Paul, L. K., & Brown, W. S. (2017). Emotional intelligence in agenesis of the corpus callosum. *Archives of Clinical Neuropsychology, 32*, 267-279.

Anderson, R. C., & Klofstad, C. A. (2012). Preference for leaders with masculine voices holds in the case of feminine leadership roles. *PloS One, 7*(12), e51216.

Andrasik, F. (2006). Psychophysiological disorders: Headache as a case in point. In F. Andrasik, *Comprehensive handbook of personality and psychopathology, Vol. 2: Adult psycho-pathology.* Hoboken, NJ: John Wiley & Sons.

Anestis, M. D., Anestis, J. C., & Lilienfeld, S. O. (2011). When it comes to evaluating psychodynamic therapy, the devil is in the details. *American Psychologist, 66*, 149-151.

Anguela, X. M., & High, K. A. (2019). Entering the modern era of gene therapy. *Annual Review of Medicine, 70*, 273-288.

Anwar, F., Fry, D. P., & Grigfaitytė, I. (2018). Aggression prevention and reduction in diverse cultures and contexts. *Current Opinion in Psychology, 19*, 49-54. doi:10.1016/j.copsyc.2017.03.029.

Aoued, H. S., Sannigrahi, S., Doshi, N., Morrison, F. G., Linsenbaum, H., Hunter, S. C., et al. (2019). Reversing behavioral, neuroanatomical, and germline influences of intergenerational stress. *Biological Psychiatry, 85*(3), 248-256.

APA Working Group on Stress and Health Disparities. (2017). Stress and health disparities: Contexts, mechanisms, and interventions among racial/ethnic minority and low-socioeconomic status populations. Retrieved from http://www.apa.org/pi/health-disparities/resources/stress-report.aspx

Apanovich, A. M., McCarthy, D., & Salovey, P. (2003). Using message framing to motivate HIV testing among low-income, ethnic minority women. *Health Psychology, 22*, 88-94.

Appelbaum, P. S., Scurich, N., & Raad, R. (2015). Effects of behavioral genetic evidence on perceptions of criminal responsibility and appropriate punishment. *Psychology, Public Policy, and Law, 21*, 134-144.

Apple, D. M., Fonseca, R. S., & Kokovay, E. (2017). The role of adult neurogenesis in psychiatric and cognitive disorders. *Brain Research, 1655*, 270-276.

Arafat, I., & Cotton, W. L. (1974). Masturbation practices of males and females. *Journal of Sex Research, 10*, 293-307.

Araujo, M. C., Dormal, M., & Schady, N. (2019). Childcare Quality and Child Development. *Journal of Human Resources, 54*(3), 656-682.

Arbuthnott, A., & Sharpe, D. (2009). The effect of physician-patient collaboration on patient adherence in non-psychiatric medicine. *Patient Education and Counseling, 77*, 60-67.

Arcaro, M. J., Schade, P. F., Vincent, J. L., Ponce, C. R., & Livingstone, M. S. (2017). Seeing faces is necessary for face-domain formation. *Nature Neuroscience, 20*, 1404-1412.

Arcelus, J., Mitchell, A. J., Wales, J., & Nielsen, S. (2011). Mortality rates in patients with anorexia nervosa and other eating disorders: A meta-analysis of 36 studies. *Archives of General Psychiatry, 68*, 724-731.

Ardila, A. (2015). A proposed neurological interpretation of language evolution. *Behavioural Neurology, 20*, 15-22.

Arena, J. G., & Tankersley, J. D. (2018). Introduction to biofeedback training for chronic pain disorders. In D. C. Turk & R. J. Gatchel (Eds.), *Psychological approaches to pain management: A practitioner's handbook* (3rd ed.), (pp. 138-159). New York: The Guilford Press.

Ariely, D., & Norton, M. I. (2009). Conceptual consumption. *Annual Review of Psychology, 60*, 475-499.

Arimoto, M., Shiomi, T., Sasanabe, R., Inagawa, S., Ueda, H., & Inafuku, S. (2011). A sheet-type device for home-monitoring sleep apneas in children. *Sleep and Biological Rhythms, 9*, 103-111.

Arlo, C. (2017). Group therapy and dialectical behavior therapy: An integrative response to a clinical case. *International Journal of Group Psychotherapy, 67*(Supp1), S13-S23.

Armbruster, D., Mueller, A., Strobel, A., Lesch, K., Kirschbaum, C., & Brocke, B. (2011). Variation in genes involved in dopamine clearance influence the startle response in older adults. *Journal of Neural Transmission, 118*, 1281-1292.

Arnett, J. (2008). The neglected 95%: Why American psychology needs to become less American. *American Psychologist, 63*, 602-614.

Arnett, J. (2011). Emerging adulthood(s): The cultural psychology of a new life stage. In L. Jensen (Ed.), *Bridging cultural and developmental approaches to psychology: New syntheses in theory, research, and policy.* New York: Oxford University Press.

Arnett, J. J. (2000). Emerging adulthood. *American Psychologist, 55*, 469-480.

Arnett, J. J. (2006). *Emerging adulthood: The winding road from the late teens through the twenties.* New York: Oxford University Press.

Arnett, J. J. (2007). Afterword: Aging out of care–Toward realizing the possibilities of emerging adulthood. *New Directions for Youth Development, 113*, 151-161.

Aronson, J., & Dee, T. (2012). Stereotype threat in the real world. In M. Inzlicht & T. Schmader (Eds.), *Stereotype threat: Theory, process, and application.* New York: Oxford University Press.

Arpaci, I., Baloğlu, M., & Kesici, Ş. (2018). The relationship among individual differences in individualism-collectivism, extraversion, and self-presentation. *Personality and Individual Differences, 121*, 89-92. doi:10.1016/j.paid.2017.09.034

Arrigoni, E., Chee, M. J. S., & Fuller, P. M. (2019). To eat or to sleep: That is a lateral hypothalamic question. *Neuropharmacology, 154*, 34-49.

Arshamian, A., Iannilli, E., Gerber, J. C., Willander, J., Persson, J., Seo, H., et al. (2013). The functional neuroanatomy of odor evoked auto-biographical memories cued by odors and words. *Neuropsychologia, 51*, 123-131.

Artistico, D., Pinto, A., Douek, J., Black, J., & Pezzuti, L. (2013). The value of removing daily obstacles via everyday problem-solving theory: Developing an applied novel procedure to increase self-efficacy for exercise. *Frontiers in Psychology, 4.* Retrieved from http://www.ncbi.nlm.nih.gov/pubmed/23372560.

Asch, S. E. (1951). Effects of group pressure upon the modification and distortion of judgments. In H. Guetzkow (Ed.), *Groups, leadership, and men.* Pittsburgh: Carnegie Press.

Associated Press (2011, September 27). Study: Murder victims disproportionately black. Accessed from http://www.msnbc.msn.com/id/20203888/ns/us_news-life/t/study-murder-victims-disproportionately-black/

Atkinson, H. (Ed.). (1997, January 21). Understanding your diagnosis. *HealthNews*, p. 3.

Atkinson, R. C., & Shiffrin, R. M. (1968). Human memory: A proposed system and its control processes. In K. W. Spence & J. T. Spence (Eds.), *The psychology of learning and motivation: Advances in research and theory* (Vol. 2). New York: Academic Press.

Attia, Z., Kapa, S., Lopez-Jimenez, F., McKie, P., Ladewig, D., et al. (2019). Screening for cardiac contractile dysfunction using an artificial intelligence-enabled electrocardiogram. *Nature Medicine, 25*, 70-74.

Aubrey, A. (2020, April 18). Who's hit hardest by COVID-19? Why obesity, stress and race all matter. National Public Radio. Downloaded from https://www.npr.org/sections/health-shots/2020/04/18/835563340/whos-hit-hardest-by-covid-19-why-obesity-stress-and-race-all-matter.

Aussilloux, C., & Bagdadli, A. (2006). Handicap mental et société: Soigner, éduquer, intégrer. Mental handicap and society. *Neuropsychiatrie de l'Enfance et de l'Adolescence, 54*, 336-340.

Austin, J. P., & Halvorson, S. A. (2019). Reducing the expert halo effect on pharmacy and therapeutics committees. *Journal of the American Medical Association, 321*(5), 453-454.

Averill, J. R. (1975). A semantic atlas of emotional concepts. *Catalog of Selected Documents in Psychology, 5*, 330.

Ayling, K., Bowden, T., Tighe, P., Todd, I., Dilnot, E. M., Negm, O. H., et al. (2017). The application of protein microarray assays in psychoneuroimmunology. *Brain, Behavior, and Immunity, 59*, 62-66.

Azeredo, A., Moreira, D., Figueiredo, P., & Barbosa, F. (2019). Delinquent behavior: Systematic review of genetic and environmental risk factors. *Clinical Child and Family Psychology Review.* https://doi.org/10.1007/s10567-019-00298-w.

Bacchiochi, J. R. (2006). Development and validation of the Malingering Discriminant Function Index (M-DFI) for the Minnesota Multiphasic Personality Inventory-2 (MMPI-2). *Dissertation Abstracts International: Section B: The Sciences and Engineering, 66*(10-B), 5673.

Baczyńska, A., & Thornton, G. C. (2017). Relationships of analytical, practical, and emotional intelligence with behavioral dimensions of performance of top managers. *International Journal of Selection and Assessment, 25*, 171-182.

Baddeley, A., & Wilson, B. (1985). Phonological coding and short-term memory in patients without speech. *Journal of Memory and Language, 24*, 490-502.

Baddeley, A. D., Allen, R. J., & Hitch, G. J. (2011). Binding in visual working memory: The role of the episodic buffer. *Neuropsychologia, 49*, 1393-1400.

Badke, M. B., Sherman, J., Boyne, P., Page, S., & Dunning, K. (2011). Tongue-based biofeedback for balance in stroke: Results of an 8-week pilot study. *Archives of Physical and Medical Rehabilitation, 92*, 1364-1370.

Bagattini, C., Mele, S., Brignani, D., & Savazzi, S. (2015). No causal effect of left hemisphere hyperactivity in the genesis of neglect-like behavior. *Neuropsychologia, 72*, 12-21.

Bagge, C., & Sher, K. (2008). Adolescent alcohol involvement and suicide attempts: Toward the development of a conceptual framework. *Clinical Psychology Review, 28*, 1283-1296.

Bagnall, D. (2010). The use of spinal cord stimulation and intrathecal drug delivery in the treatment of low back-related pain. *Physical Medicine & Rehabilitation Clinics of North America, 21*, 851-858.

Bahrick, L. E., Lickliter, R., & Castellanos, I. (2013). The development of face perception in infancy: Intersensory interference and unimodal visual facilitation. *Developmental Psychology, 49*, 1919-1930.

Bailey, J. M., Vasey, P. L., Diamond, L. M., Breedlove, S. M., Vilain, E., & Epprecht, M. (2016). Sexual orientation, controversy, and science. *Psychological Science in the Public Interest, 17*(2), 45-101.

Baker, J., & Berenbaum, H. (2007). Emotional approach and problem-focused coping: A comparison of potentially adaptive strategies. *Cognition and Emotion, 21*, 95-118.

Baker, S. E., Johnson, P. J., & Slater, D. (2007). Learned food aversion with and without an odour cue for protecting untreated baits from wild mammal foraging [Special issue: Conservation, enrichment, and animal behavior]. *Applied Animal Behaviour Science, 102*, 410-428.

Balaban, C. D., McBurney, D. H., & Affeltranger, M. A. (2005). Three distinct categories of time course of pain produced by oral capsaicin. *The Journal of Pain, 6*, 315-322.

Balconi, M., Bortolotti, A., & Crivelli, D. (2013). Self-report measures, facial feedback, and personality differences (BEES) in cooperative vs. noncooperative situations: Contribution of the mimic system to the sense of empathy. *International Journal of Psychology, 48*, 631-640.

Ball, D. (2004). Genetic approaches to alcohol dependence. *British Journal of Psychiatry, 185*, 449-451.

Balon, R. (2017). Burden of sexual dysfunction. *Journal of Sex & Marital Therapy, 43*, 49-55.

Balter, M. (2017). Schizophrenia's unyielding mysteries. *Scientific American, 316*(5), 54-61.

Bandura, A. (1986). *Social foundations of thought and action: A social cognitive theory.* Englewood Cliffs, NJ: Prentice Hall.

Bandura, A. (1994). Social cognitive theory of mass communication. In J. Bryant & D. Zillmann (Eds.), *Media effects: Advances in theory and research: LEA's communication series.* Hillsdale, NJ: Erlbaum.

Bandura, A. (1999). Social cognitive theory of personality. In D. Cervone & Y. Shod (Eds.), *The coherence of personality.* New York: Guilford.

Bandura, A. (2000). Self-efficacy: The foundation of agency. In W. J. Perrig & A. Grob (Eds.), *Control of human behavior, mental processes, and consciousness: Essays in honor of the 60th birthday of August Flammer.* Mahwah, NJ: Erlbaum.

Bandura, A. (2004). Swimming against the mainstream: The early years from chilly tributary to transformative mainstream. *Behavior Research and Therapy, 42*, 613-630.

Bandura, A. (2009). Social cognitive theory goes global. *The Psychologist, 22*, 504-506.

Bandura, A., & Cherry, L. (2019). Enlisting the power of youth for climate change. *American Psychologist.* http://dx.doi.org/10.1037/amp0000512.

Bandura, A., & Locke, E. A. (2003). Negative self-efficacy and goal effects revisited. *Journal of Applied Psychology, 88*, 87-99.

Bandura, A., Grusec, J. E., & Menlove, F. L. (1967). Vicarious extinction of avoidance behavior. *Journal of Personality and Social Psychology, 5*, 16-23.

Bandura, A., Ross, D., & Ross, S. (1963a). Imitation of film-mediated aggressive models. *Journal of Abnormal and Social Psychology, 66*, 3-11.

Bandura, A., Ross, D., & Ross, S. (1963b). Vicarious reinforcement and imitative learning. *Journal of Abnormal and Social Psychology, 67*, 601-607.

Banks, J. A. (2006). Improving race relations in schools: From theory and research to practice. *Journal of Social Issues, 62*, 607-614.

Banks, J. B., & Boals, A. (2017). Understanding the role of mind wandering in stress-related working memory impairments. *Cognition and Emotion, 31*, 1023-1030.

Barbaro, N., Boutwell, B. B., Barnes, J. C., & Shackelford, T. K. (2017). Rethinking the transmission gap: What behavioral genetics and evolutionary psychology mean for attachment theory: A comment on Verhage et al. (2016). *Psychological Bulletin, 143*, 107-113.

Barber, N. (2019). The most creative time of day. *Psychology Today.* Retrieved from https://www.psychologytoday.com/us/blog/the-human-beast/201906/the-most-creative-time-day.

Barcott, B., & Scherer, M. (2015, May 25). The great pot experiment. *Time*, pp. 38-44.

Bargh, J. A. (2014). Our unconscious mind. *Scientific American, 310*, 30-37.

Barke, D. B. (2011). Self-selection for stressful experiences. *Stress and Health: Journal of the International Society for the Investigation of Stress, 27*, 194-205.

Barker, J., & Jones, M. (2008). The effects of hypnosis on self-efficacy, affect, and soccer performance: A case study. *Journal of Clinical Sport Psychology, 2*, 127-147.

Barkley, R. (2000). *Taking charge of ADHD* (rev. ed.). New York: Guilford Press.

Barkley, R. A., Knouse, L. E., & Murphy, K. R. (2011). Correspondence and disparity in the self- and other ratings of current and childhood ADHD symptoms and impairment in adults with ADHD. *Psychological Assessment, 23*, 437-446.

Barlow, D. H. (2007). *Clinical handbook of psychological disorders: A step-by-step treatment manual* (4th ed.). New York: Guilford Press.

Barmeyer, C. I. (2004). Learning styles and their impact on cross-cultural training: An international comparison in France, Germany and Quebec. *International Journal of Intercultural Relations, 28*, 577-594.

Barnes, J. C., & Jacobs, B. A. (2013). Genetic risk for violent behavior and environmental exposure to disadvantage and violent crime: The case for gene-environment interaction. *Journal of Interpersonal Violence, 28,* 92-120.

Barnett, J. E., Wise, E. H., & Johnson-Greene, D. (2007). Informed consent: Too much of a good thing or not enough? *Professional Psychology: Research and Practice, 38,* 179-186.

Barnett, R. C. (2004). Woman and work: Where are we, where did we come from, and where are we going? [Preface]. *Journal of Social Issues, 60,* 667-674.

Barnett, S. M., Rindermann, H., Williams, W. M., & Ceci, S. J. (2011). Society and intelligence. In R. J. Sternberg & S. Kaufman (Eds.), *The Cambridge handbook of intelligence.* New York: Cambridge University Press.

Barrada, J., Abad, F., & Olea, J. (2011). Varying the valuating function and the presentable bank in computerized adaptive testing. *The Spanish Journal of Psychology, 14,* 500-508.

Barresi, J. (2007). Consciousness and intentionality. *Journal of Consciousness Studies, 14, Special issue: Concepts of Consciousness: Integrating an Emerging Science,* 77-93.

Barrett, L. (2011). *Beyond the brain: How body and environment shape animal and human minds.* Princeton, NJ: Princeton University Press.

Barrett, L. F., & Russell, J. A. (2015). An introduction to psychological construction. In L. F. Barrett & J. A. Russell (Eds.), *The psychological construction of emotion.* New York: Guilford Press.

Barrett, L. F., & Salovey, P. (Eds.). (2002). *The wisdom in feeling: Psychological processes in emotional intelligence.* New York: Guilford Press.

Barrett, L. F., Adolphs, R., Marsella, S., Martinez, A. M., & Pollak, S. D. (2019). Emotional expressions reconsidered: Challenges to inferring emotion from human facial movements. *Psychological Science in the Public Interest, 20*(1), 1-68.

Barron, F. (1990). *Creativity and psychological health: Origins of personal vitality and creative freedom.* Buffalo, NY: Creative Education Foundation.

Barry, C. T., Doucette, H., Loflin, D. C., Rivera-Hudson, N., & Herrington, L. L. (2017). "Let me take a selfie": Associations between self-photography, narcissism, and self-esteem. *Psychology of Popular Media Culture, 6,* 48-60.

Barson, J. R., Morganstern, I., & Leibowitz, S. F. (2011). Similarities in hypothalamic and mesocorticolimbic circuits regulating the overconsumption of food and alcohol. *Physiology & Behavior, 104,* 128-137.

Bartlett, F. (1932). *Remembering: A study in experimental and social psychology.* Cambridge, England: Cambridge University Press.

Bartlett, M. Y., & DeSteno, D. (2006). Gratitude and prosocial behavior: Helping when it costs you. *Psychological Science, 17,* 319-325.

Bartocci, G. (2004). Transcendence techniques and psychobiological mechanisms underlying religious experience. *Mental Health, Religion and Culture, 7,* 171-181.

Bartone, P., Roland, R., Picano, J., & Williams, T. (2008). Psychological hardiness predicts success in U.S. Army Special Forces candidates. *International Journal of Selection and Assessment, 16,* 78-81.

Barzilay, S., Feldman, D., Snir, A., Apter, A., Carli, V., Hoven, C. W., et al. (2015). The interpersonal theory of suicide and adolescent suicidal behavior. *Journal of Affective Disorders, 183,* 68-74.

Bass, E. C., Saldarriaga, L., Cunha, J., Chen, B., Santo, J. B., & Bukowski, W. M. (2018). A cross-cultural analysis of the relations of physical and relational aggression with peer victimization. *International Journal of Behavioral Development, 42*(1), 132-142.

Bassett, A. M., & Baker, C. (2015). Normal or abnormal? "Normative uncertainty" in psychiatric practice. *Journal of Medical Humanities, 36,* 89-111.

Basten, U., Hilger, K., & Fiebach, C. J. (2015). Where smart brains are different: A quantitative meta-analysis of functional and structural brain imaging studies on intelligence. *Intelligence, 51,* 10-17.

Bastian, B., Jetten, J, Hornsey, M. J., & Leknes, S. (2014). The positive consequences of pain: A biopsychosocial approach. *Personality and Social Psychology Review, 18,* 256-279.

Bateman, A. W. (2011). Commentary on "Minding the difficult patient": Mentalizing and the use of formulation in patients with borderline personality disorder comorbid with antisocial personality disorder. *Personality and Mental Health, 5,* 85-90.

Bates, E. (2005). Plasticity, localization, and language development. In S. T. Parker & J. Langer (Eds.), *Biology and knowledge revisited: From neurogenesis to psychogenesis.* Mahwah, NJ: Lawrence Erlbaum Associates.

Bates, J. E., & Pettit, G. S. (2015). Temperament, parenting, and social development. In J. E. Grusec & P. D. Hastings (Eds.), *Handbook of socialization: Theory and research* (2nd ed.). New York: Guilford Press.

Batson, C. (2011). *Altruism in humans.* New York: Oxford University Press.

Bauer, J. J., Schwab, J. R., & McAdams, D. P. (2011). Self-actualizing: Where ego development finally feels good? *Humanistic Psychologist, 39,* 121-136.

Bauer, P. J., Larkina, M., Güler, E., & Burch, M. (2019). Long-term autobiographical memory across middle childhood: Patterns, predictors, and implications for conceptualizations of childhood amnesia. *Memory, 27*(9), 1175-1193.

Baum, A., Lorduy, K., & Jenkins, F. J. (2011). The molecular biology of stress: Cellular defense, immune response, and aging. In R. J. Contrada & A. Baum (Eds.), *The handbook of stress science: Biology, psychology, and health.* New York: Springer Publishing Co.

Baumeister, R. F., & Stillman, T. (2006). Erotic plasticity: Nature, culture, gender, and sexuality. In R. D. McAnulty & M. M. Burnette (Eds.), *Sex and sexuality, Vol 1: Sexuality today: Trends and controversies.* Westport, CT: Praeger Publishers/Greenwood Publishing.

Baumeister, R. F., Ainsworth, S. E., & Vohs, K. D. (2015). Are groups more or less than the sum of their members? The moderating role of individual identification. *Behavioral and Brain Sciences.* Accessed at http://www.ncbi.nlm.nih.gov/pubmed/25936575.

Baumrind, D. (1971). Current patterns of parental authority. *Developmental Psychology, 4,* 1-104.

Baumrind, D. (2005). Patterns of parental authority and adolescent autonomy. *New Directions for Child and Adolescent Development, 108,* 61-69.

Baumrucker, S., Mingle, P., Harrington, D., Stolick, M., Carter, G. T., & Oertli, K. A. (2011). Medical marijuana and organ transplantation: Drug of abuse, or medical necessity? *American Journal of Hospice & Palliative Medicine, 28,* 130-134.

Bautista, D. M., Wilson, S. R., & Hoon, M. A. (2014). Why we scratch an itch: The molecules, cells and circuits of itch. *Nature Neuroscience, 17*(2), 175-182.

Bayliss, D. M., Jarrold, C., Baddeley, A. D., & Gunn, D. M. (2005). The relationship between short-term memory and working memory: Complex span made simple? *Memory, 13,* 414-421.

Bazalakova, M. H., Wright, J., Schneble, E. J., McDonald, M. P., Heilman, C. J., Levey, A. I., et al. (2007). Deficits in acetylcholine homeostasis, receptors and behaviors in choline transporter heterozygous mice. *Genes, Brain & Behavior, 6,* 411-424.

BBC. (2019). Opioid crisis: US drug overdose deaths drop by 5.1%. Retrieved from https://www.bbc.com/news/world-us-canada-49026223.

Beam, A. (2014, August 21). Four-bit recall. *Boston Globe,* p. 1.

Beam, C. R., & Turkheimer, E. (2013). Phenotype-environment correlations in longitudinal twin models. *Development and Psychopathology, 25,* 7-16.

Bearman, C. R., Ball, L. J., & Ormerod, T. C. (2007). The structure and function of spontaneous analogising in domain-based problem solving. *Thinking & Reasoning, 13,* 273-294.

Beauchamp, M. H., Vera-Estay, E., Morasse, F., Anderson, V., & Dooley, J. (2019). Moral reasoning and decision-making in adolescents who sustain traumatic brain injury. *Brain Injury, 33*(1), 32-39.

Beaudry, J. L., Lindsay, R. C. L., Leach, A., Mansour, J. K., Bertrand, M. I., & Kalmet, N. (2015). The effect of evidence type, identification accuracy, line-up presentation, and line-up administration on observers' perceptions of eyewitnesses. *Legal and Criminological Psychology, 20,* 343-364.

Bebermeier, S., Echterhoff, G., Bohner, G., & Hellmann, J. H. (2015). The generalization of shared reality: When communication about one target shapes evaluations of other targets. *European Journal of Social Psychology, 45*, 623-640.

Beck, A. P., & Lewis, C. M. (Eds.). (2000). *The process of group psychotherapy: Systems for analyzing change.* Washington, DC: American Psychological Association.

Beck, A. T. (1995). Cognitive therapy: Past, present, and future. In M. J. Mahoney (Ed.), *Cognitive and constructive psychotherapies: Theory, research, and practice.* New York: Springer.

Beck, A. T. (2004). Cognitive therapy, behavior therapy, psychoanalysis, and pharmacotherapy: A cognitive continuum. In A. Freeman, M. J. Mahoney, P. Devito, & D. Martin (Eds.), *Cognition and Psychotherapy* (2nd ed.). New York: Springer Publishing Co.

Beck, A. T., & Rector, N. A. (2005). Cognitive approaches to schizophrenia: Theory and therapy. *Annual Review of Clinical Psychology, 1*, 577-606.

Beck, A. T., Davis, D. D., & Freeman, A. (2015). *Cognitive therapy of personality disorders* (3rd ed.). New York: Guilford Press.

Beck, K., Javitt, D. C., & Howes, O. D. (2016). Targeting glutamate to treat schizophrenia: Lessons from recent clinical studies. *Psychopharmacology, 233*, 2425-2428.

Beck, M. (2015, June 2). Your body's witching hours. *Wall Street Journal*, pp. D1-D2.

Becker, J., Brackbill, D., & Centola, D. (2017). Network dynamics of social influence in the wisdom of crowds. *PNAS Proceedings of the National Academy of Sciences of the United States of America, 114*, 70-76.

Becker, T. (2003). Is emotional intelligence a viable concept? *Academy of Management Review, 28*, 192-195.

Beersma, D. G. M., & Gordijn, M. C. M. (2007). Circadian control of the sleep-wake cycle. *Physiology & Behavior, 90*.

Begeny, J. C., & Martens, B. K. (2007). Inclusionary education in Italy: A literature review and call for more empirical research. *Remedial and Special Education, 28*, 80-94.

Begg, D., & Langley, J. (2001). Changes in risky driving behavior from age 21 to 26 years. *Journal of Safety Research, 32*, 491-499.

Beghetto, R. A., & Kaufman, J. C. (Eds.). (2010). *Nurturing creativity in the classroom.* New York: Cambridge University Press.

Begley, S. (2019). The schizophrenic mind. Retrieved from http://www.sharonlbegley.com/the-schizophrenic-mind.

Behrendt, R. (2011). *Neuroanatomy of social behaviour: An evolutionary and psychoanalytic perspective.* London England: Karnac Books.

Behrens, M., Lendon, C., & Roe, C. (2009). A common biological mechanism in cancer and Alzheimer's disease? *Current Alzheimer Research, 6*, 196-204.

Beidel, D. C., & Turner, S. M. (2007). Etiology of social anxiety disorder. In D. C. Beidel & S. M. Turner (Eds.), *Shy children, phobic adults: Nature and treatment of social anxiety disorders* (2nd ed.). Washington, DC: American Psychological Association.

Beitel, M., Wald, L. M., Midgett, A., Green, D., Cecero, J. J., Kishon, R., & Barry, D. T. (2015). Humanistic experience and psychodynamic understanding: Empirical associations among facets of self-actualization and psychological mindedness. *Person-Centered and Experiential Psychotherapies, 14*, 137-148.

Belasen, A. T., & Fortunato, M. V. (2013). Situational motivation: Challenge the binary. In M. A. Paludi (Ed.), *Psychology for business success, Vol 1: Juggling, balancing, and integrating work and family roles and responsibilities, Vol 2: Institutional equity and compliance, Vol 3: Managing, leading, and developing employees, Vol 4: Implementing best practices in human resources.* Santa Barbara, CA: Praeger/ABC-CLIO.

Belluck, P. (2019, June 21). Lost wallet with cash will tempt its finder, often to return it full. *The New York Times*, p. 15.

Bem, D. (2012). ESP is not a psychological anomaly. *PsychCRITIQUES, 57*, 2012.

Ben-Porath, Y. S., Corey, D. M., & Tarescavage, A. M. (2017). Using the MMPI 2 RF in pre-employment evaluations of police officer candidates. In C. L. Mitchell & E. H. Dorian (Eds.), *Police psychology and its growing impact on modern law enforcement.* Hershey, PA: Information Science Reference/IGI Global.

Bench, S. W., Lench, H. C., Liew, J., Miner, K., & Flores, S. A. (2015). Gender gaps in overestimation of math performance. *Sex Roles, 72*, 536-546.

Benet-Martinez, V., Lee, F., & Leu, J. (2006). Biculturalism and cognitive complexity: Expertise in cultural representations. *Journal of Cross-Cultural Psychology, 37*, 386-407.

Benitez, P., de Carvalho Gomes, M. L., Bondioli, R., & Domeniconi, C. (2017). Mapping of inclusive strategies for students with intellectual disabilities and autism. *Psicologia Em Estudo, 22*, 81-93.

Benson, E. (2003, April). The science of sexual arousal. *Monitor on Psychology*, 50-56.

Bentwich, J., Dobronevsky, E., Aichenbaum, S., Shorer, R., Peretz, R., Khaigrekht, M., et al. (2011). Beneficial effect of repetitive transcranial magnetic stimulation combined with cognitive training for the treatment of Alzheimer's disease: A proof of concept study. *Journal of Neural Transmission, 118*, 463-471.

Beran, M. J., Smith, J., & Perdue, B. M. (2013). Language-trained chimpanzees (*Pan troglodytes*) name what they have seen but look first at what they have not seen. *Psychological Science, 24*, 660-666.

Berecki-Gisolf, J., McKenzie, S. J., Dobson, A. J., McFarlane, A., & McLaughlin, D. (2013). A history of comorbid depression and anxiety predicts new onset of heart disease. *Journal of Behavioral Medicine, 36*, 347-353.

Berends, Y. R., Tulen, J. H. M., Wierdsma, A. I., van Pelt, J., Kushner, S. A., & van Marle, H. J. C. (2019). Oxytocin, vasopressin and trust: Associations with aggressive behavior in healthy young males. *Physiology & Behavior, 204*, 180-185.

Berenson, A. (2019, January 5-6). Marijuana is more dangerous than you think. *Wall Street Journal*, p. 5.

Berger, I., Werdermann, M., Bornstein, S. R., & Steenblock, C. (2019). The adrenal gland in stress-adaptation on a cellular level. *The Journal of Steroid Biochemistry and Molecular Biology, 190*, 198-206.

Berk, L. E. (2005). Why parenting matters. In S. Olfman (Ed.), *Childhood lost: How American culture is failing our kids.* Westport, CT: Praeger Publishers/Greenwood Publishing Group.

Berke, D. S., Reidy, D. E., Miller, J. D., & Zeichner, A. (2017). Take it like a man: Gender-threatened men's experience of gender role discrepancy, emotion activation, and pain tolerance. *Psychology of Men & Masculinity, 18*, 62-69.

Berkman, L. F., Ertel, K. A., & Glymour, M. M. (2011). Aging and social intervention: Life course perspectives. In R. H. Binstock & L. K. George (Eds.), *Handbook of aging and the social sciences* (7th ed.). San Diego, CA: Elsevier Academic Press.

Berkowitz, L. (2001). On the formation and regulation of anger and aggression: A cognitive-neoassociationistic analysis. In W. G. Parrott (Ed.), *Emotions in social psychology: Essential readings.* New York: Psychology Press.

Bernard, L. L. (1924). *Instinct: A study in social psychology.* New York: Holt.

Bernstein, D., & Loftus, E. (2009a). How to tell if a particular memory is true or false. *Perspectives on Psychological Science, 4*, 370-374.

Bernstein, D., & Loftus, E. (2009b). The consequences of false memories for food preferences and choices. *Perspectives on Psychological Science, 4*, 135-139.

Bernstein, E. (2011, April 19). Friendly fight: A smarter way to say "I'm angry." *Wall Street Journal*, pp. D1, D4.

Berntsen, D., & Rubin, D. C. (2004). Cultural life scripts structure recall from autobiographical memory. *Memory and Cognition, 32*, 427-442.

Berridge, K. C. (2004). Motivation concepts in behavioral neuroscience. *Physiology and Behavior, 81*, 179-209.

Bertakis, K. (2009). The influence of gender on the doctor-patient interaction. *Patient Education and Counseling, 76*, 356-360.

Bertakis, K., Franks, P., & Epstein, R. (2009). Patient-centered communication in primary care: Physician and patient gender and gender concordance. *Journal of Women's Health, 18*, 539-545.

Bertelli, M. O., Bianco, A., Rossi, A., Mancini, M., La Malfa, G., & Brown, I. (2019). Impact of severe intellectual disability on proxy instrumental assessment of quality of life. *Journal of Intellectual and Developmental Disability, 44*(3), 272-281.

Berthoud, H. R. (2002). Multiple neural systems controlling food intake and body weight. *Neuroscience and Biobehavioral Reviews, 26*, 393-428.

Best, D. (2017). Why the mechanisms of 12-step behaviour change should matter to clinicians. *Addiction, 112*, 938-939.

Betley, J. N., Xu, S., Cao, Z. H., Gong, R., Magnus, C. J., Yu, Y., et al. (2015). Neurons for hunger and thirst transmit a negative-valence teaching signal. *Nature, 521*, 180-185.

Betterton, R. T., Broad, L. M., Tsaneva-Atanasova, K., & Mellor, J. R. (2017). Acetylcholine modulates gamma frequency oscillations in the hippocampus by activation of muscarinic M1 receptors. *European Journal of Neuroscience, 45*, 1570-1585.

Beyene, Y., Gilliss, C., & Lee, K. (2007). "I take the good with the bad, and I moisturize": Defying middle age in the new millennium. *Menopause, 14*, 734-741.

Bhar, S., Gelfand, L., Schmid, S., Gallop, R., DeRubeis, R., Hollon, S., et al. (2008). Sequence of improvement in depressive symptoms across cognitive therapy and pharmacotherapy. *Journal of Affective Disorders, 110*, 161-166.

Bhatia, S. (2017). The semantic representation of prejudice and stereotypes. *Cognition, 164*, 46-60.

Bhogal, M. S., Farrelly, D., & Galbraith, N. (2019). The role of prosocial behaviors in mate choice: A critical review of the literature. *Current Psychology: A Journal for Diverse Perspectives on Diverse Psychological Issues, 38*(4), 1062-1075.

Bialystok, E. (2011). Reshaping the mind: The benefits of bilingualism. *Canadian Journal of Experimental Psychology, 65*, 229-235.

Bialystok, E., & Craik, F. I. M. (2011). Cognitive and linguistic processing in the bilingual mind. *Current Directions in Psychological Science, 19*, 19-23.

Bialystok, E., Barac, R., Blaye, A., & Poulin-Dubois, D. (2010). Word mapping and executive functioning in young monolingual and bilingual children. *Journal of Cognition and Development, 11*, 485-508.

Bian, L., Leslie, S., & Cimpian, A. (2017). Gender stereotypes about intellectual ability emerge early and influence children's interests. *Science, 355*, 389-391.

Bieberstein, A., & Roosen, J. (2015). Gender differences in the meanings associated with food hazards: A means-end chain analysis. *Food Quality and Preference, 42*, 165-176.

Bienvenu, O. J., Davydow, D. S., & Kendler, K. S. (2011). Psychiatric "diseases" versus behavioral disorders and degree of genetic influence. *Psychological Medicine: A Journal of Research in Psychiatry and the Allied Sciences, 41*, 33-40.

Bigsby, E., Monahan, J. L., & Ewoldsen, D. R. (2017). An examination of adolescent recall of anti-smoking messages: Attitudes, message type, and message perceptions. *Health Communication, 32*, 409-419.

Billiard, M. (2008). Narcolepsy: Current treatment options and future approaches. *Neuropsychiatric Disease and Treatment, 4*, 557-566.

Binet, A., & Simon, T. (1916). *The development of intelligence in children (The Binet-Simon Scale).* Baltimore: Williams & Wilkins.

Bischoff, R. J., Springer, P. R., Felix, D. S., & Hollist, C. S. (2011). Finding the heart of medical family therapy: A content analysis of medical family therapy casebook articles. *Families, Systems, & Health, 29*, 184-196.

Bittles, A. H., Bower, C., & Hussain, R. (2007). The four ages of Down syndrome. *European Journal of Public Health, 17*, 121-225.

Bjork, R. A. (2015). Forgetting as a friend of learning. In D. S. Lindsay, A. P. Yonelinas, H. I. Roediger, D. S. Lindsay, A. P. Yonelinas, & H. I. Roediger (Eds.), *Remembering: Attributions, processes, and control in human memory: Essays in honor of Larry Jacoby.* New York: Psychology Press.

Bjorklund, D. F. (2018). A metatheory for cognitive development (or "Piaget is dead" revisited). *Child Development, 89*(6), 2288-2302.

Bjornsdottir, E., Keenan, B. T., Eysteinsdottir, B., Arnardottir, E. S., Janson, C., Gislason, T., et al. (2015). Quality of life among untreated sleep apnea patients compared with the general population and changes after treatment with positive airway pressure. *Journal of Sleep Research, 24*, 328-338.

Bjornstad, R. (2006). Learned helplessness, discouraged workers, and multiple unemployment equilibria. *Journal of Socio-Economics, 35*, 458-475.

Black, A. L., & McCafferty, D. (1998, July 3-5). The age of contentment. *USA Weekend*, 4-6.

Black, B. M., & Weisz, A. N. (2004). Dating violence: A qualitative analysis of Mexican American youths' views. *Journal of Ethnic and Cultural Diversity in Social Work, 13*, 69-90.

Blackmore, S. (2018, September). Decoding the puzzle of human consciousness. *Scientific American*, pp. 49-53.

Blackwell, L. S., Rodriguez, S., & Guerra-Carrillo, B. (2015). Intelligence as a malleable construct. In S. Goldstein, D. Princiotta, & J. A. Naglieri (Eds.), *Handbook of intelligence: Evolutionary theory, historical perspective, and current concepts.* New York: Springer Science + Business Media.

Blagrove, M., Edwards, C., van Rijn, E., Reid, A., Malinowski, J., Bennett, P., et al. (2019). Insight from the consideration of REM dreams, non-REM dreams, and daydreams. *Psychology of Consciousness: Theory, Research, and Practice, 6*(2), 138-162.

Blain-Arcaro, C., & Vaillancourt, T. (2019). Longitudinal associations between externalizing problems and symptoms of depression in children and adolescents. *Journal of Clinical Child & Adolescent Psychology, 48*(1), 108-119.

Blake, A. B., & Castel, A. D. (2019). Memory and availability-biased metacognitive illusions for flags of varying familiarity. *Memory & Cognition, 47*(2), 365-382.

Blakeslee, (1992, September 29). Radical brain surgery, the earlier the better, offers epileptics hope. *The New York Times*, p. C3.

Blanton, H., Jaccard, J., & Burrows, C. N. (2015). Implications of the Implicit Association Test D-transformation for psychological assessment. *Assessment, 22*, 429-440.

Blass, T. (1996). Attribution of responsibility and trust in the Milgram obedience experiment. *Journal of Applied Social Psychology, 26*, 1529-1535.

Blass, T. (2004). *The man who shocked the world: The life and legacy of Stanley Milgram.* New York: Basic Books.

Blass, T. (2009). From New Haven to Santa Clara: A historical perspective on the Milgram obedience experiments. *American Psychologist, 64*, 37-45.

Blatter, K., & Cajochen, C. (2007). Circadian rhythms in cognitive performance: Methodological constraints, protocols, theoretical underpinnings. *Physiology & Behavior, 90*, 196-208.

Blechner, M. J. (2013). New ways of conceptualizing and working with dreams. *Contemporary Psychoanalysis, 49*, 259-275.

Bloom, P. N., McBride, C. M., & Pollak, K. I. (2006). Recruiting teen smokers in shopping malls to a smoking-cessation program using the foot-in-the-door technique. *Journal of Applied Social Psychology, 36*, 1129-1144.

Blum, D. (2002). *Love at goon park: Harry Harlow and the science of affection.* Cambridge, MA: Perseus.

Blum, H. P. (2011). To what extent do you privilege dream interpretation in relation to other forms of mental representations? *International Journal of Psychoanalysis, 92*, 275-277.

Blumen, H. M., Rajaram, S., & Henkel, L. (2013). The applied value of collaborative memory research in aging: Considerations for broadening the scope. *Journal of Applied Research in Memory and Cognition, 2*, 133-135.

Blumenthal, H., Leen-Feldner, E. W., Babson, K. A., Gahr, J. L., Trainor, C. D., & Frala, J. L. (2011). Elevated social anxiety among early maturing girls. *Developmental Psychology, 47*, 1133-1140.

Boag, S. (2015). Repression, defence, and the psychology of science. In S. Boag, L. W. Brakel, & V. Talvitie (Eds.), *Philosophy, science, and psychoanalysis: A critical meeting.* London: Karnac Books.

Boag, S. (2017). On dreams and motivation: Comparison of Freud's and Hobson's views. *Frontiers in Psychology, 7*, 1-13.

Boag, S., Brakel, L. W., & Talvitie, V. (2015). *Philosophy, science, and psychoanalysis: A critical meeting.* London, England: Karnac Books.

Boake, C. (2008). Clinical neuropsychology. *Professional Psychology: Research and Practice, 39*, 234-239.

Boarini, R., Laslier, J., & Robin, S. (2009). Interpersonal comparisons of utility in bargaining: Evidence from a transcontinental ultimatum game. *Theory and Decision, 67*, 341-373.

Bode, C., de Ridder, D. T., Kuijer, R. G., & Bensing, J. M. (2007). Effects of an intervention promoting proactive coping competencies in middle and late adulthood. *Gerontologist, 47*, 42-51.

Boden, J. M., Fergusson, D. M., & Horwood, L. J. (2007). Anxiety disorders and suicidal behaviours in adolescence and young adulthood: Findings from a longitudinal study. *Psychological Medicine, 37,* 431-440.

Boeve-de Pauw, J., Donche, V., & Van Petegem, P. (2011). Adolescents' environmental worldview and personality: An explorative study. *Journal of Environmental Psychology, 31,* 109-117.

Bogaert, A. F., Visser, B. A., & Pozzebon, J. A. (2015). Gender differences in object of desire self-consciousness sexual fantasies. *Archives of Sexual Behavior, 44*(8), 2299-2310.

Bohn, C., Aderka, I. M., Schreiber, F., Stangier, U., & Hofmann, S. G. (2013). Sudden gains in cognitive therapy and interpersonal therapy for social anxiety disorder. *Journal of Consulting and Clinical Psychology, 81,* 177-182.

Bolkan, S. (2015). Intellectually stimulating students' intrinsic motivation: The mediating influence of affective learning and student engagement. *Communication Reports, 28,* 80-91.

Boller, F. (2004). Rational basis of rehabilitation following cerebral lesions: A review of the concept of cerebral plasticity. *Functional Neurology: New Trends in Adaptive and Behavioral Disorders, 19,* 65-72.

Bonanno, G. A. (2004). Loss, trauma, and human resilience: Have we underestimated the human capacity to thrive after extremely aversive events? *American Psychologist, 59,* 20-28.

Bonini, L. (2017). The extended mirror neuron network: Anatomy, origin, and functions. *The Neuroscientist, 23,* 56-67.

Bonta, B., D. (1997). Cooperation and competition in peaceful societies. *Psychological Bulletin, 121,* 299-320.

Borgmann-Winter, K. E., Wang, K., Bandyopadhyay, S., Torshizi, A. D., Blair, I. A., & Hahn, C.-G. (2019). The proteome and its dynamics: A missing piece for integrative multi-omics in schizophrenia. *Schizophrenia Research.* https://doi.org/10.1016/j.schres.2019.07.025.

Bornstein, M. H., & Lansford, J. E. (2019). Culture and family functioning. In B. H. Fiese, M. Celano, K. Deater-Deckard, E. N. Jouriles, & M. A. Whisman (Eds.), *APA handbook of contemporary family psychology: Applications and broad impact of family psychology., Vol. 2.* (pp. 417-436). Washington, DC: American Psychological Association.

Bornstein, R. F. (2003). Psychodynamic models of personality. In T. Millon & M. J. Lerner (Eds.), *Handbook of psychology: Personality and social psychology* (Vol. 5). New York: Wiley.

Boroditsky, L. (2010, July 24-25). Lost in translation. *Wall Street Journal,* p. W3.

Boser, U. (2017). *Learn better: Mastering the skills for success in life, business, and school, or, how to become an expert in just about anything.* Emmaus, PA: Rodale Books.

Bosquet Enlow, M., Petty, C. R., Svelnys, C., Gusman, M., Huezo, M., Malin, A., et al. (2019). Differential effects of stress exposures, caregiving quality, and temperament in early life on working memory versus inhibitory control in preschool-aged children. *Developmental Neuropsychology, 44*(4), 339-356.

Bossarte, R. M., & Swahn, M. H. (2011). The associations between early alcohol use and suicide attempts among adolescents with a history of major depression. *Addictive Behaviors, 36.*

Bosson, J. K., & Vandello, J. A. (2011). Precarious manhood and its links to action and aggression. *Current Directions in Psychological Science, 20,* 82-86.

Bouchard, T. J., Jr. (2004). Genetic influence on human psychological traits: A survey. *Current Directions in Psychological Science, 13,* 148-151.

Bouchard, T. J., Jr., Segal, N. L., Tellegen, A., McGue, M., Keyes, M., & Krueger, R. (2004). Genetic influence on social attitudes: Another challenge to psychology from behavior genetics. In L. F. DiLalla (Ed.), *Behavior genetics principles: Perspectives in development, personality, and psychopathology.* Washington, DC: American Psychological Association.

Bourne, L. E., Dominowski, R. L., Loftus, E. F., & Healy, A. F. (1986). *Cognitive processes* (2nd ed.). Englewood Cliffs, NJ: Prentice Hall.

Bouton, M. E., Todd, T. P., Vurbic, D., & Winterbauer, N. E. (2011). Renewal after the extinction of free operant behavior. *Learning & Behavior, 39,* 57-67.

Bouvard, M., & Roulin, J. (2017). Exploratory factor analysis of the French version of the Big Five Questionnaire for Children (BFQ-C). *Swiss Journal of Psychology, 76,* 125-130.

Bouvard, M., Fournet, N., Denis, A., Sixdenier, A., & Clark, D. (2017). Intrusive thoughts in patients with obsessive compulsive disorder and non-clinical participants: A comparison using the International Intrusive Thought Interview Schedule. *Cognitive Behaviour Therapy, 46,* 287-299.

Boxer, P., Huesmann, L., Bushman, B., O'Brien, M., & Moceri, D. (2009). The role of violent media preference in cumulative developmental risk for violence and general aggression. *Journal of Youth and Adolescence, 38,* 417-428.

Boyd-Wilson, B. M., McClure, J., & Walkey, E. H. (2004). Are well-being and illusory perceptions linked? The answer may be yes, but. . . . *Australian Journal of Psychology, 56,* 1-9.

Boylan, J. M., & Ryff, C. D. (2015). Psychological well-being and metabolic syndrome: Findings from the Midlife in the United States national sample. *Psychosomatic Medicine, 77,* 548-558.

Boyle, G. J. (2019). Overarching personality paradigm: A neo-Cattellian psychometric model. *Personality and Individual Differences, 147,* 317-325.

Boyle, G. J., Goldman, R., Svoboda, J. S., & Fernandez, E. (2002). Male circumcision: Pain, trauma and psychosexual sequelae. *Journal of Health Psychology, 7,* 329-343.

Boyle, S. H., Williams, R. B., Mark, D. B., Brummett, B. H., Siegler, I. C., & Barefoot, J. C. (2005). Hostility, age, and mortality in a sample of cardiac patients. *American Journal of Cardiology, 96,* 64-72.

Braasch, M., Buchwald, P., & Hobfoll, S. (2019). Commerce and crossover of resources in Facebook groups—A qualitative study. *Computers in Human Behavior, 99,* 101-108.

Bradford, A. C., & Bradford, W. D. (2017). Factors driving the diffusion of medical marijuana legalisation in the United States. *Drugs: Education, Prevention & Policy, 24,* 75-84.

Bradshaw, A. (2019). Temperature and civil conflict. *Nature Human Behaviour, 3*(6), 548-548.

Brafman, A. H. (2011). *Fostering independence: Helping and caring in psychodynamic therapies.* London: Karnac Books.

Brailey, C. D., & Slatton, B. C. (2019). Women, work, and inequality in the US: Revising the second shift. *Journal of Sociology, 7*(1), 29-35.

Brambilla, P., Cipriani, A., Hotopf, M., & Barbui, C. (2005). Side-effect profile of fluoxetine in comparison with other SSRIs, tricyclic and newer antidepressants: A meta-analysis of clinical trial data. *Pharmacopsychiatry, 38,* 69-77.

Brandao, T., Tavares, R., Schulz, M. S., & Matos, P. M. (2015). Measuring emotion regulation and emotional expression in breast cancer patients: A systematic review. *Clinical Psychology Review, 43,* 114-127.

Brandon, M., & Saffran, J. R. (2011). Apparent motion enhances visual rhythm discrimination in infancy. *Attention, Perception, & Psychophysics, 73,* 1016-1020.

Brandwatch. (2019, June 1). 53 incredible Facebook statistics and facts. Downloaded from https://www.brandwatch.com/blog/facebook-statistics/.

Brang, D., Rouw, R., Ramachandran, V. S., & Coulson, S. (2011). Similarly shaped letters evoke similar colors in grapheme-color synesthesia. *Neuropsychologia, 49,* 1355-1358.

Brant, A. M., Munakata, Y., Boomsma, D. I., DeFries, J. C., Haworth, C. A., Keller, M. C., et al. (2013). The nature and nurture of high IQ: An extended sensitive period for intellectual development. *Psychological Science, 24,* 1487-1495.

Brasic, J. R. (2002). Conversion disorder in childhood. *German Journal of Psychiatry, 5,* 54-61.

Brausch, A. M., & Gutierrez, P. M. (2009). Differences in non-suicidal self-injury and suicide attempts in adolescents. *Journal of Youth and Adolescence, 21,* 46-51.

Brazelton, T. B. (1969). *Infants and mothers: Differences in development.* New York: Dell.

Breland, K., & Breland, M. (1966). *Animal behavior.* New York: Macmillan.

Brennan, P. (2011). Pheromones: Fact or fantasy? *Ethology, 117,* 265-266.

Breslin, C. W., & Safer, M. A. (2011). Effects of event valence on long-term memory for two baseball championship games. *Psychological Science, 20,* 1-5.

Brewer, M. B. (2007). The social psychology of intergroup relations: Social categorization, ingroup bias, and outgroup prejudice. In A. W. Kruglanski & E. Higgins (Eds.), *Social psychology: Handbook of basic principles* (2nd ed.). New York: Guilford Press.

Bridgman, T., Cummings, S., & Ballard, J. (2019). Who built Maslow's pyramid? A history of the creation of management studies' most famous symbol and its implications for management education. *Academy of Management Learning & Education, 18.*

Brody, J. (2008, May 20). Trying to break nicotine's grip. *The New York Times,* p. E9.

Brody, J. (2019, April 30). Virtual reality as therapy for pain. *The New York Times,* p. D7.

Brody, S., & Costa, R. M. (2017). Vaginal orgasm is associated with indices of women's better psychological, intimate relationship, and psychophysiological function. *Canadian Journal of Human Sexuality, 26,* 1-4.

Brody, S., & Weiss, P. (2015). Erectile dysfunction and premature ejaculation: Interrelationships and psychosexual factors. *Journal of Sexual Medicine, 12,* 398-404.

Broeders, R., van den Bos, K., Müller, P. A., & Ham, J. (2011). Should I save or should I not kill? How people solve moral dilemmas depends on which rule is most accessible. *Journal of Experimental Social Psychology, 47,* 923-934.

Bronson, P., & Merryman, A. (2009). *NurtureShock.* New York: Twelve.

Bronstein, M. V., Pennycook, G., Bear, A., Rand, D. G., & Cannon, T. D. (2019). Belief in fake news is associated with delusionality, dogmatism, religious fundamentalism, and reduced analytic thinking. *Journal of Applied Research in Memory and Cognition, 8(1),* 108-117.

Broockman, D., & Kalla, J. (2016). Durably reducing transphobia: A field experiment on door-to-door canvassing. *Science, 352,* 220-224.

Brown, E. (2001, September 17). The World Health Organization takes on big tobacco (but don't hold your breath): Anti-smoking advocates are mounting a global campaign: It's going to be a long, hard fight. *Forbes,* pp. 37-41.

Brown, M. W., & Banks, P. J. (2015). In search of a recognition memory engram. *Neuroscience and Biobehavioral Reviews, 50,* 12-28.

Brown, M., Chodzen, G., Mihelicova, M., & Collins, K. (2017). Applying a time-patterned typology of homelessness among individuals with mental illness. *American Journal of Community Psychology, 59,* 306-315.

Brown, P. (1986). Simbu aggression and the drive to win. *Anthropolitical Quarterly, 59,* 165-170.

Brown, P. K., & Wald, G. (1964). Visual pigments in single rod and cones of the human retina. *Science, 144,* 45-52.

Brown, R. (1958). How shall a thing be called? *Psychological Review, 65,* 14-21.

Brown, R. D., Goldstein, E., & Bjorklund, D. F. (2000). The history and zeitgeist of the repressed-false-memory debate: Scientific and sociological perspectives on suggestibility and childhood memory. In D. F. Bjorklund (Ed.), *False-memory creation in children and adults: Theory, research, and implications.* Mahwah, NJ: Lawrence Erlbaum.

Brown, R. J. (2006). Different types of "dissociation" have different psychological mechanisms. *Journal of Trauma Dissociation, 6,* 7-28.

Brown, S., Martinez, M. J., & Parsons, L. M. (2006). Music and language side by side in the brain: A PET study of the generation of melodies and sentences. *Journal of Neuroscience, 23,* 2791-2803.

Brown-Chidsey, R., & Andren, K. J. (Eds.). (2015). *Assessment for intervention, second edition: A problem-solving approach,* New York: Guilford Press.

Browne, J., Penn, D. L., Meyer-Kalos, P. S., Mueser, K. T., Estroff, S. E., Brunette, M. F., et al. (2017). Psychological well-being and mental health recovery in the NIMH RAISE early treatment program. *Schizophrenia Research, 185,* 167-172.

Brownlee, J. (2019). Cognitive shortcuts and public support for intervention. *Journal of Conflict Resolution.* Advance online publication https://doi.org/10.1177/0022002719854210.

Brucker, B., Ehlis, A., Häußinger, F. B., Fallgatter, A. J., & Gerjets, P. (2015). Watching corresponding gestures facilitates learning with animations by activating human mirror-neurons: An fNIRS study. *Learning and Instruction, 36,* 27-37.

Bruehl, S., Burns, J. W., Gupta, R., Buvanendran, A., Chont, M., Orlowska, D., et al. (2017). Do resting plasma β-endorphin levels predict responses to opioid analgesics? *Clinical Journal of Pain, 33,* 12-20.

Bruggeman, H., Yonas, A., & Konczak, J. (2007). The processing of linear perspective and binocular information for action and perception. *Neuropsychologia, 45,* 1420-1426.

Bruni, L., Pelligra, V., Reggiani, T., & Rizzolli, M. (2019). The pied piper: Prizes, incentives, and motivation crowding-in. *Journal of Business Ethics,* 1-16.

Bruno, A., Celebre, L., Torre, G., Pandolfo, G., Mento, C., Cedro, C., et al. (2019). Focus on disruptive mood dysregulation disorder: A review of the literature. *Psychiatry Research, 279,* 323-330.

Bruno, D. (2016, November 23). An electric shock therapy stops self-harm among the autistic, but at what cost? *Washington Post Magazine.* Accessed from https://www.washingtonpost.com/lifestyle/magazine/an-electric-shock-therapy-stops-self-harm-among-the-autistic-but-at-what-cost/2016/11/21/b9b06c44-8f2c-11e6-9c85-ac42097b8cc0_story.html?utm_term=.1b9a9a3266b4.

Bruton, A. M., Shearer, D. A., & Mellalieu, S. D. (2019). Who said "there is no 'I' in team"? The effects of observational learning content level on efficacy beliefs in groups. *Psychology of Sport and Exercise, 45,* 101563.

Bryant, R. M., Coker, A. D., Durodoye, B. A., McCollum, V. J., Pack-Brown, S. P., Constantine, M. G., & O'Bryant, B. J. (2005). Having our say: African American women, diversity, and counseling. *Journal of Counseling and Development, 83,* 313-319.

Bub, K. L., Buckhalt, J. A., & El-Sheikh, M. (2011). Children's sleep and cognitive performance: A cross-domain analysis of change over time. *Developmental Psychology, 47(6),* 1504-1514.

Buchanan, T., & Selmon, N. (2008). Race and gender differences in self-efficacy: Assessing the role of gender role attitudes and family background. *Sex Roles, 58,* 822-836.

Buchert, R., Thomasius, R., Wilke, F., Petersen, K., Nebeling, B., Obrocki, J., et al. (2004). A voxel-based PET investigation of the long-term effects of "ecstasy" consumption on brain serotonin transporters. *American Journal of Psychiatry, 161,* 1181-1189.

Buckner, J. D., & Shah, S. M. (2015). Fitting in and feeling fine: Conformity and coping motives differentially mediate the relationship between social anxiety and drinking problems for men and women. *Addiction Research & Theory, 23,* 231-237.

Budenz, A., Purtle, J., Klassen, A., Yom-Tov, E., Yudell, M., & Massey, P. (2018). The case of a mass shooting and violence-related mental illness stigma on twitter. *Stigma and Health.* https://doi-org.silk.library.umass.edu/10.1037/sah0000155.

Buerkle, C. (2011). Masters of their domain: Seinfeld and the discipline of mediated men's sexual economy. In E. Watson & M. E. Shaw (Eds.), *Performing American masculinities: The 21st-century man in popular culture.* Bloomington, IN: Indiana University Press.

Buggio, L., Facchin, F., Chiappa, L., Barbara, G., Brambilla, M., & Vercellini, P. (2019). Psychosexual consequences of female genital mutilation and the impact of reconstructive surgery: A narrative review. *Health Equity, 3(1),* 36-46.

Buhrmester, M., Kwang, T., & Gosling, S. D. (2011). Amazon's Mechanical Turk: A new source of inexpensive, yet high-quality, data? *Perspectives on Psychological Science, 6,* 3-5.

Bulf, H., Johnson, S. P., & Valenza, E. (2011). Visual statistical learning in the newborn infant. *Cognition, 121,* 127-132.

Bunce, J. A. (2015). Incorporating ecology and social system into formal hypotheses to guide field studies of color vision in primates. *American Journal of Primatology, 77,* 516-526.

Buon, M., Habib, M., & Frey, D. (2017). Moral development: Conflicts and compromises. In J. A. Sommerville & J. Decety (Eds.), *Social cognition: Development across the life span.* New York: Routledge/Taylor & Francis Group.

Burbach, M. E., Matkin, G. S., & Fritz, S. M. (2004). Teaching critical thinking in an introductory leadership course utilizing active learning strategies: A confirmatory study. *College Student Journal, 38,* 482-493.

Burchinal, M. R., Roberts, J. E., & Riggins, R., Jr. (2000). Relating quality of center-based child care to early cognitive and language development longitudinally. *Child Development, 71,* 338-357.

Bureau of Labor Statistics, U.S. Department of Labor. (2017, March 8). Women's median earnings 82 percent of men's in 2016. *The Economics Daily.* Accessed at https://www.bls.gov/opub/ted/2017/womens-median-earnings-82-percent-of-mens-in-2016.htm.

Bureau, J., Martin, J., Yurkowski, K., Schmiedel, S., Quan, J., Moss, E., et al. (2017). Correlates of child-father and child-mother attachment in the preschool years. *Attachment & Human Development, 19,* 130-150.

Burger, J. M. (2009). Replicating Milgram: Would people still obey today? *American Psychologist, 64,* 1-11.

Burland, J. P., Lepley, A. S., Cormier, M., DiStefano, L. J., Arciero, R., & Lepley, L. K. (2019). Learned helplessness after anterior cruciate ligament reconstruction: An altered neuro-cognitive state? *Sports Medicine, 49*(5), 647-657.

Burns, G. W. (2017). *101 stories for enhancing happiness and well-being: Using metaphors in positive psychology and therapy.* New York: Routledge/Taylor & Francis Group.

Burns, N. R., Bryan, J., & Nettelbeck, T. (2006). Ginkgo biloba: No robust effect on cognitive abilities or mood in healthy young or older adults. *Human Psychopharmacology: Clinical and Experimental, 21,* 27-37.

Burri, A., Spector, T., & Qazi, R. (2015). Common genetic factors among sexual orientation, gender nonconformity, and number of sex partners in female twins: Implications for the evolution of homosexuality. *Journal of Sexual Medicine, 12,* 1004-1011.

Burt, S. A., Plaisance, K. S., & Hambrick, D. Z. (2019). Understanding "what could be": A call for "experimental behavioral genetics." *Behavior Genetics, 49*(2), 235-243.

Burton, L., Bensimon, E., Allimant, J., Kinsman, R., Levin, A., Kovacs, L., et al. (2013). Relationship of prosody perception to personality and aggression. *Current Psychology: A Journal for Diverse Perspectives on Diverse Psychological Issues, 32,* 275-280.

Buscemi, V., Chang, W.-J., Liston, M. B., McAuley, J. H., & Schabrun, S. M. (2019). The role of perceived stress and life stressors in the development of chronic musculoskeletal pain disorders: A systematic review. *The Journal of Pain.* https://doi.org/10.1016/j.jpain.2019.02.008.

Busch, A. J., Morey, L. C., & Hopwood, C. J. (2017). Exploring the assessment of the DSM-5 alternative model for personality disorders with the personality assessment inventory. *Journal of Personality Assessment, 99,* 211-218.

Bush, J. (2008). Viability of virtual reality exposure therapy as a treatment alternative. *Computers in Human Behavior, 24,* 1032-1040.

Buss, A. H. (2011). *Pathways to individuality: Evolution and development of personality traits.* Washington, DC: American Psychological Association.

Buss, D. (2003). *Evolutionary psychology.* Boston: Allyn & Bacon.

Buss, D. M. (2001). Human nature and culture: An evolutionary psychological perspective. *Journal of Personality, 69,* 955-978.

Buss, D. M., Abbott, M., & Angleitner, A. (1990). International preferences in selecting mates: A study of 37 cultures. *Journal of Cross-Cultural Psychology, 21,* 5-47.

Bustillo, J. R., Jones, T., Chen, H., Lemke, N., Abbott, C., Qualls, C., et al. (2017). Glutamatergic and neuronal dysfunction in gray and white matter: A spectroscopic imaging study in a large schizophrenia sample. *Schizophrenia Bulletin, 43,* 611-619.

Butcher, J. N. (2011). *A beginner's guide to the MMPI-2* (3rd ed.). Washington, DC: American Psychological Association.

Butler, L. T., & Berry, D. C. (2004). Understanding the relationship between repetition priming and mere exposure. *British Journal of Psychology, 95,* 467-487.

Buysse, D. J., Germain, A., Moul, D. E., Franzen, P. L., Brar, L. K., Fletcher, M. E., et al. (2011). Efficacy of brief behavioral treatment for chronic insomnia in older adults. *Archives of Internal Medicine, 171,* 887-895.

Buzi, R., Weinman, M., & Smith, P. (2007). The relationship between adolescent depression and a history of sexual abuse. *Adolescence, 42*(168), 679-688.

Bylund, E., & Athanasopoulos, P. (2017). The Whorfian time warp: Representing duration through the language hourglass. *Journal of Experimental Psychology: General, 146,* 911-916.

Byrne, B. M., & Watkins, D. (2003). The issue of measurement invariance revisited. *Journal of Cross-Cultural Psychology, 34,* 155-175.

Cabioglu, M., Ergene, N., & Tan, Ü. (2007). Smoking cessation after acupuncture treatment. *International Journal of Neuroscience, 117,* 571-578.

Cacioppo, J. T., & Decety, J. (2009). What are the brain mechanisms on which psychological processes are based? *Perspectives on Psychological Science, 4,* 10-18.

Cadenhead, K., & Braff, D. L. (1995). Neurophysiology of schizophrenia: Attention, information processing, and inhibitory processes in schizophrenia. In J. A. Den Boer, H. G. M. Westenberg, & H. M. van Praag (Eds.), *Advances in the neurobiology of schizophrenia.* Oxford, England: John Wiley & Sons.

Caelian, C. F. (2006). The role of perfectionism and stress in the suicidal behaviour of depressed adolescents. *Dissertation Abstracts International: Section B: The Sciences and Engineering, 66*(12-B), 6915.

Callahan, M. P., & Zukowski, K. T. (2019). Reactions to transgender women and men in public restrooms: Correlates and gender

differences. *Journal of Homosexuality, 66*(1), 117-138.

Calvert, S. L., Appelbaum, M., Dodge, K. A., Graham, S., Nagayama Hall, G. C., Hamby, S., et al. (2017). The American Psychological Association Task Force assessment of violent video games: Science in the service of public interest. *American Psychologist, 72,* 126-143.

Cameron, C. D., Spring, V. L., & Todd, A. R. (2017). The empathy impulse: A multinomial model of intentional and unintentional empathy for pain. *Emotion, 17,* 395-411.

Cameron, O. G. (2002). *Visceral sensory neuroscience: Interoception.* London: Oxford University Press.

Campagnoli, C., & Domini, F. (2019). Does depth-cue combination yield identical biases in perception and grasping? *Journal of Experimental Psychology: Human Perception and Performance, 45*(5), 659-680.

Campbell, R. (2008). The psychological impact of rape victims. *American Psychologist, 63,* 702-717.

Campos, R. C. (2011). "It might be what I am": Looking at the use of Rorschach in psychological assessment. *Journal of Projective Psychology & Mental Health, 18,* 28-38.

Cannas Aghedu, F., Veneziani, C. A., Manari, T., Feybesse, C., & Bisiacchi, P. S. (2019). Assessing passionate love: Italian validation of the PLS (reduced version). *Sexual and Relationship Therapy,* 1-12.

Cannon, W. B. (1929). Organization for physiological homeostatics. *Physiological Review, 9,* 280-289.

Cantarero, K., Gamian-Wilk, M., & Dolinski, D. (2017). Being inconsistent and compliant: The moderating role of the preference for consistency in the door-in-the-face technique. *Personality and Individual Differences, 115,* 54-57.

Canton, M., Gall, D. L., Feillet, F., Bonnemains, C., & Roy, A. (2019). Neuropsychological profile of children with early and continuously treated phenylketonuria: Systematic review and future approaches. *Journal of the International Neuropsychological Society, 25*(6), 624-643.

Cantor, D., Fisher, B., Chibnall, S., Harps, S., Townsend, R., Thomas, G., et al. (2019, October 15). Report on the AAU campus climate survey on sexual assault and misconduct. Washington, DC: Association of American Universities.

Cao, R., Nosofsky, R. M., & Shiffrin, R. M. (2017). The development of automaticity in short-term memory search: Item-response learning and category learning. *Journal of Experimental Psychology: Learning, Memory, and Cognition, 43,* 669-679.

Capraro, V., & Sippel, J. (2017). Gender differences in moral judgment and the evaluation of gender-specified moral agents. *Cognitive Processing, 18*(4), 399-405.

Caputi, T. L., & McLellan, A. T. (2017). Truth and DARE: Is DARE's new Keepin' It REAL curriculum suitable for American nationwide implementation? *Drugs: Education, Prevention & Policy, 24*(1), 49-57.

Carbon, C., & Ditye, T. (2011). Sustained effects of adaptation on the perception of familiar faces. *Journal of Experimental Psychology: Human Perception and Performance, 37,* 615-625.

Carcea, I., & Froemke, R. C. (2019). Biological mechanisms for observational learning. *Current Opinion in Neurobiology, 54,* 178-185.

Carciofo, R., Song, N., Du, F., Wang, M. M., & Zhang, K. (2017). Metacognitive beliefs mediate the relationship between mind wandering and negative affect. *Personality and Individual Differences, 107,* 78-87.

Card, N. A. (2017). Developmental methodology: I. Developmental methodology as a central subdiscipline of developmental science. *Monographs of the Society for Research in Child Development, 82,* 7-12.

Cardemil, E. V., Pinedo, T. M., & Miller, I. W. (2005). Developing a culturally appropriate depression prevention program: The family coping skills program. *Cultural Diversity and Ethnic Minority Psychology, 11,* 99-112.

Carey, B. (2015, October 20). New approach may alleviate schizophrenia. *The New York Times,* p. A1.

Carey, B. (2016, May 30). After thriving in combat tours, veterans are struggling at home. *The New York Times,* pp. A1, A3.

Carhart-Harris, R. (2007). Speed > Ecstasy > Ritalin: The science of amphetamines. *Journal of Psychopharmacology, 21,* 225.

Carleton, R. N., Duranceau, S., Freeston, M. H., Boelen, P. A., McCabe, R. E., & Antony, M. M. (2014). "But it might be a heart attack": Intolerance of uncertainty and panic disorder symptoms. *Journal of Anxiety Disorders, 28,* 463-470.

Carlstedt, R. A. (2017). Sports performance. In G. R. Elkins, G. R. Elkins (Eds.), *Handbook of medical and psychological hypnosis: Foundations, applications, and professional issues.* New York: Springer Publishing Co.

Carmichael, S. L., Ma, C., Feldkamp, M. L., Shaw, G. M., & National Birth Defects Prevention Study. (2019). Comparing usual dietary intakes among subgroups of mothers in the year before pregnancy. *Public Health Reports, 134*(2), 155-163.

Carnagey, N., Anderson, C. A., & Bushman, B. J. (2007). The effect of video game violence on physiological desensitization to real-life violence. *Journal of Experimental Social Psychology, 43,* 489-496.

Carnagey, N., Anderson, C., & Bartholow, B. (2007). Media violence and social neuroscience: New questions and new opportunities. *Current Directions in Psychological Science, 16,* 178-182.

Carnevale, M., Luna, D., & Lerman, D. (2017). Brand linguistics: A theory-driven framework for the study of language in branding.

International Journal of Research in Marketing, 34(2), 572-591.

Carpenter, S. (2002). What can resolve the paradox of mental health disparities? *APA Monitor, 33,* 18.

Carpenter, S. M., & Niedenthal, P. M. (2019). Disrupting facial action increases risk taking. *Emotion.* http://dx.doi.org/10.1037/emo0000597.

Carr, C. M., Wolchik, S. A., Tein, J. Y., & Sandler, I. (2019). Mother-adolescent and father-adolescent relationships after divorce: Relations with emerging adults' romantic attachment. *Journal of Divorce & Remarriage, 60*(3), 194-210.

Carr, P., & Steele, C. (2009). Stereotype threat and inflexible perseverance in problem solving. *Journal of Experimental Social Psychology, 45,* 853-859.

Carr, T. (2019, June). Real pain relief, now! *Consumer Reports,* 24-33.

Carrillo, M., Ricci, L., Coppersmith, G., & Melloni, R. (2009). The effect of increased serotonergic neurotransmission on aggression: A critical meta-analytical review of preclinical studies. *Psychopharmacology, 205,* 349-368.

Carroll, D. W. (2017). The ethics of memory research. *PsycCRITIQUES, 62,* 15-22.

Cartwright, R., Agargum, M. Y., & Kirkby, J. (2006). Relation of dreams to waking concerns. *Psychiatry Research, 141,* 261-270.

Caruso, E. (2008). Use of experienced retrieval ease in self and social judgments. *Journal of Experimental Social Psychology, 44,* 148-155.

Carvalho, J., & Nobre, P. (2011). Biopsychosocial determinants of men's sexual desire: Testing an integrative model. *Journal of Sexual Medicine, 8,* 754-763.

Carver, C., & Scheier, M. (2002). Coping processes and adjustment to chronic illness. In A. Christensen & M. Antoni (Eds.), *Chronic physical disorders: Behavioral medicine's perspective.* Malden, MA: Blackwell Publishers.

Casad, B. J. (2007). Gender stereotype violation among job applicants: An examination of theory and measurement. *Dissertation Abstracts International: Section B: The Sciences and Engineering, 67*(7-B), 4154.

Casasola, M. (2011). Infant spatial categorization from an information processing approach. In L. M. Oakes, C. H. Cashon, M. Casasola, & D. H. Rakison (Eds.), *Infant perception and cognition: Recent advances, emerging theories, and future directions.* New York: Oxford University Press.

Cassells, J. V. S. (2007). The virtuous roles of truth and justice in integral dialogue: Research, theory, and model practice of the evolution of collective consciousness. *Dissertation Abstracts International Section A: Humanities and Social Sciences, 67*(10-A), 4005.

Cassino, D., & Besen, C. Y. (2019). Race, threat, and workplace sexual harassment: The dynamics of harassment in the United States, 1997-2016. *Gender, Work and Organization.* https://doi.org/10.1111/gwao.12394.

Catalano, S. M. (2006, September). Criminal victimization, 2005. *Bureau of Justice Statistics Bulletin.* Washington, DC: Bureau of Justice Statistics.

Catmur, C., & Heyes, C. (2019). Mirroring "meaningful" actions: Sensorimotor learning modulates imitation of goal-directed actions. *The Quarterly Journal of Experimental Psychology, 72*(2), 322-334.

Catrysse, L., Gijbels, D., & Donche, V. (2019). A systematic review on the conceptualization and operationalization of students' levels of processing in functional magnetic resonance imaging studies. *Mind, Brain, and Education, 13*(3), 198-210.

Cattell, R. B., Cattell, A. K., & Cattell, H. E. P. (2000). *The sixteen personality factor™ (16PF ®) questionnaire.* Champaign, IL: Institute for Personality and Ability Testing.

Cauce, A. M. (2007). Bringing community psychology home: The leadership, community and values initiative. *American Journal of Community Psychology, 39,* 1-11.

Cavallini, E., Pagnin, A., & Vecchi, T. (2003). Aging and everyday memory: The beneficial effect of memory training. *Archives of Gerontology & Geriatrics, 37,* 241-257.

Cecchini, M. P., Knaapila, A., Hoffmann, E., Boschi, F., Hummel, T., & Iannilli, E. (2019). A cross-cultural survey of umami familiarity in European countries. *Food Quality and Preference, 74,* 172-178.

Celi, L.A.G., Fraser, H.S.F., Nikore, V., Osorio, J.S., & Paik, K. (2017). *Global health informatics: Principles of eHealth and mHealth to improve quality of care.* Cambridge, MA: MIT Press.

Center for Collegiate Mental Health. (2019, January). *2018 Annual Report* (Publication no. STA 19-180).

Centers for Disease Control and Prevention. (2018). 2017 STD Surveillance Report . Atlanta: U.S. Department of Health and Human Services. doi: 10.15620/cdc.59237external icon.

Centers for Disease Control and Prevention (CDC) (2013). Adult cigarette smoking in the United States: Current estimate. Retrieved from http://www.cdc.gov/tobacco/data statistics/fact sheets/adult data/cig smoking/.

Centers for Disease Control and Prevention (CDC) (2019). Current cigarette smoking among adults in the United States. Retrieved from http://www.cdc.gov/tobacco/data statistics/fact sheets/adult data/cig smoking/.

Centers for Disease Control and Prevention (CDC). (2000). *Suicide prevention fact sheet.* Atlanta: National Center for Injury Prevention and Control.

Centers for Disease Control and Prevention (CDC). (2015, April 16). E-cigarette use triples among middle and high school students in just one year. Press release. Retrieved from http://www.cdc.gov/media/releases/2015/p0416-e-cigarette-use.html.

Centers for Disease Control and Prevention (CDC). (2015, April 16). E-cigarette use triples among middle and high school students in just one year. Press release. Retrieved from http://www.cdc.gov/media/releases/2015/p0416-e-cigarette-use.html.

Centers for Disease Control and Prevention (CDC). (2019). Current cigarette smoking among adults in the United States. Retrieved from http://www.cdc.gov/tobacco/data_statistics/fact_sheets/adult_data/cig_smoking/.

Centers for Disease Control and Prevention. (2010, October 5). Binge drinking. *VitalSigns.*

Centers for Disease Control and Prevention. (2011). *The national intimate partner and sexual violence survey.* Washington, DC: Author.

Centers for Disease Control and Prevention. (2013). *HIV in the United States: At a glance.* Atlanta: CDC.

Centers for Disease Control and Prevention. (2013). *STD surveillance tables.* Atlanta: Author.

Chamberlain, K., & Zika, S. (1990). The minor events approach to stress: Support for the use of daily hassles. *British Journal of Psychology, 81,* 469-481.

Chamberlain, S. R., Menzies, L., Hampshire, A., Suckling, J., Fineberg, N. A., del Campo, N., et al. (2008). Orbitofrontal dysfunction in patients with obsessive-compulsive disorder and their unaffected relatives. *Science, 321,* 421-422.

Chan, M. (2016, June 20). Revisiting Andrea Yates 15 years after she drowned her children. *Time.* Downloaded from https://time.com/4375398/andrea-yates-15-years-drown-children/.

Chandler, J., Paolacci, G., Peer, E., Mueller, P., & Ratliff, K. A. (2015). Using nonnaive participants can reduce effect sizes. *Psychological Science, 26,* 1131-1139.

Chandra, A., Mosher, W. D., & Copen, C. (2011, March). Sexual behavior, sexual attraction, and sexual identity in the United States: Data from the 2006-2008 National Survey of Family Growth. *National Health Statistics Report, 36.*

Chang, L., & Geary, D. C. (2007). The future of psychology: Evolutionary approach to scientific psychology [Special issue: Evolutionary psychology]. *Acta Psychologica Sinica, 39,* 381-382.

Chang, Y.-T., Lin, S., Meng, L., & Fan, Y.-T. (2018). Atypical temporal activation pattern and central-right brain compensation during semantic judgment task in children with early left brain damage. *Brain and Language, 177-178,* 37-43.

Chang, Y.-W., Hsu, P.-Y., Wang, Y., & Chang, P.-Y. (2019). Integration of online and offline health services: The role of doctor-patient online interaction. *Patient Education and Counseling.* https://doi.org/10.1016/j.pec.2019.04.018.

Chao, M. M., Takeuchi, R., & Farh, J. (2017). Enhancing cultural intelligence: The roles of implicit culture beliefs and adjustment. *Personnel Psychology, 70,* 257-292.

Chao, R. (2011). Managing stress and maintaining well-being: Social support, problem-focused coping, and avoidant coping. *Journal of Counseling & Development, 89,* 338-348.

Chapman, J. (2006). Anxiety and defective decision making: An elaboration of the groupthink model. *Management Decision, 44,* 1391-1404.

Chapman, L. J., & Chapman, J. P. (1973). *Disordered thought in schizophrenia* (p. 3). New York: Appleton-Century-Crofts.

Chapman, S. C., & Wu, L. (2015). Epidemiology and demography of illicit drug use and drug use disorders among adults aged 50 and older. In I. Crome, L. Wu, R. Rao, & P. Crome, (Eds.), *Substance use and older people.* New York: Wiley-Blackwell.

Charlesworth, T. E. S., & Banaji, M. R. (2019). Patterns of implicit and explicit attitudes: I. Long-term change and stability from 2007 to 2016. *Psychological Science, 30*(2), 174-192.

Chavez, P. R., Nelson, D. E., Naimi, T. S., & Brewer, R. D. (2011). Impact of a new gender-specific definition for binge drinking on prevalence estimates for women. *American Journal of Preventive Medicine, 40,* 468-471.

Chen, C., & Stevenson, H. W. (1995). Motivation and mathematics achievement: A comparative study of Asian-American, Caucasian-American, and East Asian high school students. *Child Development, 66,* 1215-1234.

Chen, C., & Zhang, L. (2011). Temperament, personality and achievement goals among Chinese adolescent students. *Educational Psychology, 31,* 339-359.

Chen, R. (2014). *Cognitive development: Theories, stages and processes and challenges.* (R. Chen, Ed.). Hauppauge, NY: Nova Science Publishers.

Chen, T., Yue, G. H., Tian, Y., & Jiang, C. (2017). Baduanjin mind-body intervention improves the executive control function. *Frontiers in Psychology, 7,* 72-81.

Chen, Z., Fu, L., Peng, Y., Cai, R., & Zhou, S. (2011). The relationship among childhood abuse, parenting styles, and antisocial personality disorder tendency. *Chinese Journal of Clinical Psychology, 19,* 212-214.

Cheng, C., & Cheung, M. L. (2005). Cognitive processes underlying coping flexibility: Differentiation and integration. *Journal of Personality, 73,* 859-886.

Cheng, C. T., Ho, S. M., Liu, W. K., Hou, Y. C., Lim, L. C., Gao, S. Y., et al. (2019). Cancer-coping profile predicts long-term psychological functions and quality of life in cancer survivors. *Supportive Care in Cancer, 27*(3), 933-941.

Cheng, S., & Kwan, K. (2008). Attachment dimensions and contingencies of self-worth: The moderating role of culture. *Personality and Individual Differences, 45,* 509-514.

Cheng, Y., Diao, Q., & Behrens, J. T. (2017). A simplified version of the maximum information per time unit method in computerized adaptive testing. *Behavior Research Methods, 49,* 502-512.

Chernyak, N., Leimgruber, K. L., Dunham, Y. C., Hu, J., & Blake, P. R. (2019). Paying back people who harmed us but not people who helped us: Direct negative reciprocity precedes direct positive reciprocity in early development. *Psychological Science, 30*(9), 1273-1286.

Chesworth, B., Lanier, P., & Rizo, C. F. (2019). The association between exposure to intimate partner violence and child bullying behaviors. *Journal of Child and Family Studies, 28,* 2220-2231.

Chin, J. (2013). Eastern and Western learning styles: The paradox of Asian learners. *PsycCRITIQUES, 58,* 102-111.

Chin, T. (2015). Harmony and organizational citizenship behavior in Chinese organizations. *International Journal of Human Resource Management, 26,* 1110-1129.

Chiodo, D., Wolfe, D., Crooks, C., Hughes, R., & Jaffe, P. (2009). Impact of sexual harassment victimization by peers on subsequent adolescent victimization and adjustment: A longitudinal study. *Journal of Adolescent Health, 45,* 246-252.

Chiu, Y., Lo, S., & Hsieh, A. (2017). How colour similarity can make banner advertising effective: Insights from Gestalt theory. *Behaviour & Information Technology, 36,* 606-619.

Cho, S., Holyoak, K. J., & Cannon, T. D. (2007). Analogical reasoning in working memory: Resources shared among relational integration, interference resolution, and maintenance. *Memory & Cognition, 35,* 1445-1455.

Chodakiewitz, Y., Williams, J., Chodakiewitz, J., & Cosgrove, G. R. (2015). Ablative surgery for neuropsychiatric disorders: Past, present, future. In B. Sun & A. De Salles (Eds.), *Neurosurgical treatments for psychiatric disorders.* New York: Springer Science + Business Media.

Choi, H., Kensinger, E. A., & Rajaram, S. (2013). Emotional content enhances true but not false memory for categorized stimuli. *Memory & Cognition, 41,* 403-415.

Choi, H., Kensinger, E. A., & Rajaram, S. (2017). Mnemonic transmission, social contagion, and emergence of collective memory: Influence of emotional valence, group structure, and information distribution. *Journal of Experimental Psychology: General, 146,* 1247-1265.

Choi, K. W., Stein, M. B., Dunn, E. C., Koenen, K. C., & Smoller, J. W. (2019). Genomics and psychological resilience: A research agenda. *Molecular Psychiatry.* https://doi.org/10.1038/s41380-019-0457-6.

Chokshi, N. (2017, July 21). Teenagers recorded a drowning man and laughed. *The New York Times.*

Choma, B. L., Jagayat, A., Hodson, G., & Turner, R. (2018). Prejudice in the wake of terrorism: The role of temporal distance, ideology, and intergroup emotions. *Personality and Individual Differences, 123,* 65-75.

Chomsky, N. (1978). On the biological basis of language capacities. In G. A. Miller & E. Lennenberg (Eds.), *Psychology and biology of language and thought.* New York: Academic Press.

Chomsky, N. (1991). Linguistics and cognitive science: Problems and mysteries. In A. Kasher (Ed.), *The Chomskyan turn.* Cambridge, MA: Blackwell.

Chou, K. (2005). Everyday competence and depressive symptoms: Social support and sense of control as mediators or moderators? *Aging and Mental Health, 9,* 177-183.

Choubsaz, Y., & Gheitury, A. (2017). Is semantics affected by missing a critical period? Evidence from the Persian deaf. *Journal of Psycholinguistic Research, 46,* 77-88.

Christakis, N. A., & Fowler, J. H. (2008). The collective dynamics of smoking in a large social network. *The New England Journal of Medicine, 358,* 2249-2258.

Christensen, K. A., Aldao, A., Sheridan, M. A., & McLaughlin, K. A. (2017). Habitual reappraisal in context: Peer victimisation moderates its association with physiological reactivity to social stress. *Cognition and Emotion, 31,* 384-394.

Christensen, S. S. (2019). Escape from the diffusion of responsibility: A review and guide for nurses. *Journal of Nursing Management, 27*(2), 264-270.

Christian, C. J., Lencz, T., Robinson, D. G., Burdick, K. E., Ashtari, M., Malhotra, A. K., et al. (2008). Gray matter structural alterations in obsessive-compulsive disorder: Relationship to neuropsychological functions. *Neuroimaging, 164,* 123-131.

Christoffels, I. K., de Haan, A. M., Steenbergen, L., van den Wildenberg, W. M., & Colzato, L. S. (2015). Two is better than one: Bilingual education promotes the flexible mind. *Psychological Research, 79,* 371-379.

Chung, K.-F., Lee, C.-T., Yeung, W.-F., Chan, M.-S., Chung, E. W.-Y., & Lin, W.-L. (2018). Sleep hygiene education as a treatment of insomnia: A systematic review and meta-analysis. *Family Practice, 35*(4), 365-375.

Cialdini, R. B., & Sagarin, B. J. (2005). Principles of interpersonal influence. In T. C. Brock & M. C. Green (Eds.), *Persuasion: Psychological insights and perspectives* (2nd ed.). Thousand Oaks, CA: Sage Publications.

Cialdini, R. B., Schaller, M., Houlihan, D., Arps, K., Fultz, J., & Beaman, A. L. (1975). Reciprocal concessions procedure for inducing compliance: The door-in-the-face technique. *Journal of Personality and Social Psychology, 31,* 206-215.

Cisler, J. M., James, G. A., Tripathi, S., Mletzko, T., Heim, C., Hu, X. P., et al. (2013). Differential functional connectivity within an emotion regulation neural network among individuals resilient and susceptible to the depressogenic effects of early life stress. *Psychological Medicine, 43,* 507-518.

Clarkin, J. F., & Lenzenweger, M. F. (Eds.). (2004). *Major theories of personality disorders* (2nd ed.). New York: Guilford.

Clawson, R. C., dela Cruz, L. N., Allen, S., Wolgemuth, T., Maner, A., Dorsett, A., et al. (2019). Continuous access to snacks from weaning onwards in female rats causes weight gain, insulin insensitivity, and sustained leptin resistance in adulthood. *Physiology & Behavior, 201,* 165-174.

Clay, R. A. (2017, July/August). Women outnumber men in psychology, but not in the field's top echelons. *Monitor on Psychology,* pp. 18-19.

Cleary, A. M. (2019). The biasing nature of the tip-of-the-tongue experience: When decisions bask in the glow of the tip-of-the-tongue state. *Journal of Experimental Psychology, 148*(7), 1178-1191.

Clement, S. (2015, March 4). Millennials like to spank their kids just as much as their parents did. *Washington Post.* Retrieved from https://www.washingtonpost.com/news/wonk/wp/2015/03/05/millennials-like-to-spank-their-kids-just-as-much-as-their-parents-did.

Clements, A. M., Rimrodt, S. L., & Abel, J. R. (2006). Sex differences in cerebral laterality of language and visuospatial processing. *Brain, 8,* 150-158.

Clemons, T. L. (2006). Underachieving gifted students: A social cognitive model. *Dissertation Abstracts International Section A: Humanities and Social Sciences, 66*(9-A), 3208.

Clément-Guillotin, C., & Fontayne, P. (2011). Situational malleability of gender schema: The case of the competitive sport context. *Sex Roles, 64,* 426-439.

Coan, J. A., Schaefer, H. S., & Davidson, R. J. (2006). Lending a hand: Social regulation of the neural response to threat. *Psychological Science, 17*(12), 1032-1039.

Coats, E. J., & Feldman, R. S. (1996). Gender differences in nonverbal correlates of social status. *Personality and Social Psychology Bulletin, 22,* 1014-1022.

Cobos, P., Sanchez, M., Garcia, C., Vera, M. N., & Vila, J. (2002). Revisiting the James versus Cannon debate on emotion: Startle and autonomic modulation in patients with spinal cord injuries. *Biological Psychology, 61,* 251-269.

Cockburn, P. (2019, November 15). Erdogan's ethnic cleansing of the Kurds is still happening now—and we have Trump to thank. *The Independent.* Downloaded from https://www.independent.co.uk/voices/erdogan-turkey-kurds-border-syria-war-trump-ethnic-cleansing-a9204581.html.

Coderre, T. J. (2011). Complex regional pain syndrome: What's in a name? *The Journal of Pain, 12,* 2-12.

Coenen, V. A., Bewernick, B. H., Kayser, S., Kilian, H., Boström, J., Greschus, S., et al. (2019). Superolateral medial forebrain bundle deep brain stimulation in major depression: A gateway trial. *Neuropsychopharmacology, 44*(7), 1224.

Cohen, G. L., Garcia, J., Apfel, N., & Master, A. (2006). Reducing the racial achievement gap: A social-psychological intervention. *Science, 313,* 1307-1310.

Cohen, P., Slomkowski, C., & Robins, L. N. (Eds.). (1999). *Historical and geographical influences on psychopathology.* Mahwah, NJ: Erlbaum.

Cohen, S., Murphy, M. L. M., & Prather, A. A. (2019). Ten surprising facts about stressful life events and disease risk. *Annual Review of Psychology, 70,* 577-597.

Cohn, A., Maréchal, M., Tannenbaum, D., & Zünd, C. (2019). Civic honesty around the globe. *Science, 365,* 70-73.

Cohn, D., & Caumont, A. (2016, March 31). 10 demographic trends that are shaping the U.S. and the world. *Fact Tank: News in the Numbers.* Retrieved from http://www.pewresearch.org/fact-tank/2016/03/31/10-demographic-trends-that-are-shaping-the-u-s-and-the-world/.

Cole, S. W., Arevalo, J. M., Takahashi, R., Sloan, E. K., Lutgendorf, S. L., Sood, A. K., et al. (2010). Computational identification of gene-social environment interaction at the human IL6 locus. *Proceedings of the National Academy of Sciences of the USA, 107,* 5681-5686.

Coleman, J. A., Ingram, K. M., & Sheerin, C. M. (2019). Racial differences in posttraumatic stress disorder symptoms among African American and Caucasian male veterans. *Traumatology, 25*(4), 297-302.

Coles, R., & Stokes, G. (1985). *Sex and the American teenager.* New York: Harper & Row.

Colom, R., Haier, R. J., Head, K., Alvarez-Linera, J., Quiroga, M. A., Shih, P. C., et al. (2009). Gray matter correlates of fluid, crystallized, and spatial intelligence: Testing the P-FIT model. *Intelligence, 37,* 124-135.

Coltheart, M., Langdon, R., & McKay, R. (2007). Schizophrenia and monothematic delusions. *Schizophrenia Bulletin, 33,* 642-647.

Conforto, A. B., Luccas, R., Menezes, I. S., Machado, A. G., Mello, E. A., Assis, P. S., et al. (2019). Peripheral nerve stimulation to enhance upper limb motor function in stroke. *Stroke, 50*(Suppl 1), A120-A120.

Connolly, A. C. (2007). Concepts and their features: Can cognitive science make good on the promises of concept empiricism? *Dissertation Abstracts International: Section B: The Sciences and Engineering, 67*(7-B), 4125.

Conoley, C. W., Plumb, E. W., Hawley, K. J., Spaventa-Vancil, K. Z., & Hernández, R. J. (2015). Integrating positive psychology into family therapy: Positive family therapy. *The Counseling Psychologist, 43,* 703-733.

Conroy, J., Lin, L., & Christidis, P. (2019). How satisfied are psychology-degree holders with their job? *Monitor on Psychology,* p. 19.

Conway, M. A. (Ed.). (2002). *Levels of processing 30 years on: Special issue of memory.* Hove, UK: Psychology Press.

Cook, L. (2015, August 19). The heroin epidemic in 9 graphs. *US News & World Report.* Accessed from http://www.usnews.com/news/blogs/data-mine/2015/08/19/the-heroin-epidemic-in-9-graphs.

Cook, M. (2013). *Levels of personality* (3rd ed.). New York: Cambridge University Press.

Cook-Cottone, C., & Smith, A. (2013). Eating disorders. In C. A. Noggle & R. S. Dean (Eds.), *The neuropsychology of psychopathology*. New York: Springer Publishing Co.

Coolidge, F. L., Segal, D. L., Estey, A. J., & Neuzil, P. J. (2011). Preliminary psychometric properties of a measure of Karen Horney's Tridimensional Theory in children and adolescents. *Journal of Clinical Psychology, 67,* 383-390.

Cooper, J. (2007). *Cognitive dissonance: Fifty years of a classic theory*. Thousand Oaks, CA: Sage Publications.

Cooper, J. (2019). Cognitive dissonance: Where we've been and where we're going. *International Review of Social Psychology, 32*(1).

Cooper, M., & McLeod, J. (2011). Person-centered therapy: A pluralistic perspective. *Person-Centered and Experiential Psychotherapies, 10,* 210-223.

Cooper, Z., & Shafran, R. (2008). Cognitive behaviour therapy for eating disorders. *Behavioural and Cognitive Psychotherapy, 36,* 713-722.

Cope, D. (2001). *Virtual music*. Cambridge, MA: MIT Press.

Cope, D. (2003). Computer analysis of musical allusions. *Computer Music Journal, 27,* 11-28.

Copeland, W. E., Worthman, C., Shanahan, L., Costello, E. J., & Angold, A. (2019). Early pubertal timing and testosterone associated with higher levels of adolescent depression in girls. *Journal of the American Academy of Child & Adolescent Psychiatry*. https://doi.org/10.1016/j.jaac.2019.02.007.

Coplan, R., Reichel, M., & Rowan, K. (2009). Exploring the associations between maternal personality, child temperament, and parenting: A focus on emotions. *Personality and Individual Differences, 46,* 241-246.

Coren, S. (2004). Sensation and perception. In I. B. Weiner (Ed.), *Handbook of Psychology* (Vol. 1). Hoboken, NJ: John Wiley & Sons.

Cornelis, E., Heuvinck, N., & Majmundar, A. (2019). The ambivalence story: Using refutation to counter the negative effects of ambivalence in two-sided messages. *International Journal of Advertising,* 1-23.

Cornelis, M. C., Tordoff, M. G., El-Sohemy, A., & van Dam, R. M. (2017). Recalled taste intensity, liking and habitual intake of commonly consumed foods. *Appetite, 109,* 182-189.

Cornell, C. B. (2006). A graduated scale for determining mental age. *Dissertation Abstracts International: Section B: The Sciences and Engineering, 66*(9-B), 5121.

Cornier, M. (2011). Is your brain to blame for weight regain? *Physiology & Behavior, 104,* 608-612.

Corsello, A. (2005). The wronged man. In *The best American magazine writing, 2005*. New York: Columbia University Press.

Cosmides, L., & Tooby, J. (2004). Social exchange: The evolutionary design of a neurocognitive system. In M. S. Gazzaniga (Ed.), *Cognitive neurosciences* (3rd ed.). Cambridge, MA: MIT.

Costa, P. T., Jr., & Widiger, T. A. (Eds.). (2002). *Personality disorders and the Five-Factor Model of personality* (2nd ed.). Washington, DC: American Psychological Association.

Costa, R., & Figueiredo, B. (2011). Infant's psychophysiological profile and temperament at 3 and 12 months. *Infant Behavior & Development, 34,* 270-279.

Costanzo, R., & Miwa, T. (2006). Posttraumatic olfactory loss. *Advances in Oto-rhino-laryngology, 63,* 99-107.

Coulson, D., & Harvey, M. (2013). Scaffolding student reflection for experience-based learning: A framework. *Teaching in Higher Education, 18,* 401-413.

Council of National Psychological Associations for the Advancement of Ethnic Minority Interests. (2000, January). *Guidelines for research in ethnic minority communities*. Washington, DC: American Psychological Association.

Coutrot, A., Silva, R., Manley, E., de Cothi, W., Sami, S., Bohbot, V., et al. (2018). Global determinants of navigation ability. *Current Biology, 28,* 2861-2866.

Couturier, J., & Lock, J. (2006). Eating disorders: Anorexia nervosa, bulimia nervosa, and binge eating disorder. In T. G. Plante (Ed.), *Mental disorders of the new millennium: Biology and function* (Vol. 3). Westport, CT: Praeger Publishers/Greenwood Publishing.

Coventry, K. R., Venn, S. F., Smith, G. D., & Morley, A. M. (2003). Spatial problem solving and functional relations. *European Journal of Cognitive Psychology, 15,* 71-99.

Cowan, N. (2001). The magical number 4 in short-term memory: A reconsideration of mental storage capacity. *Behavioral and Brain Sciences, 24,* 97-185.

Cowen, A. S., & Keltner, D. (2019). What the face displays: Mapping 28 emotions conveyed by naturalistic expression. *American Psychologist*. http://dx.doi.org/10.1037/amp0000488.

Cox, J. (2003, May 6). How far would you go to save your life? *Denver Post*, p. F1.

Cox, J. C., Green, E. P., & Hennig-Schmidt, H. (2016). Experimental and behavioral economics of healthcare. *Journal of Economic Behavior & Organization, 131*(Part B), A1-A4.

Cox, J. W., Rich, S., Chui, A., Muyskens, J., & Ulmanu, M. (2018). Database: The number of children impacted by school shootings. *Washington Post*. Retrieved from https://www.washingtonpost.com/graphics/2018/local/school-shootings-database/.

Coyle, N. (2006). The hard work of living in the face of death. *Journal of Pain and Symptom Management, 32,* 266-274.

Craig, P. L. (2017). Clinical neuropsychologists. In R. J. Sternberg, (Ed.), *Career paths in psychology: Where your degree can take you* (3rd ed.). Washington, DC: American Psychological Association.

Craighero, L., Leo, I., Umilta, C., & Simion, F. (2011). Newborns' preference for goal-directed actions. *Cognition, 120,* 26-32.

Craik, F., & Lockhart, R. (2008). Levels of processing and Zinchenko's approach to memory research. *Journal of Russian & East European Psychology, 46,* 52-60.

Crano, W. D., Brewer, M. B., & Lac, A. (2015). *Principles and methods of social research* (3rd ed.). New York: Routledge/Taylor & Francis Group.

Cranston, C. C., Miller, K. E., Davis, J. L., & Rhudy, J. L. (2017). Preliminary validation of a brief measure of the frequency and severity of nightmares: The Trauma-Related Nightmare Survey. *Journal of Trauma & Dissociation, 18,* 88-99.

Crede, M. (2018). What shall we do about grit? A critical review of what we know and what we don't know. *Educational Researcher, 47*(9), 606-611.

Creel, S. C., & Bregman, M. R. (2011). How talker identity relates to language processing. *Language and Linguistics Compass, 5,* 190-204.

Creery, J., Oudiette, D., Antony, J., & Paller, K. (2015). Targeted memory reactivation during sleep depends on prior learning. *Sleep, 38,* 755-763.

Crespo, R., & Mesurado, B. (2015, August). Happiness economics, eudaimonia and positive psychology: From happiness economics to flourishing economics. *Journal of Happiness Studies, 16*(4), 931-946.

Criswell, H., Ming, Z., Kelm, M., & Breese, G. (2008). Brain regional differences in the effect of ethanol on GABA release from presynaptic terminals. *Journal of Pharmacology and Experimental Therapeutics, 326,* 596-603.

Critelli, J., & Bivona, J. (2008). Women's erotic rape fantasies: An evaluation of theory and research. *Journal of Sex Research, 45,* 57-70.

Crockford, C., Wittig, R. M., & Zuberbühler, K. (2015). An intentional vocalization draws others' attention: A playback experiment with wild chimpanzees. *Animal Cognition, 18,* 581-591.

Croom, A. M. (2015). Aristotelian moral psychology and the situationist challenge. *Polish Psychological Bulletin, 46,* 262-277.

Crosnoe, R., & Elder, G. H., Jr. (2002). Successful adaptation in the later years: A life course approach to aging. *Social Psychology Quarterly, 65,* 309-328.

Cross, C. P., & Campbell, A. (2011). Women's aggression. *Aggression and Violent Behavior, 16,* 390-398.

Crouse, K. (2018, February 14). Men's skating has an open secret: Starvation. *The New York Times*, p. A1.

Crowne, K. (2013). Cultural exposure, emotional intelligence, and cultural intelligence: An exploratory study. *International Journal of Cross-Cultural Management, 13*(1), 5-22.

Crum, A. J., & Langer, E. J. (2007). Mind-set matters: Exercise and the placebo effect. *Psychological Science, 18,* 165-171.

Crönlein, T., Lehner, A., Schüssler, P., Geisler, P., Rupprecht, R., & Wetter, T. C. (2019). Changes in subjective-objective sleep discrepancy following inpatient cognitive behavior therapy for insomnia. *Behavior Therapy*. http://dx.doi.org/10.1016/j.beth.2019.03.002.

Cuddy, A. J. C., Fiske, S. T., & Glick, P. (2004). When professionals become mothers, warmth doesn't cut the ice. *Journal of Social Issues, 60,* 701-718.

Cuijpers, P., Karyotaki, E., Reijnders, M., & Ebert, D. D. (2019). Was Eysenck right after all? A reassessment of the effects of psychotherapy for adult depression. *Epidemiology and Psychiatric Sciences, 28*(1), 21-30.

Cuijpers, P., van Straten, A., Andersson, G., & van Oppen, P. (2008). Psychotherapy for depression in adults: A meta-analysis of comparative outcome studies. *Journal of Consulting and Clinical Psychology, 76,* 909-922.

Culhane-Pera, K. A., Borkan, J. M., & Patten, S. (2007). Culture and ethnicity. In O. J. Z. Sahler & J. E. Carr (Eds.), *The behavioral sciences and health care* (2nd rev. and updated ed.). Ashland, OH: Hogrefe & Huber Publishers.

Cummings, A., Ceponiene, R., & Koyama, A. (2006). Auditory semantic networks for words and natural sounds. *Brain Research, 1115,* 92-107.

Cummings, J. L. (2019). Assessing US racial and gender differences in happiness, 1972-2016: An intersectional approach. *Journal of Happiness Studies: An Interdisciplinary Forum on Subjective Well-Being.*

Cunningham, P. (2006). Early years teachers and the influence of Piaget: Evidence from oral history. *Early Years An International Journal of Research and Development, 26,* 5-16.

Ćurković, M., Kosec, A., & Savic, A. (2019). Re-evaluation of significance and the implications of placebo effect in antidepressant therapy. *Frontiers in Psychiatry, 10,* 143.

Curthoys, I. S. (2017). The new vestibular stimuli: Sound and vibration–anatomical, physiological and clinical evidence. *Experimental Brain Research, 235,* 957-972.

da Cunha-Bang, S., Fisher, P. M., Hjordt, L. V., Holst, K., & Knudsen, G. M. (2019). Amygdala reactivity to fearful faces correlates positively with impulsive aggression. *Social Neuroscience, 14*(2), 162-172.

Daftary, F., & Meri, J. W. (2002). *Culture and memory in medieval Islam.* London: I. B. Tauris.

Dai, D. Y., & Wang, X. (2007). The role of need for cognition and reader beliefs in text comprehension and interest development. *Contemporary Educational Psychology, 32,* 332-347.

Dakin, E. K., & Areán, P. (2013). Patient perspectives on the benefits of psychotherapy for late-life depression. *American Journal of Geriatric Psychiatry, 21,* 155-163.

Dalal, A. K., & Misra, G. (2006). Psychology of health and well-being: Some emerging perspectives [Special issue: Psychology of health and well-being]. *Psychological Studies, 51,* 91-104.

Damaske, S. (2011). A "major career woman"? How women develop early expectations about work. *Gender & Society, 25,* 409-430.

Damian, R. I., Spengler, M., Sutu, A., & Roberts, B. W. (2019). Sixteen going on sixty-six: A longitudinal study of personality stability and change across 50 years. *Journal of Personality and Social Psychology, 117*(3), 674-695.

Damjanovic, L., Meyer, M., & Sepulveda, F. (2017). Raising the alarm: Individual differences in the perceptual awareness of masked facial expressions. *Brain and Cognition, 114,* 1-10.

Dani, J. A., & Montague, P. (2007). Disrupting addiction through the loss of drug-associated internal states. *Nature Neuroscience, 10,* 403-404.

Daniels, C. W., & Sanabria, F. (2017). Interval timing under a behavioral microscope: Dissociating motivational and timing processes in fixed-interval performance. *Learning & Behavior, 45,* 29-48.

Danner, D., Hagemann, D., Schankin, A., Hager, M., & Funke, J. (2011). Beyond IQ: A latent state-trait analysis of general intelligence, dynamic decision making, and implicit learning. *Intelligence, 39,* 323-334.

Danovitch, J. H. (2019). Growing up with Google: How children's understanding and use of Internet-based devices relates to cognitive development. *Human Behavior and Emerging Technologies, 1*(2), 81-90.

Dard, R. F., Dahan, L., & Rampon, C. (2019). Targeting hippocampal adult neurogenesis using transcription factors to reduce Alzheimer's disease-associated memory impairments. *Hippocampus, 29*(7), 579-586.

Dare, J. S. (2011). Transitions in midlife women's lives: Contemporary experiences. *Health Care for Women International, 32,* 111-133.

Das, A. (2007). Masturbation in the United States. *Journal of Sex & Marital Therapy, 33,* 301-317.

Das, A., Parish, W., & Laumann, E. (2009). Masturbation in urban China. *Archives of Sexual Behavior, 38,* 108-120.

Das, J. P. (2015). Search for intelligence by PASSing g. *Canadian Psychology/Psychologie Canadienne, 56,* 39-45.

Dasborough, M., & Harvey, P. (2017). Schadenfreude: The (not so) secret joy of another's misfortune. *Journal of Business Ethics, 141,* 693-707.

Datar, A. (2017). The more the heavier? Family size and childhood obesity in the U.S. *Social Science & Medicine, 180,* 143-151.

Davern, M. (2013). Nonresponse rates are a problematic indicator of nonresponse bias in survey research. *Health Services Research, 48,* 905-912.

David, E. R., & Derthick, A. O. (2018). *The psychology of oppression.* New York: Springer Publishing Co.

Davidson, J. (2016, August 11). With 500,000 female genital mutilation survivors or at risk in U.S., it's not just someone else's problem. *Washington Post.* Accessed from https://www.washingtonpost.com/news/powerpost/wp/2016/08/11/with-500000-female-genital-mutilation-survivors-or-at-risk-in-u-s-its-not-just-someone-elses-problem/?utm_term=.1fa2e2862173.

Davidson-Kelly, K., Schaefer, R. S., Moran, N., & Overy, K. (2015). "Total inner memory": Deliberate uses of multimodal musical imagery during performance preparation. *Psychomusicology: Music, Mind, and Brain, 25,* 83-92.

Davies, S., Jackson, P., Lewis, G., Hood, S., Nutt, D., & Potokar, J. (2008). Is the association of hypertension and panic disorder explained by clustering of autonomic panic symptoms in hypertensive patients? *Journal of Affective Disorders, 111,* 344-350.

Davis, K., Christodoulou, J., Seider, S., & Gardner, H. (2011). The theory of multiple intelligences. In R. J. Sternberg & S. Kaufman (Eds.), *The Cambridge handbook of intelligence.* New York: Cambridge University Press.

Davis, L. J. (2009, June 15). Sotomayor and the New Haven firefighters case: More myths than facts. *Washington Times,* p. A04.

Davis, S. R. (2007). The nose knows best. *PsycCRITIQUES, 52,* 22-31.

Dawkins, L., Ford, A., Bauld, L., Balaban, S., Tyler, A., & Cox, S. (2019). A cross sectional survey of smoking characteristics and quitting behaviour from a sample of homeless adults in Great Britain. *Addictive Behaviors, 95,* 35-40.

Dawson, S. J., Fretz, K. M., & Chivers, M. L. (2017). Visual attention patterns of women with androphilic and gynephilic sexual attractions. *Archives of Sexual Behavior, 46,* 141-153.

Day, A. L., & Livingstone, H. A. (2003). Gender differences in perceptions of stressors and utilization of social support among university students. *Canadian Journal of Behavioural Science, 35,* 73-83.

Day, R. D., & Lamb, M. E. (2004). *Conceptualizing and measuring father involvement.* Mahwah, NJ: Lawrence Erlbaum Associates.

de Abreu, C. N., & Filho, R. C. (2017). Anorexia nervosa and bulimia nervosa–A psychotherapeutic cognitive-constructivist approach. *International Review Of Psychiatry, 29,* 248-253.

De Brigard, F., Brady, T. F., Ruzic, L., & Schacter, D. L. (2017). Tracking the emergence of memories: A category-learning paradigm to explore schema-driven recognition. *Memory & Cognition, 45,* 105-120.

De Bruin, K. (2019). The impact of inclusive education reforms on students with disability: an international comparison. *International Journal of Inclusive Education, 23*(7-8), 1-16.

de Bruïne, G.,Vredeveldt, & van Koppen, P. (2018). Cross-cultural differences in object recognition: Comparing asylum seekers from Sub-Saharan Africa and a matched Western European control group. *Applied Cognitive Psychology,* 1-11.

De Dreu, C. W., Greer, L. L., Van Kleef, G. A., Shalvi, S., & Handgraaf, M. J. (2011). Oxytocin promotes human ethnocentrism. *PNAS Proceedings of the National Academy of Sciences of the United States of America, 108,* 1262-1266.

de Gusmao, C. M., Pollak, L. E., & Sharma, N. (2017). Neuropsychological and psychiatric outcome of GPi-deep brain stimulation in dystonia. *Brain Stimulation, 10,* 994-996.

de Jong, R., Lommen, M. J., de Jong, P. J., & Nauta, M. H. (2019). Using multiple contexts and retrieval cues in exposure-based therapy to prevent relapse in anxiety disorders. *Cognitive and Behavioral Practice, 26*(1), 154-165.

de Klerk, C. C., Bulgarelli, C., Hamilton, A., & Southgate, V. (2019). Selective facial mimicry of native over foreign speakers in preverbal infants. *Journal of Experimental Child Psychology, 183*, 33-47.

De Los Reyes, A., Lerner, M. D., Keeley, L. M., Weber, R. J., Drabick, D. A., Rabinowitz, J., et al. (2019). Improving interpretability of subjective assessments about psychological phenomena: A review and cross-cultural meta-analysis. *Review of General Psychology, 23*(3), 293-319.

De Meyer, H., Beckers, T., Tripp, G., & van der Oord, S. (2019). Reinforcement contingency learning in children with ADHD: Back to the basics of behavior therapy. *Journal of Abnormal Child Psychology.* https://doi.org/10.1007/s10802-019-00572-z.

de Sousa, A. F., Cowansage, K. K., Zutshi, I., Cardozo, L. M., Yoo, E. J., Leutgeb, S., & Mayford, M. (2019). Optogenetic reactivation of memory ensembles in the retrosplenial cortex induces systems consolidation. *PNAS Proceedings of the National Academy of Sciences of the United States of America, 116*(17), 8576-8581.

de Sousa, D. F. M., Gonçalves, M. L. L., Politti, F., de Paula Lovisetto, R. D., Fernandes, K. P. S., Bussadori, S. K., et al. (2019). Photobiomodulation with simultaneous use of red and infrared light emitting diodes in the treatment of temporomandibular disorder: Study protocol for a randomized, controlled and double-blind clinical trial. *Medicine, 98*(6), e14391.

de Visser, E. J., Monfort, S. S., Goodyear, K., Lu, L., O'Hara, M., Lee, M. R., et al. (2017). A little anthropomorphism goes a long way: Effects of oxytocin on trust, compliance, and team performance with automated agents. *Human Factors, 59*, 116-133.

de Visser, R., Richters, J., Rissel, C., Grulich, A., Simpson, J., Rodrigues, D., et al. (2019). Romantic jealousy: A test of social cognitive and evolutionary models in a population-representative sample of adults. *The Journal of Sex Research, 0*(0), 1-10. doi: https://doi.org/10.1080/00224499.2019.1613482

de Voogd, L. D., Klumpers, F., Fernández, G., & Hermans, E. J. (2017). Intrinsic functional connectivity between amygdala and hippocampus during rest predicts enhanced memory under stress. *Psychoneuroendocrinology, 75*, 192-202.

de Vries, D. A., & Kühne, R. (2015). Facebook and self-perception: Individual susceptibility to negative social comparison on Facebook. *Personality and Individual Differences, 86*, 217-221.

de Waal, F. B. M. (2014). Hard-wired for good? *Science, 347*, 379.

Deacon, B. J., & Spielmans, G. I. (2017). Is the efficacy of "antidepressant" medications overrated?. In S. O. Lilienfeld & I. D. Waldman (Eds.), *Psychological science under scrutiny: Recent challenges and proposed solutions.* Hoboken, NJ: Wiley-Blackwell.

Dean, K. K., & Koenig, A. M. (2019). Cross-cultural differences and similarities in attribution. In K. D. Keith (Ed.). *Cross-Cultural Psychology: Contemporary Themes and Perspectives.* Hoboken, NJ: John Wiley & Sons.

DeAngelis, D., & Monahan, J. (2008). Professional credentials and professional regulations: Social work professional development. In B. W. White, K. M. Sowers, & C. N. Dulmus (Eds.), *Comprehensive handbook of social work and social welfare, Vol. 1: The profession of social work.* Hoboken, NJ: John Wiley & Sons.

DeAngelis, T. (2016). Behavioral therapy works best for insomnia. *Monitor on Psychology, 47*, 18-19.

DeAngelis, T. (2016, September). Preventing medical errors. *Monitor on Psychology,* pp. 48-52.

Dearing, E., McCartney, K., & Taylor, B. (2009). Does higher quality early child care promote low-income children's math and reading achievement in middle childhood? *Child Development, 80*, 1329-1349.

Deater-Deckard, K., Ivy, L., & Smith, J. (2005). Resilience in gene-environment transactions. In S. Goldstein & R. B. Brooks (Eds.), *Handbook of resilience in children.* New York: Kluwer Academic/Plenum Publishers.

Debatin, T. (2019). A revised mental energy hypothesis of the *g* factor in light of recent neuroscience. *Review of General Psychology, 23*(2), 201-210.

DeBlaere, C., Watson, L. B., & Langrehr, K. J. (2018). Intersectionality applied: Intersectionality is as intersectionality does. In C. B. Travis & J. W. White (Eds.), *APA handbook of the psychology of women: Volume 1: History, theory, and battlegrounds* (pp. 567-584). Washington, DC: American Psychological Association.

Debnath, R., Salo, V.C., Buzzell, G.A., Yoo, K.H., & Fox, N.A., 2019. Mu rhythm desynchronization is specific to action execution and observation: Evidence from time-frequency and connectivity analysis. *Neuroimage, 184*, 496-507. https://doi.org/10.1016/j.neuroimage.2018.09.053.

DeBord, K. A., Fischer, A. R., Bieschke, K. J., & Perez, R. M. (2017). *Handbook of sexual orientation and gender diversity in counseling and psychotherapy.* Washington, DC: American Psychological Association.

DeGaton, J. F., Weed, S., & Jensen, L. (1996). Understanding gender differences in adolescent sexuality. *Adolescence, 31*, 217-231.

deGroot, A. (1978). *Thought and choice in chess.* Paris: Mouton de Gruyter.

deGroot, A. D. (1966). Perception and memory versus thought: Some old ideas and recent findings. In B. Kleinmuntz (Ed.), *Problem solving: Research, method, and theory.* New York: Wiley.

Del Giudice, M. (2011). Alone in the dark? Modeling the conditions for visual experience in human fetuses. *Developmental Psychobiology, 53*, 214-219.

del Rosal, E., Alonso, L., & Moreno, R. (2006). Simulation of habituation to simple and multiple stimuli. *Behavioural Processes, 73*, 272-277.

Delacollette, N., Dumont, M., Sarlet, M., & Dardenne, B. (2013). Benevolent sexism, men's advantages and the prescription of warmth to women. *Sex Roles, 68*, 296-310.

DeLamater, J. D., & Sill, M. (2005). Sexual desire in later life. *Journal of Sex Research, 42*, 138-149.

Delcourt, M. A. B., Cornell, D. G., & Goldberg, M. D. (2007). Cognitive and affective learning outcomes of gifted elementary school students. *The Gifted Child Quarterly, 51*, 359-382.

Dell, P. F. (2013). Three dimensions of dissociative amnesia. *Journal of Trauma & Dissociation, 14*, 25-39.

DeLoache, J., & LoBue, V. (2009). The narrow fellow in the grass: Human infants associate snakes and fear. *Developmental Science, 12*, 201-207.

Demaree, H. A., & Everhart, D. E. (2004). Healthy high-hostiles: Reduced para-sympathetic activity and decreased sympathovagal flexibility during negative emotional processing. *Personality and Individual Differences, 36*, 457-469.

DeMaris, A. (2013). Burning the candle at both ends: Extramarital sex as a precursor of marital disruption. *Journal of Family Issues, 34*, 1474-1499.

Dement, W. C., & Wolpert, E. A. (1958). The relation of eye movements, body mobility, and external stimuli to dream content. *Journal of Experimental Psychology, 55*, 543-553.

Dender, A., & Stagnitti, K. (2011). Development of the Indigenous Child-Initiated Pretend Play Assessment: Selection of play materials and administration. *Australian Occupational Therapy Journal, 58*, 34-42.

Deng, C., & Georgiou, G. K. (2015). Establishing measurement invariance of the cognitive assessment system across cultures. In T. C. Papadopoulos, R. K. Parrila, & J. R. Kirby (Eds.), *Cognition, intelligence, and achievement: A tribute to J. P. Das.* San Diego, CA: Elsevier Academic Press.

Denmark, G. L., & Fernandez, L. C. (1993). Historical development of the psychology of women. In F. L. Denmark & M. A. Paludi (Eds.), *A handbook of issues and theories.* Westport, CT: Greenwood Press.

Dennis, S. (2011). Smoking causes creative responses: On state antismoking policy and resilient habits. *Critical Public Health, 21*, 25-35.

Densley, J., & Peterson, J. (2018). Group aggression. *Current Opinion in Psychology, 1943-48.* doi:10.1016/j.copsyc.2017.03.031.

DePaolo, J., Gravina, N. E., & Harvey, C. (2019). Using a behavioral intervention to improve performance of a women's college lacrosse team. *Behavior Analysis in Practice, 12*(2), 407-411.

Deregowski, J. B. (1973). Illusion and culture. In R. L. Gregory & G. H. Combrich (Eds.), *Illusion in nature and art.* New York: Scribner.

Dernbach, K., & Marshall, M. (2001). Pouring beer on troubled waters: Alcohol and violence in the Papua New Guinea Highlands during the 1980s. *Contemporary Drug Problems: An Interdisciplinary Quarterly, 28*, 3-47.

DeRobertis, E. M., & Bland, A. M. (2019). Lifespan human development and "the humanistic perspective": A contribution toward inclusion. *The Humanistic Psychologist.* http://dx.doi.org/10.1037/hum0000141.

Deroy, O., & Spence, C. (2013). Are we all born synaesthetic? Examining the neonatal synaesthesia hypothesis. *Neuroscience and Biobehavioral Reviews, 37*, 1240-1253.

Deshields, T., Tibbs, T., Fan, M. Y., & Taylor, M. (2006). Differences in patterns of depression after treatment for breast cancer. *Psycho-Oncology, 15*(5), 398-406.

Després, O., Lithfous, S., Tromp, D., Pebayle, T., & Dufour, A. (2017). Gamma oscillatory activity is impaired in episodic memory encoding with age. *Neurobiology of Aging, 52*, 53-65.

Deutsch, M. (1994). Constructive conflict resolution: Principles, training, and research. *Journal of Social Issues, 50*, 13-32.

Devos, T. (2011). The role of race in American politics: Lessons learned from the 2008 presidential election. In G. S. Parks & M. W. Hughey (Eds.), *The Obamas and a (post) racial America?* New York: Oxford University Press.

Dhillon, S., Yang, L., & Curran, M. (2008). Spotlight on bupropion in major depressive disorder. *CNS Drugs, 22*, 613-617.

Di Fabio, A., & Palazzeschi, L. (2009). An in-depth look at scholastic success: Fluid intelligence, personality traits or emotional intelligence? *Personality and Individual Differences, 46*, 581-585.

Di Ieva, A., Esteban, F. J., Grizzi, F., Klonowski, W., & Martín-Landrove, M. (2015). Fractals in the neurosciences, part II: Clinical applications and future perspectives. *The Neuroscientist, 21*, 30-43.

Diamond, M. (2009). Human intersexuality: Difference or disorder? *Archives of Sexual Behavior, 38*, 172.

Dias, A. M., & van Deusen, A. (2011). A new neurofeedback protocol for depression. *Spanish Journal of Psychology, 14*, 374-384.

Diaz, A., & Bell, M. (2011). Information processing efficiency and regulation at five months. *Infant Behavior & Development, 34*, 239-247.

Dickinson, D. L., & Oxoby, R. J. (2011). Cognitive dissonance, pessimism, and behavioral spillover effects. *Journal of Economic Psychology, 32*, 295-306.

Diemand-Yauman, C., Oppenheimer, D. M., & Vaughan, E. B. (2010), Fortune favors the bold (and the italicized): Effects of disfluency on educational outcomes. *Cognition, 118*(1), 111-115.

Diener, E., & Seligman, M. E. P. (2004). Beyond money: Toward an economy of well-being. *Psychological Science in the Public Interest, 5*, 1-31.

Diener, E., Lucas, R. E., & Scollon, C. N. (2006). Beyond the hedonic treadmill: Revising the adaptation theory of well-being. *American Psychologist, 61*, 305-314.

Diener, M., Isabella, R., Behunin, M., & Wong, M. (2008). Attachment to mothers and fathers during middle childhood: Associations with child gender, grade, and competence. *Social Development, 17*, 84-101.

Dierolf, A. M., Fechtner, J., Böhnke, R., Wolf, O. T., & Naumann, E. (2017). Influence of acute stress on response inhibition in healthy men: An ERP study. *Psychophysiology, 54*, 684-695.

Digdon, N. (2017). The Little Albert controversy: Intuition, confirmation bias, and logic. *History of Psychology.* Accessed from https://www.ncbi.nlm.nih.gov/pubmed/28125246.

Dijksterhuis, A., Chartrand, T. L., & Aarts, H. (2007). Effects of priming and perception on social behavior and goal pursuit. *Frontiers of Social Psychology, 17*, 33-40.

DiJulio, B., Norton, M., Craighill, P., Clement, P., & Brodie, M. (2015, June 12). Survey of current and recent college students on sexual assault. *Washington Post/Kaiser Family Foundation Survey Project.*

Dill, K., & Thill, K. (2007). Video game characters and the socialization of gender roles: Young people's perceptions mirror sexist media depictions. *Sex Roles, 57*, 851-864.

Dillard, J. P., & Shen, L. (2007). Self-report measures of discrete emotions. In R. A. Reynolds, R. Woods, & J. D. Baker (Eds.), *Handbook of research on electronic surveys and measurements.* Hershey, PA: Idea Group Reference/IGI Global, 2007.

Diller, L. (2017, January 17). The United States of Adderall. *Huffington Post.* Accessed from http://www.huffingtonpost.com/larry-diller/the-united-states-of-adderall_b_8914480.html.

Dimaggio, G., D'Urzo, M., Pasinetti, M., Salvatore, G., Lysaker, P. H., Catania, D., & Popolo, R. (2015). Metacognitive interpersonal therapy for co-occurrent avoidant personality disorder and substance abuse. *Journal of Clinical Psychology, 71*, 157-166.

Dimaggio, G., Salvatore, G., MacBeth, A., Ottavi, P., Buonocore, L., & Popolo, R. (2017). Metacognitive interpersonal therapy for personality disorders: A case study series. *Journal of Contemporary Psychotherapy, 47*, 11-21.

Dingfelder, S. (2011). Reflecting on narcissism. *Monitor on Psychology, 42*, 64-68.

Diniz, B. S., Butters, M. A., Albert, S. M., Dew, M., & Reynolds, C. (2013). Late-life depression and risk of vascular dementia and Alzheimer's disease: Systematic review and meta-analysis of community-based cohort studies. *British Journal of Psychiatry, 202*, 329-335.

Dirie, W. (2011). *Desert flower.* New York: William Morrow.

Dittrich, W. H., Johansen, T., & Fineberg, N. A. (2011). Cognitive Assessment Instrument of Obsessions and Compulsions (CAIOV-13)—A new 13-item scale for evaluating functional impairment associated with OCD. *Psychiatry Research, 187*, 283-290.

Dixon, R. A., & Cohen, A. L. (2003). Cognitive development in adulthood. In R. M. Lerner, M. A. Easterbrooks, & J. Mistry (Eds.), *Handbook of psychology: Developmental psychology* (Vol. 6). New York: Wiley.

Dixon, R. A., McFall, G., Whitehead, B. P., & Dolcos, S. (2013). Cognitive development in adulthood and aging. In R. M. Lerner, M. Easterbrooks, J. Mistry, & I. B. Weiner (Eds.), *Handbook of psychology, Vol. 6: Developmental psychology* (2nd ed.). Hoboken, NJ: John Wiley & Sons Inc.

Dixon, R. A., Rust, T. B., & Feltmate, S. E. (2007). Memory and aging: Selected research directions and application issues. *Canadian Psychology Psychologie Canadienne, 48*, 67-76.

Djapo, N., Kolenovic-Djapo, J., Djokic, R., & Fako, I. (2011). Relationship between Cattell's 16PF and fluid and crystallized intelligence. *Personality and Individual Differences, 51*, 63-67.

Do, V. T. (2006). Asian American men and the media: The relationship between ethnic identity, self-esteem, and the endorsement of stereotypes. *Dissertation Abstracts International: Section B: The Sciences and Engineering, 67*(6-B), 3446.

Dobbins, I. G., & Kantner, J. (2019). The language of accurate recognition memory. *Cognition, 192*, 103988.

Dockrell, J. E., & Marshall, C. R. (2015). Measurement issues: Assessing language skills in young children. *Child and Adolescent Mental Health, 20*, 116-125.

Dodes, L. (2015). *The sober truth: Debunking the bad science behind 12-step programs and the rehab industry.* New York: Beacon Press.

Dodge, K. A. (2004). The nature-nurture debate and public policy [Special issue: 50th anniversary issue, part 2: The maturing of the human development sciences–Appraising past, present, and prospective agendas]. *Merrill-Palmer Quarterly: Journal of Developmental Psychology, 50*, 418-427.

Dohnke, B., Weiss-Gerlach, E., & Spies, C. D. (2011). Social influences on the motivation to quit smoking: Main and moderating effects of social norms. *Addictive Behaviors, 36*, 286-293.

Doi, T. (1990). The cultural assumptions of psychoanalysis. In J. W. Stigler, R. A. Shweder, & G. Herdt (Eds.), *Cultural psychology: Essays on comparative human development.* New York: Cambridge University Press.

Dolan, R. J. (2002). Emotion, cognition, and behavior. *Science, 298*, 1191-1194.

Dolinski, D. (2011). A rock or a hard place: The foot-in-the-face technique for inducing compliance without pressure. *Journal of Applied Social Psychology, 41*, 1514-1537.

Dollinger, S. J. (2003). Need for uniqueness, need for cognition and creativity. *Journal of Creative Behavior, 37*, 99-116.

Domhoff, G. W. (2011). The neural substrate for dreaming: Is it a subsystem of the default network? *Consciousness and Cognition, 20*, 1163-1174.

Domschke, K. (2013). Clinical and molecular genetics of psychotic depression. *Schizophrenia Bulletin, 39,* 766-775.

Domènech-Abella, J., Mundó, J., Haro, J. M., & Rubio-Valera, M. (2019). Anxiety, depression, loneliness and social network in the elderly: Longitudinal associations from The Irish Longitudinal Study on Ageing (TILDA). *Journal of Affective Disorders, 246,* 82-88.

Donahoe, J. W., & Vegas, R. (2004). Pavlovian conditioning: The CS-UR relation. *Journal of Experimental Psychology: Animal Behavior Processes, 30,* 17-33.

Dong, G., Wu, L., Wang, Z., Wang, Y., Du, X., & Potenza, M. N. (2018). Diffusion-weighted MRI measures suggest increased white-matter integrity in Internet gaming disorder: Evidence from the comparison with recreational Internet game users. *Addictive Behaviors, 81,* 32-38.

Doty, R. L., Green, P. A., Ram, C., & Yankell, S. L. (1982). Communication of gender from human breath odors: Relationship to perceived intensity and pleasantness. *Hormones and Behavior, 16,* 13-22.

Doty, R. L., Tourbier, I., Ng, V., Neff, J., Armstrong, D., Battistini, M., et al. (2015). Influences of hormone replacement therapy on olfactory and cognitive function in post-menopausal women. *Neurobiology of Aging, 36,* 2053-2059.

Douglas, V. J., Kwan, M. Y., Minnich, A. M., & Gordon, K. H. (2019). The interaction of sociocultural attitudes and gender on disordered eating. *Journal of Clinical Psychology.* https://doi.org/10.1002/jclp.22835.

Douthit, K. Z., & Russotti, J. (2017). Biology of marginality: A neurophysiological exploration of the social and cultural foundations of psychological health. In T. A. Field, L. K. Jones, L. A. Russell-Chapin, T. A. Field, L. K. Jones, & L. A. Russell-Chapin (Eds.), *Neurocounseling: Brain-based clinical approaches.* Alexandria, VA: American Counseling Association.

Dovidio, J. F., Piliavin, J. A., Schroeder, D. A., & Penner, L. A. (2006). *The social psychology of prosocial behavior.* Mahwah, NJ: Lawrence Erlbaum Associates.

Drakatos, P., Marples, L., Muza, R., Higgins, S., Nesbitt, A., Dongol, E. M., et al. (2019). Video polysomnographic findings in non-rapid eye movement parasomnia. *Journal of Sleep Research, 28*(2), 1-8.

Draper, K. (2019, August 6). Video games get blame, despite lack of evidence. *The New York Times,* p. 13.

Draper, K. & Kepner, T. (2019, August 31). Autopsy finds that Angels' Skaggs had ingested opioids and alcohol. *The New York Times,* p. B14.

Drerup, M. L., & Ahmed-Jauregui, S. (2019). Online delivery of cognitive behavioral therapy-insomnia: Considerations and controversies. *Sleep Medicine Clinics, 14*(2), 283-290.

Dresler, M., Shirer, W. R., Konrad, B. N., Muller, N. C., Wagner, I. C., Fernandez, G., et al. (2017). Mnemonic training reshapes brain networks to support superior memory. *Neuron, 93*(5), 1227-1235.

Dresler, T., Guhn, A., Tupak, S. V., Ehlis, A., Herrmann, M. J., Fallgatter, A. J., et al. (2013). Revise the revised? New dimensions of the neuroanatomical hypothesis of panic disorder. *Journal of Neural Transmission, 120,* 3-29.

Drewes, A. A. (2005). Play in selected cultures: Diversity and universality. In E. Gil & A. A. Drewes (Eds.), *Cultural issues in play therapy.* New York: Guilford Press.

Driessen, E., Van, H. L., Peen, J., Don, F. J., Twisk, J. R., Cuijpers, P., et al. (2017). Cognitive-behavioral versus psychodynamic therapy for major depression: Secondary outcomes of a randomized clinical trial. *Journal of Consulting and Clinical Psychology, 85,* 653-663.

Dryden, W., & David, D. (2008). Rational emotive behavior therapy: Current status. *Journal of Cognitive Psychotherapy, 22,* 195-209.

Duckworth, A. (2016). *Grit: The power of passion and perseverance.* New York: Scribner/Simon & Schuster.

Dudai, Y. (2011). The engram revisited: On the elusive permanence of memory. In S. Nalbantian, P. M. Matthews, & J. L. McClelland (Eds.), *The memory process: Neuroscientific and humanistic perspectives.* Cambridge, MA: MIT Press.

Dufford, A. J., Bianco, H., & Kim, P. (2019). Socioeconomic disadvantage, brain morphometry, and attentional bias to threat in middle childhood. *Cognitive, Affective & Behavioral Neuroscience, 19*(2), 309-326.

Duffy, F., Sharpe, H., & Schwannauer, M. (2019). Review: The effectiveness of interpersonal psychotherapy for adolescents with depression a systematic review and meta-analysis. *Child and Adolescent Mental Health, 24*(4), 307-317.

Dugger, C. W. (1996, December 28). Tug of taboos: African genital rite vs. U.S. law. *The New York Times,* pp. 1, 9.

Dugger, C. W. (2013, July 22). Genital cutting found in decline in many nations. *The New York Times,* p. A1.

Duke, M., & Nowicki, S., Jr. (1979). *Abnormal psychology: Perspectives on being different.* Monterey, CA: Brooks/Cole.

Duncker, K. (1945). On problem solving. *Psychological Monographs, 58* (5, whole no. 270).

Dunkley, D. M., Lewkowski, M., Lee, I. A., Preacher, K. J., Zuroff, D. C., Berg, J., et al. (2017). Daily stress, coping, and negative and positive affect in depression: Complex trigger and maintenance patterns. *Behavior Therapy, 48,* 349-365.

Dunn, E. C., Soare, T. W., Zhu, Y., Simpkin, A. J., Suderman, M. J., Klengel, T., et al. (2019). Sensitive periods for the effect of childhood adversity on DNA methylation: Results from a prospective, longitudinal study. *Biological Psychiatry, 85*(10), 838-849.

Dunning, D. (2019). The best option illusion in self and social assessment. *Self and Identity, 18*(4), 349-362.

Durbin, A., Nisenbaum, R., Kopp, B., O'Campo, P., Hwang, S. W., & Stergiopoulos, V. (2019). Are resilience and perceived stress related to social support and housing stability among homeless adults with mental illness? *Health & Social Care in the Community, 27*(4), 1053-1062.

Dweck, C. S. (2017). Is psychology headed in the right direction? Yes, no, and maybe. *Perspectives on Psychological Science, 12,* 656-659.

Dweck, C. S., & Yeager, D. S. (2018). Mindsets change the imagined and actual future. In G. Oettingen, A. T. Sevincer, & P. Gollwitzer (Eds.), *The psychology of thinking about the future.* New York: Guilford Press.

Dweck, C. S., & Yeager, D. S. (2019). Mindsets: A view from two eras. *Perspectives on Psychological Science, 14*(3), 481-496.

Dwyer, C. (2020, April 8). New York City's Latinx residents hit ardest by coronavirus deaths. National Public Radio. Downloaded from https://www.npr.org/2020/04/08/829726964/new-york-citys-latinx-residents-hit-hardest-by-coronavirus-deaths.

Eagly, A. H., & Wood, W. (2013). The nature-nurture debates: 25 years of challenges in understanding the psychology of gender. *Perspectives on Psychological Science, 8,* 340-357.

Eagly, A. S. (2016). Psychology of gender: Nature and nurture working together. In R. J. Sternberg, S. T. Fiske, & D. J. Foss (Eds.), *Scientists making a difference: One hundred eminent behavioral and brain scientists talk about their most important contributions.* New York: Cambridge University Press.

Eaker, E. D., Sullivan, L. M., Kelly-Hayes, M., D'Agostino, R. B., Sr., & Benjamin, E. J. (2004). Anger and hostility predict the development of atrial fibrillation in men in the Framingham Offspring Study. *Circulation, 109,* 1267-1271.

Ebigbo, P. O., Lekwas, E. C., & Chukwunenyem, N. F. (2015). Brain fag: New perspectives from case observations. *Transcultural Psychiatry, 52,* 311-330.

Ebrahimian, Z., Karimi, Z., Khoshnoud, M. J., Namavar, M. R., Daraei, B., & Haidari, M. R. (2017). Behavioral and stereological analysis of the effects of intermittent feeding diet on the orally administrated MDMA ("ecstasy") in mice. *Innovations in Clinical Neuroscience, 14,* 40-52.

Ecenbarger, W. (1993, April 1). America's new merchants of death. *Reader's Digest,* p. 50.

Eckardt, M. H. (2005). Karen Horney: A portrait: The 120th anniversary, Karen Horney, September 16, 1885. *American Journal of Psychoanalysis, 65,* 95-101.

Ecker, U. H., Tay, J., & Brown, G. A. (2015). Effects of prestudy and poststudy rest on memory: Support for temporal interference accounts of forgetting. *Psychonomic Bulletin & Review, 22,* 772-778.

Edoka, I. P., Petrou, S., & Ramchandani, P. G. (2011). Healthcare costs of paternal depression in the postnatal period. *Journal of Affective Disorders, 133,* 356-360.

Edwards, C., Edwards, A., Stoll, B., Lin, X., & Massey, N. (2019). Evaluations of an artificial intelligence instructor's voice: Social identity theory in human-robot interactions. *Computers in Human Behavior, 90,* 357-362.

Edwards, M. S., Moore, P., Champion, J. C., & Edwards, E. J. (2015). Effects of trait anxiety and situational stress on attentional shifting are buffered by working memory capacity. *Anxiety, Stress & Coping: An International Journal, 28,* 1-16.

Efklides, A., & Moraitou, D. (2013). *A positive psychology perspective on quality of life.* New York: Springer Science + Business Media.

Egan, K. (2005). Students' development in theory and practice: The doubtful role of research. *Harvard Educational Review, 75,* 25-41.

Egan, K. J., Knutson, K. L., Pereira, A. C., & von Schantz, M. (2017). The role of race and ethnicity in sleep, circadian rhythms and cardiovascular health. *Sleep Medicine Reviews, 33,* 70-78.

Egervari, G., Ciccocioppo, R., Jentsch, J. D., & Hurd, Y. L. (2017). Shaping vulnerability to addiction—the contribution of behavior, neural circuits and molecular mechanisms. *Neuroscience and Biobehavioral Reviews.* Accessed from http://www.sciencedirect.com/science/article/pii/S0149763417300866.

Eggertson L. (2010). Lancet retracts 12-year-old article linking autism to MMR vaccines. *CMAJ : Canadian Medical Association journal = Journal de l'Association Medicale Canadienne, 182*(4), E199-E200.

Ehde, D. M., Dillworth, T. M., & Turner, J. A. (2014). Cognitive-behavioral therapy for individuals with chronic pain: Efficacy, innovations, and directions for research. *American Psychologist, 69,* 153-177.

Einarsson, C., & Granstroem, K. (2002). Gender-biased interaction in the classroom: The influence of gender and age in the relationship between teacher and pupil. *Scandinavian Journal of Educational Research, 46,* 117-127.

Eizenberg, M. M., & Zaslavsky, O. (2004). Students' verification strategies for combinatorial problems. *Mathematical Thinking and Learning, 6,* 15-36.

Ekman, P. (1972). Universals and cultural differences in facial expressions of emotion. In J. Cole (Ed.), *Darwin and facial expression: A century of research in review.* New York: Academic Press.

Ekman, P. (1994b). Strong evidence for universals in facial expressions: A reply to Russell's mistaken critique. *Psychological Bulletin, 115,* 268-287.

Ekman, P. (2003). *Emotions revealed: Recognizing faces and feelings to improve communication and emotional life.* New York: Times Books.

Ekman, P. (2007). *Emotions revealed* (2nd ed.). New York: Holt.

Ekman, P., Levenson, R. W., & Friesen, W. V. (1983). Autonomic nervous system activity distinguishes among emotions. *Science, 223,* 1208-1210.

Ekonomou, A., Savva, G. M., Brayne, C., Forster, G., Francis, P. T., Johnson, M., et al. (2015). Stage-specific changes in neurogenic and glial markers in Alzheimer's disease. *Biological Psychiatry, 77,* 711-719.

Elen, M., D'Heer, E., Geuens, M., & Vermeir, I. (2013). The influence of mood on attitude-behavior consistency. *Journal of Business Research, 66,* 917-923.

Elias, V. L., Fullerton, A. S., & Simpson, J. M. (2015). Long-term changes in attitudes toward premarital sex in the United States: Reexamining the role of cohort replacement. *Journal of Sex Research, 52,* 129-139.

Eljamel, S. (2015). Ablative surgery for depression. In B. Sun & A. De Salles (Eds.), *Neurosurgical treatments for psychiatric disorders.* New York: Springer Science + Business Media.

Elkins, D. (2009). Why humanistic psychology lost its power and influence in American psychology: Implications for advancing humanistic psychology. *Journal of Humanistic Psychology, 49,* 267-291.

Ellins, E., Halcox, J., Donald, A., Field, B., Brydon, L., Deanfield, J., & Steptoe, A. (2008). Arterial stiffness and inflammatory response to psychophysiological stress. *Brain, Behavior, and Immunity, 22,* 941-948.

Elliot, A. J., Dweck, C. S., & Yeager, D. S. (2017). *Handbook of competence and motivation: Theory and application* (2nd ed.). New York: Guilford Press.

Ellis, A. (1974). *Growth through reason.* Hollywood, CA: Wilshire Books.

Ellis, A. (2002). *Overcoming resistance: A rational emotive behavior therapy integrated approach* (2nd ed.). New York: Springer.

Ellis, A. (2004). Expanding the ABCs of rational emotive behavior therapy. In A. Freeman, M. J. Mahoney, P. Devito, & D. Martin (Eds.), *Cognition and psychotherapy* (2nd ed.). New York: Springer Publishing Co.

Elmlinger, S. L., Schwade, J. A., & Goldstein, M. H. (2019). The ecology of prelinguistic vocal learning: Parents simplify the structure of their speech in response to babbling. *Journal of Child Language,* 1-14. doi:10.1017/S0305000919000291.

Emmett, J., & McGee, D. (2013). Extrinsic motivation for large-scale assessments: A case study of a student achievement program at one urban high school. *The High School Journal, 96,* 116-137.

Emre, M. (2019). *The personality brokers.* NY: Doubleday.

Endendijk, J. J., Groeneveld, M. G., van der Pol, L. D., van Berkel, S. R., Hallers-Haalboom, E. T., Bakermans-Kranenburg, M. J., et al. (2017). Gender differences in child aggression: Relations with gender-differentiated parenting and parents' gender-role stereotypes. *Child Development, 88,* 299-316.

Enge, L. R., Lupo, A. K., & Zárate, M. A. (2015). Neurocognitive mechanisms of prejudice formation: The role of time-dependent memory consolidation. *Psychological Science, 26,* 964-971.

Engel, U., Jann, B., Lynn, P., Scherpenzeel, A., & Sturgis, P. (2015). *Improving survey methods: Lessons from recent research.* New York: Routledge/Taylor & Francis Group.

Engen, T. (1987). Remembering odors and their names. *American Scientist, 75,* 497-503.

Epatko, L. (2018, April 16). This summer camp helps kids reach across the Israeli-Palestinian divide. *PBS News Hour.* Accessed from https://www.pbs.org/newshour/world/seeds-of-peace-empowers-its-young-leaders-to-confront-conflict-around-the-world.

Erb, J., Henry, M. J., Eisner, F., & Obleser, J. (2013). The brain dynamics of rapid perceptual adaptation to adverse listening conditions. *Journal of Neuroscience, 33,* 10688-10697.

Erickson, R. (2008). A study of the science of taste: On the origins and influence of the core ideas. *Behavioral and Brain Sciences, 31,* 59-75.

Erikson, E. H. (1963). *Childhood and society.* New York: Norton.

Ervik, S., Abdelnoor, M., & Heier, M. S. (2006). Health-related quality of life in narcolepsy. *Acta Neurologica Scandinavica, 114,* 198-204.

Erzurumluoglu, A. M., Liu, M., Jackson, V. E., Barnes, D. R., Datta, G., Melbourne, C. A., et al. (2019). Meta-analysis of up to 622,409 individuals identifies 40 novel smoking behaviours associated genetic loci. *Molecular Psychiatry.* https://doi.org/10.1038/s41380-018-0313-0.

Esparham, A. E., & Dilts, J. J. (2019). Integrative management of pediatric primary headaches. *Pediatric Annals, 48*(6), e231-e235.

Espinola, M., DeVinney, H., & Steinberg, A. (2017). Women at midlife. In K. A. Kendall-Tackett, L. M. Ruglass, K. A. Kendall-Tackett, & L. M. Ruglass (Eds.), *Women's mental health across the lifespan: Challenges, vulnerabilities, and strengths.* New York: Routledge/Taylor & Francis Group.

Etienne, J. (2013). Thoughts on how to regulate behaviours: An overview of the current debate. *British Journal of Guidance & Counselling, 41,* 36-45.

Etxeberria, I., Etxebarria, I., & Urdaneta, E. (2019). Subjective well-being among the oldest old: The role of personality traits. *Personality and Individual Differences, 146,* 209-216.

Etzrodt, C. M. (2013). Ethical considerations of therapeutic hypnosis and children. *American Journal of Clinical Hypnosis, 55,* 370-377.

Euler, M. J., Weisend, M. P., Jung, R. E., Thoma, R. J., & Yeo, R. A. (2015). Reliable activation to novel stimuli predicts higher fluid intelligence. *Neuroimage, 114,* 311-319.

Evcik, D., Kavuncu, V., Cakir, T., Subasi, V., & Yaman, M. (2007). Laser therapy in the treatment of carpal tunnel syndrome: A randomized controlled trial. *Photomedical Laser Surgery, 25,* 34-39.

Everly, G. S., Jr., & Lating, J. M. (2007). Psychotherapy: A cognitive perspective. In A. Monat, R. S. Lazarus, & G. Reevy (Eds.), *The Praeger handbook on stress and coping* (Vol. 2). Westport, CT: Praeger Publishers/Greenwood Publishing.

Eysenck, H. J. (1995). *Eysenck on extraversion.* New York: Wiley.

Fabian, M. (2019). The coalescence of being: A model of the self-actualisation process. *Journal of Happiness Studies: An Interdisciplinary Forum on Subjective Well-Being.* https://doi.org/10.1007/s10902-019-00141-7.

Fadjukoff, P., Feldt, T., Kokko, K., & Pulkkinen, L. (2019). Identity status change within personal style clusters: A longitudinal perspective from early adulthood to midlife. *Identity, 19*(1), 1-17.

Fadus, M. C., Odunsi, O. T., & Squeglia, L. M. (2019). Race, ethnicity, and culture in the medical record: Implicit bias or patient advocacy? *Academic Psychiatry*, 1-5.

Fagan, J. F., & Holland, C. R. (2002). Equal opportunity and racial differences in IQ. *Intelligence, 30*, 361-387.

Fagan, J. F., & Holland, C. R. (2007). Racial equality in intelligence: Predictions from a theory of intelligence as processing. *Intelligence, 35*, 319-334.

Fagan, J. F., & Holland, C. R. (2009). Culture-fair prediction of academic achievement. *Intelligence, 37*, 62-67.

Fagan, J., & Press, J. (2008). Father influences on employed mothers' work-family balance. *Journal of Family Issues, 29*, 1136-1160.

Fagelson, M., & Baguley, D. M. (2018). Hyperacusis: Past, present, and future. In *Hyperacusis and disorders of sound intolerance: Clinical and research perspectives.* San Diego, CA: Plural Publishing.

Fairfield, H. (2012, February 4). Clues to a troubling gap. *The New York Times*, p. S1.

Falasca, N. W., D'Ascenzo, S., Di Domenico, A., Onofrj, M., Tommasi, L., Laeng, B., et al. (2015). Hemispheric lateralization in top-down attention during spatial relation processing: A Granger causal model approach. *European Journal of Neuroscience, 41*, 912-922.

Falbe, J., Thompson, H. R., Patel, A., & Madsen, K. A. (2019). Potentially addictive properties of sugar-sweetened beverages among adolescents. *Appetite, 133*, 130-137.

Faniko, K., Ellemers, N., Derks, B., & Lorenzi-Cioldi, F. (2017). Nothing changes, really: Why women who break through the glass ceiling end up reinforcing it. *Personality and Social Psychology Bulletin, 43*, 638-651.

Farnsworth, D. L. (2015). Identical twins raised apart. *Teaching Statistics, 37*, 1-6.

Farrell, A. K., Simpson, J. A., Carlson, E. A., Englund, M. M., & Sung, S. (2017). The impact of stress at different life stages on physical health and the buffering effects of maternal sensitivity. *Health Psychology, 36*, 35-44.

Faupel, A., Herrick, E., & Sharp, P. M. (2018). *Anger management: A practical guide for teachers* (3rd ed.). New York: Routledge/Taylor & Francis Group.

Fayek, A. (2017). *Understanding classical psychoanalysis: Freudian concepts in contemporary practice.* New York: Routledge/Taylor & Francis Group.

Fearing, V. G., & Clark, J. (Eds.). (2000). *Individuals in context: A practical guide to client-centered practice.* Chicago: Slack Publishing.

Federal Bureau of Investigation (2019, September 30). FBI releases 2018 crime statistics. News release. Downloaded from https://www.fbi.gov/news/pressrel/press-releases/fbi-releases-2018-crime-statistics.

Fedyk, M. (2017). *The social turn in moral psychology.* Cambridge, MA: MIT Press.

Feld, G. B., & Born, J. (2017). Sculpting memory during sleep: Concurrent consolidation and forgetting. *Current Opinion in Neurobiology, 44*, 20-27.

Feldman, D. H. (2003). Cognitive development in childhood. In R. M. Lerner, M. A. Easterbrooks, & J. Mistry (Eds.), *Handbook of psychology: Developmental psychology* (Vol. 6). New York: Wiley.

Feldman, D. H. (2004). Piaget's stages: The unfinished symphony of cognitive development. *New Ideas in Psychology, 22*, 175-231.

Feldman, R. S. (2013). *P.O.W.E.R. learning: Foundations of student success.* New York: McGraw-Hill.

Feldman, R. S. (2017). *P.O.W.E.R. Learning: Strategies for success in college and life.* New York: McGraw-Hill.

Felson, R. B., & Tedeschi, J.T. (Eds.). (1993). *Aggression and violence: Social interactionist perspectives.* Washington, DC: American Psychological Association.

Feng, B., Bell, R. A., Jerant, A. F., & Kravitz, R. L. (2011). What do doctors say when prescribing medications? An examination of medical recommendations from a communication perspective. *Health Communication, 26*, 286-296.

Fenter, V. L. (2006). Concerns about Prozac and direct-to-consumer advertising of prescription drugs. *International Journal of Risk & Safety in Medicine, 18*, 1-7.

Ferguson, C. J. (2015). "Everybody knows psychology is not a real science": Public perceptions of psychology and how we can improve our relationship with policymakers, the scientific community, and the general public. *American Psychologist, 70*, 527-542.

Ferguson, C. J. (2015a). Does media violence predict societal violence? It depends on what you look at and when. *Journal of Communication, 65*, E1-E22.

Ferguson, C. J. (2015b). Do angry birds make for angry children? A meta-analysis of video game influences on children's and adolescents' aggression, mental health, prosocial behavior, and academic performance. *Psychological Science*, 1-22.

Ferguson, C. J., & Beresin, E. (2017). Social science's curious war with pop culture and how it was lost: The media violence debate and the risks it holds for social science. *Preventive Medicine: An International Journal Devoted to Practice and Theory, 99*, 69-76.

Ferguson, C. J., & Wang, J. C. K. (2019). Aggressive video games are not a risk factor for future aggression in youth: A longitudinal study. *Journal of Youth and Adolescence, 48*(8), 1439-1451.

Ferjan Ramírez, N., Lytle, S. R., Fish, M., & Kuhl, P. K. (2019). Parent coaching at 6 and 10 months improves language outcomes at 14 months: A randomized controlled trial. *Developmental Science, 22*(3), e12762.

Fernald, R. D. (2015). Social behaviour: Can it change the brain? *Animal Behaviour, 103*, 259-265.

Fernyhough, C. (2017). Talking to ourselves. *Scientific American, 317*, 74-79.

Ferranti, J. (2015). DSM-5: Development and implementation. In C. Scott (Ed.), *DSM-5® and the law: Changes and challenges.* New York: Oxford University Press.

Ferring, D., Tournier, I., & Mancini, D. (2015). "The closer you get . . .": Age, attitudes and self-serving evaluations about older drivers. *European Journal of Ageing, 12*(3), 229-238.

Festinger, D., Marlowe, D., Croft, J., Dugosh, K., Arabia, P., & Benasutti, K. (2009). Monetary incentives improve recall of research consent information: It pays to remember. *Experimental and Clinical Psychopharmacology, 17*, 99-104.

Festinger, L. (1957). *A theory of cognitive dissonance.* Stanford, CA: Stanford University Press.

Festinger, L., & Carlsmith, J. M. (1959). Cognitive consequences of forced compliance. *Journal of Abnormal and Social Psychology, 58*, 203-210.

Festini, S. B., & Reuter-Lorenz, P. A. (2017). Rehearsal of to-be-remembered items is unnecessary to perform directed forgetting within working memory: Support for an active control mechanism. *Journal of Experimental Psychology: Learning, Memory, and Cognition, 43*, 94-108.

Fetvadjiev, V. H., Meiring, D., van de Vijver, F. R., Nel, J. A., Sekaja, L., & Laher, S. (2018). Personality and behavior prediction and consistency across cultures: A multimethod study of Blacks and Whites in South Africa. *Journal of Personality and Social Psychology, 114*(3), 465-481. doi:10.1037/pspp0000129.

Fevang, S. E., Hysing, M., Sommerfelt, K., & Elgen, I. (2017). Mental health assessed by the strengths and difficulties questionnaire for children born extremely preterm without severe disabilities at 11 years of age: A Norwegian, national population-based study. *European Child & Adolescent Psychiatry.* Accessed from https://www.ncbi.nlm.nih.gov/pubmed/28585081.

Fichtenberg, C. M., & Glantz, S. A. (2006). Association of the California tobacco control program with declines in cigarette consumption and mortality from heart disease. In K. E. Warner (Ed.), *Tobacco control policy.* San Francisco, CA: Jossey-Bass.

Fields, R.D. (2016). *Why we snap: Understanding the rage circuit in your brain.* New York: Penguin.

Figen, A. (2011). The relationship between test anxiety and learned helplessness. *Social Behavior and Personality, 39,* 101-112.

Filbey, M. (2019). *The neuroscience of addiction.* Cambridge, England: Cambridge University Press.

Filip, M., Lukavská, K., & Šolcová, I. P. (2019). Dialogical and integrated self in late adulthood: Examining two adaptive ways of growing old. *The International Journal of Aging and Human Development.* https://doi.org/10.1177/0091415019831445.

Filippello, P., Sorrenti, L., Buzzai, C., & Costa, S. (2015). Perceived parental psychological control and learned helplessness: The role of school self-efficacy. *School Mental Health, 7*(4), 298-310.

Filippi, C. A., Cannon, E. N., Fox, N. A., Thorpe, S. G., Ferrari, P. F., & Woodward, A. L. (2016). Motor system activation predicts goal imitation in 7-month-old infants. *Psychological Science, 27*(5), 675-684.

Finan, P. H., Zautra, A. J., & Wershba, R. (2011). The dynamics of emotion in adaptation to stress. In R. J. Contrada & A. Baum (Eds.), *The handbook of stress science: Biology, psychology, and health.* New York: Springer Publishing Co.

Fine, C. (2010). *Delusions of gender: How our minds, society, and neurosexism create difference.* New York: W. W. Norton & Co.

Fine, R., & Fine, L. (2003). *Basic chess endings.* New York: Random House.

Fingelkurts, A., Fingelkurts, A. A., & Kallio, S. (2007). Hypnosis induces a changed composition of brain oscillations in EEG: A case study. *Contemporary Hypnosis, 24,* 3-18.

Fink, B., Manning, J. T., & Williams, J. H. G. (2007). The 2nd to 4th digit ratio and developmental psychopathology in school-aged children. *Personality and Individual Differences, 42,* 369-379.

Fink, S. (2017, July 28). Two C.I.A. psychologists can face trial, judge rules. *The New York Times,* p. A18.

Finke, M. S., Howe, J. S., & Huston, S. J. (2017). Old age and the decline in financial literacy. *Management Science, 63,* 213-230.

Finkelhor, D., & Jones, L. M. (2004, January). Explanations for the decline in child sexual abuse cases. *Juvenile Justice Bulletin.*

Finkelstein, M. (2009). Intrinsic vs. extrinsic motivational orientations and the volunteer process. *Personality and Individual Differences, 46,* 653-658.

Finkler, K. (2004). Traditional healers in Mexico: The effectiveness of spiritual practices. In U. P. Gielen, J. M. Fish, & J. G. Draguns (Eds.), *Handbook of culture, therapy, and healing.* Mahwah, NJ: Lawrence Erlbaum Associates.

Finlay, F. O., Jones, R., & Coleman, J. (2002). Is puberty getting earlier? The views of doctors and teachers. *Child: Care, Health and Development, 28,* 205-209.

Finn, A. (2011). Jungian analytical theory. In D. Capuzzi & D. R. Gross (Eds.), *Counseling and psychotherapy* (5th ed.). Alexandria, VA: American Counseling Association.

Finn, K. (2015). Sequelae of cannabis as medicine. *Pain Medicine, 16,* 1447-1449.

Fischer, I. (2011). Several eyes for an eye: The impact of biased perceptions and noise on conflict escalation patterns. *Peace and Conflict: Journal of Peace Psychology, 17,* 77-84.

Fischer, P., Krueger, J. I., Greitemeyer, T., Vogrincic, C., Kastenmüller, A., Frey, D., & Kainbacher, M. (2011). The bystander-effect: A meta-analytic review on bystander intervention in dangerous and non-dangerous emergencies. *Psychological Bulletin, 137,* 517-537.

Fishbach, A., Dhar, R., & Zhang, Y. (2006). Subgoals as substitutes or complements: The role of goal accessibility. *Journal of Personality and Social Psychology, 91,* 232-242.

Fisher, A. K., Moore, D. J., Simmons, C., & Allen, S. C. (2017). Teaching social workers about microaggressions to enhance understanding of subtle racism. *Journal of Human Behavior in the Social Environment, 27*(4), 346-355.

Fisher, C. B. (2003). *Decoding the ethics code: A practical guide for psychologists.* Thousand Oaks, CA: Sage.

Fisher, G. G., & Barnes-Farrell, J. L. (2013). Use of archival data in occupational health psychology research. In R. R. Sinclair, M. Wang, & L. E. Tetrick (Eds.), *Research methods in occupational health psychology: Measurement, design, and data analysis.* New York: Routledge/Taylor & Francis Group.

Fisher, R. J., & Kelman, H. C. (2011). Perceptions in conflict. In D. Bar-Tal, (Ed.), *Intergroup conflicts and their resolution: A social psychological perspective.* New York: Psychology Press.

Fiske, S. T. (2017). Going in many right directions, all at once. *Perspectives on Psychology, 12,* 652-655.

Flannelly, K. J. (2017). *Religious beliefs, evolutionary psychiatry, and mental health in America: Evolutionary threat assessment systems theory.* Cham, Switzerland: Springer International Publishing.

Fleming, J. (2000). Affirmative action and standardized test scores. *Journal of Negro Education, 69,* 27-37.

Flohr, E. R., Erwin, E., Croy, I., & Hummel, T. (2017). Sad man's nose: Emotion induction and olfactory perception. *Emotion, 17,* 369-378.

Flynn, J. R. (2009). *What is intelligence? Beyond the Flynn effect* (Expanded paperback ed.). Cambridge, England: Cambridge University Press.

Foderaro, L. W. (2006, February 16). Westchester lawyer, his memory lost, is found in Chicago shelter after 6 months. *The New York Times,* p. B3.

Folkman, S., & Moskowitz, J. T. (2000). Stress, positive emotion, and coping. *Current Directions in Psychological Science, 9,* 115-118.

Folkman, S., & Moskowitz, J. T. (2004). Coping: Pitfalls and promise. *Annual Review of Psychology, 55,* 745-774.

Forbus, K. D., Liang, C., & Rabkina, I. (2017). Representation and computation in cognitive models. *Topics in Cognitive Science, 9*(3), 694-718.

Forer, B. (1949). The fallacy of personal validation: A classroom demonstration of gullibility. *Journal of Abnormal and Social Psychology, 44,* 118-123.

Ford, B. Q., & Gross, J. J. (2019). Why beliefs about emotion matter: An emotion-regulation perspective. *Current Directions in Psychological Science, 28*(1), 74-81.

Forgas, J. P., & Laham, S. M. (2005). The interaction between affect and motivation in social judgments and behavior. In J. P. Forgas, K. P. Williams, & S. M. Laham (Eds.), *Social motivation: Conscious and unconscious processes.* New York: Cambridge University Press.

Forgas, J. P., & Laham, S. M. (2017). Halo effects. In R. F. Pohl (Ed.), *Cognitive illusions: Intriguing phenomena in thinking, judgment and memory.* New York: Routledge/Taylor & Francis Group.

Forsdike, K., & Pirotta, M. (2019). St John's wort for depression: Scoping review about perceptions and use by general practitioners in clinical practice. *Journal of Pharmacy and Pharmacology, 71*(1), 117-128.

Forsman, J., Masterman, T., Ahlner, J., Isacsson, G., & Hedström, A. K. (2019). Selective serotonin re-uptake inhibitors and the risk of violent suicide: A nationwide postmortem study. *European Journal of Clinical Pharmacology, 75*(3), 393-400.

Forson, T.S. (2018, February 21.) Who is African-American? Definition evolves as USA does. *USA Today.* Retrieved from https://www.usatoday.com/story/news/nation-now/2018/02/21/black-history-african-american-definition/1002344001/.

Forsythe, A. (2019). *Key thinkers in individual differences: Ideas on personality and intelligence.* New York: Routledge.

Fost, J. (2015). Are there psychological species? *Review of Philosophy and Psychology, 6,* 293-315.

Foster, K. M. (2005). Introduction: John Uzo Ogbu (1939-2003): How do you ensure the fair consideration of a complex ancestor? Multiple approaches to assessing the work and legacy of John Uzo Ogbu. *International Journal of Qualitative Studies in Education, 18,* 559-564.

Foulds, J., Gandhi, K. K., Steinberg, M. B., Richardson, D. L., Williams, J. M., Burke, M. V., & Rhoads, G. G. (2006). Factors associated with quitting smoking at a tobacco dependence treatment clinic. *American Journal of Health Behavior, 30,* 400-412.

Fountas, K. N., & Smith, J. R. (2007). Historical evolution of stereotactic amygdalotomy for the management of severe aggression. *Journal of Neurosurgery, 106,* 716-713.

Fowler, G., Cope, C., Michalski, D., Christidis, P., Lin, L., & Conroy, J. (2018). Women outnumber men in psychology graduate programs. *Monitor in Psychology,* p. 21.

Fox, S., & Spector, P. E. (2000). Relations of emotional intelligence, practical intelligence, general intelligence, and trait affectivity with interview outcomes: It's not all just "G." *Journal of Organizational Behavior, 21*, 203-220.

Frances, A. (2013). *Saving normal: An insider's revolt against out-of-control psychiatric diagnosis, DSM-5, Big Pharma, and the medicalization of ordinary life.* New York: Morrow.

Francis, G., Cummins, B., Kim, J., Grzeczkowski, L., & Thunell, E. (2019). The moon size illusion does not improve perceptual judgments. *Consciousness and Cognition, 73,* 102754.

Francis, M. M., Hummer, T. A., Vohs, J. L., Yung, M. G., Visco, A. C., Mehdiyoun, N. F., et al. (2019). Cognitive effects of bilateral high frequency repetitive transcranial magnetic stimulation in early phase psychosis: A pilot study. *Brain Imaging and Behavior, 13*(3), 852-861.

Frank, K., & Hou, F. (2015). Source-country gender roles and the division of labor within immigrant families. *Journal of Marriage and Family, 77,* 557-574.

Frank, S., Goldwater, S., & Keller, F. (2013). Adding sentence types to a model of syntactic category acquisition. *Topics in Cognitive Science, 5,* 495-521.

Franklin, A., Pilling, M., & Davies, I. (2005). The nature of infant color categorization: Evidence from eye movements on a target decision task. *Journal of Experimental Child Psychology, 91,* 227-248.

Franklin, T. B., & Mansuy, I. M. (2011). The involvement of epigenetic defects in mental retardation. *Neurobiology of Learning and Memory, 96,* 61-67.

Franko, D. L., & Roehrig, J. P. (2011). African American body images. In T. F. Cash & L. Smolak (Eds.), *Body image: A handbook of science, practice, and prevention* (2nd ed.). New York: Guilford Press.

Frawley, T. (2008). Gender schema and prejudicial recall: How children misremember, fabricate, and distort gendered picture book information. *Journal of Research in Childhood Education, 22,* 291-303.

Freedberg, D. (2011). Memory in art: History and the neuroscience of response. In S. Nalbantian, P. M. Matthews, & J. L. McClelland (Eds.), *The memory process: Neuroscientific and humanistic perspectives.* Cambridge, MA: MIT Press.

Freedman, J. L., & Fraser, S. C. (1966). Compliance without pressure: The foot-in-the-door technique. *Journal of Personality and Social Psychology, 4,* 195-202.

Freedman, M. R., & Waldrop, J. (2011). Freshman orientation sessions can teach incoming students about healthful lifestyles. *Journal of Nutrition Education and Behavior, 43,* 69-70.

Freeman, J. (2013). The long-term effects of families and educational provision on gifted children. *Educational and Child Psychology, 30*(2), 7-17.

Freeman, J. E. (2006). Psychology of race and ethnicity. In W. Buskit & S. F. Davis (Eds.), *Handbook of the teaching of psychology.* Malden, MA: Blackwell Publishing.

French, S., Coleman, B., & DiLorenzo, M. (2013). Linking racial identity, ethnic identity, and racial-ethnic socialization: A tale of three race-ethnicities. *Identity: An International Journal of Theory and Research, 13,* 1-45.

Fresco, D. M. (2013). Tending the garden and harvesting the fruits of behavior therapy. *Behavior Therapy, 44,* 177-179.

Freud, S. (1900). *Group psychology and the analysis of the ego.* London: Hogarth.

Freud, S. (1922/1959). *Group psychology and the analysis of the ego.* London: Hogarth.

Frey, W. H. (2018). The US will become "minority white" in 2045, Census projects. Brookings Institute. Retrieved from https://www.brookings.edu/blog/the-avenue/2018/03/14/the-us-will-become-minority-white-in-2045-census-projects/.

Frias-Navarro, D., García, L., Garcia-Banda, G., Pascual-Soler, M., & Badenes-Ribera, L. (2018). Attitudinal change toward same-sex parents: The effect of the explanation of the etiology of the homosexual sexual orientation. *Sexuality Research and Social Policy, 15*(4), 516-529.

Friborg, O., Barlaug, D., Martinussen, M., Rosenvinge, J. H., & Hjemdal, O. (2005). Resilience in relation to personality and intelligence. *International Journal of Methods in Psychiatric Research, 14,* 29-42.

Friborg, O., Hjemdal, O., & Rosenvinge, J. H. (2006). Resilience as a moderator of pain and stress. *Journal of Psychosomatic Research, 61,* 213-219.

Friedman, J. N. W., Oltmanns, T. F., & Turkheimer, E. (2007). Interpersonal perception and personality disorders: Utilization of a thin slice approach. *Journal of Research in Personality, 11,* 667-688.

Frijda, N. H. (2005). Emotion experience. *Cognition and Emotion, 19,* 473-497.

Frodl, T., Janowitz, D., Schmaal, L., Tozzi, L., Dobrowolny, H., Stein, D. J., et al. (2017). Childhood adversity impacts on brain subcortical structures relevant to depression. *Journal of Psychiatric Research, 86,* 58-65.

Frosch, A. (2011). The effect of frequency and duration on psychoanalytic outcome: A moment in time. *Psychoanalytic Review, 98,* 11-38.

Frost, J. C., Molinari, V., Dobbs, D., Edgar, V. B., Jones, K. S., Pietz, C., & Badana, A. N. S. (2019). Who gets certified by the American Board of Professional Psychology and why: A diversity survey. *Journal of Clinical Psychology, 17*(10), 1820-1837.

Fryling, M. J. (2017). The functional independence of Skinner's verbal operants: Conceptual and applied implications. *Behavioral Interventions, 32,* 70-78.

Fuhrman, O., McCormick, K., Chen, E., Jiang, H., Shu, D., Mao, S., et al. (2011). How linguistic and cultural forces shape conceptions of time: English and Mandarin time in 3D. *Cognitive Science: A Multidisciplinary Journal, 7,* 1305-1328.

Fujita, K., Nakamura, N., Watanabe, S., & Ushitani, T. (2017). Comparative visual illusions: Evolutionary, cross-cultural, and developmental perspectives. In J. Call, G. M. Burghardt, I. M. Pepperberg, C. T. Snowdon, & T. Zentall (Eds.), *APA handbook of comparative psychology: Perception, learning, and cognition.* Washington, DC: American Psychological Association.

Furnham, A., & Swami, V. (2007). Perception of female buttocks and breast size in profile. *Social Behavior and Personality, 35,* 1-8.

Furumoto, L., & Scarborough, E. (2002). Placing women in the history of psychology: The first American women psychologists. In W. E. Pickren (Ed.), *Evolving perspectives on the history of psychology.* Washington, DC: American Psychological Association.

Furuyashiki, T., & Kitaoka, S. (2019). Neural mechanisms underlying adaptive and maladaptive consequences of stress: Roles of dopaminergic and inflammatory responses. *Psychiatry and Clinical Neurosciences.* https://doi.org/10.1111/pcn.12901.

Fusari, A., & Ballesteros, S. (2008). Identification of odors of edible and nonedible stimuli as affected by age and gender. *Behavior Research Methods, 40,* 752-759.

Fusaro, M., Tieri, G., & Aglioti, S. M. (2019). Influence of cognitive stance and physical perspective on subjective and autonomic reactivity to observed pain and pleasure: An immersive virtual reality study. *Consciousness and Cognition: An International Journal, 67,* 86-97.

Föcking, M., Doyle, B., Munawar, N., Dillon, E. T., Cotter, D., & Cagney, G. (2019). Epigenetic factors in schizophrenia: Mechanisms and experimental approaches. *Molecular Neuropsychiatry, 5*(1), 6-12.

Gaab, J., Rohleder, N., Nater, U. M., & Ehlert, U. (2005). Psychological determinants of the cortisol stress response: The role of anticipatory cognitive appraisal. *Psychoneuroendocrinology, 30,* 599-610.

Gabbiadini, A., & Greitemeyer, T. (2017). Uncovering the association between strategy video games and self-regulation: A correlational study. *Personality and Individual Differences, 104,* 129-136

Gable, S.L., Hopper, E.A., Schooler, J.W. (2019). When the muses strike: Creative ideas of physicists and writers routinely occur during mind wandering. *Psychological Science,* 1-9.

Gadbois, S. A., & Sturgeon, R. D. (2011). Academic self-handicapping: Relationships with learning specific and general self-perceptions and academic performance over time. *British Journal of Educational Psychology, 81,* 207-222.

Gade, M., Souza, A. S., Druey, M. D., & Oberauer, K. (2017). Analogous selection processes in declarative and procedural working memory: N-2 list-repetition and task-repetition costs. *Memory & Cognition, 45,* 26-39.

Gafner, G. (2013). Review of *Subliminal: How your unconscious mind rules your behavior. American Journal of Clinical Hypnosis, 56,* 192-193.

Gainotti, G. (2019). Emotions and the right hemisphere: Can new data clarify old models? *The Neuroscientist, 25*(3), 258-270.

Galambos, N. L., Fang, S., Krahn, H. J., Johnson, M. D., & Lachman, M. E. (2015). Up, not down: The age curve in happiness from early adulthood to midlife in two longitudinal studies. *Developmental Psychology, 51*(11), 1664-1671.

Galanter, M., III. (2018). Combining medically assisted treatment and twelve-step programming: A perspective and review. *The American Journal of Drug and Alcohol Abuse, 44*(2), 151-159.

Galdi, G. (2015). Celebrating the 75th anniversary of the *American Journal of Psychoanalysis. American Journal of Psychoanalysis, 75*, 1-2.

Galef, D. (2001). The information you provide is anonymous, but what was your name again? *Chronicle of Higher Education, 47*, p. B5.

Gallese, V., Gernsbacher, M. A., Heyes, C., Hickok, G., & Iacoboni, M. (2011). Mirror neuron forum. *Perspectives on Psychological Science, 6*, 369-407.

Gallo, M. M. (2015). *"No one helped": Kitty Genovese, New York City, and the myth of urban apathy.* New York: Cornell University Press.

Gandolphe, M., & El Haj, M. (2017). Flashbulb memories of the Paris attacks. *Scandinavian Journal of Psychology, 58*, 199-204.

Ganna, A., Verweij, K. J. H., Nivard, M. G., Maier, R., Wedow, R., et al. (2019, August 30). Large-scale GWAS reveals insights into the genetic architecture of same-sex sexual behavior. *Science, 365*.

Gao, Y., Schneider, B., & Li, L. (2017). The effects of the binocular disparity differences between targets and maskers on visual search. *Attention, Perception, & Psychophysics, 79*, 459-472.

Garber, M. (2020, April 30). *Groundhog Day* was a horror movie all along. *The Atlantic.* Downloaded from https://www.theatlantic.com/culture/archive/2020/04/groundhog-day-horror-movie-quarantine/610867/, April 30, 2020.

Garcia, C. E. (2019). Belonging in a predominantly White institution: The role of membership in Latina/o sororities and fraternities. *Journal of Diversity in Higher Education,* doi:10.1037/dhe0000126.

Garcia, J. (2003). Psychology is not an enclave. In R. J. Sternberg (Ed.), *Psychologists defying the crowd: Stories of those who battled the establishment and won.* Washington, DC: American Psychological Association.

Garcia, S. M., Weaver, K., Moskowitz, G. B., & Darley, J. M. (2002). Crowded minds: The implicit bystander effect. *Journal of Personality and Social Psychology, 83*, 843-853.

García-Herrero, S., Mariscal, M. A., Gutiérrez, J. M., & Ritzel, D. O. (2013). Using Bayesian networks to analyze occupational stress caused by work demands: Preventing stress through social support. *Accident Analysis and Prevention, 57*, 114-123.

Gardini, S., Cornoldi, C., De Beni, R., & Venneri, A. (2009). Cognitive and neuronal processes involved in sequential generation of general and specific mental images. *Psychological Research/Psychologische Forschung, 73*, 633-643.

Gardner, B., & O'Connor, D. (2008). A review of the cognitive effects of electroconvulsive therapy in older adults. *Journal of ECT, 24*, 68-80.

Gardner, E. P., & Kandel, E. R. (2000). Touch. In E. R. Kandel, J. H. Schwartz, & T. M. Jessell (Eds.), *Principles of neural science* (4th ed.). New York: McGraw-Hill.

Gardner, F., & Moore, Z. (2008). Understanding clinical anger and violence: The anger avoidance model. *Behavior Modification, 32*, 897-912.

Gardner, H. (1999). *Intelligence reframed: Multiple intelligences for the 21st century.* New York: Basic Books.

Gardner, H. (2000). The giftedness matrix: A developmental perspective. In R. C. Friedman & B. M. Shore (Eds.), *Talents unfolding: Cognition and development.* Washington, DC: American Psychological Association.

Garfield, J. (2014). Sad psychosurgery. *Brain: A Journal of Neurology, 137*, 1262-1265.

Garfin, D. R., Holman, E. A., & Silver, R. C. (2015). Cumulative exposure to prior collective trauma and acute stress responses to the Boston marathon bombings. *Psychological Science, 26*, 675-683.

Gariépy, G., Riehm, K. E., Whitehead, R. D., Doré, I., & Elgar, F. J. (2019). Teenage night owls or early birds? Chronotype and the mental health of adolescents. *Journal of Sleep Research, 28*(3), 1-8.

Garlow, S. J., Purselle, D. C., & Heninger, M. (2007). Cocaine and alcohol use preceding suicide in African American and White adolescents. *Journal of Psychiatric Research, 41*, 530-536.

Garrigan, P., & Kellman, P. (2008). Perceptual learning depends on perceptual constancy. *PNAS Proceedings of the National Academy of Sciences of the United States of America, 105*, 2248-2253.

Garwick, G. B. (2007). Intelligence-related terms in mental retardation, learning disability, and gifted/talented professional usage, 1983-2001: The 1992 mental retardation redefinition as natural experiment. *Dissertation Abstracts International Section A: Humanities and Social Sciences, 67*(9-A), 3296.

Gatchel, R. J., & Weisberg, J. N. (2000). *Personality characteristics of patients with pain.* Washington, DC: APA Books.

Gates, G. J. (2017). How many people are lesbian, gay, bisexual, and transgender? Williams Institute. Downloaded from https://williamsinstitute.law.ucla.edu/wp-content/uploads/Gates-How-Many-People-LGBT-Apr-2011.pdf.

Gaudiano, B. A., & Miller, I. W. (2013). The evidence-based practice of psychotherapy. *Clinical Psychology Review, 33*, 813-824.

Geher, G. (2019). *Own your psychology major!* Washington, DC: American Psychological Association

Gelbard-Sagiv, H., Mukamel, R., Harel, M., Malach, R., & Fried, I. (2008). Internally generated reactivation of single neurons in human hippocampus during free recall. *Science, 322*, 96-101.

Gelfand, M. M. (2000). Sexuality among older women. *Journal of Women's Health and Gender Based Medicine, 9*(Suppl. 1), S15-S20.

Geller, E. S. (2011). Psychological science and safety: Large-scale success at preventing occupational injuries and fatalities. *Psychological Science, 20*, 109-114.

Gelstein, S., Yeshurun, Y., Rozenkrantz, L., Shusha, S., Frumin, I., Roth, Y., et al. (2011). Human tears contain a chemosignal. *Science, 331*, 226-230.

Geniole, S. N., Procyshyn, T. L., Marley, N., Ortiz, T. L., Bird, B. M., Marcellus, A. L., et al. (2019). Using a psychopharmacogenetic approach to identify the pathways through which—and the people for whom—testosterone promotes aggression. *Psychological Science, 30*(4), 481-494.

Genovese, J. E. C. (2006). Piaget, pedagogy, and evolutionary psychology. *Evolutionary Psychology, 4*, 2127-2137.

Genter, D. (2016). Language as cognitive tool kit: How language supports relational thought. *American Psychologist, 71*, 650-657.

Gentner, D., Goldin, S., & Goldin-Meadow, S. (Eds.). (2003). *Language in mind: Advances in the study of language and cognition.* Cambridge, MA: MIT.

Gercama, I., & Jones, T. (2020, April 2). Alternative morning rituals offer comfort and closure during an outbreak. National Public Radio. Downloaded from https://www.npr.org/sections/goatsandsoda/2020/04/02/793951420/new-mourning-rituals-offer-comfort-and-closure-during-an-outbreak.

Gerdes, A., Uhl, G., & Alpers, G. (2009). Spiders are special: Fear and disgust evoked by pictures of arthropods. *Evolution and Human Behavior, 30*, 66-73.

Gershkoff-Stowe, L., Connell, B., & Smith, L. (2006). Priming overgeneralizations in two- and four-year-old children. *Journal of Child Language, 33*, 461-486.

Gershoff, E. (2017, November 16). Spanking linked to increase in children's behavior problems. *Association for Psychological Science.* Retrieved from https://www.psychological-science.org/news/releases/spanking-linked-to-increase-in-childrens-behavior-problems.html.

Gershoff, E., & Grogan-Kaylor, A. (2016). Spanking and child outcomes: Old controversies and new meta-analyses. *Journal of Family Psychology, 30*, 453-469.

Gershoff, E., Sattler, K., & Ansari, A. (2018). Strengthening causal estimates for links between spanking and children's externalizing behavior problems. *Psychological Science, 29*, 110-120.

Gerstel, N. (2005). In search of time. *Science, 308*, 204-205.

Getner, D., & Holyoak, K. J. (1997). Reasoning and learning by analogy. *American Psychologist, 52,* 32-34.

Geurten, M., Willems, S., Germain, S., & Meulemans, T. (2015). Less is more: The availability heuristic in early childhood. *British Journal of Developmental Psychology, 33,* 405-410.

Geyer, T., Gokce, A., & Müller, H. J. (2011). Reinforcement of inhibitory positional priming by spatial working memory contents. *Acta Psychologica, 137,* 235-242.

Ghahramani, Z. (2015). Probabilistic machine learning and artificial intelligence. *Nature, 521*(7553), 452-459.

Ghavami, N., & Peplau, L. (2013). An intersectional analysis of gender and ethnic stereotypes: Testing three hypotheses. *Psychology of Women Quarterly, 37,* 113-127.

Giacobbi, P. R. Jr., Lynn, T. K., Wetherington, J. M., Jenkins, J., Bodendorf, M., & Langley, B. (2004). Stress and coping during the transition to university for first-year female athletes. *Sports Psychologist, 18,* 1-20.

Giacomini, M., Baylis, F., & Robert, J. (2007). Banking on it: Public policy and the ethics of stem cell research and development. *Social Sciences Medicine, 22,* 88-84.

Gialopsos, B. M. (2017). Sexual violence in academia: Policy, theory, and prevention considerations. *Journal of School Violence, 16,* 141-147.

Gianaros, P. J., & Wager, T. D. (2015). Brain-body pathways linking psychological stress and physical health. *Current Directions In Psychological Science, 24,* 313-321.

Giannakakis, A., & Fritsche, I. (2011). Social identities, group norms, and threat: On the malleability of ingroup bias. *Personality and Social Psychology Bulletin, 37,* 82-93.

Giannopoulos, V. L., & Vella-Brodrick, D. A. (2011). Effects of positive interventions and orientations to happiness on subjective well-being. *Journal of Positive Psychology, 6,* 95-105.

Gibb, K., Tunbridge, D., Chua, A., & Frederickson, N. (2007). Pathways to inclusion: Moving from special school to mainstream. *Educational Psychology in Practice, 23,* 109-127.

Gibbs, J. C. (2013) *Moral development and reality: Beyond the theories of Kohlberg, Hoffman, and Haidt* (3rd ed.) New York: Oxford University Press.

Gibbs, N. (2005, August 8). Being 13. *Time,* pp. 41-55.

Gibbs, W. W. (2002). From mouth to mind. *Scientific American, 287.* 26.

Gibson, S. (2013). Milgram's obedience experiments: A rhetorical analysis. *British Journal of Social Psychology, 52,* 290-309.

Gignac, G. E., & Zajenkowski, M. (2019). People tend to overestimate their romantic partner's intelligence even more than their own. *Intelligence, 73,* 41-51.

Gignac, G. E., Bartulovich, A., & Salleo, E. (2019). Maximum effort may not be required for valid intelligence test score interpretations. *Intelligence, 75,* 73-84.

Gilbert, P. D. (2007). Spirituality and mental health: A very preliminary overview. *Current Opinions in Psychiatry, 20,* 594-598.

Gilboa, A., Winocur, G., & Rosenbaum, R. S. (2006). Hippocampal contributions to recollection in retrograde and anterograde amnesia. *Hippocampus, 16,* 966-980.

Gillam, B., Palmisano, S. A., & Govan, D. G. (2011). Depth interval estimates from motion parallax and binocular disparity beyond interaction space. *Perception, 40,* 39-49.

Gillan, C. M., & Sahakian, B. J. (2015). Which is the driver, the obsessions or the compulsions, in OCD? *Neuropsychopharmacology, 40,* 247-248.

Gilligan, C. (1996). The centrality of relationships in psychological development: A puzzle, some evidence, and a theory. In G. G. Noam & K. W. Fischer (Eds.), *Development and vulnerability in close relationships.* Hillsdale, NJ: Erlbaum.

Gilligan, C. (2004). Recovering psyche: Reflections on life-history and history. *Annual of Psychoanalysis, 32,* 131-147.

Gilligan, J. (2019). Why we should universalize the insanity defense and replace punishment with therapy and education. *Aggression and Violent Behavior, 46,* 225-231.

Gingrich, J.A., Malm, H., Ansorge, M.S., Brown, A., Sourander, A., Suri, D., et al. (2017). New insights into how serotonin selective reuptake inhibitors shape the developing brain. *Brain Defects Research, 109,* 924-932.

Giovenco, D.P., & Delnevo, C.D. (2018). Prevalence of population smoking cessation by electronic cigarette use status in a national sample of recent smokers. *Addictive Behaviors, 76,* 129-134.

Gizer, I. R., Ehlers, C. L., Vieten, C., Seaton-Smith, K. L., Feiler, H. S., Lee, J. V., et al. (2011). Linkage scan of alcohol dependence in the UCSF Family Alcoholism Study. *Drug and Alcohol Dependence, 113,* 125-132.

Glachet, O., Moustafa, A. A., Gallouj, K., & El Haj, M. (2019). Smell your memories: Positive effect of odor exposure on recent and remote autobiographical memories in Alzheimer's disease. *Journal of Clinical and Experimental Neuropsychology, 41*(6), 555-564.

Gladwell, M. (2004, September 20). Annals of psychology: Personality, plus how corporations figure out who you are. *The New Yorker,* 42-45.

Glaser, G. (2015, April.) The irrationality of Alcoholics Anonymous. *The Atlantic.* Downloaded from https://www.theatlantic.com/magazine/archive/2015/04/the-irrationality-of-alcoholics-anonymous/386255/.

Glass, K., Flory, K., Hankin, B., Kloos, B., & Turecki, G. (2009). Are coping strategies, social support, and hope associated with psychological distress among Hurricane Katrina survivors? *Journal of Social and Clinical Psychology, 28,* 779-795.

Glass, O. M., Forester, B. P., & Hermida, A. P. (2017). Electroconvulsive therapy (ECT) for treating agitation in dementia (major neurocognitive disorder)—A promising option. *International Psychogeriatrics, 29,* 717-726.

Glicksohn, J., & Nahari, G. (2007). Interacting personality traits? Smoking as a test case. *European Journal of Personality, 21,* 225-234.

Glisky, E. L. (2007). Changes in cognitive function in human aging. In D. R. Riddle (Ed.), *Brain aging: Models, methods, and mechanisms.* Boca Raton, FL: CRC Press.

Golden, W. L. (2006). Hypnotherapy for anxiety, phobias and psychophysiological disorders. In R. A. Chapman (Ed.), *The clinical use of hypnosis in cognitive behavior therapy: A practitioner's casebook.* New York: Springer Publishing.

Golder, S. A., & Macy, M. W. (2011). Diurnal and seasonal mood vary with work, sleep, and day length across diverse cultures. *Science, 333,* 1878-1881.

Goldey, K. L., & van Anders, S. M. (2011). Sexy thoughts: Effects of sexual cognitions on testosterone, cortisol, and arousal in women. *Hormones and Behavior, 59,* 754-764.

Goldhammer, H., Krinsky, L., & Keuroghlian, A. S. (2019). Meeting the behavioral health needs of LGBT older adults. *Journal of the American Geriatrics Society.* https://doi.org/10.1111/jgs.15974.

Goldstein, I. (2000). Female sexual arousal disorder: New insights. *International Journal of Impotence Research, 12*(Suppl. 4), S152-S157.

Goldstein, J., Ross, D. A., & Moreno De Luca, D. (2019). Found in translation: Autism genetics and the quest for its Rosetta Stone. *Biological Psychiatry, 85*(7), e29-e30.

Goldstein, S. N. (2006). The exploration of spirituality and identity status in adolescence. *Dissertation Abstracts International: Section B: The Sciences and Engineering, 67*(6-B), 3481.

Golimbet, V. E., Alfimova, M. V., Gritsenko, I. K., & Ebstein, R. P. (2007). Relationship between dopamine system genes and extraversion and novelty seeking. *Neuroscience Behavior and Physiology, 37,* 601-606.

Gong, D., Yao, Y., Gan, X., Peng, Y., Ma, W., & Yao, D. (2019). A reduction in video gaming time produced a decrease in brain activity. *Frontiers in Human Neuroscience, 13,* 134.

Gontkovsky, S. T. (2005). Neurobiological bases and neuropsychological correlates of aggression and violence. In J. P. Morgan (Ed.), *Psychology of aggression.* Hauppauge, NY: Nova Science Publishers.

Gonzalez, M., Ateah, C. A., Durrant, J. E., & Feldgaier, S. (2019). The impact of the Triple P Seminar Series on Canadian parents' use of physical punishment, non-physical punishment and non-punitive responses. *Behaviour Change, 36*(2), 102-120.

González-Torres, M. A., & Fernandez-Rivas, A. (2015). Self-identity and gender differences. In M. Sáenz-Herrero (Ed.), *Psychopathology in women: Incorporating gender perspective into* descriptive psychopathology. Cham, Switzerland: Springer International Publishing.

Goode, Erica. (1999, April 13). "If things taste bad, "phantoms" may be at work." *The New York Times*.

Goodman, G. S., Gonzalves, L., & Wolpe, S. (2019). False memories and true memories of childhood trauma: Balancing the risks. *Clinical Psychological Science, 7*(1), 29-31.

Goodman, G., & Quas, J. (2008). Repeated interviews and children's memory: It's more than just how many. *Current Directions in Psychological Science, 17,* 386-390.

Goodwin, R., Costa, P., & Adonu, J. (2004). Social support and its consequences: "Positive" and "deficiency" values and their implications for support and self-esteem. *British Journal of Social Psychology, 43,* 465-474.

Gooren, L. (2006). The biology of human psychosexual differentiation. *Hormones and Behavior, 50,* 589-601.

Gopie, N., Craik, F. M., & Hasher, L. (2011). A double dissociation of implicit and explicit memory in younger and older adults. *Psychological Science, 22,* 634-640.

Gopnik, A. (2017). Making AI more human. *Scientific American, 316,* 60-65.

Gopnik, A., & Griffiths, T. (2017, August 20). What happens to creativity as we age? *The New York Times,* p. SR9.

Gopnik, A., Griffiths, T. L., & Lucas, C. G. (2015). When younger learners can be better (or at least more open-minded) than older ones. *Current Directions in Psychological Science, 24*(2), 87-92.

Gordon, J. K., Andersen, K., Perez, G., & Finnegan, E. (2019). How old do you think I am? Speech-language predictors of perceived age and communicative competence. *Journal of Speech, Language, and Hearing Research, 62*(7), 2455-2472.

Goriounova, N. A., & Mansvelder, H. D. (2019). Genes, cells and brain areas of intelligence. *Frontiers in human neuroscience, 13,* 44.

Gorton, R. N., & Erickson-Schroth, L. (2017). Hormonal and surgical treatment options for transgender men (female-to-male). *Psychiatric Clinics of North America, 40,* 79-97.

Gossop, M., Stewart, D., & Marsden, J. (2008). Attendance at Narcotics Anonymous and Alcoholics Anonymous meetings, frequency of attendance and substance use outcomes after residential treatment for drug dependence: A 5-year follow-up study. *Addiction, 103,* 119-125.

Goswami, I., & Urminsky, O. (2017). The dynamic effect of incentives on postreward task engagement. *Journal of Experimental Psychology: General, 146,* 1-19.

Gotlib, I. H., Krasnoperova, E., Yue, D. N., & Joorman, J. (2004). Attentional biases for negative interpersonal stimuli in clinical depression. *Journal of Abnormal Psychology, 113,* 127-135.

Goto, T., Ishibashi, Y., Kajimura, S., Oka, R., & Kusumi, T. (2015). Development of free will and determinism scale in Japanese. *Japanese Journal of Psychology, 86,* 32-41.

Gottesman, I. I., & Hanson, D. R. (2005). Human development: Biological and genetic processes. *Annual Review of Psychology, 56,* 263-286.

Gotts, S. J., Jo, H., Wallace, G. L., Saad, Z. S., Cox, R. W., & Martin, A. (2013). Two distinct forms of functional lateralization in the human brain. *PNAS Proceedings of the National Academy of Sciences of the United States of America, 110,* E3435-E3444.

Gould, T. W., Dominguez, B., de Winter, F., Yeo, G. W., Liu, P., Sundararaman, B., et al. (2019). Glial cells maintain synapses by inhibiting an activity-dependent retrograde protease signal. *PLoS Genetics, 15*(3), e1007948.

Goyal, M. S., Blazey, T. M., Su, Y., Couture, L. E., Durbin, T. J., Bateman, R. J., Benzinger, T. L., et al. (2019). Persistent metabolic youth in the aging female brain. *Proceedings of the National Academy of Sciences , 116*(8), 3251-3255.

Goyal, N., Adams, M., Cyr, T. G., Maass, A., & Miller, J. G. (2019). Norm-based spontaneous categorization: Cultural norms shape meaning and memory. *Journal of Personality and Social Psychology.* http://dx.doi.org/10.1037/pspi0000188.

Grady, C. L., St-Laurent, M., & Burianová, H. (2015). Age differences in brain activity related to unsuccessful declarative memory retrieval. *Brain Research, 161,* 230-47.

Grady, D., & Altman, L. K. (2008, December 29). Lessons for other smokers in Obama's efforts to quit. *The New York Times,* p. A12.

Graf, N., Brown, A., & Patten, E. (2019). The narrowing, but persistent, gender gap in pay. *FactTank,* Pew Research Center. Retrieved from https://www.pewresearch.org/fact-tank/2019/03/22/gender-pay-gap-facts/

Graff, T. C., Luke, S. G., & Birmingham, W. C. (2019). Supportive hand-holding attenuates pupillary responses to stress in adult couples. *PLOS One, 14*(2), e0212703.

Grahek, N. (2007). *Feeling pain and being in pain* (2nd ed.). Cambridge, MA: MIT Press.

Granic, I., Hollenstein, T., & Dishion, T. (2003). Longitudinal analysis of flexibility and reorganization in early adolescence: A dynamic systems study of family interactions. *Developmental Psychology, 39,* 606-617.

Granic, I., Lobel, A., & Engels, R. E. (2014). The benefits of playing video games. *American Psychologist, 69,* 66-78.

Grann, J. D. (2007). Confidence in knowledge past: An empirical basis for a differential decay theory of very long-term memory monitoring. *Dissertation Abstracts International Section A: Humanities and Social Sciences, 67,* 2462.

Grant, A. (2008). Does intrinsic motivation fuel the prosocial fire? Motivational synergy in predicting persistence, performance, and productivity. *Journal of Applied Psychology, 93,* 48-58.

Grant, D. M., & Wingate, L. R. (2011). Cognitive-behavioral therapy. In C. Silverstein (Ed.), *The initial psychotherapy interview: A gay man seeks treatment.* Amsterdam, Netherlands: Elsevier.

Gray, G. C. (2006). The regulation of corporate violations: Punishment, compliance, and the blurring of responsibility. *British Journal of Criminology, 46,* 875-892.

Gray, J. R., Chabris, C. F., & Braver, T. S. (2003). Neural mechanisms of general fluid intelligence. *Nature: Neurosciences, 6*(3), 316-322.

Grebelsky-Lichtman, T., & Katz, R. (2019). When a man debates a woman: Trump vs. Clinton in the first mixed gender presidential debates. *Journal of Gender Studies, 6*(28), 699-719.

Greene, N. R., & Naveh-Benjamin, M. (2020). A specificity principle of memory: Evidence from aging and associative memory. *Psychological Science, 31*(3), 316-331.

Green, J., Lynn, S., & Montgomery, G. (2008). Gender-related differences in hypnosis-based treatments for smoking: A follow-up meta-analysis. *American Journal of Clinical Hypnosis, 50,* 259-271.

Green, J. P., & Lynn, S. J. (2019). *Cognitive-behavioral therapy, mindfulness, and hypnosis for smoking cessation: A scientifically informed intervention.* Hoboken, NJ: Wiley-Blackwell.

Greenberg, L. S. (2015). Working with primary emotions. In L. S. Greenberg, *Emotion-focused therapy: Coaching clients to work through their feelings* (2nd ed.). Washington, DC: American Psychological Association.

Greenberg, P. E., Fournier, A. A., Sisitsky, T., Pike, C. T., & Kessler, R. C. (2015). The economic burden of adults with major depressive disorder in the United States (2005 and 2010). *The Journal of clinical psychiatry, 76*(2), 155-162.

Greenberg, R., & Goldman, E. (2009). Antidepressants, psychotherapy or their combination: Weighing options for depression treatments. *Journal of Contemporary Psychotherapy, 39,* 83-91.

Greenberg, S., & Stephens-Davidowitz, S. (2019, April 6). You underestimate yourself. *The New York Times,* p. SR-2.

Greene, J. D., & Paxton, J. M. (2009). Patterns of neural activity associated with honest and dishonest moral decisions. *PNAS Proceedings of the National Academy of Sciences of the United States of America, 106*(30), 12506-12511.

Greene, K. M., & Maggs, J. L. (2017). Academic time during college: Associations with mood, tiredness, and binge drinking across days and semesters. *Journal of Adolescence, 56,* 24-33.

Greenfield, B. L., & Tonigan, J. S. (2013). The general Alcoholics Anonymous tools of recovery: The adoption of 12-step practices and beliefs. *Psychology of Addictive Behaviors, 27*(3), 553-561.

Greenspan, S. (2006). Functional concepts in mental retardation: Finding the natural essence of an artificial category. *Exceptionality, 14,* 205-224.

Greenwald, T. (2019, April 30). What exactly is artificial intelligence, anyway? *Wall Street Journal*, p. R2.

Greer, R. D., Dudek-Singer, J., & Gautreaux, G. (2006). Observational learning. *International Journal of Psychology, 41*, 486-499.

Gregory, R. L. (1978). *The psychology of seeing* (3rd ed.). New York: McGraw-Hill.

Gregory, R. L. (2008). Emmert's Law and the moon illusion. *Spatial Vision, 21*, 407-720.

Gregory, S. (1856). *Facts for young women*. Boston: George Gregory.

Gregory, S. S. (1994, March 21). At risk of mutilation. *Time*, pp. 45-46.

Greitemeyer, T., & Sagioglou, C. (2017). Increasing wealth inequality may increase interpersonal hostility: The relationship between personal relative deprivation and aggression. *Journal of Social Psychology, 157*(6), 766-776.

Greitemeyer, T., & Sagioglou, C. (2019). The experience of deprivation: Does relative more than absolute status predict hostility? *British Journal of Social Psychology, 58*(3), 515-533.

Grenfell-Essam, R., Ward, G., & Tan, L. (2013). The role of rehearsal on the output order of immediate free recall of short and long lists. *Journal of Experimental Psychology: Learning, Memory, and Cognition, 39*, 317-347.

Griffith, T. L., Sawyer, J. E., & Poole, M. S. (2019). Systems savvy: Practical intelligence for transformation of sociotechnical systems. *Group Decision and Negotiation*. https://doi.org/10.1007/s10726-019-09619-4

Grigg-Damberger, M. M. (2017). Ontogeny of sleep and its functions in infancy, childhood, and adolescence. In S. Nevšímalová, O. Bruni, S. Nevšímalová, & O. Bruni (Eds.), *Sleep disorders in children*. Cham, Switzerland: Springer International Publishing.

Griggs, R. A. (2015a). Psychology's lost boy: Will the real Little Albert please stand up? *Teaching of Psychology, 42*, 14-18.

Griggs, R. A. (2015b). The Kitty Genovese story in introductory psychology textbooks: Fifty years later. *Teaching of Psychology, 42*, 149-152.

Griggs, R. A. (2017). Milgram's obedience study: A contentious classic reinterpreted. *Teaching of Psychology, 44*, 32-37.

Grigorenko, E. (2009). Speaking genes or genes for speaking? Deciphering the genetics of speech and language. *Journal of Child Psychology and Psychiatry, 50*, 116-125.

Grigorenko, E. L., & Dozier, M. (2013). Introduction to the special section on genomics. *Child Development, 84*, 6-16.

Grimm, J. W. (2011). Craving. In M. C. Olmstead (Ed.), *Animal models of drug addiction*. Totowa, NJ: Humana Press.

Grinberg, N., Joseph, K., Friedland, L., Swire-Thompson, B., & Lazer, D. (2019). Fake news on Twitter during the 2016 US presidential election. *Science, 363*(6425), 374-378.

Gros, D. F., Merrifield, C., Rowa, K., Szafranski, D. D., Young, L., & McCabe, R. E. (2019). A naturalistic comparison of group transdiagnostic behaviour therapy (TBT) and disorder-specific cognitive behavioural therapy groups for the affective disorders. *Behavioural and Cognitive Psychotherapy, 47*(1), 39-51.

Gross, D. M. (2006). *The secret history of emotion: From Aristotle's rhetoric to modern brain science*. Chicago: University of Chicago Press.

Gross, G., & Weiss, E. L. (2018). A call to the helping disciplines to deconstruct diversity and race: An essay on the social constructions of the "other." *International Journal for the Advancement of Counselling*, doi:10.1007/s10447-018-9344-0.

Grosso, M. (2015). The "transmission" model of mind and body: A brief history. In E. F. Kelly, A. Crabtree, & P. Marshall (Eds.), *Beyond physicalism: Toward reconciliation of science and spirituality*. Lanham, MD: Rowman & Littlefield.

Grover, S., & Helliwell, J. F. (2019). How's life at home? New evidence on marriage and the set point for happiness. *Journal of Happiness Studies: An Interdisciplinary Forum on Subjective Well-Being, 20*, 373-390.

Groves, R. M., Singer, E., Lepkowski, J. M., Heeringa, S. G., & Alwin, D. F. (2004). Survey methodology. In S. J. House, F. T. Juster, R. L. Kahn, H. Schuman, & E. Singer (Eds.), *A telescope on society: Survey research and social science at the University of Michigan and beyond*. Ann Arbor, MI: University of Michigan Press.

Gruber, J., Saxbe, D., Bushman, B. J., McNamara, T., & Rhodes, M. (2019). How can psychological science contribute to a healthier, happier, and more sustainable world? *Perspectives on Psychological Science, 14*(1), 3-6.

Gruber, R. P., & Block, R. A. (2017). Perception of scenes in different sensory modalities: A result of modal completion. *American Journal of Psychology, 130*, 23-34.

Gruber, T. R. (2013). Nature, nurture, and knowledge acquisition. *International Journal of Human-Computer Studies, 71*, 191-194.

Grundy, D. (2015). Principles and standards for reporting animal experiments in the *Journal of Physiology* and *Experimental Physiology*. *Journal of Physiology, 593*, 2547-2549.

Grøntvedt, T. V., Kennair, L. E. O., & Bendixen, M. (2019). How intercourse frequency is affected by relationship length, relationship quality, and sexual strategies using couple data. *Evolutionary Behavioral Sciences*. http://dx.doi.org/10.1037/ebs0000173.

Grünbaum, A. (2015). Critique of psychoanalysis. In S. Boag, L. W. Brakel, & V. Talvitie (Eds.), *Philosophy, science, and psychoanalysis: A critical meeting*. London: Karnac Books.

Grünert, U., Jusuf, P. R., Lee, S. S., & Nguyen, D. (2011). Bipolar input to melanopsin containing ganglion cells in primate retina. *Visual Neuroscience, 28*, 39-50.

Gu, C., Warkentin, S., Mais, L. A., & Carnell, S. (2017). Ethnic differences in parental feeding behaviors in UK parents of preschoolers. *Appetite, 113*, 398-404.

Guadagno, R. E., & Cialdini, R. B. (2002). Online persuasion: An examination of gender differences in computer-mediated interpersonal influence [Special issue: Groups and Internet]. *Group Dynamics, 6*, 38-51.

Guida, A., Tardieu, H., Le Bohec, O., & Nicolas, S. (2013). Are schemas sufficient to interpret the personalization effect? Only if long-term working memory backs up. *European Review of Applied Psychology/Revue Européenne De Psychologie Appliquée, 63*, 99-107.

Guidelines for the treatment of animals in behavioural research and teaching. (2017). *Animal Behaviour, 123*, i-ix.

Gun Violence Archive. (2019, November 15). Downloaded from https://www.gunviolencearchive.org/.

Guo, Y. (2019). Sexual double standards in white and Asian Americans: Ethnicity, gender, and acculturation. *Sexuality & Culture, 23*(1), 57-95.

Gupta, A., Love, A., Kilpatrick, L. A., Labus, J. S., Bhatt, R., Chang, L., et al. (2017). Morphological brain measures of cortico-limbic inhibition related to resilience. *Journal of Neuroscience Research, 95*(9), 1760-1775. doi: 10.1002/jnr.24007.

Gupta, M. A. (2013). Review of somatic symptoms in post-traumatic stress disorder. *International Review of Psychiatry, 25*, 86-99.

Gurney, A., Dienes, Z., & Scott, R. B. (2019). Hypnotic suggestibility is unaffected by a challenging inhibitory task or mental exhaustion. *Psychology of Consciousness: Theory, Research, and Practice*. http://dx.doi.org/10.1037/cns0000186.

Gurven, M., Fuerstenberg, E., Trumble, B., Stieglitz, J., Beheim, B., Davis, H., & Kaplan, H. (2017). Cognitive performance across the life course of Bolivian forager-farmers with limited schooling. *Developmental Psychology, 53*(1), 160-176.

Guttmacher Institute (2012). Facts on American teens' sources of information about sex. Accessed at http://www.guttmacher.org/pubs/FB-Teen-Sex-Ed.html.

Guéguen, N., Marchand, M., Pascual, A., & Lourel, M. (2008). Foot-in-the-door technique using a courtship request: A field experiment. *Psychological Reports, 103*, 529-534.

Gülbetekin, E. (2019). Is there any hemispheric asymmetry difference for processing religious stimuli in people with high and low religious attitude? *Psychology of Religion and Spirituality*. Advance online publication. https://doi.org/10.1037/rel0000264

Haas, H. S., Fuerst, M. P., Tönz, P., & Gubser-Ernst, J. (2015). Analyzing the psychological and social contents of evidence—Experimental comparison between guessing, naturalistic observation, and systematic analysis. *Journal of Forensic Sciences, 60*, 659-668.

Haberstick, B. C., Schmitz, S., Young, S. E., & Hewitt, J. K. (2005). Contributions of genes and environments to stability and change in externalizing and internalizing problems during elementary and middle school. *Behavior Genetics, 35,* 381–396.

Hadad, B., Maurer, D., & Lewis, T. L. (2017). The role of early visual input in the development of contour interpolation: The case of subjective contours. *Developmental Science, 20,* 25–32.

Hadiwijaya, H., Klimstra, T. A., Vermunt, J. K., Branje, S. T., & Meeus, W. J. (2017). On the development of harmony, turbulence, and independence in parent-adolescent relationships: A five-wave longitudinal study. *Journal of Youth and Adolescence, 46,* 1772–1788.

Hadke, I., Karia, S., & De Sousa, A. (2015). Hallucinations in patients with schizophrenia attending a tertiary psychiatry hospital. *Arab Journal of Psychiatry, 26*(1), 68–73.

Hagelskamp, C., Hughes, D., Yoshikawa, H., & Chaudry, A. (2011). Negotiating motherhood and work: A typology of role identity associations among low-income, urban women. *Community, Work & Family, 14,* 335–366.

Hagger, M. S., & Hamilton, K. (2019). Grit and self-discipline as predictors of effort and academic attainment. *British Journal of Educational Psychology, 89*(2), 324–342.

Hagmann-von Arx, P., Lemola, S., & Grob, A. (2018). Does IQ = IQ? Comparability of intelligence test scores in typically developing children. *Assessment, 25*(6), 691–701.

Haier, R. J. (2003). Brain imaging studies of intelligence: Individual differences and neurobiology. In R. J. Sternberg & J. Lautrey (Eds.), *Models of intelligence: International perspectives.* Washington, DC: American Psychological Association.

Haier, R. J. (2011). Biological basis of intelligence. In R. J. Sternberg & S. Kaufman (Eds.), *The Cambridge handbook of intelligence.* New York: Cambridge University Press.

Haig, B. D. (2018). The importance of scientific method for psychological science. *Psychology, Crime & Law, 25*(6), 527–541.

Hajek, P., Phillips-Waller, A., Przulj, D. , Pesola, F. et al. (2019). A randomized trial of e-cigarettes versus nicotine-replacement therapy. *New England Journal of Medicine, 380,* 629–637.

Hales, C. M., Carroll, M. D., Fryar, C. D., & Ogden, C. L. (2017). Prevalence of obesity among adults and youth: United States, 2015–2016. *NCHS Data Brief, 288.* Retrieved from https://www.cdc.gov/nchs/data/databriefs/db288.pdf.

Halford, S. (2006). Collapsing the boundaries? Fatherhood, organization and home-working. *Gender, Work & Organization, 13,* 383–402.

Halkitis, P. (2009). *Methamphetamine addiction: Biological foundations, psychological factors, and social consequences.* Washington, DC: American Psychological Association.

Hall, G. C. N. (1996). *Theory-based assessment, treatment, and prevention of sexual aggression.* New York: Oxford University Press.

Hall, J. A., Schlegel, K., Castro, V. L., & Back, M. (2019). What laypeople think the Big Five trait labels mean. *Journal of Research in Personality, 78,* 268–285.

Hall, P. J., Chong, C., McNaughton, N., & Corr, P. J. (2011). An economic perspective on the reinforcement sensitivity theory of personality. *Personality and Individual Differences, 51,* 242–247.

Hallit, S., Hajj, A., Sacre, H., Al Karaki, G., Malaeb, D., Kheir, N., et al. (2019). Impact of sleep disorders and other factors on the quality of life in general population: A cross-sectional study. *Journal of Nervous and Mental Disease, 207*(5), 333–339.

Halpern, D. F. (2010, December, 3). How neuro-mythologies support sex role stereotypes. *Science, 330,* 1320–1322.

Halpern, D. F. (2011). *Sex differences in cognitive abilities* (4th ed.). New York: Psychology Press.

Halpert, J. (2003, April 28). What do patients want? *Newsweek,* pp. 63–64.

Hamani, Y., Sciaki-Tamir, Y., Deri-Hasid, R., Miller-Pogrund, T., Milwidsky, A., & Haimov-Kochman, R. (2007). Misconceptions about oral contraception pills among adolescents and physicians. *Human Reproduction, 22,* 3078–3083.

Hambleton, R. K. (2006). Psychometric models, test designs and item types for the next generation of educational and psychological tests. In D. Bartram & R. K. Hambleton (Eds.), *Computer-based testing and the Internet: Issues and advances.* New York: John Wiley & Sons.

Hambleton, R. K., & Zenisky, A. L. (2013). Reporting test scores in more meaningful ways: A research-based approach to score report design. In K. F. Geisinger, B. A. Bracken, J. F. Carlson, J. C. Hansen, N. R. Kuncel, S. P. Reise, & M. C. Rodriguez (Eds.), *APA handbook of testing and assessment in psychology, Vol. 3: Testing and assessment in school psychology and education.* Washington, DC: American Psychological Association.

Hamel, L., Lopes, L., Munana, C., & Brodie, M. (2019, September 16). *The Kaiser Family Foundation/Washington Post Climate Change Survey.* Downloaded from https://www.kff.org/other/report/the-kaiser-family-foundation-washington-post-climate-change-survey/, September 16, 2019.

Hamer, M., Taylor, A., & Steptoe, A. (2006). The effect of acute aerobic exercise on stress-related blood pressure responses: A systematic review and meta-analysis. *Bi Psychology, 71,* 183–190.

Hamilton, A. C., & Martin, R. C. (2007). Semantic short-term memory deficits and resolution of interference: A case for inhibition? In D. S. Gorfein & C. M. Macleod (Eds.), *Inhibition in cognition.* Washington, DC: American Psychological Association.

Hamilton, L. K., Joppé, S. E., Cochard, L. M., & Fernandes, K. L. (2013). Aging and neurogenesis in the adult forebrain: What we have learned and where we should go from here. *European Journal of Neuroscience, 37,* 1978–1986.

Han, P., Fark, T., de Wijk, R. A., Roudnitzky, N., Iannilli, E., Seo, H.-S., & Hummel, T. (2019). Modulation of sensory perception of cheese attributes intensity and texture liking via ortho- and retro-nasal odors. *Food Quality and Preference, 73,* 1–7.

Han, S., & Ma, Y. (2014). Cultural differences in human brain activity: A quantitative meta-analysis. *NeuroImage, 99,* 293–300.

Han, S., & Ma, Y. (2015). A culture-behavior-brain loop model of human development. *Trends in Cognitive Sciences, 19*(11), 666–676.

Hangley, B. (2018, September). Are you still in there? *Readers' Digest,* pp. 90–97.

Hangya, B., Tihanyi, B. T., Entz, L., Fabo, D., Erőss, L., Wittner, L., et al. (2011). Complex propagation patterns characterize human cortical activity during slow-wave sleep. *Journal of Neuroscience, 31,* 8770–8779.

Hanna-Pladdy, B., Pahwa, R., & Lyons, K. E. (2015). Paradoxical effect of dopamine medication on cognition in Parkinson's disease: Relationship to side of motor onset. *Journal of the International Neuropsychological Society, 21,* 259–270.

Harden, R., Oaklander, A., Burton, A. W., Perez, R. M., Richardson, K., Swan, M., et al. (2013). Complex regional pain syndrome: Practical diagnostic and treatment guidelines, 4th edition. *Pain Medicine, 14,* 180–229.

Harding, D. J., & Jencks, C. (2003). Changing attitudes toward premarital sex: Cohort, period, and aging effects. *Public Opinion Quarterly, 67,* 211–226.

Hardt, J., Sidor, A., Nickel, R., Kappis, B., Petrak, P., & Egle, U. (2008). Childhood adversities and suicide attempts: A retrospective study. *Journal of Family Violence, 23,* 713–718.

Hardt, O., Nader, K., & Nadel, L. (2013). Decay happens: The role of active forgetting in memory. *Trends in Cognitive Sciences, 17,* 111–120.

Hardy, L. T. (2007). Attachment theory and reactive attachment disorder: Theoretical perspectives and treatment implications. *Journal of Child and Adolescent Psychiatric Nursing, 20,* 27–39.

Haridi, M., Weyn Banningh, S., Clé, M., Leu-Semenescu, S., Vidailhet, M., & Arnulf, I. (2017). Is there a common motor dysregulation in sleepwalking and REM sleep behaviour disorder? *Journal of Sleep Research. 26*(5), 614–622.

Hariri, A. R. (2015). *Looking inside the disordered brain: An introduction to the functional neuroanatomy of psychopathology.* Sunderland, MA: Sinauer Associates.

Harlow, H. F., & Zimmerman, R. R. (1959). Affectional responses in the infant monkey. *Science, 130,* 421–432.

Harlow, J. M. (1869). Recovery from the passage of an iron bar through the head. *Massachusetts Medical Society Publication, 2,* 329–347.

Harmer, C. J., Duman, R. S., & Cowen, P. J. (2017). How do antidepressants work? New perspectives for refining future treatment approaches. *The Lancet Psychiatry, 4,* 409–418.

Harmon-Jones, E., Harmon-Jones, C., & Levy, N. (2015). An action-based model of cognitive-dissonance processes. *Current Directions in Psychological Science, 24,* 184–189.

Harper, T. (1978, November 15). It's not true about people 65 or over. *Green Bay Press-Gazette* (Wisconsin), p. D-1.

Hart, B., & Risley, T. R. (1997). Use of language by three-year-old children. Courtesy of Drs. Betty Hart and Todd Risley, University of Kansas.

Hartanto, A., & Yang, H. (2019). Does early active bilingualism enhance inhibitory control and monitoring? A propensity-matching analysis. *Journal of Experimental Psychology: Learning, Memory, and Cognition, 45*(2), 360–378.

Hartanto, A., Toh, W. X., & Yang, H. (2018). Bilingualism narrows socioeconomic disparities in executive functions and self-regulatory behaviors during early childhood: Evidence from the early childhood longitudinal study. *Child Development.* https://doi-org.silk.library.umass.edu/10.1111/cdev.13032.

Hartmann, E., & Benum, K. (2019). Rorschach assessment of two distinctive personality states of a person with dissociative identity disorder. *Journal of Personality Assessment, 101*(2), 213–228.

Hartshorne, J., & Germine, L. (2015). When does cognitive functioning peak? The asynchronous rise and fall of different cognitive abilities across the life span. *Psychological Science, 26,* 433–443.

Harvey, J. H., Wenzel, A., & Sprecher, S. (Eds.). (2004). *The handbook of sexuality in close relationships.* Mahwah, NJ: Lawrence Erlbaum Associates.

Harvie, D. S., Moseley, G. L., Hillier, S. L., & Meulders, A. (2017). Classical conditioning differences associated with chronic pain: A systematic review. *The Journal of Pain, 18*(8), 889–898.

Hasnain, N. N., Ansari, S., & Sethi, S. (2011). Life satisfaction and self esteem in married and unmarried working women. *Journal of the Indian Academy of Applied Psychology, 37,* 316–319.

Hass, R. W. (2017). Tracking the dynamics of divergent thinking via semantic distance: Analytic methods and theoretical implications. *Memory & Cognition, 45,* 233–244.

Hassouneh, D., Alcala-Moss, A., & McNeff, E. (2011). Practical strategies for promoting full inclusion of individuals with disabilities in community-based participatory intervention research. *Research in Nursing & Health, 34,* 253–265.

Hastings, R. P., & Oakford, S. (2003). Student teachers' attitudes towards the inclusion of children with special needs. *Educational Psychology, 23,* 87–94.

Hattori, S., Kishida, I., Suda, A., Miyauchi, M., Shiraishi, Y., Fujibayashi, M., et al. (2017). Effects of four atypical antipsychotics on autonomic nervous system activity in schizophrenia. *Schizophrenia Research.* Accessed at https://www.ncbi.nlm.nih.gov/pubmed/28709776.

Hauke, C. (2006). The unconscious: Personal and collective. In R. K. Papadopoulos (Ed.), *The handbook of Jungian psychology: Theory, practice and applications.* New York: Routledge.

Havermans, R. C., Mulkens, S., Nederkoorn, C., & Jansen, A. (2007). The efficacy of cue exposure with response prevention in extinguishing drug and alcohol cue reactivity. *Behavioral Interventions, 22,* 121–135.

Haviland-Jones, J. M., & Wilson, P. J. (2008). A "nose" for emotion: Emotional information and challenges in odors and semiochemicals. In M. Lewis, J. M. Haviland-Jones, & L. G. Barrett (Eds.), *Handbook of emotions* (3rd ed.). New York: Guilford Press.

Hayes, S. C. (2015). Humanistic psychology and contextual behavioral perspectives. In K. J. Schneider, J. F. Pierson, & J. T. Bugental (Eds.), *The handbook of humanistic psychology: Theory, research, and practice* (2nd ed.). Thousand Oaks, CA: Sage Publications, Inc.

Hayes, W. M., & Wedell, D. H. (2020). Modeling the role of feelings in the Iowa Gambling Task. *Decision, 7*(1), 67–89. https://doi.org/10.1037/dec0000116.

Hayflick, L. (2007). Biological aging is no longer an unsolved problem. *Annals of the New York Academy of Sciences, 1100,* 1–13.

Hays, P. A. (2008). *Addressing cultural complexities in practice: Assessment, diagnosis, and therapy* (2nd ed.). Washington, DC: American Psychological Association.

Hayward, R., & Elliott, M. (2011). Subjective and objective fit in religious congregations: Implications for well-being. *Group Processes & Intergroup Relations, 14,* 127–139.

Heath, M., & Manzone, J. (2017). Manual estimations of functionally graspable target objects adhere to Weber's law. *Experimental Brain Research, 235,* 1701–1707.

Heathcote, A., Coleman, J. R., Eidels, A., Watson, J. M., Houpt, J., & Strayer, D. L. (2015). Working memory's workload capacity. *Memory & Cognition, 43,* 973–989.

Heatherton, T., & Sargent, J. (2009). Does watching smoking in movies promote teenage smoking? *Current Directions in Psychological Science, 18,* 63–67.

Hecht, J. M. (2007). *The happiness myth: Why what we think is right is wrong. A history of what really makes us happy.* New York: HarperSanFrancisco/HarperCollins.

Hedegaard, H., Miniño, A. M., & Warner, M. (2018). Drug overdose deaths in the United States, 1999–2017. NCHS Data Brief, no. 329. Hyattsville, MD: National Center for Health Statistics. Retrieved from https://www.cdc.gov/nchs/data/databriefs/db329-h.pdf.

Hedges, D. W., Brown, B. L., Shwalk, D. A., Godfrey, K., & Larcher, A. M. (2007). The efficacy of selective serotonin reuptake inhibitors in adult social anxiety disorder: A meta-analysis of double-blind, placebo-controlled trials. *Journal of Psychopharmacology, 21,* 102–111.

Heffernan, M. E., & Fraley, R. C. (2015). How early experiences shape attraction, partner preferences, and attachment dynamics. In V. Zayas & C. Hazan (Eds.), *Bases of adult attachment: Linking brain, mind and behavior.* New York: Springer Science + Business Media.

Hegarty, P. (2007). From genius inverts to gendered intelligence: Lewis Terman and the power of the norm [Special issue: Power matters: Knowledge politics in the history of psychology]. *History of Psychology, 10,* 132–155.

Hegarty, P., & Massey, S. (2007). Anti-homosexual prejudice . . . as opposed to what? Queer theory and the social psychology of anti-homosexual attitudes. *Journal of Homosexuality, 52,* 47–71.

Heilman, R. M., & Kusev, P. (2017). The gender pay gap: Can behavioral economics provide useful insights? *Frontiers in Psychology, 8,* 22–32.

Heim, S., Stumme, J., Bittner, N., Jockwitz, C., Amunts, K., & Caspers, S. (2019). Bilingualism and "brain reserve": A matter of age. *Neurobiology of Aging, 81,* 157–165.

Heinrichs, R. W. (2005). The primacy of cognition in schizophrenia. *American Psychologist, 60,* 229–242.

Heintz, M. M., Brander, S. M., & White, J. W. (2015). Endocrine disrupting compounds alter risk-taking behavior in guppies (Poecilia reticulata). *Ethology, 121,* 480–491.

Heitzmann, C. A., Merluzzi, T. V., Jean-Pierre, P., Roscoe, J. A., Kirsh, K. L., & Passik, S. D. (2011). Assessing self-efficacy for coping with cancer: Development and psychometric analysis of the brief version of the Cancer Behavior Inventory (CBI-B). *Psycho-Oncology, 20,* 302–312.

Helgeson, V. S. (2015). Gender and personality. In M. Mikulincer, P. R. Shaver, M. L. Cooper, & R. J. Larsen (Eds.), *APA handbook of personality and social psychology, Volume 4: Personality processes and individual differences.* Washington, DC: American Psychological Association.

Helgeson, V. S., & Zajdel, M. (2017). Adjusting to chronic health conditions. *Annual Review of Psychology, 68,* 545–571.

Heller, H. C., Ruby, N. F., Rolls, A., Makam, M., & Colas, D. (2014). Adaptive and pathological inhibition of neuroplasticity associated with circadian rhythms and sleep. *Behavioral Neuroscience, 128,* 273–282.

Henckes, N. (2011). Reforming psychiatric institutions in the mid-twentieth century: A framework for analysis. *History of Psychiatry, 22,* 164–181.

Hennessy, M. B., & Shair, H. N. (2017). Filial attachment: Development, mechanisms, and consequences. In J. Call, G. M. Burghardt,

I. M. Pepperberg, C. T. Snowdon, & T. Zentall (Eds.), *APA handbook of comparative psychology: Basic concepts, methods, neural substrate, and behavior*. Washington, DC: American Psychological Association.

Hennig-Fast, K., Meister, F., Frodl, T., Beraldi, A., Padberg, F., Engel, R., et al. (2008). The case of persistent retrograde amnesia following a dissociative fugue: Neuropsychological and neurofunctional underpinnings of loss of autobiographical memory and self-awareness. *Neuropsychologia, 46*(12), 2993-3005.

Henningsen, D. D., Henningsen, M. L., & Eden, J. (2006). Examining the symptoms of groupthink and retrospective sensemaking. *Small Group Research, 37*, 36-64.

Henrich, J., Heine, S., and Norenzayan, A. (2010). The weirdest people in the world? *Behavioral and Brain Sciences, 33*, 61-83.

Henshall, C., Cipriani, A., Ruvolo, D., Macdonald, O., Wolters, L., & Koychev, I. (2019). Implementing a digital clinical decision support tool for side effects of antipsychotics: a focus group study. *Evidence-Based Mental Health, 22*(2), 56-60.

Herbenick, D., Reece, M., Sanders, S., Dodge, B., Ghassemi, A., & Fortenberry, J. (2009). Prevalence and characteristics of vibrator use by women in the United States: Results from a nationally representative study. *Journal of Sexual Medicine, 6*, 1857-1866.

Herbert, W. (2011). *On second thought: Outsmarting your mind's hard-wired habits*. New York: Broadway.

Hermans, D., Boddez, Y., & Vervliet, B. (Accepted/In press). The experimental study of mental health problems—Building on Watson & Rayner (1920). In G. Davey (Ed.), *Classical Studies in Clinical Psychology*. Thousand Oaks, CA: Sage Publishing.

Hernández-Orallo, J. (2017). *The measure of all minds: Evaluating natural and artificial intelligence*. New York: Cambridge University Press.

Herrnstein, R. J., & Murray, D. (1994). *The bell curve*. New York: Free Press.

Herskovits, M. (2018). *Acculturation: A study of culture contact*. New York: Moat Portultis.

Herting, M. M., & Sowell, E. R. (2017). Puberty and structural brain development in humans. *Frontiers in Neuroendocrinology, 44*, 122-137.

Hertlein, K. M., Weeks, G. R., & Gambescia, N. (2007). The treatment of hypoactive sexual desire disorder: An intersystem approach. In L. VandeCreek, F. L. Peterson, Jr., & J. W. Bley (Eds.), *Innovations in clinical practice: Focus on sexual health*. Sarasota, FL: Professional Resource Press/Professional Resource Exchange.

Hertzog, C., Kramer, A., Wilson, R., & Lindenberger, U. (2008). Enrichment effects on adult cognitive development: Can the functional capacity of older adults be preserved and enhanced? *Psychological Science in the Public Interest, 9*, 1-65.

Herzberg, L. (2009). Direction, causation, and appraisal theories of emotion. *Philosophical Psychology, 22*, 167-186.

Herzog, H. (2017). The ethics of behavioral research using animals: A classroom exercise. In J. R. Stowell & W. E. Addison (Eds.), *Activities for teaching statistics and research methods: A guide for psychology instructors*. Washington, DC: American Psychological Association.

Hetzel-Riggin, M. D. (2017). A study of the impact of informed consent procedures on participant responses in trauma-related research. *Journal of Loss and Trauma, 22*, 36-46.

Heward, W. L., & Orlansky, M. D. (1988). *Exceptional children* (3rd ed.). Columbus, OH: Merrill.

Hickok, G. (2015, May 10). Rhythms of the brain. *The New York Times*, p. SR 9.

Higgs, S. (2015). Social norms and their influence on eating behaviours. *Appetite, 86*, 38-44.

Hilbert, S., Schwaighofer, M., Zech, A., Sarubin, N., Arendasy, M., & Bühner, M. (2017). Working memory tasks train working memory but not reasoning: A material- and operation-specific investigation of transfer from working memory practice. *Intelligence, 61*, 102-114.

Hilger, K., Ekman, M., Fiebach, C. J., & Basten, U. (2017). Efficient hubs in the intelligent brain: Nodal efficiency of hub regions in the salience network is associated with general intelligence. *Intelligence, 60*, 10-25.

Hill, B. D., Foster, J. D., Elliott, E. M., Shelton, J., McCain, J., & Gouvier, W. (2013). Need for cognition is related to higher general intelligence, fluid intelligence, and crystallized intelligence, but not working memory. *Journal of Research in Personality, 47*, 22-25.

Hilton, R. C., Rengasamy, M., Mansoor, B., He, J., Mayes, T., Emslie, G. J., et al. (2013). Impact of treatments for depression on comorbid anxiety, attentional, and behavioral symptoms in adolescents with selective serotonin reuptake inhibitor-resistant depression. *Journal of the American Academy of Child & Adolescent Psychiatry, 52*, 482-492.

Hines, M. (2004). *Brain gender*. New York: Oxford University Press.

Hines, M., & Alexander, G. (2008). Monkeys, girls, boys and toys: A confirmation letter regarding sex differences in toy preferences: Striking parallels between monkeys and humans. *Hormones and Behavior, 54*, 478-479.

Hinterberger, T., Schöner, J., & Halsband, U. (2011). Analysis of electrophysiological state patterns and changes during hypnosis induction. *International Journal of Clinical and Experimental Hypnosis, 59*, 165-179.

Hipp, T. N., Bellis, A. L., Goodnight, B. L., Brennan, C. L., Swartout, K. M., & Cook, S. L. (2017). Justifying sexual assault: Anonymous perpetrators speak out online. *Psychology of Violence, 7*, 82-90.

Hirnstein, M., Hugdahl, K., & Hausmann, M. (2019). Cognitive sex differences and hemispheric asymmetry: A critical review of 40 years of research. *Laterality: Asymmetries of Body, Brain and Cognition, 24*(2), 204-252.

Hirschberger, G., Pyszczynski, T., & Ein-Dor, T. (2010). An ever-dying people: The existential underpinnings of Israelis' perceptions of war and conflict. *Cahiers Internationaux de Psychologie Sociale, 87*(3), 443-457. doi:10.3917/cips.087.0443.

Hirst, W., Phelps, E. A., Meksin, R., Vaidya, C. J., Johnson, M. K., Mitchell, K. J., et al. (2015). A ten-year follow-up of a study of memory for the attack of September 11, 2001: Flashbulb memories and memories for flashbulb events. *Journal of Experimental Psychology: General, 144*, 604-623.

Ho, S. M. Y., Saltel, P., Machavoine, J., Rapoport-Hubschman, N., & Spiegel, D. (2004). Cross-cultural aspects of cancer care. In National Institutes of Health and Stanford University School of Medicine, *Cancer, culture, and communication*. New York: Kluwer Academic/Plenum Publishers.

Hobson, J. A. (2005). In bed with Mark Solms? What a nightmare! A reply to Domhoff (2005). *Dreaming, 15*, 21-29.

Hobson, J. A. (2007). States of conciseness: Normal and abnormal variation. In P. D. Zelazo, M. Moscovitch, & E. Thompson (Eds.), *The Cambridge handbook of consciousness*. London: Cambridge University Press.

Hobson, K. (2011, March 28). How can you help the medicine go down? *Wall Street Journal*, p. R10.

Hochschild, A. (2001, February). A generation without public passion. *Atlantic Monthly*, pp. 33-42.

Hoenen, M., Lübke, K. T., & Pause, B. M. (2017). Sensitivity of the human mirror neuron system for abstract traces of actions: An EEG-study. *Biological Psychology, 124*, 57-64.

Hofeditz, M., Nienaber, A., Dysvik, A., & Schewe, G. (2017). "Want to" versus "have to": Intrinsic and extrinsic motivators as predictors of compliance behavior intention. *Human Resource Management, 56*, 25-49.

Hofer, J., & Busch, H. (2019). Women in power-themed tasks: Need for power predicts task enjoyment and power stress. *Motivation and Emotion*. https://doi.org/10.1007/s11031-019-09782-w.

Hofer, J., Busch, H., Raihala, C., Šolcová, I. P., & Tavel, P. (2017). The higher your implicit affiliation-intimacy motive, the more loneliness can turn you into a social cynic: A cross-cultural study. *Journal of Personality, 85*, 179-191.

Hoff, E. (2003). Language development in childhood. In R. M. Lerner, M. A. Easterbrooks, & J. Mistry. (Eds.), *Handbook of psychology: Developmental psychology* (Vol. 6). New York: Wiley.

Hoff, E. (2008). *Language development*. New York: Wadsworth.

Hoffman J. (2018, November 17). One drag on a Juul hooked a teenager for years. *The New York Times*, p. A1.

Hoffman, J. (2020, April 2). Here to help: Online resources for help with sobriety. *The New York Times*, p. A3.

Hofmann, S. G. (2007). Enhancing exposure-based therapy from a translational research perspective. *Behaviour Research and Therapy, 45,* 1987-2001.

Hofmann, W., Gschwendner, T., Castelli, L., & Schmitt, M. (2008). Implicit and explicit attitudes and interracial interaction: The moderating role of situationally available control resources. *Group Processes & Intergroup Relations, 11,* 69-87.

Hogan, J., Davies, S., & Hogan, R. (2007). Generalizing personality-based validity evidence. In S. M. McPhail (Ed.), *Alternative validation strategies: Developing new and leveraging existing validity evidence.* Hoboken, NJ: John Wiley & Sons.

Hogg, M. A. (2006). Social identity theory. In P. J. Burke (Ed.), *Contemporary social psychological theories.* Palo Alto, CA: Stanford University Press.

Hogue, J. V. & Mills, J.S. (2019). The effects of active social media engagement with peers on body image in young women. *Body Image, 28,* 1-5.

Holbrook, E., Puram, S., See, R., Tripp, A., & Nair, D. (2018). Induction of smell through transethmoid electrical stimulation of the olfactory bulb. *International Forum of Allergy and Rhinology, 9,* 158-164.

Holden, C. (2003). Deconstructing schizophrenia. *Science, 299,* 333-335.

Holden, C. (2007). Embryonic stem cells. Stem cell science advances as politics stall. *Science, 316,* 1825.

Holland, J. C., & Lewis, S. (2001). *The human side of cancer: Living with hope, coping with uncertainty.* New York: Quill.

Holleran, S., Mehl, M., & Levitt, S. (2009). Eavesdropping on social life: The accuracy of stranger ratings of daily behavior from thin slices of natural conversations. *Journal of Research in Personality, 43,* 660-672.

Hollingworth, H. L. (1943/1990). *Leta Stetter Hollingworth: A biography.* Boston: Anker.

Hollins, K. (2007). Consequences of antenatal mental health problems for child health and development. *Current Opinions on Obstetric Gynecology, 19,* 568-573.

Holloway, L. (2000, December 16). Chief of New York City schools plans to revamp bilingual study. *The New York Times,* p. A1.

Holmes, A. (2017). Drug addictions: New insight into causes, comorbidity and potential treatments. *Genes, Brain & Behavior, 16,* 5-7.

Holtyn, A. F., & Lattal, K. A. (2013). Briefly delayed reinforcement effects on variable "ratio and yoked" interval schedule performance. *Journal of the Experimental Analysis of Behavior, 100,* 198-210.

Holtz, J. (2011). *Applied clinical neuropsychology: An introduction.* New York: Springer Publishing Co.

Holzhauer, C. G., Wemm, S., & Wulfert, E. (2017). Distress tolerance and physiological reactivity to stress predict women's problematic alcohol use. *Experimental and Clinical Psychopharmacology, 25,* 156-165.

Hongchun, W., & Ming, L. (2006). About the research on suggestibility and false memory. *Psychological Science (China), 29,* 905-908.

Hoobler, J. M., Lemmon, G., & Wayne, S. J. (2011). Women's underrepresentation in upper management: New insights on a persistent problem. *Organizational Dynamics, 40,* 151-156.

Hope, M. O., Taylor, R. J., Nguyen, A. W., & Chatters, L. M. (2019). Church support among African American and black Caribbean adolescents. *Journal of Child and Family Studies,* 1-14.

Hopkins-Doyle, A., Sutton, R. M., Douglas, K. M., & Calogero, R. M. (2019). Flattering to deceive: Why people misunderstand benevolent sexism. *Journal of Personality and Social Psychology, 116*(2), 167-192.

Hopper, J., & Lisak, D. (2014, December 9). Why rape and trauma survivors have fragmented and incomplete memories. *Time.* Accessed from http://time.com/3625414/rape-trauma-brain-memory/.

Hopwood, C., Newman, D., Donnellan, M., Markowitz, J., Grilo, C., Sanislow, C., et al. (2009). The stability of personality traits in individuals with borderline personality disorder. *Journal of Abnormal Psychology, 118,* 806-815.

Horesh, D., Solomon, Z., Zerach, G., & Ein-Dor, T. (2011). Delayed-onset PTSD among war veterans: The role of life events throughout the life cycle. *Social Psychiatry and Psychiatric Epidemiology, 46,* 863-870.

Hori, H., Teraishi, T., Sasayama, D., Matsuo, J., Kawamoto, Y., Kinoshita, Y., & Kunugi, H. (2011). Relationships between season of birth, schizotypy, temperament, character and neurocognition in a non-clinical population. *Psychiatry Research, 189,* 388-397.

Horiguchi, H., Winawer, J., Dougherty, R. F., & Wandell, B. A. (2013). Human trichromacy revisited. *Proceedings of the National Academy of Sciences, 110,* 199-106.

Horney, K. (1937). *Neurotic personality of our times.* New York: Norton.

Hornsveld, R. J., Zwets, A. J., Leenaars, E. M., Kraaimaat, F. W., Bout, R., Lagro-Janssen, T. M., & Kanters, T. (2018). Violent female offenders compared with violent male offenders on psychological determinants of aggressive behavior. *International Journal of Offender Therapy and Comparative Criminology, 62*(2), 450-467. doi:10.1177/0306624X16648109.

Horton, C. L. (2011). Recall and recognition of dreams and waking events: A diary paradigm. *International Journal of Dream Research, 4,* 8-16.

Horton, K. D., Wilson, D. E., Vonk, J., Kirby, S. L., & Nielsen, T. (2005). Measuring automatic retrieval: A comparison of implicit memory, process dissociation, and speeded response procedures. *Acta Psychologica, 119,* 235-263.

Houghtalen, R. P., & Talbot, N. (2007). Dissociative disorders and cognitive disorders. In O. J. Z. Sahler & J. E. Carr (Eds.), *The behavioral sciences and health care* (2nd rev. and updated ed.). Ashland, OH: Hogrefe & Huber Publishers.

Hounkpatin, H. O., Wood, A. M., Boyce, C. J., & Dunn, G. (2015). An existential-humanistic view of personality change: Co-occurring changes with psychological well-being in a 10 year cohort study. *Social Indicators Research, 121,* 455-470.

Houri, A. K., & Sullivan, A. L. (2019). Relations of social-emotional functioning and kindergarten academic achievement in children of immigrants. *Psychology in the Schools.* https://doi-org.silk.library.umass.edu/10.1002/pits.22281.

Houwen, J., Moorthaemer, B. J. E., Lucassen, P. L. B. J., Akkermans, R. P., Assendelft, W. J. J., olde Hartman, T. C., et al. (2019). The association between patients' expectations and experiences of task-, affect- and therapy-oriented communication and their anxiety in medically unexplained symptoms consultations. *Health Expectations: An International Journal of Public Participation in Health Care & Health Policy, 22*(3), 338-347.

Howard, D. J. (2019). A dual process theory explanation for door-in-the-face effectiveness. *Basic and Applied Social Psychology, 41,* 1-14.

Howe, M. L. (2011). The adaptive nature of memory and its illusions. *Psychological Science, 20,* 312-315.

Howell, E. F. (2011). *Understanding and treating dissociative identity disorder: A relational approach.* New York: Routledge/Taylor & Francis Group.

Howes, O., & Kapur, S. (2009). The dopamine hypothesis of schizophrenia: Version III—The final common pathway. *Schizophrenia Bulletin, 35,* 549-562.

Howes, O. D., McCutcheon, R., Owen, M. J., & Murray, R. M. (2017). The role of genes, stress, and dopamine in the development of schizophrenia. *Biological Psychiatry, 81*(1), 9-20.

Hu, J. (2019). *Prominence and locality in grammar: The syntax and semantics of wh-questions and reflexives.* New York: Routledge.

Huang, H., & Kashubeck-West, S. (2015). Exposure, agency, perceived threat, and guilt as predictors of posttraumatic stress disorder in veterans. *Journal of Counseling & Development, 93,* 3-13.

Huang, L. M., Sacchi, D. M., & Sherman, J. W. (2017). On the formation of context-based person impressions. *Journal of Experimental Social Psychology, 68,* 146-156.

Huang, S., Etkin, J., & Jin, L. (2017). How winning changes motivation in multiphase competitions. *Journal of Personality and Social Psychology, 112,* 813-837.

Huang, W. (2019). A psychological perspective on extrasensory perception. In N. Rezaei & A. Saghazadeh, (Eds). *Biophysics and neurophysiology of the sixth sense.* Cham, Switzerland: Springer.

Hubbard, K., O'Neill, A., & Cheakalos, C. (1999, April 12). Out of control. *People,* pp. 52-72.

Hubel, D. H., & Wiesel, T. N. (2004). *Brain and visual perception: The story of a 25-year collaboration.* New York: Oxford University Press.

Huckins, L. M., Hatzikotoulas, K., Southam, L., Thornton, L. M., Steinberg, J., Aguilera-McKay, F., et al. (2018). Investigation of common, low-frequency and rare genome-wide variation in anorexia nervosa. *Molecular Psychiatry, 23*(5), 1169-1180.

Hudson, C. G. (2019). Deinstitutionalization of mental hospitals and rates of psychiatric disability: An international study. *Health & Place, 56,* 70-79.

Hudson, J. I., Coit, C. E., Lalonde, J. K., & Pope, H. G. (2012). By how much will the proposed new DSM-5 criteria increase the prevalence of binge eating disorder? *International Journal of Easting Disorders, 45,* 139-141.

Hudson, W. (1960). Pictorial depth perception in subcultural groups in Africa. *Journal of Social Psychology, 52,* 183-208.

Hudspeth, A. J. (2013). The inner ear. In E. R. Kandel, J. H. Schwartz, & T. M. Jessell (Eds.), *Principles of neural science* (5th ed.). New York: McGraw-Hill.

Huerta, M., Cortina, L. M., & Pang, J. S. (2006). Sex and power in the academy: Modeling sexual harassment in the lives of college women. *Personality and Social Psychology Bulletin, 32,* 616-628.

Hugdahl, K., Thomsen, T., & Ersland, L. (2006). Sex differences in visuo-spatial processing: An fMRI study of mental rotation. *Neuropsychologia, 44,* 1575-1583.

Hugenberg, K., & Sacco, D. (2008). Social categorization and stereotyping: How social categorization biases person perception and face memory. *Social and Personality Psychology Compass, 2,* 1052-1072.

Hui, A., He, M., & Wong, W. (2019). Understanding the development of creativity across the life span. In J. Kaufman & R. Sternberg (Eds.), *The Cambridge handbook of creativity* (2nd ed.). Cambridge, England: Cambridge University Press.

Hull, C. L. (1943). *Principles of behavior.* New York: Appleton-Century-Crofts.

Human, L. J., & Biesanz, J. C. (2011). Through the looking glass clearly: Accuracy and assumed similarity in well-adjusted individuals' first impressions. *Journal of Personality and Social Psychology, 100,* 349-364.

Hummer, T. A., & McClintock, M. K. (2009). Putative human pheromone androstadienone attunes the mind specifically to emotional information. *Hormones and Behavior, 55,* 548-559.

Humphrey, N., Curran, A., & Morris, E. (2007). Emotional intelligence and education: A critical review. *Educational Psychology, 27,* 235-254.

Humphreys, K., Blodgett, J. C., & Wagner, T. H. (2014). Estimating the efficacy of Alcoholics Anonymous without self-selection bias: An instrumental variables re-analysis of randomized clinical trials. *Alcoholism: Clinical and Experimental Research, 38*(11), 2688-2694.

Hunt, E. (1994). Problem solving. In R. J. Sternberg (Ed.), *Thinking and problem solving: Handbook of perception and cognition* (2nd ed.). San Diego, CA: Academic Press.

Hunt, J. S. (2017). Studying the effects of race, ethnicity, and culture on jury behavior. In M. B. Kovera & M. B. Kovera (Eds.), *The psychology of juries.* Washington, DC: American Psychological Association.

Hunt, J. S., Seifert, A. L., & Armenta, B. E. (2006). Stereotypes and prejudice as dynamic constructs: Reminders about the nature of inter-group bias from the hurricane Katrina relief efforts. *Analyses of Social Issues and Public Policy, 6,* 237-253.

Hunt, M. (1974). *Sexual behaviors in the 1970s.* New York: Dell.

Huprich, S. K., & Nelson, S. M. (2015). Advancing the assessment of personality pathology with the Cognitive-Affective Processing System. *Journal of Personality Assessment, 97,* 467-477.

Hurley, D. B., & Kwon, P. (2013). Savoring helps most when you have little: Interaction between savoring the moment and uplifts on positive affect and satisfaction with life. *Journal of Happiness Studies, 14,* 1261-1271.

Hurschler, M. A., Liem, F., Oechslin, M., Stämpfli, P., & Meyer, M. (2015). fMRI reveals lateralized pattern of brain activity modulated by the metrics of stimuli during auditory rhyme processing. *Brain and Language, 14,* 741-750.

Husain, O. (2015). From persecution to depression: A case of chronic depression—Associating the Rorschach, the TAT, and Winnicott. *Journal of Personality Assessment, 97,* 230-240.

Huston, J. P., Silva, M., Komorowski, M., Schulz, D., & Topic, B. (2013). Animal models of extinction-induced depression: Loss of reward and its consequences. *Neuroscience and Biobehavioral Reviews, 37*(9A), 2059-2070.

Hutchinson, B., & Mitchell, M. (2019, January). 50 years of test (un)fairness: Lessons for machine learning. In *Proceedings of the Conference on Fairness, Accountability, and Transparency* (pp. 49-58). ACM.

Huttunen-Lenz, M., Hansen, S., Larsen, T. M., Christensen, P., Drummen, M., Adam, T., et al. (2019). The PREVIEW study: Supporting behavior change in an international intervention study among participants with pre-diabetes. *European Journal of Health Psychology, 26*(1), 10-20.

Hviid, A., Hansen, J. V., Frisch, M., & Melbye, M. (2019). Measles, mumps, rubella vaccination and autism: A nationwide cohort. *Annals of Internal Medicine, 170*(8):513-520. doi: 10.7326/M18-2101.

Hwang, E., Kim, H., Lee, S., Kim, M., Lee, S., Han, S., et al. (2017). Loganin enhances long-term potentiation and recovers scopolamine-induced learning and memory impairments. *Physiology & Behavior, 171,* 243-248.

Hwang, J., Lee, C., & Lee, E. (2019). Gender norms and housework time allocation among dual-earner couples. *Labour Economics, 57,* 102-116.

Hyde, J., Mezulis, A. H., & Abramson, L. Y. (2008). The ABCs of depression: Integrating affective, biological, and cognitive models to explain the emergence of the gender difference in depression. *Psychological Review, 115,* 291-313.

Hyde, J. S. (2005). The gender similarities hypothesis. *American Psychologist, 50,* 581-592.

Hyde, J. S., & Mertz, J. E. (2009). Gender, culture, and mathematics performance. *Proceedings of the National Academy of Sciences of the United States of America, 106,* 8801-8807.

Hyde, J. S., Lindberg, S. M., Linn, M. C., Ellis, A. B., & Williams, C. C. (2008). Gender similarities characterize math performance. *Science, 321,* 494-495

Hyman, B. T. (2011). Amyloid-dependent and amyloid-independent stages of Alzheimer disease. *Archives of Neurology, 68,* 1662-1664.

Høglend, P. P., Dahl, H. S., Hersoug, A. G., Lorentzen, S. S., & Perry, J. C. (2011). Long-term effects of transference interpretation in dynamic psychotherapy of personality disorders. *European Psychiatry, 26,* 419-424.

Ibbotson, P. , & Tomasello, M. (2016). Language in a new key. *Scientific American, 315,* 70-75.

Idås, T., Backholm, K., & Korhonen, J. (2019). Trauma in the newsroom: Social support, post-traumatic stress and post-traumatic growth among journalists working with terror. *European Journal of Psychotraumatology, 10*(1).

Iglesias, A. (2005). Awake-alert hypnosis in the treatment of panic disorder: A case report. *American Journal of Clinical Hypnosis, 47,* 249-257.

Igo, S. E. (2006). Review of a telescope on society: Survey research and social science at the University of Michigan and beyond. *Journal of the History of the Behavioral Sciences, 42,* 95-96.

Ijeoma, O. B., & Oladipo, A. I. (2019). Efficacy of systematic desensitization therapy on academic boredom among adolescents in Edo state secondary schools. *Journal of Educational and Social Research, 9*(2), 83-89.

Iliceto, P., D'Antuono, L., Cassarà, L., Giacolini, T., Sabatello, U., & Candilera, G. (2017). Obsessive-compulsive tendencies, self/other perception, personality, and suicidal ideation in a non-clinical sample. *Psychiatric Quarterly, 88,* 411-422.

Ingraham, C. (2019, March 29). The share of Americans not having sex has reached a record high. *Washington Post.* Retrieved from https://www.washingtonpost.com/business/2019/03/29/share-americans-not-having-sex-has-reached-record-high/.

Inoue, T., Abekawa, T., Nakagawa, S., Suzuki, K., Tanaka, T., Kitaichi, Y., et al. (2011). Long-term naturalistic follow-up of lithium augmentation: Relevance to bipolarity. *Journal of Affective Disorders, 129,* 64-67.

Institute of Medicine (US) Immunization Safety Review Committee (2004). *Immunization Safety Review: Vaccines and Autism.* Washington, DC: National Academies Press.

International Human Genome Sequencing Consortium. (2003). *International Consortium completes Human Genome Project.* Bethesda, MD: National Human Genome Research Institute.

Irwin, M. (2008). Human psychoneuroimmunology: 20 years of discovery. *Brain, Behavior, and Immunity, 22,* 129-139.

Irwin, R. R. (2006). Spiritual development in adulthood: Key concepts and models. In C. Hoare (Ed.), *Handbook of adult development and learning.* New York: Oxford University Press.

Isbell, L. M., & Tyler, J. M. (2003). Teaching students about in-group favoritism and the minimal groups paradigm. *Teaching of Psychology, 30,* 127-130.

Ishikawa, S., Okajima, I., Matsuoka, H., & Sakano, Y. (2007). Cognitive behavioural therapy for anxiety disorders in children and adolescents: A meta-analysis. *Child and Adolescent Mental Health, 12,* 164-172.

Islam, R. F. (2019). Revisiting the universality of multiple intelligences theory in English writing classroom: Putting theory into practice. *ELS Journal on Interdisciplinary Studies in Humanities, 2*(1), 148-155.

Iverson, P., Kuhl, P. K., Reiko, A. Y., Diesch, E., Tohkura, Y., Ketterman, A., et al. (2003). A perceptual interference account of acquisition difficulties for non-native phonemes. *Cognition, 87,* B47-B57.

Ivtzan, I., Gardner, H. E., Bernard, I., Sekhon, M., & Hart, R. (2013). Wellbeing through self-fulfilment: Examining developmental aspects of self-actualization. *The Humanistic Psychologist, 41,* 119-132.

Izard, C. E. (1994). Innate and universal facial expressions: Evidence from developmental and cross-cultural research. *Psychological Bulletin, 115,* 288-299.

Izuhara, M., Hashioka, S., Sato, T., Nishikoori, H., Koike, M., Matsuda, H., et al. (2019, June 4). The effectiveness of electroconvulsive therapy for psychiatric symptoms and cognitive fluctuations similar to dementia with Lewy bodies: A case report. *Psychogeriatrics,*doi: 10.1111/psyg.12465.

Jablonka, E. (2017). The evolution of linguistic communication: Piagetian insights. In N. Budwig, E. Turiel, P. D. Zelazo, N. Budwig, E. Turiel, & P. D. Zelazo (Eds.), *New perspectives on human development.* New York: Cambridge University Press.

Jack, R. E., & Schyns, P. G. (2017). Toward a social psychophysics of face communication. *Annual Review of Psychology, 68,* 269-297.

Jackson, A. S., Sui, X., Hébert, J. R., Church, T. S., & Blair, S. N. (2009). Role of lifestyle and aging on the longitudinal change in cardiorespiratory fitness. *Archives of Internal Medicine, 169*(19), 1781-1787. doi:10.1001/archinternmed.2009.312.

Jackson, J. D. (2006). Trauma, attachment, and coping: Pathways to resilience. *Dissertation Abstracts International: Section B: The Sciences and Engineering, 67*(1-B), 547.

Jackson, M. L., Gunzelmann, G., Whitney, P., Hinson, J. M., Belenky, G., Rabat, A., et al. (2013). Deconstructing and reconstructing cognitive performance in sleep deprivation. *Sleep Medicine Reviews, 17,* 215-225.

Jacob, B. C. (2011). Testosterone replacement therapy in males with erectile dysfunction. *Journal of Pharmacy Practice, 24,* 298-306.

Jacob, K. S. (2014). DSM-5 and culture: The need to move towards a shared model of care within a more equal patient-physican partnership. *Asian Journal of Psychiatry, 7,* 89-91.

Jacob, K. S., Kumar, P. S., Gayathri, K., Abraham, S., & Prince, M. J. (2007). The diagnosis of dementia in the community [Special issue: Focus on psychogeriatrics in the developing world]. *International Psychogeriatrics, 19,* 669-678.

Jacobs, A., & Richtel, M. (2017, September 18). How big business got Brazil hooked on junk foods. *The New York Times.* Accessed from https://www.nytimes.com/interactive/2017/09/16/health/brazil-obesity-nestle.html?emc=edit_ta_20170917&nl=top-stories&nlid=15802952&ref=headline&_r=0.

Jacobs, E. G., Kroenke, C., Lin, J., Epel, E. S., Kenna, H. A., Blackburn, E. H., et al. (2013). Accelerated cell aging in female APOE-4 carriers: Implications for hormone therapy use. *Plos ONE, 8,* 103-111.

Jacobs, J. A., & Gerson, K. (2004). *The time divide: Work, family, and gender inequality.* Cambridge, MA: Harvard University Press.

Jacobs, M., Roesch, S., Wonderlich, S., Crosby, R., Thornton, L., Wilfley, D., et al. (2009). Anorexia nervosa trios: Behavioral profiles of individuals with anorexia nervosa and their parents. *Psychological Medicine, 39,* 451-461.

Jacobsen, P. B., Prasad, R., Villani, J., Lee, C.-M., Rochlin, D., Scheuter, C., et al. (2019). The role of economic analyses in promoting adoption of behavioral and psychosocial interventions in clinical settings. *Health Psychology, 38*(8), 680-688.

Jacobson, S. W., Stanton, M. E., Dodge, N. C., Pienaar, M., Fuller, D. S., Molteno, C. D., et al. (2011). Impaired delay and trace eyeblink conditioning in school-age children with fetal alcohol syndrome. *Alcoholism: Clinical and Experimental Research, 35,* 250-264.

Jacoby, J., & Schwartz, G. W. (2017). Three small-receptive-field ganglion cells in the mouse retina are distinctly tuned to size, speed, and object motion. *Journal of Neuroscience, 37,* 610-625.

Jacoby, L. L., & Wahlheim, C. N. (2013). On the importance of looking back: The role of recursive remindings in recency judgments and cued recall. *Memory & Cognition, 41,* 625-637.

Jacoby-Senghor, D. S., Sinclair, S., & Smith, C. T. (2015). When bias binds: Effect of implicit outgroup bias on ingroup affiliation. *Journal of Personality and Social Psychology, 109*(3), 415-433.

Jain, S., Malinowski, M., Chopra, P., Varshney, V., & Deer, T. (2019). Intrathecal drug delivery for pain management: recent advances and future developments. *Expert Opinion on Drug Delivery,* https://doi.org/10.1080/17425247.2019.1642870.

James, W. (1890). *The principles of psychology.* New York: Holt.

James, W. (2015). The principles of psychology (excerpt). In T. Alter & Y. Nagasawa (Eds.), *Consciousness in the physical world: Perspectives on Russellian monism.* New York: Oxford University Press.

Jamieson, G. A. (2007). *Hypnosis and conscious states: The cognitive neuroscience perspective.* New York: Oxford University Press.

Jamison, K. R. (1995). *An unquiet mind: A memoir of moods and madness.* New York: Knopf.

Jannini, E. A., McMahon, C. G., & Waldinger, M. D. (2013). *Premature ejaculation: From etiology to diagnosis and treatment.* New York: Springer-Verlag Publishing.

Jarlais, D. C. D., Arasteh, K., & Perlis, T. (2007). The transition from injection to non-injection drug use: Long-term outcomes among heroin and cocaine users in New York City. *Addiction, 102,* 778-785.

Jarrold, C., & Tam, H. (2011). Rehearsal and the development of working memory. In P. Barrouillet & V. Gaillard (Eds.), *Cognitive development and working memory: A dialogue between neo-Piagetian theories and cognitive approaches.* New York: Psychology Press.

Jauhar, S., Hayes, J., Goodwin, G. M., Baldwin, D. S., Cowen, P. J., & Nutt, D. J. (2019). Antidepressants, withdrawal, and addiction; where are we now? *Journal of Psychopharmacology, 33*(6), 655-659.

Javaid, A. (2017). In the shadows: Making sense of gay male rape victims' silence, suffering, and invisibility. *International Journal of Sexual Health, 29*(4), 279-291.

Jay, M. (2017). *Supernormal: The untold story of adversity and resilience.* New York: Twelve.

Jayne, K. M., Purswell, K. E., & Stulmaker, H. L. (2019). Facilitating congruence, empathy, and unconditional positive regard through therapeutic limit-setting: Attitudinal conditions limit-setting model (ACLM). *International Journal of Play Therapy.* http://dx.doi.org/10.1037/pla0000101.

Jeffery, A. J. (2015). Two behavioral hypotheses for the evolution of male homosexuality in humans. In T. K. Shackelford & R. D. Hansen (Eds.), *The evolution of sexuality.* Cham, Switzerland: Springer International Publishing.

Jelen, L. A., King, S., Horne, C. M., Lythgoe, D. J., Young, A. H., & Stone, J. M. (2019). Functional magnetic resonance spectroscopy in patients with schizophrenia and bipolar affective disorder: Glutamate dynamics in the anterior cingulate cortex during a working memory task. *European Neuropsychopharmacology, 29*(2), 222-234.

Jenkins, S. R. (1994). Need for power and women's careers over 14 years: Structural power, job satisfaction, and motive change. *Journal of Personality and Social Psychology, 66,* 155-165.

Jennings, D. J., Alonso, E., Mondragón, E., Franssen, M., & Bonardi, C. (2013). The effect of stimulus distribution form on the acquisition and rate of conditioned responding: Implications for theory. *Journal of Experimental*

Psychology: Animal Behavior Processes, 39, 233-248.

Jensen, M. P., & Patterson, D. R. (2014). Hypnotic approaches for chronic pain management: Clinical implications of recent research findings. *American Psychologist, 69,* 167-177.

Jensen, M. P., & Turk, D. C. (2014). Contributions of psychology to the understanding and treatment of people with chronic pain: Why it matters to ALL psychologists. *American Psychologist, 69,* 105-118.

Jewanski, J., Simner, J., Day, S. A., Rothen, N., & Ward, J. (2019). The "golden age" of synesthesia inquiry in the late nineteenth century (1876-1895). *Journal of the History of the Neurosciences,* 1-28.

Jia, C., & Hegg, C. C. (2015). Effect of IP3R3 and NPY on age-related declines in olfactory stem cell proliferation. *Neurobiology of Aging, 36,* 1045-1056.

Jia, H., Zack, M. M., & Thompson, W. W. (2011). State quality-adjusted life expectancy for U.S. adults from 1993 to 2008. *Quality of Life Research: An International Journal of Quality of Life Aspects of Treatment, Care & Rehabilitation, 20,* 853-863.

Jiang, S., Miao, B., & Chen, Y. (2017). Prolonged duration of isoflurane anesthesia impairs spatial recognition memory through the activation of JNK1/2 in the hippocampus of mice. *Neuroreport: For Rapid Communication of Neuroscience Research, 28,* 386-390.

Jin, B., & Kim, J. (2017). Grit, basic needs satisfaction, and subjective well-being. *Journal of Individual Differences, 38*(1), 29-35.

Jin, J., Pei, G., & Ma, Q. (2019). They are what you hear in media reports: The racial stereotypes toward Uyghurs activated by media. *Frontiers in Neuroscience, 13,* 168.

Joe, G. W., Flynn, P. M., & Broome, K. M. (2007). Patterns of drug use and expectations in methadone patients. *Addictive Behaviors, 32,* 1640-1656.

Joel, D., & McCarthy, M.M. (2017). Incorporating sex as a biological variable in neuropsychiatric research: Where are we now and where should we be? *Neuropsychopharmacology, 42,* 379-385.

John-Steiner, V., & Mahn, H. (2003). Sociocultural contexts for teaching and learning. In W. M. Reynolds & G. E. Miller (Eds.), *Handbook of psychology: Educational psychology* (Vol. 7). New York: Wiley.

Johnsdotter, S., & Essén, B. (2005). It is only a tradition: Making sense of Swedish Somalis' narratives of female circumcision and avoiding submission to hegemonic political discourse. *Critical Social Policy, 25,* 577-589.

Johnson, C. Y. (2014, January 17). Finding a way to erase harmful memories. *Boston Globe,* p. 1.

Johnson, G. B. (2000). *The Living World* (p. 600). Boston: McGraw-Hill.

Johnson, H. D. (2004). Gender, grade and relationship differences in emotional closeness within adolescent friendships. *Adolescence, 39,* 243-255.

Johnson, W., & Deary, I. J. (2011). Placing inspection time, reaction time, and perceptual speed in the broader context of cognitive ability: The VPR model in the Lothian Birth Cohort 1936. *Intelligence, 39,* 405-417.

Johnson-Laird, P. N. (2006). *How we reason.* Oxford, England: Oxford University Press.

Johnston, E., & Olson, L. (2015). *The feeling brain: The biology and psychology of emotions.* New York: W. W. Norton & Co.

Johnston, L. D., Miech, R. A., O'Malley, P. M., Bachman, J. G., & Schulenberg, J. E. (2016, December 13). Teen use of any illicit drug other than marijuana at new low, same true for alcohol. Ann Arbor, MI: University of Michigan News Service. Accessed from http://www.monitoringthefuture.org.

Johnston, L. D., O'Malley, P. M., Bachman, J. G., & Schulenberg, J. E. (2009). *Monitoring the Future national results on adolescent drug use: Overview of key findings, 2008* (NIH Publication No. 09-7401). Bethesda, MD: National Institute on Drug Abuse.

Johnston, L. D., O'Malley, P. M., Miech, R. A., Bachman, J. G., & Schulenberg, J. E. (2017). *Monitoring the Future national survey results on drug use, 1975-2016: Overview, key findings on adolescent drug use.* Ann Arbor, MI: Institute for Social Research.

Johnston, M. V. (2004). Clinical disorders of brain plasticity. *Brain and Development, 26,* 73-80.

Jones, A. L. (2006). The contemporary psychoanalyst: Karen Horney's theory applied in today's culture. *PsycCRITIQUES, 51,* 127-134.

Jones, C. (2020, May 13). Student anxiety, depression increase during school closures. *EdSource.* Downloaded from https://edsource.org/2020/student-anxiety-depression-increasing-during-school-closures-survey-finds/631224, May 18, 2020.

Jones, D. (2010). A WEIRD view of human nature skews psychologists' studies. *Science, 328,* 1627.

Jones, J. E., & Corp, E. S. (2003). Effect of naltrexone on food intake and body weight in Syrian hamsters depends on metabolic status. *Physiology and Behavior, 78,* 67-72.

Jones, J. M. (2007). Exposure to chronic community violence: Resilience in African American children. *Journal of Black Psychology, 33,* 125-149.

Jones, R. K., Darroch, J. E., & Singh, S. (2005). Religious differentials in the sexual and reproductive behaviors of young women in the United States. *Journal of Adolescent Health, 36,* 279-288.

Jones, S. W., Weitlauf, J., Danhauer, S. C., Qi, L., Zaslavsky, O., Wassertheil-Smoller, S., et al. (2017). Prospective data from the Women's Health Initiative on depressive symptoms, stress, and inflammation. *Journal of Health Psychology, 22,* 457-464.

Joo, M., & Park, S. W. (2019). Depression is associated with negativity in TAT narratives: The mediating role of agency. *Current Psychology: A Journal for Diverse Perspectives on Diverse Psychological Issues.* https://doi.org/10.1007/s12144-019-00245-6.

Jordan-Young, R. M. (2010). *Brain storm: The flaws in the science of sex differences.* Cambridge, MA: Harvard University Press.

Joseph, S. (2019). Why we need a more humanistic positive organizational scholarship: Carl Rogers' person-centered approach as a challenge to neoliberalism. *The Humanistic Psychologist.* http://dx.doi.org/10.1037/hum0000151

Jost, J. T., Kay, A. C., & Thorisdottir, H. (2009). *Social and psychological bases of ideology and system justification.* New York: Oxford University Press.

Jovanović, D., Stanojević, P., & Stanojević, D. (2011). Motives for, and attitudes about, driving-related anger and aggressive driving. *Social Behavior and Personality, 39,* 755-764.

Joyce, J. (1934). *Ulysses.* New York: Random House.

Jung, C. G. (1961). *Freud and psychoanalysis.* New York: Pantheon.

Jung, J., & Chang, D. (2017). Types of creativity—Fostering multiple intelligences in design convergence talents. *Thinking Skills and Creativity, 23,* 101-111.

Justman, S. (2011). From medicine to psychotherapy: The placebo effect. *History of the Human Sciences, 24,* 95-107.

Jónsson, H., Kristensen, M., & Arendt, M. (2015). Intensive cognitive behavioural therapy for obsessive-compulsive disorder: A systematic review and meta-analysis. *Journal of Obsessive-Compulsive and Related Disorders, 6,* 83-96.

Kafali, H. Y., Bildik, T., Bora, E., Yuncu, Z., & Erermis, H. S. (2019). Distinguishing prodromal stage of bipolar disorder and early onset schizophrenia spectrum disorders during adolescence. *Psychiatry Research, 275,* 315-325.

Kahn, K. B., Lee, J. K., Renauer, B., Henning, K. R., & Stewart, G. (2017). The effects of perceived phenotypic racial stereotypicality and social identity threat on racial minorities' attitudes about police. *Journal of Social Psychology, 157,* 416-428.

Kahn, R. E., Frick, P. J., Youngstrom, E. A., Kogos Youngstrom, J., Feeny, N. C., & Findling, R. L. (2013). Distinguishing primary and secondary variants of callous-unemotional traits among adolescents in a clinic-referred sample. *Psychological Assessment, 25,* 966-978.

Kaiser Family Foundation. (2014, April). The HIV/AIDS epidemic in the United States. Menlo Park, CA: Author.

Kaiser, B. L., Thomas, G. R., & Bowers, B. J. (2017). A case study of engaging hard-to-reach participants in the research process: Community Advisors on Research Design and Strategies (CARDS)®. *Research in Nursing & Health, 40,* 70-79.

Kalanthroff, E., Anholt, G. E., Keren, R., & Henik, A. (2013). What should I (not) do? Control over irrelevant tasks in obsessive-compulsive disorder patients. *Clinical Neuropsychiatry: Journal of Treatment Evaluation, 10* (Suppl. 1) 61-64.

Kalka, D. (2016). Quality of life and proactive coping with stress in a group of middle adulthood women with type 2 diabetes. *Polish Psychological Bulletin, 47,* 327-337.

Kalodner, C. R. (2011). Cognitive-behavioral theories. In D. Capuzzi & D. R. Gross (Eds.),

Counseling and psychotherapy (5th ed.). Alexandria, VA: American Counseling Association.

Kamens, S. R. (2011). On the proposed sexual and gender identity diagnoses for DSM-5: History and controversies. *Humanistic Psychologist, 39,* 37-59.

Kamimori, G. H., McLellan, T. M., Tate, C. M., Voss, D. M., Niro, P., & Lieberman, H. R. (2015). Caffeine improves reaction time, vigilance and logical reasoning during extended periods with restricted opportunities for sleep. *Psychopharmacology, 232,* 2031-2042.

Kandala, N. B., Ezejimofor, M. C., Uthman, O. A., & Komba, P. (2018). Secular trends in the prevalence of female genital mutilation/cutting among girls: A systematic analysis. *BMJ Global Health, 3*(5), e000549. doi:10.1136/bmjgh-2017-000549.

Kandler, C., Riemann, R., & Angleitner, A. (2013). Patterns and sources of continuity and change of energetic and temporal aspects of temperament in adulthood: A longitudinal twin study of self- and peer reports. *Developmental Psychology, 49,* 1739-1753.

Kane, J. M., Robinson, D. G., Schooler, N. R., Mueser, K. T., Penn, D. L., Rosenheck, R. A., et al. (2016). Comprehensive versus usual community care for first-episode psychosis: 2-year outcomes from the NIMH RAISE Early Treatment Program. *American Journal of Psychiatry, 173,* 362-372.

Kanel, D., Al-Wasity, S., Stefanov, K., & Pollick, F. E. (2019). Empathy to emotional voices and the use of real-time fMRI to enhance activation of the anterior insula. *NeuroImage, 198,* 53-62.

Kanoski, S. E., Hayes, M. R., Greenwald, H. S., Fortin, S. M., Gianessi, C. A., Gilbert, J. R., et al. (2011). Hippocampal leptin signaling reduces food intake and modulates food-related memory processing. *Neuropsychopharmacology, 36,* 1859-1870.

Kantrowitz, B., & Underwood, A. (2007, June 25). The teen drinking dilemma. *Newsweek,* pp. 36-37.

Kao, D. (2011). Message sidedness in advertising: The moderating roles of need for cognition and time pressure in persuasion. *Scandinavian Journal of Psychology, 52,* 329-340.

Kaposi, D. (2017). The resistance experiments: Morality, authority and obedience in Stanley Milgram's account. *Journal for the Theory of Social Behaviour.* Accessed from http://onlinelibrary.wiley.com/doi/10.1111/jtsb.12137/abstract.

Karabulut, S., Korkmaz Bayramov, K., Bayramov, R., Ozdemir, F., Topaloglu, T., Ergen, E., et al. (2019). Effects of post-learning REM sleep deprivation on hippocampal plasticity-related genes and microRNA in mice. *Behavioural Brain Research, 361,* 7-13.

Karaszewski, B. (2008). Sub-neocortical brain: A mechanical tool for creative generation? *Trends in Cognitive Sciences, 12,* 171-172.

Karlson, C. W., Gallagher, M. W., Olson, C. A., & Hamilton, N. A. (2013). Insomnia symptoms and well-being: Longitudinal follow-up. *Health Psychology, 32,* 311-319.

Kasemsap, K. (2017). Mastering cognitive neuroscience and social neuroscience perspectives in the information age. In M. A. Dos Santos (Ed.), *Applying neuroscience to business practice.* Hershey, PA: Business Science Reference/IGI Global.

Kassam, K. S., Gilbert, D. T., Swencionis, J. K., & Wilson, T. D. (2009). Misconceptions of memory: The Scooter Libby effect. *Psychological Science, 20,* 551-552.

Kassel, J. D., Evatt, D. P., Greenstein, J. E., Wardle, M. C., Yates, M. C., & Veilleux, J. C. (2007). The acute effects of nicotine on positive and negative affect in adolescent smokers. *Journal of Abnormal Psychology, 116,* 543-553.

Kassin, S. M. (2017). The killing of Kitty Genovese: What else does this case tell us? *Perspectives on Psychological Science, 12,* 374-381.

Kassin, S. M., Redlich, A. D., Alceste, F., & Luke, T. J. (2018). On the general acceptance of confessions research: Opinions of the scientific community. *American Psychologist, 73,* 63-80.

Kato, N. (2009). Neurophysiological mechanisms of electroconvulsive therapy for depression. *Neuroscience Research, 64,* 3-11.

Katz, J. (2017, June 5). Drug deaths in America are rising faster than ever. *The New York Times.* Accessed from https://www.nytimes.com/interactive/2017/06/05/upshot/opioid-epidemic-drug-overdose-deaths-are-rising-faster-than-ever.html.

Katz, M. (2001). The implications of revising Freud's empiricism for drive theory. *Psychoanalysis and Contemporary Thought, 24,* 253-272.

Kaufman, A., Johnson, C., & Liu, X. (2008). A CHC theory-based analysis of age differences on cognitive abilities and academic skills at ages 22 to 90 years. *Journal of Psychoeducational Assessment, 26,* 350-381.

Kaufman, J. C., & Baer, J. (2006). *Creativity and reason in cognitive development.* New York: Cambridge University Press.

Kaufman, J. C., & Plucker, J. A. (2011). Intelligence and creativity. In R. J. Sternberg & S. Kaufman (Eds.), *The Cambridge handbook of intelligence.* New York: Cambridge University Press.

Kaufman, J. C., Kaufman, S., & Plucker, J. A. (2013). Contemporary theories of intelligence. In D. Reisberg (Ed.), *The Oxford handbook of cognitive psychology.* New York: Oxford University Press.

Kauten, R. L., Lui, J. L., Stary, A. K., & Barry, C. T. (2015). "Purging my friends list. Good luck making the cut": Perceptions of narcissism on Facebook. *Computers in Human Behavior, 51,* 244-254.

Kavaliers, M., Ossenkopp, K. P., & Choleris, E. (2019). Social neuroscience of disgust. *Genes, Brain and Behavior, 18*(1), e12508.

Kawakami, N., & Miura, E. (2015). Image or real? Altering the mental imagery of subliminal stimuli differentiates explicit and implicit attitudes. *Imagination, Cognition and Personality, 34,* 259-269.

Kawashima, H., Izaki, Y., & Grace, A. A. (2006). Cooperativity between hippocampal-pre-frontal short-term plasticity through associative long-term potentiation. *Brain Research, 1109,* 37-44.

Kazantseva, A., Gaysina, D., Kutlumbetova, Y., Kanzafarova, R., Malykh, S., Lobaskova, M., et al. (2015). Brain derived neurotrophic factor gene (BDNF) and personality traits: The modifying effect of season of birth and sex. *Progress in Neuro-Psychopharmacology & Biological Psychiatry, 56,* 58-65.

Kazar, D. B. (2006). Forensic psychology: Did we leave anything out? *PsycCRITIQUES, 51,* 88-97.

Kazdin, A. (2008). Evidence-based treatment and practice: New opportunities to bridge clinical research and practice, enhance the knowledge base, and improve patient care. *American Psychologist, 63,* 146-159.

Keating, D. P., & Clark, L. V. (1980). Development of physical and social reasoning in adolescence. *Developmental Psychology, 16,* 23-30.

Kecmanovic, J. (2020, April 27). Could therapy ease your coronavirus stress? How to decide, what to expect and where to find it. *Washington Post.* Downloaded from https://www.washingtonpost.com/lifestyle/wellness/finding-therapy-coronavirus-stress-anxiety-anger/2020/04/25/4c00dd3c-866d-11ea-a3eb-e9fc93160703_story.html.

Keer, M., van den Putte, B., Neijens, P., & de Wit, J. (2013). The influence of affective and cognitive arguments on message judgement and attitude change: The moderating effects of meta-bases and structural bases. *Psychology & Health, 28,* 895-908.

Keillor, J. M., Barrett, A. M., Crucian, G. P., Kortenkamp, S., & Heilman, K. M. (2002). Emotional experience and perception in the absence of facial feedback. *Journal of the International Neuropsychological Society, 8,* 130-135.

Kekäläinen, T., Freund, A. M., Sipilä, S., & Kokko, K. (2019). Cross-sectional and longitudinal associations between leisure time physical activity, mental well-being and subjective health in middle adulthood. *Applied Research in Quality of Life,* 1-18.

Keller, J. (2007). Stereotype threat in classroom settings: The interactive effect of domain identification, task difficulty and stereotype threat on female students' math performance. *British Journal of Educational Psychology, 77,* 323-338.

Kelley, H. (1950). The warm-cold variable in first impressions of persons. *Journal of Personality and Social Psychology, 18,* 431-439.

Kelly, J. B. (2000). Children's adjustment in conflicted marriage and divorce: A decade review of research. *Journal of the American Academy of Child & Adolescent Psychiatry, 39,* 963-973.

Keltikangas-Järvinen, L., Räikkönen, K., Ekelund, J., & Peltonen, L. (2004). Nature and nurture in novelty seeking. *Molecular Psychiatry, 9,* 308-311.

Kempermann, G. (2011). Seven principles in the regulation of adult neurogenesis. *European Journal of Neuroscience, 33,* 1018-1024.

Kemps, E., & Tiggemann, M. (2007). Reducing the vividness and emotional impact of distressing autobiographical memories: The importance of modality-specific interference. *Memory, 15*, 412-422.

Kendler, K. S., & Schaffner, K. F. (2011). The dopamine hypothesis of schizophrenia: An historical and philosophical analysis. *Philosophy, Psychiatry, & Psychology, 18*, 41-63.

Kendler, K., Halberstadt, L., Butera, F., Myers, J., Bouchard, T., & Ekman, P. (2008). The similarity of facial expressions in response to emotion-inducing films in reared-apart twins. *Psychological Medicine, 38*(10), 1475-1483.

Kendler, K. S., Aggen, S. H., Gillespie, N., Neale, M. C., Knudsen, G. P., Krueger, R. F., et al. (2017). The genetic and environmental sources of resemblance between normative personality and personality disorder traits. *Journal of Personality Disorders, 31*, 193-207.

Kenett, Y. N., Levi, E., Anaki, D., & Faust, M. (2017). The semantic distance task: Quantifying semantic distance with semantic network path length. *Journal of Experimental Psychology: Learning, Memory, and Cognition, 43*, 1470-1489.

Kennedy, C. E., Moore, P. J., Peterson, R. A., Katzman, M. A., Vermani, M., & Charmak, W. D. (2011). What makes people anxious about pain? How personality and perception combine to determine pain anxiety responses in clinical and non-clinical populations. *Anxiety, Stress & Coping: An International Journal, 24*, 179-200.

Kennedy, D. O., & Haskell, C. F. (2011). Cerebral blood flow and behavioural effects of caffeine in habitual and non-habitual consumers of caffeine: A near infrared spectroscopy study. *Biological Psychology, 86*, 296-305.

Kennedy, J. E. (2004). A proposal and challenge for proponents and skeptics of psi. *Journal of Parapsychology, 68*, 157-167.

Kennison, S. M., & Bowers, J. (2011). Illustrating brain lateralisation in a naturalistic observation of cell-phone use. *Psychology Learning & Teaching, 10*, 46-51.

Keppler, J. (2017, May 3). Shedding light on the fundamental mechanism underlying hypnotic analgesia. *Annals of Palliative Medicine*, pii: apm. 2017.04.03. doi: 10.21037/apm.2017.04.03.

Kerr, E. (2020, April 27). How college students manage coronavirus. *US. News & World Report.* Downloaded from https://www.usnews.com/education/best-colleges/articles/how-college-students-are-managing-coronavirus-stress, May 18, 2020.

Kertz, S. J., Koran, J., Stevens, K. T., & Björgvinsson, T. (2015). Repetitive negative thinking predicts depression and anxiety symptom improvement during brief cognitive behavioral therapy. *Behaviour Research and Therapy, 68*, 54-63.

Keränen, T., Halkoaho, A., Itkonen, E., & Pietilä, A. (2015). Placebo-controlled clinical trials: How trial documents justify the use of randomisation and placebo. *BMC Medical Ethics, 16*, 88-96.

Kesebir, P., & Diener, E. (2008). In pursuit of happiness: Empirical answers to philosophical questions. *Perspectives on Psychological Science, 3*, 117-125.

Keshavarz, M. (2017). Glial cells as key elements in the pathophysiology and treatment of bipolar disorder. *Acta Neuropsychiatrica, 29*, 140-152.

Kessler, R. C., & Wang, P. S. (2008). The descriptive epidemiology of commonly occurring mental disorders in the United States. *Annual Review of Public Health, 29*, 115-129.

Ketisch, T., & Jones, R. A. (2013). Review of "ADHD diagnosis & management." *American Journal of Family Therapy, 41*, 272-274.

Khazaal, Y., Chatton, A., Claeys, F., Ribordy, F., Zullino, D., & Cabanac, M. (2008). Antipsychotic drug and body weight set-point. *Physiology & Behavior, 95*, 157-160.

Khedr, E. M., Omran, E. A., Ismail, N. M., El-Hammady, D. H., Goma, S. H., Kotb, H., et al. (2017). Effects of transcranial direct current stimulation on pain, mood and serum endorphin level in the treatment of fibromyalgia: A double blinded, randomized clinical trial. *Brain Stimulation, 10*(5), 893-90.

Khera, A. V., Chaffin, M., Wade, K. H., Zahid, S., Brancale, J., Xia, R., et al. (2019). Polygenic prediction of weight and obesity trajectories from birth to adulthood. *Cell, 177*(3), 587-596.

Kidd, E., & Lum, J. (2008). Sex differences in past tense overregularization. *Developmental Science, 11*, 882-889.

Kihlstrom, J. F. (2005a). Dissociative disorders. *Annual Review of Clinical Psychology, 1*, 227-253.

Kihlstrom, J. F. (2005b). Is hypnosis an altered state of consciousness or what? Comment. *Contemporary Hypnosis, 22*, 34-38.

Kim, D. R., Pesiridou, A., & O'Reardon, J. P. (2009). Transcranial magnetic stimulation in the treatment of psychiatric disorders. *Current Psychiatry Reports, 11*, 447-52.

Kim, H., Clark, D., & Dionne, R. (2009). Genetic contributions to clinical pain and analgesia: Avoiding pitfalls in genetic research. *The Journal of Pain, 10*, 663-693.

Kim, N. (2008). The moon illusion and the size-distance paradox. In S. Cummins-Sebree, M. A. Riley, & K. Shockley (Eds.), *Studies in perception and action IX: Fourteenth International Conference on Perception and Action.* Mahwah, NJ: Lawrence Erlbaum Associates.

Kim, S., Polari, A., Melville, F., Moller, B., Kim, J., Amminger, P., et al. (2017). Are current labeling terms suitable for people who are at risk of psychosis? *Schizophrenia Research, 188*, 172-177.

Kim, Y., & Yoon, H. (2017). Common and distinct brain networks underlying panic and social anxiety disorders. *Progress in Neuro-Psychopharmacology & Biological Psychiatry.* Accessed from https://www.ncbi.nlm.nih.gov/pubmed/28642079.

Kim-Cohen, J., Caspi, A., & Moffitt, T. E. (2003). Prior juvenile diagnoses in adults with mental disorder: Developmental follow-back of a prospective-longitudinal cohort. *Archives of General Psychiatry, 60*, 709-717.

Kimbrel, N. A. (2007). A model of the development and maintenance of generalized social phobia. *Clinical Psychological Review, 8*, 69-75.

King-Casas, B., Sharp, C., Lomax-Bream, L., Lohrenz, T., Fonagy, P., & Montague, P. R. (2008). The rupture and repair of cooperation in borderline personality disorder. *Science, 321*, 806-810.

Kinsey, A. C., Pomeroy, W. B., & Martin, C. E. (1948). *Sexual behavior in the human male.* Philadelphia: Saunders.

Kinsey, A. C., Pomeroy, W. B., Martin, C. E., & Gebhard, P. H. (1953). *Sexual behavior in the human female.* Philadelphia: Saunders.

Kirk, E. P., Jacobsen, D. J., Gibson, C., Hill, J. O., & Donnelly, J. E. (2003). Time course for changes in aerobic capacity and body composition in overweight men and women in response to long-term exercise: The Midwest exercise trial (MET). *International Journal of Obesity, 27*, 912-919.

Kirsch, I., Lynn, S. J., Vigorito, M., & Miller, R. R. (2004). The role of cognition in classical and operant conditioning. *Journal of Clinical Psychology, 60*, 369-392.

Kirzinger, A, Kearney, A., Hamel, L., & Brodie, M. (2020, April 2). KFF Health tracking poll— early April 2020: The impact of coronavirus on life in America. KFF Health Tracking Poll. Kaiser Family Foundation.

Kisely, S., Chang, A., Crowe, J., Galletly, C., Jenkins, P., Loi, S., et al. (2015). Getting started in research: Systematic reviews and meta-analyses. *Australasian Psychiatry, 23*, 16-21.

Kish, S., Fitzmaurice, P., Boileau, I., Schmunk, G., Ang, L., Furukawa, Y., et al. (2009). Brain serotonin transporter in human methamphetamine users. *Psychopharmacology, 202*, 649-661.

Kitayama, S. (2017). Journal of Personality and Social Psychology: Attitudes and social cognition. *Journal of Personality and Social Psychology, 112*, 357-360.

Kivipelto, M. & Hakansson, K. (2017). A rare success against Alzheimer's. *Scientific American, 316*, 32-37.

Kivlighan, D. M., Goldberg, S. B., Abbas, M., Pace, B. T., Yulish, N. E., Thomas, J. G., et al. (2015). The enduring effects of psychodynamic treatments vis-à-vis alternative treatments: A multilevel longitudinal meta-analysis. *Clinical Psychology Review, 40*, 1-14.

Kizilirmak, J. M., Galvao Gomes da Silva, J., Imamoglu, F., & Richardson-Klavehn, A. (2015). Generation and the subjective feeling of "aha!" are independently related to learning from insight. *Psychological Research, 80*(6), 1059-1074.

Klein, K. M., Apple, K. J., & Kahn, A. S. (2011). Attributions of blame and responsibility in sexual harassment: Reexamining a psychological model. *Law and Human Behavior, 35*, 92-103.

Kleinplatz, P. J., Moser, C., & Lev, A. (2013). Sex and gender identity disorders. In G. Stricker, T. A. Widiger, & I. B. Weiner (Eds.), *Handbook of psychology, Vol. 8: Clinical psychology* (2nd ed.). Hoboken, NJ: John Wiley & Sons Inc.

Kluck, A. (2008). Family factors in the development of disordered eating: Integrating dynamic and behavioral explanations. *Eating Behaviors, 9*, 471-483.

Kluger, J. (2001, April 2). Fear not! *Time*, pp. 51-62.

Kluger, J. (2013, July 29). The power of the bilingual brain. *Time*, 42-47.

Kluger, J. (2018, October 24). Strong and smart, service monkeys give a helping hand to people with quadriplegia, *Time*. Retrieved from https://time.com/longform/service-monkeys-quadriplegia/.

Kluger, J. (2019, June 24). The vaccine battlegrounds. *Time*, pp. 38-43.

Knight, S. C., & Meyer, R. G. (2007). Forensic hypnosis. In A. M. Goldstein (Ed.), *Forensic psychology: Emerging topics and expanding roles.* Hoboken, NJ: John Wiley & Sons.

Knight, W. (2019, July 31). Instead of practicing, this AI mastered chess by reading about it. *MIT Technology Review.* Downloaded from https://www.technologyreview.com/s/614043/instead-of-practicing-this-ai-mastered-chess-by-reading-about-it/. August 28, 2019.

Knutson, D., & Koch, J. M. (2019). Person-centered therapy as applied to work with transgender and gender diverse clients. *Journal of Humanistic Psychology*, 0022167818791082.

Koch, C., & Greenfield, S. (2007). How does consciousness happen? *Scientific American, 297*(4), 76-83.

Koch, J. (2003). Gender issues in the classroom. In W. M. Reynolds & G. E. Miller (Eds.), *Handbook of psychology: Educational psychology* (Vol. 7). New York: Wiley.

Kochli, D. E., Thompson, E. C., Fricke, E. A., Postle, A. F., & Quinn, J. J. (2015). The amygdala is critical for trace, delay, and contextual fear conditioning. *Learning & Memory, 22*, 92-100.

Kogstad, R. E., Ekeland, T. J., & Hummelvoll, J. K. (2011). In defence of a humanistic approach to mental health care: Recovery processes investigated with the help of clients' narratives on turning points and processes of gradual change. *Journal of Psychiatric and Mental Health Nursing, 18*, 479-486.

Koh, E., Stauss, K., Coustaut, C., & Forrest, C. (2017). Generational impact of single-parent scholarships: Educational achievement of children in single-parent families. *Journal of Family Issues, 38*, 607-632.

Kohlberg, L. (1984). *The psychology of moral development: Essays on moral development* (Vol. 2). San Francisco: Harper & Row.

Kohlberg, L., & Ryncarz, R. A. (1990). Beyond justice reasoning: Moral development and consideration of a seventh stage. In C. N. Alexander & E. J. Langer (Eds.), *Higher stages of human development: Perspectives on adult growth.* New York: Oxford University Press.

Kojima, M., & Kangawa, K. (2008). Structure and function of ghrelin. *Results & Problems in Cell Differentiation, 46*, 89-115.

Kolb, B., Gibb, R., & Robinson, T. E. (2003). Brain plasticity and behavior. *Current Directions in Psychological Science, 12*, 1-5.

Komarovskaya, I., Loper, A., Warren, J., & Jackson, S. (2011). Exploring gender differences in trauma exposure and the emergence of symptoms of PTSD among incarcerated men and women. *Journal of Forensic Psychiatry & Psychology, 22*, 395-410.

Konijnenberg, E., den Braber, A., ten Kate, M., Tomassen, J., Mulder, S. D., Yaqub, M., et al. (2019). Association of amyloid pathology with memory performance and cognitive complaints in cognitively normal older adults: A monozygotic twin study. *Neurobiology of Aging, 77*, 58-65.

Konishi, K., & Bohbot, V. D. (2013). Spatial navigational strategies correlate with gray matter in the hippocampus of healthy older adults tested in a virtual maze. *Frontiers in Aging Neuroscience, 5.*

Koper, R. J., & Jaasma, M. A. (2001). Interpersonal style: Are human social orientations guided by generalized interpersonal needs? *Communications Reports, 14,* 117-129.

Korcha, R. A., Polcin, D. L., Bond, J. C., Lapp, W. M., & Galloway, G. (2011). Substance use and motivation: A longitudinal perspective. *American Journal of Drug and Alcohol Abuse, 37*, 48-53.

Korotkov, D., Perunovic, M., Claybourn, M., Fraser, I., Houlihan, M., Macdonald, M., & Korotkov, K. (2011). The Type B behavior pattern as a moderating variable of the relationship between stressor chronicity and health behavior. *Journal of Health Psychology, 16*, 397-409.

Korur, F., Toker, S., & Eryılmaz, A. (2016). Effects of the integrated online advance organizer teaching materials on students' science achievement and attitude. *Journal of Science Education and Technology* [serial online], *25*(4), 628-640.

Kosinski, M., Matz, S. C., Gosling, S. D., Popov, V., & Stillwell, D. (2015). Facebook as a research tool for the social sciences. *American Psychologist, 70*, 543-556.

Koss, M. P. (1993). Rape: Scope, impact, interventions, and public policy responses. *American Psychologist, 48*, 1062-1069.

Koss, M. P. (2011). Hidden, unacknowledged, acquaintance, and date rape: Looking back, looking forward. *Psychology of Women Quarterly, 35*, 348-354.

Kosslyn, S. M., & Miller, G. W. (2013). *Top brain, bottom brain: Surprising insights into how you think.* New York: Simon & Schuster.

Kotre, J., & Hall, E. (1990). *Seasons of life.* Boston: Little, Brown.

Kounios, J., Fleck, J. I., Green, D. L., Payne, L., Stevenson, J. L., Bowden, E. M., et al. (2008). The origins of insight in resting-state brain activity. *Neuropsychologia, 46*, 281-291.

Kouros, C. D., & Papp, L. M. (2019). Couples' perceptions of each other's daily affect: Empathic accuracy, assumed similarity, and indirect accuracy. *Family Process, 58*(1), 179-196.

Kowalik, J., Weller, J., Venter, J., & Drachman, D. (2011). Cognitive behavioral therapy for the treatment of pediatric posttraumatic stress disorder: A review and meta-analysis. *Journal of Behavior Therapy and Experimental Psychiatry, 42*, 405-413.

Kozulin, A., Gindis, B., Ageyev, V. S., & Miller, S. M. (2003). *Vygotsky's educational theory in cultural context.* New York: Cambridge University Press.

Koçak, O., Özpolat, A., Atbaşoğlu, C., & Çiçek, M. (2011). Cognitive control of a simple mental image in patients with obsessive-compulsive disorder. *Brain and Cognition, 76*, 390-399.

Krassner, A. M., Gartstein, M. A., Park, C., Dragan, W. Ł., Lecannelier, F., & Putnam, S. P. (2017). East-west, collectivist-individualist: A cross-cultural examination of temperament in toddlers from Chile, Poland, South Korea, and the U.S. *European Journal of Developmental Psychology, 14*(4), 449-464. doi:10.1080/17405629.2016.1236722.

Krause, A. J., Simon, E. B., Mander, B. A., Greer, S. M., Saletin, J. M., Goldstein-Piekarski, et al. (2017). The sleep-deprived human brain. *Nature Reviews Neuroscience, 18*(7), 404-418.

Krause, M., Civelek, M., Romanoski, C., & Fang, Y. (2019). Human genetics in vascular mechanotransduction and metabolism. *Arteriosclerosis, Thrombosis, and Vascular Biology, 39*(Suppl.1), A162-A162.

Krauth-Gruber, S., & Bonnot, V. (2019). Collective guilt, moral outrage, and support for helping the poor: A matter of system versus in-group responsibility framing. *Journal of Community & Applied Social Psychology.* Advance online publication. https://doi.org/10.1002/casp.2428.

Krautheim, J. T., Dannlowski, U., Steines, M., Neziroğlu, G., Acosta, H., Sommer, J., et al. (2019). Intergroup empathy: Enhanced neural resonance for ingroup facial emotion in a shared neural production-perception network. *NeuroImage, 194*, 182-190.

Kreher, D., Holcomb, P., Goff, D., & Kuperberg, G. (2008). Neural evidence for faster and further automatic spreading activation in schizophrenic thought disorder. *Schizophrenia Bulletin, 34*, 473-482.

Kreiczer-Levy, S. (2019). Parents and adult children: The elusive boundaries of the legal family. *Law and Social Inquiry, 44*(2), 519-525.

Kreppner, J., Rutter, M., Marvin, R., O'Connor, T., & Sonuga-Barke, E. (2011). Assessing the concept of the 'insecure-other' category in the Cassidy-Marvin scheme: Changes between 4 and 6 years in the English and Romanian adoptee study. *Social Development, 20*, 1-16.

Kreuger, A. (2007). Are we having fun yet? Categorizing and evaluating changes in time allocation. *Brookings Papers on Economic Activity*, (Vol. 2), 38, 193-218.

Kromer, M., & Parry, J. A. (2019). The Clinton effect? The (non)impact of a high-profile candidate on gender stereotypes. *Social Science Quarterly.* https://doi.org/10.1111/ssqu.12701.

Krueger, K., & Dayan, P. (2009). Flexible shaping: How learning in small steps helps. *Cognition, 110*, 380-394.

Krumhuber, E. G., & Scherer, K. R. (2011). Affect bursts: Dynamic patterns of facial expression. *Emotion, 11*, 825-841.

Krupić, F., Čustović, S., Jašarević, M., Šadić, S., Fazlić, M., Grbic, K., & Samuelsson, K. (2019). Ethnic differences in the perception of pain: A systematic review of qualitative and quantitative research. *Medicinski Glasnik, 16*(1), 108-114 .

Krüger, O., Korsten, P., & Hoffman, J. I. (2017). The rise of behavioral genetics and the transition to behavioral genomics and beyond. In J. Call, G. M. Burghardt, I. M. Pepperberg, C. T. Snowdon, & T. Zentall (Eds.), *APA handbook of comparative psychology: Basic concepts, methods, neural substrate, and behavior.* Washington, DC: American Psychological Association.

Kubanek, J., Snyder, L. H., & Abrams, R. A. (2015). Reward and punishment act as distinct factors in guiding behavior. *Cognition, 139*, 154-167.

Kucewicz, M. T., Berry, B. M., Miller, L. R., Khadjevand, F., Ezzyat, Y., Stein, J. M., et al. (2018). Evidence for verbal memory enhancement with electrical brain stimulation in the lateral temporal cortex. *Brain: A Journal of Neurology, 141*(4), 971-978.

Kulik, L., & Sadeh, I. (2015). Explaining fathers' involvement in childcare: An ecological approach. *Community, Work & Family, 18*, 19-40.

Kumari, S., & Joshi, S. (2013). Neonatal outcomes in women with depression during pregnancy. *Journal of Projective Psychology & Mental Health, 20*, 141-145.

Kuncel, N. R., & Beatty, A. S. (2013). Thinking at work: Intelligence, critical thinking, job knowledge, and reasoning. In K. F. Geisinger, B. A. Bracken, J. F. Carlson, J. C. Hansen, N. R. Kuncel, S. P. Reise, & M. C. Rodriguez (Eds.), *APA handbook of testing and assessment in psychology, Vol. 1: Test theory and testing and assessment in industrial and organizational psychology.* Washington, DC: American Psychological Association.

Kuosmanen, K., Rovio, S., Kivipelto, M., Tuomilehto, J., Nissinen, A., & Kulmala, J. (2016). Determinants of self-rated health and self-rated physical fitness in middle and old age. *European Journal of Mental Health, 11*(1-2), 128-143.

Kupfer, D. J., Kuhl, E. A., & Regier, D. A. (2013). DSM-5—The future arrived. *JAMA: Journal of the American Medical Association, 309*, 1691-1692.

Kupferschmidt, K. (2019, July 12). Psychologist aims to study diverse minds, not WEIRDos. *Science, 365*, p. 110.

Kupfersmid, J. (2019). Freud's clinical theories then and now. *Psychodynamic Psychiatry, 47*(1), 81-97.

Kurdziel, L., Duclos, K., & Spencer, R. M. C. (2013). Sleep spindles in midday naps

enhance learning in preschool children. *PNAS Early Edition*, 1-6.

Kuriyama, K., Stickgold, R., & Walker, M. P. (2004). Sleep-dependent learning and motor-skill complexity. *Learning and Memory, 11*, 705-713.

Kushlev, K., Dunn, E. W., & Lucas, R. E. (2015). Higher income is associated with less daily sadness but not more daily happiness. *Social Psychological and Personality Science, 6*, 483-489.

Kuther, T. L., & Burnell, K. (2019). A life span developmental perspective on psychosocial development in midlife. *Adultspan Journal, 18*(1), 27-39.

Kwang, T., Crockett, E. E., Sanchez, D. T., & Swann, W. B., Jr. (2013). Men seek social standing, women seek companionship: Sex differences in deriving self-worth from relationships. *Psychological Science, 24*, 1142-1150.

Kwon, K., Bingham, G., Lewsader, J., Jeon, H., & Elicker, J. (2013). Structured task versus free play: The influence of social context on parenting quality, toddlers' engagement with parents and play behaviors, and parent-toddler language use. *Child & Youth Care Forum, 42*, 207-224.

Kwong, A. S., López-López, J. A., Hammerton, G., Manley, D., Timpson, N. J., Leckie, G., et al. (2019). Genetic and environmental risk factors associated with trajectories of depression symptoms from adolescence to young adulthood. *JAMA Network Open, 2*(6), e196587-e196587.

Kyaga, S., Landén, M., Boman, M., Hultman, C. M., Långström, N., & Lichtenstein, P. (2013). Mental illness, suicide and creativity: 40-year prospective total population study. *Journal of Psychiatric Research, 47*, 83-90.

Kyllonen, P., & Kell, H. (2017). What is fluid intelligence? Can it be improved? In M. Rosén, K. Yang Hansen, U. Wolff, M. Rosén, K. Yang Hansen, & U. Wolff (Eds.), *Cognitive abilities and educational outcomes: A festschrift in honour of Jan-Eric Gustafsson.* Cham, Switzerland: Springer International Publishing.

Köhler, W. (1927). *The mentality of apes.* London: Routledge & Kegan Paul.

Kübler-Ross, E. (1969). *On death and dying.* New York: Macmillan.

LaBar, K. (2007). Beyond fear: Emotional memory mechanisms in the human brain. *Current Directions in Psychological Science, 16*, 173-177.

Labrecque, L. T., & Whisman, M. A. (2017). Attitudes toward and prevalence of extramarital sex and descriptions of extramarital partners in the 21st century. *Journal of Family Psychology, 31*(7), 952-957.

Labrecque, N., & Cermakian, N. (2015). Circadian clocks in the immune system. *Journal of Biological Rhythms, 30*, 277-290.

Laddis, A., Dell, P. F., & Korzekwa, M. (2017). Comparing the symptoms and mechanisms of "dissociation" in dissociative identity disorder and borderline personality disorder. *Journal of Trauma & Dissociation, 18*, 139-173.

Laederach-Hofmann, K., & Messerli-Buergy, N. (2007). Chest pain, angina pectoris, panic disorder, and Syndrome X. In J. Jordan, B. Barde, & A. M. Zeiher (Eds.), *Contributions toward evidence-based psychocardiology: A systematic review of the literature.* Washington, DC: American Psychological Association.

LaFrance, M., & Harris, J. L. (2004). Gender and verbal and nonverbal communication. In M. A. Paludi (Ed.), *Praeger guide to the psychology of gender.* Westport, CT: Praeger Publishers/ Greenwood Publishing Group.

Lagacé-Séguin, D. G., & d'Entremont, M. L. (2006). The role of child negative affect in the relations between parenting styles and play. *Early Child Development and Care, 176*, 461-477.

Lahti, J., Räikkönen, K., Ekelund, J., Peltonen, L., Raitakari, O. T., & Keltikangas-Järvinen, L. (2005). Novelty seeking: Interaction between parental alcohol use and dopamine D4 receptor gene exon III polymorphism over 17 years. *Psychiatric Genetics, 15*, 133-139.

Lai, C. H. (2019). The neural markers of MRI to differentiate depression and panic disorder. *Progress in Neuro-Psychopharmacology and Biological Psychiatry, 91*, 72-78.

Lai, C. K., & Banaji, M. R. (2020). The psychology of implicit intergroup bias and the prospect of change. In D. Allen & R. Somanathan (Eds.), *Difference without Domination: Pursuing Justice in Diverse Democracies.* Chicago: University of Chicago Press.

Lake, C. J., Carlson, J., Rose, A., & Chlevin-Thiele, C. (2019). Trust in name brand assessments: The case of the Myers-Briggs Type Indicator. *The Psychologist-Manager Journal, 22*(2), 91-107.

Lal, S. (2002). Giving children security: Mamie Phipps Clark and the racialization of child psychology. *American Psychologist, 57*, 20-28.

Lalasz, C. B., & Weigel, D. J. (2011). Understanding the relationship between gender and extradyadic relations: The mediating role of sensation seeking on intentions to engage in sexual infidelity. *Personality and Individual Differences, 50*, 1079-1083.

LaLumiere, R. T., & Kalivas, P. W. (2013). Motivational systems: Rewards and incentive value. In R. J. Nelson, S. Y. Mizumori, & I. B. Weiner (Eds.), *Handbook of psychology, Vol. 3: Behavioral neuroscience* (2nd ed.). New York: John Wiley & Sons Ltd.

Lambert, W. W. (1971). *Comparative perspectives on social psychology.* Boston: Little, Brown.

Lamborn, S. D., & Groh, K. (2009). A four-part model of autonomy during emerging adulthood: Associations with adjustment. *International Journal of Behavioral Development, 33*, 393-401.

Lampard, A. M., Byrne, S. M., McLean, N., & Fursland, A. (2011). An evaluation of the enhanced cognitive-behavioural model of bulimia nervosa. *Behaviour Research and Therapy, 49*, 529-535.

Lanciano, T., Curci, A., Mastandrea, S., & Sartori, G. (2013). Do automatic mental associations detect a flashbulb memory? *Memory, 21,* 482-493.

Landro, L. (2010, May 11). New ways to treat pain. *Wall Street Journal,* p. D1-D2.

Landro, L. (2011, April 26). "Use only as directed" isn't easy. *Wall Street Journal,* pp. D1-D2.

Landry, S. H., Zucker, T. A., Taylor, H. B., Swank, P. R., Williams, J. M., Assel, M., et al. (2013). Enhancing early child care quality and learning for toddlers at risk: The responsive early childhood program. *Developmental Psychology, 50*(2), 526-541.

Lane, K. A., Banaji, M. R., Nosek, B. A., & Greenwald, A. G. (Eds.). (2007). Understanding and using the Implicit Association Test: IV: What we know (so far) about the method. In B. Wittenbrink & N. Schwarz (Eds.), *Implicit measures of attitudes.* New York: Guilford Press.

Lang, A. J., Sorrell, J. T., & Rodgers, C. S. (2006). Anxiety sensitivity as a predictor of labor pain. *European Journal of Pain, 10,* 263-270.

Lang, P. J., & Bradley, M. M. (2013). Appetitive and defensive motivation: Goal-directed or goal-determined? *Emotion Review, 5,* 230-234.

Langa, M. E., & Gone, J. P. (2019). Cultural context in DSM diagnosis: An American Indian case illustration of contradictory trends. *Transcultural psychiatry,* https://doi.org/10.1177/1363461519832473.

Langan-Fox, J., & Grant, S. (2006). The Thematic Apperception Test: Toward a standard measure of the big three motives. *Journal of Personality Assessment, 87,* 277-291.

Langdridge, D., & Butt, T. (2004). The fundamental attribution error: A phenomenological critique. *British Journal of Social Psychology, 43,* 357-369.

Lange, J., & Boecker, L. (2019). Schadenfreude as social-functional dominance regulator. *Emotion, 19*(3), 489-502.

Langford, J. S., Pitts, R. C., & Hughes, C. E. (2019). Assessing functions of stimuli associated with rich-to-lean transitions using a choice procedure. *Journal of the Experimental Analysis of Behavior.* https://doi.org/10.1002/jeab.540.

Langlois, F., Langlois, M., Carpentier, A. C., Brown, C., Lemieux, S., & Hivert, M. (2011). Ghrelin levels are associated with hunger as measured by the Three-Factor Eating Questionnaire in healthy young adults. *Physiology & Behavior, 104,* 373-377.

Langreth, R. (2000, May 1). Every little bit helps: How even moderate exercise can have a big impact on your health. *Wall Street Journal,* p. R5.

Lansford, J. E., Sharma, C., Malone, P. S., Woodlief, D., Dodge, K. A., Oburu, P., et al. (2014). Corporal punishment, maternal warmth, and child adjustment: A longitudinal study in eight countries. *Journal of Clinical Child and Adolescent Psychology, 43*(4), 670-685.

Lanza, S. T., & Collins, L. M. (2002). Pubertal timing and the onset of substance use in females during early adolescence. *Prevention Science, 3,* 69-82.

Laplane, L., Mantovani, P., Adolphs, R., Chang, H., Mantovani, A., McFall-Ngai, M., et al. (2019). Opinion: Why science needs philosophy. *Proceedings of the National Academy of Sciences, 116*(10), 3948-3952.

LaPointe, L. L. (2013). *Paul Broca and the origins of language in the brain.* San Diego, CA: Plural Publishing.

Larsen, E. F. (2014). Good teens turned addicts. *Choices.* Accessed from http://www.huffingtonpost.com/2014/09/24/teens-turned-drug-addicts_n_5877306.html.

Larsen, R. J., & Buss, D. M. (2006). *Personality psychology: Domains of knowledge about human nature with PowerWeb* (2nd ed.). New York: McGraw-Hill.

Lasalvia, A. (2015). DSM-5 two years later: Facts, myths and some key open issues. *Epidemiology and Psychiatric Sciences, 24,* 185-187.

Latané, B., & Darley, J. M. (1970). *The unresponsive bystander: Why doesn't he help?* New York: Appleton-Century-Crofts.

Lattal, K. A., Cançado, C. X., Cook, J. E., Kincaid, S. L., Nighbor, T. D., & Oliver, A. C. (2017). On defining resurgence. *Behavioural Processes, 141*(Part 1), 85-91.

Lauer, E. E., Martin, S. B., & Zakrajsek, R. A. (2019). ISCORE: Using technology and imagery to enhance performance of closed motor skills. *Strategies, 32*(3), 19-24.

Lauriello, J., & Rahman, T. (2015). Schizophrenia spectrum and other psychotic disorders. In L. W. Roberts & A. K. Louie (Eds.), *Study Guide to DSM-5®.* Arlington, VA: American Psychiatric Publishing, Inc.

Lavazza, A., & Manzotti, R. (2013). An externalist approach to creativity: Discovery versus recombination. *Mind & Society, 12,* 61-72.

Lavenex, P., & Lavenex, P. (2009). Spatial memory and the monkey hippocampus: Not all space is created equal. *Hippocampus, 19,* 8-19.

Lavigne, K. M., Rapin, L. A., Metzak, P. D., Whitman, J. C., Jung, K., Dohen, M., et al. (2015). Left-dominant temporal-frontal hypercoupling in schizophrenia patients with hallucinations during speech perception. *Schizophrenia Bulletin, 41,* 259-267.

Lazarus, A. A. (1997). *Brief but comprehensive psychotherapy: The multimodal way.* New York: Springer.

Lazarus, R. S. (1995). Emotions express a social relationship, but it is an individual mind that creates them. *Psychological Inquiry, 6,* 253-265.

Lazear, E.P. (2017, June 26). The surprising factor for immigrant success. *Wall Street Journal.* Accessed from https://www.wsj.com/articles/the-surprising-factor-for-immigrant-success-1498517898.

Lazer, D. M. J., Baum, M. A., Benkler, Y., Berinsky, A. J., Greenhill, K. M., Menczer, F., et al. (2018, March 9). The science of fake news. *Science, 359*(6380), 1094-1096.

Le Maner-Idrissi, G., & Renault, L. (2006). Développement du 'schéma de genre': Une asymétrie entre filles et garçons? Are there sex differences in the acquisition of a gender schema? *Enfance, 58,* 251-265.

Leahey, T. M., Bond, D. S., Raynor, H., Roye, D., Vithiananthan, S., Ryder, B. A., et al. (2012). Effects of bariatric surgery on food cravings: Do food cravings and the consumption of craved foods "normalize" after surgery? *Surgery for Obesity and Related Diseases: Official Journal of the American Society for Bariatric Surgery, 8*(1), 84-91.

Leahy, R. L. (2015). Emotional schema therapy. In N. C. Thoma & D. McKay (Eds.), *Working with emotion in cognitive-behavioral therapy: Techniques for clinical practice.* New York: Guilford Press.

Leander, N. P., Stroebe, W., Kreienkamp, J., Agostini, M., Gordijn, E., & Kruglanski, A. W. (2019). Mass shootings and the salience of guns as means of compensation for thwarted goals. *Journal of Personality and Social Psychology, 116*(5), 704-723.

Leaper, C., & Ayres, M. (2007). A meta-analytic review of gender variations in adults' language use: Talkativeness, affiliative speech, and assertive speech. *Personality and Social Psychology Review, 11,* 328-363.

Leaper, C., & Friedman, C. K. (2007). The socialization of gender. In J. E. Grusec & P. D. Hastings (Eds.), *Handbook of socialization: Theory and research.* New York: Guilford Press.

Leaper, C., Brown, C., & Ayres, M. M. (2013). Adolescent girls' cognitive appraisals of coping responses to sexual harassment. *Psychology in the Schools, 50,* 969-986.

Lee, A., Isaac, M., & Janca, A. (2007). Posttraumatic stress disorder and terrorism. In A. Monat, R. S. Lazarus, & G. Reevy (Eds.), *The Praeger handbook on stress and coping* (Vol. 1). Westport, CT: Praeger Publishers/Greenwood Publishing Group.

Lee, A. Y., & Aaker, J. L. (2004). Bringing the frame into focus: The influence of regulatory fit on processing fluency and persuasion. *Journal of Personality and Social Psychology, 86,* 205-218.

Lee, A. Y., Reynolds, K. D., Stacy, A., Niu, Z., & Xie, B. (2019). Family functioning, moods, and binge eating among urban adolescents. *Journal of Behavioral Medicine, 42*(3), 511-521.

Lee, D., Kleinman, J., & Kleinman, A. (2007). Rethinking depression: An ethnographic study of the experiences of depression among Chinese. *Harvard Review of Psychiatry, 15,* 1-8.

Lee, E., & Troop-Gordon, W. (2011). Peer processes and gender role development: Changes in gender atypicality related to negative peer treatment and children's friendships. *Sex Roles, 64,* 90-102.

Lee, F. H., & Raja, S. N. (2011). Complementary and alternative medicine in chronic pain. *Pain, 152,* 28-30.

Lee, J. F., & Chin, A. C. (2019). Are females and males equitably represented? A study of early readers. *Linguistics and Education, 49,* 52-61.

Lee, J. J., McGue, M., Iacono, W. G., Michael, A. M., & Chabris, C. F. (2019). The causal influence of brain size on human intelligence: Evidence from within-family phenotypic associations and GWAS modeling. *Intelligence, 75,* 48-58.

Lee, J. Q., McDonald, R. J., & Sutherland, R. J. (2019). Hippocampal damage causes retrograde amnesia and slower acquisition of a cue-place discrimination in a concurrent cue-place water task in rats. *Neuroscience, 412,* 131-143.

Lee, K-F. (2017, June 25). The real threat of artificial intelligence. *The New York Times,* p. SR4.

Lee, S., & Mason, M. (2019). Effectiveness of brief DBT-informed group therapy on psychological resilience: A preliminary naturalistic study. *Journal of College Student Psychotherapy, 33*(1), 25-37.

Lee, S., Moon, S. I., & Feeley, T. H. (2019). The "that's-not-all" compliance-gaining technique: When does it work? *Social Influence,* 1-15.

Lee, S. A., & Liang, Y. J. (2019). Robotic foot-in-the-door: Using sequential-request persuasive strategies in human-robot interaction. *Computers in Human Behavior, 90,* 351-356.

Lee, T. T. C., Taylor, A. M., Holbert, A. M., & Graham, J. R. (2019). MMPI-2-RF predictors of interpersonal relationship characteristics in committed couples. *Psychological Assessment.* http://dx.doi.org/10.1037/pas0000735

Leeman, R. F., Fischler, C., & Rozin, P. (2011). Medical doctors' attitudes and beliefs about diet and health are more like those of their lay countrymen (France, Germany, Italy, UK and USA) than those of doctors in other countries. *Appetite, 56,* 558-563.

Legault, J., Fang, S. Y., Lan, Y. J., & Li, P. (2019). Structural brain changes as a function of second language vocabulary training: Effects of learning context. *Brain and cognition, 134,* 90-102.

Lehman, D. R., & Taylor, S. E. (1988). Date with an earthquake: Coping with a probable, unpredictable disaster. *Personality and Social Psychology Bulletin, 13,* 546-555.

Lehrer, J. (2012, April 13). When memory commits an injustice. *Wall Street Journal,* p. C18.

Lehrman, S. (2007). Going beyond X and Y. *Scientific American, 296,* 40-41.

Leiblum, S. R., & Chivers, M. L. (2007). Normal and persistent genital arousal in women: New perspectives. *Journal of Sex & Marital Therapy, 33,* 357-373.

Leigh, J. H., Zinkhan, G. M., & Swaminathan, V. (2006). Dimensional relationships of recall and recognition measures with selected cognitive and affective aspects of print ads. *Journal of Advertising, 35,* 105-122.

Leising, D., Scharloth, J., Lohse, O., & Wood, D. (2014). What types of terms do people use when describing an individual's personality? *Psychological Science, 25,* 1787-1794.

Leitner, L. M. (2007). Diversity issues, postmodernism, and psychodynamic therapy. *PsycCRITIQUES, 52,* n.p.

Lemay, E., & Clark, M. (2008). How the head liberates the heart: Projection of communal responsiveness guides relationship promotion. *Journal of Personality and Social Psychology, 94,* 647-671.

Lemay, E. P., Jr., Clark, M. S., & Feeney, B. C. (2007). Projection of responsiveness to needs and the construction of satisfying communal relationships. *Journal of Personality and Social Psychology, 92,* 834-853.

Lemogne, C., Consoli, S. M., Geoffroy-Perez, B., Coeuret-Pellicer, M., Nabi, H., Melchior, M., et al. (2013). Personality and the risk of cancer: A 16-year follow-up study of the GAZEL cohort. *Psychosomatic Medicine, 75,* 262-271.

Lenzenweger, M. F., & Dworkin, R. H. (Eds.). (1998). *The origins and development of schizophrenia: Advances in experimental psychopathology.* Washington, DC: American Psychological Association.

Leong, C., Alessi-Severini, S., Enns, M. W., Nie, Y., Sareen, J., Bolton, et al. (2017). Cerebrovascular, cardiovascular, and mortality events in new users of selective serotonin reuptake inhibitors and serotonin norepinephrine reuptake inhibitors: A propensity score-matched population-based study. *Journal of Clinical Psychopharmacology, 37,* 332-340.

Lepore, J. (2009, November 9). Why is American history so murderous? *The New Yorker.*

Leppänen, J. M., Moulson, M. C., Vogel-Farley, V. K., & Nelson, C. A. (2007). An ERP study of emotional face processing in the adult and infant brain. *Child Development, 78,* 232-245.

Leskinen, E. A., Rabelo, V. C., & Cortina, L. M. (2015). Gender stereotyping and harassment: A "catch-22" for women in the workplace. *Psychology, Public Policy, and Law, 21,* 192-204.

Lester, K. J., Coleman, J. I., Roberts, S., Keers, R., Breen, G., Bögels, S., et al. (2017). Genetic variation in the endocannabinoid system and response to cognitive behavior therapy for child anxiety disorders. *American Journal of Medical Genetics Part B: Neuropsychiatric Genetics, 174,* 144-155.

Leszcz, M., Pain, C., Hunter, J., Maunder, R., & Ravitz, P. (2015). *Achieving psychotherapy effectiveness.* New York: W. W. Norton & Co.

Leung, A. K., & Chiu, C. (2010). Multicultural experience, idea receptiveness, and creativity. *Journal of Cross-Cultural Psychology, 41*(5-6), 723-741.

LeVay, S. (2011). *Gay, straight, and the reason why: The science of sexual orientation.* New York: Oxford University Press.

Levi, A., Chan, K. K., & Pence, D. (2006). Real men do not read labels: The effects of masculinity and involvement on college students' food decisions. *Journal of American College Health, 55,* 91-98.

Levin, R. J. (2007). Sexual activity, health and well-being—the beneficial roles of coitus and masturbation. *Sexual and Relationship Therapy, 22,* 135-148.

Levine, C. S., Miyamoto, Y., Markus, H. R., Rigotti, A., Boylan, J. M., Park, J., et al. (2016). Culture and healthy eating: The role of independence and interdependence in the United States and Japan. *Personality and Social Psychology Bulletin, 42*(10), 1335-1348.

Levine, J. M., & Moreland, R. L. (2006). Small groups: An overview. In J. M. Levine & R. L. Moreland (Eds.), *Small groups.* New York: Psychology Press.

Levine, L. E., & Munsch, J. (2011). *Child development: An active learning approach.* Thousand Oaks, CA: Sage Publications, Inc.

Levine, R. (2019). A group analyst's perspective on the Trump-Clinton election and aftermath. *International Journal of Group Psychotherapy, 69*(2), 192-220.

Levine, S. Z. (2011). Elaboration on the association between IQ and parental SES with subsequent crime. *Personality and Individual Differences, 50,* 1233-1237.

Levine, S. Z., & Rabinowitz, J. (2007). Revisiting the 5 dimensions of the Positive and Negative Syndrome Scale. *Journal of Clinical Psychopharmacology, 27,* 431-436.

Levinson, D. (1992). *The seasons of a woman's life.* New York: Knopf.

Levinson, D. J. (1990). A theory of life structure development in adulthood. In C. N. Alexander & E. J. Langer (Eds.), *Higher stages of human development: Perspectives on adult growth.* New York: Oxford University Press.

Levy, B. (1996). Improving memory in old age through implicit self-stereotyping. *Journal of Personality and Social Psychology, 71,* 1092-1107.

Levy, B. R., & Myers, L. M. (2004). Preventive health behaviors influenced by self-perceptions of aging. *Preventive Medicine: An International Journal Devoted to Practice and Theory, 39,* 625-629.

Levy, I., & Adam, K.-M. (2018). Online commenting about a victim of female-on-male rape: The case of Shia LaBeouf's sexual victimization. *Sex Roles: A Journal of Research, 79*(9-10), 578-593.

Levy, S. (2019). Youth and the opioid epidemic. *Pediatrics, 143*(2), e20182752.

Lewellyn, K. B., & Muller-Kahle, M. I. (2019). The corporate board glass ceiling: The role of empowerment and culture in shaping board gender diversity. *Journal of Business Ethics.* https://doi.org/10.1007/s10551-019-04116-9.

Lewin, T. (2003, December 22). For more people in their 20s and 30s, going home is easier because they never left. *The New York Times,* p. A27.

Lewinsohn, P. M., Petit, J. W., Joiner, T. E., Jr., & Seeley, J. R. (2003). The symptomatic expression of major depressive disorder in adolescents and young adults. *Journal of Abnormal Psychology, 112,* 244-252.

Lewis, C., & Lamb, M. (2011). The role of parent-child relationships in child development. In M. E. Lamb & M. H. Bornstein (Eds.), *Social and personality development: An advanced textbook.* New York: Psychology Press.

Lewis, C. E., Thomas, K. F., Dodge, N. C., Molteno, C. D., Meintjes, E. M., Jacobson, J. L., et al. (2015). Verbal learning and memory impairment in children with fetal alcohol spectrum disorders. *Alcoholism: Clinical and Experimental Research, 39*, 724-732.

Lewis, D. G., Al-Shawaf, L., Conroy-Beam, D., Asao, K., & Buss, D. M. (2017). Evolutionary psychology: A how-to guide. *American Psychologist, 72*(4), 353-373.

Lewis, T., & Umbreit, M. (2015). A humanistic approach to mediation and dialogue: An evolving transformative practice. *Conflict Resolution Quarterly, 33*(1), 3-17.

Li, A., Bagger, J., & Cropanzano, R. (2017). The impact of stereotypes and supervisor perceptions of employee work-family conflict on job performance ratings. *Human Relations, 70*, 119-145.

Li, B., Piriz, J., Mirrione, M., Chung, C., Proulx, C. D., Schulz, D., et al. (2011). Synaptic potentiation onto habenula neurons in learned helplessness model of depression. *Nature, 470*, 535-539.

Li, M. D., Lou, X., Chen, G., Ma, J. Z., & Elston, R. C. (2008). Gene-gene interactions among CHRNA4, CHRNB2, BDNF, and NTRK2 in nicotine dependence. *Biological Psychiatry, 64*, 951-957.

Li, T. K., Volkow, N. D., & Baler, R. D. (2007). The biological bases of nicotine and alcohol co-addiction. *Biological Psychiatry, 61*, 1-3.

Li, X., Chen, L., Ma, R., Wang, H., Wan, L., Bu, J., et al. (2019). The neural mechanisms of immediate and follow-up of the treatment effect of hypnosis on smoking craving. *Brain Imaging and Behavior.* https://doi.org/10.1007/s11682-019-00072-0.

Li, Y., Hofstetter, C. R., Wahlgren, D., Irvin, V., Chhay, D., & Hovell, M. F. (2015). Social networks and immigration stress among first-generation Mandarin-speaking Chinese immigrants in Los Angeles. *International Journal of Social Welfare, 24*, 170-181.

Li, Y., Zuo, Y., Yu, P., Ping, X., & Cui, C. (2015). Role of basolateral amygdala dopamine D2 receptors in impulsive choice in acute cocaine-treated rats. *Behavioural Brain Research, 287*, 187-195.

Li, Z., Yu, J., Yang, X., & Zhu, L. (2019). Associations between empathy and altruistic sharing behavior in Chinese adults. *The Journal of General Psychology, 146*(1), 1-16.

Libedinsky, C., & Livingstone, M. (2011). Role of prefrontal cortex in conscious visual perception. *Journal of Neuroscience, 31*, 64-69.

Liben, L. S., & Bigler, R. S. (2002). The development course of gender differentiations: Conceptualizing, measuring, and evaluation constructs and pathways. *Monographs of the Society for Research in Child Development, 67*, 148-167.

Licis, A. K., Desruisseau, D. M., Yamada, K. A., Duntley, S. P., & Gurnett, C. A. (2011). Novel genetic findings in an extended family pedigree with sleepwalking. *Neurology, 76*, 49-52.

Lick, D. J., Durso, L. E., & Johnson, K. L. (2013). Minority stress and physical health among sexual minorities. *Perspectives on Psychological Science, 8*, 521-548.

Liebelt, E., Rabinowitz, S., Nathan, I., & Bruland, P. (2017). Telehealth as means to diagnose and treat opioid abuse. Healthcare Information and Management Systems Society. Retrieved from https://www.himss.org/news/telehealth-means-diagnose-and-treat-opioid-abuse.

Lieberman, M. D. (2007). Social cognitive neuro-science: A review of core processes. *Annual Review of Psychology, 58*, 259-289.

Lieberman, P. (2015). A tangled tale of circuits, evolution, and language. *PsycCRITIQUES, 60*, 88-97.

Liechti, M. E., Dolder, P. C., & Schmid, Y. (2017). Alterations of consciousness and mystical-type experiences after acute LSD in humans. *Psychopharmacology, 234*, 1499-1510.

Liedl, A., Müller, J., Morina, N., Karl, A., Denke, C., & Knaevelsrud, C. (2011). Physical activity within a CBT intervention improves coping with pain in traumatized refugees: Results of a randomized controlled design. *Pain Medicine, 12*, 138-145.

Liem, G. D. (2015). Academic and social achievement goals: Their additive, interactive, and specialized effects on school functioning. *British Journal of Educational Psychology, 86*, 37-56.

Lien, Y. W., Chu, R. L., Jen, C. H., & Wu, C. H. (2006). Do Chinese commit neither fundamental attribution error nor ultimate attribution error? *Chinese Journal of Psychology, 48*, 163-181.

Lilienfeld, S. O. (2007). Psychological treatments that cause harm. *Perspectives on Psychological Science, 2*, 53-58.

Lilienfeld, S. O. (2012). Further sources of our field's embattled public reputation. *American Psychologist*, 808-809.

Lilienfeld, S. O. (2017). Microaggressions: Strong claims, inadequate evidence. *Perspectives on Psychological Science, 12*, 138-169.

Lilienfeld, S. O. (2019). Microaggression research and application: clarifications, corrections, and common ground. *Perspectives on Psychological Science, 15*(1), 27-37.

Lillard, A. S., & Woolley, J. D. (2015). Grounded in reality: How children make sense of the unreal. *Cognitive Development, 34*, 111-114.

Lillo-Crespo, M., Forner-Ruiz, M., Riquelme-Galindo, J., Ruiz-Fernández, D., & García-Sanjuan, S. (2019). Chess practice as a protective factor in dementia. *International Journal of Environmental Research and Public Health, 16*(12), 2116.

Lim, A., & Okuno, H. G. (2015). A recipe for empathy: Integrating the mirror system, insula, somatosensory cortex and motherese. *International Journal of Social Robotics, 7*, 35-49.

Limberg, B. (2015). Nature vs. nurture. . . again: Examining the interplay between genetics and the environment. *PsycCRITIQUES, 60*, 88-98.

Lin, C. H., & Lin, H. M. (2007). What price do you ask for the "extra one"? A social value orientation perspective. *Social Behavior and Personality, 35*, 9-18.

Lin, I., Wang, S., Chu, I., Lu, Y., Lee, C., Lin, T., & Fan, S. (2017). The association of Type D personality with heart rate variability and lipid profiles among patients with coronary artery disease. *International Journal of Behavioral Medicine, 24*, 101-109.

Lin, J., Arthurs, J., & Reilly, S. (2017). Conditioned taste aversions: From poisons to pain to drugs of abuse. *Psychonomic Bulletin & Review, 24*, 335-351.

Lin, L., McCormack, H., Kruczkowski, L., & Berg, M. B. (2015). How women's perceptions of peer weight preferences are related to drive for thinness. *Sex Roles, 72*, 117-126.

Lin, L., Stamm, K., & Christidis, P. (2018, February). How diverse is the psychology workforce? *Monitor on Psychology*, p. 19.

Lin, X., Xie, S., & Li, H. (2019). Chinese mothers' and fathers' involvement in toddler play activity: Type variations and gender differences. *Early Child Development and Care, 189*(2), 179-190.

Lin, Y., Li, K., Sung, W., Ko, H., Tzeng, O. L., Hung, D. L., et al. (2011). The relationship between development of attention and learning in children: A cognitive neuroscience approach. *Bulletin of Educational Psychology, 42*, 517-542.

Lindberg, L. D., Maddow-Zimet, I., & Marcell, A. V. (2019). Prevalence of sexual initiation before age 13 years among male adolescents and young adults in the United States. *JAMA Pediatrics, 173*(6), 553-560.

Lindblad, F., Lindahl, M., & Theorell, T. (2006). Physiological stress reactions in 6th and 9th graders during test performance. *Stress and Health: Journal of the International Society for the Investigation of Stress, 22*, 189-195.

Lindemann, O., & Bekkering, H. (2009). Object manipulation and motion perception: Evidence of an influence of action planning on visual processing. *Journal of Experimental Psychology: Human Perception and Performance, 35*, 1062-1071.

Lindley, L. D. (2006). The paradox of self-efficacy: Research with diverse populations. *Journal of Career Assessment, 14*, 143-160.

Lindorff, M. (2005). Determinants of received social support: Who gives what to managers? *Journal of Social and Personal Relationships, 22*, 323-337.

Lindsay, P. H., & Norman, D. A. (1977). *Human information processing* (2nd ed.). New York: Academic Press.

Linley, P. (2013). Human strengths and well-being: Finding the best within us at the intersection of eudaimonic philosophy, humanistic psychology, and positive psychology. In A. S. Waterman (Ed.), *The best within us: Positive psychology perspectives on eudaimonia*. Washington, DC: American Psychological Association.

Liou, A. P., Paziuk, M., Luevano, J. M., Jr, Machineni, S., Turnbaugh, P. J., & Kaplan, L. M. (2013). Conserved shifts in the gut microbiota due to gastric bypass reduce host weight and adiposity. *Science Translational Medicine, 5*(178), 178ra41.

Lips, H. M. (2003). *A new psychology of women: Gender, culture, and ethnicity.* New York: McGraw-Hill.

Little, K., Ramssen, E., Welchko, R., Volberg, V., Roland, C., & Cassin, B. (2009). Decreased brain dopamine cell numbers in human cocaine users. *Psychiatry Research, 168,* 173-180.

Liu, J., Ying, Z., & Zhang, S. (2015). A rate function approach to computerized adaptive testing for cognitive diagnosis. *Psychometrika, 80,* 468-490

Liu, L., He, S. Z., & Wu, Y. (2007). An analysis of the characteristics of single parent families with different structures and their children. *Chinese Journal of Clinical Psychology, 15,* 68-70.

Liu, Y., Meng, J., Yao, M., Ye, Q., Fan, B., & Peng, W. (2019). Hearing other's pain is associated with sensitivity to physical pain: An ERP study. *Biological psychology, 145,* 150-158.

Livingstone, A. G., Spears, R., Manstead, A. R., Bruder, M., & Shepherd, L. (2011). We feel, therefore we are: Emotion as a basis for self-categorization and social action. *Emotion, 11,* 754-767.

Llorca-Mestre, A., Samper-García, P., Malonda-Vidal, E., & Cortés-Tomás, M. T. (2017). Parenting style and peer attachment as predictors of emotional instability in children. *Social Behavior and Personality, 45,* 677-694.

Lobato, M. I., Koff, W. J., & Manenti, C. (2006). Follow-up of sex reassignment surgery in transsexuals: A Brazilian cohort. *Archives of Sexual Behavior, 35,* 711-715.

Lobban, F., Barrowclough, C., & Jones, S. (2006). Does expressed emotion need to be understood within a more systemic framework? An examination of discrepancies in appraisals between patients diagnosed with schizophrenia and their relatives. *Social Psychiatry and Psychiatric Epidemiology, 41,* 50-55.

Lobo, I., & Harris, R. (2008). GABAa receptors and alcohol. *Pharmacology, Biochemistry and Behavior, 90,* 90-94.

Loehlin, J. C., Bartels, M., Boomsma, D. I., Bratko, D., Martin, N. G., Nichols, R. C., et al. (2015). Is there a genetic correlation between general factors of intelligence and personality? *Twin Research and Human Genetics, 18,* 234-242.

Lofholm, N. (2003, May 6). Climber's kin share relief: Ralston saw 4 options, they say; death wasn't one of them. *Denver Post,* p. A1.

Loftus, E. F., & Palmer, J. C. (1974). Reconstruction of automobile destruction: An example of the interface between language and memory. *Journal of Verbal Learning and Verbal Behavior, 13,* 585-589.

Lombaard, N., & Naudé, L. (2017). "Breaking the cycle": Black adolescents' experiences of being stereotyped during identity development. *Journal of Psychology in Africa, 27,* 185-190.

London, B. (2013, October 16). From a child bride who was circumcised at five to woman of the year: Extraordinary story of Somali supermodel who starred in James Bond film. *Mail Online.* Retrieved from http://www.dailymail.co.uk/femail/article-2461477/Waris-Dirie-fights-female-circumcision-receives-Woman-Year-Campaigning-award.html.

Longo, M. R., Trippier, S., Vagnoni, E., & Lourenco, S. F. (2015). Right hemisphere control of visuospatial attention in near space. *Neuropsychologia, 70,* 350-357.

Lorenz, K. (1966). *On aggression.* New York: Harcourt Brace Jovanovich.

Lorenz, K. (1974). *Civilized man's eight deadly sins.* New York: Harcourt Brace Jovanovich.

Loriedo, C., & Di Leone, F. G. (2017). Conversion disorder. In G. R. Elkins (Ed.), *Handbook of medical and psychological hypnosis: Foundations, applications, and professional issues.* New York: Springer Publishing Co.

Lovett, I. (2019, April 13-14). One teenager killed himself, then six more followed. *Wall Street Journal,* pp. A1, A12.

Loving, T., Crockett, E., & Paxson, A. (2009). Passionate love and relationship thinkers: Experimental evidence for acute cortisol elevations in women. *Psychoneuroendocrinology, 34,* 939-946.

Lowe, P., Humphreys, C., & Williams, S. J. (2007). Night terrors: Women's experiences of (not) sleeping where there is domestic violence. *Violence against Women, 13,* 549-561.

Lowry, M., & Bryant, J. (2019). Blue is in the eye of the beholder: A cross-linguistic study on color perception and memory. *Journal of Psycholinguistic Research, 48*(1), 163-179.

Lozano, A., & Mayberg, H. (2015). Treating depression at the source: Electrical stimulation deep within the brain may alleviate devastating mood. *Scientific American, 312,* 68-73.

Lu, S. (2015, February.) Erasing bad memories. *Monitor on Psychology,* pp. 41-45.

Lucas, H. D., Creery, J. D., Hu, X., & Paller, K. A. (2019). Grappling with implicit social bias: A perspective from memory research. *Neuroscience, 406,* 684-697.

Luchins, A. S. (1946). Classroom experiments on mental set. *American Journal of Psychology, 59,* 295-298.

Lucini, F. A., Del Ferraro, G., Sigman, M., & Makse, H. A. (2019). How the brain transitions from conscious to subliminal perception. *Neuroscience, 411,* 280-290.

Lueck, J. A., Costantini, R., & Knobloch, M. (2019). The making of an addiction: Examining psychological determinants of prescription stimulant abuse among college students. *Health Communication.* Advance online publication. https://doi.org/10.1080/10410236.2019.1598743

Lui, P. P. (2019). College alcohol beliefs: Measurement invariance, mean differences, and correlations with alcohol use outcomes across sociodemographic groups. *Journal of Counseling Psychology, 66*(4), 487-495.

Lun, V. M., & Bond, M. H. (2006). Achieving relationship harmony in groups and its consequence for group performance. *Asian Journal of Social Psychology, 9,* 195-202.

Lunde, S. J., Vuust, P., Garza-Villarreal, E. A., & Vase, L. (2019). Music-induced analgesia: How does music relieve pain? *Pain, 160*(5), 989-993.

Lundgren, H., Kroon, B., & Poell, R. F. (2019). Pigeonholing or learning instrument? Test takers' reactions to personality testing in management development. *European Journal of Training and Development, 43*(3/4), 354-374.

Luo, J., He, K., Andolina, I. M., Li, X., Yin, J., Chen, Z., et al. (2019). Going with the flow: The neural mechanisms underlying illusions of complex-flow motion. *The Journal of Neuroscience, 39*(14), 2664-2685.

Luo, S., & Zhang, G. (2009). What leads to romantic attraction: Similarity, reciprocity, security, or beauty? Evidence from a speed-dating study. *Journal of Personality, 77,* 933-964.

Luong, G., Rauers, A., & Fingerman, K. L. (2015). The multifaceted nature of late-life socialization: Older adults as agents and targets of socialization. In J. E. Grusec & P. D. Hastings (Eds.), *Handbook of socialization: Theory and research* (2nd ed.). New York: Guilford Press.

Luria, A. R. (1968). *The mind of a mnemonist.* Cambridge, MA: Basic Books.

Lurie, K., Robinson, A., & Pecsenye, M. (2005). *Cracking the GRE 2006.* New York: Random House.

Luscomb, B. (2018). The divorce rate Is dropping. That may not actually be good news. *Time.* Downloaded from https://time.com/5434949/divorce-rate-children-marriage-benefits/.

Lutgendorf, S. K., & Andersen, B. L. (2015). Biobehavioral approaches to cancer progression and survival: Mechanisms and interventions. *American Psychologist, 70,* 186-197.

Luttrell, A., Petty, R. E., & Xu, M. (2017). Replicating and fixing failed replications: The case of need for cognition and argument quality. *Journal of Experimental Social Psychology, 69,* 178-183.

Lutz, C. K., & Novak, M. A. (2005). Environmental enrichment for nonhuman primates: Theory and application. *ILAR Journal, 46,* 178-191.

Luxton, D. D. (2016). An introduction to artificial intelligence in behavioral and mental health care. In D. D. Luxton (Ed.), *Artificial intelligence in behavioral and mental health care.* San Diego, CA: Elsevier Academic Press.

Lynn, S. J., Krackow, E., Loftus, E. F., Locke, T. G., & Lilienfeld, S. O. (2015). Constructing the past: Problematic memory recovery techniques in psychotherapy. In S. O. Lilienfeld, S. J. Lynn, & J. M. Lohr (Eds.), *Science and pseudoscience in clinical psychology* (2nd ed.). New York: Guilford Press.

Lynn, S. J., Laurence, J., & Kirsch, I. (2015). Hypnosis, suggestion, and suggestibility: An integrative model. *American Journal of Clinical Hypnosis, 57,* 314–329.

Lynn, S. J., Maxwell, R., Merckelbach, H., Lilienfeld, S. O., van Heugten-van der Kloet, D., & Miskovic, V. (2019). Dissociation and its disorders: Competing modjanetels, future directions, and a way forward. *Clinical Psychology Review,* 101755.

Lyons, H., Giordano, P. C., Manning, W. D., & Longmore, M. A. (2011). Identity, peer relationships, and adolescent girls' sexual behavior: An exploration of the contemporary double standard. *Journal of Sex Research, 48,* 437–449.

López, G., & Bialik, K. (2017, May 3.). Key findings about U.S. immigrants. *Fact Tank: News in the Numbers.* http://www.pewresearch.org/fact-tank/2017/05/03/key-findings-about-u-s-immigrants/.

López-Pérez, B., & Ambrona, T. (2015). The role of cognitive emotion regulation on the vicarious emotional response. *Motivation and Emotion, 39,* 299–308.

López-Pérez, B., Carrera, P., Oceja, L., Ambrona, T., & Stocks, E. (2017). Sympathy and tenderness as components of dispositional empathic concern: Predicting helping and caring behaviors. *Current Psychology: A Journal for Diverse Perspectives on Diverse Psychological Issues.* Accessed from https://link.springer.com/article/10.1007/s12144-017-9615-7.

Macaluso, E., & Driver, J. (2005). Multisensory spatial interactions. a window onto functional integration in the human brain. *Trends in Neurosciences, 28, Issue 5,* 264–271.

Macaluso, E., Frith, C. D., & Driver, J. (2000). Modulation of human visual cortex by crossmodal spatial attention. *Science, 289,* 1206–1208.

Macauda, G., Ellis, A. W., Grabherr, L., Francesco, R. B., & Mast, F. W. (2019). Canal-otolith interactions alter the perception of self-motion direction. *Attention, Perception, & Psychophysics, 81*(5), 1698–1714.

Maccoby, E. E., & Jacklin, C. N. (1974). *The psychology of sex differences.* Palo Alto, CA: Stanford University Press.

Macduff, I. (2006). Your pace or mine? Culture, time and negotiation. *Negotiation Journal, 22,* 31–45.

Mace, J. H., Bernas, R. S., & Clevinger, A. (2015). Individual differences in recognising involuntary autobiographical memories: Impact on the reporting of abstract cues. *Memory, 23,* 445–452.

Mack, J. (2003). *The museum of the mind.* London: British Museum Publications.

Mack, M. L., Love, B. C., & Preston, A. R. (2016). Dynamic updating of hippocampal object representations reflects new conceptual knowledge. *PNAS Proceedings of the National Academy of Sciences of the United States of America, 113,* 13203–13208.

MacKay, D. M. (2019). The earthquake that reshaped the intellectual landscape of memory, mind and brain: Case H. M. In MacPherson, S. E. & Sala, S. D. (Eds). *Cases of amnesia: Contributions to understanding memory and the brain,* New York: Routledge.

Mackay, J., & Eriksen, M. (2002). *The tobacco atlas.* Geneva, Switzerland: World Health Organization.

Mackey, A. P., Finn, A. S., Leonard, J. A., Jacoby-Senghor, D. S., West, M. R., Gabrieli, C. F. O., et al. (2015). Neuroanatomical correlates of the income-achievement gap. *Psychological Science,* 1–9.

MacLennan, A. (2009). Evidence-based review of therapies at the menopause. *International Journal of Evidence-Based Healthcare, 7,* 112–123.

MacLennan, B. J. (2017). Neural networks, learning, and intelligence. In J. Call, G. M. Burghardt, I. M. Pepperberg, C. T. Snowdon, & T. Zentall (Eds.), *APA handbook of comparative psychology: Basic concepts, methods, neural substrate, and behavior.* Washington, DC: American Psychological Association.

MacNeilage, P. F., Rogers, L. J., & Vallortigara, G. (2009). Origins of the left and right brain. *Scientific American, 301,* 60–67.

MacPhee, D., & Prendergast, S. (2019). Room for improvement: Girls' and boys' home environments are still gendered. *Sex Roles, 80*(5–6), 332–346.

Madden, D. J. (2007). Aging and visual attention. *Current Directions in Psychological Science, 16,* 70–74.

Maddi, S. R. (2007). The story of hardiness: Twenty years of theorizing, research, and practice. In A. Monat, R. S. Lazarus, & G. Reevy (Eds.), *The Praeger handbook on stress and coping* (Vol. 2). Westport, CT: Praeger Publishers/Greenwood Publishing.

Maddi, S. R., Khoshaba, D. M., Harvey, R. H., Fazel, M., & Resurreccion, N. (2011). The personality construct of hardiness, V: Relationships with the construction of existential meaning in life. *Journal of Humanistic Psychology, 51,* 369–388.

Maddock, R. J., Buonocore, M. H., Miller, A. R., Yoon, J. H., Soosman, S. K., & Unruh, A. M. (2013). Abnormal activity-dependent brain lactate and glutamate + glutamine responses in panic disorder. *Biological Psychiatry, 73,* 1111–1119.

Mader, S. S. (2000). *Biology* (6th ed.). Boston: McGraw-Hill.

Madon, S., Willard, J., & Guyll, M. (2006). Self-fulfilling prophecy effects of mothers' beliefs on children's alcohol use: Accumulation, dissipation, and stability over time. *Journal of Personality and Social Psychology, 90,* 911–926.

Magee, S. R., Bublitz, M. H., Orazine, C., Brush, B., Salisbury, A., Niaura, R., et al. (2013). The relationship between maternal-fetal attachment and cigarette smoking over pregnancy. *Maternal and Child Health Journal, 18*(4), 1017–1022.

Magee, W., & Upenieks, L. (2019). Gender differences in self-esteem, unvarnished self-evaluation, future orientation, self-enhancement and self-derogation in a US national sample. *Personality and Individual Differences, 149,* 66–77.

Magida, A. J. (2006). *Opening the doors of wonder: Reflections on religious rites of passage.* Berkeley, CA: University of California Press.

Magis, D., & Schoenen, J. (2011). Treatment of migraine: Update on new therapies. *Current Opinions in Neurology, 24,* 203–210.

Magley, V. J. (2002). Coping with sexual harassment: Reconceptualizing women's resistance. *Journal of Personality and Social Psychology, 83,* 930–946.

Magoni, M., Bassani, L., Okong, P., Kituuka, P., Germinario, E. P., Giuliano, M., et al. (2005). Mode of infant feeding and HIV infection in children in a program for prevention of mother-to-child transmission in Uganda. *AIDS, 19,* 433–437.

Magoon, M., & Critchfield, T. (2008). Concurrent schedules of positive and negative reinforcement: Differential-impact and differential-outcomes hypotheses. *Journal of the Experimental Analysis of Behavior, 90,* 1–22.

Magruder, K., & Yeager, D. (2009). The prevalence of PTSD across war eras and the effect of deployment on PTSD: A systematic review and meta-analysis. *Psychiatric Annals, 39,* 778–788.

Maguen, S., Li, Y., Madden, E., Seal, K. H., Neylan, T. C., Patterson, O. V., et al. (2019). Factors associated with completing evidence-based psychotherapy for PTSD among veterans in a national healthcare system. *Psychiatry Research, 274,* 112–128.

Maguire, E., Woollett, K., & Spiers, H. (2006) London taxi drivers and bus drivers: A structural MRI and neuropsychological analysis. *Hippocampus, 16,* 1091–1101.

Maher, B. (2015). The anatomy of obedience. *Nature, 523,* 408–409.

Mahesh, A. (2019). The US misunderstanding of India during the 1971 South Asia crisis. *Journal of Arts and Humanities, 8*(5), 19–31.

Majeres, R. L. (2007). Sex differences in phonological coding: Alphabet transformation speed. *Intelligence, 35,* 335–346.

Majlesi, K., Lundborg, P., Black, S., & Devereux, P. (2019). Poor little rich kids? The role of nature versus nurture in wealth and other economic outcomes and behaviors. *Review of Economic Studies.* https://doi.org/10.1093/restud/rdz038.

Major, J. S. (2019). *Anti-Terrorism; Forensic Science; Psychology in Police Investigations.* London: Routledge.

Major, J. T., Johnson, W., & Bouchard, T. J. (2011). The dependability of the general factor of intelligence: Why small, single-factor models do not adequately represent *g. Intelligence, 39,* 418–433.

Malamuth, N. M., Linz, D., Heavey, C. L., & Barnes, G. (1995). Using the confluence model of sexual aggression to predict men's conflict with women: A 10-year follow-up study. *Journal of Personality and Social Psychology, 69*, 353-369.

Malin, D. H., Schaar, K. L., Izygon, J. J., Nghiem, D. M., Jabitta, S. Y., Henceroth, M. M., et al. (2015). Validation and scopolamine-reversal of latent learning in the water maze utilizing a revised direct platform placement procedure. *Pharmacology, Biochemistry and Behavior, 13*, 590-96.

Malloy, L. C., Brubacher, S. P., & Lamb, M. E. (2011). Expected consequences of disclosure revealed in investigative interviews with suspected victims of child sexual abuse. *Applied Developmental Science, 15*, 8-19.

Malouff, J. M., & Rooke, S. E. (2013). Expert-recommended warnings for medical marijuana. *Substance Abuse, 34*, 92-93.

Manca, S., Altoè, G., Schultz, P. W., & Fornara, F. (2019). The persuasive route to sustainable mobility: Elaboration likelihood model and emotions predict implicit attitudes. *Environment and Behavior.* https://doi.org/10.1177/0013916518820898.

Mancinelli, R., Binetti, R., & Ceccanti, M. (2007). Woman, alcohol and environment: Emerging risks for health. *Neuroscience & Biobehavioral Reviews, 31*, 246-253.

Manjhi, A., & Purty, S. (2017). Response to the blank card of Thematic Apperception Test (TAT) and its correlation with personality factors. *Journal of Projective Psychology & Mental Health, 24*, 52-56.

Manly, J., & Echemendia, R. (2007). Race-specific norms: Using the model of hypertension to understand issues of race, culture, and education in neuropsychology. *Archives of Clinical Neuropsychology, 22*, 319-325.

Mann, R. E., & Hollin, C. R. (2007). Sexual offenders' explanations for their offending. *Journal of Sexual Aggression, 13*, 3-9.

Mannarini, T., Talò, C., & Rochira, A. (2017). How diverse is this community? Sense of community, ethnic prejudice, and perceived ethnic heterogeneity. *Journal of Community and Applied Social Psychology, 27*(3), 181-195.

Mannerström, R., Muotka, J., & Salmela-Aro, K. (2019). Associations between identity processes and success in developmental tasks during the transition from emerging to young adulthood. *Journal of Youth Studies.* https://doi.org/10.1080/13676261.2019.1571179

Manni, R., & Terzaghi, M. (2013). Dreaming and enacting dreams in nonrapid eye movement and rapid eye movement parasomnia: A step toward a unifying view within distinct patterns? *Sleep Medicine, 14*, 387-388.

Manor, J. K., & Gailliot, M. T. (2007). Altruism and egoism: Prosocial motivations for helping depend on relationship context. *European Journal of Social Psychology, 37*, 347-358.

Mansson, K. N., Salami, A., Frick, A., Carlbring, P., Andersson, G., Furmark, T., & Boraxbekk, C. J. (2016). Neuroplasticity in response to cognitive behavior therapy for social anxiety

disorder. *Translational Psychiatry, 6*, e727. doi: 10.1038/tp.2015.218.

Manstead, A. S. R., & Wagner, H. L. (2004). *Experience emotion.* Cambridge, England: Cambridge University Press.

Manzo, L., Gómez, M. J., Callejas-Aguilera, J. E., Fernández-Teruel, A., Papini, M. R., & Torres, C. (2015). Partial reinforcement reduces vulnerability to anti-anxiety self-medication during appetitive extinction. *International Journal of Comparative Psychology, 28*, 22-30.

Marchman, V. A., Ashland, M. D., Loi, E. C., Adams, K. A., Fernald, A., & Feldman, H. M. (2019). Predictors of early vocabulary growth in children born preterm and full term: A study of processing speed and medical complications. *Child Neuropsychology*, 1-21.

Maresh, E. L., Stim, J. J., Voorhis, A. C., Kang, S. S., Luciana, M., Sponheim, S. R., et al. (2019). Neurophysiological correlates of cognitive control and approach motivation abnormalities in adolescent bipolar disorders. *Cognitive, Affective & Behavioral Neuroscience, 19*(3), 677-691.

Marks, I. M. (2004). The Nobel prize award in physiology to Ivan Petrovich Pavlov-1904. *Australian and New Zealand Journal of Psychiatry, 38*, 674-677.

Markus, H. R. (2007). Sociocultural psychology: The dynamic interdependence among self systems and social systems. In S. Kitayama & D. Cohen (Eds.), *Handbook of cultural psychology.* New York: Guilford Press.

Markus, H., & Kitayama, S. (2003). Culture, self, and the reality of the social. *Psychological Inquiry, 14*, 277-283.

Markus, H., & Kitayama, S. (2010). Cultures and selves: A cycle of mutual constitution. *Perspectives on Psychological Science, 5*, 420-430.

Markus, K. A., & Borsboom, D. (2013). *Frontiers of test validity theory: Measurement, causation, and meaning.* New York: Routledge/Taylor & Francis Group.

Marques, A. H., Bjørke-Monsen, A., Teixeira, A. L., & Silverman, M. N. (2015). Maternal stress, nutrition and physical activity: Impact on immune function, CNS development and psychopathology. *Brain Research, 161*, 728-46.

Marsh, B. (2008, February 24). A growing cloud over the planet. *The New York Times*, p. WK4.

Marsh, H. W., Hau, K. T., & Sung, R. Y. T. (2007). Childhood obesity, gender, actual-ideal body image discrepancies, and physical self-concept in Hong Kong children: Cultural differences in the value of moderation. *Developmental Psychology, 43*, 647-662.

Marshall, J. R. (2011). Ultimate causes and the evolution of altruism. *Behavioral Ecology and Sociobiology, 65*, 503-512.

Marshall, K., Laing, D. G., & Jinks, A. L. (2006). The capacity of humans to identify components in complex odor-taste mixtures. *Chemical Senses, 31*, 539-545.

Marshall, L., & Born, J. (2007). The contribution of sleep to hippocampus-dependent memory

consolidation. *Trends in Cognitive Sciences, 11*(10), 442-450.

Marshall, M. K. (2007). The critical factors of coaching practice leading to successful coaching outcomes. *Dissertation Abstracts International: Section B: The Sciences and Engineering, 67*(7-B), 4092.

Marshall, R. D., Bryant, R. A., Amsel, L., Suh, E. J., Cook, J. M., & Neria, Y. (2007). The psychology of ongoing threat: Relative risk appraisal, the September 11 attacks and terrorism-related fears. *American Psychologist, 62*, 304-316.

Martelle, S., Hanley, C., & Yoshino K. (2003, January 28). "Sopranos" scenario in slaying? *Los Angeles Times*, p. B1.

Martin, D., Katalinic, N., Hadzi-Pavlovic, D., Ingram, A., Ingram, N., Simpson, B., et al. (2019). Cognitive effects of brief and ultrabrief pulse bitemporal electroconvulsive therapy: A randomised controlled proof-of-concept trial. *Psychological Medicine*, 1-8.

Martin, E. A., & Kerns, J. G. (2011). The influence of positive mood on different aspects of cognitive control. *Cognition and Emotion, 25*, 265-279.

Martin, K. K., & North, A. C. (2015). Diffusion of responsibility on social networking sites. *Computers in Human Behavior, 44*, 124-131.

Martin, L., & Pullum, G. K. (1991). *The great Eskimo vocabulary hoax.* Chicago: University of Chicago Press.

Marulanda, D., & Radtke, H. L. (2019). Men pursuing an undergraduate psychology degree: What's masculinity got to do with it? *Sex Roles, 81*(5-6), 338-354.

Marwha, D., Halari, M., & Eliot, L. (2017). Meta-analysis reveals a lack of sexual dimorphism in human amygdala volume. *NeuroImage, 147*, 282-288.

Mashour, G. A., Walker, E. E., & Martuza, R. L. (2005). Psychosurgery: Past, present, and future. *Brain Research Reviews, 48*, 409-419.

Maslow, A. H. (1970). *Motivation and personality.* New York: Harper & Row.

Maslow, A. H. (1987). *Motivation and personality* (3rd ed.). New York: Harper & Row.

Mason, M. (1995). *The making of Victorian sexuality.* New York: Oxford University Press.

Mason, T. B., Maduro, R. S., Derlega, V. J., Hacker, D. S., Winstead, B. A., & Haywood, J. E. (2017). Individual differences in the impact of vicarious racism: African American students react to the George Zimmerman trial. *Cultural Diversity and Ethnic Minority Psychology, 23*, 174-184.

Massadi, O. A., López, M., Tschöp, M., Diéguez, C., & Nogueiras, R. (2017). Current understanding of the hypothalamic ghrelin pathways inducing appetite and adiposity. *Trends In Neurosciences, 40*, 167-180.

Massé-Alarie, H., Beaulieu, L., Preuss, R., & Schneider, C. (2017). The side of chronic low back pain matters: Evidence from the primary motor cortex excitability and the postural adjustments of multifidi muscles. *Experimental Brain Research, 235*, 647-659.

Mast, F. W., & Kosslyn, S. M. (2002). Visual mental images can be ambiguous: Insights from individual differences in spatial transformation abilities. *Cognition, 86*, 57-70.

Masters, W. H., & Johnson, V. E. (1966). *Human sexual response.* Boston: Little, Brown.

Masters, W. H., & Johnson, V. E. (1979). *Homosexuality in perspective.* Boston: Little, Brown.

Mather, M. B., & vanderWeele, T. J. (2019). Finding common ground in meta-analysis "wars" on violent video games. *Perspectives on Psychological Science, 14*, 705-708.

Mathes, E. W. (2019). An evolutionary perspective on Kohlberg's theory of moral development. *Current Psychology*, 1-14.

Mathews, H. L., & Janusek, L. (2011). Epigenetics and psychoneuroimmunology: Mechanisms and models. *Brain, Behavior, and Immunity, 25*, 25-39.

Matsumoto, D. (2002). Methodological requirements to test a possible in-group advantage in judging emotions across cultures: Comment on Elfenbein and Ambady (2002) and evidence. *Psychological Bulletin, 128*, 236-242.

Mattan, B. D., Kubota, J. T., & Cloutier, J. (2017). How social status shapes person perception and evaluation: A social neuroscience perspective. *Perspectives on Psychological Science, 12*, 468-507.

Mattan, B. D., Wei, K. Y., Cloutier, J., & Kubota, J. T. (2018). The social neuroscience of race-based and status-based prejudice. *Current Opinion in Psychology, 24*, 27-34.

Mattys, S. L., Seymour, F. F., Attwood, A. S., & Munafò, M. R. (2013). Effects of acute anxiety induction on speech perception: Are anxious listeners distracted listeners? *Psychological Science, 24*, 1606-1608.

Maturana, M. J., Pudell, C., Targa, A. S., Rodrigues, L. S., Noseda, A. D., Fortes, et al. (2015). REM sleep deprivation reverses neurochemical and other depressive-like alterations induced by olfactory bulbectomy. *Molecular Neurobiology, 51*, 349-360.

Maurer, D., Lewis, T. L., Brent, H. P., & Levin, A. V. (1999). Rapid improvement in the acuity of infants after visual input. *Science, 286*, 108-110.

Mayer, D., Simetin, I. P., Rodin, U., Benjak, T., Puntarić, E., & Puntarić, I. (2015). The impacts of media messaging and age and sex variance on adolescent smoking habits in Croatia. *Journal of Addiction Medicine, 9*, 147-154.

Mayer, J. D., Salovey, P., & Caruso, D. R. (2004). Emotional intelligence: Theory, findings, and implications. *Psychological Inquiry, 15*, 197-215.

Mayer, J. D., Salovey, P., & Caruso, D. R. (2008). Emotional intelligence: New ability or eclectic traits? *American Psychologist, 63*, 503-517.

Mayer, R. E. (2013). Problem solving. In D. Reisberg (Ed.), *The Oxford handbook of cognitive psychology.* New York: Oxford University Press.

Maynard, A. E., & Martini, M. I. (2005). *Learning in cultural context: Family, peers, and school.* New York: Kluwer Academic/Plenum Publishers.

Mays, J. C., & Newman, A. (2020, April 9). Black and Hispanic New Yorkers are twice as likely as whites to succumb. *The New York Times,* p. A16.

Mays, V. M., & Ghavami, N. (2018). History, aspirations, and transformations of intersectionality: Focusing on gender. In C. B. Travis & J. W. White (Eds.), *APA handbook of the psychology of women: Volume 1: History, theory, and battlegrounds.* Washington, DC: American Psychological Association.

Mazzoni, G., Clark, A., De Bartolo, A., Guerrini, C., Nahouli, Z., Duzzi, D., et al. (2019). Brain activation in highly superior autobiographical memory: The role of the praecuneus in the autobiographical memory retrieval network. *Cortex: A Journal Devoted to the Study of the Nervous System and Behavior, 120*, 588-602. https://doi.org/10.1016/j.cortex.2019.02.020.

McAdams, D. P., Diamond, A., de St. Aubin, E., & Mansfield, E. (1997). Stories of commitment: The psychosocial construction of generative lives. *Journal of Personality and Social Psychology, 72*, 678-694.

McAleavey, A. A., Youn, S. J., Xiao, H., Castonguay, L. G., Hayes, J. A., & Locke, B. D. (2019). Effectiveness of routine psychotherapy: Method matters. *Psychotherapy Research, 29*(2), 139-156.

McArthur, B. A., Burke, T. A., Connolly, S. L., Olino, T. M., Lumley, M. N., Abramson, L. Y., et al. (2019). A longitudinal investigation of cognitive self-schemas across adolescent development. *Journal of Youth and Adolescence, 48*(3), 635-647.

McCabe, B., Lee, D., & Viray, T. (2019). Does ethnicity moderate the link between drinking norms and binge drinking in college students? *International Journal of Mental Health and Addiction.* https://doi.org/10.1007/s11469-018-0036-0.

McCabe, M. (2009). Anorgasmia in women. *Journal of Family Psychotherapy, 20*, 177-197.

McCaffery, J. (2019, April 1). A wingman for life. *Reader's Digest.*

McCann, J. T., Lynn, S. J., Lilienfeld, S. O., Shindler, K. L., & Hammond Natof, T. R. (2015). The science and pseudoscience of expert testimony. In S. O. Lilienfeld, S. J. Lynn, & J. M. Lohr (Eds.), *Science and pseudoscience in clinical psychology* (2nd ed.). New York: Guilford Press.

McCarrey, A. C., & Resnick, S. M. (2015). Postmenopausal hormone therapy and cognition. *Hormones and Behavior, 74*, 167-172.

McCarthy, J. (2005). Individualism and collectivism: What do they have to do with counseling? *Journal of Multicultural Counseling and Development, 33*, 108-117.

McCarthy, J., & Brown, A. (2015, March 2). Getting more sleep linked to higher well-being. Gallup Poll. Accessed from http://www.gallup.com/poll/1181583/getting-sleep-linked-higher.aspx.

McCarthy, R. J., & Skowronski, J. J. (2011). You're getting warmer: Level of construal affects the impact of central traits on impression formation. *Journal of Experimental Social Psychology, 47*, 1304-1307.

McCaul, K. D., Johnson, R. J., & Rothman, A. J. (2002). The effects of framing and action instructions on whether older adults obtain flu shots. *Health Psychology, 21*, 624-628.

McCauley, R. N., & Henrich, J. (2006). Susceptibility to the Müller-Lyer illusion, theory-neutral observation, and the diachronic penetrability of the visual input. *Philosophical Psychology, 19*, 79-101.

McClelland, D. C. (1985). How motives, skills, and values determine what people do. *American Psychologist, 40*, 812-825.

McClelland, D. C., Atkinson, J. W., Clark, R. A., & Lowell, E. L. (1953). *The achievement motive.* New York: Appleton-Century-Crofts.

McCluskey, U., & O'Toole, M. (2019). *Transference and countertransference from an attachment perspective: A guide to clinical practice.* New York: Routledge.

McConkey, R., Sadowsky, M., & Shellard, A. (2019). An international survey of obesity and underweight in youth and adults with intellectual disabilities. *Journal of Intellectual and Developmental Disability, 44*(3), 374-382.

McConnell, A. R., & Rydell, R. J. (2019). The Implicit Association Test: Implications for understanding consumer behavior. In F. R. Kardes, P. M. Herr, & N. Schwarz (Eds.), *Handbook of research methods in consumer psychology.* New York: Routledge.

McCormick, J. (2019, April 1). What AI can tell from listening to you. *Wall Street Journal.* https://www.wsj.com/articles/what-ai-can-tell-from-listening-to-you-11554169408.

McCrae, R. R., Kurtz, J. E., Yamagata, S., & Terracciano, A. (2011). Internal consistency, retest reliability, and their implications for personality scale validity. *Personality and Social Psychology Review, 15*, 28-50.

McCredie, M. N., & Morey, L. C. (2019). Convergence between Thematic Apperception Test and self-report: Another look at some old questions. *Journal of Clinical Psychology.* https://doi-org.silk.library.umass.edu/10.1002/jclp.22826.

McCrink, K., & Wynn, K. (2007). Ratio abstraction by 6-month-old infants. *Psychological Science, 18*, 740-745.

McCulloch, K., Lachner Bass, N., Dial, H., Hiscock, M., & Jansen, B. (2017). Interaction of attention and acoustic factors in dichotic listening for fused words. *Laterality: Asymmetries of Body, Brain and Cognition, 22*, 473-494.

McDaniel, M. A., Maier, S. F., & Einstein, G. O. (2002). "Brain specific" nutrients: A memory cure? *Psychological Science in the Public Interest, 3*, 12-18.

McDermott, M. S., Beard, E., Brose, L. S., West, R., & McEwen, A. (2013). Factors associated with differences in quit rates between "specialist" and "community" stop-smoking practitioners in the English stop-smoking services. *Nicotine & Tobacco Research, 15*, 1239-1247.

McDonald, A. R., Muraskin, J., Van Dam, N. T., Froehlich, C., Puccio, B., Pellman, J., et al. (2017). The real-time fMRI neurofeedback based stratification of Default Network Regulation Neuroimaging data repository. *Neuroimage, 146,* 157-170.

McDonald, H. E., & Hirt, E. R. (1997). When expectancy meets desire: Motivational effects in reconstructive memory. *Journal of Personality and Social Psychology, 72,* 5-23.

McDougall, W. (1908). *Introduction to social psychology.* London: Methuen.

McElreath, R., Wallin, A., & Fasolo, B. (2013). The evolutionary rationality of social learning. In R. Hertwig & U. Hoffrage (Eds.), *Simple heuristics in a social world.* New York: Oxford University Press.

McElroy, S. L., Guerdjikova, A. I., Mori, N., & Romo-Nava, F. (2019). Progress in developing pharmacologic agents to treat bulimia nervosa. *CNS drugs, 33*(1), 31-46.

McGaugh, J. L, & LePort, A. (2014). Remembrance of all things past. *Scientific American, 310,* 41-45.

McGilvray, J. (Ed.). (2004). *The Cambridge companion to Chomsky.* Oxford, England: Cambridge University Press.

McGinn, D. (2003, June 9). Testing, testing: The new job search. *Time,* pp. 36-38.

McGinty, J. C. (2019, September 14-15). To lower suicides methods matter. *Wall Street Journal,* p. A2.

McGinty, J.C. (2019, June 22-23). Divorces are down, unless you're 55 or older. *Wall Street Journal,* p. A2.

McGregor, K. K., & Capone, N. C. (2004). Genetic and environmental interactions in determining the early lexicon: Evidence from a set of trizygotic quadruplets. *Journal of Child Language, 31,* 311-337.

McGuigan, S., Zhou, S. H., Brosnan, M. B., Thyagarajan, D., Bellgrove, M. A., & Chong, T. T. (2019). Dopamine restores cognitive motivation in Parkinson's disease. *Brain, 142*(3), 719-732.

McIntyre, K., Korn, J., & Matsuo, H. (2008). Sweating the small stuff: How different types of hassles result in the experience of stress. *Stress and Health: Journal of the International Society for the Investigation of Stress, 24,* 383-392.

McKenna, K., Goodrich, L., Forbes, P. W., & Ibeziako, P. (2019). Pilot study to examine the clinical utility of biofeedback in solid organ transplant. *Clinical Practice in Pediatric Psychology, 7*(2), 127-139.

McKetton, L., DeSimone, K., & Schneider, K. A. (2019). Larger auditory cortical area and broader frequency tuning underlie absolute pitch. *The Journal of Neuroscience, 39*(15), 2930-2937.

McKinley, J. C. Jr. (2013, September 12). Overdoses of "Molly" led to Electric Zoo deaths. *The New York Times.* Accessed from http://artsbeat.blogs.nytimes.com/2013/09/12/overdoses-of-molly-led-to-electric-zoo-deaths/.

McLay, R. N., Baird, A., Webb-Murphy, J., Deal, W., Tran, L., Anson, H., et al. (2017). A randomized, head-to-head study of virtual reality exposure therapy for posttraumatic stress disorder. *Cyberpsychology, Behavior, and Social Networking, 20,* 218-224.

McLean, C. P., Su, Y., Carpenter, J. K., & Foa, E. B. (2017). Changes in PTSD and depression during prolonged exposure and client-centered therapy for PTSD in adolescents. *Journal of Clinical Child And adolescent Psychology, 46,* 500-510.

McLeod, J. (2015). Happiness, wellbeing and self-esteem: Public feelings and educational projects. In K. Wright & J. McLeod (Eds.), *Rethinking youth wellbeing: Critical perspectives.* New York: Springer Science + Business Media.

McNamara, T. P. (2013). Semantic memory and priming. In A. F. Healy, R. W. Proctor, & I. B. Weiner (Eds.), *Handbook of psychology, Vol. 4: Experimental psychology* (2nd ed.). Hoboken, NJ: John Wiley & Sons Inc.

McRobbie, L.R. (2018, November 28). How culture shapes your mind—and your mental illness *Boston Globe.* Downloaded from https://www.bostonglobe.com/ideas/2018/11/28/how-culture-shapes-your-mind-and-your-mental-illness/sMl-hWP5LGSOvQAFd83I3qN/story.html.

McSpadden, K. (2015, May 14). You now have a shorter attention span than a goldfish. *Time.*

McTeague, L. M., Lang, P. J., Laplante, M., & Bradley, M. M. (2011). Aversive imagery in panic disorder: Agoraphobia severity, comorbidity, and defensive physiology. *Biological Psychiatry, 70,* 415-424.

Mehl, M. R., Vazire, S., Ramirez-Esparza, N., Slatcher, R. B., & Pennebaker, J. W. (2007). Are women really more talkative than men? *Science, 317,* 82.

Meier, B., & Rothen, N. (2015). Developing synaesthesia: A primer. *Frontiers in Human Neuroscience, 9,* 211.

Meltzer, A. L., Makhanova, A., Hicks, L. L., French, J. E., McNulty, J. K., & Bradbury, T. N. (2017). Quantifying the sexual afterglow: The lingering benefits of sex and their implications for pair-bonded relationships. *Psychological Science, 28*(5), 587-598.

Meltzoff, A. N. (1996). The human infant as imitative generalist: A 20-year progress report on infant imitation with implications for comparative psychology. In C. M. Heyes & B. G. Galef, Jr. (Eds.), *Social learning in animals: The roots of culture.* San Diego, CA: Academic Press.

Meltzoff, J., & Cooper, H. (2018). *Critical thinking about research: Psychology and related fields,* 2nd ed. Washington, DC: American Psychological Association.

Melzack, R., & Katz, J. (2001). The McGill Pain Questionnaire: Appraisal and current status. In D. Turk & R. Melzack (Eds.), *Handbook of pain assessment* (2nd ed.). New York: Guilford Press.

Mendle, J., Moore, S. R., Briley, D. A., & Harden, K. P. (2016). Puberty, socioeconomic status, and depression in girls: Evidence for gene × environment interactions. *Clinical Psychological Science, 4*(1), 3-16.

Mendoza-Pérez, J. C., Ortiz-Hernández, L., & Lozano-Verduzco, I. (2019). Sexual practices among a sample of young lesbian and bisexual women from Mexico: An exploratory study. *International Journal of Sexual Health, 31*(2), 154-163.

Menolascino, N., & Jenkins, L. N. (2018). Predicting bystander intervention among middle school students. *School Psychology Quarterly, 33*(2), 305-313.

Menon, J. M. L., Nolten, C., Achterberg, E. J. M., Joosten, R. N. J. M. A., Dematteis, M., Feenstra, M. G. P., et al. (2019). Brain microdialysate monoamines in relation to circadian rhythms, sleep, and sleep deprivation—a systematic review, network meta-analysis, and new primary data. *Journal of Circadian Rhythms, 17*(1), 1. DOI: http://doi.org/10.5334/jcr.174.

Mensah, F. K., Bayer, J. K., Wake, M., Carlin, J. B., Allen, N. B., & Patton, G. C. (2013). Early puberty and childhood social and behavioral adjustment. *Journal of Adolescent Health, 53,* 118-124.

Meraji, S.M., & Hodges, L. (2020, April 6). How to get therapy when you can't leave the house. National Public Radio. Downloaded from https://www.npr.org/2020/04/03/826726628/how-to-get-therapy-when-you-cant-leave-the-house.

Mercadillo, R. E., Díaz, J., Pasaye, E. H., & Barrios, F. A. (2011). Perception of suffering and compassion experience: Brain gender disparities. *Brain and Cognition, 76,* 5-14.

Mercier, H. (2017). Confirmation bias—Myside bias. In R. F. Pohl (Ed.), *Cognitive illusions: Intriguing phenomena in thinking, judgment and memory.* New York: Routledge/Taylor & Francis Group.

Merikangas, K. R., Ames, M., Cui, L., Stang, P. E., Ustun, T. B., VonKorff, M., et al. (2007). The impact of comorbidity of mental and physical conditions on role disability in the US adult household population. *Archives of General Psychiatry, 64,* 1180-1188.

Mesoudi, A. (2011). Evolutionary psychology meets cultural psychology. *Journal of Evolutionary Psychology, 9,* 83-87.

Messner, M., Reinhard, M., & Sporer, S. (2008). Compliance through direct persuasive appeals: The moderating role of communicator's attractiveness in interpersonal persuasion. *Social Influence, 3,* 67-83.

Meston, C. M. (2003). Validation of the female sexual function index (FSFI) in women with female orgasmic disorder and in women with hypoactive sexual desire disorder. *Journal of Sex and Marital Therapy, 29,* 39-46.

Metz, C. (2017, July 31). Therapy in a dose of illusion. *The New York Times,* pp. B1, B4.

Michael, R. T., Gagnon, J. H., Laumann, E. O., & Kolata, G. (1994). *Sex in America: A definitive survey.* Boston: Little, Brown.

Micheau, J., & Marighetto, A. (2011). Acetylcholine and memory: A long, complex and chaotic but still living relationship. *Behavioural Brain Research, 221,* 424-429.

Midanik, L. T., Tam, T. W., & Weisner, C. (2007). Concurrent and simultaneous drug and alcohol use: Results of the 2000 national alcohol survey. *Drug and Alcohol Dependence, 90,* 72-80.

Miech, R. A., Johnston, L. D., O'Malley, P. M., Bachman, J. G., Schulenberg, J. E., & Patrick, M. E. (2019). *Monitoring the Future national survey results on drug use, 1975-2018: Volume I, Secondary school students.* Ann Arbor, MI: Institute for Social Research, University of Michigan. Available at http://monitoringthe-future.org/pubs.html#monographs.

Mignon, A., & Mollaret, P. (2002). Applying the affordance conception of traits: A person perception study. *Personality and Social Psychology Bulletin, 28,* 1327-1334.

Miguez, G., Witnauer, J. E., & Miller, R. R. (2011). The role of contextual associations in producing the partial reinforcement acquisition deficit. *Journal of Experimental Psychology: Animal Behavior Processes, 37,* 88-97.

Mihalca, L., Mengelkamp, C., & Schnotz, W. (2017). Accuracy of metacognitive judgments as a moderator of learner control effectiveness in problem-solving tasks. *Metacognition and Learning.* Accessed from https://link.springer.com/article/10.1007/s11409-017-9173-2.

Mihura, J. L., Bombel, G., Dumitrascu, N., Roy, M., & Meadows, E. A. (2019). Why we need a formal systematic approach to validating psychological tests: The case of the Rorschach Comprehensive System. *Journal of Personality Assessment, 101*(4), 374-392.

Mika, V. S., Wood, P. R., Weiss, B. D., & Trevino, L. (2007). Ask Me 3: Improving communication in a Hispanic pediatric outpatient practice. *American Journal of Behavioral Health, 31,* S115-S121.

Miles, P., Schaufeli, W. B., & van den Bos, K. (2011). When weak groups are strong: How low cohesion groups allow individuals to act according to their personal absence tolerance norms. *Social Justice Research, 24,* 207-230.

Milgram, S. (2005). *Obedience to authority.* New York: Pinter & Martin.

Miller, C., & Williams, A. (2011). Ethical guidelines in research. In J. C. Thomas & M. Hersen (Eds.), *Understanding research in clinical and counseling psychology* (2nd ed.). New York: Routledge/Taylor & Francis Group.

Miller, C. C. (2018, August 11). The glass ceiling built at home, where daughters do more chores. *The New York Times,* p. B2.

Miller, G. (2008). The roots of morality. *Science, 320,* 734-737.

Miller, G. E., Chen, E., & Parker, K. J. (2011). Psychological stress in childhood and susceptibility to the chronic diseases of aging: Moving toward a model of behavioral and biological mechanisms. *Psychological Bulletin, 137,* 959-997.

Miller, J. A., & Leffard, S. A. (2007). Behavioral assessment. In S. R. Smith & L. Handler (Eds.), *The clinical assessment of children and adolescents: A practitioner's handbook.* Mahwah, NJ: Lawrence Erlbaum Associates.

Miller, L. A., McIntire, S. A., & Lovler, R. L. (2011). *Foundations of psychological testing: A practical problem* (3rd ed.). Thousand Oaks, CA: Sage Publications, Inc.

Miller, N., Perich, T., & Meade, T. (2019). Depression, mania and self-reported creativity in bipolar disorder. *Psychiatry Research, 276,* 129-133.

Mills, J. (2013). Jung's metaphysics. *International Journal of Jungian Studies, 5,* 19-43.

Mills, M. C. (2019, August 30). How do genes affect same-sex behavior? *Science, 365,* 869-870.

Mills, M. J. (2011). Associations among achievement measures and their collective prediction of work involvement. *Personality and Individual Differences, 50,* 360-364.

Milne, M. R., Qian, L., Turnbull, M. T., Kinna, G., Collins, B. M., Teasdale, R. D., et al. (2019). Downregulation of SNX27 expression does not exacerbate amyloidogenesis in the APP/PS1 Alzheimer's disease mouse model. *Neurobiology of Aging, 77,* 144-153.

Milner, B. (1966). Amnesia following operation on temporal lobes. In C. W. M. Whitty & P. Zangwill (Eds.), *Amnesia.* London: Butterworth.

Milner, B. (2005). The medial temporal-lobe amnesic syndrome. *Psychiatric Clinics of North America, 28,* 599-611.

Milos, G., Baur, V., Schumacher, S., Kuenzli, C., Schnyder, U., Mueller-Pfeiffer, C., et al. (2017). How fat will it make me? Estimation of weight gain in anorexia nervosa. *Appetite, 114,* 368-373.

Miner-Rubino, K., & Cortina, L. M. (2007). Beyond targets: Consequences of vicarious exposure to misogyny at work. *Journal of Applied Psychology, 92,* 1254-1269.

Miner-Rubino, K., Winter, D. G., & Stewart, A. J. (2004). Gender, social class, and the subjective experience of aging: Self-perceived personality change from early adulthood to late midlife. *Personality and Social Psychology Bulletin, 30,* 1599-1610.

Minică, C. C., Mbarek, H., Pool, R., Dolan, C. V., Boomsma, D. I., & Vink, J. M. (2017). Pathways to smoking behaviours: Biological insights from the Tobacco and Genetics Consortium meta-analysis. *Molecular Psychiatry, 22,* 82-88.

Mintz, A., & Wayne, C. (2014). Group decision making in conflict: From groupthink to polythink in the war in Iraq. In P. T. Coleman, M. Deutsch, & E. C. Marcus (Eds.), *The handbook of conflict resolution: Theory and practice* (3rd ed.). San Francisco, CA: Jossey-Bass.

Miquel, J. (2006). Integración de teorías del envejecimiento (parte I). Integration of theories of aging. *Revista Espanola de Geriatria y Gerontologia, 41,* 55-63.

Mirambo, M. M., Aboud, S., Majigo, M., Groß, U., & Mshana, S. E. (2019). Adverse pregnancy outcomes among pregnant women with acute rubella infections in Mwanza City, Tanzania. *International Journal of Infectious Diseases, 78,* 72-77

Mirzairad, R., Haydari, A., Pasha, R., Ehteshamzadeh, P., & Makvandi, B. (2017). The relationship between perfectionism and psychological distress with the mediation of coping styles and self-esteem. *International Journal of Mental Health and Addiction, 15,* 614-620.

Mischel, W. (2004). Toward an integrative science of the person. *Annual Review of Psychology, 55,* 1-22.

Mischel, W. (2009). From Personality and Assessment (1968) to Personality Science, 2009. *Journal of Research in Personality, 43,* 282-290.

Mischel, W., & Shoda, Y. (2008). Toward a unified theory of personality: Integrating dispositions and processing dynamics within the cognitive-affective processing system. In O. P. Oliver, R. W. Robins, & L. A. Pervin (Eds.), *Handbook of personality psychology: Theory and research* (3rd ed.). New York: Guilford Press.

Mitchell, W. J., Ho, C.-C., Patel, H., & MacDorman, K. F. (2011). Does social desirability bias favor humans? Explicit-implicit evaluations of synthesized speech support a new HCI model of impression management. *Computers in Human Behavior, 27*(1), 402-412.

Mitte, K. (2005). Meta-analysis of cognitive-behavioral treatments for generalized anxiety disorder: A comparison with pharmacotherapy. *Psychological Bulletin, 131,* 785-795.

Miyatsu, T., & McDaniel, M. A. (2019). Adding the keyword mnemonic to retrieval practice: A potent combination for foreign language vocabulary learning? *Memory & Cognition, 47*(4), 1-16.

Mizrahi, R., Agid, O., Borlido, C., Suridjan, I., Rusjan, P., Houle, S., et al. (2011). Effects of antipsychotics on D3 receptors: A clinical PET study in first episode antipsychotic naive patients with schizophrenia using [11C]-(+)-PHNO. *Schizophrenia Research, 131,* 63-68.

Modak, T., Bhad, R., & Rao, R. (2019). A rare case of physical dependence with psychedelic LSD—A case report. *Journal of Substance Use, 24*(4), 347-349.

Moen, K. C., Miller, J. K., & Lloyd, M. E. (2017). Selective attention meets spontaneous recognition memory: Evidence for effects at retrieval. *Consciousness and Cognition: An International Journal, 49,* 181-189.

Moen, P. (2015). An institutional/organizational turn: Getting to work-life quality and gender equality. *Work and Occupations, 42,* 174-182.

Moffitt, T. E., Caspi, A., & Rutter, M. (2006). Measured gene-environment interactions in psychopathology: Concepts, research strategies, and implications for research, intervention, and public understanding of genetics. *Perspectives on Psychological Science, 1,* 5-27.

Moghaddam, F. M. (2008). The materialist view: From realistic conflict theory to evolutionary psychology. In F. M. Moghaddam (Ed.), *Multiculturalism and intergroup relations: Psychological implications for democracy in global.* Washington, DC: American Psychological Association.

Mograss, M., Guillem, F., Brazzini-Poisson, V., & Godbout, R. (2009). The effects of total sleep deprivation on recognition memory processes: A study of event-related potential. *Neurobiology of Learning and Memory, 91,* 343–352.

Mohr, C., & Messina, S. (2015). Brain dysfunctions, psychopathologies, and body image distortions: Propositions for a possible common cause. *European Psychologist, 20,* 72–81.

Mokdad, A. H., Brewer, R. D., & Naimi, T. (2007). Binge drinking is a problem that cannot be ignored. *Preventive Medicine: An International Journal Devoted to Practice and Theory, 44,* 303–304.

Molina, M., Sann, C., David, M., Touré, Y., Guillois, B., & Jouen, F. (2015). Active touch in late-preterm and early-term neonates. *Developmental Psychobiology, 57,* 322–335.

Mollen, S., Engelen, S., Kessels, L. E., & van den Putte, B. (2017). Short and sweet: The persuasive effects of message framing and temporal context in antismoking warning labels. *Journal of Health Communication, 22,* 20–28.

Monaghan, P., & Fletcher, M. (2019). Do sound symbolism effects for written words relate to individual phonemes or to phoneme features? *Language and Cognition, 11*(2), 235–255.

Monk, T. H., Buysse, D. J., Billy, B. D., Fletcher, M. E., Kennedy, K. S., Schlarb, et al. (2011). Circadian type and bed-timing regularity in 654 retired seniors: Correlations with subjective sleep measures. *Sleep, 34,* 235–239.

Monteleone, P., Martiadis, V., & Maj, M. (2011). Circadian rhythms and treatment implications in depression. *Progress in Neuro-Psychopharmacology & Biological Psychiatry, 35,* 1569–1574.

Montgomery, K. L. (2011). Living with panic, worry, and fear: Anxiety disorders. In C. Franklin & R. Fong (Eds.), *The church leader's counseling resource book: A guide to mental health and social problems.* New York: Oxford University Press.

Montgomery, M. (2020, March 15). DC's bars were packed despite coronavirus. We asked people why they went out. *Washingtonian.* Downloaded from https://www.washingtonian.com/2020/03/15/dcs-bars-were-packed-despite-coronavirus-we-asked-people-why-they-went-out/ March 17, 2020.

Moodley, R., Gielen, U. P., & Wu, R. (2013). *Handbook of counseling and psychotherapy in an international context.* New York: Routledge/Taylor & Francis Group.

Moody, R. L., Starks, T. J., Grov, C., & Parsons, J. T. (2017). Internalized homophobia and drug use in a national cohort of gay and bisexual men: Examining depression, sexual anxiety, and gay community attachment as mediating factors. *Archives of Sexual Behavior.* Accessed from https://www.ncbi.nlm.nih.gov/pubmed/28608294.

Moon, C., Lagercrantz, H., & Kuhl, P. (2013). Language experienced in utero affects vowel perception after birth: A two-country study. *Acta Paediatrica, 102,* 156–160.

Moore, A. A., Lapato, D. M., Brotman, M. A., Leibenluft, E., Aggen, S. H., Hettema, J. M., et al. (2019). Heritability, stability, and prevalence of tonic and phasic irritability as indicators of disruptive mood dysregulation disorder. *Journal of Child Psychology and Psychiatry, 60*(9), 1032–1041.

Moore, D. G., Goodwin, J. E., & George, R. (2007). Infants perceive human point-light displays as solid forms. *Cognition, 104,* 377–396.

Moore, D. W. (2005, June 16). Three in four Americans believe in paranormal. Gallup News Service.

Moore, E. S., Wilkie, W. L., & Desrochers, D. M. (2017). All in the family? Parental roles in the epidemic of childhood obesity. *Journal of Consumer Research, 43,* 824–859.

Mora, M., Urdaneta, E., & Chaya, C. (2019). Effect of personality on the emotional response elicited by wines. *Food Quality and Preference, 76,* 39–46.

Mora-Giral, M., Raich-Escursell, R. M., Segues, C. V., Torras-Claras, A. J., & Huon, G. (2004). Bulimia symptoms and risk factors in university students. *Eating and Weight Disorders, 9,* 163–169.

Morad, Y., Barkana, Y., Zadok, D., Hartstein, M., Pras, E., & Bar-Dayan, Y. (2009). Ocular parameters as an objective tool for the assessment of truck drivers fatigue. *Accident Analysis and Prevention, 41,* 856–860.

Morcom, A. M., & Friston, K. J. (2011). Decoding episodic memory in ageing: A Bayesian analysis of activity patterns predicting memory. *Neuroimage, 33,* 88–91.

Moreno-Gómez, F. N., Véliz, G., Rojas, M., Martínez, C., Olmedo, R., Panussis, F., et al. (2017). Music training and education slow the deterioration of music perception produced by presbycusis in the elderly. *Frontiers in Aging Neuroscience, 9,* 1–10.

Moretz, M., & McKay, D. (2009). The role of perfectionism in obsessive-compulsive symptoms: "Not just right" experiences and checking compulsions. *Journal of Anxiety Disorders, 23,* 640–644.

Morgan, A. A., Marsiske, M., & Whitfield, K. E. (2008). Characterizing and explaining differences in cognitive test performance between African American and European American older adults. *Experimental Aging Research, 34,* 80–100.

Morris, B. (2018, September 10). Most teens prefer to chat online rather than in person. *Wall Street Journal.* Retrieved from https://www.wsj.com/articles/most-teens-prefer-to-chat-online-than-in-person-survey-finds-1536597971.

Morris, S. Y. (2017, May 25). What does it mean to have hyperthymesia or highly superior autobiographical memory (HSAM)? *HealthLine.* Retrieved from http://www.healthline.com/health/hyperthymesia#overview1.

Morrone, A. S., & Pintrich, P. R. (2006). Achievement motivation. In G. G. Bear & K. M. Minke (Eds.), *Children's needs III: Development, prevention, and intervention.* Washington, DC: National Association of School Psychologists.

Moscoso, S. C., Chaves, S. S., & Argilaga, M. T. A. (2013). Reporting a program evaluation: Needs, program plan, intervention, and decisions. *International Journal of Clinical and Health Psychology, 13,* 58–66.

Mosher, C. E., Winger, J. G., Given, B. A., Helft, P. R., & O'Neil, B. H. (2015). Mental health outcomes during colorectal cancer survivorship: A review of the literature. *Psycho-Oncology, 25*(11), 1261–1270.

Moskowitz, D. S., Sutton, R., Zuroff, D. C., & Young, S. N. (2015). Fetal exposure to androgens, as indicated by digit ratios (2D:4D), increases men's agreeableness with women. *Personality and Individual Differences, 75,* 97–101.

Motley, M. T. (1987, February). What I meant to say. *Psychology Today,* pp. 25–28.

Motta, M., Callaghan, T., & Sylvester, S. (2018). Knowing less but presuming more: Dunning-Kruger effects and the endorsement of anti-vaccine policy attitudes. *Social Science & Medicine, 211,* 274–281.

Moulding, R., Nedeljkovic, M., Kyrios, M., Osborne, D., & Mogan, C. (2017). Short-term cognitive-behavioural group treatment for hoarding disorder: A naturalistic treatment outcome study. *Clinical Psychology & Psychotherapy, 24,* 235–244.

Moynihan, A. B., Igou, E. R., & van Tilburg, W. P. (2017). Free, connected, and meaningful: Free will beliefs promote meaningfulness through belongingness. *Personality and Individual Differences, 107,* 54–65.

Mueller, C. E. (2009). Protective factors as barriers to depression in gifted and nongifted adolescents. *Gifted Child Quarterly, 53,* 3–14.

Mullane, M. P., Martens, B. K., Baxter, E. L., & Steeg, D. V. (2017). Children's preference for mixed- versus fixed-ratio schedules of reinforcement: A translational study of risky choice. *Journal of the Experimental Analysis of Behavior, 107,* 161–175.

Mullangi, S., & Jagsi, R. (2019). Imposter syndrome: Treat the cause, not the symptom. *JAMA, 322*(5), 403–404.

Mumphrey, M. B., Hao, Z., Townsend, R. L., Patterson, L. M., Münzberg, H., Morrison, C. D., et al. (2016). Eating in mice with gastric bypass surgery causes exaggerated activation of brainstem anorexia circuit. *International Journal of Obesity, 40*(6), 921–928.

Mungan, E., Peynircioğlu, Z. F., & Halpern, A. R. (2011). Levels-of-processing effects on "remember" responses in recognition for familiar and unfamiliar tunes. *The American Journal of Psychology, 124,* 37–48.

Munjiza, J., Britvic, D., Radman, M., & Crawford, M. J. (2017). Severe war-related trauma and personality pathology: A case-control study. *BMC Psychiatry, 17,* 22–28.

Munro, C., Randell, L., & Lawrie, S. M. (2017). An integrative bio-psycho-social theory of anorexia nervosa. *Clinical Psychology & Psychotherapy, 24,* 1–21.

Munson, B., & Babel, M. (2019). The phonetics of sex and gender. In W. F. Katz & P. F. Assmann (Eds.), *The Routledge Handbook of Phonetics*. New York: Routledge.

Murayama, K., & Kitagami, S. (2013). Consolidation power of extrinsic rewards: Reward cues enhance long-term memory for irrelevant past events. *Journal of Experimental Psychology: General, 143*, 15-20.

Murphy, H. (2019, March 28). A woman, 71, doesn't feel pain. Now scientists know why: A mutation. *The New York Times*, p. A7.

Murphy, N. A., Hall, J. A., Ruben, M. A., Frauendorfer, D., Schmid Mast, M., Johnson, K. E., et al. (2019). Predictive validity of thin-slice nonverbal behavior from social interactions. *Personality and Social Psychology Bulletin, 45*(7), 983-993.

Murphy, S. (2019, September 27). "Whitey" Bulger's girlfriend Catherine Greig living with his relatives in Hingham. *Boston Globe*. Downloaded from https://www.bostonglobe.com/metro/2019/09/27/whitey-bulger-girlfriend-living-with-his-relatives-hingham/oqdRdiX7u5Ez4cTZr4Kb0O/story.html.

Murray, B. (2002, June). Good news for bachelor's grads. *Monitor on Psychology*, pp. 30-32.

Murray, S. B., Quintana, D. S., Loeb, K. L., Griffiths, S., & Le Grange, D. (2019). Treatment outcomes for anorexia nervosa: A systematic review and meta-analysis of randomized controlled trials. *Psychological medicine, 49*(4), 535-544.

Murthy, P., Kudlur, S., George, S., & Mathew, G. (2009). A clinical overview of fetal alcohol syndrome. *Addictive Disorders & Their Treatment, 8*, 1-12.

Musetti, A., & Corsano, P. (2019). Multidimensional self-esteem and secrecy from friends during adolescence: The mediating role of loneliness. *Current Psychology: A Journal for Diverse Perspectives on Diverse Psychological Issues*. https://doi.org/10.1007/s12144-019-00180-6.

Myers and Briggs Foundation. (2019). MBTI basics. Downloaded from https://www.myersbriggs.org/my-mbti-personality-type/mbti-basics/home.htm?bhcp=1.

Myers, L. L. (2007). Anorexia nervosa, bulimia nervosa, and binge eating disorder. In B. A. Thyer & J. S. Wodarski (Eds.), *Social work in mental health: An evidence-based approach*. Hoboken, NJ: John Wiley & Sons.

Myrtek, M. (2007). Type A behavior and hostility as independent risk factors for coronary heart disease. In J. Jordan, B. Barde, & A. M. Zeiher (Eds.), *Contributions toward evidence-based psychocardiology: A systematic review of the literature*. Washington, DC: American Psychological Association.

Mõttus, R., Briley, D. A., Zheng, A., Mann, F. D., Engelhardt, L. E., Tackett, J. L., et al. (2019). Kids becoming less alike: A behavioral genetic analysis of developmental increases in personality variance from childhood to adolescence. *Journal of Personality and Social Psychology, 117*(3), 635-658.

Møller, A. R. (2011). Anatomy and physiology of the auditory system. In A. R. Møller, B. Langguth, D. DeRidder, & T. Kleinjung (Eds.), *Textbook of tinnitus*. New York: Springer Science + Business Media.

Müller, M., Bosy-Wesphal, A., & Heymsfield, S. B. (2010). Is there evidence for a set point that regulates human body weight? *F1000 Medicine Reports, 2*, 59.

Nader, E. G., Kleinman, A., Gomes, B., Bruscagin, C., Santos, B., Nicoletti, M., et al. (2013). Negative expressed emotion best discriminates families with bipolar disorder children. *Journal of Affective Disorders, 148*, 418-423.

Nagda, B. A., Tropp, L. R., & Paluck, E. L. (2006). Looking back as we look ahead: Integrating research, theory, and practice on intergroup relations. *Journal of Social Research, 62*, 439-451.

Naglieri, J. A., LeBuffe, P. A., & Ross, K. M. (2013). Measuring resilience in children: From theory to practice. In S. Goldstein & R. B. Brooks (Eds.), *Handbook of resilience in children* (2nd ed.). New York: Springer Science + Business Media.

Nagy, T. F. (2011). Informed consent. In T. F. Nagy (Ed.), *Essential ethics for psychologists: A primer for understanding and mastering core issues*. Washington, DC: American Psychological Association.

Nakamura, Y., Goto, T. K., Tokumori, K., Yoshiura, T., Kobayashi, K., Nakamura, Y., et al. (2011). Localization of brain activation by umami taste in humans. *Brain Research, 1390*, 156-163.

Nakhate, K. T., Subhedar, N. K., & Kokare, D. M. (2019). Involvement of neuropeptide CART in the central effects of insulin on feeding and body weight. *Pharmacology, Biochemistry and Behavior, 181*, 101-109.

Nalbantian, S. (2011). Autobiographical memory in modernist literature and neuroscience. In S. Nalbantian, P. M. Matthews, & J. L. McClelland (Eds.), *The memory process: Neuroscientific and humanistic perspectives*. Cambridge, MA: MIT Press.

Narrow, W. E., Rae, D. S., Robins, L. N., & Regier, D. A. (2002). Revised prevalence estimates of mental disorders in the United States: Using a clinical significance criterion to reconcile 2 surveys' estimates. *Archives of General Psychiatry, 59*, 115-123.

Nass, C. and Brave, S. 2005. *Wired for speech: How voice activates and advances the human-computer relationship*. Cambridge, MA: MIT Press.

National Eating Disorders Association. (2019). Identity and eating disorders. Accessed from https://www.nationaleatingdisorders.org/identity-eating-disorders.

National Institute of Child Health and Human Development (NICHD) Early Child Care Research Network. (1999). Child care and mother-child interaction in the first 3 years of life. *Psychology, 35*, 1399-1413.

National Institute of Child Health and Human Development (NICHD) Early Child Care

Research Network. (2001). Child-care and family predictors of preschool attachment and stability from infancy. *Development Psychology, 37*, 847-862.

National Institute of Child Health and Human Development (NICHD) Early Child Care Research Network. (2006). Child-care effect sizes for the NICHD study of early child care and youth development. *American Psychologist, 61*, 99-116.

National Institute of Mental Health (NIMH). (2019). Suicide. Downloaded from https://www.nimh.nih.gov/health/statistics/suicide.shtml.

National Institute on Drug Abuse. (2018). What is the scope of cocaine use in the United States? Downloaded from https://www.drugabuse.gov/publications/research-reports/cocaine/what-scope-cocaine-use-in-united-states.

National Institute on Drug Abuse. (2019). What are some signs and symptoms of someone with a drug use problem? Bethesda, MD: National Institutes of Health. Retrieved from https://easyread.drugabuse.gov/content/what-are-some-signs-and-symptoms-someone-drug-use-problem.

National Institutes of Health. (2015, November 24). Talking to your doctor. Retrieved from https://www.nih.gov/institutes-nih/nih-office-director/office-communications-public-liaison/clear-communication/talking-your-doctor.

National Prevention Information Network. (2011). *STDs today*. Retrieved from http://www.cdcnpin.org/scripts/std/std.asp.

National Research Council. (2001). *Eager to learn: Educating our preschoolers*. Washington, DC: National Academy Press.

National Sexual Violence Resource Center. (2019). Get statistics. Downloaded from https://www.nsvrc.org/node/4737.

Natsuaki, M. N., Samuels, D., & Leve, L. D. (2015). Puberty, identity, and context: A biopsychosocial perspective on internalizing psychopathology in early adolescent girls. In K. C. McLean & M. Syed (Eds.), *The Oxford handbook of identity development*. New York: Oxford University Press.

Neal, D., Matson, J. L., & Belva, B. C. (2013). An examination of the reliability of a new observation measure for autism spectrum disorders: The autism spectrum disorder observation for children. *Research in Autism Spectrum Disorders, 7*, 29-34.

Nedelec, J. L. (2017). A multi-level analysis of the effect of interviewer characteristics on survey respondents' reports of sensitive topics. *Personality and Individual Differences, 107*, 96-101.

Neibergall, N. C., Swanson, A. J., & Sánchez, F. J. (2019). Hormones, sexual orientation, and gender identity. In L. L. Welling & T. K. Shackelford, (Eds.), *The Oxford handbook of evolutionary psychology and behavioral endocrinology*. New York: Oxford University Press.

Nelson, D. L., Kitto, K., Galea, D., McEvoy, C. L., & Bruza, P. D. (2013). How activation, entanglement, and searching a semantic network contribute to event memory. *Memory & Cognition, 41,* 797-819.

Nelson, G., & MacLeod, T. (2017). The evolution of housing for people with serious mental illness. In J. Sylvestre, G. Nelson, T. Aubry, J. Sylvestre, G. Nelson, T. Aubry (Eds.), *Housing, citizenship, and communities for people with serious mental illness: Theory, research, practice, and policy perspectives.* New York: Oxford University Press.

Nelson, T. D. (2013). The neurobiology of stereotyping and prejudice. In D. D. Franks & J. H. Turner (Eds.), *Handbook of neurosociology.* New York: Springer Science + Business Media.

Nelson, W. M., III, & Finch, A. J., Jr. (2000). Managing anger in youth: A cognitive-behavioral intervention approach. In P. C. Kendall (Ed.), *Child & adolescent therapy: Cognitive-behavioral procedures* (2nd ed.). New York: Guilford Press.

Nepi, L. D., Fioravanti, J., Nannini, P., & Peru, A. (2015). Social acceptance and the choosing of favourite classmates: A comparison between students with special educational needs and typically developing students in a context of full inclusion. *British Journal of Special Education, 42*(3), 320-337.

Neria, Y., DiGrande, L., & Adams, G. G. (2011). Postraumatic stress disorder following the September 11, 2001, terrorist attacks. *American Psychologist, 66,* 429-446.

Nestoriuc, Y., Martin, A., Rief, W., & Andrasik, F. (2008). Biofeedback treatment for headache disorders: A comprehensive efficacy review. *Applied Psychophysiology and Biofeedback, 33,* 125-140.

Nettles, M. T. (2019). History of testing in the United States: Higher education. *The ANNALS of the American Academy of Political and Social Science, 683*(1), 38-55.

Neufang, S., Geiger, M. J., Homola, G. A., Mahr, M., Schiele, M. A., Gehrmann, A., et al. (2019). Cognitive-behavioral therapy effects on alerting network activity and effective connectivity in panic disorder. *European Archives of Psychiatry and Clinical Neuroscience, 269*(5), 587-598.

Newby-Clark, I. R., & Ross, M. (2003). Conceiving the past and future. *Personality and Social Psychology Bulletin, 29,* 807-818.

Newman, C. F., Leahy, R. L., Beck, A. T., Reilly-Harrington, N. A., & Gyulai, L. (2002). *Bipolar disorder: A cognitive therapy approach.* Washington, DC: American Psychological Association.

Newman, M., & Bakay, R. (2008). Therapeutic potentials of human embryonic stem cells in Parkinson's disease. *Neurotherapeutics, 5,* 237-251.

Newman, S. D., Willoughby, G., & Pruce, B. (2011). The effect of problem structure on problem-solving: An fMRI study of word versus number problems. *Brain Research, 30,* 88-96.

Ng, E., Lipsman, N., Hamani, C., Lozano, A., Kennedy, S., & Giacobbe, P. (2019). Adverse childhood experiences and deep brain stimulation outcomes for treatment resistant depression. *Brain Stimulation: Basic, Translational, and Clinical Research in Neuromodulation, 12*(2), 548.

Ng, Q. X., Venkatanarayanan, N., & Ho, C. X. (2017). Clinical use of Hypericum perforatum (St. John's wort) in depression: A meta-analysis. *Journal of Affective Disorders, 210,* 211-221.

Nguyen, H. D., Le, H., & Boles, T. (2010). Individualism-collectivism and co-operation: A cross-society and cross-level examination. *Negotiation and Conflict Management Research, 3,* 179-204.

Nguyen, J., Deng, Y., & Reinhart, R. M. G. (2018). Brain-state determines learning improvements after transcranial alternating-current stimulation to frontal cortex. *Brain Stimulation, 11*(4), 723-726.

Niccols, A. (2007). Fetal alcohol syndrome and the developing socio-emotional brain. *Brain Cognition, 65,* 135-142.

Nichols, S. (2011). Experimental philosophy and the problem of free will. *Science, 331,* 1401-1403.

Nicklaus, S., & Schwartz, C. (2019). Early influencing factors on the development of sensory and food preferences. *Current Opinion in Clinical Nutrition & Metabolic Care, 22*(3), 230-235.

Niedenthal, P. M. (2007). Embodying emotion. *Science, 316,* 1002-1005.

Nielsen, S. R., Boye, K., Bastiaanse, R., & Lange, V. M. (2019). The production of grammatical and lexical determiners in Broca's aphasia. *Language, Cognition and Neuroscience.* https://doi.org/10.1080/23273798.2019.1616104.

Nielsen, T., O'Reilly, C., Carr, M., Dumel, G., Godin, I., Solomonova, E., et al. (2015). Overnight improvements in two REM sleep-sensitive tasks are associated with both REM and NREM sleep changes, sleep spindle features, and awakenings for dream recall. *Neurobiology of Learning and Memory, 122,* 88-97.

Nijboer, T. C. W., te Pas, S. F., & van der Smagt, M. J. (2011). Detecting gradual visual changes in colour and brightness agnosia: A double dissociation. *NeuroReport: For Rapid Communication of Neuroscience Research, 22,* 175-180.

Nimrod, G., & Kleiber, D. A. (2007). Reconsidering change and continuity in later life: Toward an innovation theory of successful aging. *International Journal of Human Development, 65,* 1-22.

Nisbet, E. K., Zelenski, J. M., & Murphy, S. A. (2011). Happiness is in our nature: Exploring nature relatedness as a contributor to subjective well-being. *Journal of Happiness Studies, 12,* 303-322.

Nisbett, R. E. (2007, December 9). All brains are the same color. *The New York Times,* p. E11.

Nisbett, R. E. (2009). All brains are the same color. *Association for Psychological Science Observer, 22*(3), 20-21.

Nisbett, R. E., & Cohen, D. (1996). *Culture of honor: The psychology of violence in the South.* Boulder, CO: Westview Press.

Nishida, M., Pearsall, J., Buckner, R., & Walker, M. (2009). REM sleep, prefrontal theta, and the consolidation of human emotional memory. *Cerebral Cortex, 19,* 1158-1166.

Nishimura, T., Kawamura, S., & Sakurai, S. (2011). Autonomous motivation and meta-cognitive strategies as predictors of academic performance: Does intrinsic motivation predict academic performance? *Japanese Journal of Educational Psychology, 59,* 77-87.

Nishino, S. (2007). Clinical and neurobiological aspects of narcolepsy. *Sleep Medicine, 8,* 373-399.

Nolen-Hoeksema, S. (2020). *Abnormal psychology* (8th ed.). New York: McGraw-Hill.

Norcia, A. M., Pei, F., Bonneh, Y., Hou, C., Sampath, V., & Petter, M. W. (2005). Development of sensitivity to texture and contour information in the human infant. *Journal of Cognitive Neuroscience, 17,* 569-579.

Norcross, J. C. (2002). Empirically supported therapy relationships. In J. C. Norcross (Ed.), *Psychotherapy relationships that work: Therapist contributions and responsiveness to patients.* New York: Oxford University Press.

Norcross, J. C., Beutler, L. E., & Levant, R. F. (2006). *Evidence-based practices in mental health: Debate and dialogue on the fundamental questions.* Washington, DC: American Psychological Association.

Norlander, T., Von Schedvin, H., & Archer, T. (2005). Thriving as a function of affective personality: Relation to personality factors, coping strategies and stress. *Anxiety, Stress & Coping: An International Journal, 18,* 105-116.

Norman D., & Randle, A. (2019, July 1). "Gay," "femme," "nonbinary": How identity shaped the lives of these 10 New Yorkers. *The New York Times.* Retrieved from https://www.nytimes.com/interactive/2019/07/01/nyregion/nyc-pride-portraits.html.

North, M. M., & North, S. M. (2017). Virtual reality therapy for treatment of psychological disorders. In M. M. Maheu, K. P. Drude, & S. D. Wright (Eds.), *Career paths in telemental health.* Cham, Switzerland: Springer International Publishing.

Norton, D., Heath, D., & Ventura, D. (2013). Finding creativity in an artificial artist. *Journal of Creative Behavior, 47,* 106-124.

Norton, P. J., & Price, E. C. (2007). A meta-analytic review of adult cognitive-behavioral treatment outcome across the anxiety disorders. *Journal of Nervous and Mental Disease, 195,* 521-531.

Nosek, C. L., Kerr, C. W., Woodworth, J., Wright, S. T., Grant, P. C., Kuszczak, S. M., et al. (2015). End-of-life dreams and visions: A qualitative perspective from hospice patients. *American Journal of Hospice & Palliative Medicine, 32,* 269-274.

Nourouzpour, N., Salomonczyk, D., Cressman, E. K., & Henriques, D. Y. (2015). Retention of proprioceptive recalibration following visuomotor adaptation. *Experimental Brain Research, 233,* 1019-1029.

Nouwens, P. G., Lucas, R., Embregts, P. M., & van Nieuwenhuizen, C. (2017). In plain sight but still invisible: A structured case analysis of people with mild intellectual disability or borderline intellectual functioning. *Journal of Intellectual and Developmental Disability, 42,* 36-44.

Novotney, A. (2017). A growing wave of online therapy. *Monitor on Psychology, 48,* 48.

Nowak, A., Deutsch, M., Bartkowski, W., & Solomon, S. (2010). From crude law to civil relations: The dynamics and potential resolution of intractable conflict. *Peace and Conflict: Journal of Peace Psychology, 16,* 189-209.

Nowakowski, M. E., McCabe, R. E., & Busse, J. W. (2019). Cognitive behavioral therapy to reduce persistent postsurgical pain following internal fixation of extremity fractures (COPE): Rationale for a randomized controlled trial. *Canadian Journal of Pain, 3*(2), 59-68.

Nurnberger, J. I., Jr., & Bierut, L. J. (2007). Seeking the connections: Alcoholism and our genes. *Scientific American, 296*(4), 46-53.

Nussbaum, A. D., & Steele, C. M. (2007). Situational disengagement and persistence in the face of adversity. *Journal of Experimental Social Psychology, 43,* 127-134.

Nyaradi, A., Li, J., Hickling, S., Foster, J., & Oddy, W. H. (2013). The role of nutrition in children's neurocognitive development, from pregnancy through childhood. *Frontiers in Human Neuroscience, 7,* 97.

Nygaard, E., Slinning, K., Moe, V., & Walhovd, K. B. (2017). Cognitive function of youths born to mothers with opioid and poly-substance abuse problems during pregnancy. *Child Neuropsychology, 23,* 159-187.

Nærland, T., Bakke, K. A., Storvik, S., Warner, G., & Howlin, P. (2017). Age and gender-related differences in emotional and behavioural problems and autistic features in children and adolescents with Down syndrome: A survey-based study of 674 individuals. *Journal of Intellectual Disability Research, 61,* 594-603.

O'Leary, A. P., & Sloutsky, V. M. (2017). Carving metacognition at its joints: Protracted development of component processes. *Child Development, 88,* 1015-1032.

Oberauer, K., Awh, E., & Sutterer, D. W. (2017). The role of long-term memory in a test of visual working memory: Proactive facilitation but no proactive interference. *Journal of Experimental Psychology: Learning, Memory, and Cognition, 43,* 1-22.

Occhionero, M. (2004). Mental processes and the brain during dreams. *Dreaming, 14,* 54-64.

Occhionero'Brien, W. H., & Young, K. M. (2013). Assessment of psychopathology: Behavioral approaches. In J. R. Graham, J. A. Naglieri, & I. B. Weiner (Eds.), *Handbook of psychology, Vol. 10: Assessment psychology* (2nd ed.). Hoboken, NJ: John Wiley & Sons Inc.

Offer, D., Kaiz, M., Howard, K. I., & Bennett, E. S. (2000). The altering of reported experiences. *Journal of the American Academy of Child & Adolescent Psychiatry, 39,* 735-742.

Ogbu, J. U. (2003). *Black American students in an affluent suburb: A study of academic disengagement.* New Jersey: Lawrence Erlbaum.

Ogden, C. L., Carroll, M. D, Kit, B. K., & Flegal, K. M. (2014). Prevalence of childhood and adult obesity in the United States, 2011-2012. *Journal of the American Medical Association, 311,* 806-814.

Ohira, T., Hozawa, A., Iribarren, C., Daviglus, M. L., Matthews, K. A., Gross, M. D., & Jacobs, D. R. Jr. (2007). Longitudinal association of serum carotenoids and tocopherols with hostility: The CARDIA study. *American Journal of Epidemiology, 18,* 235-241.

Ojagbemi, A., Bello, T., & Gureje, O. (2018). Gender differential in social and economic predictors of incident major depressive disorder in the Ibadan Study of Ageing. *Social Psychiatry and Psychiatric Epidemiology: The International Journal for Research in Social and Genetic Epidemiology and Mental Health Services, 53*(4), 351-361.

Ojha, H., & Pramanick, M. (2009). Effects of age on intensity and priority of life needs. *Journal of the Indian Academy of Applied Psychology, 35,* 131-136.

Okada, K., Nakao, T., Sanematsu, H., Murayama, K., Honda, S., Tomita, M., et al. (2015). Biological heterogeneity of obsessive-compulsive disorder: A voxel-based morphometric study based on dimensional assessment. *Psychiatry and Clinical Neurosciences, 69,* 411-421.

Okely, J. A., Weiss, A., & Gale, C. R. (2018). The interaction between individualism and wellbeing in predicting mortality: Survey of Health Ageing and Retirement in Europe. *Journal of Behavioral Medicine, 41*(1), 1-11. doi:10.1007/s10865-017-9871-x.

Olatunji, B. (2008). New directions in research on health anxiety and hypochondriasis: Commentary on a timely special series. *Journal of Cognitive Psychotherapy, 22,* 183-190.

Oliver, M. B., & Hyde, J. S. (1993). Gender differences in sexuality: A meta-analysis. *Psychological Bulletin, 114,* 29-51.

Olson, D. H., & DeFrain, J. (2014). *Marriages and families: Intimacy, diversity, and strengths.* New York: McGraw-Hill.

Olulade, O. A., Jamal, N. I., Koo, D. S., Perfetti, C. A., LaSasso, C., & Eden, G. F. (2016). Neuroanatomical evidence in support of the bilingual advantage theory. *Cerebral Cortex, 26*(7), 3196-3204.

Ong, J. C. (2017). Insomnia: The problem of sleeplessness. In J. C. Ong, *Mindfulness-based therapy for insomnia.* Washington, DC: American Psychological Association.

Open Science Collaboration. (2015, August 28). Estimating the reproducibility of psychological science. *Science, 349.*

Opendak, M., Gould, E., & Sullivan, R. (2017). Early life adversity during the infant sensitive period for attachment: Programming of behavioral neurobiology of threat processing and social behavior. *Developmental Cognitive Neuroscience, 25,* 145-159.

Opler, M., Perrin, M., Kleinhaus, K., & Malaspina, D. (2008). Factors in the etiology of schizophrenia: Genes, parental age, and environment. *Primary Psychiatry, 15,* 37-45.

Organization for Economic Cooperation and Development (OECD). (2018). The resilience of students with an immigrant background: Factors that shape well-being. *OECD Reviews of Migrant Education.* https://doi.org/10.1787/9789264292093-en.

Ornat, S. L., & Gallo, P. (2004). Acquisition, learning, or development of language? Skinner's "Verbal behavior" revisited. *Spanish Journal of Psychology, 7,* 161-170.

Orwin, R. G., & Condray, D. S. (1984). Smith and Glass' psychotherapy conclusions need further probing: On Landman and Dawes' re-analysis. *American Psychologist, 39,* 71-72.

Orúzar, H., Miranda, R., Oriol, X., & Montserrat, C. (2019). Self-control and subjective-wellbeing of adolescents in residential care: The moderator role of experienced happiness and daily-life activities with caregivers. *Children and Youth Services Review, 98,* 125-131.

Öst, L.-G., & Ollendick, T. H. (2017). Brief, intensive and concentrated cognitive behavioral treatments for anxiety disorders in children: A systematic review and meta-analysis. *Behaviour Research and Therapy, 97,* 134-145.

Osth, A. F., & Farrell, S. (2019). Using response time distributions and race models to characterize primacy and recency effects in free recall initiation. *Psychological Review, 126*(4), 578-609.

Ostojic-Aitkens, D., Brooker, B., & Miller, C. J. (2019). Using ecological momentary assessments to evaluate extant measures of mind wandering. *Psychological Assessment, 31*(6), 817-827.

Otgaar, H., Howe, M. L., & Muris, P. (2017). Maltreatment increases spontaneous false memories but decreases suggestion-induced false memories in children. *British Journal of Developmental Psychology, 35*(3), 376-391.

Otters, R. V., & Hollander, J. F. (2015). Leaving home and boomerang decisions: A family simulation protocol. *Marriage & Family Review, 51,* 39-58.

Ouimet, A., Gawronski, B., & Dozois, D. (2009). Cognitive vulnerability to anxiety: A review and an integrative model. *Clinical Psychology Review, 29,* 459-470.

Oviedo-Joekes, E., Brissette, S., Marsh, D. C., Lauzon, P., Guh, D., Anis, A., et al. (2009). Diacetylmorphine versus methadone for the treatment of opioid addiction. *New England Journal of Medicine, 361,* 777-786.

Owen, D. (2019, May 13). Volumetrics. *New Yorker,* pp. 26-31.

Ozana, A., & Ganel, T. (2019). Obeying the law: Speed-precision tradeoffs and the adherence to Weber's law in 2D grasping. *Experimental Brain Research, 237*(8), 2011-2021.

Özdemir, V., Dove, E. S., Gürsoy, U. K., Şardaş, S., Yıldırım, A., Yılmaz, Ş. G., et al. (2017). Personalized medicine beyond genomics: Alternative futures in big data–Proteomics, environtome and the social proteome. *Journal of Neural Transmission, 124*, 25–32.

Ozier, E. M., Taylor, V. J., & Murphy, M. C. (2019). The cognitive effects of experiencing and observing subtle racial discrimination. *Journal of Social Issues*. https://doi-org.silk.library.umass.edu/10.1111/josi.12349.

O'Keefe, P., & Rodgers, J. L. (2019). The corrosive influence of the Flynn effect on age normed tests. *Multivariate behavioral research, 54*(1), 155–155.

Paciorek, A., & Williams, J. N. (2015). Semantic generalization in implicit language learning. *Journal of Experimental Psychology: Learning, Memory, and Cognition, 41*, 989–1002.

Packer, D. (2009). Avoiding groupthink: Whereas weakly identified members remain silent, strongly identified members dissent about collective problems. *Psychological Science, 20*, 546–548.

Padgett, D. K., Stanhope, V., & Henwood, B. F. (2011). Housing-first services for homeless adults with co-occurring disorders: An evidence-based practice. In M. Roberts-DeGennaro & S. J. Fogel (Eds.), *Using evidence to inform practice for community and organizational change*. Chicago: Lyceum Books.

Pagano, M. E., White, W. L., Kelly, J. F., Stout, R. L., & Tonigan, J. S. (2013). The 10-year course of Alcoholics Anonymous participation and long-term outcomes: A follow-up study of outpatient subjects in Project MATCH. *Substance Abuse, 34*, 51–59.

Pager, D., & Shepherd, H. (2008). The sociology of discrimination: Racial discrimination in employment, housing, credit, and consumer markets. *Annual Review of Sociology, 34*, 181–209.

Pahlke, E., Hyde, J., & Mertz, J. E. (2013). The effects of single-sex compared with coeducational schooling on mathematics and science achievement: Data from Korea. *Journal of Educational Psychology, 105*, 444–452.

Palamar, J. J., Rutherford, C., & Keyes, K. M. (2019). "Flakka" use among high school seniors in the United States. *Drug and Alcohol Dependence, 196*, 86–90.

Palfi, B., Moga, G., Lush, P., Scott, R. B., & Dienes, Z. (2019). Can hypnotic suggestibility be measured online? *Psychological Research*. https://doi.org/10.1007/s00426-019-01162-w

Paller, K.A., & Oudiette, D. (2018, November). Sleep learning gets real. *Scientific American*, pp. 28–31.

Palmiter, R. (2015). Hunger logic. *Nature Neuroscience, 18*, 789–791.

Paniagua, F. A. (2000). *Diagnosis in a multicultural context: A casebook for mental health professionals*. Thousand Oaks, CA: Sage.

Papoiu, A., Nattkemper, L., Sanders, K., Kraft, R., Chan, Y-H, Coghill, R., et al. (2013). Brain's reward circuits mediate itch relief. A functional MRI study of active scratching.*PLoS ONE 8*(12): e82389.

Pappano, L. (2019). America's colleges struggle to envision the future of diversity on campus. *The Hechinger Report*. Downloaded from https://hechingerreport.org/whither-diversity/.

Pardini, D., White, H. R., Xiong, S., Bechtold, J., Chung, T., Loeber, R., et al. (2015). Unfazed or dazed and confused: Does early adolescent marijuana use cause sustained impairments in attention and academic functioning? *Journal of Abnormal Child Psychology, 43*(7), 1203–1217.

Parent, M. C., Gobble, T. D., & Rochlen, A. (2019). Social media behavior, toxic masculinity, and depression. *Psychology of Men & Masculinities, 20*(3), 277–287.

Parish, C. L., & Arenas, E. (2007). Stem-cell-based strategies for the treatment of Parkinson's disease. *Neurodegenerative Disease, 4*, 339–347.

Park, A. (2011, March 7). Healing the hurt. *Time*, 64–71.

Park, D. C. (2007). Eating disorders: A call to arms. *American Psychologist, 62*, 158.

Park, E., McCoy, T. P., Erausquin, J. T., & Bartlett, R. (2018). Trajectories of risk behaviors across adolescence and young adulthood: The role of race and ethnicity. *Addictive Behaviors, 76*, 1–7.

Park, H., & Antonioni, D. (2007). Personality, reciprocity, and strength of conflict resolution strategy. *Journal of Research in Personality, 41*, 110–125.

Park, H., & Raymo, J. M. (2013). Divorce in Korea: Trends and educational differentials. *Journal of Marriage and Family, 75*, 110–126.

Park, H., Yun, I., & Walsh, A. (2017). Early puberty, school context, and delinquency among South Korean girls. *International Journal of Offender Therapy and Comparative Criminology, 61*(7), 795–818.

Park, J., Park, K., & Dubinsky, A. J. (2011). Impact of retailer image on private brand attitude: Halo effect and summary construct. *Australian Journal of Psychology, 63*, 173–183.

Park, P., Kang, H., Sanderson, T. M., Bortolotto, Z. A., Georgiou, J., Zhuo, M., et al. (2019). On the role of calcium-permeable AMPARs in long-term potentiation and synaptic tagging in the rodent hippocampus. *Frontiers in Synaptic Neuroscience, 11*, 4.

Parke, B. N. (2003). *Discovering programs for talent development*. Thousand Oaks, CA: Corwin Press.

Parke, M. R., Seo, M., & Sherf, E. N. (2015). Regulating and facilitating: The role of emotional intelligence in maintaining and using positive affect for creativity. *Journal of Applied Psychology, 100*, 917–934.

Parkinson, J., Garfinkel, S., Critchley, H., Dienes, Z., & Seth, A. K. (2017). Don't make me angry, you wouldn't like me when I'm angry: Volitional choices to act or inhibit are modulated by subliminal perception of emotional faces. *Cognitive, Affective & Behavioral Neuroscience, 17*, 252–268.

Parra, A., & Argibay, J. C. (2007). Comparing psychics and non-psychics through a "token-object" forced-choice ESP test. *Journal of the Society for Psychical Research, 71*, 80–90.

Parris, B. A. (2017). The role of frontal executive functions in hypnosis and hypnotic suggestibility. *Psychology of Consciousness: Theory, Research, and Practice, 4*, 211–229.

Parrish, E. M., Kim, N. S., Woodberry, K. A., & Friedman, Y. M. (2019). Clinical high risk for psychosis: The effects of labelling on public stigma in a undergraduate population. *Early Intervention in Psychiatry, 13*(4), 874–881.

Parrott, A. C., Downey, L. A., Roberts, C. A., Montgomery, C., Bruno, R., & Fox, H. C. (2017). Recreational 3,4-methylenedioxy-methamphetamine or 'ecstasy': Current perspective and future research prospects. *Journal of Psychpharmacology*. doi: 10.1177/0269881117711922.

Passos, V. L., Berger, M. P. F., & Tan, F. E. (2007). Test design optimization in CAT early stage with the nominal response model. *Applied Psychological Measurement, 31*, 213–232.

Paterson, H. M., Kemp, R. I., & Ng, J. R. (2011). Combating co-witness contamination: Attempting to decrease the negative effects of discussion on eyewitness memory. *Applied Cognitive Psychology, 25*, 43–52.

Patten, S. B., Williams, J. A., Lavorato, D. H., Bulloch, A. M., Fiest, K. M., Wang, J. L., et al. (2017). Seasonal variation in major depressive episode prevalence in Canada. *Epidemiology and Psychiatric Sciences, 26*, 169–176.

Patterson, T. G., & Joseph, S. (2013). Unconditional positive self-regard. In M. E. Bernard (Ed.), *The strength of self-acceptance: Theory, practice and research*. New York: Springer Science + Business Media.

Paul, A. M. (2004). *Cult of personality: How personality tests are leading us to miseducate our children, mismanage our companies and misunderstand ourselves*. New York: Free Press.

Paulmann, S., Jessen, S., & Kotz, S. A. (2009). Investigating the multimodal nature of human communication: Insights from ERPs. *Journal of Psychophysiology, 23*, 63–76.

Pavot, W., & Diener, E. (2013). Happiness experienced: The science of subjective well-being. In S. A. David, I. Boniwell, & A. Conley Ayers (Eds.), *The Oxford handbook of happiness*. New York: Oxford University Press.

Pavão, R., Tort, A. L., & Amaral, O. B. (2015). Multifactoriality in psychiatric disorders: A computational study of schizophrenia. *Schizophrenia Bulletin, 41*, 980–988.

Pawluski, J. L., Li, M., & Lonstein, J. S. (2019). Serotonin and motherhood: From molecules to mood. *Frontiers in Neuroendocrinology*. doi: 10.1016/j.yfrne.2019.03.001.

Payne, K., & Marcus, D. (2008). The efficacy of group psychotherapy for older adult clients: A meta-analysis. *Group Dynamics: Theory, Research, and Practice, 12*, 268–278.

Pearce, R. R., & Lin, Z. (2007). Chinese American post-secondary achievement and attainment: A cultural and structural analysis. *Educational Review, 59*, 19–36.

Pearson, A. R., Dovidio, J. F., & Pratto, E. (2007). Racial prejudice, intergroup hate, and blatant and subtle bias of whites toward blacks in legal decision making in the United States. *International Journal of Psychology & Psychological Therapy, 7,* 125-134.

Pearson, G. D. H., & Knobloch-Westerwick, S. (2019). Is the confirmation bias bubble larger online? Pre-election confirmation bias in selective exposure to online versus print political information. *Mass Communication & Society, 22*(4), 466-486.

Pedersen, P. B., Draguns, J. G., Lonner, W. J., & Trimble, J. E. (Eds.). (2002). *Counseling across cultures* (5th ed.). Thousand Oaks, CA: Sage.

Pedraza, O., & Mungas, D. (2008). Measurement in cross-cultural neuropsychology. *Neuropsychology Review, 18,* 184-193.

Pekrun, R. (2017). Emotion and achievement during adolescence. *Child Development Perspectives, 11,* 215-222.

Pellegrini, A. D., Bohn-Gettler, C. M., Dupuis, D., Hickey, M., Roseth, C., & Solberg, D. (2010). An empirical examination of sex differences in scoring preschool children's aggression. *Journal of Experimental Child Psychology, 109,* 232-238.

Pempek, T., Yermolayeva, Y., & Calvert, S. (2009). College students' social networking experiences on Facebook. *Journal of Applied Developmental Psychology, 30,* 227-238.

Pendyam, S., Bravo-Rivera, C., Burgos-Robles, A., Sotres-Bayon, F., Quirk, G. J., & Nair, S. S. (2013). Fear signaling in the prelimbic-amygdala circuit: A computational modeling and recording study. *Journal of Neurophysiology, 110,* 844-861.

Penhollow, T. M., Young, M., & Nnaka, T. (2017). Alcohol use, hooking-up, condom use: Is there a sexual double standard? *American Journal of Health Behavior, 41,* 92-103.

Penley, J. A., Tomaka, J., & Wiebe, J. S. (2002). The association of coping to physical and psychological health outcomes: A meta-analytic review. *Journal of Behavioral Medicine, 25,* 551-603.

Penlington, C., Urbanek, M., & Barker, S. (2019). Psychological theories of pain. *Primary Dental Journal, 7*(4), 24-29.

Penn, D. L., Corrigan, P. W., Bentall, R. P., Racenstein, J. M., & Newman, L. (1997). Social cognition in schizophrenia. *Psychological Bulletin, 121,* 114-132.

Pennequin, V., Questel, F., Delaville, E., Delugre, M., & Maintenant, C. (2019). Metacognition and emotional regulation in children from 8 to 12 years old. *British Journal of Educational Psychology.* https://doi.org/10.1111/bjep.12305.

Perogamvros, L., & Schwartz, S. (2015). Sleep and emotional functions. In P. Meerlo, R. M. Benca, & T. Abel (Eds.), *Sleep, neuronal plasticity and brain function.* New York: Springer-Verlag Publishing.

Perovic, S., & Radenovic, L. (2011). Fine-tuning nativism: The "nurtured nature" and innate cognitive structures. *Phenomenology and the Cognitive Sciences, 10,* 399-417.

Perrier, M., & Ginis, K. M. (2017). Narrative interventions for health screening behaviours: A systematic review. *Journal of Health Psychology, 22,* 375-393.

Perrin, A., & Anderson , M. (2019). Share of U.S. adults using social media, including Facebook, is mostly unchanged since 2018. Pew Research Center. Downloaded from https://www.pewresearch.org/fact-tank/2019/04/10/share-of-u-s-adults-using-social-media-including-facebook-is-mostly-unchanged-since-2018/.

Perry, G. (2013). *Behind the shock machine.* New York: New Press.

Pervin, L. A. (2003). *The science of personality* (2nd ed.). London: Oxford University Press.

Pessoa, L. (2011). Reprint of: Emotion and cognition and the amygdala: From "what is it?" to "what's to be done?" *Neuropsychologia, 49,* 681-694.

Peterfi, Z., McGinty, D., Sarai, E., & Szymusiak, R. (2010). Growth hormone-releasing hormone activates sleep regulatory neurons of the rat preoptic hypothalamus. *American Journal of Physiology: Regulatory, Integrative and Comparative Physiology, 298,* R147-R156.

Peters, E. N., Rosenberry, Z. R., Schauer, G. L., O'Grady, K. E., & Johnson, P. S. (2017). Marijuana and tobacco cigarettes: Estimating their behavioral economic relationship using purchasing tasks. *Experimental and Clinical Psychopharmacology, 25*(3), 208-215.

Peters, E., Hess, T. M., Västfjäll, D., & Auman, C. (2007). Adult age differences in dual information processes. *Perspectives on Psychological Science, 2,* 1-23.

Peters, P., Van Der Heijden, B., Spurk, D., De Vos, A., & Klaassen, R. (2019). Please don't look at me that way. An empirical study into the effects of age-based (meta-) stereotyping on employability enhancement among supermarket workers. *Frontiers in Psychology, 10,* 249.

Petersen, A. (2011, August 23). A sleep battle of the sexes. *Wall Street Journal,* pp. D1, D4.

Peterson, A. (2018, August 14). Short-term therapy programs for quick relief. *The New York Times,* p. D-3.

Peterson, C. (2000). The future of optimism. *American Psychologist, 55,* 44-55.

Peterson, L. R., & Peterson, M. J. (1959). Short-term retention of individual items. *Journal of Experimental Psychology, 58,* 193-198.

Petersson, K. M., Silva, C., Castro-Caldas, A., Ingvar, M., & Reis, A. (2007). Literacy: A cultural influence on functional left-right differences in the inferior parietal cortex. *European Journal of Neuroscience, 26,* 791-799.

Petrill, S. A., & Deater-Deckard, K. (2004). The heritability of general cognitive ability: A within-family adoption design. *Intelligence, 32,* 403-409.

Pettigrew, T. F., & Tropp, L. R. (2006). A meta-analytic test of intergroup contact theory. *Journal of Personality and Social Psychology, 90,* 751-783.

Pezoulas, V. C., Zervakis, M., Michelogiannis, S., & Klados, M. A. (2017). Resting-state functional connectivity and network analysis of cerebellum with respect to crystallized IQ and gender. *Frontiers in Human Neuroscience, 11,* 1-10.

Pfaff, D. W. (2014). *The altruistic brain: How we are naturally good.* Oxford: Oxford University Press.

Phalen, P. L., Dimaggio, G., Popolo, R., & Lysaker, P. H. (2017). Aspects of Theory of Mind that attenuate the relationship between persecutory delusions and social functioning in schizophrenia spectrum disorders. *Journal of Behavior Therapy and Experimental Psychiatry, 56,* 65-70.

Phillips, M. (2013, December 12). The lobotomy files. *Wall Street Journal,* p. A1.

Phillips, W. L. (2019). Cross-cultural differences in visual perception of color, illusions, depth, and pictures. *Cross-Cultural Psychology: Contemporary Themes and Perspectives,* 287-308.

Philpot, R., Liebst, R., Suonpera, L., Bernasco, M., Lindegaard, W., & Rosenkrantz, M. (2019). Would I be helped? Cross-national CCTV footage shows that intervention is the norm in public conflicts. *American Psychologist.* Advance online publication. doi:10.1037/amp0000469.

Phinney, J. S. (2003). Ethnic identity and acculturation. In K. M. Chun, O. Balls, & P. Organista (Eds.), *Acculturation: Advances in theory, measurement, and applied research.* Washington, DC: American Psychological Association.

Phua, J., Jin, S. V., & Kim, J. (. (2017). Uses and gratifications of social networking sites for bridging and bonding social capital: A comparison of Facebook, Twitter, Instagram, and Snapchat. *Computers in Human Behavior, 72,* 115-122.

Phukhachee, T., Maneewongvatana, S., Angsuwatanakul, T., Iramina, K., & Kaewkamnerd-pong, B. (2019). Investigating the effect of intrinsic motivation on alpha desynchronization using sample entropy. *Entropy, 21*(3), 237.

Pi-Sunyer, X. (2003). A clinical view of the obesity problem. *Science, 299,* 859-860.

Piaget, J. (1970). Piaget's theory. In P. H. Mussen (Ed.), *Carmichael's manual of child psychology* (3rd ed., Vol. I). New York: Wiley.

Piaget, J., & Inhelder, B. (1958). *The growth of logical thinking from childhood to adolescence* (A. Parsons & S. Seagrin, Trans.). New York: Basic Books.

Pickel, K. (2009). The weapon focus effect on memory for female versus male perpetrators. *Memory, 17,* 664-678.

Pickering, G. J., & Gordon, R. (2006). Perception of mouthfeel sensations elicited by red wine are associated with sensitivity to 6-N-propylthiouracil. *Journal of Sensory Studies, 21,* 249-265.

Pieper, J., Chang, D. G., Mahasin, S. Z., Swan, A. R., Quinto, A. A., Nichols, S. L., et al. (2019). Brain amygdala volume increases in veterans and active-duty military personnel with combat-related posttraumatic stress disorder and mild traumatic brain injury. *Journal of Head Trauma Rehabilitation.* Advance online publication. doi: 10.1097/HTR.0000000000000492.

Pietromonaco, P., & Collins, N. L. (2017). Interpersonal mechanisms linking close relationships to health. *American Psychologist, 72,* 531-542.

Pietschnig, J., & Voracek, M. (2015). One century of global IQ gains: A formal meta-analysis of the Flynn effect (1909-2013). *Perspectives on Psychological Science, 10*(3), 282-306.

Pijnenborg, G. M., Timmerman, M. E., Derks, E. M., Fleischhacker, W. W., Kahn, R. S., & Aleman, A. (2015). Differential effects of antipsychotic drugs on insight in first episode schizophrenia: Data from the European First-Episode Schizophrenia Trial (EUFEST). *European Neuropsychopharmacology, 25,* 808-816.

Pillai, A., Schooler, N. R., Peter, D., Looney, S. W., Goff, D. C., Kopelowicz, A., et al. (2018). Predicting relapse in schizophrenia: Is BDNF a plausible biological marker? *Schizophrenia Research, 193,* 263-268.

Pillay, S. S., Rogowska, J., Gruber, S. A., Simpson, N., & Yurgelun-Todd, D. A. (2007). Recognition of happy facial affect in panic disorder: an fMRI study. *Journal of Anxiety Disorders, 21,* 381-393.

Pinal, D., Zurrón, M., & Díaz, F. (2015). Age-related changes in brain activity are specific for high order cognitive processes during successful encoding of information in working memory. *Frontiers in Aging Neuroscience, 7,* 88-97.

Pincus, T., & Morley, S. (2001). Cognitive processing bias in chronic pain: A review and integration. *Psychological Bulletin, 127,* 599-617.

Pinker, S. (1994). *The language instinct.* New York: William Morrow.

Pinker, S. (2004). Clarifying the logical problem of language acquisition. *Journal of Child Language, 31,* 949-953.

Pinker, S. (2019, July 18). Bystanders who intervene in an attack. *Wall Street Journal,* p. C2.

Pinker, S., & Jackendoff, R. (2005). The faculty of language: What's special about it? *Cognition, 96,* 201-236.

Pinkerton, S. D., Bogart, L. M., Cecil, H., & Abramson, P. R. (2002). Factors associated with masturbation in a collegiate sample. *Journal of Psychology and Human Sexuality, 14,* 103-121.

Pinky, P. D., Bloemer, J., Smith, W. D., Moore, T., Hong, H., Suppiramaniam, V., et al. (2019). Prenatal cannabinoid exposure and altered neurotransmission. *Neuropharmacology, 149,* 181-194.

Pinquart, M., & Kauser, R. (2017). Do the associations of parenting styles with behavior problems and academic achievement vary by culture? Results from a meta-analysis. *Cultural Diversity and Ethnic Minority Psychology.* Accessed from https://www.ncbi.nlm.nih.gov/pubmed/28394165.

Pisarik, C. T., Rowell, P., & Currie, L. K. (2013). Work-related daydreams: A qualitative content analysis. *Journal of Career Development, 40,* 87-106.

Planalp, E. M., & Goldsmith, H. H. (2019). Observed profiles of infant temperament: Stability, heritability, and associations with parenting. *Child Development.* https://doi.org/10.1111/cdev.13277.

Plante, C., & Anderson, C.A. (2017). Global warming and violent behavior. *APS Observer,* pp. 29-32.

Plemmons, G., Hall, M., Doupnik, S., Gay, J., Brown, C., Browning, W., et al. (2018). Hospitalization for suicide ideation or attempt: 2008-2015. *Pediatrics, 141*(6), 1-10.

Plomin, R. (2005). Finding genes in child psychology and psychiatry: When are we going to be there? *Journal of Child Psychology and Psychiatry, 46,* 1030-1038.

Plomin, R. (2009). The nature of nurture. In K. McCartney & R. A. Weinberg (Eds.), *Experience and development: A festschrift in honor of Sandra Wood Scarr.* New York: Psychology Press.

Plomin, R., & McGuffin, P. (2003). Psychopathology in the postgenomic era. *Annual Review of Psychology, 54,* 205-228.

Pluess, M., & Belsky, J. (2009). Differential susceptibility to rearing experience: The case of childcare. *Journal of Child Psychology and Psychiatry, 50,* 396-404.

Plötner, M., Over, H., Carpenter, M., & Tomasello, M. (2015). Young children show the bystander effect in helping situations. *Psychological Science, 26*(4), 499-506.

Poirier, M., Saint-Aubin, J., Mair, A., Tehan, G., & Tolan, A. (2015). Order recall in verbal short-term memory: The role of semantic networks. *Memory & Cognition, 43,* 489-499.

Polivy, J., Herman, C. P., & Boivin, M. (2005). Eating disorders. In J. E. Maddux & B. A. Winstead (Eds.), *Psychopathology: Foundations for a contemporary understanding.* Mahwah, NJ: Lawrence Erlbaum Associates.

Pollan, M. (2018). *How to change your mind: What the new science of psychedelics teaches us about consciousness, dying, addiction, depression, and transcendence.* New York: Penguin.

Polonsky, D. C. (2006). Review of the big book of masturbation: From angst to zeal. *Journal of Sex & Marital Therapy, 32,* 75-78.

Ponterotto, J. G., Utsey, S. O., & Pedersen, P. B. (2006). *Preventing prejudice: A guide for counselors, educators, and parents.* Thousand Oaks, CA: Sage Publications.

Pontzer, H. (2017). Exercise paradox. *Scientific American, 316,* 28-31.

Pool, E., Rehme, A. K., Fink, G. R., Eickhoff, S. B., & Grefkes, C. (2013). Network dynamics engaged in the modulation of motor behavior in healthy subjects. *Neuroimage, 88,* 68-76.

Popov, V, Marevic, I., Rummel, J., & Reder, L.M. (2019). Forgetting is a feature, not a bug: Intentionally forgetting some things helps us remember others by freeing up working memory resources. *Psychological Science,* 1-15.

Popp, D., Donovan, R. A., & Crawford, M. (2003). Gender, race, and speech style stereotypes. *Sex Roles, 48,* 317-325.

Porcerelli, J. H., Bornstein, R. F., Porcerelli, D., & Arterbery, V. E. (2015). The complex role of personality in cancer treatment: Impact of dependency-detachment on health status, distress, and physician-patient relationship. *Journal of Nervous and Mental Disease, 203,* 264-268.

Porkka-Heiskanen, T. (2013). Sleep homeostasis. *Current Opinion in Neurobiology, 23,* 799-805.

Posada, G., & Trumbell, J. M. (2017). Universality and cultural specificity in child-mother attachment relationships: In search of answers. In S. Gojman-de-Millan, C. Herreman, & L. A. Sroufe (Eds.), *Attachment across clinical and cultural perspectives: A relational psychoanalytic approach.* New York: Routledge/Taylor & Francis Group.

Post, C., & Leuner, B. (2019). The maternal reward system in postpartum depression. *Archives of Women's Mental Health, 22*(3), 417-429.

Post, J. M. (2015, April). Terrorism and right-wing extremism: The changing face of terrorism and political violence in the 21st century: The virtual community of hatred. (Special issue: Violence in America: Part II.) *International Journal of Group Psychotherapy, 65*(2), 243-271.

Potash, J. S. (2015). Archetypal aesthetics: Viewing art through states of consciousness. *International Journal of Jungian Studies, 7,* 139-153.

Pottick, K. J., Kirk, S. A., Hsieh, D. K., & Tian, X. (2007). Judging mental disorder in youths: Effects of client, clinician, and contextual differences. *Journal of Consulting Clinical Psychology, 75,* 1-8.

Pow, A. M., & Cashwell, C. S. (2017). Posttraumatic stress disorder and emotion-focused coping among disaster mental health counselors. *Journal of Counseling & Development, 95*(3), 322-331.

Pow, J. L., Baumeister, A. A., Hawkins, M. F., Cohen, A. S., & Garand, J. C. (2015). Deinstitutionalization of American public hospitals for the mentally ill before and after the introduction of antipsychotic medications. *Harvard Review of Psychiatry, 23,* 176-187.

Powell, L. H. (2006). Review of marital and sexual lifestyles in the United States: Attitudes, behaviors, and relationships in social context. *Family Relations, 55,* 149.

Powers, K. D. (2006). An analysis of Kohlbergian moral development in relationship to biblical factors of morality in seminary students (Lawrence Kohlberg). *Dissertation Abstracts International: Section B: The Sciences and Engineering, 67*(6-B), 3485.

Powers, K. L., Brooks, P. J., Aldrich, N. J., Palladino, M. A., & Alfieri, L. (2013). Effects of video-game play on information processing: A meta-analytic investigation. *Psychonomic Bulletin & Review, 20,* 1055-1079.

Pozzan, L., & Valian, V. (2017). Asking questions in child English: Evidence for early abstract representations. *Language Acquisition: A Journal of Developmental Linguistics, 24,* 209-233.

Prasser, J., Schecklmann, M., Poeppl, T. B., Frank, E., Kreuzer, P. M., Hajak, G., et al. (2015). Bilateral prefrontal rTMS and theta burst TMS as an add-on treatment for depression: A randomized placebo controlled trial. *World Journal of Biological Psychiatry, 16,* 57-65.

Pratkanis, A. R. (2007). Social influence analysis: An index of tactics. In A. R. Pratkanis (Ed.), *The science of social influence: Advances and future progress.* New York: Psychology Press.

Pratkanis, A. R., Epley, N., & Savitsky, K. (2007). Issue 12: Is subliminal persuasion a myth? In J. A. Nier (Ed.), *Taking sides: Clashing views in social psychology* (2nd ed.). New York: McGraw-Hill.

Pratt, H. D., Phillips, E. L., Greydanus, D. E., & Patel, D. R. (2003). Eating disorders in the adolescent population: Future directions [Special issue: Eating disorders in adolescents]. *Journal of Adolescent Research, 18,* 297-317.

Pratt, L. A., & Brody, D. J. (2014). Depression in the U.S. household population, 2009-2012. NCHS data brief, no. 172. Hyattsville, MD: National Center for Health Statistics.

Pratt, M. W. & Matsuba, M. K. (2019). *The life story, domains of identity, and personality development in emerging adulthood.* New York: Oxford University Press.

Pratto, F., Lee, I., Tan, J. Y., & Pitpitan, E. Y. (2011). Power basis theory: A psychoecological approach to power. In D. Dunning (Ed.), *Social motivation.* New York: Psychology Press.

Prayag, A. S., Najjar, R. P., & Gronfier, C. (2019). Melatonin suppression is exquisitely sensitive to light and primarily driven by melanopsin in humans. *Journal of Pineal Research: Molecular, Biological, Physiological and Clinical Aspects of Melatonin, 66*(4), 1-8.

Pretsch, J., Heckmann, N., Flunger, B., & Schmitt, M. (2013). Agree or disagree? Influences on consensus in personality judgments. *European Journal of Psychological Assessment.* Retrieved from http://psycnet.apa.org/psycinfo/2013-30588-001/.

Price, M. (2008, September). Against doctors' orders. *Monitor on Psychology,* pp. 34-36.

Priester, J. R., & Petty, R. E. (2011). The pot-holed path to happiness, possibly paved with money: A research dialogue. *Journal of Consumer Psychology, 21,* 113-114.

Prieto, J. T., McEwen, D., Davidson, A. J., Al-Tayyib, A., Gawenus, L., Sangareddy, S. R. P., et al. (2019). Monitoring opioid addiction and treatment: Do you know if your population is engaged? *Drug and Alcohol Dependence, 202,* 56-60.

Prince, C. V. (2005). Homosexuality, transvestism and transsexuality: Reflections on their etymology and differentiation. *International Journal of Transgenderism, 8,* 15-18.

Prinz, J. J. (2007). Emotion: Competing theories and philosophical issues. In P. Thagard (Ed.), *Philosophy of psychology and cognitive science.* Amsterdam, Netherlands: North Holland/Elsevier.

Prior, K. N., & Bond, M. J. (2017). Patterns of "abnormal" illness behavior among healthy individuals. *American Journal of Health Behavior, 41,* 139-146.

Proffitt, D. R. (2006). Distance perception. *Current Directions in Psychological Science, 15,* 131-139.

Prohovnik, I., Skudlarski, P., Fulbright, R. K., Gore, J. C., & Wexler, B. E. (2004). Functional MRI changes before and after onset of reported emotions. *Psychiatry Research: Neuroimaging, 132,* 239-250.

Proudfoot, D. (2009). Meaning and mind: Wittgenstein's relevance for the "does language shape thought?" debate. *New Ideas in Psychology, 27,* 163-183.

Proyer, R. T., Gander, F., Wellenzohn, S., & Ruch, W. (2013). What good are character strengths beyond subjective well-being? The contribution of the good character on self-reported health-oriented behavior, physical fitness, and the subjective health status. *Journal of Positive Psychology, 8,* 222-232.

Prus, A. J., Mooney-Leber, S. M., Berquist, M. I., Pehrson, A. L., Porter, N. P., & Porter, J. H. (2015). The antidepressant drugs fluoxetine and duloxetine produce anxiolytic-like effects in a schedule-induced polydipsia paradigm in rats: Enhancement of fluoxetine's effects by the a2 adrenoceptor antagonist yohimbine. *Behavioural Pharmacology, 26,* 489-494.

Ptak, R., & Lazeyras, F. (2019). Functional connectivity and the failure to retrieve meaning from shape in visual object agnosia. *Brain and Cognition, 131,* 94-101.

Puca, R. M. (2005). The influence of the achievement motive on probability estimates in pre- and post-decisional action phases. *Journal of Research in Personality, 39,* 245-262.

Purdy, S. C., Sharma, M. M., Munro, K. J., & Morgan, C. A. (2013). Stimulus level effects on speech-evoked obligatory cortical auditory evoked potentials in infants with normal hearing. *Clinical Neurophysiology, 124,* 474-480.

Pérez-Leroux, A. T., Pirvulescu, M., & Roberge, Y. (2011). Topicalization and object omission in child language. *First Language, 31,* 280-299.

Qu, C., Zhang, A., & Chen, Q. (2013). Monetary effects on fear conditioning. *Psychological Reports, 112,* 353-364.

Quartana, P. J., & Burns, J. W. (2007). Painful consequences of anger suppression. *Emotion, 7,* 400-414.

Quinn, K., Pacella, M. L., Dickson-Gomez, J., & Nydegger, L. A. (2017). Childhood adversity and the continued exposure to trauma and violence among adolescent gang members. *American Journal of Community Psychology, 59,* 36-49.

Quinn, P. C., Lee, K., & Pascalis, O. (2018). Perception of face race by infants: Five developmental changes. *Child Development, 12,* 204-209.

Quinn, T. C., & Overbaugh, J. (2005). HIV/AIDS in women: An expanding epidemic. *Science, 308,* 1582-1583.

Quintana, S. M., Aboud, F. E., & Chao, R. K. (2006). Race, ethnicity, and culture in child development: Contemporary research and future directions. *Child Development, 77,* 1129-1141.

Rabin, J. (2004). Quantification of color vision with cone contrast sensitivity. *Visual Neuroscience, 21,* 483-485.

Rabin, R. C. (2013, August 13). A glut of antidepressants. *The New York Times,* p. D4.

Racine, S. E., VanHuysse, J. L., Keel, P. K., Burt, S. A., Neale, M. C., Boker, S., et al. (2017). Eating disorder-specific risk factors moderate the relationship between negative urgency and binge eating: A behavioral genetic investigation. *Journal of Abnormal Psychology, 126,* 481-494.

Radford, J. (2019, June 17). Key findings about U.S. immigrants. Pew Research Center. Downloaded from https://www.pewresearch.org/fact-tank/2019/06/17/key-findings-about-u-s-immigrants/, September 14, 2019.

Radvansky, G. A. (2010). *Human memory.* New York: Psychology Press.

Radvansky, G. A., Pettijohn, K. A., & Kim, J. (2015). Walking through doorways causes forgetting: Younger and older adults. *Psychology and Aging, 30,* 259-265.

Raffin, E., Richard, N., Giraux, P., & Reilly, K. T. (2016). Primary motor cortex changes after amputation correlate with phantom limb pain and the ability to move the phantom limb. *Neuroimage, 130,* 134-144.

Ragins, B., & Winkel, D. E. (2011). Gender, emotion and power in work relationships. *Human Resource Management Review, 21,* 377-393.

Ragland, J. D., Layher, E., Hannula, D. E., Niendam, T.A., Lesh, T.A., Solomon, M., et al. (2015). Impact of schizophrenia on anterior and posterior hippocampus during memory for complex scenes. *Neuroimage Clinics, 13,* 82-88.

Rahman, Q., & Yusuf, S. (2015). Lateralization for processing facial emotions in gay men, heterosexual men, and heterosexual women. *Archives of Sexual Behavior, 44,* 1405-1413.

Rahman, Q., Kumari, V., & Wilson, G. D. (2003). Sexual orientation-related differences in pre-pulse inhibition of the human startle response. *Behavioral Neuroscience, 117,* 1096-1102.

Rajecki, D. W., & Borden, V. M. H. (2011). Psychology degrees: Employment, wage, and career trajectory consequences. *Perspectives on Psychological Science, 6,* 321-335.

Rajsic, J., Wilson, D. E., & Pratt, J. (2015). Confirmation bias in visual search. *Journal of Experimental Psychology: Human Perception and Performance. 41*(5), 1353-1364.

Ramachandran, Vilayanur S., and Edward M. Hubbard. (2006). Hearing colors, tasting shapes. *Scientific American, 16,* 76-83.

Ramchand, R., Jaycox, L., Ebener, P., Gilbert, M. L., Barnes-Proby, D., & Goutam, P. (2017). Characteristics and proximal outcomes of calls made to suicide crisis hotlines in California: Variability across centers. *Crisis: The Journal of Crisis Intervention and Suicide Prevention, 38*(1), 26-35.

Ramos, R. A., Ferguson, C. J., Frailing, K., & Romero-Ramirez, M. (2013). Comfortably numb or just yet another movie? Media violence exposure does not reduce viewer empathy for victims of real violence among primarily Hispanic viewers. *Psychology of Popular Media Culture, 2,* 2-10.

Randall, D. K. (2012, August 4-5). Decoding the science of sleep. *Wall Street Journal,* pp. C1-C2.

Randolph-Seng, B., & Nielsen, M. E. (2009). Opening the doors of perception: Priming altered states of consciousness outside of conscious awareness. *Archiv für Religionspsychologie/Archive for the Psychology of Religions, 31,* 237-260.

Rangell, L. (2007). *The road to unity in psychoanalytic theory.* Lanham, MD: Jason Aronson.

Ranscombe, P. (2019). The PET and the pendulum: investigating hypnosis and the brain. *The Lancet Psychiatry, 6*(6), 475-476.

Rapaport, M., Nierenberg, A. A., Howland, R., Dording, C., Schettler, P. J., & Mischoulon, D. (2011). The treatment of minor depression with St. John's wort or citalopram: Failure to show benefit over placebo. *Journal of Psychiatric Research, 45,* 931-941.

Rasch, B., Buchel, C., Gais, S., & Born, J. (2007). Odor cues during slow-wave sleep prompt declarative memory consolidation. *Science, 315,* 1426.

Raskin, N. J., & Rogers, C. R. (1989). Person-centered therapy. In R. J. Corsini & D. Wedding (Eds.), *Current psychotherapies* (4th ed.). Itasca, IL: F. E. Peacock.

Rassin, E., & Muris, P. (2007). Abnormal and normal obsessions: A reconsideration. *Behaviour Research and Therapy, 45,* 1065-1070.

Rastrelli, G., Cipriani, S., Corona, G., Vignozzi, L., & Maggi, M. (2019). Clinical characteristics of men complaining of premature ejaculation together with erectile dysfunction: A cross-sectional study. *Andrology, 7*(2), 163-171.

Ravallion, M., & Lokshin, M. (2010). Who cares about relative deprivation? *Journal of Economic Behavior & Organization, 73*(2), 171-185. doi:10.1016/j.jebo.2009.08.008.

Ravicz, M.M., Perdue, K.L., Westerlund, A., Vanderwert, R.E. and Nelson, C.A. (2015). Infants' neural responses to facial emotion in the prefrontal cortex are correlated with temperament: A functional near-infrared spectroscopy study. *Frontiers in Psychology. 6,* 922.

Ravindran, A., Richter, M., Jain, T., Ravindran, L., Rector, N., & Farb, N. (2019). Functional connectivity in obsessive-compulsive disorder and its subtypes. *Psychological medicine,* 1-9.

Ray, J. V., Thornton, L. C., Frick, P. J., Steinberg, L., & Cauffman, E. (2015). Impulse control and callous-unemotional traits distinguish patterns of delinquency and substance use in justice involved adolescents: Examining the moderating role of neighborhood context. *Journal of Abnormal Child Psychology, 43*(9), 1190-1203.

Ray, L., Bryan, A., MacKillop, J., McGeary, J., Hesterberg, K., & Hutchison, K. (2009). The dopamine D4 receptor gene exon III polymorphism, problematic alcohol use and novelty seeking: Direct and mediated genetic effects. *Addiction Biology, 14,* 238-244.

Ray, L. A., & Hutchison, K. E. (2007). Effects of naltrexone on alcohol sensitivity and genetic moderators of medication response: A double-blind placebo-controlled study. *Archives of General Psychiatry, 64,* 1069-1077.

Ray, R., Loughead, J., Wang, Z., Detre, J., Yang, E., Gur, R., et al. (2008). Neuroimaging, genetics and the treatment of nicotine addiction. *Behavioural Brain Research, 193,* 159-169.

Raz, A. (2007). Suggestibility and hypnotizability: Mind the gap. *American Journal of Clinical Hypnosis, 49,* 205-210.

Raznahan, A., Lee, Y., Stidd, R., Long, R., Greenstein, D., Clasen, L., et al. (2010). Longitudinally mapping the influence of sex and androgen signaling on the dynamics of human cortical maturation in adolescence. *Proceedings of the National Academy of Sciences, 107,* 16988-16993.

Rea, L.M., & Parker, R.A. (2014). *Designing and conducting survey research: A comprehensive guide* (4th ed.). New York: Jossey-Bass.

Reddy, P. H., Amakiri, N., Tran, J., & Kubosumi, A. (2019). Amyloid beta and microRNAs in Alzheimer's disease. *Frontiers in Neuroscience, 13,* 430.

Reddy, S. (2013, March 19). People who taste too much. *Wall Street Journal,* p. D1.

Reddy, S. (2013, September 3). A field guide to the perfect nap. *Wall Street Journal,* pp. D1-D2.

Reddy, S. (2015, May 19.) How doctors break bad news. *Wall Street Journal,* pp. D1, D4.

Reddy, S. (2016, May 10). When daydreaming becomes a problem. *Wall Street Journal,* pp. D1, D4.

Reddy, S. (2019, July 1). Challenging the stigma of "shock therapy." *Wall Street Journal,* p. A14.

Redford, M. A. (2017). Sound categories or phonemes? *British Journal of Psychology, 108,* 34-36.

Redick, T. S., Unsworth, N., Kane, M. J., & Hambrick, D. Z. (2017). Don't shoot the messenger: Still no evidence that video-game experience is related to cognitive abilities–A reply to Green et al (2017). *Psychological Science, 28*(5), 683-686.

Redick, T. S., Wiemers, E. A., & Engle, R. W. (2019). The role of proactive interference in working memory training and transfer. *Psychological Research,* 1-20.

Redish, A. D. (2004). Addiction as a computational process gone awry. *Science, 306,* 1944-1947.

Redshaw, M., & Martin, C. (2013). Babies, "bonding" and ideas about parental "attachment."
Journal of Reproductive and Infant Psychology, 31, 219-221.

Reed, P. (2007). Response rate and sensitivity to the molar feedback function relating response and reinforcement rate on VI+ schedules of reinforcement. *Journal of Experimental Psychology: Animal Behavior Processes, 33,* 428-439.

Reed, S. K. (2017). Problem solving. In S. F. Chipman, (Ed.), *The Oxford handbook of cognitive science.* New York: Oxford University Press.

Rees, P., & Seaton, N. (2011). Psychologists' response to crises: International perspectives. *School Psychology International, 32,* 73-94.

Regnerus, M., Price, J., & Gordon, D. (2017). Masturbation and partnered sex: Substitutes or complements? *Archives of Sexual Behavior, 46*(7), 2111-2121.

Rehan, W., Antfolk, J., Johansson, A., & Santtila, P. (2019). Do single experiences of childhood abuse increase psychopathology symptoms in adulthood? *Journal of Interpersonal Violence, 34*(5), 1021-1038.

Reich, D. (2018, March 23). 'Race' in the age of modern genetics. *The New York Times,* p. SR1.

Reichenberg, A., & Harvey, P. D. (2007). Neuropsychological impairments in schizophrenia: Integration of performance-based and brain imaging findings. *Psychological Bulletin, 133,* 212-223.

Reichenberg, A., Harvey, P., Bowie, C., Mojtabai, R., Rabinowitz, J., Heaton, R., et al. (2009). Neuropsychological function and dysfunction in schizophrenia and psychotic affective disorders. *Schizophrenia Bulletin, 35,* 1022-1029.

Reid, J. L., Martin, A., & Brooks-Gunn, J. (2017). Low-income parents' adult interactions at childcare centres. *Early Child Development and Care, 187,* 138-151.

Reid, J. R., MacLeod, J., & Robertson, J. R. (2010). Cannabis and the lung. *Journal of the Royal College of Physicians, 40,* 328 -334.

Reijonen, J. H., Pratt, H. D., Patel, D. R., & Greydanus, D. E. (2003). Eating disorders in the adolescent population: An overview [Special issue: Eating disorders in adolescents]. *Journal of Adolescent Research, 18,* 209-222.

Reilly, E. D., Rackley, K. R., & Awad, G. H. (2017). Perceptions of male and female STEM aptitude: The moderating effect of benevolent and hostile sexism. *Journal of Career Development, 44,* 159-173.

Reilly, M. T., Noronha, A., Goldman, D., & Koob, G. F. (2017). Genetic studies of alcohol dependence in the context of the addiction cycle. *Neuropharmacology, 12,* 23-21.

Reilly, T., & Waterhouse, J. (2007). Altered sleep-wake cycles and food intake: The Ramadan model. *Physiology & Behavior, 90,* 219-228.

Reiner, R. (2008). Integrating a portable biofeedback device into clinical practice for patients with anxiety disorders: Results of a pilot study. *Applied Psychophysiology and Biofeedback, 33,* 55-61.

Reinisch, J. M., Mortensen, E. L., & Sanders, S. A. (2017). Prenatal exposure to progesterone affects sexual orientation in humans. *Archives of Sexual Behavior, 46*(5), 1239-1249.

Reisberg, D. (1997). *Cognition: Exploring the science of the mind.* New York: Norton.

Reisberg, D. (2009). *Cognition: Exploring the science of the mind.* New York: Norton.

Reisberg, D. (2013). Mental images. In D. Reisberg (Ed.), *The Oxford handbook of cognitive psychology.* New York: Oxford University Press.

Reisner, A. D., Piel, J., & Makey, M. (2013). Competency to stand trial and defendants who lack insight into their mental illness. *Journal of the American Academy of Psychiatry and the Law, 41*, 85-91.

Reks, S., Sheaves, B., & Freeman, D. (2017, July 15.) Nightmares in the general population: Identifying potential causal factors. *Social Psychiatry and Psychiatric Epidemiology.*doi: 10.1007/s00127-017-1408-7.

Remington, G., Foussias, G., Fervaha, G., & Agid, O. (2014). Schizophrenia, cognition, and psychosis. *JAMA Psychiatry, 71*, 336-337.

Ren, X., Wang, T., & Jarrold, C. (2016). Individual differences in frequency of inner speech: Differential relations with cognitive and non-cognitive factors. *Frontiers in Psychology, 7*, 1675.

Renshaw, D. C. (2006). Male and female circumcision today. *The Family Journal, 14*, 283-285.

Rentzou, K., Slutsky, R., Tuul, M., Gol-Guven, M., Kragh-Muller, G., Foerch, D. F., et al. (2019). Preschool teachers' conceptualizations and uses of play across eight countries. *Early Childhood Education Journal, 47*(1), 1-14.

Repp, B. H., & Knoblich, G. (2007). Action can affect auditory perception. *Psychological Science, 18*, 6-7.

Ressler, R. L., & Maren, S. (2019). Synaptic encoding of fear memories in the amygdala. *Current Opinion in Neurobiology, 54*, 54-59.

Reynolds, C. A., & Maughan, E. D. (2015). Telehealth in the school setting: An integrative review. *Journal of School Nursing, 31*, 44-53.

Reynolds, C. R., & Ramsay, M. C. (2003). Bias in psychological assessment: An empirical review and recommendations. In J. R. Graham & J. A. Naglieri (Eds.), *Handbook of psychology: Assessment psychology* (Vol. 10). New York: Wiley.

Reznikova, T. N., Seliverstova, N. A., Kataeva, G. V., Aroev, R. A., Ilves, A. G., & Kuznetsova, A. K. (2015). Functional activity of brain structures and predisposition to aggression in patients with lingering diseases of the CNS. *Human Physiology, 41*, 27-33.

Ribas-Fernandes, J. J. F., Shahnazian, D., Holroyd, C. B., & Botvinick, M. M. (2019). Subgoal- and goal-related reward prediction errors in medial prefrontal cortex. *Journal of Cognitive Neuroscience, 31*(1), 8-23.

Riccelli, R., Toschi, N., Nigro, S., Terracciano, A. & Passamonti, L. (2017). Surface-based morphometry reveals the neuroanatomical basis of the five-factor model of personality. *Social Cognitive and Affective Neuroscience, 12*, 671-684

Rice, C. (2009). Prevalence of autism spectrum disorders–Autism and Developmental Disabilities Monitoring Network, United States, 2006. *MMWR, 58*(SS10), 1-20.

Richard, D. C. S., & Lauterbach, D. (Eds.). (2006). *Handbook of exposure therapies.* New York: Academic Press.

Richards, C. (2011). Transsexualism and existentialism. *Existential Analysis, 22*(2), 272-279.

Richards, R. (2006). Frank Barron and the study of creativity: A voice that lives on. *Journal of Humanistic Psychology, 46*, 352-370.

Richardson, D., & Hammock, G. S. (2011). Is it aggression? Perceptions of and motivations for passive and psychological aggression. In J. P. Forgas, A. W. Kruglanski, & K. D. Williams (Eds.), *The psychology of social conflict and aggression.* New York: Psychology Press.

Richmond, A. S., Broussard, K. A., Sterns, J. L., Sanders, K. K., & Shardy, J. C. (2015). Who are we studying? Sample diversity in teaching of psychology research. *Teaching of Psychology, 42*, 218-226.

Ricker, T. J., Sandry, J., Vergauwe, E., & Cowan, N. (2019). Do familiar memory items decay? *Journal of Experimental Psychology: Learning, Memory, and Cognition.* http://dx.doi.org/10.1037/xlm0000719.

Rideout, V. (2018). The Common Sense census: Media use by tweens and teens. Common Sense Media. Retrieved from https://www.commonsensemedia.org/sites/default/files/uploads/research/census.researchreport.pdf.

Rieber, R. W., & Robinson, D. K. (2006). Review of the essential Vygotsky. *Journal of the History of the Behavioral Sciences, 42*, 178-180.

Riener, C. (2019). New approaches and debates on top-down perceptual processing. *Teaching of Psychology, 46*(3), 267-272.

Rigby, L., & Waite, S. (2007). Group therapy for self-esteem: Using creative approaches and metaphor as clinical tools. *Behavioural and Cognitive Psychotherapy, 35*, 361-364.

Rimmele, J. M., Sussman, E., & Poeppel, D. (2015). The role of temporal structure in the investigation of sensory memory, auditory scene analysis, and speech perception: A healthy-aging perspective. *International Journal of Psychophysiology, 95*, 175-183.

Rinaman, L., Banihashemi, L., & Koehnle, T. J. (2011). Early life experience shapes the functional organization of stress-responsive visceral circuits. *Physiology & Behavior, 104*, 632-640.

Rindermann, H., Becker, D., & Coyle, T. R. (2017). Survey of expert opinion on intelligence: The Flynn effect and the future of intelligence. *Personality and Individual Differences, 106*, 242-247.

Rindone, H. G. (2015). Methamphetamine addiction. In R. L. Smith (Ed.), *Treatment strategies for substance and process addictions.* Alexandria, VA: American Counseling Association.

Riniolo, T. C., Koledin, M., Drakulic, G. M., & Payne, R. A. (2003). An archival study of eyewitness memory of the Titanic's final plunge. *Journal of General Psychology, 130*, 89-95.

Rinn, W. E. (1991). Neuropsychology of facial expression. In R. S. Feldman & B. Rimé (Eds.), *Fundamentals of non-verbal behavior.* Cambridge, England: Cambridge University Press.

Ripley, A. (2005, March 7). Who says a woman can't be Einstein? *Time,* pp. 51-60.

Risen, J. (2015, August 8). Association bars psychologists from ties to U.S. national security interrogations. *The New York Times,* p. A11.

Ritchie, H, & Roser, M. (2018, April). Mental health. Our World in Data. Downloaded from https://ourworldindata.org/mental-health.

Rizzi, T. S., & Posthuma, D. (2013). Genes and intelligence. In D. Reisberg (Ed.), *The Oxford handbook of cognitive psychology.* New York: Oxford University Press.

Robb, M. B. (2019). *The new normal: Parents, teens, screens, and sleep in the United States.* San Francisco, CA: Common Sense Media.

Robbins, M. L., Wright, R. C., María López, A., & Weihs, K. (2019). Interpersonal positive reframing in the daily lives of couples coping with breast cancer. *Journal of Psychosocial Oncology, 37*(2), 160-177.

Robbins, T. W., Vaghi, M. M., & Banca, P. (2019). Obsessive-compulsive disorder: Puzzles and prospects. *Neuron, 102*(1), 27-47.

Roberts, R. M., Neate, G. M., & Gierasch, A. (2017). Implicit attitudes towards people with visible difference: Findings from an Implicit Association Test. *Psychology, Health & Medicine, 22*, 352-358.

Robinson, D. N. (2007). Theoretical psychology: What is it and who needs it? *Theory & Psychology, 17*, 187-198.

Robinson, N. M. (2003). Two wrongs do not make a right: Sacrificing the needs of gifted students does not solve society's unsolved problems. *Journal for the Education of the Gifted, 26*, 251-273.

Robinson, T. N., Banda, J. A., Hale, L., Lu, A. S., Fleming-Milici, F., Calvert, S. L., et al. (2017). Screen media exposure and obesity in children and adolescents. *Pediatrics, 140*(Supplement 2), S97-S101.

Robinson-Papp, J., George, M. C., Dorfman, D., & Simpson, D. M. (2015). Barriers to chronic pain measurement: A qualitative study of patient perspectives. *Pain Medicine, 16*, 1256-1264.

Robson, H., Grube, M., Lambon Ralph, M. A., Griffiths, T. D., & Sage, K. (2013). Fundamental deficits of auditory perception in Wernicke's aphasia. *Cortex: A Journal Devoted to the Study of the Nervous System and Behavior, 40*(7), 1808-1822.

Rodrigues, L., & Girandola, F. (2017). Self-prophecies and cognitive dissonance: Habit, norms and justification of past behavior. *North American Journal of Psychology, 19*, 65-86.

Rodrigues-Amorim, D., Rivera-Baltanás, T., López, M., Spuch, C., Olivares, J. M., & Agís-Balboa, R. C. (2017). Schizophrenia: A review of potential biomarkers. *Journal of Psychiatric Research, 93,* 37–49.

Roediger, H. L., III, & McCabe, D. P. (2007). Evaluating experimental research: Critical issues. In R. J. Sternberg, H. L. Roediger, III, & D. F. Halpern (Eds.), *Critical thinking in psychology.* New York: Cambridge University Press.

Roen, K. (2019). Intersex or diverse sex development: Critical review of psychosocial health care research and indications for practice. *Journal of Sex Research, 56*(4–5), 511–528.

Roffman, R. A. (2013). Legalization of marijuana: Unraveling quandaries for the addiction professional. *Frontiers in Psychiatry, 4,* 88–93.

Rogalsky, C., Love, T., Driscoll, D., Anderson, S. W., & Hickok, G. (2011). Are mirror neurons the basis of speech perception? Evidence from five cases with damage to the purported human mirror system. *Neurocase, 17,* 178–187.

Rogers, B., & Naumenko, O. (2015). The new moon illusion and the role of perspective in the perception of straight and parallel lines. *Attention, Perception, & Psychophysics, 77,* 249–257.

Rogers, C. R. (1951). *Client-centered therapy.* Boston: Houghton-Mifflin.

Rogers, C. R. (1971). A theory of personality. In S. Maddi (Ed.), *Perspectives on personality.* Boston: Little, Brown.

Rogers, C. R. (1995). *A way of being.* Boston: Houghton Mifflin.

Rogers, J. M. (2009). Tobacco and pregnancy: Overview of exposures and effects. *Birth Defects Research Part C: Embryo Today, 84,* 152–160.

Rogers, S. (2007). The underlying mechanisms of semantic memory loss in Alzheimer's disease and semantic dementia. *Dissertation Abstracts International: Section B: The Sciences and Engineering, 67*(10-B), 5591.

Rogoff, B., Coppens, A. D., Alcalá, L., Aceves-Azuara, I., Ruvalcaba, O., López, A., et al. (2017). Noticing learners' strengths through cultural research. *Perspectives on Psychological Science, 12*(5), 876–888.

Rohan, K. J., Meyerhoff, J., Ho, S.-Y., Roecklein, K. A., Nillni, Y. I., Hillhouse, J. J., et al. (2019). A measure of cognitions specific to seasonal depression: Development and validation of the Seasonal Beliefs Questionnaire. *Psychological Assessment, 31*(7), 925–938.

Roid, G., Nellis, L., & McLellan, M. (2003). Assessment with the Leiter International Performance Scale–Revised and the S-BIT. In R. S. McCallum & R. Steve (Eds.), *Handbook of nonverbal assessment.* New York: Kluwer Academic/Plenum Publishers.

Rolles-Abraham, K.L. (2020, April 27). How my patients and I struggle with remote mental health treatment during circuit breaker. *TODAY.* Downloaded from https://www.today-online.com/commentary/how-patients-and-i-struggle-remote-mental-health-treatment-covid-19-circuit-breaker.

Rolls, E. T. (2011). Functions of human emotional memory: The brain and emotion. In S.

Nalbantian, P. M. Matthews, & J. L. McClelland (Eds.), *The memory process: Neuroscientific and humanistic perspectives.* Cambridge, MA: MIT Press.

Rom, S. A., Miller, L., & Peluso, J. (2009). Playing the game: Psychological factors in surviving cancer. *International Journal of Emergency Mental Health, 11,* 25–36.

Romani, C., Palermo, L., MacDonald, A., Limback, E., Hall, S. K., & Geberhiwot, T. (2017). The impact of phenylalanine levels on cognitive outcomes in adults with phenylketonuria: Effects across tasks and developmental stages. *Neuropsychology, 31,* 242–254.

Romero-Guevara, R., Cencetti, F., Donati, C., & Bruni, P. (2015). Sphingosine 1-phosphate signaling pathway in inner ear biology. New therapeutic strategies for hearing loss? *Frontiers in Aging Neuroscience, 7,* 101–111.

Romero-Lebrón, E., Oviedo, D. M. A., Elias, D., Vrech, D. E., & Peretti, A. V. (2019). Effect of the mating plug on female chemical attractiveness and mating acceptance in a scorpion. *Ethology, 125*(4), 184–194.

Roncero, C., Daigre, C., Gonzalvo, B., Valero, S., Castells, X., Grau-López, L., et al. (2013). Risk factors for cocaine-induced psychosis in cocaine-dependent patients. *European Psychiatry, 28,* 141–146.

Ronconi, L., Casartelli, L., Carna, S., Molteni, M., Arrigoni, F., & Borgatti, R. (2017). When one is enough: Impaired multisensory integration in cerebellar agenesis. *Cerebral Cortex, 27,* 2041–2051

Rooke, S. E., & Hine, D. W. (2011). A dual process account of adolescent and adult binge drinking. *Addictive Behaviors, 36,* 341–346.

Rooney, E. J. (2019). Considering the costs: Adopting a judicial test for the least restrictive environment mandate of the Individuals with Disabilities Education Act. *Journal of Legislation, 45*(2), 298.

Roos, V., & Zaaiman, R. (2017). Active ageing as positive intervention: Some unintended consequences. In C. Proctor (Ed.), *Positive psychology interventions in practice.* Cham, Switzerland: Springer International Publishing.

Rorschach, H. (1924). *Psychodiagnosis: A diagnostic test based on perception.* New York: Grune & Stratton.

Rosellini, A. J., Stein, M. B., Colpe, L. J., Heeringa, S. G., Petukhova, M. V., Sampson, N. A., et al. (2015). Approximating a DSM-5 diagnosis of PTSD using DSM-IV criteria. *Depression and Anxiety, 32,* 493–501.

Rosen, N. O., Dubé, J. P., Corsini-Munt, S., & Muise, A. (2019). Partners experience consequences, too: A comparison of the sexual, relational, and psychological adjustment of women with sexual interest/arousal disorder and their partners to control couples. *The Journal of Sexual Medicine, 16*(1), 83–95.

Rosenberg, L., & Park, S. (2002). Verbal and spatial functions across the menstrual cycle in healthy young women. *Psychoneuroendocrinology, 27,* 834–841.

Rosenblatt, P. C. (2013). The concept of complicated grief: Lessons from other cultures. In M. Stroebe, H. Schut, & J. van den Bout (Eds.), *Complicated grief: Scientific foundations for health care professionals.* New York: Routledge/Taylor & Francis Group.

Rosenbloom, T., & Wolf, Y. (2002). Sensation seeking and detection of risky road signals: A developmental perspective. *Accident Analysis and Prevention, 34,* 569–580.

Rosenfeld, , R., Gaston, S., Spivak, H., & Irazola, S. (2017, November). Assessing and responding to the recent homicide rise in the United States. Washington, DC: National Institute of Justice.

Rosenfeld, M. J., & Thomas, R. J. (2012). Searching for a mate: The rise of the Internet as a social intermediary. *American Sociological Review, 77,* 523–547.

Rosenhan, D. L. (1973). On being sane in insane places. *Science, 179,* 250–258.

Rosenstein, D. S., & Horowitz, H. A. (1996). Adolescent attachment and psychopathology. *Journal of Consulting and Clinical Psychology, 64,* 244–253.

Rosenström, T., Ystrom, E., Torvik, F. A., Czajkowski, N. O., Gillespie, N. A., Aggen, S. H., et al. (2017). Genetic and environmental structure of DSM-IV criteria for antisocial personality disorder: A twin study. *Behavior Genetics, 47,* 265–277.

Rosenthal, N. F. (2003). *The emotional revolution: How the new science of feeling can transform your life.* New York: Citadel.

Rosenthal, R. (2003). Covert communication in laboratories, classrooms, and the truly real world. *Current Directions in Psychological Science, 12,* 151–154.

Rosenthal-von der Pütten, A. M., Hastall, M. R., Köcher, S., Meske, C., Heinrich, T., Labrenz, F., et al. (2019). "Likes" as social rewards: Their role in online social comparison and decisions to like other people's selfies. *Computers in Human Behavior, 92,* 76–86.

Rosner, H. (2001, April 30). The science of O. *New York Magazine,* pp. 25–31.

Ross, C. A. (2015). When to suspect and how to diagnose dissociative identity disorder. *Journal of EMDR Practice and Research, 9,* 114–120.

Ross, E. D., Gupta, S. S., Adnan, A. M., Holden, T. L., Havlicek, J., & Radhakrishnan, S. (2019). Neurophysiology of spontaneous facial expressions: II. Motor control of the right and left face is partially independent in adults. *Cortex: A Journal Devoted to the Study of the Nervous System and Behavior, 111,* 164–182.

Ross, J. (2006). Sleep on a problem . . . It works like a dream. *The Psychologist, 19,* 738–740.

Ross, L. A., Molholm, S., Blanco, D., Gomez-Ramirez, M., Saint-Amour, D., & Foxe, J. J. (2011). The development of multisensory speech perception continues into the late childhood years. *European Journal of Neuroscience, 33,* 2329–2337.

Ross, P. E. (2004). Draining the language out of color. *Scientific American, 290*(4), 46–51.

Rossato, M., Pagano, C., & Vettor, R. (2008). The cannabinoid system and male reproductive functions. *Journal of Neuroendocrinology, 20,* 90–93.

Rossi-Arnaud, C., Cestari, V., Marques, V. S., Gabrielli, G. B., & Spataro, P. (2017). Collaboration in implicit memory: Evidence from word-fragment completion and category exemplar generation. *Psychological Research, 81,* 55–65.

Rotan, L. W., & Ospina-Kammerer, V. (2007). *Mindbody medicine: Foundations and practical applications.* New York: Routledge/Taylor & Francis Group.

Rouder, J. N., Morey, R. D., & Province, J. M. (2013). A Bayes factor meta-analysis of recent extrasensory perception experiments: Comment on Storm, Tressoldi, and Di Risio (2010). *Psychological Bulletin, 139,* 241–247.

Roughton, R. E. (2002). Rethinking homosexuality: What it teaches us about psychoanalysis. *Journal of the American Psychoanalytic Association, 50,* 733–763.

Routtenberg, A., & Lindy, J. (1965). Effects of the availability of rewarding septal and hypothalamic stimulation on bar pressing for food under conditions of deprivation. *Journal of Comparative and Physiological Psychology, 60,* 158–161.

Roy, M., Moreau, N., Rousseau, C., Mercier, A., Wilson, A., & Atlani-Duault, L. (2019). Ebola and localized blame on social media: Analysis of Twitter and Facebook conversations during the 2014–2015 Ebola epidemic. *Culture, Medicine, and Psychiatry: An International Journal of Cross-Cultural Health Research.* https://doi.org/10.1007/s11013-019-09635-8.

Royzman, E. B., Cassidy, K. W., & Baron, J. (2003). "I know, you know": Epistemic egocentrism in children and adults. *Review of General Psychology, 7,* 38–65.

Rozin, P., Kabnick, K., Pete, E., Fischler, C., & Shields, C. (2003). The ecology of eating: Smaller portion sizes in France than in the United States help explain the French paradox. *Psychological Science, 14,* 450–454.

Rubin, D. C., Schrauf, R. W., Gulgoz, S., & Naka, M. (2007). Cross-cultural variability of component processes in autobiographical remembering: Japan, Turkey, and the USA. *Memory, 15,* 536–547.

Ruiz, M. R. (2015). Behaviourisms: Radical behaviourism and critical inquiry. In I. Parker & I. Parker (Eds.), *Handbook of critical psychology.* New York: Routledge/Taylor & Francis Group.

Rulison, K. L., & Loken, E. (2009). I've fallen and I can't get up: Can high-ability students recover from early mistakes in CAT? *Applied Psychological Measurement, 33,* 83–101.

Runevitch, J. (2019, February 28). Total recall: An IU grad's rare ability creates a map to almost every day of her life. WTHR-TV. Retrieved from https://www.wthr.com/article/total-recall-iu-grads-rare-ability-creates-map-almost-every-day-her-life.

Rushton, J. P., & Jensen, A. R. (2006). The totality of available evidence shows the race IQ gap still remains. *Psychological Science, 17,* 921–922.

Russell, M. J., Masuda, T., Hioki, K., & Singhal, A. (2019). Culture and neuroscience: How Japanese and European Canadians process social context in close and acquaintance relationships. *Social Neuroscience, 14*(4), 484–498.

Russo, N. (1981). Women in psychology. In L. T. Benjamin, Jr. & K. D. Lowman (Eds.), *Activities handbook for the teaching of psychology.* Washington, DC: American Psychological Association.

Rutherford, B., Rose, S., Sneed, J., & Roose, S. (2009, April). Study design affects participant expectations: A survey. *Journal of Clinical Psychopharmacology, 29,* 179–181.

Rutland, A., & Killen, M. (2015). A developmental science approach to reducing prejudice and social exclusion: Intergroup processes, social-cognitive development, and moral reasoning. *Social Issues and Policy Review, 9,* 121–154.

Rutter, M. (2002). Nature, nurture, and development: From evangelism through science toward policy and practice. *Child Development, 73,* 1–21.

Ryan, R. M., & Deci, E. L. (2011). A self-determination theory perspective on social, institutional, cultural, and economic supports for autonomy and their importance for well-being. In V. I. Chirkov, R. M. Ryan, & K. M. Sheldon (Eds.), *Human autonomy in cross-cultural context: Perspectives on the psychology of agency, freedom, and well-being.* New York: Springer Science + Business Media.

Ryan, R. M., & Deci, E. L. (2017). *Self-determination theory: Basic psychological needs in motivation, development, and wellness.* New York: Guilford Press.

Rymer, R. (1994). *Genie: A scientific tragedy.* New York: Penguin.

Sa, M. (2015). Mood and personality disorders. In G. M. Kapalka (Ed.), *Treating disruptive disorders: A guide to psychological, pharmacological, and combined therapies.* New York: Routledge/Taylor & Francis Group.

Saarimäki, H., Gotsopoulos, A., Jaaskelainen, I. P., Lampinen, J., Vuilleumier, P., Hari, R., et al. (2016). Discrete neural signatures of basic emotions. *Cerebral Cortex, 26*(6), 2563–2573.

Sachs-Ericsson, N., Joiner, T., Plant, E. A., & Blazer, D. G. (2005). The influence of depression on cognitive decline in community-dwelling elderly persons. *American Journal of Geriatric Psychiatry, 13,* 402–408.

Sachse, P., Beermann, U., Martini, M., Maran, T., Domeier, M., & Furtner, M. R. (2017). "The world is upside down"–The Innsbruck goggle experiments of Theodor Erismann (1883–1961) and Ivo Kohler (1915–1985). *Cortex: A Journal Devoted to the Study of the Nervous System and Behavior, 92,* 222–232.

Sachser, R. M., Haubrich, J., Lunardi, P. S., & de Oliveira Alvares, L. (2017). Forgetting of what was once learned: Exploring the role of postsynaptic ionotropic glutamate receptors still remains. *Psychological Science, 17,* 921–922.

on memory formation, maintenance, and decay. *Neuropharmacology, 112*(Part A), 94–103.

Sacks, O. (2003, July 28). The mind's eye. *The New Yorker,* pp. 48–59.

Sadeghi-Nejad, H., & Watson, R. (2008). Premature ejaculation: Current medical treatment and new directions. *Journal of Sexual Medicine, 5,* 1037–1050.

Sadeh, N., Bounoua, N., & Javdani, S. (2019). Psychopathic traits, pubertal timing, and mental health functioning in justice-involved adolescents. *Personality and Individual Differences, 145,* 52–57.

Safdar, S., & Kosakowska-Berezecka, N. (2015). *Psychology of gender through the lens of culture: Theories and applications.* Cham, Switzerland: Springer International Publishing.

Sahakian, B. J., & Gottwald, J. (2017). *Sex, lies, & brain scans: How fMRI reveals what really goes on in our minds.* New York: Oxford University Press.

Sakellaridi, S., Christopoulos, V., Aflalo, T., Pejsa, K., Rosario, E., Ouellette, D., Pouratian, N., & Andersen, R. (2019). Intrinsic variable learning for brain-machine interface control by human anterior intraparietal cortex. *Neuron, 102,* 694–705.

Salazar, L. F., Crosby, R. A., & DiClemente, R. J. (2015). Experimental research designs. In L. F. Salazar, R. A. Crosby, & R. J. DiClemente (Eds.), *Research methods in health promotion* (2nd ed.). San Francisco: Jossey-Bass.

Salgado, D. M., Quinlin, K. J., & Zlotnick, C. (2007). The relationship of lifetime polysubstance dependence to trauma exposure, symptomatology, and psychosocial functioning in incarcerated women with comorbid PTSD and substance use disorder. *Journal of Trauma Dissociation, 8,* 9–26.

Salles, A., Bohn, K. M., & Moss, C. F. (2019). Auditory communication processing in bats: What we know and where to go. *Behavioral Neuroscience, 133*(3), 305–319.

Sallquist, J., Eisenberg, N., Spinrad, T. L., Eggum, N. D., & Gaertner, B. (2009). Assessment of preschoolers' positive empathy: Concurrent and longitudinal relations with positive emotion, social competence, and sympathy. *Journal of Positive Psychology, 4,* 223–233.

Salmon, C. (2017). Long-term romantic relationships: Adaptationist approaches. *Evolutionary Behavioral Sciences, 11,* 121–130.

Salvi, V., Fagiolini, A., Swartz, H., Maina, G., & Frank, E. (2008). The use of antidepressants in bipolar disorder. *Journal of Clinical Psychiatry, 69,* 1307–1318.

Sammut, G., & Buhagiar, L. J. (2017). The sociocultural determination of planned behaviour. *Integrative Psychological & Behavioral Science, 51,* 164–170.

Samoilov, V., & Zayas, V. (2007). Ivan Petrovich Pavlov (1849–1936). *Journal of the History of the Neurosciences, 16,* 74–89.

Samuel, D. B., Carroll, K. M., Rounsaville, B. J., & Ball, S. A. (2013). Personality disorders as maladaptive, extreme variants of normal personality: Borderline personality disorder and neuroticism in a substance using sample. *Journal of Personality Disorders, 27,* 625-635.

Sanders, C., Sadoski, M., van Walsum, K., Bramson, R., Wiprud, R., & Fossum, T. (2008). Learning basic surgical skills with mental imagery: Using the simulation centre in the mind. *Medical Education, 42,* 607-612.

Sandford, S. (2017). Freud, Bion and Kant: Epistemology and anthropology in *The Interpretation of Dreams. International Journal of Psychoanalysis, 98,* 91-110.

Sandman, C. A. (2015). Mysteries of the human fetus revealed. *Monographs of the Society for Research in Child Development, 80,* 124-137.

Sanes, J. R., & Masland, R. H. (2015). The types of retinal ganglion cells: Current status and implications for neuronal classification. *Annual Review of Neuroscience, 38,* 221-246.

Sang-hun, C. (2017, September 21). Kim's rejoinder to Trump's rocket man: "Mentally deranged U.S. dotard." *The New York Times.* Retrieved from https://www.nytimes.com/2017/09/21/world/asia/kim-trump-rocketman-dotard.html.

Santarnecchi, E., Rossi, S., & Rossi, A. (2015). The smarter, the stronger: Intelligence level correlates with brain resilience to systematic insults. *Cortex: A Journal Devoted to the Study of the Nervous System and Behavior, 64,* 293-309.

Santelli, J., Carter, M., Orr, M., & Dittus, P. (2009). Trends in sexual risk behaviors, by nonsexual risk behavior involvement, U.S. high school students, 1991-2007. *Journal of Adolescent Health, 44,* 372-379.

Santoro, A., Frankland, P. W., & Richards, B. A. (2016). Memory transformation enhances reinforcement learning in dynamic environments. *The Journal of Neuroscience, 36*(48), 12228-12242.

Santos, B. G., Carey, R. J., & Carrera, M. P. (2017). The acquisition, extinction and spontaneous recovery of Pavlovian drug conditioning induced by post-trial dopaminergic stimulation/inhibition. *Pharmacology, Biochemistry and Behavior, 156,* 24-29.

Santtila, P., Wager, I., Witting, K., Harlaar, N., Jern, P., Johansson, A., et al. (2008). Discrepancies between sexual desire and sexual activity: Gender differences and associations with relationship satisfaction. *Journal of Sex & Marital Therapy, 34,* 31-44.

Saper, C. B. (2013). The neurobiology of sleep. *CONTINUUM: Lifelong Learning in Neurology, 19,* 19-31.

Sarmiento, I. (2011). Rape stereotypes and labeling: Awareness of victimization and trauma. *Psychological Reports, 108,* 141-148.

Sarsour, K., Sheridan, M., Jutte, D., Nuru-Jeter, A., Hinshaw, S., & Boyce, W. (2011). Family socioeconomic status and child executive functions: The roles of language, home environment, and single parenthood. *Journal of the International Neuropsychological Society, 17,* 120-132.

Sarubin, N., Hilbert, S., Naumann, F., Zill, P., Wimmer, A., Nothdurfter, C., et al. (2017).

The sex-dependent role of the glucocorticoid receptor in depression: Variations in the NR3C1 gene are associated with major depressive disorder in women but not in men. *European Archives of Psychiatry and Clinical Neuroscience, 267,* 123-133.

Sasayama, D., Washizuka, S., & Honda, H. (2016). Effective treatment of night terrors and sleepwalking with ramelteon. *Journal of Child and Adolescent Psychopharmacology, 26*(10), 948.

Sato, A., Matsuo, A., & Kitazaki, M. (2019). Social contingency modulates the perceived distance between self and other. *Cognition, 192,* 104006.

Saucier, G., & Srivastava, S. (2015). What makes a good structural model of personality? Evaluating the big five and alternatives. In M. Mikulincer, P. R. Shaver, M. L. Cooper, & R. J. Larsen (Eds.), *APA handbook of personality and social psychology, Volume 4: Personality processes and individual differences.* Washington, DC: American Psychological Association.

Sauer, J. D., Palmer, M. A., & Brewer, N. (2019). Pitfalls in using eyewitness confidence to diagnose the accuracy of an individual identification decision. *Psychology, Public Policy, and Law, 25*(3), 147.

Saunders, B. T., Yager, L. M., & Robinson, T. E. (2013). Preclinical studies shed light on individual variation in addiction vulnerability. *Neuropsychopharmacology, 38,* 249-250.

Sauter, S. L., & Hurrell, J. J. (2017). Occupational health contributions to the development and promise of occupational health psychology. *Journal of Occupational Health Psychology, 22,* 251-258.

Savage, J., & Yancey, C. (2008). The effects of media violence exposure on criminal aggression: A meta-analysis. *Criminal Justice and Behavior, 35,* 772-791.

Savage-Rumbaugh, E. S., Toth, N., & Schick, K. (2007). Kanzi learns to knap stone tools. In D. A. Washburn (Ed.), *Primate perspectives on behavior and cognition.* Washington, DC: American Psychological Association.

Savazzi, S., Fabri, M., Rubboli, G., Paggi, A., Tassinari, C. A., & Marzi, C. A. (2007). Interhemispheric transfer following callosotomy in humans: Role of the superior colliculus. *Neuropsychologia, 45,* 2417-2427.

Saville, B. (2009). Performance under competitive and self-competitive fixed-interval schedules of reinforcement. *The Psychological Record, 59,* 21-38.

Sawa, A., & Snyder, S. H. (2002). Schizophrenia: Diverse approaches to a complex disease. *Science, 296,* 692-695.

Saywitz, K. J., Wells, C. R., Larson, R. P., & Hobbs, S. D. (2019). Effects of interviewer support on children's memory and suggestibility: Systematic review and meta-analyses of experimental research. *Trauma, Violence, & Abuse, 20*(1), 22-39.

Scalzo, S., Bowden, S., & Hillbom, M. (2015). Wernicke-Korsakoff syndrome. In J. Svanberg, A. Withall, B. Draper, & S. Bowden (Eds.),

Alcohol and the adult brain. New York: Psychology Press.

Scarborough, J. (2019). Understanding gendered realities: Mothers and father roles in family based therapy for adolescent eating disorders. *Clinical Social Work Journal,* 1-13.

Scarella, T. M., Boland, R. J., & Barsky, A. J. (2019). Illness anxiety disorder: Psychopathology, epidemiology, clinical cbnharacteristics, and treatment. *Psychosomatic Medicine, 81*(5), 398-407.

Scarr, S., & Weinberg, R. A. (1976). I.Q. test performance of black children adopted by white families. *American Psychologist, 31,* 726-739.

Scaturo, D. J. (2004). Fundamental clinical dilemmas in contemporary group psychotherapy. *Group Analysis, 37,* 201-217.

Scelfo, J. (2015, February 8). They. *The New York Times,* p. ED18.

Schachter, R. (2011). Using the group in cognitive group therapy. *Group, 35,* 135-149.

Schachter, S., & Singer, J. E. (1962). Cognitive, social, and physiological determinants of emotional state. *Psychological Review, 69,* 379-399.

Schachter, S., & Singer, J. E. (2001). Cognitive, social, and psychological determinants of emotional state. In W. G. Parrott, (Ed.), *Emotions in social psychology: Essential readings.* New York: Psychology Press.

Schaefer, E. G., Halldorson, M. K., & Dizon-Reynante, C. (2011). TV or not TV? Does the immediacy of viewing images of a momentous news event affect the quality and stability of flashbulb memories? *Memory, 19,* 251-266.

Schaie, K. W. (2005b). What can we learn from longitudinal studies of adult development? *Research in Human Development, 2,* 133-158.

Schaller, M., & Crandall, C. S. (Eds.). (2004). *The psychological foundations of culture.* Mahwah, NJ: Lawrence Erlbaum Associates.

Scharrer, E., & Ramasubramanian, S. (2015). Intervening in the media's influence on stereotypes of race and ethnicity: The role of media literacy education. *Journal of Social Issues, 41,* 171-185.

Schencker, L. (2017, June 17). World's first and America's first IVF babies meet in Chicago for first time. *Chicago Tribune.* Retrieved from https://www.chicagotribune.com/business/ct-first-ivf-babies-meet-0617-biz-20170616-story.html.

Schepers, P., & van den Berg, P. T. (2007). Social factors of work-environment creativity. *Journal of Business and Psychology, 21,* 407-428.

Schermer, J., Johnson, A. M., Vernon, P. A., & Jang, K. L. (2011). The relationship between personality and self-report abilities: A behavior-genetic analysis. *Journal of Individual Differences, 32,* 47-53.

Schier, L. A., Hyde, K. M., & Spector, A. C. (2019). Conditioned taste aversion versus avoidance: A re-examination of the separate processes hypothesis. *PloS one, 14*(6), e0217458.

Scheier, M. F., Carver, C. S., & Bridges, M. W. (1994). Distinguishing optimism from neuroticism (and trait anxiety, self-mastery, and self-esteem): A reevaluation of the Life Orientation Test.

Schiff, R., & Vakil, E. (2015). Age differences in cognitive skill learning, retention and transfer: The case of the Tower of Hanoi puzzle. *Learning and Individual Differences, 39,* 164-171.

Schilling, O. K., & Diehl, M. (2015). Psychological vulnerability to daily stressors in old age: Results of short-term longitudinal studies. *Zeitschrift Für Gerontologie Und Geriatrie, 48,* 517-523.

Schlichting, M. L., & Frankland, P. W. (2017). Memory allocation and integration in rodents and humans. *Current Opinion in Behavioral Sciences, 17,* 90-98.

Schlinger, H. D. (2015). Behavior analysis and behavioral neuroscience. *Frontiers in Human Neuroscience, 9,* 98-105

Schlinger, H. R. (2011). Skinner as missionary and prophet: A review of Burrhus F. Skinner: Shaper of behaviour. *Journal of Applied Behavior Analysis, 44,* 217-225.

Schmidt, J. P. (2006). The discovery of neurotransmitters: A fascinating story and a scientific object lesson. *PsycCRITIQUES, 61,* 101-115.

Schmidt, J., Klusmann, U., Lüdtke, O., Möller, J., & Kunter, M. (2017). What makes good and bad days for beginning teachers? A diary study on daily uplifts and hassles. *Contemporary Educational Psychology, 48,* 85-97.

Schnall, S., Haidt, J., Clore, G. L., & Jordan, A. H. (2008). Disgust as embodied moral judgment. *Personality and Social Psychology Bulletin, 34,* 1096-1109.

Schneiderman, N., McIntosh, R. C., & Antoni, M. H. (2019). Psychosocial risk and management of physical diseases. *Journal of Behavioral Medicine, 42*(1), 16-33.

Schnell, K., & Herpertz, S. C. (2007). Effects of dialectic-behavioral-therapy on the neural correlates of affective hyperarousal in borderline personality disorder. *Journal of Psychiatric Research, 41,* 837-847.

Schnupp, J., Nelken, I., & King, A. (2011). *Auditory neuroscience: Making sense of sound.* Cambridge, MA: MIT Press.

Schoch, S. F., Cordi, M. J., Schredl, M., & Rasch, B. (2019). The effect of dream report collection and dream incorporation on memory consolidation during sleep. *Journal of Sleep Research, 28*(1), 1-8.

Schofield, W., & Vaughan-Jackson, P. (1913). *What a boy should know.* New York: Cassell.

Schooler, L. J., & Hertwig, R. (2012). How forgetting aids heuristic inference. In G. Gigerenzer, R. Hertwig, & T. Pachur (Eds.), *Heuristics: The foundations of adaptive behavior.* New York: Oxford University Press.

Schredl, M., & Piel, E. (2005). Gender differences in dreaming: Are they stable over time? *Personality and Individual Differences, 39,* 309-316.

Schredl, M., & Reinhard, I. (2011). Gender differences in nightmare frequency: A meta-analysis. *Sleep Medicine Reviews, 15,* 115-121.

Schreurs, B. G., Smith-Bell, C. A., & Burhans, L. B. (2011). Classical conditioning and conditioning-specific reflex modification of rabbit heart rate as a function of unconditioned stimulus location. *Behavioral Neuroscience, 125,* 604-612.

Schroers, M., Prigot, J., & Fagen, J. (2007). The effect of a salient odor context on memory retrieval in young infants. *Infant Behavior & Development, 30,* 685-689.

Schultheiss, O. C., & Schiepe-Tiska, A. (2013). The role of the dorsoanterior striatum in implicit motivation: The case of the need for power. *Frontiers in Human Neuroscience, 7.* Retrieved from http://www.ncbi.nlm.nih.gov/pubmed/23626531.

Schurger, A., Sarigiannidis, I., Naccache, L., Sitt, J. D., & Dehaene, S. (2015). Cortical activity is more stable when sensory stimuli are consciously perceived. *PNAS Proceedings of the National Academy of Sciences of the United States of America, 112,* E2083-E2092.

Schwartz, B. (2008). Working memory load differentially affects tip-of-the-tongue states and feeling-of-knowing judgments. *Memory & Cognition, 36,* 9-19.

Schwartz, B. L. (2002). The phenomenology of naturally-occurring tip-of-the-tongue states: A diary study. In S. P. Shohov (Ed.), *Advances in psychology research* (Vol. 8). Huntington, NY: Nova.

Schwartz, B. L., & Metcalfe, J. (2011) Tip-of-the-tongue (TOT) states: Retrieval, behavior, and experience. *Memory & Cognition, 39,* 737-749.

Schwartz, J. M., & Begley, S. (2002). *The mind and the brain: Neuroplasticity and the power of mental force.* New York: Regan Books/Harper Collins.

Schwartz, J., & Wald, M. L. (2003). NASA's curse? "Groupthink" is 30 years old, and still going strong. *The New York Times,* p. C1.

Schwartz, P., Maynard, A., & Uzelac, S. (2008). Adolescent egocentrism: A contemporary view. *Adolescence, 43*(171), 441-448.

Schwartz, S. J., Donnellan, M., Ravert, R. D., Luyckx, K., & Zamboanga, B. L. (2013). Identity development, personality, and well-being in adolescence and emerging adulthood: Theory, research, and recent advances. In R. M. Lerner, M. Easterbrooks, J. Mistry, & I. B. Weiner (Eds.), *Handbook of psychology, Vol. 6: Developmental psychology* (2nd ed.). Hoboken, NJ: John Wiley & Sons Inc.

Schwartz, S. J., Meca, A., Ward, C., Szabó, Á., Benet-Martínez, V., Lorenzo-Blanco, E. I., et al. (2019). Biculturalism dynamics: A daily diary study of bicultural identity and psychosocial functioning. *Journal of Applied Developmental Psychology, 62,* 26-37. https://doi-org.silk.library.umass.edu/10.1016/j.appdev.2018.12.007.

Schwartzmant, R. J., Alexander, G. M., & Grothusen, J. R. (2011). The use of ketamine

in complex regional pain syndrome: Possible mechanisms. *Expert Review of Neurotherapeutics, 11,* 719-734.

Schwarzer, R., & Luszczynska, A. (2013). Stressful life events. In A. M. Nezu, C. Nezu, P. A. Geller, & I. B. Weiner (Eds.), *Handbook of psychology, Vol. 9: Health psychology* (2nd ed.). Hoboken, NJ: John Wiley & Sons Inc.

Schwenkreis, P., El Tom, S., Ragert, P., Pleger, B., Tegenthoff, M., & Dinse, H. (2007). Assessment of sensorimotor cortical representation asymmetries and motor skills in violin players. *European Journal of Neuroscience, 26,* 3291-3302.

Schäfer, L., Mehler, L., Hähner, A., Walliczek, U., Hummel, T., & Croy, I. (2019). Sexual desire after olfactory loss: Quantitative and qualitative reports of patients with smell disorders. *Physiology & Behavior, 201,* 64-69.

Sciutto, M., & Eisenberg, M. (2007). Evaluating the evidence for and against the overdiagnosis of ADHD. *Journal of Attention Disorders, 11,* 106-113.

Scott, K. M., de Jonge, P., Stein, D. J., & Kessler, R. C. (Eds.). (2018). *Mental disorders around the world: Facts and figures from the WHO World Mental Health Surveys.* New York: Cambridge University Press.

Scull, A. (2015). *Madness in civilization: A cultural history of insanity, from the Bible to Freud, from the madhouse to modern medicine.* Princeton, NJ: Princeton University Press.

Searight, H. (2013). Deinstitutionalization of people with mental illness: A failed policy that could have succeeded. *PsycCRITIQUES, 58,* 88-94

Searls, D. (2017). *The inkblots: Hermann Rorschach, his iconic test, and the power of seeing.* New York: Crown Publishers/Random House.

Sebastiani, L., Castellani, E., & D'Alessandro, L. (2011). Emotion processing without awareness: Features detection or significance evaluation? *International Journal of Psychophysiology, 80,* 150-156.

Seeman, P. (2011). All roads to schizophrenia lead to dopamine supersensitivity and elevated dopamine D2(high) receptors. *CNS Neuroscience & Therapeutics, 17,* 118-132.

Segall, M. H. (1988). Cultural roots of aggressive behavior. In M. Bond (Ed.), *The cross-cultural challenge to social psychology.* Newbury Park, CA: Sage.

Segall, M. H., Campbell, D. T., & Herskovits, M. J. (1966). *The influence of culture on visual perception.* New York: Bobbs-Merrill.

Sejunaite, K., Lanza, C., & Riepe, M. W. (2019). Everyday memory in healthy aging: Porous but not distorted. *Frontiers in Aging Neuroscience, 11.*

Seligman, M. E. (2007). *What you can change . . . and what you can't: The complete guide to successful self-improvement.* New York: Vintage.

Seligman, M. E. P. (1995). The effectiveness of psychotherapy: The Consumer Reports study. *American Psychologist, 50,* 965-974.

Sell, C., Möller, H., & Taubner, S. (2017). Effectiveness of integrative imagery- and trance-based psychodynamic therapies: Guided imagery psychotherapy and hypnopsycho-therapy. *Journal of Psychotherapy Integration*. Accessed at http://psycnet.apa.org/record/2017-07863-001.

Selove, R. (2007). The glass is half full: Current knowledge about pediatric cancer and sickle cell anemia. *PsycCRITIQUES, 52*, 88-99.

Selsky, A. (1997, February 16). African males face circumcision rite. *Boston Globe*, p. C7.

Selye, H. (1976). *The stress of life*. New York: McGraw-Hill.

Selye, H. (1993). History of the stress concept. In L. Goldberger & S. Breznitz (Eds.), *Handbook of stress: Theoretical and clinical aspects* (2nd ed.). New York: Free Press.

Semin, G. R., & Garrido, M. V. (2013). A systemic approach to impression formation: From verbal to multimodal processes. In J. P. Forgas, K. Fiedler, & C. Sedikides (Eds.), *Social thinking and interpersonal behavior*. New York: Psychology Press.

Semler, C. N., & Harvey, A. G. (2005). Misperception of sleep can adversely affect daytime functioning in insomnia. *Behaviour Research and Therapy, 43*, 843-856.

Semykina, A., & Linz, S. J. (2007). Gender differences in personality and earnings: Evidence from Russia. *Journal of Economic Psychology, 28*, 387-410.

Senden, M., Emmerling, T. C., Van Hoof, R., Frost, M. A., & Goebel, R. (2019). Reconstructing imagined letters from early visual cortex reveals tight topographic correspondence between visual mental imagery and perception. *Brain Structure and Function, 224*(3), 1167-1183.

Senholzi, K. B., & Kubota, J. T. (2016). The neural mechanisms of prejudice intervention. In J. R. Absher & J. Cloutier (Eds.), *Neuroimaging personality, social cognition, and character*. San Diego, CA: Elsevier Academic Press.

Senholzi, K. B., Depue, B. E., Correll, J., Banich, M. T., & Ito, T. A. (2015). Brain activation underlying threat detection to targets of different races. *Social Neuroscience, 10*, 651-662.

Seow, Y.-X., Ong, P. K. C., & Huang, D. (2016). Odor-specific loss of smell sensitivity with age as revealed by the Specific Sensitivity test. *Chemical Senses, 41*, 487-495.

Seroczynski, A. D., Jacquez, F. M., & Cole, D. A. (2003). Depression and suicide during adolescence. In G. R. Adams & M. D. Berzonsky (Eds.), *Blackwell handbook of adolescence*. Malden, MA: Blackwell Publishers.

Serpell, R. (2000). Intelligence and culture. In R. Sternberg (Ed.), *Handbook of intelligence*. Cambridge, England: Cambridge University Press.

Serretti, A. (2017). Genetics and pharmacogenetics of mood disorders. *Psychiatria Polska, 51*, 197-203.

Servick, K. (2014). New support for "gay gene." *Science, 346*, 900.

Servick, K. (2018, August 31). Social science studies get a "generous" test. *Science*, 836.

Sezgin, F., & Erdogan, O. (2015). Academic optimism, hope and zest for work as predictors of teacher self-efficacy and perceived success.

Kuram Ve Uygulamada Eğitim Bilimleri, 15, 7-19.

Shafer, V. L., & Garrido-Nag, K. (2007). The neurodevelopmental bases of language. In E. Hoff & M. Shatz (Eds.), *Blackwell handbook of language development*. Malden, MA: Blackwell Publishing.

Shah, A. S., Young, J., & Vieira, K. (2014). Long-term Suboxone treatment and its benefit on long-term remission for opiate dependence. *African Journal of Psychiatry, 17*, 1-4.

Shain, S. (2019, June 17). Making a decision doesn't have to be so hard. *The New York Times*, p. B7.

Shaked, A., & Clore, G. (2017). Breaking the world to make it whole again: Attribution in the construction of emotion. *Emotion Review, 9*(1), 27-35.

Shakya, H., & Christakis, N. (2017). Association of Facebook use with compromised well-being: A longitudinal study. *American Journal of Epidemiology, 185*, 203-211.

Shanahan, L., Copeland, W. E., Worthman, C. M., Erkanli, A., Angold, A., & Costello, E. (2013). Sex-differentiated changes in C-reactive protein from ages 9 to 21: The contributions of BMI and physical/sexual maturation. *Psychoneuroendocrinology, 38*, 2209-2217.

Shaner, L., Kelly, L., Rockwell, D., & Curtis, D. (2017). Calm abiding: The lived experience of the practice of long-term meditation. *Journal of Humanistic Psychology, 57*, 98-121.

Shang, X., Kallmann, M., & Arif, A. S. (2019, March). Effects of virtual agent gender on user performance and preference in a VR training program. In K. Arai & R. Bhatia (Eds.), *Advances in Information and Communication*. Cham, Switzerland: Springer.

Shapira-Berman, O. (2019). That which was "not": Some thoughts regarding Oedipus's modern conflicts. *Psychoanalytic Review, 106*(3), 247-271.

Sharifian, N., & Zahodne, L. B. (2019). Social media bytes: Daily associations between social media use and everyday memory failures across the adult life span. *The Journals of Gerontology: Series B.* https://doi.org/10.1093/geronb/gbz005.

Sheahan, C. L., Pozzulo, J. D., Reed, J. E., & Pica, E. (2017). The role of familiarity with the defendant, type of descriptor discrepancy, and eyewitness age on mock jurors' perceptions of eyewitness testimony. *Journal of Police and Criminal Psychology*. Accessed from https://link.springer.com/article/10.1007/s11896-017-9232-2.

Shehab, A. S., Brent, D., & Maalouf, F. T. (2016). Neurocognitive changes in selective serotonin reuptake inhibitors–Treated adolescents with depression. *Journal of Child and Adolescent Psychopharmacology, 26*, 713-720.

Shehata-Dieler, W., Ehrmann-Mueller, D., Wermke, P., Voit, V., Cebulla, M., & Wermke, K. (2013). Pre-speech diagnosis in hearing-impaired infants: How auditory experience

affects early vocal development. *Speech, Language and Hearing, 16*, 99-106.

Sheldon, K. M., & Lucas, R. E. (Eds.) (2014). *Stability of happiness: Theories and evidence on whether happiness can change*. San Diego, CA: Elsevier Academic Press.

Shellenbarger, S. (2012, August 22). Are you a hero or a bystander? *Wall Street Journal*, p. D1.

Shellenbarger, S. (2013, April 3). Tactics to spark creativity. *Wall Street Journal*, pp. D1-D2.

Shellenbarger, S. (2019, January 24). The secret benefits of forgetting. *Wall Street Journal*, A12.

Shepperd, J., Malone, W., & Sweeny, K. (2008). Exploring causes of the self-serving bias. *Social and Personality Psychology Compass, 2*, 895-908.

Sherblom, S. (2008). The legacy of the "care challenge": Re-envisioning the outcome of the justice-care debate. *Journal of Moral Education, 37*, 81-98.

Sherman, S. L., Allen, E. G., Bean, L. H., & Freeman, S. B. (2007). Epidemiology of Down syndrome [Special issue: Down syndrome]. *Mental Retardation and Developmental Disabilities Research Reviews, 13*, 221-227.

Shibata, K., Sasaki, Y., Bang, J. W., Walsh, E. G., Machizawa, M. G., Tamaki, M., et al. (2017). Overlearning hyperstabilizes a skill by rapidly making neurochemical processing inhibitory-dominant. *Nature Neuroscience, 20*, 470-475.

Shifren, J. L., Crandall, C. J., & Manson, J. E. (2019). Menopausal Hormone Therapy. *JAMA, 321*(24), 2458-2459.

Shimono, K., & Wade, N. J. (2002). Monocular alignment in different depth planes. *Vision Research, 42*, 1127-1135.

Shin, A. C., Zheng, H., Townsend, R. L., Patterson, L. M., Holmes, G. M., & Berthoud, H. R. (2013). Longitudinal assessment of food intake, fecal energy loss, and energy expenditure after Roux-en-Y gastric bypass surgery in high-fat-fed obese rats. *Obesity Surgery, 23*(4), 531-540.

Shin, D. W., Roter, D. L., Roh, Y. K., Hahm, S. K., Cho, B., & Park, H. (2015). Physician gender and patient centered communication: The moderating effect of psychosocial and biomedical case characteristics. *Patient Education and Counseling, 98*, 55-60.

Shin, H. B., & Kominski, R. A. 2010. *Language Use in the United States: 2007*. American Community Survey Reports, ACS-12. Washington, DC: U.S. Census Bureau.

Shin, J. E., Suh, E. M., Li, N. P., Eo, K., Chong, S. C., & Tsai, M. H. (2019). Darling, get closer to me: Spatial proximity amplifies interpersonal liking. *Personality and Social Psychology Bulletin, 45*(2), 300-309.

Shirai, F., & Hayashi-Takagi, A. (2017). Optogenetics: Applications in psychiatric research. *Psychiatry and Clinical Neurosciences, 71*, 363-372.

Shirayama, Y., & Hashimoto, K. (2017). Effects of a single bilateral infusion of R-ketamine in the rat brain regions of a learned helplessness model of depression. *European Archives of Psychiatry and Clinical Neuroscience, 267,* 177-182.

Shnabel, N., Purdie-Vaughns, V., Cook, J. E., Garcia, J., & Cohen, G. L. (2013). Demystifying values-affirmation interventions: Writing about social belonging is a key to buffering against identity threat. *Personality and Social Psychology Bulletin, 39,* 663-676.

Shogren, K. A., & Wehmeyer, M. L. (2017). Problem solving. In M. L. Wehmeyer, K. A. Shogren, T. D. Little, & S. J. Lopez (Eds.), *Development of self-determination through the life-course.* New York: Springer Science + Business Media.

Shors, T. J. (2009). Saving new brain cells. *Scientific American, 500,* 47-54.

Shrestha, L. B., & Heisler, E. J. (2011). The changing demographic profile of the United States. Congressional Research Service. Retrieved from www.fas.org/sgp/crs/misc/RL32701.pdf.

Shulman, J. L., & Horne, S. G. (2006). Guilty or not? A path model of women's sexual force fantasies. *Journal of Sex Research, 43,* 368-377.

Shurkin, J. N. (1992). *Terman's kids: The groundbreaking study of how the gifted grow up.* Boston: Little, Brown.

Shweder, R. A. (1994). You're not sick, you're just in love: Emotion as an interpretive system. In P. Ekman & R. J. Davidson (Eds.), *The nature of emotion: Fundamental questions.* New York: Oxford

Sibunruang, H., Capezio, A., & Restubog, S. D. (2015). In pursuit of success: The differential moderating effects of political skill on the relationships among career-related psychological needs and ingratiation. *Journal of Career Assessment, 23,* 336-348.

Sidman, M. (2006). The distinction between positive and negative reinforcement: Some additional considerations. *Behavior Analyst, 29,* 135-139.

Sielski, R., Rief, W., & Glombiewski, J. A. (2017). Efficacy of biofeedback in chronic back pain: A meta-analysis. *International Journal of Behavioral Medicine, 24,* 25-41.

Siemer, M., Mauss I., & Gross, J. J. (2007). Same situation–different emotions: How appraisals shape our emotions. *Emotion, 7,* 592-600.

Siemerkus, J., Tomiello, S., & Stephan, K. E. (2019). Bayesian inference and hallucinations in schizophrenia. *Brain, 142*(8), 2178-2181.

Sierra-Mercado, D., & Lazaro-Munoz, G. (2018). Enhance diversity among researchers to promote participant trust in precision medicine research. *American Journal of Bioethics, 18,* 44-46

Sifrit, K. J. (2006). The effects of aging and cognitive decrements on simulated driving performance. *Dissertation Abstracts International: Section B: The Sciences and Engineering, 67,* 2863.

Sikka, P., Revonsuo, A., Sandman, N., Tuominen, J., & Valli, K. (2017). Dream emotions: A comparison of home dream reports with laboratory early and late REM dream reports. *Journal of Sleep Research.* Accessed from https://www.ncbi.nlm.nih.gov/pubmed/28568911.

Sikkema, K. J., Ranby, K. W., Meade, C. S., Hansen, N. B., Wilson, P. A., & Kochman, A. (2013). Reductions in traumatic stress following a coping intervention were mediated by decreases in avoidant coping for people living with HIV/AIDS and childhood sexual abuse. *Journal of Consulting and Clinical Psychology, 81,* 274-283.

Silva, M. T. A., Gonçalves, E. L., & Garcia-Mijares, M. (2007). Neural events in the reinforcement contingency. *Behavior Analyst, 30,* 17-30.

Silverstein, M. L. (2007). Rorschach test findings at the beginning of treatment and 2 years later, with a 30-year follow-up. *Journal of Personality Assessment, 88,* 131-143.

Simon, D. (2018, October 31). Whitey Bulger met a violent end after a lifetime of brutality. CNN. Retrieved from https://www.cnn.com/2018/10/31/us/james-whitey-bulger/index.html.

Simon, E. B., Maron-Katz, A., Lahav, N., Shamir, R., & Hendler, T. (2017). Tired and misconnected: A breakdown of brain modularity following sleep deprivation. *Human Brain Mapping, 38,* 3300-3314.

Simon, E. B., Oren, N., Sharon, H., Kirschner, A., Goldway, N., Okon-Singer, H., et al. (2015). Losing neutrality: The neural basis of impaired emotional control without sleep. *Journal of Neuroscience, 35*(38), 13194-13205.

Simon, S., & Hoyt, C. (2008). Exploring the gender gap in support for a woman for president. *Analyses of Social Issues and Public Policy, 8,* 157-181.

Simonton, D. K. (2009). Varieties of (scientific) creativity: A hierarchical model of domain-specific disposition, development, and achievement. *Perspectives on Psychological Science, 4,* 441-452.

Simonton, D. K. (2014). The mad-genius paradox: Can creative people be more mentally healthy but highly creative people more mentally ill? *Perspectives on Psychological Science, 9,* 470-480.

Simães, C., Gomes, A. R., & Costa, P. (2019). A multigroup analysis of the effect of cognitive appraisal on nurses' psychological distress. *Nursing Research, 68*(3), E1-E11.

Sinclair, R. R., Waitsman, M. C., Oliver, C. M., & Deese, M. (2013). Personality and psychological resilience in military personnel. In R. R. Sinclair & T. W. Britt (Eds.), *Building psychological resilience in military personnel: Theory and practice.* Washington, DC: American Psychological Association.

Singer, B. F., Bryan, M. A., Popov, P., Robinson, T. E., & Aragona, B. J. (2017). Rapid induction of dopamine sensitization in the nucleus accumbens shell induced by a single injection of cocaine. *Behavioural Brain Research, 324,* 66-70.

Singer, L. T., & Richardson, G. A. (2011). Introduction to "Understanding developmental consequences of prenatal drug exposure: Biological and environmental effects and their interactions." *Neurotoxicology and Teratology, 33,* 5-8.

Singh, R. D., Jimerson, S. R., Renshaw, T., Saeki, E., Hart, S. R., Earhart, J., et al. (2011). A summary and synthesis of contemporary empirical evidence regarding the effects of the Drug Abuse Resistance Education Program (D.A.R.E.). *Contemporary School Psychology, 15,* 93-102.

Singh, S., Wulf, D., Samara, R., & Cuca, Y. P. (2000). Gender differences in the timing of first intercourse: Data from 14 countries. *International Family Planning Perspectives, 26,* 21-28, 43.

Sininger, Y. S., & Cone-Wesson, B. (2004). Asymmetric cochlear processing mimics hemispheric specialization. *Science, 305,* 1581.

Sininger, Y. S., & Cone-Wesson, B. (2006). Lateral asymmetry in the ABR of neonates: Evidence and mechanisms. *Hearing Research, 212,* 203-211.

Sivec, H. J., Montesano, V. L., Skubby, D., Knepp, K. A., & Munetz, M. R. (2017). Cognitive behavioral therapy for psychosis (CBT-p) delivered in a community mental health setting: A case comparison of clients receiving CBT informed strategies by case managers prior to therapy. *Community Mental Health Journal, 53,* 134-142.

Skinner, B. F. (1957). *Verbal behavior.* New York: Appleton-Century-Crofts.

Skinner, B. F. (1975). The steep and thorny road to a science of behavior. *American Psychologist, 30,* 42-49.

Skolnick, P., Popik, P., & Trullas, R. (2009). Glutamate-based antidepressants: 20 years on. *Trends in Pharmacological Science, 30,* 563-569.

Śledziński, P., Zeyland, J., Slomski, R., & Nowak-Terpiłowska, A. (2019). The adverse effects of marijuana use: The present state and future directions. *Journal of Child & Adolescent Substance Abuse, 28*(2), 65-72.

Sleigh, J. W., Leslie, K., Davidson, A. J., Amor, D. J., Diakumis, P., Lukic, V., et al. (2019). Genetic analysis of patients who experienced awareness with recall while under general anesthesia. *Anesthesiology.* https://doi.org/10.1097/ALN.0000000000002877.

Slocombe, K. E., Waller, B. M., & Liebal, K. (2011). The language void: The need for multimodality in primate communication research. *Animal Behaviour, 81,* 919-924.

Slotboom, A., Hendriks, J., & Verbruggen, J. (2011). Contrasting adolescent female and male sexual aggression: A self-report study on prevalence and predictors of sexual aggression. *Journal of Sexual Aggression, 17,* 15-33.

Ślusarczyk, E., & Niedzwienska, A. (2013). A naturalistic study of prospective memory in preschoolers: The role of task interruption and motivation. *Cognitive Development, 28,* 179-192.

Smart, R. G. (2007). Review of introduction to addictive behaviours. *Addiction, 102,* 831.

Smetana, J. G. (2005). Adolescent-parent conflict: Resistance and subversion as developmental process. In L. Nucci (Ed.), *Conflict, contradiction, and contrarian elements in moral development and education.* Mahwah, NJ: Lawrence Erlbaum Associates.

Smetana, J., Daddis, C., & Chuang, S. (2003). "Clean your room!" A longitudinal investigation of adolescent-parent conflict and conflict resolution in middle-class African American families. *Journal of Adolescent Research, 18,* 631-650.

Šmigelskas, K., Žemaitienė, N., Julkunen, J., & Kauhanen, J. (2015). Type A behavior pattern is not a predictor of premature mortality. *International Journal of Behavioral Medicine, 22,* 161-169.

Smith, C. (2006). Symposium V–Sleep and learning: New developments [Special issue: Methods and learning in functional MRI]. *Brain and Cognition, 60,* 331-332.

Smith, C. A., & Lazarus, R. S. (2001). Appraisal components, core relational themes, and the emotions. In W. G. Parrott (Ed.), *Emotions in social psychology: Essential readings.* Philadelphia: Psychology Press.

Smith, C. D., Chebrolu, J., Wekstein, D. R., Schmitt, F. A., & Markesbery, W. R. (2007). Age and gender effects on human brain anatomy: A voxel-based morphometric study in healthy elderly. *Neurobiology of Aging, 28,* 1057-1087.

Smith, D. E., Springer, C. M., & Barrett, S. (2011). Physical discipline and socioemotional adjustment among Jamaican adolescents. *Journal of Family Violence, 26,* 51-61.

Smith, E. P., Witherspoon, D. P., Hart, M., & Davidson, W. S. (2017). The dynamic and interactive role of theory in community psychology research, practice, and policy. In M. A. Bond, I. Serrano-García, C. B. Keys, & M. Shinn (Eds.), *APA handbook of community psychology: Methods for community research and action for diverse groups and issues.* Washington, DC: American Psychological Association.

Smith, E. S., Geissler, S. A., Schallert, T., & Lee, H. J. (2013). The role of central amygdala dopamine in disengagement behavior. *Behavioral Neuroscience, 127,* 164-174.

Smith, M. L., Glass, G. V., & Miller, T. I. (1980). *The benefits of psychotherapy.* Baltimore: The Johns Hopkins University Press.

Smith, N. A., Folland, N. A., Martinez, D. M., & Trainor, L. J. (2017). Multisensory object perception in infancy: 4-month-olds perceive a mistuned harmonic as a separate auditory and visual object. *Cognition, 164,* 1-7.

Smith, R. A., & Weber, A. L. (2005). Applying social psychology in everyday life. In F. W. Schneider, J. A. Gruman, & L. M. Coutts (Eds.), *Applied social psychology: Understanding and addressing social and practical problems.* Thousand Oaks, CA: Sage Publications.

Smith, S. (2019, July 2). Preschool genius: Meet the Farragut 5-year-old that has a higher IQ than most people. WBIR-TV. Retrieved from https://www.wbir.com/article/news/local/watercooler/preschool-genius-meet-the-farragut-5-year-old-that-has-a-higher-iq-than-most-people/51-41596720-e185-48a5-993e-f252ad8dfeef.

Smith, S. G., Zhang, X., Basile, K. C., Merrick, M. T., Wang, J., Kresnow, M., et al. (2018). The National Intimate Partner and Sexual Violence Survey (NISVS): 2015 data brief–Updated release. Atlanta: National Center for Injury Prevention and Control, Centers for Disease Control and Prevention.

Smith, T. J., & Hillner, B. E. (2019). The cost of pain. *JAMA Network Open, 2*(4):e191532.

Smith, T. W., & Son, J. (2013). *Trends in public attitudes about sexual morality.* Chicago: NORC at the University of Chicago.

Smrtnik-Vitulić, H., & Zupančič, M. (2011). Personality traits as a predictor of academic achievement in adolescents. *Educational Studies, 37,* 127-140.

Snowdon, C. T. (2017). Learning from monkey "talk." *Science, 355,* 1120-1122.

Snyder, J., Cramer, A., & Afrank, J. (2005). The contributions of ineffective discipline and parental hostile attributions of child misbehavior to the development of conduct problems at home and school. *Developmental Psychology, 41,* 30-41.

Snyder, M. D., & Dwyer, P. C. (2013). Altruism and prosocial behavior. In H. Tennen, J. Suls, & I. B. Weiner (Eds.). *Handbook of psychology, Vol. 5: Personality and social psychology* (2nd ed.). Hoboken, NJ: John Wiley & Sons.

Sodian, B. (2011). Theory of mind in infancy. *Child Development Perspectives, 5,* 39-43.

Sohlberg, J. (2019). Elections are (not) exciting: Need for cognition and electoral behaviour. *Scandinavian Political Studies, 42*(2), 138-150.

Sohr-Preston, S. L., & Scaramella, L. V. (2006). Implications of timing of maternal depressive symptoms for early cognitive and language development. *Clinical Child and Family Psychology Review, 9,* 65-83.

Šolcová, I. P., & Lačev, A. (2017). Differences in male and female subjective experience and physiological reactions to emotional stimuli. *International Journal of Psychophysiology, 117,* 75-82.

Solesio-Jofre, E., Lorenzo-López, L., Gutiérrez, R., López-Frutos, J., Ruiz-Vargas, J., & Maestú, F. (2011). Age effects on retroactive interference during working memory maintenance. *Biological Psychology, 88,* 72-82.

Solomon, A. (2020, April 12). Don't ignore clinical mental illness. *The New York Times,* p. SR10.

Solomonia, R. O., & McCabe, B. J. (2015). Molecular mechanisms of memory in imprinting. *Neuroscience and Biobehavioral Reviews, 50,* 56-69.

Somers, T. J., Moseley, G., Keefe, F. J., & Kothadia, S. M. (2011). Neuroimaging of pain: A psychosocial perspective. In R. A. Cohen & L. H. Sweet (Eds.), *Brain imaging in behavioral medicine and clinical neuroscience.* New York: Springer Science + Business Media.

Sood, A. B., & Linker, J. (2017). Proximal influences on the trajectory of suicidal behaviors and suicide during the transition from adolescence to young adulthood. *Child and Adolescent Psychiatric Clinics of North America, 26,* 235-251.

Soorya, L. V., Carpenter, L., & Romanczyk, R. G. (2011). Applied behavior analysis. In E. Hollander, A. Kolevzon, & J. T. Coyle (Eds.), *Textbook of autism spectrum disorders.* Arlington, VA: American Psychiatric Publishing, Inc.

Sori, C. E. (Ed.). (2006). *Engaging children in family therapy: Creative approaches to integrating theory and research in clinical practice.* New York: Routledge/Taylor & Francis Group.

Soussignan, R. (2002). Duchenne smile, emotional experience, and automatic reactivity: A test of the facial feedback hypothesis. *Emotion, 2,* 52-74.

South, S. C., Reichborn-Kjennerud, T., Eaton, N. R., & Krueger, R. F. (2013). Genetics of personality. In H. Tennen, J. Suls, & I. B. Weiner (Eds.), *Handbook of psychology, Vol. 5: Personality and social psychology* (2nd ed.). Hoboken, NJ: John Wiley & Sons Inc.

South, S., & Krueger, R. (2008). An interactionist perspective on genetic and environmental contributions to personality. *Social and Personality Psychology Compass, 2,* 929-948.

Spackman, M. P., Fujiki, M., & Brinton, B. (2006). Understanding emotions in context: The effects of language impairment on children's ability to infer emotional reactions. *International Journal of Language & Communication Disorders, 41,* 173-188.

Sparks, S. D. (2007). Foundation: Gifted poor students given short shrift. *Education Daily, 40,* 3.

Sparrow, B., Liu, J., & Wegner, D. M. (2011). Google effects on memory: cognitive consequences of having information at our fingertips. *Science, 333,* 776-778.

Spaulding, S. (2013). Mirror neurons and social cognition. *Mind & Language, 28,* 233-257.

Special issue: The dopamine hypothesis of schizophrenia. (2017). *Biological Psychiatry, 81*(1), 1

Speirs-Neumeister, K. L., & Finch, H. (2006). Perfectionism in high-ability students: Relational precursors and influences on achievement motivation. *Gifted Child Quarterly, 50,* 238-251.

Spence, C., Auvray, M., & Smith, B. (2015). Confusing tastes with flavours. In D. Stokes, M. Matthen, & S. Biggs (Eds.), *Perception and its modalities.* New York: Oxford University Press.

Spence, M. J., & DeCasper, A. J. (1982, March). *Human fetuses perceive maternal speech.* Paper presented at the meeting of the International Conference on Infant Studies, Austin, TX.

Spence-Cochran, K., & Pearl, C. (2006). Moving toward full inclusion. In P. Wehman (Ed.), *Life beyond the classroom: Transition strategies for young people with disabilities* (4th ed.). Baltimore: Paul H. Brookes Publishing.

Spencer, S. J., Fein, S., Zanna, M. P., & Olson, J. M. (Eds.). (2003). *Motivated social perception: The Ontario Symposium* (Vol. 9). Mahwah, NJ: Erlbaum.

Sperling, G. (1960). The information available in brief visual presentation. *Psychological Monographs, 74,* 29.

Sperner-Unterweger, B., & Fuchs, D. (2015). Schizophrenia and psychoneuroimmunology: An integrative view. *Current Opinion in Psychiatry, 28,* 201-206.

Sperry, R. (1982). Some effects of disconnecting the cerebral hemispheres. *Science, 217,* 1223-1226.

Spiegel, D. (2014). Minding the body: Psychotherapy and cancer survival. *British Journal of Health Psychology, 19,* 465-485.

Spiegel, D. (2015). Hypnosis and pain control. In T. R. Deer, M. S. Leong, & A. L. Ray (Eds.), *Treatment of chronic pain by integrative approaches: The American Academy of Pain Medicine textbook on patient management.* New York: Springer Science + Business Media.

Spitzer, R. L., Skodol, A. E., Gibbon, M., & Williams, J. B. W. (1983). *Psychopathology: A case book.* New York: McGraw-Hill.

Sprecher, S., & Hatfield, E. (1996). Premarital sexual standards among U.S. college students: Comparison with Russian and Japanese students. *Archives of Sexual Behavior, 25,* 261-288.

Sprecher, S., & Regan, P. C. (2002). Liking some things (in some people) more than others: Partner preferences in romantic relationships and friendships. *Journal of Social and Personal Relationships, 19,* 436-481.

Sprecher, S., Treger, S., & Sakaluk, J. K. (2013). Premarital sexual standards and sociosexuality: Gender, ethnicity, and cohort differences. *Archives of Sexual Behavior, 42*(8), 1395-1405.

Squire, L. R., Clark, R. E., & Bayley, P. J. (2004). Medial temporal lobe function and memory. In M. S. Gazzaniga (Ed.), *Cognitive neurosciences* (3rd ed.). Cambridge, MA: MIT.

Srinivasan, M., Al-Mughairy, S., Foushee, R., & Barner, D. (2017). Learning language from within: Children use semantic generalizations to infer word meanings. *Cognition, 159,* 11-24.

Stacks, A., Oshio, T., Gerard, J., & Roe, J. (2009). The moderating effect of parental warmth on the association between spanking and child aggression: A longitudinal approach. *Infant and Child Development, 18,* 178-194.

Stainton, T., & Clare, I. C. H. (2012). Human rights and intellectual disabilities: An emergent theoretical paradigm? *Journal of Intellectual Disability Research, 56,* 1011-1013.

Stam, G. (2015). Changes in thinking for speaking: A longitudinal case study. *Modern Language Journal, 99*(Suppl 1), 83-99.

Stam, K., Verbakel, E., & Graaf, P. M. (2013). Do values matter? The impact of work ethic and traditional gender role values on female labour market supply. *Social Indicators Research, 116,* 593-610.

Stangier, U., Schramm, E., Heidenreich, T., Berger, M., & Clark, D. M. (2011). Cognitive therapy vs. interpersonal psychotherapy in social anxiety disorder: A randomized controlled trial. *Archives of General Psychiatry, 68,* 692-700.

Staniewski, M. W., & Awruk, K. (2019). Entrepreneurial success and achievement motivation—A preliminary report on a validation study of the Questionnaire of Entrepreneurial Success. *Journal of Business Research, 101,* 433-440.

Stankov, L. (2003). Complexity in human intelligence. In R. J. Sternberg, J. Lautrey, & T. I. Lubart (Eds.), *Models of intelligence: International perspectives.* Washington, DC: American Psychological Association.

Stanley, M. L., Henne, P., Iyengar, V., Sinnott-Armstrong, W., & De Brigard, F. (2017). I'm not the person I used to be: The self and autobiographical memories of immoral actions. *Journal of Experimental Psychology: General, 116,* 884-895.

Stanojevic, S., Mitic, K., & Vujic, V. (2007). Exposure to acute physical and psychological stress alters the response of rat macrophages to corticosterone, neuropeptide Y and beta-endorphin. *International Journal on the Biology of Stress, 10,* 65-73.

Stapleton, P., Crighton, G. J., Carter, B., & Pidgeon, A. (2017). Self-esteem and body image in females: The mediating role of self-compassion and appearance contingent self-worth. *The Humanistic Psychologist, 45*(3), 238-257.

Starcevic, V., Berle, D., Milicevic, D., Hannan, A., Pamplugh, C., & Eslick, G. D. (2007). Pathological worry, anxiety disorders and the impact of co-occurrence with depressive and other anxiety disorders. *Journal of Anxiety Disorders, 21,* 1016-1027.

Startup, M., Bucci, S., & Langdon, R. (2009). Delusions of reference: A new theoretical model. *Cognitive Neuropsychiatry, 14,* 110-126.

Staub E. (2019). Promoting healing and reconciliation in Rwanda, and generating active bystandership by police to stop unnecessary harm by fellow officers. *Perspectives on Psychological Science, 14*(1), 60-64. doi:10.1177/1745691618809384.

Staub, E. (2011). *Overcoming evil: Genocide, violent conflict, and terrorism.* New York: Oxford University Press.

Staub, E. (2018). Preventing violence and promoting active bystandership and peace: My life in research and applications. *Peace and Conflict: Journal of Peace Psychology, 24*(1), 95-111.

Staub, E., Pearlman, L., & Bilali, R. (2010). Understanding the roots and impact of violence and psychological recovery as avenues to reconciliation after mass violence and intractable conflict: Applications to national leaders, journalists, community groups, public education through radio, and children. In G. Salomon & E. Cairns (Eds.), *Handbook on peace education.* New York: Psychology Press.

Staudt, M. D., Herring, E. Z., Gao, K., Miller, J. P., & Sweet, J. A. (2019). Evolution in the treatment of psychiatric disorders: from psychosurgery to psychopharmacology to neuromodulation. *Frontiers in Neuroscience, 13.*

Stech, E. P., Lim, J., Upton, E. L., & Newby, J. M. (2019, July 15). Internet-delivered cognitive behavioral therapy for panic disorder with or without agoraphobia: A systematic review and meta-analysis. *Cognitive Behaviour Therapy,* 1-24.

Steele, J. D., Christmas, D., Eljamel, M. S., & Matthews, K. (2007). Anterior cingulotomy for major depression: clinical outcome and relationship to lesion characteristics. *Biological Psychiatry, 12,* 127-134.

Stein, L. A. R., & Graham, J. R. (2005). Ability of substance abusers to escape detection on the Minnesota Multiphasic Personality Inventory- Adolescent (MMPI-A) in a juvenile correctional facility. *Assessment, 12,* 28-39.

Stein, R., & Swan, A. B. (2019). Evaluating the validity of Myers-Briggs Type Indicator theory: A teaching tool and window into intuitive psychology. *Social and Personality Psychology Compass.* https://doi-org.silk.library.umass.edu/10.1111/spc3.12434.

Steinbeis, N., Crone, E., Blakemore, S., & Kadosh, K. C. (2017). Development holds the key to understanding the interplay of nature versus nurture in shaping the individual. *Developmental Cognitive Neuroscience, 25,* 1-4.

Steinberg, L. (2007). Risk taking in adolescence: New perspectives from brain and behavioral science. *Current Directions in Psychological Science, 16,* 55-59.

Steinberg, L. (2016). Commentary on special issue on the adolescent brain: Redefining adolescence. *Neuroscience and Biobehavioral Reviews, 70,* 343-346.

Steinfeld, C., Ellison, N., & Lampe, C. (2008). Social capital, self-esteem, and use of online social network sites: A longitudinal analysis. *Journal of Applied Developmental Psychology, 29,* 434-445.

Steinhubl, S. R., Wineinger, N. E., Patel, S., Boeldt, D. L., Mackellar, G., Porter, V., et al. (2015). Cardiovascular and nervous system changes during meditation. *Frontiers in Human Neuroscience, 9,* 88-97.

Steinmetz, K. (2015, March 6). States battle over bathroom access for transgender people. *Time.* Accessed from http://time.com/3734714/transgender-bathroom-bills-lgbtdiscrimination/.

Steinmetz, K. (2017, March, 27). Infinite identities. *Time,* pp. 49-54.

Steinmetz, N. A., Koch, C., Harris, K. D., & Carandini, M. (2018). Challenges and opportunities for large-scale electrophysiology with Neuropixels probes. *Current Opinion in Neurobiology, 50,* 92-100.

Steins-Loeber, S., Madjarova, R., Lörsch, F., Herpertz, S. C., Flor, H., & Duka, T. (2019). An experimental study on spontaneous recovery of conditioned reward expectancies and instrumental responding in humans. *Behaviour Research and Therapy, 118*, 54-64.

Stemler, S. E., & Sternberg, R. J. (2006). Using situational judgment tests to measure practical intelligence. In J. A. Weekley & R. E. Ployhart (Eds.), *Situational judgment tests: Theory, measurement, and application*. Mahwah, NJ: Lawrence Erlbaum Associates.

Stemler, S. E., Sternberg, R. J., Grigorenko, E. L., Jarvin, L., & Sharpes, K. (2009). Using the theory of successful intelligence as a framework for developing assessments in AP physics. *Contemporary Educational Psychology, 34*, 195-209.

Stenbacka, L., & Vanni, S. (2007). fMRI of peripheral visual field representation. *Clinical Neurophysiology, 108*, 1303-1314.

Stern, E., & Silbersweig, D. A. (2001). Advances in functional neuroimaging methodology for the study of brain systems underlying human neuropsychological function and dysfunction. In D. A. Silbersweig & E. Stern (Eds.), *Neuropsychology and functional neuroimaging: Convergence, advances and new directions*. Amsterdam, Netherlands: Swets and Zeitlinger.

Sternberg, R. J. (1998). *Successful intelligence: How practical and creative intelligence determine success in life*. New York: Plume.

Sternberg, R. J. (2000). Intelligence and wisdom. In R. J. Sternberg et al. (Eds.), *Handbook of intelligence*. New York: Cambridge University Press.

Sternberg, R. J. (2004). A triangular theory of love. In H. T. Reis & C. E. Rusbult (Eds.), *Close relationships: Key readings*. Philadelphia, PA: Taylor & Francis.

Sternberg, R. J. (2006). A duplex theory of love. In R. J. Sternberg (Ed.), *The new psychology of love*. New Haven, CT: Yale University Press.

Sternberg, R. J. (2011). Individual differences in cognitive development. In U. Goswami (Ed.), *The Wiley-Blackwell handbook of childhood cognitive development* (2nd ed.). New York: Wiley-Blackwell.

Sternberg, R. J. (2013). What is cognitive education? *Journal of Cognitive Education and Psychology, 12*(1), 45-58.

Sternberg, R. J. (2015). Multiple intelligences in the new age of thinking. In S. Goldstein, D. Princiotta, & J. A. Naglieri (Eds.), *Handbook of intelligence: Evolutionary theory, historical perspective, and current concepts*. New York: Springer Science + Business Media.

Sternberg, R. J. (2017). *Career paths in psychology: Where your degree can take you* (3rd ed.). Washington, DC: American Psychological Association.

Sternberg, R. J., & Jarvin, L. (2003). Alfred Binet's contributions as a paradigm for impact in psychology. In R. J. Sternberg (Ed.), *The anatomy of impact: What makes the great works of psychology great*. Washington, DC: American Psychological Association.

Sternberg, R. J., & Pretz, J. E. (2005). *Cognition and intelligence: Identifying the mechanisms of the mind*. New York: Cambridge University Press.

Sternberg, R. J., Grigorenko, E. L., & Kidd, K. K. (2005). Intelligence, race, and genetics. *American Psychologist, 60*, 46-59.

Sternberg, R. J., Hojjat, M., & Barnes, M. L. (2001). Empirical aspects of a theory of love as a story. *European Journal of Personality, 15*, 1-20.

Sternberg, R. J., Jarvin, L., & Grigorenko, E. L. (2011). *Explorations in giftedness*. New York: Cambridge University Press.

Sternberg, R. J., Kaufman, J. C., & Pretz, J. E. (2004). A propulsion model of creative leadership [Special issue: Creativity in the workplace]. *Creativity and Innovation Management, 13*, 145-153.

Sternberg, R. J., Kaufman, J. C., & Roberts, A. M. (2019). The relation of creativity to intelligence and wisdom. In Kaufman, J. C & Sternberg, R. J. (Eds.), *The Cambridge handbook of creativity* (2nd ed.). New York: Cambridge University Press.

Sternson, S. M., Betley, J., & Cao, Z. (2013). Neural circuits and motivational processes for hunger. *Current Opinion in Neurobiology, 23*, 353-360.

Stetka, B. (2019, January). Mind over meal: Does weight-loss surgery rewire gut-brain connections? *Scientific American*, 47-51.

Stettler, N., Stallings, V. A., Troxel, A. B., Zhao, J. Z., Schinnar, R., Nelson, S. E., et al. (2005). Weight gain in the first week of life and overweight in adulthood. *Circulation, 111*, 1897-1903.

Stevens, C. F. (2015). Novel neural circuit mechanism for visual edge detection. *PNAS Proceedings of the National Academy of Sciences of the United States of America, 112*, 875-880.

Stevens, G. (2015). Black psychology: Resistance, reclamation, and redefinition. In I. Parker & I. Parker (Eds.), *Handbook of critical psychology*. New York: Routledge/Taylor & Francis Group.

Stevens, T., Brevers, D., Chambers, C. D., Lavric, A., McLaren, I. L., Mertens, M., et al. (2015). How does response inhibition influence decision making when gambling? *Journal of Experimental Psychology: Applied, 21*, 15-36.

Stevenson, H. W., Lee, S., & Mu, X. (2000). Successful achievement in mathematics: China and the United States. In C. F. M. van Lieshout & P. G. Heymans (Eds.), *Developing talent across the life span*. New York: Psychology Press.

Stewart, C. E., Lee, S. Y., Hogstrom, A., & Williams, M. (2017). Diversify and conquer: A call to promote minority representation in clinical psychology. *Behavior Therapist, 40*, 74-79.

Stewart, N., Ungemach, C., Harris, A., Bartels, D., Newell, B., Paolacci, G., & Chandler, J. (2015). The average laboratory samples a population of 7,300 Amazon Mechanical Turk workers. *Judgment & Decision Making, 10*, 479-491.

Stey, P. C., Lapsley, D., & McKeever, M. O. (2013). Moral judgement in adolescents: Age differences in applying and justifying three principles of harm. *European Journal of Developmental Psychology, 10*, 206-220.

Stickgold, R. (2015). Why we sleep. *Scientific American, 313*(4), 52-57.

Stickgold, R., Hobson, J. A., Fosse, R., & Fosse, M. (2001). Sleep, learning, and dreams: Off-line memory reprocessing. *Science, 294*, 1052-1057.

Stickley, T., & Nickeas, R. (2006). Becoming one person: Living with dissociative identity disorder. *Journal of Psychiatric and Mental Health Nursing, 13*, 180-187.

Stifter, C. A., Dollar, J. M., & Cipriano, E. A. (2011). Temperament and emotion regulation: The role of autonomic nervous system reactivity. *Developmental Psychobiology, 53*, 266-279.

Stix, G. (2011). The neuroscience of true grit. *Scientific American, 304*, 28-33.

Stockdale, M. S., & Sagrestano, L. M. (2011). Resources for targets of sexual harassment. In M. A. Paludi, C. R. Paludi, & E. R. DeSouza (Eds.), *Praeger handbook on understanding and preventing workplace discrimination* (Vols. 1 & 2). Santa Barbara, CA: Praeger/ABC-CLIO.

Stocks, E., Lishner, D., & Decker, S. (2009). Altruism or psychological escape: Why does empathy promote prosocial behavior? *European Journal of Social Psychology, 39*, 649-665.

Stockton, R., Morran, D. K., & Krieger, K. (2004). An overview of current research and best practices for training beginning group leaders. In J. L. DeLucia-Waack, D. A. Gerrity, C. R. Kalodner, & M. T. Riva (Eds.), *Handbook of group counseling and psychotherapy*. Thousand Oaks, CA: Sage Publications.

Stoll, O. (2019). Peak performance, the runner's high, and flow. In M. H. Anshel, S. J. Petruzzello, & E. E. Labbé (Eds.), *APA handbook of sport and exercise psychology, Vol. 2: Exercise psychology*. Washington, DC: American Psychological Association.

Stolorow, R. D., & Stolorow, B. A. (2013). Blues and emotional trauma. *Clinical Social Work Journal, 41*, 5-10.

Stone, C. A. (2015). Neuro/cognitive and sociocultural perspectives on language and literacy disabilities: Moving from parallel play to productive cooperation. In R. H. Bahr & E. R. Silliman (Eds.), *Routledge handbook of communication disorders*. New York: Routledge/Taylor & Francis Group.

Stone, D. L., & Rosopa, P. J. (2017). The advantages and limitations of using meta-analysis in human resource management research. *Human Resource Management Review, 27*, 1-7.

Stone, J. (2002). Battling doubt by avoiding practice: The effects of stereotype threat on self-handicapping in white athletes. *Personality and Social Psychology Bulletin, 28*, 1667-1678.

Stone, J., Moskowitz, G. B., Zestcott, C. A., & Wolsiefer, K. J. (2019). Testing active learning workshops for reducing implicit stereotyping of Hispanics by majority and minority group medical students. *Stigma and Health*. http://dx.doi.org/10.1037/sah0000179.

Stopa, L., Denton, R., Wingfield, M., & Taylor, K. (2013). The fear of others: A qualitative analysis of interpersonal threat in social phobia and paranoia. *Behavioural and Cognitive Psychotherapy, 41*, 188-209.

Stoppelbein, L., McRae, E., & Greening, L. (2017). A longitudinal study of hardiness as a buffer for posttraumatic stress symptoms in mothers of children with cancer. *Clinical Practice in Pediatric Psychology, 5*, 149-160.

Storm, L., & Ertel, S. (2001). Does psi exist? Comments on Milton and Wiseman's (1999) meta-analysis of Ganzfeld's research. *Psychological Bulletin, 127*, 424-433.

Storm, L., & Rock, A. J. (2015). Dreaming of psi: A narrative review and meta-analysis of dream-ESP studies at the Maimonides Dream Laboratory and beyond. In J. A. Davies & D. B. Pitchford (Eds.), *Stanley Krippner: A life of dreams, myths, and visions: Essays on his contributions and influence*. New York: University Professors Press.

Stowell, J. R., Robles, T. F., & Kane, H. S. (2013). Psychoneuroimmunology: Mechanisms, individual differences, and interventions. In A. M. Nezu, C. Nezu, P. A. Geller, & I. B. Weiner (Eds.), *Handbook of psychology, Vol. 9: Health psychology* (2nd ed.) Hoboken, NJ: John Wiley & Sons Inc.

Strange, D., Clifasefi, S., & Garry, M. (2007). False memories. In M. Garry & H. Hayne (Eds.), *Do justice and let the sky fall: Elizabeth Loftus and her contributions to science, law, and academic freedom*. Mahwah, NJ: Lawrence Erlbaum Associates.

Strathern, A., & Stewart, P. J. (2003). *Landscape, memory and history: Anthropological perspectives*. London: Pluto Press.

Strayer, D. L., & Drews, F. A. (2007). Cell-phone-induced driver distraction. *Current Directions in Psychological Science, 16*, 128-131.

Strenze, T. (2015). Intelligence and success. In S. Goldstein, D. Princiotta, & J. A. Naglieri (Eds.), *Handbook of intelligence: Evolutionary theory, historical perspective, and current concepts*. New York: Springer Science + Business Media.

Striano, T., & Vaish, A. (2006). Seven- to 9-month-old infants use facial expressions to interpret others' actions. *British Journal of Developmental Psychology, 24*, 753-760.

Striegel, R. H., Bedrosian, R., Wang, C., & Schwartz, S. (2011). Why men should be included in research on binge eating: Results from a comparison of psychosocial impairment in men and women. *International Journal of Eating Disorder, 45*, 233-240.

Striegel-Moore, R., & Bulik, C. M. (2007). Risk factors for eating disorders. *American Psychologist, 62*, 181-198.

Strogatz, S. (2018, January 8). One giant step for a chess-playing machine. *The New York Times*, p. D1.

Strong, T., & Tomm, K. (2007). Family therapy as re-coordinating and moving on together. *Journal of Systemic Therapies, 26*, 42-54.

Stålhammar, J., Nordlund, A., & Wallin, A. (2015). An example of exceptional practice effects in the verbal domain. *Neurocase, 21*, 162-168.

Stöllberger, C., Koller, J., Finsterer, J., Schauer, D., & Ehrlich, M. (2019). Anterograde amnesia as a manifestation of acute type A aortic dissection. *International Journal of Angiology*. DOI: 10.1055/s-0039-1693029.

Subrahmanyam, K., Reich, S., Waechter, N., & Espinoza, G. (2008). Online and offline social networks: Use of social networking sites by emerging adults. *Journal of Applied Developmental Psychology, 29*, 420-433.

Substance Abuse and Mental Health Services Administration. (2014). *Results from the 2013 National Survey on Drug Use and Health: Mental Health Findings*, NSDUH Series H-49, HHS Publication No. (SMA) 14-4887. Rockville, MD: Author.

Substance Abuse and Mental Health Services Administration. (2019). Key substance use and mental health indicators in the United States: Results from the 2018 National Survey on Drug Use and Health (HHS Publication No. PEP19-5068, NSDUH Series H-54). Rockville, MD: Center for Behavioral Health Statistics and Quality, Substance Abuse and Mental Health Services Administration. Retrieved from https://www.samhsa.gov/data/.

Sue, D. W. (2017). Microaggressions and "evidence": Empirical or experiential reality? *Perspectives on Psychological Science, 12*, 170-172.

Sue, D. W., & Sue, D. (1990). *Counseling the culturally different: Theory and practice* (2nd ed.). Oxford, England: John Wiley & Sons.

Suen, H.K. (2015). Technical Brief Kuder Career Interests Assessment® - Likert 2015 (KCIA-L 2015). Downloaded from http://www.kuder.com/webres/File/Technical%20Briefs/KCIA-L%202015%20Technical%20Brief.pdf?_cldee=ZmVsZG1hbkBwc3ljaC51bWFzcy5lZHU%3d&recipientid=lead-2aa47b3dbbc-fe91180ea005056a4665b-ea83342043f04f-f280eeca01c617d635&utm_source=ClickDimensions&utm_medium=email&utm_campaign=Kuder.com%20Form%20%E2%80%93%20KCIA%20Likert%20Technical%20Brief&esid=89615f06-9e6c-4c0a-a192-898b61900b0f.

Suh, E. M. (2002). Culture, identity consistency, and subjective well-being. *Journal of Personality & Social Psychology, 83*, 1378-1391.

Suhail, K., & Chaudhry, H. R. (2004). Predictors of subjective well-being in an Eastern Muslim culture. *Journal of Social and Clinical Psychology, 23*, 359-376.

Suizzo, M.-A., & Bornstein, M. H. (2006). French and European American child-mother play: Culture and gender considerations. *International Journal of Behavioral Development, 30*, 498-508.

Sullivan, E. L., Smith, S. M., & Grove, K. L. (2011). Perinatal exposure to high-fat diet programs energy balance, metabolism and behavior in adulthood. *Neuroendocrinology, 93*, 1-8.

Summa, K. C., & Turek, F. W. (2015). The clocks within us. *Scientific American, 312*, 51-55.

Summers, M. (2000). *Everything in its place*. New York: Putnam.

Summers, S. J., Schabrun, S. M., Marinovic, W., & Chipchase, L. S. (2017). Peripheral electrical stimulation increases corticomotor excitability and enhances the rate of visuomotor adaptation. *Behavioural Brain Research, 322*(Part A), 42-50

Sun, J., Schwartz, H. A., Son, Y., Kern, M. L., & Vazire, S. (2019). The language of well-being: Tracking fluctuations in emotion experience through everyday speech. *Journal of Personality and Social Psychology*. https://doi.org/10.1037/pspp0000244.

Sun, L. H. (2019, September 5). Contaminant found in marijuana vaping products linked to deadly lung illnesses, tests show. *Washington Post*. Downloaded from https://www.washingtonpost.com/health/2019/09/05/contaminant-found-vaping-products-linked-deadly-lung-illnesses-state-federal-labs-show/.

Sun, X., Niu, G., You, Z., Zhou, Z., & Tang, Y. (2017). "Gender, negative life events and coping on different stages of depression severity: A cross-sectional study among Chinese university students". Corrigendum. *Journal of Affective Disorders, 215*, 102.

Sun, Y., Giacobbe, P., Tang, C. W., Barr, M. S., Rajji, T., Kennedy, S. H., et al. (2015). Deep brain stimulation modulates gamma oscillations and theta-gamma coupling in treatment resistant depression. *Brain Stimulation, 6*, 1033-1042.

Sunshine, J. E., Meo, N., Kassebaum, N. J., Collison, M. L., Mokdad, A. H., & Naghavi, M. (2019). Association of adverse effects of medical treatment with mortality in the United States: A secondary analysis of the Global Burden of Diseases, Injuries, and Risk Factors Study. *JAMA Network Open, 2*(1):e187041. doi:10.1001/jamanetworkopen.2018.7041.

Super, C. M. (1980). Cognitive development: Looking across at growing up. In C. M. Super & S. Harakness (Eds.), *New directions for child development: Anthropological perspectives on child development*. San Francisco: Jossey-Bass.

Surya, S., Bishnoi, R. J., & Shashank, R. B. (2019). Balancing medical ethics to consider involuntary administration of electroconvulsive therapy. *The Journal of ECT, 35*(3), 150-151.

Sutherland, S. (2016). The maddening sensation of itch. *Scientific American, 314*, 39-43.

Sutin, A. R., & Robins, R. W. (2007). Phenomenology of autobiographical memories: The Memory Experiences Questionnaire. *Memory, 15*, 390-411.

Suzuki, L. A., Short, E. L., & Lee, C. S. (2011). Racial and ethnic group differences in intelligence in the United States: Multicultural perspectives. In R. J. Sternberg & S. Kaufman (Eds.), *The Cambridge handbook of intelligence.* New York: Cambridge University Press.

Suárez-Orozco, M. M., & Suárez-Orozco, C. (2018, September 20). Like it or not, immigrant children are our future. *Washington Post.* Downloaded from https://www.washingtonpost.com/news/theworldpost/wp/2018/09/20/immigrant/.

Swain, R. A., Kerr, A. L., & Thompson, R. F. (2011). The cerebellum: A neural system for the study of reinforcement learning. *Frontiers in Behavioral Neuroscience, 18,* 89-96.

Sweeney, M. M., Meredith, S. E., Juliano, L. M., Evatt, D. P., & Griffiths, R. R. (2019). A randomized controlled trial of a manual-only treatment for reduction and cessation of problematic caffeine use. *Drug and Alcohol Dependence, 195,* 45-51.

Szegedy Maszak, M. (2003, January 13). The sound of unsound minds. *U.S. News & World Report,* pp. 45-46.

Sørensen, S. Ø. (2017). The performativity of choice: Postfeminist perspectives on work-life balance. *Gender, Work and Organization, 24*(3), 297-313.

Tadmor, C. T. (2007). Biculturalism: The plus side of leaving home? The effects of second-culture exposure on integrative complexity and its consequences for overseas performance. *Dissertation Abstracts International Section A: Humanities and Social Sciences, 67*(8-A), 3068.

Taibbi, R. (2018). *Brief therapy with couples and families in crisis.* New York: Routledge/Taylor & Francis Group.

Tajfel, H., & Turner, J. C. (2004). The social identity theory of intergroup behavior. In J. T. Jost & J. Sidanius (Eds.), *Political psychology: Key readings.* New York: Psychology Press.

Tajfel, H., & Turner, J. C. (2010). An integrative theory of intergroup conflict. In T. Postmes & N. R. Branscombe (Eds.), *Rediscovering social.* New York: Psychology Press.

Takahashi, M., Nakata, A., Haratani, T., Ogawa, Y., & Arito, H. (2004). Post-lunch nap as a worksite intervention to promote alertness on the job. *Ergonomics, 47,* 1003-1013.

Takamiya, S., Yuki, S., Hirokawa, J., Manabe, H., & Sakurai, Y. (2019). Dynamics of memory engrams. *Neuroscience Research.* https://doi.org/10.1016/j.neures.2019.03.005

Taki, Y., Thyreau, B., Kinomura, S., Sato, K., Goto, R., Wu, K., et al. (2013). A longitudinal study of age and gender related annual rate of volume changes in regional gray matter in healthy adults. *Human Brain Mapping, 34,* 2292-2301.

Takizawa, T., Kondo, T., & Sakihara, S. (2007). Stress buffering effects of social support on depressive symptoms in middle age: Reciprocity and community mental health: Corrigendum. *Psychiatry and Clinical Neurosciences, 61,* 336-337.

Takooshian, H., Gielen, U. P., Plous, S., Rich, G. J., & Velayo, R. S. (2016). Internationalizing undergraduate psychology education: Trends, techniques, and technologies. *American Psychologist, 71,* 136-147.

Tal-Or, N., & Papirman, Y. (2007). The fundamental attribution error in attributing fictional figures' characteristics to the actors. *Media Psychology, 9,* 331-345.

Talarico, J. (2009). Freshman flashbulbs: Memories of unique and first-time events in starting college. *Memory, 17,* 256-265.

Talarico, J. M., Bohn, A., & Wessel, I. (2019). The role of event relevance and congruence to social groups in flashbulb memory formation. *Memory, 27,* 985-997.

Talarico, J., & Rubin, D. (2007). Flashbulb memories are special after all; in phenomenology, not accuracy. *Applied Cognitive Psychology, 21,* 557-578.

Talukdar, S., & Shastri, J. (2006). Contributory and adverse factors in social development of young children. *Psychological Studies, 51,* 294-303.

Tam, S. E., Bonardi, C., & Robinson, J. (2015). Relative recency influences object-in-context memory. *Behavioural Brain Research, 281,* 250-257.

Tamannaeifar, M., & Shahmirzaei, S. (2019). Prediction of academic resilience based on coping styles and personality traits. *Journal of Practice in Clinical Psychology, 7*(1), 1-9.

Tamini, B., Bojhd, F., & Yazdani, S. (2011). Love types, psychological well-being and self-concept. *Journal of the Indian Academy of Applied Psychology, 37,* 169-178.

Tan, G., Rintala, D. H., Jensen, M. P., Richards, J. S., Holmes, S. A., Parachuri, R., et al. (2011). Efficacy of cranial electrotherapy stimulation for neuropathic pain following spinal cord injury: a multi-site randomized controlled trial with a secondary 6-month open-label phase. *Journal of Spinal Cord Medicine, 34,* 285-296.

Tan, L., Yu, J., & Tan, L. (2015). Causes and consequences of microRNA dysregulation in neurodegenerative diseases. *Molecular Neurobiology, 51,* 1249-1262.

Tanaka, C., Matsui, M., Uematsu, A., Noguchi, K., & Miyawaki, T. (2012). Developmental trajectories of the fronto-temporal lobes from infancy to early adulthood in healthy individuals. *Developmental Neuroscience, 34*(6), 477-487.

Tanaka-Matsumi, J. (2019). Culture and psychotherapy: Searching for an empirically supported relationship. In K. D. Keith (Ed.), *Cross-cultural psychology: Contemporary themes and perspectives* (2nd ed.). Hoboken, NJ: John Wiley & Sons, Inc.

Tandon, R., Gaebel, W., Barch, D. M., Bustillo, J., Gur, R. E., Heckers, S., et al. (2013). Definition and description of schizophrenia in the DSM-5. *Schizophrenia Research, 150*(1), 3-10.

Tang, Y., Zhao, L., Lou, Y., Shi, Y., Fang, R., Lin, X., et al. (2018). Brain structure differences between Chinese and Caucasian cohorts: A comprehensive morphometry study. *Human Brain Mapping, 39*(5), 2147-2155.

Tanida, Y., Nakayama, M., & Saito, S. (2019). The interaction between temporal grouping and phonotactic chunking in short-term serial order memory for novel verbal sequences. *Memory, 27*(4), 507-518.

Tao, K. W., & Gloria, A. M. (2019). Should I stay or should I go? The role of impostorism in STEM persistence. *Psychology of Women Quarterly, 43*(2), 151-164.

Tappin, B. M., McKay, R. T., & Abrams, D. (2017). Choosing the right level of analysis: Stereotypes shape social reality via collective action. *Behavioral and Brain Sciences, 40.* Accessed from https://www.ncbi.nlm.nih.gov/pubmed/28327226.

Tasker, F. (2005). Lesbian mothers, gay fathers, and their children: A review. *Journal of Developmental and Behavioral Pediatrics, 26,* 224-240.

Tassone, D., Reed, A. E., & Carstensen, L. L. (2019). Time may heal wounds: Aging and life regrets. *Psychology and Aging.* Advance online publication. http://dx.doi.org/10.1037/pag0000381.

Tavernise, S. (2015, April 17). Teenagers pick up e-cigarettes as old-school smoking declines. *The New York Times,* p. A1.

Taylor, F., & Bryant, R. A. (2007). The tendency to suppress, inhibiting thoughts, and dream rebound. *Behaviour Research and Therapy, 45,* 163-168.

Taylor, M. A., & Bisson, J. B. (2019). Changes in cognitive function: Practical and theoretical considerations for training the aging workforce. *Human Resource Management Review.* Advance online publication https://doi.org/10.1016/j.hrmr.2019.02.001.

Taylor, S. (2015). *Health psychology* (9th ed.). New York: McGraw-Hill.

Taylor, S. E., Kemeny, M. E., Reed, G. M., Bower, J. E., & Gruenewald, T. L. (2000). Psychological resources, positive illusions, and health. *American Psychologist, 55,* 99-109.

Tazouti, Y., & Jarlégan, A. (2019). The mediating effects of parental self-efficacy and parental involvement on the link between family socioeconomic status and children's academic achievement. *Journal of Family Studies, 25*(3), 250-266.

Teague, R. (2013). The American view of Freud's couch. *PsycCRITIQUES, 58,* 12-21.

Tedeschi, R. G., Blevins, C. L., & Riffle, O. M. (2017). Posttraumatic growth: A brief history and evaluation. In M. A. Warren & S. I. Donaldson (Eds.), *Scientific advances in positive psychology.* Santa Barbara, CA: Praeger/ABC-CLIO.

Tellis, G. J., MacInnis, D. J., Tirunillai, S., & Zhang, Y. (2019). What drives virality (sharing) of online digital content? The critical role of information, emotion, and brand prominence. *Journal of Marketing, 83*(4), 1-20.

ten Cate, C. (2017). Assessing the uniqueness of language: Animal grammatical abilities take center stage. *Psychonomic Bulletin & Review, 24*, 91-96.

Tenenbaum, H. R., & Leaper, C. (2002). Are parents' gender schemas related to their children's gender-related cognitions? A meta-analysis. *Developmental Psychology, 38*, 615-630.

Teovanović, P., Knežević, G., & Stankov, L. (2015). Individual differences in cognitive biases: Evidence against one-factor theory of rationality. *Intelligence, 50*, 75-86.

Thaler, L. (2015). Using sound to get around: Discoveries in human echolocation. *APS Observer, 28*, 24-27.

Thaler, N. S., Thames, A. D., Cagigas, X. E., & Norman, M. A. (2015). IQ testing and the African American client. In L. T. Benuto & B. D. Leany (Eds.), *Guide to psychological assessment with African Americans.* New York: Springer Science + Business Media.

Tharp, R. G. (1989). Psychocultural variables and constants: Effects on teaching and learning in schools [Special issue: Children and their development: Knowledge base, research agenda, and social policy application]. *American Psychologist, 44*, 349-359.

Thase, M. E. (2013). Comparative effectiveness of psychodynamic psychotherapy and cognitive-behavioral therapy: It's about time, and what's next? *American Journal of Psychiatry, 170*, 953-956.

Thatcher, D. L., & Clark, D. B. (2006). Adolescent alcohol abuse and dependence: Development, diagnosis, treatment and outcomes. *Current Psychiatry Reviews, 2*, 159-177.

Theriault, J., Krause, P., & Young, L. (2017). Know thy enemy: Education about terrorism improves social attitudes toward terrorists. *Journal of Experimental Psychology: General, 146*(3), 305-317.

Thompson, A. K., & Wolpaw, J. R. (2015). Restoring walking after spinal cord injury: Operant conditioning of spinal reflexes can help. *The Neuroscientist, 21*(2), 203-215.

Thompson, M. (2015, April 6.) Unlocking the secrets of PTSD. *Time*, pp. 41-43.

Thompson, T., Terhune, D. B., Oram, C., Sharangparni, J., Rouf, R., Solmi, M., et al. (2019). The effectiveness of hypnosis for pain relief: A systematic review and meta-analysis of 85 controlled experimental trials. *Neuroscience and Biobehavioral Reviews, 99*, 298-310.

Thorkildsen, T. A. (2006). An empirical exploration of language and thought. *PsycCRITIQUES, 51*, n.p.

Thorndike, E. L. (1932). *The fundamentals of learning.* New York: Teachers College.

Thornton, A., & Young-DeMarco, L. (2001). Four decades of trends in attitudes toward family issues in the United States: The 1960s through the 1990s. *Journal of Marriage and the Family, 63*, 1009-1017.

Thrailkill, E. A., & Bouton, M. E. (2017). Effects of outcome devaluation on instrumental behaviors in a discriminated heterogeneous chain. *Journal of Experimental Psychology: Animal Learning and Cognition, 43*, 88-95.

Thrash, T. M., & Elliot, A. J. (2002). Implicit and self-attributed achievement motives: Concordance and predictive validity. *Journal of Personality, 70*, 729-755.

Thurman, S. M., & Lu, H. (2013). Physical and biological constraints govern perceived animacy of scrambled human forms. *Psychological Science, 24*, 1133-1141.

Tien, L., Davis, A., Arnold, T. H., & Benjamin, G. H. (2012). *Ethics for psychologists: A casebook approach.* Thousand Oaks, CA: Sage Publications.

Tillema, E. S. (2019). Students' solution of arrangement problems and their connection to Cartesian product problems. *Mathematical Thinking and Learning*, 1-33.

Tingley, K. (2016, March 20). Sixth sense. *The New York Times Magazine*, p. MM52.

Tippin, J., Sparks, J., & Rizzo, M. (2009). Visual vigilance in drivers with obstructive sleep apnea. *Journal of Psychosomatic Research, 67*, 143-151.

Tobajas, J., Gómez-Ramírez, P., María-Mojica, P., Navas, I., García-Fernández, A. J., Ferreras, P., et al. (2019). Selection of new chemicals to be used in conditioned aversion for non-lethal predation control. *Behavioural Processes, 166*, 103905.

Todorov, A., Fiske, S., & Prentice, D. (Eds.). (2011). *Social neuroscience: Toward understanding the underpinnings of the social mind.* New York: Oxford University Press

Tokutsu, Y., Umene-Nakano, W., Shinkai, T., Yoshimura, R., Okamoto, T., Katsuki, A., et al. (2013). Follow-up study on electroconvulsive therapy in treatment-resistant depressed patients after remission: A chart review. *Clinical Psychopharmacology and Neuroscience, 11*, 34-38.

Tolman, E. C., & Honzik, C. H. (1930). Introduction and removal of reward and maze performance in rats. *University of California Publications in Psychology, 4*, 257-275.

Tolnai, S., Beutelmann, R., & Klump, G. M. (2017). Effect of preceding stimulation on sound localization and its representation in the auditory midbrain. *European Journal of Neuroscience, 45*, 460-471.

Tomasello, M. (2019). The role of roles in uniquely human cognition and sociality. *Journal for the Theory of Social Behaviour.* Accessed from https://doi-org.silk.library. umass.edu/10.1111/jtsb.12223.

Tommasi, L. (2009). Mechanisms and functions of brain and behavioural asymmetries. *Philosophical Transactions of the Royal Society B, 364*, 855-859.

Tonidandel, S., Quinones, M. A., & Adams, A. A. (2002). Computer-adaptive testing: The impact of test characteristics on perceived performance and test takers' reactions. *Journal of Applied Psychology, 87*, 320-332.

Tonnaer, F., Cima, M., & Arntz, A. (2019). Explosive matters: Does venting anger reduce or increase aggression? Differences in anger venting effects in violent offenders. *Journal of Aggression, Maltreatment & Trauma*, 1-17.

Tononi, G., & Cirelli, C. (2013). Perchance to prune. *Scientific American, 309*(2), 34-39.

Tononi, G., & Koch, C. (2008). The neural correlates of consciousness: An update. In A Kingstone & M. B. Miller (Eds.), *The year in cognitive neuroscience.* Malden, MA: Blackwell Publishing.

Topol, E. J. (2019). High-performance medicine: the convergence of human and artificial intelligence. *Nature medicine, 25*(1), 44.

Torrey, E. F., & Yolken, R. H. (2019). Schizophrenia as a pseudogenetic disease: A call for more gene-environmental studies. *Psychiatry Research, 278*, 146-150.

Tosto, M. G., Hayiou-Thomas, M. E., Harlaar, N., Prom-Wormley, E., Dale, P. S., & Plomin, R. (2017). The genetic architecture of oral language, reading fluency, and reading comprehension: A twin study from 7 to 16 years. *Developmental Psychology, 53*, 1115-1129.

Toto, H. S. A., Piffer, D., Khaleefa, O. H., Bader, R. A. S. A. T., Bakhiet, S. F. A., Lynn, R., et al. (2019). A study of the heritability of intelligence in Sudan. *Journal of Biosocial Science, 51*(2), 307-311.

Towns, C. R. (2017). The science and ethics of cell-based therapies for Parkinson's disease. *Parkinsonism & Related Disorders, 34*, 1-6.

Tracy, J. L., & Robins, R. W. (2004). Show your pride: Evidence for a discrete emotion expression. *Psychological Science, 15*, 194-197.

Tramontana, J. (2011). *Sports hypnosis in practice: Scripts, strategies and case examples.* Norwalk, CT: Crown House Publishing Limited.

Travis, F. (2006). From I to I: Concepts of self on a object-referral/self referral continuum. In A. P. Prescott (Ed.), *The concept of self in psychology.* Hauppauge, NY: Nova Science Publishers.

Travis, F., Haaga, D. A., Hagelin, J., Tanner, M., Nidich, S., Gaylord-King, C., et al. (2009). Effects of transcendental meditation practice on brain functioning and stress reactivity in college students. *International Journal of Psychopathy, 71*, 170-176.

Treatment Advocacy Center. (2016). Serious mental illness and homelessness. Downloaded from https://www.treatmentadvocacycenter.org/storage/documents/backgrounders/smi-and-homelessness.pdf.

Tremaroli, V., Karlsson, F., Werling, M., Ståhlman, M., Kovatcheva-Datchary, P., Olbers, T., et al. (2015). Roux-en-Y gastric bypass and vertical banded gastroplasty induce long-term changes on the human gut microbiome contributing to fat mass regulation. *Cell Metabolism, 22*(2), 228-238.

Tremblay, A. (2004). Dietary fat and body weight set point. *Nutrition Review, 62*(7, Pt 2), S75-S77.

Triandis, H. C. (2011). Culture and self-deception: A theoretical perspective. *Social Behavior and Personality, 39*, 3-14.

Triscari, M., Faraci, P., D'Angelo, V., Urso, V., & Catalisano, D. (2011). Two treatments for fear of flying compared: Cognitive behavioral therapy combined with systematic desensitization or eye movement desensitization and reprocessing (EMDR). *Aviation Psychology and Applied Human Factors, 1*, 9–14.

Tropp, L. R., & Bianchi, R. A. (2006). Valuing diversity and interest in intergroup contact. *Journal of Social Issues, 62*, 533–551.

Trujillo-Pisanty, I., Hernandez, G., Moreau-Debord, I., Cossette, M. P., Conover, K., Cheer, J. F., et al. (2011). Cannabinoid receptor blockade reduces the opportunity cost at which rats maintain operant performance for rewarding brain stimulation. *Journal of Neuroscience, 31*, 5426–5430.

Trull, T. J., & Widiger, T. A. (2003). Personality disorders. In G. Stricker, T. A. Widiger, & I. B. Wiener (Eds.), *Handbook of psychology: Clinical psychology* (Vol. 8). New York: Wiley.

Tschentscher, N., & Hauk, O. (2017). Frontal cortex supports the early structuring of multiple solution steps in symbolic problem-solving. *Journal of Cognitive Neuroscience, 29*, 114–124.

Tsemberis, S., & Macnaughton, E. (2017). Homelessness and challenges of community care. In N. Okkels, C. B. Kristiansen, & P. Munk-Jørgensen (Eds.), *Mental health and illness in the city*. New York: Springer Science + Business Media.

Tseng, W. S. (2003). *Clinician's guide to cultural psychiatry*. San Diego, CA: Elsevier Publishing.

Tsenkova, V., Boylan, J., & Ryff, C. (2013). Stress eating and health. Findings from MIDUS, a national study of US adults. *Appetite, 69*, 151–155.

Tsukasaki, T., & Ishii, K. (2004). Linguistic-cultural relativity of cognition: Rethinking the Sapir-Whorf hypothesis. *Japanese Psychological Review, 47*, 173–186.

Tucker, C. M., & Herman, K. C. (2002). Using culturally sensitive theories and research to meet the academic needs of low-income African American children. *American Psychologist, 57*, 762–773.

Tucker-Drob, E. M., Brandmaier, A. M., & Lindenberger, U. (2019). Coupled cognitive changes in adulthood: A meta-analysis. *Psychological Bulletin, 145*(3), 273–301.

Tuckey, M. R., Searle, B. J., Boyd, C. M., Winefield, A. H., & Winefield, H. R. (2015). Hindrances are not threats: Advancing the multidimensionality of work stress. *Journal of Occupational Health Psychology, 20*, 131–147.

Tuerk, P. W., Yoder, M., Grubaugh, A., Myrick, H., Hamner, M., & Acierno, R. (2011). Prolonged exposure therapy for combat-related posttraumatic stress disorder: An examination of treatment effectiveness for veterans of the wars in Afghanistan and Iraq. *Journal of Anxiety Disorders, 25*, 397–403.

Tummala-Narra, P. (2016). *Psychoanalytic theory and cultural competence in psychotherapy*. Washington, DC: American Psychological Association.

Tunstall, B. J., Verendeev, A., & Kearns, D. N. (2013). Outcome specificity in deepened extinction may limit treatment feasibility: Co-presentation of a food cue interferes with extinction of cue-elicited cocaine seeking.

Drug and Alcohol Dependence. Retrieved from http://www.ncbi.nlm.nih.gov/pubmed/24071568.

Turner, M. E., Pratkanis, A. R., & Struckman, C. K. (2007). Groupthink as social identity maintenance. In C. K. Struckman (Ed.), *The science of social influence: Advances and future progress*. New York: Psychology Press.

Turner, S., Taillieu, T., Cheung, K., & Afifi, T. O. (2017). The relationship between childhood sexual abuse and mental health outcomes among males: Results from a nationally representative United States sample. *Child Abuse & Neglect, 66*, 64–72.

Turri, M. G. (2015). Transference and katharsis, Freud to Aristotle. *International Journal of Psychoanalysis, 96*, 369–387.

Tuszynski, M. H. (2007). Nerve growth factor gene therapy in Alzheimer's disease. *Alzheimer's Disease and Associated Disorders, 21*, 179–189.

Tutwiler, S., Lin, M., & Chang, C. (2013). The use of a gesture-based system for teaching multiple intelligences: A pilot study. *British Journal of Educational Technology, 44*, E133–E138.

Tversky, A., & Kahneman, D. (1987). Rational choice and the framing of decisions. In R. Hogarth & M. Reder (Eds.), *Rational choice: The contrast between economics and psychology*. Chicago: University of Chicago Press.

Twenge, J. M. (2013). Does online social media lead to social connection or social disconnection? *Journal of College and Character, 14*, 11–20.

Twenge, J. M., & Kasser, T. (2013). Generational changes in materialism and work centrality, 1976–2007: Associations with temporal changes in societal insecurity and materialistic role-modeling. *Personality and Social Psychology Bulletin, 34*, 17–31.

Twenge, J. M., Cooper, A. B., Joiner, T. E., Duffy, M. E., & Binau, S. G. (2019). Age, period, and cohort trends in mood disorder indicators and suicide-related outcomes in a nationally representative dataset, 2005–2017. *Journal of Abnormal Psychology, 128*(3), 185–199.

Twenge, J. M., Hisler, G. C., & Krizan, Z. (2019). Associations between screen time and sleep duration are primarily driven by portable electronic devices: Evidence from a population-based study of US children ages 0–17. *Sleep Medicine, 56*, 211–218.

Twenge, J. M., Martin, G. N., & Campbell, W. K. (2018). Decreases in psychological well-being among American adolescents after 2012 and links to screen time during the rise of smartphone technology. *Emotion, 18*(6), 765–780.

Twining, R. C., Wheeler, D. S., Ebben, A. L., Jacobsen, A. J., Robble, M. A., Mantsch, J. R., & Wheeler, R. A. (2015). Aversive stimuli drive drug seeking in a state of low dopamine tone. *Biological Psychiatry, 77*, 895–902.

Tyrer, H., Tyrer, P., Lisseman-Stones, Y., McAllister, S., Cooper, S., Salkovskis, P., et al. (2015). Therapist differences in a randomised trial of the outcome of cognitive behaviour therapy for health anxiety in medical

patients. *International Journal of Nursing Studies, 52*, 686–694.

U.S. Bureau of Labor Statistics. (2007). *American time use survey*. Washington, DC: Author.

U.S. Bureau of Labor Statistics. (2013, April 26). Employment characteristics of families–2012. Washington, DC: Author.

U.S. Census Bureau. (2016). The majority of children live with two parents. Census Bureau Reports. Downloaded from https://www.census.gov/newsroom/press-releases/2016/cb16-192.html.

U.S. Census Bureau. (2017, September 14). New American community survey statistics for income, poverty and health insurance available for states and local areas. Release Number CB17-157. Retrieved from https://www.census.gov/newsroom/press-releases/2017/acs-single-year.html?CID=CBSM+ACS16.

U.S. Census Bureau. (2019, June 20.) A more diverse nation. Downloaded from https://www.census.gov/library/visualizations/2019/comm/age-race-distribution.html.

U.S. Department of Health and Human Services. (2016). E-cigarette use among youth and young adults. A report of the Surgeon General. Atlanta, GA: U.S. Department of Health and Human Services, Centers for Disease Control and Prevention, National Center for Chronic Disease Prevention and Health Promotion, Office on Smoking and Health.

U.S. Senate Select Committee on Intelligence. (2004, July 7). *Report of the U.S. intelligence community's prewar intelligence assessments on Iraq*. Retrieved from https://www.hsdl.org/?abstract&did=448158.

Ullman, S. E., & Townsend, S. M. (2007). Barriers to working with sexual assault survivors: A qualitative study of rape crisis center workers. *Violence Against Women, 13*, 412–443.

UNAIDS. (December 2013). 2013 AIDS epidemic update. Geneva, Switzerland: United Nations Programme on HIV/AIDS.

UNESCO. (2019). I'd blush if I could: Closing gender divides in digital skills through education. Retrieved from https://en.unesco.org/Id-blush-if-I-could.

Unsworth, N., Redick, T. S., McMillan, B. D., Hambrick, D. Z., Kane, M. J., & Engle, R. W. (2015). Is playing video games related to cognitive abilities? *Psychological Science, 26*(6), 759–774.

Urban, J. B., & Linver, M. R. (2019). *Building a career outside academia: A guide for doctoral students in the behavioral and social sciences.* (J. B. Urban & M. R. Linver, Eds.). Washington, DC: American Psychological Association.

Urlacher, B. R. (2008). Walking out of two-level social traps (with a little help from my friends). *Simulation & Gaming, 39*, 453–464.

Ursprung, W. W., Sanouri, A., & DiFranza, J. R. (2009). The loss of autonomy over smoking in relation to lifetime cigarette consumption. *Addictive Behaviors, 22*, 12–19.

Uylings, H. B. M. (2006). Development of the human cortex and the concept of "critical" or "sensitive" periods. *Language Learning, 56,* 59–90.

Vadivel, K., & Ganesh, G. (2019). Enhancing the student's understanding of place theory of hearing using a sonometer. *International Journal of Physiology, 7*(1), 39–41.

Vagianos, A. (2015, February 19). 1 in 3 women has been sexually harassed at work, according to survey. *Huffington Post.* Accessed at http://www.huffingtonpost.com/2015/02/19/1-in-3-women-sexually-harassed-work-cosmopolitan_n_6713814.html.

Vaillant, G. E., & Vaillant, C. O. (1990). Natural history of male psychological health: XII. A 46-year study of predictors of successful aging at age 65. *American Journal of Psychiatry, 147,* 31–37.

Valencia, R. R., & Suzuki, L. A. (2003). *Intelligence testing and minority students: Foundations, performance factors, and assessment issues.* Thousand Oaks, CA: Sage.

Valenzuela, V., Martínez, G., Duran-Aniotz, C., & Hetz, C. (2016). Gene therapy to target ER stress in brain diseases. *Brain Research, 1648*(Part B), 561–570.

Vally, Z., & D'Souza, C. G. (2019). Abstinence from social media use, subjective well-being, stress, and loneliness. *Perspectives in Psychiatric Care.* https://doi.org/10.1111/ppc.12431.

Valois, R. F., Zullig, K. J., & Hunter, A. A. (2013). Association between adolescent suicide ideation, suicide attempts and emotional self efficacy. *Journal of Child and Family Studies, 24,* 237–248.

Valsecchi, M., Caziot, B., Backus, B. T., & Gegenfurtner, K. R. (2013). The role of binocular disparity in rapid scene and pattern recognition. *I-Perception, 4*(2), 254–262.

Valyear, M. D., Villaruel, F. R., & Chaudhri, N. (2017). Alcohol-seeking and relapse: A focus on incentive salience and contextual conditioning. *Behavioural Processes, 141*(Part 1), 26–32.

Van Belle, V., Pelckmans, K., Suykens, J. A. K., & Van Huffel, S. (2011). Learning transformation models for ranking and survival analysis. *Journal of Machine Learning Research, 12,* 819–862.

Van Damme, C., Deschrijver, E., Van Geert, E., & Hoorens, V. (2017). When praising yourself insults others: Self-superiority claims provoke aggression. *Personality and Social Psychology Bulletin, 43,* 1008–1019.

Van den Wildenberg, W. P. M., & Van der Molen, M. W. (2004). Developmental trends in simple and selective inhibition of compatible and incompatible responses. *Journal of Experimental Child Psychology, 87,* 201–220.

Van der Zee, E. A., Platt, B. B., & Riedel, G. G. (2011). Acetylcholine: Future research and perspectives. *Behavioural Brain Research, 221,* 583–586.

Van Deurzen, E., Craig, E., Längle, A., Schneider, K. J., Tantam, D., & du Plock, S. (Eds.). (2019). *The Wiley world handbook of existential therapy.* Hoboken, NJ: Wiley Blackwell.

van Dijk, W. W., Ouwerkerk, J. W., Wesseling, Y. M., & van Koningsbruggen, G. M. (2011). Towards understanding pleasure at the misfortunes of others: The impact of self-evaluation threat on schadenfreude. *Cognition and Emotion, 25,* 360–368.

van Marle, K., & Wynn, K. (2009). Infants' auditory enumeration: Evidence for analog magnitudes in the small number range. *Cognition, 111,* 302–316.

van Nieuwenhuijzen, M., Vriens, A., Scheepmaker, M., Smit, M., & Porton, E. (2011). The development of a diagnostic instrument to measure social information processing in children with mild to borderline intellectual disabilities. *Research in Developmental Disabilities, 32,* 358–370.

Van Overwalle, F., & Siebler, F. (2005). A connectionist model of attitude formation and change. *Personality and Social Psychology Review, 9,* 231–274.

Van Rosmalen, L., Van der Veer, R., & Van der Horst, F. (2015). Ainsworth's strange situation procedure: The origin of an instrument. *Journal of the History of the Behavioral Sciences, 51,* 261–284.

van Soelen, I. C., Brouwer, R. M., van Leeuwen, M., Kahn, R. S., Pol, H., & Boomsma, D. I. (2011). Heritability of verbal and performance intelligence in a pediatric longitudinal sample. *Twin Research and Human Genetics, 14,* 119–128.

van Wesel, F., Boeije, H., & Hoijtink, H. (2013). Use of hypotheses for analysis of variance models: Challenging the current practice. *Quality & Quantity: International Journal of Methodology, 47,* 137–150.

Vandbakk, M., Olaff, H. S., & Holth, P. (2019). Conditioned reinforcement: The effectiveness of stimulus–stimulus pairing and operant discrimination procedures. *The Psychological Record, 69*(1), 67–81.

Vandell, D. L., Burchinal, M. R., Belsky, J., Owen, M. T., Friedman, S. L., Clarke-Stewart, A., et al. (2005). *Early child care and children's development in the primary grades: Follow-up results from the NICHD Study of Early Child Care.* Paper presented at the biennial meeting of the Society for Research in Child Development, Atlanta, GA.

Vandervert, L. R., Schimpf, P. H., & Liu, H. (2007). How working memory and the cerebellum collaborate to produce creativity and innovation. *Creativity Research Journal, 19,* 1–18.

Vandierendonck, A., & Szmalec, A. (Eds.). (2011). *Spatial working memory.* New York: Psychology Press.

Vanheule, S., Desmet, M., Rosseel, Y., & Meganck, R. (2006). Core transference themes in depression. *Journal of Affective Disorders, 91,* 71–75.

Vanis, J. (2019, August 30). Controversial MCAS question hurt scores of some black students, study finds. *Boston Globe.* Downloaded from https://www.bostonglobe.com/metro/2019/08/30/controversial-mcas-question-hurt-scores-some-black-students-study-concludes/EmGOOQgiGVNpHvrp8W5ATK/story.html-l?s_campaign=breakingnews:newsletter.

Varkevisser, R. D. M., van Stralen, M. M., Kroeze, W., Ket, J. C. F., & Steenhuis, I. H. M. (2019). Determinants of weight loss maintenance: A systematic review. *Obesity Reviews, 20*(2), 171–211.

Varma, R. (2018). US science and engineering workforce: Underrepresentation of women and minorities. *American Behavioral Scientist, 62*(5), 692–697.

Varma, S. (2007). A computational model of Tower of Hanoi problem solving. *Dissertation Abstracts International: Section B: The Sciences and Engineering, 67*(8-B), 4736.

Vasudeva, K., Vodovotz, Y., Azhar, N., Barclay, D., Janjic, J. M., & Pollock, J. A. (2015). In vivo and systems biology studies implicate IL-18 as a central mediator in chronic pain. *Journal of Neuroimmunology, 28,* 343–349.

Vaughan-Graham, J., Patterson, K., Zabjek, K., & Cott, C. A. (2019). Important movement concepts: Clinical versus neuroscience perspectives. *Motor Control, 23*(3), 273–293.

Vaughn Becker, D., & Neuberg, S. L. (2019). Pushing archetypal representational systems further. *Psychological Inquiry, 30*(2), 103–109.

Vega, C. P. (2006). The effects of therapeutic components on at-risk middle school children's grades and attendance: An archival study of an after-school prevention program. *Dissertation Abstracts International: Section B: The Sciences and Engineering, 66,* 4504.

Velentzas, K., Heinen, T., & Schack, T. (2011). Routine integration strategies and their effects on volleyball serve performance and players' movement mental representation. *Journal of Applied Sport Psychology, 23,* 209–222.

Vellacott, J. (2007). Resilience: A psychoanalytic exploration. *British Journal of Psychotherapy, 23,* 163–170.

Velotti, P., Garofalo, C., Dimaggio, G., & Fonagy, P. (2019). Mindfulness, alexithymia, and empathy moderate relations between trait aggression and antisocial personality disorder traits. *Mindfulness, 10*(6), 1082–1090.

Veltman, M. W. M., & Browne, K. D. (2001). Three decades of child maltreatment research: Implications for the school years. *Trauma Violence and Abuse, 2,* 215–239.

Vera-Estay, E., Dooley, J. J., & Beauchamp, M. H. (2015). Cognitive underpinnings of moral reasoning in adolescence: The contribution of executive functions. *Journal of Moral Education, 44,* 17–33.

Verdon, B. (2011). The case of thematic tests adapted to older adults: On the importance of differentiating latent and manifest contents in projective tests. *Rorschachiana, 32,* 46–71.

Verhaeghen, P., Aikman, S. N., & Van Gulick, A. E. (2011). Prime and prejudice: Co-occurrence in the culture as a source of automatic stereotype priming. *British Journal of Social Psychology, 50,* 501–518.

Verona, E., & Sullivan, E. (2008). Emotional catharsis and aggression revisited: Heart rate reduction following aggressive responding. *Emotion, 8,* 331–340.

Verschueren, M., Rassart, J., Claes, L., Moons, P., & Luyckx, K. (2017). Identity statuses throughout adolescence and emerging adulthood: A large-scale study into gender, age, and contextual differences. *Psychologica Belgica, 57*, 32-42.

Vesely, A. K., Saklofske, D. H., & Leschied, A. W. (2013). Teachers–The vital resource: The contribution of emotional intelligence to teacher efficacy and well-being. *Canadian Journal of School Psychology, 28*, 71-89.

Vicari, S., Pontillo, M., & Armando, M. (2013). Neurodevelopmental and psychiatric issues in Down's syndrome: Assessment and intervention. *Psychiatric Genetics, 23*, 95-107.

Vicario, C. M., Kuran, K. A., & Urgesi, C. (2019). Does hunger sharpen senses? A psychophysics investigation on the effects of appetite in the timing of reinforcement-oriented actions. *Psychological Research, 83*(3), 395-405.

Vieira, E. M., & Freire, J. C. (2006). Alteridade e psicologia humanista: Uma leitura ética da abordagem centrada na pessoa. Alterity and humanistic psychology: An ethical reading of the person-centered approach. *Estudos de Psicologia, 23*, 425-432.

Villafaina, S., Collado-Mateo, D., Cano-Plasencia, R., Gusi, N., & Fuentes, J. P. (2019). Electroencephalographic response of chess players in decision-making processes under time pressure. *Physiology & Behavior, 198*, 140-143. https://doi.org/10.1016/j.physbeh.2018.10.017.

Villarosa, L. (2002, December 3). To prevent sexual abuse, abusers step forward. *The New York Times*, p. B1.

Vincent, J. (2019, March 20). Google's next Doodle uses AI to generate music in the style of Johann Sebastian Bach. *The Verge*. Downloaded from https://www.theverge.com/2019/3/20/18274077/google-doodle-johann-sebastian-bach-birthday-ai-machine-learning.

Vincus, A. A., Ringwalt, C., Harris, M. S., & Shamblen, S. R. (2010). A short-term, quasi-experimental evaluation of D.A.R.E.'s revised elementary school curriculum. *Journal of Drug Education, 40*, 37-49.

Vitello, P. (2006, June 12). A ring tone meant to fall on deaf ears. *The New York Times*, p. A1.

Vlassova, A., & Pearson, J. (2013). Look before you leap: Sensory memory improves decision making. *Psychological Science, 24*, 1635-1643.

Vleioras, G., & Bosma, H. A. (2005). Are identity styles important for psychological well-being? *Journal of Adolescence, 28*, 397-409.

Vogt, D., Rizvi, S., Shipherd, J., & Resick, P. (2008). Longitudinal investigation of reciprocal relationship between stress reactions and hardiness. *Personality and Social Psychology Bulletin, 34*, 61-73.

Voiß, P., Höxtermann, M. D., Dobos, G., & Cramer, H. (2019). The use of mind-body medicine among US individuals with sleep problems: Analysis of the 2017 National Health Interview Survey data. *Sleep Medicine, 56*, 151-156.

Volterra, V., Caselli, M. C., Capirci, O., Tonucci, F., & Vicari, S. (2003). Early linguistic abilities of Italian children with Williams syndrome [Special issue: Williams syndrome]. *Developmental Neuropsychology, 23*, 33-58.

Voruganti, L. P., Awad, A. G., Parker, B., Forrest, C., Usmani, Y., Fernando, M. L. D., et al. (2007). Cognition, functioning and quality of life in schizophrenia treatment: Results of a one-year randomized controlled trial of olanzapine and quetiapine. *Schizophrenia Research, 96*, 146-155.

Vosoughi, S., Roy, D., & Aral, S. (2018). The spread of true and fale news online. *Science, 359*, 1146-1151.

Vrieze, S. I., McGue, M., Miller, M. B., Hicks, B. M., & Iacono, W. G. (2013). Three mutually informative ways to understand the genetic relationships among behavioral disinhibition, alcohol use, drug use, nicotine use/dependence, and their co-occurrence: Twin biometry, GCTA, and genome-wide scoring. *Behavior Genetics, 43*, 97-107.

Vukasović, T., & Bratko, D. (2015). Heritability of personality: A meta-analysis of behavior genetic studies. *Psychological Bulletin, 141*, 769-785.

Vygotsky, L. S. (1926/1997). *Educational psychology*. Delray Beach, FL: St. Lucie Press.

Vöhringer, I. A., Kolling, T., Graf, F., Poloczek, S., Fassbender, I., Freitag, C., et al. (2017). The development of implicit memory from infancy to childhood: On average performance levels and interindividual differences. *Child Development*. Accessed from https://www.ncbi.nlm.nih.gov/pubmed/28220933.

Wabitsch, M., Funcke, J., Lennerz, B., Kuhnle-Krahl, U., Lahr, G., Debatin, K., & Fischer-Posovszky, P. (2015). Biologically inactive leptin and early-onset extreme obesity. *The New England Journal of Medicine, 372*, 48-54.

Wagemans, J., Elder, J. H., Kubovy, M., Palmer, S. E., Peterson, M. A., Singh, M., et al. (2012). A century of Gestalt psychology in visual perception: I. Perceptual grouping and figure–ground organization. *Psychological Bulletin, 138*, 1172-1217.

Wagner, R. K. (2002). Smart people doing dumb things: The case of managerial incompetence. In R. J. Sternberg (Ed.), *Why smart people can be so stupid*. New Haven, CT: Yale University Press.

Wagner, R. K. (2011). Practical intelligence. In R. J. Sternberg & S. Kaufman (Eds.), *The Cambridge handbook of intelligence*. New York: Cambridge University Press.

Wagstaff, G. (2009). Is there a future for investigative hypnosis? *Journal of Investigative Psychology and Offender Profiling, 6*, 43-57.

Wagstaff, G. F., Wheatcroft, J. M., & Jones, A. (2011). Are high hypnotizables especially vulnerable to false memory effects? A socio-cognitive perspective. *International Journal of Clinical and Experimental Hypnosis, 59*, 310-326.

Waismeyer, A., & Meltzoff, A. N. (2017). Learning to make things happen: Infants' observational learning of social and physical causal events. *Journal of Experimental Child Psychology, 162*, 58-71.

Wakefield, J. C. (2013). DSM-5: An overview of changes and controversies. *Clinical Social Work Journal, 41*, 139-154.

Walker, L., & Frimer, J. (2009). The song remains the same: Rebuttal to Sherblom's re-envisioning of the legacy of the care challenge. *Journal of Moral Education, 38*, 53-68.

Walker, M. P., & van der Helm, E. (2009). Overnight therapy? The role of sleep in emotional brain processing. *Psychological Bulletin, 135*, 731-748.

Walker, W. R., Skowronski, J. J., & Thompson, C. P. (2003). Consolidation of long-term memory: Evidence and alternatives. *Review of General Psychology, 7*, 203-210.

Wallace, L. S., Chisolm, D. J., Abdel-Rasoul, M., & DeVoe, J. E. (2013). Survey mode matters: Adults' self-reported statistical confidence, ability to obtain health information, and perceptions of patient-health-care provider communication. *Journal of Health Psychology, 18*, 1036-1045.

Wallen, K., & Lloyd, E. A. (2011). Female sexual arousal: genital anatomy and orgasm in intercourse. *Hormonal Behavior, 59*, 780-792.

Wallis, C. (2019, June). Is pot any good for pain? *Scientific American*, p. 20.

Walsh, R., & Shapiro, S. L. (2006). The meeting of meditative disciplines and Western psychology. *American Psychologist, 61*, 227-239.

Walton, G. M., & Cohen, G. L. (2011). A brief social-belonging intervention improves academic and health outcomes of minority students. *Science, 331*, 1447-1451.

Walton, J. R., Murphy, C., & Bartram, L. (2017). Childhood behavioral problems–Attention-deficit/hyperactivity disorder (ADHD). In W. O'Donohue, L. James, & C. Snipes (Eds.), *Practical strategies and tools to promote treatment engagement*. Cham, Switzerland: Springer International Publishing.

Wampold, B. E. (2019). A smorgasbord of PTSD treatments: What does this say about integration? *Journal of Psychotherapy Integration, 29*(1), 65.

Wampold, B. E. (2019). *The basics of psychotherapy: An introduction to theory and practice* (2nd ed.). Washington, DC: American Psychological Association.

Wan, C., & Chiu, C. (2011). Culture as intersubjective representations of values. In A. Y. Leung, C. Chiu, & Y. Hong (Eds.), *Cultural processes: A social psychological perspective*. New York: Cambridge University Press.

Wang, A., & Clark, D. A. (2002). Haunting thoughts: The problem of obsessive mental intrusions [Special issue: Intrusions in cognitive behavioral therapy]. *Journal of Cognitive Psychotherapy, 16*, 193-208.

Wang, D. (2019). A study of the relationship between narcissism, extraversion, body-esteem, social comparison orientation and selfie-editing behavior on social networking sites. *Personality and Individual Differences, 146*, 127-129.

Wang, F., Kameda, M., Yasuhara, T., Tajiri, N., Kikuchi, Y., Liang, H. B., et al. (2011). GDNF-pretreatment enhances the survival of neural stem cells following transplantation in a rat model of Parkinson's disease. *Neuroscience Research, 18*, 202-211.

Wang, J. X., Rogers, L. M., Gross, E. Z., Ryals, A. J., Dokucu, M. E., Brandstatt, Hermiller, M. S., et al. (2014). Targeted enhancement of cortical-hippocampal brain networks and associative memory. *Science, 345*(6200), 1054-1057.

Wang, M. T., & Kenny, S. (2013). Longitudinal links between fathers' and mothers' harsh verbal discipline and adolescents' conduct problems and depressive symptoms. *Child Development, 85*(3), 908-923.

Wang, M., Chen, W., Zhang, C., & Deng, X. (2017). Personality types and scholarly creativity in undergraduate students: The mediating roles of creative styles. *Personality and Individual Differences, 105*, 170-174.

Wang, P. S., Aguilar-Gaxiola, S., Alonso, J., Angermeyer, M. C., Borges, G., Bromet, E. J., et al. (2007). Use of mental health services for anxiety, mood, and substance disorders in 17 countries in the WHO World Mental Health Surveys. *Lancet, 370*, 841-850.

Wang, Q. (2004). The emergence of cultural self-constructs: Autobiographical memory and self-description in European American and Chinese children. *Developmental Psychology, 40*, 3-15.

Wang, Q., & Conway, M. A. (2006). Autobiographical memory, self, and culture. In L-G. Nilsson & N. Ohta, *Memory and society: Psychological perspectives*. New York: Psychology Press.

Wang, Q., Peterson, C., Khuu, A., Reid, C. P., Maxwell, K. L., & Vincent, J. M. (2019). Looking at the past through a telescope: Adults postdated their earliest childhood memories. *Memory, 27*(1), 19-27.

Wang, R., Liu, H., Jiang, J., & Song, Y. (2017). Will materialism lead to happiness? A longitudinal analysis of the mediating role of psychological needs satisfaction. *Personality and Individual Differences, 105*, 312-317.

Wang, V. O., & Sue, S. (2005). In the eye of the storm: Race and genomics in research and practice. *American Psychologist, 60*, 37-45.

Wang, X., Lu, T., Snider, R. K., & Liang, L. (2005). Sustained firing in auditory cortex evoked by preferred stimuli. *Nature, 435*, 341-346.

Wang, Y., & Sloan, F. A. (2018). Present bias and health. *Journal of Risk and Uncertainty, 57*(2), 177-198.

Wang, Y., & Zhong, Z. (2015). Effects of frustration situation and resilience on implicit aggression. *Chinese Journal of Clinical Psychology, 23*, 209-212.

Wannez, S., Heine, L., Thonnard, M., Gosseries, O., & Laureys, S. (2017). The repetition of behavioral assessments in diagnosis of disorders of consciousness. *Annals of Neurology, 81*, 883-889.

Warach, B., Josephs, L., & Gorman, B. S. (2019). Are cheaters sexual hypocrites? Sexual hypocrisy, the self-serving bias, and personality style. *Personality and Social Psychology Bulletin.* doi: 10.1177/0146167219833392.

Ward, L. M. (2011). The thalamic dynamic core theory of conscious experience. *Consciousness and Cognition: An International Journal, 20*, 464-486.

Ward-Baker, P. D. (2007). The remarkable oldest old: A new vision of aging. *Dissertation Abstracts International Section A: Humanities and Social Sciences, 67*(8-A), 3115.

Wark, B., Lundstrom, B., & Fairhall, A. (2007). Sensory adaptation. *Current Opinion in Neurobiology, 17*, 423-429.

Warmbold-Brann, K., Burns, M. K., Preast, J. L., Taylor, C. N., & Aguilar, L. N. (2017). Meta-analysis of the effects of academic interventions and modifications on student behavior outcomes. *School Psychology Quarterly, 32*(3), 291-305.

Warne, R. T. (2019). An evaluation (and vindication?) of Lewis Terman: What the father of gifted education can teach the 21st century. *Gifted Child Quarterly, 63*(1), 3-21.

Warne, R. T., & Liu, J. K. (2017). Income differences among grade skippers and non-grade skippers across genders in the Terman sample, 1936-1976. *Learning and Instruction, 47*, 1-12.

Wasserman, J. D. (2018). A history of intelligence assessment: The unfinished tapestry. In D. P. Flanagan & E. M. McDonough (Eds.), *Contemporary intellectual assessment: Theories, tests, and issues* (4th ed.). New York: The Guilford Press.

Waters, A. M., Theresiana, C., Neumann, D. L., & Craske, M. G. (2017). Developmental differences in aversive conditioning, extinction, and reinstatement: A study with children, adolescents, and adults. *Journal of Experimental Child Psychology, 159*, 263-278.

Watkins, C. (2007). *Date rape*. Farmington Hills, MI: Greenhaven Press.

Watson, J. B. (1924). *Behaviorism*. New York: W.W. Norton & Company.

Watson, J. C., Goldman, R. N., & Greenberg, L. S. (2011). Humanistic and experiential theories of psychotherapy. In J. C. Norcross, G. R. VandenBos, & D. K. Freedheim (Eds.), *History of psychotherapy: Continuity and change* (2nd ed.). Washington, DC: American Psychological Association.

Watson, P. J., Brymer, M. J., & Bonanno, G. A. (2011). Postdisaster psychological intervention since 9/11. *American Psychologist, 66*, 482-494.

Watters, E. (2010, January 10). The Americanization of mental illness. *The New York Times*, p. C2.

Watts, S., Kirkman, E., Bieler, D., Bjarnason, S., Franke, A., Gupta, R., et al. (2019). Guidelines for using animal models in blast injury research. *Journal of the Royal Army Medical Corps, 165*(1), 38-40.

Waxman, S. (2009). Learning from infants' first verbs. *Monographs of the Society for Research in Child Development, 74*, 127-132.

Weaver, K. (2019, May 6). Man drowns near Denison Dam trying to save two children. KXII. https://www.kxii.com/content/news/Possible-drowning-near-Denison-Dam-509511041.html.

Weber, J. M. (2019). Individuals matter, but the situation's the thing: The case for a habitual situational lens in leadership and organizational decision-making. *Organizational Dynamics*. https://doi.org/ 10.1016/j.orgdyn.2019.03.003.

Weber, L., & Dwoskin, E. (2014, September 30). As personality tests multiply, employers are split. *Wall Street Journal*, pp. A1, A12.

Wechsler, H., Lee, J. E., Nelson, T. F., & Kuo, M. (2002). Underage college students' drinking behavior, access to alcohol, and the influence of deterrence policies. *Journal of American College Health, 50*, 223-236.

Weck, F., Bleichhardt, G., Witthöft, M., & Hiller, W. (2011). Explicit and implicit anxiety: Differences between patients with hypochondriasis, patients with anxiety disorders, and healthy controls. *Cognitive Therapy and Research, 35*, 317-325.

Weeks, M., & Lupfer, M. B. (2004). Complicating race: The relationship between prejudice, race, and social class categorizations. *Personality and Social Psychology Bulletin, 30*, 972-984.

Wehrle, R., Kaufmann, C., Wetter, T. C., Holsboer, F., Auer, D. P., Pollmacher, T., et al. (2007). Functional microstates within human REM sleep. First evidence from fMRI of a thalamocortical network specific for phasic REM periods. *European Journal of Neuroscience, 25*, 863-871.

Wehrum, S., Klucken, T., Kagerer, S., Walter, B., Hermann, A., Vaitl, D., et al. (2013). Gender commonalities and differences in the neural processing of visual sexual stimuli. *Journal of Sexual Medicine, 10*, 1328-1342.

Weidemann, C. T., Kragel, J. E., Lega, B. C., Worrell, G. A., Sperling, M. R., Sharan, A. D., et al. (2019). Neural activity reveals interactions between episodic and semantic memory systems during retrieval. *Journal of Experimental Psychology: General, 148*(1), 1.

Weimann, J., Knabe, A., & Schöb, R. (2015). *Measuring happiness: The economics of well-being*. Cambridge, MA: MIT Press.

Weinberg, M. S., Williams, C. J., & Pryor, D. W. (1991, February 27). Personal communication. Indiana University, Bloomington.

Weiner, R. D., & Falcone, G. (2011). Electroconvulsive therapy: How effective is it? *Journal of the American Psychiatric Nurses Association, 17*, 217-218.

Weinschenk, A. C., Dawes, C. T., Kandler, C., Bell, E., & Riemann, R. (2019). New evidence on the link between genes, psychological traits, and political engagement. *Politics and the Life Sciences, 38*(1), 1-13.

Weinstein, L. (2007). Selected genetic disorders affecting Ashkenazi Jewish families. *Family & Community Health, 30,* 50-62.

Weinstein, M., Glei, D. A., Yamazaki, A., & Ming-Cheng, C. (2004). The role of intergenerational relations in the association between life stressors and depressive symptoms. *Research on Aging, 26,* 511-530.

Weintraub, K. (2019, April). Aroma therapy. *Scientific American,* 9-10.

Weir, K. (2016). The science of naps. *Monitor on Psychology, 47,* 48-51.

Weir, K. (2016, April). New insights on eating disorders. *Monitor on Psychology,* pp. 36-40.

Weir, K. (2016, March). The risks of earlier puberty. *Monitor on Psychology,* pp. 41-44.

Weiss, A., Bates, T., & Luciano, M. (2008). Happiness is a personal(ity) thing: The genetics of personality and well-being in a representative sample. *Psychological Science, 19,* 205-210.

Weissman, M. M., Bland, R. C., Canino, G. J., Faravelli, C., Greenwald, S., Hwu, H. G., et al. (1997). Cross-national epidemiology of major depression and bipolar disorder. *Journal of the American Medical Association, 276,* 293-299.

Weissman, M., Markowitz, J., & Klerman, G. L. (2007). *Clinician's quick guide to interpersonal psychotherapy.* New York: Oxford University Press.

Weisz, C., & Quinn, D. M. (2018). Stigmatized identities, psychological distress, and physical health: Intersections of homelessness and race. *Stigma and Health, 3*(3), 229-240.

Welkowitz, L. A., Struening, E. L., Pittman, J., Guardino, M., & Welkowitz, J. (2000). Obsessive-compulsive disorder and comorbid anxiety problems in a national anxiety screening sample. *Journal of Anxiety Disorders, 14,* 471-482.

Weller, P. D., Anderson, M. C., Gomez-Ariza, C. J., & Bajo, M. T. (2013). On the status of cue independence as a criterion for memory inhibition. *Journal of Experimental Psychology: Learning, Memory, and Cognition, 39,* 1232-1245.

Wen, M., Butler, L. T., & Koutstaal, W. (2013). Improving insight and non-insight problem solving with brief interventions. *British Journal of Psychology, 104,* 97-118.

Wendt, D. C., Gone, J. P., & Nagata, D. K. (2015). Potentially harmful therapy and multicultural counseling: Bridging two disciplinary discourses ψ. *The Counseling Psychologist, 43*(3), 334-358.

Wenzel, A. (2011). Obsessions and compulsions. In A. Wenzel & S. Stuart (Eds.), *Anxiety in childbearing women: Diagnosis and treatment.* Washington, DC: American Psychological Association.

Wenzel, A., Zetocha, K., & Ferraro, R. F. (2007). Depth of processing and recall of threat material in fearful and nonfearful individuals. *Anxiety, Stress & Coping: An International Journal, 20,* 223-237.

Werhane, P. H., Pincus Hartman, L., Archer, C., Englehardt, E. E., & Pritchard, M. S. (2013). *Obstacles to ethical decision-making: Mental models, Milgram and the problem of obedience.* New York: Cambridge University Press.

Werker, J. F., & Tees, R. C. (2005). Speech perception as a window for understanding plasticity and commitment in language systems of the brain. *Developmental Psychobiology, 46,* 233-234.

Werner, J. S., Pinna, B., & Spillmann, L. (2007). Illusory color and the brain. *Scientific American, 296,* 90-96.

Wertheimer, M. (1923). Untersuchungen zur Lehre von der Gestalt, II. *Psychol. Forsch., 5,* 301-350. In R. Beardsley & M. Wertheimer (Eds.) (1958), *Readings in perception.* New York: Van Nostrand.

Wertz, J., Belsky, J., Moffitt, T. E., Belsky, D. W., Harrington, H., Avinun, R., et al. (2019). Genetics of nurture: A test of the hypothesis that parents' genetics predict their observed caregiving. *Developmental Psychology, 55*(7), 1461-1472.

West, D. S., Harvey-Berino, J., & Raczynski, J. M. (2004). Behavioral aspects of obesity, dietary intake, and chronic disease. In J. M. Raczynski & L. C. Leviton (Eds.), *Handbook of clinical health psychology: Vol. 2. Disorders of behavior and health.* Washington, DC: American Psychological Association.

West, R. L., Bagwell, D. K., & Dark-Freudeman, A. (2007). Self-efficacy and memory aging: The impact of a memory intervention based on self-efficacy. *Neuropsychological Development and Cognition, B, Aging and Neuropsychological Cognition, 14,* 1-28.

Westen, D., Novotny, C. M., & Thompson-Brenner, H. (2004). The empirical status of empirically supported psychotherapies: Assumptions, findings, and reporting in controlled clinical trials. *Psychological Bulletin, 130,* 631-663.

Wester, A. J., van Herten, J. C., Egger, J. M., & Kessels, R. C. (2013). Applicability of the Rivermead Behavioural Memory Test-Third Edition (RBMT-3) in Korsakoff's syndrome and chronic alcoholics. *Neuropsychiatric Disease and Treatment, 9,* 202-212.

Westerhausen, R., Moosmann, M., Alho, K., Medvedev, S., Hämäläinen, H., & Hugdahl, K. (2009). Top-down and bottom-up interaction: Manipulating the dichotic listening ear advantage. *Brain Research, 1250,* 183-189.

Westerterp, K. R. (2006). Perception, passive overfeeding and energy metabolism. *Physiology & Behavior, 89,* 62-65.

Westmarland, N., & Alderson, S. (2013). The health, mental health, and well-being benefits of rape crisis counseling. *Journal of Interpersonal Violence, 28,* 3265-3282.

Wettstein, M., Wahl, H.-W., Siebert, J., & Schröder, J. (2019). Still more to learn about late-life cognitive development: How personality and health predict 20-year cognitive trajectories. *Psychology and Aging, 34*(5), 714-728.

Whillans, A. V., & Dunn, E. W. (2019). Valuing time over money is associated with greater social connection. *Journal of Social and Personal Relationships, 36*(8), 2549-2565.

Whillans, A.V., Dunn, E.W., Smeets, Pl., Bekkers, R., & Norton, M.I. (2017). Buying time promotes happiness, *PNAS, 114,* 8523-8527.

Whisman, M., & Snyder, D. (2007). Sexual infidelity in a national survey of American women: Differences in prevalence and correlates as a function of method of assessment. *Journal of Family Psychology, 21,* 14-154.

Whitaker, R. (2009). Deinstitutionalization and neuroleptics: The myth and reality. In Y. O. Alanen, M. González de Chávez, A. S. Silver, B. Martindale, Y. O. Alanen, M. González de Chávez, et al. (Eds.), *Psychotherapeutic approaches to schizophrenic psychoses: Past, present and future.* New York: Routledge/Taylor & Francis Group.

Whitbourne, S. (2010). *The search for fulfillment.* New York: Ballantine.

Whitbourne, S. K. (2000). The normal aging process. In S. K. Whitbourne & S. Krauss (Eds.), *Psychopathology in later adulthood.* New York: Wiley.

Whitbourne, S. K., Zuschlag, M. K., Elliot, L. B., & Waterman, A. S. (1992). Psychosocial development in adulthood: A 22-year sequential study. *Journal of Personality and Social Psychology, 63,* 260-271.

White, F. A., Harvey, L. J., & Abu-Rayya, H. M. (2015). Improving intergroup relations in the Internet Age: A critical review. *Review of General Psychology, 19,* 129-139.

White, K. (2013). Remembering and forgetting. In G. J. Madden, W. V. Dube, T. D. Hackenberg, G. P. Hanley, & K. A. Lattal (Eds.), *APA handbook of behavior analysis, Vol. 1: Methods and principles.* Washington, DC: American Psychological Association.

White, L. (2007). Linguistic theory, universal grammar, and second language acquisition. In B. Van Patten & J. Williams (Eds.), *Theories in second language acquisition: An introduction.* Mahwah, NJ: Lawrence Erlbaum Associates.

White, R. G., Jain, S., Orr, D. R., & Read, U. M. (2017). *The Palgrave handbook of sociocultural perspectives on global mental health.* New York: Palgrave Macmillan.

White, R. K. (2004). Misperception and war. *Peace and Conflict: Journal of Peace Psychology, 10,* 399-409.

Whitebread, D., Coltman, P., Jameson, H., & Lander, R. (2009). Play, cognition and self-regulation: What exactly are children learning when they learn through play? *Educational and Child Psychology, 26,* 40-52.

Whiting, B. B. (1965). Sex identity conflict and physical violence: A comparative study. *American Anthropologist, 67,* 123-140.

Whitney, P. G., & Green, J. A. (2011). Changes in infants' affect related to the onset of independent locomotion. *Infant Behavior & Development, 34,* 459-466.

Whitton, L., Cosgrove, D., Clarkson, C., Harold, D., Kendall, K., Richards, A., et al. (2016). Cognitive analysis of schizophrenia risk genes that function as epigenetic regulators of gene expression. *American Journal of Medical Genetics Part B: Neuropsychiatric Genetics, 171*, 1170–1179.

Whorf, B. L. (1956). *Language, thought, and reality.* New York: Wiley.

Wicks, S., Berger, Z., & Camic, P. M. (2019). It's how I am . . . it's what I am . . . it's a part of who I am: A narrative exploration of the impact of adolescent-onset chronic illness on identity formation in young people. *Clinical Child Psychology and Psychiatry, 24*(1), 40–52.

Widaman, K. (2009). Phenylketonuria in children and mothers: Genes, environments, behavior. *Current Directions in Psychological Science, 18*, 48–52.

Widiger, T. A. (2015). Assessment of DSM-5 personality disorder. *Journal of Personality Assessment, 97*, 456–466.

Wiech, K. (2016). Deconstructing the sensation of pain: The influence of cognitive processes on pain perception. *Science, 354*, 584–587.

Wiederman, M. W. (2011). Body image and sexual functioning. In T. F. Cash & L. Smolak (Eds.), *Body image: A handbook of science, practice, and prevention* (2nd ed.). New York: Guilford Press.

Wiedman, C. (2019). Rewarding collaborative research: Role congruity bias and the gender pay gap in academe. *Journal of Business Ethics.* Advance online publication. https://doi.org/10.1007/s10551-019-04165-0.

Wieth, M., & Zacks, R. (2011). Time of day effects on problem solving: When the non-optimal is optimal. *Thinking & Reasoning, 17*, 387–401.

Wiggins, B. J., & Chrisopherson, C. D. (2019). The replication crisis in psychology: An overview for theoretical and philosophical psychology. *Journal of Theoretical and Philosophical Psychology, 39*, 202–217.

Wilcox, C. E., Calhoun, V. D., Rachakonda, S., Claus, E. D., Littlewood, R. A., Mickey, J., et al. (2017). Functional network connectivity predicts treatment outcome during treatment of nicotine use disorder. *Psychiatry Research: Neuroimaging, 26*, 545-53.

Wildavsky, B. (2000, September 4). A blow to bilingual education. *U.S. News & World Report*, pp. 22–28.

Wilde, D. J. (2011). *Jung's personality theory quantified.* New York: Springer-Verlag Publishing.

Wiley, J., & Jarosz, A. F. (2012). Working memory capacity, attentional focus, and problem solving. *Current Directions in Psychological Science, 21*, 258–262.

Wilkin, L., & Haddock, B. (2011). Functional fitness of older adults. *Activities, Adaptation & Aging, 35*, 197–209.

Wilkinson, H. A. (2009). Cingulotomy. *Journal of Neurosurgery, 110*, 607–611.

Williams, C. L., & Butcher, J. N. (2011). The nuts and bolts: Administering, scoring, and augmenting MMPI-A assessments. In C. L.

Williams & J. N. Butcher (Eds.), *A beginner's guide to the MMPI–A.* Washington, DC: American Psychological Association.

Williams, I. L., & Mee-Lee, D. (2019). Inside the black box of traditional treatment programs: Clearing the air on the original literary teachings of Alcoholics Anonymous (AA). *Addiction Research & Theory, 27*(5), 412–419.

Williams, J. E., & Best, D. L. (1990). *Measuring sex stereotypes: A multinational study.* Newbury Park, CA: Sage.

Williams, J. E., Paton, C. C., Siegler, I. C., Eigenbrodt, M. L., Nieto, F. J., & Tyroler, H. A. (2000). Anger proneness predicts coronary heart disease risk: Prospective analysis from the Atherosclerosis Risk in Communities (ARIC) Study. *Circulation, 101*, 2034–2039.

Williams, M. T. (2019). Microaggressions: Clarification, evidence, and impact. *Perspectives on Psychological Science, 15*(1), 3–26.

Williams, R. H., Black, S. W., Thomas, A. M., Piquet, J., Cauli, B., & Kilduff, T. S. (2019). Excitation of cortical nNOS/NK1R neurons by hypocretin 1 is independent of sleep homeostasis. *Cerebral Cortex, 29*(3), 1090–1108.

Williams, R. L. (2013). Overview of the Flynn effect. *Intelligence, 41*, 753–764.

Williamson, P., McLeskey, J., & Hoppey, D. (2006). Educating students with mental retardation in general education classrooms. *Exceptional Children, 72*, 347–361.

Willis, J. (2017). Moving toward extremism: Group polarization in the laboratory and the world. In S. C. Cloninger & S. A. Leibo, S. C. (Eds.), *Understanding angry groups: Multidisciplinary perspectives on their motivations and effects on society.* Santa Barbara, CA: Praeger/ABC-CLIO.

Wills, K. E. (2013). Sickle cell disease. In I. Baron & C. Rey-Casserly (Eds.), *Pediatric neuropsychology: Medical advances and lifespan outcomes.* New York: Oxford University Press.

Wills, T., Sargent, J., Stoolmiller, M., Gibbons, F., & Gerrard, M. (2008). Movie smoking exposure and smoking onset: A longitudinal study of mediation processes in a representative sample of U.S. adolescents. *Psychology of Addictive Behaviors, 22*, 269–277.

Wilmot, J. H., Puhger, K., & Wiltgen, B. J. (2019). Acute disruption of the dorsal hippocampus impairs the encoding and retrieval of trace fear memories. *Frontiers in Behavioral Neuroscience, 13*, 116.

Wilson, J. H., & Joye, S. W. (2017). Demonstrating interobserver reliability in naturalistic settings. In J. R. Stowell & W. E. Addison (Eds.), *Activities for teaching statistics and research methods: A guide for psychology instructors.* Washington, DC: American Psychological Association.

Wilson, T. D. (2006). The power of social psychological interventions. *Science, 313*, 1251–1252.

Wilson, T. G., Grilo, C. M., & Vitousek, K. M. (2007). Psychological treatment of eating

disorders [Special issue: Eating disorders]. *American Psychologist, 62*, 199–216.

Wimber, M., Alink, A., Charest, I., Kriegeskorte, N., & Anderson, M. C. (2015). Retrieval induces adaptive forgetting of competing memories via cortical pattern suppression. *Nature Neuroscience, 18*(4), 582–589.

Wimmer, M. C., Maras, K. L., Robinson, E. J., & Thomas, C. (2016). The format of children's mental images: Evidence from mental scanning. *Cognition, 154*, 49–54.

Winberg, M. (2019, July 5). Sonic devices target teenagers in Philadelphia. National Public Radio. https://www.npr.org/2019/07/05/738860218/sonic-devices-target-teenagers-in-philadelphia.

Winner, E. (2003). Creativity and talent. In M. H. Bornstein & L. Davidson (Eds.), *Well-being: Positive development across the life course.* Mahwah, NJ: Lawrence Erlbaum.

Winston, C. N., Maher, H., & Easvaradoss, V. (2017). Needs and values: An exploration. *The Humanistic Psychologist, 45*(3), 295–311.

Winter, D. G. (2007). The role of motivation, responsibility, and integrative complexity in crisis escalation: Comparative studies of war and peace crises. *Journal of Personality and Social Psychology, 92*, 920–937.

Winter, D. G. (2016). Taming power: Generative historical consciousness. *American Psychologist, 71*, 160–174.

Wiseman, R., & Greening, E. (2002). The mind machine: A mass participation experiment into the possible existence of extra-sensory perception. *British Journal of Psychology, 93*, 487–499.

Wishart, D., Somoray, K., & Rowland, B. (2017). Role of thrill and adventure seeking in risky work-related driving behaviours. *Personality and Individual Differences, 104*, 362–367.

Witt, C. M., Jena, S., & Brinkhaus, B. (2006). Acupuncture for patients with chronic neck pain. *Pain, 125*, 98–106.

Wittig, S. M., & Rodriguez, C. M. (2019). Emerging behavior problems: Bidirectional relations between maternal and paternal parenting styles with infant temperament. *Developmental Psychology, 55*(6): 1199–1210.

Wixted, J. T., & Carpenter, S. K. (2007). The Wickelgren power law and the Ebbinghaus savings function. *Psychological Science, 18*, 133–134.

Wixted, J. T., & Wells, G. L. (2017). The relationship between eyewitness confidence and identification accuracy: A new synthesis. *Psychological Science in the Public Interest, 18*(1), 10–65.

Wixted, J. T., Mickes, L., Clark, S. E., Gronlund, S. D., & Roediger, H. L., III. (2015, September). Initial eyewitness confidence reliably predicts eyewitness identification accuracy. *American Psychologist, 70*(6), 515–526. http://dx.doi.org/10.1037/a0039510.

Wlodarczyk, A., Basabe, N., Páez, D., Villagrán, L., & Reyes, C. (2017). Individual and collective posttraumatic growth in victims of natural disasters: A multidimensional perspective. *Journal of Loss and Trauma, 22*(5), 371-384.

Wojciechowska, L. (2017). Subjectivity and generativity in midlife. *Polish Psychological Bulletin, 48*, 38-43.

Wolf, A. J., Guyer, M. J., & Sharpe, L. (2010). Repressed memories in a controversial conviction. *Journal of the American Academy of Psychiatry Law, 38*, 607-609.

Wolfe, E., & Walker, C. (2019, November 19). In 46 weeks this year, there have been 45 school shootings. CNN. Downloaded from https://www.cnn.com/2019/11/15/ us/2019-us-school-shootings-trnd/index.html.

Wolk, D. A., Das, S. R., Mueller, S. G., Weiner, M. W., & Yushkevich, P. A. (2017). Medial temporal lobe subregional morphometry using high resolution MRI in Alzheimer's disease. *Neurobiology of Aging, 49*, 204-213.

Wolman, D. (2012). The split brain: A tale of two halves. *Nature, 483*, 260-263.

Wombacher, K., Matig, J. J., Sheff, S. E., & Scott, A. M. (2019). "It just kind of happens": College students' rationalizations for blackout drinking. *Health Communication, 34*(1), 1-10.

Wong, N., Sarver, D. E., & Beidel, D. C. (2011). Quality of life impairments among adults with social phobia: The impact of subtype. *Journal of Anxiety Disorders, 14*, 88-95.

Wood, W., & Eagly, A. H. (2002). A cross-cultural analysis of the behavior of women and men: Implications for the origins of sex differences. *Psychological Bulletin, 128*, 699-727.

Wood, W., & Eagly, A. H. (2015). Two traditions of research on gender identity. *Sex Roles, 73*, 461-473.

Woodruff, S. I., Conway, T. L., & Edwards, C. C. (2007). Sociodemographic and smoking-related psychosocial predictors of smoking behavior change among high school smokers. *Addictive Behaviors, 33*, 354-358.

Woods, S. C., Schwartz, M. W., Baskin, D. G., & Seeley, R. J. (2000). Food intake and the regulation of body weight. *Annual Review of Psychology, 51*, 255-277.

Woodson, S. R. J. (2006). Relationships between sleepiness and emotion experience: An experimental investigation of the role of subjective sleepiness in the generation of positive and negative emotions. *Dissertation Abstracts International: Section B: The Sciences and Engineering, 67*(5-B), 2849.

Woollett, K., & Maguire, E. (2009). Navigational expertise may compromise anterograde associative memory. *Neuropsychologia, 47*, 1088-1095.

World Health Organization. (2019). Guidelines on physical activity, sedentary behaviour and sleep for children under 5 years of age. https://apps.who.int/iris/handle/10665/ 311664.

World Health Organization. (2019a). Smoking fact sheet. Retrieved from https://www.who. int/news-room/fact-sheets/detail/tobacco.

World Health Organization (2019b). *WHO report on the global tobacco epidemic.* Geneva: Author.

Wretman, C. J. (2016). Saving Satir: Contemporary perspectives on the change process model. *Social Work, 61*, 61-68.

Wright, A. C. (2017). The current state and future of factor analysis in personality disorder research. *Personality Disorders: Theory, Research, and Treatment, 8*, 14-25.

Wright, A. C., Zalewski, M., Hallquist, M. N., Hipwell, A. E., & Stepp, S. D. (2016). Developmental trajectories of borderline personality disorder symptoms and psychosocial functioning in adolescence. *Journal of Personality Disorders, 30*, 351-372.

Wright, D. S., Nash, R. A., & Wade, K. A. (2015). Encouraging eyewitnesses to falsely corroborate allegations: Effects of rapport-building and incriminating evidence. *Psychology, Crime & Law, 21*, 648-660.

Wrosch, C., Bauer, I., & Scheier, M. (2005). Regret and quality of life across the adult life span: The influence of disengagement and available future goals. *Psychology and Aging, 20*, 657-670.

Wrzesniewski, K., & Chylinska, J. (2007). Assessment of coping styles and strategies with school-related stress. *School Psychology International, 28*, 179-194.

Wróbel, M., & Królewiak, K. (2017). Do we feel the same way if we think the same way? Shared attitudes and the social induction of affect. *Basic and Applied Social Psychology, 39*, 19-37.

Wu, N., Hou, Y., Wang, Q., & Yu, C. (2018). Intergenerational transmission of educational aspirations in Chinese families: Identifying mediators and moderators. *Journal of Youth and Adolescence*, doi:10.1007/s10964-018-0820-y.

Wu, Y. (2013). An empirical study of narrative imagery in implicit and explicit contexts. *Computers in Human Behavior, 29*, 1580-1589.

Wynn, K., Bloom, P., & Chiang, W. C. (2002). Enumeration of collective entities by 5-month-old infants. *Cognition, 83*, B55-B62.

Wyra, M., Lawson, M. J., & Hungi, N. (2007). The mnemonic keyword method: The effects of bidirectional retrieval training and of ability to image on foreign language vocabulary recall. *Learning and Instruction, 17*, 360-371.

Wyrofsky, R. R., Reyes, B. A., Zhang, X. Y., Bhatnagar, S., Kirby, L. G., & Van Bockstaele, E. J. (2019). Endocannabinoids, stress signaling, and the locus coeruleus-norepinephrine system. *Neurobiology of Stress*. DOI: 10.1016/j.ynstr.2019.100176.

Xi, J., Lee, M., LeSuer, W., Barr, P., Newton, K., & Poloma, M. (2017). Altruism and existential well-being. *Applied Research in Quality of Life, 12*, 67-88.

Xiang, J., & Stanley, S. J. (2017). From online to offline: Exploring the role of e-health consumption, patient involvement, and patient-centered communication on perceptions of health care quality. *Computers in Human Behavior, 70*, 446-452.

Xiang, P., Zhang, H., Geng, L., Zhou, K., & Wu, Y. (2019). Individualist-collectivist differences in climate change inaction: The role of perceived intractability. *Frontiers in Psychology, 10*.

Xiao, N. G., Quinn, P. C., Liu, S., Ge, L., Pascalis, O., & Lee, K. (2015). Eye tracking reveals a crucial role for facial motion in recognition of faces by infants. *Developmental Psychology, 51*, 744-757.

Xiao, Z., Yan, H., Wang, Z., Zou, Z., Xu, Y., Chen, J., et al. (2006). Trauma and dissociation in China. *American Journal of Psychiatry, 163*, 1388-1391.

Xie, G., & Johnson, J. Q. (2015). Examining the third-person effect of baseline omission in numerical comparison: The role of consumer persuasion knowledge. *Psychology & Marketing, 32*, 438-449.

Xie, T. T., Wang, T. Z., Wei, Y. P., & Ye, E. C. (2019). Declarative memory affects procedural memory: The role of semantic association and sequence matching. *Psychology of Sport and Exercise, 43*, 253-260.

Yadav, R., Yadav, R. K., Sarvottam, K. & Netam, R. (2017). Framingham Risk Score and estimated 10-year cardiovascular disease risk reduction by a short-term yoga-based life-style intervention. *Journal of Alternative Complement Medicine, 23*(9), 730-737.

Yagi, M., Hirano, Y., Nakazato, M., Nemoto, K., Ishikawa, K., Sutoh, C., et al. (2017). Relationship between symptom dimensions and white matter alterations in obsessive-compulsive disorder. *Acta Neuropsychiatrica, 29*, 153-163.

Yagoda, B. (2018, September). Your lying mind: The cognitive biases tricking you brain. *The Atlantic*.

Yamada, R., & Itsukushima, Y. (2013). The schema provokes a disparity of false recollection between actions and objects in an everyday scene. *Scandinavian Journal of Psychology, 54*, 276-282.

Yamawaki, N., Darby, R., & Queiroz, A. (2007). The moderating role of ambivalent sexism: The influence of power status on perception of rape victim and rapist. *Journal of Social Psychology, 147*, 41-56.

Yanakieva, S., Polychroni, N., Family, N., Williams, L. T. J., Luke, D. P., & Terhune, D. B. (2019). The effects of microdose LSD on time perception: A randomised, double-blind, placebo-controlled trial. *Psychopharmacology, 236*(4), 1159-1170.

Yang, C., Crain, S., Berwick, R. C., Chomsky, N., & Bolhuis, J. J. (2017). The growth of language: Universal grammar, experience, and principles of computation. *Neuroscience and Biobehavioral Reviews*. Accessed from http://www. sciencedirect.com/science/article/pii/ S0149763416305656.

Yang, D., Bushnell, E. W., Buchanan, D. W., & Sobel, D. M. (2013). Infants' use of contextual cues in the generalization of effective actions from imitation. *Journal of Experimental Child Psychology , 116*, 510-531.

Yang, J., Hou, C., Ma, N., Liu, J., Zhang, Y., Zhou, J., et al. (2007). Enriched environment treatment restores impaired hippocampal synaptic plasticity and cognitive deficits induced by prenatal chronic stress. *Neurobiology of Learning and Memory, 87,* 257-263.

Yang, L.-L., Zhao, D., Kong, L.-L., Sun, Y.-Q., Wang, Z.-Y., Gao, Y.-Y., et al. (2019). High-frequency repetitive transcranial magnetic stimulation (rTMS) improves neurocognitive function in bipolar disorder. *Journal of Affective Disorders, 246,* 851-856.

Yang, N., Gelaye, B., Zhong, Q., Rondon, M. B., Sanchez, S. E., & Williams, M. A. (2016). Serum brain-derived neurotrophic factor (BDNF) concentrations in pregnant women with post-traumatic stress disorder and comorbid depression. *Archives of Women's Mental Health, 19,* 979-986.

Yang, Q., Song, D., & Qing, H. (2017). Neural changes in Alzheimer's disease from circuit to molecule: Perspective of optogenetics. *Neuroscience and Biobehavioral Reviews, 79,* 110-118.

Yano, J. M., Yu, K., Donaldson, G. P., Shastri, G. G., Ann, P., Ma, L., et al. (2015). Indigenous bacteria from the gut microbiota regulate host serotonin biosynthesis. *Cell, 161(2),* 264-276.

Yapko, M. D. (2006). Utilizing hypnosis in addressing ruminative depression-related insomnia. In M. D. Yapko (Ed.), *Hypnosis and treating depression: Applications in clinical practice.* New York: Routledge/Taylor & Francis Group.

Yarkoni, T. (2015). Neurobiological substrates of personality: A critical overview. In M. Mikulincer, P. R. Shaver, M. L. Cooper, & R. J. Larsen (Eds.), *APA handbook of personality and social psychology, Volume 4: Personality processes and individual differences.* Washington, DC: American Psychological Association.

Yelderman, L. A., & Miller, M. K. (2017). Religious fundamentalism, religiosity, and priming: Effects on attitudes, perceptions, and mock jurors' decisions in an insanity defense case. *Psychology, Crime & Law, 23,* 147-170.

Yelderman, L. A., Joseph, J. J., West, M. P., & Butler, E. (2019). Mass shootings in the United States: Understanding the importance of mental health and firearm considerations. *Psychology, Public Policy, and Law, 25(3),* 212-223.

Yeomans, M. R., Tepper, B. J., & Ritezschel, J. (2007). Human hedonic responses to sweetness: Role of taste genetics and anatomy. *Physiology & Behavior, 91,* 264-273.

Yesilyaprak, B., Kisac, I., & Sanlier, N. (2007). Stress symptoms and nutritional status among survivors of the Marmara region earthquakes in Turkey. *Journal of Loss & Trauma, 12,* 1-8.

Yi, X., Plucker, J. A., & Guo, J. (2015). Modeling influences on divergent thinking and artistic creativity. *Thinking Skills and Creativity, 16,* 62-68.

Yildirim, F., & Barnett, R. V. (2017). Comparing the effects of specific variables on passionate love among young people: A cross-cultural

study. In N. R. Silton (Ed.), *Family dynamics and romantic relationships in a changing society.* Hershey, PA: Information Science Reference/IGI Global.

Yim, D., & Rudoy, J. (2013). Implicit statistical learning and language skills in bilingual children. *Journal of Speech, Language, and Hearing Research, 56,* 310-322.

Yoder, R. M., Goebel, E. A., Köppen, J. R., Blankenship, P. A., Blackwell, A. A., & Wallace, D. G. (2015). Otolithic information is required for homing in the mouse. *Hippocampus, 25,* 890-899.

Yoo, H., & Castro, K. S. (2011). Does nativity status matter in the relationship between perceived racism and academic performance of Asian American college students? *Journal of College Student Development, 52,* 234-245.

Yoo, H., & Pituc, S. T. (2013). Assessments of perceived racial stereotypes, discrimination, and racism. In K. F. Geisinger, B. A. Bracken, J. F. Carlson, J. C. Hansen, N. R. Kuncel, S. P. Reise, & M. C. Rodriguez (Eds.), *APA handbook of testing and assessment in psychology, Vol. 2: Testing and assessment in clinical and counseling psychology.* Washington, DC: American Psychological Association.

Yost, M. R., & Zurbriggen, E. L. (2006). Gender differences in the enactment of sociosexuality: An examination of implicit social motives, sexual fantasies, coercive sexual attitudes, and aggressive sexual behavior. *Journal of Sex Research, 43,* 163-173.

Young, G. (2017). *Revising the APA ethics code.* Cham, Switzerland: Springer International Publishing.

Young, K. D., Misaki, M., Harmer, C. J., Victor, T., Zotev, V., Phillips, R., et al. (2017). Real-time functional magnetic resonance imaging amygdala neurofeedback changes positive information processing in major depressive disorder. *Biological Psychiatry, 82(8),* 578-586.

Young, N. L., Kuss, D. J., Griffiths, M. D., & Howard, C. J. (2017). Passive Facebook use, Facebook addiction, and associations with escapism: An experimental vignette study. *Computers in Human Behavior, 71,* 24-31.

Young, R., Subramanian, R., Miles, S., Hinnant, A., & Andsager, J. L. (2017). Social representation of cyberbullying and adolescent suicide: A mixed-method analysis of news stories. *Health Communication, 32(9),* 1082-1092.

Yuen, E. K., Koterba, E. A., Stasio, M. J., Patrick, R. B., Gangi, C., Ash, P., et al. (2019). The effects of Facebook on mood in emerging adults. *Psychology of Popular Media Culture, 8(3),* 198-206.

Yıldız, M., Orak, U., Walker, M. H., & Solakoglu, O. (2019). Suicide contagion, gender, and suicide attempts among adolescents. *Death studies, 43(6),* 365-371.

Zacks, J. (2008). Neuroimaging studies of mental rotation: A meta-analysis and review. *Journal of Cognitive Neuroscience, 20,* 1-19.

Zahl-Olsen, R., Thuen, F., & Espehaug, B. (2019). Divorce and Remarriage in Norway: A Prospective Cohort Study Between 1981

and 2013. *Journal of Divorce & Remarriage,* 1-12.

Zahn, N., Sellbom, M., Pymont, C., & Schenk, P. W. (2017). Associations between MMPI-2-RF scale scores and self-reported personality disorder criteria in a private practice sample. *Journal of Psychopathology and Behavioral Assessment, 39(4),* 723-741.

Zahnow, R., McVeigh, J., Ferris, J., & Winstock, A. (2017). Adverse effects, health service engagement, and service satisfaction among anabolic androgenic steroid users. *Contemporary Drug Problems: An Interdisciplinary Quarterly, 44,* 69-83.

Zaitsu, W. (2007). The effect of fear on eyewitness' retrieval in recognition memory. *Japanese Journal of Psychology, 77,* 504-511.

Zajonc, R. B. (2001). Mere exposure: A gateway to the subliminal. *Current Directions in Psychological Science, 10,* 224-228.

Zamarian, L., Högl, B., Delazer, M., Hingerl, K., Gabelia, D., Mitterling, T., et al. (2015). Subjective deficits of attention, cognition and depression in patients with narcolepsy. *Sleep Medicine, 16,* 45-51.

Zambrano-Sánchez, E., Martinez-Cortés, J., Poblano, A., Dehesa-Moreno, M., Vázquez-Urbano, F., & del Río-Carlos, Y. (2019). Maternal smoking during pregnancy and physiological anxiety in children with attention deficit hyperactivity disorder. *Applied Neuropsychology: Child.* https://doi.org/10.1080/21622965.2019.1632708.

Zappasodi, F., Perrucci, M. G., Saggino, A., Croce, P., Mercuri, P., Romanelli, R., et al. (2019). EEG microstates distinguish between cognitive components of fluid reasoning. *NeuroImage, 189,* 560-573.

Zell, E., Krizan, Z., & Teeter, S. R. (2015). Evaluating gender similarities and differences using metasynthesis. *American Psychology, 50,* 10-20.

Zeng, L., Proctor, R. W., & Salvendy, G. (2011). Can traditional divergent thinking tests be trusted in measuring and predicting real-world creativity? *Creativity Research Journal, 23,* 24-37.

Zhang, D., Guo, T., Pan, H., Hou, J., Feng, Z., Yang, L., et al. (2019). Judging a book by its cover: The effect of facial perception on centrality in social networks. In WWW '19, *The World Wide Web Conference.*

Zhang, D., He, Z., Chen, Y., & Wei, Z. (2016). Deficits of unconscious emotional processing in patients with major depression: An ERP study. *Journal of Affective Disorders, 199,* 13-20.

Zhang, J., Chen, H., Kornreich, R., & Yu, C. (2019). Prenatal diagnosis of Tay-Sachs disease. In B. Levy (Ed.). *Prenatal Diagnosis.* New York: Humana Press.

Zhang, W., & Guo, B. (2017). Resolving defence mechanisms: A perspective based on dissipative structure theory. *International Journal of Psychoanalysis, 98,* 457-472.

Zhao, F., Li, S., Li, T., & Yu, G. (2019). Does stereotype threat deteriorate academic performance of high school students with learning disabilities? The buffering role of psychological disengagement. *Journal of Learning Disabilities, 52*(4), 312-323.

Zhao, K., & Smillie, L. D. (2015). The role of interpersonal traits in social decision making: Exploring sources of behavioral heterogeneity in economic games. *Personality and Social Psychology Review, 19*, 277-302.

Zheng, D., Ni, X. L., & Luo, Y. J. (2019). Selfie posting on social networking sites and female adolescents' self-objectification: The moderating role of imaginary audience ideation. *Sex Roles, 80*(5-6), 325-331.

Zhou, Y., Li, H., Siddiqui, N., Caudle, Y., Zhang, H., Elgazzar, M., & Yin, D. (2017). Hematopoietic stem progenitor cells prevent chronic stress-induced lymphocyte apoptosis. *Journal of Neuroimmunology, 309*, 72-76.

Zhou, Z., & Buck, L. B. (2006). Combinatorial effects of odorant mixes in olfactory cortex. *Science, 311*, 1477-1481.

Zhou, Z., Liu, Q., & Davis, R. L. (2005). Complex regulation of spiral ganglion neuron firing patterns by neurotrophin-3. *Journal of Neuroscience, 25*, 7558-7566.

Zickar, M. J. (2015). Digging through dust: Historiography for the organizational sciences. *Journal of Business and Psychology, 30*, 1-14.

Zigler, E., Bennett-Gates, D., Hodapp, R., & Henrich, C. (2002). Assessing personality traits of individuals with mental retardation. *American Journal on Mental Retardation, 107*, 181-193.

Zilbergeld, B., & Ellison, C. R. (1980). Desire discrepancies and arousal problems in sex therapy. In S. R. Leiblum & L. A. Pervin (Eds.), *Principles and practices of sex therapy.* New York: Guilford.

Zizzari, Z. V., Engl, T., Lorenz, S., van Straalen, N. M., Ellers, J., & Groot, A. T. (2017). Love at first sniff: A spermatophore-associated pheromone mediates partner attraction in a collembolan species. *Animal Behaviour, 124*, 221-227.

Zuberi, T., Patterson, E. J., & Stewart, Q. T. (2015). Race, methodology, and social construction in the genomic era. *Annals of the American Academy of Political and Social Science, 661*(1), 109-127.

Zuger, A. (2005, November 10). Doctors learn how to say what no one wants to hear. *The New York Times*, p. S1.

Zvyagintsev, M., Clemens, B., Chechko, N., Mathiak, K. A., Sack, A. T., & Mathiak, K. (2013). Brain networks underlying mental imagery of auditory and visual information. *European Journal of Neuroscience, 37*, 1421-1434.

Zyoud, S. H., Sweileh, W. M., Awang, R., & Al-Jabi, S. W. (2018). Global trends in research related to social media in psychology: Mapping and bibliometric analysis. *International Journal of Mental Health Systems, 12*, doi:10.1186/s13033-018-0182-6.

Name Index

Subject Index

Note: Page numbers followed by *f* indicate figures.